The Orders and Tractates of the Talmud

SEDER ZERA'IM *1 volume*

Berakoth, Pe'ah, Demai, Kil'ayim, Shebi'ith, Terumoth, Ma'aseroth, Ma'aser Sheni, Ḥallah, 'Orlah, Bikkurim

SEDER MO'ED *4 volumes*

1: Shabbath
2: 'Erubin, Pesaḥim
3: Yoma, Sukkah, Beẓah
4: Rosh Hashanah, Ta'anith, Sheḳalim, Megillah, Mo'ed Ḳaṭan, Ḥagigah

SEDER NASHIM *4 volumes*

1: Yebamoth
2: Kethuboth
3: Nedarim, Nazir, Soṭah
4: Giṭṭin, Ḳiddushin

SEDER NEZIḲIN *4 volumes*

1: Baba Ḳamma, Baba Meẓi'a
2: Baba Bathra
3: Sanhedrin
4: 'Abodah Zarah, Horayoth, Shebu'oth, Makkoth, 'Eduyyoth, Aboth

SEDER ḲODASHIM *3 volumes*

1: Zebaḥim, Menaḥoth
2: Ḥullin
Bekoroth, 'Arakin, Temurah, Kerithoth, Me'ilah, Tamid, Middoth, Ḳinnim

SEDER ṬOHOROTH *1 volume*

Niddah, Kelim, Oholoth, Nega'im, Parah, Ṭohoroth, Miḳwaoth, Makshirin, Zabim, Ṭebul Yom, Yadayim, 'Uḳẓin

INDEX *1 volume*

THIS SPECIAL LIMITED ANNIVERSARY EDITION OF
THE BABYLONIAN TALMUD IN ENGLISH
HAS BEEN PUBLISHED BY THE SONCINO PRESS
AND PRINTED AND BOUND AT THE
OXFORD UNIVERSITY PRESS
COINCIDING WITH THE QUINCENTENARY OF
BOTH HOUSES

THE BABYLONIAN TALMUD

SEDER NASHIM

VOLUME II

KETHUBOTH

THE BABYLONIAN TALMUD

SEDER NASHIM

IN FOUR VOLUMES

II

TRANSLATED INTO ENGLISH
WITH NOTES, GLOSSARY AND INDICES
UNDER THE EDITORSHIP OF

RABBI DR I. EPSTEIN

B.A., Ph.D., D. Lit.

THE SONCINO PRESS
LONDON

FIRST PUBLISHED 1936

Printed in Great Britain
at the University Press, Oxford
by Eric Buckley
Printer to the University

KETHUBOTH

TRANSLATED INTO ENGLISH

WITH NOTES, GLOSSARY

AND INDICES

PAGES 1 TO 198

BY

RABBI DR SAMUEL DAICHES
BARRISTER AT LAW

PAGES 198 TO THE END

BY

REV. DR ISRAEL W. SLOTKI, M. A., Litt. D.

PREFATORY NOTE BY THE EDITOR

The Editor desires to state that the translation of the several Tractates, and the notes thereon, are the work of the individual contributors and that he has not attempted to secure general uniformity in style or mode of rendering. He has, nevertheless, revised and supplemented, at his own discretion, their interpretation and elucidation of the original text, and has himself added the footnotes in square brackets containing alternative explanations and matter of historical and geographical interest.

ISIDORE EPSTEIN

CONTENTS

INTRODUCTION

Kethuboth,[1] the second Tractate of the Order of Nashim, deals in the main with the laws relating to married life in its various aspects and manifestations, enumerating, discussing and defining the privileges and duties of husband and wife in their mutual relationship from the day of their betrothal. Cognate subjects, such as questions of immoral conduct and infidelity, and the relative rights of a father and husband, and other topics bearing directly or indirectly upon the main theme are introduced as amplifications, illustrations and elucidations or as part of the arguments and discussions.

CHAPTER I, beginning with the institution of marriage, fixes the week-days on which marriages are to be solemnized and determines the form and number of, and the restrictions applicable to, the benedictions ordained for the occasion. The minimum amounts of the *kethubah* to which virgins, widows, divorcees or other women belonging to the various strata of social and religious life are entitled, and the conditions governing the forfeiture of her *kethubah* by a wife in the absence of her virginity, are duly indicated. The age at which a child may be admitted as a proselyte and the circumstances in which this is allowed are incidentally introduced. Other subjects dealt with include the questions of the reliability of a woman's testimony concerning the status or the innocence of a man with whom she had had intercourse and the conditions in which a ravished girl is not necessarily debarred from marrying a priest.

(1) כְּתוּבּוֹת is the pl. of the noun כְּתוּבָּה (rt. כתב, 'to write') prob. of the form פְּעֻלָּה with *waw* in place of the *kubbuz*. If it is regarded as the particip. pass. fem. pl. of כתב the vocalization should be כְּתוּבוֹת. The noun denotes generally anything that 'is written', but in a technical or legal connotation it is applied to (*a*) a marriage deed, (*b*) the statutory sum that is due to a wife in the event of her husband's death or on being divorced, or (*c*) a wife's jointure or settlement which her husband assigns to her voluntarily or in return for assets that she brings to him on marriage. As the laws and discussions relating to these and cognate subjects constitute its main body the entire Tractate assumed the name of *Kethuboth*.

CHAPTER II deals with disputes on the amount of a *kethubah,* arising from a disagreement between husband and wife as to whether the latter was married as a virgin or a widow. This is followed by an enumeration of the conditions under which witnesses to a deed may invalidate their signatures, and a discussion of the following questions: In what circumstances a woman's word is accepted when she states that she is divorced or that, though she had been a captive, she had remained undefiled; when a man is believed to be a priest on his own evidence, and when a woman imprisoned by heathens is permitted, and when forbidden, to her husband. The principle is laid down that no one may testify concerning oneself, and priests' wives in a town that was taken by troops of siege are forbidden to their husbands unless independent evidence in their favour is forthcoming. An enumeration of cases where grown up persons are believed when testifying to what they had seen in their childhood concludes the chapter.

CHAPTER III lays down the laws of compensation, fines and penalties relating to the violation or seduction of certain classes of women, a distinction being drawn between these and others in whose case some or none of the forms of compensation or fines are applicable, and a discussion is included on the question of the imposition of two penalties for one act involving two offences. How compensation is computed, when a fine is due to the victim herself and when it is to be paid to her father or son are other subjects discussed, and the principle is enunciated that any fines or payments exceeding the actual cost of the damage done need not be paid on one's own evidence.

CHAPTER IV discusses the rights of a father to his young daughter's acquisitions or possessions, such as fines, briefly discussed in the previous chapter, compensation, *kethubah*, finds and the proceeds of her handiwork; the claims of a husband to some of these rights and the duties he assumes in return; the relative rights of a father and husband; whether a father is legally or morally obliged to maintain his children, and the duties and privileges of brothers when a young sister claims maintenance out of their deceased father's estate; from what date distraint for a *kethubah* or a deed of sale may be exercised; the penalties of a betrothed proselyte who played the harlot and those of the man who wrongly accused his wife of an immoral act; and the privileges of a wife and her children under the statutory rules of the *kethubah* though the document was not properly drawn up or was never written. A number of the famous enactments of Usha are quoted and discussed.

CHAPTER V proceeds to lay down the rules in relation to additions to, and deductions from, the statutory *kethubah*, the wife's right in this connection to distraint and its limitations, the different periods allowed to several classes of women for the preparation of their marriage outfits and the times when they are eligible to eat *terumah* if their intended husbands or levirs are priests. Under what conditions a husband may consecrate a wife's handiwork, the services a wife must perform for her husband, how long she must suckle her child, the times for marital intercourse, the penalties if one of the parties refuses the other his or her conjugal rights, and the minimum of food and clothing a husband must allow his wife if he maintains her through an agent, are among the other subjects discussed and determined.

CHAPTER VI defines a husband's rights to his wife's property, handiwork and acquisitions, and gives the ratio between the additional jointure which he must assign to her in her *kethubah* and the capital in money or kind which she brings to him on marriage. The amount of the dowry that a daughter may expect from her father or from his estate after his death, and the extent to which she may recover it from assigned property, are duly indicated; and the duty of providing for the marriages of orphans and for the general necessities, and even luxuries, of the poor is discussed in some detail, emphasis being laid on the preservation of the dignity and self-respect of the recipients. Other subjects dealt with include those of a father-in-law who promised a certain amount to his son-in-law and of a father who deposited a sum of money with a trustee for the benefit of his daughter, who wishes it to be handed over to her husband.

CHAPTER VII is concerned with the laws governing the relations between, or separation of a husband and wife where he, by making a vow, seeks to prevent her from deriving any benefit from him, from eating a particular kind of fruit, from enjoying any particular pleasure or from fulfilling any of her legitimate desires, and enumerates cases of morally or physically defective women who may be divorced without a *kethubah*, and of men who on account of their objectionable bodily condition or occupation may be compelled to divorce their wives.

Chapter VIII deals with the disposal of money, goods, slaves, or landed property inherited by a wife, or a widow awaiting the levirate marriage or *ḥaliẓah* (v. Glos.) by her deceased husband's brother, and describes the circumstances in which the inheritance belongs to the woman or the man. The limitations of a husband's claim to the return of expenses incurred in the amelioration of his wife's property are also laid down.

Chapter IX contains a variety of subjects: The forms and modes of a husband's renunciation of his rights to his wife's property, and the legal consequences resulting therefrom; the relative claims of a wife, creditor and heirs to the estate of a deceased man; an oath of honest dealing that may be exacted from a wife who trades for, or administers the estate of her husband, and the forms and modes of exemption from it; the oath that may be required from a woman who impaired her *kethubah* and from one distraining on orphans' property; the laws governing the right to the collection of a *kethubah* where the woman produced her letter of divorce and her *kethubah*, one of the documents, two of each or two of the former and one of the latter and *vice versa*. The chapter concludes with a statement on the validity of the *kethubah* of the wife of a minor, and a proselyte who was converted at the same time as her husband, and with a discussion on the validity in such cases of the additional jointure.

Chapter X determines the priority of the claims to the recovery of their *kethubahs* and to exemption from oath of two or more wives who were married to the same husband, the relative rights of their respective heirs, and the legal position in the event of the surrender by one of the women of her claim to distrain on the buyer of her deceased husband's estate. These laws give rise to a discussion on the respective rights of creditors holding bonds that bear different dates.

CHAPTER XI sets out the rights and duties of a widow in relation to her late husband's orphans; lays down laws affecting the validity or invalidity of the action of a wife who sells her deceased husband's estate, and of Beth din or agents who sell any estate, at a higher or lower price than the market value. Classes of women not entitled to a *kethubah*, maintenance or any of the other privileges of a wife and those who are entitled to some of these privileges are enumerated.

CHAPTER XII circumscribes the extent and limitation of the obligations of a man towards his wife's daughter whom he had undertaken to maintain for a certain number of years, and of heirs towards the widow of their father, and the periods within which a widow's *kethubah* must be claimed by herself and her heirs respectively.

CHAPTER XIII records the rulings of two famous Jerusalem Judges on the claim to maintenance by the wife of an absent husband; on the refunding of the expenses of a person who, without any authorization, has supplied her with maintenance; on the priority of sons and daughters respectively where the estate left by their father was large or small; and on the legal demand from her intended husband of a woman whose father failed to pay the sum he had promised him. Incidentally are mentioned other rulings by the same Judges on pleas that cannot be regarded as an admission of part of a claim; the trustworthiness of a witness who signed a deed of sale and then contested the ownership of the holder of the deed; the rights of the man the path to whose field was lost during his absence abroad; the invalidity of a bond of indebtedness where the debtor produced a later deed shewing that the creditor had sold to him a field of his, and the respective claims of two persons who produced bonds of indebtedness against each other. The serious consequences of taking bribes and the meticulous care it is necessary to exercise in order to escape temptation are duly described and illustrated. The currency in which certain *kethubahs* must be paid is discussed, and Judaea, Transjordan and Galilee are declared to be distinct countries so that a wife may refuse her husband's wish to leave one of these to settle in another. The superiority of Palestine over all other lands and of Jerusalem over all other towns is proclaimed and illustrated.

The *Aggadic* material of the Tractate includes midrashic and homiletic interpretations of Scripture and stories and incidents pointing morals.

The work of the righteous is regarded as greater than that of creation; and the manner in which R. Gamaliel set an example of simplicity in burial is related (Ch. I).

Some wedding songs and a number of feats performed by Rabbis for the entertainment of the bride and bridegroom are recorded, and the opinion is expressed that one can never praise too highly a bride's charm or virtues. The order of precedence in attending on the dead, on a bride and on a king is indicated and it is also laid down when even engagement in the study of the Torah must give way to attendance on the dead or to participation in wedding festivities (Ch. II).

In the matter of charity one is advised to spend not more than a fifth of his wealth lest by too much liberality he become impoverished and fall a burden upon the public funds. Popular remedies for scorpion bites and the sting of bees are mentioned and some rules are laid down as to the age when a child's education should begin and at what successive ages he may start on Scripture and Mishnah. The Psalmist's praise of him who does righteousness 'at all times' is variously applied to the man who maintains his own children, who brings up orphans in his house or who studies the Torah and teaches it to others. (Ch IV).

The opinion that a wife should be taken merely for the sake of her beauty, or for the sake of children or merely for the sake of wearing her finery, and the extent of the influence of the diet of an expectant mother on her child is referred to, and the romance of the marriage of the shepherd Akiba with the daughter of Ben Kalba Sabu'a and his subsequent attainment to the highest rank of scholarship and affluence is given at considerable length (Ch. V).

The story of the daughter of the wealthy Naḳdimon b. Gorion, whose marriage settlement amounted to a million gold *denarii* and who was eventually reduced to abject poverty is told, the loss of the family's fortune being attributed to Naḳdimon's self-glorification when assisting the poor or to his failing to give in accordance with his means (Ch. VI).

How R. Joshua b. Levi visited Paradise and succeeded for a while in depriving the Angel of Death of his knife is related (Ch. VII) and the closing scenes of the life of R. Judah I, his last wishes and instructions, and his burial and mourning are graphically described (Ch. XII).

The circumstances in which *Seder Eliyyahu Rabbah* and *Seder Eliyyahu Zuṭa* (v. *infra* fol. 106*a*) came to light, quotations from Ben Sira, the love and adoration of Palestine, the merit and dignity of scholars, the marvellous events and manifestations in the days of the Messiah and other eschatological matters are embodied in the last chapter.

Among medieval commentators on which the notes are based, Rashi takes first place and the Tosafists follow though at a very great distance. Of moderns, L. Goldschmidt, M. Jastrow and J. Levy must be specially mentioned.

Thanks are due to Professor Edward Robertson, D.D., D.Litt. for kindly reading the proofs, to my son Judah J. Slotki, M.A., who, besides compiling the indices, read through the entire MS. and made a number of valuable suggestions, and to my daughters, Deborah and Shulamith Rose, who prepared the typescript for the press and assisted in the checking of the proofs. I must also express appreciation of the sympathetic interest in my work shewn by the librarians of the Manchester University and the John Rylands Libraries by whom most of the books required for this work were generously supplied.

I. W. SLOTKI

The indices of this Tractate have been compiled by Judah J. Slotki, M.A.

KETHUBOTH

CHAPTER I

MISHNAH. [2*a*] A MAIDEN IS MARRIED[1] ON THE FOURTH DAY [OF THE WEEK] AND A WIDOW ON THE FIFTH DAY, FOR TWICE IN THE WEEK THE COURTS OF JUSTICE[2] SIT IN THE TOWNS, ON THE SECOND DAY [OF THE WEEK] AND ON THE FIFTH DAY, SO THAT IF HE [THE HUSBAND] HAD A CLAIM AS TO THE VIRGINITY [OF THE MAIDEN-BRIDE] HE COULD GO EARLY [ON THE MORNING OF THE FIFTH DAY OF THE WEEK] TO THE COURT OF JUSTICE.

GEMARA. R. Joseph said: Rab Judah said [that] Samuel said: Why did they [the Rabbis] say, A MAIDEN IS MARRIED ON THE FOURTH DAY? Because we have learned:[3] 'If the time [appointed for the marriage] arrived and they[4] were not married,[5] they[4] eat of his [food][6] and they eat[7] of *terumah*'[8]—you might think that if the time arrived on the first day in the week he would have to supply her with food, therefore have we learned, A MAIDEN IS MARRIED ON THE FOURTH DAY.[9] Said R. Joseph: Lord of Abraham![10] He [Samuel] attaches a Mishnah which was taught, to a Mishnah which was not taught! Which was taught and which was not taught? This was taught and this was taught!—But [put it this way]: he attaches a Mishnah, the reason of which was

(1) Lit., 'is taken' as wife. (2) Lit., 'houses of judgment (law, justice)'. (3) V. *infra* 57*a*. (4) The maiden or the widow. (5) The marriage did not take place through the man's fault. (6) The man has to maintain them. (7) If the man (the bridegroom) is a priest. (8) The priest's share of the crop, v. Glos. (9) And thus to teach that it is not his fault that he does not marry her on the first day in the week, because the Rabbis ordained that he has to wait with the marriage till the fourth day (in the case of a maiden), or the fifth day (in the case of a widow). (10) An exclamation, like 'O, God!' (v. Rashi *ad loc.*).

explained,[1] to a Mishnah, the reason of which was not explained.[2] But if it was said,[3] it was said thus; Rab Judah said [that] Samuel said: Why did they say, A MAIDEN IS MARRIED ON THE FOURTH DAY? Because IF HE HAD A CLAIM AS TO THE VIRGINITY HE COULD GO EARLY [NEXT MORNING] TO THE COURT OF JUSTICE—well, let her be married on the first day in the week, so that if he had a claim as to virginity he could go early [on the morning of the second day of the week] to the court of justice! [The answer is:] The Sages watched over the interests[4] of the daughters of Israel so that [the bridegroom] should prepare for the [wedding-] feast three days, [namely] on the first day in the week, the second day in the week, and the third day in the week, and on the fourth day he marries her. And now that we have learned *'shakedu'*,[5] that [Mishnah] which we have learned: If the time arrived and they were not married, they eat of his [food] and they eat of *terumah,* [is to be understood as implying that if] the time arrived on the first day in the week, since he cannot marry [her, on the first day of the week, on account of the ordinance], he does not give her food [on the three days, from the first day of the week to the fourth day]. Therefore[6] [R. Joseph concludes], if he became ill or she became ill, or she became menstruous,[7] he does not give her food.

Some [scholars] there are who put this as a question: If he became ill, what is [the law]?[8] [Shall I say:] There,[9] the reason [he need not support her,] is because he is forced,[10] and here, he is also forced?[11] Or [shall I say] perhaps, there,[12] he is forced[13] by an

(1) Our Mishnah: SO THAT . . . HE COULD GO EARLY TO THE COURT OF JUSTICE. (2) V. *infra* 57a. (3) The saying of Samuel. (4) Lit., 'ordinance', 'improvement'. (5) 'They (the Sages) watched', etc.—the principle just stated. (6) Since we find that the bride has no claim to maintenance where he is not to blame for the delay in the marriage. (7) After the time for the marriage had arrived and the marriage cannot take place through one of these causes. (8) Lit., 'how is it?' (9) When the appointed date of the marriage falls on the first day of the week; v. *infra* 57a. (10) By the ordinance of the scholars, according to which he must wait till the fourth day of the week (שקדו). (11) By his illness to postpone the marriage. (12) When the appointed date of the marriage falls on the first day of the week. (13) To postpone the marriage.

ordinance which the Rabbis ordained,[1] [but] here, [he is] not?[2] And if you will say:[3] If he became ill he supplies her with food, [then the question would still be:] if she became ill, what is [the law]? Can he say unto her, 'I am here ready to marry you'? Or, perhaps, she can say unto him, 'His field[4] has been flooded'?[5] And if you will say [that] she can say to him [when she falls ill], 'His field has been flooded,' [then the question is,] if she became menstruous, what is [the law]? During her regular time there is no question [2*b*] that she cannot say to him, 'His field has been flooded'. When is the question asked? [If she became menstruous] not during her regular time, what is [the law]? Since it is not during her regular time, she can say unto him, 'His field has been flooded'? Or, perhaps, since there are women who change their periods, it is as if it was her regular time? R. Aḥai explained:[6] [We learnt:] 'When the time came and they were not married, they eat of his food and they eat of *terumah*.'[7] It does not state, 'They [the men] did not marry them [the women]' but [it says] 'They [the women] were not married.' In what case? If they prevent,[8] why do they eat of his food and eat of the *terumah?* Hence, you must say [must you not],[9] that they were forced as in this case,[10] and it states 'they eat of his food and they eat of *terumah*'?—R. Ashi said: Indeed I can say[11] [that] in the case of an accident[12] she does not eat [of his].[13] And [here][14] they [the men] prevented.[15] And by right he ought to have stated, 'they [the men] did not marry [the women].'[16] But

(1) And therefore he need not support her. (2) I.e., in this case he would have to support her since the postponement of the marriage is due to his illness. (3) Lit., 'And if you may be able (or, find it possible) to say.' (4) Another reading is 'thy field'. The sense is, of course, the same. (5) I.e., it is his bad luck that she became ill, and consequently he must support her. (6) I.e., 'answered'. (7) Mishnah 57*a*; v. *supra*. (8) If the women cause the hindrance to the marriage taking place now. (9) Lit., 'but is it not'. (10) Lit., 'as in this manner', that is, when menstruation appeared outside the regular time. (11) Lit., 'always I say unto thee'. (12) As irregular menstruation (v. n. 10). The accident is a mishap that comes from the woman. (13) Lit., 'every accident, she does not eat.' (14) In the Mishnah quoted by R. Aḥai. (15) The marriage from taking place now. (16) And not 'they (the women) were not married'.

since the first clause[1] speaks of them [the women] the latter clause also speaks of them [the women]?[2]

Raba said: And with regard to divorce[3] it is not so.[4] Accordingly Raba holds [that] accident is no plea in regard to divorce.[5] Whence does Raba get this [rule]? Shall I say, from what we have learned: 'Behold this is thy bill of divorce if I come not [back] from now until twelve months,'[6] and he died within the twelve months, there is no divorce.[7] [And we would conclude from this that only if] he died there is no divorce,[8] but if he became ill[9] there is a divorce![10] But perhaps indeed I might say [that] if he became ill there would also be no divorce,[11] and [the Mishnah][12] lets us hear just this [rule], that there is no divorce after death.[13] [That] there is no divorce after death, a previous Mishnah[14] teaches: 'Behold, this is thy bill of divorce if I die,' [or] 'behold, this is thy bill of divorce from this illness,'[15] [or] 'behold, this is thy bill of divorce after [my] death,' he has not said anything.[16] [But] perhaps [that[17] is] to exclude from that[18] of our teachers, for it has been taught: Our teachers allowed her to marry again.[19] And we said: Who

(1) Of the Mishnah, quoted by R. Aḥai; v. *infra* 57*a*. (2) I.e., since that Mishnah speaks in the first clause of 'maiden' and 'widow', it uses in the clause that follows the passive 'they were not married' the subjects of which are the 'maiden' and the 'widow'. To use the active 'they did not marry', referring to the men, would have required more words in that clause. (3) Lit., 'deeds (of divorce).' (4) I.e., an accident, as explained *infra*, does not invalidate a divorce. (5) Lit., 'there is no accident with divorce'. (6) These words the husband says to the wife. 'From now until twelve months' means 'within twelve months'. (7) Lit., 'it is not a *Get*,' (v. Glos.) that is, the divorce does not take effect; v. Giṭ. 76*b*. (8) Because there can be no divorce after death. (9) And he could not come back within the twelve months through his illness. (10) Which proves that we do not admit a plea of *force majeure* to invalidate a *Get*. (11) For the plea of accident does apply to divorce. (12) Giṭ. 76*b*. (13) And no other deduction, e.g., as to illness, is to be made from that Mishnah. (14) Giṭ. 72*a*. Lit., 'beginning', 'first clause', denoting here a previous Mishnah. (15) This phrase is not clear. V. Rashi here and Giṭ. 72*a*. The phrase seems to mean, 'If I die from this illness.' V. Tosaf. *a.l.* (16) I.e., his words have no effect. (17) I.e., the Mishnah of Giṭ. 76*b* quoted above. (18) I.e., from the view of our teachers. If this is the object of (the first clause of) the Mishnah of Giṭ. 76*b*, Raba cannot deduce from this Mishnah that if he (the husband) became ill the divorce took effect; v. *supra*, also note 9. (19) 'Our teachers' regard her as

are 'our teachers'? Rab Judah said [that] Samuel said: The court that allowed the oil [of the heathen];[1] they[2] hold like R. Jose who said, 'the date of the document shows it.'[3] But from the later clause:[4] '[This is thy bill of divorce][5] from now if I come not [back] from now [and] until twelve months', and he died within the twelve months, it is a divorce. [And we may deduce] 'if he died', and the same rule applies if he became ill.[6] [But] perhaps [the divorce is effective] only when he died, because it was not pleasing to him that she should become subject to[7] the *yabam!*[8]—But [the deduction can be made] from this: There was a certain [man][9] who said unto them:[10] 'If I do not come [back] from now until thirty days it shall be a divorce.'[11] He came [back] at the end of thirty days but the ferry stopped him.[12] He said unto them,[13] 'Look, I have come [back]; look, I have come [back]!'[14] Said Samuel: This is not regarded as having come back.[15] But perhaps an accident which is frequent[16] is different,[17] for since he ought to have stipulated it[18] and he did not stipulate it, he injured himself![19]—But [we

divorced (against the Mishnah) and allow her to marry again without *ḥaliẓah*. If she is regarded as a widow and she has no children she requires *ḥaliẓah* before she can re-marry. As to *ḥaliẓah* v. Deut. XXV. 5-10, and Glos.

(1) V. A.Z. 36*a* and 37*a*. (2) I.e., the members of the court of justice. (3) [B.B. 136*a*; and so here the date inserted for the *Get* is intended to make it effective from the time of the delivery thereof. For further notes v. Giṭ. (Sonc. ed.) p. 136]. (4) I.e., Raba deduces the rule that the plea of accident does not apply to divorce from the second clause of the Mishnah, cf. Giṭ. 76*b*. (5) V. Giṭ. 76*b*. (6) And he could not come back on account of his illness. (7) Lit., 'that she should fall before' (the *yabam*). (8) The husband's brother, who, if she was regarded as a widow (and not as divorced), would have to marry her or let her perform *ḥaliẓah*. (9) A husband. (10) Certain persons who might be witnesses. (11) I.e., the bill of divorce given now shall become effective. (12) The ferry was on the other side of the river and he could not get across, and he was thus prevented (by this accident) from arriving in his town within the thirty days. (13) To persons standing near by. (14) The divorce should therefore not take effect. (15) Lit., 'Its name is not "come back"'—the divorce, therefore, takes effect. This proves that *force majeure* is no plea in regard to *Get*. (16) I.e., an accident which is likely to occur, as the ferry being on the other side of the river. (17) Does not bar the divorce from becoming effective. (18) That if the ferry should be on the other side of the river and he could not get across and come into his town, it should be regarded

must say] Raba expressed an opinion of his own:[1] On account of the chaste women and on account of the loose women.[2] On account of the chaste women,[3] because if you will say that it should not be a divorce,[4] [3a] sometimes [it may happen] that he was not held back by an accident,[5] and she would think that he was held back by an accident[6] and she would be tied, and sit.[7] And on account of the loose women, because if you will say [that] it should not be a divorce, sometimes [it may happen] that he was held back by an accident[8] and she would say[9] that he was not held back by an accident[10] and she would go and get married, and the result would be[11] [that] the divorce was invalid[12] and her children [from the second marriage] would be bastards.[13] But is it possible[14] that

as if he had arrived in the town and come back within the meaning of his condition, which would thus be regarded as not fulfilled, and the divorce would, consequently, not take effect. (19) He has himself to blame. The attempted deduction from the ferry case is therefore refuted.

(1) Since the rule of Raba, that an accident is no bar to the effectiveness of the divorce, cannot be derived from any Mishnah or from the ferry case, it is attributed to himself, that is to his own reasoning. (2) By 'loose women' are meant women who would not be particular about marrying again even if the validity of the divorce was not established. (3) The divorce should be effective. (4) That the divorce should not become effective because of the accident. (5) Lit. 'that he was not forced.' The divorce would therefore certainly be effective. (6) And the divorce would, in her view, not take effect (if the rule would have been that an accident is a bar to the divorce becoming effective). (7) Lit., 'and she will be tied'. I.e., she would regard herself as tied to her absent husband and would not marry again. An *'agunah* is 'a woman tied to an absent husband'. The Rabbis endeavoured to prevent the state of *'agunah;* v. Giṭ. 33*a*. (8) And the divorce would not take effect. (9) The use of 'she would say' here in contradistinction to 'she would think' in the case of the 'chaste women' is no doubt intentional. She (the loose woman) would *say* this, although she would not *think* so in her heart. (10) In which case the divorce would become effective. (11) Lit., 'and it is found.' (12) If the divorce should not become effective because of an accident. (13) The children of a married woman and a man who is not her husband are bastards, *mamzerim;* v. Yeb. 49*a*. This would be the case if the divorce would not become effective because of an accident and the first husband should turn up and say that he was held back by an accident. To prevent such evil results Raba established the rule that an accident should not be a bar to the divorce taking effect. (14) Lit., 'and is there anything?'

according to the law of the Bible it would not be a divorce[1] and on account of 'the chaste women' and on account of the 'loose women' we should allow a married woman[2] to the world?[3]—Yes, every one who betroths in accordance with the sense of the Rabbis he betroths,[4] and the Rabbis have annulled his betrothal.[5] Said Rabina to R. Ashi: This might be well[6] [if] he betrothed her with money,[7] [but if] he betrothed [her] by act of marriage, what can one say [then]?—The Rabbis have made[8] his act of marriage non-marital.[9]

Some, [however,] say[10] [as follows]: Raba said: And so [also] with regard to divorce. Accordingly Raba holds [that the plea of] accident applies to divorce.[11] An objection was raised: 'Behold this is thy bill of divorce if I come not [back] from now [and] until twelve months,' and he died within the twelve months, there is no divorce. [Now] if he dies there is no divorce, but if he became ill there would be a divorce!—Indeed I might say [unto thee] that if he became ill there would be no divorce either, and [the Mishnah] lets us hear just this [rule]: that there is no divorce after death. [That] there is no divorce after death a previous Mishnah teaches! —Perhaps [that is] to exclude from that of our teachers. Come and hear:[12] 'From now if I have not come [back] from now [and]

(1) [The plea of *force majeure* as recognized in the Bible, v. Deut. XXII, 26.] (2) Lit., 'the wife of a man.' (3) I.e., to marry another man. (4) Lit., 'he sanctifies,' 'he consecrates.' To sanctify, to consecrate a woman to oneself means to marry her. *Ḳiddushin* 'sanctifications' means 'betrothal,' 'marriage.' I.e., every one who marries a woman marries her on the basis that the marriage is sanctioned by the law of the Rabbis. (5) Lit., 'and the Rabbis have caused the betrothal to be released from him,' that is retrospectively. As the marriage is subject to the sanction of the Rabbis, the Rabbis can, if the necessity arises, annul the marriage. Such a necessity has arisen when an accident would be a bar to the divorce becoming effective. (6) The answer just given might be regarded as satisfactory. (7) V. Ḳid. 2*a*. (8) I.e., have declared it to be, or regard it. (9) Lit., 'an intercourse of prostitution.' The Rabbis have in either case the power to annul the marriage. The argument that Raba arrived at his view through his own reasoning stands. (10) Lit., 'There are some who say.' (11) According to this version, Raba holds that an accident is a bar to the divorce becoming effective. (12) From here till 'he injured himself' the text is practically identical with the corresponding text on folio 2*b*. There are only

until twelve months,' and he died within the twelve months, it is a divorce. Would not the same rule apply if he became ill? No, only if he died, because it was not pleasing to him that she should become subject to the *yabam*. Come and hear: A certain [man] said unto them: 'If I do not come [back] from now [and] until thirty days it shall be a divorce.' He came [back] at the end of thirty days but the ferry stopped him. And he said unto them, 'Look, I have come [back]; look, I have come [back]!' And Samuel said: This is not regarded as having come back!—An accident which is frequent is different, for since he ought to have stipulated it and he did not stipulate it, he injured himself.

R. Samuel b. Isaac said: They have only taught[1] since the institution of Ezra[2] and after, [according to which] the courts of justice sit[3] only on the second day and on the fifth day [of the week]. But before the institution of Ezra, when the courts of justice sat every day, a woman[4] could be married on any day. Before the institution of Ezra, what there was there was![5]—He means it thus: If there are courts of justice that sit now as before the institution of Ezra,[6] a woman may be married on any day. But what of *shakedu?*[7] [We suppose] that he[8] had [already] taken the trouble.[9] [3b] What is [the reference to] *shakedu?* [For] it has been taught: Why did they say that a maiden is married on the fourth day? Because if he had a claim as to virginity he could go early [next morning] to the court of justice. But let her be married on the first day in the week and if he had a claim as to virginity he could go early [on the morning of the second day in the week] to the court of justice?—The Sages watched over the interests of the daughters of Israel so that [the man] should prepare for the [wedding-]feast three days, the first day in the week, and the second day in the week, and the third day in the week, and on

one or two omissions and one or two slight variations. For interpretation, v. notes on the translation of 2*b*. The difference of the arguments is obvious.

(1) That a maiden marries on the fourth day of the week. (2) V. B.Ḳ. 82*a*. (3) Lit., 'are fixed.' (4) Even a maiden. (5) That is past and does not matter! (6) Every day. (7) Lit., 'we require "they watched"'. V. *supra* 2*a*. (8) The bridegroom. (9) Of preparing for the wedding.

the fourth day he marries her. And from [the time of] danger and onwards the people made it a custom to marry on the third day and the Sages did not interfere with them. And on the second day [of the week] he shall not marry; and if on account of the constraint[1] it is allowed. And one separates the bridegroom from the bride on the nights of Sabbath at the beginning,[2] because he makes a wound.[3]

What [was the] danger? If I say that they[4] said, 'a maiden that gets married on the fourth day [of the week] shall be killed', [then how state] 'they made it a custom'? We should abolish it entirely! —Said Rabbah: [That] they said, 'a maiden that gets married on the fourth day [of the week] shall have the first sexual intercourse with the prefect.'[5] [You call] this danger? [Surely] this [is a case of] constraint![6]—Because there are chaste women who would rather surrender themselves to death and [thus] come to danger. But let one expound to them[7] that [in a case of] constraint [it] is allowed?[8]—There are loose women[9] and there are also priestesses.[10] But [then] let one abolish it?[11]—A decree[12] is likely to cease, and [therefore] we do not abolish an ordinance of the Rabbis on account of a decree. If so, on the third day he [the prefect] would also come and have intercourse [with the bride]? —Out of doubt he does not move himself.[13]

[It is stated above:] 'And on the second day [of the week] he shall not marry; and if on account of the constraint it is allowed.' What constraint [is referred to]? Shall I say [that it is] that which we have said?[14] There,[15] one calls it 'danger', and here, one calls it [mere] 'constraint'! And further, there [it states], 'they made it a custom', [whilst] here, 'it is allowed'![16]—Said Raba: [it is that] they

(1) This will be explained anon. (2) If it is her first marital union. (3) By the first act of intercourse. (4) The Roman authorities. (5) *jus primae noctis;* v. *J.E.*, VII, p. 395. (6) [And no woman is enjoined to sacrifice her life in resisting this assault; v. *supra* p. 7 n. 1, v. *infra* 51*b*.] (7) The women. (8) V. n. 6. (9) Who might submit voluntarily. (10) Wives of priests who would be forbidden to their husbands even when submitting under constraint; v. *infra* 51*b*. (11) Marrying on Wednesday. (12) Of the Romans. (13) To come into town. (14) The fear of the exercise of *jus primae noctis*. (15) Earlier in the cited Baraitha. (16) [Implying that it was not an established custom.]

say 'a general has come to town'.[1] In what case? If he comes and passes by,[2] let it be delayed![3]—It is not necessary [to state this but] that he came and stayed. Let him, [then], marry on the third day [of the week]?[4]—His[5] vanguard arrived on the third day. And if you wish I may say: What is [the meaning of] 'on account of the constraint'? As it has been taught: If his bread was baked and his meat prepared and his wine mixed[6] and the father of the bridegroom[7] or the mother of the bride died,[8] they bring the dead [person] into a room and the bridegroom and the bride into the bridal chamber,[9] [4a] and he performs the dutiful marital act[10] and [then] separates [himself from her].[11] And [then] he keeps the seven days of the [wedding-]feast[12] and after that he keeps the seven days of mourning.[12] And [during] all these days he sleeps among the men and she sleeps among the women.[13] And they do not withhold ornaments[14] from the bride all the thirty days.[15] [But that is] only [if] the father of the bridegroom or the mother of the bride [died], because there is [then] no one who should prepare for them [for the wedding], but not [in case of] the reverse.[16] Rafram b. Papa said [that] R. Ḥisda said: They taught [this] only when water had [already] been put on the meat, but if water had not [yet] been put on the meat, it is to be sold. Raba said: And in a city, although water had been put on the meat, it is sold.[17] R. Papa said: And in a village, although water had not been

(1) And he would requisition the food prepared for the wedding-feast. (2) If he only passes through the town. (3) I.e., let the marriage be delayed till the *fourth day* of the following week. (4) [Instead of the second day of the week and thus give him a longer opportunity for making preparations for the wedding.] (5) The general's. (6) With water, their wine being too strong to be drunk undiluted. I.e., all the preparations for the wedding had been made. (7) [Who had to provide for the wedding-feast.] (8) [Who provided the wife with her trousseau.] (9) *Ḥuppah*, v. Glos. First the marriage and then the mourning. (10) The first intercourse. (11) [Immediately after which the burial takes place. The death of one of these parents is thus the constraint referred to. Where the death occurred on Monday the marriage is to take place immediately so as to avoid delay in the funeral.] (12) V. *infra*. (13) So that they have no intercourse. (14) 'Ornaments' means both jewellery and toilet requisites. (15) [The thirty days of semi-mourning that follow the death of a near relative.] (16) These rules do not apply. (17) Because it can be sold.

put on the meat, it is not sold.[1] But where [then] will you find [the rule] of R. Ḥisda [to apply]? Said R. Ashi: For instance, [in] Matha Meḥasia,[2] which is neither a city nor a village.[3]

It has been taught according to R. Ḥisda: If his bread was baked and his meat prepared and his wine mixed and water had been put on the meat and the father of the bridegroom or the mother of the bride died, they bring the dead [person] into a room and the bridegroom and the bride into the bridal chamber, and he performs the dutiful marital act and [then] separates [himself from her]. And [then] he keeps the seven days of the [wedding-]feast and after that he keeps the seven days of mourning. And all these days he sleeps among the men and she sleeps among the women. And so [also] if his wife became menstruous does he sleep among the men and she sleeps among the women. And they do not withhold ornaments from the bride all the thirty days. In any case he must not perform the [first] marital act on the eve of Sabbath or in the night following the Sabbath.

The Master said [above]: 'He sleeps among the men and she sleeps among the women.' This supports R. Joḥanan, for R. Joḥanan said: Although they said [that] there is no mourning on a festival, yet matters of privacy he keeps.[4] R. Joseph the son of Raba lectured in the name of Raba: They taught[5] only if he had yet no intercourse [with her],[6] but if he had [already] intercourse, his wife may sleep with him.[7] But here we deal with a case when he had intercourse, and still it teaches [that] he sleeps among the men and she sleeps among the women?—When did he[8] say [it]? With regard to his wife becoming menstruous. But it says, 'And so [also if his wife became menstruous]'![9] [4*b*]—Thus he[10] means

(1) Because it cannot be sold. (2) A place near Sura. (3) Lit., 'Which is excluded from a city and excluded from a village'. (4) [I.e., mourning customs that affect domestic relations, and thus involve no outward manifestations of grief, must be observed.] (5) That he sleeps among the men and she sleeps among the women. (6) And he may feel tempted. (7) In one room. (8) Raba. (9) And this would seem to show that there is no difference between the time of mourning and the period of menstruation. (10) The Tanna of the cited Baraitha.

to say:[1] And so [also], if his wife became menstruous and he had not yet had intercourse [with her] he sleeps among the men and she sleeps among the women. Is this [then] to say that he treats mourning more lightly than menstruation?[2] Surely. R. Isaac the son of Ḥanina said that R. Huna said: All kinds of work[3] which a wife performs for her husband, a menstruant[4] may perform for her husband, except the mixing of the cup[5] and the making[6] of the bed and the washing of his face, his hands and his feet;[7] while with regard to mourning it has been taught: Although they[8] said: No man has a right to force his wife[9] to paint [her eyes] or rouge [her face], in truth[10] they said: She mixes him the cup[11] and she makes him the bed and she washes his face, his hands and his feet?[12] — [This is] not difficult; here[13] [it speaks] of his mourning,[14] there[15] [it speaks] of her mourning.[16] But it says:[17] 'The father of the bridegroom or the mother of the bride [died]'?[18] — This refers to the rest.[19] But is there a difference between his mourning and her mourning? Surely it has been taught: If a man's father-in-law or mother-in-law died,[20] he cannot force his wife to paint [her eyes] and to rouge [her face], but he lowers his bed[21] and keeps mourning with her. And so [also] if a woman's father-in-law or mother-in-law died[22] she is not allowed to paint [her eyes] and to rouge [her face], but she lowers her bed

(1) Lit., 'thus he says.' (2) Lit., 'that mourning is lighter to him (the husband) than menstruation'. The case of menstruation is limited to where no intercourse had taken place. (3) Lit., 'all works'. (4) I.e., the wife during menstruation. (5) I.e., pouring out of wine; v. *supra* p. 10 n. 6. (6) Lit., 'spreading.' (7) Because the nearness may bring temptation; v. *infra* 61*a*. (8) The Rabbis. (9) When she is mourning for a parent. (10) Cf. B.M. 60*a*; wherever an opinion is introduced with the words, 'in truth they said,' it means to say that it is an established legal rule. (11) Cf. *infra* 61*a*. (12) This would show that he treats mourning less lightly than menstruation! (13) *Supra* 4*a*: 'he sleeps among the men and she sleeps among the women.' (14) And she might be tempted. (15) Lit., 'here.' In the Baraitha just quoted. (16) And she would resist temptation. (17) Lit., 'it teaches.' (18) This shows that there is no difference between his mourning and her mourning. (19) Lit., 'When it teaches, on the rest.'—I.e., this refers to the other points mentioned in the Baraitha on 4*a*. (20) Lit., 'he whose father-in-law or mother-in-law died.' (21) Placing the mattresses on or near the floor was a sign of mourning. (22) Lit., 'she whose father-in-law or mother-in-law died.'

and keeps mourning with him![1]—Teach with reference to his mourning 'he sleeps among the men and his wife sleeps among the women'.[2] But it says: 'And so [also]'?[3]—This refers to painting and rouging.[4] But it says 'with him'! Does this not mean,[5] with him in one bed?—No, [it means] with him in one house, and as Rab said to his son Ḥiyya: In her presence[6] keep mourning, in her absence do not keep mourning.[7] R. Ashi said: Can you compare this mourning[8] with ordinary mourning?[9] Ordinary mourning is strict and one would not deal lightly[10] with it. [But] this mourning, since the Rabbis were lenient [about it], one might deal lightly with it. What is the leniency? Shall I say, because it says he performs the dutiful act of marriage and separates [himself from her]? That is[11] because the mourning has not rested upon him[12] yet; [namely] if according to R. Eliezer, [the mourning does not begin] until the body has been taken out of the house,[13] and if according to R. Joshua, [the mourning does not begin] until the *golel*[14] has been closed![15]—But [the leniency is this,] because it says: He keeps [first] the seven days of the [wedding-]feast and after that he keeps the seven days of mourning.

The Master said: 'In any case he must not perform the [first] marital act on the eve of Sabbath or in the night following the Sabbath. It is right [that he may not perform it] on the eve of

(1) Since it does not state in the latter case that he has to sleep among the men etc., it shows that there is no difference between his mourning and her mourning. (2) And so there would be a difference between his mourning and her mourning. In his mourning there would be the precaution just stated, while in her mourning that precaution would not be required. (3) This would show that there is no difference between his mourning and her mourning. (4) In either case she does not paint or rouge. (5) Lit., 'what not?' (6) In the presence of Ḥiyya's wife who was in mourning. (7) I.e., 'with him' (or 'with her') shews that she keeps mourning with him in his presence and he keeps mourning with her in her presence. (8) Lit., 'the mourning of here', namely the mourning immediately before the marriage; v. *supra* 3*b* (bottom) and 4*a*. (9) Lit., 'mourning of the world.' (10) Lit., 'and one would not come to disregard it.' (11) Lit., 'there'. (12) Has not begun yet. (13) Lit., 'until it goes out from the door of the house.' (14) The covering stone of a tomb. 'To close the *golel*' means 'to close the tomb with the *golel*,' v. Nazir (Sonc. ed.) p. 302, n. 5. (15) Cf. M.Ḳ. 27*a*.

Sabbath, because of a wound.[1] But in the night following the Sabbath, why not?—Said R. Zera: [5a] Because of accounts.[2] Said Abaye to him: And are accounts of a religious nature forbidden?[3] Surely R. Ḥisda and R. Hamnuna both said: Accounts of a religious nature, one is allowed to calculate them on Sabbath; and R. Eleazar said: One may assign charity to the poor on Sabbath; and R. Jacob said [that] R. Joḥanan said: One may go to synagogues and to schoolhouses to watch over public affairs[4] on Sabbath; and R. Jacob the son of Idi said [that] R. Joḥanan said: One may do any work to save a life[5] on Sabbath; and R. Samuel the son of Naḥmani said [that] R. Jonathan said: One may go to theatres and circuses[6] to watch over public affairs on Sabbath; and [a scholar] of the school of Menashia taught: One may negotiate about the girls to be betrothed on Sabbath[7] and about a boy to teach him the book[8] and to teach him a trade?—But, said R. Zera, it has been prohibited[9] lest he might slaughter a fowl.[10] Said Abaye to him: But if this were so, then the Day of Atonement which fell on the second day of the week should be postponed[11] for fear[12] lest he might slaughter a fowl?[13]—There,[14] that [he has to prepare

(1) He makes a wound through the first intercourse. (2) If he will consummate the marriage in the night following the Sabbath he will give a dinner in the evening and he will make accounts (in his mind) on Sabbath as to the cost of that festive meal. (3) I.e., is it forbidden to make calculations for a religious purpose on Sabbath? (4) Lit., 'the affairs of many'. (5) Lit., 'one removes a person' from under debris. The meaning is: One may do any work on Sabbath to save a life. (6) Theatres and circuses were also places of general assemblies. In the same way public meetings were also held in synagogues and schoolhouses. (7) I.e., one may negotiate the betrothal of them on Sabbath. (8) I.e., *the* book, the Bible. (9) Lit., 'a preventive measure'. To have the first intercourse in the night following the Sabbath. (10) Lit., 'the child of a fowl', that is a young fowl. There is also the reading בו 'on it' i.e., on Sabbath for בן. He would be so busy thinking of the festive meal on Sabbath night that he might forget that it was Sabbath and slaughter a fowl for the dinner in the evening. (11) For one day; v. Rashi. (12) 'As a preventive measure'. (13) On Sabbath, since he would be busy thinking of the preparations for the meal on Sunday, which would be the eve of the Day of Atonement. On the eve of the Day of Atonement it is a religious duty to have a festive meal. (14) In the case of the Day of Atonement.

only] for himself he is not troubled [so much],[1] [but] here,[2] that [he has to prepare] for others,[3] he is troubled.[4] Or: there, he has an interval,[5] [but] here, he has no interval.[6] Now that you have come so far,[7] the eve of Sabbath[8] also is prohibited[9] for fear lest he might slaughter a fowl.[10]

The question was asked:[11] [Does the Mishnah mean:] A maiden is married on the fourth day [of the week], and the intercourse takes place on the fourth day, and we are not afraid that he might be pacified?[12] Or perhaps [the meaning is] a maiden is married on the fourth day [of the week], and the intercourse takes place on the fifth day[13] because we are afraid that he might be pacified?—Come and hear: Bar-Ḳappara taught: A maiden is married on the fourth day [of the week] and the intercourse takes place on the fifth day[13] because on it [the fifth day] the blessing for the fishes was pronounced.[14] A widow is married on the fifth day [of the week] and the intercourse takes place on the sixth day[15] because on it [the sixth day] was pronounced the blessing for man.[16] [We thus see that] the reason is on account of the blessing, but as to [his] being pacified we are not afraid. If so,[17] [in the case of] a widow also the intercourse should take place on the fifth day [of the week], because on it [the fifth day] was pronounced the blessing

(1) And he will not forget that it is Sabbath and he will not slaughter a fowl on Sabbath. (2) In the case of the wedding-feast on Sabbath night. (3) For the guests of the evening. (4) And he might forget that it is Sabbath and he might slaughter a fowl on Sabbath. (5) Sabbath night and Sunday morning. He does not have the important meal before midday or later on the day of the eve of the Atonement Day. (6) The wedding-dinner would take place on Sabbath night as soon as Sabbath is out. (7) To this result, namely that he must not perform the first intercourse in the night following the Sabbath because he might profane the Sabbath by slaughtering a fowl on Sabbath. (8) Friday night. (9) To have the first intercourse. (10) On Friday evening, after Sabbath had already begun. (11) Lit., 'it was asked by them'. (12) Lit., 'cooling off to the (his) mind.' That is, if he has intercourse on Wednesday and he has reason to complain as to virginity, his anger might cool off by Thursday morning and he might not go on Thursday to the court of justice; v. *supra 2a*. (13) I.e., Wednesday evening, which belongs to the fifth day. (14) Lit., 'said (by God).' Cf. Gen. I, 20-23, especially 22. (15) Thursday evening, v. n. 13. (16) Cf. Gen. I, 26-28, especially 28. (17) If the reason is on account of the blessing.

for the fishes?[1]—The blessing for man is better for him.[2] Or on account of 'they have watched,'[3] for it has been taught: Why did they[4] say [that] a widow is married on the fifth day [of the week] and the intercourse takes place on the sixth day? Because, if you will say that the intercourse should take place on the fifth day, in the morning[5] he will rise and go to his work;[6] therefore the Sages watched over the welfare[7] of the daughters of Israel that he should rejoice with her[8] three days, [namely] on the fifth day of the week,[9] on the eve of Sabbath[10] and [on] Sabbath.[11] What is the difference between 'the blessing' and 'they have watched'?[12] The difference is this:[13] [in the case of] a man of leisure,[14] or [in the case] when a festival falls on the eve of Sabbath.[15]

Bar-Ḳappara expounded: The work of the righteous[16] is greater than the work[17] of heaven and earth, for in [regard to] the creation of heaven and earth it is written, *Yea, My* hand *hath laid the foun-*

(1) It means this: If the reason is the blessing, why should not intercourse, in the case of a widow, take place on the same day as the marriage, namely on the fifth day? And on the fifth day there was the blessing for the fishes. And if that blessing is good enough for a maiden it should be good enough for a widow. (2) For Bar Ḳappara. He considered the blessing for man a stronger reason. In the case of a maiden it is different, as, if her intercourse should take place on Friday, we should be afraid that he might be appeased by Monday, the first court-day after Friday. Therefore the blessing for the fishes has to suffice in the case of the maiden. (3) *Shaḳedu*, v. *supra* pp. 2 and 8. The ordinance that in the case of a widow the intercourse should take place on Friday was made in the interests of the daughters of Israel. (4) The Sages. (5) The next morning. In case of a widow the marriage festivities last only one day. V. *infra* 7a bottom. (6) Lit., 'he rises unto his trade (work) and goes his way.' That is, he walks out of the house and leaves the whole wedding atmosphere behind him. This had to be prevented. (7) Lit., 'ordinance (for the welfare).' (8) With the widow-bride. (9) The day of the marriage. (10) Friday, the day of the intercourse. (11) The religious day of rest. (12) What is the difference between these two reasons? (13) Lit., 'there is between them.' (14) Lit., 'an idle man.' 'They have watched' would not apply to a man of leisure, as he need not go to work next day. But the intercourse would have to take place on Friday if the reason was 'the blessing'. (15) In which case Friday is a religious day of rest, and he would not go to work. But the reason of 'the blessing' would still operate for intercourse on Friday. (16) Pious men. (17) The creation.

dation of the earth, and My right hand *hath spread out the heavens,*[1] while in [regard to] the work of the hands of the righteous it is written, *The place which Thou hast made for Thee to dwell in, O Lord, the sanctuary, O Lord, which Thy* hands *have established.*[2] Replied[3] one Babylonian, and R. Ḥiyya [was] his name: [It is written,] *And the dry land his* hands *formed?*[4]—It is [to be] written, 'His hand'.[5] But it is written, *they formed?*[6]—Said R. Naḥman b. Isaac: 'His fingers formed,'[7] as it is written, *When I behold Thy heavens, the work of Thy fingers, the moon and the stars which Thou hast established.*[8]

An objection was raised: [It is written,] *The heavens declare the glory of God, and the work of His* hands *the firmament shows?*[9]—Thus he said:[10] The handiwork[11] of the righteous, who shews [it]?[12] The firmament. And what is it? Rain.[13]

Bar-Ḳappara [also] expounded: What [is the meaning of what] is written, *And thou shalt have a peg among thy implements?*[14] Do not read,[15] *thy implements,*[16] but 'upon thy ear';[17] [this means to say] that if a man hears an unworthy thing[18] [5b] he shall plug his finger[19] into his ears. And this is the same that R. Eleazar said: Why do the fingers of man resemble pegs? Why?[20] Shall I say because they are divided?[21] [Surely] each one has been made for its own purpose![22]

(1) Isa. XLVIII, 13. There '*My* hand' is written. (2) Ex. XV, 17. In regard to the sanctuary, which is the work of the hands of pious men, '*Thy* hands' is written. (3) I.e., objected. (4) Ps. XCV, 5. (5) [The *kethib* in some texts is ידו ('*his hand*').] (6) [In the plural, so that the subject '*hand*' must also be in the plural.] (7) 'Fingers' is implied as subject. (8) Ps. VIII, 4. (9) Ps. XIX, 2. [Thus we have 'hands' written also in connection with creation.] (10) Thus the Psalmist meant. (11) Lit., 'the work of their hands.' (12) Who tells them, announces them? (13) Rain comes because the pious pray for it. The handiwork of the righteous is called the 'work of His hands', because in the rain the work of God and the work of the righteous meet. The rain is the work of God, but it comes as the result of the good deeds of the pious, whose prayers God fulfils. (14) Deut. XXIII, 14. (15) [In the sence of 'render'.] (16) From אֲזֵן, 'implement, tool'. (17) As if from אֹזֶן, 'ear'. (18) Lit., 'a thing (or, a word) that is not worthy', not fit to be heard. (19) The finger is pointed like a peg. (20) Lit., 'what is the reason?' I.e., what is the meaning of the question? With regard to what are the fingers of man like pegs? (21) I.e., shall I say that the question is: Why are the fingers divided? They might have been joined together. (22) Lit., 'for its thing.'

For a Master said: This one[1] [is used for measuring] the span;[2] this one[3] [is used for] taking a fistful of the meal-offering,[4] this one[5] [is used for defining] the cubit measure,[6] this one[7] [is used for taking the measure of] 'a finger',[8] [and] this one[9] [is used for service with] the thumb![10]—But [the question is] why[11] [are the fingers] pointed like pegs? [The reason is] that if a man hears an unworthy thing he shall plug his fingers into his ears. [A member] of the school of R. Ishmael taught: Why is the whole ear hard and the ear-lap soft? [So] that if a man hears an unworthy thing he shall bend the ear-lap into it.[12]

Our Rabbis taught: A man shall not let his ears hear idle things,[13] because they are burnt first of [all] the organs.[14]

The question was asked: Is it allowed[15] to perform the first marital act on Sabbath?[16] Is the blood [in the womb] stored up,[17] or is it the result of a wound?[18] And if you will say[19] [that] the blood is stored up [in the womb, then the question arises:] is he concerned about the blood,[20] and it is allowed; or is he concerned

(1) The little finger. (2) I.e., the distance from the little finger to the thumb of a spread hand. (3) The finger next to the little finger. (4) קמיצה, the taking of a fistful of the meal-offering, v. Lev. II, 2. (5) The middle finger. (6) The cubit is a measure equal to the distance from the elbow to the tip of the middle finger. (7) The fourth from the little finger. (8) And also for priestly service with the 'finger'; cf. Lev. IV, 6. (9) The fifth from the little finger. (10) V. Lev. VIII, 23, 24; XIV, 14, 17, 25, 28. We thus see that every finger has a definite purpose. They therefore had to be divided and function as separate fingers! (11) Lit., 'what is the reason (that)?' (12) Into the ear. He will thus close the ear and not hear the unworthy thing. (13) Not only unworthy things, but even idle things a man should not hear, e.g., tittle-tattle. (14) Lit., 'of the limbs.' 'Because they are burnt first of (all) the organs' seems to have a figurative meaning. From hearing unworthy or idle things he may proceed to speak unworthy or idle things and then to do unworthy or idle things. The ear is thus the first organ to 'be burnt', to 'catch fire'. Cf. Prov. VI, 27-28. Cf. the English phrase, 'to burn one's fingers.' (15) Lit., 'How is it'? (16) When the intercourse could not take place before Sabbath, (Tosaf.). (17) And the intercourse would be allowed, since the blood flows out of its own accord, no wound having been made. (18) Lit., 'or is it wounded?' And the intercourse would be forbidden. (19) Lit., 'And if you should be able to say.' (20) Is his aim to release it? Lit., 'is it the blood he requires?' [According to Tosaf.: In order to see whether she is a virgin.]

with the opening,[1] and it is forbidden?[2] And if you will say [that] he is concerned with the blood and the opening comes of itself, [then the question arises:] Is the ***halachah***[3] according to R. Simeon who says: A thing which is not intended[4] is allowed; or is the ***halachah*** according to R. Judah who says: A thing which is not intended is forbidden?[5] And if you will say [that] the ***halachah*** is according to R. Judah [then the question arises], does he do damage in regard to the opening, or does he improve in regard to the opening?[6] Some say:[7] And if you will say that the blood is the result of a wound [then the question arises], is he concerned about the blood and it is forbidden,[8] or is he concerned with his own pleasure, and it is allowed? And if you will say [that] he is concerned with his own pleasure and the blood comes out of itself,[9] [then the question arises,] is the ***halachah*** according to R. Judah or is the ***halachah*** according to R. Simeon? And if you will say [that] the ***halachah*** is according to R. Judah, [then the question arises,] does he do damage by [making] the wound, or does he improve by [making] the wound? And if you will say [that] he does damage by [making] the wound, [then the question arises,] with regard to one who does damage, is the ***halachah*** according to R. Judah, [*6a*] or is the law according to R. Simeon?[10] In the

(1) Or is his aim to make an opening? (2) It is forbidden to make an opening on Sabbath. [Such an act comes under the category of 'building'.] (3) 'Adopted opinion', 'rule'. (4) An act which is in itself forbidden but is the unintended though unavoidable result of an act which is permitted. Thus one may, according to R. Simeon, push a couch on the floor, on Sabbath, if one has not the intention to make a rut in the floor, although, as a matter of fact, such a rut is made as the unavoidable result of pushing the couch. (5) R. Judah's view is opposed to that of R. Simeon; v. n. 4. (6) Is the making of the opening considered to be to the advantage or disadvantage of the woman? If it is to her disadvantage it would be allowed even according to R. Judah. [Based on the principle that an act of damage does not constitute labour in regard to Sabbath. V. Shab. 106*a*.] (7) Lit., 'there are who say', that the questions were with regard to the assumption that the blood is the result of a wound. (8) To have the intercourse on Sabbath. (9) The coming of the blood is therefore an unintended but unavoidable result of an act, the intended object of which is the pleasure. (10) According to R. Simeon he who does damage by making a wound had to bring a sin-offering; v. Shab. 106*a*.

school of Rab[1] they said: Rab allowed[2] and Samuel forbade.[2] In Nehardea[3] they said: Rab forbade and Samuel allowed. Said R. Naḥman b. Isaac: And your [mnemotechnical] sign [is]: These make it lenient for themselves, and these make it lenient for themselves.[4] But does Rab allow it? Surely R. Shimi b. Hezekiah said in the name of Rab: [As regards] that stopper of the brewing boiler, it is forbidden to squeeze it in[5] on a festival day![6]—In that [case][7] even R. Simeon admits [that it is forbidden], for Abaye and Raba, both of them say: R. Simeon admits [that it is forbidden] in [a case of] 'Let his head be cut off, and let him not die!'[8] [But] R. Ḥiyya the son of Ashi said [that] Rab said: The *halachah* is according to R. Judah,[9] and R. Ḥanan the son of Ammi [said that] Samuel said: The *halachah* is according to R. Simeon.[10] And R. Ḥiyya the son of Abin taught it without [naming the] men:[11] Rab said [that] the *halachah* is according to R. Judah, and Samuel said [that] the *halachah* is according to R. Simeon?—Still, Rab holds like R. Judah, [but] according to that version that says, 'the blood is stored up [in the womb],' he does damage in regard to the opening,[12] [and] according to that version that says, 'the blood is the result of a wound,' he does damage in [making] the wound.[12]

R. Ḥisda objected: If a girl, whose period[13] to see [blood] had not arrived yet, got married, Beth Shammai[14] say: One gives her four nights,[15] and the disciples of Hillel say: Until the wound is

(1) In Sura. Before the words 'in the school of Rab', some texts have the word 'it has been said (that)'. (2) To have the first intercourse on Sabbath. (3) The place of Samuel. (4) In Sura they said that Rab allowed it, and in Nehardea they said that Samuel allowed it. (5) Into the bottle. The stopper is made of soft material, and, if it is squeezed, the liquid absorbed in the material would come out. (6) This shows that Rab, like R. Judah, holds that a permitted action which results in a prohibited action, though the latter was not intended, is forbidden; v. p. 19, nn. 4 and 5. (7) Of the stopper in the brewing bottle. (8) 'Let his head be cut off, and let him not die!' is a dialectic term for an *absolutely unavoidable* result of an act. V. Jast., s.v. פסק. In such a case R. Simeon admits that the act leading to the forbidden act is prohibited. This applies to the stopper. Intercourse, however, is different; v. *infra* 6*b*. (9) V. p. 19, n. 5. (10) V. p. 19, n. 4. (11) I.e., without naming the authorities. (12) V. *supra* p. 19, n. 6. (13) Lit., 'time'. (14) Lit., 'the house', i.e., the school, of Shammai. (15) In which she can have intercourse with her husband.

healed up.[1] If her period to see [blood] had arrived[2] and she married, Beth Shammai say: One gives her the first night,[3] and Beth Hillel say: Until the night following the Sabbath [one gives her] four nights.[4]

[6*b*] [Now] does it not[5] mean that if he had [yet] no intercourse [with his wife] he may have intercourse [with her] even on Sabbath?[6]—Said Raba: No, except Sabbath. Said Abaye to him: But it says, 'until the night following the Sabbath [one gives her] four nights'?[7]—Only, said Raba, when he already had intercourse [with her].[8] If [it were, as you say,] after he already had intercourse, what does he let us hear?[9]—He lets us hear that it is allowed to have intercourse on Sabbath, as that [statement] of Samuel [teaches], for Samuel said: One may enter into a narrow opening on Sabbath,[10] although[11] he causes pebbles to break loose.[12]

(1) The blood that comes out is attributed to the wound and not to menstruation. Ordinarily, after the first intercourse further intercourse is forbidden until the coming out of blood, i.e., menstruation, is over. But in this case, in which the young bride had never yet had any menstruation, it is assumed that the blood is not due to menstruation but to the wound caused by the intercourse. According to Beth Shammai this assumption holds good for four nights, and according to Beth Hillel it holds good 'until the wound is healed up.' As to the definition of this phrase, v. Nid. 64*b*. V. also Nid. 65*b*, where it is finally decided that after the first coition no further intercourse must take place until the flowing of blood has stopped, even in the case of a young bride who had not yet had any menstruation. V. also *Eben ha-'Ezer*, 63, and *Yoreh De'ah*, 193. (2) But she had in fact not yet seen blood; that is, she had the maturity for it, but the maturity had not yet manifested itself. A girl has reached the period of maidenhood (puberty) when she is twelve years and one day old. When she is twelve and a half years old she has reached the state of *bogereth*, (v. Glos.), full maturity, womanhood. V. *infra* 39*a*. (3) He may repeat the intercourse during the first night. (4) Mishnah in Nid. 64*b*. (5) Lit., 'is it not?' Having quoted the Mishnah from Nid. 64*b*, R. Ḥisda proceeds to ask his question, which is based on the last statement of Beth Hillel. (6) The question presumes that 'until the night following the Sabbath (one gives her) four nights' may also mean any one of the four nights, and thus the intercourse may be first consummated on the night of Sabbath, (v. Rashi). This shews that one may have the first intercourse on Sabbath. (7) Sabbath must, therefore, be included! (8) One night before Sabbath. The intercourse on Sabbath was thus not the first. (9) What new law does the Tanna teach us? Why should he (the husband) not be allowed to have intercourse on Sabbath? (10) Lit., 'a narrow opening (or

R. Joseph objected: A bridegroom is free from the reading of *Shema'*[1] in the first night[2] until the night following the Sabbath, if he has not performed [yet] an act.[3] Is it not[4] because he is anxious to perform the marital act?[5]—Said Abaye to him: No; he is anxious because he has not had intercourse.[6] Said Raba to him: And on account of anxiety [only][7] he is free [from reading *Shema'*]? If this were so, then [if] his ship sank in the sea, he would also be free [from the reading of *Shema'*]! And should you say [that] it is really so, surely, R. Abba b. Zabda said [that] Rab said: A mourner is bound to observe all the precepts that are stated in the Torah except [that] of the *Tefillin*[8] because it is said with regard to them *'an ornament'?*[9]—But, said Raba, this[10] is a dispute of Tannaim,[11] for one [Baraitha] teaches: If he[12] did not do an act [of coition] in the first [night],[13] he is free [from reading *Shema'*] also in the second [night]; in the second [night],[14] he is free [from reading *Shema'*] also in the third [night].[15] And another [Baraitha] teaches: [In] the first and second [night] he is free, [but in] the third [night] he is obliged [to read *Shema'*].[16] And Abaye [holds that] there[17] also

breach), one may enter into it on Sabbath.' (11) Lit., 'and although.' (12) He may have, say the second intercourse on Sabbath, v. Rashi, *ad loc.*

(1) The verses, Deut. VI, 4-9; XI, 13-21; Num. XV, 37-41 which are recited daily, morning and evening. (2) Following the marriage. (3) I.e., the first intercourse. Mishnah Ber. 16*a*. (4) That he is free from the reading of *Shema'*, even on Sabbath night. (5) Lit., 'because he is anxious, because he wants to have intercourse.' Being preoccupied with a duty (*miẓwah*) he is free from another duty (*miẓwah*). (6) [Before Sabbath, and forbidden to have it on Sabbath.] (7) Mental agitation, worry. (8) *Phylacteries*, v. Glos. (9) Cf. Ezek. XXIV, 17. [The reference being there to the *Tefillin* which Ezekiel was charged not to lay aside despite his mourning for his wife. V. M.K. 15*a*.] A mourner, though very much troubled, is nevertheless not free from observing the precepts. We thus see that anxiety does not exempt one from fulfilling the various religious commandments. And so in the case of the Mishnah quoted by R. Joseph it cannot be that the bridegroom is free from the reading of *Shema'* only because of his anxiety. (10) With regard to the first intercourse on Sabbath. (11) Lit., 'this is (of) Tannaim. (12) The bridegroom. (13) After the marriage. (14) If he did not do an act in the second night either. (15) The third night (after the fourth day in the week) is Sabbath, and he is free from reading *Shema'* as he is allowed to perform the marital act for the first time. (16) The teacher of this

they][1] differ with regard to anxiety.[2] And these Tannaim [are] like those Tannaim,[3] for it has been taught [in a Baraitha]: He who marries a maiden shall not perform the first intercourse[4] on Sabbath, and the Sages allow [it]. Who are the Sages?—Said Rabbah: It is R. Simeon, who says: A thing which is not intended is allowed.[5] Said Abaye to him: But R. Simeon admits [that it is forbidden] in [a case of] 'Let his head be cut off and let him not die!'[6] Said he to him: Not like those Babylonians who are not skilled in moving aside,[7] but there are some who are skilled in moving aside.[8] If so,[9] why [give the reason of] 'anxious'?[10]—For one who is not skilled. [Then] let them say: One who is skilled is allowed [to perform the first intercourse on Sabbath], one who is not skilled is forbidden?—Most [people] are skilled.[11] Said Raba the son of R. Ḥanan to Abaye: If this were so, then why [have] groomsmen,[12] why [have] a sheet?[13]—He [Abaye] said to him: There [the groomsmen and the sheet are necessary] perhaps he will see and destroy [the tokens of her virginity].[14]

Baraitha holds that he is not allowed to perform it first on Sabbath, and therefore he is obliged to read *Shema'*. (17) In the Baraithas just quoted.

(1) The Tannaim. (2) According to the first Baraitha his anxiety caused by the fact that he is not allowed to perform the act on Sabbath frees him from reading *Shema'*. And according to the second Baraitha this anxiety does not free him from reading *Shema'*. According to the first Baraitha the case of the mourner would be different. Since anxiety is no part of the mourning observances (Rashi, *a.l.*). (3) I.e., the dispute of the Tannaim just quoted by Raba is the same as the dispute of the Tannaim of the Baraitha to be quoted now. (4) Lit., 'shall not have intercourse at the beginning.' (5) V. *supra* p. 19, n. 4. (6) V. *supra* p. 20, n. 8. (7) I.e., having intercourse with a virgin without causing a bleeding. (8) Thus no blood need come out, and 'Let his head be cut off and let him not die!' does not apply. (9) If the bridegroom is skilled in 'moving sideways'. (10) He need not be anxious about the intercourse and should not be free from reading *Shema'* on account of such anxiety. (11) Therefore the principle regarding 'Let his head be cut off and let him not die!' does not, as a rule, apply. (12) The groomsmen testify in case of need to the virginity of the bride. V. *infra* 12*a*. If the bridegroom will act in a manner that will cause no bleeding, the groomsmen will not be able to testify on the question of virginity. (13) To provide evidence of the virginity of the bride. Cf. Deut. XXII, 17. (14) It may happen that he will act in the normal manner and cause bleeding but he will destroy the tokens and maintain that the bride

R. Ammi objected:[1] He who pierces[2] an abscess on Sabbath, if [in order] to make an opening[3] to it, he is guilty,[4] but if [in order] to cause pus to come out of it [7a] he is free from punishment]?[5]—There[6] it is[7] stored up[8] and is [entirely] loose,[9] here[10] it[11] is stored up[12] but is not [entirely] loose.[13] R. Ammi allowed to have first intercourse[14] on Sabbath. Said the Rabbis to him: But her *kethubah*[15] is not written yet!—He said to them: Let her seize movable goods.[16] R. Zebid permitted to have the first intercourse on Sabbath. Some say: R. Zebid himself had the first intercourse on Sabbath. Rab Judah allowed to have the first intercourse on a festival. R. Papi said in the name of Raba: You shall not say [that] on a festival it[17] is allowed, but [that] on Sabbath it is forbidden. It is just as well allowed on Sabbath; only it happened so.[18] R. Papa said in the name of Raba: On a festival it is allowed, on Sabbath it is forbidden. Said R. Papi to R. Papa: What is your opinion? Since a wound[19] has been permitted [on a festival] for a necessity, it has been permitted also when there is no necessity? If that were so, it should be permitted to put spices on coals[20] on a festival, for since the kindling of fire has been allowed [on a festival] for a

was not a virgin; for this reason the above mentioned provisions are necessary. Where however he moved aside and made a false charge as to her virginity, the bride can plead that she is still a virgin (Rashi).

(1) V. 'Ed. (Sonc. ed.) p. 12 nn. 5-6. (2) Lit., 'loosens.' Jast.: 'manipulates.' (3) Lit., 'mouth'. (4) Of Sabbath-breaking. (5) And permitted; v. Shab. 107*a* and 3*a*. Intercourse should thus be permitted on Sabbath for the first time, even when the aim is the bleeding! (6) In the case of the abscess. (7) The blood. (8) In the abscess. (9) From the flesh. (10) In the case of the virgin-bride. (11) The blood. (12) In the womb. (13) From the walls of the womb. [Read with MS.M. 'It is neither stored up nor loose,' but the result of a wound, hence forbidden.] (14) Lit., 'to perform in the beginning'. (15) The marriage contract; lit., 'a written deed' (v. Glos.). Marital union is forbidden before the *kethubah* is written. (16) And the movable goods will be a pledge in her hand with regard to the *kethubah* until the marriage contract will be written, when all his real estate is mortgaged with regard to *kethubah*. (17) The first intercourse. (18) Lit., 'and the event that was was thus'. [The question was put to him on a festival and he declared it permissible.] (19) I.e., the making of a wound. (20) To perfume the room after dinner; v. Ber. 43*a*.

necessity, it should be allowed also when there is no necessity![1] Said he to him.[2] Concerning this[3] the Biblical verse said, *save that which every man must eat,*[4] [this means] a thing which is useful[5] for every man.[6] R. Aḥa, the son of Raba, said to R. Ashi: If this were so,[7] then if a deer happened to come to the hands of a person[8] on a festival, [shall we say that] since it is not of equal usefulness for every person,[9] is it really so that it would be forbidden to kill it? Said he[10] to him:[11] I say, 'a thing that is needful for every person,'[12] [and] a deer is needful for every person.[13] R. Jacob, the son of

(1) The meaning of the question of R. Papi to R. Papa is as follows: If a distinction is to be made, regarding the first intercourse, between Sabbath and a festival and it is to be held, as R. Papa holds in the name of Rab, that it is forbidden on Sabbath and allowed on a festival, then R. Papa must hold that, since certain work was allowed on a festival for a necessity, work should be allowed on a festival even when there is no necessity for it. It is, e.g., allowed to make a wound on a festival by slaughtering an animal for the need of food. It would, therefore, according to R. Papa, be allowed to make a wound (v. *supra 3b, 4b, 5b*) by performing the first intercourse on a festival, although there is no necessity for it, since the first intercourse can wait until after the festival. If this view were correct, then it should have been allowed to burn spices on coals on a festival, although spices are not a necessity, since the kindling of fire on a festival is allowed for a necessity. And the accepted view is that it is forbidden to put spices on coals on a festival. Consequently, if the first intercourse is forbidden on Sabbath it should be forbidden also on a festival, since it is not a necessity. R. Papa's view is therefore wrong.— Generally speaking, work that is forbidden on Sabbath is forbidden on a festival. There is an exception in the case of work necessary for preparing food. This is already indicated in Ex. XII, 16; v. Meg. 7*b*. (2) To R. Papi. (3) I.e., to avoid, or anticipate the answer to, your question. (4) Ex. XII, 16. The verse continues, '*that only may be done to you*'. (5) Literally, 'equal', 'like', 'worth'; a thing that is of equal worth for every one, namely, to eat, to do, to have. (6) The sense of the answer is this: You cannot compare the first intercourse to spices. Spices are not of equal necessity for every person. As Rashi puts it, only people who are used to luxuries desire spices. But sexual intercourse, even the first act, is a human need, which applies to all people. (7) I.e., if only work for a necessity to all is allowed on a festival. (8) Lit., 'happened to meet him.' (9) Cf. n. 6. (10) R. Ashi. (11) To R. Aḥa. (12) R. Ashi seems to emphasize the needfulness of the object, though it may not be of equal necessity to all. (13) Indeed, he answers, a deer is good for every person, and therefore, it may be slaughtered on a festival.

Idi, said: R. Joḥanan gave a decision[1] in Ẓaidan:[2] It is forbidden to perform the first intercourse on Sabbath.—And is there an instructive decision for a prohibition?[3]—Yes, we have learned in a Mishnah:[4] The school of Hillel gave a decision regarding her[5] that she[6] should be a Nazirite yet another seven years. Or indeed it is as that which has been taught: If the cord of the spinal column is severed in its larger portion [the animal is *trefa*],[7] [this is] the view of Rabbi.[8] R. Jacob says: Even if it[9] is [only] perforated [the animal is *trefa*]. Rabbi gave a decision[10] according to R. Jacob.[11]

R. Huna said: The *halachah* is not as stated by R. Jacob. R. Naḥman b. Isaac taught thus: R. Abbahu said: R. Ishmael b. Jacob, from Tyre asked R. Joḥanan in Ẓaidan, and I heard [it]: Is it allowed[12] to have the first intercourse on Sabbath? And he[13] said to him:[14] It is forbidden.—And the law is: It is allowed to have the first intercourse on Sabbath.[15]

R. Ḥelbo said [that] R. Huna said [that] R. Abba, the son of Zabda, said [that] Rab said: A maiden as well as a widow requires a benediction.[16]—But did R. Huna say so? Did not R. Huna say: A widow does not require a benediction?—It is not difficult.[17] Here[18] [it speaks] of a young man[19] who marries a widow, there[20] of a widower who marries a widow. And when a widower marries

(1) הורה means 'to teach', 'to instruct', 'to decide'. הוראה denotes a decision based on traditional teaching and (on) one's own learned deductions. One might call it 'an instructive decision.' (2) Sidon; [others: Bethsaida.] (3) I.e., does one apply the term הורה or הוראה to a prohibitory decision which need not necessarily be based on tradition or powers of deduction (Rashi). (4) Nazir 19*b*. (5) הורוה. (6) The Queen Helena of Adiabene, mother of King Monabaz. V. Nazir (Sonc. ed.) p. 66, n. 4. (7) It is forbidden to use the animal for food if the larger portion of its spinal cord was severed while the animal was alive. (8) Lit., '(these are) words of Rabbi'. Rabbi is Rabbi Judah ha-Nasi. (9) The spinal cord. (10) הורוה, v. Ḥul. 45*b*. (11) Against his own view. The view of R. Jacob was stricter than that of Rabbi. (12) Lit., 'How is it?' (13) R. Joḥanan. (14) To R. Ishmael. (15) This is the conclusion of the long argument. (16) At the celebration of the marriage, v. *P.B.* p. 299. Lit., 'laden (with) a blessing.' Cf. 'obliged to', 'bound to.' (17) There is no contradiction between the two traditions. (18) Where R. Huna says that a widow requires a benediction. (19) A young man who was never married before. (20) Where R. Huna says that a widow does not require a benediction.

a widow [a benediction] is not required? Did not R. Naḥman say: Huna b. Nathan said to me: A Tanna taught: Whence [is it derived that] the benediction of the bridegrooms[1] [has to be said] in the presence of ten [persons]? Because it is said, *And he took ten men of the elders of the city, and said: 'Sit ye down here'. And they sat down.*[2] And Boaz was a widower, who married a widow![3]—What is [the meaning of the words] 'she does not require a benediction' which R. Huna said? She does not require a benediction during all the seven days, but on one day[4] she requires a benediction. But that which has been taught:[5] 'The Sages were anxious for the welfare of the daughters of Israel, that he[6] may rejoice with her[7] three days'—how is this to be understood?[8] If [it speaks] of a young man, did you not say— seven;[9] if of a widower, did you not say—one day?[10]—If you wish, you may say [that it speaks] of a widower [and in this case] one day is for the benediction and three days are for rejoicing. And if you wish, you may say [that it speaks] of a young man [and in this case] seven [days] are for the benediction and three [days] for rejoicing.

[7*b*] An objection was raised: [It has been taught:] The benediction is said [at the celebration of the marriage] for a maiden seven [days] and for a widow one day. Is it not [to be understood that] even [in the case of] a widow who marries a young man [the benediction is said only on one day]?—No [only when the widow marries] a widower. But [if the widow marries] a young man, what [then]? Seven [days]?[11] If that is so, let it be taught:[12] The bene-

(1) Identical with the benediction mentioned above. (2) Ruth IV, 2. (3) And still the benediction was required. As to Boaz having been a widower, v. B.B. 91*a*. (4) On the day of marriage. (5) V. *supra* 5*a*. (6) The bridegroom. (7) The bride. (8) Lit., 'In what?' 'How?' (9) The benediction has to be said all the seven days following the marriage ceremony, and this implies rejoicing. That the benediction has to be said all the seven days in the case of the marriage of a young man, even if the bride is a widow, is inferred from the statement that in the case of the marriage of a widower and a widow it is not required to say the benediction all the seven days (Rashi). (10) Only on one day has the benediction to be said, and this apparently means rejoicing only on one day. (11) The benediction has to be said during seven days, just as at the marriage of a young man and a maiden! (12) I.e., it should have been taught.

diction is said for a maiden[1] seven [days], and for a widow who marries a young man[2] seven [days], and for a widow [who marries a widower][3] one day?—It taught a decided thing:[4] That there is no maiden who has less than seven [days],[5] and there is no widow who has less than one day.[6] The [above] text [says]: R. Naḥman said: Huna b. Nathan said to me: A Tanna taught: Whence [is it derived that] the benediction of the bridegrooms [has to be said] in the presence of ten [persons]? Because it is said, *And he took ten men of the elders of the city, and said: 'Sit ye down here'*.[7] But R. Abbahu said [that it is derived] from here: *In assemblies bless ye God, the Lord, from the fountain of Israel.*[8] And how does R. Naḥman expound this verse of R. Abbahu?[9]—He requires it for the same purpose as has been set out in a Baraitha:[10] R. Meir used to say: Whence [can it be derived] that even embryos in the bowels of their mothers sang[11] a song[12] by the sea?[13] Because it is said, *In assemblies bless ye God, the Lord, from the fountain of Israel.*[14] And the other one?[15]—If [that were] so, let the verse say,[16] 'from the

(1) On the occasion of the marriage of a maiden. (2) On the occasion of the marriage of a widow and a young man. (3) On the occasion of the marriage of a widow and a widower. (4) A definite thing. (5) On the occasion of the marriage of every maiden the benediction is said during the seven days following the marriage. (6) On the occasion of the marriage of a widow the benediction must be said at least on one day (the day of the marriage). Usually a widow marries a widower. (7) V. *supra 7a*. (8) Ps. LXVIII, 27. An 'assembly' consists of at least ten persons; v. Sanh. 2*a*. The '*fountain*' is regarded by R. Abbahu, Midrashically, as an allusion to the young wife. Cf. Prov. V, 18: *Let thy fountain be blessed, and have joy of the wife of thy youth*. V. also v. 15, and Isa. LI, 1. The derivation of R. Abbahu from the verse in Psalms is this: When a marriage is celebrated and a new fountain of Israel is to enrich life, a benediction has to be said in the presence of ten persons. (9) I.e., to what Midrashic use does R. Naḥman put Ps. LXVIII, 27? (10) Lit., 'to what has been taught'. (11) Lit., 'said.' (12) Probably *the* song (Ex. XV) is meant. (13) The Red Sea. (14) The derivation is: Even those who were still in '*the fountain*' of Israel sang a song unto the Lord. In vv. 23 and 26 R. Meir no doubt saw, Midrashically, allusions to the crossing of the Red Sea. Cf. especially v. 26 with Ex. XV, 20, 21. (15) R. Abbahu. How does he derive the idea of R. Meir just expounded, since he uses the verse in Ps. LXVIII for another purpose (benediction at the marriage in the presence of ten persons)? (16) I.e., the verse should have read.

womb.'[1] Why [does it say], *'from the fountain'?*[2] [To show that it is] concerning the affairs of the fountain.[3] And how does R. Abbahu expound that verse of R. Naḥman?[4]—He requires it for expounding: an Ammonite, and not an Ammonitess, a Moabite, and not a Moabitess.[5] For if you would think [that the presence of the ten men was required] for [the saying of] the benediction, would it not have been sufficient if they had not been elders?[6] And the other one?[7]—If you would think [that the verse was to be used] for that exposition, would it not have been sufficient if there had not been ten [persons]?[8]—Yes, to make the matter public[9]—and as Samuel said to R. Ḥanna of Bagdath:[10] Go out and bring me ten[11] [persons] and I will say unto thee in their presence; If one assigns [property] to an embryo, it acquires it. But the law is: If one assigns [property] to an embryo, it does not acquire it.[12]

The Rabbis taught: The benediction of the bridegrooms is said[13]

(1) 'From the womb' would indicate the presence of 'fruit of the womb', of an embryo. Cf. e.g., Gen. XXX, 2. (2) 'Fountain' does not refer to present pregnancy, to an embryo, but to the source of life in the woman without implying that there is life in it now. Therefore we can also speak of the *'fountain'* in the maiden. (3) Marriage is concerned very largely with 'the affairs of the fountain.' R. Abbahu, therefore, prefers to use the verse in Ps. LXVIII for his Midrashic exposition (benediction at the marriage in the presence of ten persons). (4) Ruth IV, 2. (5) In Deut. XXIII, 4, it is said, *An Ammonite or a Moabite shall not enter into the assembly of the Lord.* The presence of ten elders was required for the interpretation that the prohibition to enter into the assembly of the Lord, that is, to be admitted into the community of Israel, applied only to Ammonite and Moabite men and not to Ammonite or Moabite women. This interpretation made the law clear, and thus Boaz could marry Ruth the Moabitess. (6) That the presence of elders was necessary shews that the interpreting and establishing of a law was required. (7) R. Naḥman. How will he get that exposition if he uses the verse for a different purpose? (8) If the presence of the elders was required for establishing a law, then there was no need to have ten elders. A smaller number of elders would also have been sufficient. It is different, according to R. Naḥman, if the presence of the ten persons was required for saying the benediction at the marriage of Boaz and Ruth. Ten persons form a congregation; v. *supra.* (9) This is the view of R. Abbahu. (10) Bagdad, v. Rashi, Ber. 54*b*. (11) So as to make his legal pronouncement public. (12) V. B.B. 142*b*. (13) Lit., 'they bless the benediction etc.' The reference is to the benediction at the celebration of the

in the house of the bridegroom.[1] R. Judah says: Also in the house of the betrothal[2] it is said.[3] Abaye said: And in [the province of] Judah they taught [the opinion of R. Judah] because [in the province of Judah] he[4] is alone with her.[5]

Another [Baraitha] teaches: The benediction of the bridegrooms is said in the house of the bridegrooms and the benediction of betrothal in the house of betrothal. [As to] the benediction of betrothal—what does one say?[6]— Rabin b. R. Adda and Rabbah son of R. Adda both said in the name of Rab Judah: Blessed art Thou, O Lord our God, King of the Universe, who has sanctified us by his commandments and has commanded us concerning the forbidden relations and has forbidden unto us the betrothed[7] and has allowed unto us the wedded[8] through [the marriage] canopy[9] and sanctification.[10] R. Aḥa, the son of Raba, concludes it,[11] in the name of Rab Judah, [with the words]: Blessed art Thou, O Lord, who sanctifies Israel through canopy and sanctification. He who does not seal[12] [holds that] it is analogous to the blessing over fruits and to the benediction [said on performing] religious commandments.[13] And he who seals[14] [holds that] it is analogous to the *ḳiddush*.[15]

marriage held usually at the house of the bridegroom's parents as distinguished from that recited at the betrothal at the house of the parents of the bride. V. *infra*.

(1) V. *infra*. (2) On 'betrothal', v. Glos. *s.v. erusin*. (3) V. p. 29, n. 13. (4) The bridegroom. (5) The bride. Bridegroom and bride are, in the province of Judah, closeted alone after the betrothal, (v. *infra* 12a). [This is forbidden without the benediction having been previously recited. V. Kallah, I.] (6) I.e., what are the words constituting the benediction of betrothal? (7) [Betrothal (*erusin*) without marriage (*nissu'in*) does not permit the bride to the bridegroom.] (8) I.e., the women who are legally married unto their husbands. For the sake of clarity the post-Talmudic versions read: 'those who are wedded *unto us*.' V. Rashi and the Prayer-Books. (9) *Ḥuppah* v. Glos. and Ḳid. (Sonc. ed.) p. 5, n. 7. (10) חופה דקדושין together constitute the complete marriage. [*Var. lec.* (Iṭṭur and others) חופה בקדושין '*Ḥuppah* by means of *Ḳiddushin*', a preferable reading since the act *Ḳiddushin* (betrothal) took place in former days before *Ḥuppah*.] (11) The benediction; i.e., he adds a concluding portion. (12) I.e., does not add the concluding portion. (13) In those blessings there are no concluding portions. [Because their subject matter is praise and not interrupted by

Our Rabbis taught: The blessing of the bridegrooms is said in the presence of ten [persons][1] all the seven days.[2] Rab Judah said: And that is only if new guests[3] come.[4] What does one say?[5] Rab Judah said: 'Blessed art Thou, O Lord our God, King of the Universe, [8a] who has[6] created all things[7] to his glory', and[8] 'the Creator of man', and 'who has created man in his image, in the image of the likeness of his form, and has prepared unto him[9] out of himself[10] a building for ever.[11] Blessed art thou, O Lord, Creator of man'.[12] 'May the barren[13] greatly rejoice and exult[14]

words of supplication or other matter (Rashi). Tosaf.: Because they are short prayers], Cf., e.g., *P.B.* pp. 289-291, 270. (14) I.e., adds a concluding portion. (15) *Kiddush*, 'sanctification', is the special term for the benediction said at the beginning of the Sabbath or a festival. And that benediction has a concluding portion; cf. *P.B.* pp. 124, 230-231, 243. [Because apart from words of praise to God it contains matter in description of the day of rest or the festival (Rashi). Tosaf.: because it is a lengthy prayer.]

(1) Lit., 'with ten'. (2) Following the marriage. (3) Lit., 'new faces'. (4) The benediction of the bridegrooms is said, at the meal, on every day of the seven days if on every succeeding day new guests, that is guests who were not there on the previous day, come to the meal. For a pretty thought as to Sabbath being 'a new guest' v. Tosaf. *a.l.* (5) I.e., What is the text of the benediction? (6) It is common usage to translate in the Prayer Books the perfect verb 'has' in the benediction by 'hast' (created, etc.). (7) Lit., 'all'. (8) I.e., also the benediction of ('the Creator of man'). The words, 'the Creator of man' are preceded by the words, 'Blessed art Thou, O Lord our God, King of the universe,' as in the first benediction. (9) Unto man. (10) Out of man. *P.B.* 'out of his very self.' (11) Lit., 'a building even to perpetuity.' By 'a building for ever', Eve is meant. V. Rashi, *a.l.* and cf. Gen. II. 22. 'A building for ever' contains the idea of '*the mother of all living*' (Gen. III, 20). It is woman that carries the human race. *P.B.* p. 299:—'a perpetual fabric'—expresses well this idea. (12) These three benedictions are based on Gen. I and II. In the first benediction God is praised for the creation of the world ('the all'). In the second benediction God is praised for the creation of man. 'Man' is used here in the sense of 'human being'; cf. Gen. I, 27. In the third benediction God is praised for fashioning man in his image, in the image of the likeness of his form, and for preparing a perpetual building out of man himself. In creating Eve, out of man, God provided for the perpetual renewal of man, of the human being. The divine form of man and the continual re-creation of man, by ever recurring new births, in the divine form, are the subjects of praise in the third benediction while the subject of the second benediction is the creation of man generally. 'The Creator of man', in the concluding portion of the third benediction,

when her children will be gathered[1] in her midst in joy.[2] Blessed art Thou, O Lord, who maketh Zion joyful through[3] her children'[4] 'Mayest Thou make the loved[5] companions greatly to rejoice, even as of old[6] Thou didst gladden Thy creature[7] in the Garden of Eden. Blessed art Thou, O Lord, who maketh bridegroom and bride to rejoice'.[8] 'Blessed art Thou, O Lord our King, God of the universe, who has created joy and gladness, bridegroom and bride, rejoicing, song, mirth, and delight,[9] love, and brotherhood, and peace, and friendship.[10] Speedily, O Lord our God, may be heard in the cities of Judah, and in the streets of Jerusalem, the voice of joy and the voice of gladness, the voice of the bridegroom and the voice of the bride, the voice of the singing[11] of bridegrooms from their canopies[12] and of youths from their feasts[13] of song.

has already the further meaning of the creation of man as expressed in the third benediction. In this respect 'The Creator of Man', in the third benediction, differs from 'The Creator of Man' of the second benediction. This might also explain the difficulty which has been felt to exist in the relationship of these two benedictions (v. the Gemara later and Rashi *a.l.*; v. also Abrahams' Notes, *P.B.* p. ccxvi). (13) I.e., Zion; cf. Isa. LIV. (14) Cf. Isa. LXI, 10 and LXII, 5.

(1) Lit., 'at the gathering of her children.' (2) Cf. Isa. LIV, 1-3. (3) Lit., 'in', 'with'. (4) I.e., by restoring to Zion her children. This benediction seems to have arisen out of Isa. LXII. Cf. especially vv. 4 and 5. And according to Ps. CXXXVII, Jerusalem is to be remembered and set 'above my chiefest joy'; Rashi *a.l.* (fol. 8*a*). (5) I.e., the bridegroom and the bride. (6) The word מקדם in Gen. II, 8, means 'eastward'. Here it is used in the sense of 'in former times', 'of old'. (7) I.e., Adam, by giving him a wife; cf. Gen. II, 23. Adam and Eve rejoiced at their union. And so may the bridegroom and bride rejoice. (8) The last two benedictions do not begin with 'Blessed art Thou, O Lord our God, King of the universe,' because they are in fact prayers. In the first, second and third benedictions God is praised for what he had done. In the fourth as well as in the fifth benediction a *prayer* is uttered that God may cause something to happen, namely joy to Zion, or to the bridegroom and the bride. For another explanation, v. Rashi and Tosaf. *a.l.* V., however, Rashi s.v. משמח. The fifth benediction seems to have resulted from the fourth benediction. V. *supra* n. 4 and cf. Isa. LXII, 5. The two prayers, like the two ideas contained in vv. 4 and 5, were bound up with one another. (9) All these words mean 'joy'. דיצה means 'dancing with joy'. (10) Or, 'fellowship', 'companionship'. (11) Lit., 'breakings forth into song, shouts of joy'. (12) In the Hebrew text the singular is used. Canopy means here 'a bridal chamber'. Cf. Joel II, 16. (13) In the Hebrew text the singular is used.

Blessed art Thou, O Lord, who maketh the bridegroom to rejoice with[1] the bride'.[2]

Levi came[3] to the house of Rabbi to[4] the wedding-feast of R. Simeon his son [and] said five benedictions.[5] R. Assi came[3] to the house of R. Ashi to[4] the wedding-feast of Mar his son [and] said six benedictions.[6] Does it mean to say that they differ in this: that one holds that there was one formation,[7] and the other holds that there were two formations?[8]—No. All[9] agree [that] there was [only] one formation, [but they differ in this:] one holds [that] we go according[10] to the intention,[11] and the other holds [that] we go according[10] to the fact,[12] as that [statement] of Rab Judah [who] asked:[13] It is written, *And God created man in his own image,*[14] and it is written, *Male and female created He them.*[15] How is this [to be

(1) In this benediction the joy referred to is the joy of the bridegroom *with* the bride (Rashi). (2) In this benediction God is praised for the creation of joy in its various forms. Bridegroom and bride represent joy. True joy leads to love and friendship. These six benedictions are recited at Jewish weddings up to this day. The benediction over the wine is added to them, and together they are called 'the Seven Benedictions'. The loftiness of tone and the beauty of style of these benedictions are unsurpassed. The blend of Biblical strength and Midrashic sweetness seems to point to an early date. (3) Lit., 'happened to come'. (4) Lit., 'in'. A more correct translation might be, 'during'. (5) Lit., 'blessed five'. Apparently the second benediction was left out (Rashi). (6) I.e., all the six benedictions. (7) For man and woman. Therefore one benediction for the creation of man and woman is sufficient. This would be the third benediction. (8) One of man and one of woman. (9) Lit., 'the whole world.' (10) Lit., 'after'. (11) The intention was to create two human beings: man and woman. (12) Only man was formed, and woman was 'built' out of him; cf. Gen. II, 7 and 22. (13) Lit., 'to throw up a question'. (14) Gen. I, 27. (15) Gen. V, 2: It seems that R. Judah does not ask his question merely from the first five words of Gen. I, 27, and from the first three words of Gen. V, 2, for in that case there would have been no need for him to refer to Gen. V, 2, since he could have asked the question from the last words of Gen. I, 27 '*male and female he created them*' but his question is from the *whole* verse 27 in Gen. I and from the *whole* verse 2 in Gen. V. The meaning of the question would be this: Gen. I, 27 begins by saying that God created man and ends by saying that man was created as male and female. The last words of Gen. I, 27 would thus shew that there were two creations. Gen. V, 2 begins by saying that God created them male and female, and then it says, *and He blessed them and called their name Man in the day when they were created*. This verse would shew that in

understood]? [In this way:] In the beginning it was the intention[1] [of God] to create two [human beings], and in the end [only] one [human being] was created.

R. Ashi came to the house of R. Kahana.[2] The first day[3] he said all the benedictions.[4] From then and further on;[5] if there were new guests[6] he said all the benedictions, but if not [he declared] it to be merely a continuance of the same joy[7] [in which case] one says [only] the benedictions 'in whose dwelling there is joy'[8] and 'who has created'.[9] From the seventh day to the thirtieth day,[10] whether he[11] said to them[12] 'because of the wedding'[13] or whether he did not say to them 'because of the wedding', one says the benediction 'in whose dwelling there is joy'.[14] From then[15] and further on;[16] if he said to them 'because of the wedding' he says the benediction 'in whose dwelling there is joy', but not otherwise.[17] And if he says to them 'because of the wedding', until when [is this benediction said]?[18]—Said R. Papi in the name of Raba: Twelve

the end there was only one creation. In short: Gen. I, 27, begins with one creation and ends with two creations, and Gen. V, 2, begins with two creations and ends with one creation. This, it seems, is the question of Rab Judah. Rab Judah quoted the verses by quoting the first portions of the verse. He really meant to say 'etc.'—In 'Er. 18*a* and Ber. 61*a* the name is R. Abbahu. In 'Er. 18*a*, *in the image of God hath he created man*, is quoted from Gen. I, 27. In Ber. 61*a*, '*for in the image of God made he man*' (Gen. IX, 6) is quoted. This quotation apparently stands for that of Gen. I, 27. Both in 'Er. 18*a* and Ber. 61*a* '*male and female created He them*' is quoted first.

(1) Lit., 'it went up in the thought', namely of God. A sense of reverence does not allow Rab Judah to mention 'God' after 'thought'. The meaning of the answer is: At first God intended to create two human beings, man and woman (Gen. I, 27). But in the end only man was created by God, and woman was 'built' by God out of man (Gen. V, 2). (2) I.e., to the wedding-feast. (3) The first of the seven days of the wedding festivities, which began after the marriage ceremony; v. *supra* 7*b*. (4) Lit., 'he blessed all of them.' (5) Lit., 'from now'. I.e., from the second day to the end of the seven days. (6) Lit., 'new faces'; cf. *supra* 7*b*. (7) If there were new guests it would be a new occasion for joy. (8) Lit., 'the joy'. (9) The sixth benediction. (10) Lit., 'from seven to thirty.' (11) The host, as a rule the father of the bride. (12) The invited guests. (13) 'I have invited you here to dinner' (Rashi). (14) שהשמחה במעונו, v. p. 35, n. 1. (15) Lit., 'from now'. (16) I.e., after the thirty days. (17) Lit., 'if not, not'. (18) The benediction 'in whose dwelling there is joy'.

months [forming] a year.[1] And at first[2] from when?[3] Said R. Papa:

(1) I.e., the whole of the first year. The phrase 'in whose dwelling there is joy' occurs here for the first time. Commenting on this phrase Rashi says 'at the beginning of the summons (to say Grace).' The words 'in whose dwelling there is joy' are indeed used in the introduction to the Grace after meals at weddings; v. *P.B.* p. 300. Cf. also Abrahams' Notes, p. ccxviii, and Baer, *Seder Abodath Israel*, p. 563. But the question arises: was שהשמחה במעונו said before the Grace after meals in Talmudic times? In our text there is no indication that this was so. Another question is: did the whole benediction consist of the words שהשמחה במעונו? Or were they the initial words of a longer benediction? The benediction אשר ברא 'who has created' mentioned together with it is the sixth benediction, the longest of the six benedictions. One is thus very much tempted to think that שהשמחה במעונו were words of a longer benediction probably introduced by the formula 'Blessed art Thou, O Lord our God, King of the Universe' and said as a substitute for the first five benedictions. The key note of the first five benedictions is joy. Joy speaks out of every benediction; there was joy in the creation of the universe, in the creation of man, in the formation of man and woman. There is joy in the fourth and fifth benedictions. The joy in the first three benedictions is the joy of God. The joy in the fourth and fifth benedictions is also divine joy. The sixth benediction speaks of the joy created by God for man, 'Blessed art Thou, O Lord our God, King of the Universe, who has created joy and gladness,' etc. The joy of the first five benedictions is summarized by the words, 'in whose dwelling there is joy.' There is joy on high, there is joy with God. This joy is spoken of in the first five benedictions. And this joy is also expressed briefly in the words 'in whose dwelling there is joy'. The human joy, created by God, is expressed in the sixth benediction אשר ברא, while שהשמחה במעונו stands for the benediction which was a substitute for the first five benedictions. On the first day of the wedding the six benedictions were said. After the first day, if there were no new guests, two benedictions were said. After the seventh day only one benediction was said. And that benediction was 'in whose dwelling there is joy.' Man's joy began to diminish. So only God's joy was now mentioned. In the time after the Talmud שהשמחה במעונו was given a place in the introduction to the Grace after meals at weddings, instead of being said as a full benediction after Grace, because the full text of this benediction was not mentioned in the Talmud. It may be that the tradition that the full benediction (with 'Blessed art Thou,' etc.) was said, was lost. It was felt that שהשמחה במעונו was left hanging in the air and it was incorporated in the summons to say Grace; v. *P.B.*, p. 300. That the word מעון was chosen to denote the dwelling of God may be due to the fact that it is mentioned in Ḥag. 12*b* as the heavenly region in which the angels sing; v. Abrahams

From the time that they put barley into the mortar.[1] But this is not so? Did not R. Papa busy himself for his son Abba Mar[2] and say the benediction[3] from the time of the betrothal?—It was different [in the case of] R. Papa, because he took the trouble [of preparing everything for the wedding].[4] Rabina busied himself for his son[5] in the house of R. Ḥabiba and said the benediction[3] from the time of the betrothal. He said: I am sure with regard to them that they will not retract [the betrothal].[6] [But] the matter was not successful[7] and they did retract. R. Taḥlifa, son of the West,[8] came to Babylon [and] said six long benedictions.[9] But the law is not according to him. R. Ḥabiba came into the house of a circumcision[10] [and] said the benediction 'in whose dwelling there is joy.' But the law is not according to him, since they are distressed because the child has pain.

R. Naḥman said [that] Rab said: Bridegrooms are of the number, and mourners are not of the number.[11] An objection was raised:

and Baer, *loc. cit.* מעין is there spoken of as the fifth of the seven firmaments. Might there not be in it an allusion to the *five* benedictions, for which the benediction of שהשמחה במעונו is a substitute? (2) Or, 'originally,' i.e., 'before the wedding.' (3) Does one say 'in whose dwelling there is joy'.

(1) Or trough (for brewing beer), or pot (for planting barley for the wedding ceremony). The meaning of this phrase is: from the time that they begin making preparations for the wedding (v. Rashi). (2) I.e., R. Papa had his son engaged to be married. (3) 'In whose dwelling there is joy'. (4) As all preparations for the wedding and the wedding-feast were made, R. Papa felt that he could say the benediction. (5) I.e., Rabina had his son engaged (Rashi). (6) And therefore he said the benediction. (7) Lit., 'the matter was not supported (by divine help). (8) I.e., son of Palestine, Palestinian. It may be that מערבא ('West') was the name of the father of R. Taḥlifa; v. Levy, s.v. But the mention of Babylon seems to support the rendering 'son of the West', 'Palestinian'. (9) He extended the first two benedictions by making additions to them (Rashi). It is possible that 'by long' is meant the full benedictions as they are given on fol. 8*a*, in contradistinction to the short blessing שהשמחה במעונו. (10) I.e., a house in which a circumcision took place, followed by a festive meal. (11) There must be ten male persons for the recital of the six (or seven) 'benedictions of the bridegrooms'; v. *supra* 7*a* and 7*b*. The benediction of the mourners is also said in the presence of ten male persons; v. *infra* 8*b*. R. Naḥman says in the name of Rab that bridegrooms may be of the ten, but mourners may not be of the ten. There must be ten without the mourners.

Bridegrooms and mourners are of the number?—You ask [from] a Baraitha against Rab?[1] Rab is a Tanna and differs![2] It has been said: R. Isaac said [that] R. Joḥanan said: Bridegrooms are of the number, and mourners are not of the number. An objection was raised: Bridegrooms and mourners are of the number?[3]—[8b] With regard to what was that taught?[4] With regard to Grace after meals;[5] [and] with regard to what did R. Joḥanan say [this ruling]?[6] With regard to the line [of comforters].[7] But [then] what of the dictum[8] of which R. Isaac said [that] R. Joḥanan said: 'One says the benediction[9] of the bridegrooms in the presence of ten [male persons] and the bridegrooms are of the number, and [one says] the benediction of the mourners[10] in the presence of ten [male persons] and the mourners are not of the number'—is there a benediction [said] in the line [of comforters]?[11]—But [the answer is]: With regard to what did R. Joḥanan say [this ruling]?[6] with regard to the [benediction recited in the] open space.[12] But [then] what of the dictum which R. Isaac said [that] R. Joḥanan said: 'One says the benediction of the bridegrooms in the presence of ten [male persons] all the seven [days][13] and the bridegrooms are of the number, and [one says] the benediction of the mourners in the presence of ten [male persons] all the seven [days][14] and the mourn-

(1) Lit., 'You throw a Baraitha against Rab.' (2) I.e., Rab's authority is as great as that of a Tanna and he has therefore the right to differ with other Tannaim, Teachers of Mishnah or Baraitha. (3) The same question is asked against R. Joḥanan as was asked against Rab. But the answer which was effective in the case of Rab could not be given with regard to R. Joḥanan. Therefore different answers are attempted; v. *infra* 8b. (4) Lit., 'When was that taught'. In the Baraitha (that mourners are also of the number). (5) Lit., 'the benediction of food'. (6) That mourners are not of the number. (7) The line of comforters which was formed to offer consolation to the mourners after a burial, v. Sanh. 19a. (8) Lit., 'But as to this that'. (9) 'The blessing, or benediction, of the bridegrooms' has a collective sense. The six (or seven) benedictions are meant. (10) Has also a collective sense; v. *infra*. (11) Does one say benedictions in the line that is formed, after the burial of the dead, so that the friends may comfort the mourners? There only words of comfort are said, but no benedictions. In Sanh. 19a one word of comfort is mentioned: תתנחמו 'be comforted'. (12) The benedictions of the mourners were said in the open space, v. *infra*. (13) Of the wedding festivities. (14) Of mourning.

ers are not of the number—is the benediction [recited in] the open space said all the seven days?[1]—It is possible in the presence of new friends[2]—as in the case of[3] R. Ḥiyya, the son of Abba, [who was] the Bible teacher of the son[4] of Resh Laḳish, or, as some say,[5] the Mishnah teacher of the son of Resh Laḳish. [It happened as follows:] A child [of R. Ḥiyya, the son of Abba] died.[6] The first day[7] he [Resh Laḳish] did not go to him. The next day[8] he [Resh Laḳish] took with him[9] Judah the son of Naḥmani,[10] his *meturgeman*,[11] [and] said to him: Rise [and] say something[12] with regard to[13] [the death of] the child. He spoke[14] and said: [It is written,] *And the Lord saw and spurned, because of the provoking of His sons and His daughters.*[15] [This means, in] a generation [in which

(1) Lit., 'Is there a benediction of the open space all the seven days?' (2) Lit., 'Thou wilt find it in (the case of) new faces'. When new friends come to visit the mourners for the first time during the seven days, the benediction of mourners is said in the free space. (3) Lit., 'as that of.' (4) So MS.M.; cur. edd. 'sons'. (5) Lit., 'and some say.' (6) It was R. Ḥiyya's child that died and not Resh Laḳish's. Resh Laḳish went to comfort R. Ḥiyya and took his (Resh Laḳish's) *meturgeman* (v. *infra*) with him. Some scholars go wrong in the rendering of this passage. V., for instance, Levy p. 303, Bacher rightly speaks of the death of the young child of R. Ḥiyya. (7) I.e., the first day of R. Ḥiyya's mourning. (8) Lit., 'on the morrow.' (9) Lit., 'led him.' (10) Judah the son of Naḥmani, is mentioned several times as the *meturgeman* of Resh Laḳish; v. e.g. Soṭ. 37b, Giṭ. 60b, (also Tem. 14b), and Sanh. 7b. (11) 'Interpreter'. As to his function v. *J.E.*, vol. VIII, p. 521, and vol. I, p. 527, n. 1. One sentence may be quoted from the last-named article. 'In a limited sense it ('the interpreter,' Amora, or *meturgeman*) signifies the officer who stood at the side of the lecturer or presiding teacher in the academy and in meetings for public instruction, and announced loudly, and explained to the large assembly in an oratorical manner, what the teacher had just expressed briefly and in a low voice.' The *meturgeman* was, therefore, a sort of assistant lecturer. Judah the son of Naḥmani, was assistant lecturer to Resh Laḳish. He was also a good preacher who expounded well Biblical verses homiletically (cf. e.g., Sanh. 7b). He could also recite benedictions by heart. Cf. Giṭ. 60b and Tem. 14b. For these reasons apparently Resh Laḳish took with him Judah the son of Naḥmani, when he paid a visit of condolence to R. Ḥiyya, the son of Abba. Judah spoke on behalf of Resh Laḳish. (12) Lit., 'a word', 'a thing.' (13) Lit., 'corresponding to', 'vis-à-vis'. (14) Lit., 'he opened.' This probably means: he opened his mouth (and said); cf. Job III, 1. It may also mean: he opened his discourse; v. the Dictionaries of Levy and Jastrow, s.v. Here the first meaning seems to be more likely. (15) Deut. XXXII, 19.

the fathers spurn the Holy One, blessed be He, He is angry with their sons and their daughters and they die when they are young.[1] And some say [that] he [the child of R. Ḥiyya, the son of Abba, that died] was a young man[2] and that he [Judah the son of Naḥmani] said thus to him:[3] *Therefore the Lord shall have no joy in their young men, neither shall He have compassion on their fatherless and widows; for every one is profane and an evil-doer, and every mouth speaketh folly. For all this His anger is not turned away, but His hand is stretched out still.*[4] (What is the meaning[5] of '*but His hand is stretched out still*'? Said R. Ḥanan, the son of Rab:[6] All know for what purpose[7] a bride is brought into the bridal chamber, but whoever disgraces his mouth and utters[8] a word of folly—even if a [divine] decree[9] of seventy years of happiness[10] were sealed [and granted] unto him,[11] it is turned for him into evil.)—He came to comfort, [and] he grieved him?—Thus he said to him: Thou art important enough to be held responsible[12] for [the shortcomings of] the generation.[13] He[14] [then] said to him:[15] Rise [and] say something with regard to the praise of the Holy One, blessed be He. He spoke and said: The God,[16] who is great in the abundance of His greatness, mighty and strong in the multitude of awe-inspiring deeds, who reviveth the dead with his word,[17] who does great things that are unsearchable[18] and wondrous works without number.[19] Blessed art Thou, O Lord, who revivest the dead.[20] He[21] then said to him:[22] Rise [and] say

(1) Lit., 'small'. (2) I.e., a grown-up son, not a small child. (3) To R. Ḥiyya, the son of Abba. (4) Isa. IX, 16. (5) Lit., 'What?' 'Why?' (6) In Shab. 33*a*: b. Raba. (7) Lit., 'for what.' (8) Lit., 'brings forth from his mouth.' (9) Lit., 'a decree of His judgment.' (10) Lit., 'for good.' (11) I.e., even if it was decreed in heaven that he should have seventy years of happiness, cf. R.H. 16*b*. (12) Lit., 'to be seized'. (13) Cf. Shab. 33*b*: 'the righteous men are seized for (the shortcomings of) the generation.' V. Rashi *a.l.* (14) Resh Laḳish. (15) Judah the son of Naḥmani. (16) According to Rashi the words 'Blessed art Thou, O Lord our God, King of the Universe,' are to be supplemented before 'The God,' etc. (17) This phrase occurs also in the abbreviated *Amida* prayer said on Friday night, v. *P.B.* p. 120. (18) Lit., 'until there is no searching.' Cf. Ps. CXLV, 3. (19) Lit., 'until there is no number.' Cf. Ps. CXLVII, 5. The whole phrase occurs also in the evening service prayer v. *P.B.*, p. 99. (20) This benediction is, in its main ideas, reminiscent of the first three benedictions of the *Amida*. (21) Resh Laḳish. (22) Judah the son of Naḥmani.

something with regard to the mourners. He spoke and said: Our brethren, who are worn out, who are crushed by this bereavement,[1] set your heart to consider[2] this: This it is [that] stands for ever,[3] it is a path from the six days of creation.[4] Many have drunk, many will drink,[5] as the drinking of the first ones, so will be that of the last ones. Our brethren, the Lord of consolation comfort you. Blessed be He who comforteth the mourners. (Said Abaye: 'Many have drunk' he should have said, 'many will drink' one should not have said, 'the drinking of the first ones', he should have said, 'the drinking of the last ones' one should not have said, for R. Simeon, the son of Laḳish,[6] said, and so one has taught in the name of R. Jose: Man should never open his mouth to Satan.[7] Said R. Joseph: What text [shows this]? *We should have been as Sodom, we should have been like unto Gomorrah.*[8] What did He[9] reply unto him?[10] *Hear the word of the Lord, ye rulers of Sodom,* etc.[11]) He[12] [then] said to him:[13] Rise [and] say something with regard to the comforters of the mourners.[14] He spoke and said: Our brethren, bestowers of lovingkindnesses, sons of bestowers of lovingkindnesses, who hold fast to the covenant of Abraham our father[15] [for it is said, *For I have known him, to the end that he may command his children,* etc.],[16] our brethren, may the Lord of recompense pay you your reward. Blessed art Thou who payest the recompense. He[17] [then] said unto him:[18] Rise [and] say something with regard

(1) Lit., 'by this mourning.' (2) Cf. I Chron. XXII, 18. (3) Rashi adds: that all die, and you should not weep too much. (4) Lit., 'in the beginning'. (5) From the cup of sorrow. (6) I.e., Resh Laḳish. (7) That is, one should never utter ominous words and thus invite misfortune. (8) Isa. I, 9. (9) God. (10) Unto Isaiah. (11) Isa. I, 10. Because Isaiah compared the people to Sodom and Gomorrah, God addressed them as 'rulers of Sodom,' 'people of Gomorrah.' This is to illustrate how ominous words can have an evil effect. (12) Resh Laḳish. (13) Judah the son of Naḥmani. (14) The friends who came to comfort the mourners. (15) Rashi adds: who bestowed lovingkindnesses. The meaning is: who are carrying out the trust with which Abraham was charged, also for future generations; v. next note. (16) The passage is bracketed also in the original. The verse continues: *and his household after him, that they may keep the way of the Lord, to do righteousness and justice; to the end that the Lord may bring upon Abraham that which He has spoken of him;* Gen. XVIII, 19. (17) Resh Laḳish. (18) Judah the son of Naḥmani.

to the whole of Israel. He spoke and said: Master of the worlds, redeem and save, deliver [and] help Thy people Israel from pestilence,[1] and from the sword, and from plundering,[2] and from the blast, and from the mildew, and from all kinds of calamities that [may] break forth and come into[3] the world. Before we call, mayest Thou answer.[4] Blessed art Thou who stayest the plague.[5] 'Ulla

(1) Lit., 'the pestilence.' (2) Lit., 'the spoil', 'the plunder'. (3) Lit., 'to'. (4) Lit., 'and thou wilt answer'. (5) Cf. Num. XVII, 13, 15; XXV, 8; II Sam. XXIV, 21, 25; Ps. CVI, 30. It is now time to deal with one or two points arising out of what we are told on this page (folio 8*b*) about the visit of Resh Laḳish and his *meturgeman*, Judah the son of Naḥmani, to R. Ḥiyya the son of Abba, on the occasion of the death of R. Ḥiyya's child. The story of this visit was introduced in order to show that there is ברכת רחבה during all the seven days of mourning if new friends are present on each occasion. Now, what is ברכת רחבה? This question has not been answered yet. In the time of the Gaonim the tradition concerning it had faded already. In *Shiṭṭah Meḳubbeẓeth* on Keth. 8*b* three different views are quoted. The view mentioned in Naḥmanides' *Toroth ha-Adam* ed. Venice, p. 50*a*, is again different. The explanation attempted by Krauss in the *Jahrbuch der jüd.-lit. Gesellschaft*, vol. XVII (1926), pp. 238-239 (v. also Krauss, *Jahresbericht XXXVII-XXXIX Isr.-Theol. Lehranstalt* in Wien, p. 60f) is unsatisfactory. בית האבל in Kethuboth 8*b* is not inaccurate (v. *Jahrbuch*, p. 238). The emendation suggested by Krauss (*Jahresbericht*, p. 60) for מאי ברכת אבלים ברכת רחבה (Meg. 23*b*) is unacceptable. In Tractate Soferim ch. XIX ברכת רחבה is not mentioned. The quotation from Hai and Sherira in *Shiṭṭah Meḳubbeẓeth* concludes with the words: 'As much as we have heard, we never heard that the ברכת רחבה was in vogue in Babylon'. The following explanation may however be briefly submitted:—רחבה in this connection has nothing to do with רחוב public place. It is, rather, the open space behind the house (of the mourner). V. Er. 24*a-b* and Krauss, *T.A.* vol. I, p. 48, and p. 361, n. 633. ברכת רחבה would thus mean the blessing of the mourners said in the open space behind the house of the mourner. When ten or more friends came to comfort the mourner there was, at any rate in many cases, no room in the house for all the visitors, and the mourners sat in the open space behind the house and the guests assembled there, and the benedictions ברכת אבלים, were recited before the assembly in the open space. רחבה was therefore almost identical with the בית האבל. Therefore, when it is said in Meg. 23*b* מאי ברכת אבלים ברכת רחבה this statement is entirely correct. (לא אזל לגביה) can only mean that he (Resh Laḳish) did not go to him (to the mourner). The next day he did go to him, namely, to his house, or to the open space behind the house. What Krauss, *Jahrbuch*, p. 239, says

said, and some say [that] it was taught in a Baraitha: Ten cups [of wine] the scholars have instituted [to be drunk] in the house of the mourner: Three before the meal in order to open the small bowels, three during the meal in order to dissolve the food in the bowels, and four after the meal: one corresponding to 'who feedeth',[1] one corresponding to the blessing of 'the land',[1] one corresponding to 'who rebuildeth Jerusalem',[1] and one corresponding to 'who is good and doeth good'.[1] They [then] added unto them

on לגביה cannot be accepted.) The story on this page (folio 8*b*) confirms this interpretation. Resh Laḳish and his *meturgeman* went to R. Ḥiyya, that is, they went to his house, or to the open space near his house. Judah, the son of Naḥmani, delivered there a homily and recited four benedictions. And these benedictions are called ברכת רחבה and ברכת אבלים That is: The ברכת אבלים, which was recited in the רחבה, was also called ברכת רחבה and required the presence of ten new guests. Whether this ברכת רחבה required a cup of benediction is difficult to say. In *Toroth ha-Adam* p. 48*b* it says: Some say that ברכת רחבה requires a cup; cf. however ibid. 49*a*, where the view of R. Paltai seems to be that it had no 'cup' attached to it. In the story on this page (folio 8*b*) no 'cup' is mentioned. It might have been implied. It may be that the סעודת הבראה (the meal given by friends to the mourners after the funeral) also took place in this רחבה. Cf. M.Ḳ. 25*a*. The ברכת רחבה fell, apparently, early into disuse, so that in post-Talmudic times its real character was not known any more. It is difficult to see why these benedictions disappeared from use. They are beautiful in thought and language, especially benedictions 1 and 2. These two benedictions deserve to be reinstated. Another point that should be noted is this: Judah the son of Naḥmani, did not give his own sayings. The homily which he delivered was not his own. The benedictions which he recited had long been fixed. Cf. Rashi, *ad loc.* וכן סדורות על הסדר. It is strange that Graetz thinks that Judah the son of Naḥmani improvised these beautiful prayers and that these prayers shew that Judah was a fine Hebrew stylist. Judah the son of Naḥmani was a *meturgeman*, and a *meturgeman* was not expected to say original things. He knew by heart the homilies of others and the fixed benedictions, and he delivered the homilies well and he recited the benedictions well. It is interesting to note that קום אימא מילתא was said to the *Meturgeman*, although the מילתא was not his. Cf. also *Shiṭṭah Meḳubbeẓeth:* והא דאמרינן קום אימא מילתא סדורא בעלמא אמר ליה אבל הני ברכות מעיקרא איתקון

(1) 'Who feedeth' is the first benediction of Grace after meals, the blessing of 'the land' is the second, 'who rebuildeth Jerusalem' is the third, and 'who is good and doeth good' is the fourth. V. *P.B.*, pp. 280-283; cf. Ber. 48*b*.

[another] four [cups]: one in honour of the officers of the town, and one in honour of the leaders of the town, and one in honour of the Temple, and one in honour of Rabban Gamaliel. [When] they began to drink [too much] and to become intoxicated, they restored the matter to its original state.[1] What [about] Rabban Gamaliel?—As it has been taught: At first the carrying out of the dead[2] was harder for his relatives[3] than his death,[4] so that they left him[5] and ran away, until Rabban Gamaliel[6] came and adopted a simple style and they carried him out[7] in garments of linen, and [then] all the people followed his example and carried out [the dead][8] in garments of linen. Said R. Papa: And now it is the general practice [to carry out the dead] even in rough cloth worth [only] a *zuz*.[9]

R. Eleazar said: [9a] He who says, I have found an 'open opening'[10] is trusted to make her forbidden for him.[11] Why?[12] It is a double doubt:[13] It is a doubt [whether she had the intercourse with the other man while] under him,[14] or[15] [while] not under him.[16] And if you say[17] that [she had that intercourse while] under him, [there is] the [other] doubt [whether she had that intercourse] by violence or[18] by [her free] will!—It was necessary[19] [to state

(1) Lit., 'to its old state.' Cf. Sem. ch. XIV, where the text is somewhat different and the order of the 'cups' varies. (2) I.e., the funeral. (3) The relatives of the dead. (4) Because of the great expense. They buried the dead in costly garments (Rashi). (5) The dead. (6) I.e., Rabban Gamaliel II, also called Rabban Gamaliel of Jabneh. (7) For variant, cf. M.Ḳ. 27*b*. (8) For burial. (9) A silver coin, one fourth of a *sheḳel*. (10) 'An open opening' is a euphemistic expression for 'absence of virginity'. The husband, after the first intercourse with his young wife, claims that he found no virginity. (11) V. *infra*. (12) Lit., 'And why?'—The question is: Why should his wife become forbidden for him by what he said regarding the absence of her virginity? (13) Lit., 'the doubt of a doubt'. (14) Under her husband, that is, since the betrothal (*erusin*); in which case she is regarded as an adulteress who is forbidden to live with her husband. V. Sanh. 51*a*. (15) Lit., 'A doubt'. (16) Before her betrothal. (17) Lit., 'If thou wilt be found (consequently) to say.' (18) If a betrothed (or married) woman is violated by another man she does not become forbidden for her husband. V. *infra* 51*b*; v. also Deut. XXII, 25-27. (19) Lit., 'not necessary', i.e., it would not have been necessary but for the case of the wife of a priest. The meaning is: the rule applies in the case of the wife of a priest.

this rule] in the case of the wife of a priest.[1] And if you wish, you may say [that it speaks of] the wife of an Israelite,[2] and for instance when her father received the betrothal for her [when] she was less than three years and one day old.[3] What does he[4] let us hear by [this since] we have already learnt [it]:[5] 'If a man says[6] to a woman, "I have betrothed thee [to myself]", and she says, "Thou hast not betrothed me [to thyself]," she is allowed [to marry] his relatives, but he is forbidden [to marry] her relatives.'[7]—What you might have supposed is that there[8] [he causes a prohibition to himself] because it is certain to him,[9] but here it is not quite certain to him.[10] [Therefore] he[11] lets us hear [this rule].[12] But did R. Eleazar say so? Did not R. Eleazar say: The wife does not become forbidden for her husband save in the case of[13] warning[14] and seclusion,[15] and as [we find in] the occurrence that happened?[16]—But how can you [in any case] understand it?[17] Was the occurrence that happened accompanied by warning and seclusion? And again, did they[18] declare her[19] forbidden?[20]—This is no difficulty, [for] thus he[21] means to say:[22] The wife does not become forbidden for her husband save in the case of warning and seclusion, [and this we learn]

(1) If the wife of a priest was violated she was forbidden for her husband. V. *infra* 51*b*, and Yeb. 56*b*. (2) I.e., an ordinary Jew, not a priest. (3) In this case there is only one doubt: whether she was violated, or submitted by her free will. The other doubt ('under him' or 'not under him') does not arise, since in the latter case her virginity would not be affected. V. Ned. 44*b*. (4) R. Eleazar (an Amora). (5) That a man may, by his own evidence, prohibit for himself a thing or a person otherwise permitted to him. (6) Lit., 'he who says'. (7) The forbidden degrees of relatives by marriage; v. Ḳid. 65*a*. (8) Ḳid. 65*a*. (9) Lit., 'it is certainly established to him.' (10) His grievance may be imaginary. (11) R. Eleazar. (12) That he is believed. (13) Lit., 'over the affairs of'. (14) Given to the wife by the suspecting husband. (15) Of the wife with the suspected man. V. Num. V, 11ff; cf. Soṭ. 2*a* and 2*b*. (16) Lit., 'according to the deed that was'. I.e., of David and Bath-sheba; cf. II Sam. XI. This contradicts the dictum of R. Eleazar that the woman becomes forbidden on a mere charge by her husband of an 'open opening'. (17) This latter dictum of R. Eleazar. (18) The authorities. (19) Bath-sheba. (20) [For Uriah. The fact that she was allowed to marry David shews that she was not forbidden to Uriah, for it is a general rule that an adulteress is forbidden to continue with her husband as well as her paramour. Soṭ. 27*b*.] (21) R. Eleazar. (22) Lit., 'he says'.

from the occurrence that happened, because [there] there was no warning and seclusion and [therefore] she[1] was not forbidden.[2] But [the former question] is nevertheless difficult. In the [case of] warning and seclusion but not [in the case of] 'an open opening'![3] —But according to your argument[4] [the question could be asked]: [In the case of] warning and seclusion, yes, [and in the case of] witnesses,[5] no! Hence he[6] means to say thus: The wife does not become forbidden for her husband through one witness[7] but through two witnesses;[8] but in the case of warning and seclusion:[9] even through one witness,[10] and 'an open opening' is like two witnesses.[11] And if you will say: [In the case of] the occurrence that happened, why did they not declare her forbidden?[12] [The answer is:] There it was compulsion.[13] And if you wish you can say as R. Samuel the son of Naḥmani said[14] [that] R. Jonathan said: [9b] Everyone who goes out into the war of the House of David writes for his wife a deed of divorce,[15] for it is written, *And to thy brethren shalt thou bring greetings, and take their pledge.*[16] What

(1) Bath-sheba. (2) For Uriah. V. p. 44, n. 20. (3) Lit., 'warning . . . yes; an open . . . no.' I.e., the words of R. Eleazar imply that the wife would be forbidden for her husband only in case of warning and seclusion, but not in the case of 'an open opening', which contradicts his former ruling. (4) If you are to argue from the implications of R. Eleazar's words as they stand. (5) Why should the evidence of witnesses that the wife was unfaithful be weaker than warning and seclusion? Surely this cannot be! (6) R. Eleazar. (7) By the evidence of one witness that the wife was unfaithful; v. Rashi *ad loc.* (8) By the evidence of two witnesses. (9) Where there are two witnesses to the warning and seclusion. (10) If even only one witness testified to the adultery that followed she is forbidden to her husband. V. Soṭ. 2*b*. (11) I.e., the charge of an 'open opening' by her husband is on a par with the evidence of two witnesses. (12) For David, seeing that many people knew of the occurrence, and thus there were witnesses. (13) Bath-sheba could not resist the demand of the king. [And since she was thus not forbidden to Uriah, she was permitted also to David. (V. *supra* p. 44, n. 20)]. (14) Lit., 'as that which R. Samuel the son of Naḥmani said'. (15) [So that in case he falls in battle his wife should be free to marry without the necessity of *ḥaliẓah*. The *Get* would in that case take effect retrospectively from the date of its writing (Rashi). Tosaf.: He writes a *Get* without any conditions to take effect immediately.] (16) I Sam. XVII, 18.

[is the meaning of], *'and take their pledge'?* R. Joseph learnt: Things which are pledged between him and her.[1]

Abaye said: We have also learned[2] [this]:[3] A MAIDEN IS MARRIED ON THE FOURTH DAY OF THE WEEK. [This implies] only on the fourth day, but not the fifth day.[4] What is the reason? [Presumably] on account of the cooling of the temper.[5] Now in which respect [could the cooling of the mind have a bad result]? If with regard to giving her the *kethubah*,[6] let him give it to her.[7] Consequently[8] [we must say only] with regard to making her forbidden for him;[9] and [it is a case where] he puts forward a claim.[10] Is it not that he puts forward the claim of 'an open opening'?[11] — No, [it is a case where] he puts forward the claim of blood.[12]

Rab Judah said [that] Samuel said: If any one says, 'I have found an open opening', he is trusted to cause her to lose her *kethubah*. Said R. Joseph: What does he[13] let us hear? We have [already] learned [this]:[14] He who eats[15] at his father-in-law's [between the time of betrothal and the time of marriage] in Judaea,[16] without witnesses, cannot [after the marriage] raise the claim of [the loss of] virginity, because he is alone with her.[17] In Judaea he

(1) I.e., the betrothals; these thou shalt take from them by a deed of divorce (Rashi). (2) We have been taught in a Mishnah; v. *supra* 2a. (3) That the claim of 'an open opening' makes the wife forbidden for the husband. (4) Lit., 'on the fourth day, yes, on the fifth day, no.' (5) The husband might be appeased by the following Monday; cf. *supra* 2a and 5a. (6) V. Glos. (7) No harm is done by this. There is no sin involved in the payment of the marriage settlement to the wife, even if, in law, she forfeited it through her conduct. (8) Lit., 'but'. (9) If her conduct makes her forbidden for the husband for marital intercourse then the disregard of this prohibition would involve a sin. And therefore a maiden marries on the fourth day of the week so that there should be no 'cooling of the mind'. (10) I.e., the husband must have put forward a serious claim. (11) As evidence of unfaithfulness. This proves that the charge of an 'open opening' by the husband renders his wife forbidden to him. (12) I.e., he claims that there was no bleeding. And this is a more manifest sign of the absence of virginity, evidencing unfaithfulness, than 'an open opening'. (13) Rab Judah. (14) In a Mishnah; cf. *infra* 12a. (15) I.e., he who frequently visits the house of the father of his betrothed bride. (16) This was customary in Judaea. (17) And might have had intimate relations with the bride.

cannot raise this claim, but in Galilee[1] he can raise it. Now in which respect? If to make her forbidden for him, why [should he] not [be able to raise this claim] in Judaea?[2] Consequently[3] [we must say it is] to cause her to lose her *kethubah;*[4] and [it is in a case] when he raises a claim. Is it not that he raises the claim of 'an open opening'?—No, when he raises the claim of blood.[5] [10a] It was stated: Rab Naḥman said [that] Samuel said in the name of R. Simeon b. Eleazar: The scholars ordained for the daughters of Israel [as follows]: for a maiden two hundred [*zuz*[6]] and for a widow a *maneh*[7] [one hundred *zuz*].[8] And they trusted him, so that when he said, 'I have found an open opening', he is believed.[9] If so, what have the Sages accomplished with their ordinance?[10]—Said Raba: The presumption is [that] no one will take the trouble of preparing a [wedding-]feast and will then spoil it.[11] One has taught: Since it[12] is a fine [instituted] by the Sages she[13] shall collect only from the worst land[14] [of the husband's estate]. [You say] a fine! Why a fine?[15]—Say then: since it is an ordinance of the Sages,[16] she shall collect only from the worst land [of the husband's estate]. Rabban Simeon b. Gamaliel says: The *kethubah* of a wife is from the Torah.[17] But did Rabban Simeon b. Gamaliel say so? Surely it has been taught: [It is written in the Torah] *He shall pay money according to the dowry of virgins;*[18] [this teaches us that] this[19] is [as much] as the dowry of the virgins[20] and the dowry of the virgins is [as much] as

(1) In Galilee that custom (v. p. 46, n. 16) did not prevail. (2) If he is sure that he has not been intimate with her during the time of betrothal and he charges her with unfaithfulness, he renders her, by the mere charge, forbidden to him? (3) Lit., 'but'. (4) In Judaea he cannot make her lose the *kethubah*, because he might have been intimate with her during the period of betrothal. (5) And therefore Samuel's statement is necessary. (6) V. Glos. (7) V. Glos. (8) As her *kethubah*. V. *infra* 10*b*. (9) And she loses the *kethubah*. (10) If he can make her lose the *kethubah* by the claim of an 'open opening'. (11) No one will go to the trouble and expense of a wedding and then waste it all by an invented claim. If he makes such a charge, he is, no doubt, telling the truth. (12) The *kethubah*. (13) The wife. (14) Cf. also B.Ḳ. 7*b* and 8*a*. (15) Why do you call it a fine? And why should it be a fine? (16) I.e., a Rabbinical, and not a Biblical, ordinance. (17) I.e., an ordinance of the Bible. (18) Ex. XXII, 16. (19) The payment for the enticement of the virgin. (20) I.e., fifty pieces of silver, the fine inflicted for violating a virgin, v. Deut. XXII, 27.

this.[1] But,[2] the Sages found a support for [the rule that] the *kethubah* of a wife is from the Torah. Rabban Simeon b. Gamaliel says: The *kethubah* of a wife is not from the words of the Bible, but from the words of the *Soferim!*[3]—Reverse it.[4] And why does it appear to you right to reverse[5] the latter [teaching]? Reverse the former [teaching]![6]—We have [already] heard that R. Simeon the son of Gamaliel said that the *kethubah* is from the Bible, for we learnt: Rabban Simeon b. Gamaliel says: He[7] gives her[8] [the *kethubah*] in Cappadocian coins.[9] And if you wish, you may say: The whole of it[10] is [according to] Rabban Simeon b. Gamaliel, only[11] it is defective[12] and it teaches thus:[13] Here the Sages found a support for [the rule that] the *kethubah* of a wife is from the Torah. The *kethubah* of a widow [however] is not from the words of the Torah but from the words of the *Soferim*, for Rabban Simeon b. Gamaliel says: The *kethubah* of a widow is not from the words of the Torah but from the words of the *Soferim*.[14]

Someone came before R. Naḥman [and] said to him: I have found an open opening.[15] R. Naḥman answered:[16] Lash him with palm-switches; harlots[17] lie prostrate before him.[18] But it is R.

(1) The *'silver pieces'* referred to are *shekels*, not *ma'ahs*, v. *infra* 38*a*. (2) Lit., 'from here', i.e., from the phrase *'dowry of virgins'*. (3) The *Soferim*, or scribes, were the learned men who succeeded Ezra during a period of about two hundred years. Rabban Simeon b. Gamaliel therefore holds that the *kethubah* was a Rabbinical, and not a Biblical, ordinance. (4) The answer is: Reverse the reading and say that Rabban Simeon b. Gamaliel said that in the Scriptural verse mentioned is to be found a support for the rule that the *kethubah* of a wife is from the Bible, and that the first Tanna said that it was not Biblical but 'from the words of the *Soferim*'. (5) Lit., 'And why do you see that you should reverse.' (6) Where it says that Rabban Simeon b. Gamaliel holds that the *kethubah* of a wife is from the Torah. (7) The husband. (8) The wife. (9) They were more valuable than the Palestinian coins. The husband has to pay in Cappadocian coins because the *kethubah* is from the Bible; v. *infra* 110*b*. (10) Of the teaching of the Baraitha mentioned before. (11) Lit., 'and'. (12) A clause is missing. (13) I.e., the Baraitha should be read thus. (14) According to this version of the Baraitha, R. Simeon b. Gamaliel holds that the *kethubah* of the maiden-wife is Biblical and that the *kethubah* of the widow-wife is rabbinical. (15) He (the husband) raised this complaint about his newly wedded wife. (16) Lit., 'said to him', i.e., concerning him. (17) V. Levy, Vol. III,

Naḥman who said that he [the husband] is believed![1]—He is believed, but [at the same time] one lashes him with palm-switches. R. Aḥai answered: Here[2] [it speaks] of a young man,[3] there [it speaks] of one who was married before.[4]

Some one came before Rabban Gamaliel [and] said to him, I have found an 'open opening'. He [Rabban Gamaliel] answered him: Perhaps you moved aside.[5] I will give you an illustration: To what is this like? To a man who was walking in the deep darkness of the night[6] [and came to his house and found the door locked];[7] if he moves aside [the bolt[8] of the door] he finds it open, if he does not move aside [the bolt of the door] he finds it locked. Some say [that] he [R. Gamaliel] answered him thus: Perhaps you moved aside wilfully[9] and you tore away the door and the bar.[10] I will give you an illustration: To what is this like? To a man who was walking in the deep darkness of the night [and came to his house and found the door locked]; if he moves aside [the bolt of the door] wilfully[11] he finds it open, if he does

p. 2. Rashi: 'the harlots of Mabrakta'. [Mabrakta was a place in the neighbourhood of Maḥoza, v. Obermeyer, p. 177.] (18) I.e., such a man ought to be punished, for if he is such an expert in these matters he must have led an immoral life.

(1) If the husband says that he has not found virginity in his wife. Why should he then be lashed for having complained to R. Naḥman about his wife? (2) Where R. Naḥman ordered punishment. (3) Who was not married before. He would not have known if he had not had intercourse with harlots before his marriage. There R. Naḥman ordered lashing. (4) And therefore he could know without having led an immoral life. He is therefore believed and receives no lashing (Rashi). It is also possible that according to R. Aḥai both are believed. R. Aḥai only explains that it is the young man who gets the birch. (5) And thus performed the coition without tearing the hymen. V. Jast. p. 898. (6) Lit., 'in the blackness of night and darkness'; cf. Prov. VII, 9. (7) Some such words as these must be inserted. (8) 'He moved aside', and 'he did not move aside' refer apparently to the bolt of the door and not to the door itself. The simile is obvious: the bolt is compared to the membrum virile. He moved the membrum virile aside and therefore found 'an open opening'. (9) Intentionally. (10) The 'door', 'door-way', 'entrance', apparently refers to the vagina, or the entrance into the vagina, and 'the bar' to the hymen. He intentionally moved so forcibly that he tore open the entrance and swept away the hymen without feeling it. (11) The action must be intentional. The chief point of this

not move aside [the bolt of the door] wilfully he finds it locked.

Some one came before Rabban Gamaliel the son of Rabbi [and] said to him, 'My master, I have had intercourse [with my newly-wedded wife] and I have not found any blood.' She [the wife] said to him, 'My master, I was a virgin.' He said to them: Bring me that cloth.[1] They brought him the cloth, and he soaked it in water and he washed it and he found on it a good many drops of blood.[2] [Thereupon] he [Rabban Gamaliel] said to him [the husband]: Go, be happy with thy bargain.[3] Huna Mar the son of Raba of Paraziḳa,[4] said to R. Ashi: Shall we also do it?[5] He answered him: [10b] Our[6] laundry work[7] is like their[8] washing.[9] And if you will say let us do laundry work,[10] [my answer is] the smoothing stone will remove it.[11]

Someone came before Rabban Gamaliel the son of Rabbi [and] said to him, 'My master, I have had intercourse [with my newly-wedded wife] and I have not found any blood.' She [the wife] said to him, 'My master, I am still a virgin.' He [then] said to them: Bring me two handmaids, one [who is] a virgin and one who had intercourse with a man. They brought to him [two such handmaids], and he placed them upon a cask of wine. [In the case of]

version seems to be the wilful intention. The bolt of a door cannot, as a rule, be moved aside accidentally. There must be intention in the action.

(1) Upon which they spent the night. (2) The blood was covered by semen. (3) Lit., 'take possession of' a phrase in which there is also an element of joy. 'Be happy with' expresses well the spirit of the decision. Rabban Gamaliel himself was happy that he could keep together and strengthen the bond of marriage between husband and wife. (4) Faransag, near Bagdad. (5) I.e., apply in such cases the test applied by Rabban Gamaliel to the cloth. (6) Babylonian. (7) גיהוין is fine laundry work. (8) Palestinian. (9) כיבוס is plain washing. In Palestine the plain washing was better than in Babylonia, because the water in Palestine was better or because they had in Palestine better ingredients (Rashi). In order to get the same results they would have to do fine laundry work in Babylonia, and that would include smoothing the cloth with a stone, according to Rashi, with a gloss-stone. (10) Let us apply גיהוין to the cloth on which the bride and bridegroom slept. (11) The blood. In the process of גיהוין the stone with which the cloth would be smoothed would cause the drops of blood, which would be seen after plain washing, to disappear. The test of Rabban Gamaliel could therefore not be employed in Babylonia.

the one who was no more a virgin its smell[1] went through,[2] [in the case of] the virgin the smell did not go through.[3] He [then] placed this one [the young wife] also [on a cask of wine], and its smell[4] did not go through. He[5] [then] said to him:[6] Go, be happy with thy bargain.[7]—But he should have examined her from the very beginning![8]—He had heard a tradition,[9] but he had not seen it done in practice,[10] and he thought, The matter might not be certain[11] and it would not be proper[12] to deal lightly with daughters of Israel.[13]

Someone came before Rabban Gamaliel the elder [and] said to him, 'My master, I have had intercourse [with my newly-wedded wife] and I have not found any blood. She [the wife] said to him, 'My master, I am of the family of Dorkaṭi, [the women of] which have neither blood of menstruation nor blood of virginity.' Rabban Gamaliel investigated among her women relatives and he found [the facts to be] in accordance with her words. He [then] said to him: Go, be happy with thy bargain. Happy art thou that thou hast been privileged [to marry a woman] of the family of Dorkaṭi. What is [the meaning of] Dorkaṭi?—A cut-off generation.[14]—R. Ḥanina said: Vain consolation Rabban Gamaliel offered[15] to that man, for R. Ḥiyya taught: As the leaven is wholesome for the dough, so is blood wholesome for a woman. And one has [also] taught in the name of R. Meir: Every woman who has abundant blood has many children. It has been said: R. Jeremiah b. Abba said: He [Rabban Gamaliel] said to him [the husband]: Be happy with thy bargain. But R. Jose b. Abin said: He said to him: thou hast been punished with thy bargain.[16] We quite understand

(1) I.e., the smell of the wine. (2) One could smell the wine from the mouth (Rashi). (3) One could not smell the wine from the mouth. (4) I.e., the smell of the wine. (5) Rabban Gamaliel. (6) To the husband. (7) The test shewed that the wife was a virgin. (8) Why did he first have to experiment with the two handmaids. (9) That this was a reliable test. (10) Lit., 'The practice he had not seen.' (11) Lit., 'perhaps it is not certain that the matter is good,' that is, that the test would be effective. (12) Lit., 'The way of the land,' that is, the custom. (13) Therefore he carried out the test first with handmaids. (14) Heb. *Dor. Ḳaṭu'a.* (15) Lit., 'consoled him.' (16) Lit., 'Be punished with thy bargain,' that is, the marriage stands, although it is not to thy advantage.

the one who says 'Thou hast been punished' with thy bargain—this is [according to the view] of R. Ḥanina. But according to him who says 'Be happy' [with thy bargain], what is the advantage [of such a marriage]?—He [the husband] does not come to any doubt regarding menstruation.

Someone came to Rabbi [and] said, 'My master, I have had intercourse [with my newly-wedded wife] and I have not found any blood.' She said, 'My master, I was [and am] still a virgin, and it was [a period of] years of dearth.' Rabbi saw that their faces were black,[1] [and] he commanded concerning them, and they[2] brought them[3] to a bath and gave them to eat and to drink and brought them to the bridal chamber, and he had intercourse with her and found blood. He[4] [then] said to him: Go, be happy with thy bargain. Rabbi applied to them the verse:[5] *Their skin is shrivelled upon their bones; it is withered, it is become like a stick.*[6]

MISHNAH. A MAIDEN—HER KETHUBAH IS TWO HUNDRED [ZUZ],[7] AND A WIDOW—A MANEH.[8] A MAIDEN, WHO IS A WIDOW, [OR] DIVORCED, OR A ḤALUẒAH[9] FROM BETROTHAL[10]—HER KETHUBAH[11] IS TWO HUNDRED [ZUZ], AND THERE LIES AGAINST THEM THE CHARGE OF NON-VIRGINITY.[12]

GEMARA. Why [is a widow called] *'almanah'?* R. Ḥana of Bagdad said: because of the *maneh*.[13] But what can be said with

(1) From hunger. (2) Those who carried out Rabbi's commands. (3) The young couple. (4) Rabbi. (5) Lit., 'read concerning them.' (6) Lam. IV, 8. (7) V. Glos. (8) One hundred *zuz*. (9) A woman released from a leviratical marriage, by *ḥaliẓah;* v. Deut. XXV, 5-10. (10) She was only betrothed (*arusah*, v. Glos.) but not married, and became a widow or was divorced, or released by *ḥaliẓah* from marrying her deceased fiancé's brother. (11) Lit., 'their *kethubah*'. The *kethubah* of either the widow, or the divorcee, or the *ḥaliẓah*. (12) The husband who marries one of these women has a right to complain if he does not find signs of virginity. As they were only betrothed but not married they are expected to be virgins. (13) The value of the *kethubah* of a woman who married when she was a widow. This is no attempt at proper etymology.

regard to a widow from the betrothal?[1]—Because that one is called *'almanah'*[2] this one is also called *'almanah.'*[3] What can be said with regard to [the word] *'almanah'*, that is written in the Bible?[4]—[The woman] for whom the Rabbis will in future institute [the *kethubah* of] a *maneh*. But does the Bible speak of a thing which will be in the future?[5]—Yes, for it is written: *And the name of the third river is Ḥiddeḳel, that is it which goeth towards the east of Ashur,*[6] and R. Joseph learnt: Ashur, that is Seleucia. But was [Seleucia] already then in existence? But [it is mentioned] because it will exist in the future. Here also *'almanah'* is mentioned in the Bible] because it [the *kethubah* of *maneh*] will exist in the future.

R. Ḥana of Bagdad also said: The rain waters, saturates and manures [the earth] and refreshes[7] and enlarges[8] [the fruits]. Raba the son of R. Ishmael, and some say R. Yemar the son of Shelemiah, said: Which is the verse?[9] [It is this:] *Thou waterest the ridges abundantly, thou settlest the furrows thereof; thou makest it soft with showers, thou blessest the springing thereof.*[10]

R. Eleazar said: The altar removes and feeds, makes beloved, atones.[11] Have not 'atones' and 'removes' the same meaning?[12] It removes [evil decrees][13] and atones for sins. R. Ḥana of Bagdad also said: Dates warm, satisfy, act as a laxative,[14] strengthen[15] and do not make [one] delicate.

Rab said: If one has eaten dates, he should not give a legal decision. An objection was raised. Dates are wholesome morning and evening, in the afternoon they are bad, at noon they are incomparable,[16] and they remove three things: evil thought, stress

(1) The value of the *kethubah* of such a widow is two hundred *zuz*, and still she is called *'almanah'*. (2) This is no attempt at proper etymology. (3) Lit., 'One calls her.' (4) The *kethubah* was not biblically ordained for the widow; v. *supra* 10*a*. (5) Lit., 'And was the verse written for the future?' (6) Gen. II, 14. (7) Or 'softens.' (8) Lit., 'causes to extend.' (9) That can be referred to in support of R. Ḥana's saying regarding the rain. (10) Ps. LXV, 11. (11) A play on the word מזבח (altar). (12) 'Removes' apparently also refers to sins! (13) The answer is that 'removes' refers to evil decrees. (14) Lit., 'loosen', (the bowels). (15) The body. (16) I.e., very good.—Dates are good, or very good, after the meals in the morning, noon and evening. They are not good in the afternoon after a rest (Rashi).

of the bowels, and abdominal troubles!—Do we say that they are no good? They are indeed good, only for the moment [they cause] unsteadiness. It is analogous to wine, for the Master said:[1] He who has drunk[2] one-fourth [of a *log*][3] of wine shall not give a legal decision.[4] And if you wish you may say: There is no difficulty: This is before a meal and that is after a meal,[5] for Abaye said: Mother[6] told me: Dates before a meal are as an axe to the palm-tree,[7] after a meal as a bar to the door.[8] *Dasha* [door], Raba explained:[9] *derek sham*[10] ['the way there'].[11] *Darga* [stairs, ladder], Raba explained:[12] *derek gag* [the way of the roof].[13] *Puria* [bed], R. Papa explained: *sheparin we-rabin 'aleha* [because one is fruitful and multiplies on it]. R. Naḥman b. Isaac said: [11a] We will also say:[14] *ailonith* [the barren woman that is] a man-like[15] woman, who does not bear children.[16]

MISHNAH. A WOMAN PROSELYTE, A WOMAN CAPTIVE, AND A WOMAN SLAVE, WHO HAVE BEEN REDEEMED, CONVERTED, OR FREED [WHEN THEY WERE] LESS THAN THREE YEARS AND ONE DAY OLD—THEIR KETHUBAH IS TWO HUNDRED [ZUZ], AND THERE IS WITH REGARD TO THEM THE CLAIM OF [NON-]VIRGINITY.[17]

(1) The reference is to Samuel, in whose name this saying is quoted in *'Er.* 64a. (2) Lit., he who drinks. (3) *Log* is a liquid measure equal to the contents of six eggs. (4) And one-fourth of a *log* of wine is certainly wholesome. But for the moment it may make one unsteady, and therefore unfit to give legal decisions. (5) Lit., 'bread'. If one eats dates before a meal, the effect is bad and one must not give legal decisions. The passage which declares them bad speaks of a case where one eats dates after a meal. The statement itself bears this out; v. *supra* p. 53, n. 6. (6) V. Ḳid. (Sonc. ed.) p. 153. (7) That is, injurious. (8) This apparently means good. It is difficult to see the meaning of the comparison. Rashi explains: They sustain the body as the bar supports a door. (9) Lit., 'said'. (10) A play on the word. (11) Or, the way is there; or, through there. (12) Lit., 'said.' (13) Or, the way to the roof; or, the way through the roof. (14) We will make a similar etymological exposition. (15) Or ram-like. איילונית 'a woman who cannot bear children,' is connected with איל (ram). (16) I.e., who is incapable of bearing children. (17) If they had sexual intercourse before they were three years and one day old the hymen would grow

GEMARA. R. Huna said: A minor proselyte[1] is immersed[2] by the direction[3] of the court.[4] What does he let us know? That it is an advantage[5] to him and one may act for a person in his absence[6] to his advantage? [Surely] we have learned [this already]: One may act for a person in his absence to his advantage, but one cannot act for a person in his absence to his disadvantage! —What you might have supposed is that an idolator[7] prefers a life without restraint[8] because it is established for us that a slave certainly prefers a dissolute life,[9] therefore, he[10] lets us know that this is said[11] [only in the case] of a grown-up person who has already tasted sin,[12] but [in the case of] a minor, it is an advantage to him.[13] May we say that [this Mishnah] supports him:[14] A WOMAN PROSELYTE, A WOMAN CAPTIVE, AND A WOMAN SLAVE, WHO HAVE BEEN REDEEMED, CONVERTED, OR FREED [WHEN THEY WERE] LESS THAN THREE YEARS AND ONE DAY OLD [etc.]? Is it not that they immersed them[15] by the direction of the Court?[16] No, here we treat of the case of a proselyte whose sons and daughters were converted with him, so that they are satisfied with what their father does.[17]

again, and they would be virgins. V. 9*a* and 11*b* and cf. Nid. 44*b* and 45*a*.

(1) I.e., a minor who wants to become a proselyte, that is, be converted to Judaism. Prior to and for the purpose of that conversion the would-be proselyte has to undergo circumcision and immersion in water. V. Yeb. 46*a*ff. The immersion is to signify his purification. If the would-be proselyte is a minor (under thirteen years of age) and has no father to act for him, the Court can authorise his ritual immersion. (2) Lit., 'they immerse him'. (3) Lit., 'by the knowledge'. (4) Lit., 'house of judgment'. Three members constitute the court. (5) To be received into the Jewish Faith. (6) Lit., 'not in his presence'.—As the proselyte is a minor he is not, legally speaking, present. (7) Lit., 'one who worships the stars and planets.' (8) Lit., 'lawlessness, unbridled lust.'—It would therefore be a disadvantage to the minor would-be proselyte to become a Jew. (9) Cf. Giṭ. 13*a*.—This confirms the former supposition. (10) R. Huna. (11) Lit., 'these words.' (12) Lit., 'who has tasted the taste of what is forbidden'. (13) To become a Jew. (14) R. Huna. (15) The women proselytes. (16) Because they were less than three years and one day old, consequently minors. (17) The immersion of the minor proselytes therefore took place by the direction of their father and not of the Court.—This Mishnah is therefore no support for R. Huna.

R. Joseph said: When they[1] have become of age they can protest [against their conversion].[2]

Abaye asked:[3] A WOMAN PROSELYTE, A WOMAN CAPTIVE, AND A WOMAN SLAVE, WHO HAVE BEEN REDEEMED, CONVERTED OR FREED [WHEN THEY WERE] LESS THAN THREE YEARS AND ONE DAY OLD—THEIR KETHUBAH IS TWO HUNDRED [ZUZ]. Now if you indeed mean to say [that] when they have become of age they can protest [against their conversion],[4] would we give her the *kethubah* that she may go and eat [it] in her heathen state?—When she has become of age.[5] [But] when she has become of age, too, she can protest and go out![6]—As soon as she was of age one hour, and did not protest, she cannot protest any more.[7]

Raba raised an objection: These maidens receive the fine:[8] if a man has intercourse with[9] a bastard,[10] a *Nethinah*,[11] a Cuthean,[12] a proselyte, a captive, or a slave, who have been redeemed, converted, or freed [when they were] less than three years and one day old—they have to be paid the fine.[13] Now if you say [that] when they have become of age they can protest, would we give her[14] the fine that she may go and eat it in her heathen state?—When she has become of age.[15] When she has become of age too she can protest and go out![16]—As soon as she was of age one hour and did not protest she cannot protest any more.[17] Abaye did not say as Raba [said][18] [because] there[19] [where it speaks of fines

(1) The minor proselytes. (2) And leave the Jewish faith and go back to their former state without being liable to a penalty by the Jewish Court. (3) Lit., 'he raised against this a point of contradiction from a higher authority.' (4) V. note 2. (5) Only then one gives her the *kethubah*. (6) Of Judaism; why then give her the *kethubah?* (7) The *kethubah* would be given to her after 'one hour'. (8) Lit., 'These maidens to whom there is a fine'.—The fine is that for seducing a girl; v. Deut. XXII, 29. (9) Lit., 'He who came on.' (10) V. Yeb. 49*a*. (11) A descendant of the Gibeonites. V. Joshua IX, 21, 23, 27 and cf. Yeb. 78*b*. (12) A Samaritan. (13) V. *infra* 29*a*. (14) The proselyte. (15) And adhered to Jewish practice, only then she is paid the fine, v. Tosaf. (16) Of Judaism. (17) The fine would be given to her after 'one hour'. (18) Did not ask the question of Raba. (19) In the Mishnah, *infra* 29*a*.

we can say]: This is the reason:[1] that the sinner should not have any benefit.[2] Raba did not say as Abaye [said][3] because in the case of the *kethubah* [we can say that] this is the reason:[4] that it[5] should not be a light matter in his eyes to send her away.[6]

MISHNAH. WHEN A GROWN-UP MAN[7] HAS HAD SEXUAL INTERCOURSE WITH[8] A LITTLE GIRL,[9] OR WHEN A SMALL BOY[10] HAS INTERCOURSE WITH A GROWN-UP WOMAN, OR [WHEN A GIRL WAS ACCIDENTALLY] INJURED BY A PIECE OF WOOD[11]—[IN ALL THESE CASES] THEIR KETHUBAH IS TWO HUNDRED [ZUZ]; SO ACCORDING TO[12] R. MEIR. BUT THE SAGES SAY: A GIRL WHO WAS INJURED ACCIDENTALLY BY A PIECE OF WOOD—HER KETHUBAH IS A MANEH. A VIRGIN, WHO WAS A WIDOW, A DIVORCEE, OR A ḤALUẒAH FROM MARRIAGE[13]—HER[14] KETHUBAH IS A MANEH.[15] [11*b*] AND THERE IS WITH REGARD TO THEM NO CHARGE OF NON-VIRGINITY. A WOMAN PROSELYTE, A WOMAN CAPTIVE AND A WOMAN SLAVE, WHO HAVE BEEN REDEEMED, CONVERTED, OR FREED [WHEN THEY WERE] MORE THAN THREE YEARS AND ONE DAY OLD—THEIR KETHUBAH IS A MANEH, AND THERE IS WITH REGARD TO THEM NO CHARGE OF NON-VIRGINITY.

GEMARA. Rab Judah said that Rab said: A small boy who

(1) Why the fine should be paid to the seduced proselyte girl. (2) Therefore he should pay the fine in any case. But the case of the *kethubah* (in our Mishnah) is different. Therefore, Abaye asked from our Mishnah. (3) He did not ask the same question as Abaye. (4) Why the *kethubah* is paid to the woman proselyte. (5) Lit., 'she'. (6) Lit., 'to bring her out (of his house)', that is, to divorce her. Therefore he should pay the *kethubah* in any case. But the case of the fine is different. Therefore Raba asks from the Mishnah *infra* 29*a*. (7) A man who was of age. (8) Lit., 'who came on'. (9) Less than three years old. (10) Less than nine years of age. (11) Lit., 'One who was injured by wood', as a result of which she injured the hymen. (12) Lit., 'the words of'. (13) A maiden was married, and immediately after the marriage, became a widow or divorced, or a *ḥaluẓah;* v. *supra* 10*b*. (14) Lit., 'their', that is, the *kethubah* of each of them. (15) Since the marriage had taken place she is regarded as a married woman and it is assumed that she is no more a virgin.

has intercourse with a grown-up woman makes her [as though she were] injured by a piece of wood.[1] When I said it before Samuel he said: 'Injured by a piece of wood' does not apply to[2] flesh. Some teach this teaching by itself:[3] [As to] a small boy who has intercourse with a grown-up woman, Rab said, he makes her [as though she were] injured by a piece of wood; whereas Samuel said: 'Injured by a piece of wood' does not apply to flesh. R. Oshaia objected: WHEN A GROWN-UP MAN HAS HAD INTERCOURSE WITH A LITTLE GIRL, OR WHEN A SMALL BOY HAS INTERCOURSE WITH A GROWN-UP WOMAN, OR WHEN A GIRL WAS ACCIDENTALLY INJURED BY A PIECE OF WOOD—[IN ALL THESE CASES] THEIR KETHUBAH IS TWO HUNDRED [ZUZ]; SO ACCORDING TO R. MEIR. BUT THE SAGES SAY: A GIRL WHO WAS INJURED ACCIDENTALLY BY A PIECE OF WOOD—HER KETHUBAH IS A MANEH![4] Raba said. It means[5] this: When a grown-up man has intercourse with a little girl it is nothing, for when the girl is less than this,[6] it is as if one puts the finger into the eye;[7] but when a small boy has intercourse with a grown-up woman he makes her as 'a girl who is injured by a piece of wood,' and [with regard to the case of] 'a girl injured by a piece of wood,' itself, there is the difference of opinion between R. Meir and the Sages.

Rami b. Ḥama said: The difference of opinion[8] is [only] when he[9] knew her,[10] for R. Meir compares her[11] to a mature girl,[12] and

(1) Although the intercourse of a small boy is not regarded as a sexual act, nevertheless the woman is injured by it as by a piece of wood. (2) Lit., 'is not in'. (3) I.e., the difference of opinion between Rab and Samuel with regard to that question was recorded without any reference to R. Judah. (4) The Sages differ only with regard to a girl injured by a piece of wood, but not with regard to a small boy who has intercourse with a grown-up woman. This shows that the latter case cannot be compared with the former case. The Mishnah would consequently be against Rab and for Samuel. (5) Lit., 'says'. (6) Lit., 'here', that is, less than three years old. (7) I.e., tears come to the eye again and again, so does virginity come back to the little girl under three years. Cf. Nid. 45*a*. (8) Between R. Meir and the Sages. (9) The husband. (10) I.e., he knew, when he married her, that the bride was thus injured. (11) The one who was thus injured. (12) *A bogereth* (v. Glos.), a girl of full maturity, may

the Sages compare her to a woman who had intercourse with a man.[1] But if he did not know her,[2] all agree[3] that she has nothing.[4] And why does R. Meir compare her to a mature girl? Let him compare her to a woman who had intercourse with a man!—[In the case of] a woman who had intercourse with a man, a deed had been done to her by a man;[5] but in her case[6]—no deed has been done to her by a man.—And why do the Rabbis compare[7] her to a woman who had intercourse with a man? Let them compare her to a mature girl! [In the case of] a mature girl no deed whatsoever has been done to her,[8] but in her case— a deed has been done to her.[9]

'But if he did not know her, all agree that she gets nothing'.[10] R. Naḥman objected: If she says, 'I was injured by a piece of wood,' and he says, 'No, but thou hadst intercourse with a man', Rabban Gamaliel and R. Eliezer say [that] she is believed![11] But, said Raba, whether he knew her[12] and whether he did not know her,[13] according to R. Meir [her *kethubah* is] two hundred [*zuz*];[14] [whereas] according to the Rabbis, if he knew her [her *kethubah* is] a *maneh*, [if] he did not know her, she gets nothing.[15]

Raba however changed his opinion,[16] for it has been taught: How [does] the bringing out of an evil name[17] [take place]? He[18]

sometimes not have signs of virginity, (v. Yeb. 59*a*), and her *kethubah* is nevertheless two hundred *zuz*.

(1) And had no virginity. Therefore her *kethubah* is only a *maneh*, as that of a widow. (2) Did not know of the injury and thus thought that she was in her full virginity. (3) Lit., 'the words of all.' (4) Lit., 'it is nothing'.—As he was kept in ignorance of what happened to her, she does not get even a *maneh* (Rashi). (5) Lit., 'by the hands of man'. (6) Lit., 'this'. (7) Lit., 'instead of comparing'. (8) Her signs of virginity vanished through her maturity. (9) Through the piece of wood. (10) This is the concluding part of the statement. (11) V. *infra* 13*a*. This shews that she gets the *kethubah* even if he did not know that she had been thus injured. (12) I.e., knew, when he married her, that she had been injured. (13) Did not know that she was thus injured. (14) [And the author of the Mishnah which states that she is believed, will be R. Meir, and she receives two hundred *zuz*]. (15) V. n. 4. [And our Mishnah which states that she gets only a *maneh* will represent the view of the Sages in the case where he knew her]. (16) Lit., 'and Raba went back on himself.' (17) Cf. Deut. XXII, 13, 14. (18) The husband.

comes to court and says, 'I, So-and-so,[1] have not found in thy daughter the tokens of virginity.' If there are witnesses that she has been unchaste under him,[2] she gets a[3] *kethubah* of a *maneh*.[4] [But surely] if there are witnesses that she has been unchaste under him, she is to be stoned![5]—It means this: If there are witnesses that she has been unchaste under him, she has to be stoned; if she was unchaste before [the betrothal], she gets a *kethubah* of a *maneh*. Now R. Ḥiyya b. Abin said [that] R. Shesheth said: This teaches:[6] If he married her in the presumption that she is a virgin and she was found to have had intercourse with a man,[7] she gets a *kethubah* of a *maneh*. Whereupon R. Naḥman objected: 'If one marries a woman and does not find in her virginity, [and] she says, "After thou hadst betrothed me [to thyself] I was forced[8] and [thus] thy[9] field has been inundated," and he says, "No, but before I betrothed thee [unto me] [thou hadst intercourse with a man], my bargain is [thus] a mistaken one," [etc.]'[10] and [this assuredly means] she is to get nothing![11] And R. Ḥiyya b. Abin said to them: Is it possible! R. Amram and all the great ones of the age sat[12] when R. Shesheth said that teaching and they found it difficult[13] and he[14] answered: In which respect is it indeed a mistaken bargain? In respect of two hundred [*zuz*], but a *maneh* she gets [as a *kethubah*]. And you[15] say [that it means] she gets nothing! Whereupon Raba said: He who asked [this question][16] has asked well, for 'a mistaken bargain' means entirely.[17] But [then] that

(1) Lit., 'such and such a person',—the husband is addressing the father of his young wife. (2) I.e., that she had intercourse with a man after their betrothal. (3) Lit., 'there is unto her'. (4) V. *infra* 46a. (5) Lit., 'a daughter of stoning'—(Cf. Deut. XXII, 20, 21). [How then can she have a claim to a *kethubah*?] (6) Lit., 'this says'. (7) Before the betrothal. (8) By a man to have intercourse with him. (9) Lit., 'his field'. (10) V. Mishnah, *infra* 12b. (11) [I.e., the words 'my bargain is a mistaken one' imply that the husband in making this charge denies her the right to receive anything at all. This refutes R. Shesheth's view that she is entitled in such a case to one *maneh*.] (12) I.e., were present. (13) Lit., 'and it was difficult unto them'. I.e., they felt the difficulty presented by the cited Mishnah. (14) R. Shesheth. (15) R. Naḥman. (16) I.e., R. Naḥman, by asking the question from the cited Mishnah. (17) I.e., entirely a mistaken bargain and she gets nothing. The question of R. Naḥman was therefore a good question.

[other teaching] presents a difficulty.[1] Put [it] right[2] and say thus: If there are witnesses that she was unchaste under him[3] she has to be stoned, if she was unchaste before [the betrothal], she gets nothing, if she was found to be injured by a piece of wood, she has a *kethubah* of a *maneh*. But surely it was Raba who said [above that], according to the Rabbis, if he did not know her, she gets nothing![4] Hence you must conclude[5] from this[6] that Raba retracted from that [opinion].[7]

Our Rabbis taught: If the first [husband] took her [the bride] to his home for the purpose of marriage, and she has witnesses that she was not alone [with him,][8] or even if she was alone [with him], but she did not stay [with him] as much time as is needed for intercourse, the second [husband][9] cannot raise any complaint with regard to her virginity, for the first [husband] had taken her to his home [for the purpose of marriage].[10] [12a] Rabbah said: This teaches that if he married her in the presumption that she was a virgin and she was found to have had intercourse she gets a *kethubah* of a *maneh*.[11] R. Ashi said: [No,] generally, I can tell you, she receives indeed nothing; but it is different here, because the first one had married her.[12] But let us apprehend that perhaps

(1) Lit., 'That is difficult'. The Baraitha of Kethuboth 46a, which says that if she was unchaste before the betrothal she gets a *kethubah* of a *maneh*. (2) I.e., answer. (3) I.e., that she had intercourse with a man after their betrothal. (4) And this is in contradiction with what Raba said just now, namely, that if the young wife was found to be injured by a piece of wood, she has a *kethubah* of a *maneh*. (5) Lit., 'hear from this'. (6) From Raba's statement that one injured thus gets a *kethubah* of a *maneh*. (7) Expressed by Raba previously that, according to the Rabbis, if the husband did not know before the betrothal that the bride was injured, she gets no *kethubah* at all. (8) Lit., 'that she was not hidden.' (9) The woman married again after the death of, or divorce by, the first husband. (10) As she was married before, the second husband must reckon with the possibility of her having had intercourse with the first husband, in spite of the evidence which she can bring to shew that the marriage was not consummated. (11) [For evidently he relied on the evidence that the first marriage was not consummated, and thus married her on the presumption that she was a virgin, and still it is said that he cannot bring a charge against her to make her forfeit the *kethubah* of a *maneh* to which she is entitled as a widow.] (12) And there may have been intercourse and this militates against the presumption that she was a virgin on the second marriage.

she was unchaste under him![1]—Said R. Sherabia: [We] suppose he betrothed her to himself and had immediately intercourse with her.[2]

Some[3] there are who refer this[4] to our Mishnah: A VIRGIN, WHO IS A WIDOW, A DIVORCEE OR A ḤALUẒAH FROM MARRIAGE,—HER KETHUBAH[5] IS A MANEH AND THERE IS NO CLAIM OF VIRGINITY WITH REGARD TO THEM. 'A VIRGIN FROM MARRIAGE'—how is it possible?—When she was brought into the bridal chamber and no intercourse took place. Rabbah said: This teaches that if he married her in the presumption that she was a virgin and she was found to have had intercourse she gets a *kethubah* of a *maneh*.[6] R. Ashi said: [No,] indeed, I can tell you, generally she gets nothing; but it is different here, because she was brought into the bridal chamber.[7] But let us apprehend that perhaps she was unchaste under him![8]—Said R. Sherabia: When he betrothed her to himself and had immediately intercourse with her.[9] He who refers this[10] to the Baraitha,[11] how much more [would this apply] to our Mishnah.[12] But he who refers this to our Mishnah would not apply it to the Baraitha, because he could say unto her, 'I have relied upon the witnesses.'[13]

MISHNAH. HE WHO EATS WITH HIS FATHER-IN-LAW IN

(1) After the betrothal to the second husband. [Why then should he not be able to bring a charge against her so as to give witnesses an opportunity to testify as to the true facts?] (2) So that unchastity was impossible. (3) Lit., 'and some'. (4) I.e., the observations of Rabbah, R. Ashi and R. Sherabia. (5) I.e., the *kethubah* of each of them. (6) V. *supra* p. 60, n. 11. (7) [So that it is to be assumed that the marriage was consummated, v. *supra* p. 60, n. 12.] (8) After the betrothal to the second husband. (9) So that unchastity was impossible. (10) I.e., the observations of Rabbah, R. Ashi and R. Sherabia. (11) Fol. 11*b*, bottom. In the case of the Baraitha there were witnesses that there was no intercourse. (12) In the Mishnah there were no witnesses that no intercourse took place. (13) And in view of the testimony of the witnesses the presumption that she was a virgin is a strong one, so that R. Ashi's reply to Rabbah would not hold good. True, 'the first one married her,' but there are witnesses who say that no intercourse took place. Rabbah's deduction from the Baraitha would therefore be justified.

JUDAEA WITHOUT THE PRESENCE OF WITNESSES CANNOT RAISE A COMPLAINT REGARDING THE VIRGINITY, BECAUSE HE HAS BEEN ALONE WITH HER.[1]

GEMARA. Since it says[2] in the Mishnah HE WHO EATS,[3] it follows that there are places also in Judaea where one does not eat.[4] Abaye said: Conclude from this that in Judaea, too, the places differ in their custom, as it was taught: R. Judah said: In Judaea they used formerly to leave the bridegroom and the bride alone one hour before their entry into the bridal chamber, so that he may become intimate with her,[5] but in Galilee they did not do so. In Judaea they used formerly to put up two best men,[6] one for him and one for her, in order to examine the bridegroom and the bride when they enter the bridal chamber,[7] and in Galilee they did not do so. In Judaea, formerly, the best men used to sleep in the house in which the bridegroom and the bride slept, and in Galilee they did not do so. And he who did not act according to this custom could not raise the charge of non-virginity.[8] To which [does this[9] refer]? Shall I say [that it refers] to the first clause?[10] [If so,] it ought to read, 'He who acted[11] [according to this custom]!' Again[12] [if you will say that it refers] to the last clause,[13] it ought to read, 'He who was not examined!'[14]—Abaye said: Indeed [it refers] to the first clause, so read,[15] 'He who acted [according

(1) And he may have had intimate intercourse with his bride. (2) Lit., 'teaches'. (3) In the house of the father-in-law. (4) V. note 3. (5) Lit., 'that his heart may become bold,' towards her, that is that he may become used to her. V. Krauss, *T.A.* II, p. 461, n. 341. (6) Heb. *Shoshebin*, groomsman, v. B.B. (Sonc. ed.) p. 618, n. 10. (7) So that they should not deceive one another regarding the tokens of virginity (Rashi). [That would be in such localities in Judaea where the young affianced couple were not allowed to be alone before the entry into the bridal chamber. This shews that customs differed in Judaea itself.] (8) Cf. Tosef. Keth. I. (9) The last sentence from 'and' till 'virginity'. (10) In which it said that in Judaea they used to leave the bridegroom and the bride alone. (11) If he did not act according to this custom he ought to be able to raise the charge of non-virginity. (12) Lit., 'but'. (13) With regard to the examination by the best men. (14) I.e., he over whom there was no supervision by the best man; v. Rashi. (15) Lit., 'and teach'.

to this custom].' Said Raba to him: But it reads,[1] 'He who did not act!' But, said Raba, it means thus: He who did not act according to the custom of Galilee in Galilee but [acted] according to the custom of Judaea in Galilee cannot raise the claim of virginity. R. Ashi said: Indeed [it refers] to the last clause,[2] and we should read,[3] 'He who was not examined.'[4]

MISHNAH. IT IS ALL ONE WHETHER [THE WOMAN IS] AN ISRAELITISH WIDOW OR A PRIESTLY WIDOW[5]—HER KETHUBAH IS A MANEH. THE COURT OF THE PRIESTS[6] COLLECTED FOR A MAIDEN[7] FOUR HUNDRED ZUZ, AND THE SAGES DID NOT PROHIBIT [IT] TO THEM.[8]

GEMARA. A Tanna taught: And the priestly widow—her ***kethubah*** is two hundred [*zuz*]. But we have taught in our Mishnah: AN ISRAELITISH WIDOW AS WELL AS A PRIESTLY WIDOW—HER KETHUBAH IS A MANEH!—Said R. Ashi: There were two ordinances. At first they[9] ordained for a maiden four hundred *zuz* and for a widow a ***maneh***. [12b] When they[9] saw that they[10] treated them[11] lightly,[12] they[9] ordained for them[13] two hundred [*zuz*]. When they[9] saw [again] that they[14] kept away from

(1) Lit., 'teaches'. (2) With regard to the examination by the best men. (3) Lit., 'and teach'. (4) I.e., over whom there was no supervision by the best man. (5) An Israelitish widow is the widow of an ordinary Israelite who was also the daughter of an ordinary Israelite. A priestly widow is a widow who was the daughter of a priest; v. Rashi. (6) [(*a*) A court of twenty- three judges holding sessions in priestly communities (*Shiṭṭah Meḳubbeẓeth, a.l.*); (*b*) A Sanhedrin dominated by Sadducean or High-priestly elements. (V. Geiger *Urschrift*, pp. 114ff; and Büchler, *Schwartz Festschrift*).] (7) For the virgin-maiden that was the daughter of a priest; v. Rashi. (8) Lit., 'did not strike at their hand', 'protest'. [(*a*) Although the same was recorded as part of the ***kethubah*** proper and not as the extra addition, v. *infra* 54*b*, the payment thereof would be enforced; (*b*) or, although not recorded at all, the woman could collect it by virtue of the prevalent custom, v. Tosaf.] (9) The Court of the priests. (10) The husbands who married widows of priestly stock. (11) The wives. (12) And easily divorced them, because the amount of their ***kethubah*** was not high (Rashi). (13) The wives. (14) The would-be husbands.

them,[1] for they[2] said, 'Instead of marrying a priestly widow, we shall rather marry[3] the virgin-daughter of an Israelite,'[4] they restored their [former] ordinance.[5]

THE COURT OF OUR PRIESTS, etc. R. Judah said [that] Samuel said: They[6] did not say it only [regarding] the court of the priests,[7] but even the noble families[8] in Israel, if they want to do as[9] the priests do,[10] may do [so]. An objection was raised: If one wants to do as[9] the priests do,[10] for instance [if] the daughter of an Israelite [gets] married to a priest, or the daughter of a priest [gets married] to an Israelite, one may do [so]. [We would infer from this that only if] the daughter of an Israelite [gets married] to a priest, or the daughter of a priest [gets married] to an Israelite, [it is allowed to do as the priests do], because there is [then] one side of priesthood,[11] but if the daughter of an Israelite [gets married] to an Israelite, it is not [allowed to do as the priests do]![12]—The Mishnah states here a case of 'not only'; not only [is it allowed[13] in the case of] the daughter of an Israelite [getting married] to an Israelite, who cannot say to her 'I raise thee' [to a higher position];[14] but [in the case of] the daughter of an Israelite [getting married] to a priest, who can say to her, 'I raise thee [to a higher position],'[15] I might think that it is not allowed;[16] [hence] he lets us hear [that this is not so].[17]

MISHNAH. IF A MAN[18] MARRIES A WOMAN AND DOES

(1) The widows of priestly stock. (2) The would-be husbands. (3) Lit., 'we shall go and marry'. (4) Lit., 'a virgin, a daughter of an (ordinary) Israelite', seeing that both receive the same *kethubah*. (5) Lit., 'they restored their words'. (6) The scholars. (7) That the *kethubah* of the virgin-daughter of a priest could be increased to four hundred *zuz*. (8) I.e., families of distinguished birth. (9) Lit., 'according to the way', 'manner'. (10) And increase the *kethubah* to four hundred *zuz*. (11) I.e., one of them, either the bridegroom or the bride, is of the priestly family. (12) And increase the *kethubah* to four hundred *zuz*. (13) To increase the *kethubah* to four hundred *zuz*. (14) As they are both of ordinary Israelite families. (15) To the privileged position of the wife of a priest. (16) To increase the *kethubah* to four hundred *zuz*. (17) That it is allowed to increase the *kethubah* to four hundred *zuz*. (18) Lit., 'he who marries'.

NOT FIND[1] IN HER VIRGINITY [AND] SHE SAYS, 'AFTER THOU HADST BETROTHED ME [UNTO THEE] I WAS FORCED AND [SO] THY FIELD HAS BEEN INUNDATED'[2] AND HE SAYS, 'NO, BUT [IT OCCURRED] BEFORE I BETROTHED THEE [TO ME] AND MY BARGAIN WAS A MISTAKEN BARGAIN'—RABBAN GAMALIEL AND R. ELIEZER SAY [THAT] SHE IS BELIEVED, [BUT] R. JOSHUA SAYS: WE DO NOT LIVE FROM HER MOUTH,[3] BUT SHE IS IN THE PRESUMPTION OF HAVING HAD INTERCOURSE[4] BEFORE SHE WAS BETROTHED AND HAVING DECEIVED HIM, UNTIL SHE BRINGS PROOF FOR HER STATEMENT.[5]

GEMARA. It was stated: [If one person says to another person], 'I have a *maneh* in your hand,'[6] and the latter[7] says, 'I do not know[8]—Rab Judah and R. Huna say: [He is] bound [to pay],[9] and R. Naḥman and R. Joḥanan say: [he is] free [from the obligation to pay].[10] R. Huna and R. Judah say: [he is] bound [to pay], [because they hold that] in the case of 'sure', and 'perhaps', 'sure' has it.[11] R. Naḥman and R. Joḥanan say: [he is] free [from the obligation to pay] [because they hold the view]: leave[12] the money in the possession of its present owner.[13] Abaye said to R. Joseph: The opinion[14] of R. Huna and Rab Judah corresponds with the view of Samuel,[15] for we have learned: [If] she[16] was pregnant, and they said to her, 'What is the nature of this embryo?'[17] [and she

(1) Lit., 'and he did not find'. (2) I.e., it is thy loss. (3) I.e., we do not go by what she says and we do not believe her. (4) With another man. (5) Lit., 'for her words'. (6) I.e., you owe me a *maneh*. (7) Lit., 'this one'. (8) The person from whom the money is claimed neither denies nor admits the claim. (9) The person against whom the claim is made must pay the *maneh* to the claimant. (10) The person against whom the claim is made need not pay anything. (11) Lit., 'better', 'preferable'.—When one litigant asserts a certainty and the other litigant puts forward the plea of 'I do not know,' judgment is given for the one who asserts a certainty. (12) Or, let stand. (13) Lit., 'in the presumption of its owner'. The phrase here signifies: leave the money in the possession of its present holder, because, as he is the holder of the money, he is in the presumption of being its rightful owner. (14) Lit., 'This'. (15) Lit., 'it is of Samuel'. (16) An unmarried woman. (17) I.e., who is the father of this expected child?

answered], 'It is from the man So-and-so, and he is a priest,' Rabban Gamaliel and R. Eliezer say [that] she is believed. And Rab Judah said [that] Samuel said [that] the *halachah* is according to Rabban Gamaliel. And R. Samuel b. Judah said to Rab Judah: Sharpwitted one![1] You said to us in the name of Samuel [that] the *halachah* is according to Rabban Gamaliel also in the first[2] [Mishnah]. [Now what means]: 'also in the first [Mishnah]'? [Assuredly it must mean], although one could say[3] 'leave the money in the possession of its [present] owner,' [still] Rabban Gamaliel said: 'sure' has it.[4] Is it [then] to say that R. Judah and R. Huna follow the opinion of Rabban Gamaliel, and R. Naḥman and R. Joḥanan follow the opinion of R. Joshua?— R. Naḥman can answer you:[5] I even follow the opinion of[6] Rabban Gamaliel; only Rabban Gamaliel says it there[7] because there is *miggo*,[8] but what *miggo* is there here?[9] Or [again]: Rabban Gamaliel says it only there, because we say: leave her in her presumptive

(1) Heb. *Shinena*. V. B.Ḳ. (Sonc. ed.) p. 60 n. 2. (2) I.e., in our Mishnah, which is the first of the three Mishnahs in which Rabban Gamaliel and R. Eliezer say that she is believed. The first Mishnah will also include the following Mishnah, where, as in our Mishnah, the *kethubah* is the point at issue. (3) Lit., 'there is to say'. (4) [Since he accepts the woman's plea which is 'sure' in preference to the husband's which is 'doubtful'. Which shews that R. Huna and Rab Judah in their ruling follow the view of Samuel that the *halachah* follows Rabban Gamaliel.] (5) Lit., 'R. Naḥman says unto thee'. (6) Lit., 'I who say ever'. (7) Lit., 'until now Rabban Gamaliel does not say there'. (8) *Miggo*, means 'since,' 'because,' and 'in consequence of,' and is used here as a legal term, denoting 'a legal rule according to which a deponent's statement is accepted as true on the ground that, if he had intended to tell a lie, he might have invented one more advantageous to his case,' v. Jast. s.v. The *Miggo* here is this: Instead of saying that she was forced to have intercourse, she could have said that she was injured by a piece of wood. [This would be a more advantageous plea since it does not disqualify her from marrying a priest as does the plea that she had been forced. And similarly in the case of the next Mishnah she might have maintained that her accident happened after she had become betrothed to him, and thus is entitled to a *kethubah* of two hundred *zuz*, instead of pleading that it occurred before, reducing thereby her claim to a *maneh*. V. Rashi.] (9) In the case of the money claim, what *miggo* is there which we could apply to the claimant? Therefore, we say, 'leave the money in the possession of its (present) owner.'

state,[1] but here what presumptive state has he got?[2] It is also evident that [it is right] as we have answered, that R. Naḥman follows the opinion of[3] Rabban Gamaliel, [13a] for if it were [not] so, there would be a difficulty between one law and another law, for it is established for us [that] in civil matters the law is according to R. Naḥman, whereas in this [case][4] R. Judah [said] that Samuel said [that] the *halachah* is according to Rabban Gamaliel.[5] Is it not then to be concluded from this [that it is] as we have answered?[6] Conclude [so] from this.

MISHNAH. [IF] SHE[7] SAYS, 'I WAS INJURED BY A PIECE OF WOOD', AND HE SAYS, 'NO, THOU HAST HAD INTERCOURSE WITH A MAN[8]—RABBAN GAMALIEL AND R. ELIEZER SAY: SHE IS BELIEVED, AND R. JOSHUA SAYS: WE DO NOT LIVE FROM HER MOUTH,[9] BUT SHE IS IN THE PRESUMPTION OF HAVING HAD INTERCOURSE WITH A MAN,[10] UNTIL SHE BRINGS PROOF FOR HER STATEMENT.[11]

GEMARA. With regard to what are their claims?[12]—R. Joḥanan says: With regard to two hundred[13] [*zuz*] and a *maneh*.[14] R. Eleazar

(1) The presumption is that the maiden is a virgin. This presumption holds good until she had been found not to be a virgin, and this has been found only after her betrothal. Therefore she was, at the time of her betrothal, in the presumptive state of a virgin. (2) There is no presumption in favour of the claimant. The presumption is in favour of the person from whom the money is claimed, since he holds the money. (3) Lit., 'says'. (4) I.e., the case of our Mishnah. (5) That she is believed, and consequently she gets a *kethubah* of two hundred *zuz*. (6) That even R. Naḥman will follow the opinion of Rabban Gamaliel in the case of our Mishnah, that she is believed and gets a *kethubah* of two hundred *zuz*. (7) The woman whose husband complains about the absence of virginity. (8) Lit., 'thou art one (that has been) trodden by a man'. (9) I.e., we do not go by her statement. (10) Since she has no virginity. (11) Lit., 'for her words'. (12) I.e., what is the claim of the husband and what is the claim of the wife? (13) She says that she was injured and claims a *kethubah* of two hundred *zuz*, on the view of R. Meir, *supra* 11a. (14) He says that she had intercourse with another man, in which case she gets only a *maneh*; v. the statement of R. Ḥiyya b. Abin, *supra* 11b and Rabbah's statement, *supra* 12a.

says: with regard to a *maneh* and nothing.[1] R. Joḥanan says: With regard to two hundred [*zuz*] and a *maneh*, [because] he[2] shares the opinion of R. Meir who says [that] whether he knew of her or did not know of her[3] [she gets as her *kethubah*] two hundred [*zuz*]. And R. Eleazar says: With regard to a *maneh* or nothing, [because] he shares the view of the Rabbis who say [that] whether he knew of her or did not know of her,[3] [she gets as her *kethubah*] a *maneh*. It is quite right that R. Eleazar does not say as R. Joḥanan [says], because he establishes it[4] according to the Rabbis.[5] But why does not R. Joḥanan say as R. Eleazar [says]?—He holds [that when] he[6] married her in the presumption of [her being] a virgin and she is found to have had intercourse, she has a *kethubah* of a *maneh*.[7] [According to this view] here[8] he would say, 'a *maneh*,'[9] and she would say, 'a *maneh*,'[10] [and] what difference would there be between his claim and her claim?[11] [Now] it is quite right according to R. Eleazar[12] that we have stated[13] two cases,[14] one[15] to exclude the opinion of Rami b. Ḥama,[16] and one[17] to exclude the opinion of R. Ḥiyya b. Abin in the name of R. Shesheth.[18] But according to

(1) She claims a *maneh* as one who was thus injured and according to the Sages, (v. *supra* 11*a*) gets a *maneh*. He says that she had intercourse with a man and therefore gets no *kethubah* at all, on the view advanced by R. Ashi, *supra* 12*a*. (2) [I.e., The Tanna of this Mishnah shares, in the view of R. Joḥanan, the opinion of R. Meir. It cannot refer to R. Joḥanan as he would not be likely to accept the ruling of R. Meir in preference to that of the majority of the Sages (Rashi).] (3) That she was thus injured, v. *supra* 11*b*. (4) Our Mishnah. (5) Who are the majority and according to whom the law is decided. (6) The husband. (7) V. *supra*, p. 68, n. 14. (8) In our Mishnah. (9) I.e., That she is entitled only to a *maneh* because he believed her on marriage to be a virgin and found it was not so. (10) If R. Joḥanan would say as R. Eleazar says that she could only claim a *maneh* owing to her accident. (11) Hence R. Joḥanan has had to explain the Mishnah as representing the view of R. Meir. (12) Who says that if she had intercourse with a man, she gets no *kethubah* at all. (13) Lit., 'he teaches'. (14) The case of our Mishnah and that of the previous Mishnah. (15) The case of our Mishnah. (16) Who says (*supra* 11*b*) that if the husband did not know that she had an accident she gets no *kethubah* at all. (17) The case of the previous Mishnah, where the husband says 'my bargain is a mistaken one', taken to mean that the woman is entitled to no *kethubah* at all. (18) Who says that, even if she had intercourse with another man, she gets a *kethubah* of a *maneh*; v. *supra* 11*b*.

R. Johanan why are two cases necessary?[1] — One to show you the strength[2] of Rabban Gamaliel, and one to show you the strength of R. Joshua. The first case to show you the strength of R. Joshua, that, although one could say [there] *miggo*,[3] she is not believed. The second case to show you the strength of Rabban Gamaliel, that, although one cannot say [there][4] *miggo*, she is believed.

MISHNAH. [IF] THEY[5] SAW HER[6] TALKING WITH SOMEONE,[7] AND THEY SAID TO HER, 'WHAT SORT OF A MAN IS HE?[8] [AND SHE ANSWERED, 'HE IS] THE MAN SO-AND-SO AND HE IS A PRIEST — RABBAN GAMALIEL AND R. ELIEZER SAY: SHE IS BELIEVED,[9] AND R. JOSHUA SAYS: WE DO NOT LIVE FROM HER MOUTH,[10] BUT SHE IS IN THE PRESUMPTION OF HAVING HAD INTERCOURSE WITH A NATHIN[11] OR A MAMZER,[12-13] UNTIL SHE BRINGS PROOF FOR HER STATEMENT. [IF] SHE[14] WAS PREGNANT AND THEY[15] SAID UNTO HER, 'WHAT IS THE NATURE OF THIS FOETUS,'[16] [AND SHE ANSWERED, 'IT IS] FROM THE MAN SO-AND-SO AND HE IS A PRIEST' — RABBAN GAMALIEL AND R. ELIEZER SAY: SHE IS BELIEVED,[17] AND R. JOSHUA SAYS: WE DO NOT LIVE FROM HER MOUTH,[18] BUT SHE IS IN THE PRESUMPTION OF BEING PREGNANT FROM A

(1) [Only the case of the second Mishnah should have been stated as illustrating the difference of opinion between R. Gamaliel and R. Joshua in regard to the pleas of 'sure' and 'perhaps', and thus incidentally excluding the opinion of Rama b. Ḥama, whereas the case of the first Mishnah could be inferred from the second one.] (2) I.e., how strong his view is. (3) V. *supra*, p. 67, n. 8. (4) [Since on the view of R. Johanan she gets in any case two hundred *zuz*, even if the husband was unaware of the accident that happened before the betrothal, v. *supra*, p. 69. (5) People. (6) An unmarried woman. (7) A man. (8) Lit., 'what is the nature (or character) of this man'? (9) And she may marry a priest (10) I.e., we do not go by her statement. (11) V. Glos. (12) '*Mamzer*' is usually translated by 'bastard'. Marriage with a '*mamzer*' and a '*nathin*' was forbidden; v. Yeb. 78*b*. As to what constitutes a '*mamzer*' v. Yeb. 49*a*. (13) And the intercourse with a '*Nathin*' or a '*Mamzer*' makes her unfit to marry a priest. (14) An unmarried woman. (15) People. (16) V. *supra* p. 66 n. 17. (17) And she and her child are fit for priestly marriage. (18) I.e., we do not go by her statement.

NATHIN OR A MAMZER,[1] UNTIL SHE BRINGS EVIDENCE FOR HER STATEMENT.

GEMARA. What is the meaning of 'TALKING'? Ze'iri said: She was hidden.[2] R. Assi said: She had intercourse.[3] It is quite right according to Ze'iri that it says[4] 'TALKING'.[5] But according to R. Assi why [does it say] 'TALKING?'—[It is] a more appropriate[6] expression, as it is written:[7] *'She eateth,*[8] *and wipeth her mouth,*[9] *and saith, 'I have done wo wickedness.'*[10] It is quite right according to Ze'iri that he teaches [in the Mishnah] two [cases]: 'TALKING' and 'PREGNANT'.[11] But according to R. Assi, why [does the Mishnah teach] two [cases]?—One case[12] to declare her fit[13] and one case[14] to declare her daughter[15] fit.[16] That is quite right according to him who says [that] he who declares her fit declares [also] her daughter fit.[17] But according to him who says [that] he who declares her fit declares her daughter unfit,[18] what is there to say?—R. Assi holds the view of him[19] who says [that] he who declares her fit declares [also] her daughter fit.

R. Pappa said to Abaye: According to Ze'iri who said: What is 'TALKING?' She was hidden, and R. Joshua said [that] she is not believed—did not Rab say: We punish with lashes for the privacy[20] but we do not prohibit[21] on account of the privacy? Is

(1) And neither she nor her child is fit for priestly marriage. (2) 'TALKING' means: 'she was hidden' with a man, and she may have had with him intercourse. (3) 'TALKING' means: 'she had intercourse' with the man. (4) In the Mishnah. Lit., 'that he teaches'. (5) Secret talking. Talking in hiding is also 'talking'. (6) I.e., euphemistic. (7) Proverbs XXX, 20. (8) Also euphemistic expressions. (9) Also euphemistic expressions. (10) The first part of the verse reads: '*So is the way of an adulterous woman*. (11) One case of suspicion and one case of certainty. V. also Rashi. (12) The case of 'TALKING'. (13) To marry a priest, according to R. Gamaliel. (14) The case of 'pregnant'. (15) If the child that was born was a daughter. (16) To marry a priest, according to R. Gamaliel. (17) V. *infra* 13*b*. (18) [Whereas the mother has had a presumption of fitness, this cannot be said of her daughter who was born under suspicion, v. *infra* 13*b*.] (19) Lit., 'holds us'. (20) I.e., the being alone of a man with a married woman. V. Levy and Jast. s.v. יחוד. (21) The married woman to her husband. In spite of the fact that the woman was alone with another man we do not assume that misconduct took place.

it to say that it is not according to R. Joshua?[1]—You may even say [that it is according to] R. Joshua, [for] they set a higher standard in matters of priestly descent.[2]

An objection was raised: [If] they[3] saw her go in[4] with someone[5] into a secret [place] [13b] or into a ruin,[6] and they said to her, 'What sort of a man is he?' [and she answered], 'he is a priest and he is the son of the brother of my father'—Rabban Gamaliel and R. Eliezer say: She is believed. R. Joshua says: We do not live from her mouth, but she is in the presumption of having had intercourse with a *Nathin* or a *Mamzer*, until she brings proof for her statement. Now it is quite right according to Ze'iri,[7] that he teaches[8] two [cases]: into a secret [place] or into a ruin.[9] But according to R. Assi who said: She had intercourse,[10] why does it teach[11] two cases?[12]—It teaches [only] one [case]: into the secret [place] of the ruin.[13] But it teaches: into a secret [place] or into a ruin!—[But say] one [expression stands] for a ruin of a town and one [expression stands] for a ruin of a field. And they are [both][14] necessary, for if it[15] had told us [only] concerning a ruin of a town [one might have said that] in this [case] Rabban Gamaliel declares her fit because most[16] [of the men] of the town are

(1) According to R. Joshua we would not believe her and we would say that misconduct took place. Consequently, she ought to be forbidden to her husband. (2) In order to ensure the purity of the priestly families, he made the law stringent in our Mishnah. But ordinarily R. Joshua would not forbid a wife to her husband on account of her having been alone with another man. (3) People. (4) Lit., 'that she went in'. (5) I.e., with a man. (6) A deserted building. (7) According to whom 'talking secretly', or being with a man in a secret place, gives grounds for suspicion, though it does not necessarily imply intercourse. (8) In the Baraitha just quoted. (9) 'Into a secret place' does not imply misconduct, but 'into a ruin' does imply misconduct. (10) Talking secretly, or being with a man in a secret place, affords no grounds for suspicion unless there has been some evidence of misconduct. (11) In the Baraitha just quoted. (12) Since the reference here is to a case where misconduct was seen to have taken place, what matters it whether it occurred in a secret place or a ruin? (13) The Baraitha is to be understood as if the reading was 'into the secret (place) of the ruin,' and thus only one case is mentioned. (14) Both expressions. (15) In the Baraitha just quoted. (16) Lit., 'the majority'.

fit with regard to her,[1] but in [the case of] a ruin of a field, when most [of the men][2] are unfit with regard to her,[3] I might say that he agrees with R. Joshua.[4] And if it[5] had told us [only] this [case][6] [I might have said that only] in this case[7] did R. Joshua say [that she is not believed], but in that [case][8] I might say [that] he agrees with Rabban Gamaliel;[9] [therefore] it was necessary [to state both cases].

An objection was raised:[10] This[11] is a testimony with regard to which the woman is fit.[12] But R. Joshua says: She is not believed. Said R. Joshua to them:[13] Do you not agree that in the case of a woman[14] who was captured, and there are witnesses that she was captured, and she says, 'I am pure,'[15] she is not believed? They said to him, 'Yes; but what a difference there is between this case and that case.'[16] In this case[17] there are witnesses,[18] and in that case[19] there are no witnesses.[20] He said to them: In that case too[21] there are also witnesses, for her stomach reaches up to her teeth.[22] They said to him, 'Most of the idolators are unrestrained in sexual

(1) Most of the inhabitants of the town are Jews, and the intercourse with a Jew does not make her unfit to marry a priest. (2) All kinds of men resort from all parts to a ruin in the field (Rashi). (3) She might have had intercourse with a man who makes her unfit to marry a priest. (4) That she is not believed. (5) The Baraitha just quoted. (6) A ruin of a field. (7) A ruin of a field. (8) A ruin in the town. (9) That she is believed. (10) Cf. Tosef. Keth. I. This is a continuation of a passage in the Tosef. which is identical with the first part of the second case of our Mishnah: 'She was pregnant (and they said unto her, "What is the nature of this embryo" (and she answered, "It is) from the man So-and-so (and) he is a priest"'—Rabban Gamaliel and R. Eliezer say: She is believed. (11) For variants v. Tosef. *loc. cit.* (12) I.e., the woman is legally fit to give that testimony and she is believed. (13) R. Gamaliel and R. Eleazer, v. n. 10. (14) Lit., 'a woman captive'. (15) I.e., no man had intercourse with me during my captivity. (16) Lit., 'between this (woman) and this (woman)'. (17) Lit., 'to this woman'. (18) In the case of the captive woman there are witnesses that she was captured. (19) Lit., 'and to this (woman)'. (20) In the case of the pregnant woman (the case of the Tosefta and our Mishnah) there are no witnesses that she had intercourse with one who makes her unfit for marrying a priest. It is clear, especially from the wording in the Tosefta, that this whole sentence, from 'yes,' until 'witness', is spoken by Rabban Gamaliel and R. Eliezer. V. Rashi. (21) Of the pregnant woman. (22) A figurative expression for 'she is visibly pregnant'.

matters.' He said to them: 'There is no guardian against unchastity.'[1] This applies[2] only in the case of the testimony of the woman with regard to herself,[3] but in the case of the testimony of the woman with regard to her daughter, all agree that the child is a *shethuki*.'[4]—[Now] what did he[5] say unto them[6] and what did they answer him? This they said unto him: 'You have answered us with regard to the pregnant woman,[7] what will you answer us with regard to the woman [whom they saw] talking [to a man]?'[8] —He said to them: The woman [whom they saw] talking [to a man] is the same as the captive woman.[9] They said to him, 'The captive woman is different, for most of the idolators are unrestrained in sexual matters.'[10] He said to them: Here also,[11] since she hid herself,[12] there is no guardian against unchastity.[13] [Now] at all events he teaches two [cases]: The woman [whom they saw] talking [to a man] and the pregnant woman![14] [This is] a refutation

(1) No one is immune from the possibility of having forbidden sexual intercourse. And the pregnant woman may have had intercourse with one forbidden to her and may thus have become unfit for a priestly marriage. The whole passage is explained soon. (2) Lit., 'with regard to what are these words said'? When do Rabban Gamaliel and R. Eliezer hold that she is believed? (3) Her testimony with regard to herself is believed. (4) A *shethuki* (lit., 'silenced') is defined in Kid. 69*a* as one who knows his mother but does not know who his father is. Therefore, the woman herself may marry a priest, but if she gave birth to a daughter, that daughter may not marry a priest. The corresponding sentence in the Tosefta is much shorter; viz., 'This applies only to the testimony with regard to herself, but with regard to the child all agree that it is a *shethuki*'. (5) R. Joshua. (6) R. Samuel and R. Eliezer. (7) Her pregnancy is evidence against her. (8) Why should she not be believed? (9) The one case is similar to the other case. In both cases there is a strong possibility of intercourse. (10) It is not only a question of sexual intercourse, but it is also a question who it was with whom the woman had intercourse. In the case of the captive woman, she is made unfit for priestly marriage, because the men among whom she finds herself are mostly unfit for her. But not so in the case of the woman who was talking to a man, where most men are fit for her; v. *supra*. (11) In the case of the woman who was talking to another man. (12) She was talking to the man secretly. (13) And she may have had intercourse with a man who makes her unfit for a priestly marriage. (14) The 'talking woman' and the pregnant woman are, at all events, two different cases.

of R. Assi,[1] [This is indeed] a refutation.[2]—But let this difference weigh with him:[3] There[4] most of the men are unfit with regard to her, but here[5] most of the men are fit with regard to her!—This[6] supports the opinion of R. Joshua b. Levi, for R. Joshua b. Levi said: He who declares her fit[7] declares her fit even when most of the men are unfit,[8] and he who declares her unfit declares her unfit even when most of the men are fit.[9]

R. Joḥanan said: He who declares her fit declares also her daughter fit, [and] he who declares her unfit declares also her daughter unfit. And R. Eleazar said: [Even] he who declares her fit declares her daughter unfit. Rabba said: What is the reason of R. Eleazar? [This:] It is quite right [with regard to her], she has the presumption of fitness,[10] [but] her daughter has no presumption of fitness.[11] R. Eleazar objected to [the ruling of] R. Joḥanan: This only applies to the testimony of the woman with regard to herself, but in the case of the testimony of the woman with regard to her daughter, all agree that the child is a *shethuḳi*.[12] Does this not [mean] a *shethuḳi* and unfit?—No, a *shethuḳi* and fit. But is there a *shethuḳi* [who is] fit?—Yes, according to Samuel, for Samuel said: [If] ten priests are standing together and one of them goes away[13] and has intercourse [with a woman], the child is a *shethuḳi*. Now what [means here] a *shethuḳi?* Is it to say that he is 'silenced' from the property of his father?[14] This is evident! Do we know who his

(1) According to whom the case of the 'talking woman' is also a case of certain sexual intercourse. (2) I.e., R. Assi stands refuted. (3) Or, let it be a difference to him (R. Joshua). Lit., 'let it go out to him'—'let it be different to him'. (4) In the case of the captive woman. (5) In the case of the 'talking woman'. (6) The fact that R. Joshua disregards this difference. (7) Lit., 'according to the words of him who declares her fit'. (8) With regard to her, as in the case of the captive woman. (9) With regard to her, as in the case of the 'talking woman'. (10) Legal fitness. She is of legitimate birth and she is fit to marry a priest. The doubt as to the nature of the man with whom she had intercourse does not destroy the presumption of her fitness. (11) Because suspicion attaches to her very birth. If the man who is the father is unfit, then she is unfit and must not marry a priest. The doubt is sufficient to make her unfit, since there is no presumption of fitness to remove. (12) V. p. 73, n. 10 and p. 74, n. 4. (13) Lit., 'separated himself'. (14) I.e., he does not inherit the property of his (alleged) father.

father is?—It means one silences him from the rights of priesthood,[1] for it is written: *'And it shall be unto him and to his seed after him the covenant of an everlasting priesthood,*[2] [that is, only] one whose seed is legitimately descending from him, excluding this one,[3] whose seed is not legitimately descending from him.[4]

A bridal couple[5] once came before R. Joseph. She said, 'It[6] is from him',[7] and he said, [14a] 'Yes, [it is] from me.' R. Joseph said: Why should we be afraid? First,[8] he admits, and moreover, Rab Judah said [that] Samuel said: The *halachah* is according to Rabban Gamaliel.[9] Abaye said to him: And in this [case], if he did not admit, would Rabban Gamaliel declare her as fit? Did not Samuel say to Rab Judah: 'Sharp-witted one! The *halachah* is according to Rabban Gamaliel, but you should not act upon it,[10] unless most men are fit for her,' whereas here most men are unfit for her![11] —And according to your reasoning is not this [statement] in itself difficult? [First he says] 'The *halachah* [is, etc.'] [and then] 'do not act in practice [on it]'![12] Hence you must say: The one ruling applies before[13] the other after it was done,[14] and in this case also it is like 'after it was done.'[15]

Abaye asked[16] Raba: Did R. Joshua say: She is not believed? This would be in contradiction with the following: R. Joshua and R. Judah b. Bathyra testified concerning the widow[17] [of one who was] of a mixed family[18] that she is fit to marry a priest![19]—He

(1) He has no share in the rights and privileges of priesthood. (2) Num. XXV, 13. (3) The unknown father of the *shethuki*. (4) [He cannot transmit the rights of priesthood to his seed, v. Yeb. 100*b*, but as regards marriage with one of priestly stock, this *shethuki* is permitted. This shews that one may be a *shethuki* and yet fit.] (5) Lit., 'that betrothed (man) and his betrothed (woman)'. (6) The child with which she was pregnant. (7) From her fiancé. (8) Lit., 'one'. (9) That she is believed, v. *supra* 12*b*. (10) Lit., 'thou shalt not do a deed'. (11) As she is betrothed, the only man fit for her is her fiancé. To all other men she is prohibited. (12) This seems self-contradictory! (13) [If a priest comes to seek guidance in regard to such a marriage we declare it not permissible unless he was held fit for the woman.] (14) [If he did marry her without consulting the authorities he may retain her.] (15) [Since she is already betrothed we do not force the bridegroom to put her aside.] (16) Lit., 'raised (a contradiction) to'. (17) V. p. 78, n. 9. (18) עיסה means 'dough' and is also a designation for a mixed community or a mixed family, that is a community

said to him: Now is this so?[1] There[2] the woman marries, and [in that case] she examines[3] and [then] marries; but here[4] the woman misconducts herself; does she first examine and then misconduct herself?[5]

Raba said: Is the contradiction [only] between [one statement of] R. Joshua and [the other statement of] R. Joshua, [but] not[6] between [one statement of] Rabban Gamaliel and [another statement of] Rabban Gamaliel?[7] Surely the concluding clause[8] teaches: Rabban Gamaliel said to them: We accept your testimony,[9] but what can we do, since Rabban Johanan b. Zakkai decreed that no court be set up for this purpose,[10] because the priests will obey you to remove[11] but not to bring near?[12]—But, said Raba; there is no contradiction between [the statement of] Rabban Gamaliel and [the other statement of] Rabban Gamaliel, [because] there[13] it is 'sure'[14] [and] here[15] it is 'perhaps.'[16] Neither is there a contradiction between [the one statement of] R. Joshua and [the other statement of] R. Joshua, [because] there[17] there is one doubt[18] [and] here[19] there is a double doubt.[20] Therefore, according to Rabban Gamaliel the 'sure' is [so] strong[21] [a plea] that even where [there is only] one doubt[22] he declares [her] fit,[23] and the 'perhaps' is [so]

or a family with an admixture of illegitimate persons or persons of doubtful legitimacy, v. Kid. 69b. (19) [This shews that we place her on her erstwhile presumption of fitness and refuse to disqualify her for the sake of a doubt.]

(1) I.e., what a comparison! (2) In the case of 'Ed. (3) The purity of the family. (4) In the case of our Mishnah. (5) Therefore she is not believed. (6) Lit., 'is there no contradiction'. (7) And one must endeavour to explain R. Gamaliel also. (8) Of the Mishnah in 'Ed. (9) I.e., we approve of what you say. (10) [Of declaring the legitimacy of such a doubtful case.] (11) I.e., not to allow persons of doubtful legitimacy to join their families. (12) They will not obey the court if permission is given for persons of doubtful legitimacy to enter their families. V. 'Ed. (Sonc. ed.) p. 48, nn. 2-7. (13) In the case of our Mishnah. (14) She says that she is sure that she had intercourse with a legitimate person. (15) In the Mishnah in 'Ed. (16) As it is a case of עיסה the woman herself cannot say that she is sure that the family is free from illegitimate admixtures. (17) In the case of our Mishnah. (18) Whether the man with whom she had intercourse was fit or unfit (regarding the priesthood). (19) In the Mishnah in 'Ed. (20) Indeed, in the case of a widow of a member of a mixed family there are many doubts of illegitimacy. (21) I.e., important. (22) Against her. (23) For the priesthood.

weak [a plea][1] that even where there is a double doubt[2] he declares [her] unfit.[3] [And] according to R. Joshua one doubt[4] is [so] strong that even in the case where [she pleads] 'sure' he declares [her] unfit,[5] and a double doubt[6] is [so] light[7] that even in the case where [she pleads] 'perhaps' he declares [her] fit.[8]

Our Rabbis taught: Which is the widow[9] [of one] of a mixed family? When there is with regard to it[10] [no doubt] on account of *mamzeruth*,[11] *nathinuth*[12] and on account of slaves of the kings,[13] R. Meir said: [14b] I have heard that when there is none of these [defects] in the family one permits [its members] to marry into the priesthood. R. Simeon b. Eleazar said in the name of R. Meir, and R. Simeon the son of Menasia also said it:[14] Which is the widow [of one] of a mixed family? When a doubtful *ḥalal*[15] was mixed up[16] in it, [for] the Israelites know the *mamzerim* who are among them, but they do not know the *ḥalalim* who are among them.[17]

The Master said: 'Which is the widow [of one] of a mixed family? When there is with regard to it [no doubt] on account of *mamzeruth, nathinuth* and on account of slaves of the kings'.

(1) Unimportant. (2) V. p. 77, n. 20. (3) For the priesthood. (4) In the case of our Mishnah. (5) For the priesthood. (6) In the Mishnah in 'Ed. (7) Unimportant. (8) For the priesthood. In short, with Rabban Gamaliel the 'sure' outweighs one doubt, and with R. Joshua one doubt outweighs the 'sure'. (9) Who has been held to be fit for marrying a priest; Tosaf. omits 'widow'. And indeed in Tosef., Ḳid. V the word is left out. The reference will be to a girl of a mixed family and not to a widow of a member of a mixed family, v. Tosaf. [On the whole subject of עיסה v., Rosenthal F. *MGWJ* 1881, also pp. 38ff and Freund L. *Schwartz-Festschrift* p. 163ff and Graetz *op. cit.* 1879, pp. 99ff]. (10) The family. (11) *Mamzer*-ship. (12) *Nathin*-ship. For *nathin* and *mamzer* v. Glos. (13) Cf. Neh. VII, 57, and Yeb. 17b. [According to Rashi the reference is to the Herodian dynasty.] When there is no suspicion, with regard to that family, of intermarriage with *mamzerim*, *nathinim* and royal slaves. (14) Lit., 'according to his words'. (15) *Ḥalal* is one who is profaned, unfit for priesthood on account of his father's illegitimate connection. Cf. Lev. XXI, 15 and v. Ḳid. 77*a* and 77*b*. A doubtful *ḥalal* is a person about whom there is a doubt whether he is a *ḥalal* or not. (16) נטמע means 'to be mixed up beyond recognition'. V. Jast. (17) Therefore one has to be careful with regard to doubtful *ḥalalim*.

[This would show that if there is a doubt on account of] a *ḥalal* [in the family] it is fit.[1] Why should these[2] be different? [Because] these are Biblical? A *ḥalal* is also Biblical![3] And further:[4] 'R. Meir said: I have heard that when there is none of these [defects] in the family one permits [its members] to marry into the priesthood'. This is the same [as that which] the first Tanna[5] [taught]! And further:[6] 'R. Simeon b. Eleazar said in the name of R. Meir, and R. Simeon b. Menasia also said it: Which is the widow [of one] of a mixed family? When a *ḥalal* was mixed up in it, [for] the Israelites know the *mamzerim* who are among them, but they do not know the *ḥalalim* who are among them.' Surely it says in the first clause [that if there is a doubt regarding] a *ḥalal* [in the family, the family is] fit [to marry into the priesthood]! R. Joḥanan said: There is a difference between them [concerning a person who when he is called] *mamzer* protests and [when he is called] *ḥalal* is silent. The first Tanna holds [that] every person who when called 'unfit' is silent is [considered] unfit, and thus the first Tanna said: Which is the widow [of one] of a mixed family? When there is in it no one who is silent if he is called *mamzer* or *nathin*, or slave of the king, or *ḥalal*. Whereupon R. Meir said to him: This applies only to [each of] these cases[7] since [he who calls him thus is liable to] render him unfit [to enter] into [the congregation,] but he who is called a *ḥalal* and is silent,[8] is fit, and the reason he is silent is that it does not trouble him.[9] Whereupon R. Simeon b. Eleazar said to the first Tanna[10] of R. Meir: If you have heard that R. Meir declares the person fit in the case of silence, this is not when he

(1) [The widow would not be disqualified where there was a doubtful admixture of a *ḥalal* in her dead husband's family.] (2) [The marriage to any one of those enumerated in the Baraitha is Biblically forbidden and consequently renders the woman who marries the offspring of such an union unfit for a subsequent marriage to a priest, v. Yeb. 68*a*.] (3) Cf. Lev. XXI, 15, and Yeb. 68*a*. (4) Another difficulty. (5) The first statement of the Baraitha and R. Meir's are practically identical. (6) Another difficulty. (7) *Mamzer*, *nathin* and royal slave. (8) [And does not protest against the stigma attached to his descent.] (9) Since he is not excluded from the congregation. (10) That is, the teacher who transmitted the words of R. Meir and said in his name 'I have heard, etc.' and not the first Tanna of the cited Baraitha.

is called *ḥalal* and is silent, but when he is called *mamzer* and is silent, for the reason he is silent is because he says to himself; 'a *mamzer* is well-known'.[1] But [if he is called] *mamzer* and he protests, or [he is called] *ḥalal* and is silent he is unfit,[2] for the reason he is silent is because he thinks, 'it is enough if he is not excluded from the congregation'.[3]

One Baraitha taught: R. Jose says: [if he is called] *mamzer* and is silent, he is fit, and if he is called *ḥalal* and is silent, he is unfit. And another Baraitha taught: [If he is called] *ḥalal* and is silent he is fit, [but if he is called] *mamzer* and is silent, he is unfit. There is no difficulty;[4] the one[5] is according to the first Tanna in the sense of R. Meir, and the other one is according to R. Simeon b. Eleazar in the sense of R. Meir.

MISHNAH. R. JOSE SAID: IT HAPPENED THAT A GIRL WENT DOWN TO DRAW[6] WATER FROM A SPRING AND SHE WAS RAVISHED. R. JOḤANAN B. NURI SAID: IF MOST OF THE INHABITANTS[7] OF THE TOWN MARRY [THEIR DAUGHTERS] INTO THE PRIESTHOOD,[8] THIS [GIRL] MAY [ALSO] MARRY INTO THE PRIESTHOOD.[9]

GEMARA. Raba said to R. Naḥman: According to whom did R. Joḥanan b. Nuri say [this in the Mishnah?]. If according to Rabban Gamaliel, [surely] he declares as fit even when there is a majority of unfit![10] [And] if it is according to R. Joshua, [surely] he declares as unfit even when there is a majority of fit![11] —He said

(1) Lit., a *mamzer* has a voice—And since he is not regarded generally as a *mamzer* he does not think it worth while to protest against the assertion of one man. (2) For the priesthood. (3) As he is not excluded from the congregation, he does not desire any investigations into his origin (Rashi). (4) There is no contradiction between these two Baraithas. (5) The second Baraitha. (6) Lit., 'to fill'. (7) Lit., 'men'. (8) Are entitled to marry their daughters to priests. This shows that they are 'fit'. (9) Because the man with whom she had intercourse is taken to be one of the majority, and the majority consists of 'fit' men. (10) Because he places the woman on the presumption of fitness, v. *supra* 13*b*. (11) V. *supra* 13*b*.

to him: Rab Judah said [that] Rab said: [15*a*] The incident[1] happened at the springs[2] of Zepphoris, and the ruling followed R. Ammi, for R. Ammi said: and that is when a company of unfit men passed by there,[3] and also R. Jannai, for R. Jannai said: if she had intercourse at the springs she is fit for the priesthood.—Do you really mean to say at the springs?—But rather [say]: If she had intercourse at the time of [the people visiting] the springs she is fit for the priesthood. But if someone went[4] from Zepphoris and had intercourse [with her], the child is a *shethuki*.[5] This is according to the following: When R. Dimi came[6] he said that Ze'iri said [in the name of] R. Ḥanina, and some say: Ze'iri said [in the name of] R. Ḥanina:[7] One goes after the majority of [the inhabitants of] the town and one does not go after the majority of the [passing] company.—Just the reverse! These[8] move about and those[9] are stationary![10]—But [say thus]: One goes after the majority of the [inhabitants of the] town, but only when there is [also] the majority of the [passing] company with it, but one does not go after the majority of the [inhabitants of the] town alone, nor after the majority of the [passing] company alone.[11]—What is the reason?[12]—It is prohibited[13] [to go after] the majority of the [passing] company in order to prevent[14] [going after] the majority of [the inhabitants of] the town. But even [in the case of] the majority of [the inhabitants of] the town, if he went[15] to her, [let us say that] he who separates himself separates himself from the majority?[16]

(1) Related in our Mishnah. (2) קרונות, *var. lec.* (קרונה, κρήνη) 'spring', so Levy. V. also Krauss, *TA.* I 212. Jast.: 'Caravan', 'Station'. (3) [So that there were two majorities of fit persons—the majority of local inhabitants and the majority of visitors from outside]. (4) Lit., 'separated himself'. (5) V. *supra* 13*b* and Glos. (6) To Palestine.] (7) Leaving out R. Dimi. (8) The people of the passing company. (9) The inhabitants of the town. (10) Lit., 'and these are fixed and stand'.—As to the point of the question, v. *infra*. (11) I.e., there must be two majorities. (12) That we do not go after the majority of the (passing) company. (13) Lit., 'a prohibition'. (14) Lit., 'on account of'. (15) Lit., 'if they went', that is to say one of the inhabitants of the town. (16) I.e., he who comes away from a crowd, or a community is regarded as having come away from those who constitute the majority of the crowd or community. And if the majority of the town consists of fit people, we ought

—It speaks of a case[1] when she went to him,[2] so that he was stationary,[3] and R. Zera said: All that is stationary is considered as half to half.[4] But do we require two majorities? Has it not been taught: If nine [meat] shops,[5] all of them, sell ritually killed meat, and one [shop sells] meat not ritually slaughtered and he bought in[6] one of them and he does not know in which of them he bought, it is prohibited because of the doubt;[7] but if [meat] was found,[8] one goes after the majority?[9] And if you will say that [it speaks of a case] when the gates of the city are not closed,[10] so that a majority[11] came [also] from outside,[12] did not R. Zera say: even when[13] the gates of the city are closed?—Where purity of descent is concerned they[14] put up a higher standard.[15]

The text says: 'R. Zera said: All that is stationary is considered as half to half.' [This apparently means] whether it is for leniency or for strictness.[16] Whence does R. Zera take it? Shall I say from [the Baraitha which teaches that] if nine [meat] shops, all of them, sell ritually killed meat and one [shop sells] meat not ritually slaughtered and he bought in one of them[17] and he does not know in which of them he bought, it is prohibited because of the doubt; but if [meat] was found, one goes after the majority? There it is for strictness![18] But [he derives it] from [the following]: If there

to assume that the man who had intercourse with the woman was one of the majority and did not disqualify her from marrying a priest, and that no blemish attaches to the child.

(1) Lit., 'no, necessarily'. (2) Lit., 'to them'. (3) I.e., fixed in one place. (4) The rule of majority does not apply, v. *infra*. (5) Out of the ten meat-shops that are in the market. (6) Lit., 'from'. (7) Lit., 'its doubt is prohibited'. [Because the prohibited minority is in a fixed, settled place (*ḳabu'a*), v. *infra*.] (8) In the market-place, in which the ten shops are situated. (9) And the majority of the shops sell ritually killed meat. Thus we see that one single majority is sufficient. (10) [And meat is admitted from the outside.] (11) Of butchers selling ritually killed meat. (12) Lit., 'from the world'. [So that there are two majorities—the majority of local Jewish butchers and the majority of Jewish butchers from outside.] (13) Lit., 'although'. (14) The Sages. (15) And therefore two majorities are required, cf. *supra* 13*a*. (16) I.e., whether the result of this rule is lenient or strict, that is, to allow or to prohibit (whichever it may be). (17) This illustrates the principle of *ḳabu'a*, a fixed, stationary prohibition. (18) And you cannot derive from this for leniency.

were [in a certain place] nine frogs and one reptile[1] and he touches one of them and he does not know which of them he touched he is unclean because of the doubt?—There also it is for strictness![2] —But [rather] from [the following]: If there were [in a certain place] nine reptiles and one frog and he touches one of them and he does not know which of them he touched, [if this happened] on private ground he is unclean because of the doubt, [but] if this happened in a public place,[3] he is clean because of the doubt.[4]

And how do we know this[5] from the Bible?—The verse says: *And if he lie in wait for him and rise up against him,*[6] [that is to say that he is not guilty of murder] until he intended [to kill] him. And the Rabbis?—They said in the school of R. Jannai: This excludes one who throws a stone into [a group of people]. What case do you mean? Do you mean a case when there are nine idolators and one Israelite? Let it be sufficient for him[7] that the majority are idolators, [and] even if [you will say that it is considered as] half to half, [the rule is that] when there is a doubt in capital cases one takes a lenient view!—It speaks of a case when there are nine Israelites and one idolator, so that the idolator is stationary, and whatever is stationary is considered as half to half.[8]

It was stated: R. Ḥiyya b. Ashi [said that] Rab said [that] the law is according to R. Jose.[9] And R. Ḥanan b. Raba [said that] Rab said [that] it was [only] a decision for the hour.[10] R. Jeremiah argued: And for pure descent we do not require two majorities? Have we not learned: [15*b*] [If] one found in it[11] an abandoned[12] child—if the majority [of the inhabitants of the town consist of]

(1) Dead reptiles make ritually unclean, but not frogs, v. Lev. XI, 29. (2) And you cannot derive from this for leniency. (3) [On the principle that a doubtful case of uncleanness is clean if it arises in a public place but unclean if in private ground v. Soṭ. p. 140.] (4) From this Baraitha you can derive both for strictness and for leniency. (5) The rule: what is stationary is considered half to half. (6) V. Deut. XIX, 11. (7) Lit., 'let it be deduced by him'. (8) For full notes on this passage v. Sanh. (Sonc. ed.) p. 531, n. 4 and B.Ḳ. (Sonc. ed.) p. 253. (9) In our Mishnah. (10) A special decision for the occasion, regard having been had to certain circumstances, which is not to be taken as a precedent, for elsewhere two majorities are required. (11) In a town in which Israelites and non-Israelites live. (12) Lit., 'thrown away'.

non-Israelites [the child is] a non-Israelite, if the majority [of the inhabitants of the town consist of] Israelites [the child is] an Israelite, [and if the inhabitants of the town are] half to half, [the child is] an Israelite.[1] And Rab said: They have taught this only with regard to sustaining it,[2] but not with regard to pure descent. And Samuel said: [They have taught this only] with regard to removing debris[3] for its sake?[4]—That which Rab Judah said in the name of Rab[5] [namely, that] the incident happened at the springs of Zepphoris,[6] escaped his[7] attention.[8] But according to R. Ḥanan b. Raba who said [that] it was a decision for the hour,[9] it is difficult![10] He who taught this[11] did not teach that.[12]

The [above] text [says]: '[If] one found in it an abandoned child—if the majority [of the inhabitants of the town consist of] non-Israelites [the child is] a non-Israelite, if the majority [of the inhabitants of the town consist of] Israelites [the child is] an Israelite, [and if the inhabitants of the town are] half to half [the child is] an Israelite. Rab said: They have taught this only with regard to sustaining it, but not with regard to pure descent. But Samuel said: [They have taught this only] with regard to removing debris for its sake.' But did Samuel say so? Did not R. Joseph say that R. Judah said in the name of Samuel: We do not go with

(1) Mak. VII, 2. (2) [Jews are in duty bound to support their own poor.] (3) On Sabbath. (4) It would appear from this text with regard to pure descent that one majority is not sufficient. (5) Lit., '(that) Rab said'. (6) So that there were two majorities, v. *supra* p. 81, n. 3. (7) R. Jeremiah. (8) Had R. Jeremiah not overlooked this he would not have asked his question, for indeed two majorities were required for pure descent. (9) It is now being assumed that R. Ḥanan also accepted the explanation that it occurred at the springs of Zepphoris, so that there were two majorities and he regards this ruling of R. Joḥanan b. Nuri only as a special decision, but elsewhere, two majorities are not required. (10) Why does Rab say in the case of the abandoned child 'but not with regard to pure descent', which would shew that Rab requires two majorities also in other cases? (11) That Rab said here 'but not with regard to pure descent'. (12) That R. Judah said in the name of Rab that the incident happened at the springs of Zepphoris. Indeed there was only one majority there, and therefore R. Ḥanan said, 'it was a decision for the hour', v. *supra*, p. 83, n. 10. In all other cases two majorities are required.

regard to saving life after the majority?[1]—But the saying of Samuel referred[2] to the first clause: 'If the majority [of the inhabitants of the town consist of] non-Israelites [the child is] a non-Israelite.' [Upon this] Samuel said: And with regard to removing debris it is not so.[3] 'If the majority [of the inhabitants of the town consist of] non-Israelites [the child is] a non-Israelite'—for what practical purpose [is this taught]?—R. Papa said: To allow him to eat [meat of] animals not ritually slaughtered.—'If the majority [of the inhabitants of the town consists of] Israelites [the child is] an Israelite,'—for what practical purpose [is this taught]?—R. Papa said: That one returns to him a lost object.[4]—'If [the inhabitants of the town are] half to half [the child is] an Israelite'—for what practical purpose [is this taught]? Resh Laḳish said: With regard to damages.[5] How shall we imagine this case? Shall we say that an ox of ours[6] gored[7] an ox of his?[8] [In this case] let him[9] say to him,[10] 'Bring evidence that you are an Israelite—and take![11] It speaks of a case when an ox of his[12] gored an ox of ours[13]—one half he[14] pays, and with regard to the other half he says to them,[15] 'Bring evidence that I am not an Israelite and I will pay[16] you.[17]

(1) Where it is a question of saving life the minority had to be equally taken into consideration. (2) Lit., 'but when that of Samuel was said, it was said with regard'. (3) One must remove the debris from the child in any case. (4) V. B.M. (Sonc. ed.) p. 149, n. 6. (5) V. B.Ḳ. (Sonc. ed) p. 211, n. 6. (6) Belonging to Israelites. (7) Cf. Ex. XXI, 35, 36. (8) Belonging to the erstwhile abandoned child. (9) The Israelite. (10) To him who was an abandoned child. (11) The damages due to you. (12) Belonging to the erstwhile abandoned child. (13) Belonging to Israelites. (14) The erstwhile abandoned child. (15) To the Israelites. (16) Lit., 'give.' (17) The other half as well, that is full damages, v. B.Ḳ. *loc. cit.*

KETHUBOTH

CHAPTER II

MISHNAH. IF A WOMAN BECAME A WIDOW OR WAS DIVORCED[1] [AND] SHE SAYS, 'THOU DIDST MARRY ME [AS] A VIRGIN,'[2] AND HE SAYS, 'NOT SO, BUT I MARRIED THEE [AS] A WIDOW,'[3-4]—IF THERE ARE WITNESSES THAT SHE WENT OUT[5] WITH A HINUMA[6] AND HER HEAD UNCOVERED,[7] HER KETHUBAH IS TWO HUNDRED [ZUZ.][8] R. JOḤANAN THE SON OF BEROḲA SAYS: ALSO THE DISTRIBUTION OF ROASTED EARS OF CORN IS EVIDENCE.[9] AND R. JOSHUA ADMITS THAT, IF ONE SAYS[10] TO HIS FELLOW,[11] 'THIS FIELD BELONGED TO YOUR FATHER AND I BOUGHT IT FROM HIM,' HE IS BELIEVED, [16a] FOR THE MOUTH THAT BOUND IS THE MOUTH THAT LOOSENS.[12] BUT IF THERE ARE WITNESSES THAT IT[13] BELONGED TO HIS FATHER AND HE SAYS, 'I BOUGHT IT FROM HIM,' HE IS NOT BELIEVED.

GEMARA. The reason[14] is that there are witnesses,[15] but if there are no witnesses the husband is believed. Is it to say that

(1) Lit., 'the woman who became a widow or was divorced.' (2) And the *kethubah* is two hundred *zuz*. (3) And the *kethubah* is one hundred *zuz*. (4) If the woman became a widow the dispute is between her and the heir (or heirs) of the husband. (5) On her wedding day, from the house of her father to the house of her husband. (6) For the meaning of this word v. *infra* p. 95. (7) That is, her hair loosened; for the meaning of פרוע cf. Num. V, 18. (8) Because only virgin-brides went out on their wedding day with a *hinuma* and with the hair of the head loosened. (9) That she was a virgin. They used to distribute roasted ears of corn to little children at the weddings of maidens, but not of widows or divorcees. (10) Lit., 'in (the case of) one (who) says.' (11) I.e., to another man. (12) I.e., if that person had been silent the other man would not have known that the field ever belonged to his father. We have, therefore, to believe both his statements. (13) The field. (14) Of the decision given in our Mishnah that the *kethubah* of the woman is two hundred *zuz*. (15) That she went out on her wedding day with the *hinuma* and uncovered head.

the anonymous and undisputed decision[1] recorded in our Mishnah is not according to Rabban Gamaliel? For if it were according to Rabban Gamaliel, did not he say that she is believed?[2]—You may even say [that it is according to] Rabban Gamaliel; [for] Rabban Gamaliel says [it][3] only there in [a case of] 'sure' and 'perhaps',[4] but here[5] where they are both[6] sure[7] [in their statements] he[8] did not say [it][9]—But he who raised the question, how could he raise it at all?[10] Surely this is a case where they are both 'sure' [in their statements]!—Since most women get married as virgins [you might say that] it[11] is like 'sure and perhaps'.[12] This[13] may also be proved by the following reasoning, since it is stated: AND R. JOSHUA ADMITS [etc.][14] It is well if you say [that] Rabban Gamaliel admits.[15] But if you say [that] Rabban Gamaliel does not admit,[16] to whom does [then] R. Joshua admit?[17]—Do you think [that]

(1) Lit., 'we have learnt without definition.' (2) V. *supra* 12*b*. (3) That she is believed. (4) There (in the Mishnah 12*b*) the husband cannot be 'sure' with regard to his statement, while the wife can be sure. V. Rashi. (5) In our Mishnah. (6) The husband and the wife. (7) Lit., 'in sure and sure'. (8) Rabban Gamaliel. (9) That the wife is believed. The wife is not believed more than the husband. (10) The answer is so obvious. (11) The case in our Mishnah. (12) The statement of the wife is more 'sure' than that of her husband. And therefore you might say that she is believed even when there are no witnesses that she went out with a *hinuma* and her head uncovered. And as this is, apparently, not the view of our Mishnah, the questioner raised his question. (13) That Rabban Gamaliel would admit that, if there were no witnesses that she went out with a *hinuma* and her head uncovered, the husband would be believed (Rashi). (14) V. second clause of our Mishnah. (15) Lit., 'Rabban Gamaliel treats of "he admits".' I.e., It is well, if it is assumed that Rabban Gamaliel admits that, in the absence of witnesses, (v. n. 13) the husband is believed, since it is a case of 'sure' and 'sure'; in which case the author of the first clause of the Mishnah is Rabban Gamaliel, who while differing from R. Joshua in a case of 'sure' and 'perhaps' (as in the Mishnah on 12*b*), agrees here with R. Joshua, since it is a case of 'sure' and 'sure'. And, therefore, it is said in the second clause of the Mishnah 'AND R. JOSHUA ADMITS,' namely in the first clause of the Mishnah Rabban Gamaliel admits to R. Joshua, and in the second clause R. Joshua admits to Rabban Gamaliel (Rashi). (16) V. n. 15. (17) To what do the words 'AND R. JOSHUA ADMITS' refer, seeing that no mention is made previously in the Mishnah of any dispute.

R. Joshua refers to this chapter?[1] He refers to *miggo*[2] in the first chapter.[3] To which?[4] Is it to say [that he refers] to this: If she was pregnant, and they said to her, 'What is the nature of this embryo', [and she answered, 'it is] from man So-and-so and he is a priest', Rabban Gamaliel and R. Eliezer say: She is believed, [and] R. Joshua says: We do not live from her mouth?[5] What *miggo* is there in that case?[6] Behold, her stomach reaches up to her teeth![7] Again [should it refer] to this: They saw her talking with someone and they said to her: 'what is the character of this man?' [and she answered, 'it is] man So-and-so and he is a priest'. Rabban Gamaliel and R. Eliezer say: She is believed [and] R. Joshua says: We do not live from her mouth?[8] [There too,] what *miggo* is there? True, there is according to Ze'iri, who says [that] 'she was talking' means 'she was hiding herself' [with a man], [in which case she has] a *miggo*, for if she wished she could say, 'I had no intercourse,' and [still] she said, 'I had intercourse,' [therefore] she is believed. But according to R. Assi, who says [that] 'she was talking' means 'she had intercourse,' what *miggo* is there?[9] Or again [should he refer] to this: She says, 'I was injured by [a piece of] wood,' and he says, 'Not so, but thou wast trodden by a man.' Rabban Gamaliel and R. Eliezer say: She is believed, and R. Joshua says: We do not live from her mouth?[10] [There too] what *miggo* is there? True, there is according to R. Eleazer, who says that [the dispute between the husband and the wife is] with regard to a *maneh* and nothing,[11] [in which case she has] a *miggo*, for if she wished she could say, 'I was injured by a piece of wood

(1) I.e., to the first clause in the first Mishnah of this Chapter. (2) I.e., the controversy regarding *miggo* v. *supra* p. 67, n. 8. (3) Lit., 'he refers to *miggo* and he refers to the first chapter'. (4) I.e., to which case does he refer? (5) V. *supra* 13*a*, second Mishnah, second clause. (6) Lit., 'there'. (7) She could not say that she had no intercourse! What other statement could she have made which would have been more to her advantage? (8) V. *supra* 13*a*, second Mishnah, first clause. (9) She could not say that she had no intercourse since there is evidence to the contrary! What other statement could she have made which would have been more to her advantage? (10) V. *infra* 13*a*, first Mishnah. (11) V. *supra* 13*a*.

under thee,'[1] and she would get two hundred [*zuz.*],[2] and [still] she said [that she was injured] earlier,[3] [therefore] she is believed. But according to R. Johanan who says that [the dispute between the husband and the wife is] with regard to two hundred [*zuz*] and a *maneh*,[4] what *miggo* is there?[5]—But [he refers] to this: If one has married a woman and has not found in her virginity [and] she says, 'After thou hadst betrothed me [to thyself] I was violated and thy field has been inundated,' and he says, 'Not so, but [it happened] before I betrothed thee [to myself]'. Rabban Gamaliel and R. Eliezer say: She is believed, and R. Joshua says: We do not live from her mouth.[6] For [here there is] a *miggo*, because if she wished she could say, 'I was injured by a piece of wood under thee,' and [by saying this] she would not make herself unfit for the priesthood, and [still] she said, 'I have been violated', and [by saying this] she made herself unfit for the priesthood; therefore Rabban Gamaliel said that she is believed. And R. Joshua said to Rabban Gamaliel: With regard to this *miggo* here,[7] I agree with you, but with regard to that *miggo* there,[8] I differ from you. Now, this is a *miggo* and that is a *miggo*, what difference is there between this *miggo* and that *miggo*?—Here[9] there is no slaughtered ox before you, there[10] there is a slaughtered ox before you.[11]

(1) Since our betrothal. In which case she is entitled to two hundred *zuz*. (2) V. *supra* p. 69. (3) That is, before the betrothal and thus claims only a *maneh*. (4) V. *supra* p. 68. And she would get two hundred (*zuz*) if she was injured by a piece of wood, whether she was injured before or after the betrothal. (5) V. preceding note. (6) V. *supra* 12*b*. (7) The second clause of our Mishnah. The man could have been silent, therefore we believe also his second statement. (8) In the Mishnah 12*b*. (9) In the second clause of our Mishnah. (10) In the Mishnah 12*b*. (11) The phrase 'there is a slaughtered ox before you' means, there is a fact which cannot be wiped out or denied. This applies to the Mishnah 12*b*. The virginity is not there. This fact remains. According to R. Joshua in such a case a *miggo* is of no avail. But in our Mishnah the other person would not have known that the field once belonged to his father if the present holder had not told him so. This is meant by the phrase, 'There is no slaughtered ox before you.' There is no fact here if the holder of the field had not stated it. In such a case a *miggo* is applied, because we assume that the holder of the field would not have said it if he had not bought the field from the other man's father.

But since most women get married as virgins,[1] [even] if no witnesses came,[2] what of it?[3]—Rabina said: Because one can say:[4] most women marry as maidens and a minority as widows. And whenever a maiden gets married, it is spoken about,[5] [16b] and since this one was not spoken about,[6] [the presumption that she belonged to] the majority has become shaken.—But if [you maintain that] whenever a maiden gets married it is spoken about, [then even] when witnesses come,[7] what of it?[8] They are false witnesses![9]—But, said Rabina: *most* marriages of maidens are spoken about,[10] and [in the case of] this one, since it was not spoken about, [the presumption that she—the bride— belonged to] the majority has been shaken.[11]

IF THERE ARE WITNESSES THAT SHE WENT OUT WITH A HINUMA, etc. Should we not be afraid that perhaps she might produce witnesses before this court and get [her *kethubah*] paid, and [later] she might produce the written document [of the *kethubah*] before another court and get [her *kethubah*] paid [a second time] by that [document]?—R. Abbahu said: This teaches [that] one writes a quittance.[12] R. Papa said:[13] It speaks of a place in which one does not write a *kethubah* document.[14]

(1) Reverting to the argument at the beginning of this folio. (2) That she went out with a *hinuma* and uncovered head. (3) She should be regarded as having belonged to the majority and therefore having been a virgin at her marriage, so that her *kethubah* would be two hundred (*zuz*). (4) Lit., 'there is to say'. (5) Lit., 'she has a voice.' A girl's marriage is much more spoken about than a widow's marriage. A girl's marriage is also much more festive and much more public. (6) If this had been known as a maiden's marriage it would have been made public and there would have been people to come forward and give evidence that she went out with a *hinuma* and her head uncovered. (7) And say that she went out with a *hinuma* and uncovered head. (8) Since this marriage was not spoken about, one should say that she was not married as a maiden. (9) Since other people knew nothing about it. (10) Not '*all* marriages of maidens'. (11) Therefore, the presence or absence of witnesses makes all the difference. (12) [And the husband produces a quittance that he paid her the *kethubah*, cf. B.B. 171*b*.] (13) [He holds that no quittance may be written for fear of putting the lender at a disadvantage in case he loses it. What they do on payment is to tear up the bond without which the creditor cannot claim his debt.] (14) [And the woman collects her dues in the court since it is a condition enjoined by the court, v. *infra* 51*a*.]

Some refer[1] this[2] to the [following] Baraitha: If she lost her *kethubah* document, or she hid it, or it was burnt, [then the matter is as follows:] if they danced before her, played before her, passed before her the cup of [glad] tidings,[3] or the cloth of virginity[4] [and] if she has witnesses with regard to one of these [things],[5] her *kethubah* is two hundred [*zuz*]. Now should we not be afraid that perhaps she might produce witnesses before this court and get [her *kethubah*] paid and [later] she might produce the written document before another court and get [her *kethubah*] paid [a second time] by that document?—R. Abbahu said: This teaches [that] one writes a quittance. R. Papa said: It speaks of a place in which one does not write a *kethubah* document. But does it not say '[if] she lost her *kethubah* document'?[6]—[It so happened] that he wrote her [one]. But may she not after all produce it and get [her *kethubah*] paid [a second time] with it! The meaning of 'she lost [it]' is 'she lost [it] in fire.'[7] If so, it is the same as 'it was burnt!' And then, what can you say with regard to 'she hid [it]?'[8] And furthermore, why [mention] 'she lost [it]'?[9]—But [this is what the Baraitha means]: if she lost it, it is as if she had hidden it before us, and we do not give her [the *kethubah* money] until witnesses say [that] her *kethubah* document has been burnt.[10] He who refers this[11] to the Baraitha, all the more [does he refer it] to the Mishnah. But he who refers this to our Mishnah [does] not [refer it] to the Baraitha, because of the difficulty.[12]

IF THERE ARE WITNESSES, etc. Should we not be afraid that perhaps she might produce witnesses of *hinuma* before this court and get [her *kethubah*] paid and [later] she might produce [other]

(1) Lit., 'teach'. (2) The controversy of R. Abbahu and R. Papa. (3) כוס של בשורה, v. *infra*. (4) On the day of her marriage. (5) Which are only done at the marriage of a virgin. (6) And this shows that a *kethubah* document was written. (7) And she cannot produce it any more. (8) If she hid it, she can produce it. (9) As 'she lost (it)' is mentioned separately, it cannot mean 'in fire'. (10) This means that if 'she lost' it or 'she hid' it, she does not get the *kethubah* money unless she finds the document and produces it. If she says 'it was burnt,' she must produce witnesses that it was burnt. This answer is indeed unsatisfactory. (11) The controversy of R. Abbahu and R. Papa. (12) V. *supra* note 10.

witnesses of *hinuma* before another court and get [her *kethubah*] paid [a second time]?—Where it is not possible otherwise,[1] we certainly write a quittance.

[It is said above in the Baraitha]: '[If] they passed before her the cup of [glad] tidings.'[2] What is the cup of [glad] tidings? R. Adda the son of Ahaba said: One passes before her a cup of wine of *Terumah*,[3] as if to say, 'This one is worthy of eating *Terumah*.'[4] R. Papa demurred to this: Does not a widow eat *Terumah*?[5] But, said R. Papa [as if to say] 'This one is "first"[6] as *Terumah* is "first".'[7]

It has been taught: R. Judah says: One passes before her a cask of wine. R. Adda the son of Ahaba said: [If she was] a virgin one passes before her a closed one, [and if] she has had intercourse with a man one passes before her an open one. Why? Let us pass [a cask of wine] before a virgin and let us not pass [a cask of wine] at all before one who had intercourse?—[It may happen] sometimes that she has seized[8] two hundred [*zuz*] and [then] says, 'I was a virgin and they did not pass [a cask of wine] before me because they were prevented by an accident.'[9]

Our Rabbis taught: How does one dance[10] before the bride? Beth Shammai say: [17*a*] The bride as she is.[11] And Beth Hillel say: 'Beautiful and graceful bride'![12] Beth Shammai said to Beth

(1) [In a place where no *kethubah* is written, and the woman collects her dues at the court by means of witnesses, and there is the possibility for her to produce two sets of witnesses before two different courts and collect her *kethubah* twice.] (2) כוס של בשורה v. Krauss *TA*. II, p. 459. In J. Keth. II, 1, הבית של בשורות 'a barrel of glad tidings' is mentioned. (3) V. Glos. (4) That is, she is unblemished and fit to marry a priest. (5) A widow may also marry a priest. (6) I. e., she is a virgin and for the first time dedicated to married life. (7) *Terumah* is called 'first', cf. Num. XV, 20, 21; Deut. XVIII, 4. (8) If she is in possession of the two hundred *zuz* the *onus probandi* is on the other party. (9) Rashi says: They were intoxicated from the wine which they drank at the wedding, and the other party could not bring evidence to disprove her statements. But now that a cask of wine has to be passed also before one who was not a virgin, witnesses will be available to testify that in the latter case an open cask was passed before her. (10) What does one sing or recite? (11) One does not exaggerate in praising the bride. If she is not beautiful one does not say that she is. (12) Every bride has to be regarded and praised as beautiful and graceful.

Hillel: If she was lame or blind, does one say of her: 'Beautiful and graceful bride'? Whereas the Torah[1] said, *'Keep thee far from a false matter.'*[2] Said Beth Hillel to Beth Shammai: According to your words,[3] if one has made a bad purchase in the market, should one praise it[4] in his eyes or depreciate it?[5] Surely,[6] one should praise it in his eyes. Therefore,[7] the Sages said: Always should the disposition of man be pleasant with people.—When R. Dimi came,[8] he said: Thus they sing before the bride in the West:[9] no powder[10] and no paint[11] and no waving[12] [of the hair], and still a graceful gazelle.

When the Rabbis ordained R. Zera they sang before him thus: No powder and no paint and no waving [of the hair], and still a graceful gazelle. When the Rabbis ordained R. Ammi and R. Assi they sang before them thus: Such as these, such as these ordain unto us, [but] do not ordain unto us of the perverters[13] or babblers,[14] and some say: of the half-scholars[15] or one-third-scholars.[16] —When R. Abbahu came from the Academy to the court of the Emperor,[17] hand-maids[18] from the Imperial house went out towards him and sang before him thus, 'Prince of his people, leader of his nation, shining light,[19] blessed be thy coming in peace!'

They tell of R. Judah b. Ila'i that he used to take a myrtle twig and dance before the bride and say: 'Beautiful and graceful bride.' R. Samuel the son of R. Isaac danced with three [twigs].[20] R. Zera

(1) I.e., the Pentateuch, (2) Ex. XXIII, 7. (3) I.e., according to the view you have just expressed. (4) The thing purchased. (5) In the text 'in his eyes' is repeated here. (6) Lit., 'you must say'. (7) Lit., 'from here'. (8) To Babylonia. (9) I.e., Palestine. (10) כחל. A powder used for painting the eye-lids, *stibium*. (11) שרק. A paint for the face. (12) פירכום means 'making the hair beautiful' either by dyeing it or by dressing it. It may also denote making the hair into locks. V. Levy and Jast. 'Waving' is perhaps the best translation. It may also refer to painting the face. Cf. Shab. 34*a* and Jast. s.v. פרכם I. One painting refers to the eyes, one to the cheeks, and one, perhaps, to the lips. (13) I.e., immature scholars who pervert the reasons of the law (Rashi). V. Sanh. 14*a*. (14) I.e., men who cannot substantiate their decisions, who cannot argue properly (Rashi). (15) V, Levy. (16) V. Levy. On these terms v. also Sanh. (Sonc. ed.) p. 65 notes. (17) At Caesarea where he had his academy. (18) In Sanh. 14*a*, 'the matrons'. (19) Lit., 'lamp of light'. (20) [He used to throw up three twigs one after the other and catch them in turn (Rashi).]

said: The old man is putting us to shame.[1] When he[2] died,[3] a pillar of fire came between him and the whole [of the rest of the] world. And there is a tradition that a pillar of fire has made such a separation[4] only either for one in a generation or for two in a generation only.[5] R. Zera said: His twig[6] [benefited] the old man, and some say: His habit[7] [benefited] the old man, and some say: his folly[8] [benefited] the old man.—R. Aḥa took[9] her[10] on his shoulder and danced [with her]. The Rabbis said to him: May we [also] do it? He said to them: If they[11] are on you[12] like a beam,[13] [then it is] all right, and if not, [you may] not.

R. Samuel b. Naḥmani said [that] R. Jonathan said: It is allowed to look intently at the face of the bride all the seven [days][14] in order to make her beloved to her husband.[15] But the law is not according to him.

Our Rabbis taught: One causes a funeral procession[16] to make way[17] for a bridal procession,[18] and both of them[19] for the King of Israel. One tells of King Agrippa that he made way for a bride, and the Sages praised him.—They praised him— from this it would seem that he did well. Did not R. Ashi say: Even according to him, who says [that] if a Nasi forgoes his honour, his honour is forgone, if a king forgoes his honour, his honour is not forgone, for a Master said:[20] *'Thou shalt set a king over thee,'*[21] [this means] that his awe shall be over thee?[22]—It was [at] a cross-road.[23]

(1) Through his myrtle dance before the bride. (2) R. Samuel the son of R. Isaac. (3) Lit., 'when his soul was at rest'. (4) I.e., that such an apparition was seen. (5) I.e., for one man or two men in a generation. Only for very great and pious men such a phenomenon occurs. (6) With which he danced at weddings before the bride. This good deed was the cause of the apparition. (7) Of dancing before the bride. (8) Of dancing with three twigs before the bride (Rashi). The words in the text for 'twig', 'habit' and 'folly' are almost alike. (9) Lit., 'caused her to ride'. (10) The bride. (11) The brides. (12) I.e., on your shoulders. (13) I.e., awaking no sensual desire. (14) Of the wedding-week. (15) When he (the husband) sees that all look at her intently (admiring her beauty), her beauty enters his heart (Rashi). (16) Lit., 'the dead'. (17) Lit., 'to pass by'. (18) Lit., 'before a bride'. (19) Lit., 'and this and this'. (20) In Ḳid. 32*b* it says שנאמר, 'for it is said'. Here אמר מר is used referring apparently to R. Ashi. (21) Deut. XVII, 15. (22) That thou shalt respect him, v. Soṭ. (Sonc. ed.) p. 204. (23) Where Agrippa made way for a bride,

Our Rabbis taught: One interrupts[1] the study of the Torah for the sake of a funeral procession[2] and the leading[3] of the bride [under the bridal canopy]. They tell of R. Judah b. Ila'i that he interrupted the study of the Torah for the sake of a funeral procession[4] and the leading[5] of the bride [under the bridal canopy]. This applies only[6] when there are not sufficient people at the funeral procession,[7] but if there are sufficient people one does not interrupt [the study of the Torah].[8] And how many are sufficient? R. Samuel the son of Ini said in the name of Rab: Twelve thousand men and six thousand trumpets.[9] And some say: Twelve thousand[10] men and among them six thousand trumpets.[11] 'Ulla said: For instance when people form a line from the city-gate to the burial place. R. Shesheth, and some say R. Johanan said: Its taking away[12] is like its giving.[13] As its giving was in [the presence of] sixty myriads[14] [of people], so [has] its taking away [to be] in [the presence of] sixty myriads [of people]. And this is the case only[15] with regard to one who read [the Bible] and studied [the Mishnah.] [17b] But for one who taught [others] there is no limit.[16]

AND IF THERE ARE WITNESSES THAT SHE WENT OUT WITH A HINUMA etc. What is *hinuma?*— Surḥab b. Papa said in the name of Ze'iri: A myrtle-canopy.[17] R. Joḥanan said: A veil under which the bride [sometimes] slumbers.[18]

R. JOḤANAN THE SON OF BEROḲA SAYS, etc. It was taught:

and people might have thought that he had to go in the other direction.
(1) Lit., 'one abolishes', 'suspends'. (2) Lit., 'for the bringing out of the dead'. (3) Lit., 'for the bringing in'. (4) Lit., 'for the bringing out of the dead'. (5) Lit., 'for the bringing in'. (6) Lit., 'in what (case) are these words said'? (7) Lit., 'when there is not with him all his requirement'. (8) This limitation only applies to the funeral procession, but not to the leading of the bride to the canopy. (9) I.e., trumpeters. (10) So the correct reading in Meg. 29a. Our text 'thirteen thousand'. (11) I.e., trumpeters. (12) I.e., the taking away of the Torah. When a scholar dies the Torah which he knew and studied is taken away, as far as his knowledge and his study are concerned. (13) I.e., as the giving of the Torah on Sinai. (14) I.e., 600,000. (15) Lit., 'and these words (have been said)'. (16) Of the number of people attending his funeral. (17) So Rashi. V. next note. (18) So Rashi. Cf. however, Levy and Jast. s. vv. Cf. also Krauss, *T.A.*, II, p. 457, note 311, and p. 458, note 316.

This was [regarded as] a proof in Judaea; what is [the proof in] Babylonia?—Rab said: The dripping of oil on the heads[1] of the scholars.[2] R. Papa said to Abaye: Did the master speak of oil [used] for cleaning [the head]?[3]—He said to him:[4] Orphan,[5] did not your mother do the dripping of the oil on the heads of the scholars at the time[6] of the event?[7] As that [case when] one of the scholars was occupied with [the wedding of] his son in the house of Rabbah b. 'Ulla—and some say, Rabbah b. 'Ulla was occupied with [the wedding of] his son in the house of one of the scholars—and he dripped oil on the heads of the scholars at the time of the event.[8]—What [sign is there at the wedding of] a widow?—R. Joseph taught: A widow has no roasted ears of corn [distributed at her wedding].[9]

AND R. JOSHUA ADMITS THAT IF ONE SAYS TO HIS FELLOW etc. But let him[10] teach: R. Joshua admits that in [the case when] one says to his fellow, 'this field belonged to you[11] and I have bought it of you' [he is believed]?—Because he would have to teach [in] the last clause: If there are witnesses that it was his and he says, 'I have bought it of you', he is not believed.[12] [And] how shall we imagine this case? If he ate [the fruits of] it [during the] years of *ḥazakah*[13] why should he not be believed? And if he did not eat

(1) Lit., 'head'. (2) Rashi: Young scholars who were present at the wedding. This was a sign that the bride was a virgin. (3) Surely the scholars do not require such oil (Rashi). Cf. also Krauss, *TA.*, I, p. 683, n. 187. (4) Abaye. (5) I.e., one who is ignorant of this custom (Rashi). (6) Lit., 'hour'. (7) I.e., at your wedding. (8) Of the wedding. (9) And the absence of the ears of corn is the sign that she is a widow (Rashi). (10) The teacher of our Mishnah. (11) Instead of 'to your father'. [Since the reason for R. Joshua's ruling is that it is a case where there is no slaughtered ox before you, he could have illustrated it in this way (Rashi). Tosaf.: this would be a stronger case seeing that both parties are 'sure' in their plea.] (12) And this is not the case, for the reasons to be stated immediately. (13) 'To eat' the field meant 'to use and take' the fruits of the field. 'To eat' the field without anyone complaining about this meant undisturbed possession of the field. And if this undisturbed possession lasted three years without interruption it established ownership. V. B.B. 28ff. Both the holding of the land and the right accruing from it giving the title of ownership are called *ḥazakah*. 'Years of *ḥazakah*'; the term means both 'the years of holding' and 'the years

[the fruits of] it [during the] years of *ḥazaḳah* it is self-evident that he is not believed![1] — If so, with regard to his father[2] also [one could argue]: If he[3] ate [the fruits of] it [during the] years of *ḥazaḳah*, why should he not be believed?[4] And if he did not eat [the fruits of] it [during the] years of *ḥazaḳah*, it is self-evident that he is not believed! We grant you with regard to his father, [because] there may be a case, as, for instance, when he ate [the fruits of] it two [years] during the life of the father and one [year] during the life of his son.[5] And [this would be] according to R. Huna, for R. Huna

of holding that give the right and title of ownership.' 'To eat' is similar to '*usus*' in the Twelve Tables (VI, 3). In the sense of 'holding' *ḥazaḳah* is also similar to '*usus*'. In the sense of 'acquisition (of ownership) by holding for a certain period fixed by law', it is similar to '*usucapio*' in Roman Law. Ulpian says, '*Usucapio est adjectio dominii per continuationem possessionis temporis lege definita.*' '*Usucapio* is the acquisition of ownership by possession for the length of time required by law.' The full time for '*usucapio*' of lands and houses was in Roman Law (till Justinian) two years. In Talmudic Law it was three years. For the Roman Law of '*usucapio*' see, Hunter, *Roman Law*, 4th ed., p. 205ff, Muirhead, *Law of Rome*, 3rd ed., p. 132f., p. 241 and p. 380, and Moyle, *Justiniani Institutiones*, 3th ed. p. 225ff. As to *iusta causa* and *iustus titulus*, v. Moyle, *op. cit.* p. 226, n. 3; in Talmudic Law cf. Baba Bathra, fol. 41*a*, Mishnah. חזקה על ידי אכילה would correspond to *usucapio*. 'The taking by using' (*usucapio*) would after the prescribed time become 'taking (altogether), that is acquiring by use.' In Talmudic Law '*capio*' was the more dominating term. It seems that the full meaning of '*auctoritas*' in '*usus auctoritas fundi*' (in the Twelve Tables, v. Muirhead, *op. cit.* p. 132) was lost in the course of time. '*Auctoritas*' seems to mean the authority, the right of ownership acquired by the use of the soil (real property). '*Usucapio*' is not so good as '*usus auctoritas*'. '*Usucapio*' has, after all, in Roman Law two meanings, as *ḥazaḳah* in Talmudic Law. It is worthy of note that Ulpian, who came from Syria, was a contemporary of the Tannaim of the second half of the second century. Gaius also lived in the second century. אכלה is not translated by 'he had the usufruct of it', because 'usufruct' is the *right* of using and taking the fruits of property not one's own. (*Justinian's Institutes*, II, 4) v. Moyle, Engl. Translation of *Justinian's Institutes*, 4th ed., p. 47, v. also Hunter, *op. cit.*, p. 396.

(1) And since he had to teach in the last clause the case where the field belonged to 'his father', he also taught in the first clause 'this field belonged to your father.' (2) I.e., the father of the other man. (3) The claimant, i.e., the man who says, 'This field belonged to your father and I bought it of him.' (4) In the last clause of the Mishnah. (5) [And the Mishnah teaches us although he did occupy for three years he is nevertheless not believed.]

said: One does not acquire the ownership of the property of a minor by the undisturbed possession of it during the prescribed period, even if [he continued in the possession after] the minor had become of age.[1] But R. Huna comes to let us hear [what is already taught in] our Mishnah![2]—If you wish, you may say, R. Huna says, 'what is to be derived from our Mishnah by implication.'[3] And if you wish, you may say, 'he lets us hear, even if he had become of age'.[4]

But let him[5] [after all] teach with regard to himself[6] and put the case when he[7] ate [the fruits of] it two [years] in his presence[8] and one [year] in his absence,[9] and, for instance, when he[10] fled? —Because of what did he flee? If he fled because of [danger to his] life,[11] it is self-evident that he[12] is not believed, since he cannot protest![13] And if he fled because of money [matters],[14] he ought to have protested,[15] because it is established for us[16] [that] a protest in his absence[17] is a [valid] protest![18] For we have learned:

(1) V. B.M. 39*b*. For certain business transactions, the minor became of age, in Talmudic Law, when he reached the age of twenty; v. B.B. 155*a*. (2) According to the answer just given the rule stated by R. Huna is implied in the teaching of the Mishnah. (3) What R. Huna states is not said explicitly in the Mishnah. It is to be derived by implication. And R. Huna derives it and states it as a rule. (4) The rule as stated by R. Huna has an additional point, namely, 'even if he had become of age'. This cannot be derived from the Mishnah by implication. This additional point is the reason why R. Huna states the rule. (5) The teacher of our Mishnah. (6) The other man, and not the other man's father. (7)The present possessor. (8) In the presence of the other man. (9) The year in his absence does not count, as he could not protest. (10) The other man. [And thus teach us that, although he did occupy it for three years, the year he had it in the other's absence does not count, and he is not believed.] (11) He was in danger of his life in the place in which he lived. He would be afraid to protest (against the man holding his land) in his place of refuge, because he would be afraid of being pursued by those who sought his life. The fact that he did not protest during the third year would, therefore, not make the possession of the field by the present holder an undisturbed possession for the period required by the law. (12) The present possessor. (13) Cf. n. 11. (14) To avoid unpleasantness because of money-matters. (15) Wherever he is, as no personal harm would be done to him even if his place of refuge became known. (16) I.e., it is an established rule. (17) I.e., in the absence of the present holder. (18) Because the protest

There are three countries with regard to *ḥazaḳah:* Judaea, Transjordan and Galilee.[1] [If] he[2] was in Judaea and someone took possession [of his land] in Galilee, [or he[2] was] in Galilee and someone took possession [of his land] in Judaea, it is no *ḥazaḳah*[3] until he is with him in the [same] province.[4] And we asked[5] concerning it,[6] What opinion does he[7] hold? If he holds that a protest in his absence[8] is a [valid] protest,[9] this should apply also to Judaea and Galilee.[10] And if he holds [that] a protest in his absence is not a [valid] protest, it should not be [a valid protest] even if they are both in Judaea?[11] [And] R. Abba the son of Memel said: Indeed, he holds [that] a protest in his absence is a [valid] protest, but our Mishnah speaks[12] of a time of lawlessness.[13]—And why does he just speak of Judaea and Galilee?[14] [18*a*] Because [the condition of the relations between] Judaea and Galilee is usually as in time of lawlessness.[15] But let him teach: R. Joshua admits [that] when one says to his fellow, 'I borrowed from you a *maneh* and

goes from person to person until it reaches the present holder. V. B.B. 38*b*.

(1) I.e.. the three provinces of Palestine mentioned in the Mishnah are regarded as three different countries in respect of *ḥazaḳah*. (2) The owner of the land. (3) The undisturbed holding of the land for the period required by law does not acquire ownership. (4) Mishnah, B.B. 38*a*: 'in one province'. Only when both, owner and holder, are in the same province, that is in Judaea or in Galilee, v. B.B. 38*a*. (5) By way of discussion. (6) Cf. B.B. 38*a-b*. (7) The teacher of the Mishnah. (8) I.e., in the absence of the present holder. (9) Because the protest goes from person to person until it reaches the present holder, v. B.B. 38*b*. (10) I.e., if the one is in Judaea and the other is in Galilee in due course the protest made by the owner in one province will reach the holder in the other province. (11) Lit., 'even Judaea and Judaea also not'.—Even if they are in the same province, but in different places. The protest is still in his absence. (12) Lit., 'and the Mishnah they taught'. (13) In the text: הירום 'Lawlessness'. A lawlessness brought about by war or by other causes. Through the lawlessness there is no communication between the two provinces, so that the protest cannot reach the holder of the land. And if the protest cannot reach the holder of the land, the protest, if made, would have no force. And as the protest would have no force, the possession of the holder does not become an undisturbed possession. Cf. Rashbam, B.B. 38*a*. (14) Lit., 'and why are Judaea and Galilee different that he takes (them)'? The meaning of the question is: 'Lawlessness may also occur between towns in the same province.' (15) Cf. B.B. 28*a* for variants.

paid it [back] to you,' he is believed![1]—Because he would have [in that case] to teach [in] the last clause: 'If there are witnesses that he borrowed from him [a *maneh*] and he says, "I have paid it [back]" he is not believed', but it is established for us[2] [that] if one lends [money] to his fellow before[3] witnesses, he need not pay it [back] to him before witnesses.[4]—But let him [then] teach: R. Joshua admits [that] if one says to his fellow, 'I owed to your father a *maneh*[5] and I returned to him half'[6] he is believed![7]—According to whose opinion?[8] If according to the opinion of the Rabbis, surely they say [that he is regarded as] one who returns a lost thing;[9] [and] if according to R. Eliezer b. Jacob, surely he says that he must take an oath![10] For it has been taught:[11] R. Eliezer b. Jacob says: Sometimes [it may happen] that a man has to take an oath because of his own statement. How [is it]? [If one says to his fellow], 'I owed to your father a *maneh* and I returned to him half,' he must take an oath.[12] And this is [a case] where one takes an oath because of one's statement.[13] But the Sages say: He is [regarded] only as one who returns a lost thing and he is free. And does not R. Eliezer b. Jacob hold [that] one who returns a lost thing is free?[14]—Rab said: [It speaks here of a case] when a minor claimed from him.[15] But did not a Master say: One does not

(1) [The Mishnah could have illustrated the ruling of R. Joshua in a case 'where there is no ox slaughtered before you', in this way instead of by one dealing with real property and with 'your father.'] (2) I.e., it is an established rule; cf. B.B. 170*a*, Shebu. 41*b*. (3) Lit., 'with'. (4) I.e., he is believed if he says he repaid it to him in the absence of witnesses, so the Mishnah could not teach that he is not believed. (5) Lit.,.'a *maneh* to thy father in my hand', that is, thy father had a *maneh* in my hand. (6) Lit., 'and made him eat half (or a portion)', it may be that he paid him the half in kind, perhaps in goods. (7) [Since it is made entirely on his own initiative. This would be a strong point, having regard to the law that elsewhere he who admits half a claim is not believed without an oath, v. *infra*.] (8) Would that statement be. (9) Even if the admission is not made on his own initiative but made on the claim of the son, he is free from paying the other half, and from taking an oath. V. Shebu 42*a*, also 38*b*. (10) As to the other half. (11) Shebu. 42*b*. (12) As to the other half. (13) If he would not have made the statement no one would have known of his debt. (14) From taking an oath. [Surely this is against the well-established principle that he is exempt. v. Giṭ. 48*b*.] (15) His statement was therefore not entirely 'his own statement'.

take an oath because of a claim by a deaf-mute, an imbecile, or a minor?[1]—What is [meant by] 'minor'? A grown-up person, and why does he call him 'minor'? Because with regard to the affairs of his father he is [regarded as] a minor. If so, [how can you say] 'his own statement?' It is a claim [made] by others!—It is a claim [made] by others and [also] his own admission. But all claims [consist of] a claim [made] by others and one's own admission![2] —They differ here with regard to [an opinion of] Rabbah, for Rabbah said: Why did the Torah say [that] he who admits a part of the claim must take an oath? [Because] it is a presumption [that] no man is insolent in the face of his creditor. He would [indeed] like to deny the whole [debt], but he does not do it[3] because no one is [so] insolent. [18*b*] [Indeed] he would like to admit the whole of it,[4] only he does not do it in order to slip away from him [for the present],[5] and he thinks, 'as soon as I will have money I will pay it'.[6] And [therefore] the Divine Law[7] said: Impose an oath on him, so that he should admit the whole of it.[8] [Now] R. Eliezer b. Jacob holds [that] he is not insolent against him nor against his son, and therefore he is not [regarded as] one who returns a lost thing. And the Rabbis hold [that] against him he is not insolent, but against his son he might be insolent, and since he is not insolent,[9] he is [regarded as] one who returns a lost thing.[10]

MISHNAH. IF WITNESSES SAID, 'THIS[11] IS OUR HANDWRITING, BUT WE WERE FORCED,[12] WE WERE MINORS, WE WERE DISQUALIFIED WITNESSES,[13] THEY ARE BELIEVED.[14] BUT

(1) V. Shebu. 38*b*. [How then could R. Eliezer in such a case impose an oath?] (2) [All cases for which an oath is imposed are such as where the one against whom a claim is made makes a partial admission. (3) Lit., 'and this one that he does not deny it'. (4) The whole debt. (5) I.e., to postpone the matter. (6) The whole debt. (7) Lit., 'the All-Merciful'. (8) Now. (9) And admits a part of the debt. (10) And he is believed without an oath. For further notes on the whole passage v. Sheb. (Sonc. ed.) pp. 257ff. (11) The handwriting of the signatures on a document. (12) To sign. (13) Lit., 'unfit with regard to testimony'. They may have been unfit either through kinship or through their conduct (Rashi). Cf. Sanh. 27*b* and 24*b*. (14) [Since it is they who at the first

IF THERE ARE WITNESSES THAT IT IS THEIR HANDWRITING, OR THEIR HANDWRITING COMES OUT FROM ANOTHER PLACE,[1] THEY ARE NOT BELIEVED.[2]

GEMARA. Rami b. Ḥama said: They taught[3] this[4] only when they[5] said: We were forced [by threats] with regard to money,[6] but [if they said], we were forced [by threats] with regard to [our] life, they are believed. Raba said to him: Is it so? After he has once testified, he cannot again testify![7] And if you will say [that] this applies only to an oral testimony but not to testimony in a document—did not Resh Laḳish say: If witnesses are signed on a document it is as if their testimony had been examined in court?[8] No; if it has been said,[9] it has been said with regard to the first clause, [where it is stated:] THEY ARE BELIEVED. Whereupon Rami b. Ḥama said: They taught this[10] only when they[11] said, 'We were forced [by threats] with regard to [our] life,' but if they said, 'we were forced [by threats] with regard to money,' they are not believed, because no one makes himself [out to be] a wicked man.[12]

Our Rabbis taught: They[13] are not believed to disqualify[14] it.[15]

instance confirm their signatures, they are also believed in the attendant reservation made by them in regard thereto.]

(1) As when their handwriting has been confirmed on another document. (2) [Since the validity of their signatures does not depend on their present attestation the reservation is not accepted.] (3) In our Mishnah. (4) That if their handwriting is confirmed through another document they are not believed to disqualify their signature on the present document. (5) The witnesses. (6) Money threats should not have made them sign a falsehood. And they are not believed to say that they signed a falsehood, v. note 12. (7) Retracting what he testified before—By their signatures they declared the document valid, and they cannot now declare it to be invalid. (8) Therefore, what applies to oral testimony applies also to testimony in a document. (9) I.e., if Rami b. Ḥama made any statement similar to the one mentioned above. (10) That they are believed to disqualify their signature. (11) The witnesses. (12) I.e., a man's testimony against himself has no legal effect. And by saying now that money threats made them sign a false testimony, the witnesses would make themselves out to be wicked men. V. n. 6. (13) The witnesses who signed the document. (14) In the manner stated in the first clause of the Mishnah. (15) The document.

This is the view of R. Meir; but the Sages say [that] they are believed. This is right according to the Rabbis,[1] who follow[2] their principle[3] 'the mouth that bound is the mouth that loosened,'[4] but what is the reason of R. Meir?[5] I grant you [with regard to] 'DISQUALIFIED WITNESSES,'[6] [because] the creditor himself examines well [the witnesses] beforehand and [then] lets [them] sign.[7] [With regard to] 'MINORS' also [it can be explained] according to R. Simeon b. Laḳish, for Resh Laḳish[8] said: [19*a*] It is a presumption that the witnesses do not sign a document unless [everything] was done by adults.[9] But what is the reason with regard to 'FORCED?'[10]—R. Ḥisda said: R. Meir holds that if one said to witnesses, 'sign a falsehood and you will not be killed,' they should rather be killed and not sign a falsehood.[11] Raba said to him: Now, if they would come to us to ask [our] advice, we would say unto them: Go [and] sign and do not be killed, for a Master said: 'There is nothing that comes before the saving of life except idolatry, incest and bloodshed only.'[12] Now that they have signed, can we say to them: why have you signed?[13] But the reason of

(1) I.e., 'the Sages'. (2) Lit., 'as'. (3) Lit., 'their reason'. (4) I.e., the same persons who made the document valid have the power to make the document invalid, cf. Mishnah 14*b*. (5) Lit., 'but according to R. Meir, what is the reason'? (6) I.e., if they say 'we were unfit to bear testimony;' v. *supra* p. 101, n. 13. (7) They must therefore have been fit witnesses, and they cannot now say that they were unfit. (8) Abbreviated from R. Simeon b. Laḳish. (9) That is, all the parties, including the witnesses, must have been grown-up persons and not minors. Therefore, R. Meir holds that the witnesses are not allowed to say now that they were minors when they signed the document. (10) Why does R. Meir hold that, if the witnesses said 'we were forced to sign the document,' they are not believed? (11) So that even if they say that they were forced to sign a falsehood by threats with regard to their life, they make themselves out to be wicked, and this no one can do; v. p. 102, n. 12. (12) This means: everything, every religious law must yield to the preservation of life. If one is told: Transgress this or that law, otherwise you will be killed, he should transgress the law and not be killed. Only in respect of idolatry, incest and bloodshed this rule does does not apply. One should rather lose one's life than commit these transgressions; v. Sanh. 74*a*. (13) In the case of signing a document, one should sign a falsehood and not lose one's life. The witnesses should, therefore, be believed if they said, 'we were forced to sign a falsehood by threats to our life'.

R. Meir is in accordance with what R. Huna [said in the name of] Rab: for R. Huna said [that] Rab said: If he[1] admits that he has written the bond,[2] there is no need[3] to confirm it.[4]

[To revert to] the main text:[5] R. Huna said [that] Rab said: If he[6] admits that he has written the bond, there is no need to confirm it. R. Naḥman said to him: Why do you go round about?[7] If you hold with R. Meir, say: the *halachah* is according to R. Meir.[8] He[9] [then] said to him:[10] And how do you Sir, hold?[11] He[12] said to him:[13] When they come[14] before us in court,[15] we say to them: go [and] confirm your documents[16] and [then] come to court.[17]

Rab Judah said [that] Rab said: If one said: This is a [loan-] deed of trust,[18] he is not believed. Who said [it]? If the debtor said it, it is plain; why should he be believed? If the creditor said [it], may a blessing come upon him![19] And if the witnesses said [it],—[then] if their handwriting comes out from another place, it is plain that they are not believed,[20] and if their handwriting does not come out from another place, why should they not be believed?[21] (Mnemonic: *BASH*)[22] Raba said: Indeed, the debtor

(1) The debtor. (2) And that the witnesses signed it by his direction. (3) For the creditor. (4) By the witnesses; and the debtor cannot plead that he has discharged the debt as long as the creditor holds the bond. The statement of the witnesses is not necessary now. Therefore, they cannot disqualify the bond, according to R. Meir. (5) From which the above quotation has been taken. (6) The debtor. (7) Lit., 'O thou cunning man, what is the use of thy going round about?' (Jast.). (8) [Instead of making it an independent statement, thus conveying the impression that it is a ruling on which there is no disagreement among Tannaim.] (9) R. Huna. (10) R. Naḥman. (11) I.e., what is your opinion? (12) R. Naḥman. (13) R. Huna. (14) Creditors. (15) Lit., 'to law'. (16) Rashi: 'Go and seek (and bring) your witnesses and confirm it (the document)'. [As a precaution, in case the debtor, though admitting that he wrote the bond, will plead that he had discharged the debt. (17) Lit., 'and go down to law'. (18) I.e., a bill of indebtedness signed on trust, in expectation that the loan, which is stated in the bill as having been advanced, will be advanced at some future date. The debtor trusts the creditor. The document is therefore called שטר אמנה, 'a document, or deed of trust'. (19) For being so honest. (20) V. our Mishnah. (21) It is their testimony upon which the validity of the document depends. (22) *B* stands for Ra*b*a, *A* for *A*baye, and *SH* for R. A*sh*i, the names of the three Amoraim who follow now.

said [it], and [it is] according to R. Huna, for R. Huna said [that] Rab said: If he[1] admits that he has written the document, there is no need to confirm it.[2] Abaye said: Indeed, the creditor said [it], and it is a case where he would injure others.[3] And [this is] according to R. Nathan, for it has been taught:[4] R. Nathan says: Whence [do we learn that], if one has a claim of a *maneh* against his fellow and that fellow against another fellow,[5] we[6] take out [the sum of a *maneh*] from this one and give it to that one?[7] The Writ says[8] *And he shall give [it] to whom he owes [it]*.[9] R. Ashi said: Indeed, the witnesses said [it], and [it is in a case] where their handwriting does not come out from another place; and as to your question,[10] Why should they not be believed, [the answer is] as stated by R. Kahana, for R. Kahana said: It is forbidden for a man to keep[11] a [loan-] deed of trust in his house, because it is said: *Let*[12] *not unrighteousness dwell in thy tents.*[13] [19b] And R. Shesheth, the son of R. Idi, said: From [the words of] R. Kahana can be inferred[14] [that] if witnesses said, 'Our words were [regarding a matter of] trust,'[15] they are not believed, for this reason:[16] Since it is 'unrighteousness' [we say that] they must not sign on [what is] unrighteousness.[17]

(1) The debtor. (2) [And the debtor cannot now invalidate the document by saying that it is a deed of trust even in the absence of attesting witnesses.] (3) If the creditor is believed that the document is a deed of trust, he will injure others, who are his creditors, if he has no other assets. Therefore, he is not believed. (4) In a Baraitha. (5) I.e., A owes a *maneh* to B, and B owes a *maneh* to C. (6) The court. (7) The court takes a *maneh* from A and gives it to C, since B who is the creditor of A is the debtor of C. (8) תלמוד לומר, lit., 'There is a teaching in the Scriptural text to intimate (this)', v. Jast. p. 1672. (9) Num. V, 7. E.V. *'and give it unto him to whom he is guilty'*. The teaching derived from these scriptural words by R. Nathan is: restitution has to be made to him to whom restitution is due. If A owes a *maneh* to B and B owes a *maneh* to C, the debt of A to B is paid, or may be paid, to C. (10) Lit., 'what you say'. (11) Lit., 'to cause to stay'. (12) M.T. *'And let not'*. (13) Job XI, 14. (14) Lit., 'understand from this'. (15) I.e., they say that the document they signed as witnesses was a loan-deed of trust. (16) Lit., 'what is the reason?' (17) And as they had signed, they are not believed when they say that it was a deed of trust, because they cannot make out themselves to be wicked; as *supra* p. 102, n. 12.

R. Joshua b. Levi, said: It is forbidden for a man to keep a paid bill of indebtedness in his house, because it is said: *'Let not unrighteousness dwell in thy tents'*.[1] In the West[2] they said in the name of Rab: [It is said]: *If iniquity be in thy hand, put it far away.*[3] This is a [loan-] deed of trust and a deed of good-will;[4] [and it is said]: *'And let not unrighteousness dwell in thy tents'*. This is a paid bill of indebtedness. He who says [that it[5] applies to] a paid bill of indebtedness, how much more [does it apply to] a [loan-] deed of trust.[6] [And] he, who says [that it applies to] a [loan-] deed of trust, [would hold that it does not apply to] a paid bill of indebtedness,[7] because sometimes they keep it on account of the scribe's fees.[8]

It has been stated: A book[9] that is not corrected[10]—R. Ami said: Until thirty days one is allowed to keep it, from then and further on, it is forbidden to keep it, because it is said: *'Let not unrighteousness dwell in thy tents.*[11]

R. Naḥman said: If witnesses said, 'Our words were [regarding a matter of] trust,'[12] they are not believed; [if they said], 'Our words were [attended by] declaration,'[13] they are [also] not believed.[14] Mar, the son of R. Ashi, said: [if witnesses said], 'Our words were [regarding a matter of] trust,' they are not believed;

(1) Job XI, 14. (2) Palestine. (3) Job XI, 14. (4) שטר פסים. Jast.: 'a deed of sale for accommodation' [Rashb. B.B. 154*b* explains it as a deed of feigned sale arranged for the purpose of making people believe that the person in whose favour it is made out is wealthy. '*Aruch* takes it as a variant of פסטים, πίστις, 'trust', (v. J. Keth. II, 3) and simply the Greek equivalent of שטר אמנה]. (5) The prohibition to keep the document. (6) There was fraud even in its origin. (7) Lit., 'but a paid bill of indebtedness, no.' (8) Lit., 'the small coins of the scribe'—the creditor paid the scribe's fee, which the debtor has to pay. The creditor, therefore, keeps back the paid bill of indebtedness until he has collected from the debtor the scribe's fee. There is a lawful ground for keeping back the documents. (9) Of the Bible. (10) I.e., the mistakes in the manuscript had not been corrected. (11) And it is 'unrighteousness' to keep a book of the Bible with mistakes uncorrected. (12) I.e., they say that the document they signed as witnesses was a loan-deed of trust. (13) Of protest. The witnesses say that the seller protested that he was forced to sell and did not recognize the sale, and that they signed the deed in cognizance of the protest. (14) They cannot invalidate a written document.

[but if they said], 'Our words were [attended by] declaration,' they are believed, for this reason:[1] this one[2] was allowed to be written[3] and that one[4] was not allowed to be written.[5]

Raba asked of R. Naḥman: How is it [if witnesses say], 'Our words were [subject to] a condition'?[6] [Are they not believed in the case of] 'declaration' and 'trust' because[7] they invalidate[8] the document, and [in] this [case of 'condition'] they also invalidate the document? Or is perhaps 'condition' a different thing?[9]—He[10] said to him:[11] When they[12] come before us in court, we say to them: go [and] fulfil your conditions and [then] come to court.

If one witness says [that there was] a condition,[13] and one witness says [that there was] no condition R. Papa said: they both testify to a valid document and only one says [that there was] a condition, and the words of one [witness] have no value where there are two witnesses.[14] R. Huna the son of R. Joshua demurred to this: If so,[15] even if they both say [that there was a condition] [their words should] also [have no value]![16] But we say [that] they come to uproot their testimony,[17] and this one also comes to uproot his testi-

(1) Lit., 'what is the reason'. (2) The latter. (3) In order to get out the seller from his predicament. (4) The former. (5) On account of 'unrighteousness'. (6) The witnesses say, 'we signed the deed of sale, but the sale was made dependent upon a condition, which has not been fulfilled'. (7) Lit., 'this is the reason'. (8) Lit., 'uproot'. (9) [The condition in itself does not affect the validity of the document, only the non-fulfilment thereof.] (10) R. Naḥman. (11) Raba. (12) The purchasers in a transaction, the witnesses to which declare, that it was subject to a condition. (13) Attached to the transaction. (14) Lit., 'in the place of two'. (15) [Since the confirmation of the signature by the witness to the transaction is treated as a formal attestation of the document, which bars the admission of any qualifying declaration subsequent thereto.] (16) [Having once testified to the validity of the document, they cannot subsequently retract by saying that it was subject to a condition. Why then did R. Naḥman, in the case of two witnesses, insist on the purchasers fulfilling the condition?] (17) [The mere confirmation of their signatures by the witnesses does not complete their attestation of the document. This is completed in their subsequent statement that it was subject to a condition. This latter statement, however, taken in itself, is but a qualification of their former statement confirming their signatures without any direct bearing as to the validity of the document, which really depends upon the fulfilment or non-fulfilment of this condition. In this it is different from the case where the subsequent

mony.[1] And the law is according to R. Huna, the son of R. Joshua.

Our Rabbis taught: If two [witnesses] were signed on a document and died, and two [witnesses] came from the street and said, 'We know that it is their handwriting, but they were forced, they were minors, they were disqualified witnesses,' they[2] are believed. But if there are [other] witnesses that this is their handwriting, or their handwriting comes out from another place, [namely] from a document, the validity of which was challenged,[3] and which was confirmed[4] in Court,[5] they are not believed.—And we collect[6] with it as with a valid document? Why? They are two and two![7] —Said R. Shesheth: This teaches [that] contradiction[8] is the beginning of rebuttal,[9] [20a] and as witnesses can be rebutted only in their presence,[10] so can they be contradicted only in their presence.[11] R. Naḥman said to him: If they[12] had been before us

statement declares the document to have been written under protest, attacking the validity of the document itself.]

(1) So that there is only one witness on the document. (2) The two witnesses from the street. (3) Lit., 'against which one called a protest'. (4) Lit., 'strengthened'. (5) As valid. (6) Lit., 'we cause to be collected (the debt)'. (7) The two witnesses who are signed on the document and who are now dead, and the two witnesses from the street, who testify to the unfitness of the witnesses who had signed on the document. Even if their handwriting is otherwise confirmed, their testimony is counterbalanced by the testimony of the two witnesses from the street. (8) הכחשה is a denial of the subject-matter of the evidence, for which however, no retaliatory punishment is imposed, as Deut. XIX, 19 does not refer to witnesses who were contradicted on the subject-matter of their evidence, but against whom the accusation (in a sense) of an 'alibi' was proved. [The term 'alibi' is used here for convenience sake, as it deals there with the presence or absence of the witnesses of the alleged crime at the time when it was committed, rather than with the presence or the absence of the accused, as the term is generally understood.] (9) הזמה. I.e., the proving of an 'alibi', a rebuttal of evidence, whereby the witnesses are proved to be *Zomemim*, (v. Glos.). The proving of the subject-matter of the evidence to be false is a first step in a subsequent proof of an 'alibi', both being but one continued process of law, v. B.Ḳ. 73*b*. (10) In view of the retaliatory punishment which it involves, the accusation of an 'alibi' can be made only in the presence of the witnesses concerned. (11) [No evidence is accepted refuting the subject-matter of the evidence in the absence of the witnesses, and since in the case of the document they are dead, the evidence of the second set of

and [the other two witnesses] had contradicted them, it[1] would have been a contradiction,[2] and we would not have paid any attention to them,[3] because it[4] is a contradicted testimony. Now that they[5] are not here[6]—[when it could be maintained] that if they had been before us, they[7] might [even] perhaps have admitted to them[8]—should they be believed? No, said R. Naḥman; set the two [witnesses][9] against the two [witnesses][10] and leave the property[11] in the possession of its master.[12] It is analogous to the [case of the] property of a [certain] madman. A [certain] madman sold property. Two [witnesses] came [and] said [that] he sold [the property] when he was insane, and two [witnesses] came and said [that] he sold [the property] when he was sane.[13] [And] R. Ashi said: Set the two [witnesses][14] against the two [witnesses][15] and leave the property[11] in the possession of the madman. And we say [this] only when he has the ownership-right of his forefathers,[16] but if he has not the ownership-right of his forefathers, we say that he bought [the property] when he was insane and that he sold [it] when he was insane.[17]—R. Abbahu said: One rebuts[18] witnesses only in their presence, but one contradicts them also in their absence. And a rebuttal in their absence—granted

witnesses is not accepted. The evidence disqualifying the witnesses as having been forced or minors is considered הכחשה, not הזמה.] (12) The witnesses who signed the document.

(1) The testimony of the new witnesses. (2) Of the testimony of the witnesses who signed the document. (3) The witnesses who signed the document. (4) The testimony of the witnesses of the document. (5) The witnesses who signed the document. (6) They died. (7) The witnesses who signed the document. (8) To the other witnesses. I.e., there is an additional reason for disregarding the testimony of the document. The witnesses who signed the document might even have admitted that what the other witnesses said was true. (9) On the one side. (10) On the other side. (11) Lit., 'money'. (12) I.e., of him who happens to have it now. [E.g., in the case of a note of indebtedness, either the debtor, or the creditor should the latter have happened to distrain on the debtor's goods. And when the Baraitha rules that they are not believed, it means only in so far that the document is not destroyed.] (13) Lit., 'well'. (14) On the one side. (15) On the other side. (16) The ownership-right came to him from his forefathers by inheritance. (17) And the property passes to the purchaser. (18) V. *supra* p. 108 nn. 9 and 10.

that it is not an [effective] rebuttal,[1] but it is a contradiction.[2]

The Master said [above]: 'If there are witnesses that this is their handwriting, or their handwriting came out from another place, [namely] from a document which was contested and was confirmed in court, they are not believed'. [This is only] if it was contested, but not, if it was not contested.[3] This is a support[4] for R. Assi, for R. Assi said: A document[5] is confirmed only from a document, which was contested and was confirmed in Court. The Nehardeans[6] said: A document is confirmed only from two *kethuboth* or from two fields,[7] and [only] when their owners[8] used[9] them for three years, and [that] in comfort.[10] R. Shimi b. Ashi said: And [only] when it is produced by another person,[11] but not [if it is produced] by himself.[12]—Why not [if from] under his own hand? Because he may have forged [the signatures of the witnesses].[13] [If so], even when produced by another person also, perhaps he went[14] and saw[15] and forged?[16]—So clearly[17] he cannot fix [it in his mind].[18]

Our Rabbis taught: A person[19] may write [down] his testimony

(1) And they do not incur the retaliatory penalty for *Zomemim* witnesses. (2) I.e., the evidence stands contradicted. (3) Lit., 'If it is contested, yes, if it was not contested, no'. If the document was contested and confirmed in court as valid, the new witnesses are not believed; but if the document was not contested and confirmed, the new witnesses are believed. (4) Lit., 'supports'. (5) I.e., the signatures of a document. If the confirmation is made by comparing it with the signatures attached to another document. (6) The Scholars of Nehardea. (7) From signatures of the same witnesses attached to two marriage settlements or deeds of sale of fields. (8) I.e., the occupants who claim to be owners. (9) Lit., 'ate'. (10) Without anyone protesting against their holding of the fields. (11) Lit., 'it comes out from under the hands of'. I.e., when the two documents, with which the contested document is compared, were in the possession of other persons and they produced them. (12) Lit., 'from under his own hand'. I.e., if they were in the possession of the person whose document is contested. (13) In the contested document. (14) To the other persons. (15) The other documents. (16) The signatures of the witnesses on the contested document. (17) Lit., 'all that'. (18) He cannot hope to imitate the handwriting of the witnesses in the other documents, since the documents are not in front of him. By seeing the documents once or twice in the hands of others, he cannot forge the signatures. (19) Who is going to be a witness in a legal dispute.

in[1] a document[2] and may, through it,[3] give evidence even after many years. R. Huna said: Only when he remembers it[4] by[5] himself. R. Joḥanan said: Even if he does not remember it by himself.[6] Rabbah said: You may infer from [the words of] R. Joḥanan [that] if two [persons] know evidence[7] and one of them has forgotten [it], the other one may remind him[8] [of it]. They asked: [In the case of] himself[9]—what is [the law]?[10]—R. Ḥabina said: Even he himself [may do so]. Mar b. R. Ashi, said: He himself [may] not. And the law is: he himself [may] not. [20b] But if he[11] is a scholar,[12] even he himself[13] [may remind the witness].[14] As that case of R. Ashi: He knew evidence for R. Kahana, [and] he[15] said to him:[16] Does the master remember that evidence?[17] And he[18] said

(1) Lit., 'on'. (2) We would say 'on paper'. (3) עליה 'through it', 'by it', 'by means of it'. There is apparently a legal nicety in the word. Not ממנה, 'from it'. If his evidence is only from it, that is if he does not recollect the evidence even when looking at the paper, his evidence would not be valid. The written testimony should be an aid to his memory. But if it does not recall anything to him, it is valueless. (4) Part of the evidence (Rashi). (5) Lit., 'of, or from himself'. And the written testimony brings it *all* back to his mind. (6) Only after looking at the document, in which he had written his testimony at the time, he reminds himself of the facts of the case. But if he cannot now recollect anything, the written testimony has no value (Rashi). The same rule obtains in the English Law of Evidence. V. Cockle, *Cases and Statutes on the Law of Evidence*, third edition, pp. 266-7: 'A witness may refresh his memory by referring to any writing or document made by himself, at or so soon after the transaction in question that the judge considers it was fresh in his memory at the time. But it is not necessary that the witness should have any independent recollection of the fact recorded, if he is prepared to swear to it on seeing the writing or document.' V. also Powell's *Principles and Practice of the Law of Evidence*, ninth edition, pp. 169-172. On p. 169: 'A witness may refresh his memory by looking at any memorandum—(1) Which revives in his mind a recollection of the fact to which it refers.' Paragraphs (2) and (3) on p. 170 are also very interesting. (3) is 'an extreme case,' and it is difficult to say whether R. Joḥanan would have gone as far as that. (7) Knew facts of a case to which they could testify. (8) Lit., 'one reminds his fellow'. (9) I.e., the litigant. (10) Lit., 'how is it'? I.e., may the litigant remind the witness of the evidence? (11) The witness. (12) If the witness is a scholar he will know whether the reminding of the facts recalls the facts, or some of the facts, to his memory. If his memory is not aided, he will not give evidence. (13) The litigant. (14) Of the facts. (15) R. Kahana. (16) To R. Ashi. (17) I.e., do you remember those facts? (18) R. Ashi.

to him:[1] No. But was it not so and so?[2] He[3] replied: I do not know. In the end, R. Ashi reminded himself, and he gave evidence for him.[4] He[3] saw that R. Kahana was surprised,[5] [so] he[3] said to him:[6] Do you think [that] I relied upon you? I threw it upon my mind[7] and I remembered it.[8]

We learnt elsewhere:[9] Mounds which are near a town or a road, whether they are new or old, are unclean;[10] those [mounds] which are distant—if they are new,[11] they are clean,[12] and if they are old,[13] they are unclean.[14] What is near? Fifty cubits.[15] And what is old? Sixty years.[16] [This is] the view[17] of R. Meir. R. Judah says: 'near', [denotes] when there is none nearer; 'old', when one remembers it.[18] [Now] what is [meant by] a town and what is [meant by] a road? Shall I say: [by] a town is [meant] an ordinary town, [and by] a road is [meant] an ordinary road? Do we presume uncleanness out of doubt? Did not Resh Lakish say: They[19] found some pretext[20] and declared the land of Israel unclean?[21]—Said R. Zera: [By] a town is [meant] a town which is near a burial place, and [by] a road is [meant] a road [leading] to a burial place. I grant you [in the case of] a road [leading] to a burial place,[22] because sometimes it might happen [that a funeral took place] at twilight, and it chanced that they buried it[23] in the mound.[24] But [in the case of]

(1) R. Kahana. (2) R. Kahana asked R. Ashi. (3) R. Ashi. (4) For R. Kahana. (5) R. Kahana was surprised that R. Ashi gave evidence after he had said twice that he did not remember it. (6) To R. Kahana. (7) Lit., 'upon my soul'.—The meaning of these words is: I tried hard to recall the facts to my mind. (8) His own mental efforts were successful.—This story shows that a scholar may be reminded of the evidence by the litigant himself. (9) *Oh*. XVI, 2. (10) We assume that there are graves in those mounds. (11) Lit., 'new ones'. (12) If a dead body had been buried there, it would have been known. (13) Lit., 'old ones'. (14) They might have been used as burial places. (15) Or less. (16) Or more. (17) Lit., 'the words'. (18) When it originated. (19) The scholars. (20) V. Nazir (Sonc. ed.) p. 247, n. 7. (21) Why should we then presume uncleanness out of a doubt? (22) That it is regarded as unclean. (23) The dead body. (24) As the funeral took place on the eve of Sabbath at twilight they might not have had time to reach the burial place before the commencement of Sabbath, and therefore they buried the dead body in the mound. Therefore, the mound is unclean.

a town which is near a burial place—all go to the burial place![1] —Said R. Ḥanina: Because women bring there[2] their abortions and lepers[3] [bring there][4] their arms.[5] [And it is assumed that] till fifty cubits she[6] goes alone,[7] but for a longer distance[8] she takes a man with her and [then] she goes to the burial place.[9] Therefore, we do not presume uncleanness in Eretz Israel.[10] R. Ḥisda said: You may infer from [the words of] R. Meir[11] [that] one remembers[12] evidence till sixty years, for a longer[13] [period than sixty years] one does not remember. But it is not so, [for] there[14] [he does not remember the evidence after sixty years] because it[15] is not his concern,[16] but here,[17] since it is his concern, even for a longer [period[18] he] also [remembers the evidence].

MISHNAH. [IF] ONE[19] WITNESS SAYS, 'THIS IS MY HANDWRITING AND THAT IS THE HANDWRITING OF MY FELLOW,' AND THE OTHER [WITNESS] SAYS, 'THIS IS MY HANDWRITING AND THAT IS THE HANDWRITING OF MY FELLOW,' THEY ARE BELIEVED. [IF] ONE SAYS, 'THIS IS MY HANDWRITING,' AND THE OTHER SAYS, 'THIS IS MY HANDWRITING,' THEY MUST JOIN TO THEMSELVES ANOTHER [PERSON].[20] [THIS IS] THE VIEW[21] OF RABBI. BUT THE SAGES SAY: THEY NEED NOT JOIN

(1) Since the burial place is near, why should the town, then, be unclean? (2) In the mounds. (3) Lit., 'those who are afflicted with boils (leprosy)'. (4) In the mounds. (5) Or other limbs, which have been amputated or have fallen off through the disease of leprosy. (6) The woman. (7) And in that case she would bury the abortion in the mound. (8) Lit., 'more'. (9) As she takes a man to accompany her she does not mind going to the burial place and burying the abortion there. (10) Lit., 'the land of Israel'. (11) Who says, 'What is old? Sixty years.' (12) Lit., 'this evidence is remembered'. (13) Lit., 'more'. (14) In the case of the mound. (15) I.e., the matter of the origin of the mound. (16) Lit., 'not thrown upon him'. I.e., there is no reason why he should remember how the mound originated more than sixty years back. (17) In the case of a legal dispute, he is interested in the facts of which he was a witness, and, therefore, he remembers the evidence even after sixty years. (18) Than sixty years. (19) Lit., 'this'. (20) So that there should be two witnesses for each handwriting (signature). (21) Lit., 'the words'.

TO THEMSELVES ANOTHER [PERSON], BUT A PERSON IS BELIEVED TO SAY, 'THIS IS MY HANDWRITING'.[1]

GEMARA. If you should find [that] according to the view of Rabbi [21a] they[2] give evidence with regard to their handwriting,[3] according to the Sages they[4] give evidence with regard to the *maneh*[5] in the deed.[6] This is self-evident!—You might have said that Rabbi was in doubt whether they[4] testified to their signature or to the *maneh* in the deed.[7] And the difference[8] would be when one of them died. [Here] we need two witnesses[9] from the street to testify regarding it,[10] because otherwise,[11] the whole of the money less a quarter would go out[12] by the mouth[13] of one witness, and both here and there the stricter rule would prevail.[14] Therefore, he

(1) And the two witnesses thus confirm the document which they signed. (2) The witnesses. (3) Therefore the handwriting of each witness has to be confirmed by two witnesses. (4) The witnesses. (5) *Maneh* is only mentioned as an illustration. It is the transaction recorded in the deed to which they testify. This transaction might have been the loan of a *maneh*. (6) And the two witnesses testify to the transaction by each of them confirming his signature, hence the ruling of the Sages. (7) [And being in doubt, he took the more stringent view, and required that both witnesses testify to each other's signature.] (8) Whether Rabbi was sure or doubtful in his view. (9) Because of Rabbi's doubt whether the witnesses testified to their signature or to the *maneh* in the deed. (10) The signature of the dead witness. (11) Lit., 'if so'. I.e., if we should say that one witness from the street would be sufficient. (12) I.e., would be given to the claimant. (13) I.e., the evidence. (14) If Rabbi was in doubt we should require two other witnesses to give evidence regarding the signature of the dead witness. One other witness, added to the surviving witness, would not do, because the evidence of the witnesses may be (since Rabbi is in doubt) with regard to the *maneh* in the deed, and not to the signatures, in which case half of the evidence regarding the transaction would be given when the surviving witness confirms his own signature. His own confirmation of his signature is sufficient, as far as his evidence is concerned, if the object of the evidence is the transaction recorded in the deed. Half of the sum mentioned in the deed would then go to the claimant by his confirmation of his signature, in other words, by his evidence. And when he testifies, with the other new witness, regarding the signature of the dead witness, half of the other half of the sum is testified to by him, so that altogehter three-quarters of the sum mentioned in the deed would go to the claimant through the evidence of one, the surviving witness, and this is not according to the law,

teaches that it is clear to Rabbi,[1] whether the result is lenient[2] or strict.[3] For Rab Judah said [that] Rab said: If two [witnesses] are signed on a document and one of them died, two [persons] from the street are required to give evidence with regard to him.[4] In this[5] it would be lenient[6] according to Rabbi and it is strict[7] according to the Rabbis. And if there are not two, but there is only one,[8] what [then]?—Said Abaye: He[9] shall write his signature on a piece of clay[10] and place it before the court, and the court confirms it,[11] and he need not testify to his own signature,[12] and he [then] goes with that one[13] and they [together] testify to [the signature of] the other [witness].[14] And only on a piece of clay[15] but not a

which demands that no more than one half should 'go out' by the evidence of one single witness. (V. Giṭ. (Sonc. ed.) p. 57, n. 9.) Therefore, through Rabbi's doubt, we should require two other witnesses when one witness died. And when both witnesses who signed the deed are alive, each signature must be testified to by both witnesses, because there would be Rabbi's doubt that the evidence may be regarding the signatures. The result would be that in both cases, whether both witnesses are alive or one witness is dead, each signature would have to be testified to by two witnesses.

(1) That the evidence is regarding the signatures. (2) As in the case of the death of one witness. Being certain in his view that the evidence is with regard to the signatures, and not with regard to the *maneh* in the deed, Rabbi would hold that one witness from the street, added to the surviving witness, is sufficient. The surviving witness and the new witness would both testify to both signatures. There would be no question of three-quarters of the sum mentioned going out by the mouth of one witness, because in Rabbi's certain view, the evidence is with regard to the signatures and not with regard to the *maneh* in the deed. (3) In the case when both the witnesses are alive. They must testify to both signatures. (4) This is according to the Sages. (5) I.e., in this case. (6) V. n. 2. (7) As the Rabbis (the Sages) hold the view that the evidence is regarding the *maneh* in the deed, two new witnesses are required to testify to the signature of the dead witness. If there would be only one new witness and he would be added to the surviving witness, three-fourths of the sum mentioned in the deed would go out by the mouth of one witness, v. p. 114, n. 14. (8) Person from the street who recognizes the handwriting of the dead witness. (9) The surviving witness. (10) חספא 'clay', or 'a piece of clay' is reminiscent of the Babylonian clay-tablets. (11) By comparing the signature on the piece of clay with the signature in the deed. (12) In the deed. (13) The person from the street. (14) Of the dead witness. (15) Shall he (the surviving witness) write his signature.

scroll,[1] lest a bad[2] man may find it and write on it whatever he likes,[3] and we have learned: If one person produces the handwriting[4] of another person[5] that he owes him [money], he collects [the debt] from unmortgaged[6] property.[7] Rab Judah said [that] Samuel said, The *halachah* is according to the Sages.[8] This is obvious! [When there is a dispute between] one [authority] and many [authorities] the law is according to the many [authorities]!—You might have said: since the *halachah* is according to Rabbi as against one of his fellow-scholars, it is also against many of his fellow-scholars,[9] so he lets us hear[10] [otherwise].

(Mnemonic: *NaḤ, NaD, ḤaD*.)[11] R. Ḥinena b. Ḥiyya said to R. Judah, and some say [that] R. Huna b. Judah [said] to Rab Judah, and some say [that] R. Ḥiyya b. Judah [said] to Rab Judah: And did Samuel say so? Surely once a deed came out[12] from the court of Mar Samuel and there was written in it, 'Whereas R. 'Anan b. Ḥiyya came and testified to his own signature and to that of his fellow-witness,[13] namely,[14] R. Ḥanan b. Rabbah, and whereas R. Ḥanan b. Rabbah came and testified to his own signature and to that of his fellow-witness, namely R. 'Anan b. Ḥiyya,' we have verified[15] it, and we have confirmed it,[15] as it is proper![16]—He said to him: That deed belonged to orphans, and Samuel was afraid of an erring court.[17] Samuel thought: There might be someone who

(1) We would say 'but not on a sheet of paper'. It is interesting to note the use of 'piece of clay', together with the use of 'scroll'. It may be that חספא was also used, later, in the sense of 'a small piece of paper'. (2) Dishonest. (3) He may write over the signature that the signatory borrowed a certain sum of money from him. (4) A note of indebtedness signed by the other person. (5) Lit., 'he produced against him his handwriting'. (6) Lit., 'free'. (7) V. B.B. 175*b*. The surviving witness must, therefore, be careful and write his signature only on a piece of clay, or on a small piece of paper, on which there is room only for his signature. (8) In our Mishnah. (9) Lit., 'from his fellow and even from his fellows'. (10) That the *halachah* is according to the several scholars. (11) *NaḤ* stands for Hi*N*enah b. *Ḥ*iyya; *NaD* for Hu*N*ah b. Ju*D*ah; *ḤaD* for *Ḥ*iyya b. Ju*D*ah, the names of the Amoraim that follow. (12) Declared as valid. (13) Lit., 'and to the one of (the person) with him'. (14) Lit., 'and who is it?' (15) The deed. (16) We thus see that Samuel acted according to the opinion of Rabbi. (17) Of judges who might mistakenly think that in this matter the law is according to Rabbi.

held that the *halachah* is [generally] according to Rabbi as against one fellow-scholar, and not as against many of his fellow-scholars, but [that] in this[1] [the *halachah* is according to Rabbi] even as against many of his fellow-scholars,[2] I will make relief,[3] so that the orphans should not suffer any loss.

Rab Judah said [that] Samuel said: Witness and judge are joined together.[4] Rami b. Ḥama said: How excellent is this tradition! Said Raba: What is the excellence? What the witness testifies to the judge does not testify to, and what the judge testifies to the witness does not testify to?[5] And indeed, when Rami b. Ezekiel came he said: Do not heed those rules which my brother Judah[6] laid down in the name of Samuel.

[21*b*] Rabbanai, the brother of R. Ḥiyya b. Abba, came to buy sesame and he said: Thus Samuel said: Witness and judge are joined together. Amemar said: How excellent is this tradition! Said R. Ashi to Amemar: Because the father of your mother[7] praised it, you also praise it! Raba has already refuted it.

R. Safra said [that] R. Abba said [that] R. Isaac b. Samuel b. Martha said [that] R. Huna said, and some say [that] R. Huna said [that] Rab said: If three[8] sit together to confirm a deed, and two [of them] know[9] the signatures of the witnesses and one does not know,[10] before they sign,[11] they may testify[12] before him,[13] and he[14] [then] signs[15] [with them]; after they have signed, they may not testify before him and he may not sign. But do we *write*

(1) In the matter of confirming witnesses' signatures. (2) And he will not accept the confirmation. (3) I.e., I will do more than is necessary. (4) For the purpose of confirming the validity of the document, the witness testifies to his signature, and the judge to his signature endorsing the document which had been presented to court for confirmation. V. *infra*. (5) The witness testifies to the transaction (to the *maneh* in the deed according to the Sages), and the judge testifies to his own signature. (6) Rab Judah was a brother of Rami. (7) Rami b. Ḥama. (8) Three laymen may constitute themselves into a court. (9) Lit., 'recognize'. (10) The signatures. (11) A declaration that the signatures of the witnesses have been confirmed. (12) To the signatures of the witnesses. (13) Before the third judge. (14) The third judge. (15) The attestation confirming the signatures. As to the form of the attestation, v. Rashi.

[the attestation]?[1] Did not R. Papi say in the name of Raba: The judge's attestation which is written before the witnesses give evidence as to their signatures is invalid, because it looks like a lie? [And] here also it looks like a lie!—But say: Before they have written [the attestation] they may testify before him and he [then] signs [with them]; after they have written [the attestation], they may not testify before him and he may not sign. We may infer from this three things.[2] We may infer that a witness may be[3] a judge;[4] we may [also] infer that, if the judges know the signatures of the witnesses, there is no need to testify[5] before them;[6] and [again] we may infer that, if the judges do not know the signatures of the witnesses, it is necessary to give evidence before every one.[7] R. Ashi demurred to this: Agreed[8] that we may infer from it that a witness may be a judge, but [how can we infer from it that], if the judges know the signatures of the witnesses, there is no need to testify before them? Perhaps, indeed, I can say to you [that] this is necessary, but it is different here, because the telling[9] has been fulfilled before one.[10] And [further, how can we infer from it that], if the judges do not know the signatures of the witnesses, it is necessary to give evidence before every one?[11] Perhaps, indeed, I can say to you [that] this is not necessary, but it is different here, because the telling[12] would not have been fulfilled at all.[13]

R. Abba sat and reported[14] this law, that a witness may be a judge. R. Safra [then] objected to R. Abba: If three[15] saw it[16] and they are [of] the court, two[17] shall stand up and set [two] of their fellows[18] beside the one, and they[19] shall testify before them,[20] and

(1) Before the signatures of the witnesses have been testified to by the signatories or by other witnesses. (2) Lit., 'hear from this three'. (3) Lit., 'be made'. (4) [The two who first testify to the signatures of the witnesses may then act as judges, endorsing the document.] (5) To the signatures. (6) Before the judges, since no provision is made for any testimony being made before the two judges who know the signatures. (7) Of the judges, since in this case the two judges have to testify before the third judge. (8) Lit., 'it is all right'. (9) The giving of evidence. (10) Before the third judge. (11) Of the judges. (12) The giving of evidence. (13) If the two judges had not testified before the third judge. (14) Lit., 'said'. (15) Of the Sanhedrin. (16) The new moon. (17) Of them. (18) Of the Sanhedrin. (19) The two. (20) The three who form the court.

[then] they say: Hallowed is the new moon, hallowed; for one person is not believed by himself. Now, if you assume that a witness may be a judge, what do we want all this for? Let them sit in their places[1] and proclaim[2] [the new moon] is hallowed!—He said to him: That was also difficult to me, and I asked R. Isaac b. Samuel b. Martha, and R. Isaac [asked] R. Huna, and R. Huna [asked] Ḥiyya b. Rab, and Ḥiyya b. Rab [asked] Rab, and he said to them: Leave alone the testimony as to the new moon, [for it is] Biblical, and the confirmation of documents is Rabbinic.[3]

R. Abba said [that] R. Huna said [that] Rab said: If three sit to confirm a document and an objection is raised[4] against one of them,[5] they[6] may, before they have signed [the attestation], give evidence regarding him,[7] and he may [then] sign; after they have signed, they may not give evidence regarding him[8] and he may not sign. On what ground was that objection raised? If the objection was on the ground of robbery,[9] [22*a*] they are two and two.[10] [And] if it is a protest regarding family blemish,[11] [then all that is required is] merely a revealing of the matter.[12]—Indeed, I will tell you, it is a protest regarding robbery, and these say: We know of him that he has repented.[13]

(1) After they have given evidence as to the new moon. (2) Together with the third person. (3) [Whereas in a Biblical matter a witness cannot act as judge, in a Rabbinic measure, e.g., the attestation of documents, no such stringency applies.] (4) Lit., 'and one calls a protest'. [This protest was made by two, v. *infra* 26*a*.] (5) It is said that he is unfit to act as judge. (6) The other two persons. (7) That he is a fit person. (8) As they are then interested parties, it being to their discredit to have acted as judges with an unfit person. (9) On account of a robbery which he is alleged to have committed. (10) Two give evidence against him (v. n. 4), and these other two for him, and he is still inadmissible, even if the other two give evidence regarding his fitness before they signed. (11) He is said to be descended from slaves and thus unfit to act as judge. (12) A search in his genealogy can reveal whether there is any ground for the objection of the two witnesses or not, independent of the evidence of the other two. Why then should the other member of the court, after having signed, be debarred from testifying in his favour? (13) Lit., 'that he has done repentance'. Repentance implies giving back the thing robbed to its owner. [Since they do not contradict the evidence of the first set of witnesses, their testimony as to his fitness is accepted, provided it is given before they signed.]

R. Zera said: This thing I have heard from R. Abba, and if not for R. Abba of Acco, I would have forgotten it: If three sit to confirm a document and one of them dies,[1] they must write, 'We were in a session of three, and one is no more.'[2] R. Naḥman b. Isaac said: And if it is written in it: This document has been produced[3] before us [as] a court of law, more is not necessary.[4] But perhaps it was an arrogant court, and [that is] according to Samuel, for Samuel said: If two have judged,[5] their judgment is a judgment,[6] only they are called an arrogant court?[7]—When it is written in it, [e.g.] 'The court of our Master Ashi.'[8] But perhaps the scholars of the school of R. Ashi hold with Samuel?—When it is written in it, 'And our Master Ashi told us.'[9]

MISHNAH. IF A WOMAN SAYS, 'I WAS MARRIED[10] AND I AM DIVORCED', SHE IS BELIEVED, FOR THE MOUTH THAT FORBADE IS THE MOUTH THAT PERMITS. BUT IF THERE ARE WITNESSES THAT SHE WAS MARRIED, AND SHE SAYS, 'I AM DIVORCED', SHE IS NOT BELIEVED. IF SHE SAYS, 'I WAS TAKEN CAPTIVE BUT I HAVE REMAINED CLEAN,'[11] SHE IS BELIEVED, FOR THE MOUTH THAT FORBADE IS THE MOUTH THAT PERMITS. BUT IF THERE ARE WITNESSES THAT SHE WAS TAKEN CAPTIVE AND SHE SAYS, 'I HAVE REMAINED CLEAN,' SHE IS NOT BELIEVED. BUT IF THE WITNESSES CAME AFTER SHE HAD MARRIED, SHE SHALL NOT GO OUT.[12]

(1) Before they signed it. (2) So that it should be known that the document was confirmed in the presence of three judges. (3) Lit., 'has gone out'. This term also implies that the document has been found valid. (4) It is then evident that they were three, as a court of law cannot consist of less than three judges. (5) Sat as a court and pronounced judgment. (6) Their decision is valid. (7) I.e., such practices should be discouraged. (8) Under R. Ashi a court would certainly consist of three. R. Ashi's court is mentioned as a mere illustration, R. Ashi being a contemporary of R. Naḥman b. Isaac, and head of the most renowned Academy and court at Meḥasia. (9) To act as a court. And then the court would certainly consist of three. (10) Lit., 'the wife of a man'. (11) No one has had intercourse with me, and I am still fit to marry into the priesthood. (12) Lit., 'behold, this (one) shall not go out'. I.e., out

GEMARA. R. Assi said: Whence [do we know] from the Torah [the principle of] 'the mouth that forbade is the mouth that permits'? Because it is said: *'My daughter I gave to this man as a wife.'*[1] [By saying] 'to *man*', he made her forbidden,[2] [by saying] *'this'*, he made her permitted.[3] Why is a Scriptural verse necessary? It stands to reason: he made her forbidden, and he made her permitted!—The Scriptural verse is required according to what R. Huna [said that] Rab said, for R. Huna said [that] Rab said: Whence [do we know] from the Bible that the father is believed to make his daughter forbidden?[4] Because it is said: *'My daughter I gave to [this] man as his wife.'*[5] Why [is it said] *'this'?*[6]—It is required for what R. Jonah taught, for R. Jonah taught: *'My daughter I gave to this man'*: '[*To*] *this* [man]', and not to the brother-in-law.[7]

Our Rabbis taught: If a woman says, 'I am married', and then she says,[8] 'I am unmarried', she is believed. But she made herself forbidden![9]—Said Raba the son of R. Huna: When she has given a plausible reason for her words.[10] We have also a Baraitha to the same effect. If she says, 'I am married', and then she says, 'I am unmarried', she is not believed, but if she gives a plausible reason for her words, she is believed. And so it once happened with a great woman, who was great in beauty, and men were eager[11] to betroth her, and she said to them, 'I am betrothed'. After a time she became betrothed.[12] The Sages said to her: Why have you

of the house of her husband. Her second marriage is valid and she is not to be sent away.

(1) Deut. XXII, 16. (2) As he does not say to which man, he made her forbidden to all men. (3) To this man. (4) To all men except the one man to whom he says he gave her in marriage. (5) Deut. XXII, 16. He can give her as wife to this man and thus make her forbidden to all other men. (6) It is obvious that he means that man, who is putting up a claim against his newly-wedded wife. (7) The law of Deut. XXII, 13ff does not apply to the husband's brother who marries the widow of his brother (cf. Deut. XXV, 5ff) and brings against her a charge of defamation. He is not subject to the fine. V. *infra* 46*a*. (8) Lit., 'and she turned (retracted) and she said'. (9) Lit., 'a piece of prohibition'. By saying 'I am married', she declared herself to be forbidden to other men, how then can she raise this prohibition by a mere retraction? (10) Why she said, 'I am married'. (11) Lit., 'and men jumped at her'. (12) Lit., 'she stood up and betrothed herself (to a man)'.

chosen[1] to do this?[2] She answered them,[3] 'At first, when unworthy men came to me, I said, "I am betrothed"; now that worthy men come to me, I became betrothed'. And this law R. Aḥa, the prince of the castle, brought before the Sages[4] in Usha, and they said: If she gives a plausible reason for her words she is believed.

Samuel asked Rab: If [a woman] says,[5] 'I am unclean',[6] and then she says, 'I am clean',[7] what is [the law]?[8] He[9] answered him:[10] Also in this case if she gives [22b] a plausible reason for her words she is believed. He[10] learned it from him[9] forty times, and still Samuel did not act accordingly with regard to himself.

Our Rabbis taught: When two [witnesses] say [that the husband of the woman] has died, and two [witnesses] say [that] he has not died, or two [witnesses] say [that] she has been divorced, and two [witnesses] say [that] she has not been divorced, she shall not marry [again], but if she has married [again], she shall not go out. R. Menaḥem b. Jose says: She shall go out. R. Menaḥem b. Jose said: When do I say [that] she shall go out?—When witnesses[11] came and then she married, but if she married and then came witnesses,[11] she shall not go out. Now, they are two and two,[12] [and] he who has intercourse with her[13] is liable to a doubtful guilt-offering![14]—Said R. Shesheth: When she married one of her witnesses.[15] Then she herself should bring a doubtful guilt-offering!—When she says, 'I am sure'.[16]

R. Joḥanan said: When two [witnesses] say [that the husband of the woman] has died, and two [witnesses] say [that] he has not

(1) Lit., 'why hast thou seen'. (2) To say that you were betrothed. (3) Lit., 'she said to them'. (4) For consideration. (5) To her husband. (6) I.e., 'I am in the period of menstruation'. (7) Lit., 'I had no menstruation'. (8) Lit., 'How is it'. May her husband believe her second statement and have intercourse with her? (9) Rab. (10) Samuel. (11) The second set of witnesses. (12) There are two witnesses against two witnesses, and the matter, that is the death of the first husband, remains in doubt. This cannot refer to the case of divorce, v. *infra*. (13) The man who marries her now. (14) A guilt-offering to be brought when one is in doubt whether the act committed was sinful or not. (15) And he is sure that the first husband died. (16) [She has a feeling of certitude that her first husband is dead, as otherwise he would have come back to her (Rashi).]

died, she shall not marry [again], but if she has married [again], she shall not go out. When two [witnesses] say [that] she has been divorced, and two [witnesses] say [that] she has not been divorced, she shall not marry [again], and if she has married, she shall go out. What is the difference between the first case and the second case?—Abaye said: Explain it[1] [that it speaks] of one witness.[2] When one witness says [that] he has died, the Rabbis believe him as two [witnesses].[3] And [this is] according to 'Ulla, for 'Ulla said: Wherever the Torah makes one witness credible, [it is as if] there are two, whereas he who said that he has not died is one, and the words of one have no validity against two.[4] If so, [she should be allowed to marry again] from the beginning?—Because of that [saying] of R. Assi, for R. Assi said: '*Put away from thee a froward mouth, and perverse lips put far from thee*'.[5] In the second case [however] one witness says [that] she has been divorced, and one witness says [that] she has not been divorced, they [therefore] both testify to a married woman, and he who says [that] she has been divorced is one, and the words of one have no validity against two. Raba said: Indeed, they are two and two, and R. Johanan regards [as right] the words of R. Menahem b. Jose[6] in [the case of] divorce, but not in [the case of] death. Why?—In the case of death, she cannot contradict him,[7] [but] in the case of divorce, she can contradict him.[8] But would she be as

(1) The statement of R. Johanan. (2) Not two sets of witnesses testified, but one single witness in each case. (3) [The Rabbis have laid down the principle that the evidence of one witness testifying to the husband's death is sufficient; v. Yeb. 88*a*.] (4) Lit., 'and the words of one are not in the place of two'. [The evidence of the former witness, who said that he was dead, is treated as that of two witnesses, whereas that of the latter only, as that of one.] (5) Prov. IV, 24—One should try to avoid evil talk, although there is no objection to the marriage from the point of view of strict law. [R. Assi was wont to quote this verse from Prov.] (6) That she should go out. (7) If her first husband comes back she cannot say to him, 'thou art dead!' Therefore, she would not say that he is dead unless she was sure that it is so, and we believe her. (8) If the first husband comes and says that he has not divorced her, she will contradict him and say that he has divorced her. If we should believe her she would rely on the denial she could give him and would marry again, although she was still the wife of the first husband.

impudent as all that?[1] Did not R. Hamnuna say: If a woman says to her husband, 'thou hast divorced me,' she is believed, [for] the presumption is [that] a woman is not insolent before her husband?[2]—This is the case only when there are no witnesses who support her; but when there are witnesses who support her, she is indeed insolent. R. Assi says: When the witnesses say, 'he has died just now, he has divorced her just now.' Death one cannot prove,[3] divorce one can prove, for we say to her, 'if it is so, shew us thy document of divorce'.[4]

Our Rabbis taught: If two [witnesses] say that she has been betrothed, and two [witnesses] say [that] she has not been betrothed, she shall not marry, and if she has married, she shall not go out. If two [witnesses] say [that] she has been divorced, and two [witnesses] say [that] she has not been divorced, she shall not marry, and if she has married, she shall go out. [23*a*] What is the difference between the first case and the second case?—Abaye said: Explain it[5] [that it speaks] of one witness.[6] When one witness says [that] she has been betrothed and one witness says [that] she has not been betrothed, they both testify to an unmarried woman, and he who says [that] she has been betrothed is one, and the words of one have no validity against two. In the second case [where] one witness says [that] she has been divorced and one witness says [that] she has not been divorced, they both testify to a married woman, and he who says that she has been divorced is one, and the words of one have no validity against two. R. Ashi said: Indeed, they are two and two, and reverse it.[7] When two say, 'we have seen[8] that she has been betrothed', and two say, 'we have not seen that she has been betrothed, she shall not

(1) To contradict her husband in the case of divorce, even if it was not true. (2) And so we ought to believe her also in the case of divorce! (3) Therefore she need not go out if she has married again, provided it was to one of the witnesses. (4) She cannot have lost it in such a short time. And if she cannot show her document of divorce she must not marry again, and if she has married, she must go out. (5) The Baraitha just quoted. (6) For each evidence. (7) In the first case she has to go out, and in the second case she need not go out. (8) This, too, is a new element.

marry [another man], and if she has married she goes out.' [But] this is obvious! 'We have not seen' is no evidence!—It is not [so obvious], as it is needed for the case when they dwelt in one courtyard; one might say, 'if she had been betrothed it would have been known,'[1] so he lets us hear that there are people who get betrothed quietly. In the second case, when two say, 'we have seen that she has been divorced,' and two say, 'we have not seen that she has been divorced, she shall not marry again, and if she has married she shall not go out,' what does he let us hear [by this case]?[2] Although they live in the same courtyard! [But then] this is the same![3]—One might say that with regard to betrothal it happens that people get betrothed quietly, but with regard to divorce, if she had been divorced, it would have been known, so he lets us hear that there are people who get betrothed and get divorced quietly.

AND IF WITNESSES COME AFTER SHE GOT MARRIED, SHE SHALL NOT GO OUT. R. Oshaia refers it[4] to the first clause.[5] Rabbah b. Abin refers it to the second clause.[6] He who refers it to the first clause, how much more [does he refer it] to the second clause, for in the case of a captive woman they have made it lenient.[7] But he who refers it to the second clause does not refer it to the first clause.[8] Is it to say that they differ concerning the view of R. Hamnuna: that he who refers it to the first clause holds the view of R. Hamnuna,[9] and he who refers it [only] to the second clause does not hold the view of R. Hamnuna?—No, all hold the view of R. Hamnuna, and here they differ in this: one argues: When was that of R. Hamnuna said?[10] In his presence,[11] but in his absence she is impudent,[12] and one holds [that] in his absence also she is not impudent.[13]

(1) Lit., 'there is a voice in the matter'. (2) 'We have not seen' is no evidence! (3) As in the first case. (4) The sentence just quoted. (5) Of our Mishnah, referring to the claim of the woman that she was divorced. (6) Referring to her claim that she remained chaste in captivity. (7) Since it is only presumed that she may have been cohabited with. (8) Lit., 'but to the first clause, no'. (9) V. *supra* 22b. (10) I.e., with regard to what case did R. Hamnuna express that view. (11) In the presence of the husband. (12) [And therefore she would have to go out if witnesses came after she married and said that she was a married woman.] (13) And therefore she need not go out.

AND IF WITNESSES CAME AFTER SHE GOT MARRIED, etc. The father of Samuel said: 'SHE GOT MARRIED', does not mean, 'she actually got married', but 'as soon as they[1] allowed her to get married', even if she did not get married yet. But it says: 'SHE SHALL NOT GO OUT'![2]—[This means] she shall not go out from her first permission.[3]

Our Rabbis taught: When she says, 'I was taken captive, and I am pure, and I have witnesses that I am pure,' they[1] do not say: We will wait until the witnesses come, but they[1] allow her at once [to marry]. If they[1] allowed her to marry and then the witnesses came and said, 'we do not know',[4] then she shall not go out. But if witnesses of defilement[5] came, even if she has many children she shall go out.[6]

Certain women captives came once to Nehardea. The father of Samuel[7] placed watchmen with them.[8] Said Samuel to him: And who watched them till now? Said he to him: 'If they had been thy daughters wouldst thou also have spoken of them so lightly?' It was '*as an error which proceedeth from before the ruler,*'[9] and the daughters of Mar Samuel were taken captive. And they were brought[10] to the Land of Israel. They let their captors stand outside and they went in into the school of R. Ḥanina. This one[11] said, 'I was taken captive and I am pure,' and that one said, 'I was taken captive and I am pure.' [So] they[1] allowed them.[12] Then the captors entered. R. Ḥanina [thereupon] said: They are the children of a Scholar.[13] It [then] became known[14] that they were the daughters of Mar Samuel. R. Ḥanina [thereupon] said to R. Shaman b. Abba: Go and take care of thy relatives.[15] Said he to R. Ḥanina:

(1) The Court. (2) This would imply that she did get married. (3) I.e., from the permission given her by the Court to get married. That permission stands. (4) Whether she is pure or not. (5) I.e., witnesses who say that she was defiled while in captivity. (6) If the husband is a priest. (7) Abba the son of Abba. (8) To guard them until they had been redeemed. (9) V. Eccl. X, 5. The words that escaped the lips of Samuel had bad results. (10) Lit., 'and they (the captors) brought them'. (11) One of the daughters of Samuel. (12) To marry even a priest. (13) Since they left the captors outside they were their own witnesses, and the principle of 'the mouth that forbids is the mouth that permits' applied. (14) Lit., 'the matter was revealed'. (15) I.e., marry one of them. [R. Shaman was a priest and relative of Samuel (Rashi).]

But there are witnesses in the country beyond the sea![1]—Now, however, they are not before us. Witnesses are in the North,[2] and [therefore] she shall be forbidden [to marry]? [Now] the reason[3] is because no witnesses came,[4] but if witnesses came she[5] is forbidden! But did not the father of Samuel say: As soon as they allowed her to get married, even if she did not get married?[6] R. Ashi said: It was stated: Witnesses of defilement.[7]

MISHNAH. [23*b*] IF TWO WOMEN WERE TAKEN CAPTIVE, [AND NOW] ONE SAYS, 'I WAS TAKEN CAPTIVE AND I AM PURE,' AND THE OTHER ONE SAYS, 'I WAS TAKEN CAPTIVE AND I AM PURE,' THEY ARE NOT BELIEVED. BUT WHEN THEY TESTIFY TO ONE ANOTHER, THEY ARE BELIEVED.

GEMARA. Our Rabbis taught: [If she says], 'I am impure and my friend is pure,' she is believed; 'I am pure and my friend is impure', she is not believed; 'I and my friend are impure', she is believed as to herself and she is not believed as to her friend; 'I and my friend are pure'; she is believed as to her friend and she is not believed as to herself.

The Master said: '[If she says], "I am pure and my friend is impure", she is not believed'. How shall we imagine this case? If there are no witnesses,[8] why is she not believed as to herself? She says, 'I was taken captive and I am pure!'[9] Hence it is plain that there are witnesses. [Now] read the middle clause: '"I and

(1) I.e., 'There are witnesses in a far country, and they may come and testify to the daughters of Samuel having been in captivity. [And defiled; (v. Tosaf.).] (2) אסתן. Assyrian, *ištan*, 'north', v. Kid. 12*b*. (3) Why she is allowed to marry. (4) To testify, cf. n. 2. (5) I.e., each one of the daughters. (6) And if witnesses came afterwards, she may get married. (7) Only to witnesses who testify that the woman was actually defiled during her captivity, would annul the permission given for her to get married but witnesses who testify only to her having been in captivity would not affect that permission. There is then no conflict between R. Ḥanina and the father of Samuel. (8) That she and her friend were taken captive. (9) And in accordance with the principle in the Mishnah, *supra* 22*a*, she should be believed.

my friend are impure"; she is believed as to herself and she is not believed as to her friend'. But if there are witnesses, why is she not believed?[1] Hence it is plain that there are no witnesses. [Now] read the last clause: '"I and my friend are pure"; she is believed as to her friend and she is not believed as to herself'. But if there are no witnesses, why is she not believed as to herself? Hence it is plain that there are witnesses. The first clause and the last clause when there are witnesses, [and] the middle clause when there are no witnesses?—Abaye said: Yes, the first clause and the last clause when there are witnesses, [and] the middle clause when there are no witnesses. R. Papa said: The whole of it [speaks] of where there are witnesses, but there is one witness who reverses.[2] [If] she says, 'I am impure and my friend is pure', and the one witness says to her, 'thou art pure and thy friend is impure', she has declared herself forbidden,[3] [and] her friend becomes permitted through her testimony.[4] If [she says] 'I am pure and my friend is impure', and the one witness says to her, 'Thou art impure and thy friend is pure', since there are witnesses,[5] she is not believed[6] [as to herself], [and] her friend becomes permitted through the testimony[7] of the [one] witness. [If she says], 'I and my friend are impure,' and the one witness says to her, 'thou and thy friend are pure,' she has declared herself forbidden, [and] her friend becomes permitted through the testimony of the [one] witness. What need is there again for this?[8] It is [the same as in] the first part![9]—You might have said [that] they are both pure and the reason why she says so[10] is that she acts [in accordance

(1) As to her friend. (2) Her testimony. (3) V. *supra* p. 121, n. 9. (4) Lit., 'through her mouth'. [For in regard to a captive woman, *the evidence of one in favour of her chastity* is sufficient, v. *infra* 27a.] (5) That she and her friend were taken captive. (6) Lit., 'all is not as if from her', i.e., as if dependent on her, (Jast.). The fact that she was taken captive is known from the evidence of the witnesses and not only from her testimony. (7) Lit., 'mouth'. (8) The last statement. (9) [From the two cases in the first part we learn the two principles that her own evidence as to her having become impure must stand, and that the evidence of the witness in favour of chastity is sufficient.] (10) Lit., 'and this that she says so',—that they are both impure.

with the saying:] '*Let me die with the Philistines*',[1] so he lets us hear.[2] [If she says] 'I and my friend are pure', and the one witness says to her, 'Thou and thy friend are impure', since there are witnesses,[3] she is not believed,' [and] her friend becomes permitted through her testimony.[4] What need is there again for this? It is [the same as in] the very first clause![5]—You might have said [that] she is believed[6] only when she declares herself as unfit,[7] but when she declares herself as fit[8] I might say that she is not believed,[9] so he lets us hear[10] [that this is not so].

MISHNAH. AND LIKEWISE TWO MEN, [IF] ONE SAYS, 'I AM A PRIEST',[11] AND THE OTHER SAYS, 'I AM A PRIEST', THEY ARE NOT BELIEVED.[12] BUT WHEN THEY TESTIFY TO ONE ANOTHER, THEY ARE BELIEVED. R. JUDAH SAID: ONE DOES NOT RAISE [A PERSON] TO THE PRIESTHOOD THROUGH THE TESTIMONY[13] OF ONE WITNESS. R. ELEAZAR SAID: ONLY THEN, WHEN THERE ARE PEOPLE WHO OBJECT;[14] BUT WHEN THERE ARE NO PEOPLE WHO OBJECT, ONE RAISES [A PERSON] TO THE PRIESTHOOD THROUGH THE TESTIMONY OF ONE WITNESS. R. SIMEON B. GAMALIEL SAYS IN THE NAME OF R. SIMEON: THE SON OF THE CHIEF OF THE PRIESTS:[15] ONE RAISES [A PERSON] TO THE PRIESTHOOD THROUGH THE TESTIMONY OF ONE WITNESS.

(1) Judg., XVI, 30. She applies to herself and to her friend the well-known saying of Samson, that is, though she is pure she says that she is impure, so that she should be believed as to her friend, of whom she says that she is impure. (2) That she is believed as to herself but not as to her friend. (3) That she and her friend were taken captive. (4) Lit., 'through her mouth'. (5) From here we learn that one witness is believed to attest the purity of the captive woman, even if there is another one contradicting him. (6) As to her friend. (7) Impure. (8) Pure. (9) As to her friend. (10) Also the last case. (11) Of priestly stock. (12) To be given *terumah*; (v. Glos.). (13) Lit., 'mouth'. (14) Lit., 'when? In the place in which there are objectors'.—The objectors say that he is not of priestly descent or legitimate origin. (15) *Segan*, v. Sanh. (Sonc. ed.) p. 97, n. 1.

GEMARA. What need is there for all these [cases]?[1]—They are needed. For if he had stated [only the case of] 'R. Joshua admits'[2] [I might have said that only in that case is that principle applied], because there is a possible loss of money,[3] but [in the case of] 'If witnesses say this is our handwriting'[4] where there is no possible loss of money,[5] I would not say so.[6] And if he had stated [the case of] 'If witnesses say this is our handwriting', [I might have said that only in that case does that principle apply] because [their statement concerns] other people,[7] but where it concerns himself[8] [24*a*] I would not say so. And if he would let us hear these two [cases, I might have said] because [both cases deal with] money matters, but [in the case of] 'a married woman',[9] which is a matter of [sexual] prohibition,[10] I would not say so.[11]

What need is there for [the case of] 'I was taken captive and I am pure'?[12]—Because he wants to teach 'But if witnesses came afters he got married, she shall not go out'.[13]—That is quite right according to him who refers this to the second clause, but according to him who refers this to the first clause,[14] what is there to say?—Because he wants to teach [the case of] 'If two women were taken captive'.[15]—And what need is there for [the case of] 'If two women were taken captive'?—You might have said [that] we may

(1) In the preceding Mishnahs from the beginning of this chapter (*supra* 15*b*) to this last Mishnah. All these have been cases taught in illustration of the same principle of 'the mouth that forbids is the mouth that permits'. (2) *Supra* 15*b*. (3) [His first statement that 'This field belonged to thy father', carries with it a possible loss of money, and it must therefore be taken in conjunction with the subsequent statement, 'But I bought it of him'.] (4) *Supra* 18*b*. (5) [There the witnesses themselves stand to lose nothing by this statement.] (6) Lit., 'I would say, no'. I.e., I would not apply here the principle of 'the mouth that forbids is the mouth that permits', and their second statement that they acted under constraint etc. is not accepted. (7) Lit., 'because for the world'.—The statement of the witnesses does not concern themselves but others. (8) As in the case of 'R. Joshua admits'. (9) *Supra* 22*a*. (10) Matters of sexual prohibition are treated with greater strictness than money matters. (11) Therefore, the case regarding a married woman is also taught in illustration of the principle. (12) Mishnah, 22*a* second clause. (13) Ibid., concluding clause of Mishnah. (14) V. *supra* 23*a*. (15) Mishnah, *supra* 23*b*.

be afraid that they favour one another,[1] so he lets us hear [that we do not say so].[2] What need is there for [the case of] 'AND LIKEWISE TWO MEN'?[3]—Because he wants to teach the difference of opinion between R. Judah and the Rabbis.[4]

Our Rabbis taught: [If one says:] I am a priest and my friend is a priest, he is believed to the extent of allowing him to eat *terumah*,[5] but he is not believed to the extent of allowing him to marry a woman[6] until there are three, [and] two testify to one and two testify to the other. R. Judah says: He is not believed even with regard to allowing him to eat *terumah* until there are three, [and] two testify to one and two testify to the other. Is this to say that R. Judah is afraid that they might favour one another,[7] and the Rabbis are not afraid that they might favour one another? Surely [from the following Mishnah] we understand just the reverse! For we have learned: When ass-drivers[8] come to a town and one of them says, 'Mine[9] is new[10] and my friend's is old, mine is not prepared[11] and my friends is prepared'; he is not believed;[12] R. Judah says: He is believed![13]—Said R. Adda b. Ahaba, in the name of Rab: The statement must be reversed.[14] Abaye said: Indeed, there is no need to reverse it;[15] in [the case of] *demai*,[16] they[17] have made it lenient, for most of the *'amme ha-'arez*[18] separate

(1) And the two women shield one another. (2) That when the two women testify to one another's purity, they are believed. (3) The case of our Mishnah. (4) The first Tanna and R. Eliezer. (5) V. Glos. (6) Of unblemished descent. (7) By false mutual recommendations. (8) Who bring corn to a place to sell. (9) My corn. (10) New = fresh, old = not fresh. Fresh corn is not so good as corn that is not fresh. [He simply says this in depreciation of his own ware and in praise of that of his fellow.] It may also be that 'new' and 'old' are used in the sense of Lev. XXIII, 10ff., the 'new' being forbidden before the offering of the *'omer*; v. Glos. (11) I.e., the priestly dues have not been given. (12) [According to the first interpretation (n. 10) the reference is to the tithes only, and according to the second also to the prohibition of 'new' corn.] (13) This would show that the Rabbis are afraid of people favouring one another, and that R. Judah is not afraid. (14) I.e., read: R. Judah says: they are not believed, and the Rabbis say: They are believed. (15) Lit., 'do not reverse'. (16) *Demai* is produce about which there is a doubt whether the tithes therefrom have been properly taken or not; v. Glos. (17) The Sages. (18) V. Glos. They did not observe, or were under the suspicion of not observing

the tithes. Raba said: Is the question [only] of R. Judah against R. Judah? Is there no question [also] of the Rabbis against the Rabbis?[1] No, [they answer]: there is no question of R. Judah against R. Judah, as we have [just] explained,[2] [and] there is no question of the Rabbis against the Rabbis, for [the case[3] is similar to that with regard to which] R. Ḥama b. 'Uḳba said that [it speaks of] when he has his trade-tools in his hand; [24b] so here also[4] [we deal with] when he[5] has his trade-tools[6] in his hand.[7] And with regard to what[8] was that of R. Ḥama, b. 'Uḳba said?[9]—With regard to what we have learned: If a potter left his pots[10] and went down to drink [water from the river,][11] the inner ones are pure and the outer ones are impure.[12] But it has been taught[13] that these and those are impure?—Said R. Ḥama b. 'Uḳba: [it speaks of a case][14] when he had his trade-tools in his hand,[15] so that[16] the hand of all touches them.[17] But it has been taught:[18] These and those are pure?—Said R. Ḥama b. 'Uḳba: When his trade-tools are not in his hand.[19] But [then] the case that we have learnt:[20] 'The inner ones are pure and the outer ones are impure'— how is that

certain religious customs regarding tithes, levitical cleanness, etc. In spite of this suspicion it was assumed that most of them did give tithes.

(1) If you do not reverse, why should the Rabbis hold that the ass-drivers are not believed, seeing that they do not suspect mutual favouritism. (2) Lit., 'answered'. They have made it lenient with regard to *demai*. (3) Of the ass-drivers. (4) In the case of the ass-drivers. (5) Each ass-driver. (6) As the measure and leveller. (7) This shows that the ass-drivers mean to sell their corn. Therefore the Rabbis suspect them of mutual favouritism. If one praises his friend's produce in one place, the friend will praise the other one's produce in another place. And therefore the Rabbis hold that they are not believed. (8) Lit., 'where'. (9) I.e., did he give that explanation. (10) I.e., put down his pots in the street and left them unobserved. (11) These words, bracketed in the text, are missing in the Mishnah Ṭoh. VII, 1, whence this is quoted. (12) As they may have been touched by persons who do not observe the laws of purity. (13) In a Baraitha. (14) In the Baraitha. (15) And thus indicates that the pots are for sale. (16) Lit., 'because'. (17) Would-be buyers handle the pots and examine them as to their quality. Therefore, in the Baraitha, both the inner and the outer pots are impure. (18) In another Baraitha. (19) There is no indication that the pots are for sale and no one touches them. (20) In the Mishnah.

possible?[1]—When they[2] are near the public road and [they are impure] because of border stones of the public road.[3] And if you wish you may say: R. Judah and the Rabbis differ as to whether one raises [a person] from *terumah* to the status of a priest.[4]

The question was asked: What is [the law]? Does one raise[5] [a person] from documents[6] to the full status of a priest?[7]—How shall we imagine this case? If we say that it is written in it: 'I, So-and-so, a priest, have signed as witness'—who testifies to him?[8] —No, [but] it must be when it is written in it: I, So-and-so, a priest, have borrowed a *maneh* from So-and-so, and witnesses have signed [the document]. What [then] is [the law]? Do they[9] testify [only] to the *maneh* [mentioned] in the document, or do they testify to the whole matter?[10]—R. Huna and R. Ḥisda [give

(1) Neither explanation of R. Ḥama b. 'Uḳba seems to apply, since some of the pots are pure and some are impure. (2) The outer pots. (3) תפופי. Lit., 'the rubbings' (Rashi), or 'border' (Jast.). According to Rashi, big stones or pegs set up at the sides of the public road, to prevent trespassing on private property, and against which passers-by press. The outer pots are impure, because passers-by, who do not observe the laws of purity, may touch them with their garments. The inner pots the passers-by cannot reach, and therefore they are pure. (4) יוחסין lit., 'genealogical records', 'traced genealogy'; (Jast. s.v.). The word המתיחשים '*those that were reckoned by genealogy*', Ezra II, 62, refers to 'the children of the priests'. (v. 61). יוחסין means therefore primarily 'genealogical priestly records', 'traced priestly genealogy'. In our text the phrase can be rendered by 'as being of a priestly family', or as 'having the status of a priest', or, briefly, 'to the full status of a priest', and the dispute between R. Judah and the Rabbis is, if a person is seen eating *terumah*, whether he is to be regarded as a priest also in family matters and be allowed to marry a woman of unblemished descent; (v. Ḳid. 69*b*). R. Judah says 'yes', and he is therefore strict even with regard to *terumah*, and does not accept the evidence of one witness, but the Rabbis would say 'no', and are therefore lenient with regard to *terumah* (v. 24*a*). This, then, is the point at issue, and not whether we suspect mutual favouritism, which, in point of fact, all agree that we do not. [According to the Rabbis, however, we must still adopt the answer given before, that the Mishnah of Demai deals with a case when the 'ass-driver had his trade-tools in his hand' (Tosaf.)] (5) Lit., 'how is it to raise', etc. (6) In which a person is designated as a priest. (7) V. note 4. (8) Who testifies that he is in fact a priest? (9) The witnesses. (10) I.e., to the whole contents of the document and so also to the priestly status of the borrower.

opposing answers]: One says: One raises,[1] and one says: One does not raise.[1]

The question was asked.[2] What is [the law]? Does one raise [a person] from the lifting up of the hands[3] to the status of a priest?[4] This is asked according to him who says [that] one raises [a person] from *terumah* to the status of a priest,[5] and this is asked according to him who says [that] one does not raise [a person from *terumah* to the status of a priest].[6] It is asked according to him who says [that] one raises: When is this said?[7] [In the case of] *terumah*, which [if eaten by one who is not a priest] is a sin punishable with death;[8] but [in the case of] 'lifting up the hands', which [if one who is not a priest performs the pronouncing of the priestly blessing] is [only transgressing the] prohibition of a positive command,[9] [I would say] no.[10] Or perhaps there is no difference,[11] [and] it is asked according to him who says [that] one does not raise: When is this said? [In the case of] *terumah*, which is eaten in privacy;[12] but [in the case of] 'lifting up the hands,' which [is done] in public [I might say that] if he were not a priest he would not have the impudence[13] [to act as a priest]. Or perhaps there is

(1) A person from documents to the status of a priest. (2) By the members of the academy. (3) The priests lifted up their hands in pronouncing the priestly blessing. The pronouncing of the priestly blessing (v. Num. VI, 22-27) is therefore called 'Lifting up the hands'. Cf. Ta'an 26, Ber. 34*a*. (4) Should one regard him, whom he sees pronouncing the priestly blessing, as a priest in every way? (5) That is, according to R. Judah. (6) That is, according to the Rabbis. (7) Lit., '(when are) these words (said)'. (8) It is therefore to be assumed that he who eats *terumah* is a priest, as it is not presumed that a person would commit such a grave sin. (9) Lit., 'do'. The commandment of pronouncing the blessing is given only to Aaron and his sons (and descendants)—Num. VI, 23. If non-Aaronides perform this commandment, they commit a transgression, because to them this is forbidden by implication. Only priests may bless, not non-priests. The transgression of a commandment, forbidden by implication from a positive command, is treated like a positive command, and is not punishable. This transgression will therefore be sooner committed by a non-Aaronide than the sin of eating *terumah*. (10) I.e., one does not raise a person from 'lifting up the hands' to the full status of priesthood. (11) Between *terumah* and lifting up the hands. (12) And the person does not mind committing a wrong act privately. (13) Lit., 'a man would not be as impudent (or, act as impudently) as all that'.

no difference?[1]—R. Ḥisda and R. Abina [give opposing answers to this question]: One says: One raises,[2] and one says: One does not raise.

R. Naḥman b. Isaac said to Raba: What is [the law]? Does one raise [a person] from 'lifting up the hands' to the full status of a priest?—Said he to him: [With regard to this] there is a difference of opinion between R. Ḥisda and R. Abina. What is the [adopted] law? Said he to him: I know a Baraitha: For it has been taught: R. Jose said: Great[3] is presumption,[4] for it is said: *And the children of the priests: the children of Habaiah, the children of Hakkoz, the children of Barzillai, who took a wife of the daughters of Barzillai the Gileadite, and was called after their name. These sought their register, of those that were reckoned by genealogy, and they were not found; therefore were they deemed polluted and put from the priesthood. And the Tirshatha*[5] *said unto them, that they should not eat of the most holy things, till there stood up a priest with Urim and Thummim.*[6] He[7] [thus] said to them: You remain[8] in your presumptive state; what have you eaten in exile?[9] The holy things of the country.[10] So here also [you shall eat] the sacred things of the country.[11] Now if we were to assume [that] one raises [a person] from 'lifting up the hands' to the state of a priest, since these spread out their hands,[12] one might raise

(1) Between *terumah* and lifting up the hands. (2) A person from lifting up of the hands to the status of priest. (3) I.e., important. (4) חזקה; the word used here in the sense of 'presumptive continuance of a state, or condition, until evidence is produced rebutting the presumption'. V. Jast. s.v. (5) [The governor; identified with Nehemiah (Rashi).] (6) Ezra II, 61-62. (7) The Tirshatha. (8) Lit., 'behold you are'. (9) In Babylonia. (10) 'Limit,' 'boundary,' has here the technical meaning of 'country,' as distinguished from 'sanctuary and Jerusalem'. 'Sacred things of the country' are the holy things that may be consumed outside the Temple and Jerusalem, such as *terumah*, as distinct from sacrificial offerings, that must be consumed within the precincts of the Temple courtyard. (11) The Tirshatha only forbade them to eat '*the most holy things*', as sacrifices. It is therefore implied that as he allowed them to eat 'the sacred things of the country,' as *terumah*, in presumptive continuance of their former state, they would be allowed, in the same way, to perform the lifting up of the hands, which was also done in 'the country'. (12) And pronounced the priestly blessing; v. preceding note.

them?'[1]—It is different here,[2] for their presumption has been impaired.[3] For if you will not say so,[4] [then] according to him who says [that] one raises [a person] from *terumah*, since they eat *terumah*, one might raise them to the status of priests! Hence [you must say it is][5] because their presumption has been impaired.[6] [25a] If so,[7] what [do the words of R. Jose mean] 'Great is the presumption'?[8]—Till now[9] they ate [only] Rabbinical *terumah*,[10] [and] now they ate Biblical *terumah*.[11] And if you wish, you may say: now also they ate Rabbinical *terumah*[12] [and] did not eat Biblical *terumah*,[13] and when does one raise [a person] from *terumah* to the status of a priest. In the case of Biblical *terumah*, but in the case of Rabbinical *terumah* one does not raise. If so,[14] what [is the meaning of the words] 'Great is the presumption'?[15]—Although one might have forbidden [Rabbinical *terumah*] because of Biblical *terumah*,[16] this has not been forbidden. But did they not eat Biblical *terumah?* Surely it is written: *'that they should not eat of the most holy things'*, [implying] *'the most holy things'* they did not eat, but Biblical *terumah* they did eat!—[No]. He means thus: Neither [may they eat] anything that is called *'holy thing'*,[17] as it is written: *'And no stranger shall eat of the* holy *thing'*, nor anything which is called *'holy thing'*, for it is written: *'And if a priest's daughter be married unto a stranger,*

(1) To the full status of priests, that is, as being of a priestly family, v. p. 133 n. 4. (2) In the case of Ezra II, 61-63. (3) Since they must not eat 'the most holy things' and the rightful priests do eat them. One would therefore not raise them to the status of priests from lifting up their hands. But in other cases one might do so. (4) That no mistake can be made because their presumption has been impaired. (5) Lit., 'but is it not'? (6) And therefore no mistake can be made, and the same applies to the 'lifting up of hands'. (7) Lit., 'and but'. (8) How far does the presumption improve their position? Why does R. Jose lay such emphasis on it? (9) Lit., 'at first'. In Babylonia. (10) *Terumah* outside Palestine is only rabbinically ordained; v. Ḳid. 36b. (11) *Terumah* in Palestine is commanded by the law of the Bible, and the eating of such *terumah* by them was due to the importance attached to 'presumption'. (12) I.e., *terumah* on vegetables and fruits. (13) On corn, wine and oil. (14) Lit., 'and but'. (15) V. *supra* p. 135, n. 4. (16) Since on their entering the land there would be plenty of Biblical *terumah* available side by side with the Rabbinical *terumah*, through being permitted to eat the latter, they might be led to eat also of the former.] (17) Lev. XXII, 10. The reference is to *terumah*, v. Yeb. 74b.

she shall not eat of the peace-offering of the holy things'[1] — and a Master said: [that this means] that which has been set aside from the holy things she shall not eat.[2]

Come and hear: A presumption for the priesthood is constituted by the 'lifting up of the hands' in Babylonia, and the eating of the *ḥallah*[3] in Syria, and taking a share in [the priestly] gifts[4] in large cities.[5] In any case he mentions [here] the 'lifting up of the hands'; is it not with regard to the full status of the priest?[6] — No, with regard to *terumah*.[7] But he teaches [the ruling regarding *terumah*] as analogous to the eating of *ḥallah;* just as the eating of *ḥallah* [entitles a person] to the full status of a priest, so does the lifting up of the hands [entitle a person] to the full status of a priest? — No, the eating of the *ḥallah* itself merely [serves as evidence] regarding *terumah*, [for] he holds that *ḥallah* in our days[8] is Rabbinical and *terumah* is Biblical and one raises [a person] from Rabbinical *ḥallah* to Biblical *terumah*,[9] and [it is] as R. Huna, the son of R. Joshua, reversed [the words of] the Rabbis.[10]

Come and hear: A presumption for the priesthood is [constituted by] the 'lifting up of the hands' and taking a share [at the distribution of the [priestly gifts] at the threshing floors[11] in the Land of Israel;[12] in Syria and in all places to which the messengers

(1) Lev. XXII, 12. The reference is to those portions of sacrifices, the breast and shoulder of peace-offerings, (v. Lev. VII, 34), that could be partaken of by the wives of priests and their slaves; v. next note. (2) Cf. preceding note. And in Ezra II, 63, both words are used, corresponding to the two words just quoted from Lev. XXII, 10 and 12; v. Ḳid. 69*b* and Yeb. 68*b* and 87*a*. (3) The priest's share of the dough; v. Num. XV, 20. (4) V. Deut. XVIII, 3. (5) [Though these portions are permissible to non-priests, it is assumed that no one but a priest would venture to accept these publicly.] (6) I.e., in family matters; (v. *supra* p. 133, n. 4) which solves R. Naḥman b. Isaac's question. (7) [He who is seen to avail himself of any of these privileges as defined may be given *terumah*, but it cannot be used as evidence regarding marriage.] (8) Lit., 'in this time', i.e., after the destruction of the Second Temple. (9) When one is seen being given *ḥallah*, we assume he is a priest, and he may be given *terumah*. (10) V. *infra*. (11) I.e., sharing in the *terumah*. (12) [Where *terumah* was Biblical and would not be given to a person of doubtful descent, and similarly in regard to the 'lifting of hands', the presence of the Sanhedrin, who would investigate claims to priesthood, would be sufficient bar to a non-priest.]

of the new moon come[1] the 'lifting up of the hands' is evidence, but not taking a share at the threshing floors.[2] Babylonia is like Syria. R. Simeon b. Gamaliel, says: Also Alexandria in Egypt formerly, because there was there a permanent court of law.[3] In any case he teaches [here] the 'lifting up of the hands'; is it not with regard to the full status of the priest?—No, with regard to *ḥallah*. But he teaches [the rule regarding the lifting up of the hands] as analogous to taking a share at the threshing floors: just as taking a share at the threshing floors [serves as evidence] in respect of the status of a priest, so does the 'lifting up of the hands' [serve] in respect of the status of a priest!—No, taking a share at the threshing floors itself [serves as evidence only as] to *ḥallah*, for he holds that *terumah* in our days is Rabbinical and *ḥallah* is Biblical and one raises [a person] from Rabbinical *terumah* to Biblical *ḥallah*, even as the Rabbis, whom R. Huna the son of R. Joshua found [in discourse]. For R. Huna, the son of R. Joshua, found the Rabbis in the School of Rab sitting[4] and saying: Even according to him who says that *terumah* in these days is Rabbinical, *ḥallah* is Biblical, for during the seven [years] that they[5] conquered [the Land] and during the seven [years] that they distributed [it][6] there was a duty upon them [to separate] *ḥallah*, but there was no duty upon them [to separate] *terumah*. And I said to them: On the contrary, even according to him who says [that] *terumah* in these days is Biblical, *ḥallah* is Rabbinical, for it has been taught: [It is written:] '*In your coming*'.[7] If '*in your coming*'[8] you might think as soon as two or three spies had entered it? [Therefore] it is said '*in your coming*'.[9] I have spoken of the coming of *all* and not of the

(1) [V. R.H. 18*a*; informing the people the day on which the Sanhedrin had proclaimed the new moon of Nisan so that they might observe the festival of Passover on the proper day. These places had to be within fifteen days' walking distance from Jerusalem.] (2) Being outside Palestine proper *terumah* there is only of Rabbinic origin. (3) Who would investigate claims to priesthood, cf. *supra* p. 137, n. 12. (4) Rashi renders: בי רב 'house of learning', 'school', 'college'. (5) The Israelites. (6) Under Joshua. V. B.M. 89*a*. (7) בבואכם, so literally Num. XV, 18. E.V. '*When you come*'. (8) The emphasis would seem to be on '*come*'. (9) The emphasis is thus laid on '*your*'. '*Your*' means '(the coming of) all of you'.

coming of a portion of you. Now when Ezra brought them up[1] [25*b*] not all of them went up.[2]

Come and hear: A presumption for the priesthood [is constituted by] the 'lifting up of the hands' and taking a share at the threshing floors and testimony.[3] Now is testimony a presumption?[4] Hence he means thus: The 'lifting up of the hands is like a testimony'; as a testimony [raises one] to the status of a priest, so the 'lifting up of the hands' [raises one] to the status of a priest![5] —No, [what it means is] a testimony that comes on the strength of a presumption[6] is like a presumption, as when a man came once before R. Ammi [and] said to him: I am convinced that he[7] is a priest. So he said to him: What have you seen? And he answered him: He read first in the Synagogue.[8]—As[9] priest or as prominent man?[10]—After him a Levite read.[11] And R. Ammi raised him to the priesthood on the strength of his testimony.[12]

Someone came before R. Joshua b. Levi, [and] said to him: I am convinced that he[13] is a Levite. He said to him: What have you seen? He answered him: He read second in the Synagogue. As Levite or as a prominent man?—A priest read before him.[14] And R. Joshua b. Levi raised him to the status of Levite[15] on the strength of his testimony.

Someone came once before Resh Laḳish [and] said to him: I am convinced that he[16] is a priest. He said to him: What have you seen? [He answered him:] He read first in the Synagogue. He[17] asked him: Have you seen him take a share at the threshing floors?[18] —Said R. Eleazar to him. And does the priesthood cease if there

(1) To the Land of Israel. (2) And therefore *ḥallah* in these days is Rabbinical. (3) Witnesses testify that he is a priest. (4) Surely you cannot call a testimony a presumption! (5) Which answers the question of R. Naḥman b. Isaac. (6) The testimony is to a fact that postulates a presumption. (7) A certain person. Lit., 'this (man)'. (8) When called up to the Law. V. Giṭ. 59*b*. (9) Lit., 'in the presumption of'. (10) V. Giṭ. 59*b*. (11) This would show that he was a priest; v. Giṭ. 59*b*. (12) Lit., 'by his mouth'. (13) A certain person. Lit., 'this (man)'. (14) [So he must have been a Levite, v. Giṭ. 59*b*.] (15) To give him the first tithe. (16) A certain person. Lit., 'this (man)'. (17) Resh Laḳish. (18) The first answer apparently did not satisfy Resh Laḳish.

is no threshing floor there?[1]—Once they sat before R. Joḥanan [and] there came such a case before them. Resh Laḳish asked him:[2] Have you seen him take a share at the threshing floor? So R. Joḥanan said to him: And does the priesthood cease if there is no threshing floor there?—He[3] turned round, looked at R. Eleazar with displeasure[4] and said: You have heard something from the smith's son[5] and you did not say it to us in his name.[6]

Rabbi and R. Ḥiyya, one raised a son to the priesthood on the testimony of his father, and one raised a brother to the state of Levite on the testimony of his brother. It can be proved that it was Rabbi who raised the son to the priesthood on the testimony of his father, for it has been taught: If one comes and says: 'This is my son and he is a priest,' he is believed with regard to allowing him to eat *terumah*, but he is not believed with regard to allowing him to marry a woman.[7] This is the opinion[8] of Rabbi. Said R. Ḥiyya to him: If you believe him so as to allow him to eat *terumah*, believe him [also] so as to allow him to marry a woman, and if you do not believe him so as to allow him to marry a woman, do not believe him also as to allow him to eat *terumah*. He answered him: I believed him so as to allow him to eat *terumah* because it is in his hands to let him eat *terumah*,[9] but I do not believe him so as to allow him to marry a woman because it is not in his hands to let him marry a woman.[10] It is proved.[11] And since it was Rabbi who raised the son to the priesthood on the testimony of his father, [it follows that] it was R. Ḥiyya who raised the brother to the status of Levite on the testimony of his brother. But [according to] R. Ḥiyya, why is the son different that [he is] not [raised]?[12]

(1) R. Eleazar apparently regarded the first answer as sufficient. (2) The witness. (3) Resh Laḳish. (4) Rashi: with an evil eye. (5) R. Joḥanan. V. Sanh. (Sonc. ed.) p. 647, n. 8. (6) He understood that R. Eleazar had heard the phrase he had cited from R. Joḥanan, and therefore reproved him for this lack of scholarly courtesy in not mentioning his source. (7) Of unblemished descent. (8) Lit., 'the words'. (9) He can give him of his *terumah*. (10) Marriage is not in the hand of the father. (11) That it was Rabbi who promoted the son to priesthood on the testimony of his father. (12) On the testimony of his father.

Because he is related to his father. A brother, too, is related to his brother?[1]—[26a] When he was talking in his simplicity.[2] As that [story which] Rab Judah related in the name of Samuel: It happened that a man was talking in his simplicity and said: 'I remember when I was a child and rode on my father's shoulder, they brought me out from school and stripped me of my shirt and immersed me[3] so that I could eat *terumah* in the evening.'[4] And R. Ḥiyya added:[5] 'And my friends held aloof from me and called me "Joḥanan the *ḥalloth-eater*".'[6] And Rabbi raised him to the priesthood on his testimony.

It has been taught: R. Simeon b. Eleazar, says: Just as *terumah* is a presumption for the priesthood, so is the first tithe a presumption for the priesthood,[7] but he who takes a share [at the threshing floors] through the court—[this] is not a presumption.[8] The first tithe belongs to the Levite?[9]—[This is] according to R. Eleazar, the son of Azariah, for it has been taught: *Terumah* belongs to the priest, the first tithe to the Levite—this is the view of R. Akiba, R. Eleazar, the son of Azariah, says: The first tithe belongs also to the priest. [But] R. Eleazar, the son of Azariah, says: 'also to the priest'; does he say: to the priest and not to the Levite?—Yes, after Ezra had punished them.[10] But perhaps it happened that they gave it to him?[11]—Said R. Ḥisda: Here we treat of a case where we know that the father of that [person] is a priest and a rumour[12] came out concerning him that he is the son of a divorced woman[13] or a *ḥaluẓah*[14] and [yet] they gave him tithe at the threshing floor. [He could not be regarded as] a Levite,

(1) Why should he be raised on the evidence of his brother? (2) The brother, on whose statement the promotion was made, did not intend to give evidence. (3) *Terumah* had to be eaten in ritual purity. (4) [Because children are apt to rummage about in places that are not clean, and thus contract defilement.] (5) Completing the man's narrative. (6) Plur. of *Ḥallah*, v. Glos. (7) If a man is seen eating first tithe, it is presumed that he is a priest. (8) This is explained *infra*. (9) V. Num. XVIII, 24. (10) The Levites, not to be given any tithes, v. Yeb. 86*b*. (11) To the Levite; how then can first tithe constitute a presumption for priesthood? (12) Lit., 'voice'. (13) He is the offspring of a union of a priest with a divorced woman, therefore a *ḥalal*, ('*profaned*'), v. Lev. XXI, 7. (14) V. Glos.

because he was not a Levite.[1] What then could you say? That he was the son of a divorced woman or the son of a *ḥaluẓah*? [But as to this] there is no question that according to him who says [that] the first tithe is forbidden to strangers,[2] they would not have given [it] to him. For even according to him who says: The first tithe is permitted to strangers,[3] it is only to sustain them[4] but as a distribution [due to him as of right] they do not give it to him.[5]

'But he who takes a share [at the threshing floors] through the court—[this] is not a presumption.' If it is not a presumption through the court, when is it a presumption?—Said R. Shesheth: he means thus: If one shares the *terumah* in the property of his father[6] through the court, it is not a presumption.—This is obvious![7]—You might have said [that] just as those[8] [get their share of *terumah*] for eating, this one also [gets his share of *terumah*] for eating, so he lets us hear [that] those [get the *terumah*] for eating and this one for selling.[9]

R. Judah says: ONE DOES NOT RAISE [A PERSON] TO THE PRIESTHOOD ON THE TESTIMONY OF ONE WITNESS, etc. R. Simeon b. Gamaliel says the same as R. Eliezer?[10] And if you will say [that] they differ with regard to an objection raised by one person, [in] that R. Eliezer holds that an objection [may be admitted if coming from] one [person] and R. Simeon b. Gamaliel holds that an objection [must come from at least] two [persons]—did not R. Joḥanan say: All agree that an objection [must come from] at least two persons?—But we treat here of a case where the father of this [person] is a priest and a rumour[11] came out concerning him that he is the son of a divorced woman or the son of a *ḥaluẓah* and they put him down,[12] and one witness came and

(1) His father is a priest. (2) Persons who are neither priests nor Levites. (3) Cf. Yeb. 74*a*, 85*b*, and 86*a*. (4) If they are poor. (5) And since they gave him tithe at the threshing floors it shews that he is an unblemished priest. (6) After the father's death. (7) Even a *ḥalal* inherits his father. (8) The brothers. (9) He inherits the *terumah* and may sell it to rightful priests but he may not eat it, although the division took place under the direction of the court. (10) In our Mishnah. (11) Lit., 'voice'. (12) From the status of priesthood.

said, 'I know that he is a priest,'[1] [26b] and they raised him [again] and [then] came two [other witnesses] and said [that] he is the son of a divorced woman or the son of a *haluzah*, and they put him down [again], and [then] came one witness and said, 'I know that he is a priest'. [Now] all agree[2] that they[3] are joined into one testimony, and they differ as to whether we are afraid of bringing contempt on the court.[4] The first Tanna[5] holds: Since we put him down we do not raise him [again], because we are afraid of bringing contempt on the court.[6] Whereas R. Simeon b. Gamaliel, holds: we have put him down and we can raise him [again],[7] and we are not afraid of bringing contempt on the court. R. Ashi asked against this: If so, even [when there are] two and two[8] also?[9] But, said R. Ashi, they differ as to whether they[10] are joined into one testimony. And they have the same difference of opinion as these Tannaim,[11] for it has been taught: Their testimonies are not joined together unless they have both seen[12] at the same time;[13] R. Joshua b. Korha, says: Even when [they have seen] one after another. Their testimonies are not established[14] in court until they both give evidence at the same time; R. Nathan says: We hear the evidence of one to-day, and when the other one comes to-morrow we hear his evidence.[15]

(1) A rightful, unblemished priest. (2) R. Eliezer and R. Simeon b. Gamaliel. (3) The testimony of the first witness and that of the last witness, so that there are two witnesses against two witnesses. (4) If he is re-instated now, having been put down by the court twice. (5) R. Eliezer. (6) [Should he be re-instated after having been degraded twice, the court would be brought into contempt; and thus R. Eliezer says that where there have been objectors, there is renewed promotion by the evidence of one witness, namely the last.] (7) [To the priesthood, in continuance of the presumptive state which he had originally enjoyed.] (8) If two witnesses who speak in his favour come at the same time. (9) He should be not raised again in the view of R. Eliezer for fear of bringing contempt on the court. (10) The testimony of the first witness and that of the last witness, so that there are two witnesses against two witnesses. (11) The Rabbis and R. Nathan of the Baraitha that follows. (12) What they testify to. (13) At the same time and in the presence of one another. (14) Accepted as evidence. (15) Their testimonies are joined together and the two single witnesses are regarded as a pair of witnesses. R. Eliezer agrees with the Rabbis, R. Simeon b. Gamaliel with R. Nathan.

MISHNAH. IF A WOMAN WAS IMPRISONED BY HEATHENS, IF FOR THE SAKE OF MONEY, SHE IS PERMITTED TO HER HUSBAND, AND IF FOR THE PURPOSE OF [TAKING HER] LIFE,[1] SHE IS FORBIDDEN TO HER HUSBAND.

GEMARA. R. Samuel b. Isaac said [that] Rab said: They have taught [this] only when the hand of Israel is strong over the heathens,[2] but when the hand of the heathens is strong over themselves,[3] even if for the sake of money, she is forbidden to her husband. Raba raised an objection: R. Jose the priest and R. Zechariah b. ha-Kaẓẓab[4] testified regarding an Israelitish woman, who was pledged[5] in Ashkelon and her family[6] put her away,[7] and her witnesses[8] testified [concerning her] that she did not hide herself [with a man] and that she was not defiled [by a man], [that] the Sages said to them: If you believe [the witnesses] that she was pledged believe [them also] that she did not hide herself and that she was not defiled, and if you do not believe [them] that she did not hide herself and that she was not defiled, do not believe [them] that she was pledged.[9] Now Ashkelon [was a town in which] the hand of the heathens was strong over themselves and he teaches [27*a*] 'when she was pledged' but not 'when she was imprisoned'?[10]—[No] the same applies also to [the case if] she had been imprisoned, only it happened so.[11]

Some say, Raba said: We have also learned [in a Mishnah] to the same effect: R. Jose the priest and R. Zechariah b. ha-Kaẓẓab testified regarding an Israelitish woman, who was pledged in Ashkelon and her family put her away and her witnesses testified concerning her that she did not hide herself [with a man] and that

(1) And she was saved afterwards. (2) [In which case they were afraid to force the woman, lest they should forfeit their money claim.] (3) I.e., when the heathens are independent, [or a euphemism 'themselves', standing for Israelites.] (4) 'Son of the Butcher'. (5) For a debt. (6) Who were priests. (7) Disqualified her from marrying a priest for fear she might have been violated. (8) Who testified to her having been pledged. (9) V. 'Ed. VIII, 2. (10) The case of 'pledged' would be worse than that of 'imprisoned', for once the tithe for redemption had expired, the pledge remains the absolute possession of the creditor (Rashi). (11) That she had been pledged.

she was not defiled [by a man], [that] the Sages said: If you believe [the witnesses] that she was pledged believe [them also] that she did not hide herself and that she was not defiled, and if you do not believe [them] that she did not hide herself and was not defiled, do not believe [them] that she was pledged. In Ashkelon [it happened] for the sake of money, and [yet] the reason [why the Sages permitted her to her husband was] because witnesses testified concerning her, but if witnesses did not testify concerning her [she would] not [have been permitted]; and is it not [also to be supposed] that there is no difference whether she was pledged or imprisoned?[1]—No, when she was pledged it is different.[2]

Some put [this argument] in the form of a contradiction. We have learned: IF FOR THE SAKE OF MONEY SHE IS PERMITTED TO HER HUSBAND. But here is a contradiction: 'R. Jose testified etc.' [Now] in Ashkelon [it happened] for the sake of money and [yet] the reason [why she is permitted to her husband] is because witnesses testify concerning her, but if no witnesses testify concerning her, [she would] not [have been permitted]. And it is answered: R. Samuel b. Isaac said: It is no contradiction; here[3] [it speaks] when the hand of Israel is strong over the heathens, [and] there[4] when the hand of the heathens is strong over themselves.

IF FOR THE PURPOSE OF [TAKING HER] LIFE SHE IS FORBIDDEN [TO HER HUSBAND]. Rab said: As, for instance, the wives of thieves.[5] Levi said: As, for instance, the wife of Ben Dunai.[6] Hezekiah said: This is only[7] when they have [already] been sentenced to death. R. Johanan says: Even if they have not yet been sentenced to death.

MISHNAH. IF TROOPS OF SIEGE HAVE TAKEN A TOWN,

(1) This supports R. Samuel b. R. Isaac. (2) V. p. 144 n. 9. (3) In our Mishnah. (4) 'Ed. V. 2. (5) Their property and their wives were apparently confiscated (Rashi). (6) Or Dinai, a notorious bandit, v. Soṭ. (Sonc. ed.) p. 249, n. 2. (7) Lit., 'and that is'.

ALL THE PRIESTS' WIVES[1] WHO ARE IN IT ARE UNFIT.[2] IF THEY HAVE WITNESSES,[3] EVEN A SLAVE,[4] EVEN A HANDMAID,[5] THEY ARE BELIEVED. NO ONE IS BELIEVED AS TO HIMSELF.

GEMARA. There is a contradiction against this: If a reconnoitring troop comes to a town in time of peace the open casks [of wine] are forbidden[6] and the closed ones are permitted.[7] In times of war both are permitted, because they have no time to offer libations.[8]—R. Mari answered: To have intercourse they have time.[9] To offer libations they have no time. R. Isaac b. Eleazar said in the name of Hezekiah: There[10] [it speaks] of a beseiging troop of the same kingdom,[11] here[12] [it speaks] of a beseiging troop of another kingdom.[13] [Even in the case of a beseiging troop] of the same kingdom it is not possible that one of them does not run away[14] [from the rest of thet roop]![15] — Rab. Judah answered in the name of Samuel: When the guards[16] see one another.[17] [But] it is not possible that one does not sleep a little![18] —R. Levi answered: When they placed round the town chains, dogs, trunks of trees and geese.[19] R. Abba, b. Zabda said: With regard to this R. Judah Nesi'ah[20] and the Rabbis differ: one said [that] there[21] [it speaks] of a beseiging troop of the same kingdom, and here[22] of a beseiging troop of another kingdom, and he found

(1) Priestesses. (2) I.e., forbidden to their husbands, as they might have been defiled by the troops. (3) That they have not been defiled. (4) A male slave. (5) A female slave. (6) Because they may have offered libations to idols. (7) It is assumed that the troops do not touch the closed casks since they have open casks of wine. (8) V. A.Z. 70*b*. And in our Mishnah it is assumed that the troops have time to violate the women of the town. (9) They are driven by their passion. (10) In A.Z. 70*b*. (11) [Sent to suppress a rebellion. The troop is therefore self-restrained] (12) In our Mishnah. (13) An enemy troop behaves in a hostile manner, and the women of the town may have been violated. (14) *Var. lec.* 'remove his foot'. (15) And has violated a woman. (16) Appointed for the protection of the population. (17) And they can call to one another to arrest any wrongdoer. Fear of the guards would prevent assaults on women. (18) I.e., the guards may fall asleep for a little while. (19) So that any one who would attempt to run away (or slip away) would be caught. (20) The Prince. R. Judah II. (21) In A.Z. 70*b*. (22) In our Mishnah.

no difficulties, whereas one[1] raised all those questions[2] and answered [them by saying] when they placed round the town chains, dogs, trunks of trees, and geese.

R. Idi b. Abin said in the name of R. Isaac b. Ashian: If there is there one hiding place, it protects all priests' wives.[3] R. Jeremiah asked [a question]: What is [the law] if it holds only one? Do we say of each one:[4] This is the one[5] or not?—But why should it be different from [the following case]? There were two paths, one was clean[6] and one was unclean, and someone walked in one of them and [then] prepared clean things,[7] and another person came and walked in the second path and [then] prepared clean things, R. Judah says: If each one comes to ask[8] separately,[9] they are [declared] clean,[10] [but] if they both come together, they are [declared] unclean;[11] R. Jose says: In either case[12] they are [declared] unclean.[13] [Whereon] Raba, and some say R. Joḥanan said: [if they come to ask] at the same time, all agree that they are [declared] unclean, if they come one after another, all agree that they are [declared] clean; they differ only when one comes to ask for himself and for the other one; one[14] regards this as[15] [if it were] at the same time, and the other[16] regards this as [if it were] one after another. Now here[17] also, since all [women] [are declared] permitted, it is like [the case where they came] at the same time?[18]—How is this

(1) The other disputing party. (2) Raised here in the Gemara. (3) It is to be assumed of each one that she hid herself there. (4) Of the priests' wives. (5) Who hid herself there. (6) Ritually. In one of the two paths were dead bodies buried, but it is not known in which. (7) Lit., 'did purities'. I.e., touched things which were ritually pure (Rashi). If he is ritually impure he makes them ritually impure. (8) They come to ask a scholar for a decision as to the things which they touched. (9) Lit., 'this one for himself and this one for himself'. (10) I.e., the things are pure, because the two men are regarded as pure. Since they came to ask separately I say of each of them that he walked in the clean path. (11) The things are unclean, because the decision given to the men cannot be: 'you are clean', since one of the two present must have walked in the unclean path. As it is not known which it was they are both regarded as unclean and the things which they touched are unclean. (12) Lit., 'Whether So-and-so'. Whether they come separately or together. (13) V. Toh. V, 5. (14) R. Jose. (15) Lit., 'compares it to'. (16) R. Judah. (17) In the case of the priests' wives. (18) And therefore all of them should

so?[1] There[2] there is certainly an impurity,[3] [but] here[4] who says that any one[5] has been defiled?[6]

R. Ashi asked: If she[7] says, 'I have not hidden myself and I have not been defiled', what is [the law]? Do we say [27b] 'why should she lie,'[8] or do we not say it? But why should this be different from the following case? Once someone hired out an ass to a person, and he said to him, 'Do not go the way of Nehar Peḳod, where there is water,[9] go the way of Naresh, where there is no water. But he[10] went the way of Nehar Peḳod and the ass died.[11] He[10] [then] came before Raba[12] and said to him, 'Indeed, I went the way of Nehar Peḳod, but there was no water. Said Raba: 'Why should he lie?' If he wished he could say 'I went the way of Naresh.' And Abaye said to him: we do not say 'Why should he lie?' where there are witnesses.[13]—Now is this so? There there were witnesses that there certainly was water on the way of Nehar Peḳod, but here has she certainly been defiled? It is [only] a fear,[14] and in the case of a fear we say ['why should he lie?']

IF THERE ARE WITNESSES, EVEN A SLAVE, EVEN A HANDMAID, THEY ARE BELIEVED. And even her own handmaid is

be forbidden on the view of R. Jose to their husbands, if there is a hiding place in which only one can hide herself, since, when R. Judah and R. Jose differ, the law is according to R. Jose (Rashi) and since it is ruled that all the women are permitted, it is as if they all had come at one and the same time to ask for a decision.

(1) I.e., is this analogy correct? How can you compare these two cases? (2) In the case of the two paths. (3) One path was unclean. (4) In the case of the priests' wives. (5) Of the priests' wives. (6) It may be that there was no defilement at all. (7) One of the priests' wives. (8) Lit., 'Why should I lie?' Do we apply here the principle of 'Why should I lie?' If she had wished to tell a falsehood she could have said that she hid herself. She does not gain any advantage by her present statement. Therefore we should believe her entire statement. (9) Which, apparently, the ass-driver would have to cross. (10) The man who hired the ass. (11) Apparently through the fatigue of crossing the water. (12) Before whom the parties, the owner and hirer of the ass, brought their dispute. (13) It is common knowledge that there is water on the way to Nehar Peḳod, v. however, B.M. (Sonc. ed.) p. 468 and notes. (14) One is merely afraid that she may have been defiled.

believed. But there is a contradiction against this:[1] She[2] must not be alone with him[3] unless there are witnesses, even a slave, even a handmaid[4] except her own handmaid,[5] because she[6] is familiar with her own handmaid![7]—R. Papi said: In [the case of] a woman captive[8] they[9] have made it lenient. R. Papa said: In the one case[10] [it speaks of] her handmaid, in the other case[11] [it speaks of] his handmaid. But her handmaid is not believed? Does he not teach [that] no one may testify as to himself? [This would imply that] her handmaid is believed![12]—Her handmaid is like herself.[13] R. Ashi said: In both cases [it speaks of] her handmaid, but [what we maintain is that] the handmaid sees and is silent.[14] [Consequently] there,[15] where her silence makes her permitted,[16] she is not believed, but here,[17] where her silence makes her forbidden,[18] she is believed. Now also, she may come and tell a falsehood?[19]—Two [things] she would not do[20] as in the case of Mari b. Isaḳ [or as some say

(1) V. Giṭ. 73*a*. (2) The wife of a husband who gave her a divorce on condition that he dies, v. Giṭ. 73*a*. (3) With her husband between the delivery of the divorce and his death. (4) Even if a slave or a handmaid is present when husband and wife are in one room. (5) The wife's own handmaid. (6) The wife. (7) We thus see that her own handmaid cannot be a witness. This is the contradiction. For further notes v. Giṭ. (Sonc. ed.) p. 348. (8) E.g., the priests' wives in the Mishnah. (9) The Rabbis. (10) In Giṭ. 73*a*. (11) In our Mishnah. (12) Anyone but herself. (13) Therefore her own handmaid cannot be a witness. (14) I.e., all the handmaid does is: She sees what her mistress does and keeps quiet. (15) In Giṭ. 73*a*. (16) There (in Giṭ. 73*a*), if the handmaid says nothing as to any intimacy between husband and wife after the conditional divorce, she is in her permitted state. And as her handmaid is suspected of seeing a wrong done and saying nothing her silent testimony is not accepted. (17) In our Mishnah. (18) A captive woman is presumed to have been violated unless there is evidence to the contrary, consequently in order to make her mistress permitted to her husband the handmaid would have *to speak*. She would have to *say* that her mistress was not defiled. And we do not assume that she would *say* an untruth. She may be guilty of a silent falsehood, but not of a spoken falsehood. Therefore when she says that her mistress has remained pure she is believed. (19) In spite of what has just been said by R. Ashi, it is possible that out of attachment to her mistress, or for fear of her, the handmaid may come and actually tell a falsehood. Why should she then be believed? (20) To be *silent* about her mistress's defilement *and* to *say* that she was not defiled, that she would do both these things we do not assume.

of Ḥana b. Isaḳ]: To him there came a brother from Be-Ḥozae and said to him: Give me a share in the property of our father. He answered him: I do not know you. He[1] [then] came to R. Ḥisda, and he[2] said to him:[1] he[3] answered you well, for it is written:[4] *'And Joseph knew his brethren, and they knew not him.'* This teaches that he went away before he had grown a beard and he came back after growing a beard.[5] [Then] he[2] said to him:[1] Go and bring witnesses that you are his brother. He[1] answered him:[2] I have witnesses, but they are afraid of him,[6] because he is a powerful man. He[2] [then] said to the other man:[3] Go you and bring witnesses that he[1] is not thy brother. He[3] answered him:[2] Is this the law? [Surely] he who claims must produce evidence![7] He[2] said to him.[3] So I rule for you and all who are powerful like you![8] But they[9] may also come and lie?[10] Two things they[9] will not do.[11]

May we say that this difference[12] is like that between [these] Tannaim? [For it was taught in a Baraitha:] This testimony[13] a man and a woman, a boy and a girl, her father and her mother, her brother and her sister [may give], but not her son and her daughter, nor her slave and her handmaid. And [in] another [Baraitha] it was taught. All are believed to testify [for her] except herself and her husband.[14] Now the views of R. Papa and R. Ashi are [certainly] according to the difference of the Tannaim.[15] But is the view of R. Papa according to the Tannaim?[16] R. Papa

(1) The claimant. (2) R. Ḥisda. (3) Mari, or Ḥana. (4) Gen. XLII, 8. (5) It is therefore possible and even natural that your brother does not recognize you. (6) Of his brother. (7) This is the accepted rule! (8) I.e., I am the interpreter and exponent of the law. I apply the rules according to circumstances. Now that I have to deal with a man like you, Mari, I modify the rule! And he bowed to the ruling of R. Ḥisda; v. B.M. 39*b*, where the story is told more fully. (9) The witnesses. (10) Cf. B.M. 39*b*. (11) To be silent as to the truth and to tell a falsehood (12) Whether her handmaid is believed or not. (13) Regarding a captive woman. (14) Her handmaid is therefore believed. (15) R. Papa and R. Ashi would hold like the second Baraitha. (16) The view of R. Papa does not seem to agree with either Baraitha, since he makes a distinction between his handmaid and her handmaid. According to the first Baraitha no handmaid is believed, whether his or hers, and according to the second Baraitha either handmaid is believed, even hers.

can answer you: That Baraitha[1] [speaks of a case] when she[2] talked in her simplicity.[3] As that which R. Dimi said when he came: R. Ḥanan of Carthagene told a story: A case came before R. Joshua b. Levi (or as some say R. Joshua b. Levi told a story: A case came before Rabbi): Someone was talking in his simplicity and said: I and my mother were taken captives among heathens. When I went out to draw my water, my mind was on my mother.[4] [When I was out] to gather wood, my mind was on my mother. And Rabbi allowed her to marry[5] a priest[6] by [the words of] his mouth.[7]

MISHNAH. R. ZECHARIAH B. HA-KAẒẒAB[8] SAID: BY THIS TEMPLE[9] HER HAND[10] DID NOT MOVE OUT OF MY HAND[11] FROM THE TIME THAT THE HEATHENS ENTERED JERUSALEM UNTIL THEY DEPARTED. THEY[12] ANSWERED HIM: NO ONE MAY TESTIFY CONCERNING HIMSELF.[13]

GEMARA. It has been taught: And notwithstanding this[14] he appointed for her a dwelling place[15] in his court-yard, and when she was out, she went out at the head of her children,[16] and when she came in, she came in at the head of her children.[17] Abaye asked: May one do so with regard to one's divorced wife?[18] [Do I say:]

(1) The second Baraitha. (2) The handmaid. (3) She related her story quite innocently, without intending to give evidence. In such a case R. Papa would also hold that her handmaid is believed. Therefore R. Papa's view would also be according to the second Baraitha. (4) Apparently he had his eyes on her so that no one assaulted her. (5) She was a widow. (6) Lit., 'into priesthood'. (7) Relying upon the story told innocently by the son. (8) 'The Butcher'. He was a priest in Jerusalem at the time of the Roman conquest. (9) He swore by the Temple. (10) The hand of his wife. (11) I.e., she was always with him, and he knew that she remained pure. (12) The Sages. (13) As it concerns himself his testimony cannot be accepted. (14) That they did not accept this testimony, and consequently she was forbidden to him (Rashi). (15) Lit., 'a house'. (16) So that she should not be alone with her husband. (17) So that she should not be alone with her husband, v. Tosef. Keth. V. for variants. (18) May she live in the same court-yard in which her former husband lives?

There[1] it was allowed because in [the case of] a captive woman[2] they[3] made it lenient, but not here,[4] or is there no difference?—Come and hear: It has been taught: If someone has divorced his wife, she shall not get married [and live] in his neighbourhood,[5] [28a] and if he[6] was a priest she must not live with him in the [same] alley.[7] If it was a small village[8]— such a case happened, and they[3] said: A small village is considered[9] a neighbourhood.[10]

Who must give way before whom?—Come and hear· It has been taught: She must give way before him, and not he before her, but if the court-yard[11] belonged to her, he must give way before her.

The question was asked: If the court-yard belonged to both, what is [the law]? Come and hear: 'She must give way before him.' In what case?[12] If the court-yard belongs to him it is obvious; and if the court-yard belongs to her, has it not been taught: 'If the court-yard belongs to her, he gives way before her'? Hence [it must be] in a such case![13]—[No.] Perhaps [it deals with a case] when they rented [the court-yard]. How is it then?[14]—Come and hear: [It is written:] *The Lord will hurl thee away violently as a man,*[15] and Rab said:[16] moving about[17] is harder for a man than for a woman.[18]

Our Rabbis taught: If he[19] borrowed[20] from the property of her father,[21] she collects the payment only through another person.[22]

(1) In the case of R. Zechariah. (2) During the siege she was regarded as a captive woman. (3) The scholars. (4) In the case about which Abaye asks. (5) שכונה, 'a group of three houses', v. A.Z. 21a. Former friendship may lead to renewed intimacy. (6) The husband. (7) Even if she has not remarried, since a priest's divorced wife is forbidden to a priest. (8) I.e., the place in which they lived. (9) Lit., 'judged'. (10) And she must not marry and live there. (11) With the buildings in it. (12) Lit., 'of what case do we treat'? (13) Lit., 'manner'. When the court belonged to both. (14) What is the answer to the question? Lit., 'what is with regard to it'. (15) Isa. XXII, 17. (16) Referring to this verse. (17) Lit., 'hurlings about'. (18) Hence, if the court-yard belonged to both, she must give way before him. By moving from place to place, a man loses the sphere of his livelihood, while a woman can assure hers by marriage. (19) The husband who was a priest. (20) While they were married. (21) I.e., property that she brought from her father's house or that she inherited from her father after her marriage. (V. Glos. s.v. *mulug*). (22) So as to avoid personal contact between them, which may lead to familiarity.

R. Shesheth said: And if they [both] come before us to Court, we do not deal with[1] them.[2] R. Papa said: We excommunicate them. R. Huna, the son of R. Joshua, said: We even order them to be lashed. R. Naḥman said: It is taught in Ebel Rabbathi:[3] This is said only[4] when she was divorced after[5] marriage, but if she was divorced after betrothal, she may collect the payments herself, because he is not [so] familiar with her.

Once a betrothed and his [former] fiancée came before Raba, and R. Adda b. Mattena, sat before him. Raba placed a messenger[6] between them.[7] R. Adda b. Mattena said to him: Did not R. Naḥman say: 'It is taught in Ebel Rabbathi etc.'?[8]—He answered him: We see[9] that they are familiar with one another.[10] Some say: Raba did not place a messenger between them. R. Adda b. Mattena said to him: Let the Master place a messenger between them. He[11] answered him:[12] Did not R. Naḥman say: 'It is taught in Ebel Rabbathi, etc.'? He[12] said to him:[11] This only when they are not familiar with one another, but [as to] these—I see that they are familiar with one another.[10]

MISHNAH. THE FOLLOWING[13] ARE BELIEVED ON TESTIFYING WHEN THEY ARE GROWN-UP[14] TO WHAT THEY HAVE SEEN WHEN THEY WERE SMALL:[15] A PERSON IS BELIEVED ON SAYING 'THIS IS THE HANDWRITING OF MY FATHER.'[16] 'THIS IS

(1) Lit., 'we do not attach ourselves to them'. (2) She must send someone to represent her. (3) Name of a small Treatise joined to the Babylonian Talmud which deals with laws of mourning. It is also called euphemistically Semaḥoth ('Joys'). (4) Lit., 'in what (case) are these words said', i.e., when must they not meet together after divorce. R. Naḥman applied the rule stated there to collecting payments or appearing in court together. For variants v. *loc. cit.* (5) Lit., 'from'. (6) Apparently a messenger of the court, an usher. (7) Between the betrothed and his former fiancée. (8) That the law does not apply to a betrothed couple that had been divorced. (9) From our own observations now. (10) Therefore the rule stated in Ebel Rabbathi cannot hold good in this case. (11) Raba. (12) R. Adda. (13) Lit., 'and those'. (14) Lit., 'in their greatness', in their majority. (15) Lit., 'in their smallness', in their minority. (16) And the signature which was appended when he was still a minor is confirmed in court on the strength of this testimony made in his majority.

THE HANDWRITING OF MY TEACHER,' 'THIS IS THE HANDWRITING OF MY BROTHER': 'I REMEMBER THAT THAT WOMAN WENT OUT[1] WITH A HINUMA AND UNCOVERED HEAD,'[2] 'THAT THAT MAN USED TO GO OUT FROM SCHOOL[3] TO IMMERSE[4] IN ORDER TO EAT TERUMAH',[5] 'THAT HE USED TO TAKE A SHARE WITH US AT THE THRESHING FLOOR,' 'THAT THIS PLACE WAS A BETH HA-PERAS,'[6] THAT UP TO HERE WE USED TO GO ON SABBATH.[7] BUT A MAN IS NOT BELIEVED WHEN HE SAYS: SO-AND-SO HAD A WAY[8] IN THIS PLACE, THAT MAN HAD A PLACE OF STANDING UP AND LAMENTATION[9] IN THIS PLACE.

GEMARA. R. Huna b. Joshua said: [This is] only[10] when a grown up person is with him.[11] And it is necessary,[12] for if he had taught us[13] [with regard to] his father, [I might say][14] that is because he[15] was always[16] with him,[17] but [with regard to] his teacher, [he would] not [be believed]. And if he had taught us [with regard to] his teacher, [I might say][18] that is because he had reverence[19]

(1) To the marriage-ceremony. (2) Signs that she was a virgin-bride: V. *supra* 15*b* and 17*b*. (3) When we were pupils together. (4) I.e., to bathe for purification so as to be ritually fit to eat *terumah*. (5) Which shews that he is a priest, cf. *supra* 24*a*-26*a*. (6) A field in which a grave has been ploughed becomes a *beth ha-peras*, and renders unclean through contact for a distance of *half* a furrow of one hundred cubits in each direction. *Peras* = half (v. Jast.). Rashi connects it with meaning 'to break' (an area of bone splinters); Maim. with 'to extend' (an area of extension); Tosaf. Nid. 57*b* with 'to tread' (an area from which people tread aside). (7) On Sabbath it is not permitted to walk 2000 cubits beyond the outer boundary of the town. (8) I.e., a right of way. (9) *Var. lec.*, SITTING DOWN. At funerals. The funeral escort, on returning from a burial, halted on the way seven times at certain places, where they stood up and sat down on the ground to offer comfort to the mourners or to lament for the departed; v. B.B. (Sonc. ed.) p. 420, n. 4. (10) Lit., 'and that is'—Only then he is believed on testifying to what he saw as a child. (11) And we are informed that he is permitted to join the other witness in the evidence which requires the minimum of two witnesses. (12) To teach the three cases regarding the handwriting. (13) Lit., 'let us hear'. (14) That he is believed. (15) The son. (16) Lit., 'frequent'. (17) With his father; he therefore knew his handwriting well. (18) That he is believed. (19) Lit., 'fear, awe'.

for his teacher.[1] And if he had taught us these two [cases],[2] [I might say[3] with regard to] his father, that is because he was always with him, and [with regard to] his teacher, because he had reverence for him, but [with regard to] his brother, in regard to whom there is neither this nor that ground,[4] I might say [that he is] not [believed]; so he teaches us[5] [that] since the confirmation of documents[6] is [only] ordained by the Rabbis,[7] so the Rabbis have believed him regarding what the Rabbis [themselves] have ordained.

I REMEMBER THAT THAT WOMAN WENT OUT WITH A HINUMA AND UNCOVERED HEAD. What is the reason?[8]—Because most women get married as virgins, so this[9] is only a declaration.[10]

THAT THAT MAN USED TO GO OUT FROM SCHOOL TO IMMERSE IN ORDER TO EAT TERUMAH. But perhaps he was the slave of a priest?[11]—This supports R. Joshua b. Levi; for R. Joshua b. Levi said: A man is forbidden to teach his slave[12] the Torah. But is it indeed not [permitted]? Has it not been taught: If his master has borrowed from him[13] or his master made him [28b] a guardian or he put on *Tefillin*[14] in the presence of his master or he read three verses[15] in the Synagogue, he does not become free![16] —There[17] it happened that he did it with his consent;[18] [for what case] do we state [our rule]?[19] When he treats him as a child.[20]

(1) He therefore knew his handwriting well. (2) Of his father and his teacher. (3) That he is believed. (4) He is neither always with him nor does he revere him. (5) Lit., 'he lets us hear'—by stating all the three cases. (6) I.e., the attestation of signatures on documents in court. (7) V. *supra* 21b. (8) That he is believed. (9) His testimony. (10) No formal testimony of witnesses is required; a general declaration is sufficient. (11) Who is also entitled to eat *terumah*. (12) And this person was in a school, (lit., 'the house of the book') where he learned the Torah (The Book = the Bible = the Torah). Therefore he could not be a slave. (13) From his slave. (14) The Phylacteries. (15) From the Bible. (16) Lit., 'he does not go out to freedom', v. Giṭ. 70a. This shews that a slave does learn the Torah. (17) In the case just quoted. (18) It may sometimes happen that a slave is taught the Torah. (19) That it is forbidden to teach a slave the Torah. (20) And teaches him as he would teach his own children. This is forbidden. Therefore the person in the Mishnah could not be a slave.

TO IMMERSE IN ORDER TO EAT TERUMAH. [Only] with regard to Rabbinical *terumah*.[1] THAT HE WAS TAKING A SHARE WITH US AT THE THRESHING FLOOR. But perhaps he was the slave of a priest?—We have learned [this] according to him who says: One does not distribute *terumah* to a slave unless his master is with him,[2] for it has been taught: One does not distribute *terumah* to a slave unless his master is with him. This is the view of R. Judah. R. Jose says: He can say: 'If I am a priest, give me for my sake, and if I am the slave of a priest, give me for the sake of my master'. In the place of R. Judah they used to raise from *terumah* to the status of a priest; in the place of R. Jose they would not raise from *terumah* to the status of a priest.[3]

It is taught:[4] R. Eleazar, the son of R. Jose,[5] said: I have never given testimony. Once I gave testimony and they raised a slave to the priesthood through my evidence.[6] [You say] they raised! Do you indeed mean to say this? Now, if the Holy One, blessed be He, does not bring a stumbling[7] through the animals of the pious men,[8] how much less through the pious men themselves?[9]—But,[10] they wanted to raise a slave to the priesthood through my evidence. He saw it[11] in the place of R. Jose,[12] and he went and testified in the place of R. Judah.[13]

THAT THIS PLACE WAS A BETH HA-PERAS Why?[14]—Because [the law of] *beth ha-peras* is Rabbinical, for Rab Judah said in the

(1) Cf. *supra* 25a.—Only with regard to Rabbinical *terumah* is such testimony sufficient. (2) As he was alone and took a share at the threshing floor, it shews that he was a priest. (3) V. *supra* 26a-27b. And therefore they would not give a slave *terumah* in the absence of his master, lest this should be used as evidence in regard to marriage. (4) In a Baraitha. (5) V. Yeb. 99b. (6) Lit., 'through my mouth'. (7) A sin, an offence. (8) V. Giṭ. 7a. (9) And how could such an offence have been caused through R. Eleazar. (10) The case was as follows. (11) That they gave *terumah* to a person who in fact was a slave in the absence of his master. (12) Where they did not raise from *terumah* to the state of a priest. There was therefore no harm in distributing *terumah* to a slave at the threshing floor. (13) Where they raised from *terumah* to the state of a priest. They therefore thought that this man was a priest. The mistake was apparently found out in time and he was not raised. No offence was brought about through a pious man. (14) Why was this testimony sufficient?

name of Rab: One blows away [the dust from][1] the *beth ha-peras*, and goes [there]. Rab Judah b. Ammi said in the name of Rab Judah: A *beth ha-peras* which has been trodden out is clean. What is the reason?[2] It is impossible that a bone [of the size] of a barley-corn was not trodden down by the foot.[3]

UP TO HERE HE USED TO GO ON SABBATH. He holds that the [Sabbath] limits[4] are Rabbinical.

A MAN IS NOT BELIEVED WHEN HE SAYS: THAT MAN HAD A WAY IN THIS PLACE, SO-AND-SO HAD A PLACE OF STANDING UP AND LAMENTATION IN THIS PLACE. What is the reason? Money we do not extract.[5]

Our Rabbis taught:[6] A boy is believed when he says, 'Thus my father told me: this family is clean, this family is unclean.— [You say,] 'clean and unclean'! Do you indeed mean to say this?[7] But [say]: 'this family is fit[8] and this family is unfit'. 'That we have eaten at the *Ḳeẓaẓah*[9] [on the occasion of the marriage] of the daughter of So-and-so to So-and-so', 'that we used to bring *ḥallah* and [priestly] gifts[10] to the priest So-and-so'. But only through himself,[11] and not through someone else. In all these cases, if he was an heathen and he became a proselyte, a slave and he was set free, he is not believed.[12] [But] he is not believed when he says 'that man had a way in this place, that man had a place of standing up and lamention in this place'. R. Joḥanan b. Beroḳa, said. He is believed. To which [clause] does R. Joḥanan b. Beroḳa, refer? Shall I say, to the last clause? This is extracting money?[13]—But [it

(1) To see whether there are any bones there. (2) Why is it regarded as clean? (3) And by being reduced to a smaller size is no longer liable to communicate defilement. (4) I.e., the ordinance regarding the Sabbath limits for walking is Rabbinical; therefore this testimony is sufficient. (5) On the strength of that statement. In civil matters such testimony is not sufficient. (6) Cf. Tosef. Keth. III for variants. (7) 'Clean' and 'unclean' are not applicable to families. (8) Unblemished and fit to marry into priestly families. (9) 'Cutting off', 'severing family connections'; a ceremony attending the sale of an heirloom to an outsider, and the marriage of a man beneath his social rank. It is the marriage-*Ḳeẓaẓah* that is spoken of here, v. *infra*. (10) V. Deut. XVIII, 3. (11) The boy himself must have been the messenger. (12) As to what he saw when he was a heathen or a slave. (13) V. note 5.

refers] to the first clause. In all these cases, if he was a heathen and he became a proselyte, a slave and he was set free, he is not believed. R. Johanan b. Beroka says: He is believed. In what [principle] do they differ?—The first Tanna holds: Since he was a heathen he would not pay special attention to it,[1] and R. Johanan b. Beroka, holds: Since he had it in his mind to become a proselyte he would pay special attention to it.

What is ḲEẒAẒAH?—The Rabbis taught: In what manner does *ḳeẓaẓah* take place? If one of the brothers has married a woman who is unworthy of him, the members[2] of the family come together, bring a cask full of fruit, break it in the middle of the open place[3] and say. 'Brethren of the house of Israel, hear. Our brother So-and-so has married a woman who is not worthy of him, and we are afraid lest his descendants[4] will be united with our descendants. Come and take for yourselves a sign[5] for future generations, that his descendants shall not be united with our descendants'. This is *ḳeẓaẓah* with regard to which a child is believed when he testifies.

(1) To the various matters about which he testified. (2) Lit., 'the sons'. (3) רחבה v. *supra* p. 41, n. 5. Here, too, it can mean the open space before the house. (4) Lit., 'seed'. (5) As a token. They should remember what happened and tell their children, so that everyone will know to distinguish between the descendants of this brother and those of the rest of the family.

KETHUBOTH

CHAPTER III

MISHNAH. [29*a*] THESE ARE MAIDENS[1] TO WHOM THE FINE IS DUE.[2] IF ANYONE HAD INTERCOURSE WITH A MAMZERETH,[3] A NETHINAH,[4] A CUTHEAN,[5] OR WITH A PROSELYTE [MAIDEN],[6] A CAPTIVE, OR A SLAVE-WOMAN,[7] WHO WAS REDEEMED,[8] CONVERTED,[9] OR FREED [WHEN SHE WAS] UNDER THE AGE OF[10] THREE YEARS AND ONE DAY.[11] IF ONE HAD INTERCOURSE WITH HIS SISTER, WITH THE SISTER OF HIS FATHER, WITH THE SISTER OF HIS MOTHER, WITH THE SISTER OF HIS WIFE, WITH THE WIFE OF HIS BROTHER,[12] WITH THE WIFE OF THE BROTHER OF HIS FATHER, OR WITH A WOMAN DURING MENSTRUATION,[13] HE HAS TO PAY THE FINE,[14] [FOR] ALTHOUGH THESE [TRANSGRESSIONS][15] ARE PUNISHED THROUGH [THE TRANSGRESSOR] BEING CUT OFF,[16] THERE IS NOT, WITH REGARD TO THEM, A DEATH [PENALTY] [INFLICTED] BY THE COURT.[17]

(1) *Na'aroth* pl. of *na'arah*, technically, a girl between twelve years and twelve and a half years of age. (2) If a man has violated any of these maidens mentioned in our Mishnah, he must pay the fine fixed in Deut. XXII, 29. (3) Fem. of *mamzer*, v. Glos. (4) Fem. of *nathin*, v. Glos. (5) A Samaritan, v. Glos. (6) V. *supra* 11*a*. (7) A maiden. (8) In the text the word is in the plural, because it refers to a class and not to one person. (9) It is interesting to note that 'CONVERTED' comes before, although it should come after, 'FREED'. The reason is probably because it is, in Hebrew, a shorter word. Of the three words the first has three, the second four, and the fourth, five syllables, not counting the suffix '*waw*', ('and'). The sequence of the words chosen makes for symmetry. (10) Lit., 'less than'. (11) He has to pay the fine. For further notes v. *supra* 11*a*. (12) Whom the brother divorced after the betrothal. (13) And they are all maidens. (14) Lit., 'the fine is due to them'. (15) V. Lev. XVIII, 9ff. (16) From life, by premature or sudden death, *Kareth* v. Glos. Cf. Lev. XVIII, 29: *For whosoever shall do any of these abominations, even the souls that do them shall be cut off from among their people.* (17) V. e.g., Lev. XX, 9ff. Only death penalty by the court releases from the money fine, v. Gemara.

GEMARA. [Does it mean that only] these blemished maidens get the fine, [but] unblemished ones [do] not?[1]—He means it thus: These are blemished maidens who get the fine:[2] IF ANYONE HAD INTERCOURSE WITH A MAMZERETH, A NETHINAH, A CUTHEAN,[3] etc.

[Only] [the Mishnah states] a maiden [receives a fine],[4] [but not] a small girl.[5] Who is the Tanna [who taught this]? Rab Judah said in the name of Rab: It is R. Meir, for it has been taught:[6] A small child from the age of one day[7] until [the time that] she grows two hairs[8], sale applies to her,[9] but not the fine;[10] from [the time that] she grows two hairs until she becomes mature,[11] the fine applies to her, but not sale.[12] This is the view of R. Meir; for R. Meir said: Wherever sale applies,[13] the fine does not apply, and wherever the fine applies, sale does not apply. But the Sages say: A small child from the age of three years and one day until [the time that] she becomes mature—the fine applies to her.[14] [Does that mean] only the fine [and] not sale![15]—Say: [29*b*] also the fine [applies] when sale [applies].[16]

(1) The phrasing of the Mishnah seems to imply that only the following maidens which are enumerated are entitled to fines—namely, only of blemished descent. Surely that is impossible. (2) Although the fine has been fixed for unblemished maidens, whom the man could marry (v. Deut. XXII, 29), it is, the Mishnah tells us, due also to blemished maidens, whom he could not marry. That unblemished maidens get the fine need not be specially mentioned in the Mishnah. (3) He has to pay the fine. (4) Lit., 'a maiden, yes, a minor, no'. (5) A *ketannah*. A girl is so called until the age of twelve years. If a minor was violated, the fine, according to the Mishnah, is not due to her. (6) V. Tosef. Keth. (7) Tosef.: A small child from the age of three years and one day. This is, no doubt, the correct reading. In the text of the Talmud 'three years and' is missing. (8) The sign of beginning maturity. (9) The father may sell his daughter as a maid-servant; v. Ex. XXI, 7. (10) If she was violated; the word *na'arah* is used in Deut. XXII, 28, 29, excluding a minor. (11) A girl becomes mature when she is twelve and a half years old. She is then called *bogereth*, v. Glos. (12) When the girl is a *na'arah* the father has no more right to sell her. (13) Sale applies only when the girl is a *ketannah*, and the fine applies only when the girl is a *na'arah*. (14) According to the Sages, the fine is due to the girl both as a *ketannah* and a *na'arah*. In other words, the word *na'arah* in Deut. XXII, 28, 29 is not to be taken strictly. (15) Lit., 'fine, yes; sale, no'! (16) During the whole period that sale applies to a girl, the fine also

But are these [maidens][1] entitled to the fine! Why? Read here: *'and she shall be his wife'*, [that means] one who is fit to be his wife?[2] —Said Resh Laḳish: [It is written:] *'maiden'*, *'maiden'*, *'the maiden'*[3] once[4] [the word *'maiden'* is necessary] for itself,[5] once to include [those maidens, the marrying of whom involves the transgression merely of] a plain prohibitory law,[6] and once to include [those maidens, the marrying of whom involves] a transgression punishable with *kareth*.[7] R. Papa said: [It is written:][8] *'virgin'*, *'virgins'*, *'the virgins'*; once [the word *'virgin'* is necessary] for itself,[9] once to include [those virgins, the marrying of whom involves the transgression merely of] a plain prohibitory law, and once to include [those virgins, the marrying of whom involves] a transgression punishable with *kareth*. Why does R. Papa not agree with Resh Laḳish?—That [verse][10] he requires for [the same teaching] as that of Abaye, for Abaye said: If he cohabited with her[11] and she died, he is free,[12] for it is said: *'And he shall give unto the father of the maiden'*;[13]

applies to her, extending however beyond that period, till her stage of *bogereth*.

(1) Mentioned in our Mishnah. (2) Lit., 'a woman who is fit for him'. From the words of the Bible one would infer that the fine is payable only if he violated a maiden whom, in law, he could marry. But as to the maidens mentioned in the Mishnah, who are either generally prohibited to an Israelite for marriage, or there is *kareth* barring their way to marriage, (as in the case of the maidens enumerated in the second clause of the Mishnah), there should be no fine due to them. (3) In Deut. XXII, 28 *'maiden'*; verse 29: *'the maiden'*, and *'the'* in *'the maiden'* is reckoned as a separate word representing the word *'maiden'*, so that we have the word *'maiden'* written three times. To each of the three words a function is assigned in the Talmudic exposition. One *'maiden'* refers to the ordinary unblemished maidens, one *'maiden'* refers to the blemished maidens as mentioned in the first clause of the Mishnah, and one *'maiden'* refers to the maidens enumerated in the second clause of the Mishnah.—The maidens mentioned in the second part of the first clause of the Mishnah seem to occupy a position of their own. V. Tosaf. 29*a*, s.v. והבא. (4) Lit., 'one ("maiden")'. (5) For the ordinary maiden, v. note 3. (6) Lit., 'those guilty of a negative prohibition', which carries with it the punishment of flagellation only. (7) V. Glos. (8) Ex. XXII, 15, 16. There it speaks of seduction. R. Papa, apparently, puts seduction and violation on one level. (9) V. *supra* nn. 3 and 5. (10) Deut. XXII, 29. (11) By force. (12) From paying the fine. (13) The full half-verse is: *'And the man that lay with her shall give unto the father of the maiden fifty silver pieces'*. (Deut. XXII, 29.)

[this means]: To the father of a maiden,[1] but not to the father of a dead [person].[2] And why did not Resh Laḳish agree with R. Papa?—That [verse][3] he requires for an analogy,[4] for it is taught: [It is written:]—'*he shall pay money according to the dowry of virgins*,[5] [this means that] this[6] shall be like the dowry of virgins,[7] and the dowry of virgins shall be like this.[8] But Resh Laḳish also requires it[9] for [the same teaching] as that of Abaye, and R. Papa also requires it[10] for the analogy?[11]—Take therefore six words:[12] '*maiden*', '*maiden*', '*the maiden*', '*virgin*', '*virgins*', '*the virgins*': Two [are necessary] for themselves,[13] one for the teaching of Abaye, and one for the analogy, [and] two remain over: one to include [those maidens, the marrying of whom involves the transgression] of a plain prohibitory law, and one to include [those maidens, the marrying of whom involves] a transgression punishable with *kareth*.

This[14] [Mishnah] is to exclude [the view of] that Tanna.[15] For it has been taught: [It is written:] *and she shall be his wife.*[16] Simeon the Temanite says: [This means:] a woman who can become his wife;[17]

(1) I.e., of a maiden that lives.   (2) If the maiden is dead, the father cannot be called any more 'the father of the maiden'. He can only be called the father of the dead maiden, and to such the fine is not payable.   (3) Ex. XXII, 16.   (4) *Gezerah shawah*; an analogy based on similarity of expressions, v. Glos.   (5) Ex. XXII, 16.   (6) The money to be paid in the case of seduction. (Ex. XXII, 16.)   (7) By '*the dowry of virgins*' is meant, according to this teaching, the sum of money to be paid as a fine in Deut. XXII, 29, which is fifty; so here (Ex. XXII, 16) it has to be fifty.   (8) As in Ex. XXII, 16 the money consists of *shekels*, (this is derived from the special word יִשְׁקֹל, employed for '*pay*'), so in Deut. XXII, 29, the fifty have to be *shekels*.   (9) The word '*the maiden*'.   (10) The word '*the virgin*'.   (11) Both the teaching of Abaye and the analogy are important to Resh Laḳish and R. Papa.   (12) Lit., 'but six verses are written'.—Make your expositions from all the six words taken together.   (13) For the ordinary cases of seduction and violation.   (14) Our Mishnah, in which it is taught that the fine is due also in the case of the violation of maidens, the marriage with whom is prohibited, as a *mamzereth* or his sister.   (15) I.e., the author of the Baraitha. As to the Tannaim mentioned in the Baraitha, the views of both of them are excluded, v. Tosaf. *a.l.*   (16) Deut. XXII, 29.   (17) Lit., 'to whom there is "*becoming*".' But his sister cannot '*become*' his wife. The very act of marriage is impossible. No marriage, no betrothal, can take effect. V. Ḳid. 66b. Therefore the law of the fine would not apply to his sister or to any of the other five maidens mentioned in the second clause of the Mishnah.

R. Simeon b. Menassia says: [This means:] a woman who can remain his wife.[1] What difference is there between them?[2]—R. Zera said: The difference between them is with regard to a *mamzereth* and a *nethinah*. According to him who says that there must be the possibility of her '*becoming*' his wife, here[3] also there is the possibility of her '*becoming*' his wife.[4] And according to him who says that there must be the possibility of her *remaining* his wife, here[5] there is not the possibility of her *remaining* his wife.[6] But according to R. Akiba, who says: Marriage takes no effect when there is a prohibitory law against[7] it, what is the difference between them?[8]—There is a difference between them in the case of a widow who marries a high priest, and this according to R. Simai, for it is taught:[9] R. Simai says: Of all[10] R. Akiba makes *mamzerim*,[11] except [the issue of] a widow and a high priest, for the Torah says: '*he shall not take*', and '*he shall not profane*',[12] [this teaches that] he makes

(1) Lit., 'who is fitting to be retained'. He takes the word '*be*', תהיה, in the sense of 'remaining'. This excludes a *mamzereth*, for although marriage with a *mamzereth* takes effect, there is '*prohibitory law*' attached to it. (v. Ḳid. 66*b*). The marriage ought therefore to be discontinued. The *mamzereth* is thus a woman who cannot *remain* his wife. Therefore, according to R. Simeon the son of Menassia, the law of fine does not apply to her.—We thus see that our Mishnah excludes both the view of Simeon the Temanite and the view of R. Simeon the son of Menassia. (2) Between Simeon the Temanite and R. Simeon b. Menassia (Rashi). (3) In the case of *mamzereth* and *nethinah*. (4) The marriage with a *mamzereth* or *nethinah* takes effect although there is a 'prohibitory law' against it. The *mamzereth* or *nethinah* can therefore *become* his wife, although she should not *remain* his wife. In the view of Simeon the Temanite it is the possibility of her becoming his wife that matters, and therefore they are entitled to the fine. (5) In the case of *mamzereth* and *nethinah*. (6) In the view of R. Simeon b. Menassia, it is the possibility of her *remaining* his wife that matters. And since a *mamzereth* or *nethinah* cannot *remain* his wife, they are not entitled to the fine. (7) V. Yeb. 44*a* and 49*a* and v. *ibid.* 10*b* and 52*b*. (8) Between Simeon the Temanite and R. Simeon the son of Menassia. A *mamzereth* or *nethinah* could not, on this view, *become* his wife even according to R. Simeon b. Menassia; what is then the difference between him and Simeon the Temanite? (9) In a Baraitha; v. Yeb. 64*a* and 68*a*. (10) I.e., of all the issues of prohibited unions. (11) R. Akiba declares the offspring of all prohibited unions to be *mamzerim*, v. Yeb. 49*a*. (12) Lev. XXI, 14f. The two verses read: *A widow or a divorced woman, or a profane woman, or a harlot, these*

[his issue] profane,[1] but not *mamzerim*.[2] And according to R. Yeshebab, who says: Come and let us cry out against Akiba b. Joseph, who says: Whenever the marriage is forbidden in Israel[3] the child [of such marriage] is a *mamzer*,[4] what is the difference between them?[5]—The difference between them is [30a] with regard to the marriage with an Egyptian or an Edomite [woman], in which case there is a transgression [merely] of a positive law.[6]—That is all right if R. Yeshebab [by his statement] only came to exclude the view of R. Simai.[7] But if his statement was his own,[8] whenever the marriage is forbidden in Israel, the child [of such a marriage] is a *mamzer*. It would include also a marriage with regard to which a positive law has been transgressed. What is [then] the difference between them?—The difference between them is with regard to a girl, who is no more a virgin, who married a high priest.[9]

shall he not take; but a virgin of his own people shall he take to wife. And he shall not profane his seed among his people; for I am the Lord who sanctify him. Vv. 10-15 deal with the high priest.

(1) The children are only unfit for the priesthood. (2) In this case R. Akiba admits that the marriage takes effect, although there is a prohibitory law against it, so that, in this case, according to Simeon b. Menassia, though the marriage would take effect, since he could not retain her owing to the prohibition, there is no fine, whereas according to Simeon the Temanite, there is a fine. (3) Lit., 'he who has no (permission of) union in Israel'. (4) This rule would include also the marriage of a widow and a high priest and would make also the child of such a marriage a *mamzer*. (5) What difference would there be now between Simeon the Temanite and R. Simeon b. Menassia? (6) With regard to the Edomite and the Egyptian it is stated in Deut. XXIII, 9: '*The children of the third generation that are born unto them shall enter into the congregation of the Lord.*' This is a 'positive law'. That the marriage with an Edomite and an Egyptian of the second generation is forbidden is derived from this positive law. And when a prohibitory law is derived from a positive law, it is regarded as a positive law. And in such a case the marriage takes effect, although it should be discontinued. Thus we would have a difference between Simeon the Temanite and Simeon the son of Menassia. (7) If his statement refers only to R. Simai, it is limited by the words of R. Simai, and a positive law (i.e., a prohibitory law derived from a positive law) cannot be brought in. (8) And is therefore unlimited. (9) In Lev. XXI, 13 the high priest is commanded to take as his wife a virgin. If he marries a girl who is no more a virgin the marriage takes effect, although it should be discontinued. And so we have again a difference between Simeon the Temanite and R. Simeon b. Menassia.

—And why is this[1] different?[2]—It is a law which does not apply to all.[3]

R. Ḥisda said: All agree that he who has intercourse with a woman during menstruation[4] [against her will] has to pay the fine,[5] for according to him who holds that there must be the possibility of her[6] *'becoming'* his wife, there is with regard to her[7] the possibility of her *becoming* his wife,[8] and according to him who holds that there must be the possibility of her[9] *remaining* his wife, there is with regard to her[10] the possibility of her *remaining* his wife.[11]

Our [Mishnah][12] likewise excludes the view of R. Neḥunia b. ha-Ḳaneh, for it is taught: R. Neḥunia b. ha-Ḳaneh, made the Day of Atonement equal to the Sabbath with regard to payment; as [he who desecrates] the Sabbath[13] forfeits his life[14] and is free from payment,[15] so [he who desecrates] the Day of Atonement[16] forfeits

(1) Prohibition derived from a positive law. (2) From other such prohibitions (e.g., the prohibition with regard to the Edomite and Egyptian) v. p. 164, nn. 6 and 8. (3) It applies only to the high priest. Therefore it is not treated as the other prohibitory laws that are derived from positive laws, and it would not be included in the general ruling of R. Akiba even according to R. Yeshebab. (4) The last case in the second clause of our Mishnah. (5) Although the cohabitation with a woman during menstruation is prohibited and is punishable with *kareth*, v. Lev. XVIII, 19 and 29. (6) The violated maiden. (7) The menstruant woman. (8) The marriage of a woman during menstruation takes effect. The fact that cohabitation during menstruation is forbidden does not affect the validity of the marriage, cf. Yeb. 49*b* and Ḳid. 68*a*. The condition of Simeon the Temanite is therefore fulfilled. (9) The violated maiden. (10) The menstruant woman. (11) The marriage of a menstruous woman is entirely valid and may be continued. Thus the condition of R. Simeon b. Menassia is fulfilled. (12) In the second clause of which it is taught that he who violates his sister or any of the other six maidens enumerated, the intercourse with whom is punishable by *kareth*, has to pay the fine. (13) By doing forbidden work on that day. (14) I.e., he is guilty of a transgression punishable by death (by the hand of man, that is by the court), v. Ex. XXXI, 15 and XXXV, 2. (15) If, in doing the forbidden work on the Sabbath, he caused damage to someone's property (e.g., if he set fire to a stack of corn) he is free from paying for the damage done, since the transgression involves the death penalty, and where there is the death penalty, there is no payment of money, on the principle that the smaller offence, for which the payment of money is due, is

his life[1] and is free from payment. What is the reason [for the view] of R. Neḥunia b. ha-Ḳaneh?—Abaye said: It is said *'harm'*[2] [in the case of death][3] by the hand of man,[4] and it is said *'harm'*[5] [in the case of death] by the hand of heaven, [so I say:] As in the case of the *'harm'* done by the hand of man one is free from payment,[6] so also in the case of *'harm'* done by the hand of heaven, one is free from payment.[7] To this R. Adda b. Ahaba, demurred: Whence [do you know] that Jacob warned his sons[8] against cold and heat,[9]

merged in the greater offence v. *infra*. (16) By doing forbidden work on that day.

(1) I.e., he is guilty of a transgression punishable by *kareth;* v. Lev. XXIII, 29, 30. *Kareth* is a divine visitation. Compare *'And (that soul) shall be cut off from among his people'* (v. 29) with *'and I will destroy that soul from among his people'* (v. 30). *Kareth* is called in the Talmud 'death by the hand of heaven', while the death penalty, i.e., death by the court, is called 'death by the hand of man'. R. Neḥunia b. ha-Ḳaneh makes 'death by the hand of heaven' (although it is not known when it will come, and when it comes it may be regarded by some people as a natural death; cf. Sema. III, 10) equal to 'death by the hand of man' (which is executed through the Court, and all see that the penalty of death was inflicted for the transgression) and applies to it also the principle that the lesser offence is merged in the greater. On this view since the intercourses mentioned in the second clause of our Mishnah are punishable with *kareth*, the fine would not be paid. (2) אסון, Ex. XXI, 22, 23. (3) *'Harm'* in Ex. XXI, 22, 23 means (also) death as v. 23 (*'then thou shalt give life for life'*) clearly shews. (4) Cf. v. 22: *And if men strive together and hurt a woman with child* etc. (5) V. Gen. XLII, 4, also XLIV, 29. There the reference is to *'harm'* that may befall Benjamin on the journey which may result in death. V. *infra*. (6) In Ex. XXI, 22, when no death (or other *'harm'*) follows, a payment of money is made. But when death follows, the death penalty is inflicted (v. 23) and no payment of money is made. This is clear, since payment of money is only mentioned in v. 22, and in v. 23 only *'life for life'* is mentioned. (7) Abaye's reasoning is as follows: i. He proves that *'harm'* refers both to the harm done by man (including death) and to the harm caused by heaven (including death). Therefore 'death by the hand of heaven' equals 'death by the hand of man'. ii. In the case in which 'death by the hand of man' is mentioned, it is stated that the penalty of death is inflicted (*'life for life'*), and no payment of money is made. The same applies to a case where the penalty is 'death by the hand of heaven'. The analogy could only be between the two words 'harm'. Once the equality of the two kinds of death is established (through the analogy), the equality of the consequences of these two kinds of death follows. (8) In Gen. XLII, 4. (9) So Rashi; Jast. 'blowing cold winds'. The words are taken from Prov. XXII, 5.

which are by the hand of heaven?[1] Perhaps [he warned them] against lions and thieves, which are 'by the hand of man?'[2]—Is it that Jacob warned them against this and did not warn them against that? Jacob warned them against every kind of harm.[3]

[But] are cold and heat by the hand of heaven? Is it not taught: Everything is 'by the hand of heaven' except cold and heat, for it is said: *'Cold and heat are in the way of the froward; he that keepeth his soul holdeth himself far from them'?*[4] Further, are lions and thieves 'by the hand of man'? Did not R. Joseph say, and R. Ḥiyya teach: Since the day of the destruction of the Temple, although the Sanhedrin ceased,[5] the four forms of capital punishment[6] have not ceased? 'They have not ceased,' [you say]? Surely they have ceased! But [say] [30*b*] the judgment of the four forms of capital punishment has not ceased.[7] He who would have been sentenced to stoning,[8] either falls down from the roof or a wild beast treads him down.[9] He who would have been sentenced to burning, either falls into a fire[10] or a serpent bites him.[11] He who would have been sentenced to decapitation,[12] is either delivered to the government[13] or robbers come upon him.[14] He who would have been sentenced to strangulation, is either drowned in the river or dies from suffocation.[15] But reverse it: Lions and thieves are 'by the hand of heaven', and cold and heat are 'by the hand of man'.

Raba said: The reason [for the view] of R. Neḥunia b. ha-Ḳaneh, is [derived] from here:[16] [It is written:] *And if the people of the land do not all hide their eyes from that man, when he giveth of his seed unto Molech,* [*and put him not to death*]; *then I will set my face against*

(1) Cold and heat come from God. (2) Thieves are 'the hand of man'. Lions are apparently called 'the hand of man', as they are not 'the hand of heaven' in the same sense in which cold and heat are 'the hand of heaven,' v., however, *infra*. (3) Lit., 'all things'. And such harm as is 'the hand of heaven' is included. (4) Prov. XXII. 5. also A.Z. (Sonc. ed.) p. 11, n. 2. (5) And capital punishment could no longer be decreed by the Jewish Courts. (6) Lit., 'the four deaths', v. Sanh. 49*b*. (7) The punishment comes in corresponding forms. (8) To death by stoning. (9) And kills him. (10) A conflagration. (11) And the poison burns and kills him. (12) With a sword, v. Sanh. 49*b*. (13) To the Roman Government. (14) And slay him. (15) סרונכי; so Jast.; Rashi: croup. (16) From the following passage of the Bible.

that man, and against his family, and will cut him off.[1] [With these words] the Torah says:[2] My *kareth* is like your death[-penalty]; as [in the case of] your death[-penalty] one is free from payment, so [in the case of] my *kareth* one is free from payment. What is the difference between Raba and Abaye?—The difference is [with regard to] a stranger[3] who ate *terumah*.[4] According to Abaye he is free [from payment],[5] and according to Raba he is bound [to pay].[6] But is he free [from payment] according to Abaye? Did not R. Ḥisda say: R. Neḥunia b. ha-Ḳaneh admits that he who stole [forbidden] fat[7] belonging to his neighbour, and ate it, is bound [to pay],[8] because he was guilty of stealing before he came to [the transgression of] the prohibition with regard to [forbidden] fat?[9] Hence [you say that] as soon as[10] he lifted it[11] up he acquired it,[12] but he did not become guilty of the transgression[13] punishable with death until he had eaten it. Here[14] also, when he lifted it[15] up he

(1) Lev. XX, 4f. (2) I.e., God says in the Torah to Israel. (3) I.e., A non-priest. (4) If a stranger eats *terumah*, he is punished with death, not with death 'by the hand of man' but with death 'by the hand of heaven'. V. Lev. XXII, 9, 10 and cf. Sanh. 83*a*. The death 'by the hand of heaven' in this case is, however, a milder form of *kareth*. *Kareth* proper means the cutting off of the life of the transgressor and of his family. The death in the case of a stranger eating *terumah* means death similar to that of *kareth*, namely '*by the hand* of heaven,' but applied only to the offender. V. Rashi, *a.l.* Cf. also Lev. XX, 5 (*then I will set my face against that man and against his family and I will cut him off*). (5) For the *terumah*. '*Harm*' indicates any kind of death, also the milder form of death 'by the hand of heaven', as that in the case of eating *terumah*. (6) To the priest for the *terumah*. Raba derives the reason for the view of R. Neḥunia b. ha-Ḳaneh, from Lev. XX, 4, 5, and there *kareth* proper is spoken of. According to Raba, therefore, only *kareth* proper is made equal to death 'by the hand of man' with regard to one being free from payment, but not the milder form of *kareth*, of death 'by the hand of heaven, as in the case of a stranger eating *terumah*. In that case, payment must be made. (7) *Ḥeleb;* v. Lev. III, 17; VII, 23 and 25. In the latter verse *kareth* is the punishment mentioned for eating *ḥeleb*. Cf. Ker. 2*a*, 4*a-b*. (8) Although the eating of *ḥeleb* is punishable with *kareth;* v. preceding note. (9) Since the crime of stealing was committed before the sin of eating *ḥeleb*, the principle of the lesser offence being merged in the greater (v. *supra* 30*a*) does not apply. (10) Lit., 'from the time that'. (11) The *ḥeleb*. (12) And from that moment becomes liable for the theft. (13) Of eating the *ḥeleb*. (14) In the case of *terumah*. (15) The *terumah*.

acquired it, but he did not become guilty of the transgression[1] punishable with death until he had eaten it![2]—Here we treat of a case where his friend stuck it[3] into his mouth.[4] [But] even then,[5] as soon as he chewed it, he acquired it, but he is not guilty of the transgression punishable with death until he has swallowed it![6] —When [his friend] stuck it into his oesophagus.[7] How shall we imagine this case? If he can give it back,[8] let him give it back.[9] And if he cannot give it back, why should he be guilty?[10]—It speaks of a case when he can give it back only with an effort.[11] R. Papa said, When his friend put liquids of *terumah* into his mouth.[12] R. Ashi said: [it speaks of a case] when a stranger ate his own *terumah*.[13] [31a] and [at the same time] tore the silk garments of his neighbour.[14]

The [above] text [stated]: 'R. Ḥisda said: R. Neḥunia b. ha-Ḳaneh admits that, if someone stole [forbidden] fat belonging to his neighbour and ate it, he is bound [to pay], because he was guilty of stealing before he came to [the transgression of] the

(1) Of eating *terumah*. (2) And he should therefore be liable to pay for it. (3) The *terumah*. (4) So that he did not acquire it by lifting it up but only from the moment he eats it, so that the offence of stealing and of eating the *terumah* are committed simultaneously. (5) Lit., 'the end of the end'. (6) The theft is thus committed before the offence of eating the *terumah*, whereas there is no liability for eating *terumah* before he swallows it. (7) So there was no chewing. (8) I.e., if he can bring it out of his oesophagus. (9) And by failing to do so he becomes liable from that very moment for stealing it. (10) Of the transgression of eating *terumah*, seeing it was a case of *force majeure*. (11) [So that even if he had brought it up, it would have been useless. Consequently he cannot be held guilty of stealing. What he can be made liable to pay for is for actually *eating* the *terumah*. This act, however, carries with it also a death penalty which applies in this case, since he could by an effort have brought it up. As both penalties do thus arise simultaneously, he is free from payment.] (12) In this case also both penalties come at the same time; cf. previous note. (13) *Terumah* of his own produce, which he separated and was going to give to the priest. In eating it he is guilty of a transgression punishable with death 'by the hand of heaven'. (14) Ordinarily he would have to pay his neighbour for the damage done to his garments. But as here the liability to death 'by the hand of heaven' for eating the *terumah* and the obligation to pay to his neighbour for the torn silk garments come at the same time, he is free from having to make the payment to his neighbour.

prohibition with regard to [forbidden] fat.' Is it to say that he differs from R. Abin? For R. Abin said: If someone threw an arrow [on Sabbath] from the beginning of four [cubits] to the end of four [cubits[1]] and it[2] tore silk garments in its passage[3] he is free [from payment],[4] for the taking up[5] was necessary for the putting down:[6] Now here[7] also the 'lifting up' was necessary for the eating.[8]—Now, is this so?[9] There[10] 'the putting down' is impossible without the 'taking up'; but here[11] the eating is possible without the 'lifting up', for, if he likes, he can bend down and eat.[12] Or: there,[13] if he wants to take it back, he cannot take it back;[14] but here,[15] he can put it back.[16]—What is the [practical] difference between the one answer and the other answer?—The difference is: when someone carried[17] a knife in the public road[18] and it[19] tore silk garments in its passage: according to the answer that the 'putting down' is impossible without the 'taking up', here[20] also

(1) To throw an object a distance of four cubits in the public road on Sabbath is a desecration of the Sabbath, which, if done wilfully, is punishable with death 'by the hand of man' (stoning) if after a warning, and with death 'by the hand of heaven' (*kareth*), if without a warning. V. Shab. 96*b* and 100*a* and Ex. XXXI, 14. (2) The arrow. (3) I.e., in the course of its flight. (4) For the silk garments, to their owner. (5) Of the arrow. (6) It is when the object is 'put down' or comes to rest, that the act of transgressing, or of throwing, is completed. But it begins with the 'taking up' of the object. The damage to the silk garments was done between the act of 'taking up' עקירה and that of 'putting down', הנחה. The penalty of death or *kareth* is thus regarded as having come at the same time as the obligation to pay for the torn garments, and he is therefore free from payment (Rashi). (7) In the case of one stealing *ḥeleb* and eating it. (8) Therefore here also the penalty of *kareth* for eating *ḥeleb* and the obligation to pay for the *ḥeleb* to its owner come at the same time, and, according to R. Abin, he would be free from payment. (9) Is this analogy correct? (10) In the case of throwing the arrow. (11) In the case of eating *ḥeleb*. (12) Without lifting; there is therefore no analogy. Hence the liability for stealing came first from the moment of lifting. (13) In the case of throwing the arrow. (14) Once he has thrown the arrow it takes its course. (15) In the case of eating the *ḥeleb*. (16) Therefore we do not say that the eating of the *ḥeleb* begins from the time when he lifted it up. (17) Lit., 'He who causes to pass'. (18) To carry an object four cubits in the public road is a desecration of the Sabbath, v. *supra*. (19) The knife. (20) In the case of the knife.

the 'putting down' is impossible without the 'taking up'.[1] And according to the answer that he cannot take it back, here[2] he can take it back.[3]

The text [stated above]: 'R. Abin said: If someone threw [on Sabbath] an arrow from the beginning of four [cubits] to the end of four [cubits] and it tore silk garments in its passage he is free [from payment], for the "taking up" was necessary for the "putting down".' R. Bibi b. Abaye raised the following objection: If someone stole a purse[4] on Sabbath he is bound [to pay],[5] because he was guilty of stealing before he came to the [transgression of] the prohibition which is punishable with stoning,[6] but if he dragged it along he is free [from payment], because the desecration of the Sabbath and the stealing come at the same time.[7] And why?[8] Here also we should say: The lifting up is necessary for the carrying out![9]—Here we treat of a case when he lifted it up in order to hide it and changed his mind and carried it out.[10] [But] is he, in this case, guilty [of desecrating the Sabbath]? Did not R. Simeon say [that] R. Ammi said in the name of R. Joḥanan: If someone was removing objects from one corner to another corner and changed his mind and carried them out he is free [of the transgression of the desecration of the Sabbath] because the taking up was not from the outset for that [purpose]?—Do not say: in order to hide it, but say: in order to carry it out, only it speaks here of a case when he [paused and] remained standing [for a while].[11] For what

(1) And he would be free from payment, v. p. 170, n. 6. (2) In the case of the knife. (3) And he would have to pay for the torn garments. (4) With money. (5) To the owner of the purse for the loss of the purse and its contents. (6) He was guilty of stealing as soon as he lifted up the purse, and he was guilty of desecrating the Sabbath only after he carried it into the public road. And as the two guilty acts did not coincide, he is not free from payment. (7) When he got it out from the domain of the owner into the public road. (8) Why should he be bound to pay if he lifted up the purse? (9) And he should be free from payment. V. p. 170, n. 6. (10) The 'lifting up' was therefore not for the purpose of carrying out. (11) [His pause in the owner's domain completed the first act of removing, making him liable for the theft, while the liability for Sabbath desecration begins when he resumes his walk to carry it outside.]

purpose did he remain standing? If to adjust the cord on his shoulder, this is the usual way.[1]—No; [we speak of a case] where he stood still in order to rest. But how would it be if [he had remained standing] in order to adjust the cord on his shoulder? [31b] He would be free [from payment]? [If so] instead of teaching 'but if he dragged it along he is free [from payment]', let him make the distinction in the same case.[2] 'When is this said?[3] If he stood still to rest; but if [he stood still] to adjust the cord on his shoulder, he is free [from payment]'? But [answer thus:] Whose opinion is this? It is that of Ben 'Azzai, who says: Walking is like standing.[4] [But] how would it be if he threw [the purse]?[5] He would be free [from payment].[6] Let him then make the distinction in the same case,[7] thus when is it said:[8] 'When he walked,[9] but when he threw it, he is free'?—The case of dragging it along is necessary [to be stated]. You might have said that this is not the way of carrying out,[10] so he lets us hear [that it is not so]. Of what [kind of purse does it speak]? If of a large purse, this[11] is the ordinary way [of carrying it out],[12] and if of a small purse, this is not the ordinary way?[13]—In fact [it speaks] of a middle-sized [purse]. But where did he carry it to? If he carried it into the public road, there is

(1) Of one who carries a cord, and this pause cannot be regarded as an interruption. (2) In the first case stated when he lifted up the purse. (3) That the two acts are held not to coincide and he is therefore bound to pay for the purse. (4) Lit., 'he who walks is as he who stands.' It means: every pace made is a new 'lifting up' and a new 'putting down'. Therefore, the theft is committed with the first 'lifting up' of the purse, and the desecration of the Sabbath is effected when the last pace is made. The two acts therefore do not coincide and he is bound to pay. (5) He lifted up the purse and threw it into the public road. (6) Because the stealing and the desecration of the Sabbath come together: cf. the case of the arrow on *supra* 30a. (7) In the first case stated when he lifted up the purse. (8) That the two acts are not held to coincide and he is therefore bound to pay for the loss to the owner of the purse. (9) And carried out the purse in walking. (10) From one territory to another, and therefore involves no liability. (11) Dragging it along. (12) And why is it necessary to let us hear that dragging it along is a way of carrying out? It is too heavy to carry. (13) And indeed it should not be regarded as 'carrying out' and should not constitute a desecration of the Sabbath.

desecration of the Sabbath but no stealing,[1] and if he carried it into private ground, there is stealing but no desecration of the Sabbath![2]—No, it is necessary [to state it] when he carried it out to the sides[3] of the public road. According to whose view?[4] If according to [that of] R. Eliezer, who says: The sides of the public road are like the public road,[5] there is desecration of the Sabbath but no stealing[6] and if it is according to the view of the Rabbis, who say: 'The sides of the public road are not like the public road,' there is stealing but no desecration of the Sabbath?[3] —Indeed, it is according to R. Eliezer, and when R. Eliezer says: 'The sides of the public road are like the public road', it is only with regard to becoming guilty of the desecration of the Sabbath,[7] because sometimes, through the pressure of the crowd, people go in there,[8] but with regard to acquiring, one does acquire there, because the public is not often there.[9] R. Ashi said: [We speak of a case] when he lowered[10] his hand to less than three [handbreadths][11] and received it.[12] [And this is] according to Raba, for Raba said: The hand of a person is regarded as [a place of] four by four [handbreadths].[13] R. Aḥa taught so.[14] Rabina [however]

(1) Lit., 'the prohibition of Sabbath is there, the prohibition of stealing is not there'.—Without lifting it up there is no acquisition in the public road. (Rashi.) (2) Since he carried it from one private ground to another private ground next to it. 'Carrying out' is forbidden on Sabbath only from private ground to public ground or from public ground to private ground. V. Shab. 2*b* and 73*a*. (3) V. *infra*. (4) Lit., 'according to whom'? (5) V. Shab. 6*a*. (6) V. note 1. (7) Guilt of the Sabbath. (8) Lit,, 'the public press and go in there'. (9) And they have therefore more the character of private ground for the purpose of acquisition by pulling (*meshikah*, v. Glos.). (10) Lit., 'joined'. (11) From the ground. Within three handbreadths from the ground it is public territory. Cf. Shab. 97*a*. (12) Indeed he dragged the purse along into the public road, and there he put his (second) hand near the ground, less than three handbreadths, and received the purse into the hand, and his hand acquired it for him. Thus the desecration of the Sabbath and the stealing came at the same time: the former when the purse was carried out into the public road (for dragging along is carrying out), and the latter when—simultaneously—it dropped into his hand (Rashi). V. also next note. (13) For the purpose of 'taking up' and 'putting down', the place must be at least four by four handbreadths; v. Shab. 4*a*. Raba said that the hand of a person is regarded as

taught: Indeed, when he carried it out into the public road, for he acquires also in the public ground.[1] [And] they[2] differ with regard to a deduction from this Mishnah, for we have learned: If he[3] was pulling it out[4] and it died in the domain of the owner, he is free;[5] but if he lifted it up or brought it[6] out from the territory of the owner[7] and it died, he is bound [to pay].[8] Rabina makes a deduction from the first clause, and R. Aḥa makes a deduction from the second clause. Rabina makes a deduction from the first clause: 'If he was drawing it out and it died in the domain of the owner, he is free'. The reason [for his being free] is because it died in the domain of the owner, but if he had brought it out[9] from the domain of the owner[10] and it died, he would have been bound [to pay].[11] R. Aḥa makes a deduction from the second clause: 'but if he lifted it up or brought it out [etc.]' Bringing out is like lifting up; as lifting up is [an act through which the object] comes into his possession,[12] so bringing out [must be an act through which the object] comes into his possession.[13] According to R. Aḥa the

being a place of four by four handbreadths; v. Shab. 5a. And just as it is regarded as a place of four by four handbreadths for the purposes of Sabbath, it is also regarded as such a place for the purposes of acquisition. Therefore, when he received the purse into his hand, although it was lower than three handbreadths from the ground, since his hand is considered a place, in the legal sense, it is as if he had lifted up the purse above the three handbreadths from the ground and he has thus acquired it by lifting it up; the desecration of the Sabbath and the stealing come therefore at the same time (Rashi). 'Lifting' as an act of acquisition must be at least three handbreadths from the ground. V. Ḳid. (Sonc. ed.) p. 124, n. 5. (14) As R. Ashi said that there is no acquisition in a public domain except by 'lifting up'.

(1) By dragging along the purse towards him. No 'lifting up' is necessary. The person acquires the object by pulling it (*meshikah*) even in a public domain. (2) R. Aḥa and Rabina. (3) V. B.Ḳ. *l.c.* (4) Lit., 'he pulled it and went'.—He intended to steal the animal. (5) From paying to the owner for the animal, for he has not acquired it yet, since he has not taken it out from the territory of the owner and it has therefore not come into his possession. (6) The animal. (7) And by doing this he acquired the animal. (8) To the owner for the animal, v. B.Ḳ. 79a. (9) By the process of 'pulling'. (10) Even into public territory. (11) This shews that pulling an object to oneself acquires also in public territory. (12) רשות has the meaning of domain as well as of possession. (13) רשות here also means 'possession'. By being brought into his

first clause is difficult and according to Rabina the second clause is difficult?—The first clause is not difficult according to R. Aḥa, for as long as it has not come into his possession it is called: 'in the domain of the owner'.[1] The second clause is not difficult according to Rabina, for we do not say [that] bringing out is like lifting up.[2]

IF ONE HAD INTERCOURSE [BY FORCE] WITH HIS SISTER, OR WITH THE SISTER OF HIS FATHER, etc. There is a question of contradiction against this: The following persons receive [the punishment of] lashes: he who has intercourse with his sister, with the sister of his father, with the sister of his mother, with the sister of his wife, with the sister of his brother, with the wife of the brother of his father, or with a woman during menstruation,[3] [32*a*] and it is established that one does not receive lashes *and pay!*[4]—'Ulla said: There is no difficulty. Here[5] [it speaks] of his sister [who is] a maiden,[6] and there[7] [it speaks] of his sister [who is] a mature girl.[8] [But in the case of] his sister [who is] a mature girl, too, [there are damages to be paid for the] shame and deterioration?[9]—[It speaks of] an idiot.[10] But [there are still damages to be paid for] the pain?[11] [It speaks of] a girl who was seduced.[12] Now that you have come to this,[13] you can even say [that it speaks of] his sister

private domain the object comes into his possession, but not by being brought out into public territory. Therefore R. Aḥa requires the device of the person receiving the object into his hand near the ground, as R. Ashi said.

(1) Even if it is in the public road. (2) In the sense in which R. Aḥa says it. (3) Persons who commit, after a warning, a transgression punishable with *kareth* receive the punishment of lashes, v. Mak. 13*a*. (4) Since he receives lashes, according to the Mishnah just quoted, he should not pay the fine, and this would be against our Mishnah. (5) In our Mishnah. (6) A *na'arah* (v. Glos.) and the fine is payable; v. *supra* 29*a*. In this case the penalty of lashes would not be inflicted. (7) In Mak. 13*a*. (8) A *bogereth* (v. Glos.), and no fine is due; v. *supra* 29*a*. In this case the penalty of lashes is inflicted. (9) Which she has suffered, (v. *infra* 39*a*-40*b*). And there would be both lashes and payment. (10) The girl is not *compos mentis*, and thus neither shame nor deterioration applies. (11) Caused by the forced intercourse. (12) In the Mishnah Mak. 13*a*, it was not a case of violation, but of seduction; and in seduction there is no pain; v. *infra* 39*b*. (13) To say that the Mishnah Mak. speaks of seduction and not violation.

[who was] a maiden [and namely when she was] an orphan[1] and [she was] seduced.[2]

Consequently, 'Ulla holds the view that wherever there is money [to be paid] and the punishment of lashes [to be inflicted], he pays the money and does not receive the lashes.[3] Whence does 'Ulla derive this?—He derives it from [the law with regard to] one person who injures another person. Just as when one person injures another person, in which case there is money to [be paid][4] and the punishment of lashes,[5] he pays the money and does not receive the lashes,[6] so whenever there are payment of money and the punishment of lashes, he pays the money and does not receive the lashes. [But may it not be argued] it is different with [the case of] one person who injures another person because he is liable for five things?[7] And [if you will say] that [the payment of] money is lighter,[8] [one can say against this] that [here it has been excepted] from its rule [and] permitted to the Court![9] But he derives it from the refuted false witnesses.[10] Just as in the case of refuted

(1) Since her father is not alive, the damages are payable to her. (2) And having yielded to his persuasion she will not claim the damages from him; hence lashes are inflicted. (3) Since 'Ulla explains the Mishnah Mak. 13*a* as dealing with a *bogereth*, as otherwise there would be, in his view, no lashes even if he were warned beforehand, but only the payment of the fine. (4) V. Ex. XXI, 19. (5) This is deduced from Deut. XXV, 3 (Rashi). (6) V. *infra* 32*b*. (7) He has to make five kinds of payments; v. B.Ḳ. 83*b*. The payment of money in this case is therefore particularly heavy and other money payments cannot be compared with it. (8) And if in this case payment of money is to be made and no lashes are to be given, the same should indeed apply to other cases. Whether the payment is greater or smaller, it is a lighter punishment than lashes, and we see here that the lighter punishment is chosen (cf. Rashi). (9) In this case the Torah has expressly stated that the Court may administer lashes (cf. Deut. XXV, 2). But the Court may prefer, and as a rule does prefer, that the person who was injured should receive money as compensation (Cf. Tosaf. s.v. ואי). Therefore in this case the money is paid and no lashes are given. But in other cases, as in those of violation and seduction, the rule may be different. In these cases the giving of lashes is not mentioned explicitly in the Torah, and thus its permissiveness is not stated. And when in such cases the punishment of lashes and the payment of money are due, lashes are given. And you cannot derive other cases from this case. With regard to the punishment of lashes v. Mak. 13*b*. (10) Witnesses proved *zomemim*, v. *Glos*.

false witnesses, whose transgression involves the payment of money and the punishment with lashes,[1] they pay the money but do not receive the lashes,[2] so whenever there are payment of money and the punishment of lashes, he pays the money and does not receive the lashes. [But it may be argued] it is different with the case of refuted false witnesses, because they do not require a warning?[3] [And if you will say] that [the payment of] money is lighter, [one can say against this,] that they[4] have not done any deed![5]—But he derives it from both.[6] The point common to both is that there are the payment of money and the punishment of lashes, and in either case he pays the money and does not receive the lashes. So whenever there are payment of money and the punishment of lashes, he pays the money and does not receive the lashes. But [it may be argued] the point common to both is [also] that they both have a strict side?[7] And if [you will say that the payment of] money is lighter, [one can say against this] that they have both a lighter side?[8]—[32b] But 'Ulla derives it from the two words *'for'*.[9] It is written here for *he hath humbled her*[10] and it is written there: *'Eye* for *eye'*. As there[11] he pays money and does not receive lashes, so wherever there are the payment of money and the punishment of lashes, he pays money and does not receive the lashes.

R. Joḥanan said: You can even say that it[12] speaks of his sister who was a maiden. Only there[12] it speaks of a case where they warned him,[13] and here[14] it speaks of a case where they did not

(1) Cf. Mak. 4*a*. (2) V. *infra* 32*b*. (3) They are subject to the *lex talionis* without a warning. (4) The refuted false witnesses. (5) Their transgression consists in words and not in deeds. Therefore the money penalty is imposed and not that of lashes. But with regard to transgressions in deeds, it may be that the transgressor receives lashes! (6) The case of one person who injures another person and the case of the refuted false witnesses. (7) In the one case the five kinds of payment and in the other case the non-requirement of a warning. (8) In the one case the exception (v. p. 176, n. 9), and in the other case the transgression consisted of words and not of a deed. Therefore you cannot compare other cases with this case. (9) תחת. A deduction based on similarity of expressions—a *Gezerah shawah* (v. Glos.). (10) Deut. XXII, 29. (11) Ex. XXI, 24. (12) The Mishnah, Mak. 13*a*. (13) And he is therefore liable to the payment of money and the penalty of lashes, and the Mishnah in Mak.

warn him.[1] Consequently R. Joḥanan holds the view that wherever there are the payment of money and the punishment of lashes and they warned him, he receives the lashes and does not pay the money. Whence does R. Joḥanan derive this?—The verse says: *According to his guilt;*[2] [from this I infer that] you punish him because of one guilt but not because of two guilts, and immediately follow[3] the words: *Forty stripes he may give him.*[4] But behold when one person injures another person, in which case there are the payment of money and the punishment of lashes, he pays money and does not receive the lashes? And if you will say that this is only when they did not warn him, but when they warned him, he receives the lashes and does not pay—did not R. Ammi say in the name of R. Joḥanan that, if one person struck another person a blow, for which no *peruṭah*[5] can be claimed as damages,[6] he receives the lashes? How shall we imagine this case? If they did not warn him, why does he receive the lashes? Hence it is clear that they warned him, and the reason [why he receives the lashes and does not pay] is because the damages do not amount to a *peruṭah*, but if they amount to a *peruṭah* he pays the money but does not receive the lashes![7]—[It is] as R. Elai said: The Torah has expressly stated[8] that the *Zomemim* witnesses have to pay money; so [here] also the Torah has expressly stated that the person who injures another person has to pay money. With regard to what has that [teaching] of R. Elai been said?—With regard to the following:[9] 'We testify that So-and-so owes his fellow two hundred *zuz*' and they were found to be *Zomemim*, they receive the lashes and pay,[10] for it is not the verse that imposes upon

13*a* teaches us that, in that case, he receives the lashes and does not pay the money. (14) In our Mishnah.

(1) And he is not liable to the penalty of lashes, and therefore he has to pay the money. (2) Deut. XXV, 2. (3) Lit., 'and next to it'. (4) Deut. XXV, 3. This shews that when there are two guilts, or two punishments for one guilt, he receives the punishment of lashes. (5) A small coin, v. Glos. (6) Lit., 'in which there is not the value of a *peruṭah*'. (7) Which contradicts R. Joḥanan's ruling. (8) Lit., 'increased'. This means: included something by using an additional word, or additional words. (9) Mak. 4*a*. (10) The amount they wanted to make the person pay, against whom they falsely testified.

them[1] the lashes[2] which imposes upon them[1] the payment[3] [of money]. This is the view of R. Meir; and the Sages say: He who pays does not receive lashes.[4] [And] let us say: he who receives lashes does not pay?[5] [Upon that] R. Elai said: The Torah has expressly stated that the *Zomemim* witnesses have to pay more money. Where has the Torah stated this?—Consider; it is written: *'Then shall ye do unto him as he had thought to do unto his brother'*; why [is it written further,] *'hand for hand'?*[6] [This means] a thing that is given from hand to hand, and that is money. [And] the same applies to the case of[7] one person who injures another person. Consider; it is written: *'As he hath done, so shall it be done to him'*;[8] why [is it written further] *'so shall it be rendered unto him'?*[9] [This means] a thing that can be rendered,[10] and that is money.

Why does R. Johanan not say as 'Ulla?[11]—If so[12] you would abolish [the prohibitory law]: *The nakedness of thy sister thou shalt not uncover.*[13] [33a] [But could not one say] also [in the case of] one person who injures another person: If so[14] you would abolish [the prohibitory law], *'he shall not exceed, lest, if he should exceed.'*[15] [And in case of] the *Zomemim* witnesses too, [one could say]: If so you would abolish [the law]: *'then it shall be, if the guilty man deserve to be beaten.'*[16] But [you must say that in the case of] the

(1) Lit., 'brings them to'. (2) For transgressing the ninth commandment. (3) V. Deut. XIX, 19. (4) V. Mak. 4a. (5) According to the view of R. Johanan. (6) Deut. XIX, 21. (7) Lit., 'also'. (8) Lev. XXIV, 19. (9) Lev. XXIV, 20. (10) Lit., 'with regard to which there is a rendering', 'a giving'. (11) That our Mishnah speaks of the case where he had intercourse with his sister as a *na'arah*, which makes him liable to the fine and exempts him from lashes. (12) That is, if he who cohabited with his sister who is a maiden, would be free from receiving lashes after he had been warned. (13) Lev., XVIII, 9. A prohibitory law, if wilfully transgressed, and after a warning, is punishable (also) with lashes. Therefore R. Johanan holds that where there are the payment of money and the punishment of lashes, he receives the lashes and does not pay the money. Only our Mishnah speaks of a case where there was no warning, and therefore he pays the fine. (14) If, in this case, he has to pay money, he does not receive the lashes, v. *supra* 32b. (15) Deut. XXV, 3. If the lashes are not given, this law is not fulfilled. (16) Deut. XXV, 2, from which is derived the inflicting of lashes on *Zomemim* witnesses, v. Mak. 2b, and *infra*.

Zomemim witnesses it is possible to fulfil it[1] when [the witnesses testified falsely about someone[2] that he was] the son of a divorced woman or the son of a *haluzah*.[3] [Similarly in the case of] a person who injured another person, it also is possible to fulfil it[4] when he struck him a blow for which no *peruṭah* can be claimed as damages.[5] [And so you can say] also [with regard to] his sister [that] it is possible to fulfil it[6] in the case of his sister who was a mature girl![7] —R. Joḥanan can answer you: [The verse] *for he hath humbled her*[8] is required for [the same teaching] as of Abaye, for Abaye said: The verse says, '*for he hath humbled her*'. This[9] [he shall pay] for he has humbled her, [from which we infer], by implication, that there are also [to be paid damages for] shame and deterioration.[10] And 'Ulla?'[11]—He derives it from a teaching of Raba, for Raba said: The verse says: *Then the man that lay with her shall give unto the father of the maiden fifty shekels of silver;*[12] [this means that] for the enjoyment of lying [with the maiden he has to pay] fifty [shekels of silver], [and we infer], by implication, that there are also [to be paid damages for] shame and deterioration.

R. Eleazar[13] says: The *Zomemim* witnesses pay money and do not receive lashes, because they cannot be warned.[14] Raba said: You

(1) The flagellation prescribed in Deut. XXV, 2. (2) A priest. (3) V. Glos. In this case one cannot do to him as he had thought to do to others; nor is there a money fine, so he receives the lashes, v. Mak. 2a. (4) The flagellation attached to the prohibitory law of Deut. XXV, 3. (5) Where there is no money payment and so he receives the lashes, v. *supra* 32b. V. Rashi. (6) The flagellation attached to the prohibitory law of Lev. XVIII, 9. (7) As long as there is a possibility of fulfilling the law it is not abolished, as in the other two cases; thus there is no point in R. Joḥanan's objection to 'Ulla's explanation. (8) Deut. XXII, 29, from which 'Ulla derives that the fine is paid and no lashes are inflicted. (9) The fifty *shekels* of silver. (10) V. *infra* 40b. (11) Whence does he derive Abaye's deduction? (12) Deut. XXII, 29. (13) So marginal glosses to text. R. Eleazar b. Pedath, generally called in the Talmud simply R. Eleazar, was a disciple and later an associate of R. Joḥanan. Cur. edd.: R. Eliezer. (14) [No verse is required to teach that *Zomemim* witnesses pay and receive no lashes (in opposition to R. Elai *supra* p. 178) as the Talmud proceeds to explain. The case of Mak. 2a (v. *supra* note 3) is an exception since there is no possibility of applying the *lex talionis;* where however it is applicable there are no lashes (Rashi).]

may know it [from the following]:[1] When shall we warn them? Shall we warn them at first?[2] They will [then] say: We have forgotten[3]. Shall we warn them during the deed?[4] They would [then] withdraw and not give any evidence.[5] Shall we warn them at the end?[6] [Then] what has been has been.[7] Abaye demurred to this: Let us warn them immediately after they have given their evidence?[8] R. Aḥa, the son of R. Iḳa demurred: Let us warn them at first[9] and gesticulate to them [afterwards].[10] Later[11] Abaye said: What I said[12] was nothing. For if one were to say[13] that *Zomemim* witnesses require a warning, [it would follow that], if we have not warned them, we would not kill them.[14] [But then] is it possible[15] that who they wished to kill without a warning,[16]—that they should require a warning? Surely, it is necessary[17] [that the words be fulfilled,] *'then shall ye do unto him as he has thought to do unto his brother'*,[18] and this would not be [the case here]? To this R. Samma the son of R. Jeremiah demurred. But now [according to your argument], [if the witnesses testified falsely about someone[19] that he was] the son of a divorced woman or the son of a *ḥaluẓah*,[20] since this case is not included in *'as he had thought* etc.' a warning should be required![21]—The verse says: *'Ye shall have*

(1) That they cannot be warned. (2) Before they gave evidence. (3) The warning. The warning has then lapsed. (4) I.e., during the evidence. (5) Seeing that they are under suspicion they would refuse altogether to give evidence, even true evidence. (6) After they had given their evidence. (7) I.e., what they said they cannot withdraw, and there would be no point in warning them. (8) 'Within as much (time) as is required for an utterance', e.g., 'a greeting'. V. Nazir (Sonc. ed.) p. 71 n. 1. (9) Before they gave evidence. (10) I.e., during the evidence. By gesticulating we would remind the witnesses of the warning given to them at first, and they could not say, 'we have forgotten it'. (11) Or, 'another time'. (12) That the *Zomemim* witnesses should require a warning to be lashed. (13) Lit., 'if it enters thy mind'. (14) Although their false evidence, had it remained unrefuted, would have brought about the penalty of death on him against whom they testified. (15) Lit., 'is there anything (like this)?' (16) Since their evidence proved to be false, they could not have given a warning to those against whom they testified. (17) Lit., 'do we not require'? (18) Deut. XIX, 19. (19) A priest. (20) V. *supra* p. 180, n. 3. (21) [If the reason that *Zomemim* witnesses require no warning is because, otherwise, the principle *'as he had thought'* could not be applied, a warning

one manner of law';[1] [this means] a law that is equal for you all.[2]

R. Shisha, the son of R. Idi, said: That a person who injures another person pays money and does not receive the lashes is derived from this:[3] [It is written:] *And if men strive together and hurt a woman with child, so that her fruit depart.*[4] [Upon this] R. Eleazar said: The verse speaks of a striving with intent to kill, for it is written, *But if any harm follow, then thou shalt give life for life*[5]. How shall we imagine this case? If they did not warn him, why should he be killed? Hence it is obvious that he was warned, [and it is held], when one is warned regarding a severe matter[6] one also is warned for a light matter,[7] and [yet] the Torah says: *And yet no harm follow, he shall be surely fined.*[8] To this R. Ashi demurred: Whence [do we know] that when one is warned regarding a severe matter one also stands warned for a light matter? Perhaps it is not so![9] And even if we will say that it is so, whence [do we know] that [the penalty of] death is severer? [33*b*] Perhaps [the punishment with] lashes is severer, for Rab said: If they had lashed Ḥananiah, Mishael and Azariah, they would have worshipped the [golden] image?[10] R. Samma the son of R. Assi said to R. Ashi; and some say [that] R. Samma the son of R. Ashi [said] to R. Ashi: Do you not make a distinction between a beating that has a limit[11] and a beating that has no limit![12] R. Jacob from Nehar Peḳod [also]

should be required in this case which the law excepts from the application of this principle].

(1) Lev., XXIV, 22. (2) And since in most cases the *Zomemim* witnesses cannot be warned, they need not be warned in this case either. (3) And not (as *supra* 32*b*) from Lev. XXIV, 20. (4) Ex. XXI, 22. (5) Ex. XXI, 23. [*'Harm'* means 'death'; and, the verse tells us, although there was no intent of killing the woman, the blow having been directed against the other man, yet the slayer is put to death, v. Sanh. 74*a*. (6) 'Life for life.' (7) The lashes for striking a person. (8) We thus see that although there was a warning and he should be liable to being punished with the lashes, he pays the money and does not receive the lashes. (9) And since he does not stand warned for the light matter, he is not liable to the punishment with lashes, and therefore pays the fine. (10) V. Dan. III. (11) The number of lashes given by the Court is limited to forty. (12) The lashes that might have been given to Ḥananiah, Mishael and Azariah would have had no limit.

demurred:[1] That is alright according to the Rabbis who[2] hold that *life*[3] actually means [life].[4] But according to Rabbi,[5] who holds that it means money, what is there to say?[6]—But, said R. Jacob from Nehar Peḳod, in the name of Raba; [it is to be derived] from the following verse:[7] [It is written,] *'If he rise again, and walk abroad upon his staff, then shall he that smote him be quit.'*[8] Would it enter your mind that this one[9] walks about in the street and that one[10] should be killed?[11] But it teaches that they imprison him;[10] if he[9] dies, they kill him; and if he does not die, *'he shall pay for the loss of his time, and shall cause him to be thoroughly healed.'*[8] Now how shall we imagine this case? If they did not warn him, why should he be killed? Hence it is plain that they warned him, and [it is held], one who was warned for a severe matter stands warned for the lighter matter and [yet] the All-Merciful says [that if he does not die] *'he shall pay for the loss of his time, and shall cause him to be thoroughly healed'*.[12] To this R. Ashi asked: Whence [do you know] that one who was warned for a severe matter stands warned for a lighter matter? Perhaps not? And if you will even say that he does [stand warned for the lighter matter], whence [do you know] that death is severer? Perhaps [the punishment with] lashes is severer, for Rab said: If they had lashed Ḥananiah, Mishael and Azariah, they would have worshipped the [golden] image? R. Samma the son of R. Assi said to R. Ashi, and some say [that] R. Samma the son of R. Ashi [said] to R. Ashi: Do you not make

(1) I.e., against the derivation of R. Shisha, based on the exposition of R. Eleazar. (2) V. Sanh. 79a-b. (3) In Ex. XXI, 23. (4) I.e., the death penalty. In this case the text deals with an attack which was attended by a warning, and so you can make the derivation that he pays the money and does not receive the lashes, as *supra* p. 182, n. 8. (5) Sanh. 79a-b. (6) Since there is no question of a death penalty the text need not necessarily refer to a case where there was a warning, and thus affords no basis for the derivation. (7) Lit., 'from here'. (8) Ex. XXI, 19. (9) Who was smitten. (10) Who smote. (11) Surely that is impossible! If the one was not killed by the injury, the smiter would not receive the death penalty. Then why does the Torah expressly say that *'he that smote him be quit'*? (12) Although there was a warning making him liable to lashes. This shews that he pays money and does not receive the lashes.

a distinction between a beating that has a limit and a beating that has no limit?[1] R. Mari [also] demurred:[2] Whence [do you know] that [one smote the other] wilfully[3] and *'he shall be quit'* [means] from [the penalty of] death? Perhaps [one smote the other] inadvertently[4] and *'he shall be quit'* [means] from exile?[5] The difficulty remains.

Resh Laḳish said:[6] This[7] is the opinion of R. Meir,[8] who says: He receives the lashes and pays [the money].[9]—If it is according to R. Meir, [then one who violated] his daughter should also [pay the fine]?[10] And if you will say that R. Meir holds [that] one may receive the lashes and pay [the money], but does not hold [that] one may receive the death penalty[11] and pay [the money][12]—has it not been taught: If he has stolen and slaughtered [an animal] on Sabbath,[13] or has stolen and slaughtered [an animal] for idolatry,[13] or has stolen an ox that is to be stoned[14] and slaughtered it, he shall pay fourfold or fivefold.[15] This is the view of R. Meir,[16] but the Sages declare him free [from payment]?—Has it not been stated regarding this: R. Jacob said in the name of R. Joḥanan, and some say [that] R. Jeremiah said in the name of R. Simeon b. Laḳish: R. Abin and R. Elai and the whole company [of scholars] said in the name of R. Joḥanan [that it speaks of a case when] he [who stole the animal] let it be slaughtered by another person. But is

(1) For notes v. *supra* p. 182, nn. 11-12. (2) To the derivation of R. Jacob from Nehar Peḳod. (3) In which case only the penalty of death is inflicted, provided there was a warning. (4) And if he killed him he is banished to one of the cities of refuge. V. Num. XXXV, 11ff and Deut. XIX, 2ff. (5) I.e., from banishment to one of the three cities of refuge. [The text thus speaks of a case where there was no warning, and for this reason makes him liable to a fine where the blow did not result in death; where however there was a warning there would be no payment, but lashes.] (6) With regard to the question from the Mishnah in Mak. 13*a*; v. *supra* 31*b*. (7) The view of our Mishnah. (8) Lit., 'whose opinion is this? It is that of R. Meir'. (9) V. *supra* 32*b*. (10) And in the Mishnah *infra* 36*b*, it is stated that in such a case no fine is paid, because the penalty of death (by the hand of man) is attached to it. V. also *Sanh.* 75*a*. (11) Lit., 'he dies'. (12) In the text follows: 'and not'; i.e., and does he not hold that? (13) And has thus incurred the death penalty. (14) V. Ex. XXI, 28. (15) V. Ex. XXI, 37. (16) We thus see that R. Meir holds that even when there is a death penalty he pays the money.

it possible that one sins and another one is punished?[1] Raba said: The Divine law says: *and slaughter it or sell it;* [this teaches that] as the sale is [effected] through [the participation of] another person, so [may] the slaughtering [of the animal] be through another person. In the School of R. Ishmael it was taught: [the word] *'or'* [is] to include the agent. In the School of Hezekiah it was taught: [the word] *'instead'*[1] [is] to include the agent. Mar Zuṭra demurred to this: Is it anywhere to be found that if he does [the deed] himself he is not liable[2] and if an agent does it he is liable? He himself [does not pay], not because he is not liable, but because he suffers the severer penalty. [But] if he [who stole the animal] let it be slaughtered by another person, what is the reason of the Rabbis who declare him free [from paying]?—Who are the Sages? [34*a*] R. Simeon, who says: An unfit slaughtering is not called[3] slaughtering. This might be right with regard to [the slaughtering for] idolatry and [the slaughtering of] the ox that is to be stoned, but the slaughtering on Sabbath is a fit slaughtering, for we learnt: If someone has slaughtered [an animal] on Sabbath or the Day of Atonement, although he is guilty of [a transgression for which he forfeits] his life,[4] his slaughtering is a fit one?[5]—He holds the opinion of R. Joḥanan ha-Sandalar,[6] for it has been taught: If someone has cooked on Sabbath, [if] by mistake, he may eat it, [and if] wilfully he may not eat it. This is the view of R. Meir. R. Judah says: [If] by mistake, he may eat it after the outgoing[7] of the Sabbath, [if] wilfully, he may never eat it. R. Joḥanan ha-Sandalar says: [If] wilfully, others may eat it after the outgoing of the Sabbath, but not he, [if] wilfully, neither he nor others may eat it.[8] What is the reason of R. Joḥanan ha-Sandalar? As R.

(1) Regarding the payment of money; v. Ḳid. 43*a*. (2) To pay the money. (3) Lit., 'its name is not'. An act of slaughter that does not for any reason whatsoever effect the ritual fitness of the animal to be eaten is not considered by them in the eye of the law a slaughter. (4) V. *supra* 30*a*. (5) Mishnah, Ḥul. 14a. (6) Probably 'sandal-maker'. (7) Lit., 'at the outgoing'. (8) According to R. Joḥanan ha-Sandalar what has been cooked on Sabbath wilfully must not be eaten by any Jew. The same would apply to what has been slaughtered wilfully on Sabbath. Thus one can say that the slaughtering on Sabbath is an unfit slaughtering.

Ḥiyya expounded at the entrance of the house of the Prince:[1] [It is written:] *'Ye shall keep the Sabbath therefore, for it is holy unto you'*.[2] [From this we derive:] As what is holy is forbidden to be eaten, so what has been prepared[3] on the Sabbath is forbidden to be eaten. If [so, you might say that] as what is holy is forbidden to be enjoyed,[4] so what has been prepared on the Sabbath should be forbidden to be enjoyed?—It says *'unto you'*; from this we learn: It shall belong to you.[5] You might think [that it is forbidden to eat] even [what has been prepared on the Sabbath] by mistake,[6] [therefore] it is said: *every one that profaneth it shall surely be put to death*.[7] [This teaches that only] when [the act was done] wilfully,[8] have I told thee [that it is forbidden as that which is holy] but not [if it was done] by mistake.

R. Aḥa and Rabina differ concerning this. One says: What has been prepared on Sabbath [is forbidden] according to the Bible, and one says: [only] according to the Rabbis. He who says: According to the Bible—as we have [just] explained.[9] [And] he who says: according to the Rabbis— the verse says: *'It is holy'*, [that means]: *'it'*[10] is holy, but what has been prepared on it is not holy.[11] According to him who says [that the prohibition is only] Rabbinical, what is the reason of the Rabbis who declare him[12] free?[13]—The Rabbis declare him free only with regard to other cases.[14]

But [with regard to] one who slaughtered for idolatry [one can ask:] as soon as he has cut[15] a little it[16] has become forbidden,[17] so

(1) Judah the Prince. (2) Ex. XXXI, 14. (3) Lit., 'the work of'. (4) I.e., to have any use or benefit from it. (5) Although one may not eat it, one may have other uses or benefits from it, e.g., one may sell it to one who is not a Jew and is therefore not bound by these laws. (6) If he did not know it was Sabbath (Rashi). (7) Ibid. (8) For which the death penalty is inflicted. (9) Lit., 'said'. (10) I.e., the Sabbath itself. (11) The prohibition is therefore only Rabbinical. (12) Who stole an animal and slaughtered it on Sabbath. (13) From paying four- or fivefold. Since the animal is, according to Biblical law, fit for food, it should be considered a fit slaughter. (14) Lit., 'the rest', i.e., the other two cases mentioned: the serving of idols and the ox condemned to death. (15) The throat of the animal. (16) The animal. (17) For any use as an animal slaughtered for idol worship v. Ḥul. 40a.

when he continues the slaughtering[1] he does not slaughter what is the owner's?[2]—Raba said: [it speaks of a case] when he says [that] he worships it[3] with the completion of the slaughtering. [But with regard to] the ox that is to be stoned [one can ask]: he[4] does not slaughter what is his?[5] Here we speak of a case when he[6] handed it[7] to a keeper and it caused the damage[8] in the house of the keeper[9] and it was sentenced in the house of the keeper and a thief stole it from the house of the keeper. And R. Meir holds the view of R. Jacob and holds the view of R. Simeon. He holds the view of R. Jacob who says: If the keeper returned it even after the sentence had been pronounced, it is regarded as returned.[10] And he holds the view of R. Simeon who says: that which causes [the gain or loss of] money is regarded as money.[11]

Rabbah said: Indeed [it speaks of a case] when he[12] slaughtered it himself [34*b*] and R. Meir holds the view that [though generally] one may receive the lashes and pay, one cannot receive the death penalty and pay[13] but these [cases][14] are different, because the Torah has enacted something novel in [the matter of] fine,[15]

(1) Cutting the throat of the animal until the slaughtering of the animal is complete to make it fit for food. (2) It has already become forbidden to the owner for any use and has thus ceased to be in his possession. He should therefore be free from paying four- or fivefold. (3) The idol. The idolatrous act is to take place when the slaughtering has been completed. Consequently he was slaughtering what was the owner's. (4) The thief. (5) The owner's. An ox that is to be stoned for goring a person is forbidden for any use. It is therefore regarded as not belonging any more to the owner. And he should therefore be free from paying four- or fivefold. (6) The owner. (7) The ox. (8) By killing a person. Cf. Ex. XXI, 28. (9) I.e., while in the possession of the keeper. (10) Although the condemned animal has no value, the liability of the keeper, who has to return the animal to its owner, is discharged by the keeper returning the animal to its owner. (11) Since the thief stole the condemned animal the keeper cannot return it to the owner and he has to pay to the owner the value of the animal as it was when he entrusted it to him. The ox that is to be stoned has therefore a money-value for the keeper. The thief must therefore pay the four- or fivefold. For fuller notes on the whole passage beginning from 'Resh Laḳish said' etc., 33*b*, v. B.Ḳ. (Sonc. ed.) pp. 407-410. (12) The thief. (13) Cf. *supra* 33*b*. (14) In the case of the slaughtering of the stolen animal, *supra* 33*b*. (15) A fine of four or five times the value of the animal is in itself a novel law.

and [therefore][1] he has to pay, although he has to suffer the death penalty.[2] And Rabbah follows his own principle, for Rabba said: If he had a kid which he had stolen and he slaughtered it on Sabbath, he is bound,[3] for he was already guilty of stealing before he came to the profanation[4] of the Sabbath; [but] if he stole and slaughtered it on Sabbath he is free,[5] for if there is no stealing[6] there is no slaughtering and no selling.

Rabbah said further: If he had a kid which he had stolen and had slaughtered it at the place he broke into,[7] he is bound,[8] for he was already guilty of stealing before he came to the transgression of breaking in;[9] [but] if he stole and slaughtered it in the place he broke into,[10] he is free, for if there is no stealing, there is no slaughtering and no selling. And it was necessary [to state both cases]. For if he had let us hear [the case of the] Sabbath [I would have said that he is free from payment] because its prohibition is a perpetual prohibition,[11] but [in the case of] breaking in, which is only a prohibition for the moment,[12] I might say, [that it is] not [so].[13] And if he had let us hear [the case of] breaking in [I would say that he is free from payment] because his breaking in is his warning,[14] but [with regard to the] Sabbath, [in] which [case] a warning is required, I might say that [it is] not [so].[15] [Therefore] it is necessary [to state both cases].

R. Papa said: If one had a cow that he had stolen and he slaugh-

(1) In view of the novel law in these cases. (2) Lit., 'he is killed'. (3) To pay the fine. (4) Lit., 'prohibiton'. (5) From paying the fine. (6) The crime of stealing is, as it were, wiped out by the more serious transgression of profaning the Sabbath. There is, therefore, no payment of principal. And since there is no payment of the principal, there is also no payment of the fine for the slaughtering and selling. (7) במחתרתו means here both: the place he broke into and the time of breaking into the place. This breaking in took place after the stealing of the kid, which was a separate act. Cf. Ex. XXII, 1. (8) To pay the fine. (9) In which case he may forfeit his life, v. Ex. XXII, 1. (10) Here the stealing and breaking in are one act. (11) I.e., if he has profaned the Sabbath and incurred the death penalty, this penalty can always be inflicted. (12) The thief's life is forfeit only when he is *'found breaking in'*. If he is found later his life is not forfeited, v. Ex. XXII, 2. (13) I.e., that he is not free from payment. (14) I.e., he may be killed without a warning. (15) I.e., that he is not free from payment.

tered it on Sabbath, he is liable[1] for he was already guilty of stealing before he came to the profanation of the Sabbath; if he had a cow that he borrowed and he slaughtered it[2] on Sabbath, he is free.[3] R. Aḥa the son of Raba said to R. Ashi: Does R. Papa mean to tell us[4] [that the same rule[5] applies to] a cow?—He answered him: R. Papa means to tell us [that the same rule[5] applies to] a borrowed [cow]. You might possibly think [that] because R. Papa said that he[6] becomes responsible for its food from the time of [his taking possession of the cow by] 'pulling'[7] here also he becomes responsible for any unpreventable accident [that may befall it] from the time of borrowing,[8] so he lets us hear [that it is not so].[9]

Raba said: If their father left them[10] a borrowed cow,[11] they[12] may use it during the whole period for which he borrowed it;[13] if it died,[14] they are not responsible for what happened.[15] If they thought that it belonged to their father and they slaughtered it and ate it, they pay the value of the meat at the lowest price.[16] If their father left them an obligation of property,[17] they are bound to pay. Some refer it[18] to the first case,[19]

(1) To pay the fine. (2) And thus stole it. (3) From paying the fine. For the stealing and the Sabbath desecration by means of the slaughtering were committed simultaneously. (4) Lit., 'come to let us hear'. (5) Which Rabbah applies to the kid. (6) Cf. B.M. 91*a*. (7) *Meshikah*. v. Glos. (8) I.e., before he desecrated the Sabbath. And therefore he should have to pay the fine when he slaughters it on Sabbath. (9) That the stealing coincides with the slaughtering, and he is therefore free from payment if he slaughters the borrowed cow on Sabbath. (10) I.e., to his children. (11) I.e., a cow which the father had borrowed. (12) The children. (13) Lit., 'all the days of the borrowing'. (14) Accidentally, without their fault. (15) Lit., 'for its accident'. The children are not responsible because they did not borrow it. (16) Which is generally estimated to be two-thirds of the ordinary price, cf. B.B. 146*b*. (17) אחריות נכסים, i.e., property which is a security for the payments which would have to be made. He left them (landed) property and with it the obligation which rests upon such property. The chief point in the phrase is the obligation for which such property is a security, and which was passed on to the children. (18) The last statement. (19) I.e., they are not responsible for the accident only if their father did not leave them an obligation of property.

and some refer it to the second case.[1] He who refers it to the first case, so much the more [does he refer it] to the second case, and he differs from R. Papa.[2] And he who refers it to the second case[3] does not refer it to the first case, and he agrees with R. Papa.[4]

It is alright [that] R. Johanan[5] does not say according to Resh Lakish,[6] because he wants to explain[7] it[8] according to the Rabbis. But why does not Resh Lakish say according to R. Johanan?—He will answer you: since he is free[9] if they warned him, he is also free [even] if they did not warn him.[10]

And they[11] follow their own principles,[12] for when R. Dimi came [from Palestine] he said: He who has committed inadvertently an act which, if he had committed it wilfully, would have been punishable with death or with lashes, and [which is also punishable] with something else,[13] R. Johanan says [that] he is bound,[14] and Resh Lakish says [that] he is free.[15] R. Johanan says [that] he is bound, for they did not warn him.[16] Resh Lakish says [that] he is free,[17] for since he is free if they warned him, so he is free also when they did not warn him.

Resh Lakish raised an objection against R. Johanan: [It is written]: *If no harm follow, he shall be surely fined.*[18] [35a] [Now] is

(1) When they slaughtered and ate it. (2) Who says that the obligation is incurred when the accident happens. According to the opposing view, the father left them the obligation, which therefore was incurred at the time of borrowing. (3) Where the father left them landed property, they are made to pay the full value of the meat since they ought to have been more careful. (4) Lit., 'and this is the view of R. Papa'. The obligation is incurred with the accident, and at the time of the accident there was no borrower, since the person that borrowed the cow was dead. (5) Who explains the Mishnah as dealing with a case where there was no warning, v. *supra* 32b. (6) Who explains the Mishnah as representing the view of R. Meir, v. *supra* 33b. (7) Lit., 'he puts'. (8) The Mishnah. (9) From paying the fine. (10) Since the offence carries with it the penalty of lashes, there is no money payment even where lashes are not inflicted. (11) R. Johanan and Resh Lakish. (12) Or 'opinions', stated elsewhere. (13) I.e., the payment of money. (14) To make the money payment. (15) From making the money payment. (16) And so there is no death penalty, and therefore he pays. (17) From making the money payment. (18) Ex. XXI, 22.

not real '*harm*' meant?[1] No, the law concerning 'harm' [is meant].[2] Some say: R. Joḥanan raised an objection against Resh Laḳish: [It is written] '*And if no harm follow, he shall be surely fined*'. Is not the law concerning '*harm*' [meant]?[2] No, real '*harm*' [is meant].[1]

Raba said: Is there any one who holds that he who committed inadvertently an act which, if he had committed it wilfully, would have been punishable with death [and which is also punishable with the payment of money] is bound [to make the money payment]? Has not the school of Hezekiah taught: [It is written] *He that smiteth a man . . . he that smiteth a beast*[3] [from which we infer:] As in [the case of] the killing of a beast you have made no distinction between [it being done] inadvertently and wilfully, intentionally and unintentionally, by way of going down or by way of going up,[4] so as to free him [from the payment], but [in any case] make him liable to pay, so also in [the case of] the killing of a man you shall make no distinction between [it being done] inadvertently and wilfully, intentionally and unintentionally, by way of going down or by way of going up, so as to make him liable to pay money, but to free him from paying money?[5] But when Rabin came [from Palestine], he said: [As to] him who committed inadvertently an act which, if he had committed it wilfully, would have been punishable with death [and which is also punishable with the payment of money]—all agree that he is free [from the payment of money]; they only differ when the act committed

(1) If no harm follows, that is if the woman does not die, he pays the fine. But if the woman dies, no fine is paid, even if he was not warned. This would be according to Resh Laḳish and against R. Joḥanan. (2) I.e., if the woman did not die, or if she died but he was not warned, he pays the fine. The 'law concerning *harm*' would imply warning. No warning, no death penalty, and therefore payment of money. This would accord with R. Joḥanan. (3) Lev. XXIV, 21. The whole verse reads: *And he that smiteth a beast shall pay for it; and he that smiteth a man shall be put to death.*—Smiting here means killing. (4) A distinction which obtains in the case of unintentional manslaughter with reference to the liability to take refuge, cf. Mak. 7*b*. (5) Even if the killing of the man was done inadvertently, and the death penalty is not inflicted, there is no payment of money to be made. R. Joḥanan could therefore not have said that he was bound to make the money payment, *supra* p. 190.

inadvertently would, if committed wilfully, have been punishable with lashes and something else.[1] R. Joḥanan says [that] he is bound [to make the money payment, because] only with regard to those who commit an act punishable with death, the analogy is made,[2] [but] with regard to those who commit an act punishable with lashes, the comparison is not made. [But] Resh Laḳish says [that] he is free [from making the money payment, because] the Torah has expressly included those who commit an act punishable with lashes to be as those who commit an act punishable with death. Where has the Torah included [them]?—Abaye said: [We infer it from] the double occurrence of *'wicked man'*[3] Raba said: [We infer it from] the double occurrence of *'smiting'*.[4] R. Papa said to Raba: Which *'smiting'* [do you mean]? If you mean[5] [the verse][6] *'And he that smiteth a beast shall pay for it, and he that smiteth a man shall be put to death,'* this[7] speaks[8] of the death penalty?[9]—Is it this *'smiting'; he that smiteth a beast shall pay for it: life for life* and next to it [comes] *And if a man cause a blemish in his neighbour, as he hath done so shall it be done to him?*[10] But here [the term] *'smiting'* is not mentioned![11]—We mean[12] the *effect* of *'smiting'*.[13] But this verse refers to one who injures his fellow, and one who injures his fellow has to pay damages?[14]—It if does not refer to a *'smiting'* in which there is the value of a *peruṭah*,[15] refer it[16] to a smiting in which there is

(1) The payment of money. (2) Between *he that smiteth a beast* and *he that smiteth a man;* v. *supra.* (3) A *Gezerah shawah* v. Glos. The word *'wicked'* occurs in Num. XXXV, 31 (in the case of the death penalty) and in Deut. XXV, 2 (in the case of the penalty of the lashes), and therefore an analogy is drawn between the two cases. (4) [Raba disapproves of this double analogy, but assumes that those who are liable to lashes are in every case exempt from payment directly from *'he that smiteth a beast'* and not by means of the analogy between them and those liable to the death penalty.] (5) Lit., 'if to say'. (6) Lev. XXIV, 21. (7) The second half of the verse. (8) Lit., 'is written'. (9) And offers no basis of deduction for the penalty of lashes. (10) Lev. XXIV, 19. This is taken to mean: he shall receive the lashes; v. *infra.* (11) It does not say in this verse 'If a man smiteth his neighbour'. It says *'If a man cause a blemish in his neighbour'.* (12) 'We speak of'. (13) To cause a blemish means to smite. And the smiter has to be smitten, that is, he has to receive the lashes. (14) But he does not receive lashes. (15) V. *infra 32b.* (16) I.e., the words *'so shall it be done to him'.*

not the value of a *peruṭah*.[1] [35b] Anyhow, he is not liable to pay damages?[2]—It necessarily [speaks of a case] where, while he smote him, he tore his silk garment.[3]

R. Ḥiyya said to Raba: And according to the Tanna of the school of Hezekiah, who says: [It is written] '*He that smiteth a man ... He that smiteth a beast*' [etc.,][4]—whence does he know that it[5] refers to a week-day and there is no distinction to be made?[6] Perhaps it refers to the Sabbath, [in which case] there is a distinction to be made with regard to the beast itself?[7]—This cannot be,[8] for it is written: '*And he that smiteth a beast shall pay for it; and he that smiteth a man shall be put to death.*' How shall we imagine this case? If they did not warn him, why should he, if he killed a man, be put to death? Hence it is clear that they warned him,[9] and if [it happened] on a Sabbath would he, if he smote a beast, pay for it?[10] Therefore it can only refer to[11] a week-day.[12]

R. Papa said to Abaye: According to Rabbah, who says [that] the Torah has instituted something novel in the matter of fines and [therefore] he pays although he is killed[13]—according to whom does he put our Mishnah? If according to R. Meir,[14] [the law

(1) And in this case he receives lashes and the analogy with '*he that smiteth a beast*' serves to teach, on the view of Resh Laḳish, that there is no payment even where, for one cause or another, there is no infliction of lashes. (2) Because the damages do not amount to a *peruṭah*. The verse thus affords no basis of deduction for the ruling of Resh Laḳish. (3) There the analogy is required, and we are taught that he is liable to lashes for the injury he inflicted and is free from paying for the silk garments even if the lashes are not actually inflicted (4) V. p. 191 and notes, (5) Lev. XXIV, 21. (6) Between 'inadvertently' and 'wilfully'; but there is in every case liability to payment. (7) Payment would be due only if he killed it inadvertently. If he killed it wilfully he would be liable to the death penalty on account of the desecration of the Sabbath and he would thus be free from the money payment. (8) Lit., 'this does not enter your mind'. It cannot be assumed that the verse refers to the offence having been committed on Sabbath and inadvertently. (9) I.e., he killed him wilfully. (10) Where he killed it wilfully. Surely not, seeing that he is liable to death! (11) Lit., 'but is it not?' (12) Where no distinction is made between wilful and inadvertent killing of a beast and the same absence of distinction applies *mutatis mutandis* to him who kills a man. (13) *Supra* 34b. (14) Who holds that the lesser penalty is not merged in the greater, v. *supra* 34b.

regarding] his daughter is difficult;[1] if according to R. Neḥunia b. ha-Ḳana,[2] [the law regarding] his sister is difficult;[3] [and] if according to R. Isaac[4] [the law regarding] a *mamzereth* is difficult?[5] It would be alright if he would hold like R. Joḥanan,[6] [for] he would [then] explain it[7] like R. Joḥanan.[6] But if he holds like Resh Laḳish[8] how can he explain it?[9]—He [therefore], of necessity, holds like R. Joḥanan.

R. Mattena said to Abaye: According to Resh Laḳish who says that the Torah has expressly included those who commit an act punishable with lashes to be as those who commit an act punishable with death[10]—who is the Tanna, who differs from R. Neḥunia b. ha-Ḳana?[11] It is either R. Meir[12] or R. Isaac.[13]

Our Rabbis taught: All forbidden relations and all relations forbidden in the second degree have no claim[14] to fine [for outrage][15] or to indemnity for seduction.

A woman who refuses [her husband] by *mi'un*[16] has no claim to fine [for outrage] or to indemnity for seduction. [In this case] a barren woman has no claim to fine for outrage or to indemnity for seduction. And a woman who has gone out[17] on account of an

(1) Why should there be no fine in the case of 'his daughter', (*infra* 36b). (2) Who agrees with R. Meir with regard to lashes but not with regard to *kareth*. (3) Why does our Mishnah impose a fine in the case of 'his sister' which is subject to *kareth*? (4) Who holds that offenders liable to *kareth* are not subject to lashes, v. Mak. 14a. (5) Why should there be a fine in this case which is subject to lashes. (6) That our Mishnah deals with a case where there was no warning and hence no infliction of lashes, v. *supra* 32b and 34b. (7) Our Mishnah. (8) That even where no lashes are actually inflicted, since there is a liability to lashes, there is no payment. V. *supra*. 34b. (9) Our Mishnah. (10) So that there is no payment even if the offence was committed unwittingly. (11) V. *supra* 30a. This Tanna would not exempt offenders liable to *kareth* from payments which would be in accord with our Mishnah which imposes a fine in the case of his sister—an offence involving *kareth*. (12) Who does not exempt from payment on account of the penalty of lashes, and thus although there are also lashes in the case of a sister, there is no exemption from the fine, v. *supra* 32b. (13) V. *supra* note 4. He will consequently hold that an offence with his sister is limited to *kareth* and does not carry with it any lashes and therefore no exemption from the fine. (14) Lit., 'there is not to them'. (15) Deut. XXII, 28, 29. (16) V. Glos. (17) I.e., who had to leave her husband.

evil name,[1] has no claim to fine for outrage or to indemnity for seduction. What are 'forbidden relations' and what are 'relations forbidden in the second degree'? Shall I say [that] 'forbidden relations' [36a] are really forbidden relations[2] and prohibitions of the second degree [are those relations which were forbidden] by the Rabbis?[3] Why should the latter not receive the fine since they are fit for him Biblically?—But, forbidden relations are those with regard to which one is liable to the penalty of death at the hand of the Court,[4] prohibitions of the second degree are those with regard to which there is *kareth*;[5] but in the case of prohibitions with regard to which one trespasses a plain prohibitory law,[6] they receive the fine. And whose opinion is it? [It is that of] Simeon the Temanite.[6] Some say: 'Forbidden relations' are those with regard to which one is liable to the penalty of death at the hand of the Court or *kareth*, 'prohibitions of the second degree' are those with regard to which one transgresses a plain prohibitory law. Whose opinion is this? That of R. Simeon b. Menassia.[6]

[It is said above:][7] A woman who refuses her husband by *mi'un* has no claim to fine [for outrage] or to indemnity for seduction. But any other minor has a claim [to the fine]. Whose opinion would this be? That of the Rabbis, who say: A minor receives the fine.[8] Read now the other clause: 'A barren woman has no claim to fine [for outrage] or to indemnity for seduction'. This is according to R. Meir, who says: The minor does not receive the fine; and this one came from her state as minor into the state of womanhood.[9] The first clause would then be according to the Rabbis and the last clause according to R. Meir? And if you would say that all of it is according to R. Meir, but in the case of the woman who refuses her husband by *mi'un* he holds like R. Judah[10]—does he indeed hold the view [of R. Judah]? Has it not been taught: Until

(1) Presumably with reference to Deut. XXII, 13ff. (2) Those forbidden in Lev. XVIII. (3) Lit., 'the Scribes', v. Yeb. 21a. (4) V. Lev. XX. (5) V. Lev. XVIII. (6) V. *supra* 29b. (7) *Supra* 35b. (8) V. *supra* 29a. (9) Without having been in the state of *na'arah*, since she did not have the signs of maidenhood. And only a *na'arah* receives the fine. (10) That a maiden can exercise the right of *mi'un*, v. *infra*.

when can the daughter exercise the right of *mi'un?* Until she grows two hairs[1]—[these are] the words of R. Meir. R. Judah says: Until the black is more than the white?[2]—But it is according to R. Judah,[3] and with regard to a minor he holds like R. Meir,[4] But does he[5] hold this view?[6] Did not Rab Judah say [that] Rab said: 'These are the words of R. Meir'?[7] Now if it had been so,[8] he ought to have said: 'These are the words of R. Meir and R. Judah'?—This Tanna[9] holds according to R. Meir in one thing[10] and differs from him in one thing.[11] Rafram said: What is meant by 'a woman who refuses her husband by *mi'un'?* One who is entitled to refuse.[12] Let him then teach[13] 'a minor'?—This is indeed difficult.

[It is said above:] 'A barren woman has no claim to fine [for outrage] or to indemnity for seduction'. A contradiction was raised against this: A woman who is a deaf-mute, or an idiot, or barren, has a claim to fine [for outrage], and a suit can be brought [by her husband] against her concerning her virginity. What contradiction is there? The one [Baraitha][14] is according to R. Meir[15] and the other [Baraitha] is according to the Rabbis! But he who raised the question, how could he raise it at all?[16]—He wanted to raise another contradiction: Against a woman who is a deaf-mute, or an idiot, or has reached maturity,[17] or lost her virginity through an accident, no suit can be brought concerning her virginity; against a woman who is blind or barren, a suit can be brought concerning her virginity. Symmachus says in the name of R. Meir: Against a blind woman a suit cannot be brought concerning her virginity!—Said R. Shesheth: This is not difficult: the

(1) The signs of puberty, i.e., as long as she is a minor. (2) I.e., after she has reached the state of *na'arah*, the growth of the hair having advanced. This shews that R. Meir does not agree with R. Judah in the matter of *mi'un*. (3) According to R. Judah the Baraitha can deal with a *na'arah*. (4) That she has no claim to fine; hence the ruling with regard to a naturally barren woman, v. *supra* p. 195, n. 9, (5) R. Judah. (6) Of R. Meir. (7) V. *infra* 40*b*. (8) As it has just now been said. (9) Of the Baraitha, cited *supra*. (10) That a minor has no claim to fine. (11) With regard to *mi'un*. (12) I.e., a minor. The whole Baraitha would then be according to R. Meir. (13) I.e., state expressly. (14) The former Baraitha. (15) That a minor has no claim and similarly a naturally barren woman, cf. n. 4. (16) The answer being so obvious. (17) A *bogereth*, v. Glos.

one [Baraitha] is according to R. Gamaliel and the other [Baraitha] is according to R. Joshua.[1] [But] say when does R. Gamaliel hold this view?[2] When she pleads;[3] but does he hold this view when she does not plead—Yes, since R. Gamaliel holds that she is believed, [we apply], in a case like this, [the verse], *Open thy mouth for the dumb.*[4]

'And against a woman who has reached maturity, one cannot bring a suit concerning her virginity.' Did not Rab say: To a woman who has reached maturity one gives the [whole] first night?[5] [36*b*]—If he raises the complaint with regard to the bleeding,[6] it is really so;[7] here we treat of a case where he raises the complaint of the 'open door'.[8]

[It is said above:] 'Symmachus says in the name of R. Meir: Against a blind woman a suit cannot be brought concerning her virginity'. What is the reason of Symmachus?—R. Zera said: 'because she may have struck against the ground'.[9] All the others[10] may also have struck against the ground?[11] All the others see it[12] and show it to their mothers,[13] this one does not see it and does not shew it to her mother.[14]

[It is said above]:[15] 'And a woman who goes out because of an evil name has no claim to fine [for outrage] and to indemnity for seduction'. A woman who goes out because of an evil name is

(1) V. *supra* 12*b*. According to R. Gamaliel's view, since the woman is believed on saying that she was violated after betrothal, in the case of a deaf-mute we admit this plea on her behalf and *mutatis mutandis* on the view of R. Joshua, v. *infra*. (2) That she is believed. (3) That she was forced after betrothal. (4) Prov. XXXI, 8. I.e., the Court pleads what she could have pleaded. (5) For intercourse. We assume that any bleeding that may proceed is not due to menstruation but to virginity, V. Nid. 64*b*. And this would shew that she has virginity. (6) I.e., the lack of it. (7) He is entitled to raise this complaint. (8) V. *supra* 9*a*. This complaint cannot be raised against a *bogereth*. (9) And thus lost her virginity. (10) All other girls. Lit., 'all of them'. (11) And yet a suit can be brought against them concerning their virginity. (12) I.e., notice the accidental loss of their virginity. (13) And it is known that the virginity is lost by accident and no claim arises concerning the virginity at their marriage. And if no accidental loss was made known the claim concerning virginity does arise. (14) But the accidental loss may have happened all the same. Therefore there is no virginity claim against a blind woman. (15) V. *supra* 35*b*.

liable to be stoned?[1]—R. Shesheth said: He[2] means it thus: if an evil name has gone out concerning her in her childhood[3] she has no claim to fine [for outrage] or to indemnity for seduction. R. Papa said: Infer from this [that] one does not collect [a debt] with an unsound document. How shall we imagine this case? If to say that a rumour has gone out that the document is forged, and similarly here that a rumour has gone out that she has been unchaste?—Did not Raba say [that] if the rumour has gone out in the town [that] she is unchaste one does not pay any attention to it?[4]—But [the case is that] two [persons] came and said [that] she asked them to commit with her a transgression[5] and similarly here [that] two [persons] came and said [that] he[6] said to them: Forge me [the document]. It is all right there,[7] since there are many unrestrained men.[8] But here[9]—if he[10] has been established,[11] have [therefore] all Israelites been established?[12]—Here also, since he[13] was going round searching for a forgery, I can say [that] he [himself] has forged it and written it.[14]

*MISHNAH. AND[15] IN THE FOLLOWING CASES NO FINE[16] IS INVOLVED: IF A MAN HAD INTERCOURSE WITH A FEMALE PROSELYTE, A FEMALE CAPTIVE OR A BONDWOMAN, WHO WAS RANSOMED, PROSELYTIZED OR MANUMITTED AFTER THE AGE OF[17] THREE YEARS AND A DAY.[18] R. JUDAH RULED:

(*) *The translation from here to the end of the Tractate is by the Rev. Dr. I. W. Slotki.*

(1) Cf. Deut. XXII, 20, 21. (2) The Tanna. (3) Before she was betrothed. (4) V. Giṭ. 89*b*. And the same would apply to the document. (5) To have intercourse with her. (6) The alleged creditor. (7) In the case of the woman. (8) Since she solicited two men she might have solicited other men with more success. (9) In the case of the document. (10) The alleged creditor. (11) As a forger. (12) As forgers. He may therefore not have found men who would sign a forged document. (13) The alleged creditor. (14) I.e., forged the signatures of the witnesses. (15) Cf. the previous Mishnah, *supra* 29*a*. (16) Lit., 'they have no fine', *sc.* of fifty *shekels*. (cf. Deut. XXII, 29). (17) Lit., 'more than'. (18) An age when intercourse is possible, and girls in the circumstances mentioned are likely to have succumbed to temptation or violence.

IF A FEMALE CAPTIVE WAS RANSOMED SHE IS DEEMED TO BE IN HER VIRGINITY[1] EVEN IF SHE BE OF AGE.

A MAN WHO HAD INTERCOURSE WITH HIS DAUGHTER, HIS DAUGHTER'S DAUGHTER, HIS SON'S DAUGHTER, HIS WIFE'S DAUGHTER, HER SON'S DAUGHTER OR HER DAUGHTER'S DAUGHTER INCURS NO FINE,[2] BECAUSE HE FORFEITS HIS LIFE, THE DEATH PENALTIES OF SUCH TRANSGRESSORS BEING[3] IN THE HANDS OF BETH DIN, AND HE WHO FORFEITS HIS LIFE PAYS NO MONETARY FINE FOR IT IS SAID IN SCRIPTURE, AND YET NO HARM FOLLOW HE SHALL BE SURELY FINED.[4]

GEMARA. R. Joḥanan said: Both R. Judah and R. Dosa taught the same thing. As to R. Judah [we have the ruling] just mentioned. As to R. Dosa?—It was taught: A female captive[5] may eat *terumah*;[6] so R. Dosa. 'What after all is it', said R. Dosa, 'that that Arab[7] has done to her? Has he rendered her unfit to be a priest's wife merely because he squeezed her between her breasts?'[8]

Said Raba:[9] Is it not possible that there is really no [agreement between them]?[10] R. Judah may have laid down his ruling[11] here[12] only in order that the sinner may gain no advantage,[13] but there[14] he may hold the same opinion as the Rabbis;[15] or else: [May not]

(1) Lit., 'behold she is in her sanctity'. (2) Lit., 'they have no fine'. (3) Lit., 'because their death'. (4) Ex. XXI, 22; from which it may be inferred that if '*harm*' (i.e., death) follows no monetary fine is incurred. (5) Who was the daughter or wife of a priest. (6) Because she is not suspected of intercourse with her captors. A seduced or violated woman is regarded as a harlot who is forbidden to a priest (cf. Lev. XXI, 7) and is, therefore, also ineligible to eat *terumah*. (7) *Sc.* her captor. Arabs were ill-famed for their carnal indulgence (v. Ḳid. 49*b* and Tosaf. s.v. וכי *a.l.*). (8) Giṭ. 81*a*; cf. 'Ed. III, 6. Captors, R. Dosa maintains, only play about with their captives but do not violate them. (9) So MS.M. Cur. edd., 'Rabbah'. Cf. Tosaf. *supra* 11*a* s.v. אביי and *infra* 37*a* s.v. אמר רבה. (10) R. Judah and R. Dosa. (11) That a ransomed captive retains the status of virgin and consequently is entitled to a fine from her seducer. (12) In our Mishnah. (13) By an exemption from the statutory fine (cf. *supra* p. 198, n. 16). (14) In the case of *terumah* cited from Giṭ. 81*a*. (15) That a female captive is forbidden to a priest and is ineligible to eat *terumah*.

R. Dosa have laid down his ruling[1] only there[2] [where it concerns] *terumah* which [at the present time is only] a Rabbinical enactment,[3] but in the case of a fine which is a Pentateuchal law[4] he may well hold the same view as the Rabbis?[5]

Abaye answered him: Is R. Judah's reason here[6] 'that the sinner may gain no advantage'? Surely it was taught: R. Judah ruled, 'If a female captive was ransomed[7] she is deemed to be in her virginity,[8] and even if she is ten years old her *kethubah* is two hundred[9] *zuz*'.[10] Now how[11] [could the reason] 'that the sinner shall gain no advantage' apply[12] there?[13]—There also [a good reason exists for R. Judah's ruling, since otherwise[14] men][15] would abstain from marrying her.[16]

Could R. Judah, however, maintain the view [that a female captive] retains the status of a virgin[17] when in fact, it was taught: A man who ransoms a female captive may marry her, but he who gives evidence on her behalf[18] may not marry her,[19] and R. Judah ruled: In either case he[19] may not marry her![20]

(1) That a captive retains her status of chastity and may eat *terumah* if she is a priest's wife or daughter. (2) V. p. 199, n. 14. (3) Pentateuchally even a woman whose seduction was a certainty is permitted to eat such *terumah*. Hence no prohibition was imposed even in Rabbinic law where seduction is doubtful. (4) And subject to greater restrictions. (5) The first Tanna of our Mishnah. (6) In our Mishnah. (7) שנפדית, so MS.M. Cur. edd., שנשבית, 'was taken captive', is difficult. (8) Cf. *supra* p. 199, n. 1. (9) The statutory sum to which a virgin is entitled. A widow is entitled to one hundred *zuz* only. (10) Tosef. Keth. III. (11) Lit., 'what'. (12) Lit., 'there is'. (13) Where the husband had committed no sin. Now since this reason is here inapplicable and R. Judah nevertheless gives the captive the status of a virgin, it follows, as R. Johanan has laid down *supra*, that R. Judah maintains his view in all cases including, of course, that of *terumah* also. (14) I.e., if the captive were only allowed a *kethubah* of one hundred *zuz*. (15) On learning that her *kethubah* was not the one given to a virgin, and suspecting, therefore, that she had been seduced. (16) As such a reason, however, is inapplicable to *terumah* R. Judah, as Raba had suggested, may well be of the same opinion as the Rabbis. (17) Cf. *supra* p. 199, n. 1. (18) That she had not been seduced. (19) If he is a priest (cf. *supra* p. 199, n. 6). (20) Tosef. Yeb. IV; which proves that a female captive does lose her status of virginity. How then could R. Judah maintain in our Mishnah and in the Baraitha cited from Tosef. Keth. III that she retains the status of a virgin?

Is not this,[1] however, self-contradictory? You said, 'A man who ransoms a female captive may marry her', and then it is stated, 'He[2] who gives evidence on her behalf may not marry her'; shall he[3] not marry her [it may well be asked] because he gives also evidence on her behalf?—This is no difficulty. It is this that was meant: A man who ransoms a female captive and gives evidence on her behalf may marry her,[4] but he who merely gives evidence on her behalf may not marry her.[5]

In any case, however, does not the contradiction against R. Judah remain?[6]—R. Papa replied: Read, 'R. Judah ruled: In either case he may marry her'.

R. Huna the son of R. Joshua replied: [The reading may] still be as it was originally given,[7] but R. Judah was speaking to the Rabbis in accordance with their own ruling. 'According to my view[8] [he argued] the man may marry her in either case; but according to your view[9] it should have been laid down that in either case he may not marry her'.

And the Rabbis?[10]—'A man who ransoms a captive and gives evidence on her behalf may marry her' because no one would throw money away for nothing,[11] but 'he who merely gives evidence on her behalf may not marry her' because he may have fallen in love with her.[12]

R. Papa b. Samuel pointed out the following contradiction to R. Joseph: [37*a*] Could R. Judah hold the view that [a female

(1) The Baraitha just cited from Tosef. Yeb. (2) Implying presumably anyone, even the man who ransomed her. (3) The man who ransomed the captive and who in such circumstances is permitted to marry her. (4) Because no man would spend money on the ransom of a captive with the object of marrying her unless he was convinced of her chastity. (5) In the absence of any special effort on his part to ransom the woman while she was captive he is suspected of tendering false evidence in a desire to gratify his passions. (6) V. *supra* p. 200, n. 20. (7) I.e., that R. Judah ruled: 'He may not marry her'. (8) That a captive retains her status of chastity. (9) That a captive loses the status of a virgin. (10) On what grounds do they draw a distinction between the man who ransoms a captive and the one who only tenders evidence in her favour? (11) Cf. *supra* note 4. (12) Lit., 'put his eyes on her'. Cf. *supra* note 5.

captive] is deemed to have retained her virginity[1] when it was, in fact, taught, 'If a woman proselyte discovered [some menstrual] blood[2] on [the day of] her conversion it is sufficient, R. Judah ruled, [to reckon her Levitical uncleanness from] the time she [discovered it].[3] R. Jose ruled: She is subject to the same laws[4] as all other women[5] and, therefore, causes uncleanness [retrospectively] for twenty-four hours,[6] or [for the period] intervening between[7] [her last] examination and[7] [her previous] examination.[8] She must also wait[9] three months;[10] so R. Judah, but R. Jose permits her to be betrothed and married at once'?[11] — The other replied: You are pointing out a contradiction between a proselyte and a captive [who belong to totally different categories, since] a proselyte does not protect her honour while a captive does protect her honour.

A contradiction, however, was also pointed out between two rulings in relation to a captive.[12] For it was taught: Proselytes,[13] captives[13] or slaves[13] who were ransomed, or proselytized, or were manumitted, must wait three months[14] if they were older than three years and one day; so R. Judah. R. Jose permits immediate betrothal and marriage.[15] [The other] remained silent. 'Have you', he said to him, 'heard anything on the subject?' — 'Thus', the former replied, 'said R. Shesheth: [This is a case] where people saw that the captive was seduced'. If so[16] what could be R. Jose's reason? — Rabbah replied: R. Jose is of the opinion that a woman

(1) Cf. *supra* p. 199, n. 1. (2) Only the menstrual blood of an Israelite woman or of one who was converted to the Jewish faith causes Levitical uncleanness. (3) I.e., only such objects are deemed to be Levitically unclean as have been touched by her after, but not before her discovery. (4) Lit., 'behold she'. (5) Of the Jewish faith. (6) מעת לעת, lit., 'from time to time'. (7) Lit., 'from . . . to'. (8) Whichever period is the less; v. 'Ed. I, 1. (9) After her conversion. (10) Before she is permitted to marry; in order to make sure that she was not with child prior to her conversion. (11) From which Baraitha it follows that R. Judah suspects illicit intercourse, contrary to the statement attributed to him in our Mishnah that a captive is presumed to protect her chastity. (12) Lit., 'captive on captive'. (13) In the original the noun appears in the sing. (14) Cf. notes 9 and 10 *mutatis mutandis*. (15) V. l.c. n. 11. (16) That there is definite evidence against her chastity.

who plays the harlot makes use of an absorbent in order to prevent conception. This[1] is intelligible in the case of a proselyte, who, since her intention is to proselytize, is careful.[2] It[1] is likewise [intelligible in the case of] a captive [who is also careful][2] since she does not know whither they would take her.[3] It[1] is similarly [intelligible in the case of] a bondwoman [who might also be careful][2] when she hears from her master.[4] What, however, can be said in the case of one who is liberated on account of the loss of a tooth or an eye?[5] And were you to suggest that R. Jose did not speak[6] of an unexpected occurrence,[7] [it might be retorted,] there is the case of a woman who was outraged or seduced[8] which may happen unexpectedly and yet it was taught: A woman who has been outraged or seduced must wait three months; so R. Judah, but R. Jose permits immediate betrothal and marriage![9]—The fact, however, is, said Rabbah,[10] that R. Jose is of the opinion that a woman who plays the harlot turns over in order to prevent conception.[11] And the other?[12]—There is the apprehension that she might not have turned over properly.[13]

FOR IT IS SAID IN SCRIPTURE, AND YET NO HARM FOLLOW HE SHALL BE SURELY FINED etc. Is, however, the deduction[14] made from this text?[15] Is it not in fact made from the following

(1) Rabbah's explanation. (2) To have an absorbent in readiness in order to avoid conception and the mixing of legitimate, with illegitimate children. Lit., 'she protects herself'. (3) She makes provision (cf. preceding note) against the possibility of being sold to an Israelite master who might set her free. (4) Of her impending liberation. (5) Cf. Ex. XXI, 26f. The bondwoman, surely, could not know beforehand that such an accident would occur. (6) I.e., did not maintain his ruling that a period of three months must be allowed to pass. (7) Lit., 'of itself', when, as in the case of the loss of a tooth or an eye, the woman was not likely to have been possessed of an absorbent. (8) [Rashi does not seem to have read 'seduced' which appears here irrelevant; v. marginal Glosses.] (9) Which shows that even when the unexpected happens R. Jose requires no waiting period. (10) The reading in the parallel passage (Yeb. 35a) is 'Abaye'. (11) No absorbent is needed. Similarly in the case of a liberated captive or slave. Hence the ruling of R. Jose that no waiting period is required. (12) Why does he require a waiting period. (13) And conception might have taken place. (14) That one who suffers the death penalty is exempt from a monetary fine. (15) Lit., 'from here' *sc.* Ex. XXI, 22, cited in our Mishnah.

text:[1] *According to the measure of his crime,*[2] [which implies][3] you make him liable to a penalty[4] for one crime, but you cannot make him liable [at the same time] for two crimes?[5]—One [text[6] deals] with [the penalties of] death and money and the other[7] with [the penalties of] flogging and money.

And [both texts[8] were] needed. For if we had been told [only of that which deals with the penalties of] death and money[6] it might have been assumed [that the restriction[9] applied only to the death penalty] because it involves loss of life,[10] but not [to the penalties of] flogging and money where no loss of life is involved. And if we had been told only of flogging and money[7] it might have been assumed [that the restriction[9] applied only to flogging] because the transgression for which flogging is inflicted[11] is not very grave,[12] but not [to the penalties of] death and money where the transgression for which the death penalty is imposed[11] is very grave.[13] [Hence it was] necessary [to have both texts].

According to R. Meir, however, who ruled: 'A man may be flogged and also ordered to pay',[14] what need was there for the two texts?[15]—One[16] deals with the penalties of death and money [37*b*] and the other[17] with those of death and flogging. And [both texts[15] were] needed. For if we had been told [only of that which deals with the penalties of] death and money[16] it might have been assumed [that the restriction[18] applied to these two penalties only] because we must not inflict one penalty upon one's body and another upon one's possessions, but in the case of death and flogging, both of which are inflicted on one's body, it might have been assumed [that the flogging] is deemed to be [but] one pro-

(1) Lit., 'from there'. (2) Deut. XXV, 2, A.V. '*fault*', R.V. '*wickedness*'. (3) Since the text makes use of the sing. (4) Flogging, spoken of in the text cited. (5) By the imposition of two forms of punishment. V. *supra* 32*b* and B.Ḳ. 83*b*, Mak. 4*b*, 13*b*. (6) Deut. XXI, 22. (7) Deut. XXV, 2. (8) V. preceding notes. (9) To one penalty. (10) The punishment being so severe it alone is sufficient. (11) Lit., 'its transgression'. (12) It is sufficient, therefore, if only one penalty is inflicted. (13) And two penalties might well have been regarded as a proper measure of justice. (14) *Supra* 33*b*. The second text, therefore, cannot be applied as suggested. (15) V. *supra* notes 6 and 7. (16) Deut. XXI, 22. (17) Deut. XXV, 2. (18) To one penalty.

tracted death penalty and both may, therefore, be inflicted upon one man.[1] And if we had been told about death and flogging only [the restriction[2] might have been assumed to apply to these penalties only] because no two corporal punishments may be inflicted on the same person, but in the case of the penalties of death and money one of which is corporal and the other monetary it might have been assumed that both may be inflicted.[3] [Both texts were, therefore,] necessary.

What need was there[4] for the Scriptural text, *Moreover ye shall take no ransom for the life of a murderer?*[5]—The All-Merciful has here stated: You shall take no monetary fine from him and thus *exempt* him from the death penalty.

What was the need[6] for the Scriptural text, *And ye shall take no ransom for him that is fled to his city of refuge?*[7]—The All-Merciful has here stated: You shall take no monetary fine from him to *exempt* him from exile.[8]

But why two texts?[9]—One deals with unwitting, and the other with intentional [murder]. And [both texts] were required. For if we had been told[10] of intentional murder[11] only it might have been assumed [that the restriction[10] applied to this case only], because the transgression for which death is inflicted[12] is grave,[13] but not to the one of unintentional murder where the transgression is not so grave. And if we had been told[14] of unintentional murder[15] only it might have been assumed [that the restriction[14] applied to this

(1) Lit., 'and we shall do on him'. (2) To one penalty. (3) V. note 1. (4) Since it has been laid down that no monetary fine may be imposed upon one who suffers the death penalty. (5) Num. XXXV, 31. It is now assumed that כופר (E.V. *ransom*) signified 'a monetary fine' that is imposed upon the murderer *in addition* to his major penalty. (6) Since no monetary fine may be imposed upon one who is flogged, much less upon one who must flee to a city of refuge. *Aliter:* Since a monetary fine is not imposed upon a murderer. Cf. תוספות ישנים and Tosaf. s.v. לא *a.l.* (7) Num. XXXV, 32. Cf. *supra* n. 3. (8) *Sc.* the fleeing to a city of refuge. (9) Num. XXXV, 31 (death and money) and ibid. 32 (exile and money). As both deal with murder, could not the lesson of the one be deduced from the other? (10) That no ransom may be substituted for the death penalty. (11) Num. XXXV, 31. (12) Lit., 'its transgression'. (13) And a monetary fine is no adequate punishment. (14) Cf. *supra* note 10, *mutatis mutandis*. (15) Num. XXXV, 32.

case only] because no loss of life is involved,[1] but not to intentional murder where a loss of life[2] is involved.[3] [Both texts were consequently] required.

What was the object[4] of the Scriptural text, *And no expiation can be made for the land for the blood that is shed therein, but by the blood of him that shed it?*[5]—It was required for [the following deduction] as it was taught: Whence is it deduced that, if the murderer has been discovered after the heifer's neck had been broken,[6] he is not to be acquitted?[7] From the Scriptural text, '*And no expiation can be made for the land for the blood that is shed therein* etc.'[8]

Then what was the need[9] for the text, *So shalt thou put away the innocent blood from the midst of thee?*[10]—It is required for [the following deduction] as it was taught: Whence is it deduced that execution by the sword[11] must be at the neck? It was explicitly stated in Scripture, '*So shalt thou put away the innocent blood from the midst of thee*', all who shed blood are compared to the atoning heifer:[12] As its head is cut[13] at the neck[14] so [is the execution of] those who shed blood at the neck.[15] If [so, should not the comparison be carried further]: As there[16] [its head is cut] with an axe and at the nape of the neck so here[17] too?—R. Naḥman answered in the name of Rabbah b. Abbuha: Scripture said, *But thou shalt love thy neighbour as thyself,*[18] choose for him an easy death.[19]

What need was there[20] for the Scriptural text, *None devoted, that may be devoted of men, shall be ransomed?*[21]—It is required for [the

(1) The murderer's punishment being exile only. (2) The penalty being death. (3) And it might have been presumed that in order to save a human life ransom was allowed to be substituted. (4) In view of Num. XXXV, 31 which forbids ransom to be substituted for capital punishment. (5) Num. XXXV, 33. (6) V. Deut. XXI, 1ff. (7) Though the heifer atones for the people if the murderer is unknown. (8) V. Soṭ. 47*b*. (9) In view of the text of Num. XXXV, 33 and the deduction just made. (10) Deut. XXI, 9, forming the conclusion of the section dealing with the ceremony of the 'atoning heifer' (v. note 12). (11) Lit., 'those executed by the sword'. (12) עגלה ערופה, lit., 'the heifer whose neck was broken'. (13) Lit., 'there'. (14) V. Deut. XXI, 4. (15) Sanh. 52*b*. (16) In the case of the atoning heifer. (17) The execution of a murderer. (18) Lev. XIX, 18. (19) Pes. 75*a*, Sanh. 52*b* and 45*a*. (20) Cf. *supra* note 9. (21) The conclusion is *He shall surely be put to death*. Lev. XXVII, 29.

following] as it was taught: Whence is it deduced that, when a person was being led to his execution,[1] and someone said, 'I vow to give his value[2] [to the Temple],' his vow is null and void?[3] [From Scripture] wherein it is said, *'None devoted, that may be devoted of man, shall be redeemed'*.[4] As it might [have been presumed that the same law applied] even before his sentence had been pronounced[5] it was explicitly stated: *'Of men'*,[6] but not *'all* men'.[7]

According to R. Hanania b. 'Akabia, however, who ruled that the [age] value of such a person[8] may be vowed[9] because its price is fixed,[10] what deduction does he[11] make from the text of *'None devoted'?*[12]—He requires it for [the following deduction] as it was taught: R. Ishmael the son of R. Johanan b. Beroka said, Whereas we find that those who incur the penalty of death at the hand of heaven[13] may pay a monetary fine and thereby obtain atonement, for it is said in Scripture, *If there be laid down on him a sum of money,*[14] it might [have been assumed that] the same law applied also [to those who are sentenced to death] at the hands of men,[15] hence it was explicitly stated in the Scriptures, *'None . . . devoted*[16] *of men shall be redeemed'*. Thus we know the law only concerning[17] severe death penalties[18] since [they are imposed for offences] which cannot

(1) Lit., 'goes out to be killed'. (2) Lit., 'his valuation upon me'. Cf. Lev. XXVII, 2ff. (3) Lit., 'he said nothing'. (4) Since his life is forfeited his value is nil. (5) Lit., 'his judgment was concluded'. (6) I.e., 'a part of a man', 'an incomplete one', viz. one sentenced to death. (7) I.e., 'a full man', 'one whose life is still in his own hands', viz. a man still on trial before his sentence of death has been pronounced. (8) Who 'was led to his execution'. (9) Lit., 'he is valued', if the person who made the vow used the expression, 'I vow his *value*' not 'his *life*'. (10) In Lev. XXVII. Though his forfeited *life* has no value, his *age* (according to Lev. XXVII, 3-7) has a fixed legal value; and the vow, since it did not refer to his *life* but his *value*, is interpreted in the Biblical sense and is consequently valid. V. 'Ar. 7b. (11) Who does not apply it to a condemned man. (12) Lit., 'that . . . what does he do to it?' (13) Offenders who are not subject to the jurisdiction of a court of law (v. Sanh. 15b). (14) Ex. XXI, 30. (15) *Sc.* by a sentence of a criminal court. (16) חרם denotes dedication, excommunication and also condemnation to destruction or death. (17) Lit., 'there is not to me but', 'I have only'. (18) For offences committed intentionally.

be atoned for[1] if committed unwittingly;[2] whence, [however, is it inferred that the same law applies also to] lighter death penalties[3] seeing that [they are for offences] that may be atoned for[4] if committed unwittingly?[5] It was explicitly stated in Scripture, '*None devoted*'.[6] But could not this[7] be inferred independently from *Ye shall take no ransom*[8] which implies: You shall take no money from him to exempt him [from death]?[9] What need was there for '*None devoted*'?—Rami b. Ḥama replied: It was required. Since it might have been assumed [38a] that this[7] applied only where murder had been committed[10] in the course of an upward movement,[11] because no atonement[12] is allowed when such an act[13] was committed unwittingly,[14] but that where murder was committed in the course of a downward movement,[11] which [is an offence that] may be atoned for[12] if committed unwittingly,[14] a monetary fine may be received from him and thereby he may be exempted [from the death penalty]. Hence we were taught[15] [that in no circumstances may the death penalty be commuted for a monetary fine].

Said Raba to him,[16] Does not this[17] follow from what a Tanna of the School of Hezekiah [taught]; for a Tanna of the School of Hezekiah taught: *He that smiteth a man*[18] [was placed in juxtaposition with] *And he that smiteth a beast*[18] [to indicate that just] as in the case of the killing of[19] a beast no distinction is made whether [the act was] unwitting or presumptuous, whether intentional or unintentional, whether it was performed in the course of a down-

(1) By a sacrifice. (2) E.g. wounding one's father or stealing a man (V. Ex. XXI, 15f). (3) If they were committed intentionally. (4) By a sacrifice. (5) E.g., idolatry or adultery. (6) 'Ar. 7*b*. (7) That no ransom may be substituted for the death penalty even in the cases of lighter death penalties. (8) Num. XXXV, 31. (9) The death penalty for murder is considered of a lighter character since, the crime, if committed unwittingly, is atoned for by exile. (10) Intentionally. Lit., 'he killed him'. (11) Of the hand, body or instrument. (12) By exile. (13) Murder in the course of an upward movement of the hand or body. (14) V. Mak. 7*b*. (15) By the text, '*None devoted*' from which deduction was made *supra*. (16) Rami b. Ḥama. (17) The deduction from '*None devoted*' that, in the case of murder, the death penalty may not be commuted for a monetary fine irrespective of whether the offence had been committed in the course of an upward, or downward movement. (18) Lev. XXIV, 21. (19) Lit., 'he who kills'.

ward movement or in the course of an upward movement, in respect of exempting him from a monetary obligation[1] but in respect of imposing a monetary obligation[2] upon him,[3] so also in the case of the killing of[4] a man no distinction is to be made whether [the act was] unwitting or presumptuous, whether intentional or unintentional, whether it was performed in the course of a downward movement or in the course of an upward movement, in respect of imposing upon him a monetary obligation[5] but[6] in respect of exempting him from any monetary obligation?[7]—But, said Rami b. Ḥama, [one of the texts[8] was] required [to obviate the following assumption]: It might have been presumed that this[9] applied only where a man blinded another man's eye and thereby killed him, but that where he blinded his eye and killed him[10] by another act a monetary fine must be exacted from him.[11]

Said Raba to him:[12] Is not this[13] also deduced from [the statement of] another Tanna of the School of Hezekiah; for a Tanna of the School of Hezekiah [taught:] *Eye for eye*[14] [implies] but not an eye[15]

(1) Which in relation to the beast was *not* spoken of in the text of Lev. XXIV, 21. (2) Which *was* spoken of in the text ibid. (3) I.e., the man who killed the beast must *in all cases mentioned* pay compensation, and under no circumstance may he evade payment. (4) Lit., 'he too kills'. (5) Of which, in respect of murder, Lev. XXIV, 21 does not speak. (6) Since the text (Lev. XXIV, 21) speaks of the death penalty as the only punishment for murder. (7) V. *supra* 35a, B.Ḳ. 35a, Sanh. 79b. This shews that no distinction is made in the case of murder between a downward movement or an upward movement, but in every case no money payment can be imposed in addition to the major punishment. And the same principle must apply to the non-acceptance of a ransom in substitution for the death penalty. What need was there then for the text of '*None devoted*' (cf. *supra* p. 208, n. 16)? (8) Either '*None devoted*' or '*He that smiteth*' (cf. Rashi). (9) That no monetary penalty may be imposed upon one who is to suffer the death penalty. (10) Simultaneously (v. Rashi). (11) As compensation for the eye, in addition to the death penalty for murder. [For the obvious difficulty involved in this reply of Rami b. Ḥama, which apparently is intended to explain the purpose of the verse '*none devoted*' according to R. Ishmael b. R. Joḥanan b. Beroḳa; v. p. 210, n. 9.] (12) Rami b. Ḥama. (13) That for blinding an eye and thereby killing the man no monetary fine may be imposed in addition to the death penalty. (14) Ex. XXI, 24. (15) I.e., compensation for the loss of an eye.

and a life for an eye?[1]—[This], however, [is the explanation], said R. Ashi: [One of the texts[2] was] required [to obviate the following assumption]: It might have been presumed that since the law of a monetary fine is an anomaly[3] which the Torah has introduced, a man must pay it even though he also suffers the death penalty. Hence we were told[4] [that even a monetary fine may not be imposed in addition to a death penalty].

But according to Rabbah, who said that it is an anomaly[3] that the Torah has introduced by the enactment of the law of a monetary fine [and that therefore an offender][5] must pay his fine even though he is also to be killed,[6] what application can be made of the text '*None devoted* . . .'?[7]—He[8] holds the view of the first Tanna who [is in dispute with] R. Hanania b. 'Akabia.[9]

(1) [From this is derived that the Law could not mean actual retaliation, as there was always the danger of loss of life to the offender while his eye was blinded; and similarly, the phrase '*life for life*' implies, but not an eye and life for a life (Tosaf.)]. B.Ḳ. 84*a*. The deduction from '*He that smiteth*' since it is not needed for this case, must consequently apply to that 'when he blinded his eye and killed him by another act'; and the question arises again: What need was there for one or for the other of the two previously cited texts (v. *supra* p. 209, n. 8)? (2) V. *supra* p. 209, n. 8. (3) חידוש, lit., 'an innovation' *sc.* different from other laws. In many instances it cannot be justified on logical grounds and can only be accepted as a divine law the reason for which is beyond human comprehension. (4) By means of one of the two texts (v. *supra* p. 209, n. 8) which is not required in respect of ordinary monetary payments. (5) If his offence warrants it. (6) *Supra* 34*b*, 35*b*. (7) Which, according to his view, is not required to exclude the case just mentioned (cf. *supra* n. 4). (8) Rabbah. (9) *Supra* 37*b* where deduction is made from this text that a vow to give to the Temple the value of a person who was led to his execution, is null and void. [The whole passage is extremely difficult; v. Tosaf. The main difficulty is presented by the second answer of Rami b. Ḥama, (v. p. 209 ,n. 11). The following may be offered in explanation: To revert to the very beginning of the discussion, the Talmud, assuming that the verse '*you shall take no fine*' denotes that no money payment is to be imposed in addition to a death penalty, asked, what need was there for this verse, in view of the verse '*and yet no harm follow*' (v. p. 205). Thereupon follows the reply that this verse meant to exclude the commutation of the death penalty for money payment. Then the question arises, what need was there for R. Ishmael b. R. Joḥanan b. Beroḳa to resort, for what practically amounts to the same ruling, to the verse '*None devoted*'? To this Rami b. Ḥama, in

MISHNAH. A GIRL[1] WHO WAS BETROTHED AND THEN DIVORCED[2] IS NOT ENTITLED, SAID R. JOSE THE GALILEAN, TO RECEIVE A FINE [FROM HER VIOLATOR].[3] R. AKIBA SAID: SHE IS ENTITLED TO RECEIVE THE FINE AND, MOREOVER, THE FINE BELONGS TO HER.[4]

GEMARA. What is R. Jose the Galilean's reason?[5]—Scripture said, *That is not betrothed*[6] [is entitled to a fine],[7] one, therefore, who was betrothed is not entitled to a fine. And R. Akiba?[8]—[In the case of a girl] *that is not betrothed* [the fine is given] to her father but if she was betrothed [the fine is given] to herself.

Now then, [the expression,] *A damsel*[9] [implies] but not one

his first reply, answers that he needed this latter verse in the case where the murder was committed in a downward course. This reply, however, is rebutted by Raba, as such a contingency is already provided for in the verse *'he that smiteth* etc.' This forces Rami b. Ḥama to fall back on *the original assumption* that the verse *'you shall take no ransom'* comes to teach that no money payment may be imposed in addition to the death penalty; and as to the very first question, what need is there, in view of the verse *'and yet no harm shall follow'* for two verses to teach the same thing?—the reply is: it is necessary to provide for a case where the blinding and the killing result from two separate blows. Raba, however, objected that this contingency too was already provided for. Hence R. Ashi's reply, that the extra verse was required to extend the rule to the case of a *fine* (v. *Shiṭṭah Meḳubbeẓeth, a.l.*). This answer, however, the Talmud did not regard as satisfactory according to Rabbah, who held that a *fine* may be imposed in addition to the death penalty. On his view the verse *'you shall take no ransom'* cannot be taken as referring to the imposition of a money payment in addition to the death penalty. Consequently, he would be forced back on the alternative explanation that it serves to teach that no death penalty may be commuted for money payment and thus the question of *supra* p. 208 'what need is there of "*None devoted*"' remains. To this the answer is, that Rabbah would agree with the first Tanna who is in dispute with R. Hanania b. 'Aḳabia].

(1) *Na'arah*; v. Glos. (2) Had she not been divorced, the offender is put to death and there is consequently no fine. (3) V. Deut. XXII, 29. The reason is stated *infra*. (4) Not to her father. (5) For his ruling in our Mishnah. (6) Deut. XXII, 28. (7) *The man . . . shall give . . . fifty sheḳels* (ibid. 29). (8) How, in view of the Scriptural text cited, can he maintain that SHE IS ENTITLED TO RECEIVE THE FINE? (9) Deut. XXII, 28, Heb. *na'arah*.

who is adolescent;[1] could it here also[2] [be maintained] that [the fine is given] to herself?[3] [Likewise the expression] *virgin*[4] [implies] but not one who is no longer a virgin; would it here also[2] [be maintained] that [the fine is given] to herself?[3] Must it not consequently be admitted[5] [that the exclusion in the last mentioned case] is complete,[6] and so here also[7] it must be complete?[8]—R. Akiba can answer you: The text of[9] *'Not betrothed'* is required for [another purpose],[10] as it was taught: *'That is not betrothed'* excludes a girl[11] that was betrothed and then divorced who has no claim to a fine; so R. Jose the Galilean. R. Akiba, however, ruled: She has a claim to a fine and her fine [is given] to her father.[12] This[13] is arrived at by analogy: Since her father is entitled to have the money of her betrothal[14] and he is also entitled to have the money of her fine[15] [the two payments should be compared to one another]: As the money of her betrothal[16] belongs to her father even after she had been betrothed[17] and divorced,[18] so also the money of her fine should belong to her father even after she had been betrothed and divorced. If so[19] what was the object of the Scriptural text, *'That is not betrothed'?* It is free for the purpose of a comparison with it and an inference from it by means of a *gezerah shawah:*[20] Here[21] it is said, *'That is not betrothed'*

(1) A *bogereth* (v. Glos). (2) Since R. Akiba laid down that the exclusion of a fine that was implied by the text of *'not betrothed'* is restricted to the girl's father but that the girl herself is still entitled to it. (3) But this is absurd, since no such law is anywhere to be found. (4) Deut. XXII, 28. (5) Lit., 'but'. (6) I.e., no fine is paid either to the girl or to her father. (7) The exclusion of which R. Jose the Galilean has spoken. (8) The previous objection against R. Akiba's ruling (cf. *supra* p. 211, n. 8) thus arises again. (9) Lit., 'that'. (10) And is consequently not available for the deduction made by R. Jose the Galilean. (11) V. *supra* p. 211, n. 1. (12) The contradiction between this ruling of R. Akiba and his ruling in our Mishnah is discussed *infra*. (13) That she is entitled to the fine even after she had been betrothed. (14) V. *infra* 46*b*. (15) V. Deut. XXII, 29. (16) I.e., a second betrothal while she was still a damsel (*na'arah*). V. *supra* p. 211, n. 1. (17) To one man. (18) From him and then betrothed to the other man. (19) If one who was betrothed and divorced is also entitled to a fine. (20) V. Glos. (21) In the case of an outrage.

and elsewhere[1] it is said, *That is not betrothed,*[2] as here[3] [the fine is that of] fifty [*silver* coins][4] so is it fifty [silver coins] there[1] also; and as there[1] [the coins must be] *shekels*[5] so here[3] also they must be *shekels*.

What, however, moved[6] R. Akiba [to apply the text] of '*That is not betrothed*'[7] for a *gezerah shawah* and that of '*Virgin*' for the exclusion[8] of one who was no longer a virgin? [38*b*] Might [not one equally well] suggest that '*Virgin*' should be applied for the *gezerah shawah*[9] and '*That is not betrothed*' [should serve the purpose of] excluding[10] a girl[11] that was betrothed and divorced?—It stands to reason [that the text of] '*That is not betrothed*' should be employed for the *gezerah shawah,*[12] since such a girl[11] is still[13] designated, *A damsel that is a virgin.*[14] On the contrary; [should not the expression of] '*Virgin*' be applied for the *gezerah shawah,* since [a non-virgin] may still be described as one '*That is not betrothed*'?[15]—It stands to reason [that R. Akiba's first view[16] is to be preferred, since] the body of the one[17] had undergone a change while that of the other[18] had not.[19]

As to R. Jose the Galilean,[20] whence does he draw that logical inference?[21]—He derives it from the following where it was taught: *He shall pay money according to the dowry of virgins*[22] [implies] that this

(1) In the case of seduction. (2) Ex. XXII, 15. (3) In the case of an outrage. (4) V. Deut. XXII, 29. (5) שקלים. The text (Ex. XXII, 16) reads ישקל (lit., 'shall weigh', E.V. *pay*) which is of the same rt. as שקל (*shekel*). (6) Lit., 'you saw'. (7) Deut. XXII, 28. (8) From the right to a fine. (9) And not, as has been said, to exclude a non-virgin from her right to the fine. (10) From the right to a fine. (11) A *na'arah*. (12) So that even a girl (*na'arah*) who was once betrothed and divorced should be entitled to the fine. (13) Despite her betrothal and divorce. (14) Hence it is quite reasonable that her right to the fine shall not be lost. A non-virgin, however, who is not described as '*a damsel that is a virgin*' justly loses her right to the fine. (15) While a *na'arah* that was once betrothed and divorced and cannot so be described should not be entitled to the fine. (16) That a *na'arah* that was once betrothed and divorced is entitled to the fine and that a non-virgin is not. (17) The non-virgin. (18) Who was betrothed and divorced. (19) Cf. *supra* note 14. (20) Who, unlike R. Akiba, does not use the expression of '*That is not betrothed*' for a *gezerah shawah*. (21) Stated *supra* 38*a* ad fin., that a fine of fifty *shekels* is to be paid both in the case of seduction and that of violation. (22) Ex. XXII, 16, the case of seduction.

[payment] shall be the same sum as the *dowry of the virgins*[1] and the *dowry*[1] *of the virgins* shall be the same as this.[2]

Does not a contradiction arise between the two statements of R. Akiba?[3]—[The respective statements represent the opinions of] two Tannaim who differ as to what was the ruling of R. Akiba.

[The ruling of] R. Akiba in our Mishnah presents no difficulty since the *gezerah shawah* does not altogether deprive the Scriptural text of its ordinary meaning.[4] According to R. Akiba's ruling in the Baraitha, however, does not the *gezerah shawah* completely deprive the Scriptural text of its ordinary meaning?[5]—R. Naḥman b. Isaac replied, Read in the text:[6] *That is not a betrothed maiden.*[7] [But] is not a betrothed maiden one [for the violation of whom] the penalty of stoning [but not fine] is incurred?[8]—It might have been assumed that, since it is an anomaly[9] that the Torah had introduced by the enactment of the law of a monetary fine, an offender[10] must, therefore, pay his fine even if he is also to be executed.[11]

According to Rabbah, however, who said that it was an anomaly[9] that the Torah had introduced by the enactment of the law of a monetary fine and that an offender[10] must pay his fine even if he is also to be executed,[12] what can be said [in reply to the objection

(1) Viz. *fifty*, as specified in Deut. XXII, 29. (2) *Shekels*, as implied from Ex. XXII, 16 (cf. *supra* p. 213, n. 5). (3) In our Mishnah he laid down that the fine BELONGS TO HER while in the Baraitha (*supra* 38a) he maintains that it 'is given to her father'. (4) Because in addition to the deduction of the *gezerah shawah*, the ordinary meaning of the text, viz. that if the '*damsel . . . is not betrothed*' the fine is given '*unto the damsel's father*' but if she was once betrothed it 'BELONGS TO HER', is also in agreement with the law. (5) The implication of the ordinary meaning being that if the damsel was betrothed the fine is paid not to her father but to herself (cf. *supra* note 4.) while according to R. Akiba it 'is given to *her father*' irrespective of whether she was, or was not betrothed. (6) Deut. XXII, 28. (7) Thus excluding one *formerly* betrothed but now divorced. The consonants of the original ארשה (Aram. ארסה) may be read as אֹרָשָׂה (as M.T.) '*was* betrothed' as well as אֲרֻשָׂה 'one who *is* betrothed'. (8) Since no monetary fine may be imposed in addition to the penalty of death. What need then was there a for a Scriptural text to teach the same law? (9) Cf. *supra* p. 210, n. 3. (10) If his crime warrants it. (11) Hence the necessity in this case for the additional Scriptural text. (12) *Supra* 34a, 35b, 38a.

raised]?[1]—He[2] adopts the same view as that of R. Akiba in our Mishnah.[3]

Our Rabbis taught: To whom is the monetary fine [of an outraged virgin[4] to be given]?—To her father. Others say: To herself. But why 'to herself'?[5]—R. Ḥisda replied: We are dealing here with the case of a virgin who was once betrothed and is now divorced, and they[6] differ on the principles underlying the difference between the view of R. Akiba in our Mishnah and his view in the Baraitha.

Abaye stated: If he[7] had intercourse with her and she died,[8] he is exempt [from the fine], for in Scripture it was stated, *Then the man . . . shall give unto the damsel's father,*[9] but not unto a dead woman's father.[10]

This ruling which was so obvious to Abaye formed the subject of an enquiry by Raba.[11] For Raba enquired: Is the state of adolescence legally attainable in the grave[12] or not? 'Is the state of adolescence attainable in the grave and [the fine,[9] therefore,] belongs to her son,[13] or is perhaps the age of adolescence not attainable in the grave and [the fine, therefore,] belongs to her father? [39*a*] But is she,[14] however, capable of [normal] concep-

(1) Cf. *supra* p. 214, n. 5. The reply given by R. Naḥman b. Isaac *supra*—that the offence referred to in the text is against one who was still betrothed and that the implication is that the offender, because he is suffering the penalty of death, is exempt from the monetary fine—is untenable; since, according to Rabbah, such an offender incurs both penalties. (2) Rabbah. (3) Which, as stated *supra*, does not 'deprive the Scriptural text of its ordinary meaning'. (4) This is now assumed to mean a virgin '*that is not betrothed*' who is spoken of in Deut. XXII, 28f. (5) The Scriptural text, surely, lays down that the fine is to be given '*Unto the damsel's father*'. (6) The respective authors of the two opinions expressed in the last cited Baraitha. (7) The offender spoken of in Deut. XXII, 28f. (8) Before he was brought to trial. (9) Deut. XXII, 29. (10) V. *supra* 29*b*. (11) V. *infra* p. 217, n. 10 final clause. (12) In the case of a virgin who was violated while she was a *na'arah* (v. Glos) and died a *na'arah* but whose violator was not brought to trial until sometime later when the girl, had she been alive, would have attained the state of *bagruth*; (v. Glos). (13) If she had one. As the fine would have been payable to her and not to her father if she had been alive (v. *infra* 41*b*) so it is now payable to her son who is her legal heir. (14) A girl in her minority. In the case under discussion, which refers

tion?[1] Did not R. Bibi recite in the presence of R. Naḥman:[2] Three [categories of] women may use an absorbent[3] in their marital intercourse:[4] a minor, and an expectant and nursing mother. The minor,[5] because otherwise she might become pregnant and die. An expectant mother,[5] because otherwise she might cause her foetus to degenerate into a sandal.[6] A nursing mother,[5] because otherwise she might have to wean her child [prematurely][7] and this would result in his death.[8] And what is [the age of such] a minor?[9] From the age of eleven years and one day to the age of twelve years and one day. One who is under,[10] or over this age[11] must carry on her marital intercourse in a normal manner; so R. Meir. But the Sages said: The one as well as the other carries on her marital intercourse in a normal manner, and mercy[12] will be vouchsafed from Heaven, for it is said in the Scriptures, *The Lord preserveth the simple.*[13] And should you reply that this is a case where she conceived when she was a *na'arah* and gave birth to a child when she was still a *na'arah* [it could be objected:] Does one give birth to a child within six months [after conception]? Did not Samuel, in fact, state: The period between the age of *na'aruth*[14] and that of *bagruth*[15] is only six months? And should you suggest [that he meant to say] that there were no less but more [than six months] surely [it could be retorted] he used the expression,

to a *na'arah*, who died before she became a *bogereth* the birth of a child is possible only if conception took place while she was a minor—under twelve years of age.

(1) I.e., one that would result in the birth of a child. (2) V. Yeb. 12*b*, 100*b*, Nid. 45*a*. (3) מוך 'hackled wool or flax'. (4) To prevent conception. (5) Is permitted the use of an absorbent. (6) סנדל, lit., 'a flat fish', i.e., a fish-shaped abortion due to superfetation. (7) On account of her second conception which causes the deterioration of her breast milk. (8) וימות, so MS.M. Cur. edd. omit. (9) Who is capable of conception but is exposed thereby to danger. (10) When no conception is possible. (11) When pregnancy involves no fatal consequence. (12) To protect them from danger. (13) Ps. CXVI, 6; *sc.* those who are unable to protect themselves. From this it follows that a girl under the age of twelve is incapable of normal conception. How then could it be assumed by Raba that a *na'arah* (cf. *supra* p. 215, n. 14) might give birth to a child? (14) Abstract of '*na'arah*', (v. Glos). (15) Abstract of '*bogereth*'.

'only'![1] It must be this, then, that he[2] asked: Is the state of adolescence[3] attainable in the grave[4] and her father consequently forfeits[5] [his right],[6] or is perhaps the state of adolescence not attainable in the grave[7] and the father, therefore, does not forfeit[8] [his right]?

Mar son of R. Ashi raised the question[9] in the following manner: Does death effect adolescence[10] or not?—The question stands undecided.[11]

Raba enquired of Abaye: What [is the legal position if] he[12] had intercourse and became betrothed?[13] The other replied: Is it written in Scripture, *'Then the man ... shall give unto the father of the damsel*[14] who was not a betrothed woman'?[15] Following, however, your line of reasoning, [the first retorted, one can argue in respect] of what was taught: '[If the offender had] intercourse with her and she married [the fine] belongs to herself', is it written in Scripture, *'Then the man ... shall give unto the father of the damsel*[16] who was not a married woman'?—What a comparison![17] There[18] [the following analogy may well be made]: Since the state of ado-

(1) Which implies 'no more'. (2) Raba. (3) V. *supra* p. 215, n. 12. (4) And the fine is, therefore, payable to the deceased as if she had been alive. (V. *infra* 41*b*). (5) פקע, lit., 'bursts'. (6) To the fine. As a fine is not inheritable before it has been collected, the father cannot inherit it from his daughter, and the offender is consequently altogether exempt from payment. (7) And the deceased retains the status of a *na'arah*. (8) V. *supra* note 5. (9) Attributed (*supra* 38*b* ad fin.) to Raba. (10) I.e., does a *na'arah* (v. Glos) assume the status of adolescence the moment she dies, and her father consequently forfeits his right to the fine as if she had actually attained her adolescence in her lifetime? The former version of Raba's question differs from this in that it assumes as a certainty, contrary to Abaye's ruling, that death does not effect adolescence, the only doubt being whether adolescence is attained *in due course, in the grave*. According to this, the latter version, however, Abaye's very certainty is questioned, and the statement (*supra* p. 215) 'This ruling which was so obvious to Abaye formed the subject of enquiry by Raba' refers to this version. (11) *Teḳu* (v. Glos.) (12) The offender spoken of in Deut. XXII, 28f. (13) Before the payment was made. Does the fine still belong to her father or is it now payable to herself? (14) Deut. XXII, 29. (15) Of course not. Scripture draws no distinction between the one and the other. (16) Deut. XXII, 29. (17) Lit., 'thus, now'. (18) Marriage.

lescence liberates a daughter from her father's authority[1] and marriage also liberates a daughter from her father's authority[2] [the two may be compared to one another]: As [in the case of] adolescence, if she attains adolescence after he had intercourse with her,[3] [the fine] belongs to the girl herself,[4] so also [in the case of] marriage, if she married after he had intercourse with her,[3] [the fine] belongs to the girl herself. But as to betrothal, does it completely liberate a daughter from her father's authority? Surely we learned: [In the case of] a betrothed girl[5] her father and her husband jointly may invalidate her vows.[6]

MISHNAH. THE SEDUCER PAYS THREE FORMS [OF COMPENSATION] AND THE VIOLATOR FOUR. THE SEDUCER PAYS COMPENSATION FOR INDIGNITY AND BLEMISH[7] AND THE [STATUTORY] FINE, WHILE THE VIOLATOR PAYS AN ADDITIONAL [FORM OF COMPENSATION] IN THAT HE PAYS FOR THE PAIN.

WHAT [IS THE DIFFERENCE] BETWEEN [THE PENALTIES OF] A SEDUCER AND THOSE OF A VIOLATOR? THE VIOLATOR PAYS COMPENSATION FOR THE PAIN BUT THE SEDUCER DOES NOT PAY COMPENSATION FOR THE PAIN. THE VIOLATOR PAYS[8] FORTHWITH[9] BUT THE SEDUCER [PAYS ONLY] IF HE DISMISSES[10] HER. THE VIOLATOR MUST DRINK OUT OF HIS POT[11] BUT THE SEDUCER MAY DISMISS [THE GIRL] IF HE WISHES. WHAT IS MEANT BY[12] 'MUST DRINK OUT OF HIS POT'?

(1) It is only a minor and a *na'arah* (v. Glos) over whom a father exercises his authority (v. *infra* 46*b*). (2) The vows of a married woman may be invalidated by her husband only and not by her father. (3) While she was still a *na'arah*. (4) Since it is the *'father of the damsel'* to whom the fine is to be paid (v. Deut. XXII, 29) and not the father of the girl *who is adolescent*. (5) A *na'arah*. (6) V. Ned. 66*b* and *infra* 46*b*; which shews that a father maintains partial control over his daughter as a *na'arah* even after her betrothal. (7) This is explained *infra*. (8) To the damsel's father. (9) Even if he marries her. (10) This is explained *infra*. (11) עציץ, an earthen vessel used as a receptacle for refuse or as a plant plot; i.e., the violator must marry his victim whatever her merits or defects. (12) Lit., 'how'.

—EVEN IF SHE IS LAME, EVEN IF SHE IS BLIND AND EVEN IF SHE IS AFFLICTED WITH BOILS [HE MAY NOT DISMISS HER]. IF, HOWEVER, SHE WAS FOUND TO HAVE COMMITTED[1] AN IMMORAL ACT OR WAS UNFIT TO MARRY AN ISRAELITE[2] HE MAY NOT CONTINUE TO LIVE WITH HER, FOR IT IS SAID IN SCRIPTURE, AND UNTO HIM SHE SHALL BE FOR A WIFE,[3] [IMPLYING] A WIFE THAT IS FIT 'UNTO HIM'.

GEMARA. [For the] PAIN of what?[4]—The father of Samuel replied: For the pain [he has inflicted] when he thrust her upon the ground.

R. Zera demurred: Now then, if he had thrust her upon silk stuffs[5] would he for a similar reason[6] be exempt? And should you say that the law is so indeed,[6] was it not [it may be retorted] taught: 'R. Simeon b. Judah stated in the name of R. Simeon,[7] A violator does not pay compensation for the pain [he has inflicted] because [39*b*] the woman would ultimately have suffered the same pain from her husband, but they[8] said to him: One who is forced to intercourse cannot be compared to one who acts willingly'?[9] —[The reference,] in fact,[10] said R. Naḥman in the name of Rabbah b. Abbuha [is to the] pain of opening the feet, for so it is said in Scripture, *And hast opened thy feet to every one that passed by*.[11] But if so, the same applies to one who has been seduced?[12]—R. Naḥman replied in the name of Rabbah b. Abbuha: The case of one who has been seduced may be compared to that of a person who said to his friend, 'Tear up my silk garments and you will be free from liability'.[13] 'My'? Are

(1) Lit., 'there was found in her'. (2) Lit., 'to enter into (the congregation of) Israel', on account of her illegitimate or tainted birth. (3) So lit. Deut. XXII, 29. (4) Must the violator pay. (5) A fall which is not painful. (6) Lit., 'thus also'. (7) The parallel passage in B.Ḳ. 59*a* has 'Simeon b. Menasya'. (8) The Rabbis who differed from his view. (9) B.Ḳ. 59*a*. Now if the PAIN referred to was that caused by the thrust the first Tanna would not have spoken of pain in the case of a husband. (10) Lit., 'but'. (11) Ezek. XVI, 25. (12) Why then is a seducer exempt from paying compensation for pain. (13) By her consent to suffer the pain the woman has exempted the man from paying compensation.

they[1] not her father's?[2]—This, however, said R. Naḥman in the name of Rabbah b. Abbuha, [is the explanation]: The smart women among them declare that one who is seduced experiences no pain. But do we not see that one does experience pain?—Abaye replied: Nurse[3] told me: Like hot water on a bald head.[4] Raba said: R. Ḥisda's daughter[5] told me, Like the prick of the blood-letting lancet.[6] R. Papa said: The daughter of Abba of Sura[5] told me, Like hard crust in the jaws.[7]

THE VIOLATOR PAYS FORTHWITH BUT THE SEDUCER [PAYS ONLY] IF HE DISMISSES HER etc. WHEN HE DISMISSES HER! Is she then his wife?[8] Abaye replied: Read, 'If he does not marry her,[9] So it was also taught: Although it was laid down that the seducer pays [the statutory fine] only if he does not marry her, he must pay compensation for indignity and blemish forthwith. And [in the case of] the violator as well as [of] the seducer, she herself or her father may oppose.[10]

As regards one who has been seduced, this[11] may well be granted because it is written in Scripture, *If her father will refuse,*[12] [since from *'refusing'*][13] I would only [have known that] her father [may refuse], whence [could it be deduced that] she herself [may also refuse]?[14] It was, therefore, explicitly stated *'will refuse'*, implying either of them.[15] But as regards a violator, though one may well grant that she [may refuse him since] it is written in Scripture, *'and unto him she shall be*[16] [which implies][17] only if she is so minded, whence, however, [it may be objected] is it deduced that her father [may also object to the marriage]?—Abaye replied:

(1) The silk garments, *sc.* her chastity and all it involves (v. *infra* 46*b*). (2) How then could she grant exemption? (3) Abaye's mother died from childbirth and he was brought up by his nurse (v. Ḳid. 31*b*). (4) Slight but pleasurable pain. (5) His wife. (6) ריבדא 'puncture', כוסילתא 'lancet used for blood-letting'. (7) V. Jast. *Aliter:* 'palate' (Rashi). (8) Obviously not, since he has not legally married her. How then can the expression of dismissed be used? (9) Since the woman, her father, or the seducer himself may object to the marriage. (10) The marriage. (11) That the girl as well as her father may oppose the marriage. (12) So lit., Ex. XXII, 16. (E.v. *utterly refuse*). (13) If the verb had not been repeated. (14) To marry the seducer. (15) Lit., 'from any place'. (16) Deut. XXII, 29. (17) Since it was not stated, 'And *he* shall *take her*'.

[Her father was given the right to object] in order that the sinner[1] might not gain an advantage.[2] Raba replied; It[3] is deduced *a minori ad majus:* If a seducer who has acted against the wish of her father alone may be rejected either by herself or by her father how much more so the violator who has acted both against the wish of her father and against the wish of herself.

Raba did not give the same reply as Abaye, because, having paid the fine, [the offender can] no [longer be described as a] sinner gaining an advantage. Abaye does not give the same reply as Raba [because it may be argued:[4] In the case of] a seducer, since he himself may object [to the marriage], her father also may object to it; [but in the case of] a violator, since he himself may not object [to the marriage] her father also may have no right to object to it.

Another Baraitha taught: Although it has been laid down that the violator pays forthwith[5] she has no claim upon him[6] when he divorces her.[7] ['When he divorces her'! Can he divorce her?[8]—Read: When she demands a divorce[9] she has no claim upon him].[6] If he died, the fine is regarded as a quittance for her *kethubah*.[10] R. Jose the son of R. Judah ruled: She is entitled[11] to a *kethubah* for one *maneh*.[12]

On what principle do they[13] differ?—The Rabbis hold the view that the only reason why[14] the Rabbis instituted a *kethubah* [for a wife was] in order that the man might not find it easy[15] to divorce her,[16] but [the violator,] surely, cannot divorce her.[17] R. Jose the son of R. Judah, however, is of the opinion that this man too might torment her until she says to him, 'I do not want you'.[18]

(1) The violator. (2) Over the seducer. (3) Her father's right to oppose the marriage. (4) Against his *a minori* inference. (5) V. Our Mishnah. (6) In respect of her *kethubah*. (7) The fine he pays is regarded as a settlement of her *kethubah*, though it was her father who received the payment. (8) Of course not, since Scripture stated, *He may not put her away all his days* (Deut. XXII, 29). (9) Lit., 'when she goes out'. (10) Cf. *supra* n. 7. (11) Like a woman who married as a widow or divorcee. (12) V. Glos. (13) R. Jose the son of R. Judah and the Rabbis. (14) Lit., 'what is the reason?' (15) Lit., 'easy in his eyes'. (16) V. *infra* 54*a*. (17) Cf. *supra* note 8. Hence no *kethubah* was necessary. (18) She too must, therefore, be protected by a *kethubah*.

THE VIOLATOR MUST DRINK OUT OF HIS POT. Said Raba of Parazika[1] to R. Ashi. Consider! [The fines of a violator and a seducer] are deduced from one another,[2] [40a] why then should not this law[3] also be inferred?[4]—Scripture stated, *He shall surely pay a dowry for her to be his wife,*[5] *'her'*[6] [implies][7] only if he is so minded [need he marry her].

WHAT IS MEANT BY 'MUST DRINK OUT OF HIS POT' etc.? R. Kahana said, I submitted the following argument before R. Zebid of Nehardea:[8] Why should not the positive commandment[9] supersede the negative one?[10] And he replied to me: 'Where do we say that a positive commandment supersedes a negative one? [Only in a case], for instance, like circumcision in leprosy,[11] since otherwise it would be impossible to fulfil the positive commandment, but here, if she should say that she did not want [the man for a husband], would [the question of the performance of] the positive commandment[9] ever have arisen?'[12]

MISHNAH. IF AN ORPHAN WAS BETROTHED AND THEN

(1) Farausag, a district near Bagdad (cf. Obermeyer p. 269). (2) The former from the latter in respect of '*shekels*' and the latter from the former in respect of the number 'fifty' (v. *supra* 38a *ad fin.*). (3) That a seducer, like a violator, must marry his victim. (4) Lit., 'in respect of this thing also let them be inferred from one another'. (5) Ex. XXII, 15. (6) לו, lit., 'to him'. (7) Since it is not stated, 'And *she shall* be his wife' (cf. *supra* p. 220, n. 17). (8) Nehardea was a town on the Euphrates, situated at its junction with the Royal Canal about seventy miles north of Sura, and famous for its great academy in the days of Samuel, which was rivalled only by that of Sura. (9) *She shall be his wife* (Deut. XXII, 29). Lit., 'let the positive command come and supersede etc.'. (10) The prohibition, e.g., to marry one who WAS UNFIT TO MARRY AN ISRAELITE. (11) It is forbidden to remove leprosy by means of a surgical operation; but if the leprosy covered the place of circumcision it is permitted to perform the circumcision although the leprosy is removed in the process. Thus the positive commandment of circumcision supersedes the negative one of leprosy. (12) Obviously not, since the girl has the right of objecting to marry him. Similarly, if she happens to be one who is forbidden to marry an Israelite she is advised to object to the marriage (Rashi). [Isaiah Trani: Since the command for the performance of this positive precept is not absolute, it is not sufficiently strong to supersede a negative prohibition.]

DIVORCED, ANY MAN WHO VIOLATES HER, SAID R. ELEAZAR, IS LIABLE [TO PAY THE STATUTORY FINE][1] BUT THE MAN WHO SEDUCES HER IS EXEMPT.[2]

GEMARA. Rabbah b. Bar Ḥana stated in the name of R. Joḥanan: R. Eleazar made his statement[3] on the lines of the view of his master R. Akiba who ruled: She[4] is entitled to receive the fine, and, moreover, the fine belongs to her. How is this[5] inferred?[6]—As it was stated, IF AN ORPHAN . . . ANY MAN WHO VIOLATES HER, SAID R. ELEAZAR, IS LIABLE [TO PAY THE STATUTORY FINE] BUT THE MAN WHO SEDUCES HER IS EXEMPT, [the difficulty arises: Is not the case of] an orphan self-evident?[7] Consequently it must be this that we were taught: A girl WHO WAS BETROTHED AND THEN DIVORCED has the same status as AN ORPHAN. As [the fine of] an orphan belongs to the orphan herself so does that of a girl who was betrothed and then divorced belong to the girl herself.

R. Zera said in the name of Rabbah b. Shila who said it in the name of R. Hamnuna the Elder who had it from R. Adda b. Ahabah who had it from Rab: The *halachah* is in agreement with the ruling of R. Eleazar. Rab [in fact] designated R. Eleazar[8] as the happiest[9] of the wise men.

MISHNAH. WHAT IS [THE COMPENSATION THAT IS PAID FOR] INDIGNITY?[10] ALL DEPENDS ON THE STATUS OF THE OFFENDER AND THE OFFENDED.

[AS TO] BLEMISH,[10] SHE IS REGARDED AS IF SHE WERE A

(1) V. Deut. XXII, 29. (2) Her acquiescence in the offence is regarded as an intimation that she has renounced her claim to the fine; and since, owing to the death of her father, the fine belongs to her, she is fully entitled to remit it. (3) In our Mishnah. (4) A girl who was betrothed and then divorced (v. Mishnah, *supra* 38a). (5) That R. Eleazar follows the ruling of R. Akiba? (6) Lit., 'from what?' (7) Since she has no father the fine obviously belongs to her. What need then was there for our Mishnah? (8) R. Eleazar b. Shammu'a, a disciple of R. Akiba (v. Yeb. 62b). (9) So Jast. or 'important', 'notable' (v. Levy). (10) V. Mishnah, *supra* 39a.

BONDWOMAN TO BE SOLD IN THE MARKET PLACE [AND IT IS ESTIMATED] HOW MUCH SHE WAS WORTH[1] AND HOW MUCH SHE IS WORTH NOW.

THE STATUTORY FINE[2] IS THE SAME FOR ALL; AND ANY SUM THAT IS FIXED PENTATEUCHALLY REMAINS THE SAME FOR ALL.

GEMARA. Might it not be suggested that the All-Merciful intended the fifty *sela'*[3] to cover all the forms of compensation?[4] —R. Zera replied: [If that were so] it would be said, 'Should one who had intercourse with a princess pay fifty and one who had intercourse with the daughter of a commoner also pay only fifty?'[5] Said Abaye to him: If so, the same might be argued in respect of a slave:[6] 'Should [compensation for] a slave who perforates pearls be thirty [and that for] one who does [40*b*] needlework also be thirty?'[7]—This, however, said R. Zera, [is the proper explanation]: If two men had intercourse with her, one in a natural, and the other in an unnatural manner, it would be argued,[8] 'Should one who had intercourse with a sound woman pay fifty and one who had intercourse with a degraded woman also pay fifty?'[5]

Said Abaye to him: If so, the same might be argued in respect of a slave: 'Should [compensation for] a healthy slave be thirty [and that for] one afflicted with boils also be thirty?'[7] —This, however, said Abaye, [is the explanation]: Scripture said,[9] *Because he hath humbled her*[10] [as if to say]: These[11] [must be paid] *'because he hath humbled her'*; thus it may be inferred that

(1) Before the offence. (2) V. Mishnah, *supra* 39*a*. (3) Deut. XXII, 29. (4) Lit., 'from all things'. (5) Though the indignity of the former is undoubtedly greater. Hence it follows that, in addition to the statutory sum which the Torah has awarded to all alike, an additional sum for indignity must be paid in accordance with the status of the offended party. (6) Compensation for whom is fixed at thirty *shekels* (v. Ex. XXI, 32). (7) Though the labour value of the one is undoubtedly higher than that of the other. (8) If no compensation for indignity were paid in addition to the statutory fine. (9) In stating the reason for the statutory fine. (10) Deut. XXII, 29. (11) The fifty *shekels* mentioned.

[compensation for] indignity and blemish[1] must also be paid.[2]

Raba replied: Scripture said, *Then the man that lay with her shall give unto the damsel's father fifty* [shekels *of*] *silver;*[3] for the gratification of 'lying' [he gives] fifty. Thus it may be inferred that [compensation for] indignity and blemish must also be paid.[2]

But say [perhaps] that [compensation for indignity and blemish is paid] to her?[4]—Scripture said, *Being in her youth in her father's house,*[5] [implying that] all advantages of 'her youth' belong to her father.

[Consider,] however, that which R. Huna said in the name of Rab: 'Whence is it deduced that a daughter's handiwork belongs to her father? [From Scripture] where it is said, *And if a man sell his daughter to be a maidservant,*[6] as[7] the handiwork of a maidservant belongs to her master so does the handiwork of a daughter belong to her father'. Now what need is there[8] [it may be asked, for this text when] the law[9] can be deduced from [the text of] '*Being in her youth in her father's house*'? Consequently [it must be admitted, must it not, that] that text was written in connection only with the annulment of vows?[10] And should you suggest[11] that we might infer[12] from it,[13] [it could be retorted that,] monetary matters[14] cannot be inferred from ritual matters.[13] And should you suggest[11] that we might infer it[12] from the law of fine,[15] [it could be retorted, could it not, that,] monetary payments cannot be inferred from fines?[16]—This, however, [is the explanation]:[17] It stands to reason

(1) Which are payable in other cases of injury. (2) Lit., 'that there is'. (3) Deut. XXII, 29. (4) Since '*the damsel's father*' was mentioned (ibid.) only in respect of the fifty *shekels* of fine. (5) Num. XXX, 17. (6) Ex. XXI, 7. (7) Since '*daughter*' and '*maidservant*' are mentioned in the same verse they may be compared to one another. (8) Lit., 'wherefore to me?' (9) That a daughter's handiwork belongs to her father. (10) And, therefore, no deduction from it can be made in respect of handiwork. Similarly here also, no deduction from it could be made in respect of compensation for indignity and blemish. Thus an objection arises against Raba's explanation. (11) In justification of Raba. (12) That compensation for indignity and blemish belongs to the father. (13) The law of the annulment of vows. (14) Such as compensation. (15) As the fine belongs to her father so does her compensation. (16) The objection against Raba thus remains. (17) Why compensation for indignity and blemish is paid to the father.

that [her compensation should] belong to her father; for if he wished he could have handed her over[1] to an ugly man or to one afflicted with boils.[2]

AS TO BLEMISH, SHE IS REGARDED AS IF SHE WERE A BONDWOMAN TO BE SOLD. How is she assessed? The father of Samuel replied: It is estimated how much[3] more a man would pay for a virgin slave than[3] for a non-virgin slave to attend upon him. 'A non-virgin slave to attend upon him'! What difference does this[4] make to him?—[The meaning], however, [is this: How much more a man would pay for] a virgin slave than[3] for a non-virgin slave[3] for the purpose of marrying her to his bondman. But even if 'to his bondman', what difference does this[5] make to him?—[We are dealing here] with a bondman who gives his master satisfaction.[6]

MISHNAH. WHEREVER THE RIGHT OF SALE APPLIES NO FINE IS INCURRED[7] AND WHEREVER A FINE IS INCURRED NO RIGHT OF SALE APPLIES. IN THE CASE OF A MINOR THE RIGHT OF SALE[8] APPLIES BUT NO FINE[9] IS INCURRED;[10] IN THE CASE OF A DAMSEL[11] A FINE IS INCURRED[10] BUT NO RIGHT OF SALE[8] APPLIES. TO A DAMSEL WHO IS ADOLESCENT[12] THE RIGHT OF SALE DOES NOT APPLY NOR IS A FINE INCURRED THROUGH HER.

GEMARA. Rab Judah stated in the name of Rab: This[13] is the ruling of R. Meir, but the Sages rule: A fine is incurred[10] even

(1) As wife. (2) Thus subjecting her to indignity and blemish while he himself derives therefrom pecuniary benefit. As her indignity and blemish are in his hands he is justly entitled to compensation from the man who inflicts them upon her. (3) Lit., 'between . . . to'. (4) The virginity of a slave whom one requires for service. (5) Cf. previous note *mutatis mutandis*. The main object of a master is the acquisition of slave children. (6) And his master in return desires to give him the satisfaction of marrying a virgin. (7) This is illustrated anon. (8) By her father (cf. Ex. XXI, 7 and 'Ar. 29*b*). (9) V. Deut. XXII, 29 and Ex. XXII, 16. (10) In case of violation or seduction. (11) *Na'arah* (v. Glos.). (12) *Bogereth* (v. Glos.). (13) That IN THE CASE OF A MINOR . . . NO FINE IS INCURRED.

where the right of sale[1] applies. For it was taught: The right of sale[1] applies to a minor from the age of one day until the time when she grows two hairs,[2] but no fine is incurred through her.[3] From the time she grows two hairs until she comes of age a fine is incurred through her but no right of sale[1] applies; so R. Meir, because R. Meir has laid down: Wherever the right of sale applies no fine is incurred, and wherever a fine is incurred no right of sale applies. The Sages, however, ruled: Through a minor from the age of three years and one day until the time she becomes adolescent a fine is incurred.[4] Only a fine [you say] but not the right of sale?[5] —Read: A fine also where the right of sale applies.[6]

R. Ḥisda said: What is R. Meir's reason?[7] Scripture said, *And unto him*[8] *she shall be*[9] *for a wife;*[10] the text thus speaks of a girl who may herself contract a marriage.[11] And the Rabbis?[12] Resh Laḳish replied: Scripture said, *na'ar*[13] which[14] implies even a minor.[15]

R. Papa the son of R. Ḥanan of Be Keloḥith heard this[16] and proceeded to report it before R. Shimi b. Ashi [when the latter] said to him: You apply it[17] to that law; we apply it to the following: Resh Laḳish ruled; A man who has brought an evil name[18] upon a minor is exempt,[19] for it is said in Scripture, *And give them unto the father of the damsel,*[18] Scripture expressed the term *na'arah*[20] as plenum.[21]

(1) V. p. 226, n. 8. (2) As a sign of puberty. (3) V. p. 226, n. 10. (4) Tosef. Keth. III. Our Mishnah (v. p. 226, n. 13) must consequently represent the ruling of R. Meir. (5) But this is contrary to the Pentateuchal law (cf. p. 226, n. 8). (6) From the age of three years and one day until she grows two hairs. Under the first age limit, no fine, and above the second age limit *until she becomes adolescent*, only a fine is incurred. (7) V. *supra* p. 226, n. 13). (8) The girl through whom the fine is incurred. (9) תהיה. (10) So lit., Deut. XXII, 29. (11) Lit., 'who *causes herself* to be'. תהיה implying action on the part of the girl herself independent of that of any other person. A minor whose marriage is dependent on the will of her father is consequently excluded from the text. (12) How in view of the implication of the text could they maintain that through a minor a fine is incurred? (13) נער (So MS.M. and BaḤ). Cur. edd. נערה. (14) Since M.T. reads נער though the *ḳere* is נערה (*damsel*). (15) [The Rabbis explain this form as an example of the epicene use of a noun; cf. Gr. ὁ παῖς and ἡ παῖς, child]. (16) The deduction attributed to Resh Laḳish. (17) The deduction from נערה, נער. (18) Deut. XXII, 19. (19) From the fine of a *hundred* sheḳels *of silver* (v. ibid.). (20) נערה '*damsel*'. (21) With a '*he*' at the

R. Adda b. Ahabah demurred: Is the reason then[1] because the All-Merciful has written *na'arah*, but otherwise it would have been said that even a minor [was included], surely [it may be objected] it is written in Scripture, *But if this thing be true, and the tokens of virginity be not found in the damsel, then they shall bring out the damsel to the door of her father's house, and [the men of her city] shall stone her*,[2] while a minor is not, is she, subject to punishment?[3] — [The explanation,] however, [is that since] *na'arah* [has been written] here[4] [it may be inferred that here only is a minor excluded] but wherever Scripture uses the expression of *na'ar* even a minor is included.

MISHNAH. [41a] HE WHO DECLARES, 'I HAVE SEDUCED THE DAUGHTER OF SO-AND-SO' MUST PAY COMPENSATION FOR INDIGNITY AND BLEMISH ON HIS OWN EVIDENCE BUT NEED NOT PAY THE STATUTORY FINE.[5]

HE WHO DECLARES, 'I HAVE STOLEN' MUST MAKE RESTITUTION FOR THE PRINCIPAL ON HIS OWN EVIDENCE BUT NEED NOT REPAY DOUBLE,[6] FOURFOLD[7] OR FIVEFOLD.[7]

[HE WHO STATES,] 'MY OX HAS KILLED SO-AND-SO' OR 'THE OX OF SO-AND-SO' MUST MAKE RESTITUTION[8] ON HIS OWN EVIDENCE. [IF HE, HOWEVER, SAID,] 'MY OX HAS KILLED THE BONDMAN OF SO-AND-SO'[9] HE NEED NOT MAKE RESTITUTION ON HIS OWN EVIDENCE.[10]

THIS IS THE GENERAL RULE: WHOEVER PAYS MORE THAN THE ACTUAL COST OF THE DAMAGE HE HAS DONE[11] NEED NOT PAY IT ON HIS OWN EVIDENCE.

end, in order to exclude the minor. [This is the only place in the Pentateuch where the word is written *plene*].

(1) Why the fine of a *hundred shekels* is not payable in respect of a minor. (2) Deut. XXII, 20f. (3) A minor would consequently have been excluded even if *na'ar* had been written. (4) Where a minor, as has been proved, must be excluded. (5) Prescribed in Ex. XXII, 16, because one's own admission to having committed an act for which a fine is prescribed cannot render one liable to pay it (v. B.Ḳ. 75a). (6) V. Ex. XXII, 3. (7) V. ibid. XXI, 37. (8) V. ibid. XXI, 30, 35. (9) The fine for which is (v. ibid. 32) thirty *shekels*. (10) Cf. *supra* n. 4. (11) When evidence against him is available.

GEMARA. Why did not he[1] include 'I have violated'?[2]—He implied that this was unnecessary: It was unnecessary [to state that if a man declared,] 'I have violated', in which case he casts no reflection on the girl's character[3], that he must pay compensation for indignity and blemish on his own evidence,[4] but [if a man declared,] 'I HAVE SEDUCED', in which case he does cast a reflection on her character,[5] it might have been assumed that he does not pay [such compensation] on his own evidence,[6] hence he informs us [that he does].

Our Mishnah does not agree with the following Tanna. For it was taught: R. Simeon b. Judah stated in the name of R. Simeon, [Compensation for] indignity and blemish also a man does not pay on his own evidence[7] because he[8] cannot be trusted[9] to tarnish the character of another man's daughter.

Said R. Papa to Abaye: What [is the ruling if] she is satisfied?[10] —It is possible that her father might not be satisfied. And what if her father also is satisfied?—It is possible that the members of her family might not be satisfied. What if the members of her family are also satisfied?—It is impossible that there should not be one somewhere[11] who is not satisfied.

HE WHO DECLARES, 'I HAVE STOLEN' MUST MAKE RESTITUTION FOR THE PRINCIPAL etc. It was stated: [In respect of liability for] half damages,[12] R. Papa ruled: It is a civil obligation,[13] but R. Huna the son of R. Joshua ruled: It is penal.[14] 'R. Papa ruled:

(1) The Tanna of our Mishnah. (2) In addition to 'I HAVE SEDUCED'. (3) Since the outrage was not her fault but her misfortune. (4) As the girl's character is not called in question the man's admission may well be regarded as a true confession to satisfy his conscience and as a desire to make amends. (5) Cf. *supra* note 3 *mutatis mutandis*. (6) I.e., his compensation is to be refused on the ground that his word which casts a reflection on the girl's reputation cannot be accepted without valid proof. (7) Cf. *supra* n. 1. (8) In the absence of other valid evidence. (9) Lit., 'not all from him'. (10) To put up with the reflection in order to gain her compensation. (11) Lit., 'in a province of the sea', 'a country beyond the sea'. (12) Restitution made for damage done by the 'horn' (v. B.Ḳ. 2b) of a *tam* (v. Glos). (13) And is consequently payable on one's own evidence. (14) Lit., 'fine', and is payable only where valid evidence, other than the admission of the offender, is available (cf. *supra* p. 228, n. 5).

It is a civil obligation', for he is of the opinion that cattle as a rule[1] cannot be presumed to be safe.[2] Justice, therefore, demands that the owner should make full restitution,[3] but the All-Merciful has shown mercy towards him[4] because his cattle have not yet become *mu'ad*.[5] 'R. Huna the son of R. Joshua ruled: It is penal', for he is of the opinion that cattle as a rule are presumed to be safe.[6] Justice, therefore, demands that the owner should make no restitution at all,[7] but it was Divine Law[8] that imposed a fine upon him in order that he should exercise special care over his cattle.[9]

(Mnemonic:[10] *He damaged what, and killed a general rule.*)

We have learned: The plaintiff and the defendant[11] are involved[12] in the payment.[13] Now according to him who holds that liability for half damages is a civil obligation[14] it is perfectly correct [to say] that the plaintiff is involved in the payment,[15] but according to him who maintains that liability for half damages is penal [it may well be asked:] If he receives that which [in strict justice] is not his due how can he be involved[16] in the payment?[17]—It[18] may apply[19] only to [a loss caused by] a decrease in the value of the carcass.[20]

(1) Unless their owner takes special care to check them. (2) They might at any moment do some damage. Hence it is the duty of their owner to hold them under control. (3) For any damage done by his cattle, since such damage is the result of his carelessness (v. *supra* n. 2). (4) By releasing him from half of the payment. (5) 'Cautioned' (v. Glos). But whatever he does pay is a civil liability (v. *supra* p. 229, n. 13). (6) And no special care on the part of the owner is called for. (7) Since it was not his fault that his cattle had done the damage. (8) By ordering him to pay half damages. (9) Cf. B.Ḳ. 15*a*. (10) Containing key words occurring in the following four citations from which objections are raised against the ruling of R. Huna the son of R. Joshua. (11) Lit., 'he who suffered, and he who caused the damage'. (12) This is now assumed to imply 'loss'. (13) B.Ḳ. 14*b*. (14) And that the plaintiff should in strict justice be entitled to full compensation. (15) Since he loses (v. *supra* n. 14) a half of which is really his due. (16) Cf. *supra* n. 12. (17) Thus an objection arises against R. Huna the son of R. Joshua. (18) The statement that the plaintiff also is 'involved in the payment'. (19) Lit., 'is required'. (20) Between the date on which the animal was killed and that on which the action was tried. Such loss is borne by the plaintiff, the defendant paying only half the difference between the value of the live animal and the carcass *as it was on the day of the accident.*

[But have we not] already learned elsewhere [about] the decrease in the value of the carcass? 'To compensate for the damage'[1] means that the owner[2] must dispose of the carcass?[3]—One [of the statements deals] with a *tam*[4] and the other with a *mu'ad*.[4] And [both statements are] required. For if [that relating to] a *tam* only had been made it might have been presumed [to apply to that alone] because the animal has not yet become *mu'ad* but not to a *mu'ad* since [in the latter case the owner] has been duly warned. And if [only the statement relating to] a *mu'ad* had been made it might have been assumed [to apply to that case alone] because the owner pays full compensation[5] but not [to that of] a *tam*.[6] [Both rulings were consequently] required.

Come and hear: What is the difference [in the case of compensation for damages] between a *tam*[4] and a *mu'ad*?[4]—In the case of a *tam* half damages are paid out of its own body,[7] while in the case of a *mu'ad* full compensation is paid out of the best of the [defendant's] estate.[8] Now if[9] it were the case [that liability for half damage[10] is penal] why was it not also stated[11] that in the case of a *tam* no compensation is paid merely on one's own evidence[12] whereas in the case of a *mu'ad*[13] compensation is paid even on one's own[14] evidence?[15]—He[16] recorded [some distinctions][17] and omitted others. What [else, however], did he omit [that should justify the assumption] that he omitted this distinction also.[18]—He omitted

(1) B.Ḳ. 9*b*. (2) Of the animal that was killed, i.e., the plaintiff. (3) I.e., he must take it in part payment of his compensation, and if its value decreases it is obvious that he must bear the loss (cf. p. 230, n. 20). What need then was there to state the same ruling twice? (4) V. Glos. (5) And, therefore, no further liability is imposed upon him. (6) Where the defendant pays only half of the damages and may, therefore, be expected to bear the loss whenever the value of the carcass had decreased. (7) I.e., of the tort-feasant animal. The defendant's estate remains exempt from all liability. (8) Mishnah, B.Ḳ. 16*b*. (9) So according to Rashal and the parallel passages in B.Ḳ. 15*a*. Cur. edd. omit 'if . . . case'. (10) In the case of a *tam* (cf. *supra* p. 229, n. 12). (11) As another distinction between a *tam* and a *mu'ad*. (12) Cf. *supra* p. 229, n. 14. (13) Where the liability is civil. (14) Cf. *supra* p. 229, n. 13 and text. (15) Cf. *supra* p. 230, n. 17. (16) The Tanna of this Mishnah. (17) Between a *tam* and a *mu'ad*. (18) In an enumeration the Tanna would not have omitted just one point.

[also the payment of] half *kofer*.[1] If [the only point not mentioned] is that of[2] half *kofer* it is no omission, [41b] since that [Mishnah] may represent the view of[3] R. Jose the Galilean who ruled that [in the case of] a *tam* half *kofer* is paid.[4]

Come and hear: [A MAN WHO SAID,] 'MY OX KILLED SO-AND-SO' OR 'THE OX OF SO-AND-SO' MUST PAY COMPENSATION ON HIS OWN EVIDENCE. Now does not [this statement deal] with a *tam?*[5]—No; with a *mu'ad*. What, however, [would be the law] in the case of a *tam?* Would no liability be established by one's own evidence? Then instead of stating in the final clause, '. . . THE BONDMAN OF SO-AND-SO' HE NEED NOT MAKE RESTITUTION ON HIS OWN EVIDENCE, could not a distinction have been drawn in the very same case, thus: 'This[6] applies only to a *mu'ad* but in respect of a *tam* no liability is incurred by one's own evidence'? —The entire [Mishnah prefers to] deal with a *mu'ad*.[7]

Come and hear: THIS IS THE GENERAL RULE: WHOSOEVER PAYS MORE THAN THE ACTUAL COST OF THE DAMAGE HE HAS DONE NEED NOT PAY ON HIS OWN EVIDENCE, from which it follows,[8] [does it not, that if the payment is] less than the cost of the damage,[9] one must pay compensation even on one's own evidence?[10]—Do not infer: '[But if payment is] less than the cost of the damage [one must pay . . . on one's own evidence]',[9] but infer: '[If payment] corresponds to the actual amount of the damage

(1) 'Ransom' (v. Ex. XXI, 30) V. Glos. In the case of manslaughter a *mu'ad* pays full compensation while a *tam* does not pay even half (cf. B.Ḳ. 41a). (2) Lit., 'on account of'. (3) Lit., 'this (is) according to whom?' (4) V. B.Ḳ. 26a. The distinction mentioned (v. *supra* n. 1) does not, therefore, apply. The other distinction also, viz. that between full *kofer* for a *mu'ad* and half *kofer* for a *tam*, cannot be regarded as an omission, since it is included in the first clause which lays down that in the case of a *tam* half damages are paid and in that of a *mu'ad* full compensation is paid, a ruling which applies to *kofer* as well as to damages. Since there is no other omission, this Mishnah proves that the liability for half damage is civil as *supra*. (5) And since liability is established by one's own evidence such liability connot be penal but civil. Cf. *supra* 230, n. 17. (6) That liability is established by one's own admission. (7) To shew that even in respect of a *mu'ad* there is a case where no liability is incurred by one's own evidence. (8) Lit., 'but'. (9) Such as half damage payable in the case of a *tam*. (10) V. *supra* note 5.

one must pay compensation even on one's own evidence'. What, however, [would be the law if payment were] less than the amount of the damage?[1] Would no liability be established by one's own evidence? Then[2] why was it not stated, 'This is the general rule: Whoever does not pay an amount corresponding to the actual cost of the damage he has done pays no compensation on his own evidence', which would imply [that where compensation is] less or more[3] [it is to be paid on one's own evidence]?[4]—This is indeed a refutation.[5]

The law, however, [is that the liability for] half damage is penal. 'A refutation' [of a ruling][6] and [yet it is] the law?—Yes; for the sole basis of the refutation[7] was that[8] the statement[9] did not run, '[whoever does not pay an amount] corresponding to the actual cost of the damage he has done'; [but such a principle][10] was not regarded by him[11] as exactly accurate, since there is the liability for half damages [in the case of the damage done by] pebbles[12] concerning which there is an *halachic* tradition that the liability is civil.[13] On account of this consideration he did not adopt [the form of the expression suggested].

Now that you have laid down that liability for half damage is penal, the case of a dog that devoured lambs or that of a cat that devoured big hens is one of unusual occurrence[14] and no distress is executed in Babylon.[15] If, however, they[16] were small the occurrence

(1) V. p. 232, n. 9. (2) Instead of laying down a rule from which a wrong inference might be drawn. (3) Than the actual cost of the damage. (4) Since, however, the rule was not stated in this form it follows that liability for less than the actual cost of the damage (v. *supra* n. 1). is not payable on one's own admission. An objection thus arises against R. Huna the son of R. Joshua (cf. *supra* p. 231, n. 5). (5) The ruling, therefore, that half damages payable in the case of a *tam* is penal, stands refuted. (6) Cf. *supra* nn. 4 and 5. (7) Lit., 'what is the reason that it was refuted?' (8) Lit., 'because'. (9) In our Mishnah. (10) Which would have excluded all cases of payment for half damages. (11) The Tanna of this Mishnah. (12) Kicked up by an animal (v. B.Ḳ. 17*a* and cf. 3*b*). (13) Despite the fact that the compensation is less than the actual damage. (14) And thus coming under the category of damage by the 'horn' (v. B.Ḳ. 2*b*) which is also one of unusual occurrence. (15) Since penal liabilities may be imposed in Palestine only by a judge who is specially ordained for the purpose (*mumḥe*, v. Glos). No such judges lived in Babylon. (16) The lambs or the hens.

is a usual[1] one and distress is executed.[2] Should the plaintiff,[2] however, seize [the chattels of the defendant][3] they are not to be taken away from him.[4] Furthermore, if[5] he pleads, 'Fix for me a date [by which the defendant must come with me] to the Land of Israel,'[6] such date must be fixed for him, and if [the defendant] does not go with him he must be placed under the ban. In any case,[7] however, [the defendant] is to be placed under the ban;[8] for he is told, 'Abate your nuisance', in accordance with a dictum of R. Nathan. For it was taught:[9] R. Nathan said, Whence is it derived that a man may not breed a bad dog in his house nor place a shaking ladder in his house? [From Scripture] where it is said, *That thou bring not blood upon thine house.*[10]

(1) Falling under the category of damage by the 'tooth' (cf. B.Ḳ. 2*b*) which is also one of usual occurrence and compensation in which case is a civil liability. (2) Even in Babylon. (3) [So Rashi. R. Tam: the animal that caused the damage (Tosaf)]. (4) And he retains an amount corresponding to half the damage. (5) Where no chattels were seized. (6) Cf. *supra* p. 233, n. 15. (7) Whether the plaintiff wishes the case to be tried in the Land of Israel or not. (8) 'Until he abates the nuisance'. (So B.Ḳ. 15*b*). (9) B.Ḳ. 15*b*, 46*a*. (10) Deut. XXII, 8, referring to the duty of removing a *cause* of danger though one is *not directly* responsible for any fatal result.

KETHUBOTH

CHAPTER IV

MISHNAH. IF A GIRL[1] WAS SEDUCED [THE COMPENSATION FOR] HER INDIGNITY AND BLEMISH AS WELL AS THE STATUTORY FINE BELONG TO HER FATHER[2] [TO WHOM BELONGS ALSO THE COMPENSATION FOR] PAIN IN THE CASE OF ONE WHO WAS VIOLATED.

IF THE GIRL'S ACTION WAS TRIED[3] BEFORE HER FATHER DIED [ALL THE FORMS OF COMPENSATION] ARE DUE TO HER FATHER;[4] IF HER FATHER [SUBSEQUENTLY] DIED THEY ARE DUE TO HER BROTHERS.[5] IF HER FATHER, HOWEVER, DIED BEFORE HER ACTION WAS TRIED THEY[6] ARE DUE TO HER.[7] IF HER ACTION WAS TRIED[3] BEFORE SHE BECAME ADOLESCENT[8] [ALL FORMS OF COMPENSATION] ARE DUE TO HER FATHER; IF HER FATHER [SUBSEQUENTLY] DIED[9] THEY ARE DUE TO HER BROTHERS.[5] IF, HOWEVER, SHE BECAME ADOLESCENT BEFORE HER ACTION COULD BE TRIED THEY ARE DUE TO HER.[10] R. SIMEON RULED: IF HER FATHER DIED[11] BEFORE SHE COULD COLLECT [THE DUES] THEY BELONG TO HER.[12] [42*a*] HER HANDIWORK, HOWEVER, AND ANYTHING SHE FINDS, EVEN IF SHE HAD NOT COLLECTED [THE PROCEEDS], BELONG TO HER BROTHERS IF HER FATHER DIED.[13]

(1) *Na'arah* (v. Glos.). (2) Cf. Mishnah *supra* 39*a* and notes. (3) Lit., 'she stood before the law'. (4) In accordance with Deut. XXII, 29. (5) As heirs of their father. Once the court had ordered payment, the amount in question is considered as the 'actual property' of the father which is inherited by his sons, v. *infra* 43*a*. (6) Being still penal liabilities. (7) V. *infra* 43*a*. *Var. lec.* adds, 'R. Simeon ruled: If her father died before she could collect (the dues) they belong to her'. (8) A *bogereth* (v. Glos.). (9) Whether before or after she became adolescent. (10) Because at that age she is no longer under her father's control. (11) *Var. lec.*; 'If she became adolescent'. (12) Because the fine does not become the 'actual property' of the father by mere decision of the court, (cf. *supra* notes 5 and 7). (13) Unlike compensation, which is not due to

GEMARA. What [new law] does he teach us?[1] Have we not [already] learned: The seducer pays three forms [of compensation] and the violator four. The seducer pays compensation for indignity and blemish as well as the statutory fine, and the violator pays an additional [form of compensation] in that he pays for the pain?[2] —It was necessary [to teach us[1] that the compensation is due] TO HER FATHER.[3] [But] that [the compensation is due] to her father is also obvious, since a seducer has to pay for it? For if [it were to be given] to herself [the objection could be raised], why should the seducer pay [to her when] he acted with her consent?[4] —It was necessary [to tell us[1] of the case where] HER ACTION WAS TRIED [which is a point in] dispute between R. Simeon and the Rabbis.[5]

We have learned elsewhere: [If a man said to another] 'You have violated or seduced my daughter', and the other replied, 'I did not violate or seduce her'. 'I adjure you' [said the first] and the other responded, 'Amen', but afterwards admitted his guilt, he is liable.[6] R. Simeon, however, exempts him, for no fine is paid on one's own admission.[7] They,[8] however, said to him: Though no man pays a fine on his own admission he nevertheless pays compensation for indignity and blemish[9] on his own admission.[10]

Abaye enquired of Rabbah:[11] What is the law according to

their father before the action had been tried and decided in his daughter's favour, these are his due from the moment they come into existence. As they are consequently his 'actual property' he is entitled to transmit them to his heirs.

(1) In our Mishnah. (2) V. 39*a* for notes. (3) This was not mentioned in the Mishnah cited. (4) If then it is also obvious that the compensation is to be paid to her father what need was there for our Mishnah? (5) The first Tanna (v. our Mishnah). (6) To pay the actual amount due as well as an additional fifth (v. Lev. V, 24), and also to bring a guilt-offering. (7) As the man would have been exempt from the penal liabilities if he had himself admitted the offence in the absence of any other evidence, he must also be exempt from all liabilities (v. *supra* note 6) in the case of a denial. For it was not a civil liability (*mamon*), but a penal liability (*ḳenas*) that he had denied. (8) The Rabbis who differed from him. (9) Which are not *ḳenas* but *mamon*. (10) V. Shebu. 36*b*. (11) Rabbah b. Naḥmani who was his teacher.

R. Simeon[1] where a man said to another, 'You have violated or seduced my daughter, and I have brought you to law and you were ordered to pay me [a stipulated sum of] money' and the other replied, 'I have neither violated nor seduced her, nor have you brought me to law nor have I been ordered to pay you any money', and after he had taken an oath[2] he admitted his guilt? Is [his liability], since his action had been tried,[3] civil[4] and he consequently incurs thereby a sacrifice for [having taken a false] oath, or is it possible that, though his action had been tried, his liability[5] is still regarded as penal?[6]—The other replied: It is a civil liability and he incurs thereby the obligation to bring a sacrifice for a false oath.[7]

He[8] pointed out to him[9] the following objection: R. Simeon, said, As it might have been presumed that if a man said to another, 'You have violated or seduced my daughter' and the other replied 'I have neither violated nor seduced her', [or if the first said], 'Your ox has killed my bondman' and the other replied, 'He did not kill him', or if a bondman said to his master,[10] 'You have knocked out my tooth' or 'You have blinded my eye',[11] and he replied, 'I have not knocked it out' or 'I have not blinded it' and [the defendant] took the oath[12] but afterwards admitted his liability—it might have been presumed that he is liable,[13] hence it was explicitly stated in Scripture, *And he deal falsely with his neighbour in a matter of deposit, or of pledge, or of robbery, or have oppressed his neighbour; or have found*

(1) Who (according to the Mishnah of Shebu. cited) exempts one from liability in the case of a denial. (2) In confirmation of his denial. (3) And he was ordered to pay. (4) [Having been ordered to pay, he can no longer secure exemption by his own admission; his liability is now considered of the *mamon* class (Rashi)]. (5) Since it was originally penal. (6) [*Var. lec.* add: 'and he who confesses to a liability for a fine is exempt'. On this reading, Abaye's question was also whether his own admission, after the action had been tried, exempts him from payment; v. Tosaf.] (7) [*Var. lec.* omit: 'and he incurs . . . false oath'. In that case Rabbah's answer is given in general terms. He merely replied, 'it is a civil liability', which for the present is taken to mean that it is so both in respect of an obligation to an oath and to liability to payment; cf. n. 6, v. Tosaf.] (8) Abaye. (9) Rabbah. (10) Lit., 'his bondman said to him'. (11) In compensation for which he demands his freedom (v. Ex. XXI, 26f). Such compensation is also deemed to be penal, because a slave was regarded as his master's chattels. (12) In confirmation of his denial. (13) V. *supra* p. 236, n. 6.

that which was lost, and deal falsely therein, and swear to a lie,[1] as these are distinguished by the characteristics of being civil cases so must all [other cases where similar liabilities[2] may be incurred be distinguished by the characteristics] of being civil. These,[3] therefore, are excluded [from liability][2] since they are penal. [42*b*] Does not [this ruling refer to a man] whose action had already been tried?[4] —No, [it deals] with one whose action had not yet been tried.[5] But, surely, since the first clause deals with the case of a man whose action had been tried, would not the final clause also deal with such a case? For in the first clause it was stated: 'I only knew [that liability[6] is incurred in] cases where compensation is paid for the actual value only, whence, however, is it deduced that [such liability is also incurred in] cases where the payment is double,[7] fourfold[8] or fivefold[8] and [in those of] the violator, the seducer and the calumniator?[9] From Scripture which explicitly stated, *And commit a trespass,*[10] [implying that all such are] included'. Now, how is this statement to be understood? If [it is one referring to] a man whose action had not yet been tried [the objection could be raised:] Is double compensation payable in such circumstances?[11] It is obvious, therefore, that [the reference is to one] whose action had already been tried. And since the first clause deals with one whose action had been tried, the final clause also must deal, must it not, with one whose action had already been tried?[12]—The other replied: I could have answered you that the first clause deals with one whose action had already been tried, and the final clause with one whose

(1) Lev. V, 21f. (2) V. *supra* p. 236, n. 6. (3) The instances enumerated by R. Simeon. (4) At one court where he was ordered to pay; and he now denies his liability before another court. As R. Simeon nevertheless exempts him from liability (cf. *supra* p. 236, n. 6), an objection arises against Rabbah. (5) I.e., whose liability had not yet been legally established and the amount claimed is still '*ḳenas*' and not '*mamon*'. (6) V. *supra* p. 236, n. 6. (7) V. Ex. XXII, 3. (8) Ibid. XXI, 37. (9) Lit., 'who brought out an evil name' (V. Deut. XXII, 19). (10) Lev. V, 21, a general statement preceding the details enumerated in the following verses. (11) Certainly not. For, in the first instance, there is no proof that the man had stolen the object and, secondly, even if he had stolen it he might yet make his own confession and thereby obtain exemption from the double payment. (12) V. *supra* note 4.

action had not yet been tried and that the entire Baraitha represents the view of R. Simeon, but I would not give you forced interpretations, for, were I to do so, you might retort: Then either the first clause should begin with 'R. Simeon said' or the final clause should conclude with 'these are the words of R. Simeon'.[1] The fact, however, is that the entire [Baraitha] refers to one whose action had already been tried, the first clause being the view of the Rabbis and the final clause that of R. Simeon, and I must agree with you in regard to the sacrifice for [taking a false] oath,[2] for the All-Merciful has exempted him[3] [as may be deduced] from [the text] *And he deal falsely.*[4] When I, however, said, that 'It is a civil liability' [I was only implying that a man had the right] to transmit such a liability as an inheritance to his sons.[5]

Again he[6] raised an objection against him:[7] R. SIMEON RULED, IF HER FATHER DIED BEFORE SHE COULD COLLECT [HER DUES] THEY BELONG TO HER. Now if you maintain [that such compensation] is a civil liability in respect of being transmitted as an inheritance to one's sons, why should the compensation belong to her? Should it not, in fact, belong to the brothers?—This subject, said Raba, both Rabbah and R. Joseph found difficult for twenty-two years[8] and no solution was forthcoming. It was only when[9] R. Joseph assumed the presidency of the academy[10] that he solved it: There[11] it is different [from other penal liabilities] because Scripture said, *Then the man that lay with her shall* give *unto*

(1) Why then did R. Simeon's name appear at the beginning of the final clause, thus indicating that only that, and not the first clause represented his view? (2) That according to R. Simeon he is not liable to bring his sacrifice even if his action had already been tried. (3) Even if his action had been previously tried. (4) Lev. V, 21 (cf. *supra* p. 238, n. 1 and text). (5) [And much more so in regard to liability to payment on self admission; cf. p. 237 n. 7, v. *Shiṭṭah Meḳubbeẓeth*]. In this respect only is it deemed to be civil if the father died after the action had been tried, though the collection of the sum had not yet been effected. (6) Abaye. (7) Rabbah. (8) I.e., during all the period Rabbah occupied the presidency of the academy at Pumbeditha (cf. Ber. 64*a* and Hor. 14*a*). (9) After the death of Rabbah. (10) Cf. *supra* n. 8. (11) The case of a fine for seduction or violation spoken of in our Mishnah.

the damsel's father fifty [shekels *of*] *silver*[1] [which implies that] the Torah has not conferred upon the father the right of possession before the money had actually been handed to him; when Rabbah, however, said, 'It is a civil liability in respect of being transmitted as an inheritance to his sons' he was referring to other penal liabilities.[2] But then, in the case of a bondman it is written in Scripture, *He shall* give *unto their master thirty* shekels *of silver*,[3] would it here[4] also [be maintained that] the Torah has not conferred upon the master the right of possession before the money had actually been handed to him?—The *yitten*[5] cannot be compared[6] with *we-nathan*.[7] If so,[8] [instead of deducing the exemption from sacrifice] from the Scriptural text, *'And he deal falsely'*,[9] should not the deduction rather be made from *'Then . . . shall give'*?[10]—Raba replied: The text of *'And he deal falsely'* was required in a case, for instance, where the girl's action had been tried and then she became adolescent[11] and died, in which case[12] when the father receives[13]

(1) Deut. XXII, 29 emphasis on *'give'*. (2) [Cf. *supra* 237, n. 4). The whole passage is extremely difficult. Commentators explain that Rabbah had it on tradition that a penal liability becomes civil in respect of inheritance after action had been taken, and the whole discussion was to elucidate exactly the implications of this vague tradition; v. Tosaf. 42*a*, s.v. אמר]. (3) Ex. XXI, 32. (4) Since the verb 'to give' was used. (5) יתן which is used in Ex. XXI, 32. (6) Lit., 'alone', 'is in a separate category'. (7) ונתן (Perfect with *waw* consec.). The former indicates merely future action while the latter implies the pluperfect, 'he shall have given'. (8) That deduction may be made from Deut. XXII, 29 to the effect that the fines of a violator and a seducer have a different legal status from that of other fines in that they remain penal even after the offender had been tried. (9) Cf. *supra* p. 238, n. 1 and text. (10) Cf. *supra* n. 8. While the text beginning *'And deal falsely'* (Lev. V, 21) excludes only those liabilities which were *originally* penal but are *not so now* after the court had issued its ruling (v. *supra* 42*a*, *ad fin*.), the text of *Then . . . shall give* (Deut. XXII, 29) deals specifically with the fines of a violator and a seducer, laying down that so long as no collection of the fines had been effected, they remain penal *even after the court had issued* its ruling (v. Rashi and cf. Tosaf. *a.l.*, s.v. אי). [Although the verse *'And deal falsely'* is necessary for other penal liabilities, the fine of a violator should not have been included seeing that it belongs to a class by itself as is deduced from *'Then . . . shall give'*, v. *Shittah Mekubbezeth*]. (11) A *bogereth*. When the fine, according to R. Simeon (cf. *supra* p. 235, n. 11, and text), belongs to her. (12) Lit., 'for there'. (13) Lit., 'inherits'.

[the fine] he inherits [it] from her.[1] If so,[2] [however, how could it be said:] 'These, therefore, are excluded [from liability] since they are in fact penal' when they are in fact[3] civil?—R. Naḥman b. Isaac replied: [The meaning is], These are excluded since they were originally penal.

He[4] pointed out to him[5] another objection: R. Simeon, however, exempts him, for no fine is paid on one's own admission.[6] The reason then[7] is because his action had not been tried[8] but if it had been tried,[9] in which case he does pay,[10] even on his own admission,[11] he would incur, also, would he not, [the obligation of bringing] a sacrifice for swearing [a false oath]?[12]—R. Simeon argues with the Rabbis on the lines of their own view. According to my own view [he argued] the All-Merciful has exempted the man[13] even after he had been tried [as may be deduced] from the text '*And deal falsely*'.[14] According to your view, however, you must at least admit that [the man is exempt] if he has not yet been tried, since the claim advanced against him is penal [43*a*] and one who makes a voluntary admission in a penal case is exempt.[15] But the Rabbis are of the opinion that the claim[16] is [mainly] in respect of compensation for indignity and blemish.[17] On what principle do they[18] differ?—R. Papa replied: R. Simeon is of the opinion that a

(1) And as far as he is concerned the liability, the payment of which had been ordered by the court, is no longer penal but civil. Hence the necessity for the text of '*And he deal falsely*' to indicate that the defendant is nevertheless exempt from a sacrifice (cf. Tosaf. s.v. כי) because *originally* the liability was penal (v. Rashi). (2) That the Baraitha (*supra* 42*a*) deals with a case where the action had already been tried and that the father inherits the fine from his daughter. (3) Cf. *supra* n. 1. (4) Abaye. (5) Rabbah. (6) Mishnah cited *supra* 42*a*. (7) Why the offender is exempt. (8) Previously, before a court. For if it had been tried he could not subsequently make a voluntary admission that would exempt him. (9) By the first court, and he was ordered to pay. (10) On the ruling of the second court. (11) The money involved being no longer penal but (on account of the ruling of the first court) civil. (12) Though the sum involved was originally penal. A contradiction thus arises between this Mishnah and the Baraithas both of which speak in the name of R. Simeon. (13) From the sacrifice for a false oath. (14) Cf. *supra* 42*a ad fin*. (15) Cf. *supra* p. 236, n. 7. (16) Of the father, in the Mishnah of Shebu. 36*b*, cited *supra* 42*a*. (17) Which are civil liabilities. (18) R. Simeon and the Rabbis.

man would not leave that which is fixed[1] to claim[2] that which is not fixed,[3] while the Rabbis hold the view that no man would leave a claim[2] from which [the defendant] could not be exempt even if he made a voluntary admission[4] and advance a claim[5] from which he would be exempt[6] if he made a voluntary admission.

R. Abina enquired of R. Shesheth: To whom belongs the handiwork of a daughter who[7] is maintained[8] by her brothers?[9] Are they[10] *in loco parentis* and as in that case her handiwork belongs to her father so here also it belongs to her brothers; or [is it more reasonable that] they should not be compared to their father, for in his case she is maintained out of his own estate but here she is not maintained out of their estate?[11] —He replied: You have learned about such a case: A widow is to be maintained out of the estate of [her deceased husband's] orphans, and her handiwork belongs to them.[12] [But] are [the two cases in every way] alike? It may not be any satisfaction to a man that his widow should be liberally provided for,[13] but he might well be pleased, might he not, that his daughter should?[14]

Does this[15] imply that a man has preference for his daughter than for his widow? Surely, R. Abba said in the name of R. Jose:[16] The relationship between[17] a widow and her daughter, in the case of a small estate,[18] has been put on the same level as that of the relationship between[17] a daughter and her brothers. As in the

(1) The statutory fine, prescribed in Deut. XXII, 29. (2) Compensation for indignity and blemish. (3) Since it varies according to the status of each individual. (4) Cf. p. 241, n. 17. (5) Cf. *supra* n. 1. (6) Since it is penal. (7) In accordance with the terms of her mother's *kethubah* (v. Glos.); cf. *infra* 52*b*. (8) Until she is married. (V. *infra* 52*b*). (9) The sons of her deceased father. (10) Since they maintain her. (11) But of that which their father had left them (cf. *supra* nn. 7 and 8). (12) Mishnah, *infra* 59*b*. As the handiwork of a widow who is entitled to maintenance by the terms of her *kethubah* belongs to the sons of the deceased, so obviously does that of a daughter who is also maintained by virtue of a claim in the *kethubah* of her mother. (Cf. *supra* n. 7). (13) By retaining her handiwork for herself. הרווחה, lit., 'relief', 'comfort'. (Rt. רווח or רוח, lit., 'to be far', 'to be placed wide apart', hence 'to have space or room', 'to live in comfort'.) (14) Her handiwork may, therefore, belong to her. (15) The suggestion just made. (16) The parallel passage in B.B. 140*b* reads, 'Assi'. (17) Lit., 'at', 'at the side of'. (18) Which does not suffice for the

case of the relationship between a daughter and her brothers, the daughter is maintained[1] while the brothers can go begging at [people's] doors, so also in the case of the relationship between a widow and her daughter, the widow is maintained and the daughter can go begging at [people's] doors;[2] [which shews, does it not, that the widow is given preference]?—As regards [provision against] degradation[3] a man gives preference to his widow;[4] as regards liberal provision[5] he gives preference to his daughter.[6]

R. Joseph objected: HER HANDIWORK, HOWEVER, AND ANYTHING SHE FINDS, EVEN IF SHE HAS NOT COLLECTED [THE PROCEEDS], BELONG TO HER BROTHERS IF HER FATHER DIED. The reason[7] then is[8] that [they originated during] the lifetime of their father, but [if they originated] after his death [they would belong] to herself. Does not [this refer to a daughter] who is maintained?[9]—No; [this is a case of one] who is not maintained.[10] If she is not maintained, what need is there to state [such a case]?[11] For even according to him who ruled that a master is entitled to say to his bondman, 'Work for me and I will not maintain you'[12] the ruling applies only to a Canaanite bondman concerning whom 'With thee' was not written in Scripture, but not to a Hebrew slave concerning whom *with thee*[13] was written in Scripture. How much less [then would such a ruling apply] to one's daughter?

maintenance of the dependents of the deceased man for a period of twelve months (v. B.B. 139*b*).

(1) Out of the estate of the deceased. (2) B.B. 140*b*. (3) Begging. (4) He feels more humiliation when his widow goes begging than when his daughter does so. (5) Cf. *supra* p. 242, n. 13. (6) It is a father's wish, as a rule, that his daughter shall be enabled to save up some money for her marriage dowry. (7) Why these BELONG TO HER BROTHERS. (8) As in the case of COMPENSATION and FINE spoken of in the same Mishnah. (9) Out of her father's estate by her brothers. How then could R. Shesheth rule that the handiwork of a daughter in such circumstances belongs to her brothers? (10) Where the deceased, for instance, left no property. (11) I.e., what need was there for the author of our Mishnah to provide a text *from which we are to infer* that a daughter's handiwork and anything she finds that originated after her father's death belong to herself? (12) Giṭ. 12*a*. (13) Deut. XV, 16, *He fareth well with thee*.

—Rabbah b. 'Ulla replied: It[1] was only required in the case of a surplus.[2]

Said Raba: Did not such a great man as R. Joseph know that [sometimes there may] be a surplus when he raised his objection?[3] The fact however is, Raba explained, that R. Joseph raised his objection from our very Mishnah. For it was stated, HER HANDIWORK, HOWEVER, AND ANYTHING SHE FINDS, EVEN IF SHE HAS NOT COLLECTED [THE PROCEEDS]; but from whom [it may be asked] is she to collect anything she finds? Consequently it must be conceded that it is this that was meant: HER HANDIWORK is like ANYTHING SHE FINDS; as anything she finds belongs to her father[4] [if she finds it] during his lifetime, and to herself [if she finds it] after his death[5] so also in the case of her handiwork, [if it was done] during the lifetime of her father it belongs to her father [but if it was done] after his death it belongs to herself. Thus it may be concluded [that the ruling of R. Shesheth stands refuted].[6]

So it was also stated:[7] Rab Judah ruled in the name of Rab, The handiwork of a daughter who is maintained by her brothers belongs to herself. Said R. Kahana: What is the reason? Because it is written in Scripture *And ye make them an inheritance for your children after you,*[8] [implying]: *'them'*[9] [you may make an inheritance] *'for your children'*, but not your daughters for your children. This tells us that a man may not transmit his authority[10] over his daughter to his son.[11]

(1) The text of our Mishnah from which the inference mentioned is to be drawn (v. p. 243 n. 11). (2) *Sc.* if the daughter's earnings exceeded the cost of her maintenance. Our Mishnah was necessary for the purpose of the inference (cf. p. 243 n. 11) that the surplus also belongs to herself. (3) Of course he knew and, therefore, he could not possibly have raised an objection in the form attributed to him. (4) In return for her board. A father is under no legal obligation to maintain his daughter (v. *infra* 49a) and it was, therefore, enacted that in recognition of his consideration for her all she finds shall belong to him (v. B.M. 12b). (5) Her father's heirs can lay no claim to her finds because the board they provide for her is not an act of kindness on their part but a legal obligation, cf. *supra* p. 243, n. 7. (6) Cf. *supra* p. 243, n. 9. (7) By Amoraim. (8) Lev. XXV, 46. (9) Canaanite bondmen. (10) Lit., 'privilege', 'advantage'. (11) Hence the ruling that the handiwork of a daughter, though it belongs to her father, does not belong to her brothers.

To this Rabbah demurred: It might be suggested that the Scriptural text[1] speaks of [payments in connection with] the seduction of one's daughter, fines and mayhem![2] And so did R. Ḥanina learn: The Scriptural text[1] speaks of [payments in connection with] the seduction of one's daughter, fines and mayhem![3]

Is not mayhem injury involving bodily pain?[4]—R. Jose b. Ḥanina replied: [43b] The wound [may be supposed to] have been made in her face.[5]

Rab[6] Zera stated in the name of R. Mattena who had it from Rab: (others assert [that it was] Rabbi[6] Zera who stated in the name of R. Mattena who had it from Rab): The handiwork of a daughter who is maintained by her brothers belongs to herself, for it is written in Scripture, *And ye make them an inheritance for your children after you*[7] [implying]: *'Them'*[8] [you may make an inheritance] *'for your children'*, but not your daughters for your children. This tells us that a man may not transmit his authority over his daughter to his son.[9]

Said Abimi b. Papi to him: *Shaḳud*[10] made this statement.[11] Who is *Shaḳud?*—Samuel. But, surely, was it not Rab who made this statement?—Read: *Shaḳud* also made this statement.

Mar the son of Amemar said to R. Ashi, Thus the Nehardeans

(1) Lev. XXV, 46, from which the ruling mentioned (v. *supra* p. 244, n. 11) has been deduced. (2) Assault involving bodily injury. V. *infra* n. 3. (3) All of which are unusual income and cannot be regarded as an income that brothers might properly expect. Handiwork, however, which may normally be expected, the brothers may justly expect from their sister in return for the maintenance with which they provide her. (4) Compensation for which is not due even to her father (v. B.Ḳ. 87*b*). What need then was there to exclude his heirs? (5) As an exposed wound decreases her value, compensation is due to her father, since it is he who suffers the loss. (6) Zera travelled from Babylon to Palestine where he was ordained by R. Joḥanan and had the title of *Rabbi* conferred upon him. His former title was only *Rab*. The following statement was made by him, according to the first reading, *before*, and according to the second reading *after* his ordination. (7) Lev. XXV, 46. (8) Canaanite bondmen. (9) Cf. *supra* p. 244, n. 11. (10) שקוד 'careful speaker' (cf. Rashi *a.l.*), 'industrious scholar' (Jast.) 'studious' (Aruk). (11) The ruling and deduction reported by R. Zera.

have laid down: The law is in agreement with the ruling of R. Shesheth.[1]

R. Ashi [however] said: The law is in agreement with Rab.[2] And the law is to be decided in agreement with the view of Rab.

MISHNAH. IF A MAN GAVE HIS DAUGHTER[3] IN BETROTHAL AND SHE WAS DIVORCED, [AND THEN] HE GAVE HER [AGAIN] IN BETROTHAL AND SHE WAS LEFT A WIDOW, HER KETHUBAH[4] BELONGS TO HIM.[5] IF HE GAVE HER IN MARRIAGE AND SHE WAS DIVORCED [AND THEN] HE GAVE HER [AGAIN] IN MARRIAGE AND SHE WAS LEFT A WIDOW, HER KETHUBAH[6] BELONGS TO HER.[7] R. JUDAH SAID: THE FIRST[8] BELONGS TO HER FATHER.[9] THEY,[10] HOWEVER, SAID TO HIM: HER FATHER, AS SOON[11] AS HE GIVES HER IN MARRIAGE, LOSES ALL CONTROL OVER HER.[12]

GEMARA. The[13] reason[14] is that when HE GAVE HER IN MARRIAGE [the first time] SHE WAS DIVORCED [and that when] HE GAVE HER [AGAIN] IN MARRIAGE, SHE WAS LEFT A WIDOW [for the *first time*],[15] but if she had been left a widow twice[16] she would not have been fit to marry again. The Tanna[17] has thus indirectly laid down an anonymous ruling in agreement

(1) V. *supra* p. 242, n. 12 and text. (2) In opposition to R. Shesheth. (3) While she was a minor or a *na'arah* (v. Glos.). (4) Of the second, as well as that of the first betrothal. (5) Because the income of a daughter under the state of *bogereth* (V. Glos.) belongs to her father. (6) Whether of the first or the second marriage. (7) Because a father's control over his daughter, even if she is a minor, ceases as soon as he gives her in marriage; and since the *collection* of a *kethubah*, though not its writing, must always follow the marriage the amount collected is the rightful possession of the daughter. (8) *Sc.* the *kethubah* of the first marriage. (9) The reason is stated *infra*. (10) The Rabbis who differed from his view. (11) Cur. edd. insert in parentheses, 'if'. (12) Hence it is she who is entitled to receive her *kethubah*. (13) The interpretation of this passage is difficult and that of Rashi is here adopted (v. Tosaf. s.v. טעמא). (14) For the illustration in the second clause of the Mishnah. (15) So that it is possible for her to remarry a third time. (16) Instead of having been divorced. (17) Of our Mishnah by avoiding any unhappy illustration in which the woman cannot marry again.

with Rabbi who holds that if [a thing has happened] twice presumption is established.[1]

R. JUDAH SAID: THE FIRST BELONGS TO HER FATHER. What is R. Judah's reason?—Both Rabbah and R. Joseph explained: Since her father has acquired the right to it[2] at the time of the betrothal.[3]

Raba objected: 'R. Judah ruled that the first[4] belonged to her father; R. Judah nevertheless admitted that if a father gave his daughter in betrothal while she was still a minor and she married after she had attained adolescence he has no authority over her'.[5] But why? Might it not here also be argued,[6] 'Since her father has acquired the right to it at the time of the betrothal'?[7] The fact, however, is that if any statement [in the nature mentioned] has at all been made it must have been made in the following terms:[8] Both Rabbah and R. Joseph explained: Because it[9] was written while she was still under his authority.[10]

As to the recovery [of a *kethubah*],[11] from which date may

(1) If a woman, for instance, was widowed twice she is deemed to be a dangerous companion to men, and is, therefore, forbidden to marry again (v. Yeb. 64*b*). (2) Lit., 'them'. The plural referring generally to the two respective amounts of the statutory *kethubah*, two hundred *zuz* for a virgin and one hundred for a widow or divorcee (v. Rashi, s.v. הואיל). (3) When the daughter was still under her father's authority. In the case of the second *kethubah*, however, which is subsequent to the first marriage R. Judah agrees, of course, with the Rabbis. (4) Cf. *supra* p. 246, n. 8. (5) *Sc.* the *kethubah* belongs to herself and not to her father. (6) That the *kethubah* should belong to the father (cf. *supra* n. 5). (7) Since such argument, however, was not used the statement attributed above to Rabbah and R. Joseph cannot be authentic. (8) Lit., 'but if it was said, it was said thus'. (9) The *kethubah* for the first marriage. On the use of the pl. נכתבין cf. *supra* n. 2. [Although the liability in regard to the *kethubah* began at betrothal, it was not reduced to writing till nuptials proper; cf. Rashi. For other interpretations v. Asheri]. (10) Unlike the Rabbis who were guided by the time of the collection (cf. *supra* p. 246, n. 7) R. Judah holds that the date of the *writing* of the *kethubah* is the determining factor. Hence his ruling in our Mishnah (where the writing took place while the daughter was in her minority) that the *kethubah* is the father's property. In the Baraitha cited, however, (where the writing took place when the daughter was already adolescent, i.e., shortly before her marriage) the *kethubah* rightly belongs no longer to her father but to herself. (11) From property sold between the date of the betrothal and that on which the *kethubah* was written.

distraint be effected?[1]—R. Huna replied: The hundred[2] or the two hundred[3] from the date of the betrothal[4] and the additional jointure[5] from that of the marriage.[6] R. Assi, however, replied: The former as well as the latter [may be distrained upon only] from the date of the marriage.[7]

But could R. Huna, however, have given such a ruling?[8] Has it not been stated: If a wife produced against her husband two *kethuboth*, one for two hundred, and one for three hundred *zuz*, she may, said R. Huna, distrain from the earlier date if she wishes to collect the two hundred *zuz* [but if she desires to collect the] three hundred *zuz* she may distrain from the later date only. Now if the ruling were as stated[9] she should be entitled, should she not, to distrain to the extent of two hundred *zuz* from the earlier date and to that of one hundred from the later date?—But [even] according to your conception [it might equally be objected why] should she [not] distrain for all the five hundred *zuz*, two hundred from the earlier date and three hundred from the later date? What then is the reason why she cannot distrain for all the five hundred? [Obviously this:] Since the man did not write in her favour,[10] 'I willingly added to your credit three hundred *zuz* to the two hundred' he must have meant to imply: 'If you desired to distrain from the earlier date you would recover [no more than] two hundred, and if you desired to distrain from the later date you

(1) I.e., does the right of distraint begin on the date of the betrothal (when the man becomes Rabbinically liable for the *kethubah*) or (as in the case just dealt with) on the date the *kethubah* was written? (V. Rashi. Cf., however, Tosaf s.v. ומיגבא). (2) For a widow or a divorcee. (3) In the case of a virgin. (4) Since these amounts are statutory liabilities applicable to all. (5) Which differs according to individual arrangements, v. *infra*. (6) When the *kethubah* is written and formal acquisition (*ḳinyan* v. Glos.) is effected. (7) Having accepted the written *kethubah* that bore the later date on which her marriage took place the woman is assumed to have surrendered her rights to the statutory amount, which she had acquired earlier on betrothal, in favour of her new advantages as well as any disadvantages that were conferred by the written document. (8) Lit., 'did R. Huna say so'? That the earlier obligation (statutory *kethubah*) is recoverable from the earlier date (betrothal), and the latter one (additional jointure) from the later date (marriage). (9) V. *supra* note 8. Lit., 'there is'. (10) In her second *kethubah*.

would receive three hundred'. [44a] Here also[1] [it may similarly be said:] This is the reason why she cannot distrain [for the additional jointure from the earlier date]: Since he did not write in her favour, 'I have added a hundred *zuz* to the two hundred'[2] she [having accepted the deed] must have renounced her former lien.[3]

The Master[4] has laid down that if she wishes she may distrain with the earlier *kethubah*[5] and if she prefers she may distrain with the later one.[5] Is it then to be assumed [that this ruling] differs from that of R. Naḥman who laid down that if two deeds[6] were issued one after the other the latter cancels the former?[7]—[No, for] has it not been stated in connection with this statement that R. Papa said: R. Naḥman nevertheless admits that if the man has added[8] one palm[9] the insertion was intended as an additional privilege?[10] And here also, surely, [the husband] has added something.[11]

[To turn to] the original text.[12] R. Naḥman laid down that if two deeds were issued one after the other the latter cancels the former. Said R. Papa: R. Naḥman nevertheless admits that if the man has added one palm the insertion was intended as an additional

(1) The last cited ruling of R. Huna. (2) But has included the two hundred in the three hundred under a later date. (3) Her right to distraint does, therefore, begin on the later date only. In the case of ordinary *kethuboth*, however, to which R. Huna's first ruling refers, a special clause to the effect that the husband has *willingly added* the additional jointure to the statutory *kethubah* forms part of the contract. The woman's original rights consequently remain unimpaired (cf. *supra* p. 248, n. 8). (4) I.e., R. Huna in his second ruling, *supra* 43b. (5) Lit., 'with that'. (6) Relating to the same transaction and the same persons. (7) And the right to distrain begins with the second date. Were R. Naḥman's ruling to be applied to the case spoken of by R. Huna, would not the *second kethubah* have cancelled the first and the woman would have had no choice in the matter? (8) In the text of the second deed. (9) Or any other object or money. The addition of a palm applies to a sale, or gift of a plot of land. (10) Lit., 'he wrote it for an addition'. The deed is not thereby impaired, and it is, therefore, within the right of the holder of the deeds to distrain either with the second deed and thus recover the original as well as the addition but from the later date only, or to distrain from the first date the original alone without the addition. (11) Another hundred *zuz*. (12) Which was cited in the discussion just concluded.

privilege.[1] It is obvious [that the reason why both deeds are valid where] the first [was a deed] of sale and the second [a deed] of gift[2] [is because the action of the owner] was intended[3] to improve the other's rights,[4] as a safeguard against[5] the law of pre-emption;[6] and much more [is this[7] obvious where] the first was for a gift and the second for a sale, for it may then be presumed that the latter was written in that manner in order to safeguard the other against[5] a creditor's rights.[8] [What], however, [is the reason why] the second cancels the first where both deeds[9] were for a sale or both for a gift?—Rafram replied: Because it may be presumed that [the holder of the deeds] has admitted to the other [the invalidity of the first deed].[10] R. Aḥa replied: Because it might be presumed that [the holder of the deeds] has surrendered his security of tenure.[11] What is the practical issue between them?[12]—The disqualification of the witnesses,[13] payment of compensation for usufruct[14] and land tax.[15]

(1) V. p. 249 for notes. (2) And related to the same transaction and the same persons as the first one. (3) Lit., 'he (intended) when he wrote for him'. (4) Even though no material addition was made to the original sale. (5) Lit., 'on account of'. (6) In virtue of which the next abutting neighbour can insist on exercising the right of first purchase. This right applies to a sale but not to a gift. בר מצרא lit., 'one on the border', *sc.* the owner of an adjacent field who has the right of pre-emption. (7) The reason for the validity of both deeds. (8) Only a buyer may claim compensation from the original owner if a creditor of that owner had distrained upon the land he bought. A donee has no such right. By the writing of the second deed the owner has conferred upon the donee the additional rights of a buyer. (9) Lit., 'both of them'. (10) And willingly accepted the second though his rights of distraint were thereby restricted to the later date. (11) During the period intervening between the date of the first, and that of the second deed. (12) Rafram and R. Aḥa. (13) According to Rafram the witnesses, since they put their signatures to an invalid document, must be regarded as legally unfit for further evidence. (So Rashi. Tosaf., however, s.v. איכא, object to this view and (*a*) restrict the disqualification of the witnesses in respect of such a deed only as is held by the man who had cast aspersion on their characters or (*b*) apply the disqualification to the signatures). According to R. Aḥa, who does not question the authenticity of the deed, the character of the witnesses is not in any way affected. (14) Which the holder of the deeds enjoyed between the first and the second date. According to Rafram, the holder of the deeds must pay such compen-

What is [the decision] in respect of the *kethubah?*[1]—Come and hear what Rab Judah laid down in the name of Samuel who had it from R. Eleazar the son of R. Simeon:[2] [The statutory *kethubah* of] a *maneh*[3] or two hundred *zuz*[4] [may be distrained for] from [the date of] the betrothal but the additional jointure only from the date of the marriage. The Sages, however, ruled: The one as well as the other [may be distrained for only] from the date of the marriage. The law is that the one as well as the other [may be distrained only] from the date of the marriage.

MISHNAH. THE DAUGHTER OF A PROSELYTE WOMAN WHO BECAME A PROSELYTE TOGETHER WITH HER MOTHER[5] AND THEN[6] PLAYED THE HARLOT IS SUBJECT TO THE PENALTY[7] OF STRANGULATION,[8] BUT NOT TO[9] [STONING AT] THE DOOR OF HER FATHER'S HOUSE[10] NOR [DOES HER HUSBAND PAY THE] HUNDRED SELA'.[11] IF SHE WAS CONCEIVED IN UNHOLINESS[12] BUT HER BIRTH WAS IN HOLINESS[13] SHE IS SUBJECT TO THE PENALTY OF STONING BUT NOT TO[9] [THAT OF BRINGING HER OUT TO 'THE DOOR OF HER FATHER'S HOUSE', NOR [DOES HER HUSBAND PAY THE] HUNDRED SELA'. IF SHE WAS BOTH CONCEIVED AND BORN IN HOLINESS[13]

sation since the first deed is presumed to be invalid. According to R. Aḥa no such compensation is paid since the holder of the deeds renounced only his security of tenure but not his usufruct. (15) The original owner must pay it according to Rafram and the holder of the deeds according to R. Aḥa.

(1) I.e., 'from which date may distraint be effected?' (V. p. 247, n. 11 and 248, n. 1). (2) *Var. lec.* 'Eliezer b. Shamua' (Bomb. ed.). (3) V. Glos. (4) The respective amounts due (*a*) to a widow or divorcee, and (*b*) to a virgin. (5) Lit., 'the female proselyte whose daughter became a proselyte with her'. (6) Having become betrothed while she was still a *na'arah* (v. Glos). (7) Lit., 'behold this'. (8) The penalty prescribed for a faithless married woman. (9) Lit., 'she has not either'. (10) Prescribed in Deut. XXII, 21 for a betrothed Israelite damsel (*na'arah*) who played the harlot. (11) Due from a man who wrongfully accused his wife (v. Deut. XXII, 19). [Nor is he flagellated, the fine and the flogging being prescribed in juxtaposition to one another (Riṭba)]. (12) *Sc.* while her mother was still a heathen. (13) After her mother's conversion.

SHE IS REGARDED AS A DAUGHTER OF ISRAEL IN ALL RESPECTS.[1]

ONE[2] WHO HAD A FATHER BUT NO 'DOOR OF HER FATHER'S HOUSE',[3] OR A 'DOOR OF HER FATHER'S HOUSE' BUT NO FATHER, IS NEVERTHELESS SUBJECT TO THE PENALTY[4] OF STONING,[5] [FOR THE REGULATION, 'TO] THE DOOR OF HER FATHER'S HOUSE',[6] WAS ONLY INTENDED AS [AN INDEPENDENT] PRECEPT.[7]

GEMARA. [44b] Whence is this[8] deduced?—Resh Lakish replied: Since Scripture said, *That she die*[9] it[10] included also her who WAS CONCEIVED IN UNHOLINESS BUT HER BIRTH WAS IN HOLINESS: If so, [should not her wrongful accuser][11] also be flogged[12] and [condemned] to pay the hundred *sela'*?[13]—Scripture stated, *That she die*[14] [implying that she] was included in respect of death but not in respect of the fine.

Might it not be suggested [that Scripture intended] to include one who was both conceived and born in holiness?—Such a person is a proper Israelite woman.[15] But can it not be said that [Scripture intended] to include one conceived and born in unholiness?—If this were so what purpose would be served[16] by the expression,[17] *'In Israel'?*[18]

R. Jose b. Ḥanina ruled: A man who brought an evil name upon an orphan girl is exempt, for it is said in Scripture, *And give them*

(1) She is subject to the penalties and entitled to the privilege as prescribed in Deut. XXII, 19, 21. (2) Any daughter of Israel (Rashi) who played the harlot while she was a betrothed *na'arah*. (3) When her father, for instance, had no house. (4) Lit., 'behold this'. (5) V. *supra* note 1. (6) פתח בית אביה (Deut. XXII, 21). Cur. edd. read אב. (7) Not as an indispensable part of the penalty. (8) That IF SHE WAS CONCEIVED IN UNHOLINESS BUT HER BIRTH WAS IN HOLINESS SHE IS SUBJECT TO THE PENALTY OF STONING. (9) Deut. XXII, 21, which is superfluous after *Shall stone her with stones* (ibid.). (10) By the insertion of the superfluous expression. (11) *Supra* p. 251, n. 11. (12) In accordance with Deut. XXII, 18, v. p. 251. n. 11. (13) V. Deut. XXII, 19. (14) Ibid. 21; emphasis on *'die'*. (15) And requires no special text to include her. (16) Lit., 'what would it benefit him'. (17) Deut. XXII, 21. (18) None whatever. Hence it follows that the last mentioned was excluded.

unto the father of the damsel,[1] which excludes this girl who has no '*father*'.

R. Jose b. Abin, or it might be said, R. Jose b. Zebida, raised an objection: *If her father utterly refuse*[2] [was meant][3] to include an orphan girl in respect of the fine;[4] so R. Jose the Galilean.[5] [Why then should the orphan in this case[6] be excluded]?—He raised the objection and he himself supplied the answer: [This[7] is a case of a girl] who became an orphan after the man had intercourse with her.[8]

Rabbah[9] ruled: He[10] is guilty. Whence [did he infer this]?—From that which Ammi taught: *A virgin of Israel,*[11] but not a proselyte virgin.[12] Now if you assume that in a case of this nature[13] in Israel[14] guilt is incurred, one can well see why it was necessary for a Scriptural text to exclude proselytes. If you, however, assume that in a case of this nature in Israel[14] [the offender] is exempt [the difficulty would arise:] Now [that we know that the offender] is exempt [even if he sinned] against Israelites[14] was it any longer necessary [to mention exemption if the offence was] against proselytes?[15]

Resh Lakish ruled: A man who has brought an evil name[16] upon

(1) Ibid. 19. (2) מאן ימאן Ex. XXII, 16, dealing with a case of seduction. (3) Since the verb was repeated (v. note 2). (4) One form of the verb (ימאן) referring to the father and the other (the infin. מאן) to a girl who has no father. (5) Which shews that, though the laws in respect of seduction (Ex. XXII, 15f) are inferred from those of outrage (Deut. XXII, 28) and *vice versa*, and though in the latter case Scripture specifically stated that the fine is payable to the damsel's father (ibid. 29), an orphan is nevertheless entitled to the fine. (6) In that of an evil name. (7) The Tannaitic ruling of R. Jose the Galilean. (8) Only such an orphan is included. All others are excluded by the Scriptural mention of father. (9) In opposition to the view of R. Jose b. Ḥanina *supra*. (10) The man who brought an evil name upon an orphan. (11) Deut. XXII, 19. (12) I.e., the penalties spoken of in the Scriptural text apply only to the former and not to the latter. (13) *Sc.* that of a girl who is fatherless. A proselyte, though his or her heathen parents are alive, has the status of one who is fatherless. (14) *Sc.* an Israelite girl who is fatherless. (15) Of course not, since the latter case would be self-evident *a minori ad majus*. As exemption, however, was specified in this case it may be concluded that in that of an Israelite orphan guilt is incurred. (16) V. Deut. XXII, 19.

a minor is exempt,[1] for it is said in Scripture, *And give them unto the father of the damsel,*[2] Scripture expressed the term *na'arah*[3] as plenum.[4] To this R. Aḥa[5] b. Abba[6] demurred: Is the reason then[7] because in this case *'the na'arah'*[8] was written [in Scripture], but otherwise it would have been said that even a minor [was included], surely, [it may be objected] it is written in Scripture, *But if the thing be true, and the tokens of virginity be not found in the damsel, then they shall bring out the damsel to the door of her father's house and [the men of the city] shall stone her,*[9] while a minor is not, is she, subject to punishment?[10]—[The explanation,] however, [is that, since] *na'arah* [has been written] here[11] [it may be inferred that only where *na'arah*[12] is used is a minor excluded] but wherever Scripture uses the expression *na'ara*[13] even a minor is included.[14]

Shila taught: There are three modes [of execution] in the case of a [betrothed] damsel[15] [who played the harlot]. If witnesses appeared against her in the house of her father-in-law[16] [testifying] that she had played the harlot in her father's house[17] [45a] she is stoned at the *door of her father's house,*[18] as if to say,[19] 'See the plant that you have reared'. If witnesses came [to testify] against her in her father's house that she played the harlot in his house[17] she is stoned at the entrance of the gate of the city. If having committed the offence[20] she eventually[21] attained adolescence[22] she is condemned to strangulation.[23]

(1) From paying the prescribed fine *'of a hundred shekels'*. (2) V. Deut. XXII, 19. (3) *Damsel,* Heb. נערה. (4) With *'he'* at the end of the word. As elsewhere נערה is written נַעֲרָ (*na'ara*) defective, it is assumed that the plenum here was intended to refer to *na'arah* (v. Glos.) only, and not to a minor, v. *supra* 40*b*, and notes. (5) *Var.* 'Adda' (cf. *supra* 40*b*). (6) *Var.* 'Ahabah' (cf. l.c. and MS.M.). (7) Why the fine mentioned is not incurred where a minor is concerned. (8) הנערה, *'the . . . damsel'*. (9) Deut. XXII, 20f. (10) And a minor would consequently have been excluded even if נַעֲרָ defective had been written. (11) Where a minor is obviously excluded because she is not subject to penalties. (12) נַעֲרָה. (13) נַעֲרָ. (14) I.e., the exclusion mentioned was not necessary for the case spoken of in this context where it is obvious (v. *supra* n. 11) but for the purpose of a general deduction. (15) *Na'arah* (v. Glos.). (16) *Sc.* after her marriage. (17) While she was betrothed. (18) Cf. Deut. XXII, 21. (19) To the parents. (20) While she was a *na'arah*. (21) Before her trial. (22) V. Glos. s.v. *bogereth*. (23) The penalty prescribed for adults. Only a *na'arah* (v. Glos.) is subject to the penalty of stoning.

This[1] then implies that wherever there occurred a change in one's person, one's mode of execution also must be changed. But is not this contradicted by the following: 'If a betrothed damsel[2] played the harlot and [her husband] brought upon her an evil name[3] after she had attained adolescence,[4] he is neither to be flogged[5] nor is he to pay the hundred *sela'*,[6] but she and the witnesses who testified falsely against her[7] are hurried[8] to the place of stoning'?[9] 'She *and* the witnesses who testified falsely against her'! Can this be imagined?[10]—But [this is the meaning:] 'She[11] or[12] her witnesses[13] are hurried[8] to the place of stoning'?[14]—Raba replied: You speak [of the law relating to a husband] who brought up an evil name; but this law is different [from the others],[15] because it is an anomaly.[16] For, elsewhere, if a girl[17] entered the bridal chamber,[18] though no intercourse followed, she is condemned to strangulation if she committed adultery, but [a woman upon whom a husband] brought an evil name is condemned to stoning.[19] Said

(1) R. Shila's last mentioned ruling that the penalty of a *na'arah* who attained majority is changed from stoning to strangulation. (2) V. p. 254, n. 20. (3) V. Deut. XXII, 14. (4) *Sc.* when their marriage took place (Rashi). (5) V. ibid. 18. (6) V. ibid. 19. (7) And were proved *Zomemim* (v. Glos.). (8) מקדימין lit., 'go early', *sc.* they cannot escape their doom and might as well get it over as soon as possible (Rashi). (9) בית הסקילה, a structure twice a man's height (i.e. six cubits) from which the condemned man was thrown before he was stoned (v. Sanh. 45a [Sonc. ed.] p. 295). (10) Obviously not. If she is condemned they must be true witnesses, and if they are condemned she must be innocent. (11) If she was found guilty. (12) The *waw* of וזוממיה may be rendered 'or' as well as 'and'. (13) In the case where their falsehood was established by other witnesses. (14) Thus, at all events, it follows that despite the change in her person she is still subject to the former penalty, which is in contradiction with the ruling of Shila (v. *supra* note 1). (The penalty of a *na'arah* is stoning and that of one who is in her adolescence is only strangulation). (15) Such as the law of Shila which deals with an accusation by witnesses and not with an evil name brought by a husband. (16) Lit., 'novelty', and no comparison with, or inference from an anomalous law may be made. (17) Even a *na'arah* (v. Glos. and cf. *infra* 48b). (18) *Ḥuppah* (v. Glos.). (19) [Although had she committed the offence at the time of the defamation, i.e., after marriage, she would be strangled. This proves that in the case where the husband himself, and not witnesses, brings a charge, after marriage, of infidelity having taken place during betrothal, we do not apply the principle that the intervening

R. Huna the son of R. Joshua to Raba: Is it not possible that the All-Merciful created the anomaly only where no constitutional change had taken place,[1] but where a constitutional change had occurred[2] the All-Merciful has created no anomaly?[3]—The fact however is, explained R. Naḥman b. Isaac, [that the question whether a change in status] involves, or does not involve a change [in the penalty] is [a point in dispute between] Tannaim. For we have learned: If they[4] committed a sin before they were appointed [to their respective offices] and [then] were appointed, they are regarded[5] as laymen. R. Simeon ruled: If their sin came to their knowledge before they were appointed[6] they are liable,[7] but if after they were appointed[8] they are exempt.[9]

[45b] [But] is it not to be maintained that R. Simeon was heard to be guided by [the time of] the awareness also,[10] did you, how-

change in the woman's status effects retrospectively a change in the penalty. And it is the exception which the law makes in this case which proves the general rule to the contrary elsewhere, v. Tosaf.].

(1) As in the case just cited where the change affects only her status—from betrothal to marriage. (2) I.e., when the girl had attained her adolescence as in the case spoken of by Shila. (3) The contradiction pointed out (v. *supra* p. 255, notes 1 and 14) would consequently arise again. (4) A High Priest and a ruler whose sin-offerings differ from those of laymen. The former's offering being a bullock (Lev. IV, 3) the latter's a he-goat (ibid. 23) while that of a layman is a she-goat (ibid. 28) or a lamb (ibid. 32). (5) In respect of their sin-offerings. (6) So that both the commission of the sin and their awareness of it occurred while they were in the same status as laymen. (7) To bring sin-offerings as prescribed for laymen (v. *supra* note 4). (8) So that their sin was committed while they were still laymen and subject to one kind of offering, and their awareness set in when, as a ruler or High Priest, another kind of offering was due. (9) Completely; on account of the change in their status (Hor. 10a). Consequently it may be assumed that the first Tanna who holds that a change in status does not involve a change of offering, maintains also that a change in the person involves no change of penalty, while R. Simeon who maintains that a change of status removes the obligation of an offering, will hold all the more so that a change in the person removes a man's liability to his former penalty and thus subjects him to the penalty appropriate to his new condition, and thus Shila's teaching will be in accordance with R. Simeon. (10) I.e., the nature of an offering cannot be determined by that status alone in which a man finds himself at the time he committed his sin. If his liability to

ever, hear that he was guided by [the time of] awareness alone and not also by that of the commission of sin? For were that so,[1] should they[2] not have brought an offering in accordance with their present status, the High Priest a bullock, and the ruler a he-goat?[3] —Surely R. Johanan said to the Tanna:[4] Read, 'She is to be condemned to stoning.'[5]

But why?[6] Did not the All-Merciful[7] speak of a betrothed *'damsel'*[8] and this one is adolescent?—R. Elai replied: Scripture said, *the damsel*[9] [implying] her who was a damsel[8] *before*.[10]

Said R. Hanania to R. Elai: If so,[11] should not [the husband] also be flogged and pay the hundred *sela'*?[12]—'May the All-Merciful', the other replied, 'save us from such an opinion'.[13] 'On the contrary [the first retorted], may the All-Merciful save us from such an opinion as yours'. What, however, is the reason?[14]—R. Isaac b. Abin, or, as some say, R. Isaac b. Abba, replied: In her case it was[15] her behaviour that brought about her [punishment] but in his case it was[15] the inclination of his lips[16] that brought about his [penalties]. 'In her case it was her behaviour that brought about

that offering is to be established he must have the same status when he becomes aware of his sin. It is on this account, and not because a change of status involves a change of penalty, that R. Simeon exempts a man from an offering where he became aware of his sin after he had assumed a new status.

(1) That a change of status involves a man in the offering or penalty of his new condition, in agreement with Shila's ruling, irrespective of that man's former status in which his sin was committed. (2) Laymen who became aware of their sins after they had been appointed High Priests or rulers. (3) The answer being in the affirmative the objection against Shila again arises (v. *supra* p. 255, notes 1 and 14). (4) Who recited Shila's ruling in his presence. (5) *Sc.* despite the change in her person her penalty remains unaltered. That is, Shila's teaching is rejected. (6) I.e., why (v. *supra* note 5) is she to be stoned. (7) In prescribing the penalty of stoning. (8) *Na'arah* (v. Glos.). (9) Deut. XXII, 21 emphasis on *'the'*, הנערה with the *'he'* article. (10) *Sc.* at the time of the offence (v. *supra* note 5). (11) That the determining factor is the time of the offence. (12) The penalties prescribed in Deut. XXII, 18f. (13) An evasive reply. R. Elai held the reason to be so obvious that he refused to discuss it. Cf. the reason given *infra*. (14) Why the girl's constitutional change alters the man's penalties and not hers. (15) Lit., 'this'. (16) *Sc.* his organs of speech. It was his talk that brought an evil name upon her.

her [punishment]' and when she played the harlot she was still a *na'arah.*[1] 'But in his case it was the inclination of his lips that brought about his [penalty]'; and when does he incur his guilt? Obviously at that time,[2] and at that time she was already adolescent.

Our Rabbis taught: A betrothed damsel[1] who played the harlot is to be stoned at *'the door of her father's house'.*[3] If she had no *'door of her father's house'*[4] she is stoned at the entrance of the gate of that city. But in a town which is mostly inhabited by idolaters she is stoned at[5] the door of the court. Similarly you may say: A man who worships idols[6] is to be stoned at the gate [of the city] where he worshipped, and in a city the majority of whose inhabitants are idolaters he is stoned at the door of the court.[7]

Whence are these rulings derived?—From what our Rabbis have taught: [By the expression] *thy gates*[8] [was meant] the gate [of the city] wherein the man has worshipped. You say, 'The gate [of the city] wherein the man has worshipped', might it not mean the gate where he is tried?[9]—[Since the expression] *'thy gates'* is used below[10] and also above[11] [an analogy is to be made:] As *'thy gates'* mentioned above[12] refers to the gate [of the city] wherein he worshipped[13] so does *'thy gates'* that was mentioned below[10] refer to the gate [of the city] wherein the man had worshipped. Another interpretation: *'Thy gates'*,[8] but not the gates of idolaters.[14] [As to] that [expression of] *'thy gates'*, has not a deduction already been drawn from it?[15]—If [the purpose of the expression were only] this

(1) *Na'arah* (v. Glos.). (2) When he spread the report. (3) If the witnesses came after she had married (v. Rashi). Cf. *supra* p. 251, n. 10. (4) Cf. *supra* p. 252, n. 3. (5) Or 'outside'; cf. Tosaf. s.v. על, *a.l.* (6) MS.M., 'and in the case of idolatry'. (7) Tosef. Sanh. X. (8) Deut. XVII, 5. (9) The judges' seat was at the city gate (cf. Ruth IV, 1ff). (10) Deut. XVII, 5, which follows, and prescribes the punishment of the crime mentioned in v. 2 that precedes it. (11) Deut. XVII, 2. (12) Where the commission of the crime is spoken of. (13) Since the text specifically deals with that subject. (v. n. 12). (14) I.e., if most of the inhabitants of a city are idolaters the execution is not carried out at the gate of the city but at the court gate. (15) In the analogy *supra*. Lit., 'you have drawn it out'. How could two deductions be made from one word?

deduction[1] Scripture would have used the expression 'gate'; why '*thy gates*'? Both deductions may, therefore, be made.

Thus we obtain [rulings in respect of] idolatry,[2] whence do we [derive the law in respect of] a betrothed girl?[3] R. Abbahu replied: '*Door*'[4] is inferred from '*door*',[5] and *door*[5] from '*gate*',[6] and '*gate*'[5] from '*thy gates*'.[7]

Our Rabbis taught: [A husband] who brings up an evil name [upon his wife] is flogged[8] and he must also pay a hundred *sela'*.[9] R. Judah ruled: As to flogging, [the husband is] flogged in all circumstances; as to the hundred *sela'*, however, where he had intercourse with her[10] he pays them but if he did not have intercourse with her[11] he does not pay. They[12] differ on the same principles as those on which R. Eliezer b. Jacob and the Rabbis differed,[13] and it is this that [each of the former group] meant: [A husband] who brought an evil name [upon his wife] is flogged and he must also pay a hundred *sela'*, whether he had intercourse, or did not have intercourse with her, [this being] in agreement with the Rabbis.[14] R. Judah ruled: As to flogging [the husband is] flogged in all circumstances;[15] as to the hundred *sela'*, however, where he

(1) Lit., 'so'. (2) Since the texts cited deal with that subject. (3) *Na'arah* (v. Glos.). (4) *Door of her father's house* (Deut. XXII, 21) in the text dealing with the punishment of a betrothed girl. (5) *Door of the gate of the court* פתח שער החצר (Num. IV, 26). (6) V. *supra* n. 5. Since both nouns (פתח) '*door*', and (שער) '*gate*' are placed in juxtaposition, the analogy may be made: As '*door*' (פתח) in this text is near '*gate*' (שער) so is '*door*' in Deut. XXII, 21 (v. *supra* n. 4) to be regarded as occurring near '*gate*'. Hence the ruling that if the girl has no 'door of her father's house' she is to be stoned at the '*gate*' of the city. (7) Deut. XVII, 5, which deals with idolatry; the analogy being: As in the case of idolatry so also in that of a betrothed girl the execution takes place at the gate of the court wherever the city is inhabited by a majority of idolaters. (8) As prescribed in Deut. XXII, 18. (9) V. Deut. XXII, 19. (10) And then brought up the evil name by alleging that he had found no tokens of virginity (v. ibid. 17). (11) And his allegation is based on the evidence of witnesses. (12) The Rabbis and R. Judah. (13) *Infra*. (14) Who maintain that the Scriptural section dealing with the case of a husband who '*brought up an evil name*' upon his wife applies in all circumstances, whether intercourse did or did not take place. (15) For even where the Scriptural section under discussion does not apply, the penalty of flogging must still be inflicted on account of the infringement of the prohibition against tale bearing.

had intercourse with her he pays them but if he did not have intercourse with her he does not pay; in agreement with R. Eliezer b. Jacob.[1]

Another reading.[2] All the statement[3] is in agreement with the opinion of R. Eliezer b. Jacob[1] and it is this that [each of the former group][4] meant: [A husband] who brought an evil name [upon his wife] is flogged and he must also pay the hundred *sela'* only where he had intercourse with her.[5] R. Judah ruled: As to flogging, [the husband is] flogged in all circumstances.[6]

Can R. Judah, however, maintain that 'as to flogging, [the husband] is flogged in all circumstances' when it was taught: R. Judah ruled, If he had intercourse he is flogged but if he did not have intercourse he is not flogged?—R. Naḥman b. Isaac replied: [By the ruling of R. Judah that the husband] 'is flogged'[7] [was meant] chastisement[8] which is a Rabbinical penalty.[9] [46*a*] R. Papa replied: By the expression[10] 'If he had intercourse he is flogged',[11] which was used there,[12] the monetary fine[13] [was meant].[14] But could one describe a monetary fine as 'flogging'?—Yes, and so indeed we have learned:[15] If a man said, 'I vow to pay half of my valuation'[16] he must pay half of his valuation. R. Jose the son of R. Judah ruled: He is flogged[17] and must pay his full valuation. [And in reply to the question,] why should he be flogged? R. Papa explained: He is 'flogged'[17] by [having to pay his] full valuation.[18]

(1) Who holds that the section under discussion deals only with a case where intercourse preceded the allegation. (2) Lit., 'some there are who say'. (3) Lit., 'all of it', *sc.* the views of both the Rabbis and R. Judah. (4) V. p. 259, n. 12. (5) In full agreement with R. Eliezer b. Jacob (cf. *supra* n. 1). (6) For the reason given p. 259, n. 15; but he is exempt from the payment of the hundred *sela'*. (7) 'In all circumstances'. (8) מכת מרדות V. Glos. s.v. *makkath marduth*. (9) Pentateuchally, however, no flogging is inflicted unless intercourse preceded the charge. (10) Lit., 'what'. (11) לוקה. The rt. לקה may signify (*a*) flogging and also (*b*) the infliction of any penalty or suffering. (12) In the last cited ruling of R. Judah. (13) The hundred *shekels*. (14) The payment of the fine only is dependent on previous intercourse, but flogging is inflicted in all circumstances (v. *supra* p. 259, n. 15). (15) MS.M., 'it was taught'. Cf. 'Ar. 20*a* and Tosef. 'Ar. III. (16) V. Lev. XXVII, 2ff. (17) לוקה (cf. *supra* note 5). (18) Or 'he is punished by having to pay etc.'.

What is the reason?[1]—[The ruling[1] in the case of a vow for] a half of one's valuation[2] is a preventive measure against the possibility [of a vow for] the value of half of one's body,[3] such a half[4] being an organic part[5] on which one's life depends.[6]

Our Rabbis taught: *And they shall fine him*[7] refers to[8] a monetary fine; *And chastise him*[9] refers to[8] flogging. One can readily understand why '*And they shall fine*' refers to a monetary payment since it is written, '*And they shall fine him a hundred* shekels *of silver and give them unto the father of the damsel*';[10] whence, however, is it deduced that '*And chastise him*' refers to flogging?—R. Abbahu replied: We deduce '*Shall chastise*'[9] from '*Shall chastise*',[11] and '*Shall chastise*'[11] from '*Son*',[12] and '*Son*'[12] from '*Son*'[13] [occurring in the Scriptural text:] *Then it shall be, if the wicked man deserve*[14] *to be beaten.*[15]

Whence is the warning[16] against bringing up an evil name [upon one's wife] deduced? R. Eleazar replied: From *Thou shalt not go up and down as a talebearer.*[17] R. Nathan replied: From *Then thou shalt keep thee*[18] *from every evil thing.*[19] What is the reason that R. Eleazar does not make his deduction[20] from the latter[21] text?[19]—That text[19] he requires for [the same deduction] as [that made by] R. Phinehas b. Jair: From the text,[22] *Then thou shalt keep thee from every evil thing;*[19] R. Phinehas b. Jair deduced[20] that a man should not indulge in [morbid] thoughts by day that might lead him to uncleanness by

(1) For the payment of his full valuation when the man only vowed half of it. (2) חצי ערכו, as prescribed in Lev. XXVII, 2ff. (3) ערך חציו. (4) Lit., 'and the value of his half'. (5) MS.M. דבר Cur. edd. אבר 'limb'. (6) And where the value of such a part or limb is vowed the full valuation must be paid. (7) Deut. XXII, 19. (8) Lit., 'this'. (9) Deut. XXII, 18. (10) Deut. XXII, 19. (11) Deut. XXI, 18. (12) Ibid. (13) Ibid. XXV, 2 (v. *infra* n. 14). (14) Lit., '*son*'. (15) V. *supra* n. 13. As this text in which '*son*' occurs (v. *supra* n. 14) speaks definitely of flogging (v. Deut. XXV, 2-3) the punishment of the '*son*' spoken of in Deut. XXI, 18, concerning whom also the expression of '*chastise*' (ibid.) was used, must also be that of flogging; and since '*chastise*' (ibid.) implies flogging, '*chastise*' in Deut. XXII, 18 must also mean flogging. V. Sanh. 71*b*. (16) *Sc.* a negative precept for the transgression of which flogging is incurred. No flogging is inflicted for an offence unless there is a prohibition in regard to it. (17) Lev. XIX, 16. (18) ונשמרת the Nif. of שמר which implies a negative precept. (19) Deut. XXIII, 10. (20) Lit., 'said'. (21) Lit., 'from that'. (22) Lit., 'from here'.

night.[1] What then is the reason why R. Nathan does not make his deduction from the former[2] text?[3]—That text[3] is a warning to the court that it must not be lenient with one[4] [of the litigants] and harsh to the other.

If [a husband] did not tell the witnesses,[5] 'Come and give evidence for me' and they volunteered to give it, he[6] is not to be flogged nor is he to pay the hundred *sela'*.[7] She, however, and the witnesses who testified falsely against her are hurried[8] to the place of stoning. 'She *and* the witnesses who testified against her'! Can this be imagined?—But [this is the meaning]: 'She *or* her witnesses are hurried to the place of stoning.[8] Now the reason then[9] is because he did not even tell them [to give their evidence].[10] Had he, however, told them [he would have been subject to the prescribed penalties][11] even though he did not hire them. [This ruling thus serves the purpose] of excluding the view of R. Judah concerning whom it was taught: R. Judah ruled, [a husband] incurs no penalties[11] unless he has hired the witnesses.[12]

What is R. Judah's reason? R. Abbahu replied: An analogy is drawn between the two forms of the root 'to lay'.[13] Here[14] it is written, *And lay*[15] *wanton charges against her,*[16] and elsewhere it is written, *Neither shall ye lay*[17] *upon him interest;*[18] as there[18] [the offence is committed through the giving of] money[19] so here [also it can be committed only by the giving of] money.[20] R. Naḥman b. Isaac said, and so did R. Joseph the Zidonian recite at the

(1) The verse following (Deut. XXIII, 11) speaking of a *man . . . that is not clean . . . by night*. V. A.Z. 20*b*. (2) Lit., 'from that'. (3) Lev. XIX, 16. (4) The Heb. of Lev. XIX, 16 cited, is לא תלך רכיל the third word being composed of the letters forming the phrase רך לי 'lenient or gentle to me'. (5) Who testified that his wife comitted adultery before her marriage. (6) Though the evidence had been proved to be false. (7) V. Deut. XXII, 18f. (8) For notes v. *supra* p. 255, n. 4ff. (9) Why the husband is exempt. (10) Since the ruling runs, 'did not *tell* them', and not 'did not hire them'. (11) V. Deut. XXII, 18f. (12) Who testified that his wife committed adultery before her marriage. (13) Or 'to put'. Lit., 'it comes (from) putting (and) putting'. (14) In the case of an evil name brought up by a husband (Deut. XXII, 13ff). (15) ושם, rt. שום 'to put', 'to lay'. (16) Deut. XXII, 14. (17) תשימון, rt. שום. (18) Ex. XXII, 24. (19) Interest. (20) *Sc*. the hiring of the witnesses.

school[1] of R. Simeon b. Yoḥai: An analogy is drawn between the two forms of the root 'to lay'.[2]

R. Jeremiah raised the question: What is the ruling[3] where [the husband] hired them[4] with a piece of land?[5] What [if he hired them] for a sum less than a *peruṭah?*[6] What [if both witnesses were hired] for one *peruṭah?*

R. Ashi enquired: What [is the ruling where a husband][7] brought an evil name [upon his wife] in respect of their first marriage? What [if a levir[8] brought up an evil name] in respect of his brother's marriage?—You may at all events solve one [of these questions].[9] For R. Jonah taught: *I gave my daughter unto this man*[10] only *unto this man*[11] but not to a levir.[12]

What [is the ruling of] the Rabbis and what [is that of] R. Eliezer b. Jacob?[13]—It was taught: What constitutes[14] the bringing up of an evil name [against one's wife]?[15] If [a husband] came to the Beth din and said, 'I, So-and-so, found not in thy daughter the tokens of virginity'. If there are witnesses that she committed adultery while living with him she is entitled to a *kethubah* for a *maneh.*[16] 'If there are witnesses that she committed adultery while living with him [you say,] she is entitled to a *kethubah* for a *maneh'!* But is she not in that case subject to the penalty of stoning?[17]—It is this that was meant: If there are witnesses that she committed adultery while she was living with him she is to be stoned; if, however, she committed adultery before [her marriage] she is entitled

(1) MS.M. 'Zaidana of the school'. [Probably of Bethsaida]. (2) V. *supra* p. 262, n. 13ff. (3) According to R. Judah who laid down that a husband incurs no penalties unless he has hired the witnesses. (4) The witnesses (v. *supra* p. 262, n. 12). (5) Does R. Judah include land also under the term of 'money', or does he, since his ruling was deduced from the law of interest, restrict the price of the hiring to movables only, such as money and foodstuffs, which are specifically mentioned in connection with the laws of interest, (v. Ex. XXII, 24 and Deut. XXIII, 20). (6) V. Glos. (7) Who remarried his wife after he had once divorced her. (8) Who was under the obligation to contract levirate marriage with his deceased brother's wife (cf. Deut. XXV, 5ff). (9) The last. (10) Deut. XXII, 16. (11) I.e., the husband. (12) *Sc.* the penalties prescribed in the section apply only to the former. (13) Referred to *supra* 45*b ad fin.* (14) Lit., 'how'. (15) V. Deut. XXII, 13ff. (16) V. Glos. (17) How then could one speak of giving her a *kethubah?*

to a *kethubah* for a *maneh*.[1] If it was ascertained that the evil name had no foundation in fact[2] the husband is flogged and he must also pay a hundred *sela'* irrespective of whether he had intercourse [with her] or whether he did not have intercourse [with her]. R. Eliezer b. Jacob said: These penalties[3] apply only where he had intercourse [with her].

According to R. Eliezer b. Jacob[4] one can well understand why Scripture used the expressions, *'And go in unto her'*[5] and *'When I came nigh to her'*,[6] but according to the Rabbis[7] what [could be the meaning of] *'And go in unto her'*[5] and *'When I came nigh unto her'?*[6] *'And go in unto her'*[5] with *wanton charges*, and *'When I came nigh to her'*[6] with words.

According to R. Eliezer b. Jacob[4] one can well see why Scripture used the expression, *'I found not in thy daughter the tokens of virginity'*,[8] but according to the Rabbis[7] what [could be the sense of the expression], *'I found not in thy daughter the tokens of virginity'?—I found not for*[9] *thy daughter* witnesses to establish her claim to *tokens of virginity*.[10]

It was quite correct for Scripture, according to R. Eliezer b. Jacob,[11] to state, *And yet these are the tokens of my daughter's virginity;*[12] but according to the Rabbis[13] what could be the sense of [the expression,] *'And yet these are the tokens of my daughter's virginity'?*[12] —*And yet these are* the witnesses who establish[10] *the tokens of my daughter's virginity*.

One can well understand, according to R. Eliezer b. Jacob,[11] why Scripture wrote, *And they shall spread the garment;*[12] but according to the Rabbis[13] what [could be the sense of the instruction,]

(1) The statutory sum due to a non-virgin. (2) Lit., 'is not an evil name'. (3) Lit., 'words', the penalties prescribed in the section of Deut. XXII, 13ff. (4) Who restricts the application of the penalties (v. *supra* n. 3) to a husband with whom intercourse had taken place. (5) Deut. XXII, 13. (6) Ibid. 14. (7) Who maintain that the penalties always apply, irrespective of intercourse. (8) Deut. XXII, 17. (9) The *lamed* in לבתך may be rendered '*in*' (as E.V.) or 'for' as here expounded. (10) By refuting the evidence of the first witnesses who accused her of the offence. כשרי (read as כַּשְּׁרֵי) is to be regarded as the Piel of כשר, 'to make fit', and referring to the *action* of the witnesses who establish the fitness or honesty of the accused. (11) V. *supra* note 4. (12) Deut. XXII, 17. (13) V. *supra* note 7.

And they shall spread the garment?—R. Abbahu replied: They explain[1] [the charge] which he submitted against her;[2] as it was taught: '*And they shall spread the garment*' teaches that the witnesses of the one party and those of the other party come, and the matter is made as clear as a new garment. R. Eliezer b. Jacob said: The words are to be taken in their literal sense: [They must produce] the actual garment.[3]

R. Isaac son of R. Jacob b. Giyori sent this message in the name of R. Johanan: Although we do not find anywhere in the Torah that Scripture draws a distinction between natural and unnatural intercourse in respect of flogging or other punishments, such a distinction was made in the case of a man who brought an evil name [upon his wife];[4] for he is not held guilty unless, having had intercourse with her, [even][5] in an unnatural manner, he brought up an evil name upon her in respect of a natural intercourse.

In accordance with whose view?[6] If [it be said to be] in accordance with the view of the Rabbis [the husband, it could be retorted, should have been held guilty] even if he had no intercourse with her. If [it be said to be] in agreement with the view of R. Eliezer b. Jacob [46*b*] must not the intercourse in both cases be in a natural manner?[7]—The fact, however, is, said R. Kahana in the name of R. Johanan, that the husband is not held guilty unless he had intercourse in a natural manner and he brought up an evil name upon her in respect of a natural intercourse.

MISHNAH. A FATHER HAS AUTHORITY OVER HIS DAUGH-

(1) ופרשו (E.V., '*and they shall spread*') is rendered, 'And they shall *explain*'. פרש, 'to explain', פרש, 'to spread', *Shin* and *Sin* being interchangeable. (2) השם לה '(the allegation) which he submitted against her'. A play on the word השמלה (E.V. the *garment*) v. Tosaf. (3) As proof of the tokens. (4) Only where his witnesses accused her of illicit intercourse in a natural manner is he, when their evidence is proved to be false, liable to pay the fine of a hundred *shekels*; but where his witnesses alleged unnatural intercourse he is exempt from the fine even though their evidence was proved to be false. (5) V. Rashi. (6) Has the last mentioned statement been made? (7) Since he takes the verses literally.

TER[1] IN RESPECT OF HER BETROTHAL [WHETHER IT WAS EFFECTED] BY MONEY,[2] DEED[3] OR INTERCOURSE;[4] HE IS ENTITLED TO ANYTHING SHE FINDS AND TO HER HANDIWORK; [HE HAS THE RIGHT] OF ANNULLING HER VOWS[5] AND HE RECEIVES HER BILL OF DIVORCE;[6] BUT HE HAS NO USUFRUCT[7] DURING HER LIFETIME.[8] WHEN SHE MARRIES, THE HUSBAND SURPASSES HIM [IN HIS RIGHTS] IN THAT HE HAS[9] USUFRUCT DURING HER LIFETIME,[10] BUT HE IS ALSO UNDER THE OBLIGATION OF MAINTAINING AND RANSOMING HER[11] AND TO PROVIDE FOR HER BURIAL. R. JUDAH RULED: EVEN THE POOREST MAN IN ISRAEL MUST PROVIDE[12] NO LESS THAN TWO FLUTES AND ONE LAMENTING WOMAN.

GEMARA. 'BY MONEY'. Whence is this[13] deduced?—Rab Judah replied: Scripture said, *Then shall she go out for nothing without money,*[14] [which implies that] this master[15] receives no money[16] but that another master does receive money;[17] and who is he? Her father.[18] But might it not be suggested that it[19] belongs to her?[20] —Since[21] it is her father who contracts[22] her betrothal, as it is

(1) While she is under the age of twelve and a half years and one day. (2) *Sc.* the money belongs to him. (3) The receipt of the deed by him effects his daughter's betrothal. (4) It is within his rights to allow such an act to have the validity of a *kinyan* (v. Glos.). (5) V. Num. XXX, 4ff. (6) If she was divorced during her betrothal before attaining her adolescence (v. Glos. s.v. *bogereth*). (7) Of property that came into her possession from her mother's side. (8) Such property passes into the possession of a father as heir to his daughter only after her death. (9) In addition to the privileges enjoyed by a father. (10) Cf. *infra* 65*b*, Kid. 3*b*. (11) If she was taken captive. (12) For his wife's funeral. (13) That the money of the betrothal belongs to her father. (14) Ex. XXI, 11, referring to a Hebrew maidservant. (15) To whom a father sold his daughter (v. ibid. 7). (16) When she leaves him on becoming a *na'arah* (v. Glos. and cf. Kid. 4*a*). (17) When, on marriage, she passes out of his control. (18) Since beside the *master* spoken of in the Scriptural text (cf. Ex. XXI, 8) the daughter of an Israelite has no other master but her father. (19) The money of her betrothal. (20) The implication of the text cited merely indicating that, unlike the case of the liberation of an Israelite maidservant, her passing out of her father's control at betrothal is attended by money, without necessarily meaning that this money goes to her father. (21) Lit., 'now'. (22) Lit., 'accepts'.

written in Scripture, *I gave my daughter unto this man,*[1] would she take the money![2] But can it not be suggested that this[3] applies only to a minor[4] who has no legal right[5] [to act on her own behalf], but that a *na'arah*[6] who has such rights[7] may herself contract her betrothal, and she herself receives the money?—Scripture stated, *Being in her youth in her father's house,*[8] [implying that] all the advantages of her youth belong to her father.

[Consider], however, that which R. Huna said in the name of Rab: 'Whence is it deduced that a daughter's handiwork belongs to her father? [From Scripture] where it is said, *And if a man sell his daughter to be a maidservant,*[9] as[10] the handiwork of a maidservant belongs to her master so does the handiwork of a daughter belong to her father'.[11] Now what need was there,[12] [it may be asked, for this text when] deduction[13] could have been made from [the text of] '*Being in her youth in her father's house*'?[8] Consequently [it must be admitted, must it not, that] that text was written in connection only with the annulment of vows?[14] And should you suggest that we might infer this[15] from it,[16] [it could be retorted that] monetary matters cannot be inferred from ritual matters.[16] And should you suggest that we might infer it[15] from [the law of] fine,[17] [it could be retorted, could it not, that] monetary payments cannot be inferred from fines? And should you suggest that it[15] might be

(1) Deut. XXII, 16. (2) Of course not. Hence it must be concluded that it, as stated in our Mishnah, belongs to her father. (3) A father's right to the betrothal money of his daughter, as implied in the Scriptural text cited. (4) Though the Scriptural text referred to deals with an evil name brought upon a *na'arah* (v. Glos.) it might nevertheless be contended that the betrothal of that *na'arah* took place while she was still a minor. (5) Lit., 'a hand'. (6) V. Glos. (7) Lit., 'a hand'. (8) Num. XXX, 17. (9) Ex. XXI, 7. (10) Since '*daughter*' and '*maidservant*' appear in juxtaposition an analogy between them may be drawn. (11) *Supra* 40*b*, *infra* 47*a*, Ḳid. 8*a*. (12) Lit., 'wherefore to me'. (13) That a father is entitled to his daughter's handiwork. (14) And, therefore, no deduction from it can be made in respect of handiwork. Similarly, here also, no deduction from it could be made in respect of a father's right to his daughter's money of betrothal. The previous question, therefore, arises again. (15) That a father is entitled to his daughter's money of betrothal. (16) From the law of the annulment of vows. (17) As the fine prescribed in Deut. XXII, 19, belongs to her father so does the money.

inferred from [the law of compensation for] indignity and blemish,[1] [it could be retorted] that indignity and blemish are different,[2] since [the rights] of her father [are also, are they not], involved[3] in it?[4]—[This], however, [is the explanation]:[5] It is logical to conclude that when the All-Merciful excluded[6] [another] going out,[7] the exclusion was meant to be [understood in a manner] similar to the original.[8] But[9] one 'going out', surely, is not like that of the other: For[10] in the case of the master [the maidservant] goes entirely out of his control while in the 'going out' from the control of her father [the daughter's] transfer to the bridal chamber is still lacking?[11]—In respect of the annulment of vows, at any rate, she passes out of his control; for we have learned: In the case of a betrothed damsel[12] it is her father and her husband who jointly annul her vows.[13]

DEED OR INTERCOURSE. Whence do we [deduce this]?[14]—Scripture said, *And becometh another man's wife*[15] [from which it may

(1) Which belongs to her father (v. *supra* 40b). (2) From the case under consideration. (3) As a father has the right to dispose of the indignity and blemish of his daughter while she is still a *na'arah*, by allowing any sort of person to marry her, he is also entitled to compensation for any indignity or blemish anyone inflicted upon her without his consent. (4) The question, whence is it deduced that the money of betrothal belongs to her father, thus arises again. (5) Why deduction may be made from Ex. XXI, 11 (cf. *supra* p. 266 notes 13-20, and text). (6) Cf. *supra* p. 266 notes 15-18 and text. (7) V. *supra* p. 266, n. 17. (8) As in the original it is the *master*, and not the maidservant, who, in the absence of the specific text to the contrary, would have received the money for the latter's redemption, so in the implication it must be the *father* (who corresponds to the master), and not his daughter, who is to receive the money when she passes out of his control at betrothal (v. Rashi). [Now since we learn that her father is entitled to her betrothal money, it follows that the right to effect her betrothal is vested in him, Tosaf.]. (9) Lit., 'but that'. (10) Lit., 'there'. (11) Until her entry into the bridal chamber (*Ḥuppah*, v. Glos.) a daughter is still partially under the control of her father who is still entitled to her handiwork and remains her heir. (12) *Na'arah* (v. Glos.). (13) The father alone has no longer the right to do so. For further notes on the passage v. Ḳid. (Sonc. ed.) p. 36. (14) A father's absolute right to effect the betrothal of his young daughter (v. *supra* p. 266, nn. 3-4) by these two methods. (15) Deut. XXIV, 2; *and becometh* והיתה.

be inferred that] the various forms of betrothal[1] are to be compared to one another.[2]

HE IS ENTITLED TO ANYTHING SHE FINDS, [47a] in order [to avert] ill feeling.[3]

TO HER HANDIWORK. Whence do we deduce this?—[From that] which R. Huna quoted in the name of Rab: Whence is it deduced that a daughter's handiwork belongs to her father?—[From Scripture] where it is stated, *And if a man sell his daughter to be a maidservant,*[4] as the handiwork of a maidservant belongs to her master so does the handiwork of a daughter belong to her father.[5] But may it not be suggested that this[6] [applies only to] a minor whom he may sell, but the handiwork of a *na'arah*[7] whom he cannot sell belongs to herself?—It is but logical to assume that it should belong to her father; for should it be imagined that her handiwork does not belong to him [the objection could well be advanced against] the right[8] which the All-Merciful has conferred upon a father to consign his daughter to the bridal chamber: How could he consign her when he thereby[9] prevents her from doing her work?[10] R. Aḥai demurred: Might it not be suggested that he[11] pays her compensation [for the time] she is taken away [from her work] or else, that he consigns her during the night,[12] or else that he might consign her on Sabbaths[13] or festivals?[13]—[The fact], however, [is that in the case of] a minor no Scriptural text was necessary.[14] For since[15] he may even sell her was it at all necessary

(1) הויות lit., 'beings', 'becomings', of the same rt. היה as that of והיתה (v. *supra* p. 268, n. 15). (2) As betrothal by money is entirely in the hands of the father (to whom the money belongs, as has been shewn *supra*) so is betrothal by deed or intercourse. (3) Between father and daughter. (4) Ex. XXI, 7. (5) Cf. *supra* 40*b*, 46*b*, Ḳid. 3*b*. (6) Lit., 'these words', a father's right to his daughter's handiwork. (7) V. Glos. (8) Lit., 'but that'. (9) Lit., 'surely'. (10) During her preparations for, and the performance of the bridal chamber ceremonial. Since, however, a father does enjoy the right it must be concluded that a daughter's handiwork does belong to her father. (11) A father who consigns his daughter into the bridal chamber. (12) When people usually rest from their work. (13) On which days work is forbidden. The question thus arises again: Whence is it deduced that a daughter's handiwork belongs to her father? (14) To confer upon her father the right to her handiwork. (15) Lit., 'now'.

[to state that her handiwork belongs to him]?[1] If a Scriptural text[2] then was at all necessary [it must have been] in respect of a *na'arah*.

TO ANNUL HER VOWS. Whence do we [deduce this]?—[From Scripture] where it is written,[3] *Being in her youth in her father's house*.[4]

AND HE RECEIVES HER BILL OF DIVORCE. Whence is this deduced?—From Scripture where it is written, *And she departeth*[5] and *And becometh*,[5] 'departure'[6] being compared to 'becoming'.[7]

BUT HE HAS NO USUFRUCT DURING HER LIFETIME. Our Rabbis taught: A father has no usufruct[8] during the lifetime of his daughter.[9] R. Jose the son of R. Judah ruled: A father is entitled to usufruct[8] in the lifetime of his daughter. On what principle do they differ?—The first Tanna is of the opinion that the Rabbis were well justified in allowing usufruct to a husband, since otherwise he might refrain from ransoming [his wife].[10] What, however, can be said[11] in respect of a father? That he would refrain from ransoming her? [It is certain that] he would ransom her in any case. R. Jose the son of R. Judah, however, is of the opinion that a father also might refrain from ransoming [his daughter], for he might think: She is carrying a purse[12] about her, let her proceed to ransom herself.[13]

WHEN SHE MARRIES, THE HUSBAND SURPASSES HIM [IN HIS RIGHTS] IN THAT HE HAS USUFRUCT etc. Our Rabbis taught: If [a father] promised his daughter in writing[14] fruit,[15] clothes or other movable objects[16] that she might take[17] with her[18] from her

(1) Obviously not. (2) Viz., the superfluous word לאמה, *to be a maidservant* (Ex. XXI, 7), from which the analogy is drawn *supra*. The ordinary text deals, of course, with a minor. (3) In the section dealing with the invalidation of vows. (4) Num. XXX, 17. *'Being in her youth'* בנעוריה, *sc*. while she is yet a *na'arah* (v. Glos.). (5) Deut. XXIV, 2. (6) I.e., divorce. (7) *Sc*. a wife (cf. Deut. XXIV, 2: *Becometh . . . wife*). As a father may contract his daughter's betrothal so may he accept her divorce. (8) V. *supra* p. 266, n. 7. (9) V. l.c. n. 8. (10) Should she ever be taken captive. (11) In justification of his claim to the usufruct of his daughter's property. (12) The savings of the proceeds of her property. (13) And should her savings be insufficient he would refuse to supplement them. (14) Lit., 'wrote for her', as her dowry. (15) Detached from the ground (v. *infra*). (16) Lit., 'vessels', 'chattels'. (17) Lit., 'which shall come'. (18) On betrothal.

father's house to that of her husband, and she died,[1] her husband does not acquire these objects. In the name of R. Nathan it was stated: The husband does acquire them. Must it be assumed that they[2] differ on the same principles as those on which R. Eleazar b. Azariah and the Rabbis differed? For we learned: A woman who was widowed or divorced, either after betrothal or after marriage, is entitled to collect all[3] [that is due to her]. R. Eleazar b. Azariah ruled: [Only a woman widowed or divorced] after her marriage recovers all [that is due to her], but if after a betrothal a virgin recovers only two hundred *zuz*[4] and a widow only one *maneh*[4] [47*b*] for the man wrote [the additional jointure] for her with the sole object of marrying her.[5] [Must it then be assumed] that he who ruled that 'her husband does not acquire' [upholds the same principle] as R. Eleazar b. Azariah[6] while he[7] who ruled that 'the husband does acquire' [upholds the same principle] as the Rabbis?[8]—No; all[9] [may, in fact, hold the same view] as R. Eleazar b. Azariah.[10] [For] he who ruled, 'her husband does not acquire', [is obviously] in agreement with R. Eleazar b. Azariah.[11] And as to him[7] who ruled, 'the husband does acquire' [it may be explained that] only [in respect of undertakings] from him[12] towards her[13] did R. Eleazar b. Azariah maintain his view,[14] [for the

(1) During the period of her betrothal. (2) R. Nathan and the first Tanna. (3) I.e., her additional jointure as well as her statutory *kethubah*. (4) V. Glos., *sc*. her statutory *kethubah only*. (5) And since he did not marry her she can have no claim to it. V. *Infra* 54*b*, 89*b*; B.M. 17*b*. (6) As the latter makes the woman's right to her additional jointure dependent on marriage, so also does the former make the husband's right to the dowry his wife brings from her father's house dependent on marriage. In the opinion of both betrothal entitles one only to the prescribed statutory rights. (7) R. Nathan. (8) As they deem betrothal to be as valid as marriage in respect of conferring upon a woman the right to her additional jointure as well as to her statutory *kethubah*, so does R. Nathan deem betrothal to be conferring upon a husband the right to the dowry his wife has brought him. As the additional jointure which is included in the document of the *kethubah* is acquired on betrothal by the woman, so is the dowry which is also included in the same document acquired on betrothal by the man. (9) R. Nathan and the first Tanna. (10) Whose ruling is (as stated *infra*) the accepted law. (11) Cf. *supra* note 6. (12) A husband. (13) A wife. (14) That betrothal does not confer upon a woman the right of acquisition.

reason that] 'the man wrote [the additional jointure] for her with the sole object of marrying her',[1] but [in respect of undertakings] from her[2] towards him[3] even R. Eleazar b. Azariah may admit [that betrothal has the same force as marriage] since [undertakings of such a nature][4] are due to [a desire for] matrimonial association, and such association, surely, had taken place.[5]

HE IS ALSO UNDER THE OBLIGATION OF MAINTAINING HER etc. Our Rabbis taught: Maintenance was provided for a wife in return for her handiwork, and her burial[6] in return for her *kethubah*.[7] A husband is, therefore, entitled to usufruct. 'Usufruct'! Who mentioned it?[8]—A clause is missing, and this is the proper reading: Maintenance was provided for a wife in return for her handiwork, her ransom in return for usufruct,[9] and her burial in return for her *kethubah*;[10] a husband, therefore, is entitled to usufruct.[9]

What [was the need for] 'therefore'?[11]—It might have been presumed [that a husband] must not consume the fruits[9] but should rather leave them,[12] since, otherwise,[13] he might refrain from ransoming her, hence we were informed that that [course][14] was preferable, for sometimes [the proceeds of the fruit] might not suffice[15] and he[16] would have to ransom her at his own expense.

(1) V. *supra* p. 271, n. 5. (2) A wife. (3) A husband. (4) The dowry e.g., which her father promises to her husband. (5) By the betrothal. Hence the ruling that, in this respect, betrothal alone confers the same rights as marriage. (6) Variant, 'ransom' (*She'iltoth*). (7) Here it means the dowry (v. *supra* n. 4) which, like the statutory *kethubah* and the additional jointure, is also entered in the *kethubah* document. (8) Lit., 'their (*sc.* the fruits') name'; the first clauses of the Baraitha cited speak only of 'handiwork' and '*kethubah*' and these, surely, provide no reason for a husband's right to usufruct. (9) Of her *melog* (v. Glos.) property which was not entered in the *kethubah*. (10) V. *supra* note 7. (11) The ruling 'a husband therefore . . . usufruct' seems superfluous after the statement, 'her ransom in return for usufruct'. (12) I.e., allow their proceeds to accumulate, and thus create a fund for his wife's ransom. (13) Lit., 'if so'; were he to consume the fruit or to spend their proceeds. (14) That the husband shall enjoy usufruct and that in return for this he shall assume the obligation of ransoming his wife. (15) To cover the full amount of the ransom. Lit., 'that they be not full'. (16) Since, in accordance with the ordinance, he enjoyed usufruct and undertook the obligation of ransom. (V. *supra* note 14).

Might I not transpose [the sequence]?[1]—Abaye replied: They[2] ordained the common for the common[3] and the uncommon for the uncommon.[4]

Said Raba: The following Tanna is of the opinion that maintenance[5] is a Pentateuchal duty. For it was taught: *She'erah*[6] refers to[7] maintenance, for so it is said in Scripture, *Who also eat the* she'er[8] *of my people;*[9] Her raiment[10] [is to be understood] according to its ordinary meaning; *'Onatha*[11] refers to the time for conjugal duty[12] prescribed in the Torah,[13] for so it is said in Scripture, *If thou shalt afflict*[14] my *daughters.*[15] R. Eleazar said: *'She'erah'* refers to the prescribed time for conjugal duty,[13] for so it is said in Scripture, *None of you shall approach to any that is near of kin*[16] *to him to uncover their nakedness;*[17] *'Her raiment'* [is to be taken] according to its literal meaning; *'Onatha* refers to maintenance, for so it is said in Scripture, *And he afflicted thee,*[18] *and suffered thee to hunger.*[19] [48*a*] R. Eliezer b. Jacob interpreted: [The expressions] *She'erah kesutha,*[20] [imply]: Provide her with raiment according to her age, viz. that a man shall not provide his old wife[21] [with the raiment] of a young one nor his young wife with that of an old one. [The expressions], *Kesutha we-'Onatha*[22] [imply.] Provide her with raiment according to the season of the year,[23] viz. that he shall not give her new

(1) In the Baraitha, thus: Maintenance in return for usufruct and ransom in return for handiwork. A wife would consequently be prevented from retaining her handiwork even if she declined maintenance. (2) The Rabbis. (3) Maintenance and handiwork are both part of a person's daily routine. (4) Usufruct for ransom. It is rare that a wife should own *melog* (v. Glos.) property or that she should be carried away as a captive. Both usufruct and ransom are consequently uncommon. (5) Of a wife by her husband. (6) E.V. *Her food*, שארה (שאר with pronom suffix; v. *infra* n. 8) Ex. XXI, 10. (7) Lit., 'these'. (8) שאר, E.V. *flesh*. (9) Micah III, 3. (10) Ex. XXI, 10. (11) עונתה, R.V., *Her duty of marriage*; A.J.V., *Her conjugal rights*, Ex. XXI, 10. עונתה (rt. ענה, in Piel, 'to afflict'; v. *infra* nn. 12 and 14). (12) עונה (rt. ענה; v. *supra* n. 11). (13) Cf. *infra* 61*b*. (14) תענה (rt. ענה). (15) Gen. XXXI, 50. (16) שאר. (17) Lev. XVIII, 6. (18) ויענך (rt. ענה). (19) Deut. VIII, 3. (20) שארה כסותה (Ex. XXI, 10), 'her age, her raiment'. שאר = flesh (cf. *supra* note 8), hence 'body', 'age'. (21) Lit., 'to her'. (22) כסותה ועונתה (Ex. XXI, 10), 'her raiment and her time' עונה = 'time', 'season'. (23) Lit., 'her season'.

raiment[1] in the summer nor worn out raiment[2] in the winter.[3]

R. Joseph learnt: *Her flesh*[4] implies close bodily contact,[5] viz. that he must not treat her in the manner of the Persians who perform their conjugal duties in their clothes. This provides support for [a ruling of] R. Huna who laid down that a husband who said, 'I will not [perform conjugal duties] unless she wears her clothes and I mine', must divorce her and give her also her *kethubah*.

R. JUDAH RULED: EVEN THE POOREST MAN IN ISRAEL etc. This[6] then implies that the first Tanna is of the opinion that these[7] are not [necessary]. But how is one to imagine [the case]? If these[7] were required by the woman's status,[8] what [it may be objected could be] the reason of the first Tanna who ruled [that these[7] were] not [required]? And if these[7] were not required by the woman's status,[9] what [it may be objected could be] the reason of R. Judah?—[The ruling was] necessary only [in a case], for instance, where these were demanded by his status but not by hers. The first Tanna is of the opinion that the principle that she[10] rises with him[11] but does not go down with him[12] is applied only during her lifetime[13] but not after her death, while R. Judah maintains [that the principle applies] even after her death. R. Ḥisda laid down in the name of Mar 'Uḳba that the *halachah* is in agreement with R. Judah.

R. Ḥisda further stated in the name of Mar 'Uḳba: If a man became insane Beth din take possession[14] of his estate and provide food and clothing for his wife, sons and daughters, and for anything else.[15] Said Rabina to R. Ashi: Why should this[16] be different from that concerning which it was taught: If a man went to a

(1) Which might be too warm for her in the hot weather. (2) Being worn thin they would not provide sufficient protection from cold. (3) Lit., 'in the days of the rains'. (4) Cf. *supra* p. 273, n. 6. (5) Lit., 'nearness of flesh'. (6) Since the ruling is attributed to R. Judah. (7) Two flutes and one lamenting woman. (8) Lit. 'that it is her (*sc.* her family's) custom'. (9) Cf. *supra* n. 8 *mutatis mutandis*. (10) A wife. (11) Her husband. (12) I.e., enjoys his advantages but does not suffer his disadvantages. (13) As in the instance dealt with *infra* 61*a*. (14) Lit., 'go down into'. (15) This is explained *infra*. (16) The case dealt with by R. Huna.

country beyond the sea and his wife claimed maintenance, Beth din take possession of[1] his estate and provide food and clothing for his wife, but not for his sons and daughters or for anything else?[2] The other replied: Do you not draw a distinction between one who departs[3] deliberately and one who departs[4] without knowing it?[5]

What [is meant by] 'anything else'? — R. Ḥisda replied: Cosmetics were meant.[6] R. Joseph explained: Charity. According to him who replied, 'Cosmetics', the ruling[7] would apply with even greater force to charity.[8] He, however, who explained, 'charity' [restricts his ruling[7] to this alone] but cosmetics [he maintains] must be given to her, for [her husband] would not be pleased that she shall lose her comeliness.

R. Ḥiyya b. Abin stated in the name of R. Huna: If a man went to a country beyond the sea, and his wife died, Beth din take possession[9] of his estate and bury her in a manner befitting the dignity of his status. [You say] 'In a manner befitting the dignity of his status', and not that of her status![10] — Read, In a manner befitting his status also; and it is this that he[11] informs us: She rises with him [in his dignity] but does not go down with him [to a lower status] even after her death.

(1) This is explained *infra*. (2) *Infra* 107a. (3) From his home to a foreign country. (4) From society, *sc.* becomes insane. (5) In the former case the man could have left instructions, if he were minded to do so, that his wife and family should be provided for. Since, however, he left no such instructions, it is obvious that he had no intention of providing for them. Hence the ruling that his wife, whom he is under a legal obligation to maintain, (her claim being secured on his estate in accordance with the terms of her *kethubah*) must be provided for by the Beth din out of his estate; not however, his sons and daughters who have no legal claim upon their father's estate. Where, however, a man becomes insane it may well be assumed that it was his wish that both his wife and family shall be properly provided for out of his estate. (6) Lit., 'this'. (7) Of the Baraitha that 'anything else' was not to be provided for. (8) Since the court which has no right to provide from a man's estate for his own wife's personal enjoyments would have much less power to exact from that estate for charity. (9) Lit., 'go down into'. (10) Why should she suffer indignity on account of his lower status? (11) R. Huna.

R. Mattena ruled: A man[1] who gave instructions that when [his wife] died she shall not be buried at the expense of his estate must be obeyed.[2] What, however, is the reason [for obeying the man] when he has left instructions? Obviously because the estate falls to the orphans;[3] but the estate falls to the orphans, does it not, even if he left no instructions?[4]—[The proper reading], however, is: A man[1] who gave instructions that when he dies *he* shall not be buried at the expense of his estate[5] is not to be obeyed, for it is not within his power[6] to enrich his sons and throw himself upon the public.

MISHNAH. SHE[7] REMAINS[8] UNDER THE AUTHORITY OF HER FATHER[9] UNTIL SHE ENTERS [48*b*] UNDER THE AUTHORITY OF HER HUSBAND[10] [BY GOING INTO THE BRIDAL CHAMBER][11] AT MARRIAGE. IF HER FATHER DELIVERED HER TO THE AGENTS OF THE HUSBAND[12] SHE PASSES[13] UNDER THE AUTHORITY OF HER HUSBAND. IF HER FATHER WENT WITH HER HUSBAND'S AGENTS[14] OR IF THE FATHER'S AGENTS WENT WITH THE HUSBAND'S AGENTS[14] SHE REMAINS[13] UNDER THE AUTHORITY OF HER FATHER. IF HER FATHER'S AGENTS DELIVERED HER TO HER HUSBAND'S AGENTS[15] SHE PASSES[13] UNDER THE AUTHORITY OF HER HUSBAND.

(1) While in a dying condition. The instructions of a dying man have the force of a legally written document. (2) Having survived her husband and collected her *kethubah* a wife has no further claim upon his estate which is consequently inherited by his sons. (3) Cf. *supra* n. 2. (4) And they, of course, are under no obligation to bury the widow. (5) But at the public cost. (6) Lit., 'all from him'. (7) A *na'arah* (v. Glos.). This Mishnah is a continuation of the previous one, *supra* 46*b*. (8) לעולם, lit., 'for ever', 'always'. (9) Even after her betrothal. He is entitled to all his privileges; and, if she is the daughter of an Israelite, although betrothed to a priest, *terumah* is forbidden to her. (10) *Var. lec.* 'to the bridal chamber' (v. Tosaf. 48*a*, s.v. לעולם). (11) *Ḥuppah* (v. Glos.); cf. Rashi, *a.l.* and cf. *supra* n. 10. (12) Who were sent to bring her from her father's house to that of her husband. (13) Lit., 'behold she is'. (14) To her husband's house. (15) Neither they nor her father who sent them accompanying her to the house of her husband.

GEMARA. What [is the purport of] REMAINS?[1]—To exclude [the ruling] of an earlier[2] Mishnah where we learned: If the respective periods[3] expired[4] and they were not married[5] they are entitled to maintenance out of the man's estate[6] and [if he is a priest][7] may also eat *terumah*.[8] Therefore 'REMAINS'[9] was used.[10]

IF HER FATHER DELIVERED HER TO THE AGENTS OF THE HUSBAND SHE PASSES UNDER THE AUTHORITY OF HER HUSBAND etc. Rab ruled: Her delivery [is regarded as entry into the bridal chamber] in all respects[11] except that of *terumah*;[12] but R. Assi ruled in respect of *terumah* also.

R. Huna, (or as some say, Ḥiyya b. Rab,) raised an objection against R. Assi: She remains[9] under the authority of her father until she enters the bridal chamber.[13] 'Did I not tell you', said Rab to them,[14] 'that you should not be guided by an ambiguous statement?[15] He[16] can answer you that "her delivery" is regarded as her entry into the bridal chamber'.

Samuel, however, ruled: [Her delivery has the force of entry into the bridal chamber only in respect] of her inheritance.[17] Resh

(1) לעולם, lit., 'for ever', 'always'. The omission of לעולם would not in any way alter the actual ruling except the wording which would then read, 'She is under' etc. Why then was an apparently superfluous word inserted? (2) Lit., 'first'. (3) One of twelve months for a virgin and of thirty days for a widow (from the date their intended husbands claimed them) in which to prepare their marriage outfits. (4) Lit., 'the time arrived'. (5) Through their future husbands' delay or neglect. (6) Lit., 'eat of his'. (7) Though they are daughters of Israelites. (8) *Infra* 57a. (9) V. note 1. (10) *Sc*. despite the expiry of the prescribed period a daughter REMAINS UNDER THE AUTHORITY OF HER FATHER UNTIL etc. and is consequently forbidden to eat *terumah* (cf. *supra* p. 276, n. 9). (11) *Sc*. the man obtains all the privileges to which a husband is entitled from the moment the bride enters the bridal chamber (e.g., the right to her handiwork, heirship). (12) The woman, if she is the daughter of an Israelite, is forbidden to eat it though the man is a priest (v. *infra* 57b). (13) And until then she is forbidden to eat *terumah* (cf. *supra* p. 276, n. 9). How then could R. Assi maintain that *terumah* is permitted to her? (14) His disciple R. Huna and his son Ḥiyya. (15) איפכא, lit., 'reverse'. (16) *Sc*. R. Assi. MS.M., 'I'. (17) I.e., if she died on the way between her father's house and that of her husband, her dowry (given to her by her father) is inherited by her husband although he is not entitled to his other rights until her entrance into the bridal chamber.

Lakish ruled: [Only in respect] of her *kethubah*.[1] What is meant by 'her *kethubah*'? [If it means] that should [the woman] die he inherits it,[2] [then this ruling is, is it not,] the same as that of Samuel?[3] Rabina replied: The meaning is[4] that her [statutory] *kethubah* from a second husband[5] is only a *maneh*.[6]

Both R. Joḥanan and R. Ḥanina ruled: Her delivery [is regarded as entry into the bridal chamber] in all respects, even that of *terumah*.[7]

An objection was raised: If the father went with the agents of the husband, or if the agents of the father went with the agents of the husband, or if she had a court-yard on the way, and she entered it with him[8] to rest there for the night,[9] her father inherits from her if she died, although her *kethubah*[10] is already in the house of her husband. If, however, her father delivered her to her husband's agents, or if her father's agents delivered her to her husband's agents, or he[11] had a court-yard on the way, and she entered it with him with an intention to matrimony, her husband is her heir if she died, although her *kethubah*[10] was still in her father's house.[12] This ruling[13] applies only in respect of her inheritance[14] but in respect of *terumah* [the law is that] no woman is allowed to eat *terumah* until she enters the bridal chamber.[15] [Does not this represent] a refutation of all?[16]—This is indeed a refutation.

[But] is not this,[17] however, self-contradictory? You said, 'She entered it with him to rest for the night'. The reason [why such an act is not regarded as entry into the bridal chamber is] because [the entrance was made specifically for the purpose of] resting for the night. Had it, however, been made with no specified intention

(1) This is explained anon. (2) Viz., the dowry her father gave her which forms one of the entries in her *kethubah*. (3) V. p. 277 n. 17 (4) Lit., 'to say'. (5) If her first husband died while she was on the way with his agents. (6) V. Glos. The amount prescribed for a widow. A virgin is entitled to two hundred *zuz*. (7) Cf. *supra* p. 277, n. 12 *mutatis mutandis*. (8) Her husband. (9) With no matrimonial intention. (10) I.e., the dowry her father gave her. (11) Her husband. (12) I.e., the objects specifically assigned to her as dowry were still in her father's house. (13) That delivery to the husband's agents has the force of a marriage. (14) V. *supra* p. 277, n. 17. (15) Tosef. Keth. IV. (16) Lit., 'all of them', those (with the exception of Samuel) whose rulings differ from this Baraitha. (17) The Baraitha last mentioned.

[it would be deemed to have been made] with an intention to matrimony. Read, however, the final clause: 'She entered it with him with an intention to matrimony', from which it follows, does it not, that if the entrance was made with no specified intention [it would be deemed to have been made just] in order to rest there for the night?—R. Ashi replied: Both entrances mentioned[1] are such as were made with no specified intention, but any unspecified [entrance into] a court-yard of hers [is presumed to have been made] in order to rest there for the night while any unspecified [entrance into] a court-yard of his[2] [is presumed to have been made] with an intention to matrimony.

A Tanna taught: If a father delivered [his daughter][3] to the agents of her husband and she played the harlot[4] her penalty is that[5] of strangulation.[6] Whence is this ruling deduced?—R. Ammi b. Ḥama replied: Scripture stated,[7] *To play the harlot in her father's house,*[8] thus excluding one whom the father had delivered to the agents of the husband.

Might it not be suggested that this[8] excludes one who entered her bridal chamber but with whom no cohabitation had taken place?[9]—Raba replied: Ammi told me [that a woman[10] who entered her] bridal chamber was explicitly[11] mentioned in Scripture: *If there be a damsel that is a virgin betrothed unto a man;*[12] *'a damsel'* but not a woman who is adolescent, *'a virgin'* but not a woman with whom intercourse took place, *'betrothed'* but not one married.[13] Now what [is meant by] 'one married'? If it be suggested: One actually married, [it can be objected that such a deduction][14] would be practically the same as that of *'a virgin* but not one with whom intercourse took place'. Consequently it must be concluded[15] [that

(1) In the first and second clauses. (2) Her husband. (3) Cf. *supra* p. 276, n. 7. (4) Prior to her entry into the bridal chamber. (5) Lit., 'behold this'. (6) Like that of a married woman; not stoning which is the penalty of one betrothed. (7) In prescribing the penalty of stoning. (8) Deut. XXII, 21. (9) What proof is there that one who had not even entered the bridal chamber is also excluded? (10) Prior to marriage. (11) I.e., is deduced from a specific expression. (12) Deut. XXII, 23. (13) V. Sanh. 66*b*. (14) '*Betrothed* but not *actually* married'. (15) Lit., 'but not?'

by 'married' was meant one] who entered into the bridal chamber but with whom no intercourse took place.[1]

[49a] But might not one suggest that if she[2] returned[3] to her parental home she resumes her former status?[4]—Raba replied: A Tanna of the school of R. Ishmael has long ago settled this difficulty. For a Tanna of the school of R. Ishmael taught: What need was there for Scripture to state, *But the vow of a widow, or of her that is divorced, even everything wherewith she hath bound her soul, shall stand against her?*[5] Is she not free from the authority of her father[6] and also from that of her husband?[7] [The fact], however, is that where[8] her father had delivered her to the agents of her husband, or where the agents of her father had delivered her to the agents of her husband and, on the way,[9] she became a widow or was divorced[10] [one would not know] whether she was to be described as of[11] the house of her father[12] or as of the house of her husband;[13] hence the need for the text[14] to tell you that as soon as she has left her father's authority,[15] even if only for a short while, he may no longer annul her vows.[16]

(1) Since this text excluded such a case from the penalty of stoning no other text is required for the same purpose. Deut. XXII, 21, is consequently free for the deduction made by R. Ammi. (2) Whom HER FATHER DELIVERED TO THE AGENTS OF THE HUSBAND. (3) Before she reached her husband's house. (4) Since she is again *'in her father's house'* her penalty might again be changed from strangulation (the penalty for a married woman) to stoning (the penalty for one betrothed who is *in her father's house,* (Deut. XXII, 21). This does not exactly raise a difficulty against our Mishnah, but is an attempt merely at elucidating the law (Rashi). (5) Num. XXX, 10. (6) Since she was once married. A father's control over his daughter ceases with her marriage. (7) Being now a widow or a divorcee. Now since neither father nor husband may annul her vows it is self-evident that her vows *'stand against* her'. What need then was there for the text of Num. XXX, 10. (8) Lit., 'behold'. (9) To her husband's house. (10) And so returned to her parental home. (11) Lit., 'how I read about her'. (12) Because, not having reached her husband's house, she has not passed entirely out of her father's control. Her father should consequently be entitled to annul her vows. (13) Who is now dead or divorced. Her vows consequently, like those of any other widow or divorcee, could no longer be annulled. (14) Lit., 'but'. (15) As, for instance, where she was delivered to the husband's agents. (16) Yeb. 87*a*. As in respect of vows the woman is no longer regarded as being *'in her father's house'* so also in respect of her penalties.

Said R. Papa: We also learned [a similar ruling]:[1] A man who has intercourse with a betrothed girl incurs no penalties[2] unless she is a *na'arah*,[3] a virgin, betrothed, and in her father's house.[4] Now one can well see that '*na'arah*' excludes[5] one who is adolescent, 'virgin' excludes[5] one with whom a man has had intercourse, and '*betrothed*' excludes one who married [by entry into the bridal chamber].[6] What, [however, could the expression] 'in her father's house' exclude? Obviously this:[7] [The case where] her father delivered her to the agents of the husband.[8]

R. Naḥman b. Isaac said: We also learned [a similar ruling]:[9] Should one have intercourse with a 'married woman'[10] the latter,[11] provided she entered under the authority of her husband,[12] although no intercourse had taken place, is to be punished by strangulation.[13] 'She entered under the authority of her husband' [implies][14] in any form whatever.[15] This is conclusive proof.

MISHNAH. A FATHER[16] IS UNDER NO OBLIGATION TO MAINTAIN HIS DAUGHTER. THIS EXPOSITION[17] WAS MADE BY R. ELEAZAR B. AZARIAH[18] IN THE PRESENCE OF THE SAGES IN THE VINEYARD OF JABNEH:[19] [SINCE IT WAS ENACTED THAT] THE SONS SHALL BE HEIRS [TO THEIR MOTHER'S

(1) *Sc.* a Mishnah which supports the ruling of the Baraitha *supra* 48*b*: 'If a father delivered . . . her penalty is that of strangulation'. (2) *Sc.* the penalties prescribed in Deut. XXII, 24ff. (3) V. Glos. (4) Sanh. 66*b*. (5) Lit., 'and not'. (6) Before intercourse had taken place (cf. *supra* 48*b ad fin.*). (7) Lit., 'not, to exclude?' (8) Cf. *supra* p. 280, notes 4 and 16. (9) V. *supra* p. note 1. (10) Lit., 'the wife of a man'. (11) *Sc.* the woman. So according to MS.M. (v. *infra* n. 13). (12) So MS.M. Cur. edd. insert 'for marriage'. (13) So MS.M., הרי זו בחנק. Cur. edd. הבא עליה הרי זה בחנק. (14) Since even 'bridal chamber' was not mentioned. (15) Lit., 'in the world'; even mere delivery to the husband's agents. (16) During his lifetime. V. *infra*. (17) On the formula of the *kethubah*. (18) On the day when he was appointed President of the College (Rashi, cf. Ber. 27*b*). (19) Or Jamnia. The כרם יבנה was either the name of the school, so called because the students 'sat in rows' like 'vines in a vineyard' (Rashi), or an actual vineyard in which the scholars met (Krauss). The school of Jabneh was established by R. Joḥanan b. Zakkai during the siege of Jerusalem by Vespasian. Cf. B.B. (Sonc. ed.) p. 549, n. 4.

KETHUBAH][1] AND THE DAUGHTERS SHALL BE MAINTAINED [OUT OF THEIR FATHER'S ESTATE,[1] THE TWO CASES MAY BE COMPARED:] AS THE SONS CANNOT BE HEIRS EXCEPT AFTER THE DEATH OF THEIR FATHER, SO THE DAUGHTERS CANNOT CLAIM MAINTENANCE EXCEPT AFTER THE DEATH OF THEIR FATHER.

GEMARA. [Since it has been said that] he IS UNDER NO OBLIGATION TO MAINTAIN HIS DAUGHTER only, it follows[2] that he is under an obligation to maintain his son, [and in the case of] his daughter also, since he is only exempt from[3] *legal* OBLIGATION he is, obviously, still subject[4] to a moral duty; who, [then, it may be asked, is the author] of our Mishnah? [Is it] neither R. Meir nor R. Judah nor R. Johanan b. Beroka? For it was taught: It is a moral duty[5] to feed one's daughters, and much more so one's sons, (since the latter are engaged in the study of the Torah);[6] so R. Meir. R. Judah ruled: It is a moral duty to feed one's sons, and much more so one's daughters, (in order [to prevent their] degradation).[7] R. Johanan b. Beroka ruled: It is a legal obligation to feed one's daughters[8] after their father's death; but during the lifetime of their father neither sons nor daughters need be[9] fed.[10] Now who [could be the author of] our Mishnah? If R. Meir, he, surely, [it may be objected] ruled that [the maintenance of] sons [was only] a moral duty.[11] If R. Judah, he, surely ruled that also[12] [the maintenance of] sons [was only] a moral duty.[11] And if R. Johanan b. Beroka [should be suggested, the objection would be: Is not his opinion that] one is not even subject to[13] a moral duty?[11]—If you wish I might say [that the author is] R. Meir; if

(1) A formula to that effect must be entered in a *kethubah*, v. Mishnah *infra* 52*b*. (2) As DAUGHTER only was mentioned. (3) Lit., 'there is not'. (4) Lit., 'there is'. (5) Though after a certain age there is no legal obligation. (6) The bracketed words are the Talmudic comment on this teaching. (V. Rashb. s.v. דעסקי B.B. 141*a*). (7) In their search for a livelihood, cf. n. 6. (8) In accordance with the terms of their mother's *kethubah*. (9) Lit., 'these and these are not'. (10) Cf. Tosef. Keth. IV and B.B. 141*a*. (11) While our Mishnah implies a legal obligation. (12) נמי. This may be omitted with MS.M. (13) Lit., 'there is not'.

you wish I might say: R. Judah; and if you prefer I might say: R. Joḥanan b. Beroḳa. 'If you wish I might say [that the author is] R. Meir', and it is this that he meant:[1] A FATHER IS UNDER NO OBLIGATION TO MAINTAIN HIS DAUGHTER, and the same law applies to his son. [Maintenance], however, is a moral duty in the case of his daughter and, much more so, in the case of his sons; and the reason why[2] HIS DAUGHTER was mentioned[3] was to teach us this: [49*b*] That even in the case of his daughter[4] he is only exempt from a legal obligation but is nevertheless subject to a moral duty.[5] 'If you wish I might say: R. Judah'; and it is this that he meant:[1] A FATHER IS UNDER NO OBLIGATION TO MAINTAIN HIS DAUGHTER, and much more so[6] his son.[7] It is, however, a moral duty [to maintain] one's son and, much more so, one's daughters; and the only reason why[2] HIS DAUGHTER was mentioned[3] was to teach us this: That even [the maintenance of] one's daughter is no[8] legal obligation. 'And if you prefer I might say: R. Joḥanan b. Beroḳa', and what was meant is this: HE IS UNDER NO OBLIGATION TO MAINTAIN HIS DAUGHTER, and the same law applies to his son; and this, furthermore, means[9] that [such maintenance] is not even[8] a moral duty; only because [the maintenance of daughters] after their father's death is a legal obligation, the expression, HE IS UNDER NO OBLIGATION, was used here also.[10]

R. Elai stated in the name of Resh Laḳish who had it from R. Judah[11] b. Ḥanina: At Usha[12] it was ordained that a man

(1) In his statement in our Mishnah. (2) Lit., 'and that'. (3) And not 'son'. Cf. *supra* p. 282, n. 2 and text. (4) Who is not engaged in the study of the Torah. (5) Had 'son' been mentioned instead of DAUGHTER it might have been assumed that the maintenance of a daughter is not even a moral duty. (6) MS.M., 'and the same law applies to'. (7) Since it is easier for a man to earn his livelihood. (8) Lit., 'there is not'. (9) Lit., 'and that is the law'. (10) In fact, however, there is neither legal obligation nor moral duty. (11) Variant, 'R. Jose' (Alfasi and Rosh). (12) Usha was a town in Galilee, in the vicinity of Sepphoris and Shefar'am, where the Sanhedrin met after it left Jabneh (Jamnia). It was also the place where, after the wars of Bar Cochba, on the cessation of the religious persecutions which characterised the Hadrianic reign in the middle of the second century, an important Rabbinical synod was held. Cf. B.B. (Sonc. ed.) p. 139, n. 1; p. 141, n. 4 and p. 207, n. 3. [On the Synod of Usha v. *J.E.*, XI, 645ff.].

must maintain his sons and daughters while they are young.[1]

The question was raised: Is the law in agreement with his statement or not?—Come and hear: When people came before Rab Judah,[2] he used to tell them, 'A *Yarod*[3] bears progeny and[4] throws them upon [the tender mercies of] the townspeople'.[5]

When people came before R. Ḥisda,[2] he used to tell them, 'Turn a mortar[6] for him upside down,[7] in public and let one[8] stand [on it] and say: The raven cares[9] for its young but that man[10] does not care for his children'.[11] But does a raven care[9] for its young? Is it not written in Scripture,[12] *To the young ravens which cry?*[13]—This is no difficulty. The latter[14] applies to white ravens[15] and the former[16] to black ones.[17]

When a man[18] came before Raba he used to tell him, 'Will it please you that your children should be maintained from the charity funds?'[19]

This ruling,[20] however, has been laid down only for one who is not a wealthy man, but if the man is wealthy he may be compelled[21] even against his wish; as was the case with[22] Raba who used compulsion against R. Nathan b. Ammi[23] and extracted from him four hundred *zuz*[24] for charity.[25]

(1) Lit., 'small', under age of puberty (Rashi). (2) With the case of a father who refused to maintain his young children. (3) יארוד (Heb. תנים) 'A bird of solitary habits' (Jast.); 'dragon' or 'jackal' (Rashi). Cf. the rendering of תנים in Jer. IX, 10 by A.V. and R.V. respectively. (4) Neglecting them. (5) From which observation it follows that a judge can only censure a heartless father but has no power to compel him to provide for the maintenance of his children. (6) אסיתא, v. Krauss, *TA*, I, 447. (7) An improvised platform. (8) *Aliter*, 'him', *sc.* the father. (9) Lit., 'asks'. (10) ההוא גברא, *sc.* the father. According to the second interpretation, (*supra* note 8) the expression, as elsewhere, may refer to the speaker himself. (11) V. *supra* note 5, (12) Ps. CXLVII, 9. (13) Presumably for food; which shews that the parent neglects them. (14) Lit., 'that', the text implying neglect of the young ravens. (15) *Sc.* very young ones. These are disliked by their parents (Rashi). (16) Rab Judah's statement that ravens do care for their young. (17) Older birds. For such the parents do care. (18) Who refused to maintain his young children. (19) V. *supra* note 5. (20) That a father cannot legally be compelled to maintain his children. (21) To maintain his children. (22) Lit., 'like that of'. (23) Who was a wealthy man. (24) V. Glos. (25) How much more then may compulsion

R. Elai stated in the name of Resh Laḳish: It was enacted at Usha[1] that if a man assigned all his estate to his sons in writing, he and his wife[2] may nevertheless[3] be maintained out of it. R. Zera, or as some say, R. Samuel b. Naḥmani, demurred: Since the Rabbis went so far as to rule[4] that [in the case that follows] a widow is maintained out of her husband's estate, was there any necessity [to state that such maintenance is allowed to] the man himself and his wife? For Rabin had sent in his letter:[5] If a man died and left a widow and a daughter, his widow is to receive her maintenance from his estate?[6] If the daughter married,[7] his widow is still to receive her maintenance from his estate. If the daughter died?[8] Rab[9] Judah the son of the sister of R. Jose b. Ḥanina said: I had such a case, and it was decided[10] that his widow was to receive her maintenance from his estate.[11] [In view of this ruling we ask: Was it] necessary [to give a similar ruling[12] in respect of] the man himself[13] and his wife?—It might have been assumed [that the law applies only] there,[14] because there is no one else to provide for her,[15] but here [it might well be argued:] Let him provide for himself and for her;[16] hence we were taught [that here also the same ruling applies].

The question was raised: Is the law in agreement with his view[17] or not?—Come and hear: R. Ḥanina and R. Jonathan were once standing together when a man approached them and bending

be used against a wealthy father who refuses to provide for his own children.

(1) Cf. *supra* p. 183, n. 12. (2) Though the sons are now the legal owners of the estate. (3) By virtue of the enactment of Usha. (4) Lit., 'greater than this did they say'. (5) From Palestine to Babylon. (6) In accordance with his undertakings in her *kethubah*. (7) And the estate was transferred into her husband's ownership. (8) And her possessions were inherited by her husband who is her heir. (9) So in the parallel passage, B.B. 193a. Cur. edd., 'Rabbi'. (10) Lit., 'they said'. (11) B.B. 193*a*. (12) That despite the assignment, maintenance may be drawn from the estate. (13) Who made the assignment. (14) The case of the widow spoken of in Rabin's letter. (15) Lit., 'who may take the trouble'. Her husband being dead she would have been helpless without the allowance for her maintenance. (16) And consequently should not be allowed to draw upon the estate he assigned to his sons. (17) That of R. Elai.

down kissed R. Jonathan upon his foot. 'What [is the meaning of] this?' said R. Ḥanina to him.[1] 'This man', the other[1] replied, 'assigned his estate to his sons in writing [50a] and I compelled them to maintain him'. Now if it be conceded that this[2] was not [in accordance with the strict] law one can well understand why he[1] had to compel them,[3] but if it be contended that this[4] is the law, would it have been necessary for him [it may be objected] to compel them?[5]

R. Elai stated: It was ordained at Usha[6] that if a man wishes to spend liberally[7] he should not spend more than a fifth.[8] So it was also taught: If a man desires to spend liberally[7] he should not spend more than a fifth,[8] [since by spending more] he might himself come to be in need [of the help] of people.[9] It once happened that a man wished to spend[7] more than a fifth[8] but his friend did not allow him. Who was it?[10]—R. Yeshebab. Others say [that the man who wished to spend was] R. Yeshebab, but his friend did not allow him. And who was it?[10]—R. Akiba. R. Naḥman, or as some say, R. Aḥa b. Jacob, said: What [is the proof from] Scripture?[11] —*And of all that Thou shalt give me I will surely give the tenth*[12] *unto thee.*[13]

But the second tenth,[14] surely, is not like the first one?—R. Ashi replied: *I will . . . give a tenth of it*[15] [implies 'I will make] the second like the first'.

Said R. Shimi b. Ashi: [The number of those who report] these

(1) R. Jonathan. (2) Maintenance of their father by sons to whom he had assigned his estate. (3) He compelled them to obey the enactment of Usha though they pleaded adherence to the strict law. (4) V. *supra* note 2. (5) Naturally not, since the sons would have had no ground whatsoever on which to base their refusal. (6) V. *supra* p. 283, n. 12. (7) In charity. (8) Of his wealth. (The reason is given anon. Cf. *infra* 76b, 'Ar. 28a). (9) Lit., 'creatures'. (10) His friend. (11) That no more than a fifth may be spent on charity. (12) עשר אעשרנו (Infinitive and Imperfect), the repetition of the verb עשר ('to give a tenth') implies two tenths or one fifth. (13) Gen. XXVIII, 22. (14) Which, being taken from the nine tenths that remained after the first tenth had been given away, represents only $(\frac{1}{10} \times \frac{9}{10} =) \frac{9}{100}$ of the original capital. (15) אעשרנו, So lit. Imperfect with suffix of 3rd sing. instead of the imperfect אעשר.

traditions[1] steadily diminishes;[2] and your mnemonic[3] is '*The young*[4] *assigned in writing*[5] *and spend liberally*'.[6]

R. Isaac stated: It was ordained at Usha[7] that a man must bear[8] with his son until [he is] twelve years [of age]. From that age[9] onwards he may threaten[10] his life.[11] But could this be correct?[12] Did not Rab, in fact, say to R. Samuel b. Shilath,[13] 'Do not accept [a pupil] under the age of six; a pupil of the age of six you shall accept and stuff him like an ox'?[14]—Yes, 'stuff him like an ox', but he may not 'threaten him'[10] until after [he has reached the age of] twelve years. And if you prefer I may say: This[15] is no difficulty, since one may have referred[16] to Scripture[17] and the other to Mishnah; for Abaye stated: Nurse[18] told me that a child of six [is ripe] for Scripture; one of ten, for Mishnah; one of thirteen,[19] for a full twenty-four hours'[20] fast,[21] and, in the case of a girl,[22] [one who is of] the age of twelve.[23]

Abaye stated, Nurse[18] told me: A child of the age of six whom

(1) The enactments of Usha reported *supra* by R. Elai. (2) The first enactment was reported by three Amoraim: R. Elai, Resh Laḳish and R. Judah (or Jose) b. Ḥanina (*supra* 49*b*); the second only by two: R. Elai and Resh Laḳish (*supra* l.c.), while the third was reported by R. Elai alone. (3) An aid to the recollection of the order in which they were cited and thereby the order of the diminutions. (4) 'A man shall maintain . . . while they are *young*' (*supra* 49*b*). (5) 'If a man *assigned . . . in writing*' (supra l.c.). (6) 'If a man wishes to *spend liberally*' (the last cited enactment). (7) V. *supra* p. 183, n. 12. (8) Lit., 'roll', i.e., have patience with him, and employ gentle means to induce him to study. (9) Lit., 'from here'. (10) Lit., 'go down with him into'. (11) *Sc.* he may adopt drastic measures if his son is neglectful or indifferent. (12) Lit., 'I am not (in agreement)'. (13) A teacher of young children (v. B.B. 8*b*). (14) B.B. 21*a*. This seems to shew that the age of compulsion is six, contrary to R. Isaac's tradition which puts it at twelve. (15) Cf. *supra* n. 14. (16) Lit., 'that'. (17) Which a child should begin studying at the age of six. (18) His mother died while he was an infant, and his upbringing was entrusted to a nurse from whom he learned many proverbs and maxims, legends and folklore; v. Ḳid. 31*b*. (19) בר תליסר, v. n. 23. (20) מעת לעת, lit., 'from time to time', from a certain hour of one day to the same hour on the following day. (21) The fast of the Day of Atonement and that of the Ninth of Ab last for a *full* twenty-four hours, beginning near sunset and terminating at nightfall on the following day. (22) Who matures earlier. (23) *Sc.* twelve years and one day (Tosaf. s.v. ובת, *a.l.*, contrary to Rashi who interprets 'twelve' as 'twelfth', viz., from the age of eleven years and a

a scorpion has bitten on the day on which he has completed his sixth year does not survive [as a rule].[1] What is his remedy?—The gall of a white stork[2] in beer. This should be rubbed into the wound [and the patient] be made to drink it. A child of the age of one year whom a bee has stung on the day he has completed his first year does not survive [as a rule].[1] What is his remedy?—The creepers of a palm-tree in water. This should be rubbed in and [the patient] be made to drink it.

Said R. Kaṭṭina: Whosoever brings his son [to school] under the age of six will run after him but never overtake him.[3] Others say: His fellows will run after him but will never overtake him.[4] Both statements, however, are correct:[5] He is feeble but learned. If you prefer I might say: The former[6] applies to one[7] who is emaciated; the latter, to one[7] who is in good health.

R. Jose b. Ḥanina stated:[8] At Usha[9] it was ordained that if a woman had sold usufruct property[10] during the lifetime of her husband and then died, the husband[11] may seize it from the buyers.[12]

R. Isaac b. Joseph found R. Abbahu standing among a crowd of people.[13] 'Who', he said to him, 'is the author of the traditions of Usha?'—'R. Jose b. Ḥanina', the other informed him. He learned

day). [The text is uncertain. MS.M. and Asheri read 'and one of twelve (בר תריסר) for a full twenty four hours' fast and in the case of a little girl'. This may mean; (*a*) 'and that applies to a little girl', whereas in the case of a boy the age for a full fast begins at thirteen, or (*b*) 'and the same law applies to a girl'; v. Isaiah Trani. Tosaf. seems to have had a still shorter text with no reference to a boy; v. Tosaf. s.v. ובת].

(1) Unless the appropriate remedy is applied (Rashi). Cf., however, Tosaf. s.v. ומאי *a.l.* (2) דיה. The 'white *dayyah*' is the Talmudic interpretation of חסידה (Lev. XI, 19), E.V. *stork* (cf. Ḥul. 63*a*). (3) *Sc.* all his efforts to restore his child to normal health will be of no avail. His health remains irrevocably ruined. (4) He will always surpass them in knowledge and attainments. (5) Lit., 'they are'. (6) V. *supra* n. 3. (7) Lit., 'that'. (8) *Infra* 78*b*, B.Ḳ. 88*b*, B.M. 35*a*, 96*b*, B.B. 50*a*, 139*b*. (9) V. *supra* p. 183, n. 12. (10) *Melog* (v. Glos). (11) Who has the legal status of a buyer. (12) Since he is in the position of the earliest purchaser. (13) באוכלוסא דאינשי, so MS.M. Cur. edd. דאושא 'of Usha'. *Var. lec.* קאי בהילכתא דאושא 'engaged in teaching the laws passed at Usha' (Jast.).

this from him forty times and then it appeared to him as if he had it safely in his bag.[1]

Happy are they that keep justice, that do righteousness at all times.[2] Is it possible to do righteousness at all times?—This, explained our Rabbis of Jabneh[3] (or, as others say, R. Eliezer), refers to a man who maintains his sons and daughters[4] while they are young.[5] R. Samuel b. Naḥmani said: This[2] refers to a man who brings up an orphan boy or orphan girl in his house and enables them to marry.

Wealth and riches are in his house; and his merit endureth for ever.[6] R. Huna and R. Ḥisda [expounded the text in different ways]. One said: It applies to a man who studies the Torah[7] and teaches it to others;[8] and the other said: It applies to a man who writes the Pentateuch, the Prophets and the Hagiographa and lends them to others.[9]

And see thy children's children; peace be upon Israel.[10] R. Joshua b. Levy said: As soon as your children have children there will be peace upon Israel; for they will not be subject to *ḥaliẓah*[11] or levirate marriage.[12] R. Samuel b. Naḥmani said: As soon as your children have children[13] there will be peace for the judges of Israel, for [doubtful claimants] will not come to quarrels.[14]

THIS EXPOSITION WAS MADE BY R. ELEAZAR B. AZARIAH[15] IN THE PRESENCE OF THE SAGES etc. [50*b*] R. Joseph sat before R. Hamnuna while R. Hamnuna was sitting and discoursing: As

(1) *Sc.* would never forget it. (2) Ps. CVI, 3. (3) V. *supra* p. 181, n. 19. (4) This is a charitable act, since legally they have no claim upon him for maintenance. (5) Children being *'at all times'* dependent on their father, the text cited may well be applied to such a man. צדקה *'righteousness'* may also signify 'charity'. (6) Ps. CXII, 3. (7) Which is compared to *'wealth and riches'*. (8) His Torah is not thereby diminished so that *'wealth and riches'* (v. *supra* note 7) *'are in his house'*, and *'his merit'* for teaching other people *'endureth for ever'*. (9) Cf. *supra* notes 7 and 8 *mutatis mutandis*. The scrolls remain his, while his *'merit endureth for ever'* for enabling others to study. (10) Ps. CXXVIII, 6. (11) V. Glos. (12) Which are frequently the cause of quarrels. (13) *Sc.* legal heirs. (14) On the disposal of the estate of the deceased. (15) So MS.M. and our Mishnah *supra* 49*a*. Cur. edd. omit 'b. Azariah' from the quotation.

sons may obtain their inheritance only from landed property so may one's daughters obtain their maintenance only from landed property. All shouted at him: 'Is it only from a man who leaves land that sons inherit while from him who leaves no land his sons do not inherit?'[1] Said R. Joseph to him:[2] Might not the Master have been speaking of the *kethubah* [that is due to] male children?[3] The other[2] replied: The Master who is a great man understood precisely what I meant.[4]

R. Ḥiyya b. Joseph stated: Rab allowed maintenance [to daughters][5] from wheat[6] of *'aliyyah*.[7]

The question was raised: Was [Rab's allowance made for] a marriage outfit,[8] and by *'aliyyah* is meant,[9] 'in accordance with her father's *generous*[10] disposition', [his ruling being] in agreement with that of Samuel who laid down that in respect of marriage outfit the assessment[11] is determined by [the disposition of] the father;[12] or was it rather for actual maintenance,[13] and by *'aliyyah* was meant[9] 'in accordance with the chivalrous[14] enactments made[15] in an upper chamber',[16] for R. Isaac b. Joseph stated: In an upper chamber it

(1) Certainly not. The Torah did not restrict the laws of inheritance to landed estates only. (2) R. Hamnuna. (3) If their mother pre-deceased their father they are entitled to recover her *kethubah* from his estate over and above the shares to which they like the other sons are entitled. (4) The comparison made between the maintenance of daughters and the inheritance of sons was not, as the others who shouted assumed, the ordinary inheritance of sons, which is a Pentateuchal right, but their inheritance of their mother's *kethubah* (v. *supra* n. 3) which, like the maintenance of daughters, is merely a Rabbinical obligation undertaken by their father in accordance with the terms of the *kethubah* which he gave to their mother. Cf. *infra* 52*b*, and 91*b*. (5) In the absence of real estate. (6) *Sc.* movable property. (7) דעלייה. The noun עליה may signify either 'upper chamber' or 'best' 'generous'. The meaning is discussed anon. (8) Which is levied from movables also. (9) Lit., 'and what *'aliyyah?*' (10) Cf. *supra* n. 7. (11) For a daughter, out of her deceased father's estate. (12) *Infra* 68*a*. A bigger allowance if he was known to be generous, and a smaller one if he was known to be niggardly. (13) Which, forming one of the terms of the *kethubah*, may legally be recovered like the statutory *kethubah* itself, from landed property only. (14) Lit., 'good'. (15) In favour of daughters. (16) Cf. 'the upper chamber of Ḥananiah b. Hezekiah' (Shab. 13*b*) and v. *supra*

Our Rabbis taught: Both landed property[1] and movable property may be seized[2] for the maintenance of a wife[3] or daughters;[3] so Rabbi.[4] R. Simeon b. Eleazar ruled: Landed property may be seized for daughters[5] from sons, for daughters from daughters,[6] and for sons from sons;[6] for sons from daughters where the estate is large[7] but not where it is small.[8] Movable property[9] may be seized for sons from sons,[10] for daughters from daughters[10] and for sons from daughters, but not for daughters from sons.[11] Although we have an established rule that the *halachah* is in agreement with Rabbi [where he differs] from his colleague, the *halachah* here is in agreement with R. Simeon b. Eleazar; for Raba stated: The law is [that payment may be exacted] from landed property but not from movable property whether in respect of a *kethubah*, maintenance or marriage outfit.[12]

MISHNAH. [IF A HUSBAND] DID NOT WRITE A KETHUBAH FOR HIS WIFE[13] SHE MAY RECOVER TWO HUNDRED ZUZ[14] [IF AT MARRIAGE SHE WAS] A VIRGIN, AND ONE MANEH[14] [IF SHE WAS THEN] A WIDOW, BECAUSE [THE STATUTORY KETHUBAH] IS A CONDITION LAID DOWN BY BETH DIN.

IF HE ASSIGNED TO HER IN WRITING A FIELD THAT WAS WORTH ONE MANEH INSTEAD OF THE TWO HUNDRED ZUZ,[15] AND DID NOT WRITE IN HER FAVOUR,[13] 'ALL PROPERTY THAT

(1) Lit., 'property which has surety', *sc.* to which a claimant may resort in case of non-payment by the defendant. (2) From orphans. (3) Of their deceased father. (4) *Infra* 68*b*. (5) For their maintenance or marriage outfit. (6) *Sc.* the younger are given equal shares with the elder though the latter had taken earlier possession of their father's estate. (7) V. next note. (8) I.e., if it does not suffice for the maintenance of the sons and the daughters until they reach adolescence (Rashi. Cf. B.B. 139*b*). In such a case the estate belongs to the daughters while the sons may go begging (B.B. loc. cit.). (9) Cf. *supra* n. 1 *mutatis mutandis*. (10) V. *supra* note 6. (11) Movable assets of the deceased in the possession of his sons are regarded, as far as his daughters are concerned, as non-existent. (12) *Supra* p. 292 and *infra* 69*b*. (13) Lit., 'for her'. (14) V. Glos. (15) The statutory amount of a virgin's *kethubah*.

I POSSESS IS SURETY FOR YOUR KETHUBAH',[1] HE IS NEVERTHELESS LIABLE [FOR THE FULL AMOUNT][2] BECAUSE [THE CLAUSE MENTIONED] IS A CONDITION LAID DOWN BY BETH DIN. IF HE DID NOT WRITE IN HER FAVOUR[3] [THE CLAUSE], 'IF YOU ARE TAKEN CAPTIVE I WILL RANSOM YOU AND TAKE YOU AGAIN AS MY WIFE,'[1] OR, IN THE CASE OF A PRIEST'S WIFE,[4] 'I WILL RESTORE YOU TO YOUR PARENTAL HOME',[5] HE IS NEVERTHELESS LIABLE [TO CARRY OUT THESE OBLIGATIONS], BECAUSE [THE CLAUSE] IS A CONDITION LAID DOWN BY BETH DIN.

IF SHE IS TAKEN CAPTIVE IT IS HIS DUTY TO RANSOM HER; AND IF HE SAID, 'HERE[6] IS HER LETTER OF DIVORCE AND HER KETHUBAH LET HER RANSOM HERSELF', HE IS NOT ALLOWED [TO ACT ACCORDINGLY].[7] IF SHE SUSTAINED AN INJURY IT IS HIS DUTY TO PROVIDE FOR HER MEDICAL TREATMENT;[8] BUT IF HE SAID, 'HERE[6] IS HER LETTER OF DIVORCE AND HER KETHUBAH, LET HER HEAL HERSELF', HE IS ALLOWED [TO ACT IN ACCORDANCE WITH HIS DESIRE].

GEMARA. Whose [view is represented in our Mishnah]? It is [obviously that of] R. Meir who ruled [that the intercourse of] any man who undertakes to give a virgin less than two hundred *zuz*[9] or a widow less than a *maneh*[9] is[10] an act of prostitution;[11] for if [it be suggested that it is the view of] R. Judah, he surely, [it can be objected] ruled, [that if a husband] wished he may write out for a virgin[12] a deed for two hundred *zuz* and she writes [a quittance][13] 'I have received from you a *maneh*,' and for a widow [he may write out a deed for] a *maneh* and she writes [a quittance],

(1) This is one of the statutory clauses that a *kethubah* must contain. (2) V. p. 293, n. 15. (3) Lit., 'for her'. (4) With whom her husband (the priest) may not live again after she had been a captive and in whose favour the clause 'and take you again as wife' cannot be written. (5) Lit., 'country', 'district'. (6) Lit., 'behold'. (7) Since the obligation to ransom her is incurred as soon as she is taken captive. (8) Lit., 'to heal her'. (9) V. Glos. (10) Lit., 'behold this'. (11) *Infra* 54*b*. (12) As her *kethubah*. (13) Though she has received nothing.

'I received from you fifty *zuz*'.[1] Read, however, the final clause: IF HE ASSIGNED TO HER IN WRITING A FIELD THAT WAS WORTH ONE MANEH INSTEAD OF THE TWO HUNDRED ZUZ, AND DID NOT WRITE IN HER FAVOUR, 'ALL PROPERTY THAT I POSSESS[2] IS SURETY FOR YOUR KETHUBAH' HE IS NEVERTHELESS LIABLE [FOR THE FULL AMOUNT], BECAUSE [THE CLAUSE MENTIONED] IS A CONDITION LAID DOWN BY BETH DIN. Does not this obviously represent the view[3] of R. Judah who laid down that [the omission from a bond of the clause] pledging property[4] [is regarded as] the scribe's error?[5] for if [it be suggested that it represents the view of] R. Meir, he, surely, [it can be objected] ruled that [the omission of the clause] pledging property is not [regarded as] the scribe's error. For we have learned: If a man found notes of indebtedness [51*b*] he must not restore them[6] if they contain a clause pledging property, because the court would exact payment from such property,[7] but if they do not contain the clause pledging property, he must return them, because the court will not exact payment from the property;[8] so R. Meir. The Sages,[9] however, ruled: In either case he must not return them, because the court will exact payment from the property[10] [in any case].[11] Would then the first clause [represent the view of] R. Meir and the final clause that of R. Judah? And should you suggest that both clauses[12] [represent the view of]

(1) *Infra* 54*b*. Now since our Mishnah insists on the payment of the full amount of the *kethubah*, presumably even if the woman had surrendered her claim (corresponding to a quittance), it can only represent the view of R. Meir who disallows such a surrender and not that of R. Judah who allows it. (2) This is assumed to include even property which he disposed of subsequent to the writing of the *kethubah*. (3) Lit., 'it comes'. (4) E.g., that of the debtor to the creditor. (5) And not as the considered consent of the creditor. Despite its error the pledging clause is deemed to have been entered. (6) Either to the creditor or to the debtor. (7) Lit., 'from them', *sc.* the *nekasim* (assets). Aliter: 'Exact payment on the strength of them', *sc.* the notes. Such exaction would be an injustice to the debtor if he has paid his liabilities and it was he who had lost the paid notes. But even where the creditor admits liability collusion with the object of robbing purchasers may be suspected (v. B.M. 12*b*). (8) Cf. *supra* n. 7, *ab. init.* (9) One of whom was R. Judah, a contemporary of R. Meir. (10) Cf. *supra* note 7. (11) Mishnah, B.M. 12*b*. (12) Lit., 'all of it'.

R. Meir and that he draws a distinction between a *kethubah* and notes of indebtedness,[1] [it could be retorted] does he, indeed, draw such a distinction? Has it not been taught: For five [classes of claims] may distraint be made only on free assets;[2] they are as follows. [A claim for] produce,[3] for amelioration shewing profits,[4] for an undertaking[5] to maintain the wife's son or the wife's daughter, for a note of indebtedness wherein no lien on property had been entered, and for a woman's *kethubah* from which the clause pledging security was omitted.[6] Now what authority have you heard laying down that [the omission from a deed of a record of] a lien on property is not regarded as the scribe's error?[7] [Obviously it is] R. Meir;[8] and yet it was stated, was it not, 'a woman's *kethubah*'?[9]—If you wish, I might reply: [Our Mishnah represents the view of] R. Meir; and if you prefer I might reply: [It represents the view of] R. Judah. 'If you prefer I might reply: [It represents the view of] R. Judah', for there[10] she specifically

(1) While in the case of the latter he does not regard the omission as a scribe's error, he does so in the case of the former since the terms of a *kethubah* are governed by statutory regulations laid down by Beth din. (2) Of the defendant; but not on his sold or mortgaged property. (3) In the case, for instance, where a field with its produce was taken away from a buyer by the man from whom the seller had robbed it. The buyer who may recover the cost of the field itself from the seller's sold or mortgaged property may not recover the cost of the produce except from his free assets. Cf. Giṭ. 48*b*, B.M. 14*b*. (4) Where the buyer (cf. *supra* n. 3) incurred expense in effecting the improvements of the land. (5) Lit., 'and he who undertakes'. (6) B.Ḳ. 95*a*. (7) And that the holder of such a deed may only distrain on free assets. (8) Who must consequently be the author of the last cited Baraitha which states that 'a note of indebtedness wherein no lien on property had been entered' entitles the holder to distrain 'only on free assets'. (9) 'May be distrained only on free assets' if the clause pledging security was omitted from it. The section of our Mishnah, therefore, which states that, despite the omission of such a clause the husband is 'NEVERTHELESS LIABLE' and the *kethubah* may presumably be distrained on sold and mortgaged property also (v. *supra* p. 295, n. 2), cannot represent the view of R. Meir. How then could it be suggested that both clauses of our Mishnah (cf. *supra* p. 295, n. 12 and text) represent the view of R. Meir? (10) In the Mishnah (*infra* 54*b*) cited *supra* 51*a*, according to which the statutory sum of a *kethubah* may be reduced.

wrote in the man's favour[1] [in a quittance]: 'I received'[2] but here[3] she did not write in his favour,[1] 'I received'.[4] 'If you wish I might reply: [Our Mishnah represents the view of] R. Meir', for by the expression,[5] 'HE IS NEVERTHELESS LIABLE' [was meant liability to pay] out of his free assets.[6]

IF HE DID NOT WRITE IN HER FAVOUR etc. Samuel's father ruled: The wife of an Israelite who had been outraged is forbidden to her husband, since it may be apprehended that the act begun[7] under compulsion may have terminated[8] with her consent.[9]

Rab raised an objection against Samuel's father: [Have we not learned,] IF YOU ARE TAKEN CAPTIVE I WILL RANSOM YOU AND TAKE YOU AGAIN AS MY WIFE?[10] The other remained silent. Rab thereupon applied to Samuel's father the Scriptural text, *The princes refrained talking and laid their hand on their mouth.*[11] What, however, could he have replied?[12]—[That the law][13] was relaxed in the case of a captive.[14]

According to Samuel's father's ruling how is it possible to conceive a case of outrage which the All-Merciful deemed to be genuine?[15]—Where, for instance, witnesses testified that she cried from the commencement to the end.

[This ruling],[16] however, differs from that of Raba; for Raba laid down: Any woman, the outrage against whom began[17] under

(1) Lit., 'for him'. (2) And she has the right to renounce a portion of her claim. (3) In our Mishnah which allows the woman the full amount of her *kethubah* even if her husband had written none. (4) And the object of our Mishnah is to point out that a woman's consent to dispense with the written document of her *kethubah* is no evidence that she has surrendered her right to recover the statutory amount to which she is entitled. It is assumed rather that her indifference to the written document is due to her reliance on her statutory rights. (5) Lit., 'what . . . that was taught'. (6) His sold or mortgaged property, however, may not be distrained on, in agreement with R. Meir, since no lien on property had been recorded in the *kethubah*. (7) Lit., 'her beginning'. (8) Lit., 'and her end'. (9) And a wife who willingly played the harlot is forbidden to her husband. (10) Though a woman in captivity is usually assumed to have been outraged. (11) Job XXIX, 9. (12) Lit., 'what has he to say'. (13) Prohibiting an outraged woman to her husband. (14) Since her violation is only a suspicion. (15) Lit., 'permitted', *sc.* the woman is exempt from punishment. Cf. Deut. XXII, 26. (16) Samuel's father's. (17) Lit., 'her beginning'.

compulsion, though it terminated with her consent, and even if she said, 'Leave him alone', and that if he had not made the attack upon her she would have hired him to do it, is permitted [to her husband]. What is the reason?—He plunged[1] her into an uncontrollable passion.[2]

It was taught in agreement with Raba: *And she be not seized*[3] [only then][4] is she forbidden,[5] [from which it follows] that if she was seized[6] she is permitted.[5] But there is another class of woman who is permitted[5] even if she was not seized.[7] And who is that? Any woman who began[8] under compulsion and ended[9] with her consent.

Another Baraitha taught: '*And she be not seized*' [only then] is she forbidden[10] [from which it follows] that if she was seized[11] she is permitted.[10] But there is another class of woman who is forbidden[10] even though she was seized. And who is that? The wife of a priest.[12]

Rab Judah stated in the name of Samuel who had it from R. Ishmael: '*And she be not seized*', [then only][13] is she forbidden,[10] but if she was seized she is permitted. There is, however, another class of woman who is permitted even if she was not seized. And who is that? A woman whose betrothal was a mistaken one,[14] and who may, even if her son sits riding on her shoulder, make a declaration of refusal[15] [against her husband] and go away.

Rab Judah ruled: Women who are kidnapped[16] are permitted to

(1) Lit., 'clothed'. (2) Being a victim of her passions she is deemed to have acted under compulsion even when she professed acquiescence. (3) Num. V, 13. E.V., *neither she be taken in the act*. (4) *Sc. if she was not seized*, i.e., if she did not act under compulsion but willingly. (5) To her husband. (6) *Sc.* if she acted under compulsion. (7) But acted willingly. (8) Lit., 'her beginning'. (9) Lit., 'and her end'. (10) To her husband. (11) *Sc.* if she acted under compulsion. (12) Yeb. 56*b*. (13) V. *supra* note 4. (14) When a condition which remained unfulfilled was attached to it. In such a case the woman may leave her husband without a letter of divorce and she has the status of a *feme sole* who had never before been married. (15) V. Glos. s.v. *mi'un*. [Isaiah Trani: This is not to be taken literally. It means simply that she is permitted to marry another man without a bill of divorce]. (16) Lit., 'whom thieves steal'.

their husbands.[1] 'But', said the Rabbis to Rab Judah, 'do they[2] not bring bread to them?'[3]—[They do this] out of fear. 'Do they[2] not, however, hand them[3] their arrows?'[4]—[They do this also] out of fear. It is certain, however, that they[2] are forbidden if [the kidnappers] release them and they go to them of their own free will.

Our Rabbis taught: Royal captives[5] have the status of ordinary captives[6] but those that are kidnapped by highwaymen are not regarded as ordinary captives. Was not, the reverse, however, taught?—There is no contradiction between the rulings concerning royal captives[7] since the former refers[8] [for example] to the kingdom of Ahasuerus[9] while the latter refers[10] to the kingdom of [one like] Ben Neẓer.[11] There is also no contradiction between the two rulings concerning captives of highwaymen[12] since the former refers[10] to [a highwayman like] Ben Neẓer[11] while the latter refers[10] to an ordinary highwayman.[13]

As to Ben Neẓer, could he be called there[14] 'king' and here[15] 'highwayman'?—Yes; in comparison with Ahasuerus he was a highwayman but in comparison with an ordinary robber he was a king.

(1) Any intercourse between the kidnappers and the women is regarded as outrage since the latter would not willingly consent to intimate relations with the men they detest. (2) The kidnapped women. (3) The thieves; which shews that they live on amicable terms with the kidnappers. (4) When their camp is attacked. (5) *Sc.* women forcibly taken into the royal harem (v. Rashi). *Aliter:* Captives of the government; 'forced by (Roman) officials' (Jast.). (6) And are permitted to their husbands, in agreement with the terms of the *kethubah* (cf. our Mishnah). (7) Lit., 'kingdom on kingdom'. (8) Lit., 'that'. (9) *Sc.* one taken captive by a royal personage. Not expecting ever to be married by such a person a captive would strenuously resist intimate relations. (10) Lit., 'that'. (11) בן נצר who was a robber and self-made ruler (cf. Rashi). A woman might well entertain the hope that such a man would consent to marry her and she might consequently allow intimate relations. Ben Neẓer is identified by some authorities with Odenathus of Palmyra, who was first a robber chief and ultimately the founder of a dynasty (v. Jast.). [V. Graetz, *Geschichte*, IV p. 453ff.]. (12) Lit., 'robbery on robbery'. (13) With whom no decent woman would desire to be associated even in marriage. Intercourse with such a man must, therefore, be regarded as outrage. (14) In the second Baraitha cited. (15) The Baraitha first mentioned.

OR, IN THE CASE OF A PRIEST'S WIFE, 'I WILL RESTORE YOU TO YOUR PARENTAL HOME' etc. Abaye ruled: If a widow was married to a High Priest[1] it is the latter's duty to ransom[2] her, since one may apply to her: OR IN THE CASE OF A PRIEST'S WIFE, 'I WILL RESTORE YOU TO YOUR PARENTAL HOME',[3] [52a] but if a bastard or a *nethinah*[4] was married to an Israelite the latter is under no obligation to ransom her, since one cannot apply to her:[5] AND TAKE YOU AGAIN AS MY WIFE.[6] Raba ruled: Wherever the captivity causes the woman to be forbidden[7] [to her husband] it is his duty to ransom her[8] but where some other circumstance causes her to be forbidden to him[9] it is not his duty to ransom her.[10]

Must it be assumed [that they[11] differ on the same principles] as the following Tannaim? [For it was taught:] If a man forbade his wife by a vow [from deriving any benefit from him] and she was taken captive, he must, said R. Eliezer, ransom her[12] and give her also her *kethubah*. R. Joshua said: He must give her her *kethubah* but need not ransom her. Said R. Nathan: I asked Symmachus, 'When R. Joshua said, "He must give her her *kethubah* but need

(1) Though such a marriage is forbidden (cf. Lev. XXI, 14). (2) If she is taken captive. (3) The clause in her *kethubah* as the wife of a priest. Since her ransom would not lead to a re-union with the High Priest but only to her restoration to her parental home, he is obliged to ransom her. (4) Fem. of *nathin* (v. Glos.). (5) As the Israelite is forbidden to live with her. (6) Which is the appropriate clause entered in a *kethubah* given to the wife of an Israelite, and which cannot apply (v. *supra* n. 5) where she is one forbidden to him. (7) Lit., 'the prohibition of captivity causes her'. (8) Contrary to the opinion of Abaye, the clause entered in a *kethubah* of a priest's wife obliges the priest to ransom his wife though she becomes forbidden to him through her captivity, only if she was permitted to him before she had been taken captive. (9) As, for instance, a widow to a High Priest. (10) Because, in the case of a forbidden marriage, as the clause 'AND TAKE YOU AGAIN AS WIFE' was *originally* invalid (cf. *supra* n. 6) the clause 'RESTORE YOU TO YOUR PARENTAL HOME' also has no validity. Thus, contrary to the ruling of Abaye, Raba maintains that a High Priest is under no obligation to ransom a widow whom he married in contravention of the laws of the High Priesthood. In the case of a bastard and a *nethinah* Raba is, of course, of the same opinion as Abaye. (11) Abaye and Raba. (12) Although, owing to his vow, he would subsequently be compelled to divorce her.

not ransom her" [did he refer to a case] where her husband first made his vow against her and she was then taken captive or even to a case where she was first taken captive and he made his vow against her subsequently?'[1] And he told me, 'I did not hear [what he exactly said] but it seems [that he referred to] a case where [the husband] made the vow against her first and the woman was taken captive afterwards; for, should you suggest [that the ruling applied also to a woman who] was taken captive first and the man made his vow against her afterwards [the objection could be raised that in such a case] he might make use of a trick'.[2] Do not they[3] then differ[4] in [the case of one] who made a vow against the wife of a priest,[5] Abaye upholding the view of R. Eliezer[6] while Raba is maintaining that of R. Joshua?[7]—No;[8] here[9] we are dealing [with the case of a woman] who, for instance, made the vow herself and her husband[10] confirmed it,[11] R. Eliezer being of the opinion that it was he[12] who put his finger between her teeth[13] while R. Joshua maintains that it was she herself who put her finger between her teeth.[14]

(1) Though there is good reason to suspect that the object of his vow was to escape his responsibity of ransoming her. (2) Cf. *supra* n. 1. (3) R. Eliezer and R. Joshua. (4) Lit., 'what, not?' (5) I.e., the man who made the vow was himself a priest. It is his duty to ransom his wife, though her being prohibited to him is not due to her captivity, because the clause, 'I WILL RESTORE YOU TO YOUR PARENTAL HOME' may well be applied. Their dispute could not refer to an Israelite who made such a vow, since in that case, the clause 'AND TAKE YOU AGAIN AS MY WIFE' being inapplicable, R. Eliezer could not have imposed upon the man the duty of ransoming his wife. (6) Cf. *supra* n. 5. (7) That the husband is exempt from ransoming his wife because her prohibition to him was not caused by her captivity but by some other circumstance, viz. his vow. (8) R. Eliezer and R. Joshua do not differ on the same principles on which Abaye and Raba differed, both of them agreeing either with Abaye or with Raba. (9) Lit., 'here in what?' (10) An Israelite. (11) Explicitly or implicity. (12) By his confirmation of the vow. (13) Metaph. It is his fault that the vow remained valid. Had he desired to annul it he had the full power to do so (v. Num. XXX, 7ff). As he is thus the cause of the woman's prohibition to him and of rendering the clause in the *kethubah* inapplicable, he must pay the penalty by retaining the responsibility of ransoming her. (14) She should not have made her vow. Having made it her prohibition to her husband is her own fault. Cf. *supra* n. 13 *mutatis mutandis*.

[But] if she herself put her finger between her teeth what claim can she have to her[1] *kethubah?* And, furthermore, [it was stated]: Said R. Nathan: I asked Symmachus, 'When R. Joshua said, "He must give her her *kethubah* but need not ransom her" [did he refer to a case] where her husband first made his vow against her and she was then taken captive or even to a case where she was first taken captive and he made his vow against her subsequently?' and he told me: 'I did not hear [what he exactly said]'. Now if [this is a case] where she herself had made the vow, what difference is there [it may be asked] whether he made the vow first against her[2] and she was taken captive afterwards or whether she was first taken captive and he then made the vow?[3]—The fact is that [here[4] it is a case where] the husband made the vow against her, but Abaye explains [the dispute][5] on the lines of his view while Raba explains it on the lines of his view. 'Abaye explains the dispute on the lines of his view', thus: If a widow [was married] to a High Priest no one[6] disputes [the ruling] that it is the husband's duty to ransom her;[7] if a bastard or a *nethinah* [was married] to an Israelite no one[6] disputes the ruling that it is not his duty to ransom her;[8] if also one made a vow against the wife of a priest[9] no one[6] disputes the ruling that it is his duty to ransom her, since [the principle in this case] is identical with that of a widow [who was married] to a High Priest.[10] They[11] differ only in [respect of him who] made a vow against the wife of an Israelite,[12] R. Eliezer

(1) Lit., 'what is its doing'. (2) I.e., by confirming it. (3) In either case, since it was she who made the vow, no trick on the part of the husband can be suspected. (4) In the dispute between R. Eliezer and R. Joshua. (5) Between R. Eliezer and R. Joshua. (6) Neither R. Eliezer nor R. Joshua. Lit., 'all the world'. (7) Cf. *supra* p. 300, n. 3. The fact that she is forbidden to him for some reason other than that of her captivity being of no consequence. (8) Cf. *supra* p. 300, n. 2, and text. (9) *Sc.* a priest against his own wife. (10) In either case the clause, 'I WILL RESTORE YOU TO YOUR PARENTAL HOME' (cf. *supra* p. 300, n. 3) may well be applied after, as well as before, the woman had been taken captive. (11) R. Eliezer and R. Joshua. (12) Cf. *supra* note 9 *mutatis mutandis.* To the wife of an Israelite it was originally possible to apply the clause, 'I WILL TAKE YOU AGAIN AS MY WIFE' but now, owing to the vow, it can no longer be applied.

being guided by the woman's original status[1] while R. Joshua is guided by her subsequent status.[2] 'Raba explains it on the lines of his view', thus: If a widow [was married] to a High Priest, or a bastard or a *nethinah* to an Israelite no one[3] disputes the ruling that it is not the husband's duty to ransom her.[4] They[5] differ only in [the case where one] made a vow against either the wife of a priest or the wife of an Israelite,[6] R. Eliezer being guided by the woman's original status[1] while R. Joshua is guided by her subsequent status.[2]

IF SHE IS TAKEN CAPTIVE IT IS HIS DUTY TO RANSOM HER etc. Our Rabbis taught: If she was taken captive during the lifetime of her husband, and he died afterwards, and her husband was aware of her [captivity],[7] it is the duty of his heirs to ransom her, but if her husband was not aware of her captivity it is not the duty of his heirs to ransom her.

Levi proposed to give a practical decision[8] in agreement with this Baraitha. Said Rab to him, Thus said my uncle:[9] The law is not in agreement with that Baraitha but with the following[10] wherein it was taught: [If a woman] was taken captive after the death of her husband it is not the duty of his orphans to ransom her, and, furthermore,[11] even if she was taken captive during the lifetime of her husband, but he died subsequently, the orphans are under no obligation to ransom her, since one cannot apply to her [the clause in her *kethubah*:] AND I WILL TAKE YOU AGAIN AS MY WIFE.[12]

(1) Lit., 'goes after (the status) of the beginning'. When the clause was applicable and therefore the obligation stands. (2) Lit., 'in the end'. (3) V. *supra* p. 302, n. 6. (4) In the case of the widow to a High Priest, as her prohibition is due to a cause other than captivity, neither the clause relating to 'remarriage' nor that of 'restoring her to her parental home' is valid (cf. *supra* p. 300, n. 10); and in the case of the last mentioned because the clause, 'I WILL TAKE YOU AGAIN AS MY WIFE' could not be applied originally and cannot be applied now. (5) R. Eliezer and R. Joshua. (6) To either of whom the relevant clauses of her *kethubah* that were *originally* applicable *now, on account of the vow* which is a cause of prohibition '*other* than that of captivity'. (7) And thus incurred the liability to ransom her before he died. (8) Lit., 'to do a deed'. (9) R. Ḥiyya who was Rab's father's brother. (10) Lit., 'as that'. (11) Lit., 'and no more but'. (12) Since her husband is dead. V. Tosef. Keth. IV.

Our Rabbis taught: [If a woman] was taken captive and a demand was made upon her husband for as much as ten times her value, he must ransom her the first time. Subsequently, however, he ransoms her only if he desired to do so but need not ransom her[1] if he does not wish to do so. R. Simeon b. Gamaliel ruled: [52b] Captives must not be ransomed for more than their value, in the interests of the public.[2] [This then implies] that they must be ransomed for their actual value even though the cost of a captive's ransom[3] exceeds the amount of her *kethubah*. Has not, however, the contrary been taught: [If a woman] was taken captive, and a demand was made upon her husband for as much as ten times the amount of her *kethubah*, he must ransom her the first time. Subsequently, however, he ransoms her only if he desires to do so but need not ransom her if he does not wish to do so. R. Simeon b. Gamaliel ruled: If the price of her ransom corresponded to the amount of her *kethubah*[4] he must ransom her; if not, he[5] need not ransom her?[6]—R. Simeon b. Gamaliel upholds two lenient rules.[7]

IF SHE SUSTAINED AN INJURY IT IS HIS DUTY TO PROVIDE FOR HER MEDICAL TREATMENT. Our Rabbis taught: A widow is to be maintained from [her husband's] orphans' estate; and if she requires medical treatment, it is regarded[8] as maintenance. R. Simeon b. Gamaliel ruled: Medical treatment of a limited liability may be deducted[9] from her *kethubah* but one which has no limited

(1) At all. It is his duty to ransom her no more than once (Rashi). *Aliter:* For an exorbitant price (v. R. Ḥan. Tosaf. s.v. רצה, *a.l.*). If, however, the ransom demanded is not higher than her value he must pay it. (2) מפני תיקון העולם 'for the sake of the social order' (Jast.), lit., 'for the establishment of the world', that captors should not thereby be encouraged to demand exorbitant prices for the ransom of their captive. (3) Lit., 'her ransom'. (4) *Sc.* did not exceed it. (5) Since one cannot be expected to be liable for a single clause of a *kethubah* more than for the total amount of the *kethubah*. [Isaiah Trani: The amount of the *kethubah* here denotes the extra jointure in addition to the statutory two hundred and one hundred *zuz*]. (6) A ruling which contradicts the implication of the first Baraitha that he must ransom her 'even though the cost of a captive's ransom exceeds the amount of her *kethubah*'. (7) The price of the ransom need not exceed either (*a*) the actual value of the woman or (*b*) the amount of her *kethubah*, whichever is the less. (8) Lit., 'behold it'. (9) Lit., 'she is healed'.

liability[1] is regarded[2] as maintenance. Said R. Johanan: Blood letting in the Land of Israel[3] was regarded as medical treatment of no limited liability.[4]

R. Johanan's relatives had [to maintain] their father's wife who required daily medical treatment. When they came to R. Johanan[5] he told them: Proceed to arrange with a medical man an inclusive fee.[6] [Later, however], R. Johanan remarked: 'We have put ourselves [in the unenviable position] of[7] legal advisers'.[8] What, however, was his opinion at first,[9] and why did he change it in the end![10]—At first he thought [of the Scriptural text,] *And that thou hide not thyself from thine own flesh,*[11] but ultimately he realized [that the position of] a noted personality is different [from that of the general public].[12]

MISHNAH. [A HUSBAND WHO] DID NOT GIVE HIS WIFE IN WRITING[13] [THE FOLLOWING UNDERTAKING:] 'THE MALE CHILDREN THAT WILL BE BORN FROM OUR MARRIAGE[14] SHALL INHERIT THE MONEY OF THY KETHUBAH IN ADDITION TO THEIR SHARES WITH THEIR BROTHERS',[15] IS NEVERTHELESS

(1) If, for instance, the woman is always ailing. (2) Lit., 'behold it'. (3) Palestine. (4) Tosef. Keth. IV. (5) Seeking advice on how to escape the constant drain on their resources. (6) Lit., 'go fix something for him, for a healer'. Since their liability would thereby become limited they would be entitled to deduct it from the woman's *kethubah*. (7) Lit., 'as'. (8) עורכי הדיינין, lit., 'those who arrange (the pleas) before the judges'. It is forbidden for a judge to act, even indirectly, as legal adviser to one of the litigants, v. Aboth (Sonc. ed.) p. 6, n. 1. (9) When he gave his advice to his relatives. (10) Lit., 'and in the end what did he think?' (11) Isa. LVIII, 7, teaching the obligation of assisting one's relatives. (12) A judge must subject himself to greater restrictions in order to be free from all possible suspicion of partiality. (13) As one of the clauses of her *kethubah*. (14) Lit., 'that you will have from me'. (15) Who may be born from another wife. The effect of such a clause is that, if the woman predeceases her husband, her sons, on the death of their father (her husband), would inherit her *kethubah*, and they would recover it from their deceased father's estate, irrespective of the amount or size of the shares to which they are entitled like any of the other sons of the deceased. This clause is designated, as '*kethubath benin dikrin*' (*kethubah* of male children).

LIABLE, BECAUSE [THIS CLAUSE] IS A CONDITION LAID DOWN BY BETH DIN.

[THOUGH HE DID NOT GIVE HIS WIFE IN WRITING[1] THE UNDERTAKING:] 'THE FEMALE CHILDREN THAT WILL BE BORN FROM OUR MARRIAGE[2] SHALL DWELL IN MY HOUSE AND BE MAINTAINED OUT OF MY ESTATE UNTIL THEY SHALL BE TAKEN IN MARRIAGE'[3] HE IS NEVERTHELESS LIABLE, BECAUSE [THIS CLAUSE] IS A CONDITION LAID DOWN BY BETH DIN.

[SIMILARLY IF HE DID NOT GIVE HIS WIFE THE WRITTEN UNDERTAKING:][4] 'YOU SHALL DWELL IN MY HOUSE AND BE MAINTAINED THEREIN OUT OF MY ESTATE THROUGHOUT THE DURATION OF YOUR WIDOWHOOD', HE IS NEVERTHELESS LIABLE, BECAUSE [THIS CLAUSE ALSO] IS A CONDITION LAID DOWN BY BETH DIN. SO DID THE MEN OF JERUSALEM WRITE. THE MEN OF GALILEE WROTE IN THE SAME MANNER AS THE MEN OF JERUSALEM. THE MEN OF JUDAEA, HOWEVER, USED TO WRITE:[5] 'UNTIL THE HEIRS MAY CONSENT TO PAY YOU YOUR KETHUBAH'. THE HEIRS, CONSEQUENTLY, MAY, IF THEY WISH TO DO IT, PAY HER HER KETHUBAH AND DISMISS HER.

GEMARA. R. Johanan stated in the name of R. Simeon b. Yohai: Why was the *kethubah* for MALE CHILDREN[6] instituted?[7] In order that any man might thereby[8] be encouraged[9] to give[10] to his daughter as much as to his son. But is such a regulation found anywhere else?[11] Seeing that the All-Merciful ordained that

(1) V. p. 305, n. 13. (2) V. p. 305, n. 14. (3) Lit., 'to men'. This clause is designated as '*kethubath benan nukban*' (*kethubah* of female children). (4) As one of the clauses of her *kethubah*. (5) Immediately after the last mentioned clause. (6) Cf. *supra* p. 305, n. 15 and text. (7) *Sc.* why should not the *kethubah*, which on the death of his wife is legally inherited by the husband, be regarded as a part of his general estate and so be equally divided between all his sons? (8) By being assured that whatever dowry he may give to his daughter will remain the property of her own children and will not pass through her husband to the children of his other wives. (9) Lit., 'that a man may leap'. (10) So MS.M. Cur. edd. 'and he will write'. (11) Lit., 'is there a thing?'

'a son shall be heir; a daughter shall not',[1] would the Rabbis proceed to make a provision[2] whereby a daughter shall be the heir?—This[3] also has Scriptural sanction, for it is written, *Take ye wives, and beget sons and daughters; and take wives for your sons, and give your daughters to husbands;*[4] [now the advice to take wives for one's] sons is quite intelligible [since such marriages are] within a father's power[5] but [as to the giving of] one's daughters [the difficulty arises:] Is [such giving] within his power?[5] [Consequently[6] it must be] this that we were taught: That a father must provide for his daughter clothing and covering and must also give her a dowry[7] so that people may be anxious to woo[8] her and so proceed to marry her. And to what extent?[9] Both Abaye and Raba ruled: Up to a tenth of his wealth.

But might it not be suggested[10] [that the sons] should inherit [what their mother received] from her father[11] but not [that which was due to her] from her husband?[12]—If that were so, a father also would abstain from assigning[13] [a liberal dowry for his daughter].[14] May it then be suggested[10] that where her father had assigned a dowry[15] her husband must also enter the clause[16] but where her father did not assign any dowry[17] her husband also need not enter

(1) Cf. Num. XXVII, 8: *If a man die, and have no son, then ye shall cause his inheritance to pass unto his daughter*, from which it follows that if a man has a son his inheritance shall not pass unto his daughter. (2) Encouraging a father (cf. *supra* p. 306, n. 8) to give his daughter a liberal dowry and thus deprive his sons of property which Pentateuchally should in due course be inherited by them. (3) A father's duty to make liberal provision for his daughter. (4) Jer. XXIX, 6. (5) Lit., 'stand in his hand'. It is the man who approaches the woman, not the woman the man. (6) Since Scripture nevertheless advises fathers to *give* their *daughters* to husbands. (7) Lit., 'something'. (8) Lit., 'jump', 'leap'. (9) Must a father go on assigning a dowry for his daughter. (10) Since the *kethubah* for the male children was instituted in order to encourage a father to provide a liberal dowry for his daughter. (11) *Sc.* the dowry he gave her, which was included in her *kethubah*. (12) The statutory *kethubah* and any additional jointure her husband may have settled upon her. (13) Lit., 'and will not write'. (14) No father would be prepared to give a liberal dowry to a husband of his daughter who does not himself also allow the sons of that daughter to inherit what he had promised their mother. (15) Lit., 'wrote'. (16) Relating to the MALE CHILDREN. Lit., 'should write'. (17) Lit., 'did not write'.

the clause?[1]—The Rabbis drew no distinction.[2] But should not then[3] a daughter[4] among sons[5] also be heir?[6]—The Rabbis have treated [the *kethubah*][7] like an inheritance.[8] But should not then a daughter[4] among the other daughters[5] be heir?[9]—The Rabbis made no distinction.[10] Why then[11] is not [the *kethubah*] recoverable[12] from movables also?[13]—The Rabbis treated it like the [statutory] *kethubah*.[14] Why then should not distraint be made on sold or mortgaged property?[15]—[The expression] we learned [was] SHALL INHERIT.[16] May it then[11] be suggested [that it is recoverable] even if there was no surplus[17] of a *denar?*[18]—The Rabbis have made no enactment where the Pentateuchal law of inheritance would thereby be uprooted.

R. Papa was making arrangements for his son to be married into the house of Abba of Sura.[19] He went there to write the *kethubah* for the bride.[20] When Judah b. Meremar heard [of his arrival] he

(1) Cf. *supra* p. 307, n. 16 *mutatis mutandis*. (2) Between the two kinds of *kethubahs*, since most *kethubahs* contain records of dowries (Rashi). All *kethubahs* must consequently include the MALE CHILDREN clause also. (3) V. *supra* p. 307, n. 10. (4) Of one wife who had no sons. (5) Of another wife. (6) To her mother, as far as her *kethubah* is concerned. The same reason that applies to male children should equally apply to a daughter in the absence of sons. Why then was a 'male children' and not a similar 'female children' clause instituted? (7) In which the term 'INHERIT' was used (cf. our Mishnah). (8) No daughter may 'inherit' among sons. (9) Though she cannot be heir among sons (v. *supra* n. 8) she is well entitled, in the case of an ordinary inheritance, to be heir among daughters. Why then should she be deprived of her mother's *kethubah* (cf. *supra* n. 6, final clause)? (10) Cf. *supra* note 2. (11) V. *supra* p. 307, n. 10. (12) By the sons. (13) As stated *supra* 50a. (14) Which cannot be recovered from the movables of a deceased husband. (15) Just as the woman can collect her *kethubah* from mortgaged or sold property, so should the sons be able to recover it from such property, v. *infra* 55a. (16) And no sold or mortgaged property may be seized for an inheritance. (17) After the two 'male children' *kethubahs* had been paid (v. Mishnah *infra* 91a). (18) Whereby the Pentateuchal law of inheritance could be carried out. Why then was it stated (l.c.) that the male children *kethubahs* are not recoverable in such a case? (19) Who was his father-in-law (cf. *supra* 39b and Sanh. 14b). R. Papa's son married the sister of his father's wife. (20) Lit., 'for her'. This would include the fixing of the amount for the dowry she was to receive from her father.

went out to welcome him.[1] When, however, they reached the door [of the bride's father's house] he asked leave to depart, when [R. Papa] said to him, 'Will the Master come in with me?' [53*a*] Observing, however, that it was distasteful to him [to enter], he addressed him thus: 'What is it that you have on your mind? [Are you reluctant to enter] because Samuel said to Rab Judah, "*Shinena*,[2] keep away from[3] transfers of inheritance[4] even though they be from a bad son to a good son, because one never knows what issue will come forth from him,[5] and much more so [when the transfer is] from a son to a daughter",[6] this[7] also [I may point out] is an enactment of the Rabbis; as R. Johanan stated in the name of R. Simeon b. Yohai'.[8] The other replied, 'This enactment applies only [to one who acts] willingly;[9] does it also imply that one should be compelled so to act?'—'Did I tell you' said [R. Papa] to him, 'to come in and coerce him? What I meant was: Come in but exercise no pressure upon him'. 'My entrance', the other replied, 'would amount to compulsion'.[10] [As R. Papa, however,] urged him, he entered but, having sat down, remained silent.[11] [Abba] thought that he[12] was vexed[13] and consequently assigned[14] [to his daughter as dowry] all that he possessed. Finally, however, he said to him,[12] 'Will not the Master speak even now? By the life of the Master, I have left nothing for myself!'—'As far as I am concerned',[15] the other replied, 'even the amount you have assigned[16] has given me no pleasure'. 'This being the case',[17] the first said,

(1) Lit., 'he came; shewed himself to him'. (2) שינגא (rt. שנן, 'to sharpen'); (i) 'keen witted', (ii) 'man of iron endurance', (iii) 'long toothed' (cf. שן 'tooth') V. B.B. Sonc. ed. vol. II, p. 561, n. 14. (3) Lit., 'be not among'. (4) From persons who are legally entitled to be heirs. (5) Though the son himself is wicked his children may be righteous. (6) By giving his daughter a dowry he deprives his sons from a portion of their inheritance. (Cf. *supra* p. 307, n. 2). (7) Allowing one's daughter a dowry. (8) *Supra* 52*b*. (9) Lit., 'from his (own) mind'. (10) The father of the bride would be ashamed to offer a small dowry in the presence of a distinguished guest. (11) While R. Papa was discussing the amount of the dowry with the bride's father. (12) Judah b. Meremar who looked on in silence. (13) At the smallness of the dowry he was offering. (14) Lit., 'wrote it'. (15) Lit., 'if from me'. (16) Lit., 'that also that you wrote'. (17) Lit., 'now also'.

'I will withdraw'. 'I did not suggest', the other said, 'that you should make a rogue[1] of yourself'.

R. Yemar the Elder enquired of R. Naḥman: Does a woman who sold her *kethubah* to her husband retain the right to the *kethubah* for her male children[2] or not?[3]—Said Raba to him: Why do you not raise the same question in the case of a woman who surrendered her claim [to her *kethubah*]?[4]—'Now', the other replied, 'that I [found it necessary to] enquire [concerning a woman] who sold [her *kethubah*],[5] though [in that case] it might well be assumed [that her need for] money compelled her [to the sale; and, furthermore,] it might be said [that she is] like a person who was struck a hundred blows with a hammer,[6] was it then necessary [to raise the same question in respect of] a woman who [voluntarily] surrendered her claim [to her *kethubah*]?[7]

Raba stated: I have no doubt[8] that a woman who sells[9] her *kethubah* to strangers[10] retains the right to the male children's *kethubah*.[2] What is the reason? [It is her need for] money that has compelled her [to sell].[11] A woman [on the other hand] who

(1) הדרנא (rt. הדר 'to return') a retractor. (2) V. our Mishnah and *supra* p. 305, n. 15. (3) *Sc.* are her sons still entitled to inherit her *kethubah* as they are entitled to inherit their share in the estate of their father, or do they lose the former right on account of their mother's sale which had transferred her rights to their father from whose estate they can inherit no bigger shares than those to which his other sons are entitled? (4) Which is a more common occurrence than a sale. (5) Believing that even in such a case it is possible that the woman irrevocably loses her rights. (6) V. Golds. who compares עוכלא with Syr. אכלא 'a hammer', and renders עוכלי, 'hammer blows'. *Aliter:* They inflicted upon her a hundred strokes with a lash to which a small weight named *'ukla* was attached (Rashi). *Aliter:* I may adopt the opinion of him who said, they struck (defeated) that opinion with a hundred measures against one (a hundred arguments against, for one in favour of it). *'Ukla* (cf. איכלא) is a small measure of capacity and also of a weight (Jast.). (7) Obviously not. If she might lose her rights even when she acted under the stress of circumstances, there can be no question that she loses them when she willingly surrenders them. (8) Lit., 'it is plain to me'. (9) For a mere trifle, since, to the buyers the transaction is of a highly speculative and doubtful value. V. *infra* n. 10. (10) Who recover it only if she is divorced or if she survives her husband, but lose it completely if she predeceases him and he inherits it. (11) Not her indifference to the

surrenders her claim [to her *kethubah*] in favour of her husband does not retain the right to the male children's *kethubah*. What is the reason? She has lightheartedly surrendered her claims.[1] [Is, however, a woman,] Raba enquired, who sells her *kethubah* to her husband treated as one who sells it to strangers,[2] or as one who renounces it in favour of her husband?[3] After he raised the question he himself solved it: [The law concerning] a woman who sells her *kethubah* to her husband is the same as that of one who sells it to strangers.[2]

R. Idi b. Abin raised an objection: [We learned]: If she[4] died, neither the heirs of the one husband nor the heirs of the other are entitled to inherit her *kethubah*.[5] And in considering the difficulty, 'How does the question of a *kethubah* at all arise?'[6] R. Papa replied, 'The *kethubah* of the male children [was meant]'.[7] But why?[8] Could not one[9] argue here also:[10] 'Her passion has overpowered

welfare of her sons. On this account, therefore (v. *infra* n. 1), she does not lose her rights on behalf of her sons.

(1) And, having thereby shewn her complete indifference to the interests of her sons, her surrender is deemed to be final and irrevocable. (2) Since in both cases she sells it for a mere trifle, the husband's purchase being no less of a speculation than that of strangers (cf. p. 310, nn. 9-10). For should she predecease him, her *kethubah* would in any case be inherited by him; and the only advantage he might possibly derive from his purchase is the knowledge that his sons would benefit from it if he predeceased his wife. As, in fact, he did not predecease her his purchase fully assumes the same nature as that of strangers, and her male children inherit her *kethubah*. (3) Since the *kethubah* is actually in his possession (which is not the case with strangers) and she consented to sell him all her rights. (4) A woman whose husband went to a country beyond the sea and who, on being told by one witness that her husband was dead, contracted a marriage, and her first husband subsequently returned. (5) Yeb. 87*b*. (6) Lit., 'what is its doing?' How could her children submit any claim to her *kethubah* when she herself, as stated earlier in the Mishnah cited (Yeb. l.c.), is not entitled to one? (7) Yeb. 91*a*; *sc.* if the woman predeceased her two husbands, who in consequence inherited her estate, her children have no claim to her *kethubah* and receive shares equal to those of their paternal brothers. (8) Should her children be deprived of the *kethubah* of their mother? (9) Since it has been said above that the reason why the woman does not lose her right to the *kethubah* for her male children is because it was her need that compelled her to sell it. (10) In the case of the woman who married a second husband on the evidence of one witness.

her'?[1]—There[2] [the loss of her *kethubah*] is a penalty that the Rabbis have imposed upon her.[3]

Rabin b. Ḥanina once sat [at his studies] before R. Ḥisda and in the course of the session he laid down in the name of R. Eleazar: A woman who surrenders her *kethubah* to her husband is not entitled to maintenance.[4] The other[5] said to him: Had you not spoken to me in the name of a great man I would have told you: *Whoso rewardeth evil for good, evil shall not depart from his house.*[6]

R. Naḥman and 'Ulla and Abimi son of R. Papi once sat at their studies, and R. Ḥiyya b. Ammi was sitting with them when there came before them a man whose betrothed wife had died.[7] 'Go and bury her', they said to him, 'or pay her *kethubah* on her account'.[8] Said R. Ḥiyya to them, We have a teaching:[9] In the case of a betrothed wife[10] [the husband] is subject neither to the laws of *onan*,[11] nor may he defile himself for her;[12] and she likewise[13] is not subject to the laws of *onan*,[14] nor may she defile herself for him;[15] if she dies he is not her heir,[16] but if he dies she collects her *kethubah*.[17] Now the reason [why she collects her *kethubah* is] because it

(1) And this compelled her to marry again. Now since she acted under compulsion her children should not be deprived of her *kethubah*. (2) V. p. 311, n. 10. (3) For marrying again on insufficient evidence (that of one witness) before instituting further inquiries to verify his evidence. (4) During her widowhood. As she surrendered her *kethubah* she surrendered thereby all her rights, including that of maintenance, that are contained therein. (5) R. Ḥisda. (6) Prov. XVII, 13. (7) Before her marriage. (8) [The reference is to the statutory amount of the *kethubah*, these Rabbis being of the opinion that the husband has been allowed to retain the *kethubah* of his deceased wife for the expenses he incurred in the burial.] (9) A Baraitha. Cf. *infra* p. 313, n. 1. (10) Before her marriage. (11) V. Glos. Unlike an *onan* whose married wife died, he may partake of holy food. (12) If he is a priest (cf. Lev. XXI, 1f). (13) If he died. (14) She also is permitted to partake of holy food. (15) During a festival when not only priests but also Israelites and women are forbidden to attend on the corpses of those who are not their near relatives (v. R.H. 16*b*). *Aliter:* Nor is she under an *obligation* to defile herself for him. (Cf. Rashi *a.l.* and Yeb. 29*b*. s.v. ולא מיטמאה; and Tosaf. loc. cit. s.v. לא). (16) To the dowry her father gave her. (17) Yeb. 29*b*, 43*b*, *infra* 89*b*. Both the statutory amount and any additional jointure, if he provided her with a *kethubah* on betrothal (cf. *infra* 89*b*.

was he who died; had she, however, died she would not have been entitled to any *kethubah*.[1] What is the reason?[2]—R. Hoshaia replied: Because one cannot apply to her: 'If you will be married to another man you will receive what is prescribed for you'.[3]

When Rabin came[4] he stated in the name of Resh Laḳish: If a betrothed woman died, she is not entitled to a *kethubah*. Said Abaye to them:[5] Go and tell him: [53b] 'You are deprived of your benefaction;[6] it is cast upon the thorns',[7] for R. Hoshaia has already expounded his traditional teachings[8] in Babylon.[9]

THE FEMALE CHILDREN THAT WILL BE BORN FROM OUR MARRIAGE etc. Rab[10] taught: Until they shall be taken in marriage;[11] but Levi taught: Until they shall attain adolescence.[12] [Would daughters then be maintained] according to Rab although they attained adolescence, and according[13] to Levi even though they married?[14]—The fact, however, [is that where a daughter] attained adolescence though she was not married or where she was married

(1) Contrary to the ruling *supra* that the man must either bury his betrothed wife or pay to her account the amount of her *kethubah*. (2) For the man's exemption from the duty of burying his wife despite the statutory amount of her *kethubah* which he inherits. (3) This is one of the clauses of a *kethubah* (v. Yeb. 117*a*). Since this clause can obviously have no effect except when a husband predeceases his wife or when she is divorced by him, the *kethubah* cannot be regarded as the wife's property whenever she predeceases her husband, and he, consequently, cannot be regarded as inheriting it from her. [As to the teaching *supra* 47*b* that the husband inherits the *kethubah* in return for her burial, the reference is to the dowry, v. *supra* p. 272, n. 7 and cf. p. 312, n. 8. (4) From Palestine to Babylon. (5) Those present at the college. (6) Or 'recognition' (v. Rashi). (7) שקילא טיבותך שדיא אחיזרי, a proverb. The information whereby he intended to benefit the students was of no use to them. *Aliter:* Your good-natured information is taken and thrown over the hedge (slight adaptation from Jast.). *Aliter:* Take your favours and throw them in the bush, v. B.M. Sonc. ed. p. 377. (8) Which included the one reported by Rabin. (9) They were in no need, therefore, to wait for the Palestinian report of Rabin. (10) In dealing with this clause in the *kethubah*. (11) Lit., 'to men'. Cf. our Mishnah which agrees with Rab's ruling. (12) V. Glos. s.v. *bogereth*. (13) So MS.M. Cur. edd., 'and Levi'. (14) Surely not; since either of these conditions liberates a daughter from her father's control and she must in consequence lose her claim to maintenance (cf. *infra* 68*b*).

though she did not attain adolescence no one[1] disputes [the ruling that she is not entitled to maintenance]. They[2] differ only on the question of a [daughter who was] betrothed but did not attain adolescence.[3]

So also did Levi teach in his Baraitha:[4] Until they shall attain adolescence and the time for their marriages arrives. Both?[5] —What was meant is this:[6] Either they shall attain adolescence or[7] the time for their marriage[8] shall arrive.

[They[9] differ on the same principles] as the following Tannaim: How long is a daughter to be maintained? Until she is betrothed. In the name of R. Eleazar it was stated: Until she attains adolescence.

R. Joseph learnt: [Daughters must be maintained] until they become [wives]. The question was raised: Does this[10] mean becoming [wives] at marriage or becoming [wives] at betrothal?—The question must stand unanswered.[11]

Said R. Ḥisda to R. Joseph: Did you ever hear from Rab Judah whether a betrothed [orphan] is entitled to maintenance[12] or not?[13] The other replied: I have not actually heard it, but it may logically be concluded that she is not entitled, because [her future husband], having betrothed her, would not allow[14] her to be degraded.[15] 'If

(1) Lit., 'all the world'. V. *infra* n. 2. (2) Rab and Levi. (3) According to Rab she is maintained only until betrothal though by that time she may still be under age, and according to Levi, either adolescence or marriage deprives her of her rights to maintenance. (4) Levi, like R. Ḥiyya and R. Oshaia, was the compiler of six orders of Baraithoth corresponding to the six orders of the Mishnah compiled by R. Judah the Patriarch. (5) Cf. p. 313, n. 14. (6) Lit., 'but'. (7) The '*Waw*' in ויםטי may be rendered, 'and' as well as 'or'. (8) A period of twelve months from the time her intended husband had claimed her, in the case of a virgin, and one of thirty days in the case of a widow (v. Mishnah *infra* 57a). (9) Rab and Levi. (10) The expression 'become (wives)' in R. Joseph's statement. (11) Teḳu, v. Glos. (12) By her brothers, out of their deceased father's estate. (13) [He wished to know according to which of the two Tannaim, whose views have just been cited, was the law to be fixed (Tosaf.)] (14) Lit., 'it would not be pleasing to him'. (15) As the maintenance of an orphan daughter by her brothers was ordained in order to prevent her degradation (v. *supra* 49a) it cannot be enforced in this case where no degradation is to be expected.

you have not actually heard this', [R. Ḥisda] retorted 'it may logically be concluded that she is entitled, for [her intended husband], not being sure of her,[1] would not throw his money away for nothing'.[2]

Another reading:[3] He[4] replied: I have not actually heard it, but it may logically be concluded that she is entitled [to maintenance]; for [her intended husband], not being sure of her, would not throw his money away for nothing. The other[5] retorted: If you have not actually heard this it may logically be concluded that she is not entitled to maintenance; because [her future husband], having betrothed her, would not allow her to be degraded.

(Mnemonic of the men:[6] *SHaK ZaRaP*.[7] [Subjects:] She *refused* and a *sister-in-law* of the *second degree* is *betrothed* and he *outraged* her.)

R. Shesheth was asked: Is a minor who exercised her right of refusal[8] entitled to maintenance[9] or not?[10]—You, replied R. Shesheth, have learned this: A widow[11] in her father's house, a divorced woman[11] in her father's house or a woman[11] who was awaiting the decision of a levir[12] in her father's house is entitled to maintenance. R. Judah ruled: [Only a woman who] is still in her father's house is entitled to maintenance but [a woman who] is no longer in her father's house is not entitled to maintenance. [Now is not] R. Judah's ruling exactly the same as that of the first Tanna?[13] Consequently it may be concluded that[14] the difference between

(1) A betrothal does not always lead to marriage. (2) As he would not maintain her, the duty (for the reason stated *supra* p. 314, n. 15) devolves upon her brothers. (3) Reversing the respective views of R. Joseph and R. Ḥisda. (4) R. Joseph. (5) R. Ḥisda. (6) Who raised the following questions. (7) *SH*esheth, La*K*ish, Ela*Z*ar, *R*aba, *P*apa. (8) V. Glos. s.v. *mi'un*. (9) By her brothers, out of their deceased father's estate. (10) The point of the question is whether (*a*) the declaration of refusal to live with her husband dissolved her marriage retrospectively and she resumes in consequence the status of one who was never married and is, therefore, entitled to maintenance until she reaches her adolescence; or (*b*) since her marriage had once removed her from her father's control, in consequence of which she has lost her right to maintenance, her subsequent declaration of refusal cannot again restore to her the right she had once lost. (11) Who had been only betrothed but had never married. (12) *Shomereth yabam*, v. Glos. (13) Who also spoke only of a woman 'in her father's house'. Wherein, then, do they differ? (14) Lit., 'what, not?'

them is the case of a minor who had exercised her right of refusal,[1] the first Tanna being of the opinion that she is entitled [to maintenance][2] while R. Judah upholds the view that she is not entitled to it.[3]

Resh Laḳish enquired: Is the daughter of a sister-in-law[4] entitled to maintenance[5] or not? Has she no claim to it, since the Master said,[6] Her *kethubah* is a charge on the estate of her first husband[7] or is it possible that she is entitled to it since the Rabbis have enacted that whenever she[8] is unable to collect her *kethubah* from [the estate of] the first, she may recover it from that of the second?[9]—The question must remain unanswered.[10]

R. Eleazar enquired: Is the daughter of a forbidden relative of the second degree of incest[11] entitled to maintenance[12] or not? [54a] Has she no claim to maintenance[13] since [her mother] is not entitled to a *kethubah*, or is it likely that the Rabbis have imposed a penalty only upon her mother who had committed a transgression but not upon her who had committed no transgression?—This remains unanswered.[10]

Raba asked: Is the daughter of a betrothed wife entitled to

(1) V. Glos. s.v. *mi'un*. (2) Cf. p. 315, n. 10. By mentioning a 'widow (cf. *supra* n. 11) in her father's house' the first Tanna meant to include also the minor who exercised her right of refusal who is thereby restored to the status of one who had never been married and had always been 'in her father's house'. (3) V. *supra* p. 315, n. 10. He ruled, 'who is *still* in her father's house', *sc.* who has never left it to be married, is entitled to maintenance; not, however, one who had once been married though that marriage had taken place during minority. (4) Whom the levir married in fulfilment of the law of the levirate marriage (v. Deut. XXV, 5). (5) By her brothers, out of their deceased father's estate. (6) Yeb. 85*a*. (7) This refers to the sister-in-law. That is to say the mother of the daughter in question. As her *kethubah* cannot be made a charge upon the estate of her second husband (her original brother-in-law), so cannot the maintenance of her daughter, which is one of the obligations undertaken in the same document. (8) The sister-in-law. (9) Cf. *supra* n. 8 *mutatis mutandis*. (10) Teḳu, v. Glos. (11) V. Yeb. 20*a*, 21*a*. (12) Out of the estate of her deceased father. (13) Which is only one of the obligations a man undertakes in the *kethubah* he gives to his wife.

maintenance[1] or not? Is she entitled to maintenance[2] since [her mother] is entitled to a *kethubah*[3] or is it possible that she is not entitled [to maintenance],[2] since the Rabbis have not ordained [the writing of] the *kethubah* until the time of the marriage?[4]—The question must stand unanswered.

R. Papa asked: Is the daughter of an outraged woman[5] entitled to maintenance[1] or not? According to the ruling of R. Jose the son of R. Judah, who has laid down[6] that [her mother] is entitled to recover[7] a *kethubah* for one *maneh*,[8] the question does not arise.[9] It arises only according to the ruling of the Rabbis who have laid down that the fine[10] is regarded as a quittance for her *kethubah*. What, [it may be asked, is the decision]?[11] Has she no claim to maintenance[12] since [her mother] is not entitled to a *kethubah*,[13] or might it possibly [be argued thus:] What is the reason why a *kethubah* [has been instituted for a wife]? In order that the man might not find it easy[14] to divorce her;[15] but [this man],[16] surely, cannot[17] divorce her?[18]—This must stand unanswered.

YOU SHALL DWELL IN MY HOUSE etc. R. Joseph learnt: IN MY HOUSE[19] but not in my hovel.[20] She is entitled, however, to

(1) Out of her deceased father's estate if he had sons from another wife. (2) V. *supra* p. 316, n. 13. (3) If her father had written one for her on betrothal. As he is responsible for the *kethubah* of his wife so should he be responsible for the maintenance of his daughter (v. *supra* p. 316, n. 13). (4) As the obligation of the *kethubah* does not begin before marriage, that of maintenance also does not begin earlier. (5) Whom the offender has subsequently married (v. Deut. XXII, 28f). (6) *Supra* 39*b*. (7) Out of the man's estate, though he had already paid to her father the fine prescribed in Deut. XXII, 29, v. *supra* 39*b*. (8) V. Glos. (9) As the *kethubah* is recoverable from the man's estate so is the daughter's maintenance (v. *supra* p. 316, n. 13). (10) That is paid to her father (Deut. XXII, 29). (11) As regards the daughter's maintenance. (12) V. *supra* p. 316, n. 13). (13) As the *kethubah* cannot be recovered so cannot the daughter's maintenance. (14) Lit., 'that she shall not be easy in his eyes'. (15) He cannot easily divorce her if his act involves him in the payment of the amount specified in the *kethubah*. (16) Who committed outrage. (17) V. Deut. XXII, 29. (18) Hence the ruling that the woman is not entitled to a *kethubah*. As this argument, however, does not apply to her daughter the latter may well be entitled to maintenance. (19) *Sc.* only if the deceased left a proper house must his sons provide living accommodation for his widow. (Cf. however, Jast. *infra* n. 20.) (20) בביקתי, MS.M. בבית עקתי. ביקתא = בי עקתא (v. Shab. 77*b*), 'a house of

maintenance.[1] Mar son of R. Ashi ruled: She is not entitled even to maintenance.[2] The law, however, is not in agreement with Mar son of R. Ashi.

R. Naḥman stated in the name of Samuel: If marriage was proposed to her[3] and she accepted, she is no longer entitled to maintenance.[4] [This is to imply that] if she did not accept,[5] she would not be entitled to maintenance!—R. Anan replied: This was explained to me by Mar Samuel: If she said, '[I cannot accept the proposal] out of respect for the memory of[6] So-and-so, my husband', she is entitled to maintenance; [but if she said], 'Because the men are not suitable for me,' she is not entitled to maintenance.[7]

R. Ḥisda ruled: If she[8] played the harlot she is not entitled to maintenance. R. Joseph ruled: If she painted her eyes[9] or dyed her hair[10] she is not entitled to maintenance.[11] He who ruled: 'If she played the harlot'[12] would even more so deprive her of maintenance if she paints her eyes or dyes her hair. He, however, who ruled: 'If she painted her eyes or dyed her hair'[12] would allow her maintenance[13] if she played the harlot. What is the reason?—Her passions have overpowered her.

distress', 'a poor man's house' (Rashi). If the house is too small the orphans may ask her to live elsewhere. *Aliter:* ביקתא = בקעתא, 'valley', 'group of fields', 'estate'; the widow 'must be content to live in her late husband's house with his heirs, but she cannot claim a separate residence' (Jast.).

(1) Though she is in residence in her paternal home, she does not forfeit her claim to maintenance from her late husband's estate. Though the first part of the clause of her *kethubah*, DWELL IN MY HOUSE, is not carried out, the second part, BE MAINTAINED OUT OF MY ESTATE, nevertheless remains valid. (2) As one part of the clause is inapplicable the other part also becomes void. (3) The widow. (4) Her WIDOWHOOD is deemed to have terminated thereby, and in consequence she loses the rights attached to it. (5) Whatever the reason. (6) Lit., 'on account of'. (7) The heirs cannot be compelled to continue her maintenance once she has had an offer from a man who is willing to provide for her. (8) The widow. (9) Rt. כחל, (denom. of כוחל, *stibium*, a powder applied to the eyelids), 'to paint the eyelids', cosmetically or medically (v. Jast.). (10) Rt. פרכס (denom. of פיקס, φῦκος with inserted ר), 'to adorn with paint or dye' (v. Levy). Jast. derives it from פרך, 'to rub', 'to rub with paint' (s.v. פרכס); 'dyeing the hair' (Jast. s.v. פירכוס). (11) Since it is apparent that she is not much concerned for the memory of her late husband. (12) 'She is not entitled to maintenance'. (13) Lit., 'she has'.

The law, however, is not in agreement with any of these reported rulings but with that which Rab Judah laid down in the name of Samuel: She[1] who claims her *kethubah* at court is not entitled to maintenance. But is she not entitled? Surely it was taught: If she sold her *kethubah*, pledged it, or mortgaged [the land that was pledged[2] for] her *kethubah* to a stranger, she is not entitled to maintenance. [Does not this imply] that only such[3] [acts deprive a widow of her maintenance] but not [the act of] claiming [her *kethubah* at court]?—These [acts[4] deprive her of her maintenance] whether she appeared at court or not, but the act of claiming [her *kethubah* deprives her of maintenance] only if she appeared[5] in court but does not [deprive her of it] if she did not appear at court.

SO DID THE MEN OF JERUSALEM etc. It was stated: Rab ruled, 'The *halachah* is in agreement with [the practice of] the MEN OF JUDAEA', but Samuel ruled, 'The *halachah* agrees with [the practice of] the MEN OF GALILEE'.

Babylon[6] and all its neighbouring towns[7] followed a usage in agreement with the ruling of Rab; Nehardea[8] and all its neighbouring towns[7] followed a usage agreeing with the ruling of Samuel.

A woman of Maḥuza[9] was once married to [a man of] Nehardea. When they came to R. Naḥman,[10] and he observed from her voice that she was a native of Maḥuza, he said to them, '[The decision must be in agreement with Rab, for] Babylon and all its neighbouring towns have adopted a usage in agreement with the ruling of Rab'. When, however, they pointed out to him, 'But, surely, she is married to [a man of] Nehardea,' he said to them, 'If that is the case, [the decision will be in agreement with Samuel for]

(1) The widow. (2) V. Rashi. (3) Lit., 'these, yes'. (4) Whereby the widow actually recovers her *kethubah*. (5) Lit., 'yes'. (6) [Stands here for Sura which was in the neighbourhood of the old great city of Babylon, v. Giṭ. Sonc. ed. p. 17, n. 3.] (7) So Rashi; 'her dependencies', *sc.* places following her usages (Jast.); '*seine Nachbarorte*' (Golds). (8) V. *supra* p. 222, n. 8. (9) A Jewish trading centre. One of the 'neighbouring towns' or 'dependencies' of Babylon. (10) In connection with a dispute concerning the fulfilment of the terms of the *kethubah* (v. the final clauses of our Mishnah).

Nehardea and all its neighbouring towns followed a usage agreeing with the ruling of Samuel. How far does [the usage of] Nehardea extend?—As far afield as the Nehardean *kab*[1] is in use.[2]

It was stated: [When a *kethubah* is being paid to] a widow, said Rab, assessment is made of what she wears,[3] but Samuel said: That which she wears is not assessed. Said R. Ḥiyya b. Abin: [Their opinions[4] are] reversed[5] in the case of a retainer.[6] R. Kahana taught: And so[7] [are their opinions][4] in the case of a retainer;[6] and [Rab] had laid down this mnemonic, 'Strip the widow and the orphan[8] and go out'.

R. Naḥman said: Although we have learned in a Mishnah in agreement with the view of Samuel[9] the law is in agreement with that of Rab. For we learned: Whether a man has consecrated his estate, or whether he has consecrated the valuation of himself[10] [the Temple treasurer][11] has no claim either upon the clothes of that man's wife,[12] or upon the clothes of his children, or the coloured articles that were dyed for them,[13] or any new sandals that [their father] may have bought[13] for them.[14]

Said Raba to R. Naḥman: Since, however, we have learned in a Mishnah in agreement with the view of Samuel, why does the law agree with that of Rab? The other replied: At first sight it might appear[15] to run parallel to the principle of Samuel, but if you examine it carefully [you will find that] the law, in fact, must be in agreement with [the view of] Rab. For this[16] is the

(1) V. Glos. Here a term for a dry measure in general, not the specific *kab* (Obermeyer p. 242). (2) Lit., 'spreads'. (3) *Sc.* the value of her clothes is deducted from the amount of her *kethubah*. (4) Those of Rab and Samuel. (5) Samuel ruling that the value of clothes is, and Rab maintaining that it is not to be deducted from the man's wages. (6) Or 'client' (v. Jast.), when he leaves the employ of his master who, during the period of his service, had been supplying him with his clothes. לקיט (rt. לקט 'to gather') 'gleaner', 'field labourer'. (7) As in the case of a widow. (8) *Sc.* the retainer or client. (9) Viz. that a wife's clothes are the property of her husband. (10) V. Lev. XXVII, 1ff. (11) Who comes to collect such offerings. (12) Cf. *supra* note 9. (13) Though they have not yet used them (cf. Rashi). This shews that the raiments are the property of the wife. (14) 'Ar. 24a, B.Ḳ. 102*b*. (15) לכאורה, adv., *Lamed* and *Kaf*. prefixed to the noun אורה, 'light'. (16) Lit., 'what'.

reason:[1] When he[2] bought[3] [the clothes] for her [he did so] on the assumption that she would live with him.[4] He did not, however, buy[3] them for her on the assumption that she should take them[5] and depart.[6]

A daughter-in-law of the house of Bar Eliashib was claiming her *kethubah* from orphans. When she summoned them to court and they said, 'It is degrading for us that you should come with us in such [clothes]', she went home and dressed and wrapped herself in all her garments. When they came before Rabina he told them: The law is in agreement with the ruling of Rab who laid down [that when a *kethubah* is being paid to] a widow, assessment is made of what she wears.

A man[7] once said, 'Let a bride's outfit[8] be provided for my daughter', and the price of an outfit was subsequently reduced. 'The benefit',[9] ruled R. Idi b. Abin, 'belongs to the orphans'.[10]

A man[7] once said, [54*b*] 'Four hundred *zuz*[11] [of the value of this] wine shall be given to my daughter', and the price of wine rose. 'The profit', ruled R. Joseph, 'belongs to the orphans'.[12]

Relatives of R. Johanan had [the responsibility of maintaining their] father's wife who was in the habit of consuming much[13] food. When[14] they came to R. Johanan[15] he told them, 'Go and ask your

(1) Why the Temple treasurer has no claim upon a wife's clothes though their value is rightly to be deducted from the amount she is paid in settlement of her *kethubah*. (2) The husband. (3) Or, 'transferred possession'. (4) Consequently, so long as she lives with him, they are her absolute property and no one can take them away from her. Hence the ruling of the Mishnah of 'Ar. that the Temple treasurer cannot claim them. (5) When he died. (6) Hence the ruling of Rab that their value is to be deducted from her *kethubah*. (7) On his death bed. The instructions of a person in such a condition have the force of a legally written document. (8) The cost of which was well known, all brides being similarly provided for (Rashi). (9) פורנא (rt. פרן 'to cut', hence 'to endow') 'endowment', hence 'good luck' (v. Jast.); 'surplus' (Golds.). (10) It is their duty to provide the outfit, and since they can obtain it at a reduced price the balance is theirs. (11) V. Glos. (12) Since the bequest was not a quantity of wine but a specified sum of money. (13) Lit., 'spoilt', or 'caused to diminish' (Af. of פסר). (14) During their father's lifetime. He was on the point of dying and disposing of his property (cf. p. 322, n. 1). (15) To consult him as to how they could reduce their liability.

father that he should assign a plot of land for her maintenance'.[1] When they subsequently came before Resh Lakish, he said to them, '[By such an assignment] he has increased all the more [the allowance for] her maintenance'.[2] 'But', they said to him, 'R. Johanan did not say so?' – 'Go', he told them, 'and give her [proper maintenance], otherwise[3] I shall pull R. Johanan out of your ears'. R. Johanan, when they came to him again, said to them, 'What can I do when one of equal standing[4] differs from me?' R. Abbahu stated: This was explained to me by R. Johanan: [If the husband] said,[5] 'towards maintenance' he has thereby increased [the allowance for] her maintenance;[6] but if he said,[5] 'for maintenance' he has thereby limited the allowance for her maintenance.[7]

(1) So that the liability of the heirs would thereby be limited to the value of that plot of land only. Such an assignment, of course, is valid only if it was made on one's death bed and is subject in addition to the woman's consent (V. Pe'ah, III, 7 and Rashi *a.l.*). The efficacy of R. Johanan's advice being dependent on the consent of the woman explains also why R. Johanan, despite his regrets for giving advice to relatives (*supra* 52*b*), proceeded to advise them again (v. Tosaf. *a.l.* s.v. דנייחר). In the other case his advice was effective despite the woman's wish. (2) His assignment of the land cannot deprive the widow of her right to proper maintenance, and can only be regarded as the provision of an additional source of income from which she might draw in case the maintenance the heirs provided was not on a liberal scale. (3) Lit., 'and if not'. (4) Lit., 'who is corresponding to me'. (5) When he assigned a particular plot of land for his wife's maintenance. (6) 'Towards' implying an addition to what is already due to her. (7) 'For maintenance' implying 'in return' or compensation for the maintenance to which she is entitled.

KETHUBOTH

CHAPTER V

MISHNAH. ALTHOUGH [THE SAGES] HAVE ENACTED THAT A VIRGIN COLLECTS[1] TWO HUNDRED ZUZ[2] AND A WIDOW ONE MANEH,[2] IF HE [THE HUSBAND] WISHES TO ADD, EVEN A HUNDRED MANEH, HE MAY DO SO.

[A WOMAN] WHO WAS WIDOWED OR DIVORCED, EITHER AFTER BETROTHAL OR AFTER MARRIAGE, IS ENTITLED TO COLLECT ALL [THAT IS DUE TO HER].[3] R. ELEAZAR B. AZARIAH RULED: [ONLY A WOMAN WIDOWED] AFTER HER MARRIAGE RECEIVES ALL [THAT IS DUE TO HER], BUT IF AFTER A BETROTHAL, A VIRGIN RECOVERS ONLY TWO HUNDRED ZUZ[2] AND A WIDOW ONLY ONE MANEH,[2] FOR THE MAN PROMISED[4] HER [THE ADDITIONAL JOINTURE] WITH THE SOLE OBJECT OF MARRYING HER.[5]

R. JUDAH RULED: IF [A HUSBAND] WISHES HE MAY WRITE OUT FOR A VIRGIN[1] A DEED FOR TWO HUNDRED ZUZ AND SHE WRITES [A QUITTANCE],[6] 'I HAVE RECEIVED FROM YOU A MANEH', AND FOR A WIDOW [HE MAY WRITE OUT A DEED FOR] A MANEH AND SHE WRITES [A QUITTANCE], 'I HAVE RECEIVED FROM YOU FIFTY ZUZ'. R. MEIR RULED: [THE INTERCOURSE OF] ANY MAN WHO UNDERTAKES TO GIVE A VIRGIN LESS THAN TWO HUNDRED ZUZ[2] OR A WIDOW LESS THAN A MANEH[2] IS[7] AN ACT OF PROSTITUTION.

GEMARA. [Is not this][8] obvious?—It might have been presumed that the Rabbis have fixed a limit in order that the man

(1) As her statutory *kethubah*. (2) V. Glos. (3) *Sc.* her statutory *kethubah* as well as any additional jointure her husband may have settled upon her. (4) Lit., 'wrote'. (5) And since he died before marrying her she can have no claim to it. (6) Though she has received nothing. (7) Lit., 'behold this'. (8) That A HUSBAND MAY ADD, IF HE WISHES etc.

who has no means might not be put to shame; hence we were taught [that there was no limit].

IF HE WISHES TO ADD etc. It was not stated, 'If he wishes to write',[1] but 'WISHES TO ADD'.[2] This then provides support for [a ruling which] R. Aibu stated in the name of R. Jannai. For R. Aibu stated in the name of R. Jannai: The supplementary provisions[3] [that are included] in a *kethubah* are subject to the same regulations as the statutory *kethubah*.[4] [In what respect] can this[5] matter?[6]—In respect of a woman who sells or surrenders [her *kethubah*],[7] or one who rebels,[8] one who impairs,[9] or claims [her *kethubah*],[10] or one who transgresses the Law;[11] [55a] in respect of amelioration,[12] an oath,[13] and the Sabbatical year,[14] in respect of him who assigned all his property to his sons,[15] or the recovery

(1) Which might have implied a mere gift. (2) *Sc.* to the *kethubah*, implying that the additional jointure assumes the same designation as the statutory *kethubah* itself. (3) Such as additional jointure, maintenance, or any other of the terms mentioned in the previous chapter. (4) *Infra* 104*b*. (5) The treatment of the additional jointure as the statutory *kethubah*. (6) Lit., 'it goes out (results) from it'. (7) By such an act she sells her additional jointure as well as her statutory *kethubah* though only '*kethubah*' was mentioned when the transaction took place. (8) Against her husband, by refusing conjugal rights or work (v. *infra* 63*a*). If, in consequence, reductions are made from her *kethubah* (v. loc. cit.) her additional jointure, like her statutory *kethubah*, is subject to these deductions. (9) By admitting that she had already been paid a part of her *kethubah* (*infra* 87*a*). In such a case she cannot recover the balance of the additional jointure even though that part of the *kethubah* had been left unimpaired, (v. Tosaf. s.v. ולפוגמת). (10) V. *supra* 54*a*. As she loses her maintenance by claiming her statutory *kethubah* so she loses it by claiming only her additional jointures (Rashi). (11) A woman who transgresses the Mosaic law or traditional Jewish practice may be divorced without receiving her *kethubah* (*infra* 72*a*). This applies to her additional jointure also. (12) Of the estate of the husband after his death. As the statutory *kethubah* cannot be recovered from such amelioration (v. Bek. 51*b*) so cannot the additional jointure either. (13) A woman must take an oath in respect of her additional jointure in all cases where she takes an oath in respect of her statutory *kethubah* (*infra* 87*a*). (14) In which all debts must be released (v. Deut. XV, 1ff) but not the obligation of a *kethubah* (v. Giṭ. 48*b*). The exemption applies to both the statutory *kethubah* and the additional jointure. (15) And left any fraction of land for his wife. Thereby she loses her *kethubah* (v. B.B. 132*a*) and her additional jointure also.

of payment out of real estate and from the worst part of it,[1] also in respect of [the law of a widow] while in her father's house,[2] and of the *kethubah* for male children.[3]

It was stated: The *kethubah* for the male children,[4] [the scholars of] Pumbeditha[5] ruled, may not be collected from sold or mortgaged property,[6] for we have learned,[4] 'They shall inherit';[7] and the scholars of[8] Matha Meḥasia[9] ruled: It may be collected from sold or mortgaged property, for we have learned,[4] 'They shall take'.[10] The law, however, is that it may not be collected from sold or mortgaged property, since we have learned,[4] 'They shall inherit'.[7]

Movables[11] which are available[12] [may be collected][13] without an oath;[14] but if they are not available,[15] [the *kethubah* may, the scholars of] Pumbeditha ruled, [be collected][16] without an oath[14] and the scholars[17] of Matha Meḥasia ruled: Only with an oath. The law [is that they may be collected] without an oath.

If [her husband] has set aside for her a plot of land [defining it]

(1) These restriction apply to the additional jointure as well as to the statutory *kethubah* (v. Giṭ. 48*b*). (2) She may claim her *kethubah* within twenty-five years only (v. *infra* 104*a*). This applies also to her additional jointure. There is no time limit in the case of a widow who lives in her late husband's house. (3) The children are entitled to their mother's additional jointure just as they are entitled to her statutory *kethubah* and to the dowry, which her father gave to her husband on the occasion of their marriage, and which also forms a part of the *kethubah* obligations of a husband. (4) V. Mishnah *supra* 52*b*. (5) פומבדיתא (lit., 'mouth of Beditha', one of the canals of the Euphrates), was a Babylonian town famous as a Jewish centre of learning. (6) Of the widow's late husband. (7) One *inherits free* assets only. (8) Lit., 'sons of'. (9) מתא מחסיא is a suburb of Sura in Babylonia. (10) Instead of 'they shall inherit'. This implies that the children are entitled to the *kethubah* as a gift made to them by their father at the time of his marriage with the right to seize his property wherever it may be found. (11) Pledged by a husband for the *kethubah* of his wife. (12) At the time of the man's death. (13) By the widow who, in other circumstances, is required to take an oath to the effect that her late husband had not given her some money or objects of value as a security for her *kethubah*. (14) Since it is definitely known what objects of value had been set aside for her *kethubah* there is no reason to suspect that any other objects or money also had been secretly deposited with her. (15) If, e.g., they were lost. (16) From the landed property of the deceased, since all of it is legally pledged for the *kethubah* of one's wife. (17) Lit., 'sons'.

by its four boundaries[1] [she[2] may collect from it] without an oath;[3] but if [he only defined it] by one boundary, [the scholars of] Pumbeditha ruled [that collection[4] may be made from it] without an oath,[3] but the scholars of Matha Meḥasia ruled: Only with an oath.[5] The law, however, is that collection[4] may be effected without an oath.[3]

If a man said to witnesses, 'Write out [a deed],[6] sign it and give it to a certain person',[7] and they took from him symbolic possession there is no need[8] to consult him.[9] [If, however,] no symbolic possession was taken, [the scholars of] Pumbeditha ruled, there is no need[8] to consult him,[9] but the scholars of Matha Meḥasia ruled: It is necessary to consult him. The law is that it is necessary to consult him.

R. ELEAZAR B. AZARIAH etc. It was stated: Rab and R. Nathan [differed]. One maintained that the *halachah* was in agreement with R. Eleazar b. Azariah and the other maintained that the *halachah* was not in agreement with R. Eleazar b. Azariah. You may conclude that it was R. Nathan who maintained that the *halachah* was in agreement with R. Eleazar b. Azariah[10] since R. Nathan was heard [elsewhere] to follow [the rule of] assumption,[11] he[12] having stated that the *halachah* was in agreement with R. Simeon Shezuri in the case of a man dangerously ill[13] [55b] and in that of *terumah*[14]

(1) As a special security for her *kethubah*. (2) When her husband dies. (3) Cf. *supra* p. 325, n. 14, *mutatis mutandis*. (4) V. loc. cit. n. 13. (5) As only one of the four boundaries had been indictated the plot of land cannot be regarded as a definite security, and the suspicion may be entertained that her husband may have given her some private deposit as a security for her *kethubah* (cf. *supra* p. 325, n. 13). (6) E.g., of a gift of land. (7) Lit., 'to him'. (8) Before the deed is written (Rashi). (9) Whether his instructions were seriously meant or whether he has not since changed his mind (cf. Rashi). According to some authorities the consultation relates to the question of entering a clause pledging the donor's property (cf. Tosaf. s.v. כתובו). (10) Whose opinion in our Mishnah is based on the *assumption* that THE MAN PROMISED ... WITH THE SOLE OBJECT etc. (11) Wherever a man did not *specify* his intention or motive. (12) Cur. edd. read 'R. Nathan'. In Ḥul. 75*b* the reading is 'R. Jonathan', and in Men. 30*b* 'R. Joḥanan'. (13) Who gave instructions for a letter of divorce to be written for his wife. The document may be delivered to the woman, even though its delivery was not mentioned in the instructions, because it is assumed that the dying man intended it for this purpose (v. Giṭ. 65*b*). (14) V. Glos.

of the tithe of *demai*[1] produce.[2] But does not Rab, however, follow [the rule of] assumption? Surely it was stated: As to the gift of a dying man[3] [in the deed of] which was recorded [symbolic] acquisition, the school of Rab in the name of Rab reported [that the testator] has [thereby] made him[4] ride on two harnessed horses;[5] but Samuel said: I do not know what decision to give on the matter. 'The school of Rab in the name of Rab reported [that the testator] has [thereby] made him ride on two harnessed horses', for it is like the gift of a man in good health,[6] and it is also like the gift of a dying man.[7] 'It is like the gift of a man in good health', in that, if he recovered, he cannot retract,[6] and 'it is like the gift of a dying man' in that, if he said that his loan[8] [shall be given] to X, his loan [is to be given] to X.[9] 'But Samuel said: I do not know what decision to give on the matter', since it is possible that he[10] decided not to transfer possession to him[11] except through the deed,[12] and no [possession by means of a] deed [may be acquired] after [the testator's] death![13] [56*a*]—The fact, however, is that both[14] follow [the rule of] assumption; and he who stated that the *halachah* [was so][15] was well justified, [while in

(1) V. Glos. (2) V. Dem. IV, 1. In this as in the previous case the rule of assumption is followed. Cf. p. 326, n. 10. (3) Who distributed all his estate. V. B.B. Sonc. ed. p. 658, n. 2. The verbal assignment of a dying man is valid and requires no deed or formal acquisition. (4) The recipient. (5) I.e., his claim has a double force: That of the gift of a dying man and that of legal acquisition. רכשי, pl. of ריכשא 'a harnessed or galloping horse'. (6) Owing to the symbolic acquisition that took place. (7) Cf. *supra* note 3. (8) Lit., 'my loan', a debt which someone owes him. (9) Although the money was not at that time in his possession and the gift was not made in the presence of the three parties concerned (v. B.B. 144*a*). (10) By the unnecessary symbolic acquisition. V. *infra* n. 12. (11) The donee. (12) Not merely by virtue of the legal validity of his instructions (v. *supra* note 3). (13) Hence it was difficult for Samuel to give a decision on the matter (v. B.B. Sonc. ed. p. 658, n. 11). As Rab, however, definitely ruled in favour of the donee on the *assumption* that the donor 'made him ride on two harnessed horses', it follows that Rab is guided by the rule of assumption. How then could it be implied *supra* that it was Rab who held that the *halachah* was not in agreement with R. Eleazar b. Azariah! (14) Rab and R. Nathan. (15) I.e., that it was in agreement with R. Eleazar b. Azariah.

respect of] him who stated that the *halachah* was not [so],[1] [it may be explained that] here[2] also [the ruling is based on] an assumption, that the man's object[3] [it is assumed] was the formation of a mutual attachment,[4] and such attachment has indeed been formed.[5]

R. Ḥanina[6] once sat in the presence of R. Jannai when he stated: The *halachah* is in agreement with R. Eleazar b. Azariah. [The Master] said to him, 'Go out, read your Biblical verses outside;[7] the *halachah* is not in agreement with R. Eleazar b. Azariah'.

R. Isaac b. Abdimi stated in the name of our Master:[8] The *halachah* is in agreement with R. Eleazar b. Azariah.

R. Naḥman stated in the name of Samuel: The *halachah* is in agreement with R. Eleazar b. Azariah. R. Naḥman in his own name, however, stated that the *halachah* was not in agreement with R. Eleazar b. Azariah, while the Nehardeans stated in the name of R. Naḥman that the *halachah* was in agreement with R. Eleazar b. Azariah. And though R. Naḥman uttered a curse, proclaiming, 'Such and such a fate shall befall every judge who gives a ruling in agreement with the opinion of R. Eleazar b. Azariah', the *halachah* is nevertheless in agreement with R. Eleazar b. Azariah.

And the *halachah* in practice is in accordance with the opinion of R. Eleazar b. Azariah.

Rabin enquired: What is the law[9] where the bride only entered the bridal chamber but there was no intercourse? Is the *kinyan*[10]

(1) Cf. preceding note, *mutatis mutandis*. (2) The statement *supra* against R. Eleazar b. Azariah. (3) In promising his bride an additional sum in her *kethubah*. (4) Between him and his bride. (5) Even though no marriage has taken place. The woman is, therefore, entitled to the full sum she had been promised. Hence the statement (which has been ascribed to Rab) against the ruling of R. Eleazar b. Azariah. (6) Following the reading of Ber. 30*b* BaḤ adds 'the Bible teacher'. (7) [I.e., Go teach the Bible to children instead of venturing into the realms of the *halachah*. Bible instructions were given in a place 'outside' the academy]. (8) Rab (v. Rashi) or Rabbi, i.e., R. Judah the Patriarch (v. Tosaf. *a.l.* s.v. אמר). According to Tosaf. the speaker here was the first R. Isaac b. Abdimi who was a disciple of Rabbi (cf. Shab. 40*b*) and a teacher of Rab (cf. B.B. 87*a* and Ḥul. 110*a*). (9) According to R. Eleazar b. Azariah's views in our Mishnah. (10) V. Glos. The legal and final union that may be regarded as *marriage*.

effected by the affectionate attachment in the bridal chamber[1] or is the *ḳinyan* effected by the affectionate attachment of the intercourse?[2]—Come and hear what R. Joseph learnt: 'Because he assigned[3] it to her only on account of the affectionate attachment of the first night'. Now, if you grant that it is the affectionate attachment in the bridal chamber that effects the *ḳinyan* it was correct for him to state 'the first night'. If, however, you contend that it is the affectionate attachment of the intercourse that effects the *ḳinyan*, does this [it may be objected, first] take place on the first night only and not subsequently?—What then [do you suggest]? The [affectionate attachment in the] bridal chamber? Is the bridal chamber [it may be retorted] entered[4] in the night only and not in the day time![5]—But according to your argument does intercourse take place at night and not in the day time? Surely Raba stated: If one was in a dark room [intercourse] is permitted![6]—This is no difficulty. He[7] may have taught us that it is proper conduct[8] that intercourse should be at night; but [if it is maintained that it is the affectionate attachment in the] bridal chamber [that effects the *ḳinyan*] the difficulty arises![9]—[The assumption that *ḳinyan* is effected in the] bridal chamber also presents no difficulty. Since, usually, the bridal chamber is a prelude to[10] intercourse he taught us that it was proper that [it should be entered] at night.

R. Ashi enquired: What is the law[11] where [a bride] entering the bridal chamber became menstruous?[12] If you should find [some reason] for saying that it is the affectionate attachment in the bridal chamber that effects the *ḳinyan*[13] [the question still remains whether

(1) *Ḥuppah* v. Glos. And the bride is consequently entitled to the full amount of the statutory, and the additional *kethubah*. (2) And since this has not taken place the bride can only claim the statutory minimum. (3) Lit., 'wrote'. (4) Lit., 'there is'. (5) Why then did R. Joseph mention 'night'? (6) In the day time. V. *infra* 65*b*, Shab. 86*a*. (7) R. Joseph. V. *supra* n. 5. (8) Lit., 'the way of the earth'. (9) V. *supra* n. 5. (10) Lit., 'stands for'. (11) Is the bride entitled to the additional jointure of her *kethubah*? Cf. *supra* p. 328, n. 9. (12) The bridegroom dying before intercourse had taken place. Intercourse with a menstruant is Pentateuchally forbidden. (Cf. Lev. XVIII, 19). (13) Cf. *supra* p. 328, n. 10.

this applies only to] a bridal chamber that is a prelude[1] to intercourse but not to a bridal chamber that is no prelude to intercourse,[2] or is there perhaps no difference?[3]—This remains unanswered.

R. JUDAH SAID: IF [A HUSBAND] WISHES HE MAY WRITE OUT FOR A VIRGIN etc. Does R. Judah hold the opinion that a quittance is written?[4] Surely we learned: If a person repaid part of his debt, R. Judah said, he[5] must exchange [the bond for another].[6] R. Jose said: He[7] must write a quittance for him![8]—R. Jeremiah replied: [Here it is a case] where the quittance is [written] within.[9] Abaye replied: You may even say [that here it is a case] where the quittance is not written within.[10] There[11] it is quite correct[12] [to disallow the use of a quittance, since the debtor] had undoubtedly repaid him[13] and it is possible that the quittance might be lost and that he[13] would produce the bond and thus collect [the paid portion of the debt] a second time. Here,[14] however,

(1) Lit., 'suitable'. (2) Cf. p. 329, n. 12. The bride would consequently have no claim upon the additional sum she was promised. (3) The bride being entitled in either case to the full amount. (4) By a creditor to whom part of a debt was repaid; and consequently there is no need to exchange the bond for one in which the balance only is entered. (5) The creditor. (6) In which only the balance of the original debt is entered while the first bond is destroyed. The debtor cannot be compelled to accept a quittance which he would have 'to guard from mice' and the loss of which might involve him in a claim for the repayment of the full loan. It is more equitable that the creditor should change the bond. (7) The creditor. (8) B.B. 170*b*. Such a course is advantageous to the creditor, since a bond entitles its holder to seize any real estate which the debtor has sold or mortgaged *after, but not before* the date of his bond. Were a new bond for the balance to be written, the creditor would lose his right to seize any of the debtor's property that was sold or mortgaged between the date of the original bond and that of the new one. In the opinion of R. Jose the rights of the creditor must not be impaired, while in the opinion of R. Judah equity demands that the debtor be not encumbered with the necessity of taking care of the quittance (cf. *supra* n. 6). How then could it be stated here that R. Judah allowed the writing of a quittance? (9) I.e., is entered on the *kethubah* itself, so that the husband, unlike the debtor spoken of in B.B., has no need to preserve any document. (10) Cf. *supra* n. 9. (11) The case of the payment of the part of a debt. (12) For R. Judah. (13) The creditor. (14) In our Mishnah.

did he indeed give her anything?[1] It is a mere statement that she addressed to him.[2] If, then, he preserved [the quittance] well and good;[3] and if he did not preserve it, well, it is he himself who is the cause of his own loss. One can well understand why Abaye did not give the explanation as R. Jeremiah, since it was not stated[4] that the quittance was entered within,[5] but why did not R. Jeremiah give the same explanation as Abaye?—The quittance here[6] is forbidden as a preventive measure against the [erroneous permitting of] a quittance elsewhere.[7]

The reason [for the husband's exemption[8] is apparently] because she gave him a quittance in writing.[9] If, however, [she had surrendered a portion of her *kethubah*] by word of mouth only [he would] not [have been exempt];[10] but why? This,[6] surely, is a monetary matter, and R. Judah was heard to rule that in a monetary matter one's stipulation[11] is valid. For was it not taught: If a man said to a woman, 'Behold thou art consecrated unto me[12] on condition that thou shalt have no [claim] upon me [for] food, raiment or conjugal rights', she is consecrated,[13] but the stipulation is null;[14] so R. Meir. R. Judah, however, said: In respect of monetary matters his stipulation is valid?[15]—R. Judah is of the opinion that the *kethubah* is a Rabbinical enactment,[16] and the Sages[17] have applied to their enactments[18] higher restrictions than to those of the Torah.[19] But what of the case of usufruct[20] which is a Rabbinical

(1) So MS.M. reading מידי. (2) She received no money at all from her husband. (3) Lit., 'he preserved it'. (4) In our Mishnah. (5) V. *supra* p. 330, n. 9. (6) The case of the *kethubah*. (7) A debt, for instance, where R. Judah does not allow it (cf. *supra* p. 330, n. 6). (8) From the payment of the part of the *kethubah* which his wife has surrendered (v. our Mishnah). (9) Lit., 'she wrote for him'. (10) Since our Mishnah speaks of writing. (11) Even though it deprives a person from a right to which he is Pentateuchally entitled. (12) The formula of marriage used by the bridegroom is, 'Behold thou art consecrated unto me by this ring according to the law of Moses and Israel'. (13) Becomes his lawful wife. (14) Since it is contrary to the law of the Torah. Cf. Ex. XXI, 10. (15) B.M. 51*a*, 94*a*, B.B. 126*b*. (16) Not Pentateuchal. (17) *Sc.* the Rabbis. (18) In order to prevent laxity. (19) The laws of the Torah, being universally respected, required no such additional restrictions. (20) *Melog* property (v. Glos.) to the fruit of which a husband is entitled during his lifetime while the property itself remains the possession of his wife.

law and the Rabbis nevertheless did not apply any restriction to it;[1] for we learned: R. Judah said, He[2] may for all time eat the fruit of the fruit[3] unless he wrote out for her [the undertaking], 'I have no claim whatsoever[4] upon your estates and their produce and the produce of their produce for ever';[5] [56b] and it had been established[5] that by 'writing'[6] only *saying* was meant![7]—Abaye replied: All [married women] have a *kethubah;* not all, however, have fruit. In respect of what is usual the Rabbis have applied restrictions. In respect of what is not usual, however, the Rabbis have made no restrictions.

But what of the case of ass-drivers[8] which is a common occurrence and the Rabbis have nevertheless applied no restrictions to it; for we learned: Where ass-drivers entered a town and one of them declared, 'My [produce] is new and that of my fellow is old' or 'Mine is not fit for use[9] but that of my fellow is fit', they are not believed; but R. Judah said, They are believed![10]—Abaye replied: To any Rabbinical enactment of an absolute character[11] the Rabbis have applied further restrictions, but to any Rabbinical enactment of uncertain origin[12] the Rabbis have added no further restrictions. Raba replied: They[13] relaxed the law in respect of *demai.*[14]

R. MEIR RULED . . . ANY MAN WHO . . . GIVE . . . LESS etc.

(1) A husband being allowed to surrender his right to the usufruct. (2) A husband who renounced his claim to the fruit of *melog* property. (3) The fruit produced by lands that were purchased out of the proceeds of the fruit of the original property. (4) Lit., 'judgment and words'. (5) *Infra* 83a. (6) In R. Judah's statement. (7) Lit., 'what writes? says'. Which proves that, according to R. Judah no restrictions were made even in the case of a Rabbinical law. (8) About whose imported produce it is uncertain whether it has been tithed (v. Glos. s.v. *Demai*). Such produce is only Rabbinically forbidden. (9) I.e., it had not been duly tithed. (10) Demai IV, 7, v. *supra* p. 131 notes. Which shews that, according to R. Judah, no restriction was imposed even on a Rabbinically forbidden produce. (Cf. *supra* note 8). (11) Lit., 'a certainty of their words'. (12) As in the case of *demai* where the prohibition is due to the uncertainty whether or not the produce had been tithed. (13) The Rabbis, though they applied restriction even in cases where their prohibition was due merely to an uncertainty. (14) V. Glos. The uncertainty here is so great, since most people even among the *'amme ha-'arez* (v. Glos. s.v. *'Am ha-'arez*) do give tithe, that no restrictions were applied to it.

The expression, 'WHO . . . GIVE . . . LESS' [implies][1] even [if the assignment remained a mere] stipulation.[2] Thus it follows that he[3] is of the opinion that the man's stipulation is void and that the woman receives [her full *kethubah*];[4] yet since[5] the man had said to her[6] 'You will have but a *maneh*',[7] her mind is not at ease[8] and his intercourse is regarded as an act of prostitution.[9] But, surely, R. Meir was heard to rule that any stipulation[10] which is contrary to what is written in the Torah is[11] null and void, [from which it may be inferred,[12] may it not, that if it is] but against a law of the Rabbis it is[11] valid?[13]—R. Meir holds the view that the *kethubah* is a Pentateuchal institution.

It was taught: R. Meir ruled, If any man assigns to a virgin[14] a sum less than two hundred *zuz* or to a widow less than a *maneh* his marriage is regarded as[15] an act of prostitution. R. Jose ruled: One is permitted [to contract such a marriage].[16] R. Judah ruled: If the man wished he may write out for a virgin a bond for two hundred *zuz* while she writes[17] for him, 'I have received from you a *maneh*'; and [he may write a bond] for a widow for a *maneh* while she writes[17] for him, 'I have received from you fifty *zuz*'.[18]

Is R. Jose then of the opinion that 'one is permitted [to contract

(1) Since the expression used is not 'if the virgin *received less*'. (2) While the woman in fact receives the full amount of her *kethubah*. (3) R. Meir. (4) Cf. *supra* n. 2. Lit., 'and there is to her'. (5) [Lit., 'and since'. The text is not smooth. MS.M. preserves a better reading 'but since she had (*a full kethubah*) what is the reason (of R. Meir)?'—Since he said to her etc.]. (6) The virgin who is entitled to two hundred *zuz*. (7) One hundred *zuz* (v. Glos.). (8) [Lit., 'her mind does not rest, rely upon', i.e., she contracted her marriage on the expectation of a *kethubah* of a smaller amount than the prescribed minimum.] (9) [Since the marriage was not performed in accordance with the requirements of the law, it is regarded as an act of prostitution.] (10) Lit., 'whoever makes a stipulation'. (11) Lit., 'his stipulation'. (12) Since he mentions the Torah only. (13) As a *kethubah* is an enactment of the Rabbis (v. R. Judah's view *supra* 56*a*), why is the stipulation void? (14) As her *kethubah*. (15) Lit., 'behold this'. (16) The stipulation being valid even if the woman's surrender of her right was only verbal. (17) Contrary to the opinion of R. Jose, R. Judah maintains that a verbal stipulation or undertaking against a Rabbinical measure is of no validity. (18) Half a *maneh*.

such a marriage]'?[1] This surely is contrary [to the following:] A woman's ***kethubah*** may not be made [a charge on] movable property as a social measure.[2] Said R. Jose: What social measure is this?[3] Their[4] price, surely, is not fixed and they deteriorate in value.[5] Now, did not the first Tanna also say that [a ***kethubah***] may not be made [a charge on movable property]?[6] Must he[7] not, consequently, have meant to say: This[8] applies only where he[9] accepted no responsibility;[10] but where he accepted responsibility[10] [the ***kethubah***] may be made [a charge upon them].[11] Thereupon came R. Jose to question: Even if he[9] did accept responsibility how [could the ***kethubah*** be] made [a charge upon them][12] when their price, surely, is not fixed and they deteriorate in value.[13] Now, if there,[14] where the diminution in value [of the movables] is only a possibility,[15] R. Jose provides against it, would he not even more so [adopt a similar course] here[16] where the diminution [of the ***kethubah***] is a certainty?—How now! There[17] she did not know it[18] to think of surrendering her rights;[19] but here she was well aware [of the fact][20] and has definitely surrendered her rights.

The sister of Rami b. Ḥama was married to R. Iwia [57*a*] and her ***kethubah***[21] was lost. When they came before R. Joseph[22] he

(1) I.e., one where the ***kethubah*** amounts to less than the prescribed minimum. (2) Lit., 'because of making the world right'. Movable objects may be easily lost and do not provide a reliable security for the ***kethubah***. (3) Lit., 'there is in this'. (4) Movable objects. (5) While a ***kethubah*** must always amount to a legally fixed minimum. (6) Wherein, then, does R. Jose differ from him? (7) The first Tanna. (8) That movable property provides no security for a ***kethubah***. (9) The husband. (10) For the loss of the movable property. (11) The possibility of deterioration in value being disregarded by the first Tanna. (12) Movable objects. (13) R. Jose is consequently of the opinion that it is not only against loss but also against a diminution in value that provision must be made. (14) Where movable objects are assigned as a security. (15) Lit., 'perhaps they diminish'. (16) Where the husband definitely assigned no more than half of the legal maximum. (17) V. *supra* note 14. (18) That the value would be diminished. (19) Lit., 'that she shall forgive' or 'surrender'. (20) That her husband has contracted for a sum less than her due. (21) I.e., the written marriage contract. V. Glos. (22) To obtain his ruling on the question whether she may continue to live with her husband without the ***kethubah***.

said to them, Thus said Rab Judah in the name of Samuel: This[1] is the opinion of R. Meir,[2] but the Sages ruled that a man may live with his wife without a *kethubah* for two or three years.[3] Said Abaye to him:[4] But did not R. Naḥman state in the name of Samuel that the *halachah* is in agreement with R. Meir in his preventive measures?[5]—If so, [the other replied] go and write one[6] for her.

When R. Dimi came[7] he stated in the name of R. Simeon b. Pazzi in the name of R. Joshua b. Levi who had it from Bar Ḳappara: The dispute[8] refers to the beginning,[9] but at the end[9] she cannot, according to the opinion of all, surrender[10] [any portion of her *kethubah*].[11] R. Joḥanan, however stated that their dispute extended to both cases.[12] Said R. Abbahu: [The following] was explained to me by R. Joḥanan: 'I and R. Joshua b. Levi do not dispute with one another. The "beginning" of which R. Joshua b. Levi spoke means[13] the beginning of [the meeting in] the bridal chamber, and by the "end" was meant[13] the termination of the intercourse;[14] and when I stated that the dispute extended to both

(1) That living with a wife whose *kethubah* is less than the prescribed minimum, and much more so with one who has no *kethubah* at all, is regarded as mere prostitution, even though the woman remained legally entitled to collect the full amount of her *kethubah*. (2) Who holds that since the woman is not absolutely certain that she will obtain the full amount of her *kethubah* (either in the case *supra*, because she believes the man's stipulation to be valid or, in this case, because she has no document to prove her claim) it can only be regarded as an act of prostitution (v. *supra* p. 333, n. 8). (3) I.e., for any length of time. V. Tosaf. s.v. שתים *a.l.* (4) R. Joseph. (5) The Rabbinical restrictions he added to those of the Torah. (6) A new marriage contract. (7) From Palestine to Babylon. (8) Between R. Judah and R. Jose on the question whether a verbal renouncement of the woman is valid (*supra* 56*b*). (9) This is explained *infra*. (10) By a mere verbal statement. (11) Since she has already acquired it. Only by means of a written quittance may her rights then be surrendered. (12) I.e., to the 'beginning' and 'end'. (13) Lit., 'what'. (14) R. Judah and R. Jose dispute only in respect of the period between the beginning and the conclusion of the meeting in the bridal chamber but agree that after intercourse the man's stipulation is invalid unless the woman has surrendered her rights in writing. It was, therefore, quite correct for R. Joshua b. Levi to state that 'at the end (i.e., of the intercourse), she cannot, according to the opinion of all, surrender (i.e., verbally) any part of her *kethubah*'.

cases [I meant] the beginning [of the meeting in] the bridal chamber and the end of that meeting which is the beginning of the intercourse.'[1]

When Rabin came[2] he stated in the name of R. Simeon b. Pazzi in the name of R. Joshua b. Levi who had it from Bar Ḳappara. The dispute refers only to the end, but at the beginning she may, so is the opinion of all, renounce[3] [any portion of her *kethubah*].[4] R. Joḥanan, however, stated that their dispute extended to both cases. Said R. Abbahu: This was explained to me by R. Joḥanan: 'I and R. Joshua b. Levi do not dispute with one another. The "end" of which R. Joshua b. Levi spoke meant the end of [the meeting in] the bridal chamber, and by the "beginning" was meant the beginning of [the meeting in] the bridal chamber; and when I stated that the dispute extended to both cases [I meant] the beginning,[5] and the termination of the intercourse.'

Said R. Papa: Had not R. Abbahu stated, 'This was explained to me by R. Joḥanan: "I and R. Joshua b. Levi do not dispute with one another"' I would have submitted that R. Joḥanan and R. Joshua b. Levi were in dispute while R. Dimi and Rabin[6] were not in dispute. The 'end' of which Rabin spoke might mean[7] the end of [the meeting in] the bridal chamber, and the 'beginning' of which R. Dimi spoke might mean[7] the beginning of the intercourse.[5] What does he[8] teach us thereby?[9]—It is this that he teaches us: [It is preferable to assume][10] that two Amoraim differ in their own opinions[11] rather than that two Amoraim should differ as to what was the view of another Amora.[12]

(1) To which the dispute indeed refers (cf. *supra* p. 335, n. 14). (2) From Palestine to Babylon. (3) V. *supra* p. 335, nn. 8-10. (4) Since she has not yet legally acquired it. (5) Which corresponds to the termination of the meeting in the bridal chamber. (6) Whose reports appear contradictory. (7) Lit., 'what'. (8) R. Papa. (9) In view of R. Abbahu's definite statement R. Papa's remark seems pointless. (10) Unless there is proof to the contrary. (11) It is natural and legitimate for opinions to differ. (12) In which case one of the two must be definitely wrong since the view of the Amora which both of them claim to represent could not possibly have agreed with what both of them submit. Had not R. Abbahu's statement been authoritative, coming as it did from R. Joḥanan himself, R. Papa's submission would have been preferred to his.

MISHNAH. A VIRGIN IS ALLOWED TWELVE MONTHS FROM THE [TIME HER INTENDED] HUSBAND CLAIMED HER,[1] [IN WHICH] TO PREPARE HER MARRIAGE OUTFIT.[2] AND, AS [SUCH A PERIOD] IS ALLOWED FOR THE WOMAN, SO IS IT ALLOWED FOR THE MAN FOR HIS OUTFIT.[3] FOR A WIDOW[4] THIRTY DAYS [ARE ALLOWED]. IF THE RESPECTIVE PERIODS EXPIRED[5] AND THEY WERE NOT MARRIED[6] THEY[7] ARE ENTITLED TO MAINTENANCE OUT OF THE MAN'S ESTATE[8] AND [IF HE IS A PRIEST] MAY ALSO EAT TERUMAH. R. TARFON SAID: ALL [THE SUSTENANCE] FOR SUCH A WOMAN MAY BE GIVEN OF TERUMAH.[9] R. AKIBA SAID: ONE HALF OF UNCONSECRATED FOOD[10] AND ONE HALF OF TERUMAH.[11]

A LEVIR[12] [WHO IS A PRIEST] DOES NOT CONFER [UPON HIS SISTER-IN-LAW][13] THE RIGHT OF EATING TERUMAH.[14] IF SHE[15] HAD SPENT SIX MONTHS[16] WITH[17] HER HUSBAND AND SIX MONTHS WITH[17] THE LEVIR,[18] OR EVEN [IF SHE SPENT] ALL OF THEM[19] WITH HER HUSBAND LESS ONE DAY WITH[17] THE LEVIR,[18] OR ALL OF THEM[19] WITH[17] THE LEVIR[18] LESS ONE DAY WITH HER HUSBAND,[20] SHE IS NOT PERMITTED TO EAT TERUMAH.[21] THIS[22] [WAS THE RULING ACCORDING TO] AN

(1) After their betrothal. (2) Jewels and similar ornaments (v. Rashi). (3) The preparations for the wedding dinner and the bridal chamber (v. ibid.). (4) Who is presumed to be in the possession of some trinkets and jewellery from her first marriage. (5) Lit., 'the time arrived'. (6) Owing to the man's delay (v. *supra* 2*b*). (7) The women. (8) Lit., 'they eat of his'. (9) Out of the proceeds of which she may buy unconsecrated food for consumption during the days of her Levitical uncleanness. (10) For consumption during her period of uncleanness. (11) For her use in her clean state. (12) יבם, the brother of a deceased childless husband, whose duty it is to marry the widow. (13) Who became a widow while still betrothed. (14) Prior to their marriage (v. *supra* n. 12). (15) As a betrothed virgin. (16) Of the period of twelve months that is granted to her. (17) Lit., 'in the presence of'. (18) I.e., in awaiting his marriage. (19) The twelve months. (20) [Isaiah Trani preserves a better reading, 'even if (she spent) all of them with the husband, less one day, or all of them with the levir]. (21) By virtue of her husband whose obligation to maintain her does not begin until the end of the twelve months, and even then terminates with his death. (22) That after THE RESPECTIVE PERIODS EXPIRED ... THEY ARE ENTITLED TO ... EAT TERUMAH.

EARLIER[1] MISHNAH.[2] THE COURT, HOWEVER, THAT SUCCEEDED[3] RULED: [57b] A WOMAN[4] MAY NOT EAT TERUMAH UNTIL SHE HAS ENTERED THE BRIDAL CHAMBER.[5]

GEMARA. Whence is this[6] derived?—R. Ḥisda replied: From Scripture which states, *And her brother and her mother said: 'Let the damsel abide with us* yamim,[7] *at the least ten*.[8] Now, what could be meant by *yamim*? If it be suggested 'two days',[9] do people, [it might be retorted,] speak in such a manner? [If when] they suggested to him[10] two days he said no, would they then suggest ten days? *Yamim* must consequently mean[11] *a year*, for it is written, yamim[12] *shall he have the right of redemption*.[13] But might it not be said [that *yamim* means] a month,[14] for it is written, *But a month of* yamim?[15] —I will tell you: [The meaning of] an undefined [expression of] *yamim* may well be inferred from another undefined expression of *yamim*, but no undefined expression of *yamim* may be inferred from one in connection with which *month* was specifically mentioned.

R. Zera stated that a Tanna taught: In the case of a minor,[16] either she herself or her father is empowered to postpone[17] [her marriage].[18] One can well understand why she is empowered to postpone [the marriage], but [why also her] father? If she is satisfied, what matters it to her father?—He might think this: Now she does not realize [what marriage implies] but to-morrow[19] she

(1) Lit., 'first'. (2) Cf. Sanh. Sonc. ed. p. 163, n. 7. (3) The authors of the earlier Mishnah. (4) Who is not the daughter of a priest. (5) *Ḥuppah*, v. Glos. (6) Lit., 'whence these words', that A VIRGIN IS ALLOWED TWELVE MONTHS. (7) ימים, E.V., *a few days*. (8) Gen. XXIV, 55, referring to the period the relatives of Rebekah wished her to remain with them after consenting to her marriage with Isaac. (9) The minimum of the plural. (10) Abraham's servant. (11) Lit., 'but what'. (12) E.V., *for a full year*. (13) Lev. XXV, 29. As here *yamim* means 'a year' so it does in Gen. XXIV, 55, while עשור means 'ten *months*'. (14) And עשור, 'ten days'. (15) Num. XI, 20. E.V. *a full month*. (16) Who was claimed by the man who betrothed her. (17) Lit., 'prevent'. (18) Beyond the period given in our Mishnah; until she is of age. V. Tosef. Keth. V. (19) After the marriage, when she finds her connubial duties distasteful.

will rebel [against her husband], leave him and come back to, and fall [a burden] upon me.[1]

R. Abba b. Levi stated: No arrangements may be made for marrying a minor while she is still in her minority. Arrangements[2] may, however, be made while she is a minor for marrying her when she becomes of age. Is not this obvious?—It might have been suggested that [this should not be allowed] as a precaution against the possibility of her beginning to feel anxiety at once[3] and so becoming ill. Hence we were taught [that no such possibility need be considered].

R. Huna stated: If on the day she became adolescent[4] she was betrothed, she is allowed thirty days[5] like a widow.[6]

An objection was raised: One who has attained adolescence is like one who has been claimed [by her intended husband in marriage]. Does not this imply, 'Like a virgin who was claimed'?[7]—No, like a widow who was claimed.

Come and hear: If a woman who is adolescent had waited for twelve months[8] her husband, said R. Eliezer, since he is liable for her maintenance, may also annul [her vows]![9]—Read: A woman who is adolescent[10] *or* one[11] who waited twelve months.[12]

Come and hear: If a man betrothed a virgin, whether he[13] claimed her and she held back or whether she claimed him and he[13] held

(1) He would then have to provide for her a new marriage outfit (v. Rashi). It is the privilege of a minor to leave her husband at any moment by the mere making of a formal declaration that she does not like him (v. Glos. s.v. *Mi'un*). (2) Without legal betrothal. (3) Lit., 'bring in fear from now'. (4) A *bogereth* (v. Glos.). Lit., 'she became adolescent one day'. (5) In which to prepare her marriage outfit. (6) Not the longer period of twelve months. It is assumed that on approaching adolescence a woman begins to prepare her marriage outfit, and the shorter period of one month is regarded as sufficient for completing it. (7) Who (v. our Mishnah) is allowed a period of twelve months! (8) From the time she was claimed by the man who betrothed her. (9) Ned. 70*b*, 73*b*. There is no need for her father to consent to the annulment. (Cf. Num. XXX, 4ff). From here it follows that *even one who is adolescent* is not entitled to maintenance until after the expiry of *twelve* months, which is an objection against R. Huna. (10) Who waited *thirty days*. (11) A *na'arah* (v. Glos.). (12) The difference between the two readings is represented in the original by the addition of a mere *waw*. (13) Lit., 'the (intended) husband'.

back, she is allowed twelve months[1] from the time of the claim but not from the time of the betrothal; and one who is adolescent is like one who has been claimed. How [is this to be understood]? If she was betrothed on the day she became adolescent,[2] she is allowed twelve months; while one betrothed [is sometimes allowed] thirty days.[3] Is not this a refutation against R. Huna?—It is a refutation.

What [was meant by] 'while one betrothed [is sometimes allowed] thirty days'?—R. Papa replied, It is this that was meant: If an adolescent woman was betrothed after twelve months of her adolescence have elapsed, she is allowed[1] thirty days like a widow.

IF THE RESPECTIVE PERIODS EXPIRED AND THEY WERE NOT MARRIED. 'Ulla stated: The daughter of an Israelite who is betrothed [to a priest] is, according to Pentateuchal law, permitted to eat *terumah*, for it is written in Scripture, *But if a priest buy any soul, the purchase of his money*,[4] and that [woman] also is the purchase of his money.[5] What then is the reason why [the Rabbis] ruled that she is not permitted to eat [*terumah*]? Because it might happen that when a cup [of *terumah*] will be offered[6] to her in the house of her father she might give her brother or sister[7] to drink [from it]. If so, [the same reason should apply] also where THE RESPECTIVE PERIODS EXPIRED AND THEY WERE NOT MARRIED!—In that case[8] he appoints for her a special place.[9] Now then, no [hired harvest] gleaner[10] [working] for an Israelite should be allowed to eat *terumah*, since it is possible that [the household of the Israelite] would come to eat with him!—If[11] they feed him from their own [victuals], would they eat of his?[12]

(1) For the preparation of her outfit. (2) Lit., 'she became of age one day'. (3) V. *infra* for further explanation. (4) Lev. XXII, 11. The conclusion of the verse is *he may eat of it*, i.e., of *terumah*. (5) The money, or the object of value, which the man gives to the woman as her token of betrothal, and whereby she is acquired as his wife. (6) Rt. מזג lit., 'to mix', *sc.* wine with water or spices. (7) Who are Israelites to whom the eating or drinking of *terumah* is forbidden. (8) Lit., 'there', where the priest is legally liable to maintain her. (9) Away from her father's household; thus preventing her from giving away his victuals to her relatives. (10) Who is a priest. (11) Lit., 'now'. (12) Obviously not. Hence the permissibility for the gleaner to eat his *terumah*.

R. Samuel son of Rab[1] Judah explained:[2] Owing to a bodily defect[3] [that might subsequently be detected].[4] If so, [should not the same reason] also [be applicable to a woman who] had entered the bridal chamber, but intercourse with whom did not take place?[5] —In that case[6] he arranges for her to be first examined and only then takes her in.[7] Now then, the slave of a priest,[8] bought from an Israelite, should not be allowed to eat *terumah* on account of a bodily defect[3] [that might be discovered]![9] —[The law of cancellation of a sale owing to a subsequent detection of a] bodily defect[3] does not apply to slaves. For if the defect is external [the buyer] has presumably seen it;[10] and if it is internal, since [the buyer] requires [the slave] for work only he does not mind a private defect.[11] Were [the slave] to be found to have been a thief or [58*a*] a gambler[12] the sale is still valid.[13] What else is there?[14] [Only that the slave might be found to have been] an armed robber or one proscribed by the government;[15] but such characters are generally known.[16]

(1) Wanting in MS.M. (2) The reason why the daughter of an Israelite who was betrothed to a priest is not permitted to eat *terumah* before the time her husband becomes liable to maintain her. (3) סימפון, 'an implied condition the non-fulfilment of which annuls the agreement', whence 'a bodily defect . . . not stated in the contract' (Jast.) Cf. τὸ σύμφωνον. (4) In the woman. This might be discovered before the marriage and, as a result, the betrothal would be annulled retrospectively. (5) In this case also, should a bodily defect be discovered before the consummation of the marriage the betrothal would be annulled retrospectively. Why then does our Mishnah permit the eating of *terumah* in such a case? (6) Lit., 'there'. (7) Into the bridal chamber. After entering into the chamber it may be safely assumed that he has satisfied himself that she was not suffering from any bodily defects. (8) Who eats *terumah* by virtue of being the slave of a priest. (9) And that would retrospectively annul the purchase. The slave would consequently retain the status of an Israelite's slave to whom the eating of *terumah* was all the time forbidden. (10) And since he nevertheless consented to the purchase he must have been content to overlook it. (11) The sale, therefore, cannot thereby be annulled. (12) So Tosaf. s.v. קוּבְיוּסטוּס, and cf. κυβευστής, 'gambler'; κυβευτικός, 'a crafty person' (contra Rashi's interpretation, 'kidnapper'). (13) Lit., 'he reached him'. Slaves being known to possess such characters a buyer of a slave is presumed to have accepted the inevitable. (14) That might be given as a reason for the cancellation of the sale. (15) Sentenced to death. (16) Lit., 'they have a voice', and the

Consider! Whether according to the [explanation of the one] Master[1] or according to that of the other Master[2] she[3] is not permitted to eat [*terumah*], what then is the practical difference between them?—The difference between them [is the case where her intended husband] accepted [her defects,[4] or where her father] delivered [her to the intended husband's agents][5] or went[6] [with them].[5]

R. TARFON SAID: ALL [THE SUSTENANCE] FOR SUCH A WOMAN MAY BE GIVEN OF TERUMAH etc. Abaye stated: The dispute[7] applies only to the daughter of a priest[8] who was betrothed to a priest but with respect to the daughter of an Israelite[9] who was betrothed to a priest all[10] agree [that she is supplied with] one half of unconsecrated food[11] and one half of *terumah*.

Abaye further stated: Their dispute[7] relates to one who[12] was only betrothed,[13] but in respect of a married woman[14] all[10] agree [that she is supplied with] one half of unconsecrated food[15] and one half of *terumah*.[15] So it was also taught: R. Tarfon said, All [the

buyer must have known the circumstances before he bought him and must have consented to have him despite his unsavoury character.

(1) 'Ulla. (2) R. Samuel. (3) The daughter of an Israelite who was betrothed to a priest. (4) Once he consented to overlook them he cannot again advance them as a reason for the annulment of the betrothal. In such a case R. Samuel's explanation is not applicable while that of 'Ulla is. (5) Cf. *supra* 48*b*. As she does not any longer live with her father's family 'Ulla's reason does not apply while that of R. Samuel does. (6) Himself or his agents. (7) That of R. Tarfon and R. Akiba. (8) Who is familiar with the restrictions of *terumah* and would, therefore, abstain from eating it during the days of her Levitical uncleanness when consecrated food is forbidden to her. (9) Who may be ignorant of the restrictions appertaining to *terumah*. (10) Even R. Tarfon. (11) For consumption during the days of her uncleanness. (12) Being the daughter of a priest. (13) Her father with whom she lives during the period of her betrothal might well be relied upon that, as a priest, he would duly supervise her observance of the laws of *terumah* and would, during her uncleanness, himself, or through her brothers, sell her *terumah* and purchase for her with the proceeds unconsecrated food. (14) Who does not live with her husband (cf. *infra* 64*b*). (15) Being alone she might not be able to arrange for the sale of her *terumah* during her uncleanness, and might consequently be apt to consume the consecrated food forbidden to her.

sustenance] for such a woman is given of *terumah*. R. Akiba said, One half of consecrated food and one half of *terumah*. This[1] applies only to the daughter of a priest who was betrothed to a priest, but with respect to the daughter of an Israelite who was betrothed to a priest all[2] agree [that she is supplied with] one half of unconsecrated food and one half of *terumah*. This,[1] furthermore, applies only to one who[3] was only betrothed but in respect of a married woman[4] all[2] agree [that she is supplied with] one half of unconsecrated food[5] and one half of *terumah*.[5] R. Judah b. Bathyra said, She is supplied with two thirds[6] of *terumah* and one third of unconsecrated food. R. Judah said, All [her sustenance] is given to her in *terumah*[7] and she sells it and purchases unconsecrated food out of the proceeds.[8] R. Simeon b. Gamaliel said, Wherever *terumah* was mentioned[9] [the woman] is to be given [a supply equal to] twice the quantity of unconsecrated victuals.[10] What is the practical difference between them?[11] — The difference between them [is the question of the woman's] trouble.[12]

A LEVIR [WHO IS A PRIEST] DOES NOT CONFER [UPON HIS SISTER-IN-LAW] THE RIGHT OF EATING TERUMAH. What is the reason?—The All-Merciful said, *The purchase of his money*[13] while she is the purchase of his brother.[14]

(1) The difference of opinion. (2) V. p. 342, n. 10. (3) Being the daughter of a priest. (4) V. p. 342, n. 14. (5) V. p. 342, n. 15. (6) Lit., 'portions'. (7) But, unlike R. Tarfon who allows only as much *terumah* as if it were unconsecrated victuals, R. Judah allows a larger quantity of *terumah* (which is cheaper) so that its proceeds should suffice for the purchase of the required quantity of ordinary food. (8) Lit., 'money'. (9) In the subject under discussion. (10) Tosef. Keth. V. *ab. init.* (11) R. Judah and R. Simeon b. Gamaliel. (12) In the selling of her *terumah*. It is difficult to sell *terumah* (the buyers of which, being priests only, are naturally few) and it must be offered at a very low price. To save the woman trouble R. Gamaliel allows her *terumah* double the quantity of unconsecrated victuals so that by reducing the price of the former by a half she would easily dispose of it and be able to acquire with the proceeds her required ordinary victuals. R. Judah, however, makes no provision for saving her trouble, and allows her only a slight margin of *terumah* above that of ordinary food estimated at the current prices. (13) Lev. XXII, 11, v. also *supra* p. 340, n. 5; only such may eat *terumah*. (14) She does not become his own wife before he acquired her through the levirate marriage.

IF SHE HAD SPENT SIX MONTHS WITH HER HUSBAND. Now that you stated [that even if she spent the full twelve months less one day] WITH THE HUSBAND [she is] not [permitted to eat *terumah*] is there any need [to mention also] WITH THE LEVIR?[1] —This is a case[2] [of anti-climax:] 'This, and there is no need to say that'.[3]

THIS [WAS THE RULING ACCORDING TO] AN EARLIER MISHNAH etc. What is the reason?[4]—'Ulla, or some say R. Samuel b. Judah, replied: Owing to a bodily defect [that might subsequently be detected].[5] According to 'Ulla[6] one can well understand [the respective rulings of the earlier,[7] and the later rulings],[8] the former[7] being due to the possibility that a cup [of *terumah*] might be offered[9] to her in the house of her father,[10] and the latter to [the possibility of] the detection of a bodily defect.[11] [58b] According to R. Samuel b. Judah, however, the earlier [ruling of the] Mishnah is due to [the possible detection of] a bodily defect and the later is also due to [the possible detection of] a bodily defect, what then is [the reason for] their difference?—[The principle underlying] the difference is the [efficacy of an] examination by outsiders. One Master[12] is of the opinion that an examination

(1) I.e., OR ALL OF THEM WITH THE LEVIR LESS ONE DAY WITH HER HUSBAND etc. If when *one day* only of the twelve months was not spent with the husband she does not acquire the privilege of eating *terumah*, how much less would such a privilege be acquired when *all the period* less one day was not spent with the husband! (2) Lit., 'he taught'. (3) Lit., 'this, and he need not tell this'. (4) Of the later Beth din. (5) V. *supra* p. 341, nn. 3-4. (6) Who (*supra* 75b) gave as the reason for the ruling of the earlier Mishnah that the woman might allow her relatives to drink of her cup of *terumah*. (7) Forbidding *terumah* during the first twelve months and permitting it after the expiration of that period. (8) Which extends the prohibition until the entry into the bridal chamber. (9) V. *supra* p. 340, n. 6. (10) And she might allow her relatives to drink from it (v. *supra* note 6). As this would not happen after the twelve months when the intended husband, becoming liable for her maintenance and desirous of preventing her from giving away his victuals to her relatives in her father's house, provides for her an abode of her own, the woman was permitted to eat *terumah*. (11) V. *supra* p. 341, n. 3. Hence the extension of the prohibition until the entry into the bridal chamber. (12) The author of the earlier Mishnah.

by others[1] is regarded as effective,[2] while the other Master[3] holds the opinion that an examination by others is not regarded as effective.[4]

MISHNAH. IF A MAN CONSECRATED HIS WIFE'S HANDIWORK,[5] SHE MAY NEVERTHELESS CONTINUE TO WORK AND TO CONSUME [THE PROCEEDS HERSELF].[6] [IF, HOWEVER, HE CONSECRATED] THE SURPLUS[7] [ONLY], R. MEIR RULED: IT IS DULY CONSECRATED.[8] R. JOḤANAN HA-SANDELAR RULED: IT REMAINS UNCONSECRATED.[8]

GEMARA. R. Huna stated in the name of Rab:[9] A woman is entitled to say to her husband, 'I do not wish either to be maintained by you or to work for you'. He holds the opinion that when the Rabbis regulated [the relations of husband and wife] her maintenance was fundamental[10] while [the assignment of the proceeds of] her handiwork [to her husband] was due [only to their desire for preventing] ill-feeling.[11] If, therefore, she said, 'I do not wish either to be maintained by you or to work for you', she is entitled to do so.[12]

An objection was raised: Maintenance [for a wife] was provided

(1) Lit., 'outside'. Which the man would naturally arrange at the expiry of the twelve months when he becomes liable for her maintenance. (2) I.e., after such an examination a man can no longer refuse to marry the woman on the ground of the subsequent detection in her of some bodily defect. Hence his ruling (v. *supra* p. 344, n. 7). (3) I.e., the authorities of the latter ruling. (4) And the man may cancel the engagement. Hence the prohibition to eat *terumah* until the entry into the bridal chamber when the man himself has the opportunity of ascertaining the condition of her body. (5) Which partly belongs to him (v. *infra* 64*b*). (6) The reason is given *infra*. (7) Of the proceeds in excess of the sum required for her maintenance. (8) The reason is given *infra*. (9) The Hebrew equivalent of the last five words is wanting in the corresponding passage in B.Ḳ. 8*b*. (10) Since a woman cannot always earn sufficient for her maintenance. (11) Between husband and wife. (12) As the Rabbinical enactment aimed at the benefit of the woman only, she may well decline that favour if she is so minded.

in return for her handiwork![1]—Read: Her handiwork was assigned [to her husband] in return for her maintenance.

May it be suggested that [our Mishnah] provides support for his[2] view? [It stated,] IF A MAN CONSECRATED HIS WIFE'S HANDIWORK SHE MAY NEVERTHELESS CONTINUE TO WORK AND TO CONSUME [THE PROCEEDS HERSELF]. Does not [this refer to a wife for whom her husband is able[3] to] provide maintenance?[4]—No; [it is a case where the husband is unable to] provide her maintenance. If, however, [her husband is unable to] provide her maintenance, what need was there to state [such an obvious case]?[5] Even according to him who holds that a master has the right to say to his slave, 'Work for me but I will not maintain you,'[6] such a rule applies only to a Canaanite slave concerning whom Scripture has not written 'with thee', but not to a Hebrew slave concerning whom it is written in Scripture, *With thee*,[7] how much less then [would this apply to] his wife?[8]—It[9] was necessary [as an introduction to] the final clause: [IF, HOWEVER, HE CONSECRATED] THE SURPLUS [ONLY], R. MEIR RULED: IT IS DULY CONSECRATED.[10] R. JOḤANAN HA-SANDELAR RULED: IT REMAINS UNCONSECRATED.

Now [R. Huna's ruling] is in disagreement with that of Resh Laḳish. For Resh Laḳish stated: You must not assume that R. Meir's reason[11] is because he is of the opinion that a man may consecrate that which has not yet come into existence[12] but this is R. Meir's reason: Since [a husband] has the right to compel her to work, his consecration is regarded as if he had said to her, 'May

(1) Which belongs to her husband (*supra* 47*b*). This implies that the assignment of a wife's handiwork to her husband was the original provision. (2) R. Huna's. (3) And, indeed, also desires to do so. Cf. Rashi and Tosaf. s.v. מאי. (4) And since he is nevertheless precluded from consecrating her handiwork it follows, as R. Huna ruled, that a wife is entitled to refuse maintenance and to retain her right over her work. (5) That he has no right to consecrate her handiwork which does not belong to him! (6) B.Ḳ. 87*b*, *supra* 43*a*, Giṭ. 12*a*. (7) Deut. XV, 16. (8) What need then was there to state the obvious? (9) The first clause which is indeed self-evident. (10) Though he does not maintain her. (11) For giving a husband the right of consecrating his wife's handiwork. (12) Such as the woman's work before she has performed it.

your hands[1] be consecrated to Him who created them'. But, surely, he[2] did not use such an expression![3]—Since R. Meir was heard to state that a man does not utter his words to no purpose,[4] [the expression the husband used here][5] may be regarded as if he had actually said to her, 'May your hands be consecrated to Him who created them'. But is R. Meir of the opinion that a man cannot consecrate anything that is not yet in existence? Surely it was taught: If a man said to a woman, 'Be thou betrothed unto me after I shall have become a proselyte' or 'After thou shalt have become a proselyte', 'After I shall have been set free', 'After thou shalt have been set free', 'After thy husband will have died', 'After thy sister will have died', or 'After thy brother-in-law shall have submitted to *ḥaliẓah*[6] from thee', she, R. Meir ruled, is legally betrothed![7]—From that [Baraitha] the inference[8] may indeed be drawn;[9] from this, [our Mishnah], however, it cannot be inferred.[10]

[IF, HOWEVER, HE CONSECRATED] THE SURPLUS [ONLY], R. MEIR RULED: IT IS DULY CONSECRATED. When does it become consecrated? — Both Rab and Samuel stated: The surplus becomes consecrated only after [the wife's] death.[11] R. Adda b. Ahabah stated: The surplus is consecrated while she is still alive.[12] [In considering this statement] R. Papa argued: In what circumstances?[13] If it be suggested: Where [the husband] allows her maintenance[14] and also allows her[15] a silver *ma'ah*[16] for her other

(1) Which, of course, were in existence at the time of the consecration. Thus it has been shewn that according to Resh Laḳish it is the opinion of R. Meir that a husband has the right to compel his wife to work. (2) The husband. (3) He did not say 'Your *hands*', but 'Your handiwork'. (4) V. 'Ar. 5a. (5) Since it would serve no purpose at all in the form he used it. (6) V. Glos. (7) When the respective conditions are fulfilled, though at the time of the betrothal they were still unfulfilled (Yeb. 92*b*, 93*b*, B.M. 16*b*). This then shews that a man can legally dispose even of that which is not yet in existence. (8) V. n. 7 final clause. (9) Lit., 'yes'. (10) Since the reason may well be the one given *supra* by Resh Laḳish. (11) When her husband inherits her estate. (12) As soon as it is produced. (13) Could the two opposing views be justified. (14) Whereby he acquires the right to her earnings. (15) Every week. (16) V. Glos.

requirements,[1] what [it may be retorted] is the reason of those who stated that it 'becomes consecrated only after [the wife's] death'?[2] If, however, it is a case where [the husband] does not allow her maintenance and does not allow her a silver *ma'ah* for her other requirements, what [it may be objected] is the reason of him who stated that 'it is consecrated while she is still alive'?—This is a case indeed[3] where he does allow her maintenance; but does not allow her a silver *ma'ah* for her other requirements. Rab and Samuel are of the opinion that [the Rabbis] have ordained [59a] maintenance [for a wife] in return for her handiwork,[4] and a silver *ma'ah*[5] in return for the surplus;[6] and since the husband does not give her the silver *ma'ah*, the surplus remains hers.[7] R. Adda b. Ahabah, however, is of the opinion that maintenance was ordained in return for the surplus,[6] and the silver *ma'ah* in return for her handiwork; and since [the husband] supplies her maintenance, the surplus is his. On what principle do they[8] differ?—The Masters hold that the usual[9] is for the usual,[10] and the Master holds that the fixed [sum][11] is for the fixed [quantity].[12]

An objection was raised: Maintenance [for a wife] was provided in return for her handiwork![13]—Read: In return for the surplus of her handiwork.

Come and hear: If he does not give her a silver *ma'ah* for her other requirements, her handiwork belongs to her![14]—Read: The *surplus* of her handiwork belongs to her. But, surely, in connection with

(1) Whereby he acquires the right to the surplus of her earnings in excess of the sum required for her maintenance, cf. *infra* 64b. (2) Since the husband is entitled to both her earnings and the surplus the consecration should take effect even while she is alive. (3) Lit., 'for ever'; 'always'. (4) Which belongs to the husband. (5) Every week. (6) V. *supra* p. 347, n. 14. (7) And cannot consequently be consecrated by him until after her death when he inherits it. (8) Rab and Samuel on the one hand and R. Adda b. Ahabah on the other. (9) Maintenance. (10) The proceeds of the woman's handiwork. A surplus, however, in excess of the sum required for her maintenance, is unusual. (11) The silver *ma'ah*. (12) A wife's handiwork the quantity of which is prescribed (v. *infra* 64b). (13) *Supra* 47b, 58b. An objection against R. Adda b. Ahabah. (14) *Infra* 64b; which proves that the *ma'ah* is in return for her handiwork not for the surplus. An objection against Rab and Samuel.

this statement it was taught: What [is the quantity of work that] she[1] must do for him?[2] The weight of five *sela's*[3] of warp in Judaea [etc.]![4]—It is this that was meant: What is the quantity of work [that she must do] in order that we might determine how much is her surplus? The weight of five *sela's* of warp in Judaea which is ten *sela's*[5] in Galilee.

Samuel stated: The *halachah* is in agreement with R. Joḥanan ha-Sandelar.[6] But could Samuel have made such a statement? Have we not learned: [If a woman said to her husband], '*Ḳonam*,[7] if I do aught for your mouth',[8] he[9] need not annul her vow.[10] R. Akiba, however, said: He[9] must annul it, since she might do more work than is due to him.[11] R. Joḥanan b. Nuri said: He[9] must annul her vow[12] since he might happen to divorce her[13] and she would [owing to her vow] be forbidden to return[14] to him.[15] And Samuel stated: The *halachah* is in agreement with R. Joḥanan b. Nuri?[16]—When

(1) A wife. (2) Her husband. (3) V. Glos. s.v. *Sela'*. (4) *Infra* 64*b*. This represents 'handiwork', not the surplus. How then could the insertion of 'surplus' be justified? (5) The Galilean *sela'* being equal to half that of Judaea. (6) In our Mishnah. (7) קונם, (*ḳonam*) one of the expressions of a vow. V. Glos. (8) I.e., that her husband shall be forbidden to eat anything prepared by her or purchased from the proceeds of her work. (9) The husband who is empowered to annul his wife's vows. V. Num. XXX, 7ff. (10) As a wife's work belongs to her husband she has no right to dispose of it by vow or in any other way. Her vow is, therefore, null and void and requires no invalidation. (11) More than the quantity to which he is entitled (v. *infra* 64*b*). Any work in excess of that quantity remains at the disposal of the wife who is entitled to forbid it to her husband by a vow. Hence the necessity for annulment. (12) Not only on account of the surplus as stated by R. Akiba. (13) When he loses all claim to her work, and her vow becomes effective. (14) He would not be able to remarry her because her vow would prevent her from performing for him any of the services which a wife must do for her husband. [R. Joḥanan b. Nuri is of the opinion that the surplus belongs to the husband and the woman has thus no right to forbid it to him by vow.] (15) V. Ned. 85*a* and *infra* 66*a* and 70*a*. (16) According to whom the woman's vow becomes valid *after* her divorce though at the time the vow was made the work she will do afterwards has *not yet come into existence*. From this it follows that a person may similarly consecrate anything that is not yet in existence. How, then, could Samuel who adopts this view as the *halachah* also state that the *halachah* is in agreement with R. Joḥanan ha-Sandelar according to whom a thing which is

Samuel stated, 'The *halachah* is in agreement with R. Joḥanan b. Nuri' [he referred only] to the surplus.[1] Then let him[2] specifically state, 'The *halachah* is in agreement with R. Joḥanan b. Nuri in respect of the surplus', or else 'The *halachah* is not in agreement with the first Tanna',[3] or else, 'The *halachah* is in agreement with R. Akiba![4]—But, replied R. Joseph, you speak of *ḳonamoth?*[5] *Ḳonamoth* are different. For, as a man may[6] forbid to himself the fruit of his fellow[7] so may he also consecrate[8] that which is not yet in existence.[9] Said Abaye to him:[10] It is quite logical that a man should be entitled to forbid the use of the fruit of his fellows to himself,[11] since he may also forbid his own fruit[12] to his fellow;[13] should he, however, have the right to forbid something that is not

not yet in existence cannot be consecrated? [For this can be the only reason for R. Joḥanan ha-Sandelar's view in the Mishnah according to Samuel who explained the reference in the Mishnah to be to the surplus after the wife's death (v. *supra* p. 347) which R. Joḥanan ha-Sandelar will regard as unconsecrated because, at the time when the husband consecrated his wife's handiwork, it was not yet in existence (Rashi).

(1) And not to all her work which has not yet come into existence. This answer could be easily refuted, since the same objection that has been raised against the 'handiwork' may equally be raised against the 'surplus' which also was not in existence when the vow was made. This had been waived, however, in view of the more general objection that follows (Rashi). [Tosaf: Samuel's statement that the *halachah* is like R. Joḥanan b. Nuri is limited to his view that the surplus belongs to the husband v. *supra* p. 349, n. 14]. (2) Samuel. (3) From which it would be inferred that annulment of the vow is necessary only on account of the surplus. (4) Who specifically mentioned the surplus. Since none of these expressions was used it is obvious that Samuel could not have referred to the surplus only. (5) Plural of *ḳonam*, a general term for vows which are usually introduced by *ḳonam*. (6) In making a vow. (7) Though he could not consecrate such fruit to the Sanctuary. (8) I.e., prohibit to himself by a vow. (9) I.e., seeing that he can, by means of a vow, prohibit to himself a thing which is not in his possession, he can also prohibit a thing which is not yet in existence. Hence the validity of the vow. In our Mishnah, however, where the subject is ordinary consecration to the sanctuary, *halachah* is indeed in agreement with R. Joḥanan ha-Sandelar that the consecration is invalid. (10) R. Joseph. 'To him' is wanting in MS.M. (11) By a vow. (12) To any particular person, by means of a vow, or to everybody by a general consecration to the Sanctuary. (13) He may forbid his fellow's fruit to himself as the master of his own body; and he may forbid his fruit to his fellow as the owner of his fruit.

yet in existence,[1] seeing that no man has the right[2] to forbid the fruit of his fellow to his fellow?[3]—But, replied R. Huna son of R. Joshua, [that[4] is a case] where the woman said, 'My hands shall be consecrated to Him who created them', [such consecration being valid] since her hands are in existence.[5] But even if she had said so, could she consecrate them? Are they not mortgaged to him?[6]—[This is a case] where she said,[7] 'When I shall have been divorced'.[8] But is there a consecration that could not take effect now[9] and would nevertheless become effective later?[10]—And why not? retorted R. Elai. Were a man to say to his friend, 'This field that I am selling you shall be consecrated as soon as I shall have re-purchased it from you', would it not[11] become consecrated?[12] R. Jeremiah demurred: What a comparison? There[13] [the seller] has the right to consecrate [his field];[14] here,[15] however, [the woman] has no power to divorce herself![16] This[15] is rather similar[17] to the case of a man who said to another, 'This field which I have sold to you shall become consecrated after I shall have re-purchased it from you', where it does not become consecrated.[18] R. Papa

(1) The woman's work. Neither her work (which has not yet been done) nor her right to it (which she will regain only after divorce) is yet in existence. (2) Even by a vow. (3) Certainly not. As a person has no right to do the latter, he being neither master of his fellow's body nor owner of his fruit, so he should not be entitled to do the former (v. *supra* note 1.) (4) R. Joḥanan b. Nuri's ruling which Samuel adopted as the *halachah*. (5) Whereas our Mishnah deals with the case where she consecrated her handiwork, and this is not yet in existence. (6) Her husband. How then could she consecrate that which is not hers? (7) The consecration shall take effect. (8) At that time she is again independent of her husband. (9) As in the case under discussion where the woman while living with her husband is ineligible to dispose of her work. (10) Obviously not. How then could the *halachah* be in agreement with R. Joḥanan b. Nuri? (11) When it is re-purchased. (12) It certainly would. Similarly in the case of a woman's work after she is divorced. (13) The case of the field one is about to sell. (14) Since at the time of the consecration it is still in his possession. Hence also the effectiveness of his present consecration after he had re-purchased that field. (15) In the case of the consecration of a wife's work while she is still with her husband. (16) How then could she have the power to consecrate her work even for the future? (17) Lit., 'this is not equal but'. (18) Because at the time of the consecration it was no longer in his possession.

demurred: Are the two cases at all similar? There[1] both the field itself and its produce are in the possession of the buyer, but here[2] the wife's person is in her own possession. This[2] is rather similar[3] to the case of a man who said to another, [59b] 'This field which I have mortgaged to you shall be consecrated after I have redeemed it,' where it is consecrated. R. Shisha son of R. Idi demurred: Are these cases similar? There[1] it[4] is in his[5] power to redeem it; but here[2] she has no power to divorce herself. This[2] is rather similar[3] to the case of a man who said to his fellow, 'This field which I have mortgaged to you for ten years[6] shall be consecrated when I shall have redeemed it', where it becomes consecrated. R. Ashi demurred: Are these cases similar? There[7] he[5] has the power to redeem it at least after ten years, but here[2] she has never the power to divorce herself![8]—But, replied R. Ashi, you speak of *ḳonamoth! Ḳonamoth* are different [from ordinary vows] since they effect the consecration of the body[9] itself;[10] and [the reason here[11] is the same] as that of Raba, for Raba stated: Consecration,[12] leavened food[13] and manumission[14] cancel a mortgage.[15] They[16] should then[17] become consecrated forthwith![18]—The Rabbis have imparted force to a husband's rights[19] [over his wife] so that they[16] shall not become consecrated forthwith.[20]

(1) The case of the sold field. (2) V. *supra* p. 351, n. 15. (3) V. p. 351, n. 17. (4) The mortgaged field. (5) The man who consecrated the field. (6) During which period he has no power to redeem it, as a wife has no power to divorce herself. (7) The ten years' mortgage. (8) The two cases, therefore, cannot be compared. (9) Of the animal or object consecrated. (10) In relation to the man concerned; and unlike other consecrations to the Temple Treasury, can never be redeemed. (11) For the validity of the consecration of the wife's work. (12) Of a pledged animal for the altar. (13) Which is pledged to a non-Israelite but kept in the possession of an Israelite when the time for its destruction on the Passover Eve arrives. No leaven or leavened food though pledged to a non-Jew may be kept in Jewish possession from the mid-day of Passover Eve until the conclusion of the Passover festival. (14) Of a mortgaged slave. (15) Similarly here, the consecration cancels the husband's claim upon the body or work of his wife. Hence the validity of her consecration. (16) The wife's hands. (17) V. *supra* n. 15. (18) Why then has it been stated that the consecration becomes effective only after her divorce. (19) שעבודא דבעל lit., 'the subjection or pledging to the husband'. (20) His rights, as long as she

MISHNAH. THE FOLLOWING ARE THE KINDS OF WORK WHICH A WOMAN MUST PERFORM FOR HER HUSBAND: GRINDING CORN, BAKING BREAD, WASHING CLOTHES, COOKING, SUCKLING HER CHILD, MAKING READY HIS BED AND WORKING IN WOOL. IF SHE BROUGHT HIM ONE BONDWOMAN[1] SHE NEED NOT DO ANY GRINDING OR BAKING OR WASHING. [IF SHE BROUGHT] TWO BONDWOMEN,[2] SHE NEED NOT EVEN COOK OR SUCKLE HER CHILD. IF THREE, SHE NEED NEITHER MAKE READY HIS BED NOR WORK IN WOOL. IF FOUR, SHE MAY LOUNGE[3] IN AN EASY CHAIR.[4] R. ELIEZER SAID: EVEN IF SHE BROUGHT HIM[5] A HUNDRED BONDWOMEN HE MAY[6] COMPEL HER TO WORK IN WOOL; FOR IDLENESS LEADS TO UNCHASTITY. R. SIMEON B. GAMALIEL SAID: EVEN[7] IF A MAN FORBADE HIS WIFE UNDER A VOW TO DO ANY WORK HE MUST DIVORCE HER AND GIVE HER KETHUBAH[8] TO HER FOR IDLENESS LEADS TO IDIOCY.[9]

GEMARA. GRINDING CORN! How could you imagine this?[10] —Read: Attending to[11] the grinding.[12] And if you prefer I might say: With a hand mill.

Our Mishnah[13] does not agree with the view of R. Ḥiyya. For R. Ḥiyya taught: A wife [should be taken] mainly for the sake[14]

lives with him, are not merely those of a creditor to whom an object has been mortgaged or pledged but the fuller rights of a buyer. For further notes on the whole of this passage, v. Ned. Sonc. ed. pp. 265ff.

(1) Or a sum that would purchase one. (2) Or their value. V. *supra* n. 1. (3) Lit., 'sit'. (4) I.e., she need not perform even minor services for him. She is under no obligation to leave her chair to bring him any object even from the same house (cf. Rashi). קתדרא, cf. καθέδρα, 'an easy chair', 'soft seat'. (5) Her husband. (6) Or, according to another interpretation, 'should'. (7) I.e., precautions must be taken against idleness not only in the case mentioned by R. Eliezer but also in the following where the husband himself forbade the work. (8) Thus enabling her to engage in work again. (9) שיעמום, 'stupefaction', 'dullness'. (10) A woman, surely, could not be expected to turn the sails or the wheels of a mill. (11) Lit., 'causing'. (12) She performs the accompanying services only. (13) Which imposes duties of work upon a wife. (14) Lit., 'a woman is not but'.

of her beauty; mainly for the sake[1] of children.[2] And R. Ḥiyya further taught: A wife is mainly for the wearing[1] of a woman's finery. And R. Ḥiyya further taught: He who wishes his wife to look graceful[3] should clothe her in linen garments. He who wishes his daughter to have a bright complexion,[4] let him, on the approach of her maturity, feed her with young fowls and give her milk to drink.

SUCKLING HER CHILD. Must it be assumed that our Mishnah[5] does not agree with the view of Beth Shammai? For was it not taught: If a woman vowed not to suckle her child she must, said Beth Shammai, pull the breast out of its mouth,[6] and Beth Hillel said: [Her husband] may compel her to suckle it.[7] If she was divorced he cannot compel her; but if [the child] knows her[8] [her husband] pays her the fee and may compel her to suckle it in order [to avert] danger?[9]—It may be said to be in agreement even with the view of Beth Shammai, but here[10] we are dealing with such a case, for instance, where the woman made a vow and her husband confirmed it; Beth Shammai being of the opinion that he has thereby put his finger between her teeth,[11] while Beth Hillel hold that it is she that has put her finger between her teeth.[12] Then[13] let them[14]

(1) V. p. 353, n. 14. (2) Not as a bondwoman for her husband. R. Ḥiyya agrees, however, that a wife is expected to work in wool in return for the maintenance her husband allows her. His only objection is to menial work such as the grinding of corn which has an injurious effect upon her womanly grace. V. Tosaf. s.v. תני. (3) Lit., 'to nurse', 'to make pliant', 'to make graceful'. (4) Lit., 'that he may make white'. (5) Which imposes upon a wife the duty of suckling her children. (6) I.e., her vow is valid, because she is under no obligation to suckle her child. (7) According to their view it is a mother's duty to suckle her child and her vow is, therefore, null and void. (8) And refuses to be nursed by any other woman (Rashi). [Isaiah Trani: Even if it does not refuse to be suckled by another woman, its separation from its mother, whom it has learnt to recognize, may prove injurious to the infant]. (9) Tosef. Keth. V. Since Beth Shammai maintain here that a wife is under no obligation to suckle her children (cf. *supra* n. 6) our Mishnah (cf. *supra* n. 5) obviously cannot be in agreement with their view. (10) In the cited Baraitha. (11) I.e., it is the husband's fault that the vow remained valid. He could easily have annulled it had he wished to do so. (V. Num. XXX, 7ff). (12) She should not have vowed (cf. *supra* note 7). (13) If, as now suggested, the husband has confirmed the vow the woman had made. (14) Beth Shammai and Beth Hillel.

express their disagreement as regards a *kethubah* generally.[1] Furthermore, it was taught:[2] Beth Shammai said: She need not suckle [her child]![3]—But, clearly, our Mishnah is not in agreement with the view of Beth Shammai.

'If [the child] knows her'. [60*a*] At what age?[4]—Raba in the name of R. Jeremiah b. Abba who had it from Rab replied: Three months. Samuel, however, said: Thirty days; while R. Isaac stated in the name of R. Joḥanan: Fifty days. R. Shimi b. Abaye stated: The *halachah* is in agreement with the statement of R. Isaac which was made in the name of R. Joḥanan. One can well understand [the respective views of] Rab and R. Joḥanan since they are guided by the child's keenness of perception.[5] According to Samuel, however, is such [precocity][6] at all possible?—When Rami b. Ezekiel came[7] he said, 'Pay no regard to those rules which my brother Judah laid down in the name of Samuel; for thus said Samuel: As soon as [the child][8] knows her'.[9]

A [divorced woman] once came to Samuel [declaring her refusal to suckle her son]. 'Go', he said to R. Dimi b. Joseph, 'and test her case'.[10] He went and placed her among a row of women and, taking hold of her child, carried him in front of them. When he came up to her [the child][11] looked at her face with joy,[12] but she turned her eye away from him. 'Lift up your eyes', he called to

(1) Where a woman vowed that her husband was to have no benefits from her. According to Beth Shammai she would be entitled to her *kethubah* because it is the man's fault that her vow remained valid (cf. *supra* p. 354, n. 11), while according to Beth Hillel she would receive no *kethubah* because the making of the vow was her fault (cf. p. 354, n. 12). (2) In respect of *any* woman, even one who made no vow. (3) How then could it be suggested that our Mishnah is in agreement with the view of Beth Shammai? (4) Lit., 'until how much?' i.e., at what age is a child assumed to know its mother, and to refuse in consequence to be suckled by another woman? (5) Lit., 'every one according to his sharpness'; the former fixing it at the age of three months and the latter at that of fifty days. (6) That a child should know its mother at the age of thirty days. (7) From Palestine to Babylon, v. *infra* 111*b*. (8) Whatever its age. (9) May a mother be compelled to suckle it; even after she has been divorced. She is only entitled to a fee from the child's father. (10) To ascertain whether the child knew its mother. (11) Cur. edd. חזית (fem.). Read with Bomb. ed. חזיה (masc.). (12) Af. of סוי, 'to look up with joy' (Jast.), 'to gaze longingly'.

her, 'come, take away your son'. How does a blind child know [its mother]? R. Ashi said: By the smell and the taste.[1]

Our Rabbis taught: A child must be breast fed for[2] twenty-four months. From that age onwards[3] he is to be regarded as one who sucks an abominable thing; these are the words of R. Eliezer. R. Joshua said: [He may be breast fed] even for four or five years. If, however, he ceased[4] after the twenty-four months and started again[5] he is to be regarded as sucking an abominable thing.[6]

The Master said, 'From that age onwards he is to be regarded as one who sucks an abominable thing'. But I could point out a contradiction: As it might have been presumed that human[7] milk is forbidden[8] since such [prohibition may be deduced from the following] logical argument: If in the case of a beast[9] in respect of which the law of contact[10] has been relaxed[11] [the use of] its milk has nevertheless been restricted,[12] how much more should the use of his milk be restricted in the case of a human being in respect of whom the law of contact has been restricted;[13] hence it was specifically stated, *The camel because it*[14] *cheweth the cud* [... *it is unclean unto you*],[15] only '*it*' is unclean; human milk, however, is not unclean but clean. As it might also have been presumed that only [human] milk is excluded[16] because [the use of milk] is not equally [forbidden] in all cases[17] but that [human] blood is not excluded[18] since [the prohibition of eating blood] is equally applicable in all cases,[19] hence it was specifically stated, *it*,[20] only '*it*' is forbidden; human

(1) Of the milk. (2) Lit., 'a baby sucks and continues until'. (3) If he is still breast fed. (4) Lit., 'he separated'. (5) Lit., 'and returned'. (6) Cf. Tosef. Nid. II. (7) Lit., 'those who walk on two (legs)'. (8) V. Rashi; lit., 'unclean'. (9) Of the unclean classes enumerated in Lev. XI, 4ff and Deut. XIV, 7ff. (10) By a human being. (11) Contact with a live animal, even of the unclean classes (v. *supra* n. 10), does not cause uncleanness. (12) It is forbidden for human consumption (v. Bek. 6*b*). (13) Contact with a menstruant, for instance, causes uncleanness. (14) Emphasis on '*it*' (הוא) (v. *infra* n. 20). (15) Lev. XI, 4. (16) Lit., 'I take out', *sc.* from the prohibition of consuming it. (17) The milk of a clean beast being permitted. (18) From the restriction of consuming it. (19) Even the blood of a clean beast is forbidden. (20) The second '*it*' (הוא) in Lev. IV, 11. Cf. *supra* n. 14. According to another interpretation the exclusion of blood is derived from the expression זה (E.V. *these*) at the beginning of the verse (Rashi).

blood, however, is not forbidden but permitted.[1] And [in connection with this teaching] R. Shesheth has stated: Even [a Rabbinical] ordinance of abstinence is not applicable to it![2]—This is no difficulty. The latter[3] [refers to milk] that has left [the breast][4] whereas the former[5] [refers to milk] which has not left [the breast]. [This law, however], is reversed in the case of blood,[6] as it was taught: [Human] blood which [is found] upon a loaf of bread must be scraped off and [the bread] may only then be eaten; but that which is between the teeth[7] may be sucked without any scruple.[8]

The Master stated, 'R. Joshua said: [He may be breast fed] even for four or five years'. But was it not taught that R. Joshua said: Even when [he carries] his bundle on his shoulders?[9]—Both represent the same age.[10] R. Joseph stated: The *halachah* is in agreement with R. Joshua.

It was taught: R. Marinus said, A man suffering from an attack on the chest[11] may suck milk[12] [from a beast] on the Sabbath.[13] What is the reason?—Sucking is an act of unusual[14] unloading[15]

(1) Cf. Ker. 22*a* and v. *infra* n. 6. (2) I.e., human milk is not only Pentateuchally, but also Rabbinically permitted. How then is this ruling to be harmonized with the previous Baraitha cited from Niddah which regards human milk as an 'abominable thing'? (3) Lit., 'that', the last mentioned Baraitha which permits the consumption of human milk. (4) And is collected in a utensil. (5) Which, regarding the milk as an 'abominable thing', forbids it to one older than twenty-four months. (6) As long as it remains within the body it is permitted; but as soon as it leaves it is forbidden as a preventive measure against the eating of animal blood. (7) I.e., which has not been separated from the body. (8) Ker. 21*b*. (9) I.e., even at an age when the child is capable of carrying small loads he may still be breast fed. How then is this to be reconciled with the Baraitha cited from Niddah (V. *supra* note 5)? (10) Lit., 'one size' or 'limit'. (11) גונח (rt. גנח 'to groan'), one sighing painfully under an attack *angina pectoris*. V. Jast. (12) Goat's milk which has a curative effect (v. Rashi). (13) Though the release of the milk from the animal's breast resembles the plucking of a plant from its root, or the unloading of a burden, which is forbidden on the Sabbath. (14) כלאחר יד, lit., 'as if by the back of the hand'. (15) מפרק (rt. פרק Piel, 'break down', 'detach'). Milking an animal with one's hands is regarded as direct unloading (or detaching) which on the Sabbath is Pentateuchally forbidden (cf. Shab. 95*a*); releasing the milk by sucking is an unusual or indirect unloading or detaching which is only Rabbinically forbidden.

against which, where pain[1] is involved, no preventive measure has been enacted by the Rabbis. R. Joseph stated: The *halachah* is in agreement with R. Marinus.

It was taught: Nahum the Galatian[2] stated, If rubbish[3] was collected[4] in a gutter[5] it is permissible to crush it with one's foot quietly[6] on the Sabbath, and one need have no scruples about the matter. What is the reason?— Such repair is carried out in an unusual manner[7] against which, when loss is involved,[8] the Rabbis enacted no preventive measure. R. Joseph stated: The *halachah* is in agreement with the ruling of Nahum the Galatian.

'If he ceased, however, after the twenty-four months and started again he is to be regarded as one who sucks an abominable thing'. And for how long?[9]—R. Judah b. Ḥabiba replied in the name of Samuel: For three days. Others read: R. Judah b. Ḥabiba recited[10] before Samuel: 'For three days'.

Our Rabbis taught: A nursing mother whose husband died within twenty-four months [of the birth of their child] shall neither be betrothed nor married again [60*b*] until [the completion of the] twenty-four months;[11] so R. Meir. R. Judah however, permits [remarriage] after eighteen months.[12] Said R. Nathan[13] b. Joseph: Those[14] surely, are the very words of Beth Shammai and these[15] are the very words of Beth Hillel; for Beth Shammai ruled: Twenty-four months,[16] while Beth Hillel ruled: Eighteen months![16] R. Simeon b. Gamaliel replied, I will explain:[17] According to the view[18]

(1) V. *supra* p. 357, n. 11. (2) Of Galatia or Gallia in Asia Minor. (3) Lit., 'small pieces of straw'. (4) Lit., 'that went up'. (5) And thus prevens the proper flow of the water. (6) בצנעא lit., 'privately'. (7) V. *supra* p. 357, n. 14. (8) Were the gutter to remain choked up the overflow of the water would cause damage. (9) Must the break last for the child to be regarded as having ceased to suck. (10) A Baraitha. His statement was not merely the report of a ruling of Samuel who was but an Amora. (11) Were she to marry sooner and happen to become pregnant, the child would have to be taken from her breast before the proper time. (12) The shorter period is in his opinion quite sufficient for the suckling of a child. (13) *Var. lec.* 'Jonathan' (v. Tosef. Nid. II). 14) The words of R. Meir. (15) R. Judah's words. (16) As the period during which a child must be breast fed. What then was the object of the repetition of the same views? (17) Read אפרש (v. *She'iltoth, Wayera*, III). Cur. edd. אכריע (rt. כרע, Hif. 'to over-balance', 'compromise'). (18) Lit., 'the words of him who says'.

[that a child must be breast fed for] twenty-four months[1] [a nursing mother] is permitted to marry again after twenty-one months,[2] and according to the view[3] [that it is to be breast fed for] eighteen months[4] she may marry again after fifteen months;[5] because a [nursing mother's] milk deteriorates only three months after [her conception].[6]

'Ulla stated: The *halachah* is in agreement with the ruling of R. Judah;[7] and Mar 'Ukba stated: R. Ḥanina permitted me to marry [a nursing woman] fifteen months after [the birth of her child].[8]

Abaye's metayer once came to Abaye and asked him: Is it permissible to betroth [a nursing woman] fifteen months after [her child's birth]?—The other answered him: In the first place[9] [whenever there is disagreement] between R. Meir and R. Judah the *halachah* is in agreement with the view of R. Judah;[7] and, furthermore, [in a dispute between] Beth Shammai and Beth Hillel the *halachah* is in agreement with the view of Beth Hillel;[10] and while 'Ulla said, 'The *halachah* is in agreement with R. Judah',[7] Mar 'Ukba stated, 'R. Ḥanina permitted me to marry [a nursing woman] fifteen months after [the birth of her child]', how much more then [is there no need for you to wait the longer period] since you only intend betrothal. When he[11] came to R. Joseph[12] the latter told him, 'Both Rab and Samuel ruled that [a nursing woman] must wait twenty-four months exclusive of the day on which her child was born and exclusive of the day on which she is betrothed'.[13]

(1) Beth Shammai. (2) Not, as R. Meir ruled, twenty-four. (3) Lit., 'the words of him who says'. (4) Beth Hillel. (5) And not, as R. Judah ruled, eighteen. (6) For three months, at least, after her remarriage the child's breast feeding need not be interrupted. The views of Beth Shammai and Beth Hillel thus differ from those of R. Meir and R. Judah respectively. (7) That a nursing mother need not wait more than eighteen months. (8) In agreement with the view of Beth Hillel as interpreted by R. Simeon b. Gamaliel. (9) Lit., 'one'. (10) Who, according to R. Simeon b. Gamaliel's interpretation, require a nursing mother to postpone remarriage for no longer a period than fifteen months. (11) Abaye, who was a disciple of R. Joseph. (12) To consult him on the question his metayer addressed to him. (13) Yeb. 43*a*.

Thereupon he[1] ran[2] three parasangs[3] after him, (some say, one parasang along sand mounds), but failed to overtake him.

Said Abaye: The statement made by the Rabbis that 'Even [a question about the permissibility of eating] an egg[4] with *kutha*[5] a man shall not[6] decide[7] in a district [which is under the jurisdiction] of his Master' was not due [to the view that this might] appear as an act of irreverence[8] but to the reason that [a disciple] would have no success in dealing with the matter. For I have in fact learned the tradition of Rab and Samuel and yet I did not get the opportunity of applying it.[9]

Our Rabbis taught: [If a nursing mother] gave her child to a wet nurse or weaned him, or if he died, she is permitted to marry again forthwith.[10] R. Papa and R. Huna son of R. Joshua intended to give a practical decision in accordance with this Baraitha, but an aged woman said to them, 'I have been in such a position[11] and R. Naḥman forbade me [to marry again].[12] Surely, this could not have been so;[13] for has not R. Naḥman in fact permitted [such remarriage][14] in the Exilarch's family?[15]—The family of the Exilarch was different [from ordinary people] because no nurse would break her agreement[16] with them.[17]

(1) Abaye. (2) In an attempt to stop his metayer from acting on his decision. (3) V. Glos. (4) That was found in a slaughtered fowl (v. Tosaf. s.v. אפילו *a.l.*). The question of eating a properly laid egg with milk (v. next note) could of course never arise. (5) A preserve containing milk. (6) Though the answer is simple and obvious. (7) Lit., 'solve'. (8) Against the Master. (9) When the question was addressed to him. MS.M. adds; 'because at that time I forgot it'. (10) After her husband's death. She need not wait until the period for suckling mentioned above has expired. (11) Lit., 'with me was (such) an event'. (12) Before the expiration of the period prescribed for the breast feeding of the child. (13) Lit., 'Is it so'? (14) V. *supra* n. 12. (15) The children having been entrusted to hired nurses. This actually happened in the case of his own wife Yaltha (v. *She'iltoth*, *Wayera*, XIII and cf. Golds. *a.l.*). (16) Lit., 'return', 'retract'. (17) Hence it was safe to allow their widows to remarry (note 12). In the case of ordinary people, however, the nurse might well change her mind at any moment and the child would consequently have to fall back upon the nursing of his own mother. Should she then happen to be in a state of pregnancy the child would be in danger of starvation.

Said R. Papi to them:[1] Could you not have inferred it[2] from the following? It has been taught: [A married woman] who was always anxious[3] to spend her time[4] at her paternal home,[5] or who has some angry quarrel at her husband's home,[6] or whose husband was in prison,[6] or had gone to a country beyond the sea,[7] or was old or infirm,[6] or if she herself was barren, old,[8] incapable of procreation or a minor,[8] or if she miscarried after the death of her husband, or was in any other way incapacitated for propagation, must[9] wait three months.[10] These are the words of R. Meir. R. Jose,[11] however, permits betrothal or marriage forthwith.[12] And [in connection with this] R. Naḥman stated in the name of Samuel: The *halachah* is in agreement with R. Meir in respect of his restrictive measures![13] — 'This', they[14] answered him, 'did not occur to us'. The law is [that if the child] died [remarriage by his mother] is permitted [forthwith], but if she has weaned him [her remarriage] is[15] forbidden. Mar son of R. Ashi ruled: Even if the child died [the remarriage of the mother] is forbidden, it being possible that she has killed it so as to be in a position[16] to marry. It once actually happened that a mother strangled her child. This incident, however, is no proof.[17] That woman[18] was an imbecile,

(1) R. Papa and R. Huna. (2) The decision of R. Naḥman reported by the woman. (3) Pass. particip. of רדף 'to pursue', 'be anxious'. (4) Lit., 'to go'. (5) And she was there when her husband died. (6) At the time of his death. (7) And there he died. (8) When her husband's death occurred. (9) Though in all such cases it is obvious that the woman cannot be pregnant. (10) Before remarriage or betrothal. This is a precaution against a similar marriage or betrothal on the part of a normal woman who might be pregnant. (11) This is also the reading of *She'iltoth*. The reading of Tosef. Yeb. VI, 6 and 'Erub. 47*a* is 'R. Judah'. (12) After the husband's death. Cf. Yeb. and 'Erub. l.c. (13) It is consequently forbidden for any widow to marry again before the prescribed period of three months has elapsed even where the cause of the prohibition, i.e., that of possible pregnancy, does not apply. Similarly in the case of a nursing mother remarriage would obviously be forbidden even where the child died or is otherwise independent of his mother's nursing. Why then had R. Papa and R. Huna to rely solely upon the aged woman's report? (14) R. Papa and R. Huna. (15) Since it is possible that her action was due to her desire to marry. (16) Lit., 'and went'. (17) Lit., 'and this is not'. (18) Who strangled her child.

for it is not likely that [sane] women would strangle their children.

Our Rabbis taught: If a woman was given a child to suckle[1] she must not suckle together with it either her own child or the child of any friend of hers. If she agreed to a small allowance for board she must nevertheless eat much.[2] Whilst in charge of the child[3] she must not eat things which are injurious for the milk. Now that you said [that she must] not [suckle] 'her own child' was there any need [to state] 'nor the child of any friend of hers'?—It might have been assumed that only her own child [must not be suckled] because owing to her affection for it she might supply it with more [than the other child] but that the child of a friend of hers [may well be suckled] because if she had no surplus [of milk] she would not have given any at all. Hence we were taught [that even the child of a friend must not be suckled].

'If she agreed to a small allowance for board she must nevertheless eat much'. Wherefrom?—R. Shesheth replied: From her own.[4]

'Whilst in charge of the child she must not eat things which are injurious'. What are these?—R. Kahana replied: For instance, cuscuta,[5] lichen, small fishes and earth.[6] Abaye said: Even pumpkins and quinces. R. Papa said: Even a palm's heart[7] and unripe dates.[8] R. Ashi said: Even *kamak*[9] and fish-hash. Some of these cause the flow of the milk to stop while others cause the milk to become turbid.

A woman who couples in a mill will have epileptic children. One who couples on the ground will have children with long necks. [A woman] who treads[10] on the blood[11] of an ass will have scabby[12] children. One who eats[10] mustard will have intemperate children.[13] One who eats[10] cress will have blear-eyed children. One who eats[10]

(1) Lit., 'behold that they gave her a son to give (him) suck'. (2) Of her own (v. *infra*) in order to maintain a healthy supply of milk. (3) Lit., 'with it'. (4) Cf. *supra* n. 2. (5) כשות, v. Jast., hops (Rashi). (6) Cf. *infra* p. 363, n. 4. (7) Read קורא (cf. Rashi). Cur. edd. קרא (gourd). (8) Lit., 'palm branch'. (9) כמכא, 'curdled milk', 'an appetizing sauce made of milk', (cf. Fleischer to Levy, and Jast.). (10) During her pregnancy. (11) Read דמא (Aruk.). Cur. edd., רמא. (12) Or 'bald', reading גורדני (cf. Rashi). Var. גרגרני 'gluttons', 'bibbers'. (13) Or 'gluttons'.

fish brine[1] will have children with blinking eyes.[2] One who eats[3] clay[4] will have ugly children. One who drinks[3] intoxicating liquor will have ungainly[5] children. One who eats[3] meat and drinks wine will have children [61a] of a robust constitution. One who eats[3] eggs will have children with big eyes. One who eats[3] fish will have graceful children. One who eats[3] parsley[6] will have beautiful children. One who eats coriander will have stout[7] children. One who eats ethrog[8] will have fragrant children. The daughter of King Shapur, whose mother had eaten ethrog[8] [while she was pregnant] with her, used to be presented before her father as his principal perfume.

R. Huna[9] related: R. Huna b. Ḥinena tested us [with the following question:] If she[10] says that she wishes to suckle her child and he[11] says that she shall not suckle it her wish is to be granted,[12] for she would be the sufferer.[13] What, [however, is the law] where he says that she shall suckle the child and she says that she will not suckle it? Whenever this[14] is not the practice in her family we, of course, comply with her wish; what, [however, is the law] where this is the practice in her family but not in his? Do we follow the practice of his family or that of hers? And we solved his problem from this: She[15] rises with him[16] but does not go down with him.[17] What, said R. Huna, is the Scriptural proof?[18]—*For she is a man's wife*,[19] [she is to participate] in the *rise* of her husband but not in

(1) Or 'small fish' (Rashi) in brine (Jast.). (2) Aruk (s.v. מץ), 'small eyes'. (3) During her pregnancy. (4) גרגושתא, a certain kind of reddish clay was believed to possess medicinal qualities as an astringent. Cf. Smith, *Dict. Gk. Rom. Ant.* s.v. *creta*, v. Jast. (5) Lit., 'black'. Cf. Jast. (6) כרפסא = כרפס, celery, parsley, or other green vegetables. (7) Or 'fleshy', cf. בישרא, 'flesh'. (8) אתרוגא or אתרוג, a fruit of the citrus family used (*a*) as one of the 'four kinds' constituting the ceremonial wreath on Tabernacles and also (*b*) as a preserve. (9) *Var. lec.* 'Papa' (Asheri and MS.M.). (10) The mother of a child. (11) The father. (12) Lit., '(we) listen to her'. (13) Through the accumulation of the milk in her breast. Lit., 'the pain is hers'. (14) The breast feeding of a child by its mother. (15) A wife. (16) Her husband. (17) *Supra* 48a. A wife enjoys the advantages of her husband but not his disadvantages. (18) For the statement cited. (19) Gen. XX, 3 בעולת בעל of the rt. עלה 'to go up', 'rise'.

his descent. R. Eleazar said, [The proof is] from here: *Because she*[1] *was the mother of all living*[2] she was given [to her husband][3] to *live* but not to suffer pain.

IF SHE BROUGHT HIM ONE BONDWOMAN etc. Her other duties, however, she must obviously perform; [but why?] Let her say to him, 'I brought you a wife in my place'![4]—Because he might reply, 'That bondwoman works for me and for herself, who will work for you!'

[IF SHE BROUGHT] TWO BONDWOMEN, SHE NEED NOT EVEN COOK OR SUCKLE etc. Her other duties, however, she must obviously perform; [but why]? Let her say to him, 'I brought you another wife who will work for me and for her, while the first one [will work] for you and for herself!'—Because he might reply, 'Who will do the work for our guests[5] and occasional visitors!'[6]

IF THREE, SHE NEED NEITHER MAKE READY HIS BED. Her other duties, however, she must perform; [but why]? Let her say to him, 'I brought you a third one[7] to attend upon our guests and occasional visitors!'—Because he might reply, 'The more the number of the household the more the number of guests and occasional visitors'. If so,[8] [the same plea could also be advanced] even [when the number of bondwomen was] four!—[In the case of] four bondwomen, since their number is considerable they assist one another.

R. Ḥana, or some say R. Samuel b. Naḥmani, stated: [SHE BROUGHT] does not mean that she had actually brought; but: Wherever she is in a position to bring,[9] even though she has not brought any. A Tanna taught: [A wife is entitled to the same privileges] whether she brought [a bondwoman] to him[10] or whether she saved up for one out of her income.

(1) Eve, symbolizing all married women. (2) Gen. III, 20. (3) Adam, mentioned earlier in the verse. (4) בהריקאי, abs. הריקא, lit., 'gap'. As the bondwoman takes her place she should be exempt altogether from domestic duties. (5) אורחי, guests that spend a month or a week. (6) פרחי (פרחא 'flying'), visitors who pay only a short visit. (7) Lit., 'another'. (8) If an increase in the number of bondwomen causes a corresponding increase in that of guests and visitors. (9) I.e., if she has the means. (10) Her husband.

IF FOUR, SHE MAY LOUNGE IN AN EASY CHAIR. R. Isaac b. Ḥanania[1] stated in the name of R. Huna: Although it has been said, SHE MAY LOUNGE IN AN EASY CHAIR she should[2] nevertheless fill[3] for him his cup, make ready his bed and wash his face, hands and feet.[4]

R. Isaac b. Ḥanania[5] further[6] stated in the name of R. Huna: All kinds of work which a wife performs for her husband a menstruant also may perform for her husband, with the exception of filling[7] his cup, making ready his bed and washing his face, hands and feet.[8] As to 'the making ready of his bed' Raba explained that [the prohibition] applies only in his presence but [if it is done] in his absence it does not matter.[9] With regard to 'the filling of his cup', Samuel's wife made a change[10] [by serving] him with her left hand. [The wife of] Abaye placed it[11] on the edge[12] of the wine cask. Raba's [wife placed it] at the head-side of his couch, and R. Papa's [wife put it] on his foot-stool.[13]

R. Isaac b. Ḥanania[14] further[15] stated: All [foodstuffs] may be held back from the waiter[16] except meat and wine.[17] Said R. Ḥisda: [This applies only to] fat meat and old wine. Raba said: Fat meat[18] throughout the year but old wine only in the Tammuz[19] season.[20]

R. Anan b. Taḥlifa related: I was once standing in the presence of Samuel when they brought him a dish of mushrooms, and, had

(1) MS.M., 'Ḥanina'. (2) She is not compelled but is advised (v. Rashi s.v. אבל *a.l.*). (3) מוזגת, rt. מזג 'to mix', *sc.* wine with water or spices. (4) Such personal services are calculated to nurse a husband's affections (Rash. l.c.). (5) MS.M. 'Ḥanina'. (6) Read (v. marg. note, *a.l.*) ואמר. Cur. edd. omit the *Waw*. (7) Cf. *supra* n. 3. (8) In order to prevent undue intimacy between husband and wife during her period of Levitical uncleanness. (9) Lit., 'we have nothing in it'. (10) During her 'clean days', after menstruation and prior to ritual immersion, when marital relations are still forbidden. (11) V. *supra* note 10. (12) Lit., mouth'. (13) Cf. Golds. Others: (v. Jast.) 'chair'. (14) MS.M. 'Ḥanina'. (15) V. *supra* note 6. (16) Until he has finished serving the meal. (17) Which excite his appetite and any delay in satisfying it causes him extreme pain. (18) Must not be held back. (19) תמוז, the fourth month of the Hebrew calendar corresponding to July-August. (20) When the weather is extremely hot and spicy wine is tempting.

he not given me [some of it], I would have been exposed to danger.[1] I, related R. Ashi, was once standing before R. Kahana when they brought him slices[2] of turnips in vinegar, and had he not given me some, I would have been exposed to danger.

R. Papa said: Even a fragrant date [if not tasted may expose one to danger].[1] This is the rule: Any foodstuff that has a strong flavour or an acrid taste [will expose a man to danger[1] if he is not allowed to taste of it].

Both Abbuha[3] b. Ihi and Minjamin b. Ihi [shewed consideration for their waiter] the one giving [him a portion] of every kind of dish[4] while the other gave [him a portion][5] of one kind only.[6] With the former Elijah[7] conversed, with the latter he did not.

[It was related of] two pious men, and others say of R. Mari and R. Phinehas the sons of R. Ḥisda, that one of them[8] gave [a share to his waiter][9] first[10] while the other gave him last.[11] With the one who gave [the waiter his share] first, Elijah[12] conversed; with the one, however, who gave his waiter last, Elijah did not converse.[13]

Amemar, Mar Zuṭra and R. Ashi were once sitting at the gate of King Yezdegerd[14] when the King's table-steward[15] passed them by. R. Ashi, observing that Mar Zuṭra [61*b*] turned pale in the face, took up with his finger [some food from the dish and] put it to his mouth. 'You have spoilt the King's meal' [the table-steward][16] cried. 'Why did you do such a thing?' he was asked [by the King's officers].[16] 'The man who prepared that dish',[17] he[18] replied, 'has rendered the King's food objectionable'. 'Why?' they asked him.

(1) Of faintness due to the extreme pangs of hunger excited by the flavour of the dish. (2) נרגלידי the 'upper portions'. (3) Bomb. ed., 'Abuth'. (4) As it was served. (5) At the beginning of the meal, of the first dish. (6) Keeping back the others until the conclusion of the meal. (7) The immortal prophet, the maker of peace and herald of the Messianic era. (8) Lit., 'master'. (9) Of every dish he served. (10) Before he tasted of it himself. (11) After he himself and his guests had finished their meal. (12) V. *supra* note 7. (13) By failing to give the waiter a share as soon as the various dishes were served he caused him unnecessary pain of unsatisfied desire and hunger. (14) Or Yezdjird, one of the Kings of Persia. (15) אַטּוֹרְנְגָא; compound word: 'table' and 'maker'. (16) V. Rashi. (17) Lit., 'thus'. (18) R. Ashi.

'I noticed', he replied, 'a piece of leprous swine[1] flesh in it'. They examined [the dish] but did not find [such a thing]. Thereupon he took hold of his finger and put it on it,[2] saying, 'Did you examine this part?' They examined it and found it [to be as R. Ashi had said]. 'Why did you rely upon a miracle?' the Rabbis asked him. 'I saw', he replied, 'the demon of leprosy hovering over him'.[3]

A Roman once said to a woman, 'Will you marry me?'—'No,' she replied. Thereupon[4] he brought some pomegranates, split them open and ate them in her presence. She kept on swallowing all the saliva[5] that irritated her, but he did not give her [any of the fruit] until [her body] became swollen.[6] Ultimately he said to her, 'If I cure you, will you marry me?'—'Yes', she replied. Again[4] he brought some pomegranates, split them and ate them in her presence. 'Spit out at once, and again and again',[7] he said to her, 'all saliva that irritated you'. [She did so] until [the matter] issued forth from her body in the shape of a green palm-branch; and she recovered.

AND WORKING IN WOOL. Only IN WOOL but not in flax. Whose [view then is represented in] our Mishnah?—It is that of R. Judah. For it was taught: [Her husband] may not compel her to wait[8] upon his father or upon his son, or to put straw before his beast;[9] but he may compel her to put straw before his herd.[10] R. Judah said: Nor may he compel her to work in flax because flax causes one's mouth to be sore[11] and makes one's lips stiff.[12] This refers, however, only to Roman flax.

R. ELIEZER SAID: EVEN IF SHE BROUGHT HIM A HUNDRED

(1) דָּבָר אַחֵר, lit., 'another thing', *sc.* 'something unnameable', e.g., swine, leprosy, idolatry and sodomy. (2) One of the pieces of meat. (3) Mar Zuṭra (v. Rashi). (4) Lit., 'he went'. (5) That welled up in her mouth as a result of the acrid flavour of the fruit. (6) Lit., 'it became (transparent) like glass' (v. Rashi). (7) Lit., 'spit (and) eject' (*bis*). (8) Lit., 'to stand', v. Rashi. (9) Such as a horse or an ass or (according to another interpretation) 'male beasts' (v. Rashi and cf. BaḤ *a.l.*). (10) Cattle or (according to the second interpretation in n. 9) 'female beasts'. (11) Or 'swollen', v. next note. (12) Because the spinner must frequently moisten the thread, with his saliva (v. Jast.). *Aliter:* 'the flax causes an offensive smell in the mouth and distends the lips' (cf. Rashi and Golds.).

BONDWOMEN. R. Malkio stated in the name of R. Adda b. Ahabah: The *halachah* is in agreement with R. Eliezer. Said R. Ḥanina the son of R. Iḳa: [The rulings concerning] a spit,[1] bondwomen[2] and follicles[3] [were laid down by] R. Malkio; [but those concerning] a forelock,[4] wood-ash[5] and cheese[6] [were laid down by] R. Malkia. R. Papa, however, said: [If the statement is made on] a Mishnah or a Baraitha [the author is] R. Malkia [but if on] a reported statement[7] [the author is] R. Malkio. And your mnemonic[8] is, 'The Mishnah[9] is queen'.[10] What is the practical difference between them?[11]—[The statement on] Bondwomen.[12]

R. SIMEON B. GAMALIEL SAID etc. Is not this the same view as that of the first Tanna?[13]—The practical difference between them [is the case of a woman] who plays with little cubs[14] or [is addicted to] checkers.[15]

(1) That has been used for the roasting of meat on a festival, may at the time be put aside (v. Beẓah 28*b*). (2) Whom a woman brought to her husband at her marriage (v. our Mishnah). (3) That these, even without the pubic hairs, are sufficient indication of *pubes* (v. Nid. 52*a*). (4) *Belorith* בלורית (cf. Sanh. Sonc. ed. p. 114, n. 5). An Israelite trimming the hairs of a heathen must withdraw his hand at a distance of three finger's breadth on every side of the forelock (A.Z. 29*a*). (5) אפר מקלה, is forbidden to be spread on a wound because it gives the appearance of an incised imprint (v. Mak. 21). (6) Forbidden, if made by a heathen, because it is smeared over with lard. (7) שמעתתא, an opinion or dictum of Rabbis, not recorded in a Mishnah or Baraitha, reported by their disciples or colleagues. (8) An aid to the recollection as to which statements were made by R. Malkia and R. Malkio respectively. (9) מתניתא a general term for Mishnah and Baraitha in contradiction to שמעתתא (v. *supra* note 7). (10) I.e., more authoritative than a reported statement. Malkia מלכיא whose name closely resembles (*queen*) מלכתא (and not Malkio) is to be associated with the Mishnah and the Baraitha that are designated *queen*. (11) R. Ḥanina and R. Papa. (12) Which is recorded in our Mishnah. According to R. Papa the comment on it must be that of R. Malkia (cf. *supra* note 10) while according to R. Ḥanina it is included among the statements attributed to R. Malkio, v. A.Z. 29*a*, and Mak. 21*a*. (13) R. Eliezer. What difference is there for all practical purposes whether the reason for the ruling is unchastity or idiocy? (14) V. Jast. Or 'wooden cubs', counters in a game (cf. Levy). (15) נדרשיר or נרדשיר *nardeshir*, the name of a game played on a board; 'chess' (Rashi). [So named after its inventor Ardeshir Babekan, v. Krauss *T.A.* III, p. 113]. A woman who spends her time in this manner may be

MISHNAH. IF A MAN FORBADE HIMSELF BY VOW TO HAVE INTERCOURSE WITH HIS WIFE[1] BETH SHAMMAI RULED: [SHE MUST CONSENT TO THE DEPRIVATION FOR] TWO WEEKS;[2] BETH HILLEL RULED: [ONLY FOR] ONE WEEK.[2]

STUDENTS MAY GO AWAY[3] TO STUDY THE TORAH, WITHOUT THE PERMISSION [OF THEIR WIVES FOR A PERIOD OF] THIRTY DAYS; LABOURERS [ONLY FOR] ONE WEEK.

THE TIMES FOR CONJUGAL DUTY PRESCRIBED IN THE TORAH[4] ARE: FOR MEN OF INDEPENDENCE,[5] EVERY DAY; FOR LABOURERS, TWICE A WEEK; FOR ASS-DRIVERS,[6] ONCE A WEEK; FOR CAMEL-DRIVERS,[7] ONCE IN THIRTY DAYS; FOR SAILORS,[8] ONCE IN SIX MONTHS. THESE ARE THE RULINGS OF R. ELIEZER.

GEMARA. What is the reason of Beth Shammai?[9]—They derive their ruling from [the law relating to] a woman who bears a female child.[10] And Beth Hillel?—They derive their ruling from [the law relating to] one who bears a male child.[11] Why should not Beth Hillel also derive their ruling from [the law relating to] a woman who bears a female child?[12]—If they had derived their ruling from [the law relating to] a woman who bears a child they should indeed have ruled thus, but [the fact is that] Beth Hillel derive

exposed to the temptation of unchastity but is in no danger of falling into idiocy.

(1) Lit., 'IF A MAN FORBADE BY VOW HIS WIFE FROM INTERCOURSE'. (2) After this period it is the duty of the husband either to have his vow disallowed or to release his wife by divorce. (3) From their homes. (4) Ex. XXI, 10. (5) טַיָּלִין (rt. טול, *Piel*, 'to walk about'), men who have no need to pursue an occupation to earn their living and are able 'to walk about' idly. (6) Who carry produce from the villages to town and whose occupation requires their absence from their home town during the whole of the week. (7) Who travel longer distances from their homes. (8) Whose sea voyages take them away for many months at a time. (9) Who allow TWO WEEKS. (10) Intercourse with whom is forbidden for two weeks (v. Lev. XII, 5). (11) In whose case the prohibition is restricted to one week (ibid. 2). (12) The fact that the longer period of two weeks has Pentateuchal sanction should entitle a husband to vow abstention for a similar length of time.

their ruling from [the law of] the menstruant.[1] On what principle do they[2] differ?—One[3] is of the opinion that the usual[4] [is to be inferred] from the usual,[5] and the other[6] is of the opinion that what a husband has caused[7] should be derived from that which he has caused.[8]

Rab stated: They[2] differ only in the case of one who specified [the period of abstention] but where he did not specify the period it is the opinion of both that he must divorce her forthwith and give her the *kethubah*. Samuel, however, stated: Even where the period had not been specified the husband may delay [his divorce],[9] since it might be possible for him to discover some reason[10] for [the remission of] his vow.[11] But surely, they[12] once disputed this question; for have we not learned: If a man forbade his wife by vow to have any benefit from him he may, for thirty days, appoint a steward,[13] but if for a longer period he must divorce her and give her the *kethubah*. And [in connection with this] Rab stated: This ruling applies only where he specified [the period] but where he did not specify it he must divorce her forthwith and give her the *kethubah*, while Samuel stated: Even where the period had not been specified the husband may also postpone [his divorce],[9] since it might be possible for him to discover some grounds[10] for [the annulment of his vow]?[14]—[Both disputes are] required. For if [their views] had been stated in the former[15] only it might have been assumed that only in that case did Rab maintain his view,

(1) The period of whose uncleanness is only seven days (v. Lev. XV, 19). (2) Beth Shammai and Beth Hillel. (3) Lit., 'Master', *sc.* Beth Hillel. (4) Such as a quarrel between husband and wife resulting in a vow of abstention. (5) Menstruation which is a monthly occurrence. Births are not of such regular occurrence. (6) Beth Shammai. (7) Abstention on account of his vow. (8) Birth. Menstruation is not the result of a husband's action. (9) For two weeks according to Beth Shammai or one week according to Beth Hillel. (10) פתח, lit., 'a door'; some ground on which to justify his plea that had he known it he would never have made that vow; v. Ned. 21. (11) A competent authority, if satisfied with the reason, may under such conditions disallow a vow. (12) Rab and Samuel. (13) To supply his wife's needs. (14) Cf. *supra* n. 11. Why then should Rab and Samuel unnecessarily repeat the same arguments? (15) The vow against marital duty.

since [the appointment] of a steward is not possible but that in the second case[1] where [the appointment] of a steward is possible he agrees with Samuel. And if the second case[1] only had been stated it might have been assumed that only in that case did Samuel maintain his view[2] but that in the former case[3] he agrees with Rab. [Hence both statements were] necessary.

STUDENTS MAY GO AWAY TO STUDY etc. For how long [may they go away] with the permission [of their wives]?—For as long as they desire. [62*a*] What should be the usual periods?[4]—Rab said: One month at the college[5] and one month at home; for it is said in the Scriptures, *In any matter of the courses which came in and went out month by month throughout all the months of the year.*[6] R. Joḥanan, however, said: One month at the college and two months at home; for it is said in the Scriptures, *A month they were in Lebanon and two months at home.*[7] Why does not Rab also derive his opinion from this text?[7]—The building of the holy Temple is different [from the study of the Torah] since it could be carried on by others.[8] Then why does not R. Joḥanan derive his opinion from the former text?[6]—There [the conditions were] different because every man was in receipt of relief.[9]

Rab said:[10] A sigh breaks down half of the human constitution,[11]

(1) A vow forbidding other benefits. (2) Since the appointment of a steward is feasible. (3) The vow against marital duty. (4) That students should (*a*) be permitted to be away from their wives even with their consent, and (*b*) remain at home (v. Rashi). According to one opinion the restrictions spoken of here apply to labourers only. Students are allowed greater freedom. (V. Tosaf. s.v. אלא, *a.l.*). (5) Lit., 'here'. (6) I Chron. XXVII, 1, emphasis on '*month by month*'. (7) I Kings V, 28. (8) Solomon had sufficient men for the work and required each group for no longer than one month out of every three. The study of the Torah demands more time. (9) The stipend allowed by the king. This allowance enabled a husband to provide a comfortable living for his wife who, in return, consented to his absence from home every alternate month. In the case of students, however, whose study brings no worldly reward to their wives, the period of absence from home should not exceed one month in every three. (10) The following discussion is introduced here on account of the difference of opinion between Rab and R. Joḥanan on the application of Scriptural texts, which is characteristic of this as of the previous discussion. (11) Lit., 'body'.

for it is said in Scripture, *Sigh, therefore, thou son of man; with the breaking of thy loins*[1] *and with bitterness shalt thou sigh.*[2] R. Johanan, however, said: Even all the human constitution, for it is said in Scripture, *And it shall be when they say unto thee: Wherefore sighest thou? that thou shalt say: Because of the tidings, for it cometh; and every heart shall melt, and all hands shall be slack, and every spirit shall faint, and all knees shall drip with water.*[3] As to R. Johanan, is it not also written, '*With the breaking of thy loins*'?—[The meaning of] this is that when [the breaking] begins it does so from the loins. And as to Rab, is it not also written, '*And every heart shall melt, and all hands shall be slack, and every spirit shall be faint*'?—The report of the holy Temple is different since [the calamity] was very severe.

An Israelite and an idolater were once walking together on the same road and the idolater could not keep pace with the Israelite. Reminding him of the destruction of the holy Temple [the latter] grew faint and sighed; but still the idolater was unable to keep pace with him. 'Do you not say', the idolater asked him, 'that a sigh breaks half of the human body'?—'This applies only', the other replied, 'to a fresh calamity but not to this one with which we are familiar. As people say: A woman who is accustomed to bereavements is not alarmed [when another occurs]'.

MEN OF INDEPENDENCE EVERY DAY. What is meant by *tayyalin?*[4]—Raba replied: Day students.[5] Said Abaye to him: [These are the men] of whom it is written in Scripture, *It is vain for you*[6] *that ye rise early, and sit up late, ye that eat of the bread of toil; so He giveth*[7] *unto those who chase their sleep away;*[8] and 'these',[9] R. Isaac explained, 'are the wives of the scholars,[10] who chase the sleep

(1) The loins are in the *middle* of the body. (2) Ezek. XXI, 11. (3) Ibid. 12. The prophet's sigh is accompanied by shattering effects on all parts of the body. (4) Cf. *supra* p. 369, n. 5. (5) בני פירקי, lit., 'sons of the lesson', i.e., students domiciled in the college town who are able to live in their own homes and to attend the college for lessons only. (6) This admonition is addressed to those who pursue worldly occupations. (7) Without toiling for it. (8) Ps. CXXVII, 2. E.V., *unto his beloved.* לידידו is homiletically treated as coming from the rt. נדד 'to shake', 'chase away'. (9) 'Those who chase their sleep away'. (10) תלמידי חכמים. V. Glos. s.v. *talmid hakam.*

from their eyes[1] in this world and achieve thereby the life of the world to come',[2] and yet you say, 'Day students'![3]—[The explanation], however, said Abaye, is in agreement [with a statement] of Rab who said [a man of independence is one,] for instance, like R. Samuel b. Shilath[4] who eats of his own, drinks of his own and sleeps in the shadow of his mansion[5] and a king's officer[6] never passes his door.[7] When Rabin came[8] he stated: [A man of independence is one], for instance, like the pampered men of the West.[9]

R. Abbahu[10] was once standing in a bath house, two slaves supporting him, when [the floor of] the bath house collapsed under him.[11] By chance he was near a column [upon which] he climbed[12] taking up the slaves with him.[13] R. Joḥanan was once ascending a staircase, R. Ammi and R. Assi supporting him, when the staircase collapsed under him. He himself climbed up and brought them up with him. Said the Rabbis to him, 'Since [your strength is] such, why do you require support?[14]—'Otherwise', he replied, 'what [strength] will I reserve for the time of my old age?'

FOR LABOURERS TWICE A WEEK. Was it not, however, taught:

(1) In sitting up all night waiting for the return of their husbands from the house of study. (2) As a reward for the consideration they shew to their studious husbands. Since the wives of students who come from other towns would not be expecting their husbands to return home every day, the reference must obviously be to those who live in the college town, i.e., the day students, which proves that even these remain all night at the college. (3) How could men who spend their nights in study be expected to perform the marital duty daily? (4) A teacher of children (v. *supra* 50*a*) who made an unostentatious but comfortable living. (5) אפדנא 'mansion', 'palace', i.e., his own home (cf. 'the Englishman's home is his castle'). (6) פריסתקא, MS.M. דרוקא, 'a detachment of soldiers'. (7) To exact from him service or money. As his wants were moderate, he had no need to be under obligation to anyone for his food or drink and had no need to go far to seek his livelihood. A man in such a position might well be described as a man of independence. (8) From Palestine to Babylon. (9) Palestine, which lay to the west of Babylon where this statement was made. (10) This is told in illustration of the physical strength enjoyed by the Palestinians. (11) And the three were in danger of falling into the pool of water over which the floor was built. (12) Grasping it with one hand. (13) With his other hand. (14) Lit., 'to support him'.

Labourers, once a week?—R. Jose the son of R. Ḥanina replied: This is no difficulty; the former[1] [speaks of labourers] who do their work in their own town while the latter [speaks of those] who do their work in another town. So it was also taught: Labourers [perform their marital duties] twice a week. This applies only [to those] who do their work in their own town, but for those who do their work in another town [the time is only] once a week.

FOR ASS-DRIVERS ONCE A WEEK. Rabbah son of R. Ḥanan[2] said to Abaye: Did the Tanna[3] go to all this trouble[4] to teach us [merely the law relating to] the man of independence[5] and the labourer?[6]—The other replied: No; [62b] to all.[7] But was it not stated ONCE IN SIX MONTHS?[8]—One who has bread in his basket is not like one who has no bread in his basket.[9]

Said Rabbah[10] son of R. Ḥanan to Abaye: What [is the law where] an ass-driver becomes a camel-driver?[11]—The other replied: A woman prefers one *ḳab*[12] with frivolity to ten *ḳab*[12] with abstinence.[13]

(1) Lit., 'here'. Our Mishnah. (2) MS.M., R. Ḥanin b. Papa. (3) The author of the first clause of our Mishnah, which deals with the case of a vow. (4) Lit., 'fold himself up'. (5) V. *supra* p. 369, n. 5. (6) Whose times only could be affected by an abstinence of ONE WEEK (Beth Hillel) or TWO WEEKS (Beth Shammai). The other classes of persons enumerated, whose times are once in thirty days or at longer intervals, would not thereby be affected. (7) Even in respect of the other classes a vow may be made for the specified periods only. (8) In the case of sailors. How could these be affected by an abstention of ONE WEEK OF TWO WEEKS? (9) Proverb (Yoma 18*b*. Yeb. 32*b*). The latter experiences the pangs of hunger much more than the former who can eat the bread should he decide to use it up. A sailor's wife may partially satisfy her desires by the hope that her husband may at any moment return. A vow extinguishes all her hope; and she must not, therefore, be allowed to suffer longer than the periods indicated. (10) Var. 'Raba' (MS.S. and Asheri). (11) I.e., may an ass-driver become a camel-driver without the permission of his wife, in view of the longer absence from home which the new occupation will involve. (12) V. Glos. (13) Proverb, (Soṭah 20*a*, 21*b*). A woman prefers a poor living in the enjoyment of the company of her husband to a more luxurious one in his absence. She would, therefore, rather have her husband for a longer period at home, though as a result he would be earning less, than be deprived of his company for longer periods, though as a result he would be earning more.

FOR SAILORS, ONCE IN SIX MONTHS. THESE ARE THE WORDS OF R. ELIEZER. R. Beruna[1] stated in the name of Rab:[2] The *halachah* follows R. Eliezer. R. Adda b. Ahabah, however, stated in the name of Rab: This is the view of R. Eliezer only, but the Sages ruled: Students may go away to study Torah without the permission [of their wives even for] two or three years.[3]

Raba stated: The Rabbis[4] relied on R. Adda b. Ahabah[5] and act accordingly at the risk of [losing] their lives.[6] Thus R. Reḥumi who was frequenting [the school] of Raba at Maḥuza[7] used to return home on the Eve of every Day of Atonement. On one occasion[8] he was so attracted by his subject [that he forgot to return home]. His wife was expecting [him every moment, saying,] 'He is coming soon,[9] he is coming soon'.[9] As he did not arrive she became so depressed that tears began to flow from her eyes. He was [at that moment] sitting on a roof. The roof collapsed under him and he was killed.[10]

How often[11] are scholars to perform their marital duties?—Rab Judah in the name of Samuel replied: Every Friday night.[12]

That bringeth forth its fruit in its season;[13] Rab Judah, and some say R. Huna, or again, as others say, R. Naḥman, stated: This [refers to the man] who performs his marital duty every Friday night.[14]

Judah[15] the son of R. Ḥiyya and son-in-law of R. Jannai was always spending his time[16] in the school house but every Sabbath eve[17] he came home. Whenever he arrived the people saw[18] a pillar of light moving before him. Once he was so attracted by his subject of

(1) *Var. lec.* 'Mattena' (Alfasi). (2) *Var. lec.* 'Raba' (Asheri). (3) And the *halachah* would be in agreement with the Sages who are the majority. (4) I.e., his (Raba's) contemporaries. (5) According to whose statement the Sages permitted students to leave their homes for long periods (v. *supra* n. 3). (6) I.e., they die before their time as a penalty for the neglect of their wives (v. Rashi). (7) A town on the Tigris, noted for its commerce and its large Jewish population. (8) Lit., 'one day'. (9) Lit., 'now'. (10) Lit., 'his soul rested', *sc.* came to its eternal rest. (11) Lit., 'when'. (12) Lit., 'from the eve of Sabbath to the eve of Sabbath'. (13) Ps. I, 3. (14) Cf. B.Ḳ. 82*a*. (15) MS.M., 'R. Judah'. (16) Lit., 'was going and sitting'. (17) בי שמשי, 'twilight', *sc.* of the Sabbath eve. (18) Read with MS.M., יהוו קא חזו Cur. edd., הוה ... חזי (sing.) may refer to R. Jannai.

study [that he forgot to return home]. Not seeing[1] that sign, R. Jannai said to those [around him], 'Lower[2] his bed,[3] for had Judah been alive he would not have neglected the performance of his marital duties'. This [remark] was *like an error that proceedeth from the ruler,*[4] for [in consequence] Judah's[5] soul returned to its eternal rest.

Rabbi was engaged in the arrangements for the marriage of his son into the family of R. Ḥiyya,[6] but when the *kethubah*[7] was about to be written the bride passed away.[8] 'Is there, God forbid', said Rabbi, 'any taint [in the proposed union]?'[9] An enquiry was instituted[10] into [the genealogy of the two] families [and it was discovered that] Rabbi descended from Shephatiah[11] the son of Abital[12] while R. Ḥiyya descended from Shimei a brother of David.[13]

Later[14] he[15] was engaged in preparations for the marriage of his son into the family of R. Jose b. Zimra. It was agreed that he[16] should spend twelve years at the academy.[17] When the girl was led before him[16] he said to them, 'Let it[18] be six years'. When they made her pass before him [a second time] he said, 'I would rather marry [her first] and then proceed [to the academy]'. He felt abashed[19] before his father, but the latter said to him, 'My son, you[20] have the mind of your creator;[21] for in Scripture it is written first, *Thou bringest them in and plantest them*[22] and later it is written, *And let*

(1) Cf. *supra* p. 375, n. 18. (2) Lit., 'bend', a mark of mourning for the dead. (3) מטתו. (4) Cf. Eccl. X, 5. (5) So MS.M., reading דיהודה. (6) He was about to marry R. Ḥiyya's daughter (Rashi). (7) V. Glos. (8) Lit., 'the soul of the girl rested'. V. *supra* p. 375, n. 10. (9) The unexpected death of the bride being due to providential intervention to prevent an undesirable union. (10) Lit., 'they sat and looked in'. (11) David's son (II Sam. III, 4). (12) One of David's wives (ibid.). (13) As the latter was not a descendent of the anointed king's family it was not proper for his daughter to be united in marriage with one who was. (14) Lit., 'he went'. (15) Rabbi. (16) Rabbi's son. (17) The marriage to be celebrated at the end of this period. (18) The period of study prior to the marriage. (19) On account of his apparent fickleness. (20) In being influenced by affection to shorten the courting interval and to hasten the marriage day. (21) Who also hastened the day of His union with Israel. (22) Ex. XV, 17, i.e., only after settlement in the promised land was the sanctuary (the symbol of the union between God and Israel) to be built.

them make Me a sanctuary, that I may dwell among them.[1] [After the marriage] he departed and spent twelve years at the academy. By the time he returned his wife[2] had lost the power of procreation. 'What shall we do?', said Rabbi. 'Should we order him to divorce her, it would be said: This poor soul waited in vain! Were he to marry another woman, it would be said: The latter is his wife and the other his mistress.' He prayed for mercy to be vouchsafed to her, and she recovered.

R. Ḥanania b. Ḥakinai was about to go away to the academy towards the conclusion of R. Simeon b. Yoḥai's wedding. 'Wait for me', the latter said to him, 'until I am able to join you'.[3] He, however, did not wait for him but went away alone and spent twelve years at the academy. By the time he returned the streets of the town were altered and he was unable to find the way[4] to his home. Going down to the river bank and sitting down there he heard a girl being addressed thus: 'Daughter of Ḥakinai, O, daughter of Ḥakinai, fill up your pitcher and let us go!' 'It is obvious',[5] he thought, 'that the girl is ours', and he followed her. [When they reached the house] his wife was sitting and sifting flour. She[6] lifted up her eyes and seeing him, was so overcome with joy[7] that she fainted.[8] 'O, Lord of the universe', [the husband] prayed to Him, 'this poor soul; is this her reward?'[9] And so he prayed for mercy to be vouchsafed to her and she revived.

R. Ḥama b. Bisa went away [from home and] spent twelve years at the house of study. When he returned he said, 'I will not act as did b. Ḥakina'.[10] He therefore entered the [local] house of study and sent word to his house. Meanwhile his son, R. Oshaia[11] entered,

(1) Ex. XXV, 8, i.e., while still in the wilderness. (V. p. 376, n. 22). (2) Having been separated from him for more than ten years (Rashi, cf. Yeb. 34*b*). (3) At the conclusion of the marriage festivities. (4) Lit., 'did not know (how) to go'. (5) Lit., 'infer from this'. (6) Read with MS.M., דלי. Cur. edd., דל עינה may be rendered 'he lifted up her eye' i.e., he attracted her attention. (v. Jast. s.v. סוי). (7) Cf. *supra* p. 355, n. 12. (8) Lit., 'her spirit fled'. (9) For depriving herself of her husband so many years for the sake of the Torah. (10) Who entered his house unexpectedly and thereby nearly caused the death of his wife. (11) Who was unknown to his father.

sat down before him and addressed to him a question on [one of the] subjects of study. [R. Ḥama], seeing how well versed he was in his studies, became very depressed. 'Had I been here,'[1] he said, 'I also could have had such a child'. [When] he entered his house his son came in, whereupon [the father] rose before him, believing that he wished to ask him some [further] legal questions. 'What[2] father', his wife chuckled,[3] 'stands up before a son!' Rami b. Ḥama applied to him [the following Scriptural text:] *And a threefold cord is not quickly broken*[4] is a reference to R. Oshaia, son of R. Ḥama, son of Bisa.[5]

R. Akiba was a shepherd of Ben Kalba Sabua.[6] The latter's daughter, seeing how modest and noble [the shepherd] was, said to him, 'Were I to be betrothed to you, would you go away to [study at] an academy?' 'Yes', he replied. She was then secretly betrothed to him and sent him away. When her father heard [what she had done] he drove her from his house and forbade her by a vow to have any benefit from his estate. [R. Akiba] departed, and spent twelve years at the academy. When he returned home he brought with him twelve thousand disciples. [While in his home town] he heard an old man saying to her, 'How long [63a] will you lead the life of a living widowhood?' 'If he would listen to me,' she replied, 'he would spend [in study] another twelve years'. Said [R. Akiba]: 'It is then with her consent that I am acting', and he departed again and spent another twelve years at the academy. When he finally returned he brought with him twenty-four thousand disciples. His wife heard [of his arrival] and went out to meet him, when her neighbours said to her, 'Borrow some respectable clothes and put them on', but she replied: *A righteous man regardeth the life of his beast.*[7] On approaching him she fell upon her face and kissed his feet. His attendants were about to thrust her aside, when [R. Akiba] cried to them, 'Leave her alone, mine and

(1) I.e., had he remained at home and attended to the education of his son. (2) Lit., is 'there'. (3) Lit., 'said'. (4) Eccl. IV, 12. (5) Three generations of scholars all living at the same time, v. B.B. Sonc. ed. p. 237, n. 8. (6) One of the three richest men of Jerusalem at the time of the Vespasian siege. V. Giṭ. 56a. (7) A quotation from Prov. XII, 10.

yours are hers'.[1] Her father, on hearing that a great man had come to the town, said, 'I shall go to him; perchance he will invalidate my vow'.[2] When he came to him [R. Akiba] asked, 'Would you have made your vow if you had known that he was a great man?' '[Had he known]' the other replied, 'even one chapter or even one single *halachah* [I would not have made the vow]'. He then said to him, 'I am the man'.[3] The other fell upon his face and kissed his feet and also gave him half of his wealth.[4]

The daughter of R. Akiba acted in a similar way[5] towards Ben Azzai. This is indeed an illustration of the proverb:[6] 'Ewe follows ewe; a daughter's acts are like those of her mother.'

R. Joseph the son of Raba [was] sent [by] his father to the academy under[7] R. Joseph, and they arranged for him [to stay there for] six years. Having been there three years and the eve of the Day of Atonement approaching, he said, 'I would go and see my family'. When his father heard [of his premature arrival] he took up a weapon and went out to meet him. 'You have remembered', he said to him, 'your mistress!'[8] Another version: He said to him, 'You have remembered your dove!'[9] They got involved in a quarrel and neither the one nor the other ate of the last meal before the fast.[10]

MISHNAH. IF A WIFE REBELS[11] AGAINST HER HUSBAND, HER KETHUBAH[12] MAY BE REDUCED BY SEVEN DENARII[13] A WEEK.[14] R. JUDAH SAID: SEVEN TROPAICS.[15] FOR HOW

(1) I.e., it is thanks to her suggestion and encouragement that he and, through him, his disciples, were able to acquire their knowledge. (2) Which a competent authority may under certain conditions do. (3) Lit., 'he'. (4) Lit., 'money'. (5) As her mother had done towards R. Akiba. (6) Lit., 'and this it is that people say'. (7) Lit., 'before'. (8) זונתך, lit., 'your harlot'. *Var. lec.* 'thy mate', 'thy beloved'. (9) יונתך This version is obtained by the slight interchange of a י for a ז (cf. *supra* n. 8). (10) לא איפסיק (rt. פסק, 'to separate', 'sever', 'cease') i.e., did not eat the סעודה המפסקת, the '*meal which*, so to speak, *causes one to cease*' the eating of food until the conclusion of the Day of Atonement after nightfall on the following day. (11) The term is explained in the Gemara *infra*. (12) V. Glos. (13) Plural of *denar*. V. Glos. (14) This is regarded as

LONG MAY THE REDUCTION CONTINUE TO BE MADE? UNTIL [A SUM] CORRESPONDING TO HER KETHUBAH [HAS ACCUMULATED].[1] R. JOSE SAID: REDUCTIONS MAY BE MADE CONTINUALLY UNTIL [SUCH TIME] WHEN, SHOULD AN INHERITANCE FALL TO HER FROM ELSEWHERE, [HER HUSBAND] WILL BE IN A POSITION TO COLLECT FROM HER THE [FULL AMOUNT DUE]. SIMILARLY, IF A HUSBAND REBELS AGAINST HIS WIFE, AN ADDITION OF THREE[2] DENARII A WEEK IS MADE TO HER KETHUBAH. R. JUDAH SAID: THREE TROPAICS.

GEMARA. REBELS in what [respect]?—R. Huna replied: [In respect] of conjugal union .R. Jose the son of R. Ḥanina replied: [In respect] of work.

We learned, SIMILARLY, IF A HUSBAND REBELS AGAINST HIS WIFE. Now according to him who said, '[In respect] of conjugal union' [this ruling] is quite logical and intelligible;[3] but according to him who said, '[In respect] of work', is he[4] [it may be objected] under any obligation [at all to work] for her?[5]—Yes,[6] [rebellion being possible] when he declares 'I will neither sustain nor support [my wife]'. But did not Rab state: If a man says, 'I will neither sustain nor support [my wife]', he must divorce her and give her the *kethubah?*[7]—Is it not necessary to consult him [before ordering him to divorce her]?[8]

An objection was raised: The same[9] [law[10] is applicable to a

the equivalent of the value of the seven kinds of work (*supra* 59*b*) a woman is expected to perform for her husband. (Cf. M.R. Gen. LII). (15) Half a *denar*.

(1) Then she may be divorced, and cannot claim her *kethubah*. (2) Corresponding to the three obligations of a husband, prescribed in Ex. XXI, 10. (3) Since a husband, like a wife, might sometimes decide to rebel in this respect. (4) A husband. (5) Surely not. How then, in this respect, is rebellion applicable to him? (6) I.e., his duty to maintain and support his wife corresponds to her duty to work for him. (7) *Infra* 77*a*, presumably at once, while according to our Mishnah every week AN ADDITION . . . IS MADE TO HER KETHUBAH. (8) Of course it is; since he may quite possibly be persuaded to resume his obligations. It is during this period of negotiation that the weekly additions are made to the *kethubah*. (9) Lit., '(it is) one to me'. (10) Relating to the rebellion of a wife against her husband.

woman] betrothed[1] or married, even to a menstruant, even to a sick woman and even to one who was awaiting the decision of the levir.[2] Now,[3] according to him who said, '[In respect] of conjugal union' it is quite correct to mention the sick, [63b] but according to him who said, '[In respect] of work', is a sick woman [it may be objected] fit to do work?[4]—The fact, however, is that[5] [in respect] of conjugal union all[6] agree that [a wife who refuses] is regarded as a rebellious woman.[7] They[6] differ only in respect of work. One Master is of the opinion that [for a refusal] of work [a wife] is not to be regarded as rebellious and the other Master holds the opinion [that for a refusal] of work also [a wife] is regarded as rebellious.

[To turn to] the main text.[8] If a wife rebels against her husband, her *kethubah* may be reduced by seven *denarii* a week. R. Judah said: Seven *tropaics*. Our Masters, however, took a second vote[9] [and ordained] that an announcement regarding her shall be made on four consecutive Sabbaths and that then the court shall send her [the following warning]: 'Be it known to you that even if your *kethubah* is for a hundred *maneh*[10] you have forfeited it'.[11] The same [law is applicable to a woman] betrothed or married, even to a menstruant, even to a sick woman, and even to one who was awaiting the decision of the levir.[12] Said R. Ḥiyya b. Joseph to Samuel: Is a menstruant capable of conjugal union?[13]—The other

(1) When she declares that she will refuse to marry. (2) *Infra* 64a. שומרת יבם, the widow of a man who died childless, who must either be taken in marriage by her deceased husband's brother or submit to *ḥaliẓah* (v. Glos.) from him. (3) Cur. edd. insert in parentheses: 'This is correct according to him who said "(In respect) of work"; but according to him who said "(In respect) of conjugal union", is a menstruant capable of conjugal union?—He can answer you: One who has bread in his basket is not like one who has none'. Others say, v, *infra* p. 382. (4) Naturally not. How then could she in this respect be guilty of rebellion? (5) Lit., 'but'. (6) R. Huna and R. Jose. (7) And the Baraitha cited deals with conjugal union. (8) Of the quotation, 'the same law etc.' cited *supra 63a ad fin*. (9) Lit., 'they (i.e., their votes) were counted again'. (10) V. Glos. (11) At the end of the four weeks. (12) Cf. Tosef. Keth. V., and *supra* notes 1 and 2. (13) Obviously not; she being forbidden to her husband until the conclusion of the days of her Levitical uncleanness and the seven subsequent 'clean days'.

replied: One who has bread in his basket is not like one who has no bread in his basket.[1]

Rami b. Ḥama stated: The announcement concerning her[2] is made only in the Synagogues and the houses of study. Said Raba: This may be proved by a deduction,[3] it having been taught, 'Four Sabbaths consecutively'.[4] This is decisive.[5]

Rami b. Ḥama further stated: [The warning] is sent to her[6] from the court twice, once before the announcement and once after the announcement.

R. Naḥman b. R. Ḥisda stated in his discourse: The *halachah* is in agreement with our Masters.[7] Raba remarked: This is senseless.[8] Said R. Naḥman b. Isaac to him, 'Wherein lies[9] its senselessness? I, in fact, told it to him, and it was in the name of a great man that I told it to him. And who is it? R. Jose the son of R. Ḥanina!' Whose view then is he[10] following?—The first of the undermentioned.[11] For it was stated: Raba said in the name of R. Shesheth, 'The *halachah* is that she[6] is to be consulted',[12] while R. Huna b. Judah

(1) Cf. *supra* p. 374, n. 9. The woman's declared rebellion and the man's knowledge that even during her cleanness she will remain forbidden, aggravate the pain of the deprivation and entitle him to immediate redress. (2) A woman who rebelled against her husband. (3) From the very text of the ordinance. (4) Emphasis on Sabbaths: days of rest when everybody is free from work and able to attend Synagogue and the houses of study. (5) Lit., 'infer from this'. (6) A woman who rebelled against her husband. (7) Whose ruling is recorded in the Baraitha just cited (v. *supra* p. 381, n. 12 and text). (8) בּוּרְכָּא (cf. בור 'empty', 'uncultivated'), 'a hollow, senseless statement'. The addition of the כ is on the analogy of words like ערכך (Levy). Others derive if from ברך 'cave out' (v. Jast.) (9) Lit., 'what'. (10) Raba who regarded the statement as senseless. (11) Lit., 'like that'. (12) With a view to inducing her to resume her duties; and during the negotiations, contrary to the view of our Masters, only the weekly sum mentioned is deducted from her *kethubah*. [On this interpretation which follows Rashi, Raba decides in accordance with our Mishnah against our Masters. Tosaf. explains differently: R. Naḥman, in stating that the *halachah* is with our Masters, meant to exclude thereby the view of Rami B. Ḥama regarding the two warnings. He maintained that the words of our Masters had to be taken as they stand, with no mention of any warning before the proclamation. This is however rejected by Raba, who declares, on the authority of R. Shesheth, the *halachah* to be that a warning is given prior to the proclamation. The warning will, in this case,

stated in the name of R. Shesheth, 'The *halachah* is that she is not to be consulted'.[1]

What is to be understood by 'a rebellious woman'?[2]—Amemar said: [One] who says, 'I like him[3] but wish to torment him'.[4] If she said, however, 'He is repulsive to me', no pressure is to be brought to bear upon her.[5] Mar Zuṭra ruled: Pressure is to be brought to bear upon her.[6] Such a case once occurred, and Mar Zuṭra exercised pressure upon the woman and [as a result of the reconciliation that ensued] R. Ḥanina of Sura[7] was born from the re-union. This, however,[8] was not [the right thing to do]. [The successful result] was due to the help of providence.[9]

R. Zebid's daughter-in-law rebelled [against her husband][10] and took possession of her silk [cloak].[11] Amemar, Mar Zuṭra and R. Ashi were sitting together[12] and R. Gamda sat beside them; and in the course of the session they laid down the law: [If a wife] rebels she forfeits her worn-out[13] clothing that may still be in existence. Said R. Gamda to them, 'Is it because R. Zebid is a great man that you would flatter him? Surely R. Kahana stated that Raba had only raised this question[14] but had not solved it'. Another version:[15] In the course of their session they decided: [If

be that she will lose the whole of her *kethubah* should she still prove recalcitrant after the proclamation].

(1) [On Tosaf. interpretation. (Previous note) the meaning is she is not warned before but only after the proclamation, agreeing with R. Naḥman b. R. Ḥisda]. (2) Heb. *moredeth*, whose divorce is to be delayed and deductions are in the meantime to be made from her *kethubah*. (3) Her husband. (4) In this case divorce is delayed in the hope that the weekly reductions of her *kethubah* and the persuasions used by the court will induce her to change her attitude. (5) [The husband can, if he wishes, divorce her forthwith without giving her her *kethubah*; v. Rashi and Tosaf. s.v. אבל.] (6) V. *supra* note 4. (7) Sura was the seat of the famous school of Rab, in the South of Babylonia. (8) Though the pressure in this case resulted in the birth of a great man. (9) Lit., 'assistance of heaven'. (10) [She said, 'He is repulsive to me' (Rashi) v. *infra* p. 384, n. 5]. (11) Which she had brought with her when she married, and which was assessed and entered in her *kethubah*. (12) Lit., 'sat'. (13) V. *supra* n. 11. (14) As to the forfeiture of worn-out clothes. (15) Lit., 'there are who say'.

a wife] rebels she does not forfeit her worn-out clothing[1] that may still be in existence. Said R. Gamda to them, [64a] 'Is it because R. Zebid is a great man[2] that you turn the law against him? Surely R. Kahana stated that Raba had only raised the question but had not solved it'. Now that it has not been stated what the law is,[3] [such clothing] is not to be taken away from her if she has already seized them, but if she has not yet seized them they are not to be given to her. We also make her wait twelve months, a [full] year, for her divorce,[4] and during these twelve months she receives no maintenance from her husband.[5]

R. Ṭobi b. Ḳisna stated in the name of Samuel: A certificate of rebellion may be written against a betrothed woman but no such certificate may be written against one who is awaiting the decision of the levir.[6] An objection was raised: The same [law[7] is applicable to a woman] betrothed or married, even to a menstruant, even to a sick woman and even to one who was awaiting the decision of the levir![8]—This is no contradiction. The one[9] refers to the case where the man claimed her;[10] the other[11] to that where she claimed him.[12] For R. Taḥlifa b. Abimi stated in the name of Samuel: If he claimed her[10] he is attended to;[13] if she claimed him she is not attended to.[14] To what case did you explain the statement

(1) V. *supra* p. 383, n. 11. (2) And would humbly accept the ruling. (3) Lit., 'neither thus nor thus'. (4) To afford her an opportunity of changing her attitude. (5) [Rashi and Adreth among others restrict this procedure to a rebellion out of repulsion, a case illustrated in their view by the daughter-in-law of R. Zebid (v. *supra* p. 383, n. 10). Where the rebellion was out of malice she loses her *kethubah* and dowry completely after the warning at the end of four weeks. Maim., on the other hand, applies it to rebellion out of malice. In the case of rebellion out of repulsion, she is granted a divorce immediately because 'she is not a captive to her husband that she should be forced to have intercourse with him', and though she forfeits her *kethubah*, she loses none of her dowry (v. Maim. Yad. *Ishuth* XIV, 8, and commentaries *a.l.*). In his view the case of R. Zebid's daughter-in-law was one of rebellion out of malice]. (6) *Shomereth yabam*, v. Glos. (7) Of. 'a rebellious woman'. (8) *Supra* 63a, notes. (9) The Baraitha cited (v. *supra* n. 8). (10) And she refused him. (11) Samuel's ruling reported by R. Ṭobi. (12) And he refused to marry her. (13) And he is awarded a certificate of rebellion against her. (14) She is not entitled to a certificate of rebellion against him, which would enable her to obtain the weekly additions to her

of Samuel[1] as referring? To the one where she claimed him?[2] [But if so] instead of saying[3] 'A certificate of rebellion may be written *against* a betrothed woman' it should have been said, *'on behalf of* a betrothed woman'![4]—This is no difficulty. Read, 'On behalf of a betrothed woman'.[5]

Wherein does a woman awaiting the decision of the levir differ [from the man] that no [certificate of rebellion should be issued on her behalf]? Obviously because we tell her, 'Go, you are not commanded [to marry]';[6] [but, then,] a betrothed woman also should be told, 'Go, you are not commanded [to marry]'![6] Again should [it be explained to be one] where she comes with the plea saying, 'I wish to have a staff in my hand and a spade for my burial',[7] [this then should] also apply to a woman awaiting the decision of the levir if she comes with such a plea!—[The proper explanation] then [must be this]: Both statements[8] [refer to the case] where the man claimed,[9] and yet there is no difficulty, since one[10] may refer[11] to the performance of *ḥaliẓah* and the other[12] to that of the levirate marriage. For R. Pedath stated in the name of R. Joḥanan: [If the levir] claimed her for the performance of *ḥaliẓah* his request is to be attended to,[13] but if he claimed her for the levirate marriage his request is disregarded.[14] Why [is he] not [attended to when he claims her] for the levirate marriage? Naturally because we tell him, 'Go and marry another woman'; [but then even when he claims her] for the performance of *ḥaliẓah* could we not also tell him, 'Go and marry another woman'? Again should the answer be:

kethubah (v. our Mishnah). The reason is given *infra*. Thus it has been shewn that there is a legal difference between the case where he makes the claim and between the case where she makes the claim.

(1) V. p. 384, n. 11. (2) V. p. 384, n. 12. (3) Lit., 'that'. (4) Against her husband. (5) The emendation involving only the slight change of על to ל. (6) A woman is under no obligation to propagate the race (v. Yeb. 65*b*). (7) I.e., a son who will provide for her while she is alive and arrange for her burial when she dies. (8) Lit., 'these and these', the statement reported in the name of Samuel as well as the other cited from 63*a supra*. (9) And she refused him. (10) The Baraitha cited (v. *supra* p. 384, n. 8). (11) Lit., 'here'. (12) Samuel's ruling reported by R. Ṭobi. (13) V. *supra* p. 384, n. 13. (14) The reason is given anon in the latter Mishnah cited.

[Because] he can plead, 'As she is bound to me[1] no other wife will be given me'. Here also[2] [could he not plead] 'As she is bound to me no other wife will be given to me'?—[The proper explanation] then [is this]: Both statements[3] [deal with one] who claimed her for the levirate marriage, but there is really no difficulty, one[4] being[5] in agreement with the earlier Mishnah while the other is[5] in agreement with the latter Mishnah. For we have learned: The commandment of the levirate marriage must take precedence over that of *ḥaliẓah*.[6] [This was the case] in earlier days when [levirs] had the intention of observing the commandment. Now, however, when their intention is not the fulfilment of the commandment, it has been ruled that the commandment of *ḥaliẓah* takes precedence over that of the levirate marriage.[7]

FOR HOW LONG MAY THE REDUCTION CONTINUE TO BE MADE? etc. What [is meant by] TROPAICS? R. Shesheth replied: [one tropaic is] an *istira*. And how much is an *istira*?—Half a *zuz*.[8] So it was also taught: R. Judah said: Three *tropaics* which [amount to] nine *ma'ah*[8] [the reduction being at the rate of] one *ma'ah* and a half per day.[9]

R. Ḥiyya b. Joseph asked of Samuel: In what respect is he[10] different [from his wife] that he is allowed [a reduction] for the Sabbath,[11] and in what respect is she different [from him] that she is not allowed [an addition] for the Sabbath?[12]—In her case,[13] since it is a reduction that is made, [the seventh *tropaic* the husband gains] does not have the appearance of Sabbath pay. In his case, however,[14] since it is additions that are made, [64*b*] [another addition for the seventh day] would have the appearance of Sabbath pay.

(1) By the marital bond which only *ḥaliẓah* can sever. (2) When he claims her for levirate marriage. (3) V. *supra* p. 385, n. 8. (4) V. *supra* p. 385, n. 10. (5) Lit., 'here'. (6) A woman who refused the levir's claim was, therefore, guilty of rebellion, and a certificate against her was issued to the levir. (7) No certificate of rebellion may, therefore, be issued against a woman who refuses such a marriage. (8) V. Glos. (9) The week consisting of six working days. (10) The husband. (11) Seven *tropaics* corresponding to *all* the days of the week including the Sabbath day. (12) The nine *ma'ah* at the rate of one and a half per day corresponding to six days only (cf. *supra* n. 9). (13) I.e., when the woman rebels. (14) When the man rebels against his wife.

R. Ḥiyya b. Joseph [further] asked of Samuel: What [is the reason for the distinction] between a man who rebels [against his wife] and a woman who rebels [against her husband]?[1] —The other replied, 'Go and learn it from the market of the harlots; who hires whom?'[2] Another explanation: [The manifestation of] his passions is external; hers is internal.

MISHNAH. IF A MAN[3] MAINTAINS HIS WIFE THROUGH A TRUSTEE, HE MUST GIVE HER [EVERY WEEK] NOT LESS THAN TWO ḲABS[4] OF WHEAT OR FOUR ḲABS OF BARLEY. SAID R. JOSE: ONLY R. ISHMAEL WHO LIVED NEAR EDOM[5] GRANTED HER A SUPPLY OF BARLEY.[6] HE MUST ALSO GIVE HER HALF A ḲAB OF PULSE AND HALF A LOG[4] OF OIL; AND A ḲAB OF DRIED FIGS OR A MANEH[4] OF PRESSED FIGS.[7] AND IF HE HAS NO [SUCH FRUIT] HE MUST SUPPLY HER WITH A CORRESPONDING QUANTITY OF OTHER[8] FRUIT. HE MUST ALSO PROVIDE HER WITH A BED, A MATTRESS[9] AND[10] A RUSH MAT. HE MUST ALSO GIVE HER [ONCE A YEAR] A CAP FOR HER HEAD AND A GIRDLE FOR HER LOINS; SHOES [HE MUST GIVE HER] EACH MAJOR FESTIVAL;[11] AND CLOTHING [OF THE VALUE] OF FIFTY ZUZ EVERY YEAR. SHE IS NOT TO BE GIVEN NEW [CLOTHES][12] IN THE SUMMER OR WORN-OUT CLOTHES IN THE WINTER, BUT MUST BE GIVEN THE CLOTHING [OF THE VALUE] OF FIFTY ZUZ DURING THE WINTER, AND SHE CLOTHES HERSELF WITH THEM WHEN THEY ARE WORN-OUT DURING THE SUMMER; AND THE WORN-OUT CLOTHES REMAIN

(1) I.e., why does the former lose only half a *tropaic* a day while the latter loses a full *tropaic* each day? (2) The man naturally hires the woman; which shews that the male feels the deprivation more than the female. His compensation, therefore, must be proportionately higher. (3) A husband who does not live with his wife. (4) V. Glos. (5) In the South of Palestine. (6) This is explained in the Gemara *infra*. (7) דבילה, a cake of pressed figs. The latter is sold by weight; the former by measure. (8) Lit., 'from another place'. (9) מפץ, a mat of bark or reeds. (10) The separate edd. of the Mishnah read, 'And if he has no mattress he gives her a rush mat'. (11) I.e., Passover, Pentecost and Tabernacles. (12) Which provide more warmth than outworn clothes.

HER PROPERTY.[1] HE MUST ALSO GIVE HER [EVERY WEEK] A SILVER MA'AH FOR HER [OTHER] REQUIREMENTS[2] AND SHE IS TO EAT WITH HIM ON THE NIGHT OF EVERY SABBATH.[3] IF HE DOES NOT GIVE HER A SILVER MA'AH FOR HER OTHER REQUIREMENTS, HER HANDIWORK BELONGS TO HER.[4] AND WHAT [IS THE QUANTITY OF WORK THAT] SHE MUST DO FOR HIM?[5] THE WEIGHT OF FIVE SELA'S OF WARP IN JUDAEA, WHICH AMOUNTS TO TEN SELA'S IN GALILEE,[6] OR THE WEIGHT OF TEN SELA'S OF WOOF[7] IN JUDAEA, WHICH AMOUNTS TO TWENTY SELA'S IN GALILEE.[6] IF SHE WAS NURSING [HER CHILD] HER HANDIWORK IS REDUCED AND HER MAINTENANCE IS INCREASED. ALL THIS APPLIES TO THE POOREST IN ISRAEL, BUT IN THE CASE OF A MEMBER OF THE BETTER CLASSES[8] ALL IS FIXED ACCORDING TO THE DIGNITY OF HIS POSITION.

GEMARA. Whose [view is represented in] our Mishnah?[9] [It seems to be] neither that of R. Joḥanan b. Beroḳa nor that of R. Simeon. For we learned: And what must be its[10] size? Food for two meals for each, [the quantity being] the food one eats on weekdays and not on the Sabbath; so R. Meir. R. Judah said: As on the Sabbath and not as on weekdays. And both intended to give the lenient ruling.[11] R. Joḥanan b. Beroḳa said:[12] A loaf that is

(1) Even after her husband had provided her with the new outfit. This is further discussed in the Gemara *infra*. (2) Smaller expenses. (3) I.e., Friday nights, the prescribed time for marital intercourse. (4) This is explained *supra* 59*a* as referring to the surplus. (5) Where he supplies her with the prescribed allowances. (6) The Galilean *sela'* being equal in weight to half of the Judaean *sela'*. (7) It is twice as difficult to web the warp than the woof. Hence a larger output is required of the latter than of the former. (8) מכובד, lit., 'honoured', 'respected'. (9) Which prescribed for a wife a minimum of TWO ḲABS. (10) The loaf of bread required for an *'erub teḥumin*. (v. Glos.). (11) I.e., to reduce the prescribed minimum of the *'erub*. R. Meir used to consume at a weekday meal less bread than at a Sabbath meal at which the richness of the additional Sabbath dishes tempted him to eat more bread. R. Judah, however, consumed on Sabbath, when several satisfying courses are served, less bread than he would on weekdays owing to the smaller number of courses. (12) In determining the quantity of bread required for two meals.

purchased for a *dupondium*[1] [when the cost of wheat is at the rate of] four *se'ah*[1] for a *sela'*.[1] R. Simeon said:[2] Two thirds of a loaf, three of which are made from a *kab*.[3] Half of this [loaf is the size prescribed] for a leprous house,[4] and half of its half[5] renders one's body[6] unfit;[7] and half of the half of its half to be susceptible to Levitical uncleanness.[8] Now, whose [view is that expressed in our Mishnah]?[9] If [it be suggested that it is that of] R. Joḥanan b. Beroḳa [the prescribed TWO ḲABS would only] be [sufficient for] eight [meals],[10] and if [the suggestion is that it is that of] R. Simeon [the TWO ḲABS would] be [sufficient even for] eighteen [meals].[11] —[Our Mishnah may] in fact [represent the view of] R. Joḥanan b. Beroḳa but, as R. Ḥisda said elsewhere,[12] 'Deduct a third of them for the [profit of the] shopkeeper',[13] so here[14] also take a

(1) V. Glos. (2) V. p. 388, n. 12. (3) Of wheat. (4) If a person remained in such a house (v. Lev. XIV, 33ff) for a length of time during which the quantity of bread mentioned can be consumed his clothes become unclean and require ritual washing (cf. Neg. XIII, 9). (5) If it consists of Levitically unclean food. (6) Of the person who ate it. (7) To eat *terumah* before he performs ritual immersion, v. 'Er. 82*b*. (8) [This latter passage does not occur in the Mishnah 'Er. but is introduced in the Gemara on 83*a* as a teaching by a Tanna]. (9) Where a wife is allowed a minimum of TWO ḲABS of wheat for the week. Since she must have at least two meals a day, the two *ḳabs* should provide fourteen (seven times two) meals, besides an additional one or two (respectively, according to the Rabbis or to R. Ḥidka, *infra*) for the Sabbath day. (10) According to R. Joḥanan b. Beroḳa a loaf that contains food for two meals (v. *supra* p. 388, n. 12) is one 'that is purchased for a *dupondium* when the cost of wheat is at the rate of four *se'ah* for a *sela'*. Each *sela'* = four *denarii*, each *denar* = six *ma'ahs* and each *ma'ah* = two *dupondia*. Consequently a *sela'* = ($4 \times 6 \times 2$) forty-eight *dupondia*. A *se'ah* = six *ḳabs* = twelve half-*ḳabs*. Consequently four *se'ahs* = (4×12) forty-eight half-*ḳabs*. For a *dupondium*, therefore, half a *ḳab* of wheat is obtained; and since this quantity supplies two meals each quarter of a *ḳab* provides one meal. The TWO ḲABS consequently provide only eight meals. (11) R. Simeon's minimum is 'two thirds of a loaf, three of which are made of a *ḳab*'. If two thirds represent two meals (v. *supra* p. 388, n. 12) each third represents one meal. If three loaves are made from one *ḳab*, each *ḳab* represents (3×3) nine meals. The TWO ḲABS, therefore, represent (6×9) = eighteen meals. Now since according to our Mishnah a wife must be allowed fourteen meals plus one additional meal or two for the Sabbath (v. *supra* note 9) neither the view of R. Joḥanan b. Beroḳa nor that of R. Simeon can be represented by it. (12) V. 'Er. 82*b*. (13) Though the shopkeeper buys at the rate of four

third[1] and add to them.[2] But [do not the meals] still amount only to twelve?[3]—She eats with him on Friday nights.[4] This is satisfactory according to him who explained[5] [TO EAT in our Mishnah as] actual eating. What, however, can be said according to him who explained 'eating' [to mean] intercourse? Furthermore, [would not her total number of meals still] be only thirteen?[6]—The proper answer is really this:[7] As R. Ḥisda said elsewhere,[8] 'Deduct a half for the [profit of the] shopkeeper,[9] so here[10] also take a half[11] and add to them.[12] (Does not a contradiction arise between the two statements of R. Ḥisda?[13]—There is no contradiction. One statement refers[14] to a place where [the sellers of the wheat] supply also wood[15] while the other refers[14] to a place where they do not supply the wood.)[16] If so[17] [the number of meals] is sixteen.[18] With whose [view then would our Mishnah agree]? With R. Ḥidka who ruled: A man must eat on the Sabbath four meals?[19]—It may be said to

se'ahs for a *sela'* = half a *ḳab* for a *dupondium* (v. *supra* p. 389, n. 10) he sells at a higher price, leaving for himself a profit of one third of the purchase price. For each *dupondium*, therefore, he sells only two thirds of half a *ḳab*. One third of half a *ḳab* or one sixth of a *ḳab* thus provides one meal. Two *ḳabs* therefore, would produce (2 × 6) = twelve meals. (14) In our Mishnah.

(1) The shopkeeper's profit which the husband saves by the supply of wheat instead of shop baked loaves. (2) To the presumed number of eight. Four is a third of twelve which is the number of meals two *ḳabs* provide. (3) Cf. *supra* p. 389, n. 13 *ad fin*. As, however, she requires fourteen plus one or plus two meals for the week (v. *supra* p. 389, n. 9) she is still short of three or four meals. (4) Lit., 'the nights of the Sabbath'. Friday night belongs to the Sabbath, the day always beginning with the sunset of the previous day. (5) *Infra* 65*b*. (6) The twelve mentioned (v. *supra* p. 389, n. 13 *ad fin*.) plus the one she has on Friday night. She is thus still short of a meal or meals (v. *supra* p. 389, n. 9) for the Sabbath day. (7) Lit., 'but'. (8) V. 'Er. 82*b*. (9) Cf. *supra* p. 389, n. 13 *mutatis mutandis*. (10) In our Mishnah. (11) V. *supra* note 1. (12) Cf. *supra* note 2 *mutatis mutandis*. The woman thus obtains her full number of meals. (13) Lit., 'a difficulty of R. Ḥisda against R. Ḥisda'. (14) Lit., 'that'. (15) For the baking of the bread. In such a case the shopkeeper deducts only a third for his profit. (16) And the shopkeeper sells at a profit equal to half of his purchase price to compensate himself for the cost of the wood. (17) That a half is to be added. (18) Each half *ḳab* producing four, instead of the presumed two meals, the two *ḳabs* would produce (4 × 4 =) sixteen meals. (19) Shab. 117*a*. As R. Ḥidka is in the minority, would an anonymous Mishnah

represent even the view of the Rabbis, for one meal is to be reserved for guests and occasional visitors.[1] Now that you have arrived at this position [our Mishnah] may be said to represent even the view of R. Simeon,[2] for according to the Rabbis[3] three meals should be deducted[4] for guests and occasional visitors[5] and according to R. Ḥidka[6] two only are to be deducted for guests and occasional visitors.[7]

SAID R. JOSE: ONLY . . . GRANTED A SUPPLY OF BARLEY etc. Do they eat barley at Edom only and throughout the world none is eaten?—It is this that he meant: ONLY R. ISHMAEL WHO LIVED NEAR EDOM GRANTED A SUPPLY OF BARLEY equal to twice the quantity of wheat, because the Idumean barley was of an inferior quality.

THE MAN MUST ALSO GIVE HER HALF A ḲAB OF PULSE. Wine, however, is not mentioned. This provides support for a view of R. Eleazar. For R. Eleazar stated: [65a] No allowance for wine is made for a woman.[8] And should you point out the Scriptural text, *I will go after my lovers, that give me my bread and my water, my wool and my flax, mine oil and my drink,*[9] [it may be replied that the reference is to] things which a woman desires.[10] And what are they? Jewellery.

R. Judah of Kefar Nabirya[11] (others say: of Kefar Napor[12] Ḥayil) made the following exposition: Whence is it derived that no allowance for wines is made for a woman?—[From Scripture in]

which usually represents the *halachah* agree with the opinion of an individual against that of a majority?

(1) Cf. *supra* p. 364, nn. 5-6. This leaves the woman with fifteen meals, twelve for the six weekdays and three for the Sabbath. (2) According to whom the TWO ḲABS would provide eighteen meals. (3) Who maintain that only three meals are prescribed for the Sabbath. (4) From the eighteen. (5) Cf. *supra* note 1. (6) Whose view is that for the Sabbath four meals are prescribed. (7) Leaving for the woman four Sabbath meals plus twelve for the week days. (8) Alcoholic drinks might lead her to unchastity (v. Rashi). (9) Hos. II, 7. *And my drink*, ושקויי, presumably including wine. (10) שקויי (cf. *supra* n. 9) being derived from the rt. שוק 'to long', 'desire'. (11) MS.M., נבוריא. [Neburja, identified with en-Nebraten in Upper Galilee]. (12) נפור; MS.M. נבור; marg., גבור.

which it is said, *So Hannah rose up after she had eaten*[1] *in Shiloh, and after drinking*,[2] only 'he had drunk' but she did not drink. Now, then, would you also [interpret:] *'She had eaten'*[3] that he[1] did not eat?—What we say is [that the deduction may be made] because the text has deliberately been changed. For consider: It was dealing with her, why did it change [the form]?[4] Consequently it may be deduced that it was 'he who drank' and that she did not drink.

An objection was raised: If [a woman] is accustomed [to drink] she is given [an allowance of drink]!—Where she is accustomed to drink the case is different. For R. Ḥinena b. Kahana stated in the name of Samuel, 'If she was accustomed [to drink] she is given an allowance of one cup; if she was not accustomed [to it] she is given an allowance of two cups'. What does he mean?—Abaye replied: It is this that he means: If she was in the habit [of drinking] two cups in the presence of her husband she is given one cup in his absence; if she is used [to drink] in the presence of her husband only one cup, she is given none at all in his absence. And if you prefer I might say: If she is used [to drink] she is allowed some wine for her puddings[5] only. For R. Abbahu stated in the name of R. Johanan: It happened that when the Sages granted the daughter-in-law of Naḳdimon[6] b. Gorion a weekly[7] allowance of two *se'ahs* of wine for her puddings she[8] said to them, 'May you grant such allowances to your daughters'. A Tanna taught: She was a woman awaiting the decision of the levir.[9] Hence they did not reply Amen after her.[10]

(1) אכלה. This is taken as perfect 3rd pers. fem; according to the accentuation of M.T. it is the inf. cstr. with fem. termination. (2) I Sam. I, 9. E.V., *They had drunk*. M.T. שָׁתֹה, Inf. is taken as the equivalent of שָׁתָה (3rd masc. sing.) 'he (Elkanah) had drunk'. (3) The word אָכְלָה (ibid.) instead of אָכֹל, אָכְלָם or אָכְלוֹ. (4) From the finite to the infinite. (5) ציקי קדירה (v. Jast.). Others, 'as an ingredient or seasoning of a dish' (v. Rashi and Golds.). (6) Or 'Nicodemon', 'Nicodemus', one of the three wealthiest men in Jerusalem in the days of the siege by Vespasian and Titus (v. Giṭ. 58a). (7) Lit., 'from the eve of the Sabbath to the eve of the Sabbath'. (8) In her annoyance at what she considered to be too small an allowance. (9) *Shomereth yabam*. V. Glos. (10) They did not wish their daughters ever to be placed in the position of a widow who is, moreover, subject to the decision of the levir.

A Tanna taught: One cup[1] is becoming to a woman; two are degrading, [and if she has] three she solicits publicly,[2] [but if she has] four she solicits even an ass in the street and cares not. Raba said: This was taught only [in respect of a woman] whose husband is not with her; but if her husband is with her [the objection to her drinks] does not arise.[3] But, surely, [there is the case of] Hannah whose husband was with her![4]—With a guest[5] it is different;[6] for R. Huna stated Whence is it inferred that a guest is forbidden marital union? [From Scripture in] which it is said, *And they rose up in the morning early and worshipped before the Lord, and returned, and came to their house to Ramah; and Elkanah knew Hannah his wife; and the Lord remembered her,*[7] only[8] then[9] but not before.

Ḥoma, Abaye's wife, came to Raba[10] and asked him, 'Grant me an allowance of board', and he granted her the allowance. 'Grant me [she again demanded] an allowance of wine'. 'I know', he said to her, 'that Naḥmani[11] did not drink wine'. 'By the life of the Master [I swear]', she replied, 'that he gave me to drink[12] from horns[13] like this'.[14] As she was shewing it to him her arm was uncovered and a light shone[15] upon the court. Raba rose, went home and solicited R. Ḥisda's daughter.[16] 'Who has been to-day at the court?' enquired R. Ḥisda's daughter. 'Ḥoma the wife of Abaye', he replied. Thereupon she followed her, striking her with the straps[17] of a chest[18] until she chased her out of all Maḥuza.[19] 'You

(1) Of wine. (2) Lit., 'with the mouth'. (3) Lit., 'we have not (anything) against it'. (4) And she nevertheless, as stated *supra*, abstained from drink. (5) אכסנאי (Cf. Gr. ξένος). 'stranger', 'lodger', 'guest'. (6) Hannah at the time was not in her own home but at Shiloh. (7) I Sam. I, 19. (8) Lit., 'yes'. (9) When they had come to their own home. (10) After Abaye's death (cf. Yeb. 64*b*). (11) Lit., 'my comforter', a name by which Abaye was often referred to, v. Giṭ. Sonc. ed. p. 140, n. 6. (12) משקיא לי, MS.M. Cur. edd., משקי ליה 'gave him to drink'. (13) Plural of שופרזא, 'a drinking horn' (v. Jast.) or 'deep cups' (cf. Rashi and Levy). (14) Pointing to her arm. (15) Lit., 'fell'. (16) His own wife. (17) Pl. of קולפא (rt. קלף, 'to peel') 'peeled or scrapped leather', 'a leather strap' (v. Jast.); 'a key' (Rashi). (18) שידא. Aruk, שיראי, 'silk'; בקולפא דשיראי 'with a silken strap'. Rashi: 'With the key of a chest'. (19) V. *supra* p. 319, n. 9.

have', she said to her, 'already killed three [men],[1] and now you come to kill another [man]!'

The wife of R. Joseph the son of Raba came before R. Nehemiah the son of R. Joseph and said to him, 'Grant me an allowance of board', and he granted her. 'Grant me also an allowance of wine' [she demanded], and he granted her. 'I know', he said to her, 'that the people of Maḥuza drink wine'.

The wife of R. Joseph the son of R. Menashya of Dewil[2] came before R. Joseph and said to him, 'Grant me an allowance of board', and he granted her. 'Grant me', she said, 'an allowance of wine', and he granted her. 'Grant me', she said again, 'an allowance of silks'. 'Why silks?' he asked. 'For your sake', she replied, 'and for the sake of your friend and for the sake of your associates'.[3]

HE MUST ALSO PROVIDE HER WITH A BED, A MATTRESS etc. Why[4] should he give her A MATTRESS AND A RUSH MAT?[5]—R. Papa replied: [This is done only] in a place where it is the practice to girth the bed with ropes,[6] which would hurt[7] her.

Our Rabbis taught: She[8] is not given[9] a cushion and a bolster. In the name of R. Nathan it was stated: She is given a cushion and a bolster. How is this to be understood? If it is a case where she is used to it,[10] what [it may be objected] is the reason of the first Tanna?[11] And if it is a case where she is not used to it,[10] what [it may be asked] is the reason of R. Nathan?[12]—[The statement was]

(1) Ḥoma had already thrice married and each of her husbands had died (v. Yeb. 64*b*). (2) [Perhaps Debeile in the neighbourhood of Hille (near Sura). There is also a Dabil in Armenia, v. Funk, *Monumenta Talmudica*, p. 291]. (3) To enable her to keep up her social standing in the company of her deceased husband's friends and associates. (4) Since beds were usually furnished with a skin girth (v. Rashi). (5) Which are much less comfortable for lying on than a skin girth. R. Tam (Tosaf. s.v. מפין *a.l.*) deletes MATTRESS since on account of its softness it is useful even where the bed is furnished with a skin spread. (6) Instead of the skin girth. (7) דמבגר (Af. of בגר) lit., 'which produce a roughness' (v. Jast.). According to Rashi בגר is to be taken in the sense of 'age'. The ropes cause her pain and 'age her' prematurely. (8) The wife spoken of in our Mishnah. (9) By her husband. (10) To sleep on a cushion and a bolster. (11) Who ruled that she is not to be allowed these comforts. (12) Why should her husband be expected to provide for her more comforts than she habitually requires.

necessary only in the case where it[1] was his habit but not her habit.[2] The first Tanna[3] is of the opinion that [her husband] may say to her, 'When I go away[4] I take them and when I return I bring them back with me',[5] while R. Nathan holds the opinion that she can tell him, 'It might sometimes happen [that you will return] at twilight[6] when you will be unable to bring them[7] and so you will take mine[8] and make me sleep on the ground'.[9]

HE MUST ALSO GIVE HER [ONCE A YEAR] A CAP. Said R. Papa to Abaye: [65*b*] This Tanna[10] [expects a person to be] 'stripped naked and to wear shoes'![11] 'The Tanna,' the other replied, 'was dealing[12] with a mountainous region where one cannot possibly manage with less than three pairs of shoes [a year],[13] and indirectly he informed us that these should be given to her on the occasion of a major festival so that she might derive joy from them.

AND CLOTHING [OF THE VALUE] OF FIFTY ZUZ. Abaye said: Fifty small *zuz*.[14] Whence is this deduced?— From the statement:[15] ALL THIS APPLIES TO THE POOREST IN ISRAEL, BUT IN THE CASE OF A MEMBER OF THE BETTER CLASSES ALL IS FIXED ACCORDING TO THE DIGNITY OF HIS POSITION. Now,

(1) V. p. 394, n. 10. (2) [Yet on the principle that 'she rises with him' *supra* 61*a*, she is entitled to them when she is with him (Rashi)]. (3) V. p. 394, n. 11. (4) From you. (5) Since she is not in the habit of using them she does not require them in his absence. (6) On Sabbath eve. (7) The carrying of objects is forbidden on the Sabbath, the prohibition beginning at twilight on the Friday evening. (8) The other bed clothes that he had given her or that she herself had purchased. (V. however, next note). (9) Hence R. Nathan's ruling that a husband must in all cases provide his wife with cushion and bolster. [*Var. lec.* (v. Tosaf.) omit 'so you will take mine'. On that reading the woman will argue that she would be made to sleep on the ground, even in his presence, when she is entitled to all the comfort to which he is accustomed, v. *supra* note 2]. (10) Who imposes upon a husband the duty of giving his wife shoes three times a year and clothing only once a year. (11) Proverb. By the time the woman will receive her second or third pair of shoes her clothes will be worn to tatters, and yet she would be wearing new shoes; a toilet more ludicrous than one uniformly shabby and worn out. (12) Lit., 'stands'. (13) Though clothes may conveniently last for the same period. (14) Provincial *zuz* (Rashi). A provinical, or country *zuz* was equal in value to an eighth of the town, or Tyrian *zuz*. (15) Lit., 'since it was taught'.

should one imagine [that the reference is to] fifty real *zuz*,[1] whence [it could be objected] would a poor man obtain fifty *zuz?* Consequently it must be concluded [that the meaning is] fifty small *zuz*.

SHE IS NOT TO BE GIVEN NEW etc. Our Rabbis taught: Any surplus of food[2] belongs to the husband, while any surplus of worn out clothes belongs to the woman. [You said:] 'Any surplus of worn out clothes belongs to the woman'; of what use are they to her?—Reḥaba replied: For putting on during the days of her menstruation so that she may not [by the constant wearing[3] of the same clothes] become repulsive to her husband. Abaye stated: We have a tradition that the surplus of the worn out clothes of a widow[4] belongs to her husband's heirs. For the reason in the former case[5] is that she shall not become repulsive to her husband[6] but in this case[7] let her be ever so repulsive.

HE MUST ALSO GIVE HER [EVERY WEEK] A SILVER MA'AH etc. What [is meant by] SHE IS TO EAT?—R. Naḥman replied: Actual eating. R. Ashi replied: Intercourse. We have learned: SHE IS TO EAT WITH HIM ON THE NIGHT OF EVERY SABBATH. Now, according to him[8] who said, '[actual] eating' it is quite correct to use the expression SHE IS TO EAT. According to him,[9] however, who said, 'intercourse', why [it may be asked] was the expression SHE IS TO EAT used?[10]—It is a euphemism,[11] as it is written in Scripture, *She*[12] *eateth, and wipeth her mouth, and saith: 'I have done no wickedness'*.[13]

An objection was raised: R. Simeon b. Gamaliel said, 'She is to eat with him on the night of the Sabbath and on the Sabbath [day]'. Now, according to him[14] who said, '[actual] eating', it is correct to state, 'and on the Sabbath [day]'.[15] According to him,[16] however, who said, 'intercourse', is there any intercourse on the

(1) I.e., of the Tyrian standard (cf. p. 395, n. 14). (2) I.e., if the woman did not consume all her allowance of food prescribed in our Mishnah. (3) During her clean and unclean periods. (4) Whose allowance for clothes is made by her deceased husband's heirs. (5) Lit., 'there'. (6) Lit., 'in his presence'. (7) Lit., 'here'. (8) R. Naḥman. (9) R. Ashi. (10) Cf. BaḤ. *a.l.* (11) לישנא מעליא, lit., 'a perfect or appropriate expression'. MS.M.adds, נקט, 'he took up (used)'. (12) The adulterous woman. (13) Prov. XXX, 20. (14) R. Naḥman. (15) Since one has to eat in the day time also. (16) R. Ashi.

Sabbath day? Did not R. Huna state, 'The Israelites are holy and do not have intercourse in the day-time'?[1]—But, surely, Raba stated: It is permitted in a dark room.[2]

IF SHE WAS NURSING [HER CHILD]. R. 'Ulla the Great made at the Prince's[3] door the following exposition: Although it was said:[4] 'A man is under no obligation to maintain his sons and daughters when they are minors', he must maintain them while they are very young.[5] How long?[6]—Until the age of six; in accordance [with the view of] R. Assi, for R. Assi stated: A child of the age of six is exempt[7] by the *'erub*[8] of his mother. Whence [is this[9] derived]?—From the statement: IF SHE WAS NURSING [HER CHILD] HER HANDIWORK IS REDUCED AND HER MAINTENANCE IS INCREASED. What can be the reason?[10] Surely because he[11] must eat together with her. But is it not possible [that the reason[10] is] because she is[12] ailing?—If that were the case it should have been stated, 'If she was ailing', why then [was it stated], IF SHE WAS NURSING?[13] But is it not possible that it was this that we were taught:[14] That nursing mothers are commonly ailing?[15]

It was stated: What is the addition[16] that he makes for her?[17]—R. Joshua b. Levi said: She is given an additional allowance for wine, because wine is beneficial for lactation.

(1) Shab. 86*a*, Nid. 17*a*. (2) V. Ibid. (3) The Exilarch. (4) Lit., 'that they (*sc.* the Rabbis) said'. (5) Lit., 'the small of the small'. (6) Must he maintain them. (7) יוצא, i.e., he does not require one specially prepared for himself (v. Golds.). Rashi takes יוצא in the literal sense, 'he goes out', i.e., should his father place an *'erub* in one direction and his mother in the opposite direction he would be allowed to move only in the direction his mother had chosen. In any case it follows that a child of the age of six is entirely attached to and dependent upon his mother and, consequently, just as a man must provide for his wife so must he provide for the child who is entirely dependent upon her. (8) V. Glos. (9) That a father is at all liable to maintain his young children. (10) For the increase of the maintenance. (11) The child. (12) During lactation. (13) The conclusion, therefore, must be that she was not ailing. (14) By the use of the expression, NURSING, and not 'ailing'. (15) As this is quite possible no positive proof is available that it is a father's legal duty to maintain his young children. (16) For the increase of the maintenance. (17) So BaḤ. Cur. edd. omit.

KETHUBOTH

CHAPTER VI

MISHNAH. A WIFE'S FIND AND HER HANDIWORK BELONG TO HER HUSBAND. AND [OF] HER INHERITANCE[1] HE HAS THE USUFRUCT DURING HER LIFETIME.[2] [ANY COMPENSATION FOR] AN INDIGNITY OR BLEMISH [THAT MAY HAVE BEEN INFLICTED UPON] HER BELONGS TO HER. R. JUDAH B. BATHYRA RULED: WHEN IN PRIVACY[3] SHE RECEIVES TWO-THIRDS [OF THE COMPENSATION] WHILE HE[4] RECEIVES ONE-THIRD, BUT WHEN IN PUBLIC[5] HE RECEIVES TWO-THIRDS[6] AND SHE RECEIVES ONE-THIRD. HIS SHARE IS TO BE GIVEN TO HIM FORTHWITH, BUT WITH HERS LAND IS TO BE BOUGHT AND HE[4] ENJOYS THE USUFRUCT.[7]

GEMARA. What does he[8] teach us? This surely was already learnt: A father has authority over his daughter in respect of her betrothal [whether it was effected] by money, by deed or by intercourse; he is entitled to anything she finds and to her handiwork; [he has the right] of invalidating her vows, and he receives her letter of divorce; but he has no usufruct during her lifetime. When she marries, the husband surpasses him [in his rights] in that he has usufruct during her

(1) Which she inherited from a relative (Rashi's first interpretation supported by R. Tam., Tosaf. s.v. וירושתה *a.l.*). (2) The capital, however, remains hers. (3) I.e., if the indignity was imposed in the absence of onlookers or the blemish inflicted upon a concealed part of her body. (4) Her husband. (5) I.e., if people witnessed the indignity or if the blemish was inflicted on a part of the body that is exposed. (6) Since he not only shares her indignity and degradation but, in addition, must also put up with a woman who has become disfigured. V. Rashi. (7) As is the case with all property that comes into a wife's possession after her marriage. The capital remains hers and after his death or on divorce she recovers also the right of usufruct. (8) The author of our Mishnah.

lifetime![1]—He[2] regarded this[3] as necessary [on account of the law relating to] INDIGNITY OR BLEMISH [THAT MAY HAVE BEEN INFLICTED UPON] HER, [which is the subject of] a dispute between R. Judah b. Bathyra and the Rabbis.[4]

A tanna recited in the presence of Raba: A wife's find belongs to herself; but R. Akiba ruled: [It belongs] to her husband. The other[5] said to him: Now that [in respect of the] surplus[6] [66*a*] which is her handiwork[7] R. Akiba ruled [that it belongs] to herself, how much more so her find? For we learned: [If a woman said to her husband,] '*Ḳonam,* if I do aught for your mouth', he need not invalidate her vow;[8] R. Akiba, however, said: He must invalidate it, since she might do more work than is due to him![9]—Reverse then: A wife's find belongs to her husband, but R. Akiba ruled [that it belonged] to herself. But surely, when Rabin came[10] he stated in the name of R. Joḥanan: In respect of a surplus[11] obtained through no undue exertion all[12] agree that [it belongs to the] husband, and they only differ in respect of a surplus[11] obtained through undue exertion; the first Tanna being of the opinion [that even this belongs] to her husband while R. Akiba maintains [that it belongs] to herself![13]—R. Papa replied: A find is like a surplus

(1) V. *supra* 46*b*, notes, from which it follows that a husband is entitled to all his wife's possessions enumerated in our Mishnah. Why then were the same rulings repeated here? (2) The author of our Mishnah. (3) Our Mishnah. (4) And could not have been inferred from the statement quoted. (5) Raba. (6) Of a woman's work above the amount required for her maintenance. (7) And should belong to her husband. A husband is entitled to his wife's handiwork (v. our Mishnah) in return for the maintenance he provides for her (v. *supra* 58*b*). (8) Since a wife's work, and even its surplus (v. *supra* note 6), belongs to her husband, (v. *supra* note 7) she has no right to dispose of it without his consent. Her vow, therefore, is null and void and no invalidation is required. (9) And of this surplus being her own property, she may well dispose. (For further notes v. *supra* 59*a*). How then, Raba argued, could the opinion be entertained that, according to R. Akiba, a wife's find (to which she has a greater claim than to the surplus mentioned) should belong to her husband? (10) From Palestine to Babylon. (11) V. *supra* note 6. (12) Lit., 'all the world', *sc.* R. Akiba and the Rabbis. (13) A find should naturally be regarded as a 'surplus obtained through no undue exertion', about which there is no difference of opinion. How then could it be said that the find of a wife is a point in dispute?

gained through undue exertion,[1] [concerning which there is] a difference of opinion between R. Akiba and the Rabbis.

R. Papa raised the question: What is the law where she performed for him two [kinds of work] simultaneously?[2] Rabina raised the question: What is the ruling where she did three or four [kinds of work][3] simultaneously?—These must remain undecided.[4]

[ANY COMPENSATION FOR] INDIGNITY OR BLEMISH [THAT MAY HAVE BEEN INFLICTED UPON] HER. Raba son of R. Ḥanan demurred:[5] Now then,[6] if a man insulted his fellow's mare would he also have to pay him [compensation for the] indignity? But is a horse then susceptible to insult?[7]—This, however, [is the objection:] If a man spat on his fellow's garment would he[8] also have to pay him [compensation for this] indignity? And should you say that [the ruling] is really so,[9] surely [it can be retorted] we have learned: If a man spat so that the spittle fell upon another person, or uncovered the head of a woman, or removed a cloak from a person he must pay four hundred *zuz*;[10] and R. Papa explained: This has been taught [to apply] only [where it touched] him[11] but if it touched his garment only [the offender] is exempt![12] —[An insult] to his garment involves no indignity to him, [but an insult to] his wife does involve an indignity to him.[13]

(1) Most finds are not easily obtained, and before one finds anything valuable among the deposits of the sea, for instance, many hours and days might have to be spent. (2) Acting as watchman, for instance, and spinning at the same time. (3) While doing the former (v. *supra* n. 2) she was also teaching, for instance, a lesson and hatching eggs. Are such performances regarded as ordinary, or undue exertion? (4) *Teku*, v. Glos. (5) Against R. Judah b. Bathyra (v. our Mishnah). (6) If a man is to receive compensation for an indignity or injury which he himself has not sustained. (7) Surely not. Raba's objection does not, consequently, arise. (8) Cf. *supra* n. 6. (9) That he must pay compensation. (10) Cf. B.Ḳ. 90*a*. (11) The body of the offended party. (12) Which proves conclusively that for such an offence, since it was not committed on one's person, no compensation is paid. Why then should a husband receive compensation for his wife's sufferings which he himself has not experienced? (13) Read ליה (MS.M.). Cur. edd., read לה, and the rendering (rather unsatisfactory) would be as follows: His garment feels no shame but his wife feels the indignity.

Said Rabina to R. Ashi: Now then,[1] if a man insulted a poor man of a good family where all the members of the family are involved in the indignity, must he also pay [compensation for] indignity to all the members of the family?[2]—The other replied: There[3] it is not their own persons [that are insulted]. Here, however, one's wife is [like] one's own body.

MISHNAH. IF A MAN UNDERTOOK TO GIVE A FIXED SUM OF MONEY TO HIS SON-IN-LAW AND HIS SON-IN-LAW DIED,[4] HE[5] MAY, THE SAGES RULED, SAY[6] 'I WAS WILLING TO GIVE [THE MENTIONED SUM] TO YOUR BROTHER BUT I AM UNWILLING TO GIVE IT TO YOU'.[7]

IF A WOMAN UNDERTOOK TO BRING HER HUSBAND[8] ONE THOUSAND DENARII HE MUST ASSIGN TO HER[9] A CORRESPONDING SUM OF FIFTEEN MANEH.[10] AS A CORRESPONDING SUM FOR APPRAISED GOODS,[11] HOWEVER, HE ASSIGNS[9] ONE FIFTH LESS.[12] [IF A HUSBAND IS REQUESTED TO ENTER IN HIS WIFE'S KETHUBAH:] 'GOODS ASSESSED AT ONE MANEH',

(1) If indirect insult also entitles one to compensation. (2) Certainly not. Why then should the husband receive compensation for indignity to his wife? (3) The case of indirect insult to the family. (4) Childless; so that his widow should now be married to, or perform *halizah* (v. Glos.) with his surviving brother (v. Deut. XXV, 5ff) who, in the case of his marriage with the widow, is entitled to the deceased brother's estate (v. Yeb. 40*a*). (5) The father-in-law. (6) To the surviving brother who by virtue of his right to the estate of the deceased now claims also the sum his father-in-law had promised him. (7) And the brother must, nevertheless, either submit to *halizah* from the widow or marry her. (8) On marriage. (9) As her *kethubah* (v. Glos.). (10) V. Glos. He must, in return for the profits he will be able to derive from his trading with her money, add fifty per cent to the amount his wife brought him. A *maneh* = a hundred *denarii* (or *zuz*), and fifteen *maneh* = fifteen hundred *denarii*. (11) I.e., if she brought to him, on marriage, goods instead of cash. This kind of dowry is designated *Shum* (appraisement). (12) Than the appraised value. This refers to an appraisement made during the wedding festivities when the tendency is to over-assess whatever goods the bride brings to her husband. [According to the T.J. a fifth is allowed for the wear and tear of the goods, since her husband is held responsible for them].

AND THESE ARE IN FACT WORTH A MANEH,[1] HE CAN HAVE [A CLAIM FOR] ONE MANEH ONLY.[2] [OTHERWISE,[3] IF HE IS REQUESTED TO ENTER IN THE KETHUBAH:] 'GOODS ASSESSED AT A MANEH', HIS WIFE MUST GIVE HIM [GOODS OF THE ASSESSED VALUE[3] OF] THIRTY-ONE SELA'S AND A DENAR,[4] AND IF 'AT FOUR HUNDRED [ZUZ]', SHE MUST GIVE [HIM GOODS VALUED[3] AT] FIVE HUNDRED [ZUZ.][5] WHATEVER [66b] A BRIDEGROOM ASSIGNS [TO HIS WIFE IN HER KETHUBAH] HE ASSIGNS AT ONE FIFTH LESS [THAN THE APPRAISED VALUE].[3]

GEMARA. Our Rabbis taught: There was no need to state that where the first[6] was a scholar and the second an *'am ha-'arez* [the father-in-law] can say, 'I WAS WILLING TO GIVE [THE MENTIONED SUM] TO YOUR BROTHER BUT I AM UNWILLING TO GIVE IT TO YOU', but even where the first was *'am ha-'arez* and the second a scholar he may also say so.

IF A WOMAN UNDERTOOK TO BRING TO HER HUSBAND ONE THOUSAND DENARII etc. Are not these[7] the same as the case in the first clause?[8]—He taught [first concerning a] large assessment[9] and then he taught also about a smaller assessment;[10] he

(1) I.e., if the assessment was made prior to the wedding festivities. (Cf. p. 401, n. 12). (2) He cannot claim twenty-five per cent more than the *maneh* as in the case where the valuation was made during the wedding festivities (v. *supra* note 1). (3) I.e., if the valuation was made during the wedding festivities (cf. *supra* p. 401, n. 12). (4) V. Glos. A *sela'* = four *denarii*, thirty-one *sela's* and one *denar* = (31 × 4 + 1) 125 *denarii*. A *maneh*, or a hundred *denarii*, is a fifth less than one hundred and twenty-five *denarii*. (5) [This passage is difficult, and the interpretations of it are many and varied, cf. e.g., Tosaf. s.v. שום. The explanation given follows Rashi. R. Hai Gaon, on the basis of the T.J. (v. *supra* p. 401, n. 12) explains: If she promised to bring him a dowry (*shum*) of property worth a *maneh*, which does not wear out, and is thus always actually worth a *maneh*, she need not add a fifth to it, v. *Shittah Mekubbezeth;* v. p. 406, in the case of a bar of gold]. (6) Brother who died. (7) The latter portions of our Mishnah, which contain various instances of deductions of a fifth. (So Rashi. For another interpretation v. Tosaf. s.v. תנא). (8) AS A CORRESPONDING SUM . . . HE ASSIGNS ONE FIFTH LESS, which includes all the other instances. (9) ONE THOUSAND DENARII to which the ruling AS A CORRESPONDING SUM . . .

taught about his assessment[1] and he also taught about her assessment.[2]

MISHNAH. IF A WOMAN UNDERTOOK TO BRING TO HER HUSBAND[3] READY MONEY, EVERY SELA'[4] OF HERS COUNTS[5] AS SIX DENARII.[6] THE BRIDEGROOM MUST UNDERTAKE [TO GIVE HIS WIFE][7] TEN DENARII FOR HER [PERFUME][8] BASKET IN RESPECT OF EACH MANEH.[9] R. SIMEON B. GAMALIEL SAID: IN ALL MATTERS THE LOCAL USAGE SHALL BE FOLLOWED.

GEMARA. This,[10] surely, is exactly [the same ruling as] 'He must assign to her a corresponding sum of fifteen *maneh*'.[11]—He taught first about a major transaction[12] and then taught about a minor transaction.[13] And [both rulings were] necessary. For had that of the major transaction only been taught it might have been assumed [that it applied to this only] because the profit [it brings in] is large but not to a minor transaction the profit from which is

HE ASSIGNS ONE FIFTH LESS refers. (10) GOODS ASSESSED AT A MANEH . . . THIRTY-ONE SELA'S AND A DENAR. Both cases were necessary, since some might assume that with a larger sum over-estimation is more likely while others might assume that over-estimation is more likely to take place in the case of a smaller sum.

(1) WHATEVER A BRIDEGROOM ASSIGNS . . . ONE FIFTH LESS, referring to a valuation made by *him* of goods she *had already* brought to him *before* the *kethubah* had been written. (2) IF AT FOUR HUNDRED [ZUZ] SHE MUST GIVE etc., the last three words implying that the *kethubah* had already been written and SHE MUST GIVE the required amount of goods which is naturally valued by her (or her relations) to correspond after due deduction with the amount entered in the *kethubah*. (3) On marriage. (4) Which is worth four *denarii*. (5) In respect of the corresponding amount to be entered in her *kethubah*. (6) I.e., fifty per cent is added to it as in the case of ready money mentioned in the previous Mishnah. The difference between the two cases will be explained in the Gemara *infra*. (7) Whether daily, weekly or more rarely has not been stated. (8) According to the explanation of the Gemara. (9) Which she brings on marriage. (10) The ruling in the first clause of our Mishnah. (11) V. previous Mishnah. In that case he adds fifty per cent, and so he does in this case also. Why then should the same ruling be recorded twice? (12) A thousand *denarii* in the previous Mishnah, *supra* 66*a*. (13) EVERY SELA' etc. in the Mishnah of ours.

small; [hence it was] necessary [to state the latter]. And had we been informed of that of the minor transaction only it might have been said [to apply to this only] because the expenses and responsibility[1] are small but not to a large transaction where the expenses and responsibility are great; [hence it was] necessary [to state the former].

THE BRIDEGROOM MUST UNDERTAKE [TO GIVE HIS WIFE] TEN DENARII FOR HER BASKET. What is meant by BASKET? R. Ashi replied: The perfume basket. R. Ashi further stated: This ruling applies to Jerusalem[2] only.

R. Ashi enquired: [Is the prescribed perfume allowance[3] made] in respect of each *maneh* valued or each *maneh* for which [obligation has been] accepted?[4] [And even][5] if you could find [some reason] for stating: ['In respect of each] *maneh* for which [obligation has been] accepted'[4] [the question arises: Is the allowance to be made only on] the first day or every day? Should you find [some ground] for deciding: Every day, [the question still remains whether this applies only to the] first week or to every week. Should you find [some authority] for stating: Every week, [it may be asked whether this applies only to the] first month or to every month. And should you find [some argument] for saying: Every month, [it may still be questioned whether this is applicable only to the] first year or to every year.—All this remains undecided.[6]

Rab Judah related in the name of Rab: It once happened that the daughter of Naḳdimon b. Gorion[7] was granted by the Sages[8] an allowance of four hundred gold coins in respect of her perfume basket for that particular day, and she[9] said to them, 'May you grant such allowances for your own daughters!' and they answered after her: Amen.[10]

(1) זיונא (v. Rashi). Jast., 'management, expenses and risks of business'; עיסקא זוטא דזוטר זיונא, 'a small capital the management of which is easy'. (2) Where the women were in the habit of indulging in the use of perfumes. (3) Ten *denarii* in respect of each *maneh* (v. our Mishnah). (4) By the husband in the *kethubah*. The latter (v. previous Mishnah) amount to one fifth less than the valuation. (5) V. Tosaf. s.v. ואם. (6) *Teḳu*, v. Glos. (7) Cf. *supra* 65*a* (p. 392, n. 6). (8) To whom, when her husband died, she applied for an order for an allowance out of her husband's estate. (9) In her discontent with the amount. (10) V. *supra* p. 392, n. 10 and text.

Our Rabbis taught: It once happened that R. Joḥanan b. Zakkai left Jerusalem riding upon an ass, while his disciples followed him, and he saw a girl picking barley grains in the dung of Arab cattle. As soon as she saw him she wrapped herself with her hair and stood before him. 'Master', she said to him, 'feed me'. 'My daughter', he asked her, 'who are you?' 'I am', she replied, 'the daughter of Naḳdimon b. Gorion'. 'My daughter', he said to her, 'what has become[1] of the wealth of your father's house?' 'Master', she answered him, 'is there not a proverb current in Jerusalem: "The salt[2] of money is diminution?"'[3] (Others read: Benevolence).[4] 'And where [the Master asked] is the wealth of your father-in-law's house?' 'The one', she replied, 'came and destroyed the other'.[5] 'Do you remember, Master', she said to him, 'when you signed my *kethubah?*' 'I remember', he said to his disciples, 'that when I signed the *kethubah* of this [unfortunate woman], I read therein "A million gold *denarii* from her father's house" besides [the amount] from her father-in-law's house'.[6] Thereupon R. Joḥanan b. Zakkai wept and said: 'How happy are Israel;[7] when they do the will of the Omnipresent no nation nor any language-speaking group has any power over them; but when they do not do the will of the Omnipresent he delivers them into the hands of a low people, and not only in the hands of a low people but into the power of the beasts of a low people'.

Did not Naḳdimon b. Gorion, however, practice charity? Surely it was taught: It was said of Naḳdimon b. Gorion that, when he walked from his house to the house of study, woollen clothes were [67*a*] spread beneath his feet and the poor followed behind him and rolled them up![8]—If you wish I might reply: He did it for his own glorification.[9] And if you prefer I might reply: He did not

(1) Lit., 'where did it go'. (2) I.e., the preservative, the safeguard. (3) חֶסֶר, i.e., spending it in the exercise of charitable and benevolent deeds. As the members of her family were not charitable they lost their money. (4) חֶסֶד (v. *supra* n. 3) interchange of ד with ר. (5) The two were mixed up and when the one was lost the other disappeared with it. (6) The addition made to her *kethubah* by the bridegroom. (7) Read with MS.M., אשריהם. Cur. edd., אשריכם, 'happy are you'. (8) I.e., taking the stuff away with them. (9) Such gifts are not regarded as proper charity.

act as he should have done,[1] as people say, 'In accordance with the camel is the burden'.[2]

It was taught: R. Eleazar the son of R. Zadok said, 'May I [not] behold the consolation [of Zion] if I have not seen her[3] picking barley grains among the horses' hoofs at Acco. [On seeing her plight] I applied to her this Scriptural text: *If thou know not, O thou fairest among women, go thy way forth by the footsteps of the flock and feed thy kids;*[4] read not *thy kids*[5] but thy 'bodies'.[6]

R. Shaman b. Abba stated in the name of R. Joḥanan: If a wife brought to her husband[7] [a bar of] gold, it is to be assessed and [entered in her *kethubah*] according to its actual value.[8]

An objection was raised: '[Broken pieces of] gold are like vessels'.[9] Does not this imply[10] 'like silver vessels' which wear out?[11]—No, 'like gold vessels' which do not wear out. If so, [the expression] should have been 'like vessels [made] thereof'! And, furthermore, it was taught: [A bar of] gold is like vessels; gold *denarii* are like ready money.[12] R. Simeon b. Gamaliel said: Where the usage is not to change them[13] they are valued and are [to be entered in the *kethubah*] at the rate of their actual value.[14] Now, to what is R. Simeon b. Gamaliel referring? If it be suggested [that he refers] to the final clause,[15] the inference [it may be pointed out would be] that the first Tanna maintains his opinion[16] even when the usage is not to change them, but, surely, [it may be objected]

(1) He did not give in accordance with his means. (2) The richer and the greater the man the more is expected of him. (3) The daughter of Naḳdimon b. Gorion. (4) Cant. I., 8. (5) גדיותיך. (6) גויותיך, involving the change of ו for ד. (7) On marriage. (8) No addition of fifty per cent (as in the case of ready money) and no subtraction of a fifth (as in the case of goods) are made. (9) כלים, the term is explained anon. (10) Lit., 'what, not?' (11) And consequently deteriorate in value. How then could R. Joḥanan maintain that a bar of gold is to be entered in the *kethubah* for its full value without reducing the fifth prescribed for goods? (12) Since they can be used as currency. An addition of fifty per cent in their case must, therefore, be entered in the *kethubah*. (13) In the ordinary course of trade, i.e., where they are not taken as currency. (14) And no addition (as in the case of cash) is made. Tosef. Keth. VI. (15) Gold *denarii* etc. (16) That an addition of fifty per cent is to be made (v. *supra* n. 12).

they can not be used as currency![1] It must consequently be assumed[2] [that he[3] referred] to the first clause and that it is this that was meant: [A bar of] gold is like vessels; and what [is meant by] vessels? silver vessels;[4] and R. Simeon b. Gamaliel said: It is like gold *denarii* where the usage is not to change them![5]—No;[6] he[3] may still refer to the final clause but [it is a case where] with difficulty they can be used as currency; and the principles on which they differ is this: One Master[7] holds the view that since they can be used as currency we allow her the increase[8] and the other Master[3] is of the opinion that since they can be used as currency only with difficulty, she is not to have the increase.[9]

If you prefer I might reply: All the statement[10] is that of R. Simeon b. Gamaliel, but a clause therein is missing, and the proper reading is as follows: [A bar of] gold is like vessels;[11] gold *denarii* are like ready money. This is the case only where it is the usage to change them,[12] but where it is the usage not to change them[13] they are to be valued and entered in the *kethubah* at the rate of their actual value; so R. Simeon b. Gamaliel for R. Simeon b. Gamaliel holds the view that where it is the usage not to change them they are to be valued and [entered in the *kethubah*] at the rate of their actual value. But [the difficulty] nevertheless [remains that the expression] should have been, 'like vessels [made] thereof'!—This is indeed a difficulty. And if you prefer I might reply: We are here[10] dealing with a case of broken pieces of gold.[14] R. Ashi said: [We deal here[10] with] gold leaf.[15]

(1) Lit., 'do not go out'. Why then should they be treated as ready money? (2) Lit., 'but not'. (3) R. Simeon b. Gamaliel. (4) And a reduction of a fifth is therefore to be made. (5) Cf. *supra* p. 406, n. 13. Would then R. Johanan accept the opinion of R. Simeon b. Gamaliel against that of the anonymous first Tanna? (6) R. Simeon b. Gamaliel does not refer to the first clause. (7) The first Tanna. (8) Of fifty per cent, as in the case of regular currency. (9) In the case of bar gold, however, it is generally agreed, as R. Johanan ruled, that it is to be entered into the *kethubah* at the rate of its actual value. (10) The Baraitha cited. (11) I.e., gold wares. (12) Cf. *supra* p. 406, n. 13 *mutatis mutandis*. (13) V. *supra* p. 406, n. 13. (14) Which wear away in use. Such are indeed to be treated in the same way as silver ware (as has been suggested *supra*), their price being entered in the *kethubah* after a deduction of one fifth had

R. Jannai stated: The spices of Antioch[1] are[2] like ready money.[3]

R. Samuel b. Naḥmani stated in the name of R. Joḥanan:[4] A woman[5] is entitled to seize Arabian camels in settlement of her *kethubah*.[6]

R. Papi stated: A woman[5] may seize clothes[7] manufactured at Be Mikse[8] for her *kethubah*.[9]

R. Papi further stated: A woman[5] may seize sacks made at Rodya[10] and the ropes of *Ḳamḥunya*[11] for her *kethubah*.

Raba stated: At first I said: A woman[5] is entitled to seize money bags[12] of Maḥuza[13] for her *kethubah*.[9] What was [my] reason? Because [women] relied upon them.[9] When I observed, however, that they[14] took them and went out with them into the market[15] and as soon as a plot of land came their way they purchased it with this money I formed the opinion that they rely[16] only upon land.[17]

been made. R. Joḥanan, however, who rules the entry of their actual value deals with the case of large bars which do not perceptibly wear away, and whose full value must consequently appear in the *kethubah*. (15) מַמְלָא var. מַלְלָא (v. Rashi). Tosaf., 'gold ore'; Golds., 'gold dust'. Cf. p. 407, n. 14 *mutatis mutandis*.

(1) Or Antiochene, the capital of Syria on the Orontes, founded by Seleucus Nicator. [Antioch was a trading centre for spices (v. Krauss, *T.A.*, I, p. 690)]. (2) In respect of the amount to be entered in a *kethubah*. (3) Fifty per cent is to be added to the amount the wife brings in on marriage. These spices were so famous that they could always be sold and thus easily turned into cash. (4) *Var. lec.*, 'Jonathan'. (MS.M. and Rosh). (5) A widow who advances the claim for her *kethubah* against her deceased husband's estate (v. Tosaf. s.v. גמלים). (6) Though these are movable objects, they are, owing to the ready sale they command, deemed to have been pledged for the *kethubah*. פרנא, 'settlement', 'endowment' (cf. Jast.). Rashi's interpretation, 'the profit of a third', is rejected by Tosaf. l.c. [Frankel *MGWJ*, 1861, p. 118 derives the term from the Gk. φερνή, the outfit which the bride has to bring with her]. (7) V. Rashi; 'sheets' (Jast.). (8) [A frontier town between Babylon and Arabia (Obermeyer, p. 334)]. (9) Cf. *supra* n. 6 *mutatis mutandis*. (10) Not identified. (11) [In the neighbourhood of Sura, *op. cit.* p. 296]. (12) I.e., the sums of money which they contain (Rashi). (13) A famous commercial town (v. *supra* p. 319, n. 9). (14) Widows or divorced women who seized them for their *kethubah*. (15) So MS.M. Cur. edd., omit the last three words. (16) As a guarantee for their *kethubah*. (17) Hence they should not be allowed to seize Maḥuza bags.

MISHNAH. IF A MAN GAVE HIS DAUGHTER IN MARRIAGE WITHOUT SPECIFYING ANY CONDITIONS, HE MUST GIVE HER NOT LESS THAN FIFTY ZUZ. IF THE [BRIDEGROOM] AGREED TO TAKE HER IN NAKED HE[1] MAY NOT SAY, 'WHEN I HAVE TAKEN HER INTO MY HOUSE I SHALL CLOTHE HER WITH CLOTHES OF MY OWN', BUT HE MUST PROVIDE HER WITH CLOTHING WHILE SHE IS STILL IN HER FATHER'S HOUSE. SIMILARLY IF AN ORPHAN IS GIVEN IN MARRIAGE[2] SHE MUST BE GIVEN NOT LESS THAN FIFTY ZUZ. IF [CHARITY] FUNDS ARE AVAILABLE[3] SHE IS TO BE FITTED OUT IN ACCORDANCE WITH THE DIGNITY OF HER POSITION.

GEMARA. Abaye stated: By FIFTY ZUZ small coins[4] [were meant]. Whence is this statement inferred?—From the statement in the final clause: IF [CHARITY] FUNDS ARE AVAILABLE SHE IS FITTED OUT IN ACCORDANCE WITH THE DIGNITY OF HER POSITION [concerning which], when it was asked, 'What was meant by FUNDS'.[5] Reḥaba explained: Charity funds.[6] Now if we should imagine that by FIFTY ZUZ the actual[7] [coins were meant], how much [it may be asked] ought we to give her even IF CHARITY FUNDS ARE AVAILABLE! Consequently it must be inferred that by FIFTY ZUZ small coins [were meant].

Our Rabbis taught: If an orphan boy and an orphan girl applied for maintenance,[8] the girl orphan is to be maintained first and the boy orphan afterwards,[9] because it is not unusual for a man to go begging[10] but it is unusual for a woman to do so.[11] If an orphan boy and an orphan girl [67*b*] applied for a marriage grant[12] the girl orphan is to be enabled to marry first and the boy orphan is married afterwards, because the shame of a woman is greater than that of a man.[13]

(1) Lit., 'the husband'. (2) By the guardians of the poor. (3) Lit., 'there is in the purse'. (4) V. *supra* 65*b*. (5) Lit., 'bag'. (6) Lit., 'bag of charity'. (7) I.e., the Tyrian *zuz* (v. *supra* l.c.). (8) Lit., 'who came to be maintained', out of the poor funds. (9) If the funds permit. (10) Lit., 'his way is to go about the doors'. (11) Lit., 'to go about'. (12) Out of the charity funds. Lit., 'came to be married'. (13) Tosef. Keth. VI.

Our Rabbis taught: If an orphan applied for assistance to marry,[1] a house must be rented for him, a bed must be prepared for him and [he must also be supplied with] all [household] objects [required for] his use, and then he is given a wife in marriage, for it is said in Scripture, *Sufficient for his need in that which he wanteth:*[2] *'sufficient for his need'*, refers to the house; *'in that which wanteth'*, refers to a bed and a table; *'he'*[3] refers to a wife, for so it is said in Scripture, *I will make him*[3] *a help meet unto him.*[4]

Our Rabbis taught: *'Sufficient for his need'* [implies] you are commanded to maintain him, but you are not commanded to make him rich; *'in that which he wanteth'* [includes] even a horse to ride upon and a slave to run before him. It was related about Hillel the Elder that he bought[5] for a certain poor man who was of a good family a horse to ride upon and a slave to run before him. On one occasion he could not find a slave to run before him, so he himself ran before him for three miles.

Our Rabbis taught: It once happened that the people of Upper Galilee bought for a poor member of a good family of Sepphoris[6] a pound of meat every day.[7] 'A pound of meat'! What is the greatness in this?—R. Huna replied: [It was] a pound of fowl's meat.[8] And if you prefer I might say: [They purchased] ordinary meat for a pound[9] [of money].[10] R. Ashi replied: The place was[11] a small village[12] and every day a beast had to be spoiled for his sake.[13]

A certain man once applied to[14] R. Nehemiah [for maintenance]. 'What do your meals consist of', [the Rabbi] asked him. 'Of fat meat and old wine', the other replied. 'Will you consent [the

(1) V. p. 409, n. 12. (2) Deut. XV, 8. (3) לו; lit., *'unto him'*. (4) Gen. II, 18, referring to a wife. Tosef. Keth. VI. (5) Alfasi: he hired. (6) A town on one of the Upper Galilean mountains. It was called Sepphoris צפורי (v. Meg. 6*a*) 'because it was perched on the top of a mountain like a bird', צפור. At one time it was the capital of Galilee and is identified (l.c.) with Ḳitron (Judges I, 30). V. Klein, S. מאמרים, 54ff. (7) Tosef. Pe'ah. IV. (8) Which was very expensive. (9) ליטרא, λίτρα, is both a weight, the Roman libra, and a measure of capacity. (10) The meat was so expensive. (11) Lit., 'there'. (12) Where there are no buyers. (13) All the meat that remained after his one pound had been taken off had to be thrown away for lack of buyers and consumers. (14) Lit., 'came before'.

Rabbi asked him] to live[1] with me on lentils?' [The other consented,] lived with him on lentils and died. 'Alas', [the Rabbi] said, 'for this man whom Nehemiah has killed.' On the contrary, he should [have said] 'Alas for Nehemiah who killed this man'!—[The fact], however, [is that the man himself was to blame, for] he should not have cultivated his luxurious habits to such an extent.

A man once applied to[2] Raba [for maintenance]. 'What do your meals consist of?' he asked him. 'Of fat chicken and old wine', the other replied. 'Did you not consider', [the Rabbi] asked him, 'the burden of the community?' 'Do I', the other replied, 'eat of theirs? I eat [the food] of the All-Merciful; for we learned: *The eyes of all wait for Thee, and Thou givest them their food in due season,*[3] this, since it is not said, 'in *their* season' but '*in* his[4] *season*', teaches that the Holy One, blessed be He, provides for every individual his food in accordance with his own habits'.[5] Meanwhile there arrived Raba's sister, who had not seen him for thirteen years, and brought him a fat chicken and old wine. 'What a remarkable incident!'[6] [Raba][7] exclaimed; [and then] he said to him, 'I apologize[8] to you, come and eat'.

Our Rabbis taught: If a man has no means and does not wish to be maintained [out of the poor funds] he should be granted [the sum he requires] as a loan and then it can be presented to him as a gift; so R. Meir. The Sages, however, said: It is given to him as a gift and then it is granted to him as a loan. ('As a gift'? He, surely, refuses to[9] take [gifts]! Raba replied: It is offered to him in the first instance[10] as a gift.)

If he has the means but does not want to maintain himself, [at his own expense],[11] he is given [what he needs] as a gift, and then he is made to repay it. (If 'he is made to repay it' he would, surely,

(1) שתגלגל (rt. גלל, Pilp.), lit., 'roll', i.e., 'to put up with the inconvenience'. (2) Lit., 'came before'. (3) Ps. CXLV, 15. בעתו lit., 'in *his* season'. (4) V. *supra* n. 3. (5) V. Rashi. (6) מאי דקמא, lit., 'what is that before me?' (7) So Rashi. Ar. reads, מאי דקאמא (= קָא אֲמָא 'which I said') i.e., the applicant remarked, 'This is just what I have said'. (Cf. Jast.). (8) Lit., 'I humble myself'. Rashi: 'I spoke too much'. The rt. ענה, עני, may bear either meaning. (9) Lit., 'not'. (10) Lit., 'to open'. (11) And thus leads a life of penury.

not take again!—R. Papa replied: [Repayment is claimed] after his death.) R. Simeon said: If he has the means and does not want to maintain himself [at his own expense], no one need feel any concern about him. If he has no means and does not wish to be maintained [out of the poor funds] he is told, 'Bring a pledge and you will receive [a loan]' in order to raise thereby his [drooping] spirit.[1]

Our Rabbis taught: *To lend*[2] refers to a man who has no means and is unwilling to receive his maintenance [from the poor funds] to whom [the allowance] must be given as a loan and then presented to him as a gift. *Thou shalt lend him*[3] refers to a man who has the means and does not wish to maintain himself [at his own expense] to whom [the allowance] is given as a gift and repayment is claimed from his [estate] after his death, so R. Judah. The Sages, however, said: If he has the means and does not wish to maintain himself [at his own expense] no one need feel any concern about him. To what, however, is the text *Thou shalt lend him*[4] to be applied? The Torah employs ordinary phraseology.[5]

Mar 'Uḳba had a poor man in his neighbourhood into whose door-socket he used to throw four *zuz* every day. Once[6] [the poor man] thought: 'I will go and see who does me this kindness'. On that day [it happened] that Mar 'Uḳba was late at[7] the house of study and his wife[8] was coming home with him. As soon as [the poor man] saw them moving the door he went out after them, but they fled from him and ran into a furnace from which the fire had just been swept. Mar 'Uḳba's feet were burning and his wife said to him: Raise your feet and put them on mine. As he was upset,[9]

(1) Lit., 'that his mind shall be elated or cheered'. By this offer he is made to feel that he is not treated as a pauper and he consents, therefore, ultimately to take the sum as a loan without a pledge. (2) העבט, E.V., *surely*, Deut. XV, 8. (3) תעביטנו, ibid. (4) I.e., the repetition of the verb, in the Infinitive and Imperfect (v. *supra* nn. 2 and 3), from which R. Judah derived his ruling. (5) Lit., 'spoke in the language of men', who are in the habit of repeating their words. Hence no inference may be drawn from the repetition in the text cited. (6) Lit., 'one day'. (7) So MS.M., בבי Cur. edd. לבי. (8) Who, owing to the late hour, went to meet him. (9) Lit., 'his mind weakened'. He feared that he was not providentially protected from the heat of the furnace because he was not as worthy of divine protection as his wife.

she said to him, 'I am usually at home[1] and my benefactions are direct'.[2] And what [was the reason for] all that?[3]—Because Mar Zuṭra b. Ṭobiah said in the name of Rab (others state: R. Huna[4] b. Bizna said in the name of R. Simeon the Pious; and others again state: R. Joḥanan said in the name of R. Simeon b. Yoḥai): Better had a man thrown himself into a fiery furnace than publicly put his neighbour to shame. Whence do we derive this? From [the action of] Tamar; for it is written in Scripture, *When she was brought forth*,[5] [*she sent to her father-in-law*].[6]

Mar 'Uḳba had a poor man in his neighbourhood to whom he regularly sent four hundred *zuz* on the Eve of every Day of Atonement. On one occasion[7] he sent them through his son who came back and said to him, 'He does not need [your help]'. 'What have you seen?' [his father] asked. 'I saw [the son replied] that they were spraying old wine before him'.[8] 'Is he so delicate?' [the father] said, and, doubling the amount, he sent it back to him.

When he[9] was about to die[10] he requested, 'Bring me my charity accounts'. Finding that seven thousand of Sijan[11] [gold] *denarii* were entered therein he exclaimed, 'The provisions are scanty and the road is long', and he forthwith[12] distributed half of his wealth. But how could he do such a thing?[13] Has not R. Elai stated: It was ordained at Usha that if a man wishes to spend liberally he should not spend more than a fifth?[14]—This applies only during a

(1) So that the poor had easy access to her. (2) Lit., 'near'. She gave them gifts in kind and they could forthwith derive benefit from them. He, however, was not approachable at all times and the alms he gave to the poor were not in kind but in money which had first to be spent before the poor could derive any benefit from it. His benefits, therefore, were indirect. (3) Why did they make such an effort to escape from the attention of the poor man? (4) Var., Ḥana (v. B.M. 59a). (5) To be burned (Gen. XXXVIII, 24). (6) Ibid., 25. She chose to be burned rather than publicly put her father-in-law to shame. It was only through Judah's own confession (ibid. 26) after he received her private message (ibid. 25) that she was saved. (7) Lit., 'day'. (8) קמיה, MS.M. Cur. edd., 'to him'. (9) Mar 'Uḳba'. (10) Lit., 'when his soul was (about to) come to its rest'. (11) The name of a Persian town in the district of Shiraz, v. Fleischer to Levy's *Wörterbuch* I, p. 560. (12) Lit., 'he arose'. (13) Distributing half his wealth. (14) V. *supra* 50a.

man's lifetime, since he might thereby be impoverished[1] but after death[2] this does not matter.

R. Abba used to bind money in his scarf,[3] sling it on his back, and place himself at the disposal of the poor.[4] He cast his eye, however, sideways [as a precaution] against rogues.[5]

R. Ḥanina had a poor man to whom he regularly sent four *zuz* on the Eve of every Sabbath. One day he sent that sum through his wife who came back and told him [that the man was in] no need of it. 'What [R. Ḥanina asked her] did you see?' [She replied:] I heard that he was asked, 'On what will you dine; [68a] on the silver [coloured] cloths[6] or on the gold [coloured] ones?[7]' 'It is in view of such cases' [R. Ḥanina] remarked, 'that R. Eleazar said: Come let us be grateful to the rogues for were it not for them we[8] would have been sinning every day, for it is said in Scripture, *And he cry unto the Lord against thee, and it be sin unto thee.*[9] Furthermore, R. Ḥiyya b. Rab of Difti[10] taught: R. Joshua b. Ḳorḥa said, Any one who shuts his eye against charity is like one who worships idols, for here[11] it is written, *Beware that there be not a base*[12] *thought in thy heart* etc.[*and thine eye will be evil against thy poor brother*][13] and there[14] it is written, *Certain base*[12] *fellows are gone out,*[15] as there[14] [the crime is that of] idolatry, so here also [the crime is like that of] idolatry'.[16]

(1) Lit., 'go down from his wealth'. (2) I.e., when one is on the point of dying as was the case with Mar 'Uḳba. (3) סודרא, 'scarf' or 'turban', a cloth placed over, or wound round the head, hanging down loosely upon the arms and shoulders. (4) Who undid the binding and shared the money among themselves. (5) He would nevertheless spare the poor the feelings of shame. (6) I.e., *white* linen (Rashi). (7) Silk cloths dyed. (Rashi *a.l.*; cf. also Rashi on Ezek. XVI, 16). טְלֵי or טַלֵּי may be compared with τύλη, cushion', 'pillow' (v. Levy); 'will you recline at dinner', he was asked, 'on the linen, or silken pillows?' The noun is also rendered, 'table outfit', the expressions, 'silver' and 'gold' being taken literally; 'Will you dine with the silver outfit (i.e., with the outfit used in connection with silver vessels) or with the gold outfit?' (Jast.). (8) Who do not always respond to every appeal for charity. (9) Deut. XV, 9. (10) Dibtha, below the Tigris. (11) In connection with the duty of assisting the poor. (12) בליעל. (13) Deut. XV, 9. (14) Concerning idolatry. (15) Deut. XIII, 14, the expression *base*, בליעל (v. *supra* n. 12), occuring in both cases. (16) It is only thanks to the rogues who claim charity under false pretences that we have an excuse for not responding to every appeal.

Our Rabbis taught: If a man pretends to have a blind eye, a swollen belly or a shrunken leg,[1] he will not pass out from this world before actually coming into such a condition. If a man accepts charity and is not in need of it his end [will be that] he will not pass out of the world before he comes to such a condition.

We learned elsewhere: 'He[2] may not be compelled to sell his house or his articles of service'.[3] May he not indeed?[4] Was it not taught: If he was in the habit of using gold articles he shall now use silver ones, if [he was using] silver ones let him now use copper ones?[5]—R. Zebid replied. This is no difficulty. The one[6] refers to the bed and table; the other to cups and dishes. What difference is there in the case of the cups and dishes that they are not [to be sold]? Obviously because he can say, '[The inferior quality] is repulsive to me', [but then, in respect of] a bed and table also, he might say [the cheaper article] is unacceptable to me!—Raba the son of Rabbah replied: [This[6] refers] to a silver strigil.[7] R. Papa replied: There is no difficulty; one[8] [refers to a man] before he came under the obligation of repayment,[9] and the other refers to a man[10] after he had come under the obligation of repayment.[11]

(1) V. Rashi; 'a hump' (Jast.). שוק may be rendered 'leg', 'foreleg' or 'shoulder'. The rt. קפח in *Piel* is to be taken according to Rashi's interpretation in the sense of 'binding', 'forcing', or 'outraging'. It is taken by Jast. as denom. of קָפֶּה 'to make high and arched shoulders', 'to cause or pretend to be hump-backed'. (2) One who owns less than two hundred *zuz* and wishes to take a share in the poor man's gifts. The possessor of two hundred *zuz* is forbidden to participate in the poor man's gifts. (3) Though the proceeds of such a sale would raise the man's capital above the two hundred *zuz* limit. Pe'ah VIII, 8. (4) Lit., 'and not?' (5) Which proves that a poor man is expected to sell his costlier goods before he is allowed to take alms. Why then was it stated here that he is not compelled to sell 'his article of service'? (6) The last mentioned Baraitha which orders the sale of 'articles of service'. (7) There can be no hardship in using instead one made of a cheaper metal. (8) The Mishnah from Pe'ah, according to which one is not compelled to sell his articles of service. (9) I.e., if he possessed less than two hundred *zuz* and applied for assistance before receiving any help under false pretences. As there is no claim against him he is not to be compelled to sell his article of service. (10) Who, being in possession of two hundred *zuz*, accepted alms under false pretences. (11) I.e., after it had been discovered that he did not belong to the poor

MISHNAH. IF AN ORPHAN WAS GIVEN IN MARRIAGE BY HER MOTHER OR HER BROTHERS [EVEN IF] WITH HER CONSENT[1] AND THEY ASSIGNED[2] TO HER A HUNDRED, OR FIFTY ZUZ,[3] SHE MAY, WHEN SHE ATTAINS HER MAJORITY,[4] RECOVER FROM THEM THE AMOUNT THAT WAS DUE TO HER.[5] R. JUDAH RULED: IF A MAN HAD GIVEN HIS FIRST DAUGHTER IN MARRIAGE, THE SECOND[6] MUST RECEIVE AS MUCH AS THE [FATHER] HAD GIVEN TO THE FIRST. THE SAGES, HOWEVER, SAID: SOMETIMES A MAN IS POOR AND BECOMES RICH OR RICH AND BECOMES POOR.[7] THE ESTATE SHOULD RATHER BE VALUED AND SHE[8] BE GIVEN [THE SHARE THAT IS HER DUE].

GEMARA. Samuel stated: In respect of the marriage outfit[9] the assessment[10] is to be determined by [the disposition of] the father.[11]

An objection was raised: 'The daughters are to be maintained and provided for[12] out of the estate of their father. In what manner? It is not to be said, "Had her father been alive he would have given her such and such a sum" but the estate is valued and she is given [her due share]'. Does not ['provided for' refer to] the marriage[13] outfit?[14]—R. Naḥman b. Isaac replied: No; [it refers to] her own maintenance.[15] But, surely, it was stated: 'Are to be maintained and

classes and was ordered by the court to refund all sums he had received unlawfully. In such a case, if he is unable to meet the claim otherwise, he is compelled to sell his costly articles and to content himself with the use of cheaper ones.

(1) And much more so if without her consent. (2) Lit., 'wrote'. (3) As her share in the estate of her deceased father. (4) Though she had accepted the amount during her minority. V. *supra* note 1. (5) Viz., a tenth of the estate. (6) Who marries after his death. (7) The amount he gives to his first daughter is, therefore, no criterion for his second. (8) The second daughter. (9) Of an orphan. (10) I.e., the amount to be given to the orphan on marriage out of her father's estate. (11) She is to receive a bigger or a smaller amount in accordance with her father's reputation for generosity or niggardliness. (12) This is explained anon. (13) Lit., ['the *parnasah* of her husband', *parnasah* being a technical term to denote the estate set aside for the dowry of the orphaned daughter. Frankel *MGWJ* 1861, p. 119 connects it with the Gk. φερνή cf. *supra* p. 408, n. 6]. (14) A contradiction against the ruling of Samuel. (15) Before marriage, while she is still with her brothers.

provided for'; does not one [of the expressions][1] refer to the marriage[2] outfit and the other to her own maintenance?[3]—No; the one as well as the other refers to her own maintenance,[3] and yet there is no real difficulty, for one of the expressions[1] refers[4] to food and drink and the other[4] to clothing and bedding.

We learned: THE SAGES, HOWEVER, SAID, SOMETIMES A MAN IS POOR AND BECOMES RICH OR RICH AND BECOMES POOR. THE ESTATE SHOULD RATHER BE VALUED AND SHE BE GIVEN [THE SHARE THAT IS HER DUE]. Now what is meant by POOR and RICH? If it be suggested that POOR means poor in material possessions, and RICH means rich in such possessions, the inference [should consequently be] that the first Tanna holds the opinion that even when a man was rich and became poor she is given as much as before; but, surely, [it may be objected] he has none [to give]. Must it not then [be concluded that] POOR means poor in mind[5] and RICH means rich in mind,[6] and yet it was stated, THE ESTATE SHOULD RATHER BE VALUED AND SHE BE GIVEN [THE SHARE THAT IS HER DUE], from which it clearly follows that we are not guided by the assumed disposition [of her father], and this presents an objection against Samuel![7] He[8] holds the same view as R. Judah. For we learned, R. JUDAH RULED: IF A MAN HAD GIVEN HIS FIRST DAUGHTER IN MARRIAGE, THE SECOND SHOULD RECEIVE AS MUCH AS THE [FATHER] HAD GIVEN TO THE FIRST. [Why], then, [did he not] say, 'The *halachah* is in agreement with R. Judah'?[9]—If he had said, 'The *halachah* is in agreement with R. Judah', it might have been assumed [to apply] only [where her father had actually] given her[10] in marriage, since [in that case] he has revealed his disposition, but not [to a case where] he had not given her[10] in marriage,[11] hence he[8] taught us[12]

(1) 'To be (*a*) maintained and (*b*) provided for'. (2) V. p. 416, n. 13. (3) V. p. 416, n. 15. (4) Lit., 'that'. (5) Niggardly; having the mind or disposition of a poor man. (6) Generous. (7) Who stated that the amount is determined by what is known of the disposition of her father. How, it is asked, could Samuel differ from a Mishnah? (8) Samuel. (9) Which would have been a shorter statement and would have included the name of its author also. (10) HIS FIRST DAUGHTER. (11) Since his disposition had not been revealed. (12) By his specific ruling.

that R. Judah's reason is that we are guided by our assumption [as to what was her father's disposition], there being no difference whether he had already given her[1] in marriage or whether he had not given her in marriage; the only object he[2] had[3] in mentioning [the case where a father] gave her[1] in marriage was to let you know the extent of the ruling[4] of the Rabbis[5] [who maintain] that although he had already given her[1] in marriage and had thereby revealed his disposition, we are nevertheless not to be guided by the assumption [as to what may have been the father's disposition].

Said Raba to R. Ḥisda: In our discourse we stated[6] in your name, 'The *halachah* is in agreement with R. Judah'. The other replied: May it be the will [of Providence] that you may report in your discourses all such beautiful sayings in my name. But could Raba, however, have made such a statement?[7] Surely, it was taught: Rabbi said, A daughter who is maintained by her brothers is to receive[8] a tenth of [her father's] estate;[9] and Raba stated that the law is in agreement with Rabbi![10]—This is no difficulty. The former[11] [is a case] where we have formed some opinion about him;[12] the latter[13] is one where we have not formed any opinion about him.[14] This explanation may also be supported by a process of reasoning. For R. Adda b. Ahaba stated: It once happened that Rabbi gave her[15] a twelfth of [her father's] estate. Are not the two statements contradictory?[16] Consequently[17] it must be inferred

(1) HIS FIRST DAUGHTER. (2) The compiler of our Mishnah. (3) Lit., 'and that'. (4) Lit., 'power'. (5) The Sages. (6) Or: Shall we state etc. (cf. Rashi, s.v. דרשינן, Beẓah 28*a*). (7) That the amount to be given to an orphan on marriage is determined, as R. Judah ruled, by the disposition of her father. (8) On marriage. (9) Ned. 39*b*. (10) I.e., that the amount the daughter is to receive is a legally prescribed proportion. How then could he have said that the *halachah* was in agreement with R. Judah (v. *supra* note 7)? (11) Lit., 'that', the statement that the *halachah* follows R. Judah (v. *supra* note 7). (12) The orphan's father. Knowing his disposition it is possible to determine accordingly what amount his daughter shall be allowed on marriage. (13) Lit., 'that', the law that the proportion she is to receive is always a tenth of the estate. (14) If he was unknown to the court and no one is able to supply reliable information on the point. (15) An orphan on marriage. (16) According to the former statement Rabbi allowed only one tenth while according to the latter he allowed a twelfth. (17) To reconcile the contradictory statements.

that the one[1] [refers to a father of whom] some opinion had been formed while the other[2] [refers to one of whom] we have formed no opinion. This is conclusive proof.

[To turn to] the main text.[3] Rabbi said, A daughter who is maintained by her brothers is to receive a tenth of [her father's] estate. They[4] said to Rabbi: According to your statement, if a man had ten daughters and one son the son should receive no share at all on account of[5] the daughters? He replied: What I mean is this: The first[6] [daughter] receives a tenth of the estate, the second [receives a tenth] of what [the first] had left, and the third [gets a tenth] of what [the second] had left, and then they divide again [all that they had received] into equal shares. [68*b*] But did not each one receive what was hers?[7]—It is this that was meant: If all of them wish[8] to marry at the same time they are to receive equal shares.[9] This provides support for [the opinion] of R. Mattena; for R. Mattena has said: If all of them wish to marry at the same time they are to receive one tenth. 'One tenth'! Can you imagine [such a ruling]?[10] The meaning must consequently be that[11] they are to receive their tenths at the same time.[12]

(1) The case where a twelfth had been allowed. (2) Cf. *supra* p. 418, n. 13. (3) A citation from which has been discussed *supra*. (4) The scholars at the college. (5) Lit., 'in the place of'. (6) It is at present assumed, 'the first to marry'. (7) Of course she did. Each one is entitled to a tenth of the value of the estate as it stood at the time she married. Why then should there be a new division in equal shares, which would deprive those who married earlier from what was their due? (8) Lit., 'came'. (9) After each in turn had received a tenth of the value of the estate as it stood at the moment her share was allowed to her. Since subsequently they will all pool their shares it does not matter which of them is given her share first; the only object of the allotment of the successive shares is to determine what part of the estate is to be left for the son. If there were three daughters for instance, the division would proceed as follows: One daughter would be allowed one tenth of the estate; the other $\frac{1}{10} \times \frac{9}{10}$; and the third $\frac{1}{10} \times \frac{81}{100}$. The son would, therefore, receive $1-(\frac{1}{10}-\frac{9}{100}-\frac{81}{1000}) = \frac{729}{1000}$, and each daughter would ultimately get a $\frac{271}{3 \times 1000}$ of the entire estate. (10) Certainly not. If every daughter is entitled to a tenth of the estate, several daughters, surely, should receive more than one tenth. (11) Lit., 'but'. (12) The reading being עישור כאחד instead of עישור אחד ('one tenth'). Cf. *supra* n. 9.

Our Rabbis taught: The daughters,[1] whether they had attained their adolescence before they married or whether they married before they had attained their adolescence, lose their right to maintenance[2] but not to their allowance for marriage outfit; so Rabbi. R. Simeon b. Eleazar said: If they also attained their adolescence, they lose the right to their marriage outfit.[3] How should they proceed?[4]—They hire for themselves husbands[5] and exact their outfit allowance. R. Naḥman stated: Huna told me, The law is in agreement with Rabbi.

Raba raised an objection against R. Naḥman: IF AN ORPHAN WAS GIVEN IN MARRIAGE BY HER MOTHER OR HER BROTHERS [EVEN IF] WITH HER CONSENT, AND THEY ASSIGNED TO HER A HUNDRED, OR FIFTY ZUZ, SHE MAY, WHEN SHE ATTAINS HER MAJORITY, RECOVER FROM THEM THE AMOUNT THAT WAS DUE TO HER. The reason then[6] is because she was a minor;[7] had she, however, been older[8] her right[9] would have been surrendered![10]—This is no difficulty; the one[11] is a case where she protested;[12] the other,[13] where she did not protest.[14] This expla-

(1) Of a man who left an estate and is survived by sons. (2) Because the terms of a *kethubah* provide for the maintenance of daughters only until adolesence (v. Glos. s.v. *bogereth*) or marriage, whichever is the earlier. (3) The tenth of the estate to which, as stated *supra*, a daughter is entitled. In his opinion it is only one who is a minor, *nacarah* (v. Glos.), that receives such tenth. Once she has reached her adolescence, or married as a *nacarah*, without claiming at the time her full marriage outfit, she loses her claim to it. (4) If they had not been married early and are desirous of securing their tenth before losing it through age. (5) [They hire men to declare that they would marry them (Strashun)]. (6) Why she may recover the amount prescribed for her marriage outfit. (7) At the time she married. (8) Even if she was still a *nacarah* at the time of marriage. (9) To her full claim. (10) And she would not be entitled to the balance of her marriage outfit. This anonymous Mishnah then is in agreement with the view of R. Simeon b. Eleazar. Now, since the *halachah* is usually in agreement with the anonymous Mishnah how could R. Naḥman maintain that the *halachah* is in agreement with Rabbi? (11) Rabbi's statement that she does not lose her marriage outfit. (12) When less than her due was assigned to her. (13) Our Mishnah. (14) Hence it is only a minor, who cannot surrender her rights, that may recover the balance when she becomes of age. One, however, who has passed her minority (cf. *supra* note 8) may well surrender her right. Her silence is regarded as consent.

nation may also be supported by a process of reasoning. For otherwise[1] there would arise a contradiction between two statements of Rabbi.[2] For it was taught, 'Rabbi said, A daughter who is maintained by her brothers is to receive a tenth of [her father's] estate', [which implies] only when[3] she is maintained[4] but not[5] when she is not maintained.[6] Must it not in consequence be concluded that one [statement deals with one] who protested and the other [with one] who did not protest. This proves it.

Rabina said to Raba: R. Adda b. Ahaba told us in your name, If she attained her adolescence she need not lodge a protest;[7] if she married she need not lodge a protest;[7] but if she attained her adolescence and was also married it is necessary for her to lodge a protest.[8] But could Raba have made such a statement? Surely, Raba pointed out an objection against R. Naḥman [from the Mishnah of] AN ORPHAN, and the other replied that 'the one is a case where she protested, the other where she did not protest'![9] —This is no difficulty. One[10] is a case where she is maintained[11] by them;[12] the other,[13] where she is not maintained by them.[14]

(1) Lit., 'for if so', that Rabbi maintains that in all cases a daughter on attaining adolescence does not lose the right to her marriage outfit. (2) Lit., 'that of Rabbi against that of Rabbi'. (3) Lit., 'yes'. (4) Is she to receive a tenth of the whole. (5) She is to receive no such allowance. (6) I.e., after she had attained her adolescence. How then could Rabbi also have stated that a daughter always (v. *supra* n. 1) receives her outfit? (7) Against the full, or partial loss of her marriage outfit allowance. Even without her protest she retains her right to the tenth of the estate that is due to her. (8) Otherwise she loses her claim to the marriage outfit. (9) *Supra*. Cf. *supra* p. 420, notes 11 to 14. From which it follows that once she passes her minority, though she did not attain her adolescence, a daughter loses her full claim to an outfit allowance if she did not lodge her protest on marriage. How then could it be said that according to Raba, 'if she married (provided it was before attaining her adolescence) she need not lodge a protest'? (10) Raba's ruling that 'if she married she need not lodge a protest'. (11) After her marriage. (12) Her brothers. In such a case it is to be presumed that her silence was not due to her consent to lose her outfit but to the belief that, as they continued to maintain her, they would also give her in due course the full amount of her outfit allowance. (13) The inference from our Mishnah according to which one who has passed out of her minority surrenders on marriage her right to the balance of her outfit. (14) Hence she loses the right to her outfit unless she lodged her protest.

R. Huna stated in the name of Rabbi: [The right[1] to] marriage outfit is not the same as that[2] conferred by a condition in a *kethubah*.[3] What is meant by 'is not the same as that conferred by a condition in a *kethubah*'? Should it be suggested[4] that whereas for the allowance for a marriage outfit even property pledged[5] may be seized,[6] [for the fulfilment of an obligation[2] under] the terms of a *kethubah* no pledged property[7] may be seized,[8] what [new point, it may be objected,] does this teach us? Surely it is a daily occurrence [that pledged property] is seized for marriage outfit but not for maintenance! [Should it], however, [be suggested that] whereas for a marriage outfit movable objects also may be seized, [for the fulfilment of an obligation under] a condition in a *kethubah* only real estate, but not movable objects, may be seized, [it may be objected that,] according to Rabbi, for the one as well as the other[9] [movable objects] may be seized. For it was taught: Both landed property and movable property may be seized for the maintenance of a wife or daughters;[10] so Rabbi! What, then, is meant by '[The right to] marriage outfit is not the same as that conferred by a condition in a *kethubah*'?—As it was taught: If a man[11] said that his daughters must not be maintained out of his estate he is not to be obeyed.[12] [If, however, he said, that] his daughters shall not receive their marriage outfit out of his estate he is obeyed, because [the right to] marriage outfit is not the same as that conferred by a condition in a *kethubah*[13].

(1) Of a daughter. (2) Of a daughter's maintenance. (3) Cf. *supra* 52*b*. (4) As a point of difference between the two rights. (5) By the brothers (not by the father). (6) Since it represents a fixed sum (one tenth of the estate) it had the validity of a debt incumbent upon the estate. (7) Even if it was only the brothers who pledged it (v. Giṭ. 48*b*). (8) As the amount is not a fixed quantity it has not the same force as a debt. (9) For maintenance as well as for marriage outfit. (10) And much more so for marriage outfit which has the validity of a debt (cf. *supra* nn. 6 and 8). (11) On his death bed. (12) Since even a dying man, whose verbal instructions have the validity of a legal contract, cannot annul the undertaking to maintain his daughters which he entered in the *kethubah*. (13) While the latter is obligatory upon the deceased and upon his heirs, the former has to be provided by the heirs only where the deceased did not give specific instructions to the contrary.

[69a] Rab inserted[1] [the following enquiry] between the lines[2] [of a communication[3] he sent] to Rabbi: What [is the law] where the brothers have encumbered [the estate they inherited from their father]?[4] [When the enquiry reached him] R. Ḥiyya [who] was sitting before him asked, '[Does he mean:] They sold it or pledged it?'—'What difference can this make?'[5] the other retorted. 'Whether they sold it [he continued] or pledged it, [the estate] may be seized [to meet the obligation] of marriage outfit but may not be seized for that of maintenance'.

As to Rab, however, if his enquiry [related to brothers] who sold [the estate], he should have written to him, 'sold'; and if his enquiry [related to brothers] who pledged it, he should have written to him, 'pledged'!—Rab wished to ascertain the law concerning both cases and he thought: If I write to him 'sold' [I shall get] satisfaction if he were to send [in reply] that 'the estate may be seized', since the same ruling would apply with even greater force to the case where they pledged [the estate]. If, however, he were to send me in reply that 'it may not be seized', the question [in respect of brothers] who pledged [the estate] would still remain. If, [again], I were to write to him, 'pledged' then if he sent in reply that 'the estate may not be seized' this ruling would apply with even greater force [to the case where] they sold it. Should he, however, send a reply that 'it may be seized', the question [in respect of brothers] who sold it would still remain. I will, therefore, write to him, 'encumbered' which might mean the one[6] as well as the other.[7]

R. Joḥanan, however, ruled: [An estate][8] may not be seized

(1) Lit., 'suspended'. (2) חטי, perhaps from חטט 'to dig', 'scratch' hence a line drawn with a stylus (cf. Rashi and Jast.). Aruk renders 'stitches' (cf. חוט 'thread'), and this is apparently the interpretation adopted by Tosaf. (s.v. תלה *a.l.*), the meaning being that 'among the documents that were sewn together one containing the enquiry was appended'; or, 'among the stitches holding the documents together the one containing the enquiry was inserted'. (3) A friendly letter (Rashi). (4) May it be seized by the daughters for their marriage outfit? (5) Lit., 'what goes out (results) from it?' (6) Lit., 'thus'. (7) Sold or pledged. And should there be a difference in law between the two cases, Rabbi in his reply would naturally indicate it. (8) Which the brothers sold or pledged. Cf. *supra*.

either [to meet the obligation of the] one or of the other.[1]

The question was raised: Did not R. Joḥanan hear the ruling of Rabbi, but if he had heard it he would have accepted it? Or is it possible that he heard it and did not accept it?—Come and hear what has been stated: If a man died and left two daughters and one son, and the first forestalled [the others] and took a tenth of the estate while the other did not manage to collect [her share] before the son died[2], R. Joḥanan ruled: The second[3] has surrendered her right.[4] Said R. Ḥanina: Something that is even more striking than this has been said, [viz., that an estate] may be seized[5] [to meet the obligation] of a marriage outfit though it may not be seized for that of maintenance, and you nevertheless state, 'The second has surrendered her right'?[6] Now, if that were the case,[7] he[8] should have asked him 'who said it?'[9]

—But is it not possible that he in fact did not hear it [at first][10] and when he [finally] heard he accepted it, but there[11] [the circumstances are] different, since the house [of the second daughter] has now ample provisions?[12] Said R. Yemar to R. Ashi: Now then,[13] if she[14] found anything at all, so that her house is amply provided for, would we in such a case also not give her a tenth of the estate?

---

(1) I.e., maintenance or marriage outfit. (2) And the entire estate fell to the lot of the daughters. (3) Since she did not collect her tenth while the son was alive, i.e., before she and her sister became the sole heirs. (4) A daughter may claim a tenth of the estate from a son only but not from a daughter whose rights are equal to hers. (5) Though it has been pledged or sold. (6) To her marriage oufit, even in an estate which had been neither sold nor pledged. The first sister, surely, cannot possess a stronger claim upon the estate than a buyer or a creditor. V. Giṭ. 51a. (7) That R. Joḥanan never heard Rabbi's ruling. (8) R. Joḥanan. (9) Since he did not ask him this it may be inferred that R. Joḥanan did hear Rabbi's ruling but did not accept it. For this reason also he did not withdraw his ruling in the case of the two daughters. (10) Rabbi's ruling. (11) The case of the two daughters which was discussed after he had heard Rabbi's ruling and accepted it. (12) At first she was entitled to a tenth only and now she gets a half. In such circumstances she may well be expected to surrender her claim to the tenth. Rabbi, however, deals with a case where the brothers are alive, and the daughters are entirely dependent on their tenths. (13) If the argument of additional provision is admissible. (14) The second sister.

—The other replied: I said, A house amply provided for from the same estate.[1]

Amemar ruled: A daughter[2] has [the legal status of] an heiress. Said R. Ashi to Amemar: Should it be desired to settle her claim[3] by means of a money payment such a settlement cannot be effected for the same reason?[4]—'Yes', the other replied. 'Should it be desired [the first asked] to settle her claim by [giving her] one plot of land, such a settlement cannot be effected for the same reason?'[4] —'Yes', the other replied.[5] R. Ashi, however, ruled: A daughter[6] has [the legal status of] a creditor.[7] And Amemar also withdrew his former opinion. For R. Minyomi son of R. Niḥumi stated: I was once standing before Amemar and a woman who claimed a tenth of [her deceased father's] estate appeared before him, and I observed [that it was his] opinion that if [her brothers] desired to settle with her by means of a money payment he would have agreed to the settlement.[8] For he heard the brothers say to her, 'If we had the money we would settle with you[9] by a cash payment', and he remained silent and told them nothing to the contrary.

Now that it has been said that [a daughter in her claim to her tenth][6] has the legal status of a creditor [the question arises whether she is the creditor] of the father or of the brothers. In what respect can this matter?—In respect [of allowing her] to collect [her tenth] either from their medium[10] land and without an oath,[11] or of their

(1) From which she was to receive her tenth. (2) In respect of her right to a tenth of her father's estate. (3) To the tenth of the estate. Lit., 'to remove her'. (4) Because she has the status of an heiress. Lit., 'thus also'. (5) As heiress she has the right to claim a share in the actual property her father left and in every portion of it. (6) In respect of her right to a tenth of her father's estate. (7) Her claim may, therefore, be met by a money payment or by the allotment of any plot of land of the value of a tenth of the estate that is due to her. (8) Lit., 'he would have removed (*sc.* dismissed) her'. (9) So MS.M. adding לך after סליקנא. (10) Land is classified as עידית best בינונית, medium or זיבורית worst, and payments are made from these respective qualities in accordance with the strength and validity of any particular claim. Cf. e.g., Giṭ. 48*b*. (11) That she had never taken anything from the estate. This would be the law if she were regarded as the creditor of the brothers.

worst land with an oath.[1] Now what [is the law]?—Come and hear [of the decision] of Rabina: He allowed the daughter of R. Ashi to collect [her tenth] from Mar[2] the son of R. Ashi out of his medium land, without an oath, but from the son of R. Sama[3] the son of R. Ashi out of his worst land with an oath.[4]

R. Nehemiah the son of R. Joseph sent the following message to Rabbah the son of R. Huna Zuṭa[5] of Nehardea:[6] When this woman[7] presents herself to you, authorize her to collect a tenth part of [her deceased father's] estate even from the casing of handmills.[8]

R. Ashi stated: When we were at the college of R. Kahana we authorized the collection [of a daughter's tenth] from the rent[9] of houses also.

R. Anan sent [this communication] to R. Huna, '[To] our colleague Huna, greetings.[10] When this woman[7] presents herself before you, authorize her to collect a tenth part of [her father's] estate'. [When the communication arrived,] R. Shesheth was sitting before him. 'Go', [R. Huna] said to him,[11] 'and convey[12] to him[13]

(1) If she is regarded as the father's creditor. In the latter case she would be subject to the restrictions imposed on a creditor who claims his debt from the debtor's orphans (v. Giṭ. 48*b*). (2) Who survived his father and from whom his sister claimed a portion of her tenth. (3) Who predeceased R. Ashi and whose son, on the death of his grandfather (R. Ashi), inherited his father's (R. Sama's) share and was now sued by his aunt to give her the portion of her tenth that his father as a son of R. Ashi owed her (Rashi). [Riṭba and others: R. Sama died shortly after R. Ashi, before his daughter managed to collect her tenth share in the estate]. (4) According to Rabina, then, the daughter was regarded as the debtor of her brothers (Mar and R. Sama). From the former, therefore, who was alive she consequently collected of the best and without an oath (cf. *supra* p. 425, n. 11). From the latter, however, she could only collect through his son as the creditor of his father's and was therefore subject to the restrictions of a creditor who collects from orphans (cf. *supra*, note 1). (5) *Var. lec.*, 'Zuṭi' (cf. B.B. 66*b*). (6) V. *supra* p. 222, n. 8. (7) The bearer, whose case R. Nehemiah had investigated. (8) The casing being regarded as landed estate from which her tenth may be collected. (9) The yield of the houses being legally regarded, like the houses themselves, as landed property (cf. *supra* n. 8). (10) Lit., 'peace'. (11) To R. Shesheth. (12) Lit., 'say'. (13) To R. Anan.

[the following message]—and he[1] who does not deliver the message[2] to him shall fall under the ban—"Anan, Anan, [is the collection to be made] from landed, or from movable property? And who presides at the meal in a house of mourning?"'[3] R. Shesheth went to R. Anan and said to him: The Master[4] is a teacher,[5] and R. Huna is a teacher of the teacher,[6] and he pronounced the ban against anyone who would not convey[7] [his message] to you;[8] and had he not pronounced the ban I would not have said, 'Anan, Anan, [is the collection to be made] from landed, or movable property, and who presides at the meal in a house of mourning?'[9] Thereupon, R. Anan went to Mar 'Ukba and said to him: See, Master, how R. Huna addressed[10] me as 'Anan, Anan';[11] and, furthermore, I do not know what he meant by the message he sent me on *marziḥa*.[12] The other said to him: Tell me now [69*b*] how the incident actually occurred. 'The incident', the first replied, 'happened in such and such a way'. 'A man', the other exclaimed, 'who does not know the meaning of *marziḥa* should [scarcely] presume to address[13] R. Huna as, "our colleague Huna".'

What [is the meaning of] *marziḥa?*—Mourning; for it is written in Scripture, *Thus saith the Lord: Enter not into the house of mourning*[14] etc.[15]

R. Abbahu stated: Whence is it deduced that a mourner sits at the head [of the table]?[16] [From Scripture] wherein it is said, *I chose out their way, and sat at the head,*[17] *and dwelt as a king in the army,*

(1) I.e., 'if you do not deliver the message etc.', the third person being used for euphemism. (2) I.e., using exactly the same words, lit., 'say'. (3) R. Huna was apparently offended by the tone or wording of R. Anan's communication. Hence the abusive reply. (4) R. Anan. (5) A complimentary introduction to the unpleasant message that follows. (6) I.e., R. Anan. An excuse for carrying out his instructions though they were offensive to R. Anan. (7) Lit., 'say'. (8) Lit., 'to him'. (9) The seat of honour at the meal in a house of mourning was given to the greatest scholar in the company. (10) Lit., 'sent'. (11) Without the title of 'R.' (12) מרזיחה, rendered *supra*, 'a house of mourning'. (13) Lit., 'sent'. (14) מרזח, Heb. from Aram. מרזיחה. (15) Jer. XVI, 5. (16) At the meal in a house of mourning. (17) E.V., *as chief*. ואשב ראש may bear both renderings.

as one that comforteth[1] *the mourners.*[2] But does not *yenahem*[3] mean [one who comforts] others?[4] R. Naḥman b. Isaac replied: The written form is YNḤM.[5] Mar Zuṭra said: [The deduction[6] is made] from here: *We-sar marzeah seruhim,*[7] he who is in bitterness and distracted[8] becomes the chief[9] of those that stretched themselves.[10]

Raba stated: The law [is that payment may be exacted] from landed property, but not from movable property, whether in respect of maintenance, *kethubah* or marriage outfit.[11]

MISHNAH. IF A MAN DEPOSITED[12] A SUM OF MONEY FOR HIS [UNMARRIED] DAUGHTER WITH A TRUSTEE,[13] AND [AFTER SHE WAS BETROTHED][14] SHE SAYS, 'I TRUST MY HUSBAND',[15] THE TRUSTEE MUST ACT IN ACCORDANCE WITH THE CONDITION OF HIS TRUST;[16] SO R. MEIR. R. JOSE, HOWEVER, SAID:

(1) This is explained by R. Naḥman anon. (2) Job. XXIX, 25. (3) יְנַחֵם Imperf. Piel of נחם. (4) How then could the text be said to refer to the mourner who is himself to be comforted? (5) ינחם, which may be vocalized as the Pual form *YeNuḤaM*, 'one who is comforted'. Though the text must retain its obvious meaning with the M.T. vocalization of יְנַחֵם, the possibility of reading ינחם as יְנֻחָם also permits of the Midrashic exposition (Tosaf. s.v. אמר). (6) That the mourner is to sit at the head of the table at the meal in a house of mourning. (7) וסר מרזח סרוחים, Amos. VI, 7. Midrashically, סר=שר (*chief*, i.e., 'sits at the head'), מרזח is divided into מר (*bitter*) and זח (rt. זוח, *distracted*), and סרוחים is taken to refer to the comforters who *stretch themselves* on their couches or on the ground at the feet of the mourner. (Cf. Golds.). E.V., *And the revelry of them that stretched themselves shall pass away.* (8) I.e., the mourner. (9) I.e., sits at the head of the table during the meal. (10) Before him, *sc.* those, who came to offer their condolence. (11) A Gaonite provision, תקנת הגאונים, empowers also the seizure of movable property to meet any of these obligations (cf. Tosaf. *supra* 51*a*, s.v. ממקרקעי). [This *Takkanah* has been ascribed to Hunai Gaon and dated 787, v. Epstein, L. *The Jewish Marriage*, p. 255 and Tykocinski, *Die Gaonäischen Verordnungen*, p. 35ff.]. (12) Lit., 'he who made a third', i.e., appointed a third person as trustee. (13) Cf. *supra* n. 12, instructing him to use the money after his death for the benefit of his daughter, e.g., to buy for her a field. (14) So Tosaf. (s.v. המשליש) contrary to Rashi's 'married'; v. Gemara *infra*. (15) 'And desire the money to be given to him'. (16) Lit., 'what was put in his hand as a third party'. The daughter's wish is to be disregarded and the trustee buys a field with it.

WERE [THE TRUST] ACTUALLY[1] A FIELD[2] AND SHE WISHED TO SELL IT, WOULD IT NOT BE DEEMED[3] SOLD FORTHWITH![4] THIS APPLIES TO ONE WHO IS OF AGE.[5] IN THE CASE OF A MINOR, HOWEVER, THERE IS NO VALIDITY AT ALL IN THE ACT OF A MINOR.

GEMARA. Our Rabbis taught: If a man deposited for his son-in-law with a trustee a sum of money wherewith to buy a field for his daughter, and she says, 'Let it be given to my husband', she is entitled [to have her wish fulfilled, if it was expressed] after her marriage[6] but if only after her betrothal the trustee must act according to the conditions of his trust;[7] so R. Meir. R. Jose, however, said: A woman who is of age has a right [to obtain her desire] whether [it was expressed] after her marriage or only after betrothal, but [in the case of] a minor [whether her wish was expressed] after marriage or after betrothal, the trustee must act in accordance with the conditions of his trust.[8] What is the practical difference between them?[9] If it be suggested that the practical difference between them is the case of a minor after her marriage, R. Meir holding the opinion that [even] she is entitled [to have her wish] and R. Jose comes to state that even after marriage [it is only] a woman who is of age that is entitled to have her wish[10] but not a minor, [in that case] what of[11] the final clause,[12] IN THE CASE OF A MINOR, HOWEVER, THERE IS NO VALIDITY AT ALL IN THE ACT OF A MINOR. Who [it might be asked] could have taught this? If it be suggested [that the author was] R. Jose, [it

(1) Lit., 'was not but'. (2) Not merely a sum of money with which to buy one. (3) Lit., 'behold it'. (4) Lit., 'from now', *sc*. from the moment she expressed her desire to sell it, and the same should apply where the trust consisted of a sum of money. The sum of money must consequently be at her disposal and she may give it to her husband if she desires to do so. (5) The point of this limitation is discussed in the Gemara *infra*. (6) The assumption being that the father wished the trustee to act only until his daughter's marriage. (7) V. *supra* p. 428, n. 16. (8) Tosef. Keth. VI. Cf. *supra* p. 428, n. 16. (9) R. Meir and R. Jose, i.e., does R. Meir in the Baraitha refer to a minor also or only to one who is of age? (10) Lit., 'yes'. (11) Lit., 'say'. (12) Of our Mishnah.

could be objected:] This, surely, could be inferred from the first clause; for, since R. Jose said, WERE [THE TRUST] ACTUALLY A FIELD AND SHE WISHED TO SELL IT, WOULD IT NOT BE DEEMED SOLD FORTHWITH! [it follows[1] that only] one that is of age, who is eligible to effect a sale, was meant,[2] but not a minor who is ineligible to effect a sale.[3] Consequently it must be R. Meir [who was the author of] it, and a clause is in fact missing [from our Mishnah], the proper reading being as follows:[4] 'THE TRUSTEE MUST ACT IN ACCORDANCE WITH THE CONDITIONS OF HIS TRUST. This applies only [to a woman whose desire was expressed] after her betrothal, but if after her marriage she is entitled [to have her wish]. THIS [furthermore] APPLIES TO ONE WHO IS OF AGE. IN THE CASE OF A MINOR, HOWEVER, THERE IS NO VALIDITY AT ALL IN THE ACT OF A MINOR.'[5]—[The fact], however, is that the practical difference between them is the case of one who is of age [whose wish was expressed] after her betrothal.[6]

It was stated: Rab Judah said in the name of Samuel, The *halachah* is in agreement with R. Jose. Raba in the name of R. Naḥman said, The *halachah* is in agreement with R. Meir. Ilfa[7] reclined[8] upon a sail mast[9] and[10] said: 'Should any one come and

(1) Since R. Jose gave as the reason for his ruling the consideration that *she could have sold* the field if she wished. (2) Lit., 'yes'. (3) The final clause, then, would be superfluous. (4) Lit., 'and thus he taught'. (5) Now, since R. Meir also admits that the act of a minor has no validity, his statement in the Baraitha cited that after marriage she is entitled to have her wish must refer to one who is of age and not to a minor. What, then, is the practical difference between R. Meir and R. Jose? (6) According to R. Meir her wish is to be ignored; according to R. Jose it is to be granted. Cf. *supra* p. 428, n. 14. As to a minor both agree that her request is not to be granted even if she makes it after her marriage. (7) Scholar and merchant, a contemporary of R. Joḥanan. When the latter was appointed to the presidency of the college the former was away from his home town, engaged in the pursuit of his commercial enterprises. What follows happened on his return when he was told that had he devoted more time to his studies and less to commerce the presidency would have been offered to him. V. Ta'an. 21*a*. (8) Lit., 'suspended himself' (cf. Rashi Giṭ. 32*b*, s.v. דתלי, Pesaḥ. 68*b*, s.v. ותלי). (9) Or sail-yard. Cf. Rashi. Other renderings: 'Sail, or mast of a boat', 'mastyard'. איסקריא, *ἱστοκεραία*, (perhaps from rt. סקר, 'to espy', hence 'espying place')

submit to me any statement [in the Baraithoth] of R. Ḥiyya and R. Oshaia[1] which I cannot make clear to him [with the aid] of our Mishnah I will drop from the mast[2] and drown myself'. An aged man came and recited to him [the following Baraitha:][3] If a man[4] said, 'Give my children[5] a *shekel* a week',[6] and they require a *sela'*,[7] a *sela'* is to be given to them.[8] But if he said, 'Give them no more than a *shekel*', only a *shekel* is to be given to them.[9] If, however, he gave instructions that if these died others[10] shall be his heirs in their stead, only one *sheḳel* [a week] is to be given to them, irrespective of whether he used the expression of 'give' or 'give no [more]'.[11] [Ilfa] said to him: [Do you wish to know] whose ruling this[12] is? [70a] It is that of R. Meir[13] who laid down that it is a religious obligation to carry out the instructions of a dying man.[14]

R. Ḥisda stated in the name of Mar 'Uḳba: The law is that whether [the dying man] said, 'Give' or 'give no more',[15] his children are to be given all that they require. But have we not, however, an established principle that the *halachah* is in agreement with R. Meir who laid down that it is a religious obligation to carry

'mast' or 'yard' (v. Jast.). מכותא cf. Assyr. *makua*, a kind of 'boat', 'mast' or 'sail-yard' (v. Rashi, *a.l.* and Giṭ. 36*a*, Rashb. B.B. 161*b*); 'a ship' (Aruk). In the parallel passage, Ta'an 21*a*, the reading for דמכותא is דספינתא (of a ship). (10) To prove that despite his commercial undertakings he had not forgotten his studies.

(1) These were regarded as the most authoritative of the Baraitha collections. (2) Cf. p. 430, n. 9. (3) Demanding Mishnaic authority for its rulings. V. *infra* note 12. (4) Lying on his death bed, or setting out on a long journey. (5) Out of the estate he leaves behind. (6) For their maintenance. (7) A *sela'* = two *sheḳels*. (8) Their father's mention of the smaller coin, it is assumed, was not meant to exclude the bigger one. All that he implied was that his children should be given no more than their actual weekly requirements. (9) Though they may be in need of more. (10) Whom he named. (11) Because in this case it is evident that it was his intention to economize as much as possible on the weekly maintenance of his children in order that the heirs he nominated might in due course receive as large an inheritance as possible. (12) That, though the children need more than their father had allowed them, the instructions of the deceased must be carried out. (13) Expressed in our Mishnah by the ruling that despite the request of the daughter the trustee must carry out the instructions of her deceased father. (14) Cf. Giṭ. 14*b*, 15*a* and 40*a*. (15) Cf. *supra* 69*b ad fin.*

out the instructions of a dying man?—This applies to other matters, but in this case [the father] is quite satisfied [that his children should be provided with all they need]; and in limiting their allowance,[1] his object was[2] to encourage them.[3]

We learned elsewhere: With regard to little children,[4] their purchase is a valid purchase and their sale is a valid sale in the case of movable objects.[5] Rafram explained: This has been taught in the case only where no guardian had been appointed,[6] but where a guardian had been appointed neither their purchase nor their sale has any legal validity. Whence is this inferred? From the expression, THERE IS NO VALIDITY AT ALL IN THE ACT OF A MINOR. But might not the case where a trustee[7] had been appointed be different?[8]—If so,[9] it should have been stated, 'IN THE CASE OF A MINOR, HOWEVER, a trustee must act in accordance with the conditions of his trust' what [then was the purpose of the expression,] THERE IS NO VALIDITY AT ALL IN THE ACT OF A MINOR? Hence it may be inferred [that the same law is applicable] in all cases.[10]

(1) Lit., 'and (as to) that which he said thus'. (2) Lit., 'he came'. (3) To lead a thrifty life and to make an effort to earn their livelihood. (4) Of the ages of 'nine and eight' (Rashi, *a.l.* s.v. הפעוטות), 'six and seven' (Rashb. B.B. 155*b*, s.v. אלא). (5) Transactions in landed estate, however, may be made by such only as have produced signs of puberty or have attained the age of twenty, v. Giṭ. 59*a*, 65*a*, B.B. l.c. (6) By a father or the court. (7) With definite instructions as to the use he was to make of the trust money. (8) From an ordinary guardian who is expected to use his own discretion in the best interests of the orphans. In the latter case the orphan's transaction might be deemed valid because it is not against their father's instructions and, being in the interest of the orphans, the guardian might well be presumed to have acquiesced. (9) That a distinction is to be drawn between a trustee with special instructions and an ordinary guardian. (10) Where there is a guardian, whose charge is somewhat similar to that of a trustee. Lit., 'even in the world'.

KETHUBOTH

CHAPTER VII

MISHNAH. IF A MAN FORBADE HIS WIFE BY VOW TO HAVE ANY BENEFIT FROM HIM HE MAY, [IF THE PROHIBITION IS TO LAST] NOT MORE[1] THAN THIRTY DAYS, APPOINT A STEWARD,[2] BUT IF FOR A LONGER PERIOD HE MUST DIVORCE HER[3] AND GIVE HER THE KETHUBAH. R. JUDAH RULED: IF HE WAS AN ISRAELITE[4] HE MAY KEEP HER [AS HIS WIFE IF THE PROHIBITION WAS FOR] ONE MONTH, BUT MUST DIVORCE HER AND GIVE HER THE KETHUBAH [IF IT WAS FOR] TWO MONTHS. IF HE WAS A PRIEST[5] HE MAY KEEP HER [AS HIS WIFE, IF THE PROHIBITION WAS FOR] TWO MONTHS,[6] BUT MUST DIVORCE HER AND GIVE HER THE KETHUBAH [IF IT WAS FOR] THREE.

IF A MAN FORBADE HIS WIFE BY VOW THAT SHE SHOULD NOT TASTE A CERTAIN FRUIT[7] HE MUST DIVORCE HER AND GIVE HER THE KETHUBAH. R. JUDAH RULED: IF HE WAS AN ISRAELITE[4] HE MAY KEEP HER [AS HIS WIFE, IF THE VOW WAS FOR] ONE DAY, [BUT IF FOR] TWO DAYS HE MUST DIVORCE HER AND GIVE HER THE KETHUBAH. IF, HOWEVER, HE WAS A PRIEST[5] HE MAY KEEP HER [AS HIS WIFE, IF THE VOW WAS FOR] TWO DAYS [BUT IF FOR] THREE HE MUST DIVORCE HER AND GIVE HER THE KETHUBAH.

IF A MAN FORBADE HIS WIFE BY VOW THAT SHE SHOULD NOT MAKE USE OF A CERTAIN ADORNMENT[8] HE MUST DI-

(1) Lit., 'until'. (2) To supply his wife's maintenance. (3) I.e., if the woman demands her freedom. (4) Who, unlike a priest (v. Lev. XXI, 7), may remarry his divorced wife. (5) Cf. *supra* n. 4. (6) A priest was allowed more time in order to afford him a longer period of retracting before his divorce separates her from him for ever. (7) He confirmed a vow she had made to that effect (Rashi). Though he has no right to forbid his wife the eating or tasting of any foodstuffs he may, by keeping silent when she herself makes such a vow, confirm it; v. Num. XXX, 7ff. Others: He vowed to abstain from his wife should she taste a certain fruit; v. Isaiah Trani. (8) Cf. *supra* n. 7 *mutatis mutandis*.

VORCE HER AND GIVE HER THE KETHUBAH. R. JOSE RULED: [THIS[1] APPLIES] TO POOR WOMEN IF NO TIME LIMIT[2] IS GIVEN, AND TO RICH WOMEN [IF THE TIME LIMIT[2] IS] THIRTY DAYS.

GEMARA. Since, however, he[3] is under an obligation to [maintain] her[4] how can he forbid her by a vow [to have any benefit from him]? Has he then the power[5] to cancel his obligation? Surely we have learned: [If a woman said to her husband] '*Ḳonam,* if I do aught for your mouth' he need not annul her vow;[6] from which[7] it is evident that, as she is under an obligation to him,[8] she has no right to cancel her obligation,[9] similarly here, since he is under an obligation to [maintain] her he should have no right to cancel his obligation![10]—[This,] however, [is the right explanation:] As he[11] is entitled to say to her,[12] 'Deduct [the proceeds of] your handiwork for your maintenance'[13] [70*b*] he [in making his vow] is regarded[14] as having said to her, 'Deduct [the proceeds of] your handiwork for your maintenance'.

If, however, one is to adopt the ruling R. Huna gave in the name of Rab, for R. Huna stated in the name of Rab: A wife may say to her husband, 'I would neither be maintained by, nor work [for you]', why should there be no need to annul [her vow] when she said '*Ḳonam,* if I do aught for your mouth'? Let it rather be said that as she is entitled to say, 'I would neither be maintained by nor work [for you]' she [in making her vow] might be regarded[14] as having said, 'I would neither be maintained by, nor work [for you]'?[15]—[The fact,] however, [is that] the explanation is not that

(1) That in the case of a vow against a wife's adornments, the husband MUST DIVORCE HER AND GIVE HER THE KETHUBAH. (2) To the duration of the vow. (3) A husband. (4) His wife. (5) Lit., 'all (power) as if from him?' (6) *Supra* 59*a* and notes. (7) Since no annulment is required. (8) A wife's handiwork belongs to her husband. (9) In consequence of which her vow is null and void and requires no annulment. (10) And his vow also should, therefore, be null and void. (11) A husband. (12) His wife. (13) I.e., he would neither maintain her nor expect her to give him her handiwork (v. *supra* n. 8). (14) Lit., 'is made'. (15) And her vow should be valid. Why then has it been said that her husband 'need not annul her vow'?

'he is regarded'[1] but that he actually said to her, 'Deduct your handiwork for your maintenance.' If so,[2] what need has she of a steward?[3]—[She needs one] where [the proceeds of her handiwork] do not suffice.[4] If, [however, her handiwork] does not suffice,[5] our original question arises again![6] R. Ashi replied: [This is a case] where [her handiwork] suffices for major requirements but does not suffice for minor requirements.

How is one to understand these 'minor requirements'? If the woman is in the habit of having them, they are, surely, a part of her regular requirements,[7] and if she is not used to them[8] what need has she for a steward?[9]—[The law concerning a steward] is required only where she was used [to them] in her father's house but consented to dispense with them when with her husband.[10] In such a case she can say to him, 'Hitherto, before you forbade me by a vow [to have any benefit from you], I was willing to put up with your [mode of living], but now that you have forbidden me [to enjoy any benefit from you] I am not able to put up [any longer] with your [mode of living]'. And wherein lies the difference [between a vow for more, and one for] NOT MORE THAN THIRTY DAYS?—[Within a period of] NOT MORE THAN THIRTY DAYS people would not become aware of it, and the matter would be no degradation to her; but after a longer period[11] people would hear of it, and the matter would be degrading to her.

If you prefer I might reply: [His vow[12] is valid] only if he vowed while she was merely betrothed to him.[13] But has a betrothed woman, however, any claim to maintenance?[14]—[Yes], if the time

(1) Lit., 'do not say; he is made'. (2) That her handiwork is not taken away from her. (3) The proceeds of her handiwork could be spent on her maintenance. (4) To make up the legally prescribed sum (v. *supra* 64*b*). (5) And it is, therefore, still her husband's duty to maintain her in part. (6) How can he by his vow cancel an obligation that is incumbent upon him? (7) Lit., 'she is used to them'. (8) Being mere luxuries. (9) The husband, surely, is not expected to provide for such luxuries. (10) Lit., 'roll with him', i.e., to put up with his mode of living. (11) Lit., 'more'. (12) That his wife shall not HAVE ANY BENEFIT FROM HIM. (13) When he is under no obligation to maintain her. (14) Certainly not (v. *supra* n. 13). What need then was there to state the obvious?

[for the celebration of the marriage] arrived and she was[1] not married. For we have learned: If the respective periods expired[2] and they were not married,[3] they[4] are entitled to maintenance[5] out of the man's estate, and [if he is a priest] may also eat *terumah*.[6] Wherein then lies the difference [between a vow for more, and one for] NOT MORE THAN THIRTY DAYS?—[During a period of] NOT MORE THAN THIRTY DAYS an agent[7] performs his mission; for a longer period no agent performs his mission.

And if you prefer I might reply: [The husband's vow[8] is valid] when he made it while she was betrothed to him and she was [afterwards] married.

But if she was married [afterwards] she must obviously have understood her position and accepted it![9]—[It is a case] where she pleaded, 'I thought I shall be able to bear it but now I cannot bear it'.

But granted that such a plea[10] is properly admissible[11] in respect of bodily defects;[12] is it admissible, however, in respect of maintenance?[13]—Clearly, then, we can only explain as we explained at first.

HE MAY, [IF THE PROHIBITION IS TO LAST] NOT MORE THAN THIRTY DAYS, APPOINT A STEWARD. Does not the steward, however, act on his[14] behalf?[15]—R. Huna replied: [Our Mishnah

(1) Lit., 'they were'. V. n. 2. (2) Lit., 'the time (for the respective marriages referred to *supra* 57*a*) arrived'. (3) Through the man's delay. (4) The women mentioned. (5) In accordance with a Rabbinical ordinance. (6) Mishnah *supra* 57*a*. Since in such circumstances the man is Pentateuchally under no obligation to maintain his betrothed his vow forbidding her to have any benefit is valid; and as he is obliged to maintain her in accordance with Rabbinic law he must appoint a steward to look after her maintenance. (7) The steward appointed (v. our Mishnah). (8) V. *supra* p. 435, n. 12. (9) What claim then could she advance? (10) Mistaken judgment. (11) Lit., 'that we say so'. (12) Though a woman at first consented to live with the man who suffered from such defects she may subsequently plead that she under-estimated her feeling and that now she cannot bear them (v. *infra* 77*a*). A woman may well be excused her first error of judgment in such circumstances. (13) No woman, surely, could plead that she was not aware that a person could live without food. As she has once accepted the disability she should not be entitled to change her mind. (14) The husband's. (15) Lit., 'do his mission'. The answer being in the affirmative, the

refers] to one who declared, 'Whoever will maintain [my wife] will not suffer any loss'.[1] But, even if he spoke in such a manner, is not the steward acting on his behalf? Have we not learned: If a man who was thrown into a pit cried that whosoever should hear his voice should write a letter of divorce for his wife, [the hearers][2] may lawfully[3] write, and deliver [it to his wife]?[4]—How now! there[5] the man said, 'should write';[6] but did the man here[7] say, 'should maintain'? All he said was, 'whoever will maintain'.[8]

But surely R. Ammi said: In [the case of] a fire [breaking] out on the Sabbath][9] permission was given to make the announcement 'Whosoever shall extinguish it will suffer no loss'.[10] Now what does [the expression] 'In a fire'[11] exclude? Does it not exclude a case of this kind?[12]—No; [it was meant] to exclude other acts that are forbidden on the Sabbath.[13]

Rabbah raised an objection: If a man is forbidden by a vow to have any benefit from another man, and he has nothing to eat [the other] may go to a shopkeeper with whom he is familiar and say to him, 'So-and-so is forbidden by a vow to have any benefit from me, and I do not know what to do for him'. [The shopkeeper] may then give to the one and recover the cost from the other.[14]

question arises why his agent should be allowed to do on his behalf what he himself is not allowed to do.

(1) He would reimburse him. (2) Though they have received no direct instructions. (3) Lit., 'behold these'. (4) Giṭ. 66*a*; as if they had been agents who had received direct instructions from him. Similarly the steward spoken of in our Mishnah should be regarded as the husband's agent (v. *supra* p. 436, n. 15). (5) The case of divorce. (6) A definite instruction. (7) In the matter of maintenance. (8) This is not even an indirect instruction but a mere intimation. Anyone acting on such an intimation only cannot be regarded as agent. (9) When a Jew is forbidden to do any work himself or to instruct someone else, even a Gentile, to do it for him. (10) Shab. 121*a*. (11) Implying a fire only and not other cases. (12) A person's announcement concerning compensation for the maintenance of his wife whom he himself is forbidden to maintain, or any similar announcements which might lead someone to perform on behalf of that person what he himself is forbidden to do. (13) The sanctity of the Sabbath demands greater restrictions which need not be applied to other prohibitions such as those of vows for instance. (14) Ned. 43*a*. Lit., 'gives to him and comes and takes from this'.

Only such [a suggestion][1] is permitted but not that of 'whoever will maintain [my wife] will not suffer any loss'?[2]—[The formula,] 'There is no question' is here implied:[3] There is no question [that a man may announce,] 'whoever will maintain [my wife] will not suffer any loss', since he is speaking to no one in particular;[4] but even in this case where, since he is familiar with him[5] and goes and speaks to him directly, [it might have been thought that his mere suggestion is] the same as if he had expressly told him,[5] 'You go and give him',[6] hence we were taught [that this also is permitted].

[To revert to] the main text.[7] If a man is forbidden by a vow to have any benefit from another man, and he has nothing to eat, [the other] may go to a shopkeeper with whom he is familiar and say to him, 'So-and-so is forbidden by a vow to have any benefit from me, and I do not know what to do for him'. [The shopkeeper] may then give to the one and recover the cost from the other.[8] If his[9] house is to be built, his wall to be put up or his field to be harvested [the other] may go to labourers with whom he is familiar and say to them, 'So-and-so is forbidden by a vow to have any benefit from me, and I do not know what to do for him'. They may then work for him and recover[10] their wages from the other. If they were going on the same journey and the one had with him nothing to eat, [the other][11] may give [some food] to a third[12] person as a gift and the first may take it [from that person] and eat it.[13] If no third person[12] is available, he[11] may put the food upon a stone or a wall, and say, 'Behold this is free[14] for all who desire [to take it]', and the other[15] may take it and eat it.[16] R. Jose, however,

(1) Which is rather vague and non-oommittal. (2) Which is more explicit and a committal undertaking. An objection against R. Huna. (3) Lit., 'he (the Tanna of that Mishnah) said'. (4) Lit., 'to the world'. (5) The shopkeeper. (6) And, thereby becoming his virtual agent, he should, like himself, be forbidden to supply any provisions. (7) Of the citation from Ned. 43*a*. (8) V. *supra* p. 437, n. 14. (9) The man who is forbidden to have benefit from the other by a vow. (10) Lit., 'and come and take'. (11) Benefit from whom he is forbidden to derive. (12) Lit., 'another'. (13) Cf. *infra* n. 16. (14) Lit., 'they are ownerless property'. (15) V. *supra* note 9. (16) MS.M. omits ומותר ('and it is permitted') which seems superfluous here as well as *supra*. V. *supra* n. 13.

forbids this.[1] Raba said: What is R. Jose's reason?—[It is forbidden as] a preventive measure against [71*a*] [a repetition of] the incident of Beth Horon.[2]

R. JUDAH SAID: IF HE WAS AN ISRAELITE HE MAY KEEP HER [AS HIS WIFE, IF THE PROHIBITION WAS FOR] ONE MONTH etc. Is not this the same ruling as that of the first Tanna?[3]—Abaye replied: He[4] came to teach us [the law concerning] a priest's wife.[5] Raba replied: The difference between them is a full month[6] and a defective month.[7]

Rab stated: This[8] was taught only in the case of a man who specified [the period of the prohibition], but where he did not specify, he[9] must divorce her immediately and give her the *kethubah*. Samuel, however, stated: Even where the period was not specified [the husband] need not divorce her, since it is possible that he might discover some reason[10] for [the remission of] his vow.[11] But surely they[12] had once been in dispute upon this principle; for have we not learned, 'If a man forbade his wife by vow to have intercourse, Beth Shammai ruled: [She must consent to the deprivation for] two weeks; Beth Hillel ruled: [Only for] one week';[13] and Rab stated, 'They[14] differ only in the case of a man who specified [the period of abstention] but where he did not specify the period he[15] must divorce her forthwith and give her the *kethubah*', and Samuel stated, 'Even where the period had not been specified the husband need not divorce her, since it might be possible for him to discover some reason[16] for [the annulment of] his[17] vow'?[18]—[Both disputes

(1) V. Ned. 43*a*. (2) V. Ned. Sonc. ed. p. 148f and notes. (3) Who also allowed a period of THIRTY DAYS. (4) R. Judah. (5) Of which the first Tanna does not speak. (6) Consisting of thirty days. (7) Of twenty-nine days. According to R. Judah ONE MONTH is allowed irrespective of whether it is a full or a defective one. According to the first Tanna THIRTY DAYS are invariably allowed. (8) That for a period of thirty days a steward may be appointed. (9) Though his vow might be annulled by a competent authority by the end of the thirty days. (10) Lit., 'a door'. (11) V. *supra* p. 370, nn. 10-11. (12) Rab and Samuel. (13) *Supra* 61*b*. (14) Beth Shammai and Beth Hillel. (15) According to the opinion of both. (16) V. *supra* note 10. (17) V. *supra*. p. 370, n. 11 (18) Why then should Rab and Samuel be in dispute upon the same principle here also?

were] necessary. For if [their views] had been expressed in the former case[1] it might have been assumed that only in that case did Rab maintain his view, since [the appointment] of a steward is not possible, but that in the latter case[2] where [the appointment] of a steward is possible, he agrees with Samuel. And if [their views] had been stated in the latter case[2] it might have been assumed that only in that case did Samuel maintain his view, since the appointment of a steward is possible, but that in the former case[1] he agrees with Rab. [Hence both statements were] necessary.

We learned: IF A MAN FORBADE HIS WIFE BY VOW THAT SHE SHOULD NOT TASTE A CERTAIN FRUIT, HE MUST DIVORCE HER[3] AND GIVE HER THE KETHUBAH. Now according to Rab[4] [there is no contradiction[5] since] the latter[6] may apply to a man who did not specify [the period of the prohibition] and the former[6] to a man who did specify [the period]. According to Samuel,[7] however, a contradiction arises![5]—Here we are dealing with a case, for instance, where the woman made the vow and he confirmed it;[8] R. Meir[9] holding the opinion that [the husband][10] had himself put his finger between her teeth. But does R. Meir hold the principle, 'He has himself put his finger between her teeth'? Surely it was taught: If a woman made the vow of a nazirite[11] and her husband heard of it and did not annul it, she, said R. Meir and R. Judah, has thereby put her own finger between her teeth. Therefore, if the husband wishes to annul her vow, he may do so. But if he[12] said, 'I do not want a wife who is in the habit of vowing',

(1) The prohibition of intercourse. (2) The vow forbidding other benefits. (3) Forthwith. (4) Who draws a distinction between a specified and an unspecified period. (5) Between this ruling (immediate divorce) and the earlier Mishnah (allowing a certain period to pass). (6) Lit., 'here'. (7) Who, contrary to the view of Rab (v. *supra* n. 4), draws no distinction. (8) Since if she is willing to accept her *kethubah* and leave him, she would not try to obtain the annulment of her vow. There is no advantage, therefore, in postponing the divorce. Where, however, he himself made the vow, the divorce is delayed in order to afford him an opportunity of discovering some ground for the remission of his vow. (9) Who is generally the author of an anonymous Mishnah. (10) By confirming her vow though he had the right to annul it. (11) V. Num. VI, 2ff. (12) Having once confirmed the vow.

she may be divorced without [receiving] her *kethubah*. R. Jose and R. Eleazar said: He[1] has put his finger between her teeth. Therefore, if the husband wishes to annul her vow, he may do so. But if he[2] said, 'I do not want a wife who is in the habit of vowing', he may divorce her but must give her the *kethubah!*[3]—Reverse [the views]: R. Meir and R. Judah said: 'He has put'[4] and R. Jose and R. Eleazar said: 'She has put'.[5] But is R. Jose of the opinion that it is she who put?[5] Have we not learned: R. Jose ruled: [THIS[6] APPLIES] TO POOR WOMEN IF NO TIME LIMIT IS GIVEN?[7]—Read: R. Meir and R. Jose said, 'He has put';[4] R. Judah and R. Eleazar said, 'She has put'.[5] But does R. Judah uphold the principle of 'She put'?[5] Have we not learned: R. JUDAH RULED: IF HE WAS AN ISRAELITE HE MAY KEEP HER [AS HIS WIFE, IF THE VOW WAS FOR] ONE DAY?[8]—Read: R. Meir and R. Judah and R. Jose said, 'He put',[4] and R. Eleazar said, 'She put'.[5] And should you find [some ground] for insisting that the names must appear in pairs,[9] then read: R. Meir and R. Eleazar said, 'She put',[10] and R. Judah and R. Jose said, 'He put';[11] and this anonymous Mishnah[12] is not in agreement with R. Meir.

Is R. Jose, however, of the opinion that [THIS[13] APPLIES] TO POOR WOMEN IF NO TIME LIMIT IS GIVEN; from which[14] it is evident that a husband has the right to annul[14] [such vows]?[15] This,

(1) V. *supra* p. 440, n. 10. (2) Having once confirmed the vow. (3) Which shews that R. Meir's view is that *she* and not he has put the finger between the teeth, where she makes the vow and he confirms it. (4) His finger between her teeth. (5) Her finger between her teeth. (6) That the husband must divorce her and give her the *kethubah*. (7) This referring (as has been explained *supra*) to a vow the woman had made, it follows that according to R. Jose it is the husband who puts his finger between her teeth. (8) But if for more than ONE DAY he must divorce her and give her the *kethubah*. This referring to a vow the woman has made, it follows that according to R. Judah also it is the husband who put his finger etc. (v. *supra* n. 7). (9) Lit., 'to say: He taught in pairs'. (10) Her finger between her teeth. (11) V. *supra* note 3. (12) Which follows the principle that it is the husband who 'put his finger between her teeth'. (13) That a husband must divorce his wife and also give her the *kethubah* if he has not annulled a vow she has made against the use of a certain adornment. (14) Since the husband is penalized (v. *supra* n. 13) for not annulling the vow. (15) I.e., those relating to a woman's adornments.

surely, is incongruous [with the following]. These are the vows[1] which a husband may annul: Vows which involve an affliction of soul[2] [as, for instance, if a woman said, 'I vow not to enjoy the pleasure of bathing] should I bathe'[3] [or] 'I swear that[4] I shall not bathe', [or again, 'I vow not to make use of adornments] should I make use of an adornment',[3] [or] 'I swear that[4] I shall not make use of any adornments'. R. Jose said: These are not regarded as vows involving an affliction of soul;[5] and the following are vows that involve an affliction of soul: '[I swear] that I shall not eat meat' or 'that I shall not drink wine' or 'that I shall not adorn myself [71*b*] with coloured garments'![6]—Here[7] we are dealing with matters affecting their intimate relations.[8] This explanation is satisfactory according to him who maintains that a husband may annul [vows on] matters affecting their intimate relations. What, however, can be said [in explanation] according to him who maintains that a husband may not annul [such vows]? For it was stated:[9] [As to vows on] matters affecting their intimate relations, R. Huna ruled: A husband may annul them; R. Adda b. Ahabah ruled: A husband may not annul them, for we do not find that a fox should die of the dust of his den![10]—The fact, however, is that we are here[7]

(1) So MS.M. and separate edd. of the Mishnah. Cur. edd., 'things'. (2) V. Num. XXX, 14. (3) 'Up to a certain time'. (4) Lit., 'if'. (5) Hence they may not be annulled by a husband. V. Ned. Mishnah 79*a*; cf. however next note. [The passage that follows does not occur in the Mishnah Ned. 79*a* and the source of the whole citation is consequently, according to some commentators, said to be a Baraitha (v. *Shiṭṭah Mekubbeẓeth*). Tosaf. however (s.v. הכי) on the basis of an entirely different text, omits this passage.] (6) Such vows only may be annulled by a husband. Now, in view of this ruling of R. Jose (v. *supra* n. 5), how could it be said that according to his opinion a husband may annul vows against the use of any adornments? (7) In the case of adornments referred to by R. Jose in our Mishnah. (8) Lit., 'things between him and her' (*sc.* husband and wife); a powder, for instance, for the removal of superfluous hair from unexposed parts of the body. A woman's abstention from the use of such kinds of cosmetics or adornments are regarded as things affecting their intimate relations and such vows may well be annulled by a husband, v. Ned. 79*b*. (9) Ned. 81*a*. (10) Proverb; i.e., one is not injured by an element to which one is accustomed. The husband being accustomed to his wife, cannot be harmed by her refusal to look after her body (as defined n. 8); 'pit' (Rashi)

dealing with a case, for instance, where she made her marital intercourse dependent upon her use of adornments, by saying, 'The enjoyment of your intercourse shall be forbidden to me should I ever make use of any adornment.'[1] [This explanation] is in agreement with a ruling of R. Kahana. For R. Kahana ruled, [If a woman said to her husband], 'The enjoyment of my intercourse [shall be forbidden][2] to you', he may compel her to such intercourse;[3] [if, however, she vowed,] 'The enjoyment of your intercourse [shall be forbidden][4] to me'[5] he must annul [her vow][6] because no person is to be fed with a thing that is forbidden to him.[7] But let her[8] not adorn herself and consequently not be forbidden to him![9]—If so,[10] she would be called, 'The ugly woman'.[11] But then let her adorn herself and be forbidden [intercourse] either for two weeks, according to Beth Shammai[12] or for one week according to Beth Hillel!'[13]—These[14] apply only to a case where he [the husband] has forbidden her by a vow [to have intercourse with him], because [in such circumstances] she thinks 'He may have been angry with me[15] and

or 'rubble', 'loose ground' (Jast.). Since the intimate relations of husband and wife are not affected by such a vow, the husband has no right to invalidate them. How, then, can he be penalized in the case of the adornments spoken of in our Mishnah?

(1) The annulment of such a vow is within the right of a husband. (2) By a vow. (3) Because it is not within her power to make a vow against a duty that is incumbent upon her as a married woman. (4) By a vow. (5) Such a vow is within her power to make, since it relates to her own gratification. (6) Though he is under no obligation to respect it. (7) Cf. *supra* note 1. (8) If according to R. Jose the only reason why a husband has the right to annul his wife's vows in connection with adornments (v. our Mishnah) is because she has made her marital intercourse dependent upon them. (9) Why then is a husband entitled to annul such vows? (10) If she were to dispense with her adornments. (11) An insult which she would not be able to bear, and in consequence of which she would resume the use of adornments and thus affect her marital relationship. Cf. *supra* note 1. (12) As in the case where a man forbade his wife by a vow to have intercourse with him (*supra* 61*b*). (13) Why then has it been stated that HE MUST DIVORCE HER AND GIVE HER THE KETHUBAH *forthwith?* (14) The respective rulings of Beth Shammai and Beth Hillel, which allow a certain period before a divorce can be enforced. (15) When he made his vow.

will later[1] calm down'.[2] Here, however, since she has made the vow and he remained silent,[3] she comes to the conclusion: 'Since he remained silent[3] he must indeed hate me'.[4]

R. JOSE RULED: [THIS APPLIES] TO POOR WOMEN IF NO TIME LIMIT IS GIVEN. What is the TIME LIMIT?[5]—Rab Judah citing Samuel replied: Twelve months.[6] Rabbah b. Bar Ḥana citing R. Joḥanan replied: Ten years.[6] R. Ḥisda citing Abimi replied: A festival;[7] for[8] the daughters of Israel adorn themselves on a festival.

AND TO RICH WOMEN [IF THE TIME LIMIT IS] THIRTY DAYS. Why just[9] THIRTY DAYS?—Abaye replied: Because[8] a prominent woman enjoys the scent of her cosmetics for thirty days.[10]

MISHNAH. IF A MAN FORBADE HIS WIFE[11] BY VOW THAT SHE SHALL NOT GO TO HER FATHER'S HOUSE, AND HE[12] LIVES WITH HER IN THE SAME TOWN, HE MAY KEEP [HER AS HIS WIFE, IF THE PROHIBITION WAS FOR] ONE MONTH; BUT IF FOR TWO MONTHS HE MUST DIVORCE HER AND GIVE HER ALSO THE KETHUBAH. WHERE HE, HOWEVER, LIVES IN ANOTHER TOWN, HE MAY KEEP [HER AS HIS WIFE, IF THE PROHIBITION

(1) Lit., 'now'. (2) And seek the help of an authority in obtaining its disallowance. (3) And so confirmed it. (4) She is, therefore, anxious to leave him at once. Hence the ruling in our Mishnah (cf. p. 443, n. 13). (5) During which a wife must put up with the deprivation of her adornments, and be unable to demand a divorce. (6) Only where the prohibition has been extended to a longer period can the husband be compelled to divorce his wife and to give her also her *kethubah*. (7) I.e., until the major festival next to the day on which the vow was made. The major festivals are Passover, Pentecost and Tabernacles. (8) Lit., 'for so'. (9) Lit., 'what is the difference?' (10) If, therefore, the prohibition imposed upon her by the vow is for less than that period, she does not suffer much by the deprivation of her cosmetics. (11) He confirmed a vow she had made to that effect. Though a husband has no right to impose such a vow upon his wife, he may confirm it by remaining silent when he hears that she has imposed such a vow upon herself; v. Num. XXX, 7ff; or, he vowed to abstain from his wife should she go to her father's house; cf. *supra* p. 433, n. 7. (12) Her father. [*Var. lec.* 'IF THEY', v. Rashi].

WAS FOR] ONE FESTIVAL,[1] [BUT IF FOR] THREE[2] FESTIVALS, HE MUST DIVORCE HER AND GIVE HER ALSO HER KETHUBAH. IF A MAN FORBADE HIS WIFE BY VOW[3] THAT SHE SHALL NOT VISIT A HOUSE OF MOURNING OR A HOUSE OF FEASTING, HE MUST DIVORCE HER AND GIVE HER ALSO HER KETHUBAH, BECAUSE THEREBY HE HAS CLOSED [PEOPLE'S DOORS] AGAINST HER. IF HE PLEADS, HOWEVER, [THAT HIS ACTION] WAS DUE TO SOME OTHER CAUSE[4] HE IS PERMITTED [TO FORBID HER]. IF HE SAID TO HER: '[THERE SHALL BE NO VOW] PROVIDED THAT YOU TELL[4] SO-AND-SO WHAT YOU HAVE TOLD ME' OR 'WHAT I HAVE TOLD YOU' OR 'THAT YOU SHALL FILL[4] AND POUR OUT ON THE RUBBISH HEAP', HE MUST DIVORCE HER AND GIVE HER ALSO HER KETHUBAH.

GEMARA. This, surely, is self-contradictory. You said, HE MAY KEEP [HER AS HIS WIFE, IF THE PROHIBITION WAS FOR] ONE FESTIVAL, which implies that if it was for two festivals he must divorce her and give her also her *kethubah*. But read the concluding clause, [IF FOR] THREE FESTIVALS HE MUST DIVORCE HER AND GIVE HER ALSO HER KETHUBAH, from which it follows, does it not, that if it was for two only he may keep [her as his wife]?[5] Abaye replied: The concluding clause refers to a priest's wife, and it represents the view of R. Judah.[6] Rabbah b. 'Ulla said: There is no contradiction, for one[7] refers to a woman who was anxious [to visit her parents home][8] and the other applies to one who was not anxious.[9]

(1) It was customary for daughters to visit their parents living in another town on the occasion of each major festival (v. p. 444, n. 7), and it was laid down that no hardship was involved if one such visit was omitted. (2) The question of two is discussed *infra*. (3) V. p. 444, n. 11. (4) This is explained in the Gemara. (5) How then are the two clauses to be reconciled? (6) In the Mishnah *supra* 70*a*. (7) Lit., 'here', the first clause which implies that if the prohibition is to last for two festivals the woman must be divorced and is to receive her *kethubah*. (8) רדופה, pass. particip. Kal of רדף, 'to pursue', v. next note. In the first year of her married life a woman is anxious, as soon as the first festival after her marriage approaches, to pay a visit to her paternal home where she looks forward to the enjoyment of recounting her novel experi-

Then[1] *was I in his eyes as one that found peace,*[2] R.[3] Joḥanan[4] interpreted: Like a bride[5] who was found faultless[6] in the house of her father-in-law[7] and she is anxious to go and tell of her success[8] at her paternal home.[9]

And it shall be at that day, saith the Lord, that thou shalt call me Ishi,[10] *and shalt not call me Ba'ali,*[11] R. Joḥanan interpreted: Like a bride in the house of her father-in-law[12] and not like a bride in her paternal home.[13]

IF A MAN FORBADE HIS WIFE BY VOW etc. One can well understand that in respect [of her prohibition to enter] A HOUSE OF FEASTING [72a] the reason, HE HAS CLOSED [PEOPLE'S DOORS] AGAINST HER, is applicable;[14] what [point, however,] is there [in the reason,] HE HAS CLOSED [PEOPLE'S DOORS] AGAINST HER, in the case of A HOUSE OF MOURNING?—A Tanna taught:

ences in her husband's home. If she is prevented by a vow from paying the visit at the first festival she must be given the opportunity of paying a visit not later than at the second festival. Hence if the vow is for the first two festivals, she is entitled to a divorce and to her *kethubah* also. (9) Where she is homesick and always longing to visit her parents, two festivals are considered a hardship. If she shews no such signs of homesickness there is no hardship involved unless the inhibition is for at least three festivals (Rashi). Tosaf. s.v. כאן explains differently: A woman who failed to visit her paternal home on the occasion of the first festival after her marriage is presumed to be fairly indifferent to such visits, and to be suffering no undue hardship by postponing her visit for another two festivals.

(1) *Var. lec.*, according to Tosaf. 'for it is written, *Then*'. (2) Cant. VIII, 10. (3) *Var. lec.*, according to Tosaf. 'and R.' etc. (4) *Var. lec.*, 'Jonathan'. (5) *Sc.* a woman in the first year of her married life. (6) שלמה (lit., 'whole', 'perfect') is of the same root as שלום (*peace*) in the text cited. (7) Where she lives with her husband. (8) Lit., 'her praise'. (9) Cf. *supra* p. 445, n. 8. (10) אִישִׁי, 'my husband', analogous to אישות 'matrimony', the term implying that the marital union between the parties is complete. (11) Hosea II, 18. בעלי, signifies 'my master', or 'my husband' in the sense that the man is lord over his wife. (12) I.e., after her marriage when her union with her husband is complete. (V. *supra* n. 10). (13) When her future husband is still her *ba'al* (master) and not her *Ish* (husband). Israel's relation to God, the prophet assures the people, will be intimate like that of the first mentioned bride and not cautious, reserved and uncertain like that of the latter. (14) By the confirmation of such a vow he deprives her of social enjoyments and relaxation.

To-morrow she might die and no creature would mourn for her.[1] Others read: And no creature would bury her.[2]

It was taught: R. Meir used to say: What is meant by the Scriptural text, *It is better to go to the house of mourning than to go to the house of feasting, for that is the end of all men, and the living will lay it to his heart,*[3] what, [I say, is meant by] *And the living will lay it*[4] *to his heart?* The matters relating to death. [Let him realize] that if a man mourns for other people others will also mourn for him; if he buries other people others will also bury him; if he lifts up [his voice to lament] for others, others will [lift up their voices to lament] for him; if he escorts others [to the grave] others will also escort him; if he carries others [to their last resting place] others will also carry him.

IF, HOWEVER, HE PLEADS [THAT HIS ACTION] WAS DUE TO SOME OTHER CAUSE HE IS PERMITTED. What is meant by SOME OTHER CAUSE?—Rab Judah citing Samuel replied: On account of dissolute men who frequent that place. Said R. Ashi: This applies only where [the place] has gained such a reputation; where, however, it has not gained such reputation it is not within the power of the husband [to veto it].[5]

IF HE SAID TO HER: '[THERE SHALL BE NO VOW] PROVIDED THAT YOU TELL [etc.].' [Why indeed] should she [not] tell it? —Rab Judah citing Samuel replied: [This refers to] abusive language.[6]

OR 'THAT YOU SHALL FILL AND POUR OUT ON THE RUBBISH HEAP'. [Why indeed] should she [not] do it?—Rab Judah citing Samuel replied: [Because the meaning of his request is] that she shall allow herself to be filled and then scatter it.[7] In a Baraitha it was taught: [The man's request is] that she shall fill ten jars of water and empty them on to the rubbish heap. Now according to

(1) As she had not participated in the mourning for others. (2) סופדה v. Tosef. Keth. VII and cf. *supra* n. 1 *mutatis mutandis*. *Aliter:* 'And none will care for her' (Jast.) סופנה (rt. ספן 'to hide', or 'to care for'). (3) Eccl. VII, 2. (4) Emphasis on *it*. (5) Lit., 'not as if all (the power) is from him'. (6) Lit., 'words of shame'. (7) Euphemism for vigorous exercise after intercourse in order to prevent conception.

[the explanation] of Samuel one can well see the reason why HE MUST DIVORCE HER AND GIVE HER ALSO HER KETHUBAH; according to the Baraitha, however, [the difficulty arises] what matters it to her if she does it?[1]—Rabbah b. Bar Ḥana citing R. Joḥanan replied: [She cannot be expected to do it] because she would appear like an imbecile.

R. Kahana stated: If a man placed his wife under a vow that she shall neither borrow nor lend a winnow, a sieve, a mill or an oven, he must divorce her and give her also her *kethubah*, because [should she fulfil the vow] he would give her a bad name among her neighbours. So it was also taught in a Baraitha: If a man placed his wife under a vow that she shall neither borrow nor lend a winnow, a sieve, a mill or an oven, he must divorce her and give her also her *kethubah*, because [should she comply with his desire] he would give her a bad name among her neighbours. Similarly if she vowed that she shall neither borrow nor lend a winnow, a sieve, a mill or an oven, or that she shall not weave beautiful garments for his children, she may be divorced without a *kethubah*, because [by acting on her wishes] she gives him a bad name among his neighbours.

MISHNAH. THESE ARE TO BE DIVORCED WITHOUT RECEIVING THEIR KETHUBAH: A WIFE WHO TRANSGRESSES THE LAW OF MOSES OR [ONE WHO TRANSGRESSES] JEWISH PRACTICE. AND WHAT IS [REGARDED AS A WIFE'S TRANSGRESSION AGAINST] THE LAW OF MOSES? FEEDING HER HUSBAND WITH UNTITHED FOOD,[2] HAVING INTERCOURSE WITH HIM DURING THE PERIOD OF HER MENSTRUATION,[3] NOT SETTING APART HER DOUGH OFFERING,[4] OR MAKING VOWS AND NOT FULFILLING THEM.[5] AND WHAT [IS DEEMED TO BE A WIFE'S TRANSGRESSION AGAINST] JEWISH PRACTICE? GOING OUT WITH UNCOVERED HEAD,[6] SPINNING IN THE STREET[7] OR CONVERSING WITH EVERY MAN. ABBA SAUL SAID: [SUCH

(1) Lit., 'let her do it'. (2) V. Num. XVIII, 21ff. (3) V. Lev. XVIII, 19. (4) V. Num. XV, 19ff. (5) V. Deut. XXIII, 22. (6) *Aliter:* With hair loose or unbound. (7) This is explained in the Gemara.

TRANSGRESSIONS INCLUDE] ALSO THAT OF A WIFE WHO CURSES HER HUSBAND'S PARENTS IN HIS PRESENCE. R. TARFON SAID: ALSO ONE WHO SCREAMS. AND WHO IS REGARDED A SCREAMER? A WOMAN WHOSE VOICE CAN BE HEARD BY HER NEIGHBOURS WHEN SHE SPEAKS INSIDE HER HOUSE.[1]

GEMARA. FEEDING HER HUSBAND WITH UNTITHED FOOD. How are we to understand this? If the husband knows [the fact],[2] let him abstain; if he does not know [it],[2] how did he discover it?—[This ruling was] required in the case only where she told him, 'So-and-so the priest has ritually prepared for me the pile of grain',[3] and he went and asked him and her statement was found to be untrue.

HAVING INTERCOURSE WITH HIM DURING THE PERIOD OF HER MENSTRUATION. How are we to understand this? If he was aware of her [condition] he could have abstained, if he was not aware [of it][4] he should still rely upon her, for R. Ḥinena b. Kahana stated in the name of Samuel: Whence is it deduced that the menstruant herself may [be relied upon to] count [correctly]?[5] From the Scriptural statement, *Then she shall number to herself*[6] *seven days*,[7] '*Lah* means to herself.'[8]—It was required in the case only where she said to her husband, 'So-and-so the sage told me that the blood was clean',[9] and when her husband went and asked him it was found that her statement was untrue. If you prefer I might reply on the lines of a ruling of Rab Judah who said: If a woman was known[10] among her neighbours to be a menstruant her husband[11] is flogged on her account for [having intercourse with] a menstruant.[12]

(1) This is explained in the Gemara. (2) When the food is given to him. (3) *Sc.* he has received his priestly dues. Asheri, Ṭur and Shulḥan 'Aruk omit 'priest'. Any person, by setting apart the priestly and Levitical dues, might ritually prepare the grain. (4) At the time. (5) The prescribed number of the days of her uncleanness. (6) לה. (7) Lev. XV, 28. (8) I.e., she may be implicitly trusted to count correctly. What need was there for the ruling in our Mishnah? (9) That it was not menstrual. (10) By her habit or the like. (11) If he had intercourse with her after he had been duly cautioned. (12) Ḳid. 80*a*. Our Mishnah would thus refer to a case where the neighbours informed the husband of the facts after the event.

NOT SETTING APART THE DOUGH OFFERING. How is this to be understood? If the husband was aware [of the fact] he should have abstained [from the food]; if he was not aware [of it at the time] how does he know it now?—[The ruling is to be understood as] required in the case only where she said to him, 'So-and-so the baker[1] has ritually prepared the dough[2] for me' and when the husband went and asked him her statement was found to be untrue.

OR MAKING VOWS AND NOT FULFILLING THEM; for the Master stated: One's children die on account of the sin of making vows,[3] as it is said in Scripture, *Suffer not thy mouth to cause thy flesh to sin* etc. [*wherefore should God be angry at thy voice, and destroy the work of thine hands*];[4] and what is the work of a man's hands? You must say: His sons and his daughters. R. Naḥman[5] said, [It[6] may be inferred] from the following: *In vain have I smitten your children;*[7] *'In vain'* implies, on account of vain utterances.[8]

It was taught: R. Meir said, Any man who knows that his wife makes vows and does not fulfil them should impose vows upon her again. [You say] 'Should impose vows upon her [again]'? Whereby would he reform her?[9]—But [say] he should provoke her again in order that she should make her vow in his presence[10] and he would [thus be able to] annul it.[11] They, however, said to him: No one can live with a serpent in the same basket.[12]

It was taught: R. Judah said, Any husband who knows that his wife does not [properly] set apart for him the dough offering should

(1) Lit., 'kneader'. (2) I.e., he has duly set apart the dough offering. (3) And not fulfilling them nor applying for their disallowance. (4) Eccl. V, 5. (5) Var., 'R. Naḥman b. Isaac' (Shab. 32*b*). (6) The penalty for the sin of vows. (7) Jer. II, 30. (8) Vows made but not fulfilled. (9) The imposition of an additional vow would hardly induce her to fulfil her former vows or change her habits. (10) ידירנה (Hif. of נדר) may bear this meaning, 'he shall cause her (by his provocation) to vow', as also the previously assumed meaning, 'he shall cause her to be under (*sc.* impose upon her) a vow'. (11) And so avoid the necessity of divorcing her. (12) Proverb; if it is the woman's habit to make vows and to break them it is practically impossible for her husband to be always on the look out to invalidate them. She would, despite all vigilance, manage to make vows of which he would remain ignorant. He is entitled, therefore, to insist on divorcing her.

set it apart again after her. They, however, said to him: No one can live with a serpent in the same basket.[1] He who taught it[2] in connection with this case[3] [would apply it] with even greater force to the other case;[4] he, however, who taught it in connection with the other case [applies it to that case only][5] but [not to this one,[3] because][6] it might sometimes happen that he would eat.[7]

AND WHAT [IS DEEMED TO BE A WIFE'S TRANSGRESSION AGAINST] JEWISH PRACTICE? GOING OUT WITH UNCOVERED HEAD. [Is not the prohibition against going out with] an uncovered head Pentateuchal;[8] for it is written, *And he shall uncover the woman's head,*[9] and this, it was taught at the school of R. Ishmael, was a warning to the daughters of Israel that they should not go out with uncovered[10] head?[11]—Pentateuchally [72*b*] it is quite satisfactory [if her head is covered by] her work-basket;[12] according to traditional Jewish practice, however, she is forbidden [to go out uncovered] even with her basket [on her head].

R. Assi stated in the name of R. Johanan: With a basket [on her head a woman] is not guilty of[13] [going about with] an uncovered head. In considering this statement, R. Zera pointed out this difficulty: Where [is the woman assumed to be]?[14] If it be suggested, 'In the street', [it may be objected that this is already forbidden by] Jewish practice;[15] but [if she is] in a court-yard[14] [the

(1) Cf. p. 450, n. 12 *mutatis mutandis*. (2) R. Judah's ruling which aims at avoiding a divorce. (3) The dough offering. (4) Vows. A transgression in connection with these (which are not common) is much less likely than in connection with the dough offering which has to be given from every dough that is made. If, according to R. Judah, divorce should be avoided in the latter case how much more so in the former. (5) Cf. *supra* n. 4. (6) Owing to the frequency of bread baking. (7) Bread, the dough offering from which had not been set apart. As one is more likely to commit a transgression in this case R. Judah would not seek to avoid a divorce. (8) Why then is it here described as one of mere Jewish practice? (9) Num. V. 18 (v. A.V.) R.V. and A.J.V. render 'And let the hair of the woman's head go loose'. (10) Cf. *supra* n. 9. (11) Why then was this described as traditional Jewish practice? (12) קלתה or קלת, *calathus*, 'a woven vase-shaped basket'. (13) Lit., 'there is not in her'. (14) When her head is covered by her basket only. (15) Spoken of in our Mishnah. What need then was there for R. Johanan's statement?

objection may be made that] if that were so[1] you will not leave our father Abraham a [single] daughter who could remain with her husband![2]—Abaye, or it might be said, R. Kahana, replied: [The statement refers to one who walks] from one courtyard into another by way of an alley.[3]

SPINNING IN THE STREET. Rab Judah stated in the name of Samuel: [The prohibition applies only] where she exposed her arms to the public. R. Ḥisda stated in the name of Abimi: [This applies only] where she spins rose [coloured materials, and holds them up] to her face.[4]

CONVERSING WITH EVERY MAN. Rab Judah stated in the name of Samuel: [This refers only to one] who jests with young men.

Rabbah b. Bar Hana related: I was once walking behind R. 'Ukba when I observed an Arab woman who was sitting, casting her spindle and spinning a rose [coloured material which she held up] to her face.[5] When she saw us she detached the spindle [from the thread], threw it down and said to me, 'Young man, hand me my[6] spindle'. Referring to her[7] R. 'Uḳba made a statement. What was that statement?—Rabina replied: He spoke of her as a woman SPINNING IN THE STREET. The Rabbis said: He spoke of her as one CONVERSING WITH EVERY MAN.

ABBA SAUL SAID: [SUCH TRANSGRESSIONS INCLUDE] ALSO THAT OF A WIFE WHO CURSES HER HUSBAND'S PARENTS IN HIS PRESENCE. Rab Judah said in the name of Samuel: [This[8]

(1) That otherwise the law of 'uncovered head' applies also in a court-yard. (2) Since all married women go about in their court-yards with uncovered heads. (3) Into which the two courts open out. An alley, since fewer people frequent it, would not have been included in the restrictions spoken of in our Mishnah in respect of a public street, yet it is not considered sufficiently private to allow the woman to go about there with 'uncovered head'. Hence the necessity for the specific ruling of R. Joḥanan. (4) That it might reflect the rose colour. וֶרֶד 'rose'. (V. Tosaf. s.v. בטווה). *Aliter:* 'Spins with a rose in her hair', reading ווֶרֶד 'and a rose' (Maim.). *Aliter:* 'Spins with the thread lowered in front of her face' (euphemism), reading וְרָד rt. רדד, 'to flatten', 'lower' (Rashi). *Var. lec.* וְיוֹרֵד (rt. ירד) 'to go down', 'descend' (cf. Jast. and Golds.). (5) Cf. *supra* n. 4. (6) Reading פלכאי (Aruch). Cur. edd., פלך. (7) Lit., 'on her' or 'it'. (8) The expression המקללת . . . בפניו, WHO CURSES. . . . IN HIS PRESENCE.

includes also] one who curses his parents in the presence of his offspring;[1] and your mnemonic sign[2] is, *Ephraim and Manasseh,*[3] *even as Reuben and Simeon,*[4] *shall be mine.*[5] Rabbah[6] explained:[7] When she said[8] in the presence of her husband's son, 'May a lion devour your grandfather'.[9]

R. TARFON SAID: ALSO ONE WHO SCREAMS. What is meant by a screamer?—Rab Judah replied in the name of Samuel: One who speaks aloud[10] on marital matters. In a Baraitha it was taught: [By screams was meant a wife] whose voice[11] during her intercourse in one court can be heard in another court. But should not this, then,[12] have been taught in the Mishnah[13] among defects?[14]—Clearly we must revert to the original explanation.[15]

MISHNAH. IF A MAN BETROTHED A WOMAN ON CONDITION THAT SHE WAS NOT SUBJECT TO ANY VOWS AND SHE WAS FOUND TO BE UNDER A VOW,[16] HER BETROTHAL IS INVALID. IF HE MARRIED HER[17] WITHOUT MAKING ANY CONDITIONS AND SHE WAS FOUND TO BE UNDER A VOW,[16] SHE MAY BE DIVORCED WITHOUT RECEIVING HER KETHUBAH.

[IF A WOMAN WAS BETROTHED] ON CONDITION THAT SHE HAS NO BODILY DEFECTS, AND SHE WAS FOUND TO HAVE SUCH DEFECTS, HER BETROTHAL IS INVALID. IF HE MARRIED HER WITHOUT MAKING ANY CONDITIONS AND SHE WAS FOUND TO HAVE BODILY DEFECTS, SHE MAY BE DIVORCED

(1) MS.M. יולדיו בפני מולדיו; Cur. edd. יולידיו בפני מולידיו. (2) To aid in the recollection that one's offspring is like oneself. (3) Jacob's grandchildren. (4) His own children. (5) Gen. XLVIII, 5. (6) Var., 'Raba'. (7) The cursing of which Samuel spoke. (8) [V. Tosaf. s.v. יולידיו; cur. edd. add 'to him']. (9) V. Rashi, and Tosaf. *loc. cit.* (10) Lit., 'makes her voice heard'. (11) Her screams of pain caused by the copulation. (12) Since her screaming is due to a bodily defect. (13) *Infra 77a.* (14) Of course it should. Such a case in our Mishnah is out of place. (15) That given in the name of Samuel. (16) Lit., 'and vows were found upon her'. (17) Lit., 'he took her, in (his house)'. It will be explained *infra* whether this does or does not refer to the preceding case.

WITHOUT A KETHUBAH. ALL DEFECTS WHICH DISQUALIFY PRIESTS[1] DISQUALIFY WOMEN ALSO.[2]

GEMARA. We have [in fact] learned [the same Mishnah] also in [the Tractate] Ḳiddushin.[3] [But] here[4] [the laws][5] were required [in respect of] ***kethuboth***,[6] and the laws concerning betrothal[7] were stated on account of those of the ***kethubah***; there[8] the laws in respect of betrothal were required, and those concerning ***kethuboth***[5] were stated on account of those of betrothal.

R. Joḥanan said in the name of R. Simeon b. Jehozadak: They[9] spoke only of the following vows. That she would not eat meat, that she would not drink wine or that she would not adorn herself with coloured garments. So it was also taught elsewhere: They spoke of such vows as involve an affliction of the soul, [namely,] that she would not eat meat, that she would not drink wine or that she would not adorn herself with coloured garments.

In dealing with this subject R. Papa raised this difficulty: What does it[10] refer to? If it be suggested [that it refers] to the first clause[11] [it might be retorted that] since the husband objects [to vows] even other kinds of vows[12] should also be included! —[It refers] only to the final clause.[13] R. Ashi said: It may in fact refer to the first clause,[11] but in respect of the vows to which people usually take exception[14] his objection is valid;[15] in respect of vows to which people do not as a rule take exception his objection has no validity.

It was stated: If a man betrothed a woman on condition [that she was under no vow] and married her without attaching any

(1) From the Temple service (cf. Lev. XXI, 17ff). (2) From marriage. If such a woman married she may be divorced without a *kethubah*. (3) In Ḳid. 50*a*. (4) Since our tractate is dealing with the laws of *kethubah*. (5) DIVORCED WITHOUT A KETHUBAH (*bis*). (6) Plural of *kethubah*. (7) HER BETROTHAL IS INVALID. (8) In the tractate of Ḳid. 50*a*. (9) The Rabbis in our Mishnah. (10) The definition of vows given in the name of R. Simeon b. Jehozadak. (11) Where the husband explicitly expressed his objection to betroth a woman who was under a vow. (12) Lit., 'all words', 'things'. (13) Where the husband had made no conditions. (14) Such as those mentioned in R. Simeon b. Jehozadak's definition. (15) And the betrothal, therefore, is invalid.

conditions, it is necessary, Rab ruled, that she[1] shall obtain from him a letter of divorce; and Samuel ruled: It is not necessary for her to obtain a letter of divorce from him.[2] Said Abaye: [73*a*] It must not be suggested that Rab's reason[3] is that, because the man has married her without attaching any conditions, he has entirely dispensed with his former condition.[4] Rab's reason rather is that no man treats his intercourse as a mere act of prostitution.[5]

Surely they[6] once disputed on such a principle.[7] For it was stated: Where [an orphan] minor[8] who did not[9] exercise her right of *mi'un*[10] and who, when she came of age, left[11] [her husband][12] and married [another man], Rab ruled: She requires no letter of divorce from her second husband,[13] and Samuel ruled: She requires a letter of divorce from her second husband![14]—[Both disputes were]

(1) If it was found that she was under a vow, and the man consequently refuses to live with her. (2) Cf. Yeb. 110*a*. (3) For regarding the marriage as valid. (4) And consequently he must not only divorce her but must give her her *kethubah* also. (5) The consummation of the marriage was, therefore, a legal act necessitating a divorce for its annulment. In respect of the monetary obligation, however, the man still adheres to his original condition which she did not fulfil, and he cannot consequently be expected to give her also her *kethubah*. (6) Rab and Samuel. (7) I.e., whether intercourse after a conditional betrothal (the case spoken of *supra* 72*b*), or a legally imperfect marriage or betrothal (the case cited *infra* from Yeb. 109*b*) has the force of a valid and proper marriage to require the divorce for its annulment. (8) Who was given in marriage by her mother or brothers. (9) While she was still in her minority. (10) V. Glos. (11) Lit., 'stood up'. (12) With whom she had intercourse after she had come of age. (13) Because, according to Rab, her second marriage was null and void owing to the *kinyan* (v. Glos.) effected by the intercourse of the first husband when she came of age. (V. *supra* n. 12). Being well aware that the original marriage which took place during the woman's minority had no legal force, the man is presumed to have intended his intercourse after she had attained her majority to effect the required legal *kinyan* of marriage. (14) Yeb. 109*b*; because any act of intercourse on the part of the first husband, even after the woman had attained her majority, was carried out in reliance on the original betrothal which, having taken place while she was a minor, had no validity. Her betrothal to the second is, therefore, valid and must be annulled by a proper divorce. Though it may be added, Samuel admits that she is prohibited to the second husband, having regard to the fact that she did not exercise her right until she reached her majority (v. Nid. 52*a*). This prohibition

necessary. For if the latter[1] only had been stated, it might have been assumed that Rab adhered to his opinion[2] in that case only because no condition was attached [to the betrothal],[3] but that in the former case,[4] where a condition was attached [to the betrothal],[5] he agrees with Samuel.[6] And if the former case[4] only had been stated, it might have been assumed that in that case only[7] did Samuel maintain his view[8] but that in the latter[1] he agrees with Rab.[9] [Hence both were] required.

We have learned: IF HE MARRIED HER WITHOUT MAKING ANY CONDITION AND SHE WAS FOUND TO BE UNDER A VOW, SHE MAY BE DIVORCED WITHOUT RECEIVING HER KETHUBAH [which[10] implies that] it is only her *kethubah* that she cannot claim but that she nevertheless requires a letter of divorce. Now does not this[11] refer to one who has betrothed a woman on condition [that she was under no vow][12] and married her without making any condition?[13] This then[14] represents an objection against Samuel![15]

is nevertheless only Rabbinical and consequently has no bearing on the question of the divorce, the purpose of which is to sever a union which is Pentateuchally binding. According to Rab, however, (v. *supra* p. 455, n. 13) the prohibition of the woman to her second husband is not merely Rabbinical but is, in fact, Pentateuchal. Why then should Rab and Samuel dispute on the same principle twice?

(1) Lit., 'that', the dispute in the case of the minor, cited from Yeb. 109b. (2) That the intercourse of the first husband is regarded as a *kinyan*. (3) And the husband may, therefore, be presumed to be anxious to give to the union all the necessary validity of a proper marriage (cf. *supra* p. 455, n. 13). (4) That stated *supra* 72*b*. (5) And the husband naturally believes that the woman, since she consented to the marriage, was in a position to fulfil it. (6) That, as it never occured to the husband (v. *supra* n. 5) that his original betrothal was in any way invalid, and as he did not, therefore, betroth her by subsequent cohabitation, no divorce is required. (7) Since a condition was attached to the original betrothal. (8) That the marriage, owing to its dependence on the original condition, is invalid. (9) That, since no conditions were made, the intercourse of the first husband after her attaining majority has the validity of a *kinyan*, and no divorce from the second is required. (10) Since the *kethubah* was excluded and not the letter of divorce. (11) The second clause of our Mishnah. (12) I.e., the case spoken of in the first and previous clause, the second clause of the Mishnah being dependent on the first. (13) Which is the case in dispute between Rab and Samuel. (14) The answer being apparently in the affirmative,

[73*b*]—No; [this[1] refers to one who] betrothed her without attaching a condition and also married her without attaching a condition.[2] If, however, one betrothed a woman on a certain condition and subsequently married her without attaching a condition would she, [according to our Mishnah], indeed[3] require no divorce?[4] If so, then, instead of stating, IF A MAN BETROTHED A WOMAN ON THE CONDITION THAT SHE WAS NOT SUBJECT TO ANY VOWS AND SHE WAS FOUND TO BE UNDER A VOW, HER BETROTHAL IS INVALID,[5] it should rather have been stated: If a man married a woman without attaching a condition and she was found to be under a vow, her betrothal is invalid, and [it would be evident, would it not, that this[6] applies] even more so to the former?[7]—It is really this reading that was meant:[8] IF A MAN BETROTHED A WOMAN ON THE CONDITION THAT SHE WAS NOT SUBJECT TO ANY VOWS, and then he married her without making any conditions, AND SHE WAS FOUND TO BE UNDER A VOW, HER BETROTHAL IS INVALID; if, however, he betrothed her without making any conditions and also MARRIED HER WITHOUT MAKING ANY CONDITIONS, SHE MAY BE DIVORCED WITHOUT RECEIVING HER KETHUBAH; it is only her *kethubah* that she cannot claim but it is necessary for her to obtain a divorce. But why has she no claim to her *kethubah?* Because, [apparently], he[9] could plead, 'I do not want a wife that is in the habit of making vows',[10] but if that is the case there should be no need for her to

and the implication being that a divorce is required. (15) Who ruled (*supra* 72*b ad. fin.*) that no divorce is necessary.

(1) The second clause of our Mishnah. (2) I.e., the second clause of our Mishnah is not dependent on the first one. (3) Lit., 'thus'. (4) This would seem to follow from the interpretation of our Mishnah just advanced on behalf of Samuel. (5) A form of expression which, omitting all reference to marriage, might imply that if she was subsequently married unconditionally a divorce is required. (6) That the betrothal is invalid and that consequently no divorce is required. (7) The case enunciated in the present form of our Mishnah where the betrothal was not followed by marriage. (8) Lit., 'thus also he said'. (9) Should he be ordered to pay the *kethubah*. (10) And her betrothal is, therefore, invalid as if the man had advanced such a plea at the actual time of the betrothal.

obtain a divorce either![1]—Rabbah replied: It is only according to Rabbinical law that she requires a divorce. So also said R. Ḥisda: It is only in accordance with the Rabbinical law that she requires a divorce. Raba replied: The Tanna[2] was really in doubt.[3] [Hence he adopted] the lenient view in monetary matters[4] and the stricter one[5] in the case of prohibitions.[6]

Rabbah stated: They[7] differ only in the case of an error[8] [affecting] two women,[9] but where an error [affects] one woman[10] all agree[11] that she requires no divorce from him.[12] Said Abaye:[13] But our Mishnah, surely, is one which [has been assumed[14] to refer to] an error [affecting] one woman but was nevertheless adduced as an objection![15] If, however, such a statement was made at all it must have been made in this form: Rabbah stated: They[16] differ only in

(1) Cf. p. 457, n. 10. Rab's view that 'no man treats his intercourse as a mere act of prostitution' (*supra* 73*a*) cannot be advanced here in reply, since Samuel, whose views are the subject of the present discussion, does not admit it. (2) Of our Mishnah. (3) As to whether the presumption that, as a rule, one does not want to live with a wife who is in the habit of making vows is sufficient reason for regarding the betrothal of such a woman as null and void. (4) I.e., the *kethubah*. As the woman's claim to it is of a doubtful nature, her husband who is the possessor of the money cannot be made to pay it. (5) That a divorce is necessary if she wishes to remarry. (6) It is forbidden to live with another man's wife. (7) Rab and Samuel, *supra* 72*b*, *ad fin*. (8) I.e., the man believed that the woman was under no vow while in fact she was. (9) The first of whom a man betrothed on the condition that she was under no vow and the second of whom he afterwards married without making any condition and subsequently found that she was under a vow. Samuel regards the non-conditional marriage of the second as invalid because the man is presumed to have married her on the same condition as that on which he betrothed the first. Rab, however, maintains that it is quite possible that the man was so attracted by the second woman that he was willing to dispense with his terms. (10) Whom the man betrothed on a certain condition and afterwards married without making any condition. (11) Even Rab. (12) Since the man has made it clear at the betrothal that he objected to live with her if she were encumbered with any vows. (13) Rashal deletes 'to him', which appears in brackets in cur. edd. (14) *Supra* 73*a ad fin*. (15) Against Samuel (l.c.); which shews, contrary to Rabbah's assumption, that even in the case of a mistake in respect of one woman, some authorities maintain that a divorce is required. (16) Rab and Samuel, *supra* 72*b ad fin*.

the case of an error [affecting] a woman [who is in a position] similar [to that of one of] two women,[1] but in the case of an error [affecting] merely one woman[2] all agree[3] that she requires no divorce from him.[4]

Abaye raised an objection against him:[5] If a man betrothed a woman in error[6] or [with something worth] less than a *perutah*,[7] and, similarly, if a minor betrothed a woman, even if any [of them] has subsequently sent presents[8] [to the woman], her betrothal is invalid,[9] because he has sent these gifts on account of the original betrothal.[10] If, however, they[11] had intercourse they have thereby effected legal *kinyan*. R. Simeon b. Judah in the name of R. Ishmael said: Even if they had intercourse they effect no *kinyan*.[12] Now here, surely, it is an error [affecting] only one woman and they[13] nevertheless differ. Would you not [admit that by 'error' is meant] an error in respect of vows?[14]—No; [what was meant is] an error in

(1) One, for instance, who was betrothed on a certain condition, was then divorced and subsequently married with no condition. In such a case Rab maintains that a divorce is required as in the case of the second woman where two women were involved (cf. *supra* p. 458, n. 9), while Samuel maintains that no divorce is required because the man's condition at the betrothal is regarded as a permanent declaration that he would not live with a woman who was in the habit of making vows and, since this condition renders the marriage null and void, no divorce is required to annul such a marriage. (2) I.e., one whose marriage had followed her betrothal, and no divorce had intervened, so that the man may well be presumed to have consummated marriage on the same terms as those he laid down at the betrothal. (3) Even Rab. (4) In raising the objection against Samuel *supra* our Mishnah was assumed to deal with 'a woman who was in a position similar to that of two women' (cf. *supra* n. 1). (5) Rabbah. (6) This, at present, is presumed to mean that the woman was under a vow and the man was at the time unaware of it. (7) V. Glos. (8) *Sablonoth*; v. Kid. Sonc. ed. p. 254, n. 4. (9) Although the presents, if specifically given as a token of betrothal, would effect a valid *kinyan* of betrothal. (10) And since that betrothal is invalid the gifts cannot effect the necessary *kinyan*. (11) Any of those mentioned whose betrothal is invalid. (12) Tosef. Kid. IV. (13) R. Ishmael and the first Tanna. (14) Cf. *supra* note 6. This proves that one authority at least (viz. the first Tanna) regards a non-conditional marriage as valid though it followed a conditional betrothal. How then could Rabbah maintain, according to the second version, that in such a case all agree that, as the marriage is invalid, no divorce is required.

respect of that which was worth less than a *peruṭah*.[1] —But was not 'less than than a *peruṭah*' explicitly mentioned: 'If a man betrothed a woman in error or [with something worth] less than a *peruṭah*'?[2] —[The latter part is] really an explanation [of the former:] What is meant by 'If a man betrothed a woman in error'? If, for instance, he betrothed her with 'something worth less than a *peruṭah*'.

On what principle do they[3] differ?[4] —One Master[5] holds the view that everyone is aware that with less than the value of a *peruṭah* no betrothal can be effected, and consequently any man having intercourse [after such an invalid act] determines [to do so] for the purpose of betrothal. The other Master,[6] however, holds the view that not everyone is aware that with less than the value of a *peruṭah* no betrothal can be effected, and when a man has intercourse [after such an act[7] he does so] in reliance on his first betrothal.[8]

He raised [another] objection against him:[9] [If a man said to a woman,] 'I am having intercourse with you on the condition that my father will consent',[10] she is betrothed to him even if his father did not consent. R. Simeon b. Judah, however, stated in the name

(1) The man, at the time of betrothal, having been under the erroneous impression that *ḳinyan* may be effected by such an insignificant sum. Since this law is generally known it may well be presumed that subsequent intercourse was intended as *ḳinyan*. In the case of an error in respect of vows, however, subsequent intercourse cannot alter the invalidity of the betrothal since during the performance of the latter act the man may still have been under the impression that his wife was not restricted by any vow. The general opinion, therefore, is, Rabbah may well maintain, that no divorce is in this case required. (2) Is it likely that the same law should be repeated in the same context? (3) R. Ishmael and the first Tanna. (4) On the previous assumption (that the 'error' referred to the conditional betrothal of a woman who was under a vow) the principles underlying this dispute might be those upheld *supra* by Rab and Samuel respectively. On the present assumption, however, (that the 'error' refers to a betrothal attempted with less than a *peruṭah*) the difficulty arises (cf. *supra* note 1) 'on what principles do they differ?' *sc.* how could R. Ishmael maintain his view that 'even if they had cohabited they effect no *ḳinyan*'? (5) The first Tanna. (6) R. Ishmael. (7) Which he believes to be a valid betrothal. (8) Which was in fact invalid and in consequence of which the cohabitation constitutes no *ḳinyan*. (9) Rabbah. (10) To the union.

of R. Simeon, If his father consented she is betrothed but if his father did not consent she is not betrothed.[1] Now here, surely, it is a case similar to that of an error affecting one woman[2] and they[3] nevertheless differ![4]—They differ in this case[5] on the following points.[6] One Master[7] holds the opinion that [the expression] 'On the condition that my father consents' implies, 'On condition that my father will remain silent', and [the betrothal is valid] because, surely, his father remained silent. And the other Master[8] holds the opinion [that the meaning of the expression is] that his father will say, 'yes', and [the betrothal is invalid] because his father in fact did not say, 'yes'.

He raised [a further] objection against him.[9] The Sages agree with R. Eliezer[10] in respect of a minor whom her father had given in marriage and who was divorced,[11] [in consequence of which] she is regarded as an 'orphan' in her father's lifetime,[12] and who was then remarried,[13] that she must perform *halizah*[14] but may not[15] contract the levirate marriage because her divorce was a perfectly legal divorce,[16] but her remarriage was not a perfectly legal remarriage.[17] This,[18] however, applies only where he[19] divorced her while she was a minor[20] and remarried her while she was still a

(1) Giṭ. 25*b*. (2) Since in both cases a condition was attached to the betrothal, merely one woman is involved, and no divorce intervened between betrothal and intercourse. (3) R. Simeon and the first Tanna. (4) R. Simeon maintaining that the intercourse is a valid *kinyan*, and a divorce is consequently required. How then (cf. *supra* p. 459, n. 14 *mutatis mutandis*) could Rabbah assert that in such a case all agree that no divorce is necessary? (5) Lit., 'there'. (6) Not on the principle underlying Rabbah's assertion. (7) The first Tanna. (8) R. Simeon. (9) Rabbah. (10) The reading in the parallel passage, Yeb. 109*a*, is 'Eleazar'. (11) Her father having received the letter of divorce on her behalf. (12) Like an orphan, she has no father to give her away in marriage, because though alive he has lost his right to do so after he has given her in marriage once. (13) Lit., 'he (the first husband from whom she was divorced) married her again'. While she was still in her minority when her actions have no legal validity. (14) V. Glos. (15) If her husband died childless and was survived by a brother. (16) And as the divorcee of his brother she is forbidden to the levir under the penalty of *kareth* (v. Glos.). (17) Cf. *supra* n. 13. (18) That the Sages admit that the minor in question may not contract the levirate marriage. (19) Her first husband. (20) The validity of the divorce

minor;[1] but if he[2] divorced her while she was a minor[3] and re-married her while she was still a minor and she became of age while she was still with him, and then he died,[4] she must either perform *ḥaliẓah* or contract the levirate marriage.[5] [74a] In the name of R. Eliezer,[6] however, it was stated: She[7] must perform *ḥaliẓah* but may not contract the levirate marriage.[8] Now, here,[9] surely, it is a case similar to that of an error[10] affecting merely one woman and they[11] nevertheless differ![12] — In that case[13] also [it may be said that][14] they[11] differ on the following principles.[15] One Master[16]

being due to the fact that her father has accepted the letter of divorce on her behalf.

(1) When neither she nor her father (cf. *supra* p. 461, n. 12) had the right to contract the marriage; and her husband died while she was still in her minority so that no intercourse at all had taken place when she came of age. (2) Her first husband. (3) V. p. 461, n. 20. (4) So that it was possible for intercourse to take place when she was already in her majority. (5) Because the act of intercourse after she had come of age constituted a legal *ḳinyan* of marriage, and she became thereby the legally married wife of the deceased. (6) V. *supra* p. 461, n. 10. (7) Whom the first husband remarried 'while she was still a minor and she came of age while she was with him, and then he died' (cf. Rashi, second version, s.v. ה"ד *a.l.*). *Aliter:* Even if she was remarried after she came of age, or was divorced and remarried after she came of age, R. Eliezer's reason being that preventive measures were necessary against the possibility of erroneously allowing one who was an 'orphan in the lifetime of her father' to contract levirate marriage. If the former interpretation is adopted the author of the Baraitha here cited would be in disagreement with the one in Yeb. 109a (v. Rashi l.c.); if the latter interpretation is adopted, the reading of cur. edd. *infra* is to be emended (v. *infra* note 14). (8) V. Yeb. 109a where this passage occurs with some slight variations. (9) Where remarriage took place 'while she was still a minor and she came of age while she was with him'. (10) The error of believing the betrothal of the minor to be valid. (11) The Sages and R. Eliezer. (12) The Sages maintaining that levirate marriage may be contracted; which proves that the intercourse that took place when she was of age is regarded as a valid *ḳinyan*. As the same principle applies also to the case of error in respect of a woman under a vow (*supra*) an objection arises against Rabbah (cf. *supra* p. 459, n. 14). (13) Lit., 'there'. (14) If the second interpretation (*supra* note 7) is adopted the reading is to be emended to: Every one knows that the betrothal of a minor is invalid, but where one betrothed a woman on a certain condition and then had intercourse he does so in reliance on this condition (v. Rashi). (15) Not on the one underlying the case of which Rabbah spoke. (16) The view expressed by the Sages.

maintains that everyone is aware that there is no validity in the betrothal of a minor and, consequently, any man having intercourse [after such an invalid act] determines that his intercourse shall serve the purpose of a betrothal.[1] The other Master,[2] however, maintains that not everyone is aware that there is no validity in the betrothal of a minor, and when a man has intercourse [after such an act[3] he does so] in reliance on his original betrothal.[4]

[So][5] it was also stated: R. Aḥa b. Jacob stated in the name of R. Joḥanan, If a man betrothed a woman on a certain condition and then had intercourse with her, she,[6] it is the opinion of all, requires no letter of divorce from him.

R. Aḥa the son of R. Iḳa, his[7] sister's son[8] raised an objection against him: A *ḥaliẓah* under a false pretext[9] is valid; and what is 'a *ḥaliẓah* under a false pretext'? Resh Laḳish explained: Where a levir is told, 'Submit to her *ḥaliẓah* and you will thereby wed her'. Said R. Joḥanan to him:[10] I am in the habit of repeating [a Baraitha,] 'Whether he[11] had the intention[12] [of performing the commandment of *ḥaliẓah*] and she had no such intention, or whether she had such intention and he had not, her *ḥaliẓah* is invalid, it being necessary[13] that both shall [at the same time] have such intention', and you say that her *ḥaliẓah* is valid?[14] But, said R. Joḥanan, [this is the meaning:][15] When a levir is told, 'Submit to her *ḥaliẓah* on the con-

(1) Hence the validity of the marriage and the permissibility of a levirate marriage. (2) R. Eliezer. (3) Which he believes to be a valid betrothal. (4) Which in fact was invalid. Hence the invalidity of the marriage etc. (cf. *supra* note 1). (5) In agreement with Rabbah who stated (*supra* 73*b*) that 'in the case of an error affecting merely one woman all agree that she requires no divorce from him'. (6) If the condition has not been fulfilled. (7) R. Aḥa b. Jacob's. (8) MS.M. reads 'son of the sister of Resh Laḳish'. (9) מוטעת (rt. טעה, Hof'al.) lit., 'misled'. (10) Resh Laḳish. Cur. edd. omit 'to him' which is the reading of MS.M. (11) The levir. (12) When he submitted to *ḥaliẓah*. (13) Lit., 'until'. (14) If the levir, according to the interpretation of Resh Laḳish, performed the *ḥaliẓah* in order to effect thereby a *ḳinyan* of marriage, he obviously did not intend to perform the commandment of *ḥaliẓah* the very purpose of which is not the union of the woman with, but her separation from, the levir. And, since there was no intention to perform the commandment, how could such a *ḥaliẓah* be valid? (15) Of 'a *ḥaliẓah* under a false pretext'.

dition that she gives you two hundred *zuz*'.[1] Thus[2] it clearly follows that as soon as a man has performed an act[3] he has thereby dispensed with his condition, [why then should it not be said] here also that as soon as the man has intercourse he has thereby dispensed with his condition?[4]—The other replied: Young hopeful,[5] do you speak sensibly?[6] Consider: Whence do we derive [the law of the validity of] any condition? [Obviously] from the condition in respect of the sons of Gad and the sons of Reuben;[7] [hence it is only] a condition that may be carried out through an agent, as was the case there,[8] that is regarded as a valid condition; but one which cannot be carried out through an agent,[9] as was the case there, is not regarded as a valid condition.[10] But is not intercourse[11] an act which cannot be performed through an agent as was the case there[8] and yet a condition in connection with it is valid?[12]—The reason[13] there is because the various forms of betrothal[14] were compared to one another.[15]

(1) V. Glos. Even if the promised sum was not paid to the levir the *ḥaliẓah* is nevertheless valid. Tosef. Yeb. XII, Yeb. 106*a*. (2) Since the non-fulfilment of the condition does not invalidate the *ḥaliẓah*. (3) [Without emphasizing at the time that he does so in reliance on the condition (v. Tosaf.).] (4) And the woman should, therefore, become his lawful wife. How then could R. Aḥa b. Jacob maintain in the name of R. Joḥanan that a betrothal, on a certain condition that has not been fulfilled, is invalid and no divorce is required even if intercourse followed the betrothal? (5) Lit., 'son of the school house'. (6) Lit., 'beautiful'. (7) V. Num. XXXII, 29, 30 and Ḳid. 61*a*. (8) Moses instructed Joshua to act, so to speak, as his agent in carrying out the condition he had made (v. Num. XXXII, 28ff). (9) *Ḥaliẓah*, for instance. The levir cannot instruct an agent to submit to *ḥaliẓah* on his behalf when the sum promised shall have been handed to him. (10) As the condition is null and void the act of *ḥaliẓah* remains valid despite the unfulfilled condition. Where, however, the condition was valid, as in the case of the betrothal spoken of by R. Aḥa b. Jacob, the non-fulfilment of the condition renders the betrothal null and void and no subsequent intercourse can be regarded as an annulment of the condition and confirmation of the betrothal. (11) When it was intended as a *ḳinyan* of marriage. (12) As was stated in the passage quoted from Giṭ. 25*b* (*supra* 73*b*). (13) For the validity of the condition. (14) הויות (rt. היה) lit., 'beings', 'becomings'. היה is the rt. of והיתה (Deut. XXIV, 2), *and she becometh . . . wife*. A woman may become a man's wife either by receiving from him (*a*) money (or its equivalent in kind) or (*b*) a deed or (*c*) by cohabitation (Ḳid. 2*a*). (15) As a

R. 'Ulla b. Abba in the name of 'Ulla in the name of R. Eleazar stated: If a man betrothed a woman by a loan[1] and then had intercourse with her, or on a certain condition[2] and then had intercourse with her, or with less than the value of a *peruṭah*[3] and then had intercourse with her, she,[4] it is the opinion of all, requires from him a letter of divorce.[5]

R. Joseph b. Abba, in the name of R. Menahem in the name of R. Ammi stated: If a man betrothed a woman with something worth less than a *peruṭah*[3] and then had intercourse with her, she[4] requires a letter of divorce from him.[5] It is only in this case[6] that no one could be mistaken,[7] but in the case of the others[8] a man may be mistaken.[9]

R. Kahana stated in the name of 'Ulla: If a man betrothed a woman on a certain condition[2] and then had intercourse with her, she[4] requires a divorce from him.[5] Such a case once occurred and the Sages could find no legal ground[10] for releasing the woman without a letter of divorce. [This is meant] to exclude [the ruling] of the following Tanna. For Rab Judah stated in the name of Samuel in the name of R. Ishmael: *And she be not seized*[11] [only

condition in connection with (*a*) and (*b*) (which may be performed through an agent) is valid, so also is one in connection with (*c*).

(1) Which she owed him. Such betrothal is invalid because loaned money may be spent, while a betrothal cannot be valid unless money or its equivalent (v. p, 464, n. 15) was actually given to the woman at the time of the betrothal (v. Ḳid. 6*b*). (2) Which was not fulfilled. (3) V. Glos. The minimum sum for a betrothal to be valid is a *peruṭah*. (4) If the union is to be dissolved. (5) Because a man, it is assumed, would not allow his intercourse to deteriorate into a mere act of prostitution. (6) Betrothal with less than a *peruṭah*. (7) That the betrothal was valid. Knowing his act to be invalid he determines to effect the *ḳinyan* of the marriage through his subsequent intercourse. Hence the necessity for a divorce to dissolve it. (8) Betrothal by a loan or on a certain condition, spoken of *supra* in the name of R. Eleazar. (9) He might be under the impression that a loan may effect a valid betrothal or that the condition he had made had been fulfilled. As his intercourse would consequently be based on his erroneous presumption of the validity of the betrothal the union would have no validity and, contrary to the view expressed in the name of R. Eleazar (v. *supra* n. 8), no divorce to dissolve it would be required. (10) Lit., 'there was no power'. (11) Num. V, 13, E.V., *neither she be taken in the act.*

then[1] is she] forbidden;[2] if, however, she was seized[3] she is permitted.[2] There is, however, another [kind of woman] who is permitted[2] even though she was not seized.[4] And who is she? A woman whose betrothal was a mistaken one[5] and who may, even if her son sits riding on her shoulder, [74b] make a declaration of refusal[6] [against her husband] and go away.[7]

Our Rabbis taught: If she[8] went to a Sage [after her betrothal] and he disallowed her vow her betrothal is valid. [If one[9] went] to a physician who cured her, her betrothal is invalid. What is the difference between the act of the Sage and that of the physician?[10] — A Sage annuls[11] the vow retrospectively[12] while a physician effects the cure only from that moment onwards.[13] But was it not, however, taught, [that if she[14] went] to a Sage and he disallowed her vow or to a physician and he cured her, her betrothal is invalid?[15] — Rabbah[16] replied: There is no contradiction. The former[17] represents the view of R. Meir; the latter[18] represents that of R. Eleazar. 'The former represents the view of R. Meir', who holds that a man does not mind[19] his wife's being exposed to the publicity[20] of a court of

(1) Only if she was *'not seized'*, i.e., she did not act under compulsion but willingly (cf. Yeb. 56*b*). (2) To her husband. (3) I.e., if she acted under compulsion. (4) Cf. *supra* n. 1. (5) I.e., when a condition that was attached to it remained unfulfilled. In such a case the woman may leave her husband without a letter of divorce and is free to marry any other man. (6) I.e., she requires no formal letter of divorce. (7) V. *supra* 51*b*. The practical ruling of the Sages, as reported by R. Kahana in the name of 'Ulla, shews that the ruling of R. Ishmael was not adopted. (8) The woman who was under a vow at the time of her betrothal. (9) The woman who was afflicted with a bodily defect at the time of her betrothal. (10) I. e., why is the betrothal valid in the case of the former and not in that of the latter? (11) Lit., 'uproots'. (12) So that the woman, at the time of her betrothal, was virtually under no vow. Hence the validity of the betrothal. (13) Since the woman at the time of the betrothal was still suffering from her affliction the betrothal was effected under a false assumption and is therefore invalid. (14) V. *supra* note 8. (15) How is this statement to be reconciled with the previous one according to which disallowance of a vow by a Sage renders the preceding betrothal valid? (16) V. Marg. glos. Cur. edd., 'Raba'. (17) The ruling that the betrothal is valid if a Sage disallowed the vow. (18) That even where a Sage had disallowed the vow the betrothal is invalid. (19) Lit., 'Is willing'. (20) שתתבזה, lit., 'that she shall be disgraced'.

law.[1] 'The latter represents that of R. Eleazar' who holds that no man wants his wife to be exposed to the publicity[2] of a court of law.[3] What is the source[4] [of these statements]?[5]—[The following] where we learned: If a man divorced his wife on account of a vow [she had made] he may not remarry her,[6] nor may he remarry his wife [if he divorced her] on account of a bad name.[7] R. Judah ruled: In the case of a vow that was made in the presence of many people[8] he may not remarry her,[9] but if it was not made in the presence of many people he may remarry her.[10] R. Meir ruled: In the case of a vow [the disallowance of which] necessitates the investigation of a Sage[11] her husband may not remarry her,[12] but if it does not require

(1) By applying in person to the Sage for the disallowance of her vow. It is assumed, therefore, that a man has no objection to betrothing a woman who is under a vow, since she may subsequently apply to a Sage for a disallowance. (2) V. p. 466, n. 20. (3) Consequently, if he had known that she was under a vow he would not have betrothed her. Hence the invalidity of the betrothal. (4) Lit., 'it'. (5) Attributed to R. Meir and R. Eleazar respectively. (6) Because, according to one opinion (v. Giṭ. 45*b*), it is possible that after the woman had obtained from a Sage the disallowance of her vow and had married another man, her first husband might regret his action in divorcing her and, advancing the plea that he would not have divorced her had he known that her vow could be disallowed, might impair thereby the validity of her second marriage. By the enactment that 'he may not re-marry her' a husband is naturally induced to institute all the necessary enquiries and to consider very carefully his course before he decides upon divorce, and should he nevertheless divorce her and then plead that he was unaware that her vow could be disallowed, his plea might well be disregarded. According to another opinion (Giṭ. l.c.) the prohibition to marry a woman in the circumstances mentioned is a penalty, and a warning to women to abstain from making vows. (7) Immoral conduct. For the reason cf. *supra* note 6 *mutatis mutandis*. As a vow may be disallowed so may a bad name turn out to be unfounded, and the first husband might then try to impair the validity of the second marriage. According to the second opinion (v. *supra* note 6 *ad fin.*) the prohibition is a penalty for, and a warning against, lax morality and ill-reputed associations. (8) Lit., 'of which many knew', cf. *infra* 75*a ab init.* (9) Since such a vow can never be disallowed (v. *infra* p. 468, n. 6 and text). R. Judah adopts the second reason (*supra* note 6). (10) Because, since the disallowance of such a vow is permitted, no penalty has been imposed upon the woman. (11) I.e., if it is of the class of vows which a husband is not entitled to invalidate. (12) R. Meir, maintaining that *a husband does not mind his wife's*

the investigation of a Sage[1] he may remarry her.[2] R. Eleazar said:[3] The prohibition against [remarriage where the disallowance of the vow] required [the investigation of a Sage][4] was ordained only on account [of a vow] which requires [no such investigation].[5] (What is R. Judah's reason?[6] Because it is written in Scripture, [75a] *And the children of Israel smote them not, because the princes of the congregation had sworn unto them.*[7] And what is considered 'many'? R. Naḥman b. Isaac said: Three [men]; [for the expression of] *'days'*[8] implies two [days] and *'many'*[8] three. R. Isaac replied: Ten; [for the term] congregation[9] was applied to them.)[10] [Now] 'R. Meir ruled: In the case of a vow [the disallowance of which] necessitates the investigation of a Sage he may not remarry her' [and] 'R. Eleazar said: The prohibition [against remarriage where the disallowance of the vow] required [the investigation of a Sage] was ordained only on account [of a vow] which required [no such investigation]',[11] on what principles do they[12] differ?—R. Meir holds the view that 'a man does not mind his wife's being exposed to the publicity of a court of law' and R. Eleazar holds the view that 'no man wants his wife to be exposed to the publicity of a court of law'.[13]

being exposed to the publicity of a court of law forbids remarriage on account of the first reason *supra* p. 467, n. 6, since the first husband might plead that if he had known that the vow could be disallowed by a Sage he would not have consented to give a divorce.

(1) I.e., if the vow was of a class the invalidation of which is within the husband's rights. (2) Because in this case the husband cannot advance the plea that the divorce was due to a misunderstanding (cf. *supra* p. 467, n. 6 and note 12). (3) Cur. edd. insert in parentheses, 'Whether it requires or whether it does not require he may not remarry her' (cf. the reading in Giṭ. 45*b*, Rashal and Asheri). (4) V. p. 467, n. 11. (5) V. *supra* note 1. Since in the latter case the husband might plead that he was not aware that he had the right to disallow the vow. In the former case, however, no such plea can be advanced because *no man would consent that his wife should be exposed to the publicity of a court of law*. V. Giṭ. 45*b*. (6) For ruling that a vow that was made in public (v. *supra* p. 467, nn. 8 and 9) may not be disallowed. (7) Josh. IX, 18; the oath could not be annulled because it was taken in public. (8) Referring to Lev. XV, 25. Cf. Nid. 73*a*. (9) עדה (Josh. ibid.). (10) And a *congregation* consists of not less than ten men. (11) Cf. *supra* p. 467, nn. 11ff. (12) R. Meir and R. Eleazar. Cf. *supra* p. 466, nn. 19ff. (13) The source of the statements (v. *supra* p. 467, n. 5)

Raba replied:[1] Here[2] we are dealing with the case of a woman from a noted family in which case the man[3] could say,[4] 'I have no wish to be forbidden to marry her relatives'.[5] If so,[6] [consider] the final clause where it is stated, 'But if he[7] went[8] to a Sage who disallowed his vow or to a physician who cured him, his betrothal of the woman is valid', [why, it may be asked, was it not] stated, 'the betrothal is invalid' and[9] explained,[10] 'Here we are dealing with the case of a man from a noted family concerning whom the woman[11] might plead, 'I have no wish to be forbidden to marry his relatives'?[12] — A woman is satisfied with any sort [of husband] as Resh Laḳish said. For Resh Laḳish stated: 'It is preferable to live in grief[13] than to dwell in widowhood'.[14] Abaye said: With a husband [of the size of an] ant her seat is placed among the great.[15] R. Papa said: Though her husband be a carder[16] she calls

has thus been shewn. For further notes on the passage v. Giṭ. (Sonc. ed.) pp. 200ff.

(1) In explanation of the contradiction pointed out *supra* 74*b*. (2) The second Baraitha which rules that the betrothal is invalid even if a Sage has disallowed the vow. (3) Even according to R. Meir who maintains that a husband does not mind his wife's appearance before a court of law one may still be objecting to live with a wife who is restricted by a vow. (4) In his desire to avoid a divorce and to obtain the retrospective annulment of his betrothal (v. following note). (5) Her mother and sister who are forbidden to marry the man who divorced her. He may insist that he wishes to retain the privilege of marrying these women members of a noted family though he objected to the particular one who restricted herself by a vow. By obtaining the annulment of the betrothal he does not place his wife under the category of a divorcee and he retains, in consequence, the right of marrying her relatives. Hence the ruling (even according to R. Meir) that the betrothal is invalid. (6) If Raba's explanation is to be accepted. (7) A man who betrothed a woman on the condition that he was under no vow or that he suffered no bodily defects. (8) After the betrothal (9) In order to reconcile the two clauses. (10) On the lines followed by Raba in the first clause. (11) Cf. *supra* n. 3 *mutatis mutandis*. (12) Cf. *mutatis mutandis*, *supra* nn. 4 and 5. (13) Or 'together', 'as husband and wife'. V. following note. (14) Yeb. 118*b*. This is a woman's maxim. She prefers a married life of unhappiness and misery to a happy and prosperous life in solitude. טַן דו (adv.) 'with a load of grief', 'in trouble' (Jast.) *Aliter*: (Cf. *supra* n. 13) טַן דו 'two bodies' (Rashi); 'two persons' (Levy). (15) A woman's opinion of a married life (v. Yeb. l.c.). הָרָאתָא pl. of חֵרְתָּא, 'a free woman'. (16) נפסא, 'flax-beater' (Rashi), 'a watchman of vegetables' (Aruch.), i.e., of a poor and humble occupation.

him to the threshold and sits down [at his side].[1] R. Ashi said: Even if her husband is only a cabbage-head[2] she requires no lentils[3] for her pot.[4]

A Tanna taught: But all such women[5] play the harlot and attribute the consequences[6] to their husbands.

ALL DEFECTS WHICH DISQUALIFY etc. A Tanna taught: To these[7] were added[8] [excessive] perspiration, a mole and offensive breath.[9] Do these, then, not cause a disqualification in respect of priests? Surely we have learned,[10] 'The old, the sick and the filthy'[11] and we have also learned, 'These defects whether permanent or transitory, render human beings[12] unfit [for the Temple service]![13] —R. Jose b. Ḥanina replied: This is no contradiction. The former refers to perspiration that can be removed;[14] the latter, to perspiration that cannot be removed.[15]

R. Ashi said [in reply]: You are pointing out a contradiction between 'perspiration' and 'one who is filthy' [which in fact are not alike, for] there, in the case of priests,[16] it is possible to remove the perspiration[17] by the aid of sour wine, and it is also possible [to remove] an offensive breath by holding pepper in one's mouth and thus performing the Temple service, but in the case of

(1) To shew her friends that she is a married woman. She is proud to be in the company of a husband however humble his occupation and social status. (2) קלוסא, i.e., 'dull', 'ugly' (v. Jast.); 'of a tainted family' (Rashi). (3) I.e., even a cheap vegetable. (4) A woman is content to dispense even with the cheapest enjoyments for the sake of a married life. (5) Who marry the unlovely types enumerated. (6) Lit., 'and hang on'. (7) The defects that disqualify priests (v. Bek. 43*a*). (8) In the case of women (v. our Mishnah). (9) Lit., 'smell of the mouth'. (10) In respect of defects that render animals unfit for the altar (Bek. 41*a*). (11) Under which term, it is at present assumed, excessive perspiration and offensive breath are included. (12) *Sc.* priests. (13) Bek. 43*a*. How then could it be said *supra* that excessive perspiration and offensive breath are not included among those that disqualify a priest? (14) By the application of water (v. Tosaf. s.v. כאן). *Aliter:* That may be cured (v. Tosaf. loc. cit.). (15) Cf. *supra* n. 14 *mutatis mutandis*. (16) Who were not described as 'filthy', but as suffering from excessive perspiration or offensive breath. R. Ashi, contrary to the previous assumption (v. *supra* note 11), draws a distinction between 'filthy' which implies a chronic state of the body and the two others which are only minor defects. (17) Even if water could not remove it.

a wife[1] [such devices are for all practical purposes] impossible.[2]

What kind of a mole is here meant? If one overgrown with hair, it would cause disqualification in both cases;[3] if one with no hair, [then, again], if it is a large one it causes disqualification in both cases[3] and if it is a small one it causes no disqualification in either; for it was taught: A mole which is overgrown with hair is regarded as a bodily defect; if with no hair it is only deemed to be a bodily defect when large but when small it is no defect; and what is meant by large? R. Simeon b. Gamaliel explained: The size of an Italian *issar!*[4]—R. Jose the son of R. Ḥanina said: One which is situated on her forehead.[5] [If it was on] her forehead he[6] must have seen it and acquiesced![7]—R. Papa replied: It is one that was situated under her bonnet and is sometimes exposed and sometimes not.

R. Ḥisda said: I heard the following statement from a great man (And who is he? R. Shila). If a dog bit her[8] and the spot of the bite turned into a scar [such a scar] is considered a bodily defect.

R. Ḥisda further stated: A harsh voice in a woman is a bodily defect; since it is said in Scripture, *For sweet is thy voice, and thy countenance is comely.*[9]

R. Nathan of Bira learnt: [The space] of one handbreadth between a woman's breasts.[10] R. Aḥa the son of Raba intended to explain in the presence of R. Ashi [that this statement meant that '[the space of] a handbreadth' is to [a woman's] advantage,[11] but R. Ashi said to him: This[12] was taught in connection with bodily defects. And what space [is deemed normal]? Abaye replied: [A space of] three fingers.

It was taught: R. Nathan said, It is a bodily defect if a woman's

(1) With whom a husband is constantly in contact. (2) Hence the ruling that even such minor defects render a betrothal invalid. (3) Lit., 'here and here', in the case of a priest and in that of a wife. (4) V. Glos. The question then arises: What kind of a mole was meant in the Baraitha *supra* where it is mentioned among the three defects of a wife that do not disqualify a priest. (5) And is small in size and without hair. (6) The man who betrothed her. (7) How then could a mole in such circumstances be regarded as a defect that causes the invalidity of the betrothal? (8) Any woman. (9) Cant. II, 14. (10) This is explained anon. (11) But if it was bigger or smaller it is to be regarded as a defect. (12) R. Nathan's statement.

breasts are bigger than those of others. By how much?—R. Meyasha the grandson of R. Joshua b. Levi replied in the name of R. Joshua b. Levi: By one handbreadth. Is such a deformity, however, possible?[1]—Yes; for Rabbah b. Bar Ḥana related, I saw an Arab woman who flung her breasts over her back and nursed her child.

But[2] *of Zion it shall be said: 'This man and that*[3] *was born in her; and the Most High Himself doth establish her;*[4] R. Meyasha, grandson of R. Joshua b. Levi, explained: Both[5] he who was born therein and he who looks forward to seeing it.[6]

Said Abaye: And one of them[7] is as good as two of us.[8] Said Raba: When one of us, however, goes up there[9] he is as good as two of them. For [you have the case of] R. Jeremiah who, while here,[10] did not understand what the Rabbis were saying, but when he went up there he was able to refer to us as 'The stupid Babylonians'.[11]

MISHNAH. IF SHE[12] WAS AFFLICTED WITH BODILY DEFECTS WHILE SHE WAS STILL IN HER FATHER'S HOUSE,[13] HER FATHER[14] MUST PRODUCE PROOF THAT THESE DEFECTS AROSE AFTER SHE HAD BEEN BETROTHED AND [THAT, CONSEQUENTLY, IT WAS THE] HUSBAND'S FIELD THAT WAS INUNDATED.[15] IF SHE CAME UNDER THE AUTHORITY OF HER HUSBAND,[16] THE HUSBAND[17] MUST PRODUCE PROOF THAT

(1) Lit., 'is there such a kind'. (2) The following paragraph, though irrelevant to the subject under discussion, is inserted here because of its author, R. Meyasha, who is also the author of the previous statement. (3) איש ואיש, lit., '*man and man*'. (4) Ps. LXXXVII, 5. (5) The inference is derived from the repetition of *man* (v. *supra* n. 3). (6) Will be acclaimed as a son of Zion. (7) The man of Zion, i.e., the Palestinians (Rashi). (8) Babylonians. (9) To Palestine. (10) In Babylon. (11) Cf. Men. 42*a*. (12) A betrothed woman. (13) I.e., before she married and went to live with her husband. (14) If his daughter is to be entitled to her *kethubah* from the man who betrothed her and refused to marry her on account of her defects. (15) Metaph. It is the husband's misfortune that the woman who had no such defects prior to her betrothal is now afflicted with them. (16) I.e., if the defects were discovered after the marriage. (17) Should he, on account of her defects, desire to divorce her and to deny her the *kethubah*.

THESE DEFECTS WERE UPON HER BEFORE SHE HAD BEEN BETROTHED AND [THAT CONSEQUENTLY] HIS BARGAIN WAS MADE IN ERROR. THIS IS THE RULING OF R. MEIR. THE SAGES, HOWEVER, RULED: THIS[1] APPLIES ONLY TO CONCEALED BODILY DEFECTS; [75*b*] BUT IN RESPECT OF DEFECTS THAT ARE EXPOSED HE[2] CANNOT ADVANCE ANY VALID PLEA.[3] AND IF THERE WAS A BATH-HOUSE IN THE TOWN HE CANNOT ADVANCE ANY VALID PLEA[3] EVEN AGAINST CONCEALED BODILY DEFECTS, BECAUSE HE [IS ASSUMED TO HAVE HAD HER] EXAMINED BY HIS WOMEN RELATIVES.[4]

GEMARA. The reason then[5] is because the father produced proof, but if he produced no proof,[6] the husband is believed.[7] Whose [view consequently is here[8] expressed]? [Obviously] that of R. Joshua who stated, 'Our life is not dependent on her statement'.[9] Now read the final clause: IF SHE CAME UNDER THE AUTHORITY OF THE HUSBAND, THE HUSBAND MUST PRODUCE PROOF, the reason then[10] is because the husband produced proof, but if he produced no proof,[11] the father is believed,[12] a ruling which

(1) The validity of a husband's plea that HIS BARGAIN WAS MADE IN ERROR. (2) Since he was in a position to see them. (3) That he was not aware of these defects. (4) He must have known, therefore, of the defects, and acquiesced. (5) Why in the first clause of our Mishnah the woman who was divorced after a betrothal is entitled to her *kethubah*. (6) So that it is unknown when the defects first arose. (7) If he pleads that the woman was afflicted with the defects prior to her betrothal; and he, as the possessor of the money, is consequently exempt from paying the *kethubah* as is the law in respect of all monetary claims where the possessor cannot be deprived of his money without legal proof of the claim advanced against him. (8) In the implication that the law is to be decided in favour of the husband who is the *possessor* of the money and not in favour of the woman who, since she was born without bodily defects, has the claim of *presumptive soundness of body*. (9) I.e., we do not rely on the woman's assertion, *supra* 12*b*, where the time she had been outraged is a matter of dispute between her and her husband. Though the woman has in her favour the claim of the *presumptive chastity of her body* she, nevertheless, cannot obtain her *kethubah* because of her husband's stronger claim as the *possessor* of the amount of the *kethubah*. (10) Why the woman does not receive her *kethubah*. (11) So that it is unknown when the defects first arose. (12) Cf. *supra* note 7 *mutatis*

expresses the view of R. Gamaliel who stated that the woman is believed![1] — R. Eleazar replied: The contradiction[2] [is evident]; he who taught the one did not teach the other.[3]

Raba said: It must not be assumed that R. Joshua[4] is never guided by the principle of the presumptive soundness of the body, for the fact is[5] that R. Joshua is not guided by that principle only where it is opposed by the principle of possession.[6] Where, however, the principle of possession is not applicable R. Joshua is guided by that of the soundness of the body; for it was taught: If the bright spot[7] preceded the white hair, he[8] is unclean; if the reverse, he is clean. [If the order is in] doubt, he is unclean; but R. Joshua said: It darkened.[9] What is meant by 'It darkened'? Rabbah replied: [It is as though the spot] darkened[10] [and, therefore,] he is clean.[11]

Raba explained:[12] The first clause [is a case of] 'Here[13] they[14] were found and here they must have arisen'[15] and so is the final clause:

mutandis; the woman's presumptive soundness of body being regarded as a superior claim to that of the husband possessor of the amount of the *kethubah.*

(1) *Supra* 12*b*. Cf. *supra* p. 473, n. 9 *mutatis mutandis* and p. 473, n. 12. A contradiction thus arises between the first and the second clause of our Mishnah. (2) תברא. *Aliter:* (rt. תבר 'to break') Divide or sever (the two clauses). R. Ḥan. (v. Tosaf. s.v. תברא). regards תברא as an imprecation. (3) The first clause represents the view of R. Joshua who maintains the same view in the case spoken of in the second clause, while the second clause expresses the view of R. Gamaliel who maintains it in the case of the first clause also, neither of them drawing a distinction between a woman who was still in her father's house and one who was already under the authority of her husband. (4) Cf. *supra* p. 473, nn 7-8. (5) Lit., 'but'. (6) Lit., 'presumptive possession of the money'. (7) In leprosy. V. Lev. XIII, 2-4. (8) The man afflicted. (9) Neg. IV, 11. (10) Cf. Lev. XIII, 6: *If the plague be dim (or dark) . . . then the priest shall pronounce him clean.* (11) Thus it has been shewn that R. Joshua, since he ruled that a doubtful case of leprosy is clean, is guided by the principle of the presumptive soundness of the human body wherever it is not opposed by the principle of possession. (12) The apparent contradiction between the first and the second clause of our Mishnah (cf. *supra* note 1). (13) In the FATHER'S HOUSE. (14) The BODILY DEFECTS of the woman. (15) And it is owing to this principle only that the onus of producing proof was thrown upon the father. Otherwise, he would have been believed without proof, in agreement with the view of R. Gamaliel, which is the adopted *halachah* (v. *supra* 12*b*), because his claim is

Here[1] they[2] were found and here they must have arisen.[3] Abaye raised an objection against him:[4] IF SHE CAME UNDER THE AUTHORITY OF THE HUSBAND, THE HUSBAND MUST PRODUCE PROOF THAT THESE DEFECTS WERE UPON HER BEFORE SHE HAD BEEN BETROTHED[5] AND [THAT, CONSEQUENTLY,] HIS BARGAIN WAS MADE IN ERROR; [Thus only if she had the defects] BEFORE SHE HAD BEEN BETROTHED [is the husband's plea] accepted,[6] [but if they were seen upon her] only after she had been betrothed[7] [his plea would] not [be accepted]. But why? Let it be said,[8] 'Here they were found and here they must have arisen'![9] —The other[4] replied: [The principle[10] cannot be applied if the defects were discovered] after she had been betrothed because it may be taken for granted that no man drinks out of a cup[11] unless he has first examined it; and this man[12] must consequently have seen [the defects] and acquiesced.[13] If so,[14] [the same principle should apply] also to one [who had defects] prior to her betrothal. [Since,] however, [it is not applied], the presumption must be that no man is reconciled to bodily defects, [why then is it not presumed] here[15] also that no man is reconciled to bodily defects?— This, however, is the explanation: [The principle[10] cannot be applied to defects discovered] after she had been betrothed because two [principles] are [opposed to it:] The presumptive soundness of the woman's body[16] and the presumption that no man

supported by the principle of his daughter's presumptive soundness of body.

(1) In the husband's house. (2) The BODILY DEFECTS of the woman. (3) The two clauses of our Mishnah thus present no contradiction, both expressing the view of R. Gamaliel (cf. *supra* p. 474, n. 15). (4) Raba. (5) תתארס. The reading in our Mishnah is נתארסה a change of tense and form that does not materially affect the meaning of the phrase. (6) Lit., 'yes'. (7) Although she was still in her father's house. (8) If Raba's explanation is correct. (9) Since this principle, however, is not adopted in the final clause, how could Raba's explanation be upheld? (10) 'Here they were found etc.'. (11) Euphemism. (12) Since he had married the woman. (13) Hence the inadmissibility of the principle, 'Here they were found etc.'. (14) If the principle of the 'presumptive examination of the cup' is the determining factor in favour of the woman. (15) In the final clause where the proof established the existence of the defects after betrothal while the woman was still in her father's house. (16) Lit. 'place the body upon its strength'.

drinks out of a cup unless he has first examined it and that this man must, consequently, have seen [the defects] and acquiesced. What possible objection can you raise?[1] Is it the presumption that no man is reconciled to bodily defects? [But this] is only [76a] one principle[2] against two principles,[3] and one against two cannot be upheld.[4] [But where the defects were discovered] before betrothal, the principle of the presumptive soundness of her body cannot be applied,[5] and all that remains is[6] the presumption that no man drinks out of a cup unless he has first examined it and that this man must consequently have seen [the defects] and acquiesced, [but to this it can be retorted:] On the contrary, the presumption is that no man is reconciled to bodily defects, and consequently the money is to remain in the possession of its holder.[7]

R. Ashi explained:[8] The [claim in the] first clause[9] [is analogous to the claim] 'You owe my father a *maneh*',[10] but that in the final clause[11] [is analogous to the claim] 'You owe me a *maneh*'.[12]

(1) Against deciding, on the basis of the two principles, in favour of the woman. (2) In favour of the man. The principle of possession is of no consequence here because it is completely disregarded when opposed by that of the presumptive soundness of the body. (3) Which are in favour of the woman. (4) Hence the ruling in her favour. (5) Since proof was adduced that she was afflicted with the defects prior to her betrothal. (6) Lit. 'what is there?' in favour of the woman's claim. (7) In the absence of the presumption of the soundness of body (cf. *supra* n. 5) the principle of possession is a determining factor (cf. *supra* note 2), and thus, being added to that of a man's irreconcilableness to bodily defects, two principles in favour of the man are opposed to one in favour of the woman. Hence the ruling in favour of the man. (8) The apparent contradiction between the first and second clause of our Mishnah (cf. *supra* p. 474, n. 1). (9) Since the *kethubah* of a betrothed woman, as a *na'arah* (v. Glos.), unlike that of a married one, belongs to her father and not to herself. (10) Where the presumptive soundness of the claimant's daughter's body, not being that of the claimant herself, cannot override the principle of possession which is in favour of the husband. Hence the necessity for the father to produce the proof. (11) Dealing with a married woman. (12) In which case (cf. *supra* note 9 *mutatis mutandis*), the presumptive soundness of the body of the woman who is herself the claimant is sufficient to establish her claim. Hence it is for the husband to produce the necessary proof. Thus it is possible to assume that both the clauses of our Mishnah under discussion represent the view of

R. Aḥa the son of R. Awya raised an objection against R. Ashi: R. Meir[1] admits that in respect of bodily defects[2] likely to have come[3] with her from her father's house it is the father who must produce the proof.[4] But why?[5] Is [not this[6] analogous to the claim,] 'You owe me a *maneh*'?[7]—Here[4] we are dealing with the case of a woman who had a superfluous limb.[8] [But if] she had a superfluous limb[9] what proof could be brought?[10]—Proof that the man has seen it[11] and acquiesced.

Rab Judah stated in the name of Samuel: If a man exchanged a cow for [another man's] ass, and the owner of the ass pulled[12] the cow[13] but the owner of the cow did not manage to pull[14] the ass before the ass died, it is for the owner of the ass to produce proof that his ass was alive at the time the cow was pulled.[15] And the Tanna [of our Mishnah who taught about] a bride[16] supports this ruling. Which [ruling concerning the] bride?[17] If it be suggested:

R. Gamaliel who ruled that the presumptive soundness of body overrides the principle of possession.

(1) Though he stated in our Mishnah that if the defects were discovered after the woman CAME UNDER THE AUTHORITY OF HER HUSBAND it is the latter that MUST PRODUCE PROOF. (2) The reference is at present assumed to be to any kind of defect. (3) Lit., 'that are likely to come'. (4) Tosef. Keth. VII. (5) Should the father have to produce the proof. (6) According to R. Ashi's explanation. (7) The woman being married and the *kethubah* belonging to her, the presumptive soundness of her body should be sufficient to establish her claim. (8) Not, as has been presumed by R. Aḥa, with one who was afflicted with any *defect*. A superfluous limb does not grow after betrothal. Being a congenital defect, the principle of the presumptive soundness of the body cannot be applied. (9) Which is obviously congenital. (10) In support of her claim to her *kethubah*. (11) Prior to betrothal or marriage. (12) Pulling, *meshikah* (v. Glos.) is one of the forms of acquiring legal possession. (13) While the ass still remained on his premises. (14) To take it to his premises. (15) If such proof is produced the former owner of the cow must bear the loss, because the legal acquisition by one of the parties of one of two objects exchanged places upon the other party the responsibility for any accident that might happen to the other object even though he did not himself formally acquire it (v. Ḳid. 28*a*). (16) Concerning whose defects a similar doubt exists. In the case of the exchanged animals it is uncertain whether the ass died before or after the acquisition of the cow; in the case of the bride it is uncertain whether she had her defects before or after her betrothal. (17) Provides the support.

[76b] The one concerning a bride IN HER FATHER'S HOUSE,[1] are the two cases [it may be objected] alike? There it is the father[2] who produces the proof and *receives*[3] [the *kethubah* from the husband][4] while here it is the owner of the ass[5] who produces the proof and *retains* [the cow],[6]—R. Abba replied: [The ruling concerning a] bride in her father-in-law's house.[7] But [the two cases] are still unlike, for there it is the husband who produces the proof[8] and thereby *impairs* the presumptive right of the father,[9] while here it is the owner of the ass who produces the proof[10] and thereby *confirms* his presumptive right![11]—R. Naḥman b. Isaac replied: [The support is derived from the case of the] bride IN HER FATHER'S

(1) In the first clause; the assumption being that, in agreement with R. Eleazar (*supra* 75b), it represents the view of R. Joshua, and that the father must produce the proof even where the defects were discovered after marriage and the doubt did not arise until after the bride had come under the authority of her husband. (Cf. Rashi, *a.l.* and *infra* s.v. אליבא, *ad fin.*). Similarly in the case of the exchange of the animals the owner of the ass must produce proof though the doubt occurred after his *meshikah* of the cow had transferred the ass to the responsibility of the other party. (2) The *claimant*. (3) Lit., 'brings out'. (4) Which is the usual rule: The claimant produces the proof and receives his due. (5) The *defendant*. (6) Contrary to the usual rule (v. *supra* n. 4). How then could it be asserted that the latter is supported by the former? (7) I.e., the second clause of our Mishnah provides the support; the assumption being with R. Eleazar (*supra* 75b), that it represents the view of R. Gamaliel and that the husband must produce the proof even where the defects were discovered prior to marriage, while the bride was still in her parental home, and her *kethubah* still belonged to her father. (Cf. Rashi a.l. and *infra* s.v. אליבא *ad fin.*). The support is adduced thus: If in this case where the doubt first arose while the bride was still under her father's authority (i.e., in the claimant's possession) it is the husband, who is the defendant, that must produce the proof, how much more so in the case of the exchange of the animals where the doubt arose in the house of the defendant (the owner of the ass) that the latter must produce the proof. (8) That she had the defects prior to her betrothal. (9) The presumption of the woman's soundness of body. (10) That the ass was alive at the time the cow was acquired by him. (11) The presumption that the ass that was alive prior to the acquisition of the cow was also alive during the time the cow was acquired. How then could a case in which the proof rightly serves the purpose of *impairing a presumptive right* be taken as support to one in which the proof is adduced to *confirm* a presumptive right?

HOUSE in respect of her token of betrothal.[1] And, furthermore, it need not be said [that this[2] applies only] in accordance with him who holds [that a token of] betrothal is not unreturnable[3] but [it holds good] even according to him who maintains [that a token of] betrothal is unreturnable, since his ruling relates only to *certain* betrothal, but [not] to *doubtful* betrothal [where the father may retain the token] only[4] if he produces proof but not otherwise.[5]

An objection was raised: If a needle was found in the thick walls of the second stomach [of a ritually killed beast, and it protrudes only] from one of its sides,[6] the beast is fit [for human consumption,[7] but if it protruded] from both sides, the beast is unfit for human consumption.[8] If a drop of blood was found on [the needle] it is certain that [the wound was inflicted] before the ritual killing;[9] if no drop of blood was found on it, it is certain that [the wound was made] after the killing.[10] If the top[11] of the wound was covered with a crust, it is certain that [the wounding occurred] three days prior to the killing;[12] if the top[11] of the wound was not covered with

(1) In the first clause of our Mishnah where the proof must be produced by the father (cf. *supra* p. 478, n. 1 *mutatis mutandis*) though it serves also the purpose of enabling him *to retain* the money, or object of value, that was given as the token of the betrothal of the bride. Similarly in the case of the exchange of the animals, the owner of the ass produces the proof and *retains* the cow. (2) That proof is required to enable the father to *retain the token of betrothal.* (3) Lit., 'given for sinking', i.e., that it is not returned under any conditions whatsoever (v. B.B. 145*a*). Since it is 'not unreturnable', it is not in the father's full possession and he might well be expected to have to produce the proof. (4) Lit., 'yes'. (5) Lit., 'if not, not'. (6) The inner side of the stomach. Owing to the thickness of its folds it is quite possible that the needle merely pricked, but did not pierce through the stomach wall. (7) Since the wound caused by the needle was not fatal. (8) *Ṭrefa* (v. Glos.). A perforation of the stomach is a fatal wound which renders the afflicted animal unfit for human consumption even if it was ritually killed before it could die of the wound. (9) And the beast is, therefore, unfit for human consumption (cf. *supra* n. 8). (10) When it could not affect the life of the beast which, in consequence, remains fit for consumption. (11) Lit., 'mouth'. (12) And should a butcher buy the beast within the three days it is a bargain made in error which he may cancel and claim the refunding of his purchase money.

a crust,[1] it is for the claimant to produce the proof.[2] Now if the butcher[3] had already paid the price he[4] would have to produce the required proof and so *obtain the refund* [of his money]; but why? Let the owner of the beast rather produce the proof and retain [the purchase money]![5]—[This is a case] where the butcher[3] has not yet paid the price.[6] But how can such an absolute assertion[7] be made?[8]—[This] however, [will dispose of the difficulty:] For when Rami b. Ezekiel came he said, 'Pay no regard to those rules which my brother Judah laid down in the name of Samuel; for thus said Samuel: He in whose domain the doubt first arose[9] must produce the proof; and the Tanna [of our Mishnah who taught about] the bride[10] provides support for this ruling.[11]

An objection was raised: If a needle was found in the thick walls of the second stomach etc.[12] Now,[13] if the butcher[3] has not yet paid the purchase price it would be the owner of the beast[13] who would have to produce the proof and so obtain [its price] from [the

(1) And the vendor pleads that the wound was made after the sale when the beast was in the possession of the buyer, while the buyer insists that it was made prior to the sale when it was still in the vendor's possession. (2) Ḥul. 50*b*. (3) *Sc*. the buyer. (4) Being the claimant. (5) As in the case spoken of by Samuel (*supra* 76*a*), where the owner of the ass produces the proof and *retains* the cow. Since, however, the law here is not so, an objection arises against Samuel's ruling. (6) So that the vendor is the claimant. Hence it is for the butcher, who is the defendant, to produce the proof and thus retain his money. (7) That the butcher always buys on credit and that he is, therefore, always the defendant. (8) A butcher, surely, does not always buy on credit and our Baraitha does not mention buyer at all but claimant, irrespective of whether he happens to be the buyer or the vendor. (9) I.e., the owner of the cow, since the doubt first arose after the owner of the ass had acquired the cow and thereby transferred the responsibility for the ass to the former owner of the cow. (10) That if the doubt concerning the first appearance of her defects arose while she was in her paternal home her father must produce the proof, and that if it arose when she was already under the authority of her husband it is the husband who must produce the proof. (11) Samuel, according to the present explanation, would hold the same opinion as Raba who stated (*supra* 75*b*) that the first as well as the second clause of our Mishnah represents the view of one Tanna, viz. that of R. Joshua. (12) *Supra*, cited from Ḥul. 50*b*. (13) Since it has been laid down that the claimant must produce the proof.

butcher]; but why? [Has not] the doubt arisen [when the beast was already] in the possession of the butcher?[1]—[This is a case] where the butcher has already paid the price.[2] But how can such a categorical statement[3] be made?[4]—It is the usual practice that so long as one man does not pay the price the other does not give his beast.

THE SAGES, HOWEVER, RULED: THIS APPLIES ONLY TO CONCEALED BODILY DEFECTS. R. Naḥman stated: [77a] Epilepsy[5] is regarded as [one of the] concealed bodily defects.[6] This, however, applies only to attacks which occur at regular periods,[7] but if they are irregular [epilepsy is regarded] as [one of the] exposed bodily defects.[8]

MISHNAH. A MAN IN WHOM BODILY DEFECTS HAVE ARISEN CANNOT BE COMPELLED TO DIVORCE [HIS WIFE]. R. SIMEON B. GAMALIEL SAID: THIS APPLIES ONLY TO MINOR DEFECTS, BUT IN RESPECT OF MAJOR DEFECTS[9] HE CAN BE COMPELLED TO DIVORCE HER.

GEMARA. Rab Judah recited: 'HAVE ARISEN';[10] Ḥiyya b. Rab recited: '*Were*'.[11] He who recited 'HAVE ARISEN' [holds that the ruling applies] with even more force [where the defects] '*were*',[11] since [in the latter case the woman] was aware of the facts and

(1) Of course it has, since the needle could not have been found before the beast had been killed. Now if Rami b. Ezekiel's report in the name of Samuel is to be regarded as authentic, the butcher should have been the party to produce the proof. (2) And it is the butcher in fact from whom the proof is expected. (3) That the butcher invariably buys for cash and that he is therefore always the claimant. (4) Does not a butcher sometimes take on credit? (5) נכפה, 'one who is epileptic'. כפה in Nif. 'to be overtaken by a demon'. (6) Because a woman may conceal her epilepsy by remaining indoors when the attack comes on. (7) In such a case she can avoid appearing in public when she feels the approach of the attack. (8) V. Our Mishnah. (9) The nature of these is explained in the Gemara. (10) I.e., that the husband's defects spoken of in our Mishnah arose *after he married* the woman. (11) Cf. *supra* n. 10, i.e., the man was afflicted with the defects *before* his marriage.

acquiesced. He, however, who recited '*Were*' [holds that the ruling does] not [apply where the defects] 'have arisen'.[1]

We learned: R. SIMEON B. GAMALIEL SAID: THIS APPLIES ONLY TO MINOR DEFECTS BUT IN RESPECT OF MAJOR DEFECTS HE CAN BE COMPELLED TO DIVORCE HER. Now, according to him who reads, 'HAVE ARISEN[2] it is quite proper to make a distinction between major defects and minor defects.[3] According to him, however, who reads, 'were', what [it may be asked] is the difference between major defects and minor ones? Was she not in fact aware [of their existence] and acquiesced?[4]—She may have thought that she would be able to tolerate them but now she finds that she is unable to tolerate them.[5]

These,[6] R. Simeon b. Gamaliel explained, are major defects: If, for instance, his eye was blinded, his hand was cut off or his leg was broken.

It was stated: R. Abba b. Jacob said in the name of R. Johanan: The *halachah* is in agreement with R. Simeon b. Gamaliel. Raba said in the name of R. Nahman: The *halachah* is in agreement with the Sages. But could R. Johanan, however, have made such a statement?[7] Surely Rabbah b. Bar Hana stated in the name of R. Johanan: Wherever R. Simeon b. Gamaliel taught in our Mishnah, the *halachah* is in agreement with his ruling except [in the cases of] 'guarantor',[8] 'Zidon'[9] and the 'latter proof'![10]—There is a dispute of Amoraim as to what was R. Johanan's view.[11]

MISHNAH. THE FOLLOWING ARE COMPELLED TO DI-

(1) Cf. *supra* p. 481, n. 10. In this case the woman might well plead that had she known that the man would later develop bodily defects she would never have consented to marry him. (2) V. *supra* p. 481, n. 10. (3) Since it is reasonable to expect a woman to object to the former but not to the latter. (4) Of course she was, the defects having arisen prior to her marriage. (5) Hence her right to claim a divorce. (6) This paragraph appears in old edd. and Alfasi (cf. BaH *a.l.*) as a Mishnah. (7) Which implies that only in this particular case is the *halachah* in agreement with R. Simeon b. Gamaliel. (8) V. B.B. 174*a*. (9) V. Git. 74*a*. (10) V. Sanh. 31*a*. (11) Rabbah b. Bar Hana maintaining that a general rule had been laid down whilst R. Abba b. Jacob disputes this.

VORCE [THEIR WIVES]: A MAN WHO IS AFFLICTED WITH BOILS, OR HAS A POLYPUS,[1] OR GATHERS [OBJECTIONABLE MATTER][2] OR IS A COPPERSMITH[2] OR A TANNER,[2] WHETHER THEY WERE [IN SUCH CONDITIONS OR POSITIONS] BEFORE THEY MARRIED OR WHETHER THEY AROSE AFTER THEY HAD MARRIED. AND CONCERNING ALL THESE R. MEIR SAID: ALTHOUGH THE MAN MADE A CONDITION WITH HER [THAT SHE ACQUIESCES IN HIS DEFECTS] SHE MAY NEVERTHELESS PLEAD, 'I THOUGHT I COULD ENDURE HIM,[3] BUT NOW I CANNOT ENDURE HIM'.[3] THE SAGES, HOWEVER, SAID: SHE MUST ENDURE [ANY SUCH PERSON] DESPITE HER WISHES, THE ONLY EXCEPTION BEING A MAN AFFLICTED WITH BOILS, BECAUSE SHE [BY HER INTERCOURSE] WILL ENERVATE HIM.

IT ONCE HAPPENED AT ZIDON THAT THERE DIED[4] A TANNER WHO HAD A BROTHER[5] WHO WAS ALSO A TANNER. THE SAGES RULED: SHE[6] MAY SAY, 'I WAS ABLE TO ENDURE[3] YOUR BROTHER BUT I CANNOT ENDURE YOU'.

GEMARA. What [is meant by one] WHO HAS A POLYPUS? —Rab Judah replied in the name of Samuel: [One who suffers from an offensive] nasal smell. In a Baraitha it was taught: [One suffering from] offensive breath.[7] R. Assi learnt in the reverse order[8] and supplied the mnemonic, 'Samuel did not cease [studying] all our chapter [with] his mouth'.[9]

WHO GATHERS. What [is meant by one] WHO GATHERS?—Rab Judah replied: One who gathers dogs' excrements.[10]

An objection was raised: 'One who gathers' means a tanner![11] —But even according to your own view,[12] would not a contra-

(1) Cf. πολύπους and v. Gemara *infra*. (2) This is explained in the Gemara. (3) Lit., 'to receive', 'accept'. (4) Without leaving any issue. (5) It is the duty of the surviving brother to contract the levirate marriage with the widow (v. Deut. XXV, 5ff). (6) The widow. (7) Lit., 'smell of the mouth'. (8) Attributing to Samuel the definition given in the Baraitha and *vice versa*. (9) *Mouth* in association with the name of Samuel suggesting that it was Samuel who interpreted POLYPUS as offensive breath from the *mouth* (cf. *supra* note 7). (10) Used for tanning. (11) Tosef. Keth. VII, which is contradictory to the definition given here by Rab Judah. (12) That 'one who gathers' means a 'tanner'.

diction arise from our Mishnah [which specifies] OR GATHERS OR IS A COPPERSMITH OR A TANNER?[1]—One may well explain why our Mishnah[1] presents no contradiction[2] because the latter[3] refers to a great tanner[4] whilst the former[5] refers to a small tanner;[6] but according to Rab Judah the contradiction remains?[7]—[The definition][8] is [a matter in dispute between] Tannaim. For it was taught: 'One who gathers' means a 'tanner'; and others say: It means 'one who gathers dogs' excrements'.[9]

OR IS A COPPERSMITH OR A TANNER. What is meant by A COPPERSMITH?—R. Ashi[10] replied: A kettle-smith.[11] Rabbah b. Bar Ḥana explained: One who digs copper from the mine.[12] It was taught in agreement with Rabbah b. Bar Ḥana: What is meant by a coppersmith? One who digs copper from the mine.[12]

Rab stated: If a husband says, 'I will neither maintain nor support [my wife]', he must divorce her and give her also her *kethubah*. R. Eleazar went and told this reported statement to Samuel [who] exclaimed, 'Make Eleazar eat barley;[13] rather than compel him to divorce her let him be compelled to maintain her'. And Rab?[14]—No one can live with a serpent in the same basket.[15] When R. Zera went up[16] he found R. Benjamin b. Japheth sitting [at the college] and reporting this[17] in the name of R. Johanan.[18] 'For this statement', he said to him, 'Eleazar was told in Babylon to eat barley'.

Rab Judah stated in the name of R. Assi:[19] We do not compel

(1) Which shews that 'tanner' and 'one who gathers' are two distinct occupations. (2) Against the Baraitha which defines 'one who gathers' as a 'tanner'. (3) Lit., 'here', the term TANNER specifically mentioned. (4) Who does not himself gather the excrements. (5) 'ONE WHO GATHERS'. (6) Who must himself gather the excrements needed for his work. (7) Cf. *supra* p. 483, n. 11. (8) Of 'one who GATHERS'. (9) Rab Judah, in differing from the Baraitha, adopted this latter definition. (10) *Var. lec.* Rab (Aruch.). (11) חשלי, pl. of חשלא, 'smith'; דודי, pl. of דודא (Bib. Heb. דוד), 'pot', 'kettle'. (12) Lit., 'cuts . . . from its root', *sc.* 'source'. (13) Like an animal, since he, by being so credulous as to accept an absurd statement, displayed no higher intelligence. (14) Why does he order divorce rather than maintenance? (15) Metaph. Divorce is, therefore, preferable. (16) From Babylon to Palestine. (17) Rab's ruling *supra*. (18) I.e., that R. Joḥanan also was of the same opinion as Rab. (19) *Var. lec.*, Rab (Asheri), R. Ashi (Alfasi).

divorce except [in the case of] those who are tainted.¹ When I mentioned this in the presence of Samuel he remarked, 'As, for instance, a widow [who was married] to a High Priest, a divorced woman or a *ḥaluzah*² to a common priest, a bastard or a *nethinah*² to an Israelite, or the daughter of an Israelite to a *nathin*² or a bastard; but if a man married a woman and lived with her ten years and she bore no child he cannot be compelled [to divorce her]'. R. Taḥlifa b. Abimi, however, stated in the name of Samuel: Even the man who married a woman and lived with her ten years and she bore no child may be compelled [to divorce her].³

We learned, THE FOLLOWING ARE COMPELLED TO DIVORCE [THEIR WIVES]: A MAN WHO IS AFFLICTED WITH BOILS OR HAS A POLYPUS. This⁴ is quite justified according to R. Assi, since only Rabbinically forbidden cases were enumerated whilst those which are Pentateuchally forbidden were omitted.⁵ According to R. Taḥlifa b. Abimi⁶ however, our Mishnah should also have stated: If a man married a woman and lived with her for ten years and she bore no child he may be compelled [to divorce her].⁷—R. Naḥman replied: This is no difficulty. For in the latter case⁸ [compulsion is exercised] by words; in the former⁹ cases, by whips.¹⁰

R. Abba demurred: *A servant will not be corrected by words!*¹¹—The

---

(1) I.e., those who are disqualified to their husbands as priests or from marrying into the congregation of Israel. [*Var. lec.*, 'We compel in the case of tainted (women)'. A man who married a woman disqualified to him is compelled to put her away (v. *Shiṭṭah Meḳubbeẓeth*). According to our text it might be suggested that Samuel's dictum is restricted to cases where the defect resides in the woman and does not exclude the cases of blemishes dealt with in our Mishnah, where the defect is in the man]. (2) V. Glos. (3) Because propagation of the species is one of the 613 commandments. (4) The omission from this list in our Mishnah of the tainted persons enumerated by Samuel. (5) As these are obvious. (6) Who, unlike R. Assi, included the man, whose wife had no child after living for ten years with him, among those who are compelled to divorce their wives. (7) Since compulsion in this case is only a Rabbinical ordinance. (8) Lit., 'that', the man whose wife had no child for ten years (v. *supra* n. 6). (9) Those enumerated in our Mishnah. (10) As the compulsion in the latter case is merely in the nature of persuasion it could not be included among the others. (11) Prov. XXIX, 19. How then would a man who refuses to carry out a decision of a court of law be moved by mere persuasion?

fact, however, explained R. Abba, is that in all these cases[1] [compulsion is exercised] by means of whips [77b] but in the former, if she said, 'I wish to be with him', she is allowed [to live with him] whilst in the latter,[2] even if she said, 'I wish to be with him', she is not allowed [to continue to live with him].[3] But behold [the case of the man who was] afflicted with boils with whom the woman is not allowed to live even if she said, 'I wish to be with him', for we learned: THE ONLY EXCEPTION BEING A MAN AFFLICTED WITH BOILS BECAUSE SHE [BY HER INTERCOURSE] WILL ENERVATE HIM, and this case was nevertheless enumerated![4]—There,[5] if she were to say, 'I will live with him under [the supervision of] witnesses',[6] she would be allowed [to remain with him] but here,[7] even if she were to say, 'I will live with him under [the supervision of] witnesses,' she would not be allowed to do so.

It was taught: R. Jose related, An old man of the inhabitants of Jerusalem told me, 'There are twenty-four [kinds of] skin disease,[8] and in respect of all these the Sages said, "Intercourse is injurious", but most of all is this the case with those afflicted with *ra'athan*'.[9] What is the cause of it?—As it was taught: If a man had intercourse immediately after being bled, he will have feeble[10] children; if intercourse took place after the man and the woman[11] had been bled they will have children afflicted with *ra'athan*. R. Papa stated: This[12] has been said only in the case where nothing was tasted [after the bleeding] but if something was tasted there can be no harm.[13]

What are the[14] symptoms?—His eyes tear, his nostrils run, spittle flows from his mouth and flies swarm about him. What is the cure?[14]

(1) The man whose wife had no child as well as those enumerated in our Mishnah. Lit., 'that and that'. (2) Lit., 'here'. V. *supra* p. 485, n. 9. (3) V. *supra* p. 485, n. 3. (4) An objection against R. Abba's explanation. (5) In the case just cited. (6) *Sc.* only to attend on him, while refraining from intercourse. (7) The case of the man whose wife had no child for ten years after their marriage. (8) Lit., 'stricken with boils'. (9) Tosef. Keth. VII, *ad fin.* ראתן (cf. רתת 'trembling'), one of the skin diseases causing nervous trembling and extreme debility of the body (v. Jast.). *Aliter:* A person having an insect in his brain (cf. Rashi). (10) Or 'nervous'. ויתיקין, rt. ותק, 'to unnerve'. (11) Lit., 'both of them'. (12) The warning against intercourse after being bled. (13) Lit., 'we have nothing against it'. (14) Lit., 'his', of the man suffering from *ra'athan*.

—Abaye said: Pila,[1] ladanum,[2] the rind of a nut tree, the shavings of a dressed hide,[3] melilot[4] and the calyx[5] of a red date-tree. These must be boiled together and carried into a house of marble,[6] and if no marble house is available they may be carried into a house [the walls of which are of the thickness] of seven bricks and a half.[7] Three hundred cups [of the mixture] must then be poured upon his[8] head until his cranium is softened, and then his brain is cut open. Four leaves of myrtle must be brought and each foot[9] [in turn] lifted up and one [leaf] placed [beneath it].[10] It[11] is then grasped with a pair of tweezers and burned; for otherwise it would return to him.[8]

R. Joḥanan issued the announcement: Beware of the flies of the man afflicted with *ra'athan*.[12]

R. Zera never sat [with such a sufferer] in the same draught. R. Eleazar never entered his tent. R. Ammi and R. Assi never ate any of the eggs coming from the alley in which he lived. R. Joshua b. Levi, however, attached himself to these [sufferers] and studied the Torah; for he said, *A lovely hind and a graceful doe,*[13] if [the Torah] bestows grace upon those who study it, would it not also protect them?

When he[14] was about to die the Angel of Death was instructed, 'Go and carry out his wish'. When he came and shewed himself to him the latter said, 'Shew me my place [in Paradise]'.—'Very well', he replied. 'Give me your knife', the other demanded, '[since, otherwise], you may frighten me on the way'. He gave it to him. On arriving there he lifted him up and shewed him [his place]. The

(1) A fragrant plant (v. Jast.). *Aliter:* polion (Rashi). *Aliter:* Penny royal (cf. Golds. '*Polei*'). (2) Or 'labdanum', λάδανον, a soft black or dark brown resinous exudation from the *Cistus* or rock rose. (3) These fall off when the hide is being smoothed. (4) Sweet scented clover. (5) מתחלא (cf. תחלא, half-ripe date), the calyx of the date when it is in its early unripe condition. (6) To shut out all draughts. (7) אריחא is of the size of half a brick, the size of the brick being three handbreadths. (8) The sufferer from *ra'athan*. (9) Of the insect (cf. Rashi's interpretation, *supra* p. 486, n. 9). (10) Thus preventing the insect from burying its feet in the brain when lifted out. (11) The insect. (12) Which are infectious. (13) Prov. V, 19, a reference to the Torah. (14) R. Joshua b. Levi.

latter jumped and dropped on the other side [of the wall].[1] He seized him by the corner of his cloak; but the other exclaimed, 'I swear that I will not go back'. Thereupon the Holy One, blessed be He, said, 'If he ever had an oath of his annulled[2] he must return;[3] but if not, he need not return'. 'Return to me my knife', he said to him; but the other would not return it to him. A *bath kol*[4] went forth and said to him, 'Return the thing to him, for it is required for the mortals'.[5]

Elijah[6] heralded him[7] proclaiming, 'Make room for the son of Levi, make room for the son of Levi'. As he[7] proceeded on his way he found R. Simeon b. Yoḥai sitting on thirteen stools[8] of gold. 'Are you', the latter asked him, 'the son of Levi?'—'Yes', he replied. 'Has a rainbow [the latter asked again] ever appeared in your lifetime?'—'Yes', he replied. 'If that is so [the other said] you are not *the* son of Levi'.[9] The fact, however, is[10] that there was no such thing [in his lifetime], but he[11] thought, 'I must take no credit for myself'.

R. Ḥanina b. Papa was his[12] friend, and when he was about to die the Angel of Death was commanded, 'Go and carry out any wish of his'. He went to his house and revealed himself to him. 'Allow me', the latter said to him, 'thirty days in which to revise my studies', for it was said,[13] 'Happy is he who comes here in full possession of his learning'. He left him, and after thirty days he appeared to him again. 'Shew me', the latter said to him 'my place [in Paradise]'. 'Very well', he replied. 'Give me your knife', the

(1) Of Paradise. (2) איתשיל (rt. שאל 'to ask' in Ithpa'el) 'to ask a competent authority for absolution from an oath or a vow'. (3) His present oath can also be annulled. (4) V. Glos. (5) Lit., 'creatures' (6) Elijah, the prophet who *went up by a whirlwind into heaven* (II Kings II, 11). (7) R. Joshua b. Levi. (8) תכתקי (v. Levy and Jast.). A more acceptable rendering might be: Sitting at thirteen tables of fine gold (cf. תכא 'a table'). (9) I.e., the saintly man concerning whom Elijah made his proclamation. The rainbow being a *token of the covenant* (Gen. IX, 12) that, though the people deserved destruction, the *waters shall no more become a flood to destroy all flesh* (ibid. 15), should not appear in the lifetime of a saint whose merit alone is sufficient to save the world from destruction (v. Rashi). (10) Lit., 'and this is not (so)'. (11) R. Joshua b. Levi. (12) The pronoun refers to the Angel of Death (Rashi) or to R. Joshua b. Levi (according to a MS.). (13) In the world to come (cf. B.B. 10*b*).

other said to him, [since otherwise], you may frighten me on the way'. 'Do you wish to treat me as your friend[1] has done?' he asked. 'Bring', the other replied, 'the Scroll of the Law and see if anything that is written therein has not been observed by me'. 'Have you attached yourself', he asked 'to the sufferers of *ra'athan* and engaged thus in the study of the Torah?'[2] Nevertheless when his soul passed to its eternal rest, a pillar of fire formed a partition between him and the world; and we have it as a tradition that such a partition by a pillar of fire is made only for a person who is unique in his generation[3] or [one] of the two [outstanding men] in his generation. R. Alexandri approached him and said, 'Do it for the honour of the Sages', but he disregarded him. 'Do it [he said] for the honour of your father's house', but he again disregarded him. 'Do it [he finally requested] for your own honour's sake' [and the pillar of fire] departed.

Abaye remarked: [The purpose of the pillar of fire was] to keep away[4] anyone who had failed to observe even a single letter[5] [of the Torah]. Said R. Adda b. Mattena to him: [This then would also] exclude the Master, since he has no battlement to his roof.[6] The fact, however, was[7] that he did have one, but the wind had thrown it down at that moment.

R. Ḥanina said: Why are there no sufferers from *ra'athan* in Babylon?—Because they eat beet[8] and drink beer containing cuscuta[9] of the *hizme*[10] shrub.

R. Joḥanan stated: Why are there no lepers in Babylon?—Because they eat beet,[8] drink beer, and bathe in the waters of the Euphrates.

(1) Cf. p. 488, nn. 11 and 12. (2) *Sc.* he was not even as pious and staunch in his faith as R. Joshua b. Levi to trust in the power of the Torah to protect him from all evil. If the latter, despite his extreme piety, did not hesitate to outwit the Angel of Death, how much more likely was he to do so. (3) Head and shoulders above them in learning and piety. (4) From attending on the deceased. (5) 'Even . . . letter' is deleted by Rashal. [On this reading render: 'Who has failed to observe (the Torah as he did)', v. Rashi]. (6) Which is a contravention of Deut. XXII, 8. (7) Lit., 'and this is not (so)'. (8) *Aliter:* Tomatoes. (9) *Instead* of the usual hops. (10) Prob. *Spira Regia* (Jast.); *αἱμασιά* is also suggested as a probable derivation.

KETHUBOTH

CHAPTER VIII

MISHNAH. [78a] IF A WOMAN CAME INTO THE POSSESSION[1] OF PROPERTY BEFORE SHE WAS BETROTHED, BETH SHAMMAI AND BETH HILLEL AGREE THAT SHE MAY[2] SELL IT OR GIVE IT AWAY AND HER ACT IS LEGALLY VALID. IF SHE CAME INTO THE POSSESSION OF THE PROPERTY AFTER SHE WAS BETROTHED, BETH SHAMMAI SAID: SHE MAY SELL IT,[2] AND BETH HILLEL SAID: SHE MAY NOT SELL IT;[2] BUT BOTH AGREE THAT IF SHE HAD SOLD IT OR GIVEN IT AWAY HER ACT IS LEGALLY VALID. R. JUDAH STATED: THE SAGES ARGUED BEFORE R. GAMALIEL, 'SINCE THE MAN[3] GAINS POSSESSION OF THE WOMAN DOES HE NOT ALSO GAIN POSSESSION OF HER PROPERTY?'[4] HE REPLIED, 'WE ARE EMBARRASSED[5] WITH REGARD TO [THE PROBLEM OF] HER NEW POSSESSIONS[6] AND DO YOU WISH TO INVOLVE US [IN THE PROBLEM OF] HER OLD ONES[7] ALSO?' IF SHE CAME INTO THE POSSESSION OF PROPERTY AFTER SHE WAS MARRIED, BOTH[8] AGREE THAT, EVEN IF SHE HAD SOLD IT OR GIVEN IT AWAY, THE HUSBAND MAY SEIZE IT FROM THE BUYERS. [IF SHE CAME INTO POSSESSION] BEFORE SHE MARRIED,[9] AND SUBSEQUENTLY MARRIED, R. GAMALIEL SAID: IF SHE[10] HAD SOLD IT OR GIVEN IT AWAY HER ACT IS LEGALLY VALID. R. ḤANINA B. AḲABIA STATED: THEY ARGUED BEFORE R. GAMALIEL,

(1) Lit., 'to whom there fell'. (2) After her betrothal and before her marriage. V. *infra.* (3) Through betrothal. (4) The application of this argument is explained in the Gemara. (5) Lit., 'ashamed'. (6) In failing to discover a reason why a husband (as stated *infra*) is entitled to seize the property which his wife had sold or given away even though she obtained it after marriage. (7) Property into the possession of which she came while she was only betrothed. (8) Beth Shammai and Beth Hillel. (9) [I.e., either before or after she was betrothed (Rashi), v. Tosaf.]. (10) After her marriage.

'SINCE THE MAN[1] GAINED POSSESSION OF THE WOMAN SHOULD HE NOT ALSO GAIN POSSESSION OF HER PROPERTY?' HE REPLIED, 'WE ARE EMBARRASSED WITH REGARD TO [THE PROBLEM OF] HER NEW POSSESSIONS AND DO YOU WISH TO INVOLVE US [IN THE PROBLEM OF] HER OLD ONES ALSO?[2] R. SIMEON DRAWS A DISTINCTION BETWEEN ONE KIND OF PROPERTY AND ANOTHER: PROPERTY THAT IS KNOWN[3] TO THE HUSBAND [THE WIFE] MAY NOT SELL, AND IF SHE HAS SOLD IT OR GIVEN IT AWAY HER ACT IS VOID; [PROPERTY, HOWEVER,] WHICH IS UNKNOWN TO THE HUSBAND SHE MAY NOT SELL, BUT IF SHE HAS SOLD IT OR GIVEN IT AWAY HER ACT IS LEGALLY VALID.

GEMARA. What is the essential difference between the first clause[4] in which they[5] do not differ and the succeeding clause[6] in which they differ?[7]—The school of R. Jannai replied: In the first clause it was into her possession that the property had come;[8] in the succeeding clause[6] the property came into his possession.[9] If, however, [it is maintained] that the property 'came into his possession' why is HER ACT LEGALLY VALID when SHE HAD SOLD [THE PROPERTY] OR GIVEN IT AWAY?—This then [is the explanation:] In the first clause the property has beyond all doubt come into her possession.[8] In the succeeding clause, [however, the property] might be said [to have come either] into her, or into his possession;[10] [hence,][11] she may not properly sell [the property, but] IF SHE HAD SOLD IT OR GIVEN IT AWAY HER ACT IS LEGALLY VALID.

(1) By marriage. (2) Cf. *supra* p. 490, nn. 5-7. (3) This is explained in the Gemara. (4) Of our Mishnah. (5) Beth Shammai and Beth Hillel., (6) Property obtained AFTER SHE WAS BETROTHED. (7) In both cases surely, she sells or gives away after betrothal when her property presumably belongs to the man who betrothed her. Cf. *infra* note 10. (8) Before betrothal she is the legal possessor of whatever is given to her. (9) Because, as it is assumed at present, after betrothal the man is the legal owner of all that the woman may have. (10) The *ḳinyan* of betrothal being regarded as that of a doubtful marriage, since it is uncertain whether marriage will follow. (11) According to Beth Hillel.

R. JUDAH STATED: [THE SAGES] ARGUED BEFORE R. GAMALIEL. The question was raised: Does R. Judah[1] refer to the case of direct permissibility[2] or also to one of *ex post facto?*[3] [78b]—Come and hear what was taught in the following. R. Judah stated: They argued before R. Gamaliel, 'Since the one woman[4] is his wife and the other[5] is his wife, just as a sale by the former[6] is invalid so also should a sale by the latter[7] be invalid'. He replied, 'We are in an embarrassed condition with regard to [the problem of] her new possessions and you wish to involve us [in the problem of] her old ones also?'[8] Thus[9] it may be inferred that he referred to a case of *ex post facto* also. This is conclusive.[10]

It was taught: R. Ḥanina b. Aḳabia said, It was not such a reply[11] that R. Gamaliel gave to the Sages,[12] but it was this that he replied, '[There is] no [comparison]; if you say [the ruling][13] is to apply to a married woman whose husband is entitled to her finds, to her handiwork and to the annulment of her vows, will you say it also applies to a betrothed woman whose husband is not entitled either to her finds or to her handiwork or to the annulment of her vows?'[14] 'Master', they said to him, '[this is quite feasible if] she effected a sale before she married;[15] what, [however, will be your ruling where] she was married and effected the sale[16] subsequently?'—'This woman also', he replied, 'may sell or give away, and her act is valid'. 'Since, however', they argued, 'he[17] gained possession

(1) In the argument he reported in the name of the Sages to invalidate her sale. (2) I.e., the ruling of Beth Shammai that if she obtained property after she was betrothed she is fully entitled to sell it or to give it away. (3) Where it is the unanimous opinion of Beth Shammai and Beth Hillel THAT IF SHE HAD SOLD IT OR GIVEN IT AWAY HER ACT IS LEGALLY VALID. (4) Lit., 'this one',—whom he married. (5) Whom he betrothed. (6) Of any property that came into her possession after marriage. (7) Of property she obtained after betrothal. (8) Cf. *supra* p. 490, nn. 5-7. Tosef. Keth. VIII. (9) Since this Baraitha speaks explicitly of a sale that had already taken place. (10) Lit., 'hear *or* infer from it'. (11) As the one contained in our Mishnah. (12) Who compared a betrothed to a married woman. (13) 'EVEN IF SHE HAD SOLD IT . . . THE HUSBAND MAY SEIZE IT FROM THE BUYERS'. (14) Only a husband and a father, acting together, may annul the vows of a betrothed woman as a *na'arah* (v. Glos.). (15) While she was only betrothed. (16) Of property that came into her possession before her marriage. (17) By the *ḳinyan* of marriage.

of the woman[1] should he not also gain possession of her property?'[2] —'We are quite embarrassed', he replied, 'about [the problem of] her new possessions and you wish to involve us [in the problem of] her old ones[3] also!' But, surely, we learned, [IF SHE CAME INTO POSSESSION] BEFORE SHE MARRIED, AND SUBSEQUENTLY MARRIED, R. GAMALIEL SAID: IF SHE HAD SOLD IT OR GAVE IT AWAY[4] HER ACT IS LEGALLY VALID![5] —R. Zebid replied, Read: She may sell or give away, and her act is valid.[6] R. Papa replied: There is no difficulty,[7] for one[8] is the view of R. Judah on R. Gamaliel's opinion[9] whilst the other[10] is the view of R. Ḥanina b. Aḳabia on R. Gamaliel's opinion.[11]

Is R. Ḥanina b. Aḳabia then in agreement with Beth Shammai?[12] —It is this that he meant: Beth Shammai and Beth Hillel did not differ at all on this point.[13]

Both Rab and Samuel stated: Whether a woman came into the possession of property before she was betrothed or whether she came into possession after she was betrothed her husband may, [if she sold it] after she married, take it away from the buyers.

(1) I.e., the right to her finds and handiwork and to the invalidation of her vows. (2) To the usufruct of which a husband is entitled during her lifetime. If her sale is valid her husband would inevitably be deprived of his right to the usufruct. (3) Cf. *supra* p. 490, nn. 5-7. (4) I.e., a case *ex post facto*. (5) From which it follows that such a sale or gift is not permitted in the first instance, a ruling which is in contradiction to that reported by R. Ḥanina in the name of R. Gamaliel. (6) [On this reading the amendment is made in the text of our Mishnah; *var. lec.*, 'Read: if she sold it or gave it away her act is valid', the change being made in the Baraitha, v. Tosaf. s.v. תני]. (7) V. *supra* n. 5. (8) Our Mishnah (cf. *supra* n. 5). (9) That even during betrothal a woman is not permitted in the first instance to sell or to give away, much less may she do so after marriage. (10) The quoted Baraitha. (11) That even a married woman may sell or give away property that came into her possession before she married. This view which R. Ḥanina did not state specifically in our Mishnah he elucidated in the Baraitha. (12) And not with Beth Hillel who ruled that even after a betrothal a woman is not permitted in the first instance to sell or give away; much less may she do so after marriage. Would then R. Ḥanina deviate from the accepted *halachah* which is in agreement with Beth Hillel? (13) But both agreed that the woman is fully entitled to sell or to give away.

In agreement with whose view [is this ruling], which is neither in agreement with that of R. Judah nor with that of R. Ḥanina b. Aḳabia?—They adopted the ruling of our Masters; for it was taught: Our Masters took a recount [of votes, and decided that] whether a woman came into the possession [of property] before she was betrothed or whether she came into its possession after she was betrothed, her husband may, [if she sold it] after she married, take it away from the buyers.[1]

AFTER SHE WAS MARRIED, BOTH AGREE. May it be suggested that here we are learning of the enactment of Usha,[2] for R. Jose the son of R. Ḥanina stated: It was enacted at Usha that if a woman sold during the lifetime of her husband *melog*[3] property,[4] and died, the husband[5] may seize it from the buyers![6]—Our Mishnah [deals with the seizure] during the woman's lifetime for the purposes of usufruct [only];[7] the enactment of Usha [refers to the seizure] of the capital after her death.[8]

R. SIMEON DRAWS A DISTINCTION BETWEEN ONE KIND OF PROPERTY [etc.]. Which kind is regarded as KNOWN, and which as UNKNOWN?—R. Jose the son of R. Ḥanina replied: KNOWN means landed property;[9] UNKNOWN, movable property. But R. Joḥanan said: Both are regarded as KNOWN, but the following is classed as UNKNOWN. Whenever a woman lives in a certain place and comes into the possession of property in a country

(1) Tosef. Keth. VIII. (2) V. *supra* p. 283, n. 12. (3) V. Glos. (4) The capital of which belongs to the woman, while its usufruct is enjoyed by the husband. (5) Who is heir to his wife and has the status of a 'prior purchaser'. (6) *Supra* 50*a*, B.Ḳ. 88*b*, B.M. 35*a*, 96*b*, B.B. 50*a*, 139*b*. The difficulty then arises: What need was there for the enactment of Usha in view of the ruling in our Mishnah? On the enactment of Usha v. Epstein, L. *The Jewish Marriage Contract*, pp. 110ff. (7) After the woman's death, however, even if she predeceased her husband, the capital would, according to our Mishnah, revert to the buyer. (8) Cf. *supra* n. 5. [Tosaf. s.v. לימא states that the Gemara could have also explained the need of the enactment of Usha to provide for the case where she inherited the property whilst betrothed, whereas the Mishnah refers only to property which fell to her after marriage]. (9) It is to be assumed that the husband in marrying her expected such property to come into her possession.

beyond the sea. So it was also taught elsewhere: The following is classed as unknown. Wherever a woman lives in a certain place and comes into the possession of property in a country beyond the sea.

A certain woman[1] wishing to deprive her [intended] husband of her estate assigned it in writing to her daughter.[2] After she married and was divorced[3] [79a] she came before R. Naḥman [to claim the return of her estate]. R. Naḥman tore up the deed.[4] R. Anan, thereupon, went to Mar 'Uḳba[5] and said to him, 'See, Master, how Naḥman the boor[6] tears up people's deeds'. 'Tell me', the other said to him, 'how exactly the incident occurred'. 'It occurred', he replied, 'in such and such a manner'. 'Do you speak', the other exclaimed, 'of a deed a woman intended as a means of evasion?[7] Thus said R. Ḥanilai b. Idi in the name of Samuel: I am an officially recognized judge,[8] and should a deed which a woman intended as a means of evasion[7] come into my hand I would tear it up.

Said Raba to R. Naḥman:[9] What in fact is the reason?[10] [Obviously] because no man would neglect himself and give his property away to others. But this would apply to strangers only, whilst to a daughter one might well give![11] —Even in the case of a daughter a woman gives preference to her own person.[12]

(1) A widow who was about to marry. (2) Intimating at the same time in the presence of witnesses that the transfer was only temporary, and that it was her wish that the estate shall revert to her on the death of her husband or on her being divorced by him. (3) And her daughter refusing to part with the gift. (4) Of the gift which the daughter produced. (5) Who was *Ab Beth Din* (v. Glos.). [The reference is to Mar 'Uḳba II, v. Funk, *Die Juden in Babylonien* I, notes p. XIV.] (6) חקלאה, lit., 'field-labourer'; 'uncultured fellow'. (7) מברחת (Hif. of ברח), lit., 'one who causes to flee' or 'to escape'. (8) He was appointed to that office by the *Resh Galutha* or Exilarch (v. Sanh. 5a). מורה הוראה, lit., 'guide for ruling', one who gives directions or decisions on questions of ritual and legal practice. (9) When he tore up the deed of gift which the daughter produced. (10) Why Samuel (upon whose ruling R. Naḥman relied) did not recognize the validity of a deed that was intended as a means of evasion. (11) On what authority then did R. Naḥman tear up the deed which had been produced by the woman's daughter? (12) And it may safely be assumed, therefore, that the gift was intended as a temporary one which was to revert

An objection was raised: If a woman desires to keep her property from her husband, how is she to proceed? She writes out[1] a deed of trust[2] to a stranger;[3] so R. Simeon b. Gamaliel.[4] But the Sages said: If he[5] wishes he may laugh at her[6] unless she wrote out for him: '[You shall acquire possession] from this day whenever I shall express[7] my consent'.[8] The reason then[9] is because she wrote out for him in the manner prescribed;[10] but had she not done so, the [fictitious] buyer would have acquired [would he not] possession of it?[11]—R. Zera replied: There is no difficulty. One ruling[12] refers to [a woman who has assigned to the stranger] all her property;[13] the other,[14] to [a woman who assigned to a stranger] a part of her property. But if the buyer does not[15] acquire her property[16] the husband[17] should acquire it![18]—Abaye replied:

to the donor as soon as the cause that impelled her to make the gift had been removed.

(1) Prior to her marriage. (2) שטר פסים (or פסים, cf. Aruch and Jast.), a deed of a feigned sale or gift with which one person entrusts (cf. פיסטים, πίστις, 'trust') another in order to make people believe (in the interests of one of the parties) that a proper sale or presentation had actually taken place. (3) Lit., 'to another', so MS.M. Cur. edd. 'to others'. (4) Who, maintaining that such a deed has no legal validity, the holder of the deed having no claim whatever upon the property specified in it, considers the fictitious transaction as a safe protection for the woman. (5) The holder of the deed. (6) I.e., he may retain possession of the property by virtue of the deed; and thus refuse to return it to her. (7) At any time in the future. (8) Tosef. Keth. IX. In this case only is the woman protected against the holder of the deed as well as against her husband. For should the latter claim the property she can evade him by expressing consent to its acquisition by the stranger; and should the stranger claim possession she can exercise her right of refusing to give her consent. (9) Why the holder of the deed cannot claim possession of the property in the case mentioned. (10) Lit., 'thus'. (11) This, then, is in contradiction to the ruling of Samuel *supra*. (12) Lit., 'that', Samuel's view. (13) Since no person would give away all his property to a stranger it is pretty obvious that the deed related to a fictitious transaction. (14) The ruling of the Sages in the Baraitha cited. (15) Where the woman's entire property had been assigned to him. (16) In consequence of which the woman remains its legal possessor. (17) Who is entitled to the usufruct of his wife's possessions during her lifetime and to her capital also after her death. (18) Why should the property be awarded to the woman?

It[1] was treated as property WHICH IS UNKNOWN TO THE HUSBAND[2] in accordance with the view of R. Simeon.[3]

MISHNAH. [IF A MARRIED WOMAN] CAME INTO THE POSSESSION OF MONEY, LAND SHOULD BE BOUGHT THEREWITH AND THE HUSBAND IS ENTITLED TO THE USUFRUCT.[4] [IF SHE CAME INTO THE POSSESSION OF] PRODUCE THAT WAS DETACHED FROM THE GROUND,[5] LAND SHOULD BE BOUGHT THEREWITH AND THE HUSBAND IS ENTITLED TO THE USUFRUCT. [IF IT WAS] PRODUCE ATTACHED TO THE GROUND, THE LAND,[6] R. MEIR RULED, IS TO BE VALUED AS TO HOW MUCH IT IS WORTH WITH THE PRODUCE[7] AND HOW MUCH WITHOUT THE PRODUCE, AND WITH THE DIFFERENCE[8] LAND SHOULD BE BOUGHT[9] AND THE HUSBAND IS ENTITLED TO ITS USUFRUCT.[10] THE SAGES, HOWEVER, RULED: ALL PRODUCE ATTACHED TO THE GROUND BELONGS TO THE HUSBAND[11] AND ONLY THAT WHICH IS DETACHED FROM IT[12] BELONGS TO THE WIFE; [WITH THE PROCEEDS OF THE LATTER] LAND IS TO BE BOUGHT AND THE HUSBAND IS ENTITLED TO THE USUFRUCT.[13]

R. SIMEON SAID: IN RESPECT OF THAT[14] WHEREIN THE

(1) Property fictitiously transferred by a woman prior to her marriage. (2) Since he believes the transaction to have been a genuine one, the husband does not expect ever to enjoy the use of the property in question. (3) Our Mishnah *ad fin*. (4) The land itself remaining in the possession of the woman. (5) I.e., after being harvested. (6) Which remains the property of the woman. (7) Which, having grown before the land came into possession of the woman, remains her property, in the opinion of R. Meir, like the land itself. (8) Lit., 'remainder', i.e., the value of the attached produce which is the property of the woman (v. *supra* note 7) and not of the husband who, according to R. Meir, is entitled only to such produce of his wife's land as grows after, but not before he had become entitled to the usufruct. (9) Thus turning the proceeds of the produce into capital. (10) The purchased land remaining the property of the wife (cf. *supra* note 4). (11) Even if it grew before he had become entitled to the usufruct of the land. (12) At the time he marries the woman, when he acquires the right to the usufruct. (13) Cf. *supra* note 4. (14) Lit., 'in the place'.

HUSBAND IS AT AN ADVANTAGE WHEN HE MARRIES HIS WIFE[1] HE IS AT A DISADVANTAGE WHEN HE DIVORCES HER[2] AND IN RESPECT OF THAT WHEREIN HE IS AT A DISADVANTAGE WHEN HE MARRIES HER HE IS AT AN ADVANTAGE WHEN HE DIVORCES HER. HOW SO? PRODUCE WHICH IS ATTACHED TO THE GROUND IS THE HUSBAND'S WHEN HE MARRIES HIS WIFE[3] AND HERS WHEN HE DIVORCES HER,[4] WHILST PRODUCE THAT IS DETACHED FROM THE GROUND IS HERS WHEN SHE MARRIES[5] BUT THE HUSBAND'S WHEN SHE IS DIVORCED.[6]

GEMARA. It is obvious[7] [that if husband and wife differ on the choice of purchase between] land and houses,[8] land [is to receive preference].[9] [If they differ on the choice between] houses and date-trees, houses [are to receive preference].[10] [If they insist respectively on] date-trees and other fruit trees, date-trees [are to receive preference].[10] [If their dispute is on] fruit trees and vines, fruit trees [are to receive preference].[10] [What, however, is the ruling if the husband desires to purchase][11] a thicket of sorb[12] or a fish pond?[13]—Some maintain that it is regarded as[14] produce;[15]

(1) Lit., 'at her entrance', *sc.* into her married state. (2) Lit., 'at her going out'. (3) If at that time they were still attached. This is in agreement with the view of the Sages *supra* and the point of difference between them and R. Simeon is discussed *infra*. (4) A divorced woman being entitled not only to the land (which was hers all the time) but also to all produce of such land that had not been detached prior to her divorce. (5) It is consequently turned into capital by purchasing therewith land to the usufruct of which the husband is entitled while the land itself remains in the possession of the woman. (6) All detached fruit belonging to the husband who is entitled to the usufruct of his wife's land. (7) When A MARRIED WOMAN CAME INTO THE POSSESSION OF MONEY which, as stated in our Mishnah, is to be invested in LAND, *sc.* a reliable profit yielding security. (8) Each insisting on his or her choice. (9) Land being a safer and better investment than houses both as regards durability (which is an advantage to the wife who remains the owner of the capital) and yield (which is an advantage to the husband who has the right of usufruct). (10) Cf. *supra* n. 9 *mutatis mutandis*. (11) Cf. *supra* n. 7. This is the interpretation of R. Tam and R. Ḥan. (V. Tosaf. s.v. כללא) contrary to Rashi. (12) Which can only be used for the cutting of its wood and which is valueless after the wood has been cut. (13) That loses all its value after the fish have been

and others maintain that it is regarded as[1] capital.[2] This is the general rule:[3] If the stump grows new shoots[4] it is regarded as capital,[5] but if the stump grows no new shoots it is regarded as produce.[6]

R. Zera stated in the name of R. Oshaia in the name of R. Jannai (others say, R. Abba stated in the name of R. Oshaia in the name of R. Jannai), If a man steals [79b] the young of a *melog*[7] beast he must pay double[8] its value to the woman.[9] In accordance with whose [view has this ruling[10] been laid down]? Is it in agreement with neither that of the Rabbis nor with that of Ḥananiah? For it was taught: The young of a *melog* beast belongs to the husband; the child of a *melog* bondwoman belongs to the wife; but Ḥananiah the son of Josiah's brother ruled, The child of a *melog* bondwoman has been given the same legal status as the young of a *melog* beast![11] —It may be said to agree even with the opinion of all,[12] for it is the produce alone that the Rabbis in their enactment have assigned to the husband but not the produce that accrues from this produce.[13]

removed. (14) Lit., 'they say concerning it'. (15) Since no capital remains (cf. *supra* p. 498, nn. 12 and 13) for the woman. Hence it is her right to veto such a purchase.

(1) Cf. *supra* n. 14. (2) Because the land of the thicket and the pond respectively remain after the sorb had been cut or the fish had been removed. Against such a purchase, therefore, the woman may not exercise her veto. (3) Laid down by the authors of the first ruling. (4) I.e., if after the first yield had been disposed of the capital continues to yield further produce or profit. (5) So R. Ḥan. (v. Tosaf. *a.l.* s.v. כללא). Cur. edd., followed by Rashi, read 'produce'. (6) V. *supra* n. 5. Cur. edd., followed by Rashi, read, 'capital'. As a thicket of sorb or a fish pond produces only one yield (cf. *supra* p. 498, nn. 12 and 13) it may not be purchased (v. *supra* p. 498, n. 7) if the woman objects (cf. *supra* n. 15). (7) V. Glos. (8) V. Ex. XXII, 6ff. (9) And not to the husband. Since a beast dies, and its yield ceases, the young must replace it as capital and is consequently the property of the wife. It may not be consumed by the husband but may be sold, and a produce-yielding object purchased with the proceeds. (10) In the statement made in the name of R. Jannai. (11) And belongs to the husband. (12) Both with that of the Rabbis and that of Ḥananiah. (13) The young is the 'produce' of the beast but the 'double' that the thief pays as restitution is the produce of that young and consequently the 'produce of the produce' of the beast. This belongs to the wife.

[The view] of Ḥananiah is quite logical on the assumption[1] that death[2] is not to be taken into consideration,[3] but [what principle is followed by] the Rabbis? If they do take into consideration the possibility of death,[4] even the young of a *melog* beast also should not [belong to the husband], and if they do not take the possibility of death into consideration,[5] then even the child of a bondwoman also [should belong to the husband]![6]—They do in fact take the possibility of death into consideration,[4] but the case of the beast is different [from that of a bondwoman] since its skin remains.[7]

R. Huna b. Ḥiyya stated in the name of Samuel: The *halachah* is in agreement with Ḥananiah. Said Raba in the name of R. Naḥman: Although Samuel said, 'The *halachah* is in agreement with Ḥananiah', Ḥananiah admits that if the woman is divorced she may pay the price [of the bondwoman's children] and take them because [they constitute] the pride of her paternal house [which she is entitled to retain].[8]

Raba stated in the name of R. Naḥman: If a woman brought to her husband[9] a goat for milking, a ewe for shearing, a hen for laying eggs, or a date-tree for producing fruit, he may go on eating [the yield of any of these][10] until the capital is consumed.

R. Naḥman stated: If a woman[9] brought to her husband a cloak[11] [its use] is [to be regarded as] produce and he may continue to use it as a covering until it is worn out.[12]

(1) Lit., 'that is'. (2) Either of the bondwoman or of the beast. (3) Hence his ruling that the child of the bondwoman, as well as the young of the beast, are to be regarded as produce which belongs to the husband, the bondwoman or the beast being regarded as the 'capital' which remains in the possession of the wife. (4) As implied by their ruling that 'the child of the *melog* bondwoman belongs to the wife' (cf. *supra* p. 499, n. 9 *mutatis mutandis*) and not to the husband. (5) As their ruling that 'the young of a *melog* beast belongs to the husband' seems to imply. (6) How then can the two rulings be reconciled? (7) And constitutes a small capital which remains the possession of the woman so that the young is treated as 'produce'. (8) Cf. Yeb. 66*b*. (9) On marriage. (10) Since milk, wool, eggs and fruit are the 'produce' of the goat, the ewe, the hen and the tree respectively and, even when the yield ceases, the woman is still left with some capital such as the skin of the goat and the ewe, the feathers of the hen or the wood of the date-tree. (11) As *melog* property. (12) The shreds being regarded as the woman's capital.

In accordance with whose view [has this statement[1] been made]?—In agreement with the following Tanna,[2] for it has been taught: Salt or sand[3] is regarded as produce;[4] a sulphur quarry or an alum-mine[5] is regarded, R. Meir said, as capital,[6] but the Rabbis said, As produce.[7]

R. SIMEON SAID: IN RESPECT OF THAT WHEREIN THE HUSBAND IS AT AN ADVANTAGE. [Is not this view of] R. Simeon identical [with that of] the first Tanna?[8]—Raba replied: The difference between them is [the case of produce that was] attached at the time of the divorce.[9]

MISHNAH. IF AGED BONDMEN OR BONDWOMEN FELL TO HER[10] [AS AN INHERITANCE] THEY MUST BE SOLD, AND LAND PURCHASED WITH THE PROCEEDS, AND THE HUSBAND CAN ENJOY THE USUFRUCT THEREOF. R. SIMEON B. GAMALIEL SAID; SHE NEED NOT SELL THEM,[11] BECAUSE THEY ARE THE PRIDE OF HER PATERNAL HOUSE.[12] IF SHE CAME INTO THE POSSESSION OF OLD OLIVE-TREES OR VINES THEY MUST BE SOLD,[13] AND LAND PURCHASED WITH THE PROCEEDS, AND THE HUSBAND CAN ENJOY THE USUFRUCT THEREOF. R. JUDAH SAID: SHE NEED NOT SELL THEM, BECAUSE THEY ARE THE PRIDE OF HER PATERNAL HOUSE.[12]

(1) Of R. Naḥman that even shreds constitute capital. (2) *Sc.* the Rabbis, *infra*, who differ from R. Meir. (3) Of *melog* property situated on the sea shore. (4) Since the yield is continual. It may, therefore, be used up by the husband. (5) The supplies of which gradually come to an end. (6) The quarry or the mine must be sold, and a constantly produce-yielding object is to be acquired with the proceeds. (7) Which may be used up by the husband. The quarry or mine constitute in their opinion the capital which remains the property of the woman. Cf. *supra* note 2. (8) The Sages, cf. *supra* p. 498, n. 3. (9) Of which the Sages did not speak in our Mishnah. While according to R. Simeon such produce belongs to the woman, the Sages assign it to the husband because it grew prior to the divorce when he was still entitled to usufruct. That produce detached at the time of divorce belongs to the husband, as R. Simeon stated, cannot, of course, be a matter in dispute. (10) A married woman. (11) Even if her husband desires it (cf. Rashi). (12) Which she is entitled to retain. (13) 'As wood' (so the separate edd. of the Mishnah).

GEMARA. R. Kahana stated in the name of Rab: They[1] differ only where [the olive-trees or vines] fell [to the woman] in her own field,[2] but [if they were] in a field that did not belong to her[3] she must, according to the opinion of all, sell them;[4] because [otherwise] the capital[5] would be destroyed.[6] To this R. Joseph demurred: Are not BONDMEN OR BONDWOMEN[7] the same as [trees in] a field that does not belong to her[8] and there is nevertheless a dispute?[9]—The fact is, if the statement[10] has at all been made it must have been made in the following terms: R. Kahana stated in the name of Rab, They[11] differ only where [the olive-trees and vines] fell [to the woman] in a field that did not belong to her[12] but [if they were] in her own field[13] it is the opinion of all that she need not sell them because [she is entitled to retain] the pride of her paternal house.

MISHNAH. HE WHO INCURRED EXPENDITURE IN CONNECTION WITH HIS WIFE'S [MELOG][14] PROPERTY, WHETHER HE SPENT MUCH AND CONSUMED[15] LITTLE, [OR SPENT] LITTLE AND CONSUMED MUCH, WHAT HE HAS SPENT HE HAS SPENT, AND WHAT HE HAS CONSUMED HE HAS CONSUMED.[16] IF HE SPENT BUT DID NOT CONSUME HE MAY TAKE AN OATH AS TO HOW MUCH HE HAS SPENT AND RECEIVE COMPENSATION.

GEMARA. How much is considered LITTLE?—R. Assi replied:

(1) The first Tanna and R. Judah in our Mishnah. (2) I.e., if she came into the possession of the trees together with land in which they grew. (3) If, for instance, her father from whom she inherited them did not own the soil and was only entitled to the trees alone until they withered. (4) In order that land or any other produce-yielding capital might be acquired with the proceeds. (5) Which should remain the permanent possession of the woman. (6) When the trees withered. (7) After whose death no capital whatsoever remains. (8) Cf. *supra* note 6. (9) Though the capital is destroyed. (10) Attributed to Rab. (11) The first Tanna and R. Judah in our Mishnah. (12) V. *supra* note 3. (13) V. *supra* note 2. (14) V. Glos. (15) By virtue of his right to its usufruct. (16) He has no claim for compensation upon his wife should he divorce her.

Even one dried fig; but this applies only where he ate it in a dignified manner.[1] Said [80*a*] R. Abba: At the school of Rab it was stated, Even the refuse[2] of dates.[3]

R. Bibi enquired: What [is the ruling in respect of] a mash of pressed dates?[4]—This stands undecided.[5]

What [is the ruling if] he did not eat it[6] in a dignified manner?[7]—'Ulla replied: On this there is a difference of opinion between two Amoraim in the West.[8] One says, The value of an *issar*;[9] and the other says, The value of a *denar*.[9]

The judges of Pumbeditha[10] stated: Rab Judah gave a practical decision[11] in [a case where the husband used up some] bundles of vine-shoots,[12] Rab Judah acting here in accordance with his own principle; for Rab Judah ruled: If he[13] ate thereof [during one of the three years] only *'uncircumcised'*[14] produce,[15] [the produce of] the Sabbatical year,[16] or the produce of mingled seed,[17] this counts [towards the three years of] *ḥazaḳah*.[18]

R. Jacob stated in the name of R. Ḥisda: If a man has incurred expenses on the *melog* property of his wife who was a minor[19] [he

(1) V. Ḳid. 45*b*. (2) שיגרא (rt. שגר 'to flow', 'to cast'). (3) After all the juice and sweetness has been pressed out, when they are practically valueless. (4) V. Jast. s.v. חובין, חובצא. (5) *Teḳu*, v. Glos. (6) The 'dried fig', *supra*. (7) I.e., what minimum quantity must one eat in such a case to be regarded as having CONSUMED LITTLE? (8) Palestine. (9) V. Glos. (10) The reference is to R. Papa b. Samuel (v. Sanh. 17*b*). (11) In favour of the wife who was divorced. (12) Of his wife's *melog* property, with which he fed his cattle. Though the shoots were hardly suitable for the purpose, Rab Judah regarded their consumption as sufficient reason for denying the husband all rights to compensation for his expenses. (13) A person who occupied a field for three years. (14) *'Orlah* (v. Glos. and cf. Lev. XIX, 23). (15) I.e., the shoots, since the fruits of *'Orlah* are forbidden for all uses. (16) Which is common property and the consumption of which is no proof of ownership. (17) *Kil'ayim* (v. Glos. and cf. Lev. XIX, 19 and Deut. XXII, 9). Only the shoots are permitted in this case also (cf. *supra* n. 15). (18) V. Glos. This shews that right of ownership may be established not only by the consumption of proper produce but also by that of mere shoots. Similarly, here, the improper feeding of one's cattle with vine-shoots is also regarded as proper consumption to exempt the woman from all responsibility for the expenses her husband had incurred on her *melog* property. (19) Who might leave him at any time by exercising her right of *mi'un* (v. Glos.).

is in the same legal position] as one who incurred expenses on the property of a stranger.[1] What is the reason?—The Rabbis have enacted this measure[2] in order that he should not allow her property to deteriorate.[3]

A woman once came into the possession of four hundred *zuz*[4] at Be-Ḥozae.[5] Her husband went thither, spent six hundred [on his journey] and brought with him the four hundred. While he was on his way back he required one *zuz* and took it out of these. When he came before R. Ammi[6] the latter ruled: What he has spent he has spent and what he used he has used.[7] Said the Rabbis to R. Ammi: Does not this[8] apply only where he consumes the produce, whilst here he used up the capital which [constituted a part of] the expenditure?—If so, he replied,[9] he is one who SPENT BUT DID NOT CONSUME, then HE MAY TAKE AN OATH AS TO HOW MUCH HE HAS SPENT AND RECEIVE HIS COMPENSATION.

HE MAY TAKE AN OATH AS TO HOW MUCH HE HAS SPENT AND RECEIVE COMPENSATION. Said R. Assi: This applies only where the appreciation corresponds to the expenditure. What exactly is the object of this[10] law?[11]—Abaye replied: That if the

(1) The minor on exercising *mi'un* must compensate her husband for any improvements he may have effected in her property, paying him at the rate given to an *aris* (v. Glos.) in that country. (2) Conferring upon the husband of a minor the rights of an *aris* in respect of any expenses on her *melog* property that he may incur. (3) Had no provision been made for enabling him to recover his expenses he, knowing that the minor might leave him at any moment by exercising her right of *mi'un*, would exploit her property to the full, spending nothing on its improvement. (4) V. Glos. (5) A town in Khuzistan, S.W. Persia. (6) Claiming his expenses. (7) Cf. our Mishnah. The benefit he has derived from the one *zuz* ('CONSUMED LITTLE') deprives him of the right to recover the six hundred *zuz* for his expenses ('HE SPENT MUCH'). (8) That if HE HAS SPENT MUCH AND CONSUMED LITTLE he cannot recover his expenses. (9) So BaḤ. (10) Lit., 'concerning what'. (11) Of R. Assi, i.e., does he lay the emphasis on TAKE AN OATH or on RECEIVE? In other words: Is it implied that the husband must swear only where the appreciation just corresponds with his outlay, but is to receive his outlay without any oath where the appreciation exceeds the outlay; or is the implication that he is to receive for his outlay no more than the value of the appreciation, and where the former exceeds the latter, he is not entitled to receive the difference even though he is willing to swear?

appreciation exceeded the expenditure he receives the sum of his outlay without an oath. Said Raba to him: If so,[1] one might be induced to act cunningly![2]—[The object of the law] however, said Raba, was that if the outlay exceeded the appreciation he is only entitled to receive that amount of his outlay which corresponds to the appreciation, and [even this can be obtained only] by an oath.[3]

The question was raised: What is the legal position where a husband has sent down[4] *arisin*[5] in his place?[6] Does [an *aris*] go down [into *melog* fields] in his reliance on the rights of the husband, [and, consequently,] when the husband forfeits his claim[7] they also[8] lose theirs, or does an *aris* possibly go down [into the *melog* fields] in his reliance on the [yield of] the land, and land, surely is usually entrusted to *arisin*?[9] To this Raba son of R. Ḥanan demurred: Wherein does this case essentially differ from that of a man who went down into a neighbour's field and planted it without the owner's authority where an assessment[10] is made and he is at a disadvantage?[11]—In that case[12] there was no other person to take the trouble;[13] but here there is the husband who should have taken the trouble.[14] What then is the decision on the matter?—R. Huna the son of R. Joshua replied: We must observe [the conditions of

(1) That in the circumstances mentioned one may obtain a sum of money without affirming his claim by an oath. (2) However small the outlay, one might claim the full value of appreciation minus a fraction, and receive it for the mere asking. (3) Confirming the amount he claims. (4) Into his wife's *melog* lands. (5) Pl. of *aris* (v. Glos.). (6) Do these *arisin*, when the woman is divorced, receive the full value of their amelioration? (7) Where, e.g., he consumed any part of the produce. (8) If they consumed any of it. (9) Had not the husband sent them, the wife would have done it herself. The *arisin* should consequently be entitled to the full refund of their share. (10) Of the appreciation. (11) B.M. 101*a*. He is repaid the amount he spent or is allowed the value of the appreciation whichever is the less. The two cases being essentially analogous, why was the question of the *arisin* at all raised? (12) That of the man who entered his neighbour's field. (13) Of planting the field. The man who undertook the work in the absence of other cultivators, and thus benefited the owner, is therefore, justly entitled to some compensation. (14) And since he would not have been entitled to any compensation if he consumed anything of the produce so also, it may well be argued, should not the *arisin*, who stepped into his place, be entitled to any compensation. Hence the enquiry.

each case]: If the husband is an *aris*,[1] the *arisin* lose all claim to compensation wherever the husband loses his claim;[2] if the husband is not an *aris* [they are entitled to compensation, since] all land is usually entrusted to *arisin*.[3]

The question was raised: What is the ruling where a husband sold [his wife's *melog*] land for usufruct?[4] Do we say that whatever he possesses[5] he may transfer to others, or is it possible that the Rabbis have by their enactment granted the usufruct to the husband only [80*b*] in order to provide for the comfort of his home but not so that he should sell it?—Judah Mar b. Meremar replied in the name of Raba: Whatever he has done is done. R. Papi[6] in the name of Raba replied: His act has no validity. Said R. Papa: The ruling reported[7] by Judah Mar b. Meremar was not explicitly stated[8] but was arrived at by inference. For a woman once brought to her husband[9] two bondwomen,[10] and the man went and married another wife and assigned to her one of them. [When the first wife] came before Raba and cried, he disregarded her. One who observed [the incident] formed the opinion [that Raba's inaction] was due to his view that whatever the husband did[11] is valid;[12] but in fact, it is not so.[13] [Usufruct has been allowed to a husband] in order to provide for the comfort of his house and here, surely, comfort was provided.[14]

And the law is that if a husband sold [his wife's *melog*] field for its usufruct[15] his act has no legal validity. What is the reason?—

(1) Capable of attending to the field himself as any experienced *aris*. (2) Since the wife might well plead that, if they had not interfered, her husband would himself have done the work. As they have only done what the husband would have done they cannot expect any higher privileges. (3) Cf. *supra* p. 505, n. 9. (4) *Sc*. that the buyer cultivated the land and enjoys its produce while the land itself remains the property of its original owner. (5) לה of cur. edd. in brackets is wanting in Alfasi. Cf. Asheri. (6) So MS.M. and BaḤ. Cur. edd., 'Papa'. (7) Lit., 'that'. (8) By Raba. (9) On marriage. (10) As *melog* property. (11) Even if he sold *melog* property. (12) Hence the statement of Judah Mar. (13) A husband has no right to sell such property. It was only in that particular case that the husband acted within his rights for the reason that follows. (14) Since the bondwoman would even now attend to general household duties. (15) V. *supra* note 4.

Abaye replied: Provision must be made against the possible deterioration of the land.[1] Raba explained: In order [to safeguard] the comfort of his house.[2] What is the practical difference between them?[3]—The practical difference between them is the case of land that was adjoining a town;[4] or else where the husband [himself] was [acting as] *aris*,[5] or else where [the husband] receives money[6] and trades therewith.[7]

MISHNAH. IF A WOMAN AWAITING THE DECISION OF THE LEVIR[8] CAME[9] INTO THE POSSESSION OF PROPERTY, BETH SHAMMAI AND BETH HILLEL AGREE THAT SHE MAY SELL IT OR GIVE IT AWAY, AND THAT HER ACT IS LEGALLY VALID.[10] IF SHE DIED, WHAT SHALL BE DONE WITH HER KETHUBAH[11] AND WITH THE PROPERTY THAT COMES IN AND GOES OUT

(1) Lit., 'we fear lest it will deteriorate'. The buyer of the usufruct, having no interest in the land itself, would exploit it to the full, neglecting its proper cultivation and use. The husband, however, who, in addition to his right to usufruct, might also, in the event of his surviving his wife, become the owner of the land itself, may well be relied upon to give it proper attention. (2) The sale of the usufruct to a stranger would deprive the household of the enjoyment of it. (3) Abaye and Raba. Is not the sale of the usufruct equally forbidden whatever the reason? (4) Where it is possible to watch the treatment meted out to the land by the buyer and to take in good time the necessary steps for its protection. In such a case Raba's reason is applicable; Abaye's is not. According to the latter the husband would be entitled to sell the usufruct. (5) He himself was looking after the land, delivering to the buyer the harvested produce. In this case also Raba's reason is applicable, but not Abaye's (cf. *supra* note 4). (6) From the buyer. (7) In this case Abaye's reason applies; but not Raba's, since the income from the trading provides for the comfort of the house. According to Raba the sale of usufruct in such a case is permitted. (8) שומרת יבם, the widow of a deceased brother during the period intervening between the death of her husband and her *haliẓah* or marriage with the levir. (9) During this waiting period (Rashi. Cf., however, Rashi on the parallel Mishnah s.v. שנפלו Yeb. 38*a*). (10) As *melog* property (v. Glos.) she has the right to dispose of it in the way she thinks fit. (11) V. Glos. Here it denotes the sum corresponding in value to the wife's dowry which is conveyed under terms of tenancy to the husband, who enters it in the marriage contract and accepts full responsibility; v. Glos. s.v. *ẓon barzel.*

WITH HER?[1] BETH SHAMMAI RULED: THE HEIRS OF HER HUSBAND[2] ARE TO SHARE IT[3] WITH THE HEIRS OF HER FATHER;[4] AND BETH HILLEL RULED: THE [ẒON BARZEL][5] PROPERTY IS TO REMAIN WITH THOSE IN WHOSE POSSESSION IT IS,[6] THE KETHUBAH[7] IS TO REMAIN IN THE POSSESSION OF THE HEIRS OF THE HUSBAND, AND THE PROPERTY WHICH GOES IN AND COMES OUT WITH HER[8] REMAINS IN THE POSSESSION OF THE HEIRS OF HER FATHER.

IF HIS[9] BROTHER[10] LEFT MONEY, LAND SHALL BE BOUGHT THEREWITH AND HE[11] SHALL ENJOY ITS USUFRUCT.[12] [IF THE DECEASED LEFT] PRODUCE THAT WAS DETACHED FROM THE GROUND, LAND SHALL BE BOUGHT [OUT OF THE PROCEEDS] AND HE[11] SHALL ENJOY ITS USUFRUCT. [IF IT WAS STILL] ATTACHED TO THE GROUND, THE LAND[13] IS TO BE ASSESSED,

(1) I.e., her *melog* property, the capital of which remains in the legal possession of the wife, the husband, who enjoys only the usufruct, accepting no responsibility for it. (2) Who is heir to his wife. 'Husband' in this context = levir. (3) I.e., the *melog* property, not the *kethubah* concerning which Beth Shammai are of the same opinion as Beth Hillel that follows. The discrepancy between the first clause in the Mishnah, where the *melog* property is declaréd definitely hers, whereas in this second clause it is considered doubtfully so, is explained in Yeb. 38*a*. (4) Since it is a matter of doubt whether the marital bond with the levir constitutes such a close relationship as that of actual marriage, the right of heirship as between her husband's heirs and her father's cannot be definitely determined. The property must, therefore, be equally divided between them. (5) V. Glos. (6) The question whether these are the heirs of the husband who had undertaken responsibility for the property, or the heirs of the wife whose capital it was originally, is dealt with in B.B. 158*b*. (7) Here (unlike *supra* p. 507, n. 11) it has its usual connotation; (*a*) the statutory sum of a hundred *zuz* for a widow and two hundred *zuz* for a virgin which is entered in all marriage contracts irrespective of any property that the wife may bring with her on marriage and (*b*) the amount which the husband adds to it over and above the value of the property which she brought to him. (8) V. *supra* note 1, (9) The levir's (v. *supra* p. 507, n. 11). (10) The deceased (v. l.c.). (11) The levir, if he contracted the levirate marriage with the widow. (12) The capital being pledged to the woman for her *kethubah* which remains a charge upon the estate of her first husband, the deceased. According to this opinion even movable possessions, such as money, are also pledged for the *kethubah*. (13) Read אותה with BaḤ *a.l.* Cur. edd. אותן refers to פירות and conveys no sense.

SAID R. MEIR, AS TO HOW MUCH IT IS WORTH[1] TOGETHER WITH THE PRODUCE AND HOW MUCH IT IS WORTH WITHOUT THE PRODUCE, AND WITH THE DIFFERENCE LAND SHALL BE BOUGHT,[2] AND HE[3] SHALL ENJOY ITS USUFRUCT. THE SAGES, HOWEVER, RULED: PRODUCE WHICH IS [STILL] ATTACHED TO THE GROUND BELONGS TO HIM,[4] BUT THAT WHICH IS DETACHED FROM THE GROUND PASSES INTO THE OWNERSHIP OF HIM WHO ṢEIZES IT FIRST.[5] IF HE [SEIZED IT] FIRST HE ACQUIRES OWNERSHIP; AND IF SHE [SEIZED IT] FIRST LAND SHALL BE BOUGHT THEREWITH AND HE[3] SHALL ENJOY ITS USUFRUCT. IF [THE LEVIR] MARRIED HER SHE IS REGARDED AS HIS WIFE IN ALL RESPECTS[4] SAVE THAT HER KETHUBAH REMAINS A CHARGE ON HER FIRST HUSBAND'S ESTATE. HE CANNOT SAY TO HER, 'BEHOLD YOUR KETHUBAH LIES ON THE TABLE', BUT ALL HIS PROPERTY[6] IS PLEDGED TO HER KETHUBAH.[7] SO, TOO, A MAN MAY NOT SAY TO HIS WIFE, 'BEHOLD YOUR KETHUBAH LIES ON THE TABLE', BUT ALL HIS PROPERTY IS PLEDGED TO HER KETHUBAH. IF HE DIVORCED HER[8] SHE IS ENTITLED ONLY TO HER KETHUBAH.[9] IF HE SUBSEQUENTLY REMARRIED HER SHE IS [TO ENJOY THE SAME RIGHTS AS] ALL OTHER WIVES, AND IS ENTITLED ONLY TO HER KETHUBAH.[4]

GEMARA. The question was raised: If a woman awaiting the decision of a levir[10] died, who is to bury her? Are her husband's

(1) היא יפה (so BaḤ). Cur. edd. הן יפין (cf. previous note). (2) R. Meir holding the view that whatever the land yielded while it was in the possession of the deceased (i.e., during his lifetime) is mortgaged for the wife's *kethubah*. (3) The levir, if he contracted the levirate marriage with the widow. (4) This is discussed in the Gemara *infra*. (5) כל הקודם זכה lit., 'whoever is first gains possession'. The same ruling applies also to money, since movables, in the opinion of the Sages, are not pledged for the *kethubah* unless the wife had seized them (cf. *infra* 84*b*). (6) Which he inherited from his deceased brother. (7) I.e., he cannot pay her out her *kethubah* and sell the rest, but must hold the whole of the deceased brother's estate as mortgaged to her *kethubah*; v. *infra* p. 512, n. 11. (8) After he had duly consummated the levirate marriage. (9) And he is at liberty to dispose of the rest of the property (v. *supra* n. 6) as he may desire. (10) Cf. *supra* p. 507, n. 8.

heirs to bury her because they inherit her *kethubah*[1] or is it possibly the heirs of her father who must bury her because they inherit the property that comes in and goes out with her?—R. Amram replied, Come and hear what was taught: If a woman awaiting the decision of a levir died, [81a] it is the duty of her heirs, even those who inherit her *kethubah*, to bury her. Said Abaye, We also have learned a [similar Mishnah]: A widow is to be maintained out of the estate of [her deceased husband's] orphans, and her handiwork belongs to them. It is not their duty, however, to bury her; it is the duty of her heirs, even those who inherit her *kethubah*, to bury her.[2] Now, what widow is it that has two kinds of heirs?[3] Obviously[4] she who is awaiting the decision of a levir.[5]

Said Raba: But could[6] he not plead, 'I am only heir to my brother; it is not my duty to bury his wife'![7]—Abaye replied: [Such a plea would be untenable] because he is approached by two alternative demands:[8] If he is heir to his brother he should bury his wife;[9] if he does not bury his wife he should return her *kethubah*.[10] [Raba] retorted, It is this that I mean: [Might he not plead], 'I am only heir to my brother; it is not my duty to bury his wife; and if [I am expected to bury her] on account of the *kethubah*[11] [I may point out that] a *kethubah* is not payable during [the husband's] lifetime'?[12]—Who is it that was heard to admit the *kethubah*

(1) Which should compensate for burial expenses (cf. *supra* 47b). (2) *Supra* 43a, *infra* 95b. (3) The expression 'her heirs, even those who inherit her *kethubah*' implies that there exists also another class of heirs who do not inherit her *kethubah*. (4) Lit., 'be saying'. (5) [The last clause is to be taken independently of the first, which cannot refer to such a widow since it speaks of orphans, v. Tosaf.]. (6) The levir who, in fact, inherits only the statutory *kethubah* and the additional jointure, which are the property of his brother, and not the *ẓon barzel*, the original property of the woman. Cf. however, Tosaf. s.v. ולימא, *a.l.* (7) It was only his brother's duty to bury his wife in return for her *kethubah* which he inherits (cf. *supra* 47b) but not his duty, since he does not inherit from the widow but from his brother. (8) Lit., 'they come to him from two sides'. (9) As his brother would have done had he survived her. (10) To her heirs. Which is conceded to a husband in return for his wife's burial expenses. (11) Cf. note 10. (12) And he, representing her husband, since it was his intention to consummate levirate marriage, is still alive.

as a text for legal exposition?[1] Beth Shammai, of course.[2] But Beth Shammai have also been heard to lay down the rule that a note of indebtedness which is due for payment is regarded as repaid.[3] For we have learned: If their husbands[4] died before they drank,[5] Beth Shammai rule that they are to receive their *kethubah* and that they need not drink,[5] and Beth Hillel rule that they either drink[5] or they do not receive their *kethubah*.[6] [Now how could it be said,] 'They either drink', when the All-Merciful said, *Then shall the man bring his wife to the priest*,[7] and he is not there? [The meaning must] consequently be: As they do not drink[8] they are not to receive their *kethubah*. Again 'Beth Shammai rule that they are to receive their *kethubah* and that they need not drink', but why [should they receive their *kethubah*]? Is not their claim of a doubtful nature,[9] it being uncertain whether she had committed adultery or not;[10] then how could an uncertainty[11] override a certainty?[12] Beth Shammai [must consequently] hold the view that 'a note of indebtedness that is due for payment is regarded as repaid'.[13] But is it not required [that the proviso], 'When thou wilt be married to another man thou wilt receive what is prescribed for thee' [be complied with], which is not the

(1) The exposition being: Since the *kethubah* contains the proviso, 'When thou wilt be married to another man, thou wilt receive what is prescribed for thee', it may be inferred that, except in the case of divorce, the *kethubah* is not payable during the lifetime of the husband, when his wife cannot 'be married to another man'. (2) V. Yeb. 117*a*. (3) Yeb. 38*b*, Soṭ. 25*a*. The amount of the debt is deemed to be in the virtual possession of the creditor. So, too, with the amount of the *kethubah* which is deemed to be in the virtual possession of the widow. The levir is consequently inheriting it not from his brother but from the widow, in return for which he must incur the obligation of burying her. (4) Of women suspected of illicit intercourse with strangers after they had been warned by their husbands. (5) The *water of bitterness*. (V. Num. V, 24). (6) Yeb. 38*b*, Soṭ. 24*a*. (7) Num. V, 15, emphasis on *man*. (8) The *water of bitterness* (v. Num. V, 24.) (9) Of course it is. (10) In the former case she loses her right to her *kethubah*; in the latter case she does not. (11) That of her claim (v. *supra* n. 10). (12) It is certain that the husband's heirs are the rightful owners of his estate. (13) So that the woman (and not the heirs) being regarded as the virtual possessor of the amount of her *kethubah*, no certainty is here overridden by an uncertainty.

case here?[1]—R. Ashi replied: A levir is also regarded as 'another man'.[2]

Raba addressed [the following message] to Abaye[3] through R. Shemaya b. Zera: Is a *kethubah*[4] indeed payable during [the levir's] lifetime? Has it not, in fact, been taught: R. Abba[5] stated, 'I asked Symmachus, "How is a man[6] who desires to sell his brother's property to proceed" [and he replied,] "If he is a priest,[7] he should prepare a banquet[8] and use persuasive means;[9] if he is an Israelite[10] he may divorce her and then marry her again".'[11] [81*b*] Now if it could be assumed that a *kethubah* is payable during the lifetime [of the levir] why should he not set aside exclusively for

(1) Since one awaiting the decision of a levir is not permitted to marry any stranger. How, then, could it be said *supra* that the *kethubah* is collected in the levir's lifetime? (2) At the moment her husband's death had set her free to marry the levir the proviso of her *kethubah* was fulfilled, and her *kethubah* is payable. (3) Who maintained *supra* that the *kethubah* is payable even during the lifetime of the levir. (4) Of a woman awaiting the decision of the levir. (5) I.e., R. Abba Arika or Rab. (6) A levir who married his deceased brother's widow for whose *kethubah* (v. our Mishnah) all the property he inherited from his deceased brother is mortgaged. (7) Who is forbidden to marry a divorced woman (v. Lev. XXI, 7). (8) For his wife, his former sister-in-law. (9) To secure her consent to sell so much of the property (v. *supra* note 6) as is in excess of the amount of her *kethubah*. If her consent cannot be obtained and he wishes to live with her he has no redress. He cannot divorce and remarry her as an Israelite may (v. *infra*) since his priesthood (v. *supra* note 7) would preclude him from marrying a woman he has once divorced. (10) Who may marry a divorced woman. (11) Adopting this course, he may either (*a*) pay her the amount of her *kethubah* as soon as she is divorced and, after selling all the property which is in excess of it, marry her again (on the condition of the first *kethubah*, v. infra 89*b*) or (*b*) he may remarry her before paying to her the amount of her *kethubah* and on remarriage give her a new one which, as all ordinary *kethuboth*, is secured not only on his present possessions but also on his future acquisitions. It is only a levir whose future acquisitions are not pledged for the *kethubah* of his deceased brother's widow (whom he marries and whose only security is the property left by her deceased husband) that is forbidden to sell the property he has inherited from that brother. Any other husband, including a levir who remarried his sister-in-law after he consummated levirate marriage and after he divorced her, since such a *kethubah* is secured by present possession and future acquisition, may well sell all his property even without his wife's consent.

her some property equal in value to the amount of the *kethubah*, and then sell the rest?[1] 'But according to your argument[2] [it might be asked] why should not the same objection[3] be raised from our Mishnah [where it was stated,] HE CANNOT SAY TO HER, "BEHOLD YOUR KETHUBAH LIES ON THE TABLE", BUT ALL HIS PROPERTY IS PLEDGED FOR HER KETHUBAH?'—'There[4] we might merely have been given a piece of good advice;[5] for, were you not to admit this, [how would you] read the final clause where it is stated, SO, TOO, A MAN MUST NOT SAY TO HIS WIFE, "BEHOLD YOUR KETHUBAH LIES ON THE TABLE", BUT ALL HIS PROPERTY IS PLEDGED FOR HER KETHUBAH, would he here also [it may be asked] not be able to sell if he wished to do so?[6] Consequently [it must be agreed that] he was there merely giving a piece of good advice;[7] and similarly here also we might merely be given a piece of good advice;[5] the statement of R. Abba, however, does present an objection!'[8]—'R. Abba's statement also does not give rise to any objection [because the restrictions on the man's liberty to sell] are due to [the desire of avoiding] hatred.'[9]

A sister-in-law once fell to the lot of a man[10] at Pumbeditha, and his [younger] brother wanted to cause her to be forbidden to marry him[11] by [forcing upon her] a letter of divorce.[12] 'What is it', [the eldest brother] said to him, 'that you have in your

(1) What need then was there for persuasion or divorce and remarriage? (2) 'Since you can see no reason against the sale of the property in excess of the *kethubah* except that a *kethubah* is not payable during the levir's lifetime'. (3) Against Abaye, *supra*. (4) In our Mishnah. (5) In the interests of the woman; but not a legal ruling. Hence no objection can arise from it. (6) Of course he could sell, since his future acquisitions are also pledged for the *kethubah* (cf. *supra* p. 512, n. 11). (7) Cf. *supra* n. 6. (8) As shewn *supra*. (9) Between husband and wife. Were he allowed to set aside a particular part of his property as surety for her *kethubah* she might misinterpret his action to be a preliminary to a permanent divorce. By adopting the measures described *supra* he makes it clear to all that the only motive for his action was his desire to sell the property. (10) The woman's husband died without issue and the duty of marrying her or submitting to her *ḥaliẓah* fell upon that man who was the eldest surviving brother of the deceased. (11) His eldest brother. (12) A divorce by one of the surviving brothers causes the widow to be forbidden to all the brothers (v. Yeb. 50*a*).

mind? [Are you troubled] because of the property[1] [that I am to inherit]?[2] I will share the property with you'. R. Joseph [in considering this case] said: Since the Rabbis have laid down that he[3] may not sell,[4] his sale is invalid even if he had already sold it.[5] For it was taught:[6] If a man died[7] and left a widow who was awaiting the decision of a levir[8] and also left a bequest of property of the value of a hundred *maneh*,[9] [the levir] must not sell the property although the widow's *kethubah* amounts only to one *maneh*, because all his property is pledged to her *kethubah*.[10] Said Abaye to him:[11] Is it so that wherever the Rabbis ruled that one must not sell, the sale is invalid, even after it had taken place? Did we not, in fact, learn: Beth Shammai said, She[12] may sell it, and Beth Hillel said, She may not sell it; but both agree that if she had sold it or given it away her act is legally valid?[13] The case was sent to R. Ḥanina b. Papi who sent [the same reply] as that of R. Joseph. On this Abaye remarked: Has R. Ḥanina b. Papi, forsooth, hung jewels[14] upon it?[15] It was then sent to R. Minyomi the son of R. Niḥumai who sent [the same reply] as Abaye[16] [and added:][17] 'Should R. Joseph give a new reason report it to me'. R. Joseph thereupon went out, investigated, and discovered that it was taught: If a man who had a monetary claim against his brother died,[18] and left a widow who had to await the decision of a levir,

(1) Of the deceased. (2) The brother who marries the widow inherits also the estate of the deceased (v. Yeb. 40*a*). (3) A levir for whose marriage (or *ḥaliẓah*) a sister-in-law is waiting. (4) The estate of his deceased brother, which he inherits. (5) Similarly, here, the share promised to the younger brother under a legal *ḳinyan* is deemed to be a sale which is invalid. (6) Cf. *infra* n. 10. (7) Without issue. (8) Cf. *supra* p. 507, n. 8. (9) V. Glos. (10) Which proves that the levir who is responsible for his sister-in-law's *kethubah* may not sell any of his deceased brother's property which he inherits. (11) R. Joseph. (12) A wife who came into the possession of property. (13) *Supra* 78*a*; which proves that a sale *ex post facto* is valid even though it was not originally permitted. (14) כיפי (כיף, כיפא 'stone') 'precious stones'. (15) He has not. His ruling is no more supported by proof or reason than that of R. Joseph, and may be equally disregarded. (16) That the sale is valid. (17) Cf. MS.M. which inserts, 'and he (also) sent (word) to them'. (18) Without issue.

[the latter][1] is not entitled to plead, 'Since I am the heir I have acquired [the amount of the debt]', but it must be taken from the levir and spent on the purchase of land and he is only entitled to its usufruct.[2] But 'is it not possible', said Abaye to him, 'that provision was made in his own interests?'[3]—'The Tanna stated', the other replied, 'that it must be "taken" from him,[4] and you say that "provision was made in his own interests"'! The case was again sent to R. Minyomi the son of R. Niḥumai who said to them: Thus said R. Joseph b. Minyomi in the name of R. Naḥman, 'This[5] is not an authentic teaching'.[6] What is the reason?[7] If it be suggested, 'Because money is a movable thing and movables are not pledged to a *kethubah*',[8] is it not possible [it might be retorted] that the statement represents the view of R. Meir who holds that movables are pledged to a *kethubah?*[9] [Should it be suggested,] however,[10] 'Because he[11] could say to her: You are not the party I have to deal with',[12] [82a] is it not possible [it might be retorted] that the statement represents the view of R. Nathan, since it was taught: R. Nathan stated, 'Whence is it deduced that if a man claims a *maneh*[13] from another, and this one [claims a similar sum] from a third, the sum is to be collected from the last [named] and handed over to the first? From Scripture, which stated,[14] *And give unto him against whom he hath trespassed'?*[15] [This], however, [is

(1) I.e., the debtor who, as brother of the deceased, marries his widow and also inherits his estate (v. *supra* p. 514, n. 4). (2) The debt in this case is similar to a sale *ex post facto*, and nevertheless it is invalid; which proves the correctness of R. Joseph's ruling. (3) Lit., 'that which was good for him they did for him'; it is more advantageous for a person when his money is invested than when it is spent. (4) Implying forcible action against his will. (5) The Baraitha discovered by R. Joseph. (6) It is spurious and not to be relied upon. (7) V. previous note. (8) And a statement that regards them as pledged to a *kethubah* must consequently be spurious. (9) Cf. Yeb. 99*a*, Ḳid. 68*b*. (10) As a reason why the statement under discussion must be considered spurious. (11) The levir. (12) He is the debtor of the deceased but not hers. Cf. *supra* n. 8 *mutatis mutandis*. (13) V. Glos. (14) Num. V, 7. (15) Emphasis on the last five words which refer to the first, who is the person against whom the *trespass* had been committed, and not to the second who is merely an intermediary who, even if the debt had been repaid to him, would also have had to transfer it to the first. Similarly in the statement under discussion the debt

the reason:][1] We find nowhere a Tanna who imposes two restrictions[2] in the matter of a *kethubah;*[3] we only find agreement either with R. Meir or with R. Nathan.[4] Raba remarked: If so, I can well understand[5] what Abaye meant when I heard him say, 'This is not an authentic teaching' and [at the time] I did not understand what [his reason] was.

A sister-in-law at Matha Meḥasia[6] once fell to the lot of a man[7] whose [younger] brother wanted to cause her to be forbidden to marry him[8] by [forcing upon her] a letter of divorce.[9] 'What is it', [the eldest brother] said to him, 'that you have in your mind? If it is on account of the property[10] [that you are troubled][11] I will share the estate with you'. 'I am afraid', the other replied, 'that you will treat me as the Pumbedithan rogue [has treated his brother]'.[12] 'If you wish', the first said to him, 'take your half at once'.[13] Said Mar son of R. Ashi: Although when R. Dimi came[14] he stated in the name of R. Joḥanan, If a man said to another, 'Go and pull[15] this cow, but it shall pass into your legal possession only after thirty days', he legally acquires it after thirty days,[16] even if it stands at the time in the meadow,[17] [in this case the younger brother cannot acquire possession of the promised share]; for there[18] it was in his power [to transfer possession at once][19] but

which the deceased claims from the levir might well be regarded as a debt due to the widow who has a claim upon the deceased.

(1) Cf. *supra* p. 515, n. 10. (2) That of R. Meir as well as that of R. Nathan. (3) Which is only a Rabbinical institution. (4) But not with both. Since the statement under discussion does impose both restrictions it must be considered spurious. (5) Lit., 'that is'. (6) A suburb of Sura. It was an important seat of learning in the days of Rab, and attained even greater fame in the first two decades of the fifth century under the guidance of R. Ashi. (7) Cf. *supra* p. 513, n. 10. (8) Cf. loc. cit. n. 11. (9) Cf. *supra* p. 513, n. 12. (10) Cf. p. 514, n. 1. (11) Cf. loc. cit. n. 2. (12) He did not keep the promise he made (*supra* 81*b*). Pumbeditha was notorious for its sharpers (cf. B.B. 46*a*, Ḥul. 127*a*). (13) Though legal acquisition could not be effected until the consummation of the levirate marriage. (14) From Palestine to Babylon. (15) Pulling, *meshikah* (v. Glos.) is one of the forms of *ḳinyan*. (16) From the moment he pulled it. (17) *Sc.*, not in the possession of the buyer. (18) In the case of the cow. (19) Hence he may legally transfer possession even after thirty days.

here[1] it is not in his power [to transfer immediate possession]. But, surely, when Rabin came[2] he stated in the name of R. Joḥanan[3] that 'he does not acquire possession'![4]—This is no difficulty: One[5] refers to a case where the seller said, 'Acquire possession[6] from now';[7] the other, where he did not say, 'Acquire from now'.

'Ulla was asked: What is the ruling where levirate marriage was consummated first and the division of the property[8] took place afterwards?[9]—The act[10] is null and void[11] [he replied]. What is the ruling [he was asked] if the division[8] took place first and the levirate marriage afterwards?[9]—The act[10] [he replied] is null and void.[11] R. Shesheth demurred: Now [that it has been said that where] levirate marriage took place first and the division[8] afterwards the act[10] is null and void, was it at all necessary [to ask the question where] the division took place first and the levirate marriage afterwards?[12]—[The respective enquiries related to] two independent incidents that occurred [at different times].[13]

When Rabin came[2] he stated in the name of Resh Laḳish: Whether levirate marriage was consummated first and the division took place afterwards, or whether the division took place first and the levirate marriage afterwards, the act is null and void. And [in fact] the law is that the act is null and void.

THE SAGES, HOWEVER, RULED: WHAT IS STILL ATTACHED

(1) In the case of the share of the younger brother. The elder brother cannot possibly convey possession of the deceased brother's estate before performing the levirate marriage, when it then passes into his possession. Hence also the invalidity of the *ḳinyan*. (2) From Palestine to Babylon. (3) In the case of the deferred acquisition of a cow, just cited. (4) Which presents a contradiction between the two rulings attributed to R. Joḥanan. (5) The first cited ruling. (6) After the thirty days. (7) I.e., retrospective possession which is valid. (8) Between the levir who married the widow and any other of the brothers. (9) Is the brother entitled to retain the property the levir has allotted to him? (10) *Sc.* the division by which the levir deprives the widow whom he married of a security for her *kethubah*. (11) And the property remains in the possession of the levir, the *kethubah* of the widow being secured on it. (12) If the division is invalid in the first case, where the *ḳinyan* might be immediate, how much more so in the second case where the *ḳinyan* can only be retrospective. (13) The second enquiry was addressed by those who did not hear of the first mentioned ruling.

TO THE GROUND BELONGS TO HIM. But why? Is not all his[1] landed estate[2] a pledge and a guarantee for her *kethubah?*—Resh Lakish replied: Read, 'Belongs to her'.[3]

IF [THE LEVIR] MARRIED HER SHE IS REGARDED AS HIS WIFE. In what respect?—R. Jose the son of R. Ḥanina replied: By this is meant that her separation from him is effected by a letter of divorce[4] and that he may marry her again.[5] [You say,] 'Her separation from him is effected by a letter of divorce'; [but] is not this obvious?—It might have been assumed that since the All-Merciful said, *And perform the duty of a husband's brother unto her,*[6] she[7] is still subject to the original levirate obligations[8] and a letter of divorce should not be enough unless [the separation had been effected] by *ḥaliẓah*, hence we were taught [that only a letter of divorce is required].

[You say,] 'He may marry her again'; [but] is not this obvious? [82b]—It might have been assumed that since he has already performed the commandment that the All-Merciful has imposed upon him she shall again resume towards him the prohibition of [marrying] a brother's wife,[9] hence we were informed [that he may remarry her]. But might it not be suggested that the law is so[10] indeed?[11]—Scripture stated, *And take her to him to wife,*[12] as soon as he has taken her she becomes his wife [in all respects].

SAVE THAT HER KETHUBAH REMAINS A CHARGE ON HER FIRST HUSBAND'S ESTATE. What is the reason?[13]—A wife has

(1) The deceased. (2) Including whatever is attached to it. (3) The Sages' dispute being limited to detached produce and money which, they maintain, as movables are not pledged to a *kethubah*. (4) Not by *ḥaliẓah* (v. Glos.) by which the bond between a levir and his sister-in-law is severed where no levirate marriage is consummated. (5) Though prior to the levirate marriage a divorced sister-in-law is forbidden to marry any of the brothers. (6) Deut. XXV, 5. (7) Since the expression of *levirate* marriage (*duty of a husband's brother*) is specifically mentioned in addition to the expression of marriage (*And take her to him to wife*, ibid.). (8) Even after the consummation of the levirate marriage. (9) Lev. XVIII, 16. (10) That *ḥaliẓah* is required and that he may not remarry her. (11) Lit., 'thus also'. (12) Deut. XXV, 5; where only the latter part of the verse, *And perform the duty of a husband's brother unto her*, would have been sufficient. (13) I.e., why should not the levir, her present husband, assume responsibility for her *kethubah*.

been given[1] to him from heaven.[2] If, however, she is unable to obtain her *kethubah* from her first husband [provision was made by the Rabbis that] she receives it from the second[3] in order that it may not be easy for him to divorce her.[4]

HE CANNOT SAY TO HER, 'BEHOLD YOUR KETHUBAH [etc.]'. What [need was there for stating] SO, TOO?[5]—It might have been suggested [that the restriction mentioned applies only] in the former case[6] because the levir does not insert [in her *kethubah* the clause] 'That which I possess and that which I will acquire',[7] but that in the latter case, where he does insert [the pledge clause,] 'That which I possess and that which I will acquire',[8] she relies upon this guarantee,[9] hence we were told [that the ruling applies in both cases].

IF HE DIVORCED HER SHE IS ENTITLED ONLY TO HER KETHUBAH. Only[10] IF HE DIVORCED HER [may he sell the property],[11] but if he did not divorce her he may not. Thus we were informed in agreement with the ruling of R. Abba.[12]

IF HE SUBSEQUENTLY REMARRIED HER SHE IS [TO ENJOY

(1) Lit., 'they caused him to acquire'. (2) She was not chosen by him but was imposed upon him by the Divine law of the levirate marriage. He cannot, therefore, be expected to undertake any monetary obligations in respect of her *kethubah*. (3) The levir who married her. (4) Lit., 'that it may not be easy in his eyes to cause her to go out'. (5) In the case of a wife. Is it not obvious that a husband's obligation towards a wife he himself has chosen cannot possibly be less than those he incurs in respect of a sister-in-law he married only in obedience to a commandment? (6) The marriage of a sister-in-law. (7) 'Shall be pledged to the *kethubah*'. So that the woman, having her security limited to the levir's possessions that were inherited from her deceased husband, would naturally suspect that by 'putting her *kethubah* on the table' the levir intends to escape his full responsibility and desires to deprive her of the possibility of collecting her *kethubah* when the occasion arises. This, as might well be expected, would create animosity between husband and wife (cf. *supra* p. 513, n. 9). (8) So that the *kethubah* is well secured. (9) And no animosity would ensue despite his 'putting of the *kethubah* on the table'. (10) Lit., 'yes'. (11) Which he inherited from the deceased and which is in excess of the amount of the *kethubah*. (12) *Supra* 81*a*, that unless the woman can be persuaded to consent to the sale of the property it may be sold only after she had been divorced.

THE SAME RIGHTS AS] ALL OTHER WIVES, AND IS ENTITLED ONLY TO HER KETHUBAH. 'IF HE SUBSEQUENTLY REMARRIED HER'! What does he thereby[1] teach us? Have we not learned: If a man divorced his wife and then remarried her, his second marriage is contracted on the terms of her first *kethubah?*[2]—It might have been assumed that the law applied only to his wife since it was he himself who wrote the *kethubah;* in the case of his sister-in-law, however, since it was not he[3] who wrote the *kethubah* for her, it might well have been assumed that where he divorced, and then remarried her the *kethubah* must come from himself, hence we were taught [that in this case also she is entitled only to the first *kethubah*].

Rab Judah stated: At first they used to give merely a written undertaking[4] in respect of [the *kethubah* of] a virgin for two hundred *zuz*[5] and in respect of that of a widow for a *maneh,*[5] and consequently[6] they grew old and could not take any wives, when Simeon b. Shetaḥ took the initiative[7] and ordained that all the property of a husband is pledged for the *kethubah* of his wife. So it was also taught elsewhere: At first they used to give merely a written undertaking[8] in respect of [the *kethubah* of] a virgin for two hundred *zuz*[5] and in respect of that of a widow for a *maneh,*[5] and consequently[6] they grew old and could not take any wives. It was then ordained that the amount of the *kethubah*[9] was to be deposited in the wife's father's house. At any time, however, when the husband was angry with her he used to tell her, 'Go to your *kethubah*'.[10] It was ordained, therefore, that the amount of the *kethubah*[9] was to be deposited in the house of her father-in-law.[11]

(1) By specifying the law in the case of a sister-in-law whom the levir had married. (2) I.e., she cannot claim a second *kethubah, infra* 89*b*; And this law one would expect to apply also to a sister-in-law. What need then was there to specify it in the case of the latter. (V. *Supra* n. 1)? (3) But her first husband. (4) Lit., 'they would write'. No clause pledging the husband's landed property being inserted in the *kethubah.* (5) V. Glos. (6) Women refusing to marry under such precarious conditions, (v. *supra* note 4). (7) Lit., 'until he came'. (8) V. *supra* note 4. (9) Lit., 'it'. (10) I.e., he could easily get rid of her since the amount of her *kethubah* was at hand and there was no need for him to make any efforts to find the money. (11) *Sc.* husband.

Wealthy women[1] converted it into silver, or gold baskets, while poor women converted it into brass[2] tubs. Still, whenever the husband had occasion to be angry with his wife he would say to her, 'Take your *kethubah* and go'.[3] It was then that[4] Simeon b. Shetaḥ ordained that the husband must insert the pledging clause, 'All my property is mortgaged to your *kethubah*'.[5]

(1) The amount of whose *kethubah* was high. In addition to the statutory sum the *kethubah* also contains additional obligations on the part of the husband corresponding to the amount the wife brought to him on marriage. (2) So Tosaf. s.v. עביט. Cur. edd. 'urine'. (3) Cf. *supra* p. 520, n. 10. (4) V. l.c. n. 7. (5) So MS.M. Cur. edd., 'to her *kethubah*'. [For a full discussion of this passage v. Epstein, L., op. cit. pp. 19ff.]

KETHUBOTH

CHAPTER IX

MISHNAH. IF A HUSBAND GIVES TO HIS WIFE A WRITTEN UNDERTAKING, 'I HAVE NO CLAIM WHATSOEVER[1] UPON YOUR ESTATES', HE MAY NEVERTHELESS ENJOY ITS USUFRUCT DURING HER LIFETIME AND, WHEN SHE DIES, HE IS HER HEIR. IF SO, WHAT WAS HIS OBJECT IN GIVING HER THE WRITTEN UNDERTAKING, 'I HAVE NO CLAIM WHATSOEVER UPON YOUR ESTATES'? THAT IF SHE SOLD THEM OR GAVE THEM AWAY HER ACT MIGHT BE VALID. IF HE WROTE, 'I HAVE NO CLAIM WHATSOEVER UPON YOUR ESTATES AND UPON THEIR PRODUCE', HE MAY NOT ENJOY THEIR USUFRUCT DURING HER LIFETIME BUT, WHEN SHE DIES, HE IS HER HEIR. R. JUDAH RULED: HE MAY IN ALL CASES ENJOY THE YIELD OF THE PRODUCE UNLESS HE WROTE OUT FOR HER [THE FOLLOWING UNDERTAKING]: 'I HAVE NO CLAIM WHATSOEVER UPON YOUR ESTATES AND UPON THEIR PRODUCE AND THE PRODUCE OF THEIR PRODUCE AND SO ON WITHOUT END.

IF HE WROTE, 'I HAVE NO CLAIM UPON YOUR ESTATES, THEIR PRODUCE AND THE PRODUCE OF THEIR PRODUCE DURING YOUR LIFETIME AND AFTER YOUR DEATH', HE MAY NEITHER ENJOY THEIR PRODUCE DURING HER LIFETIME NOR CAN HE BE HER HEIR WHEN SHE DIES. R. SIMEON B. GAMALIEL RULED: WHEN SHE DIES HE IS HER HEIR BECAUSE [BY HIS DECLARATION] HE IS MAKING A CONDITION WHICH IS CONTRARY TO WHAT IS ENJOINED IN THE TORAH[2] AND WHENEVER A MAN MAKES A CONDITION WHICH IS CONTRARY TO WHAT IS WRITTEN IN THE TORAH, HIS CONDITION IS NULL AND VOID.[3]

(1) Lit., 'no right nor claim'. (2) According to the Torah it is the husband who is the heir of his wife (v. B.B. 111*b*). (3) It is only the produce, which was granted to the husband by a Rabbinical measure, that he may renounce.

GEMARA. R. Ḥiyya taught:[1] If a husband said[2] to his wife.[3]

And if he gave her such an undertaking in writing,[4] what does it matter? Was it not taught: If a man says[5] to another,[6] 'I have no claim whatsoever on this field, I have no concern in it and I entirely dissociate myself from it',[7] his statement is of no effect?[8] —At the school of R. Jannai it was explained, [we are dealing here with the case] of a man who gave the undertaking to his wife[9] while she was still only betrothed to him,[10] [the ruling[11] being] in agreement with that of R. Kahana, that a man is at liberty to renounce beforehand an inheritance[12] which is likely to accrue to him from another source;[13] and [this ruling, furthermore, is] in agreement with a dictum of Raba, that if anyone says, 'I do not desire [to avail myself] of a regulation of the Rabbis of this kind', his desire is granted.[14] What [is meant by the expression] 'of this kind'?—As [that referred to in the statement made by] R. Huna in the name of Rab: A woman is entitled to say to her husband, 'I do not wish either to be maintained by you or to work for you'.[15]

(1) In reference to the rulings in our Mishnah. (2) Emphasis on *said*, *sc*. he can waive his rights by a mere verbal declaration. (3) *Infra* 102*b*. (4) Much less if it was only verbal. (5) Either verbally or in a written document (v. Rashi). (6) *Sc*. to his partner. (7) Lit., 'and my hand is removed from it'. (8) *Infra* 95*a*, Giṭ. 77*a*, B.B. 43*a*, 49*a*; because no man can renounce his rights by a mere verbal declaration unless by way of a gift or sale, but since there was no expression such as, 'I make the field over to you', or words to the same effect denoting a gift, the waiver is ineffective. Now since a written undertaking that omitted such an expression is invalid, how much more so would that be the case with a mere verbal utterance? An objection thus arises against R. Ḥiyya. (9) Lit., 'when he writes for her'. (10) When he has as yet no right to her property. (11) Which allows renunciation in such a case. (12) Lit., 'stipulate that he shall not inherit'. (13) *Sc*. from a stranger to whom he becomes next of kin through an act of his (such as marriage) and whose heir he becomes thereby in accordance with Rabbinic law. It is only an inheritance from a next-of-kin, or property that is already in one's possession, the rights of which cannot be waived by mere renunciation but requires (v. *supra* n. 8) the specific expressions of 'giving'. [This statement of R. Kahana is on the view that the law that the husband inherits his wife is a Rabbinic provision, v. *infra* p. 528, cf. *supra* p. 522, n. 2]. (14) Since the regulation was made for his benefit, he is at liberty to reject it. (15) Since her maintenance by her husband in return for her handiwork is a Rabbinic regulation made in favour of the woman,

If so,[1] should not [the same ruling apply to] a married woman also?[2] Abaye replied: In the case of a married woman the husband's rights have the same force as the wife's.[3] Raba said: His rights are superior to hers. This[4] is of practical significance in the case of a woman who was awaiting the decision of the levir.[5]

The question was raised: What is the ruling if symbolic *ḳinyan* was executed[6] [at the time of the renunciation]?[7]—R. Joseph replied: [The *ḳinyan* is invalid since] it related to an abstract renunciation.[8] R. Naḥman replied: [The *ḳinyan* is valid because] it related to land itself.[9] Said Abaye: R. Joseph's statement is reasonable [83*b*] where [the partner][10] lodged his protest forthwith,[11]

she is at liberty to reject it. A husband (cf. *supra* nn. 13 and 14) is similarly entitled to renounce his rights as heir to his wife, without any further formality.

(1) That the husband's right to renounce his claim upon his wife's property is due to the fact that it was for his benefit that her property was assigned to him. (2) Of course it should. Why then was it necessary for the school of R. Jannai *supra* to explain the ruling as referring to an undertaking that was given 'while she was still only betrothed to him'? (3) Lit., 'his hand is like her hand'. Since he is consequently legal possessor of the property he cannot (cf. *supra* p. 523, n. 13) waive his rights to it by mere renunciation. (4) The difference of opinion between Abaye and Raba, which does not in any way affect our present discussion since in either case a husband is regarded as the possessor of his wife's property and cannot, by a mere verbal renunciation, legally transfer it. (5) If such a woman died and left property which came into her possession either (*a*) while her husband was still alive or (*b*) after his death while she was awaiting the levir's decision, the respective rights of her heirs and her husband's heirs to such property depend on, and vary according to, the respective views of Abaye and Raba as fully discussed in Yeb. 39*a*, q.v. (6) Lit., 'they (*sc.* witnesses) acquired from him (on behalf of his partner)'. Cf. Rashi. (7) Of his share in his partner's property, spoken of in the Baraitha quoted *supra* in objection to R. Ḥiyya. Does, or does not such *ḳinyan*, it is asked, effect the legal transfer of the land despite, or because of the fact, that no expression of 'giving' (v. *supra* p. 523, n. 8) was used. [According to Tosaf. s.v. קני, the query refers to the waiving of rights by a husband to the property of his wife after marriage]. (8) Lit., 'they acquired from him (a mere verbal expression) of right and claim', which are not in his power to waive. (9) Lit., 'of the body of the land', which is, of course, a concrete object that may well be acquired by symbolic *ḳinyan*. (10) Who waived his rights. (11) As soon as the partner came to take possession of the field, he declared that he never intended to give

but if he delayed,[1] the *ḳinyan* must be regarded as relating to the land itself,[2] Amemar said, the law is that the *ḳinyan* is taken to refer to the land itself.[3] Said R. Ashi to Amemar: [Do you speak] of one who lodged his protest forthwith or of one who delayed it? 'In what respect [the other asked] does this matter?' —In respect of [determining whether the law is] in agreement with the view of R. Joseph.[4] 'I did not hear this',[5] the other replied, 'by which I mean that I do not accept it'.

IF SO, WHAT WAS HIS OBJECT IN GIVING HER THE WRITTEN UNDERTAKING etc. But[6] why should she not be able to say to him, 'You have renounced all your claims'?[7]—Abaye replied: The holder of a deed is always at a disadvantage.[8] But might it not be suggested [that he renounced his claim] upon the usufruct?[9]—Abaye replied: A young pumpkin [in hand] is better than a full-grown one [in the field].[10] But may it be suggested [that his renunciation related] to his heirship?[11] Abaye replied: Death is a common

away his share and that his renunciation was merely a way of escape from a quarrel with his partner.

(1) Lit., 'when standing', the protest being made sometime after his partner had taken possession of the field. (2) Cf. p. 524, n. 9; it being obvious that this belated protest was only the result of an afterthought, and that his original intention was to give away his share to his partner. (3) V. p. 524, n. 9. (4) *Supra* 83*a* *ad fin.* (5) The ruling of R. Joseph. Cf. MS.M. (6) If the husband's renunciation is sufficiently valid to confer legality on his wife's sale or gift. (7) I.e., even his rights to usufruct and heirship. (8) Should his claims ever conflict with those of the person in possession in whose favour the deed is always to be interpreted. In the case under discussion the wife is regarded as the 'holder of the deed' and the husband as the possessor of the rights of (i) usufruct, (ii) heirship and (iii) the seizure of any property she has sold or given away. Since his renunciation can be interpreted as referring to one of these rights only, the woman has no legal footing on which to claim 'You have renounced *all* your claims'. (9) And not upon his other rights (cf. note 7) including that of seizure of the property his wife has sold or given away. (10) Cf. 'a bird in hand is worth two in the bush' (Eng. prov.). The right to usufruct, which can be enjoyed at once, though it is of less value than the land itself, is more advantageous to a husband than the right of the seizure of property that his wife may possibly sell at some future time. The former is a certainty; the other is an eventuality. (11) Cf. *supra* n. 9 *mutatis mutandis*.

occurrence but the sale [of property by a wife] is not common;[1] and whenever a person renounces his claims [he does so] in respect of what is not a common occurrence but he does not do it in respect of that which is a common occurrence. R. Ashi replied:[2] [The husband's renunciation was] 'UPON YOUR ESTATES',[3] but not upon their produce; 'UPON YOUR[4] ESTATES', but not after your death.[5]

R. JUDAH RULED: HE MAY IN ALL CASES ENJOY THE YIELD OF THE PRODUCE [etc.]. Our Rabbis taught: The following are regarded as produce and the following as the yield of the produce respectively. If a woman brought to her husband[6] a plot of land and it yielded produce, such yield is regarded as produce. If he sold the produce and purchased land with the proceeds and that land yielded produce, such yield is regarded as the yield of the produce.

The question was raised: According to R. Judah, [is the expression] THE PRODUCE OF THEIR PRODUCE[7] the essential element,[8] or is rather WITHOUT END[9] the essential element,[10] or is it possible that both expressions are essential?[11] But should you find [some ground] for deciding [that the expression] THE PRODUCE OF THEIR PRODUCE is the essential element,[12] what need was there [it might be asked, for the mention[13] of] 'WITHOUT END'?—It is this that we were taught: So long as he renounced in her favour, in writing, the yield of the produce it is as if he had expressly written in her favour, 'without end'. But should you find [some reason] for deciding that WITHOUT END is the essential element,[14] what need was there [it might be asked, for the mention[13] of] THE PRODUCE OF THEIR PRODUCE?—It is this that

(1) A woman as a rule does not sell her ancestral possessions. (2) To the two objections just dealt with by Abaye. (3) Emphasis on ESTATES. (4) Emphasis on the pronoun. (5) When they are no longer hers. (6) On marriage. (7) And not that of WITHOUT END. (Rashi); cf. note 8 *ad fin.* (8) In the wording of the renunciation spoken of by R. Judah; and, if it was omitted, the renunciation, as far as the yield of produce is concerned, is invalid even though the expression 'without end' had been used. *Aliter:* And the renunciation is valid even though 'without end' was omitted (Tosaf. s.v. פירי). (9) And not 'the produce of the produce'. (10) Cf. *supra* n. 7, *mutatis mutandis*. (11) And if one of them was omitted the renunciation is invalid. (12) V. *supra* note 7. (13) In our Mishnah. (14) Cf. *supra* note 5.

we were taught: Although he renounced in her favour, in writing, the yield of the produce [the renunciation] is valid only[1] if he also wrote 'without end' but is invalid[2] if he did not [write it]. But if you should find some argument for giving the decision that both expressions are essential [it could be asked], what need is there for the specification[3] of both?—Both are necessary. For if only the 'yield of the produce' had been written in her favour and 'without end' had been omitted, it might have been assumed that he loses thereby his right to the enjoyment of the yield of the produce only but that he is still entitled to enjoy the produce of the yield of that produce, hence it is necessary for the expression 'without end' [to be included in the renunciation]. And if only 'without end' had been written in her favour and the 'yield of the produce' had not been specified,[3] it might have been assumed that 'without end' referred to the first produce only,[4] hence it is necessary to specify also the 'yield of the produce'.[5]

The question was raised: May a husband who wrote, in favour of his wife, the renunciation 'I have no claim whatsoever upon your estates and upon the yield of their produce', enjoy the produce itself? Has he renounced the yield of their produce only but not the produce [itself] or is it possible that he renounced all his claim? But it is quite obvious that he has renounced all his claims. For should you suggest that he only renounced his claim upon the yield of the produce but not upon the produce itself, whence [it might be objected] would arise a yield of the produce if the man had consumed the produce itself?[6]

[No, for even] according to your view, [how will you explain] the statement in our Mishnah, R. JUDAH RULED: HE MAY IN ALL CASES ENJOY THE YIELD OF THE PRODUCE etc. [Where it may equally be objected,] whence would there be a yield of the produce

(1) Lit., 'yes'. (2) Lit., 'not'. (3) In the renunciation. (4) That it is this produce, but not its yield, that he renounces for ever. (5) [All of which justifies the query as to which expression is regarded as essential according to R. Judah. The query is left unanswered, v. *infra* p. 528, n. 2]. (6) Obviously there could be none. Hence it may be concluded that the husband renounced 'all his claims'.

if she[1] has consumed the produce itself? [Your explanation,] however, [would be that the reference is to a case] where the woman had allowed [the produce] to remain;[2] here also [it may be a case] where the husband has allowed the produce to remain.[2]

R. SIMEON B. GAMALIEL RULED etc. Rab said: The *halachah* is in agreement with the ruling of R. Simeon b. Gamaliel but not because of the reason he gave. What is meant by 'the *halachah* is in agreement with the ruling of R. Simeon b. Gamaliel but not because of the reason he gave'? If it be suggested: 'The *halachah* is in agreement with the ruling of R. Simeon b. Gamaliel' in respect of his statement that WHEN SHE DIES HE IS HER HEIR, 'but not because of the reason he gave', for whereas R. Simeon b. Gamaliel is of the opinion that if A MAN MAKES A CONDITION WHICH IS CONTRARY TO WHAT IS WRITTEN IN THE TORAH, HIS CONDITION IS NULL AND VOID, Rab holds that such a condition[3] is valid[4] and [his acceptance of the ruling[5] is solely due to] his opinion that a husband's right of inheritance is a Rabbinical enactment and that the Sages have imposed upon their enactments greater restrictions than upon those of the Torah;[6] [84a] could Rab, however, [it may be retorted,] hold the opinion that one's condition [though contrary to what is written in the Torah] is valid? Has it not in fact been stated: If a man says to another, '[I sell you this object] on condition that you have no claim for overreaching against me' [the buyer], Rab ruled, has nevertheless a claim for overreaching against him,[7] and Samuel ruled, He has no claim for overreaching against him?[8]—[It is this] then [that was

(1) The wife. Cf. Rashi. Cur. edd., דאכלינהו. (2) It had for some reason remained unconsumed and a produce-yielding object had been purchased with the proceeds. [Here, too, the question remains unanswered, v. *supra* p. 527, n. 5]. (3) If it relates to monetary matters. (4) In agreement with R. Judah, *supra* 56a. (5) Of R. Simeon b. Gamaliel, that the condition is invalid in the case of the husband's heirship. (6) Not being Pentateuchal, people might be lax in their observance. Greater safeguards were, therefore, required. (7) Because the condition is contrary to the Pentateuchal injunction of אל־תונו (Lev. XXV, 14). (8) Now, since Rab recognizes the invalidity of a condition that is contrary to Pentateuchal law of overreaching, how could he be said to regard a similar condition elsewhere as valid?

meant:] 'The *halachah* is in agreement with the ruling of R. Simeon b. Gamaliel' who laid down that if A MAN MAKES A CONDITION WHICH IS CONTRARY TO WHAT IS WRITTEN IN THE TORAH, HIS CONDITION IS NULL AND VOID, 'but not because of the reason he gave', for whereas R. Simeon b. Gamaliel is of the opinion that WHEN SHE DIES HE IS HER HEIR, Rab maintains that when she dies he is not her heir.[1] But is not this in agreement with his reason[2] and not with his ruling?[3]—This then [it is that was meant:] 'The *halachah* is in agreement with the ruling of R. Simeon b. Gamaliel' who laid down that WHEN SHE DIES HE IS HER HEIR, but not 'because of the reason he gave' for, whereas R. Simeon b. Gamaliel is of the opinion that only a condition that is contrary to a Pentateuchal law is null but one that is contrary only to a Rabbinic law[4] is valid, Rab maintains that even a condition contrary to a Rabbinic law[4] is also null.[5]

But this would be in agreement, would it not, with both his reason[6] and his ruling,[7] Rab only adding [greater force to it]?[8] This then [it is that was meant:] 'The *halachah* is in agreement with R. Simeon b. Gamaliel' who laid down that WHEN SHE DIES HE IS HER HEIR, but not 'because of the reason he gave', for, whereas R. Simeon b. Gamaliel holds that a husband's right of heirship is Pentateuchal and that [it is invalid because] WHEREVER A MAN MAKES A CONDITION WHICH IS CONTRARY TO WHAT IS WRITTEN IN THE TORAH, HIS CONDITION IS NULL AND VOID, Rab maintains that a husband's right of heirship is only a Rabbinic enactment and [that the condition is nevertheless null

(1) The condition being valid because a husband's right of heirship is, in Rab's opinion, a Rabbinical enactment which has not the same force as that of a Pentateuchal law. (2) I.e., that a condition which is contrary to a Pentateuchal law is null. (3) That WHEN SHE DIES HE IS HER HEIR. The answer being in the affirmative, the facts are directly opposite to the statement made *supra* by Rab. (4) Such, e.g., as a renunciation by a husband of his rights to the usufruct of his wife's property. (5) Because in his opinion the Sages have imparted to their enactments the same force as that of a Pentateuchal law. (6) V. *supra* note 2. (7) Cf. *supra* note 3. (8) Viz., and extending R. Gamaliel's principle to a Rabbinic enactment applies it also to the usufruct. This being the case, how is Rab's statement *supra* to be understood?

because] the Sages have imparted to their enactments the same force as that of Pentateuchal laws.

But [could it be said,] that Rab is of the opinion that a husband's right of heirship is only Rabbinical when in fact we have learned:[1] R. Joḥanan b. Beroḳa ruled, 'If a husband is the heir of his wife he must [when the Jubilee year[2] arrives] return [the inheritance] to the members of her family and allow them a reduction of price';[3] and, in considering this statement, the objection was raised: What is really his[4] opinion? If he holds that a husband's right of heirship is Pentateuchal, why [it may be asked] should he return [the inheritance at all]?[5] And if [he[6] holds it to be only] Rabbinical, why [it may be objected] should [even a part of] its price be paid?[7] And Rab explained: He[6] holds in fact the opinion that a husband's right of heirship is Pentateuchal but[8] [here it is a case of a man], for instance, whose wife bequeathed to him a [family] graveyard, [and it is] in order [to avoid] a family taint[9] that the Rabbis have ruled, Let him take the price and return it; and by[10] 'allow them a reduction in price' [was meant a deduction of] the cost of his wife's grave;[11] [the return of a family graveyard being] in agreement with what was taught: If a person has sold his [family] grave, the path to this grave, his halting place,[12]

(1) Bek. 52b.   (2) Cf. Lev. XXV, 8ff.   (3) This, it is at present assumed, is the meaning of וינכה להן מן הדמים.   (4) R. Joḥanan b. Beroḳa.   (5) An inheritance to which one is Pentateuchally entitled does not return in the Jubilee Year (cf. Bek. 52b).   (6) R. Joḥanan b. Beroḳa.   (7) By the members of the wife's family. Lit., 'what is their doing?' Since the husband's right is only in Rabbinic law the members of the wife's family, who are the original owners Pentateuchally, should be entitled to the return of the inheritance to them without any monetary payment on their part.   (8) In explanation of the difficulty as to why such an inheritance should be restored in the Jubilee Year.   (9) It is derogatory for a family that strangers should be interred in their graveyard while their own members should have to seek burial in another family's graveyard.   (10) Lit., 'and what?'   (11) Since it is a husband's duty to bury his dead wife.   (12) The place where, on returning from burial, the funeral escort halts to offer, with due ceremonial, consolation to the mourners. On returning from a burial the funeral escort halted on the way at a certain station where seven times they stood up and sat down on the ground, to offer comfort and consolation to the mourners or to weep and lament for the departed.

or his place of mourning, the members of his family may come and bury him perforce,[1] in order [to avert] a slight upon the family![2] —Rab spoke here in accordance with R. Joḥanan b. Beroḳa's point of view but he himself does not uphold it.

MISHNAH. IF A MAN DIED AND LEFT A WIFE,[3] A CREDITOR,[4] AND HEIRS[5] AND HE ALSO HAD A DEPOSIT OR A LOAN IN THE POSSESSION OF OTHERS, THIS, R. TARFON RULED, SHALL BE GIVEN TO THE ONE WHO IS UNDER THE GREATEST DISADVANTAGE.[6] R. AKIBA SAID: NO PITY IS TO BE SHEWN IN A MATTER OF LAW; AND IT[7] SHALL RATHER BE GIVEN TO THE HEIRS, FOR WHEREAS ALL THE OTHERS[8] MUST TAKE AN OATH[9] THE HEIRS NEED NOT TAKE ANY OATH.[10] IF HE LEFT PRODUCE THAT WAS DETACHED FROM THE GROUND, THEN WHOEVER[11] SEIZES IT FIRST ACQUIRES POSSESSION. IF THE WIFE TOOK POSSESSION OF MORE THAN THE AMOUNT OF HER KETHUBAH, OR A CREDITOR OF MORE THAN THE VALUE OF HIS DEBT, THE BALANCE, R. TARFON RULED, SHALL BE GIVEN TO THE ONE WHO IS UNDER THE GREATEST DISADVANTAGE.[12] R. AKIBA SAID: NO PITY IS TO BE SHEWN IN A MATTER OF LAW; AND IT SHALL RATHER BE GIVEN TO THE HEIRS, FOR WHEREAS ALL THE OTHERS[8] MUST TAKE AN OATH[9] THE HEIRS NEED NOT TAKE ANY OATH.[10]

(1) They may force the buyer to take back the purchase price and so cancel the sale. (2) B.B. 100*b*, Bek. 52*b*. Cf. *supra* p. 530, n. 9. Now since Rab specifically stated here that 'a husband's right of inheritance is Pentateuchal' how could he be said to hold that such a right is only Rabbinical. (3) Who claims her *kethubah*. (4) Claiming the repayment of his debt. (5) Expecting their inheritance. (6) This is explained *infra*. (7) The deposit or the loan. (8) Widows and creditors. (9) Before they are authorized to seize any portion of the estate. (10) The inheritance passes into their possession as soon as the person whose heirs they are dies. Since they are the legal possessors, the others, whose claims have yet to be substantiated by an oath, cannot deprive them of their possessions, for the movables of orphans are not pledged to the creditors of their father. (11) The heirs, the widow or the creditor. (12) This is explained *infra*.

GEMARA. What was the object of specifying both A LOAN and a DEPOSIT?[1]—[Both were] required. For if A LOAN only had been mentioned it might have been presumed that only in that case did R. Tarfon maintain his view, because a loan is intended to be spent,[2] but that in the case of a deposit which is in existence[3] he agrees with R. Akiba.[4] And if the former[5] only had been mentioned it might have been assumed that only in that case did R. Akiba maintain his view[6] but that in the other case[7] he agrees with R. Tarfon.[8] [Hence both were] necessary.

What is meant by TO THE ONE WHO IS UNDER THE GREATEST DISADVANTAGE?—R. Jose the son of R. Ḥanina replied: To the one who is under the greatest disadvantage in respect of proof.[9] R. Joḥanan replied: [The reference is] to the *kethubah* of the wife[10] [who was given this privilege] in order to maintain pleasantness[11] [between her and her husband].[12] [This dispute is the same] as that between the following Tannaim: R. Benjamin said, To the one who is under the greatest disadvantage in respect of proof,[9] and this is the proper [course to take]; R. Eleazar said, [The reference is] to the *kethubah* of the wife[10] [who was given this privilege] in order to maintain pleasantness[11] [between her and her husband].[12]

(1) Could not the law of the one be inferred from the other? (2) The amount of the loan not being in existence at the time the man died it cannot pass into the possession of his heirs before it had been collected from the debtor. (3) At the time the depositor died, since a deposit must never be spent by the bailee. (4) That, since it is in existence, it passes into the possession of the heirs. (5) A DEPOSIT. (6) Cf. *supra* note 4. (7) A loan. (8) Cf. *supra* note 2. (9) *Sc.* the holder of the last dated bond by which such landed estate only may be seized as had been sold after that date. (10) Who, being unable to exert herself like a man in the search for any possible possessions of her husband, is regarded as 'THE ONE WHO IS UNDER THE GREATEST DISADVANTAGE'. (11) חינא, lit., 'grace'. (12) While he is alive. Her uncertainty in respect of her settlement after his death might have led to quarrels and strife. *Aliter:* That women may readily consent to marriage. Had they not been assured that they would have the first claim upon their husband's estate they might refuse all offers of marriage (cf. Rashi). *Aliter:* That women may be attractive to their husbands by their attachment and devotion which would result from the sense of security they would feel in the provision for their future (cf. T.J., Aruch and R. Ḥan. in Tosaf. s.v. לכתובת *a.l.*).

IF HE LEFT PRODUCE THAT WAS DETACHED. As to R. Akiba,[1] what was the point in discussing the BALANCE when[2] the entire estate belongs to the heirs?[3]—The law is so indeed,[4] but since R. Tarfon spoke of the BALANCE, he also mentioned the BALANCE. [84*b*]. But would R. Akiba[5] maintain that seizure[6] is never legally valid?[7]—Raba replied in the name of R. Naḥman: Seizure[8] is valid where it took place during the lifetime [of the deceased].[9]

Now according to R. Tarfon,[10] where [must the produce] be kept?[11]—Both Rab and Samuel replied: It must be heaped up and lie in a public domain, but [if it was kept] in an alley[12] no [seizure is valid]. Both R. Joḥanan and Resh Laḳish, however, said: Even [if the produce lay] in an alley [seizure is valid].

Certain judges once gave their decision in agreement with R. Tarfon, and Resh Laḳish[13] reversed their verdict. Said R. Joḥanan to him, 'You have acted as [if R. Akiba's ruling were a law] of the Torah'![14] May it be assumed that they[15] differ on this

(1) Who regards the heirs as the possessors because WHEREAS OTHERS MUST TAKE AN OATH THE HEIRS NEED NOT. (2) For the very same reason (cf. previous note). (3) The seizure on the part of the widow or a creditor of any movable portion of such property would consequently be invalid. (4) Lit., 'yes, so also'; even if the creditor or the widow has seized any portion of the estate the heirs' right to it is in no way affected and the seized property must be returned to them in its entirety. (5) V. *supra* note 1. (6) Cf. note 3. (7) This is a mere enquiry (v. Rashi). R. Tam regards it as an objection, the assumption of the invalidity of seizure being contradictory to the Mishnah *supra* 80*b*, where the woman awaiting levirate marriage, who was first to take possession of the detached produce, is declared to have acquired it; (v. Tosaf. s.v. ולרבי *a.l.*). (8) Of chattels. (9) So that the chattels had never for one moment passed into the possession of the heirs. (10) Who maintains that WHOEVER SEIZES IT FIRST ACQUIRES POSSESSION, because the heirs do not become its possessors as soon as the man dies. (11) That the seizure should be valid. (12) Which is frequented by few people. In such a spot where *meshikah* (v. Glos.) is valid (cf. B.B. 84*b*) the produce, even according to R. Tarfon, passes into the possession of the heirs as soon as its original owner dies, and seizure by any other person is invalid. (13) Who follows the ruling of R. Akiba. (14) An expression of disapproval. Only a decision which is contrary to the Torah must be reversed. A Rabbinical ruling, however, has no such force, and though a judge may be expected to act according to a certain ruling, his decision must not be reversed if he differed from it. (15) R. Joḥanan and Resh Laḳish.

principle: One Master upholds the view that if [in giving a decision] a law cited in a Mishnah had been overlooked the decision must be reversed[1] and the other Master upholds the view that if a law cited in a Mishnah had been overlooked the decision need not be reversed?[2]—No; all agree that if [in giving a decision] a law cited in a Mishnah had been overlooked the decision must be reversed, but this is the point at issue between them:[3] One Master holds that the *halachah* is in agreement with the opinion of R. Akiba [only when he differs] from a colleague of his but not from his master,[4] while the other Master holds that the *halachah* [is in agreement with him] even [if he differs] from his master. If you prefer[5] I might say: All agree that the *halachah* agrees with R. Akiba [only when he differs] from a colleague of his but not from his master. Here, however, the point at issue is this: One Master holds R. Tarfon to have been his[6] master and the other Master holds him to have been his colleague. Alternatively it might be said: All agree that he[7] was his[8] colleague; but the point at issue between them[9] is this: One Master maintains that the statement[10] was that 'The *halachah* [agrees with R. Akiba]'[11] and the other Master maintains that the statement[10] was that 'one should be inclined [in favour of a ruling of R. Akiba]'.[12]

R. Joḥanan's relatives seized in an alley a cow that belonged to orphans. When they appeared before R. Joḥanan, he said to them,

(1) Though R. Akiba's ruling is not explicitly contained in a Mishnah, but reported by Amoraim, it is considered a Mishnaic ruling since the law is in agreement with his opinion whenever it is opposed by no more than one individual. Cf. Sanh. 33*a*. (2) Is it likely, however, that any authority would uphold the latter view? (3) R. Joḥanan and Resh Laḳish. (4) R. Tarfon was sometimes regarded as the master of R. Akiba (v. *infra*). (5) Since the last mentioned view seems unlikely. (6) R. Akiba's. (7) R. Ṭarfon. (8) R. Akiba's. (9) R. Joḥanan and Resh Laḳish. (10) On the reliability of R. Akiba's rulings. (11) Hence the action of Resh Laḳish in reversing the decision of the judges mentioned. (12) I.e., a ruling of his has not the force of an *halachah* though a judge is expected to follow it rather than that of any other individual who is opposed to it. Since, however, a decision has been given to the contrary the decision must stand. Hence R. Joḥanan's objection to the action of Resh Laḳish (v. *supra* n. 11).

'Your seizure is quite lawful'. R. Simeon b. Laḳish, however, before whom they subsequently appeared, said to them, 'Go and return it'.[1] 'What can I do', said R. Joḥanan to whom they came again, 'when one of equal authority[2] differs from me?'

[A creditor] once seized an ox from the herdsman of [his debtor's] orphans. The creditor said, 'I seized it during the lifetime [of the debtor]'[3] and the herdsman said, 'He seized it after the debtor's death'.[4] They appeared before R. Naḥman who asked the herdsman, 'Have you witnesses that [the creditor] has seized it?'—'No', the other replied. [R. Naḥman thereupon] said to him: Since he could have said, 'It came into my possession through purchase'[5] he is also entitled to say, 'I seized it during the lifetime [of the debtor]'. But did not Resh Laḳish state: The law of presumptive possession is inapplicable to living creatures?[6]—The case of an ox that was entrusted to a herdsman is different [from that of other living creatures].[7]

The people of the Nasi's[8] household once seized in an alley a bondwoman belonging to orphans. At a session held by R. Abbahu, R. Ḥanina b. Papi and R. Isaac Nappaḥa in whose presence sat also R. Abba they[9] were told, 'Your seizure is quite lawful'. 'Is it', said R. Abba to them,[10] 'because these people are of the Nasi's household that you are favouring them? Surely, when

(1) In agreement with R. Akiba that seizure of movables for debt after the death of the original owner is invalid, the property having passed, at the moment he died, into the possession of his heirs. (2) V. Rashi. Lit., 'who is corresponding to me'. (3) So that it never came into the possession of the orphans. (4) Cf. *supra* note 3 *mutatis mutandis*. (5) And his statement could not be disproved on account of the absence of witnesses to testify to the seizure. (6) הגודרות, lit., 'those kept in the fold', since (*a*) they stray into other people's folds and (*b*) are sometimes taken accidentally from the pasture lands by a shepherd to whom they do not belong, (v. B.B. 36*a*, Giṭ. 20*b*). Now, since the creditor's right to the retention of the animal can only be based on that of presumptive possession, which is here inapplicable, why did Resh Laḳish allow the creditor to retain it? (7) A herdsman is presumed to take good care that his flock stray not into other people's folds, or be seized by other shepherds. (8) Judah II. (9) The people of the Nasi's household. (10) R. Abbahu and his colleagues.

certain judges once gave a decision in agreement with R. Ṭarfon Resh Laḳish reversed their decision'.[1]

Yemar b. Ḥashu had a money claim against a certain person who died and left a boat. 'Go', he said to his agent, 'and seize it'. [The latter] went and seized it, but R. Papa and R. Huna the son of R. Joshua met him and told him, 'You are seizing [the ship] on behalf of a creditor and thereby you are causing loss to others,[2] and R. Joḥanan ruled: He who seizes [a debtor's property] on behalf of a creditor and thereby causes loss to others[2] [85a] does not legally acquire it'.[3] Thereupon they[4] seized it themselves, R. Papa rowing[5] the boat while R. Huna the son of R. Joshua pulled it by the rope.[5] One Master then declared, 'I have acquired all the ship'[6] and the other similarly declared, 'I have acquired all of it'.[7] They were met by R. Phinehas b. Ammi who said to them: Both Rab and Samuel ruled that '[Seizure is valid] only if [the produce] was piled up and lay in a public domain'.[8] 'We too', they replied, 'have seized it at the main current of the river'.[9] When they appeared before Raba he said to them, 'Ye white geese[10] that strip the people of their cloaks;[11] thus ruled R. Naḥman: [The seizure is valid] only if it took place during the lifetime [of the original owner].

The men of Be-Ḥozae[12] once claimed a sum of money from Abimi the son of R. Abbahu, who sent it to them by the hand of Ḥama the son of Rabbah b. Abbahu. He duly went there and paid them, but when he asked them, 'Return to me the bond', they replied, 'This payment was made in settlement of some other claims'.[13] He

(1) *Supra.* (2) Other creditors. (3) One has no right to acquire a benefit for one man at the expense of another; v. Giṭ. 11*b*. (4) Who were also among the deceased's creditors. (5) A form of acquisition. (6) Rowing being in his opinion the proper form of acquiring legal possession of a ship. (7) Cf. *supra* n. 6 *mutatis mutandis*. (8) *Supra* 84*b*, *infra* 86*b*. The boat presumably lying at the river bank which, not being frequented by many boats, has the status of an alley, could not, therefore, be lawfully seized and acquired. (9) On which many boats ply and which has the status of a public thoroughfare where seizure is legal. (10) Metaph., 'old men'. (11) By giving a decision in their own favour and thus robbing the other creditors. (12) V. *supra* p. 504, n. 5. (13) Lit., 'these are (from other) sides'.

came before R. Abbahu [to complain] and the latter asked him, 'Have you witnesses that you have paid them?'—'No', he replied. 'Since', the former said to him, 'they could plead[1] that the payment was never made,[2] they are also entitled to plead that the payment was made in settlement of some other claims'.[3]

What is the law in respect of the agent's liability to refund?—R. Ashi replied: We have to consider the facts. If he[4] said to him, 'Secure the bond and pay the money' he[5] must refund it; [but if he[4] said,] 'Pay the money and secure the bond', he is under no obligation to refund it. The law, however, is not so. He[5] must refund it in either case, because the other[4] may well say, 'I deputed you to improve my position, not to make it worse'.

There was a certain woman with whom a case[6] of bonds was once deposited and when the heirs [of the depositor] came to claim it from her she said, 'I seized them[7] during [the depositor's] lifetime'.[8] R. Naḥman to whom she came said to her, 'Have you witnesses that it[9] was claimed from you during [the depositor's] lifetime and that you refused to return it?'—'No', she replied. 'If so', he said to her, 'your seizure is one that took place after [the owner's] death,[10] and such a seizure is invalid.[11]

A woman was once ordered[12] to take an oath[13] at the court of Raba, but when R. Ḥisda's daughter[14] said to him, 'I know that she is suspected of [taking false] oaths', Raba transferred the oath to her opponent.[15]

On another occasion R. Papa and R. Adda b. Mattena sat in his presence when a bond was brought to him. Said R. Papa to

(1) In the absence of witnesses to testify that the debt had been paid. (2) לא היו דברים מעולם, lit., 'the things never were'. (3) V. *supra* p. 536, n. 13. (4) The man who sent him. (5) The agent. (6) מלוגא (rt. מלג, 'to pluck'), a bag made of skins from which the hair has been plucked. (7) The bonds. (8) 'In payment of the debt he owed me'. (9) The case of bonds. (10) As long as he was alive the bonds were held by her as a deposit which was virtually in the possession of the depositor. (11) Since at the death of the depositor the bonds had passed directly into the possession of his heirs. (12) Lit., 'became liable'. (13) To confirm her denial of a monetary claim that had been advanced against her. (14) Raba's wife. (15) The claimant who in such a case (cf. Shebu. 44*b*) is entitled to the sum claimed on confirming it by an oath.

him, 'I know that this bond is paid up'. 'Is there', [Raba] asked him, 'any other man with the Master [to confirm the statement]?' 'No', he replied. 'Although', the other said to him, 'the Master is present [to give evidence] there is no validity [in the testimony of] one witness'.[1] Said R. Adda b. Mattena to him, 'Should not R. Papa be [deemed as reliable] as the daughter of R. Ḥisda?'[2] —'As to the daughter of R. Ḥisda [he replied] I am certain of her;[3] I am not sure, however, about the Master'.[4] Said R. Papa: Now that the Master has stated [that a judge who can assert,] 'I am certain of a person', may rely upon that person's evidence,[5] I would tear up a bond on the evidence of my son Abba Mar of whose reliability I am certain'. 'I would *tear* up'! Is such an act conceivable?[6]—He rather [meant to say,] 'I would impair a bond[7] on his evidence'.

A woman was once ordered to take[8] an oath at the court of R. Bibi b. Abaye, when her opponent suggested to them, 'Let her rather come and take the oath in our town,[9] where she might possibly feel ashamed [of her action] and confess'. 'Write out', said she to them, 'the verdict in my favour[10] so that after I shall have taken the oath it may be given to me'. 'Write it out for her', ordered R. Bibi b. Abaye. 'Because', said R. Papi, 'you are descendants of short-lived people you speak frail words;[11] surely Raba

(1) [Asheri, Alfasi and Isaiah Trani omit 'No . . . one witness'. According to this reading Raba required the confirmation by another person because R. Papa was related to one of the parties, v. Tosaf, and Strashun]. (2) Whose testimony was regarded by Raba, *supra*, as sufficient to disqualify the defendant from taking an oath. (3) That I can rely upon her evidence. (4) [Did he mean to imply that he suspected R. Papa of lying? This is unlikely in view of the discussion that follows in which R. Papa seemed to betray no resentment at the affront. Yet this is the only meaning which can be attached to the text of cur. edd. Preference is consequently to be given to the reading of Asheri and Alfasi (v. n. 1); and what Raba meant was that, as a relative, R. Papa's evidence could not be accepted]. (5) Even though no other witness is available Lit., 'it is a thing'. (6) In money matters, surely, the evidence of two witnesses is required. (7) *Sc.* the holder would have to confirm the statement in the bond by an oath before an order for repayment could be issued (Tosaf.). (8) Lit., 'become liable'. (9) So BaḤ. Cur. edd. omit 'our'. (10) זכוותא, pl. of זכותא, 'favourable judgment'. (11) Abaye was a descendant of the house of Eli

stated, 'An attestation[1] by judges that was written before the witnesses have identified their signatures is invalid',[2] from which it is evident [that such an attestation] has the appearance of a false declaration, and so here also [the verdict][3] would appear to contain a false statement'. This conclusion,[4] however, is futile[5] [as may be inferred] from a statement of R. Naḥman, who said: R. Meir ruled that even if [a husband] found it[6] on a rubbish heap, and then signed and gave it to her, it is valid; and even the Rabbis[7] differ from R. Meir only in respect of letters of divorce where it is necessary that the writing shall be done specifically in her name, but in respect of other legal documents they agree with him,[8] for R. Assi stated in the name of R. Joḥanan, 'A man may not borrow again on a bond on which he has once borrowed and which he has repaid,[9] because the obligation [incurred by the first loan][10] was cancelled;[11] the reason then is because 'the obligation was cancelled', but that [the contents of the document] have the appearance [85b] of a false statement[12] is a matter which need not be taken into consideration.

A certain man once deposited seven pearls, wrapped in a sheet,

who were condemned to die young (cf. I Sam. II, 32). ממולאי and מוליתא (rt. מלל 'to crush') 'frail things', 'frail words', 'frail or short-lived people'. A similar expression in Arabic means 'to be foolish'. Cf. B.B. 137*b*, Sonc. ed. p. 582, n. 6.

(1) Of a document, confirming the signature of the witnesses. (2) Giṭ. 26*b*, *supra* 21*b*. (3) Which the woman requested and the wording of which would have implied that when it was written she had already taken the oath. (4) That a document containing a statement which at the time of writing was not yet true is invalid even after the act it mentions has materialized. (5) Lit., 'and it is not'. (6) A letter of divorce he has prepared for his wife. (7) Who denied the validity of the document. (8) That the validity of the document (cf. *supra* n. 4) is not affected. (9) On the same day that he borrowed. Though the bond in such a case is not antedated it may not be used again. (10) Viz., the right to seize the debtor's property. (11) When it was repaid. The second loan, since no new bond was issued in connection with it, has only the force of a loan by word of mouth which does not entitle the creditor to seize any of the debtor's sold property. Should the first bond, however, be used for the second loan, the lender might unlawfully seize property to which he is not legally entitled. B.M. 17*a*. (12) The bond having been written not for the second but for the first loan.

with R. Miasha the son of the son of R. Joshua b. Levi. As R. Miasha died intestate[1] they came to R. Ammi.[2] 'In the first instance', he said to them, 'I know that R. Miasha the son of the son of R. Joshua b. Levi was not a wealthy man,[3] and secondly, does not the man[4] indicate the marks?'[5] This ruling, however, applies only to a man who was not a frequent visitor at the bailee's house,[6] but if he was a frequent visitor there [the marks he indicates are no evidence of ownership since] it might well be assumed that another person has made the deposit and he happened to see it.

A certain man once deposited a silver cup with Ḥasa; and Ḥasa died intestate.[7] R. Naḥman before whom [the heirs] appeared said to them, 'I know that Ḥasa was not a wealthy man[3] and, furthermore, does he[4] not indicate the mark?'[8] This, however, applies only to a man who was not an habitual visitor at the bailee's house,[6] but if he was a frequent visitor there [the mark he indicates is no valid proof since] it might be said that another person had deposited [the cup] and he happened to see it.

A certain man once deposited a silk cloth[9] with R. Dimi the brother of R. Safra, and R. Dimi died intestate.[1] R. Abba, to whom [the depositor] came [to submit his claim,] said to them,[10] 'In the first place I know that R. Dimi was not a wealthy man[3] and, secondly, the man is here indicating the distinguishing mark.' This, however, applies only to a man who was not a frequent visitor[6] at the bailee's house, but if he was a frequent visitor there [the indication of the mark is no valid proof since] it might well be suggested that another man deposited the object and he happened to see it.

(1) Lit., 'he did not order'. And his heirs maintained that the pearls might have belonged to the deceased from whom they inherited them. (2) To obtain his ruling on the ownership of the deposit. (3) And he could not consequently have been the owner of costly objects. (4) The depositor. (5) That the pearls were (*a*) wrapped up in a sheet and (*b*) their number was seven (Rashi. Cf., however, Tosaf. s.v. קיהיב). (6) Lit., 'that he was not in the habit of entering and going out from there'. (7) He was accidentally drowned (v. Yeb. 121*b*). (8) That it was a silver cup. (9) מטכסא cf. μέταξα, silk or silk cloth. (10) To the heirs.

A man once said[1] to those around him,[2] 'Let my estate be given to Ṭobiah', and then he died. [A man named] Ṭobiah came [to claim the estate]. 'Behold', said R. Joḥanan, 'Ṭobiah has come'.[3] Now if he said, 'Ṭobiah'[4] and 'R. Ṭobiah'[5] came, [the latter is not entitled to the estate, since] he said 'To Ṭobiah' but not 'To R. Ṭobiah'. If he,[5] however, was on familiar terms with him[6] [the estate must be given to him, since the omission of title might have been due to] the fact that he was on intimate terms with him. If two Ṭobiahs appeared,[7] one of whom was a neighbour[8] and the other a scholar, the scholar is to be given precedence.[9] If one [of the Ṭobiahs] is a relative and the other a scholar, the scholar is given precedence.[9] The question was asked: What is the position where one is a neighbour[8] and the other a relative?—Come and hear: *Better is a neighbour that is near than a brother far off.*[10] If both[11] are relatives, or both are neighbours, or both are scholars the decision is left to the discretion[12] of the judges.

Come, said Raba to the son of R. Ḥiyya b. Abin, I will tell you a fine saying of your father's:[13] Although[14] Samuel said, 'If a man sold a bond of indebtedness to another person and then he[15] released the debtor, the latter is legally released;[16] and, moreover,

(1) While he was on his death bed. (2) Lit., 'to them'. (3) *Sc.* the estate must be given to this man. (4) I.e., if he assigned his estate to a person whom he named without describing him by the title by which he is usually known. (5) A scholar of the name of Ṭobiah who bears the title 'R(abbi)'. (6) The testator. (7) Claiming the estate. (8) Of the deceased. (9) A person is assumed to be more favourably disposed towards a scholar than towards any other person. On the merit and heavenly reward of him who benefits scholars, v. Ber. 34*b*. (10) Prov. XXVII, 10. (11) Who claim the estate. (12) שורא = שוחרא, 'choice', 'singling out', 'discretion' (Jast.). *Aliter:* 'Favour', 'gift', i.e., the judges in their verdict may favour, or make a *gift* of the estate to any of the claimants they prefer (cf. R. Tam in Tosaf. s.v. שורא and Levy s.v.). *Aliter:* שורא = שדי, 'to throw', i.e., the judges must cast about for (gauge) the opinion of the testator to determine which of the claimants he preferred (Rashi). Cf. Golds. 'שורא ist unverkennbar das syn. סוודא, סודא (confabulatio, colloquium) Rat, Beschluss der Richter'. (13) Lit., 'which your father said'. (14) This is the reading in the parallel passage elsewhere (cf. B.B. 147*b*). The reading here is הא, lit., 'that', 'as to that'. (15) The seller. (16) Because the buyer of a bond is entitled only to the same rights as those of the seller and since the latter,

even [a creditor's] heir may[1] release [the debtor]' Samuel, nevertheless, admits that, where a wife brought in to her husband[2] a bond of indebtedness and then remitted it, the debt is not to be considered remitted, because her husband's rights are equal to hers.[3]

A relative of R. Naḥman once sold her *kethubah* for the goodwill.[4] She was divorced and then died. Thereupon [the buyers] came to claim [the amount of the *kethubah*] from her daughter.[5] 'Is there no one', said R. Naḥman to those around him,[6] 'who can tender her advice? [86*a*] She might remit[7] her mother's *kethubah* in favour of her father,[8] and then she may inherit it from him'.[9] When she heard this she went and remitted it [in her father's favour]. Thereupon R. Naḥman said: 'We have put ourselves in the [unenviable] position of legal advisers'.[10] What was the opinion that he held at first[11] and what made him change it afterwards?[12] —At first he thought [of the Scriptural text,] *And that thou hide not thyself from thine own flesh,*[13] but ultimately he realized that [the position of] a noted personality is different [from that of the general public].[14]

by his release of the creditor, has forfeited his claims upon the debt, the former also forfeits them; v. Ḳid., Sonc. ed. p. 239, n. 1.

(1) When he inherits the estate of the creditor. (2) On marriage. (3) Lit., 'his hand is like her hand'; hence it is not within her power to remit the debt without her husband's consent. (4) Cf. Rashi. טובת הנאה, lit., 'the goodness of a favour' (cf. the English idiom, 'a game for *love*'), i.e., receiving no full price for her *kethubah* from the buyers, who purchase it as a speculation in case her husband dies first or divorces her. Should she die first, they have no claim to the *kethubah*. (5) Who was the heir to her mother's *kethubah*. (6) Lit., 'to them'. (7) Lit., 'let her go and remit'. (8) Since, as has been stated (*supra* 85*b ad fin.*), 'even a creditor's heir may release the debtor'. The daughter is in this case the heir to a debt (the *kethubah*) which her father owed her mother who sold it to others who, like the buyers of a bond, lose all their claims upon it as soon as the heir has remitted it. (9) Upon whom the buyers have no claim. (10) עורכי הדיינין, lit., 'those who arrange (the pleas) before the judges'. A judge is forbidden to act even indirectly as legal adviser to one of the parties. Cf. Aboth I, 8, Sonc. ed. p. 6, n. 1. (11) When he tendered advice. (12) Lit., 'and in the end what did he think?' *sc.* why did he finally reproach himself for acting as 'legal adviser'? (13) Isa. LVIII, 7, implying that it is one's duty to come to the assistance of one's relative. (14) A judge, in order to be free from

[Reverting to] the main text: Samuel said, 'If a man sold a bond of indebtedness to another person, and then he released the debtor, the latter is released; and, moreover, even [a creditor's] heir may release [the debtor].'[1] Said R. Huna the son of R. Joshua: But if he[2] is clever he[3] rattles some coins in his[4] face and [the latter][5] writes the bond[6] in his[7] name.

Amemar said: He[8] who adjudicates [liability] in an action [for damage] caused indirectly would here also[9] adjudge damages[10] to the amount [recoverable] on a valid bond,[11] but he who does not adjudicate [liability] in an action for damage caused indirectly[12] would here adjudge damages only to the extent of the value of the mere scrap of paper.[13] Such[14] an action was [once tried] when through Rafram's insistence[15] R. Ashi[16] was compelled to order the collection [of damages][17] in the manner of a beam that is fit for decorative mouldings.[18]

Amemar stated in the name of R. Ḥama: If a man has against

all suspicion of partiality, must subject himself to greater restrictions and must consequently tender no legal advice whatever to one of the parties in a law-suit, even in cases where the action is not to be tried by him, v. *supra* 52*b*.

(1) V. p. 541, nn. 15ff. (2) The buyer. (3) As soon as he buys the bond and before the creditor has had time to think of remitting it to the debtor. (4) The debtor. (5) Being naturally in need of ready money. (6) For the amount involved. As soon as he buys the bond and before the creditor has time to think of remitting it to the debtor. (7) The buyer's. (8) I.e., R. Meir (cf. B.Ḳ. 100*a* f). (9) Lit., 'by it'; in the case of a bond the debt in which had been remitted to the debtor after the creditor had sold the bond of indebtedness. (10) In favour of the buyer. (11) The creditor who was the cause of the damage must compensate the buyer for his loss. (12) As to the dispute on this point v. B.Ḳ. 116*b*. (13) On which the bond is written; since the creditor might plead that he is only liable for the piece of paper which he sold. For the debt itself he is not liable since it was only indirectly that he caused the loss of it. (14) Cf., however, *infra* n. 17. (15) By his legal and scholastic arguments. (16) Who was the adjudicator in the action (cf., however, *infra* n. 17). (17) From the creditor who remitted the debt. According to another interpretation (cf. Rashi on the parallel passage, B.Ḳ. 98*b*) R. Ashi in his childhood had destroyed a bond of indebtedness, and Rafram made him pay for it in accordance with the ruling of R. Meir (v. *supra* note 8). (18) Metaph. As the beam is smooth and straight and of the best quality of wood so was the collection made to the full extent of the damage and of the best of the creditor's estate.

him the claim of his wife's *kethubah* and that of a creditor, and he owns a plot of land and has also ready money, the creditor's claim is settled by means of the ready money while the woman's claim is settled by means of the land, the creditor being treated in accordance with his rights,[1] and the wife in accordance with her rights.[2] If, however, he owns only one plot of land and it suffices to meet the claim of one only, it is to be given to the creditor;[3] it is not to be given to the wife. What is the reason?[4]—More than the man's desire to marry is the woman's desire to be married.[5]

Said R. Papa to R. Ḥama, Is it a fact that you have stated in the name of Raba: If a man, against whom there was a monetary claim owned a plot of land, and who, when his creditor approached him with the claim for repayment, replied, 'Collect your loan from the land', he is to be ordered [by the court,] 'You must yourself go and sell it, bring [the net proceeds] and deliver it to him'?[6] —'No', the other replied. 'Tell me then', [the first said to him,] 'how the incident[7] had actually occurred'. '[The debtor]' the other replied, 'alleged that his money belonged to[8] an idolater; and since he acted in an improper manner[9] he was similarly treated in an improper manner'.[10]

Said R. Kahana to R. Papa: According to the statement you

(1) As he advanced ready money he is justly entitled to ready money. (2) As her statutory *kethubah* is secured on the husband's lands she is entitled to his land only. The amount of the *kethubah* corresponding to the *ẓon barzel* (v. Glos.) property, though this might have consisted of ready money, is, like the statutory *kethubah* with which it is amalgamated, also secured on the husband's lands only. (3) If the bond of indebtedness and the *kethubah* bear the same date. Otherwise, the holder of the document bearing the earlier date takes precedence. (4) For the preference of the creditor where the documents were issued on the same date. (5) And the disadvantage in respect of the collection of her *kethubah* would not in any way deter her from marriage. If a creditor, on the other hand, were to experience undue difficulty in the collection of his debt he might decide to turn away from his door all future borrowers. (6) Is it possible that a debtor would be expected to go to all this trouble when the creditor's security was not that of ready money but of land? (7) That gave rise to the erroneous report. (8) Lit., 'attached his money to'. (9) By attempting to deprive his creditor from his due. (10) In being ordered to find a buyer for his land, though elsewhere (cf. *supra* n. 6) it is the task of the creditor to do so.

made that the repayment of [a debt to] a creditor is a religious act,[1] what is the ruling where [a debtor] said, 'I am not disposed to perform a religious act'?[2]—'We', the other replied, 'have learned: This[3] applies only to negative precepts, but in the case of positive precepts, as for instance, when a man is told, 'Make a *sukkah*'[4] and he does not make it [or, 'Perform the commandment of the] *lulab*'[5] and he does not perform it [86*b*] he is flogged[6] until his soul departeth.[7]

Rami b. Ḥama enquired of R. Ḥisda: What is the ruling where [a husband said to his wife,] 'Here is your letter of divorce but you shall be divorced thereby only after [the lapse of] thirty days', and she went and laid it down at the side of a public domain?[8] —'She', the other replied, 'is not divorced, by reason of the ruling of Rab and Samuel, both of whom have stated, 'It must be heaped up and lie in a public domain'[9] and the sides of a public domain are regarded as the public domain itself.[10] On the contrary! She should be deemed divorced by reason of a ruling of R. Naḥman, who stated in the name of Rabbah b. Abbuha, 'If a man said to

(1) V. 'Ar. 22*a*. (2) [Since, that is to say, the payment of a debt is a religious obligation, where is the sanction for the employment of compulsory measures to make one pay his debts? Others connect the question with the preceding case of one who ascribes his money to a non-Jew so as to evade payment, v. Tosaf. s.v. אמר]. (3) That flogging is administered and the sinner is thereby purged. (4) The festive booth for the Feast of Tabernacles (cf. Lev. XXIII, 34ff). (5) 'Palm-branch', the term applied to the festive wreath used in the Tabernacles ritual and consisting of four species of which the palm-branch is one (cf. Lev. XXIII, 40). (6) In an endeavour to coerce him to perform the precept. (7) Ḥul. 132*b*; if he persists in his refusal. Thus it follows that no one is at liberty to declare, 'I am not disposed to perform a religious act'. (8) Where fewer people walk, and where it remained intact until the lapse of the thirty days. Is the letter of divorce, it is asked, regarded as being still in the possession of the woman, despite its place of deposit, and the woman is consequently legally divorced, or is the spot, being at the side of a public domain, subject to the same restrictions in respect of *ḳinyan* as the public domain itself. (9) *Supra* 84*b*, 85*a*, q.v., from which it follows that an object in a public domain cannot be acquired except by a specific act of *ḳinyan*. (10) Cf. *supra* n. 9. The woman cannot consequently be regarded as being in possession of the letter of divorce and her divorce is, therefore, invalid.

another, "Pull this cow, but it shall pass into your possession only after thirty days", he legally acquires it even if it stands at the time in the meadow';[1] and a meadow presumably has, has it not, the same status as the sides of a public domain?[2]—No; a meadow has a status of its own[3] and the sides of a public domain, too, have a status of their own.[4] Another version: He[5] said to him,[6] 'She[7] is divorced by reason of a ruling of R. Naḥman,[8] the sides of a public domain having the same status as a meadow'.—'On the contrary! She should not be regarded as divorced by reason of a ruling of Rab and Samuel,[8] for have not the sides of a public domain the same status as a public domain?'—'No; a public domain has a status of its own[3] and the sides of a public domain, too, have a status of their own'.[4]

MISHNAH. IF A HUSBAND SET UP HIS WIFE AS A SHOPKEEPER[9] OR APPOINTED HER AS HIS ADMINISTRATRIX HE MAY IMPOSE UPON HER AN OATH[10] WHENEVER HE DESIRES TO DO SO. R. ELIEZER SAID: [SUCH AN OATH[10] MAY BE IMPOSED UPON HER] EVEN IN RESPECT OF HER SPINDLE AND HER DOUGH.[11]

GEMARA. The question was asked: Does R. Eliezer mean [that the oath[12] is to be imposed] by implication[13] or does he mean

(1) *Supra* 82a q.v. for notes. (2) As the cow is acquired after the specified period, though stationed in a meadow, so should the woman be deemed to be in the possession of the letter of divorce, though it lies at the side of a public domain. (3) Hence the validity of a deferred *kinyan* if at the specified period the object was within its boundaries. (4) No deferred *kinyan* being effective within such a spot. (5) R. Ḥisda. (6) Rami b. Ḥama. (7) The woman to whom her husband gave a letter of divorce stipulating that it shall take effect only after the lapse of thirty days. (8) V. *supra*. (9) That she should sell his wares. (10) That she has not dealt fraudulently with anything that had been put in her charge. (11) *Sc.* not only when she is engaged in commercial transactions, but also when she is occupied with her domestic affairs only. (V. Gemara *infra*). (12) He has spoken of in our Mishnah. (13) גלגול, lit., 'rolling', *sc.* only where the wife has to take an oath in respect of her commercial

that it may be imposed directly?[1]—Come and hear: They[2] said to R. Eliezer, 'No one can live with a serpent in the same basket'.[3] Now if you will assume that R. Eliezer meant the imposition of a direct oath[1] one can well understand the argument;[4] but if you were to suggest [that he meant the oath to be imposed] by implication only, what [it may be objected] could this[5] matter to her?[6]—She might tell him, 'Since you are so particular with me I am unable to live with you'.[7]

Come and hear:[8] If a man did not exempt his wife[9] from a vow[10] and from an oath[11] and set her up as his saleswoman or appointed her as his administratrix, he may impose upon her an oath[11] whenever he desires to do so. If, however, he did not set her up as his saleswoman and did not appoint her as his administratrix, he may not impose any oath upon her. R. Eliezer said: Although he did not set her up as his saleswoman and did not appoint her as his administratrix, he may nevertheless impose upon her an oath wherever he desires to do so, because there is no woman who was not administratrix for a short time, at least, during the lifetime of her husband, in respect of her spindle and her dough. Thereupon they said to him: No one can live with a serpent in the same basket. Thus you may infer that [R. Eliezer meant that the oath[11] may be imposed] directly. This is conclusive.

MISHNAH. [IF A HUSBAND] GAVE TO HIS WIFE AN UNDERTAKING IN WRITING, 'I HAVE NO CLAIM UPON YOU FOR

transactions may an oath in respect of her domestic occupations be added.

(1) *Sc.* even if she is attending to her domestic occupations only. (2) The Rabbis who differed from him. (3) Proverb. Serpent = cantankerous husband. (4) A wife could justly object to live with a cantankerous man who does not trust her in her domestic responsibilities. (5) The oath by implication. (6) When she has in any case to take an oath in respect of her business transactions. (7) Her refusal to live with him is not due to the actual oath but to his mistrust of her integrity. (8) An answer to the question *supra* as to what was R. Eliezer's meaning. (9) By a formal declaration. (10) E.g., 'may all the produce of the world be forbidden to me if I misappropriated any of your goods or money' (cf. Giṭ. 34b). (11) V. *supra* p. 546, n. 10.

EITHER VOW[1] OR OATH',[2] HE CANNOT IMPOSE AN OATH[3] UPON HER. HE MAY, HOWEVER, IMPOSE AN OATH UPON HER HEIRS[4] AND UPON HER LAWFUL SUCCESSORS.[5] [IF HE WROTE,] 'I HAVE NO CLAIM FOR EITHER VOW[1] OR OATH[2] EITHER UPON YOU, OR UPON YOUR HEIRS OR UPON YOUR LAWFUL SUCCESSORS', HE MAY NOT IMPOSE AN OATH EITHER UPON HER OR UPON HER HEIRS OR UPON HER LAWFUL SUCCESSORS. HIS HEIRS, HOWEVER, MAY[6] IMPOSE AN OATH UPON HER, UPON HER HEIRS OR UPON HER LAWFUL SUCCESSORS. [IF THE WRITTEN UNDERTAKING READ,] 'NEITHER I NOR MY HEIRS NOR MY LAWFUL SUCCESSORS[7] SHALL HAVE ANY CLAIM UPON YOU OR UPON YOUR HEIRS OR UPON YOUR LAWFUL SUCCESSORS FOR EITHER VOW OR OATH', NEITHER HE NOR HIS HEIRS NOR HIS LAWFUL SUCCESSORS MAY IMPOSE AN OATH EITHER UPON HER OR UPON HER HEIRS OR UPON HER LAWFUL SUCCESSORS.

IF SHE[8] WENT FROM HER HUSBAND'S GRAVE TO HER FATHER'S HOUSE,[9] OR RETURNED TO HER FATHER-IN-LAW'S HOUSE BUT WAS NOT MADE ADMINISTRATRIX, THE HEIRS ARE NOT ENTITLED TO IMPOSE AN OATH UPON HER;[10] BUT IF SHE WAS MADE ADMINISTRATRIX THE HEIRS MAY IMPOSE AN OATH UPON HER IN RESPECT OF [HER ADMINISTRATION] DURING THE SUBSEQUENT PERIOD[11] BUT NOT IN RESPECT OF THE PAST.[12]

(1) V. p. 547, n. 10. (2) V. *supra* p. 546, n. 10. (3) The nature of this oath is explained *infra*. (4) If, having been divorced by him, she died and they claim from him the amount of her *kethubah*. The oath they take affirms that the deceased had not enjoined upon them either while, or before, she was dying, nor did they find any entry among her papers that the *kethubah* was paid (v. Shebu. 45*a*). (5) People who bought her *kethubah* from her. Cf. n. 4, *mutatis mutandis*. (6) If on the death of their father the widow, her heirs or lawful successors claim from them the payment of her *kethubah*. (7) The purchasers of his estate from whom the *kethubah* is claimed in the absence of unencumbered property. (8) The woman whom her husband had granted exemption from vow and oath (v. *supra*). (9) *Sc*. she severed all connection with her husband's business affairs as soon as he was buried. (10) Even in respect of the period between her husband's death and burial. (11) Lit., 'for that which is to come', the exemption

GEMARA. What is the nature of the oath?[1]—Rab Judah replied in the name of Rab: [87a] [It is one that is incumbent] upon a woman who during the lifetime of her husband was made administratrix [of his affairs].[2] R. Naḥman replied in the name of Rabbah b. Abbuha: [It is one that is incumbent] upon a woman who impairs her *kethubah*.[3] R. Mordecai went to R. Ashi and submitted to him this argument: One can well imagine [the origin of the exemption], according to him who holds [that the oath[1] is one incumbent] upon a woman who impairs her *kethubah* [by assuming that] it occurred to the woman that she might sometime be in need of money and would draw it from her *kethubah* and would, therefore, tell her husband, 'Give me an undertaking in writing that you will impose no oath upon me'.[4] According to him, however, who holds [that the oath[1] is one incumbent] upon a woman who during the lifetime of her husband was made administratrix [of his affairs],[5] did she know [it may be objected] that he would set her up as administratrix that she should say to him, 'Give me a written undertaking that you will impose no oath upon me'?[6]—The other replied: You taught this statement[7] in

having expired at the moment the estate passed into the possession of the heirs. (12) The period of her administration prior to their father's death, when she was protected by his exemption.

(1) The exemption from which is discussed in the first clause of our Mishnah. (2) It is from such an oath only that a husband exempts his wife, but not from one which a woman incurs when she impairs her *kethubah* (v. *infra*). A husband, according to this view, only exempts his wife from an obligation which is in his power to impose upon her but not from one which she has brought upon herself. (3) By admitting that part of it has been paid to her. A woman who makes such an admission while her husband pleads that he has paid her the full amount is not entitled to receive the balance she claims except on oath, and it is the opinion of the authority cited by R. Naḥman that a husband's general exemption extends to such an oath also, much more so to that required from her as administratrix (cf. *supra* note 2). (4) And while asking for exemption from this particular oath she might at the same time ask for an exemption from both oaths. (5) Cf. *supra* note 2. (6) As she cannot be assumed to divine her husband's thoughts and intentions, the desire for such a request could naturally never arise. (7) Rab Judah's, (*supra* 86b f).

connection with that clause;[1] we teach it[2] in connection with this:[3] IF SHE WENT FROM HER HUSBAND'S GRAVE TO HER FATHER'S HOUSE, OR RETURNED TO HER FATHER-IN-LAW'S HOUSE BUT WAS NOT MADE ADMINISTRATRIX, THE HEIRS ARE NOT ENTITLED TO IMPOSE AN OATH UPON HER, BUT IF SHE WAS MADE ADMINISTRATRIX THE HEIRS MAY IMPOSE AN OATH UPON HER IN RESPECT OF [HER ADMINISTRATION] DURING THE SUBSEQUENT PERIOD BUT NOT IN CONNECTION WITH THE PAST, [and, in reply to the question as to] what exactly was meant by THE PAST, Rab Judah stated in the name of Rab: [The period] during the lifetime of her husband for which she was made administratrix [of his affairs], but in respect of [the period intervening] between death and burial an oath may be imposed upon her.[4] R. Mattena, however,[5] maintained that no oath may be imposed upon her[6] even in respect of [the period between] death and burial;[7] for the Nehardeans laid down: For poll-tax,[8] maintenance[9] and funeral expenses, an estate[10] is sold without public announcement.[11]

Said Rabbah in the name of R. Ḥiyya: [If in giving exemption to his wife a husband wrote,] 'Neither vow nor oath' it is only he who cannot impose an oath upon her, but his heirs may impose an oath upon her. [If he wrote, however,] 'Free from vow, free from oath', neither he nor his heirs may exact an oath from her,

(1) The case dealt with in the first clause of our Mishnah (cf. *supra* p. 549, n. 1). (2) I.e., you assume that R. Judah and R. Naḥman refer to one and the same clause. (3) The final clause dealing with the oath of an administratrix. (4) Cf. *supra* p. 548, n. 11. Whereas R. Naḥman refers to the first clause, Rab Judah refers to the case of an administratrix in the last clause, and so R. Mordecai's objection does not arise. (5) Differing from Rab Judah. (6) The administratrix whom her husband has exempted from oath. (7) This period also coming under the term of THE PAST. (8) On behalf of orphans. (9) Of one's widow or daughter. (10) A bequest now belonging to the orphans of the deceased. (11) Because in all these cases money is urgently needed and there is no time for the public announcement that must precede all sales effected on the order of a court. The urgency of the sale must inevitably lead to some undercutting of prices which the widow cannot possibly avoid (v. Giṭ. 52*b*). It would consequently be an act of injustice to impose upon her an oath in respect of her administration during the period between her husband's death and burial.

[since by this expression] he meant to say to her: 'Be free from the obligation of an oath'.

R. Joseph, however, stated in the name of R. Ḥiyya: [If in giving exemption to his wife a husband writes,] 'Neither vow nor oath' it is only he who cannot impose an oath upon her but his heirs may; [but if he wrote,] 'Free from vow, free from oath', both he and his heirs may exact an oath from her [since by such an expression] he thus meant to say to her: 'Clear yourself by means of an oath'.

R. Zakkai sent to Mar 'Uḳba the following message: Whether [the husband wrote,] 'Neither oath' or 'Free from oath', or whether [he wrote,] 'Neither vow', or 'Free from vow', [and he used the expression,] 'In respect of my estates',[1] he cannot impose an oath upon her, but his heirs may. [If he wrote, however,] 'In respect of these estates', neither he nor his heirs may exact an oath from her.

R. Naḥman stated in the name of Samuel in the name of Abba Saul the son of Imma Miriam: Whether [the husband wrote,] 'Neither oath' or 'Free from oath'' whether [he wrote,] 'Neither vow' or 'Free from vow', or whether [he used the expression,] 'In respect of my[1] estates' or 'In respect of these estates', neither he nor his heirs may exact an oath from her; but what can I do in view of a ruling of the Sages that anyone who comes to exact payment out of the property of orphans is not to be paid unless he first takes an oath.[2]

Others read this[3] as a Baraitha: Abba Saul the son of Imma Miriam stated: Whether [the husband wrote,] 'Neither oath' or 'Free from oath', whether [he wrote,] 'Neither vow' or 'Free from vow', or whether [he used the expression,] 'In respect of my[1] estates', or 'In respect of these estates', neither he nor his heirs may impose an oath upon her; but what can I do in view of a ruling of the Sages that anyone who comes to exact payment out of the property of orphans need not be paid unless he first takes an oath. [It was in connection with this Baraitha[4] that]

(1) Omitting the demonstrative pronoun 'these'. (2) V. B.B. 5*b*. (3) The ruling cited in the name of Abba Saul. (4) Cf. *supra* n. 3.

R. Naḥman said in the name of Samuel: The *halachah* is in agreement with the ruling of the son of Imma Miriam.

MISHNAH. A WOMAN WHO IMPAIRS[1] HER KETHUBAH IS NOT PAID[2] UNLESS SHE FIRST TAKES AN OATH.[3] IF ONE WITNESS TESTIFIES AGAINST HER THAT [HER KETHUBAH] HAS BEEN PAID,[4] SHE IS NOT BE PAID UNLESS SHE FIRST TAKES THE OATH. FROM THE PROPERTY OF ORPHANS, FROM ASSIGNED PROPERTY[5] AND [FROM THE PROPERTY OF] AN ABSENT HUSBAND[6] SHE MAY NOT RECOVER [THE PAYMENT OF HER KETHUBAH] UNLESS SHE FIRST TAKES AN OATH.[7]

HOW [ARE WE TO UNDERSTAND THE STATEMENT,] 'A WOMAN WHO IMPAIRS HER KETHUBAH'? IF HER KETHUBAH WAS FOR A THOUSAND ZUZ[8] AND [HER HUSBAND] SAID TO HER, 'YOU HAVE ALREADY RECEIVED [THE FULL AMOUNT OF] YOUR KETHUBAH', AND SHE SAYS, 'I RECEIVED ONLY A MANEH',[8] SHE IS NOT PAID [THE BALANCE] UNLESS SHE TAKES AN OATH. WHAT IS MEANT BY[9] 'IF ONE WITNESS TESTIFIES AGAINST HER THAT [HER KETHUBAH] HAS BEEN PAID'? IF HER KETHUBAH WAS FOR A THOUSAND ZUZ[8] AND WHEN [HER HUSBAND] SAID TO HER, 'YOU HAVE RECEIVED [THE FULL AMOUNT OF] YOUR KETHUBAH', SHE REPLIED, 'I HAVE NOT RECEIVED IT' WHILE ONE WITNESS TESTIFIES AGAINST HER THAT [THE KETHUBAH] HAS BEEN PAID[4] SHE IS NOT PAID UNLESS SHE FIRST TAKES AN OATH. WHAT IS MEANT BY THE EXPRESSION,[9] 'FROM ASSIGNED PROPERTY'? IF [HER HUSBAND] HAD SOLD HIS PROPERTY TO OTHERS AND SHE SEEKS TO RECOVER PAYMENT FROM THE BUYERS, SHE IS NOT PAID UNLESS SHE FIRST TAKES AN OATH. WHAT IS THE EXPLANATION OF THE EXPRESSION,[9]

(1) This is explained anon. (2) The balance she claims. (3) Affirming her claim. (4) In full (v. *infra*). (5) Mortgaged or sold. (6) Lit., 'and not in his presence', i.e., if a husband who was abroad sent a divorce to his wife and she claims her *kethubah* in his absence. (7) Which is imposed upon her by the court even if the respective defendants mentioned do not demand it. (8) V. Glos. (9) Lit., 'how'.

'FROM THE PROPERTY OF ORPHANS'? IF [HER HUSBAND] DIED AND LEFT HIS ESTATE TO HIS ORPHANS AND SHE SEEKS TO RECOVER PAYMENT FROM THE ORPHANS, SHE IS NOT PAID UNLESS SHE FIRST TAKES AN OATH. WHAT IS TO BE UNDERSTOOD BY[1] 'AN ABSENT HUSBAND'? IF HER HUSBAND WENT TO A COUNTRY BEYOND THE SEA AND SHE SEEKS TO RECOVER PAYMENT IN HIS ABSENCE,[2] SHE IS NOT PAID UNLESS SHE FIRST TAKES AN OATH. [87*b*] R. SIMEON RULED: WHENEVER[3] SHE[4] CLAIMS HER KETHUBAH THE HEIRS MAY IMPOSE AN OATH UPON HER BUT WHERE SHE DOES NOT CLAIM HER KETHUBAH THE HEIRS CANNOT IMPOSE AN OATH UPON HER.

GEMARA. Rami b. Ḥama wished to assume that the OATH[5] was Pentateuchal,[6] since [it is a case where] one [of two persons] claims two hundred [*zuz*] and the other admits one hundred [the defence] being an admission of a part of the claim,[7] and whoever admits part of a claim must[8] take an oath.[9] Said Raba: There are two objections to this assumption: In the first place, all who take an oath in accordance with Pentateuchal law take the oath and do not pay,[10] while she[11] takes the oath and receives payment. And, secondly, no oath may be imposed[8] in respect of the denial of [a claim that is] secured[12] on landed property.[13] [The fact,] however, is, said Raba, [that the oath is only] Rabbinical. As it is the person who pays that is careful to remember the details while he who receives payment is not, the Rabbis have imposed

(1) Lit., 'how'. (2) Cf. *supra* p. 552, n. 6. (3) Lit., 'all the time'. (4) The Gemara *infra* explains what R. Simeon refers to. (5) Which A WOMAN WHO IMPAIRS HER KETHUBAH must take. (6) On the difference between a Rabbinical oath and one imposed by the Torah v. Shebu. 41*a*. (7) [Read with MS.M.: for she claims of him two hundred (*zuz*) and he admits to her one hundred, so that he is admitting part of the claim]. (8) Pentateuchally. (9) That he has repaid the difference. The woman, having admitted receipt of a part of her *kethubah*, must consequently be in a similar position. (10) I.e., it is the defendant, not the claimant, who takes the oath. (11) The woman who impaired her *kethubah* and claims the balance. (12) As is a *kethubah*. (13) V. Shebu. 42*b*, B.M. 57*b*.

an oath upon her[1] that she might be careful to recollect the details.

The question was raised: What if a woman impaired her *kethubah* by [admitting that she received part payment in the presence of] witnesses? [Is it assumed that] were [her husband] to pay her [the balance] he would do it in the presence of witnesses,[2] or [is it rather assumed that] it was a mere coincidence [that witnesses were present when the first payment was made]?[3]—Come and hear:[4] All who take an oath in accordance with Pentateuchal law, take the oath and do not pay,[5] but the following take an oath and receive payment: A hired labourer,[6] a man who was robbed[7] or wounded,[8] [any claimant] whose opponent is suspected of [taking a false] oath[9] and a shopkeeper[10] with his [accounts] book,[11] and also [a creditor] who impaired his bond [the first instalment of which had been paid] in the absence of witnesses.[12] Thus only[13] [where the first instalment was paid] 'in the absence of witnesses'[14] but not where it was paid in the presence of witnesses![15]—This

(1) V. *supra* p. 553, n 11. (2) As he did in the case of the first payment. The woman would consequently be entitled to payment without taking the oath. (3) And since the man was not particular to secure witnesses on the first occasion, he might have been equally indifferent on the second occasion, and the woman would consequently have to take an oath. (4) V. Mishnah Shebu. 44*b*. (5) V. *supra* p. 553, n. 10. (6) Who swears that he has not received his wages. (7) Witnesses testifying that they saw the robber emerging from that person's house carrying an object which they could not identify. (8) The evidence shewing that the wound had been inflicted while the two men were alone in a particular spot, though no third party had witnessed the actual wounding. (9) I.e., if the defendant is known to have once before sworn falsely. (10) Who was given an order by an employer to supply a certain amount of goods to his workmen on account of their wages. (11) If the book shews that the goods had been duly supplied and the workmen deny receiving them, the shopkeeper, like the workmen, is ordered to take an oath (the former that he supplied the goods and the latter that they had not received them) and both receive payment from the employer. (12) [Add with MS.M. 'and she who impairs her *kethubah* without witnesses']. These last two mentioned cases are not found in the Mishnah (v. *supra* n. 11 *ad fin.*) and their source is a Baraitha (cf. Tosaf. s.v. ואלו *a.l.*). (13) Lit., 'yes'. (14) Must the claimant take the oath. (15) The woman, in the case under discussion, would consequently be entitled to collect the balance she claims without taking an oath.

is a case of 'there is no question . . .'[1] There is no question[2] that [when the first instalment was paid] in the presence of witnesses she must take an oath; when, however, [it was paid] in the absence of witnesses, it might be assumed that she has [the same privilege] as one who restores a lost object [to its owner][3] and should, therefore, receive payment without taking an oath. It was, therefore, taught [that the oath is nevertheless not to be dispensed with].

The question was raised: What if a woman impaired her *kethubah* [by including in the amount she admitted] sums amounting to[4] less than the value of a *peruṭah*?[5] Is it assumed that since she[6] is so careful in her statements she must be speaking the truth[7] or is it possible that she[8] is merely acting cunningly?[9]—This remains unsolved.[10]

The question was raised: What if a woman declares her [original] *kethubah* to have been less [than the amount recorded in the written document]?[11] Is it assumed that such a woman is in the same position as the woman who impaired [her *kethubah*] or is it possible [that the two cases are unlike, since] the woman who impairs [her *kethubah*] admits a part [of the sum involved][12] while this one does not admit a part [of the sum involved]?[13]—Come and hear:

(1) Lit., 'he implied (the formula): "It is not required" (to say etc.)'. (2) Lit., 'it is not required (to say that)'. (3) In such a case a person is not expected to take an oath that he had returned all that he had found. His honesty is taken for granted in view of the fact that a dishonest man would have kept the object entirely to himself. Similarly with the impaired *kethubah*. Had the woman been dishonest she need not have admitted the receipt of an instalment at all and could have collected the full amount of her *kethubah* by virtue of the written document she possesses. (4) Lit., 'less less'. (5) V. Glos. (6) By including even small and insignificant payments. (7) And should, therefore, be exempt from an oath in respect of the balance. (8) In mentioning insignificant payments. (9) She mentioned the small sums in order to give the impression of being a careful and scrupulous person while in fact the instalment or instalments she received were substantial sums. Consequently an oath should be imposed upon her. (10) *Teḳu*, v. Glos. (11) And she claims that amount; while her husband states that he had paid her all her *kethubah*. (12) The husband asserting that he paid the *full amount* and she admitting the receipt of a *part of it*. In such a case an oath may justly be imposed upon the woman. (13) Since according to her statement the *kethubah* never amounted to more than the sum she now claims.

A woman who declares that her [original] *kethubah* was less [than the amount recorded in the document] receives payment without an oath. How [is this to be understood]? If her *kethubah* was for a thousand *zuz*[1] and when her husband said to her, 'You have already received your *kethubah*,'[2] she replies, 'I have not received it,[2] but [the original *kethubah*] was only for one *maneh*,'[3] she is to receive payment without an oath.[4]

Wherewith, however, does she collect [the amount she claims]? Obviously with that document.[5] But is not that document a mere potsherd?[6]—Raba the son of Rabbah replied: [This is a case] where she states, 'There was an arrangement of mutual trust between me and him'.[7]

IF ONE WITNESS TESTIFIES AGAINST HER THAT [HER KETHUBAH] HAS BEEN PAID [etc.]. Rami b. Ḥama wished to assume that the OATH was Pentateuchal, for it is written in Scripture, *One witness shall not rise up against a man for any iniquity, or for any sin;*[8] it is only *for any iniquity or for any sin* that he may not rise up, but he may rise up [to cause the imposition upon one of the obligation] of an oath. And, furthermore, a Master has laid down: In all cases where two witnesses render a man liable to pay money, one witness renders him liable to take an oath.[9] Said Raba: There are two objections to this assumption. In the first place, all who take an oath in accordance with Pentateuchal law, do so and do not pay,[10] while she takes an oath and receives payment; and, secondly, no oath may be imposed in respect of

(1) V. Glos. (2) The amount entered in the document. (3) While the document contains a larger sum. (4) This solves the problem. (5) The *kethubah* she holds. (6) *Sc.* of no legal value, since she herself admits that the amount it records is fictitious. (7) They agreed, she states, that she would claim the smaller sum only despite the entry in the *kethubah* which shewed a larger one. This verbal agreement does not in any way affect the validity of the *kethubah* which, having been written and signed in a proper manner and attested by qualified witnesses, is a valid document on the strength of which a legal claim may well be founded; cf. *supra* 19*b*. (8) Deut. XIX, 15. (9) As two witnesses would have caused the woman to lose her *kethubah* entirely, one witness may rightly cause an oath to be imposed upon her. V. Shebu. 40*a*. (10) V. *supra* p. 553, n. 10ff.

the denial of [a claim that is] secured on landed property. [The fact], however, is, said Raba [that the oath is only] Rabbinical, [having been enacted] to appease the mind of the husband.

R. Papa said: [88a] If he[1] is clever he may bring her under the obligation[2] of a Pentateuchal oath:[3] He pays her[4] the amount of her *kethubah* in the presence of one witness, associates the first witness[5] with the second[6] and then treats his first payments[7] as a loan.[8] R. Shisha son of R. Idi demurred: How can one associate the first witness with the second one?[9]—But, said R. Shisha the son of R. Idi, [he might proceed in this manner:][10] He pays her the amount of her *kethubah* in the presence of the first witness and a second one, and then treats his first payments as a loan. R. Ashi demurred: Might she not still assert that there were two *kethubahs*?[11] —But, said R. Ashi: He might inform them[12] [of the facts].[13]

(1) The husband whose plea is supported by one witness only. (2) Lit., 'bring her to the hands of'. (3) Cf. *supra* p. 553, n. 6. (4) A second time. (5) Who saw the first payment. (6) Should she deny having had her *kethubah* paid, he presents the two witnesses in support of his claim. (7) On account of her *kethubah*. (8) Should she then deny receiving the money he may well impose upon her a Pentateuchal oath on the strength of the evidence of the first witness who was present when she received it. It is only in the case of a *kethubah* which is an hypothecary obligation (v. *supra*) that a witness cannot impose upon a defendant the Pentateuchal oath. (9) In view of the fact that the evidence of the one relates to a transaction at which the other was not present. The law of evidence demands that both witnesses testify to the same transaction. Should the woman be prepared to deny the second payment also, no Pentateuchal oath could be imposed upon her and she would thus be able to obtain a third payment also on taking a Rabbinical oath. (10) V. *supra* notes 1-8. (11) The first of which she had returned when she had received her first payment. As the first witness, who knows that the two payments were made to her in settlement of a *kethubah* would naturally corroborate her statement, the dispute would still relate to a *kethubah* and not to a loan. How then could a Pentateuchal oath be imposed upon her? (12) The two witnesses. (13) Before he makes his second payment. As the first witness would thus be aware that the second payment is made solely for the purpose of imposing upon her a Pentateuchal oath in respect of the first payment which she fraudulently denied, he would refrain from giving evidence in her favour and the man would thus be able to recover his money. Her peculiar plea that she had two *kethubahs* would naturally be disregarded in the absence of all supporting evidence.

FROM ASSIGNED PROPERTY. Elsewhere we have learned: And so also orphans cannot exact payment unless they first take an oath.[1] From whom?[2] If it be suggested, From a borrower[3] [it may be objected:] Since[4] their father would have received payment without an oath[5] should they require an oath?[6]—It is this, however, that was meant: And so also orphans cannot exact payment from orphans unless they first take an oath.[7]

R. Zeriḳa stated in the name of Rab Judah: This[8] has been taught only [in the case] where the orphans[9] stated, 'Father told us: I have borrowed and paid up'. If, however, they said, 'Father told us: I have never borrowed' [the others] cannot exact payment even if they take an oath. Raba demurred: On the contrary, wherever a man says, 'I have not borrowed', it is as if he had said, 'I have not paid'![10]—[The fact,] however, [is that] if such a statement[11] was at all made it was made in these terms: R. Zeriḳa stated in the name of Rab Judah, This[12] has been taught only [in a case] where the orphans[9] stated, 'Father told us: I have borrowed and paid up'. If, however, they said. 'Father told us: I have never borrowed', [the orphans of the creditor] may exact payment from them without an oath, because to say, 'I have not borrowed' is equivalent to saying, 'I have not paid'.

AND[13] [FROM THE PROPERTY OF] AN ABSENT HUSBAND [A WOMAN] MAY NOT RECOVER [THE PAYMENT OF HER

(1) Shebu. 45*a*. Cf. *supra* p. 548, n. 4. (2) Can they not 'exact payment etc.'. (3) Against whom they produce a bond of indebtedness bequeathed by their father. (4) Lit., 'now'. (5) As all creditors who produce a bond of indebtedness against a debtor. (6) Obviously not, since orphans would not be subject to a restriction from which their father was exempt. (7) Cf. Shebu. 47*a*. (8) That after taking an oath the orphans of a lender are entitled to receive payment of a bond they have inherited. (9) Of the borrower. (10) B.B. 6*a*, Shebu. 41*b*. If a man did not borrow he obviously did not repay; but since the bond shews that he did borrow he must obviously be ordered to pay. How then could it be said that if the orphans pleaded that their father told them that he never borrowed they are exempt from payment? (11) As the one attributed to R. Zeriḳa. (12) That the orphans cannot exact payment of a bond they have inherited unless they first take an oath. (13) V. our Mishnah. Cur. edd. add here ונפרעת. MS.M. והנפרעת.

KETHUBAH] UNLESS SHE FIRST TAKES AN OATH. R. Aḥa, the governor of the castle,[1] stated: A case[2] was once brought before R. Isaac Nappaḥa[3] at Antioch[4] and he made this statement, 'This[5] has been taught only in respect of the *kethubah* of a woman [who receives preferential treatment] in order to maintain pleasant relations[6] [between her and her husband] but not [in respect of] a creditor. Raba, however, stated in the name of R. Naḥman: Even a creditor [has been given the same privilege],[7] in order that every person shall not take his friend's money and abscond and settle in a country beyond the sea and thus [cause the creditor's] door to be shut in the face of intending borrowers.[8]

R. SIMEON RULED: WHENEVER SHE CLAIMS HER KETHUBAH etc. What is R. Simeon referring to?—R. Jeremiah replied, To this: AND[9] [FROM THE PROPERTY OF] AN ABSENT HUSBAND [A WOMAN] MAY NOT RECOVER [THE PAYMENT OF HER KETHUBAH] UNLESS SHE FIRST TAKES AN OATH [which implies that] there is no difference between [a claim] for maintenance and one for a *kethubah*;[10] and [in opposition to this ruling] R. Simeon came to lay down the rule that WHENEVER SHE CLAIMS HER KETHUBAH THE HEIRS MAY IMPOSE AN OATH UPON HER [88*b*] BUT WHERE SHE DOES NOT CLAIM HER KETHUBAH THE HEIRS CANNOT IMPOSE AN OATH UPON HER. And they[11] [in fact] differ on the same principles as those on which Ḥanan and the sons of the High Priests differed; for we learned: If a man went to a country beyond the sea and his wife claimed maintenance, she must, Ḥanan ruled, take an oath at the end[12] but not at the

(1) A surname (v. Rashi). Cf. Neh. VII, 2, where Hananiah is so described. (2) Of a claim against an absent debtor. (3) So MS.M. and BaḤ. Cur. edd. omit 'Nappaḥa'. (4) The capital of Syria, on the river Orontes. It was founded by Seleucus Nicator and was at one time named Epidaphnes. (5) That a claimant may be authorized by a court to seize the property of a defendant in the latter's absence. (6) V. *supra* p. 532, n. 11f. (7) Cf. *supra* n. 5. (8) Metaph. Undue difficulty in the collection of a debt would prevent people from risking their money in the granting of loans. (9) Cf. *supra* p. 558, n. 13. (10) For either claim the woman cannot recover from her absentee husband's property without an oath. (11) R. Simeon and the first Tanna. (12) *Sc.* when her husband dies and she claims her *kethubah*.

beginning.[1] The sons of the High Priests, however, differed from him and said that she must take an oath both at the beginning[1] and at the end.[2] R. Simeon [is thus of the same opinion] as Ḥanan while the Rabbis[3] [hold the same view] as the sons of the High Priests.

R. Shesheth demurred: Then[4] [instead of saying,] THE HEIRS MAY IMPOSE AN OATH UPON HER, it should have said, 'Beth din[5] may impose an oath upon her'!—The fact, however, is, said R. Shesheth, [that R. Simeon referred] to this:[6] If she went from her husband's grave to her father's house, or returned to her father-in-law's house but was not made administratrix, the heirs are not entitled to impose an oath upon her; but if she was made administratrix the heirs may exact an oath from her in respect of [her administration] during the subsequent period but may not exact one concerning the past;[7] and [in reference to this ruling] R. Simeon came to lay down the rule that WHENEVER SHE CLAIMS HER KETHUBAH THE HEIRS MAY EXACT AN OATH FROM HER BUT WHERE SHE DOES NOT CLAIM HER KETHUBAH THE HEIRS CANNOT IMPOSE AN OATH[8] UPON HER. And they[9] differ on the same principles as those on which Abba Saul and the Rabbis differed; for we have learned: An administrator whom the father of the orphans had appointed must take an oath,[8] but one whom the Beth din have appointed need not take an oath. Abba Saul, however, said, The rule is to be reversed: If Beth din appointed him he must take an oath but if the father of the orphans appointed him he need not take an oath.[10] R. Simeon [thus holds the same view] as Abba Saul[11] and the Rabbis [in our Mishnah hold the same view] as the Rabbis.[12] Abaye

(1) I.e., when he is still alive and she claims maintenance. (2) *Infra* 104*b*. (3) The first Tanna in our Mishnah. (4) Lit., 'that', i.e., if it is a case of a wife's claim for maintenance during her husband's lifetime. (5) The court. V. Glos. (6) The preceding Mishnah. (7) *Supra* 86*b*, q.v. for notes. (8) Affirming faithful and honest administration. (9) R. Simeon and the first Tanna. (10) Giṭ. 52*b*, q.v. for the reasons of the respective rulings. (11) Since the woman also has been appointed by the 'father of the orphans'. (12) Of the Mishnah cited.

demurred: Then[1] [rather than say,] WHEREVER SHE CLAIMS HER KETHUBAH[2] it should have said,[1] '*If*[3] she claims'.[4] The fact, however, is, said Abaye, [that R. Simeon referred] to this: [If a husband] gave to his wife an undertaking in writing, 'I renounce my claim upon you for either vow or oath', he cannot impose an oath upon her etc. [If the written undertaking read,] 'Neither I nor my heirs nor my lawful successors will have any claim upon you, or your heirs or your lawful successors for either vow or oath', neither he nor his heirs nor his lawful successors may impose an oath either upon her or upon her heirs or upon her lawful successors;[5] and [in reference to this ruling][6] R. Simeon came to lay down the rule[7] that[8] WHENEVER SHE CLAIMS HER KETHUBAH THE HEIRS MAY EXACT AN OATH FROM HER.[8]

And they[9] [consequently] differ on the same principles as those on which Abba Saul the son of Imma Miriam and the Rabbis differed,[10] R. Simeon agreeing with Abba Saul and the Rabbis [of our Mishnah] with the Rabbis.[11] R. Papa demurred: This would satisfactorily explain [the expression] WHENEVER SHE CLAIMS HER KETHUBAH.[12] What, however, can be said [in justification of] BUT WHERE SHE DOES NOT CLAIM HER KETHUBAH?[13] The fact, however, is, said R. Papa, [R. Simeon's ruling was intended] to oppose the views of both R. Eliezer and those who differed from him.[14]

(1) Since R. Simeon relaxes the law in favour of the woman. (2) Then THE HEIRS MAY IMPOSE AN OATH, an expression which implies that R. Simeon is adding a restriction. (3) I.e., *only if*. (4) 'May an oath be exacted'. 'WHENEVER SHE CLAIMS . . . THE HEIRS MAY' implies that whereas the first Tanna exempted the woman from an oath even where she claimed her *kethubah*, R. Simeon differed from him and imposed upon her an oath 'WHEREVER SHE CLAIMS'. (5) *Supra* 86*b* q.v. for notes. (6) Which exempts the woman from an oath even when she seeks to recover payment from orphans. (7) Restricting the woman's privilege. Cf. *supra* n. 2f. (8) Cf. *supra* n. 4. (9) R. Simeon and the first Tanna. (10) *Supra* 87*a*. (11) Of the Baraitha referred to. (12) Cf. *supra* note 4. The Rabbis having exempted the woman from the oath that the orphans might wish to impose upon her, R. Simeon laid down that WHEREVER etc. (13) What need was there for this statement which has no bearing on what the Rabbis have said? (14) I.e., R. Simeon differs from the views expressed in the two Mishnahs, *supra* 86*b*, and not only, as Abaye maintained, from those of the second Mishnah

MISHNAH. IF SHE[1] PRODUCED A LETTER OF DIVORCE WITHOUT A KETHUBAH[2] [89*a*] SHE IS ENTITLED TO COLLECT THE AMOUNT OF HER KETHUBAH.[3] [IF SHE, HOWEVER, PRODUCED HER] KETHUBAH WITHOUT A LETTER OF DIVORCE AND, WHILE SHE PLEADS, 'MY LETTER OF DIVORCE WAS LOST',[4] HE[5] PLEADS, 'MY QUITTANCE[6] WAS LOST', AND SO ALSO A CREDITOR WHO PRODUCED[7] A BOND OF INDEBTEDNESS THAT WAS UNACCOMPANIED BY A PROSBUL,[8] THESE[9]

only. Contrary to what has been stated in these two Mishnahs, R. Simeon laid down that a wife's liability to take an oath is not determined by the action of the husband in granting her exemption and by the terms of that exemption, but is entirely dependent on whether the woman does or does not claim her *kethubah*. (V. Rashi and Tosaf. s.v. לאפוקי *a.l.*). [On this interpretation R. Papa does not disagree with Abaye but merely adds that R. Simeon's interpretation refers also to the second clause. This is supported by MS.M. which omits: The fact is however, (lit. 'but'), said R. Papa. For other interpretations v. *Shiṭṭah Meḳubbeẓeth*].

(1) A woman who seeks to recover the amount of her *kethubah*. (2) I.e., the *written* marriage contract (v. Glos.). It is now assumed that the woman asserts that the document was lost. (3) *Sc.* the sum she claims. Should the husband plead that he already paid her that sum and that the document had been returned to him at the time and was then duly destroyed, his plea would be disregarded since the provision for a *kethubah* has the force of 'an act of a court', מעשה בית דין, and is as binding in the absence of a written document as if one had been actually in existence. Only the production of valid evidence could exempt the man from payment. Cf. B.M. 17*b*. (4) 'Before I collected my *kethubah*'. (5) The husband. (6) 'Which was given to me at the time I paid the amount of the *kethubah*'. His wife, he alleges, had produced at that time her letter of divorce only asserting that her written *kethubah* was lost. As is the procedure in such cases, he maintains, the letter of divorce was duly destroyed in order to prevent the woman from claiming therewith a second payment at another court of law, while he was furnished with a quittance as a protection for his heirs should the woman produce her *kethubah* after his death, and, denying that she was ever divorced, claim the amount of her *kethubah* as the widow of the deceased. (7) After the Sabbatical year when all debts must be released (v. Deut. XV, 2). (8) Pleading that the *prosbul* was lost, while the debtor asserts that such a document had never been made out and that he was consequently released from his debt by the Sabbatical year. פרוזבול, a form of declaration which enables a creditor to retain his rights to the collection of his debts even after the Sabbatical year. (V. Glos. and cf. Giṭ. 34*b*). (9) Lit., 'behold these'.

ARE NOT PAID. R. SIMEON B. GAMALIEL RULED: SINCE THE TIME OF DANGER[1] A WOMAN IS ENTITLED TO COLLECT HER KETHUBAH WITHOUT A LETTER OF DIVORCE AND A CREDITOR IS ENTITLED TO COLLECT [HIS DEBT] WITHOUT A PROSBUL.

GEMARA. This[2] implies [does it not] that a quittance[3] may be written;[4] for if a quittance may not be written would not the possibility have been taken into consideration that the woman might produce her *kethubah* [after her husband's death] and[5] collect therewith [a second time]?[6]—Rab replied: We are dealing[7] with a place where no *kethubah* is written.[8] Samuel, however, said: [Our Mishnah refers] also to a place where a *kethubah* is written.

May then[9] a quittance be written according to Samuel?[10]—R. Anan replied, This was explained to me by Mar Samuel:[11] Where it is the custom not to write [a *kethubah*] and [the husband] asserted, 'I have written one' it is he who must produce the proof; where it is the usage to write one and she pleads, 'He did not write one for me' it is she that must produce the proof.[12]

(1) The Hadrianic persecutions that followed the rebellion of Bar Cochba (132-135 C.E.) when all religious practices were forbidden on the penalty of death and it was hazardous to preserve a letter of divorce or a *prosbul*. (2) The ruling in our Mishnah that the amount of a *kethubah* may be collected by a woman who produces her letter of divorce only, even if, under the plea that she lost it, she does not surrender her *kethubah*. (3) In lieu of the return of the original document, such as the *kethubah* or any bond of indebtedness. (4) Despite the pleas of the defendant who objects to become the custodian of a quittance and demands the return of the original record of his obligations or, in its absence, exemption from payment. (5) As a widow (cf. *supra* p. 562, n. 6 *ad fin.*). (6) As this possibility is disregarded it follows that a quittance may well be written despite the defendant's objection. But how is this ruling to be reconciled with the accepted view of the authority (B.B. 171*b*) who holds that the defendant may rightly object to have to 'guard his quittance from mice'? (7) In our Mishnah. (8) The women relying on the general provision of the Rabbis which entitles every wife to a *kethubah*. (9) Cf. *supra* notes 2 and 3. (10) Cf. *supra* n. 9. (11) MS.M.: Samuel. (12) Samuel also is thus of the opinion that a quittance may not be written, as was laid down in B.B. 171*b*, while our Mishnah, according to his interpretation, refers both to places where

Rab[1] also withdrew from [his previously expressed opinion]. For Rab had stated: Both in a place where [a *kethubah*] is written and in one where it is not written, a letter of divorce [enables a woman to] collect her statutory[2] *kethubah* [while the written document of the] *kethubah* [enables her to] collect the additional jointure;[3] and whosoever wishes to raise any objection may come and do so.[4]

We have learned: [A WOMAN, HOWEVER, WHO PRODUCED HER] KETHUBAH WITHOUT A LETTER OF DIVORCE AND, WHILE SHE PLEADS, 'MY LETTER OF DIVORCE WAS LOST', HE PLEADS, 'MY QUITTANCE WAS LOST', AND SO ALSO A CREDITOR WHO PRODUCED A BOND OF INDEBTEDNESS WITHOUT A PROSBUL, THESE ARE NOT PAID. Now, according to Samuel[5] this statement is quite intelligible since one might interpret it as applying to a locality where it is the practice to write [no *kethubah*] and the husband pleaded, 'I did write one'. In such a case [the man] might justly be told, 'Produce your evidence', and should he fail to do so he might well be told, 'Go and pay up'.[6] According to Rab,[7] however, [the question arises,]

a *kethubah* is written as well as to those where a *kethubah* is not written. The WOMAN IS ENTITLED TO COLLECT THE AMOUNT OF HER KETHUBAH even if she fails to produce the document when, in the former case, she produced valid proof that her husband did not write one for her, and, in the latter case, where the man failed to produce valid proof that he did write one for her.

(1) Who first restricted the ruling of our Mishnah to a place where no *kethubah* is written. (2) Lit., 'root', i.e., the amount of two hundred and a hundred *zuz* to which a virgin and a widow respectively are entitled. (3) The first clause of our Mishnah thus refers to the statutory *kethubah* which may be collected with a letter of divorce, while the second clause refers to the additional jointure, both clauses applying to all localities irrespective of whether the custom of the place was to write a *kethubah* or not to write one. (4) *Sc.* no possible objection could be raised to this view, since the woman would never be able to collect more than what is her due. (5) Who allows the statutory *kethubah* as well as the additional jointure to be collected on the strength of a letter of divorce. (6) Both the additional and the statutory jointure, on the evidence of the letter of divorce. Should the woman subsequently produce a written *kethubah* without her letter of divorce, payment, as stated in our Mishnah, might justly be refused if the husband pleads that he had already paid her all that was due to her, at

granted that she[1] is not to collect her statutory *kethubah*,[2] let her at least collect the additional jointure![3]—R. Joseph replied: Here[4] we are dealing with a case where no witnesses to the divorce were present. Since [the husband] could have pleaded, 'I have not divorced her',[5] [89*b*] he is also entitled to plead, 'I have divorced her but I have already paid her the *kethubah*'.[6]

But since it was stated in the final clause, R. SIMEON B. GAMALIEL RULED: SINCE THE TIME OF DANGER A WOMAN IS ENTITLED TO COLLECT HER KETHUBAH WITHOUT A LETTER OF DIVORCE AND A CREDITOR IS ENTITLED TO COLLECT [HIS DEBT] WITHOUT A PROSBUL, [it follows that] we are dealing with a case where witnesses to the divorce are present; for had no such witnesses been present whereby could she have collected [her *kethubah*]?[7]—[The fact], however, is that the entire Mishnah represents the view of R. Simeon b. Gamaliel, but some clauses are missing, the correct reading being the following: 'NEED NOT BE PAID'. This applies only where no witnesses to the divorce are present, but if such witnesses are present she is entitled to collect her additional jointure. As to the statutory *kethubah*, if she produces her letter of divorce she may collect it, but if she does not produce her letter of divorce she may not collect it.[8] Since the time of danger, however, a woman may collect her *kethubah* even if she does not produce her letter of

the time she produced her letter of divorce, that her letter of divorce was then destroyed and that a quittance was given to him. The ruling that she NEED NOT BE PAID is consequently quite logical. (7) Who allows only the statutory *kethubah* to be collected on the production of a letter of divorce.

(1) When she produces her written *kethubah* alone. (2) Because she might have already collected it with her letter of divorce (cf. *supra* p. 564, n. 5). (3) Which is at all events due to her (cf. *supra* p. 564, n. 5). As our Mishnah, however, ruled that she NEED NOT BE PAID anything at all, an objection against Rab's view thus arises. (4) In the statement of our Mishnah under discussion. (5) And thereby procured exemption from payment of the *kethubah*. (6) His plea is accepted because by abstaining from the use of the false though convenient plea, 'I have not divorced her at all', he has established his reputation for honesty. (7) It is obvious, therefore, that witnesses were available; contrary to R. Joseph's interpretation (*supra* 89*a ad fin.*). (8) Since it is possible that she had already collected it once on the strength of her letter of divorce.

divorce, for R. SIMEON B. GAMALIEL RULED: SINCE THE TIME OF DANGER A WOMAN IS ENTITLED TO COLLECT HER KETHUBAH WITHOUT A LETTER OF DIVORCE AND A CREDITOR [IS ENTITLED TO COLLECT HIS DEBT] WITHOUT A PROSBUL'.

R. Kahana and R. Assi said to Rab: According to the ruling you have laid down that the statutory *kethubah* is collected by the letter of divorce, [the question arises,] whereby does a woman who was widowed after her marriage collect her *kethubah?* [Obviously] through the witnesses [who testify to the] death [of her husband]. Should we not, however, take into consideration the possibility that her husband might have divorced her and that she might subsequently[1] produce the letter of divorce[2] and collect[3] with it also?—[A widow may collect her *kethubah* only] if she lived with her husband.[4] But is it not possible that he might have divorced her near the time of his death?[5]—[In such a case] it is he[6] who has brought the loss upon himself.

Whereby does a woman who was widowed after her betrothal collect her *kethubah?* [Obviously] by the witnesses [who testify to the man's] death. Should we not, however, take into consideration the possibility that the man might have divorced her and that she would subsequently produce her letter of divorce and collect with it also?[7]—[This],[8] however, [is the explanation:][9] Where no other course is possible a quittance may be written.[10] For were you not to admit this [the objection might be raised even in respect of] the very witnesses [who testify to her husband's] death:[11] The possibility should be considered that the

(1) After receiving payment of her *kethubah* on the evidence of the witnesses who testified to the death of her husband. (2) Before another court. (3) Her statutory *kethubah*. (4) Where it is well known that she was not divorced by him. (5) So that the fact would remain unknown. (6) By consenting to a secret divorce. (7) The answer previously given, which well explains the case of a widow after her marriage, is inapplicable here since a betrothed man and woman do not live together. (8) And not as has been first suggested, 'where she lived with her husband'. (9) Of the difficulty pointed out by R. Kahana and R. Assi. (10) Had no quittance been allowed in such instances claimants would be deprived unjustly of their legitimate rights. (11) In localities where no *kethubah* is written.

woman might present [one pair of] witnesses to [her husband's] death before one court and so collect [her *kethubah*] and then present [another pair] before another court and collect it [again]. It must be obvious, therefore,[1] that where no other course is possible a quittance may be written.

Said Mar Ḳashisha the son of R. Ḥisda to R. Ashi: Whence is it derived that a woman who was widowed after her betrothal is entitled to a *kethubah?*[2] If it be suggested [that it may be derived] from this passage: 'A woman who was widowed or divorced either after her betrothal or after her marriage is entitled to collect all[3] [that is due to her]',[4] is it not possible [it may be retorted that this applies to a case] where the man had written a *kethubah* for her? And were you to argue, 'If he has written one for her, what need was there to tell [such an obvious rule?' It could be retorted that it serves the purpose] of rejecting the view of R. Eleazar b. Azariah who maintained that 'the man wrote the [additional jointure] for her with the sole object of marrying her'.[5] The inference too [from the Mishnah cited leads to the same conclusion].[6] For it has been stated, '[She] is entitled to collect all [that is due to her]'. Now if you agree that [this is a case where] the man had written [a *kethubah*] for her one can well understand why she 'is entitled to collect all [that is due to her]'.[7] If you submit, however, that the man did not write a *kethubah* for her,

(1) Lit., 'but it is certain'. (2) Even where the man did not write one for her. That this is the case is apparent from the previous discussion where the husband's liability has been tacitly assumed. Had not a betrothed woman been allowed a *kethubah* unless she possessed also a written document, the objection that she might collect her *kethubah* more than once could not have been advanced, since the document would have been destroyed as soon as payment had been made. (3) I.e., both her statutory *kethubah* and her additional jointure. (4) *Supra* 47*b*, 54*b*, B.M. 17*b*. (5) Cf. loc. cit., and since he died before he married her she, it might have been thought, is only entitled to her statutory *kethubah* but not to the additional jointure. Hence it was necessary for the ruling that she 'is entitled to collect all (that is due to her)'. (6) That the case dealt with is one 'where the man had actually written a *kethubah* for her'. (7) The reason being that the man had expressly promised her in writing not only the statutory *kethubah* but also the additional jointure.

what [it may be objected is the justification for the expression,] 'is entitled to collect all', seeing that she is only entitled to one hundred or two hundred[1] *zuz?*[2] [Should it,] however, [be suggested that the law[3] may be derived] from that which R. Ḥiyya b. Abin[4] taught: 'In the case of a betrothed wife[5] [a husband] is neither [subject to the laws of] *onan*[6] nor may he[7] defile himself for her,[8] and she likewise is not subject to the laws of the *onan*[9] nor is she[10] obliged[11] to defile herself for him;[12] if she died he[13] does not inherit from her though if he died she is entitled to collect the amount of her *kethubah*',[14] is it not possible [it might be retorted that this refers only to a case] where the man had written a *kethubah* for her? And should you argue, 'If he had written one for her what need was there to state [such an obvious ruling?' It might be replied that] 'it was necessary [in order to inform us that if] she died he does not inherit from her'.[15]

R. Naḥman said to R. Huna: According to Rab who laid down that a letter of divorce [enables a woman to] collect her statutory *kethubah*, is there no cause to apprehend that she might produce the letter of divorce at one court of law and collect her *kethubah* therewith and then again produce it at another court of law and

(1) One hundred if she married as a widow, and two hundred if as a virgin. (2) I.e., the statutory *kethubah* only and nothing more. (3) That a woman who was widowed after her betrothal is entitled to her *kethubah* (v. *supra* p. 567, n. 2). (4) The reading elsewhere (cf. B.M. 18*a*, Sanh. 28*b*) is 'Ammi'. (5) Before the marriage took place. (6) A mourner during the period between the death and burial of certain relatives is called *onan* (v. Glos.) and is subject to a number of restrictions. A priest whose betrothed wife died may, unlike one whose married wife died, partake of sacrificial meat or any other holy food. (7) If he is a priest. (8) Cf. Lev. XXI, 1ff. (9) She is allowed to partake of holy food. (10) Unlike a married wife whose duty it is to attend to the burial of her husband. (11) Cf. *supra* n. 10. The laws of defilement do not apply to women. Cf., however, *infra* n. 12. (12) *Aliter:* 'Nor *may* she defile herself for him', i.e., during a festival when not only priests but also Israelites and women are forbidden to attend on the corpses of those who are not their near relatives (v. R.H. 16*b*). (13) Unlike a husband who is heir to his wife (v. B.B. 111*b*). (14) Yeb. 29*b*, B.M. 18*a*. (15) Which is not obvious. And since the case where 'she died' had to be stated, the one where 'he died', though self-evident, had, by way of contrast, also to be mentioned.

collect therewith [a second time]? And should you reply that it might be torn up,[1] could she not [it may be retorted] demand, 'I need [it to be enabled] thereby[2] to marry again?—[What we do is,] we tear it up and endorse on the back of it: 'This letter of divorce has been torn by us, not because it is an invalid document but in order to prevent the woman from collecting therewith a second payment'.

MISHNAH. [A WOMAN WHO PRODUCED] TWO LETTERS OF DIVORCE AND TWO KETHUBAHS MAY[3] COLLECT PAYMENT OF THE TWO KETHUBAHS.[4] [IF SHE PRODUCES, HOWEVER,] TWO KETHUBAHS AND ONE LETTER OF DIVORCE[5] OR ONE KETHUBAH AND TWO LETTERS OF DIVORCE,[6] OR A KETHUBAH, A LETTER OF DIVORCE AND [EVIDENCE OF HER HUSBAND'S] DEATH,[7] SHE MAY COLLECT PAYMENT FOR ONE KETHUBAH ONLY, FOR ANY MAN WHO DIVORCES HIS WIFE AND THEN REMARRIES HER CONTRACTS HIS SECOND MARRIAGE ON THE CONDITION OF THE FIRST KETHUBAH.[8]

GEMARA. If she desired it, she[9] could [evidently][10] collect [payment of her *kethubah*] either with the one *kethubah* or with the other.[11] May it not then be argued that this ruling presents

(1) As soon as payment is made. (2) By using it as evidence that she had been legally divorced. (3) If the date of the first *kethubah* is earlier than that of the first divorce and that of the second *kethubah* is earlier than that of the second divorce. (4) Because it is assumed that after he had once divorced her the man had remarried her and then divorced her again. The *kethubahs* are consequently both due to her. (5) The dates of both *kethubahs* being earlier than that of the letter of divorce, so that both obviously refer to the same marriage. (6) I.e., the man married her after she had once been divorced by him, but did not write for her a second *kethubah* before he again divorced her. (7) If the order was marriage, divorce, remarriage, death. (8) I.e., that she should be entitled only to the first *kethubah*. (9) WHO PRODUCED TWO KETHUBAHS AND ONE LETTER OF DIVORCE. (10) Since our Mishnah does not specify which of the two *kethubahs* is to be used, the choice is evidently left to the woman. (11) I.e., either with the *kethubah* that bears the earlier, or with the one that bears the later date. Should she prefer to use that of the earlier date she

an objection against the ruling which R. Naḥman stated in the name of Samuel? For R. Naḥman stated in the name of Samuel: Where two bills[1] are issued one after the other[2] the latter annuls the former![3]—Has it not been stated in connection with this ruling that R. Papa said: 'R. Naḥman in fact admits that if one[4] has added in the [second] bill one palm-tree[5] [it is assumed that] he has written it[6] for the sake of that addition',[7] so also here [it is a case] where the husband has added something for her [in the second *kethubah*].[8]

Our Rabbis taught: If [a woman] produced a letter of divorce, a *kethubah* and [evidence of her husband's] death[9] [90*a*] she may, if the letter of divorce bears an earlier date than the *kethubah*,

would obviously be able to seize even such property as her husband had sold after the earlier, though prior to the later, date.

(1) Signed by the same person and referring to the same transaction. (2) *Sc.* the date on the one is later than on the other. (3) *Supra* 44*a*; and the holder of the two bills is entitled to seize only such property as the defendant had sold subsequent to the later date. This then is in contradiction, is it not, to the ruling in our Mishnah which authorizes the woman (cf. *supra* p. 569, n. 11) to make use of her earlier *kethubah*? (4) A seller or donor. (5) That was not included in the bill of the earlier date. (6) The second bill. (7) And not with the intention of annulling the first one. (8) Cf. *supra* n. 7. Hence the ruling that the woman may collect payment with either of the two *kethubahs*. She may not collect, however, with both *kethubahs* unless the second document contained a *specific insertion* to the effect that it was the husband's desire that the second one shall form an addition to the first. In the absence of such an insertion the woman may collect either (*a*) the smaller amount contained in the first *kethubah* and enjoy the right of seizing all property her husband had sold since that date or (*b*) the bigger amount in the second *kethubah* and restrict her right of seizure to such property only as had been sold after the second date. By the issue of a second *kethubah*, containing an addition to the first one without the specific insertion mentioned, a husband is assumed to have conferred upon his wife the right of *choosing* between the respective advantages and disadvantages of the two documents. Where the second *kethubah*, however, contains no addition at all, the latter document is assumed to have been intended as a cancellation of the first, since otherwise it need not have been issued, and seizure of property is restricted to the later date. (9) Claiming one *kethubah* as a divorcee from her first marriage and the other as a widow from her second marriage.

collect payment for two *kethubahs*,[1] but if the *kethubah* bears an earlier date than the letter of divorce she may collect payment of one *kethubah* only, for any man who divorces his wife and then remarries her contracts his second marriage on the condition of the first *kethubah*.

MISHNAH. [IN THE CASE OF] A MINOR WHOM HIS FATHER HAD GIVEN IN MARRIAGE, THE KETHUBAH OF HIS WIFE[2] REMAINS VALID,[3] SINCE IT IS ON THIS CONDITION THAT HE KEPT HER AS HIS WIFE. [IN THE CASE OF ONE WHO BECAME] A PROSELYTE AND HIS WIFE WITH HIM, THE KETHUBAH REMAINS VALID,[4] SINCE IT IS ON THIS CONDITION THAT HE KEPT HER AS HIS WIFE.

GEMARA. R. Huna stated: [The ruling of our Mishnah][5] was given only in respect of the *maneh*[6] or the two hundred *zuz*;[7] to the additional jointure, however, she[8] is not entitled.[9] Rab Judah, however, stated: She[10] is entitled [to receive payment for] her additional jointure also.

An objection was raised: If an additional monetary obligation was undertaken[11] the woman receives that which was added.[12] [Thus it follows, does it not, that] only if an additional monetary

(1) Since in such a case it is evident that the *kethubah* was given to her in connection with her second marriage. Her first *kethubah* she collects on the evidence of her letter of divorce. (2) The sum of two hundred *zuz* which is assigned to a virgin. (3) Even when he becomes of age, though the woman at that time is no longer a virgin. (V. Tosaf. s.v לא). The *kethubah* of a non-virgin is only one hundred *zuz*. (4) Though it was given to her before her husband became a proselyte. (5) That the wife of a minor is entitled to her *kethubah* even when he becomes of age. (6) V. Glos. (7) I.e., the statutory *kethubah* (cf. *supra* n. 3) which is a woman's due in accordance with a Rabbinical enactment and is entirely independent of the minor's will or consent. (8) The woman married to a minor. (9) Since a minor cannot legally be bound to any contract. (10) The woman who married a minor. (11) Lit., 'they renewed', *sc.* the monetary addition was undertaken by the minor after he came of age or by the intending proselyte after he had embraced Judaism. (12) Tosef. Keth. IX. It is now assumed that this refers to the additional sum only.

obligation was undertaken[1] is the woman to receive any addition[2] but if no such addition was made[3] [she does] not [receive any addition at all]?[4]—Read: '*Also* that which had been added'.[5] But surely, [in the following Baraitha] it was not taught so: 'If an additional monetary obligation was undertaken[1] the woman receives that which was added, and if no additional monetary obligation was undertaken a virgin receives two hundred *zuz* and a widow receives a *maneh*'. Is not this then an objection against Rab Judah?[6]—Rab Judah was misled by the wording of our Mishnah. He thought that the rule, 'THE KETHUBAH OF HIS WIFE REMAINS VALID', applied to the full amount;[7] but in fact it is not so. It applies to the statutory *kethubah* alone.

(1) V. p. 571, n. 11. (2) Lit., 'yes'. Cf. p. 571, n. 12. (3) After the minor came of age or the idolater had embraced Judaism. (4) An objection against Rab Judah who allows a woman even the additional jointure that a minor or an idolater may have settled upon her. (5) To the additional jointure that had been settled upon her while her husband was still an idolater or in his minority. (6) Since here it was explicitly stated that only the statutory *kethubah* may be recovered (cf. *supra* n. 4). (7) That was mentioned in the *kethubah*, i.e., the statutory *kethubah* as well as the additional jointure.

KETHUBOTH

CHAPTER X

MISHNAH. IF A MAN WAS MARRIED TO TWO WIVES AND DIED, THE FIRST [WIFE] TAKES PRECEDENCE[1] OVER THE SECOND, AND THE HEIRS[2] OF THE FIRST WIFE TAKE PRECEDENCE[3] OVER THE HEIRS OF THE SECOND. IF HE MARRIED A FIRST WIFE AND SHE DIED AND THEN HE MARRIED A SECOND WIFE AND HE HIMSELF DIED,[4] THE SECOND WIFE[5] AND HER HEIRS[6] TAKE PRECEDENCE OVER THE HEIRS OF THE FIRST WIFE.[7]

GEMARA. Since it was stated THE FIRST [WIFE] TAKES PRECEDENCE OVER THE SECOND but not 'The first wife receives payment[8] and the second does not',[9] it may be implied that if the second wife forestalled [the first] and seized [the payment of her *kethubah*] it cannot be taken away from her.[10] May it then be inferred from this ruling that if a creditor of a later date has forestalled [one of an earlier date] and distrained [on the property

(1) In respect of her claim to her *kethubah*. (2) If the women, having survived their husband, died before they had collected the payments of their *kethubahs*. (3) Cf. *supra* n. 1, *mutatis mutandis*. (4) And the sons of the first wife claim (*a*) their mother's *kethubah* to which they are entitled by virtue of the 'male children' clause (v. Mishnah *supra* 52*b*) which their father had entered in their mother's *kethubah*, or (*b*) their due share in their father's estate. (5) Who, unlike the first, has survived her husband and consequently has, in respect of her claim upon her *kethubah*, the same legal status as a creditor. (6) Who, like their mother, have the status of creditors. (7) Who predeceased her husband and consequently lost her claim to her *kethubah*, since a surviving husband is the heir of his wife, her sons' claim to her *kethubah* (v. n. 4) being treated as a claim for an inheritance (v. *supra* 55*a*) and as such must yield precedence to that of a creditor. (8) Lit., 'she has'. (9) Lit., 'has not'. (10) Since the expression of 'PRECEDENCE' only implies priority of claim but not actual and inalienable right.

of the debtor], his distraint is of legal validity?[1]—In fact it may be maintained that his distraint is of no legal validity, and as to [the phrase] TAKES PRECEDENCE, it means complete [right of seizure];[2] as we have learned: A son takes precedence over a daughter.[3]

Some there are who say: Since it was not stated, 'If the second wife forestalled [the first] and seized [the payment of her *kethubah*] it is not to be taken away from her', it may be implied that even if she has seized payment it may be taken away from her. May it then be concluded that if a creditor of a later date has forestalled [one of an earlier date] and distrained [on the property of a debtor] his distraint is of no legal validity?[4]—In fact it may be maintained that his distraint is of legal validity, only because the Tanna stated, THE SECOND WIFE AND HER HEIRS TAKE PRECEDENCE OVER THE HEIRS OF THE FIRST WIFE[5]; [90*b*] he also taught, THE FIRST WIFE TAKES PRECEDENCE OVER THE SECOND.[6]

IF A MAN MARRIED A FIRST WIFE. Three rulings may be inferred from this statement. It may be inferred that if one [wife died] during her husband's lifetime and the other after his death, [the sons of the former] are entitled to the *kethubah* of 'male children'[7] and we do not apprehend any quarrelling.[8] Whence is this inferred? Since it was stated, THE SECOND WIFE AND

(1) Lit., 'what he collected is collected'. But if this were the case there would have been no dispute on the subject *infra* 94*a*. (2) Lit., 'and what . . . he taught completely', i.e., the claim of the first wife to her *kethubah* is absolute; and, should there be no balance, the second wife would receive nothing. (3) B.B. 115*a*, where the meaning is that if there is a son he has full rights to the estate whilst a daughter has no claim of heirship upon it at all. (4) Cf. *supra* n. 1 *mutatis mutandis*. (5) Where the statement, 'If the heirs of the first forestalled the heirs of the second and seized payment it is not to be taken away from them' is inapplicable, since, in fact, it is taken away from them, the estate being mortgaged to the heirs of the second who have the status of creditors. (6) Omitting here also an expression which is inapplicable in the other case. (7) Cf. *supra* 52*b* and *supra* p. 573, n. 4. (8) Between the heirs of the second, who claim their mother's *kethubah* as creditors (cf. *supra* p. 573, n. 6) and those of the first, who claim (cf. loc. cit. n. 7) their 'male children' *kethubah* as heirs, the former disputing the right of the latter to have a larger share in the father's estate than they.

HER HEIRS TAKE PRECEDENCE OVER THE HEIRS OF THE FIRST WIFE [it follows that] they are only entitled to precedence but that if there is [a balance, the others also] take [their share]. It may also be inferred that the *kethubah* [of the second wife][1] may be regarded as the surplus[2] over the other.[3] Whence is this inferred? Since it was not stated [that payment[4] is made only] if a surplus of a *denar* remained there. Furthermore it may be inferred that a *kethubah* [claimed by virtue] of the 'male children' [clause] may not be distrained on mortgaged property;[5] for if it could be imagined that it may be distrained on mortgaged property, the sons of the first wife[6] should [be entitled to] come and distrain on [the property] of the sons of the second.[7]

To this R. Ashi demurred: Whence [these conclusions]? Might I not in fact maintain that if one [wife died] while her husband was alive, and the other after his death, [the sons of the former] are not entitled to the *kethubah* [that they claim by virtue] of the 'male children' clause, whilst the expression of[8] TAKE PRECEDENCE[9] might refer[10] to the inheritance?[11] And were you to retort:

(1) Which has the force of a debt. (2) V. Mishnah *infra* 91a. The *kethubahs* that wives' heirs receive by virtue of the 'male children' clause (*supra* 52b) is subject to a surplus of one *denar*, at least, that must remain after the *kethubahs* have been paid in full, to safeguard the application of the Pentateuchal law of succession in regard to at least part of the estate. If no such minimum surplus remains the 'male children' *kethubahs* cannot be collected and the entire estate is divided in accordance with the Pentateuchal law of succession among all the sons. (3) The *kethubah* which the heirs of the first wife claim by virtue of the 'male children' clause. The *kethubah* of the second wife which has to be paid as a debt by all the heirs (cf. *supra* p. 573, n. 5) who first inherit that amount, provides for the application of the Pentateuchal law of succession. The heirs of the first wife consequently receive their 'male children' *kethubah* and no minimum surplus of a *denar* is required as would have been the case had the second *kethubah* also been dependent on the 'male children' clause. (4) Of the 'male children' *kethubah* of the first wife. (5) I.e., it has the status of an inheritance and not that of a debt. (6) Whose claim is of an earlier date than that of the second. (7) Hence it may be inferred that their claim cannot be distrained on mortgaged property. (8) Lit., 'and what'. (9) Which implies that if there is any residue they also receive a share. (10) Lit., 'it was taught'. (11) Of their father's estate; and not to the 'male children' *kethubah*.

What was the object[1] [of the description] THE HEIRS OF THE FIRST WIFE?[2] [I might reply that] as the Tanna used the expression, THE SECOND WIFE AND HER HEIRS[3] he also spoke of THE HEIRS OF THE FIRST WIFE![4] And with reference to your conclusion that 'the *kethubah* [of the second wife] may be regarded as a surplus over the other', might I not in fact still maintain that no *kethubah* may be regarded as a surplus over the other, but here[5] it is a case where there was a surplus of a *denar!*[6]

[As to the case where] one [wife died] during her husband's lifetime and the other after his death, this is [a matter in dispute[7] between] Tannaim. For it was taught: [If a man's wives] died, one during his lifetime and the other after his death, the sons of the first wife, Ben Nannus ruled, can say to the sons of the second,[8] 'You are the sons of a creditor;[9] take your mother's *kethubah*[10] and go'.[11] R. Akiba said: The inheritance[12] has already been transferred[13] from [the sole right of inheritance by] the sons of the first wife to[14] [the joint right of inheritance by these and] the

(1) Lit., 'wherefore to me'. (2) 'OF THE FIRST WIFE' in the final clause has no point if her sons claim, not the 'male children' *kethubah* by virtue of *her* rights, but their share in their *father's* estate as *his* heirs. (3) A proper description, since it is by virtue of their mother's rights that their claim to her *kethubah* is established. (4) A mere balancing of expression which has no bearing in the latter case on the source from which their claim is derived. (5) If the PRECEDENCE spoken of refers even, as at first suggested, to the 'male children' *kethubah*. (6) Though this fact was not specifically stated in our Mishnah it may have been taken for granted in view of the ruling laid down in the following Mishnah (*infra* 91a). (7) As to whether the sons of the first wife are entitled to their mother's *kethubah* by virtue of the 'male children' clause. (8) Wherever the estate does not allow of a surplus of a *denar* above the amount of the two *kethubahs*. (9) Cf. *supra* p. 573, n. 5. (10) Which becomes due to her on the father's death, and which you inherit from her. This provides for the application of the Pentateuchal law of succession, all the heirs discharging a debt incurred by the father (cf. *supra* p. 575, n. 3). (11) The Pentateuchal law of succession having been fulfilled (v. *supra* n. 10) the sons of the first wife are entitled to the full payment of their mother's 'male children' *kethubah* out of the residue of the estate. (12) Of the *kethubah* of the first wife who predeceased her husband. (13) Lit., 'jumped', at the time the man died and was survived by his second wife. (14) Lit., 'and fell before'.

sons of the second.[1] Do they[2] not differ on the following principle: One Master[3] holds the opinion that where one [wife died] during her husband's lifetime and the other after his death [the sons of the former] are entitled to the *kethubah* [of their mother by virtue of the] 'male children' clause, and the other Master holds that where one [wife died] during a husband's lifetime and the other after his death [the sons of the former] are not entitled to the 'male children' *kethubah?*[4] Said Rabbah: I found the young scholars of the academy while they were sitting [at their studies] and arguing: All[5] [may hold the view that where] one [wife died] during her husband's lifetime and the other after his death [the sons of the former] are entitled to [their mother's] 'male children' *kethubah*, but here they[6] differ [on the principle whether the second wife's][7] *kethubah* may be regarded[8] as a surplus over the other; and the same dispute applies to [the debt] of a creditor.[9] One Master[3] holds that the [second wife's][7] *kethubah* is regarded as a surplus over the other,[8] and the same law applies to [the debt] of a creditor,[9] and the other Master holds that no one *kethubah* may be regarded as a surplus over the other, and the same law applies to [the debt] of a creditor. Thereupon I said to them: In respect of [a claim of] a creditor no one[5] disputes [the view] that [the debt] is regarded as a surplus;[10] they[2] only differ in respect of a *kethubah*.[11]

(1) I.e., the residue of the estate, remaining after the deduction of the second wife's *kethubah*, is the common inheritance of all the sons of the deceased, those of the wife who predeceased him having no claim whatsoever in respect of the 'male children' *kethubah* which is payable only where both wives predeceased their husband. (2) Ben Nannus and R. Akiba. (3) Ben Nannus. (4) V. *supra* note 1. (5) Lit., 'all the world' (v. *supra* note 2). (6) V. *supra* note 2. (7) The woman who survived her husband and whose claim has the same force as that of a creditor. (8) Where not even a *denar* remained after the claims of the two *kethubahs* had been met. (9) In the case where both wives predeceased their husband and the sons of both claim the 'male children' *kethubahs* of their mothers while the creditor lays claim to the residue. (10) And the sons of the two wives are consequently entitled to their mother's 'male children' *kethubahs* respectively. (11) Ben Nannus holds the view that the *kethubah* of a wife, who had survived her husband, has the same status as a debt and consequently (v. *supra* p. 575. n. 3) enables the sons of the first wife to collect the

To this R. Joseph demurred: If so[1] [instead of saying,] 'R. Akiba said: The inheritance has already been transferred' it should [have said,] 'If there is a surplus of a *denar* [the sons of the first wife receive their mother's *kethubah*].'[2] [The fact], however, is, said R. Joseph, that they[3] differ [on the question whether the 'male children' *kethubah* is payable where] one [wife died] during her husband's lifetime and the other after his death.[4]

These Tannaim[3] [differ on the same principle] as the following Tannaim. For it was taught: If a man married his first wife and she died and then he married his second wife and he himself died, the sons of this wife[5] may come after [her][6] death and exact their mother's *kethubah*.[7] R. Simeon ruled: If there is a surplus of one *denar*[8] both[9] receive the *kethubahs* of their mothers but if no [such surplus remains] they[9] divide [the residue][10] in equal portions. Do they[11] not differ on this principle: Whereas one Master[12]

payment of the 'male children' *kethubah* of their mother; while R. Akiba maintains that the payment of a *kethubah* is not on a par with that of any other debt; for, whereas any other debt is *paid by the heirs* to another person *after they had first inherited* that sum (v. l.c.). the amount of a *kethubah* is received by the sons themselves, in the first instance, as debtors without it having first fallen into their possession as heirs. The sons not having inherited the *kethubah*, there is no application here of the Pentateuchal law of succession. In order, therefore, that the Pentateuchal law of succession might not be superseded by the Rabbinical enactment of the 'male children' *kethubah*, it was ordained that in such a case the sons of the first wife shall lose completely their rights to the *kethubah*.

(1) That R. Akiba allows the 'male children' *kethubah* where there is a surplus. (2) The expression, however, which he actually used implies that the sons never receive their mother's *kethubah*. (3) Ben Nannus and R. Akiba. (4) As has been assumed at first (cf. *supra* p. 576, notes 7-14, and p. 577, nn. 1-4). (5) This (according to Rashi) is at present assumed to refer to the second wife who survived him and whose *kethubah* has, therefore, the status of a debt. R. Ḥan, however, reads explicitly 'the sons of the second' (v. Tosaf. *infra* 91*a* s.v. ובני). (6) V. Tosaf. l.c. (7) While the sons of the wife who predeceased her husband, as at present assumed (v. *supra* n. 5), are not entitled to their mother's *kethubah*, in virtue of the 'male children' clause. (8) After the sum of the two *kethubahs* had been deducted. (9) The sons of both wives. (10) The balance remaining after the *kethubah* of the second wife had been paid. (11) R. Simeon and the first Tanna. (12) R. Simeon.

holds that where one [wife died] during her husband's lifetime and the other after his death [the sons of the former] are entitled to the 'male children' ***kethubah***, the other Master holds that where one [wife died] during her husband's lifetime and the other after his death [the children of the former] are not entitled to the 'male children' *kethubah?*[1]—No; all[2] may agree that where one [wife died] during her husband's lifetime and the other after his death [the sons of the former] are to receive the 'male children' ***kethubah***, [91*a*] but they[2] differ here on [the question whether it is necessary for the surplus] *denar* to consist of real estate. The one Master[3] holds that only real estate is regarded as a surplus[4] but not movables[5] and the other Master[6] holds that even movables [are regarded as surplus].[7] But can you say so?[8] Have we not learned, R. Simeon ruled: Even if there was movable property[9] it is of no avail[10] unless there was landed property [of the value of] one *denar* more than [the total amount of] the two *kethubahs?*[11]—[The fact,] however, is that they[12] differ here on [the question whether] a *denar* of mortgaged property [is regarded as a surplus]. One Master[13] holds that only free property constitutes a surplus[14] but not mortgaged property, and the other Master[15] holds that mortgaged property also [constitutes a surplus]. If so,[16] [instead of stating,] 'R. Simeon ruled: *If* there is a surplus of one *denar*', should it not have been stated, '*Since* there is a surplus of one *denar*'?—The fact, however, is that they[12] differ on [the question

(1) But since the principles are the same what need was there to record two disputes on the very same principles? (2) R. Simeon and the first Tanna. (3) The first Tanna. (4) Lit., 'yes'. (5) As in the case under dispute the surplus consisted of movables the first Tanna denies the sons of the first wife all rights to their mother's *kethubah*. (6) R. Simeon. (7) Hence his ruling that where there is a surplus (even if it consists of movables) the sons of the first wife, like those of the second, are entitled to the payment of their mother's *kethubah*. (8) That R. Simeon regards movables also as a surplus. (9) Lit., 'property which has no security'. (10) As far as the calculation of a surplus is concerned. (11) V. the Mishnah *infra*. (12) R. Simeon and the first Tanna. (13) The first Tanna. (14) Lit., 'yes'. (15) R. Simeon. (16) That the Baraitha under discussion deals with a case where there is a surplus of one *denar* and that R. Simeon *relaxes* the ruling of the first Tanna by regarding that *denar* as surplus even if it represents mortgaged property.

whether a sum] less than a *denar* [constitutes a surplus]. One Master[1] is of the opinion that only a *denar* constitutes a surplus[2] but not a sum less than a *denar*, and the other Master[3] holds that even less than a *denar* [constitutes a surplus]. But did not R. Simeon, however, say 'a *denar*'? And were you to reply, 'Reverse [their views]',[4] does not the first Tanna of the Mishnah[5] [it may be retorted] also speak of a *denar*?[6]—The fact, however, [is that we must follow] on the lines of the first two explanations, and reverse [the views].[7]

Mar Zuṭra stated in the name of R. Papa: The law [is that where] one [wife died] during her husband's lifetime and the other after his death [the sons of the former] are entitled to the 'male children' *kethubah*, and that one *kethubah*[8] is regarded as the surplus over the other. [Now] granted that if we had been told that '[where] one [wife died] during her husband's lifetime and the other after his death [the sons of the former] are entitled to the "male children" *kethubah*', but had not been told that 'one *kethubah* is regarded as the surplus over the other' it might have been presumed [that the former law applied] only where the surplus amounted to a *denar* but not otherwise.[9] [Why,] however,

(1) The first Tanna. (2) Lit., 'yes'. (3) R. Simeon. (4) I.e., that in the opinion of the first Tanna the sons of the first wife are deprived of their mother's *kethubah* (cf. *supra* p. 578, n. 7) only where there is no surplus at all, but if there is one, even if of less than a *denar*, they are entitled to her *kethubah*, while according to R. Simeon they are entitled to her *kethubah* only if the surplus amounts to a *denar* (so Tosaf. s.v. וכי תימא *a.l.* contrary to Rashi). (5) *Infra*, who is in dispute with R. Simeon and who is identical with the first Tanna of the Baraitha (*supra* 90b) under discussion. (6) How then can it be suggested (cf. *supra* note 4) that the first Tanna admits a surplus of less than a *denar*? (7) Cf. *supra* note 4 *mutatis mutandis*. The first Tanna deprives the sons of the first wife of her *kethubah* only where there is no surplus at all but if there is one, even though it consists of *movables* or *mortgaged property*, they are to receive her *kethubah*, while R. Simeon allows them their mother's *kethubah* only where the *denar* surplus consists of *landed* and *free* property (cf. Tosaf. s.v. כי). The previous objection against the expressions 'if' instead of 'since' (cf. *supra* p. 579, n. 16) does not arise since R. Simeon is more restrictive than the first Tanna. (8) That is paid to the heirs of the wife who had survived her husband and whose *kethubah* has the status of a debt. (9) Lit., 'if there is a surplus of a

could we [not have] been informed [of the second law only, viz., that] 'one *kethubah* is regarded as the surplus over the other', and it would have been self-evident,[1] [would it not, that this ruling was] due to [the law that 'where] one [wife died] during her husband's lifetime and the other after his death [the sons of the former] are entitled to the "male children" *kethubah*'?[2]—If we were given the information in such a manner, [the law] might have been presumed [to apply to a case,] for instance, where a man had married three wives of whom two died during his lifetime and one after his death, and the last mentioned had given birth to a daughter who is not entitled to heirship,[3] but [not to the case where] one [wife died] during her husband's lifetime and the other after his death and the latter had given birth to a son, [since in this case] the possibility of a quarrel[4] might have to be taken into consideration,[5] hence we were taught [that even in this case one *kethubah*[6] is regarded as surplus over the other].[7]

denar, 'yes'; if not, 'not'. Hence one can well understand the necessity for the statement of the second law also.

(1) Lit., 'and I would know'. (2) Since it is such a case only, where one *kethubah* has the status of a debt, that could give rise to this law. Where both wives died during their husband's lifetime the sons of both have obviously equal rights of *inheritance* and the question of surplus to satisfy the Pentateuchal law of inheritance does not arise. (3) In respect of her father's estate. As her claim is restricted to her mother's *kethubah* alone, not being entitled to a share in the residue of her father's estate after her mother's *kethubah* had been paid, no quarrels between her and the sons of the two other wives could possibly arise on that account. Hence it is lawful for the sons whose mother's *kethubah* was larger to collect their due by pointing to the sum paid to the daughter (in settlement of her mother's *kethubah* which has the status of a *debt*) as the surplus which satisfied the Pentateuchal law of inheritance. (4) Between that son and his brothers, all of whom have the same rights to their father's estate; v. *supra* p. 574, n. 8. (5) I.e., it might have been presumed that in order to obviate such a quarrel it may have been enacted that in such a case the second *kethubah* is not regarded as a surplus and all the sons share equally, after the payment of the second *kethubah*, the residue of their father's estate. (6) V. *supra* p. 580, n. 8. (7) The possibility of a quarrel does not affect the rights of the sons of the first wife.

MISHNAH. IF A MAN WAS MARRIED TO TWO WIVES AND THEY DIED, AND SUBSEQUENTLY HE HIMSELF DIED, AND THE ORPHANS [OF ONE OF THE WIVES][1] CLAIM THEIR MOTHER'S KETHUBAH[2] [BUT THE ESTATE OF THE DECEASED HUSBAND] IS ONLY ENOUGH[3] [FOR THE SETTLEMENT OF THE] TWO KETHUBAHS[4] [ALL THE ORPHANS] RECEIVE EQUAL SHARES.[5] IF THERE WAS A SURPLUS[6] OF [A MINIMUM OF] ONE DENAR,[7] EACH GROUP OF SONS[8] RECEIVE THE KETHUBAH OF THEIR MOTHER.[9] IF THE ORPHANS [OF ONE OF THE WIVES][10] SAID, 'WE ARE OFFERING FOR OUR FATHER'S ESTATE ONE DENAR MORE [THAN THE TOTAL AMOUNT OF THE KETHUBAHS]', IN ORDER THAT THEY [MIGHT THEREBY BE ENABLED TO] TAKE THEIR MOTHER'S KETHUBAH[11] THEIR REQUEST IS DISREGARDED[12] AND[13] THE ESTATE IS [PROPERLY] VALUED AT THE BETH DIN. IF THE ESTATE INCLUDED[14] PROSPECTIVE PROPERTY,[15] IT IS NOT [REGARDED] AS [PROPERTY HELD] IN ACTUAL POSSESSION.[16] R. SIMEON RULED: EVEN IF THERE WAS MOVABLE PROPERTY[17] IT IS OF NO AVAIL[18]

(1) Whose *kethubah* was for a larger sum than that of the other. (2) As heirs of their mother, by virtue of the 'male children' clause (v. Mishnah, *supra* 52*b*); while the other heirs demand a division in equal portions on the ground that, irrespective of their mother's 'male children' *kethubahs*, as sons of the deceased they are entitled to equal shares in his estate. (3) Lit., 'and there is not there but'. (4) So that, if their demand is complied with, the brothers would be receiving their respective shares of their mother's *kethubahs* in virtue of the 'male children' clause, thus allowing no scope for the operation of the Biblical law of succession. (5) As heirs of their father with equal rights to his estate. (6) After the two *kethubahs* had been paid. (7) So that the Pentateuchal law of succession could be applied to it. (8) Lit., 'these . . . and these'. (9) And the residue of the estate (amounting to not less than one *denar*) is then divided between all the sons in equal portions. (10) V. *supra* note 1. (11) Cf. *supra* notes 4-9 and text. (12) Lit., 'they do not listen to them'. (13) Lit., 'but'. (14) Lit., 'there were there'. (15) Such, for instance, as an expected inheritance from the orphan's grandfather who survived their father, or an outstanding debt of their father's which would fall due only at some time in the future. (16) The existing estate must accordingly be divided equally amongst all the sons of the deceased though the addition of the prospective property would have provided a surplus. (17) Cf. *supra* p. 579, n. 9. (18) Cf. loc. cit. n. 10.

UNLESS THERE WAS LANDED PROPERTY [WORTH] ONE DENAR MORE THAN [THE TOTAL AMOUNT OF] THE TWO KETHUBAHS.

GEMARA. Our Rabbis taught: If one wife had[1] [a *kethubah* for] a thousand [*zuz*] and the other for five hundred, each group of sons[2] receive the *kethubah* of their mother provided a surplus of one *denar* was available; otherwise, they must divide the estate in equal proportions.

It is obvious [that if[3] the estate was] large[4] and[5] it depreciated,[6] the heirs have already[7] acquired ownership thereof.[8] What, [however, is the ruling where the estate was] small and it appreciated?[9]—Come and hear the case of the estate of the house of Bar Ẓarẓur which was small and it appreciated, and when [the heirs] came [with their suit] before R. Amram he said to them, 'It is your duty[10] to satisfy them'.[11] As they disregarded [his ruling] he said to them, 'If you will not satisfy them I will chastise you with a thorn that causes no blood to flow'.[12] Thereupon he sent them to R. Naḥman, who said to them, 'Just as [in the case where an estate was] large and it depreciated [91b] the heirs have already acquired ownership thereof, so [also where the estate was] small and it appreciated the other heirs[13] have already[14] acquired ownership thereof.[15]

(1) Lit., 'to this'. (2) Lit., 'these ... and these'. (3) At the time the father died. (4) I.e., its value exceeded the total amount of the *kethubah* by not less than a *denar*. (5) When it was valued at the court. (6) So that no surplus remained after deduction of the amounts of the *kethubahs*. (7) At the moment of their father's death, when there was a surplus (v. *supra* note 4). (8) The sons of the wife whose *kethubah* was for the larger amount are, therefore, entitled to the larger sum though at the time of the division of the property there was no longer any surplus. (9) V. *supra* notes 2-5. Are the sons who claim the larger *kethubah* now entitled to it as if the surplus had been available at the time of their father's death, or is a claim once lost never recoverable? (10) Lit., 'go'. (11) The sons of the woman whose *kethubah* was for the larger amount. (12) Metaph. He would place them under the ban. (13) Whose mother's *kethubah* was for the smaller amount. (14) At the moment their father died, when there was no surplus. (15) Cf. *supra* note 8 *mutatis mutandis*.

(Mnemonic:[1] *A thousand and a hundred duty in a* kethubah, *Jacob put up his fields by words* [*of*] *claimants.*) A man against whom there was a claim of a thousand *zuz* had two mansions each of which he sold[2] for five hundred *zuz*. The creditor thereupon came and distrained on one of them and then he was going to distrain on the other. [Whereupon the purchaser] took one thousand *zuz*, and went to [the creditor] and said to him, 'If [the one mansion] is worth to you one thousand *zuz*, well and good; but if not, take your thousand[3] *zuz* and go'.[4] Rami b. Ḥama [in dealing with the question] proposed that this case was exactly analogous to that in our Mishnah: IF THE ORPHANS [OF ONE OF THE WIVES] SAID, 'WE ARE OFFERING FOR OUR FATHER'S ESTATE ONE DENAR MORE'.[5] But Raba said to him, 'Are the two cases at all alike? There[6] the orphans[7] would be suffering a loss, but here, does the creditor suffer any loss? He only advanced a thousand *zuz* and a thousand *zuz* he receives'.

And for what amount is the *ṭirpa*[8] made out?[9]—Rabina said: For a thousand *zuz*. R. 'Awira said: For five hundred. And the law is [that the *ṭirpa* is made out] for five hundred.

A certain man against whom someone had a claim for a hundred *zuz* had two small plots of land each of which he sold[2] for fifty

(1) The words or phrases of the mnemonic correspond to striking terms in the successive rulings that follow. (2) To one person after he had incurred his debt. (3) The sum which the seller owed him. (4) I.e., 'give up both mansions'. (5) As the offer of the orphans is rejected on account of its excessive nature, so is the purchaser's demand of the excessive valuation of the one mansion also to be rejected. (6) Our Mishnah. (7) The sons of the woman whose *kethubah* was for the lesser amount. (8) טירפא (rt. טרף 'to seize'), a document issued by a court of law to a claimant (e.g., a creditor, or a purchaser on whom, as in this case, the seller's creditor has distrained) who is unable to collect his due from the defendant (in this case, the seller), authorizing him to trace his property (including any land the defendant may have sold after the liability in question had been incurred by him) for the purpose of seizing it eventually in payment of his claim. (9) Lit., 'do we write'. Where the creditor was willing to accept the one mansion from the purchaser in settlement of his claim of one thousand *zuz*, is it for the five hundred *zuz* which the purchaser has actually lost, or is it for the one thousand *zuz*, the amount of the debt he has settled?

zuz. His creditor came and distrained on one of them and then he came again to distrain on the other. [The purchaser, thereupon,] took a hundred *zuz* and went to him and said, 'If [one of the plots] is worth a hundred *zuz*[1] to you, well and good; but if not, take the one hundred *zuz* and go'.[2] R. Joseph [in considering the question] proposed to say that this was a case exactly analogous to that in our Mishnah: IF THE ORPHANS [OF ONE OF THE WIVES] SAID[3] etc. But Abaye said to him, 'Are the two cases at all alike? There the orphans would have suffered a loss, but here, what loss would [the creditor] have? He lent a hundred and receives a hundred'.

For what amount is the *ṭirpa* made out?—Rabina said: For a hundred. R. 'Awira said: For fifty. And the law is [that it is made out] for fifty.

A certain man against whom there was a claim for a hundred *zuz* died and left a small plot of land that was worth fifty *zuz*. As his creditor came and distrained on it the orphans went to him and handed to him fifty *zuz*. Thereupon he distrained on it again. When they came [with this action] before Abaye, he said to them, 'It is a moral duty incumbent upon orphans[4] to pay the debt of their father.[5] With the first payment you have performed a moral duty, and now that he has seized [the land again] his action is perfectly lawful'.[6] This ruling, however, applies only in the case where [the orphans] did not tell him,[7] 'These fifty *zuz* are for the price of the small plot of land', but if they did tell him, 'these fifty *zuz* are for the price of the small plot of land',[8] they have thereby entirely dismissed him.[9]

A certain man[10] once sold the *kethubah* of his mother[11] for a

(1) The sum which the seller owed him. (2) I.e., return both plots. (3) Cf. *supra* p. 584, nn. 5-9 *mutatis mutandis*. (4) Though such a duty cannot be enforced by a court of law. (5) As a mark of respect for his memory. (6) Since a debtor's landed property is pledged for his debts. (7) The creditor, when they paid him the first fifty *zuz*. (8) Thus pointing out that the money was not intended as a payment of the debt. (9) He cannot again seize the land which is now the absolute property of the orphans. (10) Whose mother married again after his father's death. (11) During her second husband's lifetime.

goodwill [price][1] and said to [the buyer], 'If mother comes and raises objections I shall not pay you any compensation'.[2] His mother then died having raised no objections, but he himself[3] came and objected.[4] Rami b. Ḥama [in discussing the case] proposed to decide that he[5] takes the place of his mother. Raba, however, said to him: Granted that he did not accept any responsibility for her action, did he not accept responsibility for his own action either?[6]

Rami b. Ḥama stated: If Reuben[7] sold a field to Simeon[7] without a guarantee[8] and Simeon then re-sold it to Reuben with a guarantee [92a] and Reuben's creditor[9] came and seized it from him, the law is that Simeon must proceed to offer him[10] compensation.[11] Raba, however, said to him: Granted that [Simeon] had accepted responsibility for general claims,[12] did he also accept responsibility for [claims against Reuben] himself?[13] Raba admits,

(1) טובת הנאה (cf. *supra* p. 542, n. 4). A very small price only would be paid for such a *kethubah*, the purchase of which must be in the nature of a mere speculation, since the mother might die during the lifetime of her husband who would inherit it or the son might pre-decease his mother and never come into its possession, in both of which cases the purchaser would lose all he paid. (2) Lit., 'I will not come to your rescue' (rt. פצי in Pa. 'to free', 'save', 'rescue'; 'separate by force'), i.e., he accepted no responsibility whatsoever for the safety of the money advanced. (3) As the heir of his mother. (4) Contending that as he had accepted no responsibility he may now, like his mother, himself object to the sale and thus procure the amount of the *kethubah* for himself. (5) The son. (6) Of course he did. Though he may well cancel the sale on the ground that it was invalid because it had taken place before he (the seller) was in possession of the inheritance (cf. B.M. 16*a*), he must nevertheless refund to the buyer the full price he had received whatever it may have been. (For an alternative interpretation v. Rashi *a.l.*, second explanation, and cf. Tosaf. s.v. דזבנה, *a.l.*). (7) The names of the first two sons of Jacob (cf. Gen. XXIX, 32f) are taken as fictitious names for 'seller' and 'buyer' respectively. (8) For compensation in case of distraint by a creditor. (9) By virtue of a bond the date of which was antecedent to that of the first sale. (10) Reuben. (11) As if Reuben had not been the original seller. As Simeon, who guaranteed compensation, would have to fulfil his obligation in the case of any other buyer he incurs the same liability towards Reuben who, not having given any guarantee for his sale has the same status as any other buyer. ומפצי, rt. פצי, cf. *supra* note 2. (12) Proceeding from his own creditors. (13) The answer is obviously in the negative. Simeon is undoubtedly exempt from all such claims.

however, that where Reuben inherited a field from Jacob[1] and sold it to Simeon[2] without a guarantee and Simeon then re-sold it to Reuben with a guarantee, whereupon Jacob's creditor came and seized it from him, the law is that Simeon must proceed to offer him[3] compensation.[4] What is the reason?—Jacob's creditor is regarded as any other creditor.[5]

Rami b. Ḥama [further] stated: If Reuben sold a field to Simeon with a guarantee and allowed [the price of the field] to stand[6] as a loan,[7] and when Reuben died, and his creditor came to seize it from Simeon, [the latter] satisfied him by [refunding to him the] amount,[8] the law is that Reuben's children can tell him, '[As far as] we [are concerned,] our father has left movables[9] with you, and the movables of orphans are not pledged to a creditor.'[10]

Raba remarked: If the other[11] is clever he gives them[12] a plot of land in settlement of the debt and then he collects it from them,[13] in accordance [with a ruling of] R. Naḥman who stated in the name of Rabbah b. Abbahu: If orphans collected a plot of land for their father's debt,[14] a creditor[15] may in turn collect it from them.[16]

(1) *Sc.* his father (cf. *supra* p. 586, n. 7). (2) I.e., any other person (v. loc. cit.). (3) Reuben. (4) Lit., 'and rescue him from him' (cf. *supra* p. 586, n. 2). (5) I.e., as if Jacob had been a stranger and the creditor had no claim against Reuben's *father* but against the man from whom Reuben had bought the field. Since the claim of the creditor is not *against Reuben himself* the claim against his father does not affect his right if he once sold the field without guarantee and Simeon resold it to him with a guarantee. (6) Lit., 'put up', 'established'. (7) I.e., instead of paying in cash Simeon gave him a note of indebtedness. (8) Lit., '*zuzim*', 'money', i.e., the amount of the loan which he owed to Reuben's heirs. (9) Viz., the amount of the debt. (10) Nor to the buyer who has been deprived by him of the field. Having paid a claim for which the orphans were not responsible, he must suffer the loss himself. (11) The buyer from whom the orphans now claim the price of the land which he owes. (12) The orphans. (13) By virtue of the responsibility which their father, as seller, had undertaken towards him, as buyer. Since the land comes into their possession by virtue of the debt they inherited from their father, it is deemed to be an *inheritance* which may be seized by a buyer whose purchase had been distrained on by their father's creditor. (14) Which was owing to him. (15) Who lent money to their father. (16) As if the land had been a *direct inheritance* from their father,

Rabbah[1] stated: If Reuben sold all his fields[2] to Simeon who in turn sold one field [of these] to Levi, and then Reuben's creditor appeared,[3] [the latter] may collect either from the one or from the other.[4] This law, however, applies only where [Levi] had bought [land of] medium quality, but if he bought either the best or the worst he may tell him,[5] 'It is for this reason[6] that I have taken the trouble [to buy the best or the worst because either is] land which is not available for you'.[7] And even [when he bought] medium quality the law is applicable only where [Levi] did not leave[8] medium quality of a similar nature [92*b*] but if he did leave[8] medium quality of a similar nature he may lawfully tell him,[9] 'I have left for you ample land[10] from which to collect [your debt]'.

Abaye stated: If Reuben sold a field to Simeon with a guarantee and a creditor of Reuben's came to distrain on it the law is that Reuben may proceed to litigate[11] with that creditor and [the latter] cannot say to him, 'You are no party to me'[12] for [the other can] retort, 'For whatever you will take away from him he will turn to me [to claim compensation].'[13] Others say: Even

although their acquisition of it took place after his death (cf. *supra* n. 13) as a result of the creditor's inability to meet his obligation.

(1) MS.M. reads, 'Raba', and this is also the reading in the parallel passage in B.Ḳ. 8*b*. (2) By one deed of sale (v. *infra* n. 4). (3) Claiming payment of the debt. (4) Lit., 'if he wishes he collects from this and if he wishes he etc.', i.e., either from Simeon or from Levi. Where, however, the fields were sold by Reuben under more than one deed (cf. *supra* n. 2) his creditor cannot distrain on Levi unless the field the latter had bought was the last one that Reuben had sold to Simeon. If it was not the last, Levi may refuse payment on the ground that, even after Simeon had bought that field, Reuben was still in possession of sufficient property to meet his creditor's claim, and that no creditor can distrain on property sold while free property remained in the debtor's possession. (5) The creditor who is entitled to recover his debt from the medium quality of the debtor's free, or sold property. (6) That the creditor might have no legal claim upon it. (7) Cf. *supra* n. 5. (8) With Simeon. (9) The creditor. (10) Lit., 'place'. (11) ומפצי, Cf. *supra* p. 586, n. 2. (12) Since he was distraining against Simeon and not against him who, as an uninterested party, has no right to be a pleader in the lawsuit (cf. B.Ḳ. 70*a*). (13) 'Hence I am an interested party'.

where no guarantee was given[1] the same law[2] applies, since [Reuben] may say to him,[3] 'I do not like Simeon to have any grievance against me'.

Abaye [further] stated: If Reuben sold a field to Simeon without a guarantee and there appeared against him[4] [93a] claimants[5] [disputing his title to the field][6] he[7] may withdraw before he has taken possession of it,[8] but after he had taken possession of it[9] he may no longer withdraw,[10] because [Reuben] can say to him,[7] 'You have agreed to a bag sealed with knots[11] and you got it'.[12] And from what moment is possession considered to have been effected?—As soon as he[13] sets his foot upon the landmarks.[14] Others say: Even [if the sale was made] with a guarantee the same law[15] applies, since [the seller] might say to him, 'Produce the *ṭirpa*[16] [that was issued against] you and I shall pay you'.[17]

MISHNAH. IF A MAN WHO WAS MARRIED TO THREE WIVES DIED, AND THE KETHUBAH OF ONE[18] WAS A MANEH,[19] OF THE OTHER[18] TWO HUNDRED ZUZ, AND OF THE THIRD[18] THREE HUNDRED ZUZ[20] AND THE ESTATE[21] [WAS WORTH]

(1) By Reuben to Simeon. (2) That the creditor cannot say to Reuben, 'You are no party to me'. (3) The creditor. (4) Reuben. (5) עסיקין lit., 'contestants' (v. Rashi). Others: 'disputes' (cf. Jast. s.v. עסק II). (6) *Aliter:* 'Protests against the title were issued' (v. Jast. loc. cit.). (7) Simeon. (8) If he has not yet paid for it. (9) And so legally acquired it. Legal acquisition may be effected before the price of the land had been paid, the price becoming a debt due to the seller. (10) Despite the disputes involved. (11) Rashi (B.Ḳ. 9a): A bag full of wind. (12) I.e., 'you made a purchase without proper investigation and you must bear the unpleasant consequences. (13) The buyer. (14) Of the field, to level them (v. Rashi B.M. 14b). (15) That the buyer may not withdraw after he had taken possession. (16) V. *supra* p. 584, n. 8. (17) I.e., before the court has authorized the distraint the buyer has no right to cancel the sale on the ground that he is troubled by claimants. Only when the court has given its decision in favour of the claimants, and the land was actually taken away from him, has he the right to call upon the seller for compensation. (18) Lit., 'this'. (19) A hundred *zuz* (v. Glos.). (20) And the three contracts *bore the same date*. If they bear different dates the collection of any earlier *kethubah* takes precedence over the later one. (21) Lit., 'there was'.

ONLY ONE MANEH[1] [THE SUM] IS DIVIDED EQUALLY.[2] IF THE ESTATE[3] [WAS WORTH] TWO HUNDRED ZUZ [THE CLAIMANT] OF THE MANEH RECEIVES FIFTY ZUZ[4] [AND THE CLAIMANTS RESPECTIVELY] OF THE TWO HUNDRED AND THE THREE HUNDRED ZUZ [RECEIVE EACH] THREE GOLD DENARII.[5] IF THE ESTATE[6] [WAS WORTH] THREE HUNDRED ZUZ,[7] [THE CLAIMANT] OF THE MANEH RECEIVES FIFTY ZUZ[8] AND [THE CLAIMANT] OF THE TWO HUNDRED ZUZ [RECEIVES] A MANEH[8] WHILE [THE CLAIMANT] OF THE THREE HUNDRED ZUZ [RECEIVES] SIX GOLD DENARII.[9] SIMILARLY, IF THREE PERSONS CONTRIBUTED TO A JOINT FUND[10] AND THEY HAD MADE A LOSS OR A PROFIT THEY SHARE IN THE SAME MANNER.[11]

GEMARA. [THE CLAIMANT] OF THE MANEH RECEIVES FIFTY ZUZ. Should she not be entitled to thirty-three and a third *zuz* only?[12]—Samuel replied: [Here it is a case] where the one who is entitled to the two hundred *zuz* gave a written undertaking to the woman who was entitled to one *maneh*, 'I have no claim whatsoever upon the *maneh*'.[13] But if so,[14] read the next clause: [THE CLAIMANTS RESPECTIVELY] OF THE TWO

(1) A hundred *zuz* (v. Glos.). (2) Since the three women have equal claims upon that *maneh*, the smallest *kethubah* being for no less than one *maneh*. (3) Lit., 'there was'. (4) This will be discussed in the Gemara *infra*. (5) I.e., seventy-five *zuz*. A gold *denar* = twenty-five silver *denarii* or *zuz* (v. B.M. 45*b*). The two women take equal shares in the two hundred *zuz* since the *kethubah* of either is for no less a sum and the money available is equally pledged to both. (6) Lit., 'there was'. (7) So that the first *maneh* is pledged to all the three women (cf. *supra* note 2), the second to the claimants of the two hundred and the three hundred respectively, while the third *maneh* is only pledged to the claimant of the three hundred. (8) V. *supra* note 4. (9) One hundred and fifty *zuz*. (10) Lit., 'who put into a bag' *sc*. for trading purposes. (11) In proportion to the amounts contributed. (12) I.e., a third of the first *maneh*, since she has no claim at all upon the second *maneh*. (13) Which is legally pledged to her. In that *maneh* she has only one rival claimant in the person of the woman whose *kethubah* is for three hundred. The *maneh* is consequently to be divided between the two only. (14) That the holder of the *kethubah* for the two hundred *zuz* has renounced her claim upon the first *maneh*.

HUNDRED, AND THE THREE HUNDRED ZUZ [RECEIVE EACH] THREE GOLD DENARII, [why, it may be objected, could she[1] not] tell her,[2] 'You have already renounced your claim upon[3] it'?—Because she can reply, 'I have only renounced my claim'.[4]

IF THE ESTATE [WAS WORTH] THREE HUNDRED etc. [Why should THE CLAIMANT] OF THE TWO HUNDRED ZUZ[5] RECEIVE A MANEH [when in fact] she should be entitled to seventy-five *zuz* only?[6]—Samuel replied: [Our Mishnah refers to a case] where the woman who was entitled to the three hundred *zuz* gave a written undertaking to the one who was entitled to the two hundred *zuz* and the other who was entitled to a *maneh*, 'I have no claim whatsoever upon you in respect of one *maneh*'.[7] R. Jacob of Nehar Peḳod[8] replied in the name of Rabina: The first clause deals with two acts of seizure[9] and the final clause deals with two acts of seizure.[9] 'The first clause deals with two

(1) The claimant of the three hundred *zuz*. (2) The holder of the *kethubah* for the two hundred. (3) Lit., 'you have removed yourself from'. (4) 'As far as the claimant of the *maneh* was concerned but not my legal right to a share in it', i.e., she only undertook to abstain from litigation with the claimant of the *maneh* in order to enable her thereby to obtain a half of that sum, but she had not renounced her right to a share in that *maneh* should she ever wish to assert it against the third wife, the holder of the *kethubah* for the three hundred *zuz*. She is, therefore, entitled, as far as the balance of that *maneh* is concerned, to claim a share equal to that of the third wife, which, together with her share in the second *maneh*, amounts to $(\frac{50}{2}+\frac{100}{2})$ seventy-five *zuz* or three gold *denarii*. (5) Who, as stated above, has renounced fifty *zuz* of the first *maneh*. (6) I.e., a half of the balance of fifty of the first *maneh* and a half of the second *maneh* amounting to a total of $(\frac{50}{2}+\frac{100}{2}=25+50)$ seventy-five *zuz*. The third *maneh* upon which she has no claim at all (cf. *supra* p. 590, n. 7) must, of course, be excluded from the calculations of her share. (7) While the woman whose *kethubah* was for two hundred *zuz* did not renounce any of her rights in favour of the holder of the *kethubah* for the one *maneh*. The first *maneh* is consequently divided between these two, the second *maneh* between the second and the third woman while the third *maneh* is given to the third woman only. (8) Lit., 'the river of Peḳod', a town east of Nehardea, or a district in S.E. Babylon. Peḳod is mentioned in Jer. L, 21 and Ezek. XXIII, 23. (9) I.e., the women collected the amounts mentioned in two instalments, the second of which was not available when the first was collected.

acts of seizure' viz. seventy-five *zuz* came into their hands[1] the first[2] time[3] and one hundred and twenty-five the second[2] time.[4] 'The final clause deals with two acts of seizure', viz., seventy-five came into their hands[1] the first[2] time[3] and two hundred and twenty-five the second[2] time.[5]

It was taught: This[6] is the teaching of R. Nathan. Rabbi,[7] however, said, 'I do not approve[8] of R. Nathan's views in these [cases][6] for[9] [the three wives][10] take equal shares'.[11]

SIMILARLY IF THREE PERSONS CONTRIBUTED. Samuel ruled: If two persons contributed to a joint fund,[12] one of them a *maneh*, and the other two hundred *zuz*, [93b] the profit is to be equally divided.[13]

(1) Lit., 'fell'. (2) Lit., 'one'. (3) Since each woman had a claim upon this sum the three divide it between them in equal shares, each one receiving twenty-five *zuz*. (4) The first one, having already received twenty-five *zuz*, now claims no more than seventy-five *zuz*, and since her claim to the seventy-five *zuz* is legally equal to the claims of the other two women the sum is equally divided between them and she receives a third of it, or twenty-five *zuz*, bringing up her total collection to FIFTY ZUZ. The second woman who has a claim upon the full balance of a hundred *zuz* divides the sum with the third woman each receiving fifty *zuz* which, added to the twenty-five *zuz* each received of the first *maneh*, amounts to a total of seventy-five *zuz*, or THREE GOLD DENARII. (5) Seventy-five *zuz* of these, as in the previous case (cf. *supra* n. 4), is equally divided between the three women thus allowing a total of FIFTY ZUZ for the first woman. The second one who also received twenty-five *zuz* at the first division and who still claims a balance of two hundred minus twenty-five = one hundred and seventy-five *zuz* receives twenty-five *zuz* as her share in the seventy-five *zuz* mentioned and another fifty *zuz* which is her share in the *maneh* that is equally divided between her and the third woman, thus receiving a total of twenty-five plus twenty-five plus fifty = a hundred *zuz* or a MANEH. The balance of fifty *zuz* now remaining is given to the third woman who thus receives a total of twenty-five plus twenty-five plus fifty plus fifty = one hundred and fifty = SIX GOLD DENARII. (6) The part of our Mishnah which deals with the cases of the three women. (7) R. Judah the Patriarch or Prince, compiler of the Mishnah. (8) Lit., 'see'. (9) Lit., 'but'. (10) Despite the difference in the amounts of their respective *kethubahs*. (11) The estate being equally pledged to all the three, the woman who claims the smallest amount has no less a right to it than the women who claim the bigger amounts have a right to theirs. Only in the case of contributors to a common fund are profits and losses to be

Rabbah said: It stands to reason [that Samuel's ruling applies] where an ox [was purchased][1] for ploughing and was used[2] for ploughing.[3] Where, however, an ox [was purchased] for ploughing[4] and was used[2] for slaughter[5] each of the partners[6] receives a share in proportion to his capital.[7] R. Hamnuna, however, ruled: Where an ox [was bought] for ploughing,[8] even if it was used[2] for slaughter[9] the profit must be equally divided.[10]

An objection was raised: If two persons contributed to a joint fund,[11] one of them a *maneh*, and the other, two hundred *zuz*, the profit is to be equally divided.[12] Does not this refer to an ox [bought] for ploughing and used[2] for slaughter, and [thus presenting] an objection against Rabbah?—No, it refers to an ox that was bought for ploughing and was used for ploughing.[8] What, however, [is the law where] an ox [was bought] for ploughing and used[2] for killing? Does each partner[6] [in such a case] receive a share in proportion to his capital? Then instead of stating in the final clause, 'If one man had bought [some oxen] out of his own money and the other [had bought some] out of his own money[13] and the animals were mixed up, each partner[6] receives a share in proportion to his capital',[14] could not a distinction have been made in the very same case,[15] [thus:] 'This[16] applies only where an ox was bought for ploughing and was used for ploughing, but where an ox was bought for ploughing and was

divided in proportion to the respective amounts contributed. (12) Cf. *supra* p. 590, n. 10. (13) Lit., 'for the middle'.

(1) With the joint capital. (2) Lit., 'stands'. (3) So that the share of one partner in the ox is as essential as that of the other, the animal being useless for work unless it is whole. (4) And much more so if it was purchased for slaughter. (Cf. *infra* note 7.) (5) Its value in flesh having in the meantime increased. (6) Lit., 'this . . . this'. (7) Since the carcase can be well divided. The original intention to use the animal for ploughing only (cf. *supra* note 3) does not alter the fact that in the end it was used for the purpose which admitted of division. (8) V. *supra* nn. 3 and 7. (9) Cf. *supra* n. 4 *mutatis mutandis*. (10) Lit., 'for the middle'. (11) Cf. *supra* p. 590 n. 10. (12) Tosef. Keth. X. (13) One party having bought more expensive and, therefore, much stronger animals than the other. (14) Tosef. l.c.; since stronger animals are capable of more work. (15) Spoken of in the first clause, where the two men bought an ox jointly. (16) That profits are equally divided.

used for slaughter each partner receives a share in proportion to his capital'?—It is this, in fact, that[1] was implied: 'This[2] applies only where an ox was bought for ploughing and was used for ploughing, but where an ox was bought for ploughing and was used for slaughter' the law is the same as 'if one man had bought [some oxen] out of his own money and the other [had bought some] out of his own money, and the animals were mixed up [in which case] each party receives a share in proportion to his capital'.

We learned: SIMILARLY IF THREE PERSONS CONTRIBUTED TO A JOINT FUND AND THEY MADE A LOSS OR A PROFIT THEY SHARE IN THE SAME MANNER. Does not 'THEY MADE A LOSS' mean that they made a loss on their actual transaction, and 'A PROFIT' that they made a profit on their actual transaction?[3] —R. Naḥman replied in the name of Rabbah b. Abbuha: No; they made 'A PROFIT' [owing to the issue of] new coins[4] and 'THEY MADE A LOSS' [by the deterioration of a coin into] an *istira*[5] that was only suitable for application to a bunion.[6]

MISHNAH. IF A MAN WHO WAS MARRIED TO FOUR WIVES

(1) Lit., 'thus also'. (2) That profits are equally divided. (3) Which is in contradiction to Samuel's ruling (Rashi). *Aliter:* Since it is self-evident that profits on an ox that was both bought and used for slaughter are to be divided proportionally, this ruling, being superfluous in such a case, must refer to that of an ox that was originally bought for ploughing and was only subsequently used for slaughter. Thus an objection arises against R. Hamnuna (v. Tosaf. s.v. מאי *a.l.*). (4) The older currency which the men originally invested being worth more than the new currency, so that the profit in the terms of the new currency was not made on any business transactions but on the actual coins. Since then it is the original investments that are returned to their owners the return must be in proportion to the respective original investments. Any profit, however, that is the result of business transactions is equally divided. (V. Rashi. Cf., however, Tosaf. s.v. הותירו *a.l.*) (5) A coin (v. Glos.). (6) As a cure. I.e., coins that have been withdrawn from circulation and, having lost their monetary value, are of no more use than a piece of metal. Such a loss (cf. *supra* note 4) must be borne by the two men in proportion. A trading loss, however, is, as Samuel ruled, to be equally divided.

DIED, HIS FIRST WIFE[1] TAKES PRECEDENCE[2] OVER THE SECOND, THE SECOND TAKES PRECEDENCE OVER THE THIRD AND THE THIRD OVER THE FOURTH. THE FIRST MUST TAKE AN OATH[3] [IN ORDER TO GIVE SATISFACTION] TO THE SECOND,[4] THE SECOND TO THE THIRD,[5] AND THE THIRD TO THE FOURTH,[5] WHILE THE FOURTH RECOVERS PAYMENT WITHOUT AN OATH.[6] BEN NANNUS SAID: SHOULD SHE[7] HAVE THE ADVANTAGE BECAUSE SHE IS THE LAST? SHE ALSO MAY NOT EXACT PAYMENT EXCEPT ON OATH. IF ALL [KETHUBAHS] WERE ISSUED ON THE SAME DAY THEN THE WOMAN [WHOSE KETHUBAH] PRECEDED THAT OF THE OTHER, EVEN IF ONLY BY ONE HOUR,[8] GAINS [THE FIRST RIGHT]. AND SO IT WAS THE CUSTOM IN JERUSALEM TO INSERT THE HOURS [IN SUCH DOCUMENTS]. IF ALL KETHUBAHS WERE ISSUED AT THE SAME HOUR AND THE ESTATE IS WORTH NO MORE[9] THAN A MANEH [THE WOMEN] RECEIVE EQUAL SHARES.

GEMARA. On what principle do they[10] differ?—Samuel replied: [94*a*] [Their dispute relates to a case,] for instance, where it was found that one of the fields[11] did not belong to him,[12] their point of difference[13] being the question [of the legality of the

(1) I.e., the woman whose *kethubah* bears the earliest date. (2) In respect of her claim to her *kethubah*. (3) That she had received no payments from her husband, on account of her *kethubah*, prior to his death. (4) Who might lose all her *kethubah* should no balance remain after the first had collected her due. (5) Cf. *supra* n. 4 *mutatis mutandis*. (6) If the orphans are of age. In the case of orphans who are still in their minority no one may exact payment from them except with an oath; v. *supra* 87*a*. (7) The fourth. (8) Provided the hour had been entered in the document. (9) Lit., 'and there is not there'. (10) Ben Nannus and the first Tanna. (11) Which the first three women had taken in payment of their respective *kethubahs*. (12) I.e., it was found that the deceased husband had taken it by violence from a person who might appear at any moment to claim it, and any one of the three wives, that might thus be deprived of her field, would ultimately proceed to make her claim against the field that had been reserved for the fourth wife. (13) In arguing the question whether the fourth woman may be asked by one of the other women to take an oath that she had not already collected her *kethubah* during the lifetime of their husband.

action] of a creditor of a later date who forestalled [one of an earlier date] and distrained [on the debtor's property]. The first Tanna holds that such distraint has no legal validity,[1] and Ben Nannus holds that whatever he distrained on is legally his.[2] R. Naḥman in the name of Rabbah b. Abbuha replied: Both[3] agree that the distraint [of a creditor of a later date] has no legal validity,[4] but here they differ on the question whether provision is to be made against the possibility that [the fourth woman might] allow the ground to deteriorate. One Master[5] is of the opinion that provision is to be made against the possibility that she[6] might allow the ground[7] to deteriorate,[8] and the other Master is of the opinion that no provision need be made against such a possibility. Abaye replied: The difference between them[3] is the ruling of Abaye the Elder who stated: The 'orphans' spoken of[9] are grown-ups and there is no need to say that minors[10] [are included].[11] The first Tanna[12] does not hold the view of Abaye the Elder while Ben Nannus upholds it.[13]

R. Huna stated: If two brothers or two partners had a

(1) And the creditor who holds the earlier-dated bond may consequently distrain on that property. Similarly in the case of the *kethubah* spoken of in our Mishnah, as that of the fourth woman bears the latest date, any of the other women, being in the position of earlier creditor, may distrain on her field wherever she is deprived of the field that had been allotted to her. And since the fourth may thus be deprived of her field by any of the others at any time there is no need to make sure of her claim by the imposition of an oath, and she, consequently, RECEIVES PAYMENT WITHOUT AN OATH. (2) As the fourth woman (cf. *supra* note 1) could not consequently be deprived of her field once it has been allotted to her SHE ALSO MAY NOT RECEIVE PAYMENT EXCEPT UNDER AN OATH. (3) Ben Nannus and the first Tanna. (4) Against the claims of an earlier creditor. (5) Ben Nannus. (6) The fourth woman. (7) That has been allotted to her. (8) If no oath were imposed upon her she would realize that her tenure of the property may only be temporary and would consequently exploit it to the full and neglect its amelioration. Hence the ruling that she also must take an oath before she receives payment. (9) In the Mishnah *supra* 87*a* and Shebu. 45*a*: From orphans' property she cannot recover payment except on oath. (Cf. Mishnah Giṭ. 48*b*: Payment from orphans can be received only from the poorest land). (10) Who require greater protection. (11) Cf. Giṭ. 50*a*, Shebu. 47*b*. (12) Who exempts the fourth woman from the oath. (13) Our Mishnah does not refer to the particular case which Samuel mentioned and the

lawsuit[1] against a third party[2] and one of them went with that person to law,[3] the other[4] cannot say to him,[5] 'You are not my party'[6] because[7] [the one who went to law] acted on his behalf also.[8]

R. Naḥman once visited Sura[9] and was asked what the law was in such a case.[10] He replied: This is [a case that has been stated in] our Mishnah: THE FIRST MUST TAKE AN OATH [IN ORDER TO GIVE SATISFACTION] TO THE SECOND, THE SECOND TO THE THIRD AND THE THIRD TO THE FOURTH, but it was not stated, 'the first to the third'. Now, what could be the reason?[11] Obviously[12] because [the second] has acted on her behalf also.

But are [the two cases] alike? In the latter,[13] an oath for one person is the same as an oath for a hundred,[14] but in this case[15] he[16] might well plead, 'Had I been present I would have submitted more convincing arguments'.[17] This,[18] however, applies only when he[16] was not in town [when the action was tried] but if he was in town [his plea is disregarded, since if he had any valid arguments] he ought to have come.[19]

It was stated: If two deeds[20] bearing the same date[21] [are presented in court,[22] the property in question],[23] Rab ruled, should be

oath is imposed upon the fourth woman as a protection of the orphans and not *vis-à-vis* the other women.

(1) In connection with their joint ownership. (2) Lit., 'one'. (3) And lost his case. (4) Brother or partner. (5) The third party. (6) And so demand a new trial on his share. (7) Lit., 'but'. (8) Lit., 'he did his mission'. (9) V. *supra* p. 383, n. 7. (10) Dealt with by R. Huna. (11) For exempting the first from taking an oath *vis-à-vis* the third. (12) Lit., 'not?' (13) Lit., 'there', that is our Mishnah. (14) Once the woman has declared on oath that her husband had not paid her *kethubah*, her claim to it is established irrespective of the number of women who plead that she may have been paid by her husband. (15) Lit., 'here'. (16) The brother or partner who was not present at the trial. (17) Which would have enabled him to win his case. Our Mishnah, therefore, provides no answer to the enquiry addressed to R. Naḥman. (18) That the plea, 'Had I been present etc.' is admissible. (19) To court. (20) Of a sale or a gift relating to the same property. (21) Lit., 'coming forth in one day'. (22) As the hour at which a deed was executed was not usually entered (except in Jerusalem) it cannot be determined which of the deeds is the earlier and which is the later document. (23) I.e., the property of the donor or seller respectively which the holders of the deeds claim.

divided [between the two claimants], and Samuel ruled: [The case is to be decided at] the discretion of the judges.[1] Must it be assumed that Rab follows the view of R. Meir who holds that the signatures of the witnesses make [a *Get*] effective,[2] [94b] and that Samuel follows the view of R. Eleazar who holds that the witnesses to the delivery [of a *Get*] make it effective?[3]—No, all[4] follow the view of R. Eleazar,[5] but it is the following principle on which they differ here. Rab is of the opinion that a division [between the claimants] is preferable and Samuel holds that [leaving the decision to] the discretion of the judges is preferable. But can you maintain that Rab follows the view of R. Eleazar? Surely, Rab Judah stated in the name of Rab, 'The *halachah* is in agreement with R. Eleazar in matters of divorce' [and he added,] 'When I mentioned this in Samuel's presence he said: "Also in the case of other deeds". Does not this then imply that Rab is of the opinion that in the case of deeds [the *halachah* is] not [in agreement with R. Eleazar]?'—Clearly, Rab follows the view of R. Meir and Samuel that of R. Eleazar.

An objection was raised: 'If two deeds[6] bearing the same date [are produced in court, the property in question] is to be divided. Is not this an objection against Samuel?[7]—Samuel can answer

(1) שודא דדייני, v. *supra* p. 541, n. 12. The judges are empowered to give their decision in favour of the claimant who in their opinion deserves it (so Rashi and R. Tam, Tosaf. B.B. 35*a* s.v. שודא). According to Rashb. (B.B. loc. cit.) the judges estimate which of the two claimants the seller or donor was more likely to favour. This may also be the opinion of Rashi (cf. *infra* 94*b* s.v. ושמואל *ad fin*). (2) Giṭ. 3*b*. Lit., 'the witnesses of the signature cut (the marriage union)'. In the case of a deed, too, the validity should begin on the date the signatures were attached. And since the two deeds bear the same date and no hours are specified (cf. *supra* p. 597, n. 22) the two should have the same force and there can be no other alternative but that of dividing the property equally between the two claimants. (3) Giṭ. 9*b*. The date of the signatures is immaterial. Since, therefore, it is possible that the donor or seller has delivered the one deed before he delivered the other, the judges must use their discretion in deciding which of the two claimants was the more likely to have been favoured by the deceased. (4) Lit., 'all the world', Rab and Samuel. (5) Since his ruling is the accepted law (cf. Giṭ. 86*b*). (6) V. *supra* p. 597, nn. 20-23. (7) Who maintained that it is

you: This represents the view of[1] R. Meir but I follow the view of R. Eleazar.[2]

But if this[3] represents the view of R. Meir, read the final clause: 'If he[4] wrote [a deed] for one man[5] [and then he wrote a deed for,] and delivered it to another man, the one to whom he delivered [the deed] acquires legal possession'. Now if [this[3] represents the view of] R. Meir why does he acquire possession? Did he not, in fact, lay down that the signatures of the witnesses[6] make [a *Get*] effective?[7]—This[8] [is a question which is also in dispute between] Tannaim.[9] For it was taught: And the Sages say [that the money][10] must[11] be divided,[12] while here[13] it was ruled that the trustee[14] shall use his own discretion.[15]

The mother of Rami b. Ḥama[16] gave her property in writing

left to the discretion of the judges to decide which of the claimants is to receive the property in dispute.

(1) Lit., 'this according to whom?' (2) Since Samuel has Tannaitic authority for his view he may well differ from R. Meir. (3) The Baraitha, the first clause of which has been quoted. (4) The seller or donor. (5) To whom, however, he did not deliver it until a later date (v. *infra* n. 7). (6) Not the delivery of the document. (7) And since the first deed was signed before the other, the holder of that deed should have acquired possession despite the fact that it was delivered to him after the second deed had been delivered to the other man. The Baraitha must consequently represent the view of R. Eleazar who, as is evident from the first clause, also upholds the ruling that the property in dispute must be divided. How then, in opposition to two Tannaim, could Samuel (cf. *supra* p. 598, n. 7) maintain his view? (8) The point in dispute between Rab and Samuel. (9) Cf. *supra* n. 2. (10) Which a man sent through an agent to a certain person who, however, died before the agent could deliver it to him (v. Giṭ. 14*b*). (11) If on returning the agent found that the sender also had died. (12) Between the heirs of the sender and the heirs of the payee. (13) In Babylon. (14) השליש, lit., 'the third party', i.e., the agent through whom the money was sent. The parallel passage (Giṭ. 14*b*) reads, השליח, 'the messenger'. Golds. suggests that השלי which was an abbreviation for השליח was here wrongly read השליש. (15) A ruling which is based on the same principle as that of Samuel's in respect of the judges. The ruling of the Sages is followed by Rab while that adopted by the Rabbis in Babylon is followed by Samuel. (16) Cf. B.B. 151*a* where an incident involving the same characters is recorded. The circumstances, however, are not exactly identical and the arguments involve totally different principles. The two records (v. Tosaf. s.v. אמיה) obviously deal with two different incidents.

to Rami b. Ḥama in the morning, but in the evening she gave it in writing to Mar 'Uḳba b. Ḥama.[1] Rami b. Ḥama came before R. Shesheth who confirmed him in the possession of the property. Mar 'Uḳba then appeared before R. Naḥman who similarly confirmed him in the possession of the property. R. Shesheth, thereupon, came to R. Naḥman and said to him, 'What is the reason that the Master has acted in this way?' 'And what is the reason', the other retorted, 'that the Master has acted in that way?' 'Because', the former replied, '[Rami's deed was written] first'.[2] 'Are we then', the other retorted, 'living in Jerusalem where the hours are inserted [in deeds]?'[3] 'Then why [the former asked] did the Master act in this way?'[4] '[I treated it,] the other retorted, [as a case to be decided] at the discretion of the judges'.[5] 'I too', the first said, '[treated the case as one to be decided at] the discretion of the judges'.[6] 'In the first place', the other retorted, 'I am a judge[7] and the Master is no judge, and furthermore, you did not at first come with this argument'.[8]

Two deeds [of sale][9] were once presented before R. Joseph,

(1) And it was not known to which of the two the deed was delivered first. (2) In the morning, while that of his brother was written in the evening. (3) Of course not. Since in Babylon no hours were entered in deeds it is obvious that, in accordance with the usage of the place, if two deeds were written on the same day no preference is to be given to one because it was written a few hours earlier than the other. Rami, therefore, can claim no preference over Mar 'Uḳba. (4) Since both deeds have the same force the property should have been equally divided between Rami and Mar 'Uḳba. Why was it all confirmed in the possession of the latter? (5) I.e., following the ruling of R. Eleazar that it is the witnesses to the delivery that render a deed effective, he estimated that it was Mar 'Uḳba, for whom his mother had been known to have had greater affection, to whom his deed had been delivered first. (6) And since his decision was given first, R. Naḥman should not have reversed it by relying merely on his own discretion. (7) Appointed by the Exilarch and the academy (Rashi). (8) He did not at first contend that he treated the case as one that was dependent on the discretion of the judges but submitted that Rami was entitled to the property because his deed was written first. As this submission was erroneous, since outside Jerusalem no hours were entered in deeds and the case was not tried in Jerusalem but in Babylon, his decision could well be reversed. (9) Both relating to the same field that was sold under a guarantee for indemnification.

one being dated,[1] 'On the fifth of Nisan',[2] and the other was vaguely dated, 'In Nisan'. R. Joseph confirmed the [holder of the deed which had the entry,] 'fifth of Nisan' in the possession of the property. 'And I', said the other, 'must lose?' 'You', he replied, 'are at a disadvantage, since it may be suggested that your deed was one that was written[3] on the twenty-ninth of Nisan'.[4] 'Will, then, the Master', the other asked, 'write for me [95a] a *ṭirpa*[5] [authorizing distraint on property sold][6] after the first of Iyar?'[7] 'They',[8] he replied, 'might tell you: You [are holding a deed] that was written[3] on the first of Nisan'.[9] What means of redress [can he[10] have recourse to]?[11]—They[12] write out authorizations[13] to one another.[14]

(1) Lit., 'written'. (2) The first civil month in the Hebrew calendar corresponding to March-April. (3) Lit., 'son of'. (4) I.e., the last day of the month. Hence the priority of the claim of the holder of the presumably earlier deed. (5) V. *supra* p. 584, n. 8. (6) By the same vendor. (7) The month following Nisan. Lit., 'from Iyar onwards'. However late in Nisan the deed may have been written it could not have been later than the first of the following month, and the vendee should, therefore (v. *supra* p. 600, n. 9), be entitled to distrain at least on those vendees who purchased their property from the same vendor after he had purchased his. (8) The vendees whose purchases were effected after the first of Iyar. (9) And since his deed was consequently of an earlier date than the one that was written on the 'fifth of Nisan', the holder of the latter deed was not entitled to the property which R. Joseph confirmed in his possession. 'Before distraining on our purchases', the vendees (v. *supra* n. 8) might well plead, 'claim the land which you have actually bought'. (10) The holder of the 'In Nisan' deed. (11) In view of the alternative pleadings. Should he make a claim against the holder of the deed written on the fifth of Nisan the latter could retort that 'In Nisan' meant the twenty-ninth of the month; and should he attempt to distrain on those who bought after the first of Iyar they could retort that 'In Nisan' meant the first of that month. (12) The holders of the 'In Nisan' and 'fifth of Nisan' deeds. (13) To distrain on subsequent buyers. (14) The holder of the 'In Nisan' deed is thus enabled to distrain on the subsequent vendees by virtue of his own deed or by virtue of that of the 'fifth of Nisan' held by the other. Since the vendor guaranteed to indemnify either of them he may distrain on behalf of the other if the later vendees plead that his deed was written as early as on the first of Nisan; or if, in reply to the claim of the holder of the 'fifth of Nisan' deed, they pleaded that the 'In Nisan' deed was written as late as on the twenty-ninth and that the holder of the earlier deed should consequently have distrained on him and not on them,

MISHNAH. IF A MAN WHO WAS MARRIED TO TWO WIVES SOLD HIS FIELD,[1] AND THE FIRST WIFE[2] HAD GIVEN A WRITTEN DECLARATION TO THE BUYER, 'I HAVE NO CLAIM WHATSOEVER UPON YOU', THE SECOND WIFE[3] MAY[4] DISTRAIN ON THE BUYER, AND THE FIRST WIFE[2] ON THE SECOND, AND THE BUYER ON THE FIRST WIFE,[5] AND SO THEY GO ON IN TURN UNTIL THEY ARRANGE SOME COMPROMISE BETWEEN THEM. THE SAME LAW APPLIES ALSO TO[6] A CREDITOR[7] AND TO[6] A WOMAN CREDITOR.[7]

GEMARA. What matters it even if she HAD GIVEN him A WRITTEN DECLARATION? Has it not been taught: If a man says to another, 'I have no claim whatsoever on this field, I have no concern in it and I entirely dissociate myself from it', his statement is of no effect?[8]—Here we are dealing with a case where a *ḳinyan* was executed.[9] But even if *ḳinyan* had been executed, what is the use? Could she not say, 'I merely wished to oblige my husband'?[10] Have we not, in fact, learned: If a man bought [a married woman's property][11] from her husband and then bought it also from the wife, his purchase is legally invalid.[12] Does not this[13] show clearly that the woman can plead, 'I merely wished to oblige my husband'?[10]—R. Zera replied in the name of R. Ḥisda:

who were later purchasers, he may distrain on them by virtue of his own deed.

(1) Which was pledged for the *kethubahs* of the women. (2) I.e., the woman who was married first and whose *kethubah* consequently bore the earlier date. (3) Whose claim upon the field was not in any way impaired. (4) When her husband dies. (5) Since she had renounced in his favour her claims upon that field. (6) Lit., 'and so'. (7) This is explained *infra*. (8) *Supra* 83*a* q.v. for notes, Giṭ. 77*a*. (9) Lit., 'they (*sc.* witnesses) acquired from her (on behalf of the vendee)'. Such a *ḳinyan* (as was laid down by Amemar, *supra* 83*b*) is taken to refer to the land itself and not merely to the woman's abstract renunciation. (10) *Sc.* her *ḳinyan* was not meant to be taken seriously. (11) Which (*a*) her husband inserted in her *kethubah* as a special security for the sum of that *kethubah*, apart from the general security on all his estate, or (*b*) her husband assigned to her after their wedding as special security for her *kethubah*, or (*c*) she had brought to her husband as marriage dowry and for the money value of which he had made himself responsible to her (v. B.B. 49*b* ff). (12) Giṭ. 55*b*, B.B. loc. cit. (13) The ruling that the sale is invalid.

This is no difficulty. One ruling[1] is that of R. Meir and the other[2] is that of R. Judah. For it was taught: [If a husband] drew up a deed[3] for the buyer[4] [of a field of his wife],[5] and she did not endorse it, [and then he drew up a deed] for another buyer [of a field of hers][5] and that she did endorse, she loses thereby [her claim to] her *kethubah;*[6] so R. Meir.[7] R. Judah, however, said: She may plead, 'I[8] merely meant to oblige my husband;[9] what [claim] can you have against me?'[10]

As to Rabbi,[11] however, would he allow the anonymous Mishnah here to represent the view of R. Meir and the anonymous Mishnah there[12] to represent the view of R. Judah?[13]—R. Papa replied: [Our Mishnah deals] with the case of a divorced woman,[14] and it represents the opinion of all. R. Ashi replied: Both Mishnahs[15] represent the views of R. Meir,[16] for R. Meir maintains his view[17] only there where two buyers are concerned,[18] since in such a case she may well be told, 'If you wished to oblige, you should have done so in the case of the first buyer',[19] but where only one buyer [is concerned], even R. Meir admits [that the sale is invalid],[20]

(1) That of our Mishnah. (2) The ruling that the sale is invalid. (3) Lit., 'he wrote'. (4) Lit., 'for the first'. (5) V. *supra* p. 602, n. 11. (6) If her husband has no free property left. She cannot recover her *kethubah* even from the first buyer since he might plead that when he had bought his field her husband was still left in the possession of that field which he subsequently sold to the second purchaser. (7) Because by refusing to endorse the first deed she made it clear that she had no desire to please her husband. Her action in endorsing the second deed may, therefore, be regarded as the true expression of her consent to the sale and her earnest renunciation of her claim upon the property. (8) In endorsing the second deed. (9) Cf. *supra* p. 602, n. 10. (10) Surely none. She is, therefore, entitled to recover her *kethubah* from the second buyer. (11) R. Judah the Patriarch, the Redactor of the Mishnah. (12) Giṭ. 55*b* just cited. (13) Since the *halachah* agrees as a rule with the anonymous Mishnah a contradiction would arise. (14) Who renounced her rights to the purchased field after she had been divorced, so that the plea of obliging her husband is clearly inadmissible. (15) Lit., 'all of it', our Mishnah as well as the one in Giṭ. 55*b*. (16) Both dealing with a woman who was still living with her husband. (17) That the woman loses her *kethubah*. (18) As was specifically mentioned in that Baraitha. Cf. *supra* note 7. (19) As she had not done it she cannot now plead that her object was to oblige her husband. (20) Since she may plead that she merely wished to oblige her husband.

while our Mishnah[1] [refers to a case] where [the husband had first] written out a deed for another buyer.[2]

Elsewhere we learned: Payment cannot be recovered from mortgaged property where free assets are available, even if they are only of the poorest quality.[3] The question was raised: If the free assets were blasted[4] may the mortgaged property be distrained on?—Come and hear: [If a husband] drew up a deed for the buyer [of a field of his wife] and she did not endorse it [and then he drew up a deed] for another buyer [of a field of hers] and that she did endorse, she loses thereby [her claim to] her *kethubah;* so R. Meir.[5] Now, if it could be imagined that where the free assets were blasted the mortgaged property may be distrained on [the difficulty would arise:] Granted that she lost [her right to recover] her *kethubah* from the second buyer,[6] why[7] should she not be entitled[8] to recover it, at any rate, from the first buyer?[9] —Said R. Naḥman b. Isaac:[10] The meaning of 'she loses' is that she loses [her right to recover her due] from the second buyer.[11] Said Raba: Two objections may be raised against this explanation:[12] In the first place [it may be pointed out] that [the expression of] 'she loses' implies total loss. And, furthermore, it was taught: If a man borrowed from one person and sold his property to two others, and the creditor gave a written declaration to the second buyer, 'I have no claim whatever upon you', [this creditor] has no claim whatever upon the first buyer, since the latter can tell him, 'I have left you[13] a source[14] from which to recover your

(1) Which regards the woman's renunciation as valid. (2) Whose deed she refused to endorse. Cf. *supra* p. 603, n. 7. (3) Giṭ. 48*b*. (4) After the sale of the others. (5) Cf. *supra* p. 603 notes. (6) On account of her endorsement of his purchase. (7) Since her first source of payment was no longer available. (8) As in the case of free assets that were blasted. (9) Whose purchase corresponds to the 'mortgaged property' referred to in the enquiry. Since, however, she is not allowed to distrain on the first it follows, does it not, that even if the free assets were blasted, payment cannot be recovered from mortgaged property. (10) The Baraitha quoted provides no solution to the question. (11) Her right to recover her *kethubah* from the first buyer, however, remains unimpaired. (12) Which R. Naḥman b. Isaac advanced. (13) 'When I purchased the first field'. (14) The field which the second buyer had subsequently purchased.

debt'![1]—There,[2] [it may be argued[3] that] it was he[4] who had deliberately caused the loss to himself.[5]

Said R. Yemar to R. Ashi: [95*b*] This,[6] surely, is the regular practice[7] [of the courts of law]? For did not a man once pledge a vineyard to his friend for ten years[8] but it aged after five years,[9] and [when the creditor] came to the Rabbis[10] they wrote out

(1) Similarly in the case of the woman, her *kethubah* cannot be recovered from the first buyer who might well plead that he too had left her a source from which to collect her *kethubah*. R. Naḥman b. Isaac's explanation thus stands refuted by two objections. (2) In the Baraitha cited by Raba. (3) In justification of R. Naḥman b. Isaac's explanation. So according to R. Tam and R. Ḥan (v. Tosaf. s.v. התם, *a.l.*), contrary to Rashi who regards what follows as the conclusion of Raba's arguments, v. *infra* n. 5. (4) The creditor. (5) By signing the declaration in favour of the second buyer though he was well aware that by this act he loses the only source available for the recovery of his debt. In the case of a woman, however, whose *kethubah* does not fall due for payment until *after the death* of her husband, it may well be maintained that the renunciation of her rights in favour of the second buyer, during the *lifetime* of her husband, was not regarded by her as of any practical consequence, and the loss ultimately ensuing cannot, therefore, be said to have been *deliberately* caused by herself. As the two cases are not analogous R. Naḥman b. Isaac's explanation stands unrefuted. The first objection raised by Raba remains unanswered as happens sometimes in such Talmudic discussions where only the second of two objections is dealt with. Moreover the first objection is rather feeble and may well be met by the reply that the expression 'she loses' need not necessarily imply *total* loss (so Tosaf. loc. cit.), According to Rashi 'There . . . himself', is taken by Raba as an argument against the solution of the problem that was attempted by inference from the first Baraitha, and might also be inferred from the last one quoted (cf. Golds.). 'There', i.e., in the cases dealt with in the last Baraithas, the argument runs, 'it was he', i.e., the claimant (the woman in the first case and the creditor in the second) 'who had caused the loss to himself'; and no inference can, therefore, be drawn from either of these cases in respect of the one referred to in the question where the claimant is in no way responsible for the loss of the free assets. (6) To allow creditors to distrain on mortgaged property wherever free assets are blasted. (7) Lit., 'and, surely, actions every day'. (8) The terms entered in the mortgage deed being that the creditor was to enjoy the usufruct of the vineyard during the ten years, in payment of his loan, while the vineyard itself was to return to the debtor at the end of that period without any further payment or obligation on his part. (9) I.e., ceased yielding produce before the creditor had recouped himself in full. (10) To claim the balance of the loan.

a *ṭirpa*[1] for him?[2]—There[3] also it was they[4] who caused the loss to themselves. For, having been aware that it may happen that a vineyard should age,[5] they should not have bought [any of the debtor's pledged land].[6] The law, however, is that where free assets are blasted, mortgaged property may be distrained on.

Abaye ruled: [If a man said to a woman][7] 'My estate shall be yours and after you [it shall be given] to So-and-so', and then the woman[8] married, her husband has the status of a vendee and her successor[9] has no legal claim[10] in face[11] of her husband. In agreement with whose view [was Abaye's ruling laid down]?—In agreement with the following Tanna.[12] For it has been taught: [If one man said to another,] 'My estate shall be yours and after you [it shall be given] to So-and-so' and the first recipient went down [into the estate] and sold it, the second may reclaim the estate[13] from those who bought it; so Rabbi. R. Simeon b. Gamaliel ruled: The second may receive only that which the first has left.[14] But could Abaye have laid down such a ruling? Did not Abaye in fact, say, 'Who is a cunning rogue? He who counsels[15] to sell[16] an estate[17] in accordance with the ruling of

(1) V. *supra* p. 584, n. 8. (2) And thereby enabled him to distrain on all property which the debtor had sold after the date on which the mortgage deed was written. This being the regular practice in the administration of the law, why was the question, *supra* 95*a*, at all raised? (3) The case just cited. (4) Who purchased the lands from the debtor though they were well aware that these were already pledged to the mortgagee of the vineyard. (5) And that this might happen before the expiry of the ten years in consequence of which the creditor would naturally distrain on the debtor's remaining property. (6) Having bought it they have only themselves to blame for the consequences. The regular practice of the courts in such actions has, therefore, no bearing on the case referred to in the question. (7) Who (as will be explained *infra*) was *feme sole*. (8) Lit., 'and stood up'. (9) Lit., 'to after you'. (10) Lit., 'nothing'. (11) Lit., 'place'. (12) R. Simeon b. Gamaliel. (13) After the death of the first donee who, by the terms of the gift, was entitled to the usufruct during his lifetime only but had no right to sell the estate itself. (14) B.B. 137*a*; and since the first has sold the estate the second has no rightful claim upon it. (15) So Rashb. (B.B. 137*a*). *Aliter:* Who takes counsel with himself (R. Gersh.). (16) And much more so one who sells (so according to Rashb. v. *supra* n. 15). (17) Which was given to a person with the stipulation that after his death it shall pass over to another person.

R. Simeon b. Gamaliel?[1]—Did he say, 'She *may* marry'?[2] All he said was, 'The woman married'.[3]

Abaye further stated: [If a man said to a woman,][4] 'My estate shall be yours and after you [it shall be given] to So-and-so' and the woman sold [the estate] and died, her husband[5] may seize it from the buyer, the woman's successor[6] [may seize it] from the husband,[7] and the buyer from the successor,[8] and all the estate is confirmed in the possession of the buyer.[9] But why should this case be different from the following where we learned: AND SO THEY GO ON IN TURN UNTIL THEY ARRANGE SOME COMPROMISE BETWEEN THEM?—There they are all suffering some loss[10] but here it is only the buyer who suffers the loss.[11]

Rafram went to R. Ashi and recited this argument to him: Could Abaye have laid down such a ruling?[12] Did he not, in fact, lay down: [If a man said to a woman,] 'My estate shall be yours and after you [it shall be given] to So-and-so', and then the woman

(1) Soṭah 21*b*, B.B. loc. cit. Though such a sale is morally wrong, since the donor meant the second donee to have the estate after the death of the first, it is nevertheless quite legal on the basis of the ruling of R. Simeon b. Gamaliel. Now since Abaye condemns the person who acts on the ruling of R. Simeon b. Gamaliel, would he himself base a ruling of his on this view of R. Simeon b. Gamaliel? (2) Which would have implied approval. (3) A *fait accompli*. Her action, however, though legal, is nevertheless condemned by Abaye as morally wrong. (4) Who (v. *infra*) was married. (5) Who has the status of a first buyer. (6) Cf. *supra* p. 606, n. 9. (7) Because, unlike the previous case where the woman of whom Abaye spoke was unmarried, the woman in this case (v. *supra* n. 4) was married at the time the estate was presented to her and her successor. Her husband who was not in any way mentioned by the donor is, therefore, deemed to have been implicitly excluded by the donor from all rights to, or claim upon, the estate. (8) In agreement with the ruling of R. Simeon b. Gamaliel that the first donee has the right to sell the estate. (9) It cannot again be taken away from him by the husband, since his present tenure of the estate is no longer based upon his rights as a buyer from the married woman but upon the rights derived from her successor. In the former case the husband as 'first buyer' (v. *supra* note 5) would have had right of seizure. In the latter case he has none. (10) The buyer loses some of his purchase money and the women lose portions of their *kethubah*. (11) The husband and the donees are only claiming a gift. (12) That all the estate is confirmed in the possession of the buyer.

married, her husband has the status of a vendee, and her successor has no legal claim in face of her husband?[1]—The other replied: There [it is a woman] to whom he[2] spoke while she was *feme sole*,[3] but here [we are dealing with one] to whom he[2] spoke when she was married.[4] For it is this that he meant to tell[5] her? 'Your successor only shall acquire possession; your husband shall not'.[6]

THE SAME LAW APPLIES ALSO TO A CREDITOR. A Tanna taught:[7] The same law applies to[8] a creditor and two buyers[9] and also to a woman, who was a creditor,[10] and two buyers.[11]

(1) Cf. *supra* p. 606, n. 7 and 9. (2) The donor. (3) Cf. *supra* p. 606, n. 7. (4) Cf. *supra* p. 607, n. 4. (5) Lit., 'what did he (mean) to say?' (6) Cf. *supra* 607, n. 7. (7) In explanation of our Mishnah. (8) Lit., 'and so'. (9) The *total* value of whose purchases from the debtor represents the amount of the debt. The creditor, if he renounced his claim to the extent of that portion of the debt that was secured on the second buyer's purchase, may distrain on the purchases of the first buyer who in turn distrains on the second buyer (whose purchase was that of property that was already pledged to the first in security of his purchase) who in turn distrains on the creditor (by virtue of his renunciation); and so they go on in turn until a compromise is arranged. (10) *Sc.* who claims the amount of her *kethubah*. (11) Cf. *supra* n. 9 *mutatis mutandis*.

KETHUBOTH

CHAPTER XI

MISHNAH. A WIDOW IS TO BE MAINTAINED OUT OF THE ESTATE OF [HER DECEASED HUSBAND'S] ORPHANS [AND] HER HANDIWORK BELONGS TO THEM. IT IS NOT THEIR DUTY, HOWEVER, TO BURY HER; IT IS THE DUTY OF HER HEIRS, EVEN THOSE WHO INHERIT HER KETHUBAH, TO BURY HER.

GEMARA. The question was asked: Have we learnt,[1] 'is to be maintained'[2] or 'one who is maintained'?[3] Have we learned, 'is to be maintained', in agreement with the men of Galilee,[4] so that there is no way[5] [by which the orphans] can avoid[6] maintaining her; or have we rather learned 'one who is maintained',[3] in agreement with the men of Judaea,[7] so that [the orphans,] if they wish it, need not[8] maintain her? [96*a*]—Come and hear what[9] R. Zera stated in the name of Samuel:[10] 'The find of a widow belongs to herself'. Now if you grant that what we learnt[1] was, 'one who is maintained' [this ruling is] quite justified,[11] but if you insist that what we learnt[1] was 'is to be maintained'[12] [why,[13] it

(1) In our Mishnah. (2) ניזונת, *sc.* the reading given *supra.* (3) הניזונת in which case the Mishnah means that only the handiwork of a widow, who is maintained by the orphans, belongs to them. (4) Who entered in the *kethubah* the clause: 'You shall dwell in my house and be maintained therein out of my estate throughout the duration of your widowhood' (v. Mishnah *supra* 52*b*). (5) 'To go' (cf. Jast.). (6) *Aliter:* There is no possibility of avoiding (cf. Levy). (7) Who added to the clause mentioned (*supra* n. 4), 'Until the heirs may consent to pay you your *kethubah*' (Mishnah, *supra* 52*b*). (8) If they had paid her the *kethubah.* (9) So MS.M. reading דאמר. Cur. edd. omit the *daleth.* (10) Alfasi and Asheri omitting, 'R. Zera stated' read 'Samuel stated'. (11) Our Mishnah representing the view of the men of Judaea, Samuel's ruling might be applied to a widow who (v. *supra* note 7) was not maintained by the orphans. (12) In agreement with the men of Galilee who allow the orphans no alternative. (13) In view of the fact that they must always maintain the widow as a husband must always maintain his wife.

might be objected, should they not] have the same rights as a husband, and just as in the latter case[1] a wife's find belongs to her husband, so in the former case[2] also the find of the woman[3] should belong to the heirs?[4]—I may still insist that what we have learnt[5] was 'is to be maintained'; for the reason why[6] the Rabbis have ordained that the find of a wife belonged to her husband is in order that he shall bear no grudge[7] against her, but as regards these[8] let them bear the grudge.[9]

R. Jose b. Ḥanina ruled: All manner of work which a wife must render to her husband[10] a widow must render to the orphans, with the exception of serving one's drinks,[11] making ready one's bed and washing one's face, hands or feet.[12]

R. Joshua b. Levi ruled: All manner of service that a slave must render to his master a student must render to his teacher, except that of taking off his[13] shoe.[14] Raba explained: This ruling[15] applies only to a place where he[16] is not known, but where he is known there can be no objection.[17] R. Ashi said: Even where he[16] is not known the ruling[15] applies only where he does not put on *tefillin*[18] but where he puts on *tefillin*, he may well perform such a service.[17]

R. Ḥiyya b. Abba stated in the name of R. Joḥanan. A man who deprives his student of [the privilege of] attending on him acts as if he had deprived him of [an act of] kindness, for it is said

(1) Lit., 'husband'. (2) Lit., 'here', *sc.* the case referred to by Samuel. (3) I.e., the widow. (4) As Samuel, however, ruled that it belongs to herself it must be concluded that the reading in our Mishnah is, 'one who is maintained'. (5) In our Mishnah. (6) Lit., 'what'. (7) איבה 'enmity'. (8) The orphans who are legally bound to maintain her. (9) It is only the handiwork of the widow that belongs to the orphans, in return for the maintenance she receives from them, as the handiwork of a wife, for a similar reason, belongs to her husband. (10) V. *supra* 59*b*. (11) Lit., 'mixing (the drink in his) cup'. Rt. מזג, to mix with water (to weaken its strength) or spices. (12) These are intimate services to which a husband only is entitled. (13) Lit., 'loosening', 'undoing'. (14) Only a Canaanite slave performs this menial service, and a student performing it might be mistaken for such a slave. (15) That a student should not assist his teacher in taking off his shoes. (16) The student. (17) Lit., 'we have nothing against it'. (18) V. Glos. As slaves also do not wear *tefillin* (v. Giṭ. 40*a*), his status might well be mistaken.

in Scripture, *To him that deprives*[1] *his friend*[2] *of kindness.*[3] R. Naḥman b. Isaac said: He also deprives[4] him of the fear of heaven, for it is said in Scripture, *And he forsaketh the fear of the Almighty.*[5]

R. Eleazar ruled: If a widow[6] seized movables [to provide] for her maintenance, her act is[7] valid.[8] So it was also taught: If a widow seized movables [to provide] for her maintenance, her act is[7] valid.[8] And so R. Dimi, when he came,[9] related: It once happened that the daughter-in-law of R. Shabbethai seized[10] a saddle bag[11] that was full of money,[12] and the Sages had no power to take it out of her possession.

Rabina ruled: This[13] applies only to maintenance but [movables seized] in payment of a *kethubah* may be taken away from her. Mar son of R. Ashi demurred: Wherein [is the case of seizure] for a *kethubah* different [from the other]? Is it because [the former may be distrained for] on landed property and not on movables, may not maintenance also, [it may be objected, be distrained] on landed property and not on movables? The fact, however, is that as in respect of maintenance seizure[7] is valid,[8] so it is also valid in respect of a *kethubah*.

Said R. Isaac b. Naphtali to Rabina: Thus, in agreement with your view, it has also been stated in the name of Raba.

R. Joḥanan stated in the name of R. Jose b. Zimra: A widow who allowed two or three years to pass[14] before[15] she claimed maintenance loses her maintenance. Now [that it has been said that] she loses [her maintenance after] two years, was it necessary

(1) למסס, rt. מסס 'to melt'. (2) *Sc.* the student one teaches. (3) Job VI, 14. The previous verse speaks of *help* which is homiletically applied to that of the student to his teacher. R.V. renders v. 14, *To him that is ready to faint kindness should be shewed from his friend. 'Should be shewed'* is changed by A.J.V. to '*is due*'. (4) Lit., 'breaks off'. (5) Job VI, 14; E.V., *Even to him that forsaketh* etc. [Personal attendance on scholars constitutes in itself a good education in righteous conduct and fear of the Almighty, v. Ber. 7*b*]. (6) Whose maintenance may be distrained for on landed property only (v. *supra* 69*b*). (7) *Ex post facto*. (8) Lit., 'what she seized she seized'. (9) From Palestine to Babylon. (10) From the estate of her deceased husband. (11) דסקיא, Gr. *δισάκκιον*, a bag made up of two pouches. (12) For her maintenance. (13) That the seizure of movables by a widow is *ex post facto* valid. (14) Lit., 'who delayed'. (15) Lit., 'and not'.

[to mention also] three?—This is no difficulty; the lesser number[1] refers to a poor woman while the bigger one[1] refers to a rich woman;[2] or else: The former[1] refers to a bold woman and the latter[1] to a modest woman.[3] Raba ruled: This[4] applies only to a retrospective claim,[5] but in respect of the future she is entitled [to maintenance].

R. Johanan enquired: If the orphans plead, 'We have already paid[6] [the cost of maintenance[7] in advance]', and she retorts, 'I did not receive it', who must produce the proof? [96b] Is the estate [of the deceased man] in the presumptive possession of the orphans[8] and consequently it is the widow who must produce the proof, or is the estate rather in the presumptive possession of the widow[9] and the proof must be produced by the orphans? Come and hear what Levi taught: [In a dispute on the maintenance of] a widow, the orphans must produce the proof[10] so long as she is unmarried,[11] but if she was married[12] the proof must be produced by her.[13]

R. Shimi b. Ashi said: [This point[14] is a matter in dispute between] the following[15] Tannaim: She[16] may sell [portions of her deceased husband's estate] but should specify in writing,[17] 'These I have sold for maintenance,' and 'These I have sold for the *kethubah*' [as the case may be]; so R. Judah. R. Jose, however, ruled: She[18] may sell [such portions] and need not specify the purpose[19] in writing, for in this manner she gains an advantage.[20]

(1) Lit., 'here'. (2) Who is able to live for a considerable time on her own means. Such a woman cannot be assumed to have surrendered her right to maintenance before a period of three years had elapsed. (3) Who is too shy to litigate or to go to court. Cf. *supra* n. 2 second clause. (4) The loss of maintenance. (5) For the time that has passed. (6) To the widow. (7) For the ensuing year. (8) Who are his legal heirs. (9) To whom it is pledged in accordance with an enactment of the Rabbis. (10) That they have paid her in advance. (11) Since the estate is pledged to her (v. *supra* n. 9). (12) And claims the cost of her maintenance for the time past. (13) Having married she loses the security of her former husband's estate. (14) The question of the presumptive ownership of the deceased man's estate. (15) Lit., 'as', 'like'. (16) A widow. (17) In the deeds of sale. (18) A widow. (19) Whether it was maintenance or *kethubah*. (20) Lit., 'her power is beautiful', as will be explained anon.

They[1] thus apparently[2] differ on the following point: R. Judah, who ruled that it is necessary to specify[3] the purpose,[4] holds that the [deceased man's] estate is in the presumptive possession of the orphans and that it is the widow who must produce the proof,[5] whilst R. Jose, who ruled that it was not necessary to specify the purpose, upholds the view that the estate is in the presumptive possession of the widow and that it is the orphans who must produce the proof.[6] Whence [is this[7] made so obvious]? It is quite possible that all[1] agree that the [deceased man's] estate is in the presumptive possession of his widow and that the orphans must produce the proof,[8] but R. Judah[9] is merely tendering good advice [by following which the widow] would prevent people from calling[10] her a glutton.[11] For were you not to admit this,[12] could not the question[13] raised by R. Joḥanan[14] be answered

(1) R. Judah and R. Jose. (2) Lit., 'what not'? (3) In the deeds of sale. (4) Whether it was maintenance or *kethubah*. (5) That she has not been paid the cost of maintenance. Hence it is to her advantage that the purpose of the sale should be specified. Should she fail to do so, the orphans, when she comes to claim her *kethubah* from them, might refuse payment on the ground that her sale had the purpose of recouping her for her *kethubah*. Her alternative plea, 'If so, pay me for my maintenance' could be met by the counter plea that they had already paid for it in movables, a plea which, when coming from orphans, the court must accept. (6) A specification of the purpose, therefore, would bring no advantage to her. Its omission, on the other hand, might well prove advantageous in the case where the deceased man's estate was completely consumed by the orphans and the widow had recourse to distraining on landed property which he sold during his lifetime. Submitting that her own sales had the purpose of providing for her maintenance she may legally distrain on such property which is pledged for her *kethubah*. Had she, however, specified that her sales had the purpose of recovering her *kethubah* she could no longer distrain on her husband's sold property which (v. Giṭ. 48*b*) is not pledged for her maintenance. (7) The conclusion of R. Shimi. (8) That the widow had already received the allowance for her maintenance. (9) In ruling that the widow should specify the purpose for which her sales are made. (10) Lit., 'that they shall not call'. (11) Were she to omit from the deed of sale the mention of her *kethubah* people might assume that all the proceeds of her sales were spent on her maintenance alone. As a reputed glutton her chances of a second marriage would be diminished (v. Rashi). (12) Lit., 'say so', that R. Judah in his ruling is merely tendering advice. (13) Lit., 'that'. (14) 'Who must produce the proof' (*supra 96a ad fin.*).

from the Mishnah:[1] She may sell [her deceased husband's estate] for her maintenance out of court but should enter [in the deed of sale,] 'I have sold these for maintenance'?[2] Consequently[3] it must be concluded[4] that no deduction may be made from the Mishnah[1] because therein only good advice was tendered;[5] and so also here[6] [it may similarly be submitted that R. Judah] was only tendering good advice.[5] Or else: All[7] may agree that the estate [of the deceased] is in the presumptive possession of the orphans, but R. Jose's reason[8] is exactly the same as [that given by] Abaye the Elder who stated: To what may the ruling[9] of R. Jose be compared? To [the instructions of] a dying man who said, 'Give two hundred *zuz*[10] to So-and-so, my creditor,[11] who may take them, if he wishes, in settlement of his debt or, if he prefers, he may take them as a gift', [97a] who, if he takes them as a gift, has not the same advantage [as if he had taken them for his debt].[12]

In what manner does [a widow] sell [her deceased husband's

(1) *Infra* 97b. (2) Of course it could. The reason for the requirement of a specification of the purpose of the sale that underlies R. Judah's ruling in the Baraitha should obviously hold good for the similar ruling in the Mishnah. If the reason in the former is that the estate remains in the presumptive possession of the orphans, the same reason would apply to the latter. And since a Mishnah, unlike a Baraitha, must be known to all students, R. Johanan's question would easily have been answered. (3) Since the question had to be solved from Levi's Baraitha. (4) Lit., 'but'. (5) But the presumptive possession of the estate is that of the widow. (6) In the Baraitha. (7) R. Judah and R. Jose. (8) For the ruling that the purpose of the sale need not be specified in the deed. (9) V. *supra* n. 8. משל, lit., 'simile'. (10) V. Glos. (11) Cf. B.B. 138b. (12) A debt may be distrained for on sold property, but a gift may not. Similarly with the widow, by omitting, in agreement with the ruling of R. Jose, the specification of the purpose of her sales, she retains the right to distrain on her deceased husband's sold property by advancing the plea that her own sales had been made for the purpose of her maintenance (which cannot, of course, be distrained for on such property) and that she was now seeking to recover her *kethubah* to which such property is pledged. To protect herself against the plea of the orphans that her *kethubah* also was paid out of her sales, she might arrange for witnesses to be present when the sales for her maintenance take place and when she makes a verbal declaration to that effect.

proof since] R. Papa may have acted beyond the strict requirements of the law.[1]

Come and hear: There was once a dearth at Nehardea[2] when all the people sold their mansions,[3] but when eventually wheat arrived[4] R. Naḥman told them: The law is that the mansions must be returned to their original owners!—There also the sales were made in error since it eventually became known that the ship[5] was[6] waiting in the bays.[7] If that is so,[8] how [explain] what Rami b. Samuel said to R. Naḥman, 'If [you rule] thus you will cause them[9] trouble in the future',[10] [whereupon] he replied, 'Is dearth a daily occurrence?' and to which the former retorted, 'Yes, a dearth at Nehardea is indeed a common occurrence'?[11]

And the law is that if a man sold [a plot of land][12] and [on concluding the sale] was no longer in need of money the sale may be withdrawn.

MISHNAH. A WIDOW, WHETHER [HER HUSBAND DIED]

(1) לפנים משורת הדין, lit., 'within the line of the law', i.e., he surrendered his legal right for the sake of benefiting a fellow man; v. B.Ḳ. Sonc. ed. p. 584, n. 2. (2) V. *supra* p. 222, n. 8. (3) To use the proceeds for the purchase of wheat. (4) And prices fell so that the sellers of the mansions were no longer in need of the money. (5) That carried the grain. (6) At the time the sales were effected. (7) Sheltering until the subsidence of the high water. Had these sellers been aware of the fact that the ship was so near they would never have thought of selling their mansions. Such sales may, therefore, be regarded as sales in error, which may be withdrawn. The question under discussion, however, refers to a seller who was actually in need of money when his sale was effected (v. p. 616, n. 16) and whose release came only after the sale. (8) That the reason for R. Naḥman's ruling was that the ship was already in the bays at the time the sales were arranged. So according to Rashb. (v. Tosaf. s. v. אי, *a.l.*) contra Rashi who takes this argument to be in support of the reason given for R. Naḥman's ruling. (9) The sellers. (10) Because they will not be able to find buyers. (11) Granted the frequency of *dearth* at Nehardea, the detention of the provision ships in the bays is obviously of no common occurence. Consequently it must be concluded that R. Naḥman's reason for the cancellation of the sales was not because 'the ship was in the bays' but because the sellers, though in need of money *when the sales were arranged*,

AFTER [HER] BETROTHAL[1] OR AFTER [HER] MARRIAGE[2] MAY SELL [OF HER DECEASED HUSBAND'S ESTATE] WITHOUT [THE SANCTION OF] BETH DIN. R. SIMEON RULED: [IF HER HUSBAND DIED] AFTER MARRIAGE[2] SHE MAY SELL[3] [OF HIS ESTATE] WITHOUT [THE SANCTION OF] BETH DIN,[4] [BUT IF ONLY] AFTER [HER] BETROTHAL, SHE MAY NOT SELL [ANY OF THE ESTATE] EXCEPT WITH [THE SANCTION OF] BETH DIN, SINCE SHE IS NOT ENTITLED TO MAINTENANCE, AND ONE WHO IS NOT ENTITLED TO MAINTENANCE MAY NOT SELL [SUCH PROPERTY] EXCEPT WITH [THE SANCTION OF] BETH DIN.

GEMARA. One can readily see [that the privilege[5] of a woman who was widowed] AFTER MARRIAGE is due to [her immediate need for] maintenance;[6] [97b] what, however, is the reason[7] [for conferring this privilege[8] upon one widowed] after betrothal?[9] —'Ulla replied: In order to [enhance the] attractions[10] [of matrimony].[11] R. Joḥanan replied: Because no man wants his wife to suffer the indignity [of appearing] in court. What is the practical difference between them?[12]—The practical difference between them is the case of a divorced woman. For according to him who replied, 'In order to [enhance the] attractiveness [of matrimony]' a divorced woman also may[13] claim [the privilege[14] of the provision for matrimonial] attractiveness;[10] but according to him who

had no need of the money *subsequently*, such cases *being of frequent occurrence*. (12) V. *supra* p. 616, n. 13.

(1) When her claim is restricted to that of her *kethubah* only (v. our Mishnah *infra*). (2) When she claims also maintenance. (3) For her maintenance. (4) Since she cannot be expected to starve until Beth din find time to deal with her case. (5) To SELL . . . WITHOUT THE CONSENT OF BETH DIN. (6) Cf. *supra* n. 4. (7) Of the first Tanna of our Mishnah. (8) As far as her *kethubah* is concerned. (9) Why should not a claim of this nature (cf. *supra* note 1) be subject to the jurisdiction of a court just as that of any other claimants? (10) Lit., 'grace'. (11) In the absence of the privilege some women might refuse to consent to their betrothal; v. *supra* 84a. (12) 'Ulla and R. Joḥanan. (13) Since the privilege is not dependent on the husband's feelings. (14) V. *supra* note 8.

RULED: SHE MAY SELL [THE LAND PLEDGED FOR HER KETHUBAH] EVEN IN FOUR OR FIVE INSTALMENTS[1] AND [IN THE MEANTIME][2] SHE MAY SELL [OF HER HUSBAND'S ESTATE TO PROVIDE] FOR HER MAINTENANCE WITHOUT [THE SANCTION OF] BETH DIN, ENTERING, [HOWEVER, IN THE DEED OF SALE,] 'I SOLD [THE LAND TO PROVIDE] FOR MY MAINTENANCE'.[3] A DIVORCED WOMAN, HOWEVER, MUST NOT SELL [SUCH PROPERTY] EXCEPT WITH [THE SANCTION OF] BETH DIN.

GEMARA. Who [is the author of the first ruling in] our Mishnah?[4]—It is R. Simeon. For it was taught: If a woman sold [all] her *kethubah* or pledged it, or mortgaged [the land that was pledged for] her *kethubah* to a stranger, she is not entitled to maintenance.[5] R. Simeon ruled: Even if she did not sell or pledge [all] her *kethubah*, but half of it only, she loses her maintenance.[6] Does this[7] then imply that R. Simeon holds the view that we do not regard part of the amount[8] as being legally equal to the full amount, while the Rabbis maintain that part of the amount is legally regarded as the full amount? But, [it may be objected], have we not in fact heard the reverse? For was it not taught: *And he*[9] *shall take a wife in her virginity*[10] excludes one who is adolescent[11]

(1) Lit., 'times'. (2) Before the last instalment is sold. (3) Such insertion being in certain cases advantageous for the woman (as explained *supra* 96*b*). (4) According to which a widow who sold even only part of her *kethubah* may not sell of her husband's estate without the sanction of Beth din. (5) Tosef. Keth. XI, *supra* 54*a*. If, however, she sold etc. a part of it only she is still entitled to maintenance. Cur. edd. insert here in parentheses, 'these are the words of R. Meir', a sentence which is wanting in the Tosefta. Rashi retains it. (6) Tosef. Keth. XI; as she loses her maintenance she may not sell without the sanction of Beth din. Cf. *supra* n. 4 and Rashi on our Mishnah, s.v. לא תמכור. Rashal actually inserts in the text 'and the rest she may not sell except with the sanction of Beth din', a reading which was apparently wanting in Rashi's text as well as in cur. edd., but was known to the Tosafists (v. Tosaf. s.v. מכרה). (7) The dispute between R. Simeon and the Rabbis according to which the former regards the absence of a part as the absence of the whole while the latter do not. (8) *Sc*. of the *kethubah*. Lit., '*silver*' with reference to Ex. XXII, 17. (9) A High Priest. (10) Lev. XXI, 13. (11) A *bogereth* (v. Glos.).

[some of whose] virginity is ended; so R. Meir. R. Eleazar and R. Simeon permit[1] [the marriage] of one who is adolescent?[2] —There[3] they differ [on the interpretation] of Scriptural texts,[4] R. Meir being of the opinion that *'virgin'*[5] implies even [one who retains] some of her virginity; *'her virginity'*[6] implies only one who retains all her virginity;[7] *'in her virginity'*[8] implies only[9] [when previous intercourse with her took place] in a natural manner,[10] but not when in an unnatural manner.[11] R. Eleazar and R. Simeon, however, are of the opinion that *'virgin'* would have implied a perfect virgin; *'her virginity'* implies even [one who retains] only part of her virginity; [98a] *'in her virginity'*[12] implies only one[13] whose entire virginity is intact,[14] irrespective of whether [previous intercourse with her was] of a natural or unnatural character.[15]

A certain woman[16] once seized a silver cup on account of her *kethubah*[17] and then claimed her maintenance. She appeared before Raba. He [thereupon] told the orphans, 'Proceed to provide for her maintenance; no one cares for the ruling of R. Simeon who laid down that we do not regard part of the amount as legally equal to the full amount.'

Rabbah the son of Raba sent to R. Joseph [the following

(1) A High Priest. (2) Yeb. 59a. The absence of a part of her virginity not being regarded as the absence of all virginity. Thus it follows that, while R. Simeon does not regard the absence of a part as the absence of the whole, the Rabbis do, which is the reverse of their respective views here (v. p. 621, n. 7). (3) In the Baraitha cited from Yeb. (4) Not on the question whether a part legally equals the whole. (5) בתולה. (6) בתוליה. (7) Which *excludes* the *one who is adolescent* some of whose virginity is ended. (8) בבתוליה (Lev. XXI, 13) (9) Lit., 'yes'. (10) Is she forbidden to a High Priest. (11) The superfluous ב (= *'in'*) in בבתוליה implies intercourse in the place of virginity. Unnatural intercourse with a *na'arah* (v. Glos) whereby virginity is not affected, is consequently excluded. (12) Which *includes one who is adolescent* (Lev. XXI, 13). (13) Being a *na'arah* (v. Glos.). (14) Is permitted to be married by a High Priest. (15) Yeb. 59a. She is forbidden even if it was unnatural. Her virginity must be completely intact. Cf. *supra* note 11. Thus it has been shewn that the dispute between R. Simeon and the Rabbis (*sc.* R. Meir) has no bearing on the legal relationship between the part and the whole (cf. *supra* note 4). but on the method of interpreting certain Scriptural texts. (16) A widow. (17) The amount of which exceeded the value of the cup.

enquiry:] Is a woman[1] who sells [of her deceased husband's estate] without [an authorization of] Beth din required to take an oath[2] or is she not required to take an oath?—And [why, the other replied, do you not] enquire [as to whether] a public announcement[3] [is required]?—I have no need, the first retorted, to enquire concerning a public announcement because R. Zera has stated in the name of R. Naḥman, 'If a widow assessed [her husband's estate] on her own behalf[4] her act is invalid';[5] now, how [is this statement] to be understood? If a public announcement[3] has been made [the difficulty arises,] why is her act invalid? Must we not consequently assume that there was no public announcement, and [since it was stated that] only [if the assessment was made] 'on her own behalf' is 'her act invalid' it follows, does it not, [that if she made it] on behalf of another[6] her act is valid?[7] —[No,] a public announcement may in fact have been made but [her act is nevertheless invalid] because she can be told, 'Who [authorized] you to make the assessment?'[8] as was the case with a certain man with whom corals[9] belonging to orphans had been deposited and he proceeded to assess them on his own behalf for four hundred *zuz*, and when later its price rose to six hundred *zuz*, he appeared before R. Ammi, who said to him, 'Who [authorized] you to make the assessment?'[10] And the law is that she[11] is required to take an oath,[12] but there is no need to make a public announcement.[13]

(1) A widow. (2) That she did not collect more than her due. (3) Of the intended sale of the estate, as is the procedure where the sale is ordered by the court. (4) And seized it for her *kethubah*. (5) Lit., 'she did nothing'; the orphans may at any time reclaim that land and refund her the amount of her *kethubah*. (6) I.e., she sold the estate for her *kethubah* to a third party. (7) Lit., 'what she did she did'; which shews that no public announcement is required in the case of the sale under discussion. (8) As neither the court nor the orphans had given her any such authorization the estate must remain in the legal possession of the orphans. If, however, she sells to other people her act is valid since she is fully authorized to do so. (9) כסיתא (so Rashi). Cur. edd., כיסתא 'fodder'. MS.M. כסותא 'garment'. (10) Cf. *supra* n. 8 *mutatis mutandis*. (11) A woman in the circumstances spoken of in Rabbah's enquiry *supra*. (12) V. *supra* note 2. (13) Cf. n. 3. [This implies that the assessment must nevertheless be made in the presence of an expert valuer (Trani)].

MISHNAH. IF A WIDOW WHOSE KETHUBAH WAS FOR TWO HUNDRED ZUZ SOLD[1] [A PLOT OF LAND THAT WAS] WORTH A MANEH[2] FOR TWO HUNDRED ZUZ OR ONE THAT WAS WORTH TWO HUNDRED ZUZ FOR ONE MANEH, HER KETHUBAH IS DEEMED TO HAVE BEEN THEREBY SETTLED.[3] IF HER KETHUBAH, HOWEVER, WAS FOR ONE MANEH, AND SHE SOLD [LAND THAT WAS] WORTH A MANEH AND A DENAR[2] FOR ONE MANEH, HER SALE IS VOID. EVEN THOUGH SHE DECLARED, 'I WILL RETURN THE DENAR TO THE HEIRS' HER SALE IS VOID.[4] R. SIMEON B. GAMALIEL RULED: HER SALE[3] IS ALWAYS VALID[5] UNLESS THERE WAS[6] [SO MUCH LAND] THERE AS WOULD HAVE ENABLED HER[7] TO LEAVE[8] FROM A FIELD AN AREA OF NINE ḲAB,[9] AND FROM A GARDEN THAT OF HALF A ḲAB[10] OR, ACCORDING TO R. AKIBA, A QUARTER OF A ḲAB.[10] IF HER KETHUBAH WAS FOR FOUR HUNDRED ZUZ AND SHE SOLD [PLOTS OF LAND][11] TO [THREE] PERSONS, TO EACH FOR ONE MANEH,[12] AND TO A FOURTH[13] [SHE SOLD] WHAT WAS WORTH A MANEH AND A DENAR FOR ONE MANEH,[14] [THE SALE] TO THE LAST PERSON IS VOID BUT [THE SALES] OF ALL THE OTHERS ARE VALID.

(1) From her deceased husband's estate. (2) V. Glos. (3) Because she is to blame for the loss incurred. (4) Since she had no right to sell a part of the land (representing the value of the *denar*) her entire sale is deemed to have been made in error and is, therefore, void. (5) Even if the land she sold was worth more than the amount of her *kethubah*; because she can refund the balance to the orphans. (6) Lit., 'shall be'. (7) If she had not sold for more than her due. Lit., 'sufficient', 'as much as'. (8) Exclusive or inclusive of the land she sold over and above the area representing the value of the amount that was due to her. (9) *Sc*. in which such a quantity of seed could be sown. An area of that size represents the minimum of land that can be profitably cultivated. By leaving a lesser area the woman is causing undue loss to the orphans, and her sale must consequently be annulled. If the lesser area, however, would have remained even if she had sold what was her due, her sale is valid since the orphans could not in any case have made profitable use of the residue. (10) The minimum area that can be profitably laid out as a garden. Cf. *supra* n. 9 *mutatis mutandis*. (11) From her deceased husband's estate. (12) Lit., 'to this for a *maneh* and to this for a *maneh*'. (13) Lit., 'last'. (14) So that in the last sale she disposed of more than her due.

GEMARA. Wherein does [the sale of a plot of land] THAT WAS WORTH TWO HUNDRED ZUZ FOR ONE MANEH differ [from the previous case? Is it] because she[1] might be told, 'You yourself have caused the loss'? [But, then, why should she not, where she SOLD A PLOT OF LAND THAT WAS] WORTH A MANEH FOR TWO HUNDRED ZUZ, also [be entitled to] say, 'It is I who have made the profit'?[2]—R. Naḥman replied in the name of Rabbah b. Abbuha: [98*b*] Rabbi[3] has taught here[4] that all [profits[5] belong] to the owner of the money.[6] As it was taught,[7] 'If one unit[8] was added to [the purchases made by an agent] all [the profit belongs] to the agent'; so R. Judah, but R. Jose ruled, '[The profit] is to be divided',[9] [and, in reply to the objection,] But, surely, it was taught that R. Jose ruled, All [profit belongs] to the owner of the money! Rami b. Ḥama replied: This is no difficulty for the former refers to an object that has a fixed value[10] while the latter refers to one that has no fixed[11] value.[12]

R. Papa stated: The law is that[13] [the profit made by the agent on] an object that had a fixed value must be divided,[9] but if on an object that had no fixed value all [profit belongs] to the owner of the money. What does he[14] teach us?[15]—That the reply that was given[16] is the proper one.[17]

(1) The widow who effected the sale. (2) And so have a claim to another *maneh*. (3) R. Judah I, the Patriarch, compiler of the Mishnah c. 200 C.E. (4) In our Mishnah. (5) Made by an agent. (6) Since the widow was merely acting as the agent of the orphans, who are the owners, she cannot lay any claim to the profit she made. (7) V. *infra*, n. 12. (8) Lit., 'one more'. (9) Between agent and owner; v. Tosef. Dem. VIII. (10) And, since it is not certain in whose favour the additional unit was given away by the seller, its value must be equally divided between the agent and the owner of the money. (11) So that the additional unit cannot be regarded as a gift, but as a part of the purchase, payment for which was made with the money of the owner. Hence it is the latter only who is entitled to the added unit. (12) Thus it has been shewn that our Mishnah which deals with land (something that has no fixed value) and assigns the profits to the original owner (the orphans) is in agreement with the view of R. Jose. (13) הלכתא, so cur. edd. and R. Ḥan. MS.M. and a reading approved by Tosaf. (s.v. אמר) is הלכך, 'therefore'. (14) R. Papa. (15) By his statement which is only a repetition of what has just been laid down. This question seems to imply the reading of הלכך (v. *supra* n. 13) rather

The question was raised: What [is the law where a man] said to his agent,[1] 'Sell for me a *lethek*'[2] and the latter presumed[3] to sell a *kor?*[4] [Is the agent deemed to be merely] adding to the owner's instructions and [the buyer, therefore,] acquires possession of a *lethek*, at all events, or is he rather transgressing his instructions and [the buyer, therefore,] acquires no possession of a *lethek* either?—Said R. Jacob of Nehar Pekod[5] in the name of Rabina, Come and hear: If a householder said to his agent, 'Serve a piece [of meat][6] to the guests', and the latter said to them, 'Take two',[7] and they took three,[7] all of them are guilty[8] of trespass.[9] Now if you agree [that the agent][10] was merely adding to the host's instruction one can well understand the reason why the householder is guilty of trespass. If you should maintain, however, [that the agent][10] was transgressing his instruction [the objection could well be advanced:] Why should the householder be guilty of trespass? Have we not in fact learned: If an agent performed his mission it is the householder who is guilty of trespass but if he did not perform his mission it is the agent who is guilty of trespass?[11]—Here we may be dealing with a case where the agent said to the guests, 'Take one at the desire[12] of the householder[13] and one at my own request',[12] and they took three.

Come and hear: IF HER KETHUBAH, HOWEVER, WAS FOR A MANEH, AND SHE SOLD [LAND THAT WAS] WORTH A MANEH AND A DENAR FOR A MANEH, HER SALE IS VOID.

than that of הלכתא (Tosaf.). (16) By Rami b. Hama. (17) Lit., 'that which we replied is a reply'.

(1) Lit., 'to him'. (2) *Sc.* a plot of land in which a *lethek* (= half a *kor*) of grain may be sown. (3) Lit., 'and went'. (4) V. Glos. (5) A town situated on the east of Nehardea. (6) Which was subsequently found to have been consecrated food. (7) Each. (8) The host in respect of the first, the agent in respect of the second and the guests in respect of the third. (9) Me'il. 20*a*. (10) Like the agent spoken of in the enquiry. (11) Hag. 10*b*, Kid. 42*b*, Ned. 54*a*, Me'il. 20*a*. Consequently it must be concluded, must it not, that an agent in the circumstances mentioned is deemed to have added to, and not transgressed, his instructions? (12) Lit., 'knowledge'. (13) Thus performing his mission.

Does[1] not [this mean] that SHE SOLD [LAND THAT WAS] WORTH A MANEH AND A DENAR FOR A MANEH and a *denar*,[2] and that by[1] [the expression,] 'FOR A MANEH' the *maneh* that was due to her [is meant], and by[1] EVEN[3] [one is to understand] EVEN THOUGH SHE DECLARED, 'I WILL RETURN THE DENAR TO THE HEIRS [by repurchasing for them] land of the value of a *denar*'? And was it not nevertheless stated, HER SALE IS VOID?[4] —No,[5] retorted R. Huna the son of R. Nathan, [this is a case] where [she sold] at the lower price.[6] [99a] But since the final clause[7] [deals with a case] where [she sold] at a lower price, [would not] the earlier clause[8] [naturally[9] refer to one] where [she did] not [sell] at a lower price; for has [it not] been stated in the final clause, IF HER KETHUBAH WAS FOR FOUR HUNDRED ZUZ AND SHE SOLD [PLOTS OF LAND] TO [THREE] PERSONS[10] TO EACH FOR ONE MANEH, AND TO A FOURTH[10] [SHE SOLD] WHAT WAS WORTH A MANEH AND A DENAR FOR ONE MANEH, [THE SALE] TO THE LAST PERSON IS VOID BUT [THE SALES] OF ALL THE OTHERS ARE VALID?[11]—No,[5] both the earlier and the final clause [refer to a sale] at a lower price, but[12] it is this that we were informed in the final clause: The reason [why her sale is void is] because [she sold][13] at a lower price [the property] that belonged to the orphans,[14] but [if that[15] had been done] with her own,[16] her sale is valid.[17] But is not this already inferred

(1) Lit., 'what'. (2) *Sc.* for its full price, so that no error was involved. (3) Which, in view of the fact that the *denar* obviously belongs to the orphans, is apparently meaningless. (4) As the woman is in a position similar to that of the agent spoken of in the enquiry it follows that as her sale is void so is that of the agent. (5) I.e., our Mishnah is not to be understood as suggested. (6) *Sc.* for one *maneh* only; the *error* in the sale, not the excess of the land sold, being the reason for the invalidity of the sale. [Read with MS.M. and Tosaf. בדזילא instead of בדאויל in cur. edd.]. (7) Of our Mishnah. (8) The clause just cited. (9) Since two clauses are not necessary to lay down the same principle. (10) V. our Mishnah for notes. (11) An objection against R. Huna the son of R. Nathan (cf. *supra* n. 9). (12) As to the objection (v. *supra* n. 9). (13) To the fourth person. (14) *Sc.* land that exceeded the amount that was due to her. (15) The sale of land of the value of a *maneh* and a *denar* for one *maneh* only. (16) I.e., when she was selling to the first three persons, and when the extra land for the *denar* was still hers. (17) Because the law of

from the first clause: WHOSE KETHUBAH WAS FOR TWO HUNDRED ZUZ SOLD [A PLOT OF LAND THAT WAS] WORTH A MANEH FOR TWO HUNDRED ZUZ OR ONE THAT WAS WORTH TWO HUNDRED ZUZ FOR ONE MANEH, HER KETHUBAH IS DEEMED TO HAVE BEEN THEREBY SETTLED?[1] —It might have been assumed [that the ruling[2] was applicable] there only because [by her one act] she completely severed her connection with that house,[3] but that here[4] [the sale for] the first *maneh* [should be deemed invalid] as a preventive measure against [the assumption of the validity of the sale for the] last *maneh;* hence we were informed [that the law was not so].

Some there are who say: You have no need to ask [for a ruling] where [a man said to his agent,] 'Go and sell for me a *lethek*'[5] and [the latter] sold for him a *kor,* since [in this case the agent] was undoubtedly adding to his instructions.[6] The question, however, arises as to what is the ruling where the man said to the agent, 'Go and sell for me a *kor*' and he sold for him only one *lethek.*[5] Do we [in such a case] lay down that [the agent] might tell the man, 'I have done for you that which is more advantageous to you, for [had I sold the full *kor,* and] you were no longer in need of money you could not have retracted',[7] or is it rather [held that the owner] might retort to him, 'It is no satisfaction to me that many deeds [should be held] against me'?—R. Ḥanina of Sura[8] replied, Come and hear: If one man gave to another a gold *denar*[9] and told him, 'Bring me a shirt', and the other brought

overreaching is inapplicable to landed property even where the error amounted to as much as a sixth of the value; much less when it is no more than one hundredth.

(1) Which shews that where the additional land sold constituted a part of the woman's due, her sale is valid. Cf. *supra* p. 627, n. 11. (2) That the sale is valid when the land belongs to the woman. (3) In such a case naturally no preventive measures are called for. (4) The case in the final clause. (5) V. *supra* p. 626, n. 2. (6) And the buyer is consequently entitled to the possession at least of the *lethek* (cf. *supra* 98*b*). (7) The sale consequently should be valid. (8) Cf. *supra* p. 383, n. 7. (9) Rashi: The gold *denar* = twenty-five silver *denarii,* or six *sela's* (cf. B.M. 44*b*). [Rashi probably means approximately six *sela's,* since one *sela'* = four *denarii,* or the extra *denar* may be surcharge as agio, v. Strashun].

him a shirt for three *sela's* and a cloak for three *sela's*, both are guilty of trespass.[1] Now if you admit that an agent in similar circumstances[2] has performed his mission and was only adding to his instructions, one can well see why the owner[3] is guilty of trespass.[4] If, however, you should maintain that [the agent in such circumstances] was transgressing his instructions, why should [the owner] be guilty of trespass?[5]—Here we are dealing with a case where [the agent] brought him [a shirt that was] worth six *sela's* for three.[6] If so[7] why should the agent be guilty of trespass?—On account of the cloak.[8] But if that were so,[9] read the final clause: R. Judah ruled, Even in this case[9] the owner is not guilty of trespass because he might say [to the agent,] 'I wanted a big shirt and you brought me one that is small and bad'![10]—'Bad' means[11] 'bad in respect of the price', for[12] [the owner can] tell him, 'Had you brought me one for six *sela's* [my gain would have been] even greater since it would have been worth twelve *sela's*.'[13] This[14] may also be proved by an inference. For it was stated:[15] R. Judah admits [that if the transaction was] in pulse both[16] are guilty of trespass [99*b*] because [the quantity of] pulse for a

(1) If the *denar* was found to have belonged to the sanctuary. Me'il. 21*a*. (2) Selling one *lethek* where the instruction was to sell two (a *kor*) is similar to spending on an object three *sela's* where the instruction was to spend on it six (a gold *denar*). (3) Lit., 'master of the house', *sc.* the man who gave the *denar* to the agent. (4) He is responsible for the offence since his wish had been carried out. (5) Consequently it must be inferred that the agent spoken of in the enquiry has performed his mission (cf. *supra* p. 628, n. 6). (6) Cf. *supra* note 4. (7) That the agent carried out the sender's instructions. (8) Which he bought entirely on his own responsibility. (9) That the agent bought for three *sela's* an article that was actually worth six. (10) Me'il, loc. cit. If the reply given (cf. *supra* n. 9) is to be accepted R. Judah's statement is apparently meaningless. (11) Lit., 'what'. (12) Despite the fact that the shirt bought was actually worth six *sela's*. (13) The higher the price the higher in proportion is the profit. *Aliter:* One who pays a higher price is allowed a greater discount (cf. Rashi s.v. ד״אל, and Tosaf. s.v. כל, *a.l.*). (14) That by 'bad' R. Judah meant 'bad in respect of the price', that the shirt bought for three *sela's* was actually worth six, and that the reason why the owner is not guilty of trespass is because his wish to have the advantage of the bigger purchase had not been carried out. (15) Tosef. Me'il, II. (16) The owner and the agent.

sela' [is in exactly the same proportion as] that for one *peruṭah*.[1]
This is conclusive. How is this[2] to be understood? If it be suggested [that it refers] to a place where [pulse] is sold by conjectural
estimate, does not one [it may be objected] who pays a *sela'*
obtain the commodity at a much cheaper rate?[3] — R. Papa replied:
[It refers] to a place where each *kanna*[4] is sold[5] for one *peruṭah*.[6]

Come and hear: IF HER KETHUBAH WAS FOR FOUR HUN-
DRED ZUZ AND SHE SOLD [PLOTS OF LAND] TO [THREE]
PERSONS[7] TO EACH FOR ONE MANEH, AND TO A FOURTH[7]
[SHE SOLD] WHAT WAS WORTH A MANEH AND A DENAR
FOR ONE MANEH [THE SALE] TO THE LAST PERSON IS VOID
BUT [THE SALES] OF ALL THE OTHERS ARE VALID![8] — [This[9]
is no proof, for] as R. Shisha the son of R. Idi replied[10] [that the
final clause of our Mishnah deals] with small plots of land,[11] [so it
may] in this discussion[12] also [be argued that the clause cited deals]
with small plots of land.[13]

---

(1) The smallest coin. No advantage is gained in making a bigger purchase.
The owner's wish in this case, unlike that of the shirt (cf. *supra* p. 629, n. 13)
may consequently be regarded as having been carried out. Thus it has been
shewn that the reason why R. Judah exempts the owner in the case of the shirt
is the one indicated. (Cf. p. 629, n. 14). (2) The transaction in pulse. (3) Than
one who buys for a *peruṭah* only. The more the amount spent by the buyer the
more generous the conjectural estimate of the seller. How then could it be
said (cf. *supra* n. 1) that no advantage is gained from the purchase of a larger
quantity? (4) כנא (cf. κάννα) a small measure of capacity. (5) Lit., 'measured'.
(6) V. Glos.; no advantage, therefore, is gained from the purchase of larger
quantities. Read with MS.M. דכיילי כנא כנא בפרוטה. Cur. edd., 'where they
measure with *kannai* (pl. of *kanna*) so that he tells him: Each *kanna* for a *peruṭah*'.
(7) V. our Mishnah for notes. (8) Though at the time she sold to each of the
first three persons she was in fact authorized (or entitled) to sell much more.
As these sales of the woman (which are analogous to an agent's sale of a *lethek*
when his instructions were to sell as much as a *kor*) are valid, so one would
expect the sale of the agent to be valid, and a reply is thus obtained to the
enquiry *supra* 99a. (9) Cf. *supra* note 8. (10) *Infra*. (11) Detached from
one another. (12) Lit., 'here'. (13) Cf. *supra* n. 11. In such circumstances the
woman was never expected (entitled or authorized) to sell for all the four
hundred *zuz* to one person at one and the same time. By selling the small plots
each for a price not higher than one *maneh* she is in a different legal position from
that of the agent who, in fact, was expected to sell a full *kor* while he actually

HAS BEEN DRAWN UP, THEIR SALE IS VALID EVEN IF THEY SOLD FOR TWO HUNDRED ZUZ[1] WHAT WAS WORTH ONE MANEH,[1] OR FOR ONE MANEH WHAT WAS WORTH TWO HUNDRED ZUZ.

GEMARA. The question was asked: What is the legal status of[2] an agent?[3]—[100a] Raba in the name of R. Naḥman replied: An agent [has the same status] as judges,[4] but R. Samuel b. Bisna replied in the name of R. Naḥman: As a widow.[5] 'Raba in the name of R. Naḥman replied: An agent [has the same status] as judges', for as judges do not act in their [personal interests] so does an agent not act in his [personal interests], thus excluding a widow who acts in her [own personal interests]. 'R. Samuel b. Bisna replied in the name of R. Naḥman: As a widow', for as the widow is a single individual so is an agent a single individual; thus excluding members of a court, who are many.—And the law is that an agent [has the same legal status] as a widow. But why [should this case be] different from that concerning which we learned: If a man tells his agent, 'Go and give *terumah*' the latter must give the *terumah* in accordance with the disposition of the owner, and if he does not know the owner's disposition, he should separate *terumah* in a moderate manner, viz. one fiftieth. If he reduced [the denominator by] ten or added ten to it his *terumah* is, nevertheless, valid?[6]—There[7] [the circumstances are different], for, since someone might give his *terumah* in a niggardly manner while some other might give it liberally, [the agent][8] might tell the owner, 'I deemed[9] you to be of such [a disposition]';[10]

inviting the public to inspect property put up by an order of the court for sale.

(1) V. Glos. (2) Lit. 'like whom'. (3) Who made a mistake in the sale he was instructed to effect. (4) The sale is valid if the error did not amount to a sixth (v. our Mishnah). (5) The slightest error renders the sale invalid (cf. the Mishnah *supra* 98a.) (6) Ter. IV, 4 and supra 99*b* q.v. for notes. This then shews, contrary to what was laid down above as law (cf. *supra* n. 5), that a slight error does not render an agent's act invalid. (7) In the case of an agent giving *terumah* for the owner. (8) Who gave more, or less, than the owner was inclined to give. (9) Lit., 'estimated'. (10) Niggardly or liberal as the case might be.

but here, since it was clearly an error, [the owner] might well say, 'You should have made no error'.[1]

R. Huna b. Ḥanina stated in the name of R. Naḥman: The *halachah* is in agreement with the ruling of the Sages.[2] [Can it be said,] however, that R. Naḥman does not hold [that the act of a court is invariably valid since, otherwise,] of what advantage would the power of a court be,[3] when R. Naḥman, in fact, ruled in the name of Samuel:[4] If orphans came to take their shares in their father's estate, the court must appoint for [each of] them a guardian and [these guardians] choose for [each of] them a proper share, and when [the orphans] grow up they may enter a protest [against the settlement]; but R. Naḥman in his own name, laid down: Even when they grow up they may enter no protest since, otherwise, of what advantage would the power of a court be?[3]—This is no difficulty, the former[5] [referring to a case] where the guardians made a mistake while the latter[6] [deals with one] where no error was made. If no error was made, on what grounds could [the orphans] enter their protest?—On that of the adjacent fields.[7]

When R. Dimi came[8] he stated: It once happened that Rabbi[9] acted in agreement with the ruling of the Sages[2] when Peraṭa, the son of R. Eleazar b. Peraṭa, grandson of R. Peraṭa the Great, asked him, 'If so, of what advantage would the power of a court be?'[3] And [as a result] Rabbi reversed his decision. Thus it was taught by R. Dimi. R. Safra, however, taught as follows: It once happened that Rabbi[9] desired to act in agreement with the ruling of the Sages,[2] when Peraṭa, the son of R. Eleazar b. Peraṭa, grandson of R. Peraṭa the Great, said to him, 'If so, of what

(1) Hence the invalidity of the sale however slight the error may have been. (2) The first mentioned ruling in our Mishnah. (3) I.e., the view of R. SIMEON B. GAMALIEL. (4) V. Ḳid. Sonc. ed. p. 210, notes. (5) Lit., 'that', R. Naḥman's ruling in the name of Samuel (cf. *supra* n. 2). (6) R. Naḥman's ruling in his own name (cf. *supra*, n. 3). (7) Lit., 'on (the ground of) the sides', *sc.* the unsatisfactory situation of their allotted fields owing to their distance from other fields which they already possessed. (8) From Palestine to Babylon. (9) R. Judah I, the Patriarch, compiler of the Mishnah.

advantage is the power of a court?' And[1] [as a result] Rabbi did not act as he intended.[2] Must it be assumed that they[3] differ on this principle: One master[4] holds the view that if [in giving a decision] a law cited in a Mishnah[5] has been overlooked the decision must be reversed, and the other Master[6] upholds the view[7] that it cannot be reversed?[8]—No; all[3] agree that if [in giving a decision] a law cited in a Mishnah has been overlooked the decision must be reversed, but one Master holds that the incident occurred in one way[9] while the other holds that it occurred in the other way.[9]

R. Joseph stated: If a widow sold [any of her deceased husband's estate][10] the responsibility for the indemnity falls upon the orphans,[11] and if the court sold [any such property][12] the responsibility for the indemnity again falls upon the orphans.[13] [Is not this ruling] obvious?[14]—It was not necessary [indeed in respect of] the widow,[14] but was required [in respect of] the court; for it might have been assumed [100*b*] that whoever buys from the court does so in order that he may have the benefit of a public announcement,[15] hence we were informed [that the

(1) So MS.M. (wanting in cur. edd.). (2) Lit., 'the act'. (3) R. Dimi and R. Safra. (4) R. Dimi. (5) *Sc.* that of R. Simeon b. Gamaliel, which, unlike that of the first Tanna, is also supported by a reason. (6) R. Safra. (7) Which is, however, most unlikely. (8) Had then Rabbi acted in agreement with the Sages' ruling, he would not have been able to reverse his decision. (9) Lit., 'thus'. (10) To reimburse herself for her maintenance or *kethubah*, guaranteeing indemnity to the buyer. (11) Because they are responsible for the widow's *kethubah* and maintenance, and she, in selling the estate, was merely acting as their agent. (12) For the maintenance of a widow or daughter. Cf. also *supra* n. 10 *mutatis mutandis*. (13) Cf. *supra* n. 10 *mutatis mutandis* and 97*a*. (14) Cf. *supra* n. 11. (15) Lit., 'it is with the intent that a voice may be brought out for him that he buys'. Since any sale by a court must be preceded by a public announcement, it is conceivable that if any person had a claim upon the land in question he would advance it as soon as the announcement had been made. A buyer who is presumably aware of these considerations might, therefore, be assumed to feel so secure in his purchase as to surrender his guarantee for indemnity. [*Aliter:* Whoever buys from the Beth din buys for the purpose that he might gain publicity as a man of means, without necessarily expecting any guarantee of indemnification; Strashun].

responsibility for the indemnity still remains upon the orphans].

R. SIMEON B. GAMALIEL RULED etc. To what limit [of error]?[1] —R. Huna b. Judah replied in the name of R. Shesheth: To a half.[2] So it was also taught: R. Simeon b. Gamaliel ruled, If the court sold for one *maneh* what was worth two hundred *zuz*, or for two hundred *zuz* what was worth one *maneh*, their sale is valid.

Amemar laid down in the name of R. Joseph: A court that sold [one's estate] without a [previous] public announcement are deemed[3] to have overlooked a law cited in a Mishnah and [their decision][4] must be reversed. [You say] 'Are deemed'?[3] Have they not in actual fact overlooked one, since we learned:[5] The assessment [of the property] of the orphans[6] [must be accompanied by a public announcement for a period of] thirty days, and the assessment of consecrated land[7] [for a period of] sixty days; and the announcement must be made both in the morning and in the evening?[8]—If [the ruling[9] were to be derived] from that [Mishnah alone] it might be presumed that it applied only to an agent[10] but not to a court; hence we were taught[9] [that the law applied to a court also].

R. Ashi raised an objection against Amemar: IF AN ASSESSMENT OF JUDGES WAS BY ONE SIXTH LESS, OR ONE SIXTH MORE [THAN THE ACTUAL VALUE OF THE PROPERTY], THEIR SALE IS VOID, but [it follows] if it corresponded to the actual worth of the land[11] their sale is valid. Does not this[12] [apply even to a case] where no public announcement was made?[13]—No; [it applies only to one] where an announcement was made. But since the final clause [refers to a case] where an announcement was made [must not] the first clause[14] [refer to one] where no

(1) Is the sale valid. (2) Of the actual value. (3) Lit., 'are made'. (4) Unlike an erroneous decision that does not conflict with a Mishnah, which remains in force and compensation is paid by the court. (5) In a Mishnah. (6) That is put up for sale to meet the claims of their father's widow or daughters. (7) Sold by the Temple treasurer. (8) 'Ar. 21*b*. (9) Laid down by Amemar in the name of R. Joseph. (10) Who sells orphans' property. (11) Lit., 'worth for worth', *or* 'equal for equal'. (12) The implied ruling that the sale is valid. (13) Is this then an objection against Amemar? (14) Since two adjacent clauses would not repeat the same law.

announcement was made; for in the final clause it was taught: IF A BILL FOR INSPECTION,[1] HOWEVER, HAS BEEN DRAWN UP, THEIR SALE IS VALID EVEN IF THEY SOLD FOR TWO HUNDRED ZUZ WHAT WAS WORTH ONE MANEH, OR FOR ONE MANEH WHAT WAS WORTH TWO HUNDRED ZUZ?[2]—The fact indeed is [that the first clause refers to a case] where no announcement was made, and [yet[3] there is] no difficulty, for one ruling[4] refers to objects concerning which public announcements must be made, while the other[5] refers to objects concerning which no public announcements are made, such as[6] slaves, movables and deeds. (What is the reason [why no announcement is made in the case of] slaves?—[Because if one were made] they might hear it and escape. Movables and deeds?—Because they might be stolen.) If you wish I might reply:[7] One ruling[8] refers to a time when an announcement is made while the other[5] refers to a time when no announcement is made, the Nehardeans having laid down that for poll-tax,[9] maintenance[10] and funeral expenses [an estate][11] is sold without a public announcement.[12] And if you prefer I might reply:[7] One ruling[8] applies to a place where announcements are made while the other[5] applies to one where no announcements are made, R. Naḥman having stated: Never was a bill for inspection[13] drawn up at Nehardea.[14] From this [statement][15] one implied that [the reason[16] was] because they[17] were experts in assessments; but R. Joseph b. Minyomi stated: It was explained to me by R. Naḥman [that the reason is] because

(1) Which involves, of course, a public announcement (v. *supra* p. 632, n. 12). (2) Is this then an objection against Amemar? (3) Despite the deduction which is apparently in contradiction to Amemar's ruling. (4) Lit., 'here', the ruling of Amemar. (5) The first clause of our Mishnah. (6) Lit., 'and these are objects concerning which no public announcement is made'. (7) To the objection against Amemar that was raised *supra*. (8) Lit., 'here', the ruling of Amemar. (9) On behalf of orphans. (10) Of one's widow or daughters. (11) Of a deceased, inherited by his orphans. (12) Since in all these cases money is urgently needed no time can be spared for the usual public announcement that must precede other sales ordered by a court; v. *supra* 87*a*. (13) Cf. *supra* p. 632, n. 12. (14) Cf. *supra* p. 222, n. 8. (15) Of R. Naḥman. (16) For dispensing with a bill of inspection at Nehardea. (17) The Nehardeans.

they[1] were nicknamed 'consumers of publicly auctioned estates'.[2]

Rab Judah ruled in the name of Samuel: Orphans' movables must be assessed[3] and sold forthwith.[4] R. Ḥisda ruled in the name of Abimi: They are to be sold[5] in the markets.[6] There is, however, no difference of opinion between them.[7] One speaks of a place[8] in the proximity of a market,[9] while the other deals with one[8] from which the market is far.[10]

R. Kahana had in his possession some beer that belonged to the orphan R. Mesharsheya b. Ḥilkai. He kept it until the festival,[11] saying, 'Though it might deteriorate,[12] it will have a quick sale.'[13]

Rabina had in his possession some wine belonging to the orphan Rabina the Little, his sister's son, and he had also some wine of his own which he was about to take up to Sikara.[14] When he came to R. Ashi and asked him, 'May I carry [the orphan's wine] with my own'[15] the other told him, 'You may go; it is not superior to your own'.

MISHNAH. [A MINOR] WHO EXERCISED THE RIGHT OF

(1) Who bought orphans' estates that were offered for sale after a public announcement. (2) A description of contempt. At such enforced sales the buyers usually made exorbitant profits at the expense of the helpless orphans. (3) Immediately on their father's death. (4) In order to prevent their deterioration. (5) [Read with MS.M.: They are taken to the markets, מוליכין.] (6) Or 'on market days' (cf. Rashi, s.v. דמקרב). (7) Rab Judah and R. Ḥisda. (8) Lit., 'that'. (9) *Aliter:* A time when market day is near (cf. Rashi loc. cit.). (10) *Aliter:* 'When market day is a long way off' (cf. l.c.). (11) Though beer must be classed as movables. (12) איצצתא, 'depreciation in the market' or 'deterioration of quality' (cf. Jast.). *Aliter:* 'Though it might become sour', (cf. Rashi). (13) Lit., 'will bring quick money', i.e., there will be no need to sell on credit. Cash sales, though at a comparatively small price, are preferable to sales on credit that might command a higher price. (14) [A town on the Tigris near Maḥuza, Obermeyer, p. 186]. (15) *Sc.* may a trustee undertake the risk of sea transport? [The wine could be taken from Matha Meḥasia (Sura) the home of Rabina to Sikara, either overland or by boat. The former journey, though shorter, was the more expensive and involved greater risk of breakages to the earthenware barrels in which the wine was transported, v. Obermeyer, p. 188ff.]

MI'UN,[1] A FORBIDDEN RELATIVE OF THE SECOND DEGREE,[2] OR A WOMAN WHO IS INCAPABLE OF PROCREATION IS NOT ENTITLED EITHER TO A KETHUBAH[3] OR TO THE BENEFITS[4] [OF HER MELOG[1] PROPERTY][5] OR TO MAINTENANCE,[6] OR TO HER WORN OUT ARTICLES.[7] IF THE MAN, HOWEVER, HAD MARRIED HER AT THE OUTSET ON THE UNDERSTANDING THAT SHE WAS INCAPABLE OF PROCREATION SHE IS ENTITLED TO A KETHUBAH. A WIDOW WHO WAS MARRIED TO A HIGH PRIEST,[8] A DIVORCED WOMAN OR A ḤALUẒAH[1] WHO WAS MARRIED TO A COMMON PRIEST,[9] A BASTARD OR A NETHINAH[1] WHO WAS MARRIED TO AN ISRAELITE, OR THE DAUGHTER OF AN ISRAELITE WHO WAS MARRIED TO A NATHIN,[1] OR A BASTARD IS ENTITLED TO A KETHUBAH.[10]

GEMARA. Rab taught: A minor who is released by means of a letter of divorce is not entitled to a *kethubah*[11] and, much less so, [a minor] who exercises the right of *mi'un*.[1] Samuel taught: [A minor] who exercises the right of *mi'un*[1] is not entitled to a *kethubah*,[12] but a minor who is released by a letter of divorce is entitled to her *kethubah*.[13] Samuel[14] follows his [previously

(1) V. Glos. (2) Who is forbidden by Rabbinic, though not by Pentateuchal, law (cf. Yeb. 21*a*). (3) Cf. Yeb. 113*a*, B.M. 67*a*; the first mentioned because her separation may be affected even against her husband's will, the second was penalized for contracting an unlawful marriage (cf. Yeb. 85*b*) while in the case of the last her marriage is regarded as a contract under false pretences. (4) Lit., 'fruit'. *Aliter:* Usufruct. (5) *Sc.* her husband is under no obligation to pay her ransom if she is taken captive, though in the case of a legal and normal marriage a husband must assume such obligation (in return for the usufruct of his wife's *melog* property). As this woman is not entitled to a *kethubah* she is also deprived of the right to be ransomed which is one of the terms of a *kethubah*. *Aliter:* Her husband need not refund the usufruct. (6) Cf. *supra* note 5 *mutatis mutandis*. The limitations of this ruling are dealt with *infra* 107*b*. (7) The articles which she brought to her husband on marriage and the value of which was included in her *kethubah*. If her husband has used these articles he need not compensate her for their wear or loss when she leaves him. (8) V. Lev. XXI, 13. (9) V. ibid. 7. (10) Yeb. 84*a*. (11) Since the marriage of a minor, in his opinion, has no validity and her status is that of one seduced. (12) Cf. *supra* note 3. (13) Because a divorce can be given with the husband's consent only. (14) In his ruling just cited.

expressed] principle; for he laid down: [A minor] who exercises the right of *mi'un*[1] is not entitled to a *kethubah*[2] but a minor who is released by a letter of divorce is entitled to her *kethubah*;[3] [a minor] who exercises the right of *mi'un*[1] is not [through this act] disqualified from marrying the brothers [of her husband],[4] nor is she thereby disqualified from marrying a priest,[5] but [a minor who] is released by a letter of divorce is [through this act] disqualified from marrying the brothers [of her husband][6] and also from marrying a priest;[7] [a minor] who exercises the right of *mi'un* need not wait three months[8] [101*a*] but [a minor who] was released by a letter of divorce must wait three months.[9] What does he[10] teach us when all these cases have already been taught:[11] If [a minor] has exercised the right of *mi'un* against her husband he is permitted to marry her relatives[12] and she is permitted to marry his relatives,[12] and he does not disqualify her from marrying a priest;[13] but if he gave her a letter of divorce he is forbidden to marry her relatives and she is forbidden to marry his relatives and he also disqualifies her from marrying a priest?[14]—He found it necessary [to restate these rulings in order to mention:] 'She must wait three months' which we did not learn.[15]

Must one assume [that they[16] differ on the same principles] as the following Tannaim: R. Eliezer stated, There is no validity whatsoever in the act of a minor, and her husband is entitled neither to anything she finds,[17] nor to the work of her hands,[17] nor may he invalidate her vows;[18] he is not her heir[17] and he may

(1) V. Glos. (2) Cf. *supra* p. 639, n. 3. (3) V. p. 639, n. 13. (4) V. p. 639, n. 11. (5) Since she has not the status of a divorced woman, *mi'un* dissolving the union retrospectively. (6) Because it is forbidden to marry a woman whom one's brother had divorced. (7) V. Lev. XXI, 7. (8) After *mi'un*, before contracting a second marriage, though such a period must be allowed to pass in the case of any other divorced woman or widow. Cf. *supra* n. 5. (9) As any other woman (v. *supra* note 8). (10) Samuel, in the statement cited. (11) In a Mishnah. (12) V. *supra* p. 639, n. 11. (13) Cf. note 5. (14) Yeb. 108*a*. (15) In the Mishnah of Yeb. cited. (16) Rab and Samuel. (17) To which a lawful husband is entitled. (18) Which is the privilege of a husband (cf. Num. XXX, 7ff).

not defile himself for her;[1] this being the general rule: She is in no respect regarded as his wife, except that it is necessary for her to make a declaration of refusal;[2] and R. Joshua stated, The act of a minor is valid, and her husband has the right to anything she finds[3] and to the work of her hands,[3] to invalidate her vows,[4] to be her heir,[3] and to defile himself for her;[5] the general principle being that she is regarded as his wife in every respect, except that she may leave him[2] by declaring her refusal against him?[6] Must one then assume that Rab[7] has laid down the same principle as that of R. Eliezer[8] and that Samuel[9] has laid down the same principle as that of R. Joshua?[10]—There is no difference of opinion between them[11] as to what was the view[12] of R. Eliezer;[13] they differ only in respect of the view[12] of R. Joshua. Samuel [ruled] in agreement with R. Joshua; but Rab argued that[14] R. Joshua maintained his view only there[15] [where the benefits[16] are transferred] from her to him[17] but not [where the benefits[18] are to be transferred] from him to her.[19]

OR TO HER WORN OUT ARTICLES. Said R. Huna b. Ḥiyya to

(1) If he is a priest. Only a lawful husband may (cf. Lev. XXI, 2). (2) If she wishes to marry another man. (3) Rabbinic law has conferred upon him the same rights as those of a lawful husband. Cf. p. 640, n. 17. (4) Which is the privilege of a husband (cf. Num. XXX, 7ff). (5) Even if he is a priest (cf. *supra* n. 1). Since he inherits her she is regarded as a *meth mizwah* (v. Glos.) for whom he may defile himself though Pentateuchally she is not his proper wife; v. Rashi Yeb. 108*a*. (6) And no letter of divorce is required. Yeb. 89*b*, 108*a*. (7) Who does not allow a *kethubah* to a divorced minor. (8) Who ruled: 'There is no validity whatsoever in the act of a minor'. (9) Who allows to a minor her *kethubah*. (10) Who ruled that 'the act of a minor is valid'. Is it likely, however, that Rab and Samuel who were Amoraim would engage in a dispute which is practically a mere repetition of that of Tannaim? (11) Lit., 'all the world', *sc.* Rab and Samuel. (12) Lit., 'according'. (13) I.e., even Samuel must admit that according to R. Eliezer, no *kethubah* is due to a minor *a minori ad majus* (cf. *infra* nn. 16 to 19 and text *mutatis mutandis*). (14) Lit., 'up to here'. (15) In the case cited from Yeb. (16) Inheritance, handiwork and finds. (17) A husband may well be given such privileges in order to encourage men to undertake the responsibilities of married life. (18) Such as the *kethubah* and the other privileges contained therein. (19) There is no need to hold out inducements of marriage to a woman who is assumed to be always craving for marriage.

R. Kahana: You have told us in the name of Samuel that this[1] was taught only in respect of *melog*,[2] but that to *ẓon barzel*[2] property she is entitled. R. Papa, in considering this statement, raised the point: To which [class of women did Samuel refer]? If it be suggested: To [A MINOR] WHO EXERCISED THE RIGHT OF MI'UN [the difficulty would arise:] If [the articles] are still in existence she would be entitled to receive them in either case,[3] and if they were no longer in existence she would in neither case[3] be entitled to receive them.[4] [Is the reference], then, to A WOMAN WHO IS INCAPABLE OF PROCREATION? [But here again, it may be objected:] If [the articles] were still in existence she would receive them in either case,[3] and if they no longer existed [the ruling] should be reversed: She should receive *melog* property since [the capital] always remains in her legal possession[5] but should not receive *ẓon barzel* property since [the capital] does not remain in her possession.[6] [The fact,] however, [is that the reference is] to A FORBIDDEN RELATIVE OF THE SECOND DEGREE, in whose case[7] the Rabbis have penalized the woman in respect of [what is due to her] from the man,[8] and the man in respect of [what is due to him] from the woman.[9] R. Shimi b. Ashi remarked:

(1) That the woman spoken of in our Mishnah is not entitled to compensation for the WORN OUT CLOTHES. It will be discussed anon to which of the three classes of woman mentioned Samuel referred. (2) V. Glos. (3) Whether they were *melog* or *ẓon barzel*. (4) Since, in the case of *ẓon barzel*, the husband might plead that what he used up was legally his, and in respect of *melog* also, though he had no right to use up the 'capital', he might still plead justification on the ground that it would have become his by the right of heirship if he had survived her. In either case he would be justified in his claim that the minor's right to compensation does not come into force except on divorce. (5) And the husband, therefore, had no right to use it up. (6) But in that of the husband who was consequently entitled to use it up completely. (7) Since both husband and wife are guilty of a transgression. (8) Lit., 'fined her in respect of what is his'. Viz., the *kethubah* and maintenance as well as for the wear of *melog* articles which he used up unlawfully and for which, in the case of a lawful marriage, he would have been liable to pay compensation to the woman. (9) Lit., 'fined him in respect of what is hers'. He must pay compensation for the wear of *ẓon barzel* articles which he used up, though a lawful wife cannot object to such use. [Although the woman is nor-

From R. Kahana's statement[1] it may be inferred [that if a lawful wife] brought to her husband[2] a cloak,[3] the article is [to be treated as] capital and the man may not continue to wear it until it is worn out.[4] But did not R. Naḥman, however, rule that [a cloak must be treated as] produce?[5]—He[6] differs from R. Naḥman.

IS NOT ENTITLED [. . .] TO A KETHUBAH. Samuel stated: This was taught only in respect of the *maneh*[7] and the two hundred *zuz*;[8] to the additional jointure,[9] however, she[10] is entitled. So it was also taught: The women concerning whom the Sages have ruled, 'They are not entitled to a *kethubah*' as, for instance, a minor who exercised the right of *mi'un* and the others enumerated in the same context,[11] are not entitled to the *maneh*[12] or to the two hundred *zuz*,[13] but are entitled to their additional jointures; women, however, concerning whom the Sages have ruled, 'They may be divorced without [receiving their] *kethubah*' as, for instance, [a wife who] transgresses the [Mosaic] law, and others enumerated in the same context,[14] are not entitled to their additional jointures[9] and much less to [their statutory *kethubahs* of] a *maneh*[12] or two hundred *zuz*;[13] whilst a woman who is divorced on the ground of ill repute[15] takes only[16] what is hers[17] and departs. This[18] provides support to R. Hunah who laid down: If she played the harlot [a wife] does not in consequence

mally entitled to compensation for the wear of the *ẓon barzel* property, it is still considered a fine, as legally the husband should, in this case, not be made to pay since he does not divorce of his own free will (R. Nissim). *Var. lec.*, they fined her in respect of what is hers (i.e., the *melog* property) and him in respect of what is his (i.e., the *ẓon barzel* property).]

(1) That in a forbidden marriage the woman is not entitled to compensation for worn out *melog* articles. (2) On marrying him. (3) As *melog*. (4) If he did so he must pay compensation. (5) *Supra* 79b. (6) R. Kahana. (7) The statutory *kethubah* that is due to one who married as a widow or divorcee. (8) Due to a virgin (cf. *supra* note 7 *mutatis mutandis*). (9) Which a husband settles on his wife at his own pleasure. (10) Lit., 'they', *sc.* the classes of women mentioned in our Mishnah. (11) Lit., 'and her associates'. (12) V. *supra* note 7. (13) V. *supra* n. 8. (14) Cf. *supra* n. 10 and v. Mishnah *supra* 72a. (15) Lit., 'on evil name', *sc.* of faithlessness. (16) MS.M. inserts, 'the worn out clothes'. (17) Lit., 'before her', *sc.* her *melog* property. (18) The last ruling in the cited Baraitha.

forfeit [101b] her worn out articles that are still in existence.

A tanna recited in the presence of R. Naḥman: [A wife who] played the harlot forfeits in consequence her worn out articles [though they are still] in existence. 'If she', the other said to him, 'has played the harlot, have her chattels also played the harlot?[1] Recite rather: She does not forfeit her worn out articles [that are still] in existence'. Rabbah b. Bar Ḥana stated in the name of R. Joḥanan: This[2] is the view of the unnamed R. Menaḥem,[3] but the Sages ruled: [A wife who] played the harlot does not thereby forfeit her worn out articles that are still in existence.

IF THE MAN, HOWEVER, HAD MARRIED HER etc. Said R. Huna: A woman incapable of procreation [has sometimes the status of] a wife and [sometimes she has] no such status;[4] a widow[5] [has always the status of] a proper wife. 'A woman incapable of procreation [has sometimes the status of] a wife and [sometimes she] has no such status'; if the husband knew of her [defect][6] she is entitled to a *kethubah*[7] and if he did not know of her [defect] she is not entitled to a *kethubah*. 'A widow[5] [has always the status of] a proper wife', for, whether her husband was aware of her [widowhood] or whether he was not aware of it, she is always entitled to a *kethubah*. Rab Judah, however, said: The one[8] as well as the other[9] [has sometimes the status of] a wife and [sometimes she has] no such status,[4] for [in either case] if her husband was aware of her [condition or status] she is entitled to a *kethubah* and if he was not aware of it she is not entitled to a *kethubah*. An objection was raised: If [a High Priest] married on the presumption that [the woman] was in her widowhood[10] and it was found that she had been in such a condition,[10] she is entitled to her *kethubah*.

(1) Surely not. (2) The version recited by the Tanna in the presence of R. Naḥman. (3) *Sc.* whose rulings were often quoted anonymously in the Mishnah and the Baraitha. [The reference is to R. Menaḥem b. R. Jose, v. Neg. 26*a*.] (4) Lit., 'and not a wife'. (5) Even if married to a High Priest (cf. Lev. XXI, 14). (6) Before he married her. (7) He is assumed to have acquiesced. (8) MS.M., 'one incapable of procreation'. (9) 'A widow' (so MS.M.) who was married to a High Priest. (10) Lit., 'so'.

Does not this imply that if[1] there was no presumption[2] she is not entitled to a *kethubah?*[3]—Do not infer 'that[1] if there was no such presumption' but infer [this:] If he married her on the presumption that she was not in her widowhood[4] and it was found that she had been in such a condition,[4] she is not entitled to a *kethubah*. What, however, [is the ruling where he married her] with no assumption? Is she entitled [to a *kethubah*]? Then instead of stating, 'On the presumption that [the woman] was in her widowhood[4] and it was found that she had been in such a condition,[4] she is entitled to her *kethubah*', should it not rather have been stated, 'With no assumption she is entitled to her *kethubah*'[5] and [it would have been obvious that this[6] applied] with even greater force to the former?[7] Furthermore, it was explicitly taught: If he[8] married her in the belief[9] [that she was a widow] and it was found that his belief was justified,[9] she is entitled to a *kethubah*, but if he married her with no assumption she is not entitled to a *kethubah*. [Does not this present] an objection against R. Huna?—It was our Mishnah that caused R. Huna to err. He thought that, since a distinction was drawn in the case of a woman incapable of procreation[10] and no distinction was drawn in respect of a widow, it must be inferred that a widow is entitled [to a *kethubah* even if she was married] with no assumption of her status. [In fact, however,] this is no [proper conclusion], for in stating the case of a widow the author intended to apply to it[11] the distinction drawn in the case of the woman who was incapable of procreation.[12]

(1) Lit., 'but'. (2) A case analogous to that where the High Priest was not aware of the woman's widowhood, *supra*. (3) An objection against R. Huna. (4) Lit., 'so'. (5) So BaḤ. Cur. edd. omit the last six words. (6) The woman's right to her *kethubah*. (7) Lit., 'that', where the High Priest actually presumed the woman's widowhood. (8) A High Priest. (9) בידוע, particip. pass. of ידע ('to know') with prefix. (10) 'IF THE MAN, HOWEVER, HAD MARRIED HER AT THE OUTSET . . . SHE IS ENTITLED etc.'. (11) Lit., 'stands on'. (12) Which immediately precedes it.

KETHUBOTH

CHAPTER XII

MISHNAH. IF A MAN MARRIED A WIFE AND SHE MADE AN ARRANGEMENT WITH HIM THAT HE SHOULD MAINTAIN HER DAUGHTER[1] FOR FIVE YEARS, HE MUST MAINTAIN HER FOR FIVE YEARS. IF SHE WAS [SUBSEQUENTLY][2] MARRIED TO ANOTHER MAN AND ARRANGED WITH HIM ALSO THAT HE SHOULD MAINTAIN HER DAUGHTER[1] FOR FIVE YEARS, HE, TOO, MUST MAINTAIN HER FOR FIVE YEARS. THE FIRST HUSBAND IS NOT ENTITLED TO PLEAD, 'IF SHE WILL COME TO ME I WILL MAINTAIN HER',[3] BUT HE MUST FORWARD HER MAINTENANCE TO HER AT THE PLACE WHERE HER MOTHER [LIVES].[4] SIMILARLY, THE TWO HUSBANDS CANNOT PLEAD, 'WE WILL MAINTAIN HER JOINTLY', BUT ONE MUST MAINTAIN HER AND THE OTHER ALLOW HER THE COST OF HER MAINTENANCE. IF SHE[5] MARRIED[2] HER HUSBAND MUST SUPPLY HER WITH MAINTENANCE AND THEY[6] ALLOW HER THE COST OF HER MAINTENANCE. SHOULD THEY[7] DIE, THEIR OWN DAUGHTERS ARE TO BE MAINTAINED OUT OF THEIR FREE ASSETS ONLY[8] BUT SHE[5] MUST BE MAINTAINED EVEN OUT OF ASSIGNED PROPERTY, BECAUSE SHE[9] [HAS THE SAME LEGAL STATUS] AS A CREDITOR. PRUDENT MEN USED TO WRITE,[10] 'ON CONDITION THAT I SHALL MAINTAIN YOUR DAUGHTER FOR FIVE YEARS WHILE YOU [CONTINUE TO LIVE] WITH ME'.

(1) From another husband. (2) Before the expiration of the five years. (3) *Sc.* refusing maintenance on the ground that her mother with whom she lives was no longer his wife. (4) *Var. lec.*, 'to the place of her mother' (so according to the separate edd. of the Mishnah and Alfasi). (5) The daughter. (6) Respectively; each one the full cost. (7) The two husbands (v. *supra* n. 2). (8) Cf. Giṭ. 48*b*. (9) Whose rights are based on a written bond. (10) In any agreement to maintain a wife's daughter.

GEMARA. It was stated: A man who said to his fellow, 'I owe you a *maneh*'[1] is, R. Joḥanan ruled, liable; but Resh Laḳish ruled: He is free. How is one to understand [this dispute]? If [it refers to a case] where the man said to them[2] 'You are my witnesses', what [it might be objected] is the reason of Resh Laḳish who holds him to be free?[3] If [it is a case] where he did not say to them,[2] 'You are my witnesses', what [it might equally be objected] can be the reason of R. Joḥanan who holds him liable?[4]—The fact is[5] that [the dispute relates to a case] where he did not tell them, 'You are my witnesses', but here we are[6] dealing [with the case of a person] who said to another, 'I owe you a *maneh*'[1] by [handing to him][7] a note of indebtedness.[8] R. Joḥanan ruled: He is liable, because the contents[9] of a bond[10] has the same force as if the man [who delivered it] said, 'You are my witnesses'; but Resh Laḳish ruled: He is free, because the contents[9] of a bond has no binding force.

We learned: IF A MAN MARRIED A WIFE AND SHE MADE AN AGREEMENT WITH HIM THAT HE SHALL MAINTAIN HER DAUGHTER FOR FIVE YEARS, HE MUST MAINTAIN HER FOR FIVE YEARS. Does not this refer to[11] a case like this?[12] [102*a*]—No, [our Mishnah is dealing] with deeds on verbal agreements,[13] and [the ruling[14] was necessary] in accordance with [the view] of

(1) V. Glos. (2) Those who were present at the time of his admission of the debt. (3) Such a ruling, surely, is contrary to what has been laid down in Sanh. 29*b*. (4) This, surely, is also contrary to what was taught in Sanh. 29*b*, that the admission is valid only where the debtor explicitly stated, 'You are my witnesses'. (5) Lit., 'always'. (6) Lit., 'in what are we'. (7) In the presence of witnesses. (8) In which the debt is acknowledged in the man's handwriting but is not attested by his signature nor by that of witnesses. (9) Lit., 'thing'. (10) Delivered in the presence of witnesses. (11) Lit., 'what, not?' (12) Where the husband had handed over the written agreement (cf. *supra* note 8 *mutatis mutandis*) in the presence of witnesses without specifically appointing them as such. Had the document been duly signed the ruling, being so obvious, would have been superfluous. Does this then present an objection against Resh Laḳish? (13) שטרי פסיקתא, in which the witnesses enter the terms that were verbally agreed upon between the parties and duly attach their signatures. (14) Which might appear superfluous in view of the fact that the agreement has been properly drawn up and duly signed.

R. Giddal, since R. Giddal has laid down in the name of Rab:[1]
[If[2] one man said to another,] 'How much are you giving to your
son?' [and the other replies,] 'Such and such a sum', and [when
the other asks,] 'How much are you giving to your daughter?'
[the first replies,] 'Such and such a sum', [and on the basis of this
talk] a betrothal was effected,[3] kinyan is deemed to have been
executed, these being matters concerning which kinyan is effected
by a mere verbal arrangement.[4]

Come and hear: If a man gave to a priest in writing [a statement]
that he[5] owed him five sela's[6] he must[7] pay him the five sela's
and his son is not redeemed thereby![8] — There [the law] is different
because one is under a Pentateuchal obligation [to give them]
to him.[9] If that be so, why did he write? — In order to choose for
himself a priest.[10] If that is the case[11] why is not his son redeemed?[12]
— In agreement with a ruling of 'Ulla; For 'Ulla said, Pentateuchally [the son] is redeemed as soon as [the father] gives [the note
of money indebtedness to the priest,] and the reason why the
Rabbis ruled that he was not redeemed is because a preventive
measure was enacted against the possibility of the assumption
that redemption may be effected by means of bonds [in general].[13]

Raba said: [Their[14] dispute seems to follow the same principles]

(1) Ḳid. 9b.   (2) In negotiating a marriage.   (3) Lit., 'they stood and betrothed'.
(4) No symbolic kinyan being necessary. Our Mishnah, too, deals similarly with
a verbal agreement from which symbolic kinyan was absent; and, contrary to
the opinion that an agreement without kinyan is invalid, it lays down the law
in agreement with R. Giddal.   (5) Lit., 'that I'.   (6) Or shekels. Such a sum is
due to the priest for the redemption of an Israelite's firstborn son (cf. Ex.
XIII, 13 and Num. XVIII, 16).   (7) Though the document was unsigned and
no kinyan was executed and, in consequence, should have no more legal force
than a verbal admission. This contradicts Resh Laḳish.   (8) Bek. 51a.   (9) [He
is not actually obliged Biblically to give to this particular priest, hence omit
'to him' with MS.M. which reads 'because it is Biblical'.]   (10) In the absence
of the written document the five sela's could have been given to any other
priest.   (11) That the Pentateuchal obligation confers upon a legally invalid
document the force of one that was duly signed by witnesses.   (12) A legal
bond, surely, might be regarded as a virtual payment.   (13) Other than those
in which the father of the child himself assumed the liability.   (14) R. Joḥanan
and Resh Laḳish.

as [laid down by] Tannaim: [If the guarantee] of a guarantor appears[1] below the signatures to bonds of indebtedness,[2] [the creditor] may recover his debt from [the guarantor's] free property.[3] Such a case once came before R. Ishmael who decided that [the debt] may be recovered from [the guarantor's] free property.[3] Ben Nannus, however, said to him, '[The debt may] be recovered neither from free property nor from assigned property'. 'Why?' the other asked him. 'Behold', he replied, 'this is just as if [a creditor] were [in the act of] throttling a debtor[4] in the street,[5] and his friend found him and said to him, "Leave him alone and I will pay you", [where he is undoubtedly] exempt from liability, since the loan was not made through trust in him.'[6] May it not be suggested that R. Joḥanan holds the same view as R. Ishmael while Resh Lakish holds that of Ben Nannus?—On the view of Ben Nannus there can be no difference of opinion;[7] [102b] their dispute, however, might relate to the view of R. Ishmael. R. Joḥanan is, [of course,] in agreement with R. Ishmael, while Resh Lakish [might argue:] R. Ishmael maintains his view there[8] only[9] because a Pentateuchal responsibility is involved[10] but [not] here where no Pentateuchal responsibility is involved.

The [above] text [stated]: 'R. Giddal has laid down in the name of Rab: [If one man said to another,] "How much are you giving

(1) Lit., 'which goes out'. (2) [The guarantor simply declaring 'I am guarantor' without attaching his signature (Tosaf.).] (3) But not from property which he sold or mortgaged. Since the signatures of the witnesses do not appear *below* the guarantee, the guarantor's undertaking can have no more force than a verbal promise, or a loan that has not been secured by a bond, in which case no assigned property is pledged to the creditor. (4) Lit., 'his fellow'. (5) *Sc.* using violence against him. (6) Such a guarantee is offered for the sole purpose of rescuing the debtor from the creditor's violence. It cannot be regarded as a serious guarantee to discharge the debt, since the debt was incurred before the guarantee was given, v. B.B. 175*b*. (7) I.e., even R. Joḥanan must admit that Ben Nannus differs from his ruling. For, if in the case of a guarantee which has Pentateuchal authority (v. B.B. 173*b*), Ben Nannus does not recognize the validity of a personally unattested undertaking, how much less would he recognize such an undertaking in a case like that spoken of by R. Joḥanan. (8) The case of the guarantor. (9) Lit., 'until here'. (10) The recognition of a guarantor's responsibility is (as stated *supra*) Pentateuchal.

to your son?" [and the other replied,] "Such and such a sum", and [when the other asks,] "How much are you giving to your daughter?" [the first replies,] "Such and such a sum", [and on the basis of this talk] betrothal was effected, *kinyan* is deemed to have been executed, these being matters concerning which *kinyan* is effected by a mere verbal arrangement'.[1] Said Raba: It stands to reason that Rab's ruling should apply [only] to the case of a man whose daughter was[2] a *na'arah*,[3] since the benefit [of her betrothal][4] goes to him,[5] but not to that of a *bogereth*,[3] since the benefit [of the betrothal of the latter][4] does not go to him; but, by God! Rab meant [his ruling to include] even one who is a *bogereth*. For, should you not concede this, [the objection could be put:] What benefit does the son's[6] father derive?[7] The reason consequently must be that[8] owing to the pleasure of the formation of a mutual family tie they decide to allow one another the full rights of *kinyan*.

Said Rabina to R. Ashi: Are those verbal arrangements,[9] allowed to be recorded[10] or are they not allowed to be recorded?[11] —They, the other replied, may not be recorded.[12] He[13] raised an objection against him:[14] PRUDENT MEN USED TO WRITE,[15] 'ON CONDITION THAT I SHALL MAINTAIN YOUR DAUGHTER

(1) *Supra* 102*a* q.v. for notes. (2) At the time betrothal was negotiated. (3) V. Glos. (4) *Sc.* the sum of money or object of value which the man gives to the woman as a token of betrothal which constitutes the required *kinyan*. (5) Lit., 'to his hand'. As a return for the benefit he, it may well be presumed, readily agrees that even his verbal undertaking should have the legal force of a personally attested written deed. (6) *Sc.* the bridegroom's. (7) Surely none; since the pecuniary benefit from his son's betrothal does not belong to him. (8) Lit., 'but'. (9) Lit., 'words', spoken of *supra*, in connection with which no symbolic *kinyan* was executed. (10) *Sc.* in a deed, by witnesses. (11) For, if they were to be embodied in a deed, the holder of such a deed would be enabled to distrain on assigned property to which, in the absence of symbolic *kinyan*, he is legally not entitled. [The question, according to Isaiah Trani, is whether these may be reduced to writing without the consent of both parties, either of whom may object to encumbering the property with a mortgage, v. *Shittah Mekubbezeth a.l.* and R. Nissim on Kid. 9*b* also, for other interpretations.] (12) Cf. *supra* nn. 10 and 11. (13) Rabina. (14) R. Ashi. (15) כותבין emphasis on 'WRITE'.

FOR FIVE YEARS WHILE YOU [CONTINUE TO LIVE] WITH ME'?[1] —The meaning of[2] 'WRITE' [in this context] is 'say'. Could 'saying', however, be described as 'writing'?—Yes, for so we learned: If a husband gives to his wife a written undertaking,[3] 'I have no claim whatsoever upon your estates',[4] and R. Ḥiyya taught:[5] If a husband said[6] to his wife.[7]

Come and hear: Deeds of betrothal[8] and marriage[9] may not be written except with the consent of both parties,[10] but, [it follows, that] with the consent of both parties they may be written. Does not this refer to[11] deeds based on verbal agreements?[12]—No; deeds of actual betrothal,[13] [the ruling[14] being] in agreement with R. Papa and R. Sherabya; for it was stated: If a man wrote it[15] in her name[16] but without her consent she is, said Rabbah[17] and Rabina, betrothed, but R. Papa and R. Sherabya said, She is not betrothed.[18]

Come and hear: SHOULD THEY DIE, THEIR OWN DAUGHTERS ARE TO BE MAINTAINED OUT OF THEIR FREE PROPERTY ONLY BUT SHE MUST BE MAINTAINED EVEN OUT OF ASSIGNED PROPERTY, BECAUSE SHE [HAS THE SAME LEGAL STATUS] AS A CREDITOR![19]—Here we are dealing with a case where the

(1) Though the agreement was only verbal. How then could R. Ashi maintain that verbal arrangements may not be embodied in a deed? (2) Lit., 'what'. (3) הכותב. (4) Mishnah *supra* 83*a*. (5) In reference to this Mishnah which uses the expression of writing (v. *supra* n. 3). (6) Emphasis on the word האומר. (7) Which proves that a verbal statement is sometimes described as a written one. (8) Verbal agreements between the parties on the amounts promised. (9) *Kethubah* contracts. (10) B.B. 167*b*, Ḳid. 9*b*. (11) Lit., 'what, not?' (12) Cf. *supra* p. 647, n. 13. An objection thus arises against R. Ashi who ruled that verbal agreements 'may not be recorded'. [On Trani's interpretation (*supra* p. 650, n. 11) this passage is adduced in support of R. Ashi that such deeds cannot be written without the consent of both parties. This will, however, necessitate the deletion of the words '(it follows that) with the consent of both they may be written', which words in fact do not occur in MS.M.] (13) Betrothal may be effected by a deed wherein the man enters, 'Behold thou art betrothed unto me'. (14) Which requires the consent of the woman to such a deed. (15) A deed of betrothal. (16) Or 'for her sake', that of the woman he wishes to betroth. (17) *Var.*, 'Raba' (MS.M., the parallel passage in Ḳid., and Codes). (18) Ḳid. 9*b*, 48*a*. (19) Since only a written deed would confer

man was made to confirm his obligation[1] by a *ḳinyan.*[2] If so,[3] [the same right[4] should be enjoyed, should it not, by one's own] daughters also?—[This is a case] where *ḳinyan* was executed in favour of the one[5] but not in favour of the others.[5] Whence this certainty?[6]—Since she was in existence at the time the *ḳinyan* was executed, the *ḳinyan* in her favour is effective; the other daughters,[7] however, since they were not in existence at the time the *ḳinyan* was executed, the *ḳinyan* in their favour is not effective. But do we not also deal with the case where they[8] were in existence at the time of the *ḳinyan*, this being possible where,[9] for instance, the man had divorced his wife and then remarried her?—[This] however, [is the explanation:] Since she is not covered by the provision of Beth din[10] *ḳinyan* in her case is effective; in the case of the other daughters, however, who are protected by the provision of Beth din,[10] *ḳinyan* is not effective. Are they, on that account, worse off?[11]—This, however, is the reason: In the case of his own daughters, since they are protected by the provision of Beth din,[10] it might be assumed that he entrusted them[12] with some bundles [of money].[13]

THE FIRST HUSBAND IS NOT ENTITLED TO PLEAD [etc.] R. Ḥisda stated: This[14] implies that [the place of] a daughter

upon her such a status it is obvious that such a deed was in her possession, an objection against R. Ashi (cf. *supra* n. 12).

(1) To maintain his wife's daughter. (2) Lit., 'where they acquired (symbolic) possession from his hand'. Hence the permissibility of writing a deed. (3) That the verbal agreement was under a *ḳinyan*. (4) To exact the cost of maintenance from assigned property. (5) Lit., 'to this'. (6) The Mishnah, surely, does not mention *ḳinyan* in the case of the one and omit it in that of the others. (7) Who were presumably born from the marriage contracted at the time of the *ḳinyan*. (8) The man's own daughters. (9) Lit., 'and how is this to be imagined?' (10) The clause of the *kethubah* which entitles daughters born from that marriage to maintenance. (11) The contrary might, in fact, be expected: As they enjoy the privilege of the clause in the *kethubah* (v. *supra* n. 10) they should also be entitled to the privilege of the *ḳinyan*. (12) Lit., 'caused them to seize', before he died. (13) Or valuables, to discharge his obligation on the account of their maintenance. (14) The ruling that the maintenance of one's wife's daughter must be forwarded to the place where her mother lives.

must be with her mother.[1] Whence, [however, the proof] that we are dealing here[2] with one who is of age; is it not possible that[3] we are dealing only with a minor [whose custody must be entrusted to her mother] on account of what had once happened? For it was taught: If a man died and left a young son with his mother,[4] [and while] the father's heirs demand, 'Let him be brought up with us' his mother claims, 'My son should be brought up by me', [the son] must be left with his mother, but may not be left with anyone who is entitled to be his heir.[5] Such a case[6] once occurred and [the heirs] killed him on the eve of Passover![7] —If that were so[8] it should have been stated,[9] 'To wherever she is,' [103*a*] why then was it stated, 'AT THE PLACE WHERE HER MOTHER [LIVES]'?[10] Consequently it must be inferred that [the place of] a daughter, whether she be of age or a minor, is with her mother.

THE TWO HUSBANDS CANNOT PLEAD etc. A certain man once leased his mill to another for [the consideration of the latter's services in] grinding [his corn].[11] Eventually he became rich and

(1) The brothers who maintain her are not entitled to demand that she shall live with them. (2) In our Mishnah. (3) In stating, 'WHERE HER MOTHER (LIVES)'. (4) לאמו; wanting in Bomb. ed. (5) An interested party may be suspected of murder. (6) That the child was entrusted to the care of relatives who were entitled to be his legal heirs. (7) In order to secure his property. Now since there is nothing to prove that an older daughter (who is well capable of looking after herself) must also be maintained at her mother's house and cannot be compelled to live with the brothers and receive maintenance from them, an objection arises against R. Ḥisda. [Detractors of the Talmud, it may be mentioned, professed to find in this passage an allusion to the 'ritual' murder of 'Christian' children! The absurdity of this suggestion was pointed out by Eric Bischoff in his *Talmudkatechismus*, p. 38, where he describes it as '*sinnlos*' (senseless). It is evident that this incident was recorded to emphasize the danger of entrusting a child to the care of one who stands to benefit by its death. For we see here that even the sanctity of the Festival did not deter the brothers from perpetrating a crime for the purpose of gain. This danger has also been recognized in the English Law of Insurance which lays down that a man cannot insure his child's life to derive a benefit on its death]. (8) That a daughter who is of age may be compelled to live with her brothers. (9) In our Mishnah. (10) Emphasis on MOTHER. (11) No money rental having been arranged.

bought another mill and an ass. Thereupon he said to the other, 'Until now I have had my grinding done at your place but now[1] pay me rent'.—'I shall', the other replied, 'only grind for you'.[2] Rabina [in considering the case] intended to rule that it involved the very principle that was laid down in our Mishnah: THE TWO HUSBANDS CANNOT PLEAD, 'WE WILL MAINTAIN HER JOINTLY', BUT ONE MUST MAINTAIN HER AND THE OTHER ALLOWS HER THE COST OF HER MAINTENANCE.[3] R. 'Awira, however, said to him: Are [the two cases] alike? There [the woman][4] has only one stomach, not two;[5] but here[6] [the lessee] might well tell the owner, 'Grind [in your own mill][7] and sell; grind [in mine][8] and keep'.[9] This,[10] however, has been said only in a case where [the lessee] has no [other orders for] grinding at his mill,[11] but if he has [sufficient orders for] grinding at his mill he may in such circumstances be compelled [not to act] in the manner of Sodom.[12]

MISHNAH. SHOULD A WIDOW SAY, 'I HAVE NO DESIRE TO MOVE FROM MY HUSBAND'S HOUSE', THE HEIRS CANNOT TELL HER, 'GO TO YOUR FATHER'S HOUSE AND WE WILL MAINTAIN YOU', BUT THEY MUST MAINTAIN HER IN HER HUSBAND'S HOUSE[13] AND GIVE HER A DWELLING BECOMING

(1) 'That I have another mill in which to grind my corn'. (2) But will pay no rent. (3) As in this case a cash payment must be made though originally only maintenance was undertaken so in the case of the miller a cash rental may be demanded though the original arrangement was for payment in service. (4) Spoken of in our Mishnah. (5) She cannot be expected to consume a double allowance of food. Hence there is no other alternative but that of substituting one monetary payment for one allowance of food. (6) The case of the miller. (7) The one you bought. (8) The one I hired from you. (9) A suggestion which may well be adopted by the owner without any loss to himself. (10) That the lessee cannot be compelled to pay a cash rental. (11) It would be an act of injustice to compel him to pay rent while his machinery stood idle. It is more equitable that he should be enabled to continue the original agreement whereby he is both kept employed and pays his rent. (12) The Sodomites were notorious for refusing to do any favours even when they cost them nothing. 'A dog-in-the-manger attitude' (cf. B.B. Sonc. ed. p. 62, n. 3). (13) בבית בעלה, so MS.M. Wanting in cur. edd.

HER DIGNITY. IF SHE SAID, HOWEVER, 'I HAVE NO DESIRE TO MOVE FROM MY FATHER'S HOUSE', THE HEIRS ARE ENTITLED TO SAY TO HER, 'IF YOU STAY WITH US YOU WILL HAVE YOUR MAINTENANCE, BUT IF YOU DO NOT STAY WITH US YOU WILL RECEIVE NO MAINTENANCE'. IF SHE BASED HER PLEA[1] ON THE GROUND THAT SHE WAS YOUNG AND THEY[2] WERE YOUNG,[3] THEY MUST MAINTAIN HER WHILE SHE LIVES IN THE HOUSE OF HER FATHER.

GEMARA. Our Rabbis taught:[4] [A widow] may use [her deceased huband's] dwelling as she used it during his[5] lifetime. [She may also use] the bondmen and bondwomen, the cushions and the bolsters, and the silver and gold utensils as she used them during the lifetime of her husband, for such is the written undertaking he gave her: 'And you shall dwell in my house and be maintained therein out of my estate throughout the duration of your widowhood'.[6]

R. Joseph learnt:[7] 'In my house' [implies] 'but not in my hovel'.[8]

R. Naḥman ruled: If orphans sold a widow's dwelling[9] their act is legally invalid.[10] But why [should this case be] different from that of which R. Assi spoke in the name of R. Joḥanan as follows:[11] If the male orphans forestalled [the female orphans] and sold[12] some property of a small estate[13] their sale is valid?[14]—There[15] [the property] was not pledged to any daughter[16] during [her father's] lifetime,[17] but here[18] [the dwelling]

(1) For refusing to live with the heirs. (2) The heirs, children from another wife. (3) In consequence of which she fears quarrels or temptation. (4) Cf. Tosef. Keth. XI. (5) Lit., 'her husband'. (6) Mishnah *supra* 52*b*. (7) In explaining the Mishnah cited. (8) *Supra* 54*a* q.v. for notes. (9) Which formed part of her deceased husband's estate. (10) Lit., 'they have not done anything'. (11) Lit., 'for R. Assi stated in the name of R. Joḥanan'. (12) Before the court had dealt with the case. (13) Of their deceased father, which is legally due to the daughters (cf. *infra* 108*b*). (14) Lit., 'what they sold is sold', Yeb. 67*b*, Soṭah 21*b*, B.B. 140*a*. (15) The sale of a small estate. (16) Lit., 'to her'. (17) A father is under no legal obligation to maintain his daughters. (18) A widow's dwelling.

was pledged to the widow[1] during [her husband's] lifetime.[2]

Abaye stated: We have a tradition that if a widow's dwelling[3] collapsed it is not the duty of the heirs to rebuild it.[4] So it was also taught: If a widow's dwelling[3] collapsed it is not the duty of the heirs to rebuild it.[4] Furthermore, even if she says, 'Allow me and I shall rebuild it at my own expense', she is not granted her request.[5]

Abaye asked: What [is the legal position if] she repaired it?[6] —This is undecided.[7]

IF SHE SAID, HOWEVER, 'I HAVE NO DESIRE' etc. Why should they not give her maintenance while she lives there?[8]—This supports [a statement] of R. Huna who said, 'The blessing of a house [is proportionate] to its size'.[9] Why then can they not give her according to the blessing of the house?[10]—That is so.[11]

Said R. Huna: The sayings[12] of the Sages [are a source of] blessing, wealth and healing. [As to] 'blessing', [we have] the statement just mentioned. 'Wealth'?—Because we learned: If one sold fruits to another[13] [and the buyer] pulled[14] them, though they have not yet been measured,[15] ownership is acquired. If, however, they have been measured,[16] but [the buyer] has not pulled them, ownership is not acquired. But if [the buyer] is prudent he rents the place where they are kept.[17] 'Healing'?—For we learned: A

(1) Lit., 'to her'. (2) As is evident from the Mishnah *supra* 52*b*. (3) Which formed part of her deceased husband's estate. (4) Her claim upon the dwelling terminates as soon as it is no longer fit for habitation. (5) Lit., 'they do not listen to her'. (6) The dilapidated dwelling (v. Rashi). *Aliter:* May she repair it? (V. Tosaf. s.v. הי״נ *a.l.*). Is she entitled, it is asked, to continue to live in that dwelling so long as it can be kept up by repairs or must she quit it as soon as dwelling in it becomes impossible without repairs. (7) *Teḳu*, v. Glos. (8) In her father's house. (9) Tosef. Keth. XII, B.B. 144*b*. The more the members of a household the cheaper the cost of living. (10) *Sc.* an allowance equal to the cheaper cost of her maintenance at the house of the heirs. (11) Lit., 'thus also'; she is in fact entitled to such an allowance. (12) Lit., 'tongue', 'language'. (13) The price having been agreed upon. (14) 'Pulling' (*meshikah*, v. Glos.). (15) Measuring is not an essential factor of a sale, since it merely determines the quantity sold. (16) V. B.B. 84*b* as to how and where. (17) Mishnah B.B. 84*b*. If the fruit is kept in the seller's domain the buyer who for some reason is unable to transport his purchase forthwith

man should not chew wheat and put it on his wound during the Passover because it ferments.[1]

Our Rabbis taught: When Rabbi[2] was about to depart [from this life] he said, 'I require [the presence] of my sons'. When his sons entered into his presence he instructed them: 'Take care that you shew due respect to your mother. The light[3] shall continue to burn in its usual place, the table[3] shall be laid in its usual place [and my] bed shall be spread in its usual place.[4] Joseph of Haifa and Simeon of Efrath who attended on me in my lifetime shall attend on me when I am dead'.

'Take care that you shew due respect to your mother'. Is [not this instruction] Pentateuchal, since it is written, *Honour thy father and thy mother?*[5]—She was their stepmother.[6] [Is not the commandment to honour] a stepmother[6] also Pentateuchal, for it was taught: *Honour thy father and thy mother;*[5] *'thy father'*[7] includes[8] 'thy stepmother', *'and thy mother'*[9] includes[10] 'thy stepfather',[11] and the superfluous *waw*[12] includes 'thy elder brother'? —This exposition[13] [was meant to apply] during [one's own parents'] lifetime but not after [their] death.

'The light shall continue to burn in its usual place, the table shall be laid in its usual place [and my] bed shall be spread in its usual place'.[14] What is the reason?—He used to come home again at twilight every Sabbath Eve. On a certain Sabbath Eve a neighbour came to the door speaking aloud, when his handmaid

and fears that the seller might retract and cause him financial loss, may thus protect himself by renting the spot on which the fruit is kept and thereby acquire possession of the fruit since a man's domain acquires possession for him. A buyer thus gets wealth by taking the hint of the Sages.

(1) Pesaḥ. 39*b*. From this saying one learns of a remedy for a wound. (2) R. Judah I (135-220 C.E.) the Patriarch, compiler of the Mishnah. (3) Which he used during his lifetime. (4) 'Bed shall . . . place' is wanting in MS.M. (5) Ex. XX, 12. (6) Lit., 'a father's wife'. (7) את אביך, emphasis on את, the sign of the defined accusative, which is not absolutely essential in the context. (8) Lit., 'this'. Cf., however, *Beth Joseph, Y.D.* 240 *ad fin.* where the reading is לרבות 'to include'. (9) ואת אמך cf. *supra* n. 7 *mutatis mutandis.* (10) V. *supra* note 8. (11) Lit. 'thy mother's husband'. (12) In ואת אמך. (13) Lit., 'these words', respect for step-parents. (14) V. *supra* note 4.

state, *But the kingdom gave he to Jehoram, because he was the firstborn?*[1] —The other[2] was properly representing[3] his ancestors[4] but R. Gamaliel was not properly representing[3] his ancestors.[5] Then why did Rabbi act in the manner he did?[6]—Granted that he[7] was not representing his ancestors in wisdom he was worthily representing them in his fear of sin.[8]

'Ḥanina b. Ḥama shall preside at the college'. R. Ḥanina, however, did not accept [the office] because R. Afes was by two and a half years older than he; and so R. Afes presided. R. Ḥanina sat [at his studies] outside [the lecture room],[9] and Levi came and joined him. When R. Afes went to his eternal rest[10] and R. Ḥanina took up the presidency Levi had no one to join him[11] and came in consequence to Babylon.

This description coincides with the following:[12] When Rab was told that a great man who was lame made his appearance at Nehardea[13] and held a discourse [in the course of which he] permitted [the wearing of] a wreath,[14] he said, 'It is evident[15] that R. Afes has gone to his eternal rest, and R. Ḥanina has taken over the presidency; and that Levi having had no one to join him, has come [down here].' But might not one have suggested that R. Ḥanina came to his eternal rest, that R. Afes continued in the presidency as before[16] and that Levi who had no one to join him came [therefore, to Babylon]? If you wish I might reply: Levi would have submitted to the authority of R. Afes. And if

(1) II Chron. XXI, 3. (Cf. p. 659, n. 10). What need then was there, as Levi objected, for Rabbi's specific instruction? (2) Lit., 'that', Jehoram. (3) Lit., 'fulfilling the place of'. (4) Since there was no other son possessing a superior claim. (5) His younger brother having been wiser. Hence the necessity for Rabbi's specific instructions. *Aliter:* What was his (*sc.* Levi's) difficulty? (Is it) that Scripture stated, *But the kingdom . . . the firstborn*, that (firstborn, it may be replied,) was properly representing his ancestors but R. Gamaliel etc. (cf. S. Strashun). (6) Lit., 'thus'. (7) Gamaliel. (8) Moral conception and conduct (cf. Abboth III, 11; Sonc. ed. III, 9, p. 32). (9) Since he could not recognise R. Afes as his superior. (10) Lit., 'his soul rested'. (11) Lit., 'to sit at his side'. (12) Lit., 'and that is'. (13) V. *supra* p. 222, n. 8. (14) On the Sabbath, when the carrying of objects from one domain into another is forbidden (cf. Shab. 59*b*). (15) Lit., 'infer from this'. (16) Lit., 'as he sat he sits'.

you prefer I might reply: Since [Rabbi] once said, 'Ḥanina b. Ḥama shall preside at the college', there could be no possibility of his not becoming head;[1] for about the righteous it is written in Scripture, *Thou shalt also decree a thing, and it shall be established unto thee.*[2]

Was there not R. Ḥiyya?[3]—He had already gone to his eternal rest.[4] But did not R. Ḥiyya, state, 'I saw Rabbi's sepulchre[5] and shed tears upon it'?—Reverse [the names]. But did not R. Ḥiyya state, 'On the day on which Rabbi died holiness ceased'? —Reverse [the names]. But has it not been taught: When Rabbi fell ill R. Ḥiyya entered into his presence and found him weeping. 'Master', he said to him, 'Why are you weeping? Was it not taught: '[If a man] dies smiling it is a good omen for him, if weeping it is a bad omen for him; his face upwards it is a good omen, his face downwards it is a bad omen; his face towards the public it is a good omen, towards the wall it is a bad omen; if his face is greenish it is a bad omen, if bright and ruddy it is a good omen; dying on Sabbath Eve[6] is a good omen, on the termination of the Sabbath[7] is a bad omen; dying on the Eve of the Day of Atonement is a bad omen, on the termination of the Day of Atonement[8] is a good omen; dying of diarrhoea is a good omen because most righteous men die of diarrhoea?' And the other replied, 'I weep on [account of my impending separation from] the Torah and the commandments'?[9]—If you wish I might reply: Reverse [the names]; and if you prefer I might reply: In fact there is no need to reverse [the names; but as] R. Ḥiyya was engaged in the performance of pious deeds Rabbi thought 'I will not disturb him'.[10]

(1) Lit., 'that he should not reign'. Consequently he must have survived R. Afes. (2) Job XXII, 28. (3) Who was superior to both R. Ḥanina and R. Afes. Why was he overlooked by Rabbi? (4) When Rabbi was making his testamentory appointments. (5) 'His coffin' (Rashi). (6) Being the approach of the day of rest. (7) Lit., 'at the going out of the Sabbath'. (8) One's sins having been forgiven during the day. (9) All of which proves that R. Ḥiyya was still alive when Rabbi was on his deathbed. (10) Lit., 'cause him to be idle' or 'to relax'.

This[1] is in line with the following:[2] When R. Ḥanina and R. Ḥiyya were engaged in a dispute R. Ḥanina said to R. Ḥiyya, 'Do you [venture to] dispute with me? Were the Torah, God forbid, to be forgotten in Israel, I would restore it by means of my dialectical arguments'.—'I', replied R. Ḥiyya, 'make provision that the Torah shall not be forgotten in Israel. For I bring flax seed, sow it, and weave nets [from the plant]. [With these] I hunt stags with whose flesh I feed orphans and from whose skins I prepare scrolls, and then proceed to a town where there are no teachers of young children, and write out the five Books of the Pentateuch for five children [respectively] and teach another six children respectively the six Orders of the Mishnah, and then tell each one: "Teach your section to your colleagues"'. It was this that Rabbi [had in mind when he] exclaimed, 'How great are the deeds of Ḥiyya?' Said R. Simeon b. Rabbi to him: '[Greater] even than yours?'—'Yes', he replied. 'Even', asked R. Ishmael the son of R. Jose, 'than my father's?'—'God forbid', the other replied, 'Let no such thing be [mentioned] in Israel!'[3]

'I desire', he[4] announced, 'the presence of my younger son'. R. Simeon entered into his presence and he entrusted him with the orders[5] of wisdom. 'I desire the presence of my elder son', he announced. When R. Gamaliel entered he entrusted him with the traditions and regulations[5] of the Patriarchate. 'My son', he said to him, 'conduct your patriarchate with men of high standing,[6] and cast bile among the students'.[7]

But, surely, this[8] is not proper[9] for is it not written in Scripture, *But he honoureth them that fear the Lord,*[10] and the Master said that

(1) The testimony to R. Ḥiyya's piety and public benefactions. (2) Lit., 'and that is (why)'. (3) Cf. B.M. 85*b* where the parallel passage contains some variations including the substitution of 'R. Ishmael the son of R. Jose' for 'R. Simeon b. Rabbi'. (4) Rabbi. The story of the last moments of his life, interrupted by the preceding discussions, explanations and incidents, is here resumed. (5) Plur. const. of סדר 'order', 'rules and regulations'. (6) ברמים (sing. רם, 'high', 'elevated'). Aruch reads, בדמים (דמים 'equivalent', 'compensation', 'value') 'as something precious'. (7) *Sc.* 'introduce a firm discipline in the college'. (8) Keeping scholars under a discipline which many might regard as degrading. (9) Lit., 'I am not'. (10) Ps. XV, 4.

this [text might be applied to] Jehoshaphat, King of Judah, who, on seeing a scholar, used to rise from his throne, embrace him and kiss him, and call him 'My master, my master; my teacher, my teacher'?—This is no difficulty: The latter attitude[1] [is to be adopted] in private; the former[1] in public.[2]

It was taught: Rabbi was lying [on his sickbed] at Sepphoris[3] but a [burial] place was reserved for him at Beth She'arim.[4]

Was it not, however, taught: *Justice, justice shalt thou follow*,[5] follow Rabbi to Beth She'arim?—Rabbi was [indeed] living at Beth She'arim[6] but when he fell ill[7] he was brought to Sepphoris [104*a*] because it was situated on higher ground[8] and its air was salubrious.

On the day when Rabbi died the Rabbis decreed a public fast and offered prayers for heavenly mercy. They, furthermore, announced that whoever said that Rabbi was dead would be stabbed with a sword.

Rabbi's handmaid[9] ascended the roof and prayed: 'The immortals[10] desire Rabbi [to join them] and the mortals[11] desire Rabbi [to remain with them]; may it be the will [of God] that the mortals may overpower the immortals'. When, however, she saw how often he resorted to the privy,[12] painfully taking off his *tefillin*[13] and putting them on again, she prayed: 'May it be the will [of the Almighty] that the immortals may overpower the mortals'. As the Rabbis incessantly continued[14] their prayers

(1) Lit., 'that'. (2) Scholars, like the general public, may be expected to respect the common rules and regulations and to pay homage to the Patriarch. (3) V. *supra* p. 410, n. 6. (4) Identified with (*a*) the modern Tur'an, a village situated ten kilometres E.N.E. of Sepphoris (I. S. Horowitz, *Palestine* s.v.); (*b*) Besara, mentioned in Josephus, the modern Dscheda W. of the Valley of Jezreel (Klein, S. *EJ*. 4, 427). (5) Deut. XVI, 20. (6) 'Rabbi ... She'arim' is wanting in עין יעקב edd. (7) V. B.M. 85*a*. (8) Cf. Meg. 6*a*: 'Why was it called Sepphoris (צפורי)? Because it was perched on the top of a hill like a bird' (צפור, 'bird'). (9) A famous character, known for her sagacity and learning. (10) Lit., 'those above', 'the angels'. (11) Lit., 'those below', 'lower regions'. (12) He was suffering from acute and painful diarrhoea (cf. B.M. 85*a*). (13) V. Glos. These must not be worn when the body is not in a state of perfect cleanliness. (14) Lit., 'they were not silent'.

for [heavenly] mercy she took up a jar and threw it down from the roof to the ground. [For a moment] they ceased praying[1] and the soul of Rabbi departed to its eternal rest.[2]

'Go', said the Rabbis to Bar Ḳappara, 'and investigate'.[3] He went and, finding that [Rabbi] was dead, he tore his cloak and turned the tear backwards. [On returning to the Rabbis] he began: 'The angels[4] and the mortals[5] have taken hold of the holy ark.[6] The angels overpowered the mortals and the holy ark has been captured'. 'Has he', they asked him, 'gone to his eternal rest?'—'You', he replied, 'said it; I did not say it'.

Rabbi, at the time of his passing, raised his ten fingers towards heaven[7] and said: 'Sovereign of the Universe, it is revealed and known to you that I have laboured in the study of the Torah with my ten fingers and that I did not enjoy [any worldly] benefits even with my little finger. May it be Thy will that there be peace in my [last] resting place'. A *bath ḳol*[8] echoed, announcing, ***He shall enter into peace; they shall rest on their beds.***[9]

[Does not] the context require [the singular pronoun:] 'On thy bed'?[10]—This provides support for R. Ḥiyya b. Gamda. For he stated in the name of R. Jose b. Saul: When a righteous man departs from this world the ministering angels say to the Holy One, blessed be He, 'Sovereign of the Universe, the righteous man So-and-so is coming', and he answers them, 'Let the righteous men come [from their resting places], go forth to meet him, and say to him that ***he shall enter into peace*** [and then] ***they***[11] ***shall rest on their beds***'.

R. Eleazar stated: When a righteous man departs from the world he is welcomed by[12] three companies of ministering angels. One exclaims, 'Come[13] into peace'; the other[14] exclaims, ***He who***

(1) Lit., 'they remained silent'. (2) Lit., 'rested'. (3) Rabbi's condition. (4) אראלים, lit., 'messengers' (Jast.); cf. B.H. מלאך. *Aliter:* 'God's lions' (Levy). (5) מצוקים (rt. יצק 'to cast'). *Aliter:* 'The just' (Rashi). (6) Metaph. Rabbi was known as 'our holy teacher'. (7) Lit., 'in an upward direction'. (8) V. Glos. (9) Isa. LVII, 2. (10) In harmony with the first part of the verse. [Strashun amends 'on his bed']. (11) The righteous who went out to welcome him. (12) Lit., 'go out to meet him'. (13) *Var.* 'He shall enter' (עין יעקב). (14) Lit., 'and one'.

brother,[1] and [when she became] a widow lived in her father's house. [R. Ḥiyya] maintained her for twenty-five years at her paternal home [but when] at the end [of the period] she said to him, 'Supply me with my maintenance' he told her, 'You have no [longer any claim to] maintenance'. 'Pay me [then', she said, 'my] *kethubah*'. 'You have no claim,' he replied, 'either to maintenance or to the *kethubah*'.[2] She summoned him to law before Rabbah b. Shila. 'Tell me', [the judge] said to him,[3] 'what exactly were the circumstances'. 'I maintained her', the other[3] replied, 'for twenty-five years at her paternal home and, by the life of the Master!, I carried [the stuff] to her on my shoulder'. 'What is the reason', [the judge] said to him, 'that the Rabbis[4] ruled, SO LONG AS SHE LIVES IN HER HUSBAND'S HOUSE [A WIDOW] MAY RECOVER HER KETHUBAH AT ANY TIME? Because we assume that she did not claim it in order [to save herself from] shame.[5] Similarly here also[6] [it may well be assumed] that she did not [previously] submit her claim in order [to save herself from] shame.[5] Go, and supply her [maintenance]'. [As R. Ḥiyya] disregarded [the ruling, the judge] wrote out for her an *adrakta*[7] on his property. Thereupon he came to Raba and said to him, 'See, Master, how he treated my case'.[8] 'He has given you the proper ruling', the other replied. 'If that is the case', [the widow] said to him,[9] 'let him[10] proceed to refund me the produce[11] [he has consumed] since that day[12] to date'. 'Shew me' he[9] said to her,

(1) Who died childless and whose estate was inherited by R. Ḥiyya. (2) In accordance with the ruling of the Sages in our Mishnah. (3) R. Ḥiyya. (4) *Sc.* THE SAGES. (5) Cf. *supra* p. 665, n. 16, second clause. (6) Where so much respect was shewn to her by R. Ḥiyya that he carried her foodstuffs to her on his shoulder. (7) אדרכתא (rt. דרך 'to tread'), an authorization following that of another legal document called *ṭirpa* (cf. B.B., Sonc. ed., p. 738, n. 1) which a court issues to a claimant after he had traced the defendant's property, to seize it (to 'tread' on) for the purpose of having it offered for public sale and his recovering the proceeds or the land itself at the price valued. (8) Lit., 'judged me'. (9) Raba. (10) R. Ḥiyya. (11) Of the land that was valued at a sum corresponding to that of her *kethubah*. (12) On which she received the *adrakta* (according to the opinion of Rabbah), when it was signed (according to Abaye), or when the period of the announcement of the public sale

'your *adrakta*'.[1] As he observed that it did not contain the clause,[2] 'And we have ascertained that this estate belonged to the deceased', he said to her, 'The *adrakta* is not properly drawn up'.[3] 'Let the *adrakta* be dropped', she said; 'and let me receive [the refund for the produce] from the day on which the period of the public announcement terminated[4] to date'. 'This',[5] he replied, 'applies only to a case[6] where no error has crept[7] into the *adrakta*, but where an error occurs[7] in the *adrakta* the document possesses no validity'.[8] 'But did not the Master himself lay down', she exclaimed, '[that the omission[9] of the clause] pledging property [is to be regarded as the] scribe's error?'[10]—'In this case', Raba told her, '[the omission] cannot be said to be a scribe's error, for even Rabbah b. Shila originally[11] overlooked the point'.[12] He thought: Since both belonged to him[13] what matters it [whether the widow distrains] on the one or the other.[14] But this is not [the proper view]. For sometimes [the widow] might go and improve those [lands][15] while those belonging to her husband[16] would be

terminated (according to Raba). From such date the land passes into the possession of the claimant and its produce also from that day onwards belongs to him (cf. B.M. 36*b*).

(1) V. *supra* p. 669, n. 7. (2) Lit., 'that it was not written in it'. (3) The *adrakta* referred to all R. Ḥiyya's landed property, while legally it should have been restricted to those which he inherited from his deceased brother. On his own lands the widow could have no claim whatsoever. (4) In agreement with the view of Raba (cf. *supra* p. 669, n. 12). After the claimant discovers a field that belonged to the defendant he reports to the court who value it, and arrange for a period of thirty days for the public announcement, at the end of which the claimant comes into possession (v. B.M. 35*b*). (5) That the land passes into the possession of the claimant on one of the dates mentioned (*supra* p. 669, n. 12). (6) Lit., 'these words'. (7) Lit., 'is written'. (8) Lit., 'we have not in it'; the land does not pass into the ownership of the claimant until he takes actual possession of it. (9) From a deed. (10) And is deemed to have been entered though the scribe had omitted it (B.M. 14*a*, B.B. 169*b*). Why then should an error in the *adrakta* cause its invalidity? (11) [Rightly omitted in MS.M.] (12) Lit., 'in that'. In that he had an *adrakta* made out against R. Ḥiyya's own property. (13) R. Ḥiyya. (14) R. Ḥiyya's brother's or his own. Hence he drew up the *adrakta* on all R. Ḥiyya's lands. (15) Which did not belong to her husband but to his heir and which the court handed over to her in return for her claim. (16) And were legally pledged for her *kethubah*.

allowed[1] to deteriorate and [the heir might eventually] tell her, 'Take yours[2] and return to me mine',[3] and a stigma[4] would thus fall[5] upon the court.[6]

(1) By the heir who is well aware that he can at any time re-claim his own land and transfer the property of the deceased to his widow. (2) Cf. *supra* p. 670, n. 16. (3) Cf. *supra* p. 670, n. 15. (4) Lit., 'murmur', 'reflection'. (5) Lit., 'and come to bring out'. (6) Who would be accused of carelessness or indifference in the provision they made for the widow.

KETHUBOTH

CHAPTER XIII

MISHNAH. TWO JUDGES OF CIVIL LAW[1] WERE [ADMINISTERING JUSTICE] IN JERUSALEM, ADMON AND ḤANAN B. ABISHALOM. ḤANAN LAID DOWN TWO RULINGS[2] AND ADMON LAID DOWN SEVEN:—[3]

IF A MAN WENT TO A COUNTRY BEYOND THE SEA AND HIS WIFE CLAIMED MAINTENANCE, ḤANAN RULED: [105*a*] SHE MUST TAKE AN OATH[4] AT THE END[5] BUT NOT AT THE BEGINNING.[6] THE SONS OF THE HIGH PRIESTS,[7] HOWEVER, DIFFERED FROM HIM AND RULED THAT SHE MUST TAKE AN OATH BOTH AT THE BEGINNING[6] AND AT THE END.[5] R. DOSA B. HARKINAS AGREED WITH THEIR RULING. R. JOḤANAN B. ZAKKAI SAID: ḤANAN HAS SPOKEN WELL; SHE NEED TAKE AN OATH ONLY AT THE END.[5]

GEMARA. I would point out an inconsistency: 'Three judges in cases of robbery[8] were [administering justice] in Jerusalem, Admon b. Gadai,[9] Ḥanan the Egyptian and Ḥanan b. Abishalom'. Is there not an inconsistency between 'three'[10] and 'TWO', and an inconsistency between 'CIVIL'[11] and 'robbery'?[12] One might well admit that there is no [real] inconsistency between the 'three' and the 'TWO' since he[13] may be enumerating [only those] whom he con-

(1) גזירות (plural of גזירה, 'decree', 'decision'). Var., גזילות (plural of גזילה 'robbery') v. *infra*. Cf. B.Ḳ. 58*b*, Sonc. ed. p. 340, n. 1. (2) From which the Sages differed. (3) V. *supra* n. 2. The rulings are enumerated in this Mishnah and in those following. (4) That she has no property of her husband's in her possession. (5) *Sc.* when her husband dies and she claims her ***kethubah***. (6) I.e., during his lifetime when she claims her maintenance. (7) בני כהנים גדולים. A similar description occurs in Oh. XVII, 5. Cf. *supra* p. 64, n. 6, בית דין של כהנים 'Priestly Court' or 'Court of Priests'. (8) Or any damage. (9) I.e., Admon mentioned in our Mishnah. (10) In the Baraitha cited. (11) Cf. *supra* note 1. (12) In the Baraitha cited. (13) The author of our Mishnah.

siders important[1] and omitting[2] [the one] whom he does not consider important. Does not, however, the inconsistency between 'CIVIL' and 'robbery' remain?—R. Naḥman b. Isaac replied: [Both terms may be justified on the grounds] that they[3] imposed fines[4] for acts of robbery;[5] as it was taught: If [a beast] nipped off a plant, said R. Jose, the Judges of Civil Law in Jerusalem ruled that if the plant was in its first year [the owner of the beast pays as compensation] two silver pieces,[6] if it was in its second year [he pays as compensation] four silver pieces.[7]

I point out [another] contradiction: Three judges of Civil Law were [administering justice] in Jerusalem, Admon, and Ḥanan and Naḥum?[8]—R. Papa replied: He who mentioned Naḥum was R. Nathan;[9] for it was taught: R. Nathan stated, 'Naḥum the Mede also was one of the Judges of Civil Law in Jerusalem', but the Sages did not agree with him.

Were there, however, no more [judges]? [Did not] R. Phineḥas, in fact, state on the authority of R. Oshaia that there were three hundred and ninety four courts of law[10] in Jerusalem, and an equal number of Synagogues, of Houses of Study[11] and of schools?[12]—Judges there were many, but we were speaking of Judges of Civil Law only.

Rab Judah stated in the name of R. Assi: The Judges of Civil Law in Jerusalem received their salaries out of the Temple funds[13] [at the rate of] ninety-nine *maneh*.[14] If they were not satisfied[15] they were given an increase.

[You say] 'They were not satisfied'?[15] Are we dealing with

(1) On the admissibility of another rendering v. Tosaf. s.v., דחשיב, *a.l.* (2) Lit., 'did not teach'. (3) The judges mentioned. (4) Lit., 'decreed decrees'. Hence the term 'CIVIL' גזירות (v. *supra* p. 672, n. 1) in our Mishnah. (5) גזילות (cf. *supra* p. 672, nn. 1 and 8). Hence the justification for the use of this term in the Baraitha. (6) A silver piece = one *ma'ah* or a third of a *denar*, v. Glos. (7) B.Ḳ. 58*b*. (8) Inconsistent with our Mishnah which mentions only TWO. V., however, Tosaf. s.v. דחשיב. (9) [Who considered Naḥum important, v. Maharsha]. (10) Each consisting of twenty-three judges. (11) For Mishnah and Talmud. (12) For children. (13) תרומת הלשכה, lit., 'heave-offering of the (people) to the (Temple treasure) chamber'. (14) V. Glos. (15) לא רצו, lit., 'did not want'.

wicked men?[1] The reading in fact is,[2] [If the amount was] not sufficient[3] an increase was granted to them even if they objected.[4]

Ḳarna[5] used to take one *istira*[6] from the innocent[7] party and one *istira* from the guilty party and then informed them of his decision.[8] But how could he[9] act in such a manner? Is it not written in Scripture, *And thou shalt take no gift?*[10] And should you reply that this applies only where he does not take from both [litigants] since he might [in consequence] wrest judgment, but Ḳarna, since he took [the same amount] from both parties, would not come to wrest judgment, [it can be retorted:] Is this permitted even where one would not come to wrest judgment? Was it not in fact taught: What was the purpose of the statement *And thou shalt take no gift?*[10] If to teach that one must not acquit the guilty or that one must not condemn the innocent [the objection surely could be raised]. It was already specifically stated elsewhere in Scripture, *Thou shalt not wrest judgment.*[11] Consequently it must be concluded that[2] even [where the intention is] to acquit the innocent or to condemn the guilty the Torah laid down, *And thou shalt take no gift?*[12]—This[12] applies only where [the judge] takes [the gift] as a bribe,[13] but Ḳarna took [the two *istira*] as a fee.[14] But is it permissible [for a judge to take money] as a fee? Have we not in fact learned: The legal decisions of one who takes a fee for acting as judge are null and void?[15]—This[15] applies only to a fee for pronouncing judgment, while Ḳarna was only taking compensation for loss of work.[16]

But [is a judge] permitted to take compensation for loss of work? Was it not in fact taught: Contemptible is the judge who takes a fee for pronouncing judgment; but his decision is valid?[17] Now, what is to be understood [by fee]. If it be suggested [that it means]

(1) Who expect from the public funds more than is required for a decent living. A judge's salary must not exceed the actual cost of his living (v. Rashi). (2) Lit., 'but'. (3) To provide for a decent living. (4) V. *supra* p. 673, n. 15. (5) A judge of the Exile. Cf. Sanh. 17*b*, Sonc. ed. p. 88, n. 8. (6) V. Glos. (7) *Sc.* the party in whose favour judgment was to be given. (8) Lit., 'and judged for them the law'. (9) Ḳarna. (10) Ex. XXIII, 8. (11) Deut. XVI, 19. (12) Ex. XXIII, 8. (13) *Sc.* with the intention of perverting judgment. (14) For his professional services. (15) Ḳid. 58*b*, Bek. 29*a*. (16) Lit., 'idleness'. (17) Lit., 'his judgment is judgment'.

a fee for acting as judge [the objection would arise: How could it be said,] 'his decision is valid', when in fact we have learned:[1] The legal decisions of one who takes a fee for acting as judge are null and void? Consequently it must mean[2] a fee for loss of work,[3] and yet it was stated, was it not, 'Contemptible is the judge etc.'?—This applies only to a loss of work that cannot be proved, but Ḳarna received [compensation for] loss of work that could be proved, for he was [regularly occupied in] smelling tests[4] at a wine store,[5] and for this he was paid a fee.[6] This is similar to the case[7] of R. Huna. When a lawsuit was brought to him, he used to say to the [litigants], 'Provide me with a man who will draw the water[8] in my place[9] and I will pronounce judgment for you'.

Said R. Abbahu: Come and see how blind are the eyes of those who take a bribe. If a man has pain in his eyes he pays away money to a medical man and he may be cured or he may not be cured, yet these take what is only worth one *peruṭah*[10] and blind their eyes [therewith], for it is said in Scripture, *For a gift blindeth them that have sight.*[11]

Our Rabbis taught: *For a gift doth blind the eyes of the wise,*[12] and much more so those of the foolish; *And pervert the words of the righteous,*[12] and much more so those of the wicked. Are then fools and wicked men capable of acting as judges?[13]—But it is this that is meant: '*For a gift doth blind the eyes of the wise*', even a great Sage who takes bribes will not depart from the world without [the affliction of] a dullness of the mind;[14] '*And pervert the words of the righteous*', [105*b*] even one who is righteous in every respect and takes bribes will not depart from this world without [the affliction of] confusion of mind.

(1) So BaḤ. Cur. edd. 'it was taught'. (2) Lit., 'but'. (3) Lit., 'idleness'. (4) To advise the owner as to which wine could be stored for longer and which only for shorter periods. (5) אמברא. Rashi reads the noun in the pl., 'stores'. (6) Lit., 'and they gave him a *zuz*' (v. Glos.). When acting as judge he was entitled to demand compensation for his loss. (7) Lit., 'like that'. (8) 'For the irrigation of my land'. (9) בהריקאי, cf. *supra* p. 364, n. 4. (10) The smallest coin, v. Glos. (11) Ex. XXIII, 8. (12) Deut. XVI, 19. (13) Obviously not; how then is it likely that anyone would offer them any bribe. (14) Lit., 'blindness of heart'.

When R. Dimi came[1] he related that R. Naḥman b. Kohen made the following exposition: What was meant by the Scriptural text, *The King by justice establisheth the land, but he that loveth gifts overthroweth it?* If the judge is like a king who is not in need of anything[2] he *establisheth the land*, but if he is like a priest who moves to and fro among the threshing floors,[3] he *overthroweth it*.[4]

Rabbah b. R. Shila stated: Any judge who is in the habit of borrowing[5] is unfit to pronounce judgment. This, however, applies only where he possesses nothing to lend to others, but where he possesses things to lend [his borrowing] does not matter.[6] This, however, cannot surely be correct;[7] for did not Raba borrow things from the household of Bar Merion, although they did not borrow anything from him?—There he desired to give them better standing.[8]

Raba stated: What is the reason for [the prohibition[9] against taking] a gift?[10] Because as soon as a man receives a gift from another he becomes so well disposed towards him[11] that he becomes like his own person, and no man sees himself in the wrong.[12] What [is the meaning of] *shoḥad?*[13] *She-hu ḥad.*[14]

R. Papa said: A man should not act as judge either for one whom he loves or for one whom he hates; for no man can see the guilt of one whom he loves or the merit of one whom he hates.

Abaye said: If a scholar[15] is loved by the townspeople [their love] is not due to his superiority but [to the fact] that he does not rebuke them for [neglecting] spiritual[16] matters.

Raba remarked: At first I thought that all the people of

(1) From Palestine to Babylon. (2) *Sc.* is independent of other people's help or favours. (3) Collecting his dues. (4) Cf. Sanh. 7*b*. (5) Any objects. The verb שאל, here used, does not apply to money. (6) Lit., 'we have nothing against it'. (7) Lit., 'Is it really so?' (8) His borrowing was of no benefit to himself. Lit., 'to cause them to be important'. For a similar reason Rabbah levied a contribution for charity on the orphans of the house of Bar Merion (cf. B.B. 8*a*). (9) Upon a judge. (10) Even where the judge intended to act justly. (11) Lit., 'his mind draws near to him'. (12) Lit., 'guilt'. (13) שוחד, 'gift', 'bribe'. (14) שהוא חד, 'that he (the recipient) is one (with the giver)'. This is not intended as etymology but as a word play. (15) Lit., 'one who has caught fire by (association with) Rabbis'. (16) Lit., 'of heaven'.

Mahuza[1] loved me. When I was appointed judge[2] I thought that some[3] would hate me and others[4] would love me. Having observed, however, that the man who loses[5] to-day[6] wins to-morrow I came to the conclusion that if I am loved they all love me and if I am hated they must all hate me.

Our Rabbis taught: *And thou shalt take no gift;*[7] there was no need to speak of [the prohibition of] a gift of money, but [this was meant:] Even a bribe of words[8] is also forbidden, for Scripture does not write, *And thou shalt take no gain.*[9] What is to be understood by 'a bribe of words'?[8]—As the bribe offered to Samuel.[10] He was once crossing [a river] on a board[11] when a man came up and offered him his hand.[12] 'What', [Samuel] asked him, 'is your business here?'—'I have a lawsuit', the other replied. 'I', came the reply, 'am disqualified from acting for you in the suit'.

Amemar was once engaged in the trial of an action,[13] when a bird flew down upon his head and a man approached and removed it. 'What is your business here?' [Amemar] asked him. 'I have a lawsuit', the other replied. 'I', came the reply, 'am disqualified from acting as your judge'.

Mar 'Ukba once ejected some saliva[14] and a man approached and covered it. 'What is your business here?' [Mar 'Ukba] asked him. 'I have a lawsuit', the man replied. 'I', came the reply, 'am disqualified from acting as your judge'.

R. Ishmael son of R. Jose, whose *aris*[15] was wont to bring him a basket full of fruit[16] every Friday[17] but on one occasion[18] brought it to him on a Thursday, asked the latter, 'Why the present change?'—'I have a lawsuit', the other replied, 'and thought that at the same time[19] I might bring [the fruit] to the Master'. He did not

(1) V. *supra* p. 319, n. 9. (2) In that town. (3) Who would lose their lawsuits. (4) In whose favour judgment would be given. (5) Lit., 'who is made guilty'. (6) Lit., 'now'. (7) Ex. XXIII, 8. (8) Or 'acts'. (9) בצע which would have meant a monetary bribe. (10) Lit., 'as that of Samuel'. (11) Or 'ferry'. (12) To assist him. (13) Lit., 'was sitting and deciding a law'. (14) Lit., 'threw saliva before him'. (15) Gardener-tenant (v. Glos.). (16) As rent, from R. Ishmael's garden which he cultivated. (17) מעלי שבתא, lit., 'entering of the Sabbath', *sc.* Sabbath Eve. (18) Lit., 'day'. (19) Lit., 'by the way'.

accept it from him [and] said, 'I am disqualified to act as your judge'. He thereupon appointed a couple of Rabbis to try the case for him. As he was arranging the affair[1] he [found himself] thinking, 'If he[2] wished he could plead thus, or if he preferred he might plead thus'.[3] 'Oh', he exclaimed, 'the despair that waits for those who take bribes'![4] If I, who have not taken [the fruit at all], and even if I had taken I would only have taken what is my own, am in such [a state of mind],[5] how much more [would that[5] be the state of] those who accept bribes'.

A man once brought to R. Ishmael b. Elisha[6] [a gift of] the first-fleece.[7] 'Whence', the latter asked him, 'are you?'—'From such and such a place', the other replied. 'But', [R. Ishmael] asked, 'was there no priest to whom to give it [in any of the places] between that place and this?'[8]—'I have a lawsuit', the other replied, 'and thought that at the same time[9] I would bring [the gift] to the Master'. He said to him, 'I am unfit to try your action', and refused to receive [the gift] from him. [Thereupon] he appointed two Rabbis to try his action. As he was arranging this affair[10] he [found himself] thinking, 'If he[11] wished he could plead thus, or if he preferred he might plead thus'.[12] 'Oh', he exclaimed, 'the despair that awaits those who take bribes! If I, who did not take [the gift], and even if I had taken it I would only have accepted that which is my due, am in such [a state of mind], how much more [would that be the case with] those who accept bribes'.

A man once brought to R. Anan a bale of small marsh fish.[13] 'What is your business here', the latter asked him. 'I have a lawsuit', the other replied. [R. Anan] did not accept it from him, and told him, 'I am disqualified to try your action'. 'I would

(1) Lit., 'went and came'. (2) His *aris*. (3) All possible pleadings in favour of the *aris* rose spontaneously to his mind. (4) So Jast. תיפח נפשם, lit., 'may their ghost blow out', or 'be blown' (rt. נפח 'to blow'). (5) Cf. *supra* n. 3. (6) Who was a priest and entitled to the priestly dues. (7) Cf. Deut. XVIII, 4. (8) Lit., 'from there to here'. (9) Lit., 'by the way'. (10) Lit., 'went and came'. (11) The man who offered him the priestly due. (12) Cf. *supra* notes 1-5. (13) בי גילי 'among the marshes'. *Sc.* that live among the reeds in the swamps (Jast.). [Obermeyer p. 245, n. 1 suggests בי גילי to be the name of a place, Al Kil on the Tigris].

not now request', the other said to him, 'the Master's decision [in my lawsuit]; will the Master, however, at least accept [the present] so that I may not be prevented from offering my first-fruit?[1] For it was taught: *And there came a man from Baal-shalishah, and brought the man of God bread of the first-fruits, twenty loaves of barley, and fresh ears of corn in his sack;*[2] but was Elisha[3] entitled to eat first-fruit?[4] This, however, was intended to tell you that one who brings a gift to a scholar [is doing as good a deed] as if he had offered first-fruits'. It was not my intention to accept [your gift', R. Anan] said to him, 'but now that you have given me a reason I will accept it'. Thereupon he sent him to R. Naḥman to whom he also dispatched [the following message:] 'Will the Master try [the action of] this man, for I, Anan,[5] am disqualified from acting as judge for him'. 'Since he has sent me such a message', [R. Naḥman] thought, 'he must be his relative'.[6] An orphans' lawsuit was then in progress[7] before him; and he reflected: [106*a*] The one[8] is a positive precept and the other[9] is also a positive precept, but the positive precept of shewing respect for the Torah[9] must take precedence. He, therefore, postponed[10] the orphans' case and brought up that man's suit. When the other party[11] noticed the honour he was shewing him[12] he remained speechless.[13] [Until that happened] Elijah[14] was a frequent visitor of R. Anan whom he was teaching the Order of Elijah,[15] but as soon as he[16] acted in the manner described[17] [Elijah] stayed away. He[16] spent his time[18] in fasting, and in prayers for [God's] mercy, [until Elijah] came to him again; but when he appeared he greatly

(1) Cf. Ex. XXIII, 19. (2) II Kings IV, 42. (3) Who was no priest. Tradition ascribes him to the tribe of Gad (cf. Pesaḥ. 68*a* and Rosh. *a.l.*). (4) Obviously not; why then did he accept *'first-fruits'*? (5) Wanting in MS.M. (6) It is forbidden to act as judge or witness in a relative's lawsuit. (7) Lit., 'was standing'. (8) Lit., 'that', to judge the orphan. (9) Respect for a man of learning (cf. B.Ḳ. 41*b*) and consequently also for those who are related to him. (10) Lit., 'removed', 'put aside'. (11) Lit., 'the master of his law(suit'). (12) His opponent, whom R. Naḥman presumed to be R. Anan's relative. (13) Lit., 'his plea was stopped'. (14) Cf. *supra* p. 488, n. 6. (15) סדר אליהו, a Rabbinic work of mysterious origin and authorship. (16) R. Anan. (17) Lit., 'thus'. He allowed himself to be the unconscious tool of the man who cunningly bribed him. (18) Lit., 'sat'.

frightened him. Thereupon he[1] made a box [for himself] and in it he sat before him until he concluded his Order with him. And this is [the reason] why people speak of the *Seder Eliyyahu Rabbah* and the *Seder Eliyyahu Zuṭa.*[2]

In the days[3] of R. Joseph there was a famine.[4] Said the Rabbis to R. Joseph, 'Will the Master offer prayers for [heavenly] mercy'? He replied, 'If Elisha, with whom, when the [main body of] Rabbis had departed, there still remained two thousand and two hundred Rabbis,[5] did not offer up any prayers for mercy in a time of famine,[4] should I [at such a time venture to] offer prayers for mercy? But whence is it inferred that so many remained?—[From Scripture] where it is written, *And his servant said: How should I set this before a hundred men?*[6] Now what is meant by [the expression,] '*Before a hundred men*'? If it be suggested that all[7] [was to be set] before the hundred men [one might well object that] in years of famine [all this] is rather a large quantity. Consequently it must be concluded[8] that each [loaf was set] before a hundred men.[9]

When the [main body of] Rabbis departed from the school of Rab there still remained behind one thousand and two hundred Rabbis; [when they departed] from the school of R. Huna there remained behind eight hundred Rabbis. R. Huna when delivering his discourses [was assisted] by thirteen interpreters.[10] When the Rabbis stood up after R. Huna's discourses[11] and shook out their

(1) R. Anan. (2) The former was taught when R. Anan was without, the latter when he was within, the box (Rashi). [Tosaf.: the Treatise consists of a large and small book, hence the names *Rabbah* and *Zuṭa*. Both constitute the Midrash known as *Tanna debe Eliyyahu*]. (3) Lit., 'years', a reference perhaps to the period during which he was head of the academy. (4) ריתחא, lit., 'agitation', 'excitement', hence 'anger'. Owing to God's anger the world was afflicted with famine (v. Rashi). (5) To dine with him. (6) II Kings IV, 43. (7) Lit., 'all of them', i.e., the *twenty loaves of barley and fresh ears of corn*, enumerated in the preceding verse. (8) Lit., 'but'. (9) There were *twenty loaves of barley* (II Kings II, 42), one loaf of *bread of the first-fruits* (ibid.) and one loaf of *fresh ears of corn* (ibid.), a total of twenty-two loaves. Since each loaf was set before a hundred men the total number of the men must have been (twenty-two times one hundred =) two thousand two hundred (Rashi). (10) Each of whom addressed a section of the crowded audiences, v. Glos. s.v. Amora. (11) Lit., 'sitting'.

garments the dust rose [so high] that it obscured the [light of] day, and people in Palestine[1] said, 'They have risen after the discourses of R. Huna the Babylonian'. When [the main body of] Rabbis departed from the schools of Rabbah and R. Joseph there remained four hundred Rabbis and they described themselves as orphans. When [the main body of] Rabbis departed from the school of Abaye (others say, From the school of R. Papa, while still others say, From the school of R. Ashi) there remained two hundred Rabbis, and these described themselves as orphans of the orphans.

R. Isaac b. Radifa said in the name of R. Ammi: The inspectors of [animal] blemishes[2] in Jerusalem received their wages from the Temple funds.[3] Rab Judah said in the name of Samuel: The learned men who taught the priests the laws of ritual slaughter received their fees from the Temple funds.[3] R. Giddal said in the name of Rab: The learned men who taught the priests the rules of *kemiẓah*[4] received their fees from the Temple funds.[3] Rabbah b. Bar Ḥana said in the name of R. Johanan: Book readers[5] in Jerusalem received their fees from the Temple funds.[6]

R. Naḥman said: Rab stated that the women who wove the [Temple] curtains received their wages from the Temple funds[3] but I maintain [that they received them] from the sums consecrated for Temple repairs, since the curtains were a substitute for builder's work.

An objection was raised: The women who wove the [Temple] curtains, and the house of Garmo[7] [who were in charge] of the preparation of the shewbread,[8] and the house of Abtinas[7] [who were in charge] of the preparation of the incense,[9] received their

(1) Lit., 'in the west'. (2) מבקרי מומין, lit., 'those who examine blemishes', officials whose duty it was to ascertain whether any beast was unfit as a sacrifice owing to a disqualifying blemish. (3) תרומת הלשכה, v. *supra* p. 673, n. 13. (4) קמיצה, (rt. קמץ, 'to close the hand'), 'taking a handful' from a meal-offering. Cf. e.g., Lev. II, 2 and Men. 11*a*. (5) Who check scribal errors. (6) In order to preserve the accuracy of the written word the services of the readers were placed free at the disposal of any member of the public (cf. Rashi). (7) A priestly family. (8) Cf. Ex. XXV, 30 and Yoma 38*a*. (9) Cf. Ex. XXX, 23ff and Yoma 38*a*.

wages from the Temple funds![1]—There[2] [it may be replied] the reference is [to the curtains] of the gates;[3] for R. Zera related in the name of Rab: There were thirteen curtains in the second Temple, seven corresponding to the seven gates,[4] one for the entrance to the *Hekal*,[5] one for the entrance to the *'Ulam*,[5] two[6] [at the entrance] to the *Debir*[5] and two [above them and] corresponding to them in the upper storey.[7]

Our Rabbis taught: The women who brought up their children for the [services of the red] heifer,[8] received their wages from the Temple funds. Abba Saul said: The notable[9] women of Jerusalem fed them and maintained them.

R. Huna enquired of Rab: [106b] May vessels of ministry[10] be procured[11] with the offerings consecrated to Temple repair? Are these [a part of] the equipment[12] of the altar and were, therefore,[13] purchased[14] with the offerings consecrated to Temple repair, or are they rather among the requirements of the sacrifices and were, therefore, procured[15] with the Temple funds?—'They', the other[16] replied, 'may be procured[11] with the Temple funds only'.

He raised an objection against him:[16] *And when they had made an*

(1) An objection against R. Naḥman. (2) In the Baraitha just cited. (3) Which cannot be regarded as forming a part of the structure of the building, while R. Naḥman spoke of those curtains that replaced a wall that in the first Temple formed the partition between the Holy of Holies and the *Hekal* (v. *infra* n. 5 and Yoma 51*b*). (4) Of the Temple court. (5) The *Hekal* (היכל) or 'Holy', was situated between the *'Ulam* (אולם) the Temple porch and the *Debir* (דביר), and contained the candlestick, the table for the shewbread and the golden altar. The *Debir*, or the Holy of Holies, contained the ark and the cherubim. (6) With a space of one cubit between them in place of the thickness of the wall in the first Temple (cf. *supra* note 3). (7) To form a partition between the chamber above the *Debir* and that above the *Hekal*. (8) Cf. Num. XIX, 2ff. Certain services in connection with its preparation had to be entrusted to children who from birth were brought up under conditions of scrupulous ritual purity. For this purpose the mothers had to live in specially constructed buildings from the ante-natal period until the time the children were ready for their duties. (Cf. Suk. 21*a*). (9) Rich (Rashi). (10) For use on the 'external' altar, a stone structure in the Temple court. (11) Lit., 'made'. (12) Lit., 'need', 'requirement'. (13) Since the altar was builder's work. (14) Lit., 'come'. (15) Lit., 'they were making them'. (16) Rab.

end, they brought the rest of the money[1] *before the King and Jehoiada,*[2] *whereof were made vessels for the house of the Lord, even vessels wherewith to minister*[3] etc.—The other[4] replied: He that taught you the Hagiographa did not teach you the Prophets: *But there were not made for the house of the Lord cups*[5] *etc. for they gave that to them that did the work.*[6] But if so, is there not a contradiction between the two Scriptural texts?—There is really no contradiction. The former is a case[7] where after the collections were made [for Temple repair] there remained a balance,[8] while the latter[7] is a case where no balance remained.[9] But even if there was a balance after the collection had been made, what of it?[10]—R. Abbahu replied: Beth din make a mental[11] stipulation that if they[12] be required they should be utilized for their original purpose[13] and that if [they would]not [be required] they should be [spent] on vessels of ministry.

A Tanna of the school of R. Ishmael taught: Vessels of ministry were provided[14] from the Temple funds; for it is said in Scripture, *The rest of the money,*[15] now what funds shewed a balance?[16] Obviously[17] the Temple funds.[18] But might it not be suggested that only the balance itself [could be spent on the vessels of ministry]?[19]—As Raba said,[20] *The burnt-offering*[21] implies the *first* burnt-offering,[22] so must *the money*[23] imply the *first* money.[24]

(1) That was dedicated to Temple repair. (2) '*The priest*' is in cur. edd. enclosed in parentheses. It does not appear in M.T. (3) II Chron. XXIV, 14; which proves that offerings for Temple repair may be used for the provision of vessels of ministry. An objection against Rab. (4) Rab. (5) *Sc.* vessels of ministry. (6) II Kings XII, 14-15. (7) Lit., 'here'. (8) Lit., 'they collected and left over'; hence it was permissible to procure '*vessels wherewith to minister*' with the balance. (9) Lit., 'where they collected and did not leave'. (10) Cf. *supra* n. 8 *ab init.;* how could funds collected for one purpose lawfully be used for another? (11) Lit., 'heart'. (12) The funds collected. (13) Lit., 'if they were required they were required'. (14) Lit., 'come'. (15) II Chron. XXIV, 14. (16) Lit., 'which is the money that has a remainder'. (17) Lit., 'be saying, this'. (18) Since after the current yearly expenses were met the balance was allowed to remain in the treasury. (19) But the main funds could not. (20) Pes. 58*b*, B.Ḳ. 111*a*. (21) העולה Lev. VI, 5, emphasis on the definite article. (22) *Sc.* that is offered on the altar every morning *before* all other sacrifices. (23) הכסף (II Chron. XXIV, 14) emphasis again on the definite article (cf. *supra* n. 21). (24) I.e., the income of the current year, and not only the balance. Cf. *infra* p. 684, n. 7.

An objection was raised: The incense and all congregational sacrifices were provided[1] from the Temple funds; the golden altar,[2] the frankincense[3] and the vessels of ministry were provided from the residue of the drink-offerings;[4] the altar for the burnt-offerings,[5] the chambers and the courts were provided from the funds that were dedicated for Temple repair, [and whatever was situated] outside the court walls[6] was provided out of the surplus of the Temple funds;[7] and it is this that [explains what] we learned: The city wall and its towers and all other requirements of the city were provided from the surplus of the Temple funds?[8]—This [point[9] is in fact a question at issue between] Tannaim. For we learned: What were they doing[10] with the surplus of the offerings [for the Temple funds]?[11] Beaten gold [plates that served as] a covering for [the walls and floor][12] of the Holy of Holies. R. Ishmael said: The surplus of the fruit[13] [was spent on the purchase of sacrifices] for the dry season[14] of the altar, while the surplus of the offerings [for the Temple funds] was spent upon vessels of ministry. R. Akiba said: The surplus of the offerings [for the Temple funds was spent on sacrifices] for the dry season of the altar while the surplus of the drink-offerings[4] was used for [the purchase of] the vessels of ministry. R. Ḥanina, the deputy High Priest, said: The surplus of the drink-offerings [was spent on sacrifices] for the dry season of the altar, while the surplus of the offerings [for the Temple funds was

(1) Lit., 'come'. (2) Which, since it was not attached to the ground and was movable, was not regarded as a part of the structure of the building. (3) That was placed at the side of the shewbread. The Wilna Gaon omits frankincense; v. J. Shek. IV, 3. (4) This is explained in Men. 90*a*. (5) The 'external' altar, cf. *supra* p. 682, n. 10. (6) E.g., the women's court and the city walls. (7) *Sc.* after the expenses for the current year have been met. Cf. *supra* p. 683, n. 24. (8) Shek. IV, 2. Does not this Baraitha, which lays down that vessels of ministry were provided out of the surplus of the drink-offerings contradict the teaching of the school of R. Ishmael? (9) From which funds the vessels of ministry were procured. (10) When the new year began on the first of Nisan and the funds of the previous year were no longer allowed to be used for the purchase of congregational sacrifices. (11) Of the previous year. (12) Rashi. (13) This is explained *infra*. (14) קיץ המזבח. *Sc.* when no private offerings were available and the altar lay idle; v. Shebu., Sonc. ed. p. 50, n. 3.

spent] on vessels of ministry. And neither the one nor the other[1] admitted that [there ever was a surplus] in the [proceeds of the] fruit.[2]

What is [meant by] 'fruit'?[3]—It was taught: What were they doing with the surplus of the offering [to the Temple funds]?[4] They bought fruit at a low price and sold it at a higher price, and with the profits sacrifices were purchased for the dry season of the altar; and it is this that [explains what] we learned: The surplus of the fruits was spent on sacrifices for the dry season of the altar.

What is meant by 'neither the one nor the other admitted that [there ever was a surplus] in [proceeds of the] fruit'?[5]—[The following of] which we learned: What were they doing with the surplus[6] of the Temple funds? They purchased therewith wines, oils and various kinds of fine flour, and the profit [resulting was credited] to the sacred funds; so R. Ishmael. R. Akiba said: No sale for profit is made with the sacred funds nor out of those of the poor.[7] Why [may no sales for profit be made] with sacred funds?—There must be no poverty where there is wealth. Why [is] no [sale for profit made] with the poor funds?—Because a poor man might come unexpectedly and there would be nothing to give him.

IF A MAN WENT TO A COUNTRY BEYOND THE SEA. It was stated: Rab ruled, [107*a*] An allowance for maintenance must be granted[8] to a married woman,[9] but Samuel ruled: No allowance may be granted[8] to a married woman.[9] Said Samuel: Abba[10] agrees with me [that no allowance is to be granted][11] during the first three months,[12] because no man leaves his house empty. In a case where

(1) Lit., 'and this and this', *sc.* R. Akiba and R. Ḥanina. (2) Shek. 6*a*. Thus it is shewn that the opinion expressed at the school of R. Ishmael is a question in dispute between Tannaim. (3) In the Mishnah just cited. (4) V. *supra* p. 684, n. 10. (5) *Sc.* how could they be so sure of the conditions of the market at all times? (6) Lit., 'surplus of the remainder'. (7) Shek. IV, 3. R. Akiba, and similarly R. Ḥanina (cf. *supra* n. 1), is thus of the opinion that there could never have been a surplus of the fruit since it was never sold. (8) By the court, out of her husband's estate. (9) Whose husband is away from home. אשת איש, lit., 'the wife of a man'. (10) *Sc.* Rab who was also known as Abba Arika. (11) Added by BaḤ in the text. (12) Of the husband's absence.

a report was received[1] that he[2] was dead there is no difference of opinion between them.[3] They only differ when no one heard that he[2] was dead. Rab ruled, 'An allowance for maintenance must be granted' since he[2] is under an obligation [to maintain her]; on what ground, however, did Samuel rule, 'No allowance may be granted'? —R. Zebid replied: Because it might well be assumed that he handed over to her some bundles [of valuables].[4] R. Papa replied: We must take into consideration the possibility that he told her, 'Deduct [the proceeds of] your handiwork[5] for your maintenance'.[6] What is the practical difference between them?[7]—The practical difference between them is the case of a woman who is of age[8] but [the proceeds of whose handiwork] did not suffice [for her maintenance],[9] or a minor[10] [the proceeds of whose handiwork] is sufficient [for her maintenance].[11]

We learned: IF A MAN WENT TO A COUNTRY BEYOND THE SEA AND HIS WIFE CLAIMED MAINTENANCE, ḤANAN RULED: SHE MUST TAKE AN OATH AT THE END BUT NOT AT THE BEGINNING. THE SONS OF THE HIGH PRIESTS, HOWEVER, DIFFERED FROM HIM AND RULED THAT SHE MUST TAKE AN OATH BOTH AT THE BEGINNING AND AT THE END. They thus[12] differ only in respect of the oath but [agree, do they not,] that maintenance must be given to her?[13]—Samuel explained [this to refer to a case] where a report had been received that [the absent husband] was dead.

(1) Lit., 'when they heard'. (2) The absent husband. (3) Lit., 'all the world (*sc.* Rab and Samuel) do not differ'; both agree that the woman is entitled to an allowance for maintenance. (4) Out of which to defray the cost of her maintenance. (5) Which are a husband's due. (6) And that she may have consented. (7) R. Zebid and R. Papa. (8) Whom a husband might safely entrust with valuables. (9) In consequence of which she would not have consented in return for her handiwork to forego her right to maintenance. Such a woman, according to R. Zebid, would still not be entitled to the court's ruling for her allowance, while according to R. Papa she would. (10) Whom no husband would entrust with valuables. (11) And who, in consequence, might have consented to forego her maintenance in return for her handiwork. Such a minor, according to R. Zebid, would, while according to R. Papa she would not, be entitled to the court's ruling for an allowance. (12) Lit., 'until here'. (13) An objection against Samuel.

Come and hear: If [a husband] went to a country beyond the sea and his wife claimed maintenance she must, said the sons of the High Priests, take an oath.[1] Ḥanan said: She need not take an oath. If [the husband] came, however, and declared, 'I have provided for her maintenance'[2] he is believed.[3] Here also [it may be replied] is a case where a report was received that he was dead. But, did it not say, 'If [the husband] came, however, and declared'?[4]—[The meaning of the expression is,] If he came after the report had been received.

Come and hear: If [a husband] went to a country beyond the sea, and his wife claimed maintenance, and he returned and said [to her], 'Deduct your handiwork for your maintenance', he is entitled [to withhold it]. If Beth din, however, granted the allowance before [he returned] their decision is valid.[5] Here also it is a case where a report that he had died was received.

Come and hear: If [a husband] went to a country beyond the sea and his wife claimed maintenance, Beth din take possession of[6] his estate and provide food and clothing for his wife, but not for his sons and daughters or for anything else![7]—R. Shesheth replied: [Here it is a case] where a husband maintained his wife at the hands of a trustee.[8] If so, [should not maintenance be granted to] one's sons and daughters also?[9]—[It is a case] where [a husband]

(1) Cf. *supra* p. 672, n. 4. (2) By entrusting her with some valuables. (3) If he takes the prescribed oath; and the amount allowed by the court must be refunded to him. From here it obviously follows that the court does make an allowance from an absent husband's estate, a legal practice which is contrary to Samuel's ruling. (4) A dead man, surely, could not come and make a declaration. (5) Tosef. Keth. XII. Lit., 'what they have fixed is fixed'; which proves that the court does make an allowance to a wife from her absent husband's estate, contrary to the ruling of Samuel. (6) Lit., 'go down into'. (7) This is explained *infra*. Cf. *supra* 48*a*. A contradiction thus arises (cf. *supra* n. 5) against Samuel's view. (8) Who now refuses to continue to act on his behalf. A husband's appointment of a trustee conclusively proves that he has left no valuables with his wife for her maintenance, and that he could not have asked her to retain her handiwork for her maintenance. Hence it is quite proper for Beth din to arrange for her maintenance. Where no trustee, however, is appointed Samuel's ruling holds. (9) Since it is assumed that he had

made provision for the maintenance of his wife[1] but not of his daughters.[1]

Whence this certainty?[2]—This, however, said R. Papa, [is the explanation: This is a case] where she heard from one witness that [her husband] had died. To her, since she could marry on the evidence of one witness, we must also grant maintenance; to his sons and daughters, however, since they, even if they desired it, could not be allowed to take possession of his estate on the evidence of one witness, maintenance also may not be granted. What [is meant by] 'anything else'? R. Ḥisda replied: Cosmetics. R. Joseph replied: Charity. According to him who replied, 'Cosmetics' the ruling[3] would apply with even greater force to [107b] charity[4]. He, however, who replied, 'Charity' [restricts the ruling[3] to this alone] but cosmetics [he maintains] must be given to her, for [her husband] would not be pleased that she should lose her comeliness.[5]

Come and hear: A *yebamah*[6] during the first three months is maintained out of the estate of her husband. Subsequently[7] she is not to be maintained either out of the estate of her husband or out of that of the levir. If, however, [the levir] appeared in court[8] and then absconded she is maintained out of the estate of the levir![9]—Samuel can answer you: What possibility need we take into consideration in the case of this [woman]?[10] If that of[11] [having been entrusted[12] with] bundles of valuables[13] [one could well object

entrusted the maintenance of his wife to a trustee, why not assume the same in regard to his sons and daughters?

(1) Lit., 'for this'. (2) That provision was made for the one and not for the others. The Baraitha, surely, draws no distinction. (3) That 'anything else' was not to be provided for. (4) Since a court which has no power to provide from a man's estate for his own wife's enjoyments would have much less power to exact charity from his estate. (5) *Supra* 48a. (6) A woman whose husband died without issue, and who awaits levirate marriage or *ḥaliẓah* which must not take place before the lapse of three months after her husband's death. (7) Lit., 'from now and onwards'. (8) To answer the widow's demand for marriage or *ḥaliẓah*. (9) Yeb. 41b. Is not this then (cf. *supra* p. 687, n. 5) an objection against Samuel's ruling? (10) To deprive her in consequence of her maintenance. (11) Lit., 'on account of'. (12) By the absent levir, before his departure. (13) To cover her cost of living.

that such a levir] is not well disposed towards her;[1] and if that of[2] [the remission of] her handiwork[3] [the fact is, it could be retorted, that] she is under no obligation to give it to him.[4]

Come and hear: A woman who went with her husband to a country beyond the sea and then came back and stated, 'My husband is dead', may, if she wishes, successfully claim her maintenance and, if she prefers, may equally claim her *kethubah*. [If she stated, however,] 'My husband has divorced me', she may be maintained[5] to the extent of her *kethubah!*[6]—Here also [it may be replied, it is a case] where a report was received that he had died. Then[7] why [is she maintained] only to the extent of her *kethubah?*—Because she herself has brought the loss upon herself.[8]

Come and hear: In what circumstances was it laid down that [a minor who] exercised her right of refusal[9] is not entitled to maintenance? It cannot be said, In [those of] one who lives with her husband, since [in such circumstances] her husband is under an obligation to maintain her, but [in those], for instance, [of one] whose husband went to a country beyond the sea, and she borrowed money and spent it[10] and then[11] exercised her right of refusal. Now, the reason [why she is not entitled to maintenance is obviously] because she exercised her right of refusal; had she, however, not exercised her right of refusal, maintenance would have been granted to her?[12]—Samuel can answer you: What possibility need

(1) Lit., 'his mind is not near to her', and it is, therefore, most unlikely that he left any valuables with her. (2) Lit., 'on account of'. (3) *Sc.* that he might have allowed her to retain the proceeds of her handiwork to defray therewith her cost of living. (4) Hence the indisputable right of the court to grant an allowance out of the absent levir's estate. In the case of an absent husband, however, where both possibilities must be taken into consideration, Samuel's ruling holds. (5) Out of her husband's estate, by an order of the court. (6) Because if she was in fact divorced she is well entitled to her *kethubah*, and if she was not divorced she has a rightful claim to maintenance. Now, is not this ruling (cf. *supra* p. 687, n. 5) an objection against Samuel's ruling? (7) Since the assumption is that she is a widow. (8) By declaring that she had been divorced. A divorcee is entitled to her *kethubah* but, unlike a widow, is not entitled to maintenance. (9) V. Glos. s.v. *mi'un*. (10) Lit., 'and ate'. (11) Lit., 'she stood up'. (12) Which is an objection (cf. *supra* p. 687, n. 5) against Samuel.

we provide against as far as she is concerned? If against that of[1] [having been entrusted with] bundles of valuables [it may be pointed out that] no one entrusts a minor with valuables; and if against that of [the man's remission of] her handiwork[2] [the fact is, it could be argued, that] the handiwork of a minor does not suffice [for her maintenance].[3] What is the ultimate decision?[4] When R. Dimi came[5] he related: Such a case was submitted to Rabbi at Beth She'arim[6] and he granted[7] the woman[8] an allowance for her maintenance, [while a similar case was submitted] to R. Ishmael at Sepphoris[9] and he did not grant her any maintenance. R. Joḥanan was astonished at this decision. What reason [he wondered] could R. Ishmael see that [in consequence of it] he allowed her no maintenance? Surely the sons of the High Priests and Ḥanan differed only on the question of the oath,[10] but [they all agree, do they not, that] maintenance is to be given to her?—R. Shaman b. Abba answered him: Our Master, Samuel, in Babylon has long ago explained this [as being a case] where a report had been received that [the absent husband] had died. 'You', the other remarked, 'explain so much with this reply'.

When Rabin came[5] he related: Such a case was submitted to Rabbi at Beth She'arim[6] and he did not grant the woman[8] any maintenance, [while in a similar case which was submitted] to R. Ishmael at Sepphoris[9] [the latter] granted her an allowance for her maintenance. Said R. Joḥanan: What reason could Rabbi see for not granting her an allowance, when Ḥanan and the sons of the High Priests obviously differed only in respect of the oath[10] but [agreed that] maintenance is to be given her?—R. Shaman b. Abba replied: Samuel in Babylon has long ago explained this [as being a case] where a report has been received that [the absent husband]

(1) Lit., 'on account of'. (2) V. *supra* p. 689, n. 3. (3) And she would not have agreed to release her husband from his obligation to maintain her in return for the inadequate income from her handiwork. (4) Lit., 'what is there about it?' Is maintenance to be allowed to a wife out of her absent husband's estate? (5) From Palestine to Babylon. (6) Cf. *supra* p. 663, n. 4. (7) Out of the estate of her absent husband. (8) Lit., 'her'. (9) Cf. *supra* p. 410, n. 6. (10) V. our Mishnah.

had died. 'You', the other remarked, 'explain so much with this answer'. The law, however, is in agreement with Rab,[1] and a married woman is to be granted an allowance for her maintenance. The law is also in agreement with a ruling which R. Huna laid down in the name of Rab, R. Huna having stated on the authority of Rab: A wife is within her rights when she says to her husband, 'I desire no maintenance from, and refuse to do [any work for you]'. The law, furthermore, agrees with a ruling of R. Zebid[2] in respect of glazed vessels,[3] R. Zebid having laid down: Glazed vessels[3] are permitted[4] if they are white or black,[5] but forbidden[6] if green.[7] This,[8] however, applies only to such[9] as have no cracks[10] but if they have cracks they are forbidden.[6]

MISHNAH. IF A MAN WENT TO A COUNTRY BEYOND THE SEA AND SOMEONE CAME FORWARD[11] AND MAINTAINED HIS WIFE, ḤANAN SAID: HE LOSES HIS MONEY.[12] THE SONS OF THE HIGH PRIESTS[13] DIFFERED FROM HIM AND RULED: LET HIM TAKE AN OATH AS TO HOW MUCH HE SPENT AND RECOVER IT. SAID R. DOSA B. HARKINAS: [MY OPINION IS] IN AGREEMENT WITH THEIR RULING. R. JOḤANAN B. ZAKKAI SAID:

(1) *Supra* 107*a ab init.* (2) [This is introduced here because R. Zebid figures in the above discussion; or, it is likely that both the rulings of R. Huna and R. Zebid were adopted at the same session, v. *Shiṭṭah Meḳubbeẓeth*]. (3) If earthenware. (4) For use (cf. *infra* note 5ff). (5) These kinds of glaze prevent absorption despite the porous nature of the earthenware. (6) To be used at all, if they once contained heathen foodstuffs or heathen wine of libation (*nesek*), or on the Passover if they ever contained *ḥameẓ*, any foodstuffs that were not free from leavened substances of any of the five kinds of grain (cf. Ḥal. I, 1). (7) Or 'yellow'. The last mentioned glaze, unlike the former, contains crystals of alum which increase the absorptive capacity of the potsherd (cf. A.Z. 33*b*). (8) That green (or yellow) glazed earthenware is permitted (v. *supra* note 4). (9) Lit., 'and it was not said but'. (10) In the glazed surface. (11) Lit., 'and one rose'. (12) He has no legal claim upon the husband who neither instructed him to advance the money nor promised to refund his expenses. (13) Cf. *supra* p. 672, n. 7.

ḤANAN SPOKE WELL [FOR THE MAN] PUT HIS MONEY ON A STAG'S HORN.[1]

GEMARA. Elsewhere we have learned: If a man is forbidden by a vow to have any benefit from another [108*a*] the latter may nevertheless pay for him his *shekel*,[2] repay his debt[3] and restore to him any object he may have lost; but where a reward is taken,[4] the benefit is to be given[5] to the sacred funds.[6] Now, one can well be satisfied [with the ruling that] he may 'pay for him his *shekel*' [because by this payment] he merely performs a religious act,[7] for it was taught:[8] It is lawful to withdraw[9] [from the funds of the Temple treasury] on the account of that which was lost,[10] collected[11] or about to be collected;[12] and [the ruling that he may] 'restore to him any object he may have lost' [is also intelligible since thereby] also he is performing a religious duty;[13] but [how could he be permitted to] 'repay his debt' [when thereby] he un-

(1) Metaph. He could never recover the money from the stag, nor can he recover it from the woman or her husband (cf. p. 691 n. 12). (2) His annual contribution to the fund for congregational sacrifices. According to Tosaf. (s.v. ויעל) provided it was lost on its way to the Temple treasury, v. *infra* n. 10. (3) Which he may be owing to a third party. (4) For the return of a lost object; and this man either refuses to take it or where he, too, is forbidden by vow to derive any benefit from the other man, v. Ned. 33*a*. (5) Lit., 'shall fall'. (6) Ned. 33*a*. The other may not retain the amount of the reward since it is legally due to the man from whom he is forbidden to derive any benefit. (7) And confers no benefit upon the other. (8) Cf. marginal note and Tosaf. B.M. 58*a* s.v. דתנן. Cur. edd. 'we learned'. (9) תורמין (rt. תרם 'to lift', 'separate'). Such withdrawals were made three times a year (cf. Shek. III, 1). (10) *Sc*. the man whose *shekel* was lost has a share in the sacrifices purchased out of the funds as if his contribution had actually reached the treasury. According to Tosaf. (loc. cit.); provided it had been handed by him to the Temple treasurer, and it was lost after the withdrawal in the Temple had taken place. (11) By an agent who lost it on the way. According to Tosaf., after the withdrawal in the Temple had taken place. Cf. *supra* note 10). (12) B.M. 58*a*. From the first two mentioned cases it thus follows that the man whose *shekel* was lost (cf. notes 10 and 11) gains no benefit from the generosity of the man who paid his *shekel* in the circumstances mentioned (cf. *supra* note 2). (13) And the question of conferring a benefit upon the other does not arise. His object is not the benefit of the man but the religious act.

doubtedly benefits[1] him?—R. Oshaia replied: 'This ruling[2] is that of[3] Ḥanan who said: HE LOSES HIS MONEY.[4] Raba, however, replied: The ruling[2] may be said [to agree even with the view of] the Rabbis,[5] for here[6] we are dealing [with the case of a man] who borrowed money on the condition that he does not repay it [except when he is inclined to do so].[7] It is well that Raba does not give the same reply as R. Oshaia, since [he wishes] the ruling to agree even with the opinion of the Rabbis. On what ground, however, does not R. Oshaia [wish to] give the same reply as Raba?—R. Oshaia can answer you: Granted that he[8] has no actual benefit;[9] [108b] has he not [some benefit in being spared] shame?[10] Another reading:[11] There[8] also he has benefit,[9] the benefit that he [need not] feel embarassed in the other's presence.[12]

MISHNAH. ADMON LAID DOWN SEVEN RULINGS:—[13]IF A MAN DIES AND LEAVES SONS AND DAUGHTERS, IF THE ESTATE IS LARGE,[14] THE SONS INHERIT IT AND THE DAUGHTERS ARE MAINTAINED [FROM IT][15] AND IF THE ESTATE IS SMALL,[14] THE DAUGHTERS ARE MAINTAINED FROM IT, AND THE SONS CAN GO BEGGING.[16] ADMON SAID, 'AM I TO BE THE LOSER BECAUSE

(1) קמשתרשי (rt. שרש, Hithpa.) 'to take root'. (2) That he may 'repay his debt'. (3) Lit., 'who is it?' (4) Similarly anyone who repays a stranger's debt cannot reclaim it from him. Such a debtor, it follows, is not regarded as the recipient of the amount repaid. For the same reason he cannot be regarded as the recipient of a benefit. (5) Who hold a man liable for any expenses anybody may have incurred on his behalf. (6) Lit., 'here in what?' (7) V. Ned. Sonc. ed. p. 102, n. 5. Since the creditor in such circumstances can never exact payment from the debtor, any man who repays it confers no real benefit upon him. (8) In the circumstances mentioned (cf. *supra* n. 7). (9) From the repayment of the debt. (10) Of defaulting. Of course he has. Raba's reply, therefore, is unacceptable to R. Oshaia. (11) So BaḤ and Rashal. Wanting in cur. edd. (12) [The difference between the two versions is that whereas according to the former, the sparing of a feeling of shame is not considered an actual benefit, according to the latter it is regarded as such, v. Glosses of Bezalel Ronsburg]. (13) Lit., 'said seven'. Cf. *supra* p. 672 nn. 2 and 3. (14) Lit., 'possessions are many'. The definition of 'large' and 'small' is given in B.B. Sonc. ed. p. 594. (15) Until their majority or marriage. (16) Lit., 'go about (people's) doors'.

I AM A MALE!'[1] R. GAMALIEL SAID: ADMON'S VIEW HAS MY APPROVAL.[2]

GEMARA. What does he[3] mean?[4]—Abaye replied: He means this: 'AM I TO BE THE LOSER BECAUSE I AM A MALE and capable of engaging in the study of the Torah?' Said Raba to him: Would, then, he who is engaged in the study of the Torah be entitled to heirship, while he who is not engaged in the study of the Torah not be entitled to be heir?[5]—But, said Raba, it is this that he[3] meant: 'AM I BECAUSE I AM A MALE, and entitled to be heir in the case of a large estate, TO BE THE LOSER [of my rights] in the case of a small estate?'

MISHNAH. IF A MAN CLAIMED FROM ANOTHER JARS OF OIL AND [THE LATTER] ADMITTED HIS CLAIM TO [EMPTY] JARS, ADMON RULED: SINCE HE ADMITTED A PORTION OF THE CLAIM HE MUST TAKE AN OATH,[6] BUT THE SAGES SAID: THE ADMISSION OF THE PORTION [OF THE CLAIM] IS NOT OF THE SAME KIND AS THE CLAIM.[7] R. GAMALIEL SAID: ADMON'S VIEW HAS MY APPROVAL.[2]

GEMARA. From this[8] it may be inferred that, according to the Rabbis,[9] [a man from] whom one claimed wheat and barley and he admitted the claim to the barley is exempt [from oath]. Must it then be said that this presents an objection against a ruling which R. Naḥman laid down in the name of Samuel? For R. Naḥman laid down in the name of Samuel: [A man from] whom one claimed

(1) This is explained in the Gemara. (2) Lit., 'I see the words of Admon'. (3) Admon. (4) *Sc.* what reason is there to assume that, as regards maintenance, a male should be given any preference at all over a female? (5) Obviously not. The Pentateuchal laws of inheritance, surely, draw no distinction between a learned, and an ignorant son. (6) That he owes him no oil. (7) The claim was for (*a*) jars and (*b*) oil, while the admission was in respect of the full claim of the former and of no part of the latter. (8) The statement of the Sages in our Mishnah (cf. *supra* n. 7). (9) *Sc.* THE SAGES.

wheat and barley and he admitted one of them is liable [to an oath]?[1]—Rab Judah replied in the name of Rab: [Our Mishnah deals with the case of one from] whom a certain quantity[2] [of oil] was claimed.[3] If so,[4] what could Admon's reason be?—This, however, said Raba, [is the explanation]: Both[5] [agree] that where [the claimant] said to the other, 'I have the contents[6] of ten jars of oil in your tank',[7] he claims from him the oil but not the jars, [and if he said], 'You owe me[8] ten jars full of oil', he claims both the oil and the jars; they only differ where [the claimant] said to him, 'You owe me[8] ten jars of oil'. Admon maintains that in this expression a claim for the jars also is implied, and the Rabbis[9] contend that in this expression the jars were not implied.

The reason then[10] is because 'in this expression the jars were not implied', but if the jars had been implied in this expression he would apparently have been liable [to the oath]. Must it consequently be presumed that this presents an objection against a ruling of R. Ḥiyya b. Abba? For R. Ḥiyya b. Abba[11] ruled: [A man from] whom one claimed wheat and barley, and he admitted one of them, is exempt [from an oath]?—R. Shimi b. Ashi replied: [The making of such a claim][12] is the same as if one had claimed from another a pomegranate with its peel.[13] To this Rabina demurred: A pomegranate without its peel cannot be preserved, but oil can well be preserved without jars![14]—[The fact,] however, is that[15] we are

(1) Shebu. 40*a*. (2) Lit., 'measure'. (3) JARS does not refer to the actual containers but to their measure or capacity, the jars themselves forming no part of the claim. (4) That the jars admitted formed no part of the claim. (5) Lit., 'that all the world', Admon and the Sages. (6) מלא, lit., 'fulness'. (7) בור, a receptacle in the oil press. (8) Lit., 'I have with you'. (9) *Sc.* THE SAGES. (10) Why the Sages do not regard the admission of the claim to the jars as AN ADMISSION OF THE SAME KIND AS THE CLAIM. (11) MS.M. inserts, 'in the name of R. Joḥanan'. (12) 'Jars of oil'. (13) Between the oil and the jars in which it is kept there exists a definite connection similar to that of the pomegranate and its peel; but between wheat and barley there exists no such connection. An admission of one of the two in the former cases may well be regarded as AN ADMISSION OF THE SAME KIND AS THE CLAIM though an admission of one of the two in the latter case cannot be so regarded. (14) In the tank. How then could the one pair be compared to the other? (15) Lit., 'in what?'

here[1] dealing [with the case of a man] who said to another, 'You owe me[2] ten jars of oil', and the other replied, 'The [claim for the] oil is a pure invention,[3] [and as to] the jars, too, I owe you[4] five and you have no [claim to any other] five'. Admon maintains that this expression implies a claim to the jars also and, since [the defendant] must take an oath in respect of the jars,[5] he must also take an oath by implication[6] in respect of the oil, while the Rabbis[7] are of the opinion that such an expression does not imply a claim for the jars [so that] what the one claims[8] the other did not admit, and what the latter admitted[9] the former did not claim.

MISHNAH. IF A MAN PROMISED[10] A SUM OF MONEY TO HIS [PROSPECTIVE] SON-IN-LAW AND THEN DEFAULTED,[11] [109*a*] LET [HIS DAUGHTER] REMAIN [SINGLE][12] UNTIL HER HAIR GROWS GREY.[13] ADMON RULED: SHE MAY SAY,[14] 'HAD I MYSELF PROMISED THE SUM ON MY BEHALF I WOULD REMAIN [SINGLE][12] UNTIL MY HAIR GREW GREY, BUT NOW THAT MY FATHER HAS PROMISED IT, WHAT CAN I DO? EITHER MARRY ME OR SET ME FREE'. R. GAMALIEL SAID: ADMON'S WORDS HAVE MY APPROVAL.

GEMARA. Our Mishnah does not [uphold the same view] as that of the following Tanna. For it was taught: R. Jose son of R. Judah stated, There was no difference of opinion between Admon and the Sages that, where a man promised a sum of money to his [prospective] son-in-law and then defaulted, his daughter may say[14] 'My father has promised on my behalf, what can I do?' They

(1) In our Mishnah. (2) Lit., 'I have with you'. (3) Lit., 'the things never were'. (4) Lit., 'you have'. (5) Having clearly admitted a part of the claim. (6) V. *supra* p. 549, n. 3. (7) *Sc.* THE SAGES. (8) Oil. (9) Jars. (10) Lit., 'fixed'. (11) פשט לו את הרגל, lit., 'stretched out the leg towards him', as if to say, 'Take the dust of my foot', or 'hang me by the leg, I have nothing to give you' (Rashi). (12) Unmarried and undivorced. (13) *Sc.* the son-in-law cannot be compelled either to marry her or to set her free. (14) To her prospective husband.

only[1] differ where she herself promised a sum of money on her own behalf, in which case the Sages ruled: Let her remain [single][2] until her hair grows grey, while Admon maintained that she could say, 'I thought that my father would pay for me [the promised amount], but now that my father does not pay for me, what can I do? Either marry me or set me free'. Said R. Gamaliel: Admon's words have my approval.[3]

A Tanna taught: This[4] applies only to a woman who is of age but in the case of a minor compulsion may be used. Who is to be compelled? If the father [be suggested], should [not the ruling, it may be retorted,] be reversed?[5]—But, said Raba, compulsion is exercised against the [prospective] husband that he may give her a letter of divorce.

R. Isaac b. Eleazar laid down on the authority of Hezekiah: Wherever R. Gamaliel stated, 'Admon's words have my approval', the *halachah* agrees with him. Said Raba to R. Naḥman, Even in the Baraitha?[6]—The other replied, Did we say 'In the Mishnah?' What we said was, 'Wherever R. Gamaliel stated'.[7]

Said R. Zera in the name of Rabbah b. Jeremiah: As to the two rulings which Ḥanan has laid down, the *halachah* is in agreement with him who followed his view,[8] but in respect of the seven rulings

(1) Lit., 'concerning what?' (2) Unmarried and undivorced. (3) Tosef. Keth. XII. (4) The ruling of the Baraitha. (5) If compulsion is to be resorted to, this should not be in the case of a minor whose actions have no legal validity, but in that of one who is of age, whose undertaking is legally valid (v. Strashun). (6) Just cited, where the dispute relates to a promise made by the daughter herself (cf. Rashi s.v. אפי' and Tosaf. s.v. ואפילו *a.l.*). [R. Nissim: Does this principle apply elsewhere also in a Baraitha?—though here the *halachah* has been fixed according to the version of our Mishnah]. (7) The *halachah*, apparently contradictory, being determined by the version of the Mishnah and Baraitha respectively, (cf. Tosaf. l.c.). [Cf. however n. 6]. (8) כיוצא בו, lit., 'like he who goes out with him', *sc.* R. Joḥanan b. Zakkai (cf. the Mishnahs *supra* 105*a* and 107*b*). This is discussed anon. *Aliter:* 'Like that which goes out with it', i.e., rulings similar to those laid down by Admon (v. Tosaf.) [According to Adreth a case similar to that of Admon's is provided by one who pays his fellow's debt to his creditor without his instructions, and where the claim is, say, for wheat and barley and the admission is only in regard to one of these, we have an instance similar to that of Admon].

that were laid down by Admon, the *halachah* is not in agreement with him who followed his view.[1] What does he[2] mean? If it be suggested that he means this: As to the two rulings which Ḥanan has laid down, the *halachah* is in agreement with himself and with him who followed his view,[3] and that in respect of the seven rulings that were laid down by Admon, the *halachah* is neither in agreement with himself nor with him who followed his view,[1] [it may be objected:] Did not R. Isaac b. Eleazar lay down on the authority of Hezekiah that 'wherever R. Gamaliel stated, "Admon's words have my approval", the *halachah* agrees with him'?—What he[2] meant, however, must have been this: As to the two rulings which Ḥanan has laid down, the *halachah* is in agreement with himself and with him who followed his view,[3] but in respect of the seven rulings that were laid down by Admon, the *halachah* does not agree with him who followed his view[4] but agrees with himself in all his rulings. But, surely, R. Isaac b. Eleazar laid down on the authority of Hezekiah that 'wherever R. Gamaliel stated, "Admon's words have my approval" the *halachah* agrees with him'. [Does not this imply:] Only[5] where he stated;[6] but not where he did not state?—The fact, however, is that he[2] meant this: As to the two rulings which Ḥanan has laid down, the *halachah* is in agreement with himself and with him who followed him,[3] but of the seven rulings that were laid down by Admon, there are some concerning which the *halachah* is in agreement with himself and with him who followed his view[7] while there are others concerning which the *halachah* does not agree with him[8] but with him who followed his view,[4] [the rule being that] wherever R. Gamaliel stated, 'Admon's words have my approval' is the *halachah* in agreement with him, but not elsewhere.[9]

(1) *Sc.* R. Gamaliel (cf. the Mishnahs *supra* 108*b* f). Cf. also p. 697, n. 8 *mutatis mutandis*. (2) R. Zera. (3) V. p. 697, n. 8. (4) I.e., R. Gamaliel (cf. *supra* note 1) who agreed with him in *three rulings only*, for the *halachah* agrees with Admon in all his rulings. (5) Lit., 'yes'. (6) Is the *halachah* in agreement with Admon. (7) *Sc.* the three rulings (cf. *supra* n. 4). (8) Rashal on the interpretation of Tosaf. (v. p. 697, n. 8) emends: 'agrees neither with him nor with etc.' (9) Lit., 'not those', *sc.* the rulings of Admon of which R. Gamaliel expressed no approval.

MISHNAH. IF A MAN CONTESTS [THE OWNERSHIP OF] A FIELD ON [THE DEED OF SALE OF] WHICH HE IS SIGNED AS A WITNESS,[1] ADMON RULED: [HIS CLAIM IS ADMISSIBLE BECAUSE] HE CAN SAY,[2] '[LITIGATION WITH] THE SECOND[3] IS EASIER FOR ME, SINCE THE FIRST[4] IS A MORE DIFFICULT PERSON THAN HE'.[5] THE SAGES, HOWEVER, RULED THAT HE HAS LOST HIS RIGHT.[6] IF [THE SELLER][7] MADE IT[8] A [BOUNDARY] MARK FOR ANOTHER PERSON[9] [THE CONTESTANT][10] HAS LOST HIS RIGHT.[11]

GEMARA. Abaye said: This[12] was taught only [in respect of] A WITNESS, but a judge[13] does not lose his title;[14] for R. Ḥiyya taught Witnesses may not sign a deed unless they have read it[15] [109b] but judges[16] may sign even though they have not read it.[17]

IF [THE SELLER] MADE IT A [BOUNDARY] MARK FOR ANOTHER PERSON. Abaye said: This[12] was taught only [where it was] FOR ANOTHER PERSON, but [if it was made a boundary mark] for himself[18] he does not lose his right; for he can say, 'Had I not

(1) His plea being that the seller has taken it from him by violence. (2) So separate edd. of the Mishnah, Alfasi and Asheri. (3) The buyer. (4) The seller. (5) *Sc.* he might plead that he signed as a witness, not because he acknowledged the seller to be the lawful owner, but in the hope that it would be easier for him to recover his field from the buyer than from the seller. (6) By signing the deed of sale he is presumed to have acknowledged the seller as the lawful owner of that field. (7) Whose title to the field is contested. (8) The contested field. (9) To whom he has sold a field adjacent to it. (10) Who signed as a witness to the deed of sale in which the contested field was described as the property of the seller, and given as one of the boundaries of the field sold. (11) Even according to Admon. The plea that the contestant preferred to litigate with the buyer is obviously inadmissible here, and the reason given *supra* note 6, applies. (12) The ruling that the contestant HAS LOST HIS TITLE. (13) Who attested the signatures of the witnesses to a deed of sale. (14) To the field sold and, despite his signature, may reclaim it. A judge is concerned only with the attestation of the witnesses' *signature* and not with the *contents* of the deed. (15) Since it is the contents of the deed to which they must testify. (16) Cf. *supra* n. 13. (17) A judge's signature on a deed consequently does not prove that beyond the signatures of the witnesses he was at all aware of its contents. (18) *Sc.* if the contestant himself bought a field from the man whom

done that[1] for him he would not have sold the field to me'. What [possible objection can] you have?[2] That he should have made a declaration [to that effect]? Your friend [it can be retorted] has a friend, and the friend of your friend has a friend.[3]

A certain man once made a field[4] a [boundary] mark for another person,[5] [and one of the witnesses,] having contested [its ownership,][6] died, when a guardian was appointed [over his estate].[7] The guardian came to Abaye[8] who quoted to him: 'IF [THE SELLER] MADE IT A [BOUNDARY] MARK FOR ANOTHER PERSON [THE CONTESTANT] HAS LOST HIS RIGHT'. 'If the father of the orphans had been alive', the other retorted, 'could he not have pleaded, "I have conceded to him[9] only one furrow"?'[10]—'You speak well', he said, 'for R. Joḥanan stated, If he submitted the plea, "I have conceded to you only one furrow", he is believed'. 'Proceed at any rate [Abaye later[11] told the guardian] to give him one furrow'.[12] On that [furrow, however,] there was a nursery of palm trees, and [the guardian] said to him, 'Had the father of the orphans been alive, could he not have submitted the plea, "I have re-purchased it from him"?'[13]—'You speak well', [Abaye] said to him, 'for R. Joḥanan ruled, If he submitted the plea, "I have re-purchased it from him" he is believed'.[14] Said Abaye: Anyone who appoints a guardian should

he accuses of having stolen an adjacent field from him, and the latter, inserting the field in dispute as a boundary, described it as his own.

(1) Lit., 'thus', i.e., agreed to the description of the stolen field as the property of the seller. (2) Against this plea. (3) Popular saying. The declaration would eventually reach the ears of the seller who might in consequence cancel the sale. (4) Which he was accused of having stolen. (5) To whom he had sold a field adjacent to it. (6) Cf. *supra* p. 699, n. 1. (7) To manage it for the orphans. (8) To claim the field on behalf of his wards. (9) Of the field in dispute. (10) That was immediately next to the sold field. The orphans should, therefore, be entitled to reclaim the rest of the field. (11) After proof had been adduced that the field had been stolen from the father of the orphans. (12) The minimum which the deceased must have conceded. (13) After it had been ascribed to him. (14) [The reason for this ruling, according to Rashi, is because the field is known to have belonged to the contestant and but for his signature referred to, the present occupier has no proof of his title to the field. This admission on the part of the contestant is, however, cancelled by his declaration of having repurchased the field, v. *supra* 16a.]

appoint one like this man who understands how to turn [the scales][1] in favour of orphans.

MISHNAH. IF A MAN WENT TO A COUNTRY BEYOND THE SEA AND [IN HIS ABSENCE] THE PATH TO HIS FIELD WAS LOST,[2] ADMON RULED: LET HIM WALK [TO HIS FIELD][3] BY THE SHORTEST WAY.[4] THE SAGES, HOWEVER, RULED: LET HIM EITHER PURCHASE A PATH FOR HIMSELF EVEN THOUGH IT [COST HIM] A HUNDRED MANEH OR FLY THROUGH THE AIR.

GEMARA. What is the Rabbis'[5] reason? Does not Admon speak well?[6]—Rab Judah replied in the name of Rab: [The ruling[7] refers to a field], for instance, which [the fields of] four persons surrounded on its four sides.[8] If that be so, what can be Admon's reason?[9]—Raba explained: Where four persons[10] succeeded[11] [to the adjacent fields] by virtue of the rights of four [persons respectively][12] or where four persons succeeded[11] [to them][13] by virtue of one,[12] all agree that these may turn him away.[14] They[15] only differ where one person succeeded[16] [to all the surrounding fields] by virtue of four persons.[17] Admon is of the opinion that [the claimant can say to that person,] 'At all events[18] my path is in your territory'; and the Rabbis hold the opinion [that the defendant might retort,] 'If you will keep quiet, well and good,[19] but if not I will return the

(1) Lit., 'to turn over'. (2) It being unknown in which of the surrounding fields it lay. (3) He must be allowed a short path through one of the surrounding fields. (This is further explained *infra*). (4) The minimum. He cannot claim more than what is, at all events, due to him. (5) THE SAGES. (6) The assumption now being that all the surrounding fields belonged to one person who must obviously be held responsible for the lost path. (7) In our Mishnah. (8) So that each person can shift responsibility on the others. (9) How can one be held responsible when all the four are equally involved? (10) The respective owners of the four surrounding fields. (11) Lit., 'came'. (12) *Sc.* by purchase or gift. (13) After the path was lost. (14) Cf. *supra* note 8. (15) Admon and the Sages. (16) Lit., 'came'. (17) *Sc.* by purchase or gift. (18) In whichever field the path was lost. (19) Lit., 'you will keep quiet' (*bis*). He will sell him a path at a reasonable price (cf. Rashi). V., however, Tosaf. Yeb. 37*b*, s.v. דאמר.

deeds to their respective original owners whom you will have no chance of calling to law'.[1]

A [dying man][2] once instructed [those around him] that a palm tree shall be given to his daughter, but the orphans proceeded to divide the estate and gave her no palm tree. R. Joseph [in considering the case] intended to lay down that it involved the very same principle as that of our Mishnah.[3] But Abaye said to him: Are [the two] alike? There,[4] each one can send [the claimant to the path] away;[5] but here, the palm tree is in their common possession.[6] What is their way out?[7]—They must give her a palm tree and divide [the estate] all over[8] again.

A [dying man][9] once instructed [those around him] that a palm tree shall be given to his daughter. When he died he left[10] two halves of a palm tree.[11] Sat R. Ashi [discussing the case] and grappled with this difficulty: Do people call two halves of palm trees 'a palm tree' or not?—Said R. Mordecai to R. Ashi, Thus said Abimi of Hagronia[12] in the name of Raba: People do call two halves of palm trees 'a palm tree'.[13]

MISHNAH. [110a] IF A MAN PRODUCED A BOND OF INDEBTEDNESS AGAINST ANOTHER, AND THE LATTER PRO-

(1) Lit., 'and you will not be able to talk law with them'. Cf. *supra* p. 701, n. 8. (2) The verbal instructions of one in such circumstances have the force of a legally written document. (3) Like the owners of the adjacent fields each of whom shifts the responsibility for the path on to the others, so can each brother shift the responsibility for the palm tree on to the other brothers. (4) The case in our Mishnah. (5) The one path can lie only in one person's field, and each of the defendants can, therefore, well plead that it did not lie in his. (6) Lit., 'with them', the instructions of the deceased having been given before the division of the estate, and the duty of carrying out his wish is incumbent upon all the heirs jointly. (7) Lit., 'their correction', 'redress'. (8) Lit., 'from the beginning'. (9) V. *supra* note 2. (10) Among his many palm trees. (11) *Sc.* two palm trees in each of which he owned a half, and the heirs desired to assign them to the daughter in fulfilment of their father's instructions. (12) One of the suburbs of Nehardea. (13) And the brothers can assign these to the daughter despite the greater trouble involved in their cultivation.

DUCED [A DEED OF SALE,[1] SHEWING] THAT THE FORMER HAD SOLD HIM A FIELD,[2] ADMON RULED: [THE OTHER] CAN SAY, 'HAD I OWED YOU [ANYTHING] YOU WOULD HAVE RECOVERED IT WHEN YOU SOLD ME THE FIELD'.[3] THE SAGES, HOWEVER, SAY: THIS [SELLER] MAY HAVE BEEN A PRUDENT MAN, SINCE HE MAY HAVE SOLD HIM THE LAND IN ORDER TO BE ABLE TO TAKE IT FROM HIM AS A PLEDGE.[4]

GEMARA. What is the reason of the Rabbis?[5] Does not Admon speak well?—Where [the purchase] money is paid first and the deed is written afterwards, no one disputes that the [defendant] may well say [to the claimant], 'You should have recovered your debt when you sold me the field'.[3] They only differ where the deed is written first and the purchase money is paid afterwards. Admon is of the opinion that [the claimant] should have made a declaration [of his motive],[6] while the Rabbis[5] maintain [that the claimant can retort,] 'Your friend has a friend, and the friend of your friend has a friend'.[7]

MISHNAH. IF TWO MEN PRODUCED BONDS OF INDEBTEDNESS AGAINST ONE ANOTHER,[8] ADMON RULED: [THE HOLDER OF THE LATER BOND CAN SAY TO THE OTHER,] 'HAD I OWED YOU [ANY MONEY] HOW IS IT THAT YOU BORROWED FROM ME?'[9] THE SAGES, HOWEVER, RULED: THE ONE RECOVERS HIS DEBT[10] AND THE OTHER RECOVERS HIS DEBT.[11]

(1) Bearing a later date than that of the bond. (2) And thereby he seeks to prove that either he never borrowed the sum claimed or that he repaid it prior to his purchase of the field. (3) By seizing the purchase price in payment of the debt. Since he did not do so it is obvious that he owed him nothing. (4) Movables can be hidden away. (5) THE SAGES. (6) And since he did not do so the defendant may well plead, 'HAD I OWED YOU' etc. (7) Cf. *supra* p. 700, n. 3 *mutatis mutandis*. (8) One bond bearing an earlier date than the other. (9) And this plea exempts him from payment. (10) Lit., 'bond of his debt'. (11) No balancing of amounts or exchange of bonds being allowed by the court. Each bond must be treated on its own merits and orders for distraint are given accordingly.

GEMARA. It was stated: If two men produced bonds of indebtedness against one another, R. Naḥman ruled: The one recovers his debt and the other recovers his debt.[1] R. Shesheth said: What is the point[2] in exchanging bags?[3] The one rather retains his own [money][4] and the other retains his.

All agree[5] that if both [litigants possess land of the] best,[6] medium or worst quality [distraint for each on the other is] undoubtedly a case of changing bags.[3] They differ only where one [of the litigants] has land of medium quality and the other of the worst quality. R. Naḥman is of the opinion that 'the one recovers his debt and the other recovers his debt' because in his view an assessment[7] is made on the basis of the debtor's[8] possessions,[9] [so that] the owner of the land of the worst quality proceeds to distrain on the medium quality [of the other][10] which then becomes with him the best; and the other can then proceed to take from him the worst only.[11] R. Shesheth, however, said, 'What is the point in exchanging bags?' because he is of the opinion that an assessment[12] is made on a general basis,[13] [so that] eventually when the original owner of the medium land[14] proceeds [to distrain on the property of the other][15] he will only take back his own medium land. But what [reason can] you see, according to R. Naḥman, that the owner of the worst quality of land should proceed [to

(1) V. p. 703, n. 11. (2) If the amounts of the two debts are equal (v. *infra*). (3) Metaph. If the bags are of equal weight there is no advantage to an animal in changing them from one side to the other (Jast.) or to a human being in changing the burden from one hand to the other (Levy). מטרתא, 'leather bag' (Rashi). Cf. μετρητής, 'a liquid measure', 'cask'. (4) Or property on which the other desires to distrain. (5) Lit., 'all the world', R. Naḥman and R. Shesheth. (6) Lit., 'best and best'. (7) On behalf of a creditor who distrains on the debtor's land. (8) Lit., 'of his'. (9) If the debtor, for instance, has only two kinds of land, medium and inferior quality, the former is regarded as 'best' and the creditor can only distrain on the inferior land. A creditor (cf. B.Ḳ. 7*b*) may distrain on the 'medium' land of the debtor if he possesses such, or on the 'worst'. He has no right to distrain on the 'best'. (10) Being in fact the only kind of land the other possesses. (11) He cannot reclaim the medium quality that was taken from him, since it is now regarded as its present owner's 'best' (cf. *supra* note 9). (12) V. *supra* note 7. (13) Lit., 'of all men'. (14) Lit., 'that one'. (15) Who had taken possession of his medium land.

distrain] first? Why should not rather the owner of the medium quality come first and distrain on the worst [of the other] and then let him distrain on it?[1]—[But this ruling] applies only[2] where the [holder of the worst land] submitted his claim first. But after all when they come to distrain, do they not come simultaneously?[3]—The fact, however, [is that the ruling] applies only[2] where one [of the litigants] has best and medium land, and the other has only of the worst. One Master[4] is of the opinion that an assessment[5] is made on the basis of the debtor's[6] possessions,[7] while the other Master[8] is of the opinion that an assessment[5] is made on a general basis.[9]

We have learned: THE SAGES, HOWEVER, RULED: THE ONE RECOVERS HIS DEBT AND THE OTHER RECOVERS HIS DEBT![10]—R. Naḥman explained this, according to R. Shesheth, [as referring to a case,] for instance, where one borrowed for a period of ten, and the other for one of five years.[11] But how exactly are we to understand this? If it be suggested that the first [bond][12] was for ten years and the second for five, would Admon [it may be ob-

(1) Cf. p. 704, n. 11. The other could not distrain on the medium which is now his best. (2) Lit., 'is not required but'. (3) Since both presented their bonds at court (v. our Mishnah *ab init.*). Why then should one be allowed an advantage over the other? (4) R. Naḥman. (5) V. *supra* p. 704, n. 7. (6) Lit., 'of his'. (7) Cf. *supra* p. 704, n. 9. The owner of the worst land, if allowed to distrain on the other instead of keeping his own, is at an advantage in either case, whether he distrains first or last. If he distrains first he obtains, of course, the other's medium land which, becoming his 'best', cannot be distrained on by the creditor, and the other must consequently recoup himself from his worst. If, on the other hand, the owner of the best and medium land distrains first, it is again the other's worst land (the only kind he possesses) to which he can have recourse, while the other still distrains on his medium. (8) R. Shesheth. (9) Cf. *supra* p. 704, n. 13. Where, therefore, two bonds are simultaneously presented at court and the order would naturally be made that the owner of the worst land distrains first on the other's 'medium' and that the latter then distrains on the same 'medium', the procedure would be as useless as that of 'exchanging bags'. (10) Is not this an objection against R. Shesheth? (11) So that it is advantageous to the debtor of the loan for the longer period that his bond shall not be balanced against the other's. (12) I.e., the one bearing the earlier date.

jected] have ruled [that the second can say to the first:] 'HAD I OWED YOU [ANY MONEY] HOW IS IT THAT YOU BORROWED FROM ME?' The time for payment[1] surely, had not yet arrived.[2] If, however, [it be suggested that] the first was for five years and the second for ten, how [it may again be objected] is this to be understood? If the time for payment[1] had arrived,[2] what [it may be asked] could be the reason of the Rabbis?[3] And if the time for payment[1] had not yet arrived,[2] well, payment was not yet due and what [it may again be asked] is Admon's reason?—[This ruling was] required [in that case] only where [the holder of the earlier bond][4] came [to borrow] on the day on which the five years had terminated.[5] The Masters[6] are of the opinion that it is usual to borrow money for one day[7] and the Master[8] is of the opinion that one does not borrow money for one day.[9]

Rama b. Ḥama explained: We are here[10] dealing with [a case where one of the bonds was presented by] orphans[11] who are themselves entitled to recover a debt but from whom no debt may be recovered.[12]

Was it not, however, stated, THE ONE RECOVERS HIS DEBT AND THE OTHER RECOVERS HIS DEBT?[13]—[The meaning is:] The one recovers his debt, and the other is entitled to recover it but gets nothing. Said Raba: Two objections [may be advanced] against this explanation. Firstly, it was stated, 'THE ONE RECOVERS HIS DEBT AND THE OTHER RECOVERS[13] HIS DEBT'; and, secondly, could not [the other party] allow the orphans to distrain on a plot of land [of his] and then recover it from them,[14] in accordance with [a ruling of] R. Naḥman, for R. Naḥman said in the name of Rabbah b. Abbuha: If orphans collected a plot of land for their

(1) Lit., 'its time'. (2) When the second bond was written. (3) It should be pretty obvious that the holder of the later bond should be believed since he might well plead as Admon suggested. (4) The five years' loan. (5) Payment having been due on the following day. (6) The Sages. Lit., 'master'. (7) Hence their ruling that both bonds are valid. (8) Admon. (9) Hence the admissibility of the plea, 'HAD I OWED YOU etc.' (10) In our Mishnah. (11) Who inherited it from their father. (12) If they possessed no landed property. Orphans' movables may not be distrained on. (13) Not merely, 'is entitled to recover etc.' (14) Cf. *supra* n. 12 *mutatis mutandis*.

father's debt[1] the creditor[2] may re-collect it from them?[3]—This is a difficulty.

Why could it not be explained [that this is a case] where the orphans owned land of the worst quality and the other owned best[4] and medium quality, so that the orphans proceed to distrain on his medium land[5] and allow him to distrain on their worst only? For, even though[6] an assessment[7] is made on a general basis[8] is not payment from orphans' property recovered from their worst land only?[9]—This applies only where [the creditor] has not yet seized [their property] but where[10] he had seized it[11] he may lawfully retain it.[12]

MISHNAH. [THE FOLLOWING REGIONS ARE REGARDED AS] THREE COUNTRIES IN RESPECT OF MATRIMONY:[13] JUDAEA, TRANSJORDAN AND GALILEE. [A MAN] MAY NOT TAKE OUT [HIS WIFE WITH HIM][14] FROM ONE TOWN[15] TO ANOTHER[16] OR FROM ONE CITY[17] TO ANOTHER. WITHIN THE SAME COUNTRY, HOWEVER, HE MAY TAKE HER OUT WITH HIM FROM ONE TOWN INTO ANOTHER OR FROM ONE CITY INTO ANOTHER[18] [110*b*] BUT NOT FROM A TOWN TO A CITY NOR FROM A CITY TO A TOWN.[19] [A MAN] MAY TAKE OUT [HIS WIFE WITH HIM][18] FROM AN INFERIOR[20] TO A SUPERIOR[21] DWELLING, BUT NOT FROM A SUPERIOR[21] TO AN INFERIOR[20] DWELLING. R. SIMEON B. GAMALIEL RULED: NOT EVEN FROM AN INFERIOR DWELLING

(1) Which someone owed him. (2) To whom their father owed money. (3) *Supra* 92*a*, Pes. 31*a*, B.B. 125*a*. (4) So cur. edd. and MS.M. R. Nissim and Maharsha omit. (5) To which a creditor is entitled (cf. *supra* p. 704, n. 9 second clause). (6) Lit., also'. (7) Cf. *supra* p. 704, n. 7. (8) Lit., 'of all men'. (9) V. Giṭ. 48*b*. (10) MS.M. 'but here since'. (11) As in the case under discussion where they seek to take it from him. (12) Lit., 'he seized'. (13) *Sc.* a man who married in one of these cannot compel his wife to go with him to any of the others. (14) Except with her consent. (15) כרך. (16) In another country. (17) [עיר. According to Rashi כרך is larger than עיר. According to Krauss, the former denotes a city (large or small) surrounded by a wall, v. *He'atid.* III, 1ff.] (18) Even if she objects. (19) The reason is stated *infra*. (20) Lit., 'bad'. (21) Lit., 'beautiful'.

TO A SUPERIOR DWELLING, BECAUSE THE [CHANGE TO A] SUPERIOR DWELLING PUTS [THE HUMAN BODY] TO A [SEVERE] TEST.[1]

GEMARA. One may readily grant [the justice of the ruling that a wife may not be compelled to move] FROM A CITY TO A TOWN, since everything [necessary] is obtainable in a city while not everything is obtainable in a town. On what grounds, however, [can she not be compelled to move] FROM A TOWN TO A CITY?—[This ruling] provides support for R. Jose b. Ḥanina who stated, 'Whence is it deduced that city[2] life[3] is difficult?[4] [From Scripture] where it is said, *And the people blessed all men that willingly offered themselves to dwell in Jerusalem*.[5]

R. SIMEON B. GAMALIEL RULED etc. What [is meant by] 'PUTS [THE HUMAN BODY] TO A [SEVERE] TEST'?[6]—In agreement [with a saying] of Samuel. For Samuel said: A change of diet is the beginning of bowel trouble.[7]

It is written in the Book of Ben Sira: *All the days of the poor*[8] *are evil;*[9] but are there not the Sabbaths and festivals?[10]—[The explanation, however, is] according to Samuel. For Samuel said: A change of diet is the beginning of bowel trouble.[7] Ben Sira said: The nights also.[11] Lower than [all] the roofs is his roof,[12] and on the height of mountains is his vineyard,[13] [so that] the rain of [other] roofs [pours down] upon his roof and the earth of his vineyard [is washed down] into the vineyards [of others].[14]

(1) This is further explained by Samuel *infra*. בודק, rt. בדק 'to examine', 'test', 'try'. *Aliter* (Jast.): בדק 'to penetrate'; 'the removal to a better residence (and style of living) penetrates (the body and creates disease)'. (2) Lit., 'cities'. (3) שישיבת, rt. ישב 'to sit', 'dwell'. (4) Lit., 'hard', owing to overcrowding, lack of pure country air and an insufficiency of parks and open spaces. (5) Neh. XI, 2. (6) בודק cf. *supra* note 1. (7) חולי מעים, lit., 'disease of the bowels', 'abdominal trouble'. Cf. B.B. 146*a*, Sonc. ed. p. 628 (where מעים is omitted) and Sanh. 101*a*, Sonc. ed. p. 683. (8) So A.J.V.; A.V. and R.V. '*afflicted*'. (9) Prov. XV, 15, Ben Sira XXXI, 5. (10) During which days, at least, the poor were provided with substantial meals. (11) Ben Sira loc. cit. Not only *all the days*. (12) As a poor man he is compelled to live in a low-roofed hovel. (13) Since he cannot afford a more costly vineyard in the valley. (14) Ben Sira XXXI, 6-7.

MISHNAH. [A MAN] MAY COMPEL ALL [HIS HOUSEHOLD] TO GO UP[1] [WITH HIM] TO THE LAND OF ISRAEL, BUT NONE MAY BE COMPELLED TO LEAVE IT. ALL [ONE'S HOUSEHOLD] MAY BE COMPELLED TO GO UP[1] TO JERUSALEM,[2] BUT NONE MAY BE COMPELLED TO LEAVE IT. [THIS APPLIES TO] BOTH MEN AND WOMEN.[3] IF A MAN MARRIED A WOMAN IN THE LAND OF ISRAEL AND DIVORCED HER IN THE LAND OF ISRAEL, HE MUST PAY HER [HER KETHUBAH] IN THE CURRENCY OF THE LAND OF ISRAEL. IF HE MARRIED A WOMAN IN THE LAND OF ISRAEL AND DIVORCED HER IN CAPPADOCIA HE MUST PAY HER [HER KETHUBAH] IN THE CURRENCY OF THE LAND OF ISRAEL.[4] IF HE MARRIED A WOMAN IN CAPPADOCIA AND DIVORCED HER IN THE LAND OF ISRAEL, HE MUST AGAIN PAY [HER KETHUBAH] IN THE CURRENCY OF THE LAND OF ISRAEL.[4] R. SIMEON B. GAMALIEL, HOWEVER, RULED THAT HE MUST PAY HER IN THE CAPPADOCIAN CURRENCY.

IF A MAN MARRIED A WOMAN IN CAPPADOCIA AND DIVORCED HER IN CAPPADOCIA, HE MUST PAY HER [HER KETHUBAH] IN THE CURRENCY OF CAPPADOCIA.

GEMARA. What [was the expression,] 'MAY COMPEL ALL'[5] intended to include?—To include slaves.[6] What, however, [was the expression[5] intended] to include according to him who specifically mentioned 'slaves' [in our Mishnah]?—To include [removal] from a superior dwelling to an inferior one. What [was the expression,] 'BUT NONE[7] MAY BE COMPELLED TO LEAVE IT' intended to include?—To include a slave who fled from outside the Land [of Israel] into the Land in which case his master is told,[8] 'Sell him here, and go', in order to [encourage] settlement in the

(1) Lit., 'cause to go up'. (2) From any other Palestinian place. (3) A wife also may compel her husband to live with her in Jerusalem or the Land of Israel and, if he refuses, she is entitled to demand a divorce and the payment of her *kethubah*. (4) The Cappadocian coins were dearer than the corresponding ones of the Land of Israel. (5) Emphasis on 'ALL'. (6) Hebrew slaves also may be compelled by their master to follow him to Jerusalem or to the Land of Israel. (7) Emphasis on 'NONE'. (8) Lit., 'we say to him'.

Land of Israel. What [was the expression] 'ALL[1] . . . MAY BE COMPELLED TO GO UP TO JERUSALEM' intended to include?—To include [removal] from a superior dwelling to an inferior one. What [was the expression,] 'BUT NONE[2] MAY BE COMPELLED TO LEAVE IT' intended to include?—To include even [removal] from an inferior dwelling to a superior one; only since as it was stated in the earlier clause,[3] 'NONE MAY BE COMPELLED TO LEAVE IT', it was also stated in the latter clause,[4] 'NONE MAY BE COMPELLED TO LEAVE IT'.[5]

Our Rabbis taught: If [the husband] desires[6] to go up[7] and his wife refuses[6] she must be pressed[8] to go up; and if [she does] not [consent] she may be divorced[9] without a *kethubah*. If she desires[6] to go up[7] and he refuses,[6] he must be pressed to go up; and if [he does] not [consent] he must divorce her and pay her *kethubah*. If she desires to leave[10] and he refuses to leave, she must be pressed not to leave, and if [pressure is of] no [avail] she may be divorced[9] without a *kethubah*. If he desires to leave[10] and she refuses he must be pressed not to leave, and if [coercion is of] no [avail] he must divorce her and pay her *kethubah*.[11]

IF A MAN MARRIED A WOMAN etc. Is not this self-contradictory? It was stated, IF HE MARRIED A WOMAN IN THE LAND OF ISRAEL AND DIVORCED HER IN CAPPADOCIA HE MUST PAY HER [HER KETHUBAH] IN THE CURRENCY OF THE LAND OF

(1) Emphasis on 'ALL'. (2) Emphasis on 'NONE'. (3) In reference to the Land of Israel. (4) In respect of Jerusalem. (5) Though the latter clause is, in fact, redundant, it being self-evident that if a person may be compelled to leave a superior dwelling to move to an inferior one, provided the latter is in Jerusalem, he could not *a fortiori* be compelled to leave Jerusalem even for the sake of a change from an inferior to a superior dwelling. (6) Lit., 'says'. (7) From a country outside the Land, to the Land of Israel, or from a province in the latter to Jerusalem. (8) This law does not apply to the present time owing to the risks of the journey (Tosaf. s.v. הוא *a.l.*). Rabbenu Ḥayim also maintains that living in the Land of Israel is now not a religious act owing to the difficulty and impossibility of fulfilling many of the precepts attached to the soil (Tosaf. loc. cit. q.v.). (9) Lit., 'she goes out'. (10) Jerusalem, for a provincial town in the Land of Israel, or the latter for a foreign country. (11) Tosef. Keth. XII.

ISRAEL, from which it clearly follows that we are guided by [the currency of the place where the] obligation[1] was undertaken.[2] Read, however, the concluding clause: IF HE MARRIED A WOMAN IN CAPPADOCIA AND DIVORCED HER IN THE LAND OF ISRAEL HE MUST AGAIN PAY HER [HER KETHUBAH] IN THE CURRENCY OF THE LAND OF ISRAEL, from which it follows, does it not, that we are guided by [the currency of the place] where collection is effected?[3] — Rabbah replied: [The rulings] taught here [are among those in which the claims relating to] a *kethubah* are weaker [than those of other claimants],[4] for [the author] is of the opinion that the *kethubah* is a Rabbinical enactment.[5] R. SIMEON B. GAMALIEL, HOWEVER, RULED THAT HE MUST PAY HER IN THE CAPPADOCIAN CURRENCY. He is of the opinion[6] that the *kethubah* is Pentateuchal.[7]

Our Rabbis taught: If a man produces a bond of indebtedness against another [and the place of issue] entered[8] therein was Babylon, [the debtor] must allow him to collect it in Babylonian currency. If [the place of issue] entered[8] therein was the Land of Israel he must allow him to collect it in the currency of the Land of Israel. If no place of issue was entered[8] he must, if it was presented in Babylon, pay him in Babylonian currency; and, if it was presented in the Land of Israel, he must pay him in the currency of the Land of Israel. If merely [a sum of] 'silver [pieces]'[9] was entered, the borrower may pay the other whatever he wishes.[10] [This is a ruling] which does not apply to[11] a *kethubah*.[12] To what [ruling does this[13] refer]? — R. Mesharsheya replied: To that in the

(1) To pay the *kethubah*. (2) The obligation is undertaken at marriage and collection takes place on divorce (or the man's death). (3) Cf. *supra* n. 2. (4) Cf. *supra* p. 709, n. 4, B.B. 132*b*, Sonc. ed. p. 554, n. 9, Bek. 52*a*. (5) Non-Pentateuchal (cf. *infra* n. 6 and text). (6) Contrary to the view of the first Tanna (cf. *supra* n. 5). (7) [In the Jerusalem Talmud the opinions are reversed: R. Gamaliel holds that the *kethubah* is Rabbinical, whereas the Sages consider it Biblical, the Palestinian giving preference to the Palestine coinage, v. *supra* 10*a*]. (8) Lit., 'written'. (9) No mention being made of the exact denomination. (10) Since he may assert that the figure in the bond referred to the smallest silver coin. (11) Lit., 'which is not so in'. (12) Tosef. Keth. XII. (13) The last clause.

first clause,[1] thus indicating that the law is not in agreement with[2] R. Simeon b. Gamaliel who ruled that the *kethubah* is Pentateuchal.

'If merely [a sum of] "silver [pieces]" was entered the borrower may pay the other whatever he wishes'. May not one say that [a 'silver piece' merely signified] a bar [of silver]?—R. Eleazar replied: [This is a case] where 'coin' was mentioned in the bond.[3] May not one suggest [that it signified] small change?—R. Papa replied: Small change is not made of silver.[4]

Our Rabbis taught: One should always live in the Land of Israel, even in a town most of whose inhabitants are idolaters, but let no one live outside the Land, even in a town most of whose inhabitants are Israelites; for whoever lives in the Land of Israel may be considered to have[5] a God, but whoever lives outside the Land may be regarded as one who has no God. For it is said in Scripture, *To give you the Land of Canaan, to be your God.*[6] Has he, then, who does not live in the *Land*, no God?[7] But [this is what the text intended] to tell you, that whoever lives outside the Land may be regarded as one who worships idols. Similarly it was said in Scripture in [the story of] David, *For they have driven me out this day that I should not cleave to the inheritance of the Lord, saying: Go, serve other gods.*[8] Now, whoever said to David, '*Serve other gods*'? But [the text intended] to tell you that whoever lives outside the Land[9] may be regarded as one who worships idols.[10]

R. Zera was evading Rab Judah because he desired to go up to the Land of Israel while Rab Judah had expressed [the following view:] Whoever goes up from Babylon to the Land of Israel transgresses a positive commandment, for it is said in Scripture, [111a] *They shall be carried to Babylon, and there shall they be, until the*

(1) *Sc.* unlike a creditor who, according to the first clause, is entitled to collect his due in the currency of the place of issue, a woman collects her *kethubah* in the cheaper currency only. (2) Lit., 'to bring out from'. (3) Lit., 'written in it'. (4) Lit., 'small change of silver people do not make'. Cf. B.B. 165*b* f, Sonc. ed. p. 722f. (5) Lit., 'is like as if he has'. (6) Lev. XXV, 38; implying apparently that *only in the land of Canaan* would He be their God. (7) One surely may serve God anywhere. (8) I Sam. XXVI, 19. (9) David was compelled to seek shelter from Saul in the country of Moab and the land of the Philistines. (10) Tosef. 'A.Z. V.

day that I remember them, saith the Lord.[1] And R. Zera?[2]—That text[1] refers[3] to the vessels of ministry.[4] And Rab Judah?—Another text also is available:[3] *I adjure you, O daughters of Jerusalem, by the gazelles, and by the hinds of the field,* [*that ye awaken not, nor stir up love,*[5] *until it please*]'.[6] And R. Zera?—That[7] implies that Israel shall not go up [all together as if surrounded] by a wall.[8] And Rab Judah?—Another '*I adjure you*'[9] is written in Scripture. And R. Zera?—That text is required for [an exposition] like that of R. Jose son of R. Ḥanina who said: 'What was the purpose of those three adjurations?[10]—One, that Israel shall not go up [all together as if surrounded] by a wall;[8] the second, that whereby the Holy One, blessed be He, adjured Israel that they shall not rebel against the nations of the world; and the third is that whereby the Holy One, blessed be He, adjured the idolaters that they shall not oppress Israel too much'. And Rab Judah?—It is written in Scripture, *That ye awaken not, nor stir up.*[11] And R. Zera?—That text is required for [an exposition] like that of R. Levi who stated: 'What was the purpose of those six adjurations?[12]—Three for the purposes just mentioned and the others, that [the prophets] shall not make known the end,[13] that [the people] shall not[14] delay[15] the end,[13] and that they shall not reveal the secret[16] to the idolaters'.

By the gazelles, and by the hinds of the field.[17] R. Eleazar explained:

(1) Jer. XXVII, 22. (2) How could he act against this text? (3) Lit., 'is written'. (4) Enumerated previously in the context (Jer. XXVII, 19ff). (5) For the Land of Israel. (6) Cant. II, 7. Before it pleased God to bring them back to their Land they must patiently remain in Babylon. (7) The text of Cant. II, 7. (8) Individuals, however, may well go there. Cur. edd., read בחומה. MS.M., כחומה, 'like a wall'. So also Emden and Strashun. (9) Cant. III, 5, which refers to individuals. (10) The two mentioned (Cant. II, 7, III, 5) and the one in Cant. V, 8. (11) Cant. II, 7, אם תעירו ואם תעוררו, the repetition of the root עור implies (*a*) all Israel together and (*b*) individuals. (12) Each of the three adjurations (cf. *supra* n. 10) is repeated (cf. *supra* n. 11). (13) Of the exile. The beginning of the Messianic era. (14) By their misdeeds. (15) ירחקו (rt. רחק 'to be far'). *Aliter:* Shall not regard the end (of the exile) as being too far off, and so lose hope (Maharsha). Var. ידחקו (rt. דחק 'to press'), 'force by excessive prayer'. (16) Of intercalation. *Aliter:* The secret of the reasons underlying the commandments in the Torah (Rashi). (17) Cant. II, 7.

Ho, Zion, escape, thou that dwellest with the daughter of Babylon.[1]

Abaye stated: We have a tradition that Babel[2] will not witness the sufferings[3] [that will precede the coming] of the Messiah.[4] He [also] explained it[5] to refer[6] to Huẓal[7] in Benjamin which would be named[8] the Corner of Safety.[9]

R. Eleazar stated: The dead outside the Land[10] will not be resurrected; for it is said in Scripture, *And I will set glory*[11] *in the land of the living,*[12] [implying] the dead of the land in which I have my *desire*[13] will be resurrected, but the dead [of the land] in which I have no desire will not be resurrected.

R. Abba b. Memel objected: *Thy dead shall live, my dead bodies shall arise;*[14] does not [the expression] '*Thy dead shall live*' refer to the dead of the Land of Israel, and '*My dead bodies shall arise*' to the dead outside the Land;[15] while the text,[16] *And I will give glory*[17] *in the land of the living*[12] was written of Nebuchadnezzar concerning whom the All-Merciful said, 'I will bring against them a king who is as swift as a *stag*'?[18]—The other replied: Master, I am making an ex-

(1) Zech. II, 11. (2) בבל, usually rendered 'Babylon', but v. *infra* notes 6 and 7. (3) Or 'travail'. (4) חבלי דמשיח; 'but the more correct reading is חבליה דמשיח' (Moore, G.F., *Judaism* II, 361, n. 2). חבלי המשיח 'frequent in modern Christian books is fictitious' (loc. cit.). The 'sufferings' or 'travail' are more fully described in Sanh. 97*b*, Sonc. ed. p. 654. These are the 'throes of mother Zion which is in labor to bring forth the Messiah—without metaphor, the Jewish people' (Moore, loc. cit. text). (5) The tradition as to the immunity of Babel. (6) Not, as might be assumed, to the well known Babylon (cf. *supra* note 2). (7) הוצל, a village to the north of Jerusalem between Tel Al-Ful and Nob 'the city of the priests'. It was known by many names including that of בבל (v. Horowitz, I.S., *Palèstine*, p. 73, nn. 3ff, s.v. אצל). Neubauer, (*Geogr.* p. 152) describes it as an old fortress in Palestine (v. Jast.). There was also a Huẓal in Babylonia between Nehardea and Sura. Cf. Sanh. 19*a*, Sonc. ed. p. 98, n. 3 and Berliner, *Beitr. z. Geogr.* p. 32. (8) וקרו ליה, lit., 'and they would call it'. The pronoun according to Rashi refers to the 'days of the Messiah', but this is difficult. (9) The noun הוצל is regarded here as the Hof. of נצל 'to save'. (10) Of Israel. (11) צבי. Cf. *infra* notes 13 and 18. (12) Ezek. XXVI, 20. (13) צביון containing the three letters of צבי (cf. *supra* note 11). God's care for Palestine is taken for granted. Cf. e.g., *A land which the Lord thy God careth for; the eyes of the Lord thy God are always upon it* (Deut. XI, 12). (14) Isa. XXVI, 19. (15) Of Israel. (16) Lit., 'and what'. (17) V. *supra* note 11. (18) צבי also means 'stag' (cf. *supra* note 11).

position of another Scriptural text: *He that giveth breath unto the people upon it,*[1] *and spirit to them that walk therein.*[2] But is it not written, *My dead bodies shall arise?*[3]—That was written in reference to miscarriages.[4] Now as to R. Abba b. Memel, what [is the application] he makes of the text,[5] '*He that giveth breath unto the people upon it*'?—He requires it for [an exposition] like that of R. Abbahu who stated: Even a Canaanite bondwoman who [lives] in the Land of Israel is assured of a place in[6] the world to come, [for in the context] here it is written, *Unto the people*[7] *upon it,*[8] and elsewhere it is written, *Abide ye here with*[9] *the ass*[10] [which may be rendered][11] 'people that are like an ass'.[12]

And spirit to them that work therein[8] [teaches], said R. Jeremiah b. Abba in the name of R. Joḥanan, that whoever walks four cubits in the Land of Israel is assured of a place[13] in the world to come. Now according to R. Eleazar,[14] would not the righteous outside the Land[15] be revived?[16]—R. Elai replied: [They will be revived] by rolling [to the Land of Israel]. R. Abba Sala the Great demurred: Will not the rolling be painful to the righteous?—Abaye replied: Cavities will be made for them underground.

Thou shalt carry me out of Egypt and bury me in their burying-place.[17] Ḳarna remarked: [There must be here] some inner meaning. Our father Jacob well knew that he was a righteous man in every way, and, since the dead outside the Land will also be resurrected, why did he trouble his sons?[18] Because he might possibly be unworthy to [roll through] the cavities.[19]

(1) The land of Israel. (2) Isa. XLII, 5. (3) Isa. XXVI, 19. (4) Even they will be resurrected but only in the Land of Israel. (5) Lit., 'that'. (6) Lit., 'daughter of'. (7) עַם. (8) Isa. XLII, 5. (9) עִם. (10) Gen. XXII, 5. (11) The consonants עם being the same (cf. *supra* nn. 7 and 9.) (12) *Sc.* slaves who are considered the property of the master. As the '*people*' spoken of in Isa. XLII, 5, are assured of a place in the world to come so are the 'people' referred to in Gen. XXII, 5. Moore describes this as 'a specimen of exegetical whimsicality, rather than an eccentricity of opinion' (*Judaism*, II, 380). (13) Lit., 'son of'. (14) Who based his view on Ezek. XXVI, 20, *supra*. (15) Of Israel. (16) But this, surely, is most improbable. (17) Gen. XLVII, 30. (18) To carry him to Canaan? (19) *Var. lec.*, 'because he did not accept the suffering of the pain of rolling through the cavities' (Yalḳuṭ and עין יעקב).

Similarly you read in Scripture, *And Joseph took an oath of the children of Israel, [saying . . . ye shall carry up my bones from hence]*,[1] and R. Ḥanina remarked: [There is here] an inner meaning. Joseph well knew himself to be a righteous man in every way, and, since the dead outside the Land[2] will be revived, why did he trouble his brothers [with a journey of] four hundred parasangs? Because he might possibly be unworthy to [roll through] the cavities.[3]

His brothers[4] sent [the following message] to Rabbah:[5] 'Jacob well knew that he was a righteous man in every way etc.[6] Ilfa added to this the following incident. A man was once troubled on account of [his inability to marry] a certain woman[7] and desired to go down [to her country]; but as soon as he heard this[6] he resigned himself to his unmarried state[8] until the day of his death. Although you are a great scholar [you will admit that] a man who studies on his own cannot be on a par with a man who learns from his master. And perchance you might think that you have no master [good enough for you here, we may inform you that] you have one, and he is[9] R. Joḥanan. If you are not coming up, however, beware [we advise you] of three things. Do not sit too long, for [long] sitting aggravates one's abdominal troubles;[10] do not stand for a long time, because [long] standing is injurious to the heart; and do not walk too much, because [excessive] walking is harmful to the eyes. Rather [spend] one third [of your time] in sitting, one third in standing and one third in walking. Standing is better than sitting when one has nothing to lean against'.

'Standing'! How can this be imagined in view of the statement that '[long] standing is injurious to the heart'?—What was meant in fact was this:[11] Better than sitting [111*b*] with nothing to lean against is standing with something to lean against.

And thus [his brothers][12] proceeded to say [in their message]:

(1) Gen. L, 25. (1) Of Israel. (3) V. p. 717, n. 19. (4) Who lived in Palestine and desired him to join them, (5) Rabbah b. Naḥmani who was domiciled in Pumbeditha in Babylonia (cf. *supra* p. 325, n. 5). (6) V. Ḳarna's remark *supra*. (7) Who refused to leave her home country outside Palestine to join him in Palestine. (8) Lit., 'he rolled by himself'. (9) Lit., 'and who is he?' (10) Pl. of תחתון 'nethermost', hence 'piles'. (11) Lit., 'but'. (12) V. nn. 4-5.

—'Isaac and Simeon and Oshaia were unanimous in their view that[1] the *halachah* is in agreement with R. Judah in [respect of the mating of] mules'. For it was taught: If a mule was craving for sexual gratification it must not be mated with a horse or an ass[2] but [only with one of] its own species.[3]

R. Naḥman b. Isaac stated: By 'Isaac'[4] was meant[5] R. Isaac Nappaḥa. By 'Simeon',[4] R. Simeon b. Pazzi—others say: Resh Laḳish;[6] and by 'Oshaia',[7] R. Oshaia[7] Berabbi.[8]

R. Eleazar said: The illiterate[9] will not be resurrected, for it is said in Scripture, *The dead will not live* etc.[10] So it was also taught: *The dead will not live.*[10] As this might [be assumed to refer] to all, it was specifically stated, *The lax*[11] *will not rise,*[10] [thus indicating] that the text speaks only of such a man as was lax in the study of the words of the Torah.[12] Said R. Joḥanan to him:[13] It is no satisfaction to their Master[14] that you should speak to them in this manner. That text[15] was written of a man who was so lax as[16] to worship idols. 'I', the other[17] replied, 'make an exposition [to the same effect] from another text. For it is written in Scripture, *For thy dew is as the dew of light, and the earth shall bring to life the dead,*[18] him who makes use of the '*light*' of the Torah will the '*light*' of the Torah revive, but him who makes no use of the light of the Torah[19] the light of the Torah will not revive'. Observing, however, that he[20] was distressed, he[17] said to him, 'Master, I have found for them[21] a remedy in the Pentateuch: *But ye that*

(1) Lit., 'said one thing'. (2) An act which is contrary to the law forbidding the hybridization of heterogeneous animals. (3) Tosef. Kil. I, Ḥul. 79*a*. (4) Referred to in the message *supra*. (5) Lit., 'this'. (6) *Sc.* R. Simeon b. Laḳish. (7) MS.M., Hoshaia. (8) Or 'Berebi'. A title of uncertain meaning. It denotes a scholar of any famous college or a qualified Rabbi who remained at college and acted as tutor to senior students. Cf. Mak. 5*b*, Sonc. ed. p. 25, n. 4 and Naz., Sonc. ed. p. 64, n. 1. (9) עמי הארצות pl. of '*Am ha-'areẓ* v. Glos. (10) Isa. XXVI, 14. (11) רפאים, cf. רפי, רפה 'to be *or* make lax'. A.V. and R.V. '*deceased*'; R.V. marg. and A. J. V., '*shades*'. (12) *Sc.* the illiterate (v. *supra* n. 9). (13) A. Eleazar. (14) God Who created all beings even the illiterate. (15) Isa. XXVI, 14. (16) Lit., 'who makes himself lax'. (17) R. Eleazar. (18) Isa. XXVI, 19. (19) *Sc.* the illiterate who does not engage in the study of the Torah. (20) R. Joḥanan. (21) The illiterate.

did cleave unto the Lord your God are alive every one of you this day;[1] now is it possible to '*cleave*' to the divine presence concerning which it is written in Scripture, *For the Lord thy God is a devouring fire?*[2] But [the meaning is this:] Any man who marries his daughter to a scholar, or carries on a trade on behalf of scholars,[3] or benefits scholars from his estate is regarded by Scripture[4] as if he had cleaved to the divine presence.[5] Similarly you read in Scripture, *To love the Lord thy God, [to hearken to His voice,] and to cleave unto Him.*[6] Is it possible for a human being to '*cleave*' unto the divine presence? But [what was meant is this:] Any man who marries his daughter to a scholar, or carries on a trade for scholars, or benefits scholars from his estate is regarded by Scripture as if he had cleaved to the divine presence.

R. Ḥiyya b. Joseph said: A time will come when the just will break through [the soil] and rise up in Jerusalem, for it is said in Scripture, *And they will blossom out of the city like grass of the earth*,[7] and by '*city*' only Jerusalem can be meant for it is said in Scripture, *For I will defend this city*.[8]

R. Ḥiyya b. Joseph further stated: The just in the time to come will rise [apparelled] in their own clothes.[9] [This is deduced] *a minori ad majus* from a grain of wheat. If a grain of wheat that is buried[10] naked sprouts up with many coverings how much more so the just who are buried in their shrouds.

R. Ḥiyya b. Joseph further stated: There will be a time when the Land of Israel will produce baked cakes of the purest quality[11]

(1) Deut. IV, 4, emphasis on '*cleave*'. (2) Ibid. 24. (3) Thus enabling them to devote their time to study. *Aliter:* Assigns them a share in his business as sleeping partners. V. Sanh., Sonc. ed. p. 671, n. 4. (4) Lit., 'Scripture brings up on him'. (5) The illiterate (v. *supra* p. 719, n. 19) need not, therefore, be in despair since, by practising any of these alternatives, they also will be included among the resurrected. (6) Deut. XXX, 20. (7) Ps. LXXII, 16. (8) Referring to Jerusalem. II Kings XIX, 34. (9) Which they wore during their lifetime (J.T. cited by Tosaf. s.v. בלבושיהן, *a.l.*). The noun in the present context apparently refers to the shrouds (v. Tosaf. loc. cit.) and this may also be the opinion of one authority in J.T. (cf. Marginal Glosses to text.). (10) Sown. (11) Cf. Rashi and Jast. גלוסקא, 'a brand of white flour' or 'a white and delicate bread'. (V. *infra* p. 721, nn. 2 and 3).

and silk[1] garments, for it is said in Scripture, *There will be a rich*[2] *cornfield*[3] *in the land.*[4]

Our Rabbis taught: *There will be a rich cornfield in the Land upon the top of the mountains.*[4] [From this] it was inferred that there will be a time when wheat will rise as high as a palm-tree and will grow on the top of the mountains. But in case you should think that there will be trouble in reaping it, it was specifically said in Scripture, *Its fruit shall rustle like Lebanon;*[4] the Holy One, blessed be He, will bring a wind from his treasure houses which He will cause to blow upon it. This will loosen its fine flour and a man will walk out into the field and take a mere handful[5] and, out of it, will [have sufficient provision for] his own, and his household's maintenance.

With the kidney-fat of wheat.[6] [From this] it was inferred that there will be a time when a grain of wheat will be as large as the two kidneys of a big bull. And you need not marvel at this, for a fox once made his nest in a turnip and when [the remainder of the vegetable] was weighed, it was found [to be] sixty pounds in the pound weight of Sepphoris.[7]

It was taught: R. Joseph[8] related: It once happened to a man[9] at Shiḥin[10] to whom his father had left three twigs of mustard that one of these split and was found to contain nine *ḳab* of mustard, and its timber sufficed to cover a potter's hut.

R. Simeon b. Taḥlifa[11] related. Our father left us a cabbage stack and we[12] ascended and descended it by means of a ladder.[13]

And of the blood of the grape thou drankest foaming wine.[14] It was inferred: The world to come is not like this world. In this world there is the trouble of harvesting and treading [of the grapes], but in the world to come a man will bring one grape[15] on a wagon

(1) Or 'woollen'. (2) Heb. פסת, analogous to פסים (Gen. XXXVII, 3) (E.V. *of many colours*). (3) Heb. בר signifies also 'purity'. (4) Ps. LXXII, 16. (5) פיסת ידו (cf. *supra* n. 2). (6) Deut. XXXII, 14. (7) Cf. *supra* p. 410, n. 6. (8) Read with MS.M. 'R. Jose'. (9) Ḥalafta of Sepphoris. (10) A town near Sepphoris. (11) MS.M. and others (v. Wilna Gaon), 'Ḥalafta'. (12) In order to gather its leaves. (13) בסולם. MS.M., במעלות כסולם, 'on steps as on a ladder'. (14) Deut. XXXII, 14. (15) *Aliter:* 'Stalk of grapes' (Jast.).

or a ship, put it in a corner of his house and use its contents as [if it had been] a large wine cask, while its timber[1] would be used to make fires for cooking.[2] There will be no grape that will not contain thirty kegs[3] of wine, for it is said is Scripture, *And of the blood of the grape thou drankest foaming wine,*[4] read not *'foaming'*[5] but *ḥomer.*[6]

When R. Dimi came[7] he made the following statement: What is the implication in the Scriptural text, *Binding his foal*[8] *unto the vine?*[9] There is not a vine in the Land of Israel that does not require [all the inhabitants of] one city[10] to harvest it: *And his ass's colt*[11] *unto the choice*[12] *vine,*[9] there is not even a wild[13] tree in the Land of Israel that does not produce a load of [fruit for] two she-asses.[14] In case you should imagine that it contains no wine, it was explicitly said in Scripture, *He washes his garments in wine.*[9] And since you might say that it is not red it was explicitly stated, *And of the blood of the grape thou drankest foaming wine.*[15] And in case you should say that it does not cause intoxication it was stated, *His vesture.*[16] And in case you should think that it is tasteless it was expressly stated, *His eyes shall be red*[17] *with wine,*[18] any palate that will taste it says, 'To me, to me'.[19] And since you might say that it is suitable for young people but unsuitable for old, it was explicitly stated *And his teeth white with milk;*[18] read not, *'teeth white'*[20] but 'To him who is advanced in years'.[21]

(1) The stalk of the grape. V. also p. 721, n. 15. *Aliter:* the wood of the cask which the husk had superseded (Maharsha). (2) Lit., 'under the dish'. (3) Each measuring one *se'ah* (v. *infra* n. 5). (4) Deut. XXXII, 14. (5) חֲמֶר. (6) חֹמֶר, the consonants of the two being identical. A *ḥomer* = thirty *se'ah*. (7) From Palestine to Babylon. (8) עירה, absol. עיר (v. *infra* n 10) (9) Gen. XLIX, 11. (10) Heb. עיר (v. *supra* n. 8). (11) אתונו, absol. אתון, 'she-ass'. (12) שורקה v. *infra* n. 13). (13) סרק, analogous to סורקה, the ש in שורקה (v. *supra* n. 12) being read as ס (cf. Maharsha). (14) V. *supra* n. 11. The number 'two' is perhaps derived from בני (in בני אתונו) which is taken as the pl. const. of בן and signifies no less than two. (15) Deut. XXXII, 14. Read with MS.M. and עין יעקב, *And his vesture in the blood of grapes,* which is the conclusion of Gen. XLIX, 11, the text of the present exposition. (16) סותה, derived from the rt. סות, 'to incite', 'agitate'. (17) חכלילי (v. *infra* n. 19). (18) Gen. XLIX, 12. (19) חכלילי (v. *supra* n. 17) is expounded as 'the palate (will say:) To me, to me'. (20) לְבֶן שִׁנַּיִם. (21) לְבֶן שָׁנִים lit.,

In what [sense] is the plain meaning of the text[1] to be understood?[2]—When R. Dimi came[3] he explained: The congregation of Israel said to the Holy One, blessed be He, 'Lord of the Universe, wink to me with Thine eyes,[4] which [to me will be] sweeter than wine, and shew[5] me Thy teeth which will be sweeter than milk'.[4] [This interpretation] provides support for R. Johanan who said: The man who [by smiling affectionately] shews[6] his teeth to his friend is better than one who gives him milk to drink, for it is said in Scripture, *And his teeth white with milk,*[1] read not '*teeth white*' but 'shewing the teeth'.[7]

R. Ḥiyya b. Adda[8] was the Scriptural tutor of the young children of Resh Laḳish. [On one occasion] he took a three days' holiday[9] and did not come [to teach the children]. 'Why', the other asked him when he returned, 'did you take a holiday?'—'My father', he replied, 'left me one espalier[10] and on the first day I cut from it three hundred clusters [of grapes], each cluster yielding one keg. On the second day I cut three hundred clusters, each two of which yielded one keg. On the third day I cut three hundred clusters, each three of which yielded one keg, and so I renounced my ownership of more than one half of it'. 'If you had not taken a holiday [from the Torah]', the other told him, 'it would have yielded much more'.[11]

Rami b. Ezekiel once paid a visit to Bene-berak[12] where he saw goats grazing under fig-trees, while honey was flowing from the

'to a son of years'. לבן 'white' also means 'to a son', שנים 'teeth' may also mean, by a change of vowels 'years'.

(1) Gen. XLIX, 12. (2) Lit., 'is written'. (3) From Palestine to Babylon. (4) חכלילי (cf. *supra* p. 722, nn. 17 and 19) is again read as חכ-לי-לי, but חכ is regarded as analogous to the rt. חיך 'to laugh', 'to smile affectionately', facial movements which involve the eyes and the teeth. (5) V. *infra* note 6 and text. (6) Lit., 'makes white' (cf. *supra* note 4). (7) Lit., 'whitening of the teeth' (cf. *supra* l.c.). (8) [MS.M. Abba; v. *supra* 8b]. (9) Lit., 'he relaxed'. (10) Or 'a vine trained to an espalier'. (11) *Sc.* the progressive daily decline of the yield was due to the corresponding increase in the number of days in which he failed to return to his sacred duty of teaching his pupils the word of God. (12) One of the cities in the tribe of Dan (Josh. XIX, 45); now the village Ibn Ibrak, north east of Jaffa (v. Horowitz, I.S., *Palestine* s.v.).

figs, and milk ran from them, and these mingled with each other. 'This is indeed', he remarked, '[*a land*] *flowing with milk and honey*'.[1]

R. Jacob b. Dostai related: From Lod[2] to Ono[3] [is a distance of about] three miles.[4] Once I rose up early in the morning and waded [all that way] up to my ankles in honey of the figs.

Resh Laḳish said: I myself saw the flow of the milk and honey of Sepphoris[5] and it extended [over an area of] sixteen by sixteen miles.

Rabbah b. Bar Ḥana said: I saw the flow of the milk and honey in all the Land of Israel [112a] and [the total area] was equal [to the land extending] from Be Mikse[6] to the Fort of Tulbanḳe,[7] [an area of] twenty-two parasangs in length and six parasangs in breadth.

R. Ḥelbo, R. 'Awira[8] and R. Jose b. Ḥanina once visited a certain place where a peach that was [as large] as a pot of Kefar Hino[9] was brought before them. (And how big is a pot of Kefar Hino?—Five *se'ah*.) One third [of the fruit] they ate, one third they declared free to all, and one third they put before their beasts. A year later R. Eleazar came there on a visit and [a peach] was brought to him. Taking it in his one hand[10] he exclaimed, *A fruitful land into a salt waste, for the wickedness of them that dwell therein*.[11]

R. Joshua b. Levi once visited Gabla[12] where he saw vines laden

(1) Cf. e.g., Ex. III, 8, Num. XIII, 27. (2) Or Lydda, the Roman Diospolis, W.N.W. of Jerusalem. (3) Modern Kafr Annah, between Jaffa and Lydda (v. *supra* note 2). (4) The actual distance is rather seven miles (v. Horowitz, *op. cit.*, s.v. אונו n. 1). (5) V. *supra* p. 410, n. 6. (6) V. *supra* p. 408, n. 9. (7) The latter was a place on Tel-ben-ḳaneh, one of the upper reaches of the Euphrates on the boundary between Babylonia and Palestine. Cf. Ḳid. Sonc. ed. p. 365, n. 8; Horowitz, *op. cit.* s.v. אקרא דתולבנקי; S. Funk, *Juden in Bab.* I, p. 13, n. 2. (8) MS.M. עזריה. (9) [Identified by Klein (*Beiträge*, p. 184) with Kefar Ḥananiah in Galilee]. (10) It was so small. (11) Ps. CVII, 34. (12) Biblical Gebal, a district between Ammon and Amalek (cf. Ps. LXXXIII, 8) now known as A-gibal, S.E. of the Dead Sea. This Gebal is not to be confused with Gebal, a Zidonian town in the N.W. of Palestine (v. Horowitz, *op. cit.*, s.v.).

GLOSSARY

INDEX OF SCRIPTURAL REFERENCES

GENERAL INDEX

TRANSLITERATION OF HEBREW LETTERS

ABBREVIATIONS